T0392243

United States of America, Government, Religion, Christianity, Law, Illegalities; God 1st Priority~ His Rightness, Provided Rights, Holy Bible; Not Self-Idol Selfishness.

A Right Comprehension of the USA Nation,Government System, including all the Branches, and History.

Anthony Sheffield

WESTBOW
PRESS®
A DIVISION OF THOMAS NELSON
& ZONDERVAN

WestBow Press books may be ordered through booksellers or by contacting:

WestBow Press
A Division of Thomas Nelson & Zondervan
1663 Liberty Drive
Bloomington, IN 47403
www.westbowpress.com
844-714-3454

ISBN: 978-1-5127-7436-8 (sc)
ISBN: 978-1-5127-7435-1 (e)

Library of Congress Control Number: 2017901770

Print information available on the last page.

WestBow Press rev. date: 12/10/2021

Jesus came and spoke, "Go you therefore, and teach all nations, baptizing them in the name of the Father, and of the Son, and of the Holy Spirit ~ also, be aware and know that I am with you always; even to the end of the world". Mat 28:18-20.

+++

TABLE of CONTENTS

Abbreviations..6
Format..7
Definition of Terms, Words, and Concepts...7

Chapter 1 Introductory Concerns...10
Chapter 2 Truth..14
Chapter 3 Appeal to Study and Experience...26
Chapter 4 USA Government and What It Consists of...27
Chapter 5 Covenant Contract -- Including God and Religion...27
Chapter 6 Decision Making Process for the USA Government..220
Chapter 7 Basis of Law...221
Chapter 8 What Can We Do ???...252
Chapter 9 Government System...253
Chapter 10 Evil is Illegal in the USA Which Is Intended To Put Limits To Or Stop Evil, Depending On Conditions.............267

Closing Chapter...292
List of Citations..296

+++

ABBREVIATIONS:

~~~ NOTE: Abbreviations may also apply when they are used within quotes of other Folk.

~~~ NOTE: Also Additionally to the abbreviations below~ Various different Abbreviations are used occasionally as indicated throughout the text; which are not included below.

~~~ Abbreviations are defined and explained. They are listed between the slanted double lines following: // Dates # = For most Calendar Dates the format of numbers is used, including in quoted documents. // Sometimes the word, "AND" is replaced with the symbol "&" // Law Cases are not included with their full titles. Rather they are only abbreviated with part of the case name. // 1-A = First Amendment of the USA Constitution // ANG = Anglican // AOC = Articles of Confederation // BOR = Bill of Rights of the USA // Calendar Months are Often Abbreviated, even within Quotes // (CC) = Covenant Contract, and also known as the Declaration of Independence & Constitution together as One Document; The Bill of Rights is included (18 Amendments). // CO = Congregationalist // CON = Constitution of the USA. Sometimes used with State for the State Constitution; When referring to the USA Constitution, it often also includes the 18 Amendments. // CT = Catholic // DEN = Denomination of Christianity and also named Establishments of Christianity in the~ (1-A or R-E or R~Est); or also known as the Establishment of Religion; or also rightly conceived to be Establishments of the True Religion; the True Religion is Christianity; the True Religion is defined as~ a) the True God, b) the True Mankind, c) the Basic True Doctrines of God & Mankind; "Establishment" word in the 1-A is replaced with DEN for this study. // DOC = Supporting DOC of the USA, which includes Congress Notes, and Various DOC used previously for as National Documents. // DOI = Declaration of Independence Document & Event & Activity // DT = Deist // EP = Episcopalian // EV = Evidence // EX: = Example // FFOG = Founding Fathers of National GOV (USA GOV) and USA GOV Documents, including the citizens of the USA at the time, which are a very much part of the GOV; and to be included in this abbreviation. // GOV = Government // HSC = Holy Scriptures // JW = Jew (s) // KN = Knowledge // LU = Lutheran // ME = Methodist // N GOV = National Government, or Federal or USA GOV // ND = Nondenominational Christianity // NT = New Testament of the Holy Bible // OT = Old Testament of the Holy Bible // PB = Presbyterian // PRE = President of the USA // QU = Quaker // R-E = Religious Establishment Part (First Amendment of the USA Constitution) // R~Est = Establishment of Religion // REP = Congress (Legislature) Representatives, Senate and/ or House of Reps; whether State or Federal // RW = Revolutionary War // SC = Scriptures of the Holy Bible // Scripture books of the Holy Bible use the 3 letter format. // TTT = Trials, Troubles, Temptations // USA = United States of America (sometimes US is used) // vivi = Vice Versa // VS or vs. or Vs = Verse(s) of the Holy Bible

+++

6

FORMAT

++++ The Format for the Book:

Conclusions and Evidences: The Evidences that are provided do not only prove the conclusion they are beneath, but prove other conclusions in the other Chptrs; applicable then to the total Book. The Evidences are absolute and irrefutable; doubtless. Conclusions are titled with the word "Conclusion". For each conclusion there are evidences listed. The items of evidence are listed with small titles for formats; then it may include more than one evidence with the "small title". That small title has a symbol~ "---T---". That is the format that the evidences are listed as under the conclusions that they belong to. Hence, simply read the evidences, listed as symbolized by "---T---" and the conclusions will be proved.
Sub-Conclusions are used; and they are said as "sub-conclusions".
Special Starting of paragraphs: (p) = Start of a new paragraph without indent and changing lines.
Special notes inside quotations of people other than this author: [[ ]] = Double brackets inserted with statements inside, or inside that of other peoples quotes, are from the author of this book and not part of the quotes.
Smaller Outline symbols: Small outline symbols are used under the main outline symbols as said herein.
Outline Format: This book is in outline format. The outline format used is special, as described.

DEFINITION of TERMS, WORDS, and CONCEPTS

---T--- Religion, Religious, Establishment of Religion: // This is only a short introductory note about these words. They are studied extensively and accurately later. These words are defined in various ways in this book. Past definitions, as in the AD 1700's and currently, differ sometimes. Also various definitions in the way it is used. Spiritual Moral Creature Beings sometimes use it to refer to a variety of God, or gods, and/or man joined thoughts of doctrine (teaching and manner of life) of God and man's existence together. In times past, USA GOV formation times, it explained 2 different definitions: {1} One definition was that of including a Christian denomination, or Christian secondary doctrine, or Christian expression. This was its definition in many instances of it. In both the Clauses of the First Amendment it is defined as "Christian Denomination" (secondary doctrine and expression and organization) when it says, "Establishment of Religion". Religion is True Religion, which is the True God, True Mankind, True Basic Doctrines of God & Mankind. In other words, True Religion vivi False. {2} The second way Spiritual Moral Beings used the word was in its general sense definition~ "a doctrine (teaching and manner of life) of God and man's existence together; religions about God both true and false". Therefore carefulness affection will have to be exercised in reading as to realize what definition is being used. Furthermore, there are differences identified by the FFOG about True & False Religion; sometimes the word Religion was used as referring to True Religion without putting the word True with it.

<u>God & Male Soldier & Female Maiden Symbol</u>: This is a previous version USA symbol. On the opposite side of this (which is not shown as included herein) is a pyramid & eye symbol, with the eye being that of God's presence (and his providence) as a priority to the Nation. The motto at top says~ "In Vindiciam Libertatis" - In Defense of Liberty; and the motto at bottom says~ "Virtus sola invicta" - Only Virtue Unconquered. The male is a soldier with one hand having ribbons, colored black & white. A dove is in one hand of the female; a maiden. This is not a complete study of this symbol.

<u>Eagle Symbol</u>: This is a previous version of the current Eagle~ (USA Symbol). The Eagle represents GOD himself in many Holy Scriptures; see Exodus 19:4. The Eagle claws have an olive branch and wheat bushel, defined as "Peace" -&- "Bread"; which are spirit -&- body. This symbol comes from the Christian Holy Bible.

8

<u>The Rebellion to Tyrants is Obedience to God Symbol</u>: This is a previous version of the current Pyramid and Eye. This was a symbol for the USA Declaration of Independence and Basis of the Great Seal symbol. This is from the Holy Bible (Exodus - Deuteronomy); of Israel departing Egypt and God's defense against, and defeat of Pharoh and the Egyptian army at the Red Sea; who attempted to enslave the saints and Moses~ abuse from the government. In the sky is a cloud & fire which was God's presence (including guidance) expressed to the Israelites; which is in addition to God's indwelling each person that conditionated. This symbol reads, "Rebellion to Tyrants is Obedience to God" ~ which clearly shows the Nations foreparents application of putting God 1st priority over human government. The current version of the Great Seal symbol (also included herein this book below) used the Holy Bible record, but changed the picture to be the Pyramid and Eye of God.

The Pyramid and Eye Symbol: This is the Great Seal of the USA. The pyramid and eye are part of the same Holy Bible record as the previous Symbol Version~ "Rebellion to Tyrants is Obedience to God".   The Pyramid was, previous to the Cathedrals (of Christianity), the largest building built by man on Earth; and many which are in Egypt, especially the largest pyramid on Earth.   The pyramid is used on this symbol for 2 intentions~ of building a national governmental system and of governmental abuse that Egypt did to Israel. The eye, above the pyramid, is God's; and though God's eye is unseen (God is a Spirit, John4:24) and omni-present, yet he saw the situation, and delivered the Old Testament saints from Egypt's (governmental or national) abuse. // No symbol was ever used by the Nation's foreparents that did not have connection to the Holy Bible.

------------------ Chapter 1 ,,,,,,,,,,, INTRODUCTORY CONCERNS --------------

++++ COST: The cost of righteousness has been and is great. Christ paid the atonement for the pardon of our sin and the right to repentance and a new start. If you desire a friend, then let me ask you if there can be a better friend than Christ Jesus ? He will do anything for you !!! This is not to support hedonism, rather Truth. HSC tells of Christ's great love: Rom 5:7-8~"For rarely for a righteous man will one die: yet perhaps for a good man some would even dare to die. But God expresses His love toward us, in that, while we were yet sinners, Christ died for us". Additionally, all Spiritual Moral Beings, existing in this world of Probationary TTT, have their frail body of skin & bones, or tissues & bone; are extremely weak and have not enough ability to stop death, nor stop eternal time, nor stop weakening, nor stop dangers to the body. We need a Friend like the Lord Jesus. Now many people have died for the righteous principles of the USA; and for the Lord. Righteousness was not based on opinions of the USA creature folk; rather of conscience, of God, or rightness, of love, of defending the Right against the evil. I personally have had, at least, 5 great uncles give time, energy, and a great amount of fright and courage in the military during WWII, including one physically died. // John Adams died on the 50th USA anniversary, July 4, 1826. What a day to die. This is not to say anything of partiality of any sort, but that to share that some of us are descendants of Samuel & John Adams (including John Quincy Adams) {These people helped design & start the USA Nation & system}. Actually, USA people are all products of their efforts. And plainly we are all related by Creation, and by Adam & Eve, and by Noah's 3 sons. This country, USA, is what God has given. Christ Jesus, Divine Providence, Supreme Judge, Creator, God worked for it. This is His cost and His work. // Prayer and self-denial (fasting) was a regular part of the USA, not only privately, but societally. Both the USA, as a total Nation & States, made a regular practice to plead for societal prayers; and self-denials were included. How many are these in number ?? Thousands; That is right, thousands. This was part of the formation before, during, and after, of the USA development, and of which was centered around God's presence and Holy Bible studies. // John Adams wrote "Posterity! You will never know how much it cost the present generation to preserve your freedom! I hope you will make good use of it! If you do not, I shall repent in Heaven that I ever took half the pains to preserve it!". Now what of Christ's Work in the Nation; and how does He feel and think of our FFOG and of His Own work ?? HSC~ +Heb 6:10 For God is not unrighteous to forget your work and labor of love, which you have showed toward his name ~KJV; For God is not unjust so as to overlook your work and the love that you have shown for his name ~ESV". The lovely NAME that is included, and in many ways, the one and only~ "God, Creator, Supreme Ruler, Divine Providence, Lord Jesus Christ". God is love.

++++ NATION is a DESIRE & INTENTION/ PURPOSE of GOD: Following are some Holy Scriptures and Notes on Nation: // The word Nation(s) is in the Holy Bible at least 500 times. // Nation is part of the Gospels Great Commission: Mat28:19; Mar13:10; Luk24:47, "Go you therefore, and teach all nations, baptizing them in the name of the Father, and of the Son, and of the Holy Ghost; the gospel must first be published among all nations; that repentance and remission of sins should be preached in his name among all nations". // The Appointment of~ Eternal Dwelling Place Discernment Judgment Time~ shall include nations: Mat25:32 "before Him shall be gathered all nations: and He shall separate them one from another, as a shepherd divideth his sheep from the goats". // God desires a Holy nation: Exo19:6; 1Pet2:9, "And you shall be to Me a kingdom of priests, and an holy nation". // Prayer, or Communion, with God is the Main Intention/ Purpose of a nation: Mar11:17; Deu4:7, "For what nation is there so great, who hath God so nigh to them, as the LORD our God is in all things that we call on him for? Jesus saying ,,,Is it not written, My house shall be called of all nations the house of prayer?". // The Devil/ demons want to deceive, destroy, and assist evil in the nations: Rev20:3; Joh10:10; 1Joh3:8, "And cast him into the bottomless pit, and shut him up, and set a seal on him, that he should deceive the nations no more; has come to destroy; he that sinneth is of the devil". // Jesus desires Joy, Love, Peace in a Nation: Deu32:43; 1Cor13:8; Isa26:3, "Rejoice, O you nations; Charity never faileth: they whose thoughts are kept on the Lord, He shall keep in perfect peace". // God desires to bless nations: Gal3:8 "the scripture, foreseeing that God ,,,In you shall all nations be blessed." // God is God over all nations. His Greatness is, by a comparison with the Material Substance~ as all the water of the Earth is compared to a drop of water in a bucket, ~or~ as the Universe is compared to a piece of dust; ~And~ compared using the spiritual, (unseen), are the thoughts of God and His Being and His ability to Create every Being and Material as compared to nothing, and negative nothing: Isa 40:15, 17 "Behold, the nations are as a drop of a bucket, and are counted as the small dust of the

11

balance; All nations before him are as nothing; and they are counted to him less than nothing, and vanity." // Sin or Righteousness (obedience to God's commands) is the blessing or cursing on a nation: Jer4:2; Mat6:33; Psa9:17; 66:7, "The LORD liveth, in truth, in judgment, and in righteousness; and the nations shall bless themselves in Him, and in Him shall they glory; Seek first the Kingdom of God and His righteousness; The wicked shall be turned into hell, and all the nations that forget God; his eyes behold the nations: let not the rebellious exalt themselves".

++++ EVIL SPEAKING (ES): This is going to be a little strange to say, but there is much to be said here. ES is various forms. Christ Jesus does have promises regarding ES. A thought or feeling comes in, or resides in, and so be it in; it may lay in consciousness for awhile, though it may, and best if evil not to; stop the thought and attend to Christ 2Cor10:5. But let that evil rise up to the top and set its wings of waves of sound by the pole of the tongue, and others will see its colors. When such ES occurs then such gets the attention from the Universe Guardian, who manages providence. HSC has the words as Principle Law~ "Evil Speaking".

++++ GOD WANTS GOVERNMENT SOMEHOW: Gen 8-9; Rom 13:1-6; 1Tim 2:1-5; 1Pet 2:13-14; Pro 29. He desires it to be Divine or God centered. If Spiritual Conscience Folk would only follow Christ and obey Him, including GOV Officials or system, then there would be no problem.

++++ 2 Books that are good to read on politics are by William Godbey and Roy Williams (258)(259).

++++ PEACE / WAR: Jesus words, "I did not come to bring peace; I came not for war; I came for war; I came for peace." To commune in prayer, press to the Lord's heart peaceably, and increase in the spiritual kingdom with heart development. But this world is a prepatory place for eternity, and 2 very direct forces are in battle~ they do exist. Even though the eye of man is the work of deceit to refuse truth and look idolatrously at the material things in front of them; Or seductions to influence our thoughts, feelings, affections, concepts, perceptions, ideas and definition of good, evil, and free will. Evil is not unified; and yet unified; Angelic evil are unified with one intention/ purpose~ destroy; and however they do that, they care not. Obviously they would prefer you serve and worship them (idolatrous Evil Beings); but whether you support a monkey story or some other deceit; they'll take it and try it. Wiles of the Demons (Eph 6). Nevertheless, the non-unified status of the world, as there is so much falsity; much of which does not agree to each other. The demons are standing at the ladder and are trying to pull spiritual moral Beings to hell with them. // Now no person should desire war. However the FFOG did study HSC. And these vses as follows show defensive war for safety of life of people in the national security. Exo32; Num 25; 31; 1Sam15; 2Chr23.

++++ WORLDLINESS: It is common knowledge but uncommon application, and common denial, to not come out of the evil world, and not get the evil world attitudes out; as I heard one Christian say it. Sports mania, fashions, trends, evil worldly activities, materialism, vain activities all and more, are surmounting problems on the spiritual status of the internal and external until we do not distinguish/ discern the ways of God.

++++ LAW Of LAND is BASIS of EITHER PEACE and ASSISTANCE TO CHRISTIANS or OPPOSITION: Abraham, Joseph, Moses, Egypt in the Holy Bible, Elijah, Elisha, David, Solomon, Daniel, 3 Hebrew Men, Israelites in the Holy Bible, Vs in NT, Rome's and Christian history since the time of Christ, Europe's turmoil, the Revolutionary War and its cause~ all these because of evils.

++++ Rainbow: We have this amazing spectrum of color that shines brightly in the sky with brilliant blended rays. Should we not take lessons from this kindly display and be encouraged to do our best to be a positive assistance for rightness. God put this in the sky as a reminder of love & evil. Gen9:13-15.

++++ RESPONSIBILITY: Spiritual Conscience Beings will be responsible to God. We may decide good or evil, but we will be responsible for that decision.

++++ RELIGION: We categorize nations in various ways. By their GOV system, location, "race", etc. Religion is one way, the most priority. There are Islam, heathen, Hindu, Christian, etc.

++++ HISTORY (H): What also herein is, is much H. H that is not common knowledge. H that is accurate. H that does not sail a person out to foggy sight and perceptions. H that is concerned with our dear fore-fathers & mothers and the labors that they worked to leave us what was right.

++++ GOVERNMENT & RIGHTEOUSNESS: Martin Luther, part of the Reformation, said he doubted a Christian GOV could ever exist for a whole nation because Spirit Moral folks are often evil not wanting it; and because the Holy Bible shares Christ has a narrow following whichas many like the Broad Way with the wolfs, demons, and evil. Even the religious atmosphere, including parts of Christianity, is inclusive of many falsities and false professors.

++++ GRAMMAR / INABILITY / ENHANCEMENT / NEGLECT / DIFFICULTY To FRAME WITHOUT OFFERING OPPOSITIONAL OPPORTUNITIES: One main reason for this Book and such is the Grammar and inability of the FFOG. It is one thing to change a GOV of a nation; another thing to deceitfully change it; another thing to oppose it; and so on. In the formation of the USA, there was inability to word things in words without great detail to say or form an exacting operation of a GOV. If they said things a specific way, then Beings of evil might put a "spin", change, on the words and begin oppositional activities. They furthermore did not know how, or what exact GOV form to do. They were in much study & prayer. Thus the words they used are general principle words, Principle Law, and are without doubt, have some exegesis involved and subterfuge (difficulty perceiving, conceiving). Thus if exacting dimensions and applications of every sort were given then we would not be having this discussion; or that is, parts of this discussion. And there has been a wrong study and misinterpretation of the words & DOC; sometimes a deficient study or no study.

++++ CHRISTIAN: If Spiritual Moral Beings would assist the Lord Jesus, then this booklet would not be necessary. But evil exists, is active, aggressive somewhat, and requires counteraction; Vain however is the end of it. (Luke 16).

++++ THANKFULNESS, CONSIDERACY, DISHONOR, OTHER BEINGs, and PARENTS: It should be a common attitude of all people to be thankful and to express such honor to other Beings for their work. Will you spit at others work? Christ honored work of foreparents, such as Abraham, Isaac, and Jacob, Rahab, Sarah, Abigail, Mary, John, Paul. And we are to Honor our Parents; and to be unselfish and consider and care for others work. And shall we dishonor and be unthankful to our FFOG for all that right which they did? Shall a person move in to a nice place of shelter, a house, with good foundations and good structure and be protected and have place to habitat and then turn to the builders who worked so hard and spit in their face??

++++ STATEHOOD APPLICATION of GOD: God, Creator, Supreme Ruler, Divine Providence, Lord Jesus Christ, Christianity, Christian DEN is also to be a very significant part of State GOV.

++++ REASONING, CONSCIENCE, and HONESTY TESTS: What we are about to engage in, is as all on earth should recognize, realize, and be alert to; is that our Spiritual Moral Beings existence is on the testing ground of good & evil. Obvious enough. Honesty to truth or lies is easy enough; if one can overcome the inciting or appeals with the pressure of peers; or of money or of hardships. Reasoning tests can be a little more strenuous. Not as difficult if with communion with Christ. However, evidently, some have shared, for EX, that they have experienced difficulty with "evolution". I do not know how they could have a problem with this subject; with an application of a Reasoning Test. Anyhow there are multiple voices, philosophies, religions, and so on, all saying they are right; or some saying their wrong yet inviting to such. Christ said there would be~ Reasoning Problems; and that we must be careful to be honest and maintain a clear conscience, Heb10:22. Reasoning will not void the truth, nor support falsities. What will it be?

++++ ENGLAND or BRITAIN: This Nation has had some negatives done, by only a limited part of the Spiritual folk living there in the past, and is mentioned herein; this does not share names, only some of the national actions as part of public history. However be sure that such does not subtract from the many wonderful actionshould activity done. They have many Christian Cathedrals & Churches & Activities and Spiritual Moral Beings in that land; They have helped many other nations including the USA multiple times, and brought civilization and Christianity (Methodism, Holiness Clubs, Quakers, Salvation Army, Presbyterian, etc.) many times to many nations, including assisting Israel to become a Nation again in the AD 1900's. May Christ assist them to always honor Him and may He bless them and may they know His love. And every nation. Amen!!!

++++ SPIRIT: Who is a spirit? You? I? who? What is a spirit? Affections, emotions, desire, will, conscience, thoughts, reasoning, Intention/ purpose, decisional discernment ability. Good to know ourselves. The FFOG very well knew of the Great Spirit that was existent in every space in the entire world; Although they were confronted with many areas of concern. It is best if the foundation of our Creatorship as a spirit be considerately and affectionately remembered with our concern for governmental subjects.

++++ TIME is a VALUABLE PART: When we are in discussion of Proof and Evidences, the time of occurrence is a very important part. Because some enactment or law is made in the later AD 1800's or early 1900's, for EX, does not equal that such is evidence to support that the GOV should be such and such. Not so. That is not the establishment times of the USA. If a law is made supporting the true USA GOV basis, then it remains as legal. But any actions done after the establishment of the USA GOV and its true basis is an illegal conduct; is against the USA GOV; is a form of treason, lying, stealing, and deceit. The time frame of the building or constructing of the USA is from approx. AD 1400-1870; and surely does not oppose or contradict. Also, or more summarized AD 1400-1800. Incidents occurring in the GOV currently are not the construction or building of it. Amendment options were made available for~ building destruction. The implementation and application of it is the current experience. However this is not what is essentially occurring.

++++ Intention/Purpose Clarification: This Book does not worship any particular people from history. Nor does it claim that some did not have some faults or fail ever in life. Rather the work was provided to the Nation for the said Causes. The Intention/ purpose is to put God 1st Priority, as a Being in Himself; and other Beings to receive all goodness & love.

++++ SOME Whys (Intentions/purposes) of the Book: There are many strange teachings RE our nation. Such as about the CON, the DOI, the various philosophies in the public schools, and etc. The good governments protected Christian lives through history. The cost of our FFOG is a defensive-able work and concern. Posterity is a value to us. Shall we not have a happy nation ? Does God know what Happiness is best ???

++++ RELIGION: For the GOV to abuse religion was a major concern of the FFOG. They knew history and were experiencing the abuse of a pretense in religion at the time. These following are some of the Abuses of religion (only generally stated here, not specifically) that the FFOG were concerned about: A~ false religion; A~ by not applying true religion yet saying they do; A~ by not having true religion; A~ by abusing those that have true religion. Hence, the FFoG constructed some principles that need included; or the GOV will be evil. // An evil GOV is a non-religious GOV. This was well proven and documented by the FFOG. Those thoughts of Truth were constantly maintained by the FFOG.

++++ WHICH ARE YOU ??? Innocently Mistaken? Neglectfully Mistaken? Innocently Deceived? Self Deceived? Knowledgeable ? Now we are all one or two plus of these. Many are engaged and activated in these internal states. Spirit Moral Beings as they are, with such heart characteristics, can be helped about such; if they desire; intend/ purpose. A main question and concern is: God & the CC.

+++

--------------- Chapter 2 ,,,,,,,,,, TRUTH --------------

====== [CONCLUSION]: TRUTH Or LIES (INTENDED/ PURPOSED, NOT INTENDED/ PURPOSELY, Or MISTAKENLY; some of which are INCLUDED):

---T--- The DOI -- "WE HOLD THESE TRUTHS TO BE SELF-EVIDENT".
---T--- From various Congress meeting notes: "Letters of Delegates to Congress: Volume 19 ~ 8/1, 1782 ~ 3/11, 1783 Elias Boudinot to Susan Boudinot -- founded on the TRUTH OF THE GOSPEL ,,,I can assure you in all the Sincerity of TRUTH" - "Letters of Delegates to Congress: Volume 1 - 8/1774 - 8/1775 John Sullivan to John Langdon - Read it with Attention - Consider it well - IT IS THE TRUTH AND THE TRUTH WILL SET YOU FREE" - "Journal of the Congress of the Confederate States of America, 1861-1865 [Volume 5] ,,,4/9, 1862. ,,,We heartily assent to the great FUNDAMENTAL TRUTH" - "The Debates in the Several State Conventions on the Adoption of the Federal Constitution [Elliot's Debates, Volume 1] ,,, Had not your own hearts borne testimony to THIS TRUTH" - "Journals of the Continental Congress, 1774-1789 - At the same time it is a SOLEMN TRUTH" -

"Journal of the Senate of the US of America, 1789-1793 - In full persuasion OF THIS TRUTH" - "Journal of the Senate of the US of America, 1789-1793 - since there is no TRUTH more thoroughly established" - "Journal of the Senate of the US of America, 1789-1793 - the whole greater TRUTH in the result" - "Journals of the Continental Congress, 1774-1789 - pleased to continue to us the light of GOSPEL TRUTHS," - "Journal of the Senate of the US of America, 1789-1793 - Priveleges and Advantages you have above what other Children have, of learning to read and write, of being taught the meaning of the GREAT TRUTHS OF THE BIBLE" - "Journal of the Senate of the US of America, 1789-1793, 1/11, 1790, The Senate assembled: present as on Friday. A message from the President of the US, by Mr. Lear, his Secretary, was read, as followeth: Gentlemen of the Senate: ,,,To the President of the US: Sir: We, the Senate of the US, return you our thanks,,, resuming our deliberations, in the present session, for the public good; and every exertion on our part shall be made to realize, and secure to our country, those blessings, which a GRACIOUS PROVIDENCE has placed within her reach ,,,[[note these terms from the DOI]] ,,,preservation of a free CON: the measures of GOV should, therefore, be calculated to strengthen the confidence that is due to that important TRUTH. ,,,the basis of the wealth and strength of our confederated Republic, must be the frequent subject of our deliberation, and shall be advanced by all proper means in our power ,,,Our cares and efforts shall be directed to the welfare of our country; and we have the most perfect dependence upon your co-operating with us, on all occasions, in such measures as will insure to our fellow citizens the blessings which they have a Right to expect from a free, efficient, and equal, government."

---T--- <u>TRUTH is SUPPORTED and BASIS of USA GOV by FFOG:</u> // "Journal of the Senate of the US of America, Apr 5, 1792, The consideration of the motion made yesterday, "that a committee be appointed ,,,to the Board of Commissioners ,,,that this be done either by actual experiments under the parallel of 45° of latitude complete, or by actual experiments, rectified by due allowances, under any other parallel, where a superiority of means for accurate experiment may promise on the whole greater TRUTH in the result". // "Letters of Delegates to Congress: Volume 10 - 6/1, 1778 - 9/30, 1778 - ,,,still a knowledge of our own rights, and attention to our own interests, and a SACRED respect for the dignity of human nature, have given us to understand the TRUE PRINCIPLES which ought, and which therefore shall, sway our conduct. You begin with the amiable expressions of humanity, the earnest desire of tranquility and peace. A better introduction to Americans could not be devised. ,,,we once laid our liberties ,,,And England, unhappy England, will remember with deep contrition, that these powers have been rendered of no avail by a conduct unprecedented in the annals of mankind. Had your royal master condescended to listen to the PRAYER of millions, he had not thus have sent you. Had moderation swayed what we were proud to call mother country, "her full-blown dignity would not have broken down under her." You tell us that "all parties may draw some degree of consolation, and even auspicious hope, from recollection." We wish this most sincerely for the sake of all parties. America, even in the moment of subjugation, would have been consoled by conscious VIRTUE, and her hope was and is in the justice of her cause, and the JUSTICE of the ALMIGHTY. These are sources of hope and of consolation, which neither time nor chance can alter or take away. You mention "the mutual benefits and consideration of EVILs, that may naturally contribute to determine our resolutions." ,,,a LINE OF CONDUCT EQUAL TO THE DELICACY OF YOUR FEELINGS. You could not but know that men, who sincerely love freedom, disdain the consideration of all EVILs necessary to attain it. Had not your own hearts borne testimony to this TRUTH, you might have learnt it from the annals of your history ,,,of that HOLY land ,,,contempt by every HONEST Whig in America ,,,a RELIGION in common with you: the RELIGION of America is the RELIGION of all mankind. Any person may WORSHIP in the manner he thinks most agreeable to the DEITY; [[Christian DEN referred to; Now observe here that Christian is the Deity; Now the Deity is the Christian God]] and if he behaves as a good citizen, no one concerns himself as to his faith or adorations, neither have we the least solicitude to exalt any one SECT or profession above another. [[DEN referred to]] I am extremely sorry to find in your letter some sentences, which reflect upon the character of his most CHRISTIAN Majesty. It certainly is not kind, or consistent with the principles of philanthropy you profess ,,,a gentleman's character ,,,and that too a near neighbour, and not long since an intimate brother, who besides hath lately given you the most solid additional proofs of his pacific disposition, and with an unparalleled sincerity, which would do honour to other Princes, declared to your court, unasked, the nature and effect of a treaty he had just entered into with these States. Neither is it quite according to the rules of politeness to use such terms in addressing yourselves to Congress, when you well knew that he was their good and faithful ally. It is indeed TRUE, as you justly observe, that he hath at times been at enmity with his Britannic Majesty, by which we suffered some inconveniences: but these flowed rather from our connection with you than any ill-will towards us: At the same time it is a solemn TRUTH, worthy of your serious attention, that you did not commence the present war, a war in which we have suffered infinitely more than by any former contest, a fierce, a bloody, I am sorry to add, an unprovoked and cruel war. ,,,For the TRUTH of these positions I appeal, gentlemen, to your own knowledge. I know it is very hard for you to part with what you have accustomed yourselves, from your earliest infancy, to call your colonies. I pity your situation, and therefore I excuse the little aberrations from TRUTH which your letter contains. At the same time it is possible that you may have been misinformed. For I will not suppose that your letter was intended to delude the people of these States ,,,assurance given that America had reserved a right of admitting even you to a similar treaty, you must be convinced of the TRUTH of my assertions ,,,propositions? ,,,we call GOD and the world to witness that the EVILs ,,,We again make our SOLEMN appeal to the GOD of HEAVEN to decide between you and us. And we PRAY that in the doubtful scale of battle we may be successful, as we have justice on our side, and that the MERCIFUL SAVIOUR ,,,".

---T--- <u>TRUTH is FREQUENTLY RELATED TO and RECEIVED FROM and VALUED as GOD:</u> // Truth is supported by the USA GOV and non-truth is not supported as a relation to GOD: "Letters of Delegates to Congress: Volume 10- 6/1, 1778 - 9/30, 1778 ,,,Morris ,,,Sir William Howe (Or, In His Absence, Sir Henry Dinton), William Eden, And George Johnstone. TRUSTY and well-beloved servants of your SACRED MASTER, in whom HE is well pleased. As you are sent to America for the express purpose of treating with anybody and anything, you will pardon an address from one who DISDAINS TO FLATTER those whom he loves. Should you therefore deign to read this address, your chaste ears will not be offended with the language of adulation, a language you despise. I have seen your most elegant and most excellent letter "to his Excellency Henry Laurens, the President, and other Members of the Congress." As that body have thought your propositions unworthy their particular regard, it may be some satisfaction to your curiosity, and tend to appease the offended SPIRIT of negotiation, if one out of the many individuals on this great Continent should speak to you the sentiments of America. Sentiments which your own good sense hath doubtless suggested, and which are repeated only to convince you that, notwithstanding the narrow ground of ,,,still a knowledge of our own rights, and attention to our own interests, and a SACRED respect for the dignity of human nature, have given us to understand the TRUE PRINCIPLES which ought, and which therefore shall, sway our conduct. You begin with the amiable expressions of humanity, the earnest desire of tranquility and peace. A better introduction to Americans could not be devised. For the sake of the latter, we once laid our liberties ,,,You tell us you have powers unprecedented in the annals of your history. And England, unhappy England, will remember with deep contrition, that these powers have been rendered of no avail by a conduct unprecedented in the annals of mankind. Had your royal master condescended to listen to the PRAYER of millions, he had not thus have sent you. ,,,We wish THIS MOST SINCERELY for the sake of all parties. America, even in the moment of subjugation, would have been consoled by conscious virtue, and her hope was and is in the justice of her cause, and the justice of the ALMIGHTY. These are sources of hope and of consolation, which neither time nor chance can alter or take away. You mention "the mutual benefits and consideration of EVILs, that may naturally contribute to determine our resolutions." As to the former, you know too well that we could derive no benefit from an union with you, nor will I, by deducing the reasons to evince this, cast an insult upon your understandings. As to the latter, it were to be wished you had preserved a line of conduct equal to the delicacy of your feelings. You could not but know that men, who sincerely love freedom, disdain the consideration of all EVILs necessary to attain it. Had not your own hearts borne testimony to this TRUTH, you might have learnt it from the annals of your history. ,,,But should those instances be insufficient, we PRAY you to read the unconquered mind of America ,,,Upon a supposition, however ,,,your countrymen shall be taught wisdom by experience, and learn from past misfortunes to pursue their TRUE interests ,,,To revive MUTUAL AFFECTION is utterly impossible. We freely forgive you, but it is not in nature that you should forgive us. ,,,Onondagas and Tuscaroras. But we will not offend a courtly ear by the recital of those disgusting scenes. Besides this, it might give pain to that humanity which hath, as you observe, prompted your overtures to dwell upon the splendid victories obtained by a licentious soldiery over unarmed men in defenceless villages, their wanton devastations, their deliberate murders, or to inspect those scenes of carnage painted by the wild excesses of savage rage. These amiable traits of national conduct cannot but revive in our bosoms that partial affection we once felt for everything which bore the name of Englishman. As to the common benefits of naturalization, it is a matter we conceive to be of the most SOVEREIGN indifference ,,,On the other hand, such of your subjects as shall be driven by the iron hand of Oppression to seek for refuge among those whom they now persecute, will certainly be admitted to the benefits of naturalization. WE LABOUR TO REAR AN ASYLUM FOR MANKIND, and regret that circumstances will not permit you, Gentlemen, to contribute to a design so very agreeable to your several tempers and dispositions. But further, your Excellencies say, "we will concur to extend every freedom to trade that our respective interests can require." Unfortunately there is a little difference in these interests, which you might not have found it very easy to reconcile, had the Congress been disposed to risque their heads by listening to terms, which I have the honour to assure you are treated with ineffable contempt by every HONEST Whig in America. ,,,or circumscribe it, at their pleasure, for what they might call our respective interests. But I TRUST it would not be to our mutual satisfaction. YOUR "EARNEST DESIRE to stop the farther effusion of blood, and the calamities of war," ,,,We cannot but admire the generosity of soul, which prompts you "to agree that no military force shall be kept up in the different States of North-America without the consent of the general Congress or particular Assemblies,,, do most SOLEMNLY promise [[also observe the use of oaths before God beginning before the CON]] and assure you ,,,consent of the general Congress, and that of the legislatures of those States ,,,assure you that the Congress have not consented, and probably will not consent ,,, And such treaty ,,,so that the British States throughout North-America acting with us, in peace and war, under one common SOVEREIGN, may have the irrevokable enjoyment of every privilege that is short of a total separation of interests, or consistent with that union of force on which the safety of our common RELIGION [[Christianity is here referred to; and religious words from the Holy Bible]] and liberty depends." Let me assure you, gentlemen, that the power of the respective legislatures in each particular State is already most fully established, and on the most solid foundations ,,,you have exposed yourselves to the fatigues and hazards of a disagreeable voyage, and more disagreeable negociation, hath abundant resources wherewith to defend her liberties now ,,,As the States of North-America mean to possess the irrevokable enjoyment of their privileges ,,, Your Excellencies will, I hope, excuse me when I differ from you, as to our having a RELIGION in common with you: the RELIGION of America is the RELIGION of all mankind. Any person may worship in the manner he thinks most agreeable to the Deity; and if he behaves as a good citizen, no one concerns himself as to his faith or adorations, neither have we the least solicitude to exalt any one SECT or profession above another. I am extremely sorry to find in your letter some sentences, which reflect upon the character of his most CHRISTIAN Majesty. ,,,and that too a near neighbour, and not long since an intimate brother, who besides hath lately given you the MOST SOLID ADDITIONAL PROOFS of his pacific disposition, and with an unparalleled sincerity, which would do honour to other Princes, declared to your court, unasked, the nature and effect of a treaty he had just entered into with these States. Neither is it quite according to the rules of politeness to use such terms in addressing yourselves to Congress, when you well knew that he was THEIR GOOD AND FAITHFUL ally. It is indeed TRUE, as you justly observe, that he hath at times been at enmity with his Britannic Majesty, by which we suffered some inconveniences: but these flowed rather from our connection with you than any ill-will towards us: At the same time it is a solemn TRUTH, worthy of your serious attention, that you did not commence the present war, a war in which we have suffered infinitely more than by any former contest, a fierce, a bloody, I am sorry to add, an unprovoked and cruel war. That you did not commence this, I say, because of any connection between us and our present ally; but, on the contrary, as soon as you perceived that the treaty was in agitation ,,,At present America, being engaged in a war with Great Britain, will probably obtain the most honourable terms of peace, in consequence of her friendly connection with France. For the TRUTH of these positions I appeal, gentlemen, to your own knowledge. I know it is very hard for you to part with what you have accustomed yourselves, from your earliest infancy, to call your colonies. I pity your situation, and therefore I excuse the little abberations from TRUTH which your letter contains. At the same time it is possible that you may have been misinformed. For I will not suppose that your letter was intended to DELUDE the people of these States. Such unmanly disingenuous artifices have of late been exerted with so little effect, that prudence, if not probity, would prevent a repetition. To UNDECEIVE YOU, therefore, I take the liberty of assuring your Excellencies, from the very best intelligence, that what you call "the present form of the French offers to North-America," in other words the treaties of alliance and commerce between his most CHRISTIAN Majesty and these States, were not made in consequence of any plans of accommodation concerted in Great-Britain, nor with a view to prolong this destructive war. If you consider that these treaties were actually concluded ,,,and that much time must necessarily have been consumed in adjusting compacts of such intricacy and importance, and further ,,,and the assurance given that America had reserved a right of admitting even you to a similar treaty, you must be convinced of the TRUTH of my assertions. The FACT is ,,,supposition that Congress had acceded to your propositions, and then I ask two questions. ,,,Americans are apt to compare things together, and to reason. The second question I ask is, What security could you give that the British Parliament would ratify your compacts? ,,,has not treated us with too GREAT TENDERNESS. ,,,For your use I subjoin the following creed of every good American. I believe that in every kingdom, state, or empire there must be, from the necessity of the thing, one supreme legislative power, with authority to bind every part in all cases, the proper object of human laws. I believe that to be bound by laws, to which he does not consent by himself or by his representative ,,,utterly inconsistent with every idea of liberty, for the defence of which I have SOLEMNLY pledged my life and fortune to my countrymen; and this engagement I will SACREDly adhere to so long as I shall live. Amen ,,,acknowledge the independence of America, and as Ambassadors ,,,You have told the Congress, "If, after the time that may be necessary to consider this communication, and transmit your answer, the horrors and devastations of war should continue, we call GOD and the world to witness that the EVILs, which must follow, are not to be imputed to Great-Britain." I wish you had spared your protestation. Matters of this kind may appear to you in a trivial light, as meer ornamental flowers of rhetoric, but they are serious things registered in the high chancery of HEAVEN. Remember the awful abuse of words like these by General Burgoyne, and remember his fate. There is ONE ABOVE US, who will take exemplary vengeance for every insult upon his MAJESTY. You know that the cause of America is just. You know that she contends for that freedom, to which all men are entitled. That SHE CONTENDS AGAINST OPPRESSION, RAPINE, AND MORE THAN SAVAGE BARBARITY. The blood of the innocent is upon your hands, and all the waters of the ocean will not wash it away. We again make our solemn appeal to the GOD of HEAVEN to decide between you and us. And we PRAY that in the doubtful scale of battle we may be successful, as we have justice on our side, and that the MERCIFUL SAVIOUR of the world may forgive our oppressors. I am, my LORDS and Gentlemen, The friend of human nature, And one who glories in the title of, An AMERICAN ,,,as "An American." ,,,in the Pennsylvania Packet on July 21, Sept. 19 ,,,Draft Letter to Lord Howe, June 6, 1778,,,".

---T--- <u>TRUTH BASIC APPEAL:</u> Some basics on truth are extremely important to consider. Truth is for help not hurt. There is too much fiction, pretending, movies, and artificial in our society. People are mixing up real & unreal, good & bad, true & false. If we do not get our senses straightened soon, we will have right upside down. We must call on the Lord, and study to discern, and have our senses trained to discern between good & evil. HSC~ Hebrews 4-5.

---T--- <u>Truth is a vital, extreme necessity to Life</u>; or Death: We cannot live without it. Plain fact and common knowledge, but rejected much. It should be very well known by all. TRUTH is a necessary requirement. // Truth: To deny truth is like a ship without a sail on a storm driven sea. // People do not care much whether they are really right or wrong~ it is becoming as such. Sure, people care to be right; It is a basic desire, or tendency to want to be right. However, with evil affections involved, we may want to take our stand as being right when we are actually wrong; because of some relevant intention/ purpose. Sometimes Spiritual Moral Beings say they are right when wrong because of some selfish care. The Lord says this: Pro12:5, 15; 14:12; 16:25 "The way of a fool is right in his own eyes: but he that hearkeneth to counsel is wise ,,,There is a way which seemeth right to a man, but the end thereof are the ways of death ,,,There is a way that seemeth right to a man, but the end thereof are the ways of death." That is a decisive subject. The way that the Lord Jesus wants it is as such: "The thoughts of the righteous are right: but the counsels of the wicked are deceit".

---T--- <u>The Truth is More Than Some Thoughts in our Mind Based on the Definition of Truth:</u> These thoughts are the representation of truth and hold the truth in them. Truth holds the mind & heart together. Truth is mainly a Being; That Being is God. We do not want to separate the Holy Trinity, but we will use Jesus as the Representative of all Three; Jesus said (Joh14:6), "I am the Truth". Thus, to be internally assured of truth, we must go to the origin; The source, or cause, of truth is the subject here. It is impossible to think of anything without a cause. Everything has a cause. What is truth's cause? A Being!! Jesus. Truth did not only come about by a sudden wind blowing in the air; It is not a thing; It is not a piece of paper. Truth is a Person, a Being, Jesus, the very God Himself.

---T--- <u>Truth is Invisible as God is Invisible</u>: "God is a Spirit". John4:24. Such is why God is invisible; because He is a Being, and Beings are invisible. Forms or bodies are not Beings. To know God requires to know Him as a Spirit. Joh4:24.

---T--- <u>TRUTH was the basis for the FFOG GOV Establishment and Their Personal Life</u>. None would say they were going to base the GOV on a lie; nor mistake of truth; including application to their personal life. // Now truth is not relative; This does not say, though that there may not be an exacting of what truth to apply to the GOV as related to which areas to govern, and how to apply such. Nevertheless, the general intention/ purpose and application that they did create was based on truth.

---T--- <u>Definition of Truth</u>: // Loyalty- duty to be faithful; agreeable; apply, to what is right; // Trustworthy- deserving trust; able to be trusted; veracity; // Sincerity- honest; open: motive is not pretentious; // Reality- actual being or existence, as opposed to an imaginary, idealized, or false nature- independent of people's knowledge or perception of them; // Genuine; original, not artificial or synthetic; // Authentic- genuine; original, as opposed to fakery or reproduction; // Honesty~ not cheating, lying, or breaking the law; // Fact- something based on evidence; // Correctness- No errors; // Accuracy- No errors; precise; // Evidence- proof; of the existence or truth of something; or that helps somebody to come to a particular conclusion; // Right- correct: accurate; agreeable with the facts or Evidence; // Constant- remaining the same; not varying with change in other things; // Not FALSE- not conforming to facts or truth; deliberate deception; mistaken; artificial or not genuine; incorrect; // Lawful- authorized by law: permitted or recognized by law; // Legitimate- proof that something is lawful: that a claim or action is lawful or reasonable; // Absolutes- unchangeable, always true; irrefutable; // Perfect- without errors, flaws, or faults; complete; whole; lacking nothing essential; excellent or ideal in every way; // Pure- free from contamination; no impurities; // Definite- clear; precise; distinct; fixed; certain; unquestionable; unmistakable; // Certainty- something inevitable; a conclusion that is beyond doubt; // Actual- real; existing as fact; // Real- actual being or existence, as opposed to an imaginary, idealized, or false nature; independent of people's knowledge or perception of them; genuine; original, not artificial or synthetic, not relative; // Impartial- having no direct involvement or interest; not self-idolatry; not selfishness; not favoring one person or side more than another; // Not dependent on anything; without reference to anything else; without relation to anything else.

---T--- <u>Evidence or Proof defined</u>: Evidence that serves to prove a fact or the truth of something. It is beyond all doubt and irrefutable. Thus, a conclusion can be made that is true, therefore absolute.

---T--- <u>Conclusions &Truth</u>: To make conclusions we have the process as follows: a decision based on facts: a decision made after study of the relevant facts or evidence; the part of a thought for which evidence is presented.

---T--- <u>TRUTH ~or~ FALSE (LIES)</u>: Now, please dear reader, the decision comes down to you, to be honest with the conclusions. What is your intention/ purpose? Truth has no options. What does this explain? That truth is truth and that is all the truth there is. The truth must be accepted or there is no truth. If something is not true, it is untrue. If something is untrue, it is a lie. So it comes down to either truth or lies. It is truth or untruth, truth or lies. Let us not belittle this decision or minimize it; nor be careless or negligent. Let us arise with diligence and priority intention/ purpose. It is either truth or lies, dear heart. Lies may be mistakenly accepted; or deliberately accepted; or negligently accepted. Yet either way they are lies or falsities. An honest, mistaken person may go to heaven and have accepted lies. But the lies will not continue, and all work for lies will have been futile and in opposition to truth (JESUS). The negligent person, who accepts lies, we will leave in God's decision. But the position scares me. The intentional person, who accepts lies intentionally, I strongly plead a warning. Love your neighbor as yourself. This is a command of God. It is an obvious principle that we should all practice. // If you have something to tell to another Spirit Moral Being, especially about a subject of truth or rightness, then you want another person to listen. You only want to share it with them because (intention/ purpose) them to advance in blessing and avoid harm and hurt. But if they do not listen, then a responsibility is to them. Observe the SC: Mar6:11, "And whosoever shall not receive you, nor hear you, when you depart therefrom, shake off the dust under your feet for a testimony against them. Verily I say to you, it shall be more tolerable for Sodom and Gomorrah in the day of judgment, than for that city". Is God making it our responsibility to care for others as we want to be cared for here? Obviously He is.

---T--- <u>Some Bad Heart Attitudes Which Resist The Light</u>: // Ignoring, is a form of scorning. If we ignore some Being trying to tell us truth, then we scorn them; express disrespect. // Maybe a truth thought came to consciousness of the person; time after time, time after time, came to consciousness. Insensitivity, dullness of hearing, hard-heartedness, or such; or refusal to truth; pushed over it, and over it, and over it. Some Spiritual Conscience folk use reasonings against the truth; or they do not apply the reasoning laws based on truth; rather applied falsity reasoning. God has warned in Pro3:5-6 about this sort of reasoning; "do not rely on your own reasoning" (without God); This is a reference, not to the Truth Laws in our mind & conscience, and not to the reasoning at creation which also can be developed in study, but rather to the reasoning that is self-centered. This self-centered reasoning has self as god, or some other idol; yet it connects to self. Therefore it becomes a warped sort of thinking. The mind does not work right when self is king.

---T--- <u>Truth or Lies, my friend</u>: This is our option, and a decision must be made.

---T--- <u>REASONING, PLEASURE, TRUTH</u>: "There is a way which seemeth right to a man: but the end thereof are the ways of death." (Pro14:12; 16:25). This combination is a real prescription for good or for evil. Our reasoning may include the subject of airplanes, clothes washing machines, computers, and so on. We may reason on self, self-denial, God, others, pride, humility, the definition of it all. Some things, in thinking, we have to only trust the heart of God that it is best; and we will not know the definition or reasoning, nor intention/ purpose of it at this time. God is God, and that is all I want; intention/ purpose. Pleasure is involved in various sources and ways. Lusts and desires. Imaginations and self-exaltation. Some may even take pleasure in making themselves look humble before others. Truth is the overall King; He reigns over the reasoning and pleasure; makes explanation of it all; He is in character and in thinking and in material matters; He is in Spirit, spirit, the mind as a tool, and the body; He is the King, and the only option other than lies- falsities. True or False. Pleasure cannot be set against the reasoning of truth inside us~ The Moral Spiritual Laws. Reasoning cannot twist itself against Truth Laws that make reasoning, reasoning. If reasoning is not reasoning, it may be called a form of reasoning, but it is the branch called insanity, or confusion, or contradiction, etc. Pleasure can try to strike at the feelings of fun to go against the thoughts of goodness. This will cause our Being to not be "whole."; we will malfunction; It is a ruining of our personality; we will self-destruct. An automobile may run without any effort or reasoning for awhile. It may seem fun since nothing needed extra time or effort to put oil, water, air, and tires. However, in time, the automobile will be destroyed. No sound, eye, desire, lust, body, or self-pleasure should be able to outwit the Truth that is in our thoughts; and from God. No warped sense of reasoning such as insanity, confusion, or contradiction should be made to outwit truth.

---T--- <u>The Tree - Gen2:17</u>: "But of the tree of the knowledge of good and evil, you shall not eat of it: for in the day that you eatest thereof you shall surely die." Jesus said, "a tree is known by its fruit." The tree grows that which it is; that which it is, is what is its fruit. The tree remind us of the Fall, the sin, and God's atonement; And that nothing inside us should reach out to get more or other than that of wanting God.

---T--- <u>TRUTH & SPIRIT LAWS</u>: These are Self-Evident Laws existing in our hearts & minds; written there by Jehovah Almighty Himself; in the faculty of our comprehension & reasoning & conscience. Jesus asked the Pharisees, "why reason you in your hearts?" in Mar2:8; 8:17; Luk5:22. The reasoning or conceptional faculty is part of our heart. Our heart is the same as our spirit. For instance~ who would not know the truth of such a law as this: "A statement cannot be both true and false". It may be that extra training, or a right desire, or a decision is needed to start in the right direction. Then an eternal dwelling place is connected to what we do with truth & spirit. If a person is insane, then it is either their fault or not. Now if any of these Truth Laws or Interpretation Laws are not written on our comprehension or reasoning or conscience, then they are in the Holy Bible as Revealed; expressed. The Holy Bible relates to all Spiritual Reasoning Beings. Please consider a few of the Basic Truth Laws Or Interpretation Rules for The Book Of Truth. God is very able to keep stacking the lines and precepts so high that it becomes an irrefutable evidence. They have Scriptural basis, as God provided Truth or Interpretation Rules within His Book. Such includes the following vses: Isa28; 1:18, 2Pet1:20; 3:15-16; Rev22:16-25; 2Tim2:15; 3:16; Mat4:4; 5:17-20; 6:31-33; 15:6; Joh10:35; 5:39; 7:17; Rom3:31; 10; 12:1-2; Mar7:8; 1Cor2; 13; 1The5:21; 3:31; Psal119:126; 66:18.

---T--- <u>Add All the Lines Together to Learn What it Says</u>: "line on line, precept on precept, line on line, precept on precept, here a little, there a little." (Isa28). This explains that we observe and include what all the statements say on a specific subject and then make a conclusion.

---T--- <u>Cannot Exclude Parts</u>: Evidence is what the DOCs provide; and history evidence from the FFOG.

---T--- <u>Cannot Add Outside Subjects; and Definitions Cannot be Inserted to What the Words and Sentence or Statement Say</u>: This then is not accepting the truth law, but contrarily making a different one.

---T--- <u>Requires To Be Spiritual; Know God (Jesus & Holy Spirit); and Intend/ Purpose & Decide to Commune with Him</u>: "Come to Me; In Spirit; For God has revealed them to us by his Spirit" (Mat11; Joh4:24; 1Cor2:10); (Note -this is the most important rule). The Heart is also the Spirit- "With the heart man believeth to rightness." (Rom10). Study with the heart, not only the head. We are trying to learn about God and His presence, not a machine. If you do not want God, then what about truth?

---T--- <u>Every Word has a Use for Us and is to be Considered/Included</u>: If a word or fact is omitted then the definition is changed.

---T--- <u>One Statement Cannot Contradict Another One if the Right Explanation is Conceived; if it Does, Then a Different Definition or Explanation to Comprehend it (Unity rule)</u>: The DOCs cannot be separated or broken in pieces; divided. The conclusion is wrong if it makes one contradict another.

---T--- <u>The Laws of Language Must be Affectionately Cared for</u>: Definitions, noun, verb, adjective, pronoun etc. A sentence is a complete unit of thought.

---T--- <u>A part of the Statements or DOCs Cannot be Made Void, or to Say Nothing, or be Subtracted, or to Have None Effect or Not Apply</u>: If one makes a conclusion that voids out a part, then the conclusion is wrong.

---T--- <u>To Be Defined as Not Explaining Nothing</u>: The statements explain, or are defined as what they say; nothing is NOT what they say.

---T--- <u>Deranged, Demented, Depraved</u>: Any Spiritual Moral Being with any rightness and love should not desire this state of Being.

---T--- <u>Laws of Nature (Creation) and of God</u>: This is a truth.

---T--- <u>Little things are Important to God and to be Considered, Every One of Them</u>: It is well said that, "there are sometimes jots and tittles between right and wrong, seemingly small and therefore not small but great." The jot and tittle are the smallest symbols in the Hebrew language. (Mat 5).

---T--- <u>Degree of Evidence Rule</u>: After compiling all the DOCs and statements on a given subject, the majority of the texts will provide evidence that then allows a conclusion decision as to what the explanation is. "Prove all things" 1The5:21. No conclusion can be accepted that is not proved.

---T--- <u>Study Principle</u>: Time is required for study. Meditation is required. The light of reason is required. God will do His part if you will do your part, and that is study. "Study to show yourself approved to God, a workman" 2Tim2:15. Research and compilation on a decided subject(s); to know what is said. Study includes, the studying of the DOCs, our experiences, and sensing of God's presence, all of which are in the spiritual realm. Study also includes the study of creation and providences.

---T--- <u>Righteous Principle</u>: God never writes towards an unrighteous intention or purpose. The FFOG did not purpose to establish unrightness. If it is an unrighteous conclusion, it is not God's. "Seek you first the kingdom of God and his righteousness." Mat6:33.

---T--- <u>Reasonableness Principle</u>: God never gives conclusions of confusion. He is reasonable. He may be strange to us at times, but it will make perfect sense after all the facts are known. "God is not the author of confusion; Come let us reason together; acceptable to God, which is your reasonable service; Do not lean on your own reasoning; God's thoughts are not your thoughts." {1Cor14:33; Isa1:18; 55; Pro3:5-6}. However, to know, we must be saved from our SELF-centeredness in intention/ purpose reasoning or thoughts or ideas or knowledge. Light or the gift of reason is from God. This does not equal, that we do not use our comprehension and reasoning; Truth Laws are in these from creation. What it does explain, is that we do not have self as the rule book, or alone in our thinking, or law book; neither reasoning for self idolatry, nor against God.

---T--- <u>TRUE / FALSE Rule</u>: Statements should not be made false when arriving at a conclusion as to the explanation; or such is in error. The statement must remain true and not be made false. The statement must be true in context and in the statement itself as a "stand-alone" statement. All statements must be kept true. If one is corrupted, and it is connected to other statements, then that interpretation is put on those statements. "A little leaven leaveneth the whole lump." Gal5:9.

---T--- <u>Distortion of the Total by Distortion of the Part(s)</u>: Parts cannot be untrue. If there are parts of the total that are untrue, or falsely made to be untrue, then it effects the total.

---T--- <u>Interpolation</u>: Cannot make a statement say what is not said; written. Cannot insert a definition in to it that does not exist. If the explanation that is inserted in the statement contradicts the statement itself, the definition is wrong and cannot be inserted. No other statement has a basis to offend and insert a possible definition on another statement which contradicts the statement itself or as it reads as a "stand-alone" statement. Interpolation is probably as good a word, as any, for the definition of some of the thinking processes of some Beings. Interpolation is defined as follows: 1- to change or corrupt (as a text) by inserting new and foreign matter; 2- to insert (words) into a text or into a conversation; 3- to insert between other things or parts; 4- to estimate values of (a function) between two known values; 5- to make insertions.

---T--- <u>Strange Way to Talk</u>: Some things are strangely said sometimes. Things are written oddly; in other words, the use of words is strange; or the expressions used to describe; subjects seem to be mixed together sometimes. Some expressions are difficult to perceive in some parts. However, we need to avoid coming at things with a preconceived desire. Sometimes laws (absolute) do not allow for variation; but other times a principle does allow for variation. Strange is better said~ to be unknown. Also not to be assumed, or presumed.

---T--- <u>Self-Evident</u>: Recollect that the fact that truth is necessary for life.

---T--- <u>Heart Requirements Attitudinal to Learn</u>: Humility, honesty, willingness, and rightness. God cannot teach anyone who refuses to be honest, supports evil, has pride, or is unwilling or dishonest. "God resisteth the proud." Jam4. God will not teach them who do not want Him seriously- "If you criest after wisdom as for silver; whosoever will; If any man will do his will, he shall know of the doctrine, whether it be of God, or whether I speak of myself." Pro2; Joh7:17.

---T--- <u>Cooperation is God's Way</u>: Babies are born with a two-part work: one of God's & one of man's; bread is put on the table by both God & man; salvation is part of God's work & part of mans work; so as sanctification. Same with study. You have a part & God has a part. God will not do your part, and you cannot do His part. If you refuse to study, God will refuse to teach. To study is to want and support that want with action; to apply intention/ purpose.

---T--- <u>INTENTION/ Purpose Law</u>: Intents must be considered for they are the purpose of the total action; and without which the action can be interpreted even to be evil. This is the most priority Law; together with the Will & Decisions. More study of this is included later. // Do not make more of a statement than it is intended or purposed for, or states. // Do not make less of a statement than it is intended or purposed for, or states. // No action is conducted without purpose or intent. So the action may be examined, but the intent is more of reality than the action, for it determines whether the person is right or wrong in heart. The body action is only the expression of the intent action.

---T--- <u>Falsification Definition</u>: No statement should be made to be false. All SC is true. Therefore any conclusion on a subject in SC must include all related SCs on the subject; and they must be true. If any are made false, then the wrong conclusion is made on the subject.

---T--- <u>Faction</u>: This is to submit fiction as it is fact. Applications of this are noticed as occurring today, by the Rejection of DOCs of the USA, and of Historical DOCs.

---T--- <u>DO NOT Comprehend</u>: God feels good when we trust Him even when we do not comprehend, but are faithful and obedient all the while. He honors us or shares His glory; or knowledge and mysteries; and His self and splendorous things. It takes a desire, intention/ purpose, and study to know them. What good is it to one who does not desire Him or want Him; does not intend/ purpose Him; and who will not take some time to study His Being; does not care enough to study. Adam Clarke Commentary writes: "the majesty of God ,,,must be seriously studied to be understood, in order that the truth may be more prized when it is discovered. And if it be God's glory thus partially to conceal His purposes ,,,there, face to face: here we know in part; but there we shall know as we also are known". 1Cor13.

---T--- <u>FALSITY ERRORS, LIES, DECEIT, (Sins or Mistakes):</u> // No Basis or Proof for Conclusion. 1The5:21 says, "prove all things". // Direct Conflict with Truth: The false conclusions went in direct opposition to proof. Truth Laws provide enough evidence. // Distortion of the Total by Distortion of the Part: If one part is corrupted, and it is connected to another part, it will insert that conclusion on that other part. The part that is forced does not actually say what it is forced to say. Then this same process is repeated~ forcing the corrupted part (a false conclusion on a part in the beginning) on another part; until the total is corrupted. "A little leaven leaveneth the whole lump", Gal5:9. // A wrong conclusion in one part effects a conclusion in another part. The person will have to force the other pieces to correspond; to fit in their definitions instead of letting them stand; or to be true statements in themselves. This may be how people get to having so many areas of falsities.

---T--- <u>Application Law:</u> The Statements apply to wherever they are said to apply. They do not apply where they are Not said to apply. They do not apply where they say they are not to apply to.

---T--- <u>Law of Deceit or Rejection to Observe Closely the Truth:</u> Following is a statement in the CON with the word "construed". This defined is: "To loosely interpret; to deduce that which is not there; to make inferences or insert what does not exist; infinitive omission". +The CON states~ "and nothing in this CON shall be so construed as to Prejudice,,,". Falsities relate to Construing and also Prejudiceness.

---T--- <u>The Experience of God as a Spirit (Witness of the Spirit):</u> The experience with God as a Spirit; the extreme value, need, and privilege of this experiential Christianity. Feelings: Of course we do not want to ignore the feelings of our Being; these are extremely significant. Feelings come from the body, and from the Spirit, and so on. This is a valuable part of us, and of the Lord, as any are. But we must not let the wrong feelings influence us to falsity. Demons can influence our feelings, even put their demented feelings in to us, as God allows. How vital to beware here and search our Being and search out ourselves; and be in the light of the Lord. Guard our thoughts and interior Being in each part. Intention/ purpose & the Will & decisions can control feelings; actually they are a form of feelings also.

---T--- <u>Define Terms:</u> This is the cry of the comprehending. Cry out for comprehension and wisdom, saith the Lord. Pro1-4. We should ask- what is the definition of a word? Many of the false Interpreters, and Etc., do Not define their Terms (Words & Statements).

---T--- <u>Carefulness:</u> Conclusions about Divine things require extreme carefulness; such is a self-evident principle. Our eternal home, for one, depends on it.

---T--- <u>Confusion Law:</u> Beware or be confused. Clarity.

---T--- <u>Clarity Law:</u> Make the way plain and right.

---T--- <u>Law of Contradiction:</u> // One Statement cannot contradict another. // No statement can be both true and false. Note the Light of Nature, or conscience and reasoning. Those who inevitably accept falsities are deceived. All non-truth is a lie, and this lie will cause the heart to become insensitive and hardened to God's presence & expressions. // This is a law written on our hearts, in our reasoning and conscience~ from creation. It is part of truth, in our Being, from our Creator, that makes us higher than the animals; and in the image of God. It is also found in Holy SC, in hundreds of places. Some of the vses have already been shown. // The Law of Contradiction has many aspects; following are some of them. // One part cannot contradict another. // A statement cannot be both true and false~ a statement (idea, proposition, vs, sentence) must be true as it is without any explanation inserted into it. It may not be the complete explanation. // It must be true by itself. When fitting a statement into the subject of study as a total, it cannot be made false in itself. // No explanation can be inserted in to a statement, with extra thoughts, to say something different than what it says by itself; or this also makes it false. All statements shall be true and valid. // EX: When a statement is intended/ purposed to be accepted as the controlling statement in a DOC, where it is documental truth. // A false conclusion may show some statements as being true, in other words, to be a true statement in itself; however the statement may really be only true with a false definition of a word that the false conclusion maintains as the real definition; including that if a rejection occurs of a word definition that includes all the explanation that it has, and/or limits the word to a part definition. A few SC references for the Law of Contradiction are as follows: Heb12:3; 7:7; Act13:45; 17:2; 18:4; Mic6:1-2. // Cautionary to Law of Contradiction, is that, this law must be applied carefully. It is not to make a statement say that which it does not. And it cannot be applied to subjects without knowing all the facts or parts; or having no knowledge on the function of the subject; or without knowing the intention/ purpose. Many subjects have such detail that this Law cannot be applied because all the options are not known, and therefore contradictions cannot be known.

---T--- <u>Addition or Adding Rule or Law:</u> No definition can be added to make a statement say what it does not say. No other statements may be added to add more explanations to the subject than what are included in the statement by direct reference of principle law.

---T--- <u>Omission or Subtraction Law or Rule:</u> For the conclusion to be complete, accurate, and fully comprehensive, all statements on a specific subject should be included. No statements or words on a subject can be subtracted if they are to be included.

---T--- <u>CONCLUSIONS:</u> Eccl2:13 "Let us hear the conclusion of the whole matter." Or what is the conclusion of all the pieces? What is all the conclusion of this world of good & evil? A conclusion is the last step in a reasoning process. It has been proved, now you make a conclusion. A conclusion is a complete thought that has a subject and something to say about the subject; or that the subject exists. A conclusion is a decision about a subject referencing evidence; the evidence proved it.

---T--- TRUTH: In Our Constitution Constructed as a Being: These Truth Laws are in our Constitution construction: They include Truth Moral Laws and Truth Reasoning Laws. Self-Evident Laws. I have read that they are sometimes called intuition and sometimes other names. It is very needful to know this. Generally I call them Truth Laws of Morality and of Reasoning; but specifically I call them "Self Evident Truth Laws Written on Heart & Mind". Abbreviated in this Book as SETLWHM. // There are other ones in our Being, but these are some discussed specifically in this Book. // Reasoning (R) Faculty used for Necessity and Bad Attitudes of Reasoning: Some Reasoning Beings have tried to so set aside reason, or devalue reason, and to such extent that they have become nearly insane. Others have so valued or idolized it that they become heady and are not intelligent as they claim at all. R is necessary in that we must have some comprehension to not be insane, to have faith, to test revelations, to perceive evidence, to know what we are doing, to have knowledge, and is actually involved in everything. // The Laws are called Self-Evident Laws because they require no evidence; but are the source of evidence themselves. These assist us to know what is truth and what is not. Also, Truth must have a start. EX: If we were to do an experiment on, say, gravity, then we would eventually discover the source of it must be God; we keep observing the causes of it until we find the "first Cause". So it is with truth. We do not keep going back and back and back infinitely; in other words, unlimited returning back and back; but rather there comes a point when the Truth Foundation is found; the stopping point going backwards; or the starting point coming forwards. Thus it is with Self Evident Truth Laws Written on Heart & Mind. They are the Evidence for other evidences and truths that come from them. We do not go infinitely (unlimitedly without stopping) in reverse nor infinitely (unlimitedly) without a start of basis.

---T--- EVIDENCE (Proof) LAWS (A part of the Truth Laws): The Free Will is free to decide to agree and accept truth. However the Will is not free to remove the responsibility to the truth. The mind and all the parts of our internal spirit are constituted, or constructed, with truth. Self-evidence is there, and also other evidences. We must aim our intention/ purpose to God as a Being and His truth as a value. If we do not affectionately care for the truth then it will not help us rather hurt us; the Truth will always, at some time, apply to us; whether we agree or not. Such as when God expresses Himself "knocking"; or we observe creation and by self-evidence know there must be a Creator. Thus the internal, our Being, cannot resist the Truth existing as the Truth. The EV is there and the Will cannot deny it nor remove the responsibility for it. An individual may try to construct lies (deceptions, etc.) but the responsibility and truth remains in them; and will urge them occasionally and constantly together with the calls or invitations of God. One may deny or refuse to agree or accept, but the responsibility and truth confronts them; their reasoning faculty and conscience. The affections, desires, and Will must either inevitably change or they will inevitably be condemned. The Will, affections, desires must have a right intention/ purpose; or a wrong contention or opposition to the truth laws inside and evidences of such; that have been experienced and/or that do exist interiorly, and the responsibility there-from. But the truth, the responsibility, and the evidences will not change one small amount. EV (or Proof) Laws are in our constitution construction and they cannot be denied. The Lord has commanded and made us responsible to realize the Proof (EV) and to study such; and accept such truth. EV (proof) is part of truth. 1The5:21; Eph5:13; Rom12:1-2~ "Prove ALL things; whatever doth make manifest (prove), is light; proving what is acceptable" . Any area that you agree to a lie on, will go to the judgment of God. Hopefully God arrives at the conclusion that you for some innocent reason of intention/ purpose, such as an innocent lack of time, or not actually very mentally able in the area, or were not trained enough or missed something innocently; and then He dismisses it as such. If not eternity is the residence for evil affections, desires, intention/ purpose, and Will decisions. We are not free to deny truth or the EV thereof and responsibility thereof. // FFOG said, "To prove this, let facts be submitted to a candid world." // List of some Evidences: Events in history continue occurring: Holidays; Common Knowledge of today; Self-Evidence Truth Laws written on Heart and Mind; The purpose of the Thanksgiving Holiday; Escape from other governments who opposed true Christianity; the Holy Bible; DOCs; CC (DOI & CON).

---T--- TRUTH & REVELATION: Although truth is in our constitution, by creation construction, there is Truth revealed; that is truth from God on many subjects that we will not have without His revelation. Revealing is an expression from God to teach; it is teaching us that which we do not know. // Regarding self & truth: "Lean not to our own understanding"-Pro3:5-6. Self cannot be on the throne; cannot be the reference point unless it is the Truth Laws created in us by God. We must have God as the primary reference point in our thinking. All else is idolatry!!! It is selfishness. The DOI put "God" as "GOD". // The Holy Bible is God's teaching; reavealings of KN.

---T--- Reasoning's Strangely False: Truth or lies. Observe the reasoning's and feelings of those who failed. Myself have failed. Carnal or reprobate reasoning must be avoided. The 4 Gospels in the Holy Bible tell us some. Luk23:39-43 tells of a thief on the cross that refused Christ, saying, 'if you be Christ save us and yourself"; which agreed with that of the other mockers standing nearby. Why did he not realize Christ was innocent as the other thief, that was on the other cross, did? Why did he not study the subject for honesty? Reasonings. Gen2-3~ tells that Eve kept agreeing along with Satan every time he reasoned out another evil reasoning; against truth or GOD; her desire began to change, and then she intended & decided. Mat13:55~ tells that the Pharisees rejected truth directly for to maintain a doctrine of lies; one time they hastily concluded, 'this is only Joseph the carpenter's son'~ when actually it was Jesus Lord God Messiah. So what if there are questions. God is God, is He not? Cannot He solve the problem? Shall we not trust Him, and conclude for truth; why not seek His presence & Truth?

---T--- <u>TRUTH is REQUIRED For OUR EXISTENCE</u>: // We must realize truth. // Without truth- += there is no explanation to anything or anyone; += no explanation to existence; += no absolutes; += no certainty; += no reality; += none of the distinctions that make up the definition of truth as is seen herein; += no agreement between any Being; in-fact, to enhance on this, there is anarchy, wars, strife, divisions, craziness, and a complete madhouse; += insanity, craziness, wildness, lost state of Being, every way and any way, maniacism; += no way to measure, no standard, no references. // Remember the tests for truth are in all parts of its definition, and includes experience of God; our Creator & Truth, and without Him we cannot exist. // Promises (a few about Truth)- Pro12:19; Psa145:18~ "The lip of truth shall be established for ever: but a lying tongue is but for a moment. The LORD is nigh to all them that call on him, to all that call on him in truth". // Pragmatism ,"Does it work", or "Relativity". Truth King, is not relative. Sometimes King Love forgoes honest mistakes of His subjects on situations of truth in doctrine or such; but the Truth, fact, remains that it was nevertheless a lie. Truth is not measured by saying, for EX, the truth to "live righteous" can be changed. Truth will not diminish or change with how people are living or what they do; neither diminished by a person experiencing such and such defeat, or problem keeping victory, or having failed. God is amazingly merciful! Whether acknowledged rightly in the past, or presently not experiencing well, come UP to the Truth, our standard.

---T--- <u>REASONING (R) LAWS & TESTS</u>: Included in our tests, because that 'God shall have a tried people' (Psa66:10); are those of the R. It is not only obvious from experience, but is all too obvious by observation of the Spiritual Moral people around, history, and all the lies. One Spiritual Moral person~ +=thinks distance is a situation to God so they let a dark cloud gloom over them; possibly some feeling from an evil spirit; +=Others look at the weeds and the apparent disorder of the things on the earth, and conclude evolutionary ideas; +=Others think God is unfair, as to children, double-standard measurements, the justice in this world, the suffering, the various trials, troubles, the pain that may come on the innocent, etc. Remember Eve? (Gen2-3) It hurt God's heart that she turned to evil. Creativity is good but caution must be exercised in our ideas. It is valuable to side with God, remembering that He is perfect love, will always do right, will not neglect duty, gave all on the cross as an all-consuming expression to prove His heart, Love, character. We observe the reasoning failures all around, in the churches, in society, in various deceits and falsities; errors on many doctrinal areas. And refusals to be corrected, either by Christ's humble servant or by God Himself (A Spirit), nor by self-evidence.

---T--- <u>Value of ALL This TRUTH, Witness Expressions of SPIRIT, DOCTRINAL Subjects, Making STRAIGHT the LORD's WAY</u>: It has been said that souls may be lost by activities of the church as much as by sin. Obviously the church activity would therefore be sin, essentially. And that is why God's Presence & Truth is valuable; adding the care of each heart and the Lord's Being to be experienced more. Col3:9 "Lie not one to another, seeing that you have put on the new man".

---T--- <u>LAW of EXCLUSION / INCLUSION (Grouping or Categorizing)</u>: Whenever something is included as a group and categorized as a group with all the things (spirit or material) in the world, then it is~ +=inclusive of some things & +=exclusive of some "things". The group that is categorized is given some definitions or characteristics or features identified that make it included in the group; and which are different from excluded things of the group. // Patrick Henry (in a letter to his daughter AD 1796) wrote, "bad men cannot make good citizens. It is impossible that a nation of infidels or idolaters would be a nation of freemen"; and "I think of religion of infinitely higher importance than politics", and defended that he was a Christian. // Thus infidels and idolaters are 2 oppositional or contrary states of heart to Christianity; one being a rejecter (infidel) and the other being a selector of other gods (idolater). The situation is what the GOV is based, not that all Spiritual Moral Beings are not valuable to the Lord or the USA.

---T--- <u>SINFUL & CARNAL MIND SIGNS</u>: Such minds do not trust, accept, or search the total of the evidence (EX: Holy Bible); only accept parts; look for ways to subtract parts; mix of truth with falsities; reject truth; reject laws of truth; add parts, etc.

---T--- <u>LIES (Falsities & Deceit)</u>: There are debates occurring as to interpretation of the USA CON. People can generally agree on what the text of the Constitution or law says, but they often have problems about interpretation. Falsity is not the answer for pleasure.

---T--- <u>Communication, Word, or Grammar (Word Law) Laws:</u> Statement (Sentence Law) Law and Word Definition Law needs to be clarified. A statement (sentence) made is binding; it is truth that binds together to form a complete thought; it makes KN and KN makes responsibility. A statement (sentence) is defined as from the Capitol letter until the period (.) of the sentence. It must be respected. It must by itself, alone, be True if from God; for it is impossible for God to lie (Heb6:18). Carnality puts a question mark where God puts a period. Changing God's statements is not allowed. God, the Holy Spirit or Jesus will never contradict their own WORD's. Christ said, "man,,, lives not by bread alone, but by every WORD ,,,of God; It is WRITTEN" Mat4:4. // Law of Definitions. // Word Definition Law.

---T--- <u>MISINTERPETING A Book or TEXT</u>: Any sane person knows not to be careless; esp. with Divine subjects. The USA GOV, or all mankind are sourced from Divinity; and the CC (DOI & CON) brought in the Divinity with "God" & "Lord Jesus".

---T--- <u>SPIRIT (Heart) & TRUTH</u>: Truth has been defined extensively. Further attention will assist us by observing the connection of truth & Spirit; that Truth is a Person indeed as Christ said He was the truth. John4. What is a spirit? A thought, a feeling, an affection, a will, a self-consciousness, a reasoning and judgment, an intention/ purpose, and the conscience. What is truth? A thought and a thought is a Being; "as a man thinketh in his heart, so is he", Pro23:7; thought is what a person's heart or spirit is made of, and out of (along with all the other parts); "My Words are Spirit", John6:63. All thoughts or truth has its source with God, as a Being; it is in His construction constitution, what He is made of.

Thus accepting a thought of truth is accepting Jesus; and if we reject it we kill Jesus out of us; depending on the subject, and etc. The seed (Him) of the sower, wants to germinate intensely. A SC statement (Truth thought) is Jesus. // GOD WANTS US TO Receive (facts): not be overcome with evil desires (lusts) or ignore or dismiss it; or accept lies.

---T--- <u>DISORDER - A Result of Sin.</u>

---T--- <u>HABITS:</u> A false conclusion, LIE, agreed or accepted and repeated and/or practiced for a long period of time; such as thinking a wrong thing (thought, motive, feeling, intention, desire, etc.) is not wrong, or that it is right. Or thinking wrong at first, and for awhile, knowing it was wrong, and then applying it in life to agree to it and activating it in your intentions, decisions, desires, and/or body actions; the effects will give it a superficial appearance; can also effect various feelings, to encourage the Will that the falsity subject is acceptable and not to be rejected; of being right or true, (in reality it is not); and feelings will accept; and demons may join to make all the more feel right; but these thoughts, and interior workings, and feelings, are not of God; nor are they truth. The Habit will eventually make it feel and appear true, in reasoning and feeling. How extremely valuable the spiritual realm. AMEN!!

---T--- <u>COMPARISON Rule:</u> With what? with Spirit & with truth.

---T--- <u>Everything the FFOG Intended/ purposed To Do They Intended/ purposed to be TRUE.</u>

---T--- <u>TRUTH (Facts):</u> A reminder is that Truth are facts and facts are truth; and The USA is supported and based on truth (facts): The CC states~ "We hold these truths to be self-evident ,,,To prove this, let facts be submitted to a candid world." Now the fact that Truth is our basis and God, then the following Truth Laws will Absolutely Require their application. All the truths that are in the DOI, CON, DOC, History, in our Spirit, and such are required to apply and with priority; priority is a truth. These are all truths and must be recognized as such, accepted as, valued as, and applied as Truth. The fact is that the Truth is to be supported and we are not to go astray of it or lie (at best innocent deception or mistakenly believe a lie). Truth says to not agree to every doctrine about God or mans' existence or religion. Truth and its existence and value is self-evident; we inherently know this and are responsible for such.

---T--- <u>DOCUMENTARY EVIDENCE or DOCUMENTS of THE USA:</u> These include DOCs such as Journals of Congress; DOI; CON; Judicial Cases; Letters of GOV Officers; William Blackstone's Commentaries on Law; AOC; the Holy Bible; Historical events; etc.

---T--- <u>HISTORY is an EVIDENCE:</u> Carefulness to study history, research, conceptions. Truth is a priority subject~ "Letters of Delegates to Congress: Volume 1 - Aug1774 - Aug1775 ,,,Oct. 9. 1774 ,,,I believe if it was moved and seconded that We should. come to a Resolution that Three and two make five We should be entertained with Logick and Rhetorick, Law, History, Politicks and Mathematicks, concerning the Subject for two whole days, and then We should pass the Resolution unanimously in the Affirmative. ,,,This Day I went to Dr. Allisons Meeting in the Forenoon and heard the Dr.- a good Discourse upon the LORDS SUPPER. This is a Presbyterian Meeting. I confess I am not fond of the Presbyterian Meetings in this Town. I had rather go to CHURCH. We have better Sermons, better PRAYERS, better Speakers, softer, sweeter Musick, and genteeler Company. And I must confess, that the Episcopal CHURCH is quite as agreable to my Taste as the Presbyterian. They are both Slaves to the Domination of the Priesthood. I like the Congregational Way best -next to that the Independent. This afternoon, led by Curiosity and good Company I strolled away to Mother CHURCH, or rather Grandmother CHURCH, I mean the Romish Chappell. Heard a good, short, MORAL Essay upon the Duty of Parents to their Children, founded in Justice and Charity, to take care of their Interests temporal and SPIRITual. This Afternoons Entertainment was to me, most awfull and affecting. The poor Wretches, fingering their Beads, chanting Latin, not a Word of which they understood, their Pater Nosters and Ave Maria's. Their Holy Water-their Crossing themselves perpetually--their Bowing to the Name of JESUS, wherever they hear it- their Bowings, and Kneelings, and Genuflections before the Altar. The Dress of the Priest was rich with Lace -his Pulpit was Velvet and Gold. The Altar Piece was very rich -little Images and Crucifixes about- Wax Candles lighted up. But how shall I describe the Picture of our SAVIOUR in a Frame of Marble over the Altar at full Length upon the Cross, in the Agonies, and the Blood dropping and streaming from his Wounds. The Musick consisting of an organ, and a Choir of singers, went all the Afternoon, excepting sermon Time, and the Assembly chanted--most sweetly and exquisitely. Here is every Thing which can lay hold of the Eye, Ear, and Imagination. Every Thing which can charm and beWITCH the simple and ignorant. I wonder how Luther ever broke the spell,,,". // From Congress CON meeting notes, Table of Contents, History was studied: "Confederacies; Amphictyonic; European ,,,".

---T--- <u>Other State GOV Activity Was Used To Construct the USA GOV:</u> This remark is from the Congress Notes, Table of Contents: "Rhode Island, her Conduct; Elections; TRUE Construction of the Clause,,,". This is only one State or Colony of many that was used as studies for knowledge.

---T--- <u>PRINCIPLE LAW TRUTH:</u> USA, CC (DOI & CON) support PRINCIPLE LAW. // The principles, for EX: of the Holy Bible, as in any subject, are given for an intention/ purpose. // The Law of Contradiction cannot void them, break them, or ignore them. // They must be included, felt, thanked for. // Principle Law is a branch (part) of law that consists in principles that are as statutory law (commands or rules), that may not only specifically apply to one part of life, but rather are to be applied to all parts of life; whether in thinking, feeling, activities, places of attendance, words, actions, dress, intention, etc. Principle Law~ Other words or terms for Principle Law is Guiding Laws, Guiding Rules, Maxims, Proverbs, Universal Truths, etc. All applications are not specified in a Principle Law; but it is of such a design that it can be applied to all parts of life; or discerned as to where and when to apply. Thus in every part, the principle law or guiding rule is applied to that part as a test or guide to determine, discern, decide, if it be good or evil, or truth or lie. // Language difficulty existed at times in USA history. Sometimes general words (Principle Law words) provide more flexibility. Thus there was concern to make abuse limited by Principle Law languages, when conflicting ideas and possible abuse can occur with specific words; this concern with abuse of language was shared by the FFOG; considerations with the writing of the USA DOCs. // EV from John Witherspoon stating~ "reason by tracing facts upwards or reason downward form metaphysical principles". The word "metaphysical" is a word for "spirit". // EV from Congress Meeting notes, 1778-88 ",,,it is very evident that there is a great necessity for perspicuity. In the sweeping clause, there are words which are not plain and evident. It says ,,,this CON, and the laws of the United States which shall be made in pursuance thereof, &c., shall be the supreme law of the land? The word pursuance is equivocal and ambiguous; a plainer word would be better. They may pursue bad as well as good measures, and therefore the word is improper; it authorizes bad measures ,,,(p) Mr. Chairman, I knew that many gentlemen in this Convention were not perfectly satisfied with every article of this CON; but I did not expect that so many would object to this clause. The CON must be the supreme law of the land; otherwise, it would be in the power of any one state to counteract the other states, and withdraw itself from the Union. The laws made in pursuance thereof by Congress ought to be the supreme law of the land; otherwise, anyone state might repeal the laws of the Union at large. Without this clause, the whole CON would be a piece of blank paper. Every treaty should be the supreme law of the land; without this, any one state might involve the whole Union in war. The worthy member who was last up has started an objection which I cannot answer. I do not know a word in the English language so good as the word pursuance, to express the idea <u>meant and intended</u> by the CON. Can any one understand the sentence any other way than this? When Congress makes a law in virtue of their constitutional authority, it will be an actual law. I do not know a more expressive or a better way of representing the idea by words. Every law consistent with the CON will have been made in pursuance of the powers granted by it. Every usurpation or law repugnant to it cannot have been made in pursuance of its powers. The latter will be nugatory and void. I am at a loss to know what he means by saying the laws of the Union will be unalterable. Are laws as immutable as constitutions? Can any thing be more absurd than assimilating the one to the other? The idea is not warranted by the CON, nor consistent with reason." ~See those concerns about usage of such wording? // Here are more from Congress Meeting Notes in 1788 in forming the CON: ",,,It is the goodness of the Constitution we are to examine. We are to exercise our own judgments, and act independently. And as I conceive we are not out of the Union, I hope this CON will not be adopted till amendments are made ,,,It is too unlimited, in my opinion. It may be exercised to the public good, but may also be perverted to a different purpose. Should we get those who will attend to our interest, we should be safe under any Constitution, or without any. If we send men of a different disposition, we shall be in danger. Let us give them only such powers as are necessary for the good of the community." ~See that tells of a concern of the loose wording~ principle wording of the CON; which may be good in some applications and bad in others; and the concern that Christian people in USA GOV Office. // Statements from the "Congress Notes, Table of Contents" for the CON: "Concern over the general principle statements - Sweeping Clause, not plain - EQUIVOCAL AND AMBIGUOUS ,,,System extensive, involving the Principles of Federal GOV ,,,12 Principle on which the CON was formed ,,,102,,, Cognizance of Controversies, 159 ,,,Mr Caldwell - MAXIMS, FUNDAMENTAL PRINCIPLES ,,,".

---T--- <u>TRUTH & RIGHTEOUSNESS:</u> Responsibility to love and accept Truth; not only like it. Also, to love rightness & hate evil. Many Spiritual Moral people have been unashamed, and without hesitation or fear, defiantly or smoothly either way, directly deny truth. They say, "I do not care, I think it is this way; we think it explains such and such"; etc. and so on. They defy or deny or ignore or reject; and excuse all the Laws of Truth for interpretation.

---T--- <u>TRUTH: 3 Methods of Interpreting the CON have been Sometimes Recommended:</u> {1} "Strict Construction" - interprets the DOC to define exactly what it states and no more and no less. Sometimes this method is called Fixed DOC. {2} "Historical approach" - interprets the CON by analyzing its history and what was intended at the time of its writing. {3} "Liberal approach" - views the CON as a 'Living' DOC in the sense that words and phrases must be interpreted in consideration of our modern desires, needs, and not the <u>intent</u> of authors. In concern for such, Justice Scalia opposed the Living DOC method as a philosophy of "conventional fallacy" in which the meaning of the CON is interpreted "...from age to age [as] whatever the society (or perhaps the Court) thinks it ought to mean." ~and at a meeting of the Federalist Society, according to the Associated Press, shared that (as paraphrased)~ it is very wrong thinking to believe that The CON is a living organism because it is a legal DOC which says something and does not say other things. // Now let us be clear with clarity that the strict sense (Strict Construction Method) is the only sense or the DOC is useless. Truth Laws must be applied, or the words are not true. // To use the "Liberal Approach": +Then we would be establishing a different GOV system. This is not using the CON then, but rather making a different GOV. To this, no permission has been given to the USA GOV; not from God nor others. A "Revolution" should occur then if we do not want to use the CC (CON & DOI). Furthermore, the "Liberal Approach" is actually saying "anything goes"; loose morality. This method would remove Truth; "Absolutely" no way to prove what any person(s) might desire to say that they think that it says or applies. This is a form of confusion, insanity, and anarchy. +The "Historical Approach" is to be considered with the "Strict Construction" because some of the principles are not fully explained. All college and professionals know that supporting DOCs are important to interpret what the "Main" DOC is saying on some parts. A short and concise statement of figure may be placed on the paper. But what all was considered or went in to that number or statement. Furthermore Historical DOCs are further EV to support the "Strict Statement"; so as to provide the correct interpretation, definition, and application of such "Main" DOC. Additionally, some of the words may be different in definition, in usage, and in application.

--------- Chapter 3 ,,,,,,,,,, APPEAL to STUDY and EXPERIENCE ------------

++++ APPEAL TO STUDY and SEEK IN EXPERIENCE by PRAYER by SPIRITUAL SENSES by INNER MAN: // What has God commanded, instructed ? "study", 2Tim2:15. // Now study is defined in the Greek (1c) as: to use speed; be prompt; be earnest; diligence; endeavor; labor. In English (1a): busy oneself with; apply oneself; apply the mind to knowledge and understanding; investigation; careful attention; examination; critical exam; meditate; ponder. // What does this explain? CASUAL READING (esp. of the Holy Bible) Misses; is an offense against the lord's command and way to help us. // Seeking also includes, to desire; to observe God's ways; observe by experience; observe responses from God; be alert; respond to God's word and presence; be still sometimes, and let or be active and let; intention/ purpose. // Study God's voice, Holy Bible, interpretation, what subject is being instructed. // We seek for what we desire, intend/ purpose, or want. // Seek in experience God's presence and voice. Sometimes no Church is available, or at least a true one. Maybe there is no Holy Bible or a complete one. There are many areas in life where the guidance of God is needed and no specific Holy Bible vs. is given. The Holy Bible is not made to worship, although it is a sacred instrument; but is intended/ purposed to lead to God in Presence, Spirit. Thoughts must be directed, affections pure, intentions/purposes, and a will to seek God and rightness. To want His guidance; to Seek God's will in providence, in Spirit, in HSC, in all His expressions. He is manager of Providence. Without prayer, one is no Christian and cannot survive long as a Christian. Pro3:5-6 is an excellent promise of God's presence and guidance; a very intense fervent and serious practice of God's presence:~ "trust in the Lord with all your heart and mind; and do not rely on your own reasoning (self alone, "own"); but in all your ways (thoughts too, 2Cor10:5) know, recognize, acknowledge, bring to attention, bring to consciousness God and He will direct and make plain your paths". Psa16:8 says~ "I have set the Lord always before me". Go slow, no haste and set out to work and faith it happen. If we seek, by intention/ purpose, God (want Him; to do right to Him & mankind); then God approves. Heb11:6 tells us to look at the unseen, not seen; God is more real than the demons, more real than the people around, and always right and caring. Let us claim and focus attention, bring to our consciousness, this armor!! // Experience of consciousness is such a significant and serious activity that it cannot be said enough. All we do is conscious experience; consciousness is our existence; it is compared to looking at the wall with a picture on it; it has a view, an unseen view to our existence; sense signals. Doctrine and groups of Moral people that only have some creed thoughts, and then live life without really seriously and intently and reality-wise Not experiencing God, as by communing, learning, and experiencing the light radiating from His Being regularly, are highly mistaken; missing the greatest, most splendid life of all. And the fact of needing help in the experience of temptations, trials, and providential situations, which God, who does not miss the sparrow fall, will neither miss nor be passive, or careless about! // Seeking is to be continuous. // Proof & Carefulness: Some Do Not's: +Non-seriousness, or careless with HSCs. +A thinking that HSC explains such and such only because some think it to be so; or only because other Beings say it so. +Do not feel need of EV. +Refuse to admit to EV when proved. +J.C. Ryle had this to say on PROVING: "Helped the reformation; also called, Right of the Private Judgment; It is Armor; Necessity; Discernment requires proving; Isa8:19~ by the law and by the testimony; 1Cor10:15~ judge what I say; infinite evils by absence of this attitude; go to hell if we do not exercise this; cannot believe what church tells you; do not sit still and accept evil or unknown". +C. Finney & friends assisted the 2nd Great Awakening, with the Salvation Army; which brought God's presence. They studied & communed with God; for EV. They got most of the Christian Doctrines right (accurate). The 1st Great Awakening was more helped by the Moravian Movement & Methodists (earlier group) than any other. // Pro21:30~ "There is no wisdom nor understanding nor counsel against the LORD".

++

---------- Chapter 4 ,,,,,,,,,, USA GOVERNMENT and WHAT IT Consists of
----

++++++++ USA GOVERNMENT And WHAT IT CONSISTS Of WITH ITS PARTS: a] Consisting of Beings: = 5 Beings or Groups of Beings: 1) God, 2) Executive, 3) Legislative (Congress), 4) Judicial, 5) Citizens ~&~ b] Consisting of Basic Operational (Functioning) Parts: = 7 Parts: 1) God, 2) Law, (CC included), 3) Decisions with Intentions/purposes, 4) Executive, 5) Legislative (Congress), 6) Judicial, 7) Citizenship (all Beings in the Nation). // Some of these parts (Beings & Functions) are not fully known, and/or included, and/or valued by many Beings. Thus, such leaves the thinking obscure, dark, confusing, or unknown as what is involved and what to do.

++

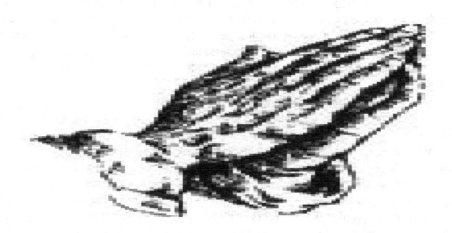

----------- Chapter 5 ,,,,,,,,,, COVENANT CONTRACT ---- Including God and
Religion -----------

====== [Conclusions Proved in this Chapter]:   The MAIN CONCLUSION: THE DECLARATION Of INDEPENDENCE (DOI) and THE CONSTITUTION (CON) is A COVENANT CONTRACT Between God and Government (Executive, Legislative, Judicial, Citizenry) and is The RULING DOC of the USA: ~~~~~~~ {Including Additionally These 5 Connecting Conclusions Proved in this Chapter}: [Conclusions]: [1] Amendments; What They Truly Are;   [2] The Declaration of Independence and The USA Constitution are Godly, Christian Religious Documents; ~and~   [3] They are One Document, or Joint Document, (a Total; a Unit; Each as a Part); ~and~   [4] The DOI is the Ruling (OverRuling or Managing or Controlling) Document of these Two Documents;   ~and~   [5] The CON is a Sub-Document of the DOI Not an Opposition, nor Subtraction, nor Voiding Document to the DOI:

--- Starting Notes:
-------- Covenant Contract is abbreviated as - (CC)
-------- Copies of the Declaration of Independence and the Constitution: I have not herein included a complete copy of the DOI or CON or BOR. However they are quoted much herein. And they are an extremely significant basis reference for this Book and our GOV structure. Thus it is recommended to get copies for your personal library.

++

====== [MAIN CONCLUSION]: THE DECLARATION Of INDEPENDENCE (DOI) And THE CONSTITUTION (CON) IS A COVENANT CONTRACT BETWEEN GOD And GOVERNMENT (EXECUTIVE, LEGISLATIVE, JUDICIAL, CITIZENRY) And Is THE RULING DOC Of THE USA: ~~~ THE LORD OUR GOD MADE A COVENANT WITH US; KNOW THEREFORE That The LORD YOUR GOD, HE Is GOD, THE FAITHFUL GOD, WHICH KEEPETH COVENANT And MERCY With THEM That LOVE HIM And KEEP HIS COMMANDMENTS To A THOUSAND GENERATIONS; I WILL FOR THEIR SAKES REMEMBER The COVENANT Of THEIR ANCESTORS, WHOM I BROUGHT FORTH OUT Of The LAND,,,, Deu 5:2; 7:9; Lev 26:45 ~~~ And Definitions of Covenant Contract (CC):

---T--- Documentary Evidence or Documents of The USA: // These include DOCs such as Journals of Congress; DOI; USA CON; Judicial Cases; Letters of GOV Officers; William Blackstone's Commentaries on Law; Articles of Confederation (the DOC that the CON came from); the Holy Bible; Historical events; The States Documents (which were used in constructing the other documents at times), etc.
---T--- *The USA Government is that of* 5 Being(s), or Groups of Beings (parties) and 7 Parts (as shown in Chpt 4): Such includes God. They are Spiritual Moral Beings.
---T--- *Documental Agreements: The CC is the DOCUMENTAL* Agreements of The USA GOV: // The definition of agreement is (1a): "the fact of agreeing; to consent or accede to; say "yes"; to be in accord; to be of the same opinion; concur; terms; to arrive at a satisfactory understanding; an understanding or arrangement between two or more people, countries, etc.; a contract; settled or determined by mutual consent". // Thus we observe, now obviously, that an agreement was surely the situation with these DOCs. The REPs did that which was agreed by the citizens; and the citizens agreed to hire them as REPs; and the REPs agreed to construct the DOCs that would do that which all the citizens stated that they agreed to. // Agreement is defined as a contract.
---T--- *Following are parts from the DOI -- the Declaration of Independence* -- Some of its Statements: // "A Declaration by the Representatives of the US of America, In Congress Assembled". This is a Declaration, or a proclaiming, of the Covenant Contract that they are entering; or making. // Declaration is defined as (1a): "announcement; formal statement; proclamation". The "Declaration of Independence" is also included in the Dictionary (1a) as: "the formal statement ,,,". And what are they stating, or declaring? +That they are a nation of people of God; +that God is the 1st Priority Being of the GOV; +and that no man or man-made GOV system shall usurp (be before, or take from) the Rights given from God. +What God, is the Christian God; and only God. {all others are gods, or a negative nothing}. // DOI Statements~ ",,,assume, among the powers of the earth, the separate and equal station to which the laws of nature and of nature's God entitle them, a decent respect to the opinions of mankind requires that they should declare the causes [[God is the 1st Cause as the Law of Causes]] which impel them to the separation. We hold these *truths* to be *self-evident* - that all men are created equal; that they are endowed by their Creator [[Creator God identified again]] with certain inalienable rights; that among these are life, liberty, and the pursuit of happiness. That to secure these rights, governments are instituted among men, deriving their just powers from the consent of the governed; that whenever any form of GOV becomes destructive of these ends [[the ends are (intentions/purposes) to God]] it is the Right of the people to alter or abolish it, and to institute a new GOV, laying its foundations on such principles [[principles including that God is God and no idolatry; Principle Laws herein]], and organizing its powers in such form, as to them shall seem most likely to effect their safety and happiness." Now see that statement? They are declaring, making formal statements, that: +God is their 1st priority Ruler or Governor, And, +their Rights come from God, And, +No man or man GOV system shall take the Rights from them, And,

+If any man or man made GOV system tries to take the Rights from God then they are Not to Obey such, And, +that GOV systems are to be made with God and to secure the Rights given from God to men; and thus not oppose them. // The GOV is to respect, with care affection, the subjects (people) in it's domain as God created Beings. That we are all of equal status and importance; loved equally. // DOI Statement~ "Prudence, indeed, will dictate that governments long established should not be changed for light and transient causes;". That statement says that, +Included is carefulness, rightness, and seriousness; Excluded is carelessness, evil, and folly. They are having to oppose a GOV of Spiritual Moral Beings. And the intention/ purpose is stated; which such cause is identified as~ +God to be the Supreme Ruler, +Men to be treated Right & loving, +and Evil opposed. // DOI Statements~ "and, accordingly, all experience hath shown that mankind are more disposed to suffer, while evils are sufferable, than to right themselves by abolishing the forms to which they are accustomed. But when a long train of abuses and usurpations, pursuing invariably the same object, evinces a design to reduce them under absolute despotism, it is their right, it is their duty, to throw off future security." There you read their formal statement that evil is not to be part of the USA GOV; and that anti-Christian God activity is not to be submitted to, or obeyed. Evil is to be limited; it is to have limitations put on it. This is the inclusion of God with the exclusions of unlimited evil. // DOI Statements~ "Such has been the patient sufferance of these colonies, and such is now the necessity which constrains them to alter their former systems of GOV. The history of the present king of Great Britain is a history of repeated injuries and usurpations, all having in direct object the establishment of an absolute tyranny over these states. To prove this, let facts be submitted to a candid world." Then a List from 1 to 27 of sins - evils - done by the British GOV Folk against the USA are stated; and each one is a support of God, Truth, Good vs. Evil; it is included in the DOI DOC. (I did not include the list here for you; see the DOI). // DOI Statement~ "a tyrant, is unfit to be the ruler of a free people". This statement formally declares that, +Free-will against Tyranny, +Evil is opposed & to be limited, +God is to be the Ruler, not men, +True Love is desired, not Tyranny. // DOI Statements~ "Nor have we been wanting in our attentions to our British brethren. We have warned them, from time to time, of attempts by their legislature to extend an unwarrantable jurisdiction over us. We have reminded them of the circumstances of our emigration and settlement here. We have appealed to their native justice and magnanimity, and we have conjured them by the ties of our common kindred to disavow these usurpations, which would inevitably interrupt our connections and correspondence. They, too, have been deaf to the voice of justice and of consanguinity. We must, therefore, acquiesce in the necessity which denounces our separation, and hold them as we hold the rest of mankind - enemies in war; in peace, friends." This is formally declaring that they have been patient and made the warnings; and that their intentions/purposes have been clarified, communicated, reasonable, kind, long-suffering, communicating and open hearted, and been willing to work together. However the evil has continued. // DOI Statement~ "We, therefore, the representatives of the US of America in general Congress assembled, appealing to the Supreme Judge of the world for the rectitude of our intentions". Reading that formal written statement prays again to God as the Governor of all Spiritual Moral Beings and material things; and that they are forming a nation that has God as its Ruler Governor. Also state their intentions to~ +be Right with God, +do right actions, +include God, +not do evil against God and men, +prayer as appeal for a covenant contract with God as the Supreme Judge. // DOI Statements~ "do, in the name and by the authority of the good people of these colonies, solemnly publish and declare that these united colonies are, and of right ought to be, free and independent States; that they are absolved from all allegiance to the British crown, and that all political connection between them and the state of Great Britain is, and ought to be, totally dissolved, and that, as free and independent States, they have full power to levy war, conclude peace, contract alliances, establish commerce, and do all other acts and things which independent states may of right do.". See here them stating a separation from evil. The word SOLEMN is defined as a religious sacred word that identifies again that God is the reason for their separation and freedom from Britain. // DOI Statements~ "And for the support of this Declaration, with a firm reliance on the protection of Divine Providence, we mutually pledge to each other our lives, our fortunes, and our sacred honor. The foregoing declaration was, by order of Congress, engrossed, and signed by the following members: See signatures.". Prayer again here is stated. And in that prayer is a declaring their intentions/ purposes to God; for a covenant contract with God; and with a pledge to God; with a reliance on God, the Divine, and a pledging to Him their all and obedience. // Thus the DOI part of the Covenant Contract is clearly entered and made as the Beginning or Start formation of a new Nation~ under~ "God, Creator, Supreme Judge, Divine Providence". They stated their agreements with Him in 4 instances by using His name in the DOI Document; God is included and priority.

---T--- Covenants, Compacts, History, National Systems studied by our Faithful Friends from cite (2)(2a): // Mr. Gibbs & Mr. Newcombe (2) share~ "The Puritans created Bible-based commonwealths in order to practice a representative government that was modeled on their church covenants". // William Blackstone, from England, (2)(& in His commentaries) shares~ "Law, in its most general and comprehensive sense, signifies a rule of action, and is applied indiscriminately to all kinds of action, whether animate or inanimate, rational or irrational. Thus we say, the laws of motion, of gravitation, of optics, or mechanics, as well as the laws of nature and of nations. And it is that rule of action which is prescribed by some superior, and which the inferior is bound to obey. Thus, when the Supreme Being formed the universe, and created matter out of nothing, He impressed certain principles upon that matter,,,,. Man, considered as a creature, must necessarily be subject to the laws of his Creator, for he is entirely a dependent being. A being, independent of any other, has not rule to pursue but such as he prescribes to himself; but a state of dependence will inevitably oblige the inferior to take the will of him on whom he depends as the rule of his conduct; not, indeed, in every particular, but in all those points wherein his dependence consists,,, consequently as man depends ,,,upon his Maker for everything, it is necessary that he should in all points conform to his Maker's will. This will of his Maker is called the law of nature.,,,, These are the eternal, immutable laws of good and evil, to which the Creator Himself in all his dispensations conforms; and which He has enabled human reason to discover,,,,. Such, among others, are these principles: that we should live honestly, should hurt nobody, and should render to every one his due; to which three general precepts Justinian has reduced the whole doctrine of law,,,,. This law of nature being,,, dictated by God Himself, is of course superior in obligation to any other. It is binding over all the globe, in all countries, and at all times. No human laws are of any validity if contrary to this; and such of them as are valid derive all their force and all their authority, mediately or immediately, from this original". // Mr. David Gibbs, Jr. & III, (2a) share~ "Many critics of Christianity's influence in America note the Constitution does not mention God or the Bible. The Truth is that it didn't need to because the Declaration of Independence had already declared twelve years earlier that its basic principles of freedom, justice, and dependence on God came from the Bible. The Constitution merely added to that foundational document the rules by which its founding principles would be put into practice".

---T--- <u>Supporting DOCs & Supporting</u> Records & Supporting Recorded Events: // These all support that the DOI & CON are a Covenant Contract.

---T--- *<u>They DID NOT declare, say, they are EXCLUDING God; Nor</u>* to be evil (sin), nor to disobey God, nor to commit idolatry: // Rather they DID declare that they are making an agreement to construct and establish a Nation WITH God, Creator, Supreme Judge, Divine Providence, Lord Jesus Christ; and to have His Laws of Creation (Nature) as their rule. This is the Covenant Contract.

---T--- <u>They Declared, Formal Statements, That They (all Branches) Will</u>: // Include~ YOUR~ "laws of nature", & Not Exclude natural laws without YOU God; (Laws of Creation); // Include~ YOU~ "natures God", and NOT Nature itself without YOU God; // Include~ YOU~ the "Creator" of mankind, NOT the creature without YOU the Creator; // Include~ YOU~ the "Supreme Judge", NOT men's discernment without YOU God; // Include~ YOUR~ care of "Divine Providence"; or ~YOU~ to care for us as our Divine Protector~ "Divine Providence", and NOT we do our self-centered life without YOUR Providential Care GOD.

---T--- *<u>DOI &CON referenced as a Covenant Contract with God,</u>* & Christianity, in the Congress Meeting Notes of 1788: // "They certainly have no authority to interfere in the establishment of any religion whatsoever; and I am astonished that any gentleman should conceive they have. Is there any power given to Congress in matters of religion? Can they pass a single act to impair our religious liberties? If they could, it would be a just cause of alarm. If they could, sir, no man would have more horror against it than myself. Happily, no sect here is superior to another. [[DEN]]~ As long as this is the case, we shall be free from those persecutions and distractions with which other countries have been torn. If any future Congress should pass an act concerning the religion of the country, [[this refers to one God, not many gods]]~ it would be an act which they are not authorized to pass, by the CON, and which the people would not obey. Every one would ask, "Who authorized the GOV to pass such an act? It is not warranted by the CON, and is barefaced usurpation." The power to make treaties can never be supposed to include a right to establish a foreign religion among ourselves, though it might authorize a toleration of others ,,,pagans ,,,Mahometans ,,,". // This here rejects~ +falsity gods; +falsity religions, such as Mahometans; +having no god, such as pagans. It supports a~ +Contract of Constitutional Law; +Having God in the Contract. Therefore it is a Covenant Contract.

---T--- <u>The Basis of the USA GOV is Not to be Totally Dependent</u> on Spiritual Creatures in Office; Rather on GOD: // FFOG Patrick Henry in CON congress meetings stated~ "Where are your checks in this GOV? Your strong holds [[a Christian term in the Holy Bible]]~ will be in the nabs of your enemies: it is on a supposition that our American governors shall be honest, that all the good qualities of this GOV are founded: But its defective, and imperfect construction, puts it in their power to perpetrate the worst of mischief's, should they be bad men: And, Sir, would not all the world, from the Eastern to the Western hemisphere, blame our distracted folly in resting our rights upon the contingency of our rulers being good or bad. Shew me that age and country where the rights and liberties of the people were placed on the sole chance of their rulers being good men, without a consequent loss of liberty?" (86).

---T--- *<u>"SUPREME Judge"; the SUPERIOR BEING~ GOD:</u>* // The DOI states God as the Supreme Judge. Now this is His Position over the USA. // The USA GOV is to include and submit to God. Because God is the Supreme Judge, He is the Superior of ALL men; therefore He must be the Superior to the USA GOV; this is stated in the DOI, CON (CC) and all supporting DOCs.

---T--- <u>"CREATOR" of the USA</u>: // The CC DOI claims God as Creator of all. Now if God is the Creator of the Universe, then He is the Creator of this Earth; and if Creator of the Earth, then He is the Creator of the USA Land & Creatures. Therefore He OWNS the USA equally as any person owns their Clay Bowl that they eat their food with. // God has ownership Rights.

---T--- <u>God is the "DIVINE PROVIDENCE"</u>: // Divine Providence is explaining by declaration (a formal statement) in the DOI, that God is the Controller, or the Manager, or the OverRuler~ of all activities, of all Spirit Creatures, of all material substance, of all the world, of all the Universe. Therefore the USA is to include Him as such.

---T--- <u>GOD is GOD as DECLARED (Formal Statement) in the DOI:</u> // Therefore God is God of the USA; to be included; not excluded. // Included as God, not included as a bug on the ground. Thus NO Idolatry.

---T--- <u>"Rights" & Priority of GOD; the Supreme Judge:</u> // Some Rights are Not to be submitted to any form of GOV with men in position. This is one intention/ reason why the DOI and Independence was initiated; to tell England that we have "rights" from God which NO MAN NOR MAN GOV can take from us. Thus these Rights are priority to all men; and therefore GOD MUST BE THE RULER of the USA GOV.

---T--- <u>COMPACT</u>: // <u>The USA GOV is based on a Compact</u>; actually it is a Compact. This word is included in many places in USA DOC. // A Compact is defined as a contractual agreement that includes God. // Statements in the DOC of Congress Meeting Notes of AD 1788 in forming the CON stated that the DOI & CON replaced a Compact: "It was cried out that we were in a most desperate situation, and that Congress could not discharge any of their most Sacred Contracts. I believe it to be the case ,,,The Confederation was binding on all the states ,,,The states are all bound together by the Confederation, and the rest cannot break from us without violating the most SOLEMN COMPACT. If they break that, they will this." // A "Solemn Compact" includes God. A Compact includes God, and using the word Solemn is extra degree to include God in contract. // The word Compact is used many times in the DOC of the USA. We will see more in this study.

---T--- *Statements from Virginia State* GOV, in their formal DOC & State CON; That they knew and agreed to the USA GOV CON; that it was a CC, or Compact; that God was to be included: // "The Virginia Resolution, 12/24, 1798 Resolved, That the General Assembly of Virginia, doth unequivocally express a firm resolution to maintain and defend the CON of the US, and the CON of this State, against every aggression either foreign or domestic, and that they will support the GOV of the US in all measures warranted by the former. ,,,That this Assembly doth explicitly and peremptorily declare, that it views the powers of the federal GOV, as resulting from the <u>COMPACT, *to which the states are parties*</u>; as limited by the plain sense and intention of the *instrument constituting the compact*; as no further valid that they are authorized by the grants *enumerated in that compact*; and that in case of a deliberate, palpable, and dangerous exercise of other powers, *not granted by the said compact,* the states who are parties thereto, have the right, and are in duty bound, to interpose for arresting the progress of the evil, and for maintaining within their respective limits, the authorities, rights and liberties appertaining to them." (14a). Thus, the USA DOI & CON (CC) was very well known as a Covenant Contract, or Compact. All the members knew it because they signed it. A Compact is defined as a contractual agreement that includes God.

---T--- *Statements from Kentucky State GOV &* CON that the USA GOV CON was a compact; that God was included: // "Resolved, That this commonwealth considers the federal union, upon the terms and for the *purposes specified in the late compact, as* conducive to the liberty and happiness of the several states: That it does now unequivocally declare its *attachment to the Union,* and *to that compact, agreeable* to its obvious and *real intention,* and will be among the last to seek its dissolution: That if those who administer the general GOV be permitted to transgress the *limits fixed by that compact, by* a total disregard to the special delegations of power therein contained, annihilation of the state GOVs, and the erection upon their ruins, of a general consolidated GOV, will be the inevitable consequence: That the principle and construction contended for by sundry of the state legislatures, that the general GOV is the exclusive judge of the extent of the powers delegated to it, stop nothing short of despotism; since the discretion of those who administer the GOV, and not the constitution, would be the measure of their powers: That the several *states who formed that instrument, being sovereign and independent, have the unquestionable right to judge of* its infraction; and that a nullification, by those sovereignties, of all unauthorized acts done under colour of that instrument, is the rightful remedy: That this commonwealth does upon the most deliberate reconsideration declare, that the said alien and sedition laws, are in their opinion, palpable violations of the said CON; and however cheerfully it may be disposed to surrender its opinion to a majority of its sister states in matters of ordinary or doubtful policy; yet, in momentous regulations like the present, which so vitally wound the best rights of the citizen, it would consider a silent acquiescence as highly criminal: That <u>although this commonwealth as a party to the federal compact; will bow to the laws of the Union</u>". // A Compact is defined as a contractual agreement that includes God.

---T--- *The Word "Union" is used often in referring* to the CC agreement: // Union is defined as: "A uniting or being united; combination; fusion; grouping together of nations, states, political groups, etc, for some purpose; marrying or being married". Such a "Union" as identified is the "Union" that was accomplished as done by the CC, with the DOI starting it, which plainly states God's Names on it. // Union is not applied to the tree & the leaf. It is applied to the CC & Spiritual Creatures. // This Term is found many times in the DOC of the USA; and referring to such as this.

---T--- <u>COVENANT CONTRACT</u>: // <u>What is a Covenant</u> Contract (CC) ?: It is a contract made with one of the persons, or entities, or Beings included, as required, to be God. Actually a Covenant is a contract. Right terms need stated because of a need to increase full comprehension; And because we need to know what we are to do as the full conditions (expectations, requirements) of the agreement. // Conditions are part of a covenant contract - agreement. All Beings agree to do something and then are bound, or responsible to do, and/or not do, something. // A Covenant is a special form of a Contract where one of the Beings (parties) is God; as stated earlier. // A Marriage Covenant is a contract that includes the man, woman, and God; not only the man & woman. // Contract parts and definitions are as follows {note abbrev~ Contracts (Ct); Agreements, (Ag)}:~ // A Ct is an Ag. Not all Ags are Cts. However all Cts are a form of an Ag; in other words, they include all the parts of an Ag. An Ag that has all the parts of a Ct is a Ct. +And hence, if people assert that the DOI & CON are only an Ag, and not a contract, such is in error; Because the DOI & CON have a contractual agreement~ because all the parts of a Ct exist. // A Ct is an Ag that becomes, or is legally binding. // A Ct is a legally binding set of promises (or promise). // The law requires the parties (Beings) to perform the promises of the Ct. // Nonperformance of the promises of the Ct is called, "breach". There are various intention/ purposes that people do not do what a Ct says; and one is~ because of a "lie". // The 3 necessary parts of a Ct are, - 1) Offer, 2) Acceptance, and 3) Consideration, (also known as that which is given for the offer, in exchange). Conditions are parts; which these parts are also called~ conditions. // Offer is the item, or service, or activity, or thing offered. This is coming from a Being, (parties), to another Being(s). // Acceptance is accomplished by one of the Beings (parties) of the Ct in agreeing with and accepting the Offer; the offer from the other Being. // A Ct is formed by various ways; such as for one way is an Ag: +One method is called an Implied Ct. This is where even though every detail is not written out for the Ct, the Ct exists; and is nevertheless regarded as a legal Ct; because there is a good or sufficient basis to make a Ct. EX: of this would be where 2 persons were in practice of doing business, and then they made an Ag that was not all written out in detail, but nevertheless made. Therefore since on the basis that they were in practice of doing business regularly, this Ag would be considered a Ct. +Another method to form a Ct is by "Express", or "Written Contract" method. This is where all the details are written out. +Another method is~ Oral Cts. +Another method is~ Written Cts. Written Cts may not be written extremely proficient but are nevertheless a Ct. An Express Written Contract has all the details written. // A Ct states that a person(s) will do such and such, in exchange for such and such. // "Consideration" is better known as the motive (intention/ purpose); or price or value which the offer is given for. EX: I will give you an "offer" for a "consideration"; a price or motive, or benefit, etc. // Cts are enforceable by law, if they can be proven. // A Ct is an Ag and often called an Ag. // A Ct includes parties (Beings); identification of Beings or parties; duties; description of goods, services, or things, or the item or activity of value exchanged; and signatures of the Beings (parties). All these things are called conditions. // Cts create a Law. It remains the law until the Ct is changed or fulfilled. // A Ct requires that the Beings (parties) be sane, sober, of age enough to fully comprehend, and responsible of their Being faculties and such. // Contract Defined (1a)(1b): "to draw together; an agreement between two or more entities to do something, esp, one formally set forth in writing; and enforceable by law; compact; covenant; a DOC containing the terms of a contract; to bargain; to make an agreement as between 2 or more persons; an agreement or covenant between two or more persons, in which each party binds himself to do or forbear some act, and each acquires a right to what the other promises; a mutual promise upon lawful consideration or promise upon lawful consideration or cause, which binds the parties to a performance; a bargain; a compact. Contracts are executory or executed; The writing which contains the agreement of parties with the terms and conditions, and which serves as a proof of the obligation". // All Ags are a Ct; or a form of such. Remember an Ag is a Ct when the parts of a contract are included; which parts are as such~ that of 2 or more entities (Beings) making promises to each other of offers and acceptance; The parts of Offer, Value or consideration, Acceptance. // The words in the DOI & CON~ that of "Union" and "Treaty"~ are other words for the same; in other words, these are a form of agreement; as Union & Treaty are special Agreements or special contracts, with specific special names. // The CC (DOI & CON) were intended/ purposed to be binding; and to be an Ag. Observe what all the work and such that the FFOG included, as put as a value~ as consideration, or giving: All their possessions, life in defensive war, the lives of other Beings (citizens), everything they had and were. Promises were claimed by God, as coming from God to us, as towards the citizens (REPs included). And promises were made to God from the citizens (REPs Included). *Thus promises, made as such, is the definition of a contract.* The terms were stated. Also consideration or price (value) was stated; even though this part of a Ct is not necessary for a Ct to exist. The REPs and citizens offered their ALL to make the nation; and they offered their ALL to God. The acceptance was made to be a righteous nation; and to accept or receive the Rights from God. And that these Rights would be not abused but INCLUDE GOD as GOD. // As a USA GOV, we cannot INCLUDE and EXCLUDE God at the same time; as by Contract. // What are these Covenant Contract Terms or Conditions? The Contract is with the USA as a Nation. +This pertains to every decision of the laws and activities of physical matter that occurs on the USA Soil; to a specific extent & about specific subjects. +The Spiritual or unseen is not to be controlled by the USA GOV. +However the USA GOV and State GOV was not to promote or allow evil physical activity on the USA Soil; it is TO BE LIMITED. +Evil includes false religion and false Christianity that commits sin against the 10 commandments. +The doctrines of Christianity were not to be meddled with or controlled by the USA GOV. +Rather Christianity was to be encouraged and supported to itself; to work itself out; to be free and let IT solve itself; Its doctrines, Its practices, etc. // The USA GOV is~ +not to make or control Christianity in all its affairs; to be Christian and support Christianity; +cannot include & exclude God at the same time on any decision of physical activity. // This also states that the USA GOV cannot separate; To separate applies as to what they do and/or what they do not; in other words, they cannot separate from the DOI & CON, the CC; this (separation) is to not be part of the Nation; the USA. // The USA GOV cannot exclude Christianity in everything; It actually must include Christianity in everything; If it excludes Christianity then it begins or initiates opposition; To oppose Christianity is to Breach and commit treason against the CC (DOI & CON). +Public Physical activity is to be monitored with regards to whether it is Christian or not; this, as such stated, is the only area where the USA GOV is to manage all situations; this applies to the limits on evil; and to business activity. +No anti-God or anti-Christ physical activity is to be promoted or allowed on USA Soil in public; Now what is such physical activity? It is discerned and measured as relating to the 10 commandments and the True God, Christ Jesus, including the Holy Bible.

---T--- *TREATY: The DOI & CON (CC) is also called a* Treaty: // The Treaty is between God & the 4 Branches as identified. // A Treaty is defined as: "Any agreement or contract; the documents embodying such an agreement" (1a). // The DOC following is one example of many that state the CC as a Treaty: Congress Meeting notes, 1778-88 ~ "it is very evident that,,, The CON must be the supreme law of the land; otherwise, it would be in the power of any one state to counteract the other states, and withdraw itself from the Union. The laws made in pursuance thereof by Congress ought to be the supreme law of the land; otherwise, anyone state might repeal the laws of the Union at large. Without this clause, the whole CON would be a piece of blank paper. Every TREATY should be the supreme law of the land,,,".

---T--- *Ruling DOC & Constitutional Law: // This Covenant Contract (CC) was* made public as a Ruling Document. This is what is called Constitutional Law. // More studies on Constitutional Laws are through this Book. // It was made Public for the Intention/ purpose to be a Ruling DOC.

32

---T--- *THE CC is to be Basis of the Laws* of the USA: // It is stated in both the DOI & CON. // This is what is said in the CON: "This CON, and the Laws of the United States which shall be made in Pursuance thereof ,,,or which shall be made, under the Authority of the United States, shall be the supreme Law of the Land." This statement is written 2 (Two) Times in the CON. // The DOI states that, "We hold these truths to be self-evident - that all men are created equal; that they are endowed by their Creator with certain inalienable rights; that among these are life, liberty, and the pursuit of happiness. That to secure these rights, governments are instituted among men, deriving their just powers from the consent of the governed; that whenever any form of GOV becomes destructive of these ends [[the ends are (intentions/ purposes) granted by having God as God; over all mankind]] it is the Right of the people to alter or abolish it, and to institute a new GOV, laying its foundations on such principles, and organizing its powers in such form, as to them shall seem most likely to effect their safety and happiness."

---T--- Responsibility to Maintain the Rules of The DOI & CON Covenant Contract with God: // A contract is binding by law (definition of a contract). A contract makes one responsible by the Law. BOTH~ the DOI & CON~ clearly state that the USA is responsible; and that the Creature citizens are responsible to do such Laws: +In the CON~ "This CON, and the Laws of the United States which shall be made in Pursuance thereof; ,,,or which shall be made, under the Authority of the United States, shall be the supreme Law of the Land." +In the DOI~ "Natures Law and Natures God ,,,Rights ,,,abolish ,,,government ,,,Supreme Judge ,,,". // Responsibility in the CC is Stated; this is another part that a covenant contract consist of.

---T--- SACRED Honor to God: "We pledge our ,,,SACRED Honor": // These are the words in the DOI. // The definition of "Sacred" is: "Make a compact; consecrated to or belonging to God; Holy; of or connected with religion or religious rites; regarded with the same respect and reverence accorded holy things" (1a). // This also proves again that the DOI & CON is a Covenant Compact or Contract; That it includes God & religion. // They decided not their words triflingly, but carefully. They intently/ purposely put their life on the line, at risk of death; and all their material possessions. // Sacred is a word that includes God. Note that it says that they are making a sacred pledge. This is that which is consecrated to God.

---T--- Word Laws; Word Definition Law: The CC Truthfully Defines GOD as Included: // Definitions following are from cite (1a). These are also the Definitions that the Supporting DOCs and FFOG used. +=The word "God" is defined as: "Monotheistic Creator; ruler of the universe; eternal; infinite; all powerful; all-knowing; Supreme Being; Almighty; Deity; Magistrate; Supreme Divinity; Divine Father; Jesus Christ; Holy Trinity". +="Supreme Judge or Ruler" is defined as: "God; Jesus Christ; Holy Trinity; highest in Rank, authority; dominant; ultimate; final authority; God that Rules or GOVERNS; authoritative regulation for conduct or action; authority on regulations of a GOV and, or religion; Reign". +="DIVINE" is defined as: "Given or inspired by God, Sacred, Holy; Devoted; religious; theological; Jesus Christ; Holy Trinity". +="Providence" is defined as: "In theology, the care and superintendence which God exercises over his creatures. He that acknowledges a creation and denies a providence, involves himself in a palpable contradiction; for the same power which caused a thing to exist is necessary to continue its existence. Some persons admit a general providence, but deny a particular providence, not considering that a general providence consists of particulars. A belief in divine providence, is a source of great consolation to good men. By divine providence is often understood God himself". +="Creator" is defined as: "The One Who Created All that exists; God". +="Lord" "Jesus Christ" is defined as: "Supreme Authority; God; Jehoshua; Messiah; Anointed".

---T--- To Make a CC with God is to Include Him as God: // Therefore to include God is to include Him as a Being. And what is a Being? God's Being includes His will, thoughts, desires, intention/ purposes, Supreme Conscience, feelings, affections, etc. This is Him as a Being.

---T--- To Include God in a CC is to Include Him in All Parts of the Nation: // God is to be included in all parts of the USA GOV. The GOV is part of the Nation. A GOV cannot oppose God and Include God. This is a contradiction. If parts start to exclude Him then that part of the Nation is excluding Him; then if it increases then more parts exclude Him. Therefore Publicity cannot exclude Him.

---T--- The Laws in this Contract Covenant (CC) Cannot be Destroyed; God lives Forever: // They cannot be altered, void, changed, deleted, or rejected. They may be clarified. // The Amendment clause is explained later in this chapter. // The DOI is Principle Laws: Such Principle Laws are made to stay as a Reference Basis. They are not to be changed in any way. They were constructed to remain as compared to a foundation of a building; such a foundation was to remain as that to be built on; not to be destroyed; only added, not subtracted.

---T--- Michael Farris is a Constitution Attorney that has a book with some legal Truth in it; including this statement: "By basing our right to be a free nation upon God's law, we were also saying ,,,that we owed obedience to the law that allowed us to be ,,,a country ,,,By-laws must be interpreted to be in agreement with the Charter,,,---,,,the Declaration of Independence ,,,the CON of the US must be in agreement with the Declaration" (69).

---T--- Constitutional Law: // Constitution Law includes some parts as following; such is studied more through this Book; including the history of it. // Constitutional Law is the use of a Contract of some sort; which constructs a Foundational Basis for the GOV of a nation. // It is Based of Centered or Referenced to a DOC; It Starts, Activates, and Stops according to the DOC; it functions or operates totally by the DOC. It does not oppose or disagree with the DOC. // It is a DOC containing fundamental laws: a DOC or statute outlining the basic laws or principles by which a country or organization is governed. // It is a written statement(s) of fundamental laws outlining the basic laws or principles by which a country or organization is governed. // Not all nation states have codified constitutions. Most, if not all, have some form of law of the land, which generally is a written form. These may consist of various laws, including customary law, conventional, statutory law, judge-made law, international rules, norms, religious laws, etc. // The United Kingdom, Britain, has had fundamental Laws; ~ law that is composed of statute, case law, and convention law; similar to Constitutional Law; and in all reality, forms of Constitutional Law. Many countries in the world have had the same or similar. Britain's law system has had a Biblical base of which will not be discussed at this time; but later. However it included such as the Magna Charta and Bill of Rights. These are discussed later. // John Locke was an encouragement towards the Fundamental Constitutional Principle. He stated, a "Right of the individual is, that the individual can do anything but that which is forbidden by law, while the state may do nothing but that which is authorized by law". What he is saying is, that an individual has liberty or freedom to do all; They have liberty to do; They have no laws against doing; They only have some laws of "Do Nots". Also what he is saying is, that the Government can not do anything; They only have liberty or freedom to Do Not; They cannot do anything without first asking permission to do it; They have laws against doing; They only have permission to enforce, or do, that of the Do Nots. +This Rule of Law, that John Locke states, is what the CON is based on. What is that? This doctrine, Rule of Law, dictates that GOV must be conducted according to law. // This Law of the CC includes GOD.

---T--- _Constitutional Law Includes a CC; &_ is Not a Democracy: // A Democracy, or a Total Democracy, is where the majority population of the people is the law; and is without Constitutional Laws. However the USA laws are based referenced to Constitutional Laws, and on Christianity and overruling, with Checks & Balances. In other words, a CC. // FFoG state such as follows~,,, // James Madison~ "Democracies have ever been spectacles of turbulence and contention ,,,incompatible with personal security, or the rights of property ,,,short in their lives ,,,violent in their deaths" (202). // John Adams~ "Remember, democracy never lasts long,,, soon wastes, exhausts, and murders itself. There never was a democracy yet that did not commit suicide" and "will soon degenerate into an anarchy ,,,that every man will do what is right in his own eyes and no man's life or property or reputation or liberty will be secure,,, wanton pleasures ,,,capricious will ,,,execrable cruelty of one or a very few" (169a). // Fisher Ames~ "A democracy is a volcano which conceals the fiery materials of its own destruction ,,,known propensity of a democracy is to licentiousness (excessive license) which the ambitious call, and ignorant believe to be liberty" (29). // Gouverneur Morris~ "We have seen the tumult of democracy terminate ,,,as it has everywhere terminated, in despotism ,,,savage and wild ,,,bring down the virtuous and wise to the level of folly and guilt" (219).

---T--- _Constitutional Law proves with Evidence that Constitutional_ Law includes that of a Contract; that with God.

---T--- The AOC which the CON replaced was a Compact (Covenant Contract); & The CON continues that AOC Compact (Covenant Contract); with God: // Statements in the DOC of Congress Meeting Notes of AD 1788 in forming the CON stated that the COMPACT, or AOC, continues to remain in effect; That the CON is only making the Compact better. These are the statements~ "It was cried out that we were in a most desperate situation, and that Congress could not discharge any of their most Sacred Contracts. I believe it to be the case ,,,The Confederation was binding on all the states ,,,The states are all bound together by the Confederation, and the rest cannot break from us without violating the most SOLEMN COMPACT. If they break that, they will this." // Compact is defined as a Covenant Contract with God; as studied herein. // The "Solemn Compact" includes the reference of the seriousness of the breaking. It was identified as a "Solemn Compact"; which is to make it a covenant with God Himself, thus sacred and serious. // They then shared that if they will break this, then they will break the other, because they are both Solemn Compacts (contracts). Once one is broken, an ease of conscience to break another. Breaking is a word related to contracts. // This states that No lesser value was placed on the CON being less than the AOC.

---T--- Not a Democracy in Totality as FFOG declare; Rather a CC with God: // A CC is part of the GOV. To have a total Democracy would be to have only the Vote. // FFOG state~ +John Quincy Adams, "The experience of all former ages had shown that of all human governments, democracy was the most unstable, fluctuating and short-lived" (220). +Benjamin Rush, "A simple democracy ,,,is one of the greatest evils" (97). +Noah Webster, ",,,democracy ,,,there are ,,,tumults and disorders ,,,generally a bad GOV,,, often the most tyrannical GOV on earth" (221). +Zephaniah Swift, ",,,more a GOV resembles a pure democracy the more they abound with disorder and confusion." (141a). +Daniel Webster proclaimed that we need to keep the American Constitution; and that if not then such good things happen rarely and we may not get it back, and there would be anarchy through the world.

---T--- DOCs before the DOI & CON were Christian Godly DOCs; & Also so were the Events & Activities of the USA: // This is EV that they intended positive care to include God. // Such DOCs include the following: +AD 1606 Virginia Charter; +AD 1620 Mayflower Compact; +AD 1629 Massachusetts Bay Colony Charter; +AD 1639 Connecticut Fundamental Orders; +AD 1643 New England United Colonies Charter (139a). // Most other Charters and DOCs were similar. // USA Supreme Judge, John Marshall (AD 1833) says, "One great object of the colonial charters was avowedly the propagation of the Christian faith" (257); +USA Supreme Judge Earl Warren says, "I believe that no one can read the history of our country without realizing that the Good Book and the spirit of the Savior have from the beginning been our guiding ,,,Whether we look to the first Charter ,,,the same objective is present: A Christian land governed by Christian principles" (Time Magazine, Feb 15, 1954). // Early in the USA formation time period, Sir Richard Sutton read a copy of a letter from an American Governor to a Trade Board, and he said, "If you ask an American, 'Who is his master?' he will tell you he has none-nor any governor but Jesus Christ" (256). // Mississippi Supreme Court, in AD 1950's, says, "Our great country is denominated a Christian nation ,,,Our state has even sometimes been referred to ,,,as being in the "Bible Belt". It cannot be denied that much of the legislative philosophy of this state and nation has been inspired by the Golden Rule and the Sermon on the Mount and other portions of the Holy Scriptures".

---T--- It is a Violation of Rights, an Offense against, & a Disrespect of our FFOG & their Work to Destroy the (CC): // The Holy Bible says Jehovah-Immanuel states (KJV Bible): Deu19:14; 27:17, "You shall not remove your neighbor's landmark, which they of old time have set in your inheritance, which you shall inherit in the land that the LORD your God giveth you,,,; Cursed be he that removeth his neighbor's landmark. And all the people shall say, Amen."

---T--- BREACH of~ Covenant or Contract Agreement: // CC (DOI & CON) are also an instrument of Agreement as a form of Covenant or Contract, because they include parts that state that they are not to be Breached; that is they have wording that states that the agreement is not to be violated. Violation is part of the definition of Breach. To oppose (including contradict) is to breach a contract; or violate. Such is illegality to the USA; and to the God of the contracts (covenant).

---T--- Student John Eidsmoe verifies that these documents are covenants and contracts (9).

---T--- The Covenant Contract (DOI with it's CON) establishes a Contractual Covenant Agreement between 5 Beings, or groups of Beings: // Those 5 Beings or groups of Beings are: God, (including His religion), Citizens, Legislative, Executive, Judicial Branches~ (GOV).

---T--- Word FEDERAL is defined as (1a)(1b): // "compact; treaty; of or formed by a compact; designating or of a union of states, which each member agrees to subordinate its governmental power to that of the central authority in certain specified common affairs; Pertaining to a league or contract; derived from an agreement or covenant between parties". // This word was put in to use and applied to the USA GOV by the FFOG in the time period of the DOI & CON (CC).

---T--- The Federal System was Constructed Similar to the State Systems they had already Constructed: // Many States had Covenant Contracts. As is defined, CC is a Contract which includes God. And God was included in the State GOV systems.

---T--- DOI & CON Establish Christ's Christian Subjects : // DOI & CON Laws include following: +DOI and specific laws may not be overruled by majority vote; +Cannot be reversed by voting for ungodly; +It is illegal to vote for the ungodly; +Support of the Holy Bible; +Creation supported; +Evil is illegal; limited; +Despotism - tyrannical or dictatorship; absolute rulers with unlimited powers and abusive; +Powers of GOV come from "God, Creator, Supreme Judge, Divine Providence"; +Tyranny opposed; +Invasion of the Rights of people; +Abuse of GOV is the judges making the laws; +Supreme Judge is God, not man; Supreme is the Highest or most Priority; +Divine Providence is God as our main Provider and Manager of all the Nation; +Creator of all the Nations Material Substance & Spiritual Creatures; +God is God, not Idolatry.

---T--- The Preamble of the CON States that it is Intentioned to Apply God's DOI: // The Preamble states - "We the people of the United States, in order to form a more perfect Union, establish justice, insure domestic Tranquility, provide for the common defense, promote the General Welfare, and secure the Blessings of Liberty, to ourselves and our Posterity, do ordain and establish this CON for the United States of America.". // The DOI is based on GOD; a Covenant with God by Prayer and Written.

---T--- The word "Blessings" in the CON is a word of Christ's Christianity; & the Rights stated in the DOI are those that come from God: // Thus this is EV that God is in both the DOI & CON; and that the DOI & CON go together.

---T--- The word, "ordain" is a godly Holy Bible Christian word; it relates to the priesthood of the OT. // This is part of what the CC do to the spiritual citizens of the USA; It makes them as ordained Priests; priests of the nation and of their personal homes. This concept comes from the Holy Bible. Priest is in the definition of the word "Ordain". It is a "ministerial function". // Such priestliness frees the citizens from Tyranny; putting them directly in God's care as priority. This was compared to the abuse that the Israelites received from Egypt in the OT~ Exo-Deu.

---T--- DOI & CON are a CC with God: // Congress Meeting notes, 1778-88~ "it is very evident that there is a great necessity for perspicuity. In the sweeping clause, there are words which are not plain and evident. It says that "this CON, and the laws of the United States which shall be made in,,, The Constitution must be the supreme law of the land; otherwise, it would be in the power of any one state to counteract the other states, and withdraw itself from the Union. The laws made in pursuance thereof by Congress ought to be the supreme law of the land; otherwise, anyone state might repeal the laws of the Union at large. Without this clause, the whole CON would be a piece of blank paper. Every treaty should be the supreme law of the land; [[A treaty is a contract]] without this, any one state might involve the whole Union in war,,, I do not know a word in the English language so good as the word pursuance, to express the idea meant and intended by the Constitution. Can any one understand the sentence any other way than this? When Congress makes a law in virtue of their constitutional authority, it will be an actual law. I do not know a more expressive or a better way of representing the idea by words. Every law consistent with the Constitution will have been made in pursuance of the powers granted by it. Every usurpation or law repugnant to it cannot have been made in pursuance of its powers. The latter will be nugatory and void. I am at a loss to know what he means by saying the laws of the Union will be unalterable. Are laws as immutable as constitutions? Can any thing be more absurd than assimilating the one to the other? The idea is not warranted by the CON, nor consistent with reason." // This is stating that these are applicable as Contracts to Rule the Nation and that they include God; that the DOI is agreed to and continued as the start of the Nation DOC.

---T--- Created Citizens Responsibility to support Christ's Christianity as part of the GOV: // FFOG John Adams says, "We electors have an important constitutional power placed in our hands ,,,a check upon two branches of the legislature,,, necessary to every subject (citizen) ,,,be in some degree a statesman and to examine and judge ,,,political principles and measures ,,,Let us examine them with a sober ,,,Christian spirit." (169a). +The "elector" and "subject" is the citizen. Hence a Contract with God included.

---T--- <u>From the Congress Meeting Notes Table</u> of Contents, AD 1788, in forming the CON: // "CONSTITUTION MUST BE THE SUPREME LAW, ... 150; Mr. LOCKE -- Constitution grants unlimited Powers,,," // This is Contractual Language.

---T--- <u>Contract Language~ From Congress CON Meeting Notes, Table of Contents</u>: // "Laws supreme; Obligation of Contracts ,,,190".

---T--- *<u>Checks & Balances for God: // The USA System developed</u>* a "Checks & Balances" system because of the sin potentiality (sometimes called), or tendency to evil, or at least the potential of each spiritual person to do evil; or that mankind is temptable to evil; that Creatures in "powerful" positions are potentially dangerous; that we live in a world of good & evil. // Ideally the FFOG knew, as we know, that God, Christ Jesus, being perfect would be the perfect Ruler. However how God and we get that done to mankind is an issue. Thus a "Checks & Balances" system. // Here is the current problem~ God, Christ Jesus and Christianity, is the Check that some Spiritual Creatures are trying to remove and oppose. THE DOI & CON, which include~ God, Supreme Ruler, Creator, Divine Providence, Lord Jesus Christ, the Christian Oath, or Oath to God, and other Holy Biblical subjects, such as religion, is to be put as first priority; NOT IDOLATRY; in the USA and STATE GOV Decisions & activities.

---T--- <u>Compact & Union words both are Covenant Contract EV</u>; they are used repeatedly in DOCs: // From Congress CON Meeting Notes, Table of Contents: "Resolved, That Congress consider the Confederation as a compact between the several States for mutual good: That the Union, under the authority of that Compact, has a right to demand the duties stipulated to be performed by each state, expressed by the Articles of the said Compact". ~That is the AOC DOC; that the CON replaced. The CON continues the AOC; thus it continues the Compact and Union.

---T--- <u>Without the CC (DOI & CON) we are</u> only a group of confused Spiritual Immoral wild Creatures without any known order of organization: // Confusion: If a group of Spiritual Beings want to organize together, then they must communicate. Communication is by words; and then we may either share the word by mouth, and all agree; and also write it on paper, in such an agreement. (Agreements are Covenants and Contracts). Thus this communication was agreed to by the FFOG (the 5 Branches), and written~ the CC.

---T--- <u>The CC (DOI & CON) have Binding Ability & are stated</u> as Applicable to the Nation & as Together: // From Congress CON Meeting Notes, Table of Contents: "LAWS CONSISTENT WITH THE CONSTITUTION BINDING ON THE PEOPLE; POWERS usurped; Powers intended to be given, legal without new Authority, &c ,,,179". // Thus note that the laws of the land were to agree with the DOI & CON; which plainly clarify that these are the overruling DOC of the USA; and has all the definitions and applications of a Covenant Contract. // Binding is a Contractual Term.

---T--- <u>THE 7 CONDITIONS STATED In The CC (DOI & CON)</u>: // NOW note that this CC (DOI & CON), with clarity, with plainness, with absoluteness~ establishes the Laws of the USA to be based on; that is the Governing, or ruling organization - law making society of order - is to be based on these factors as Follows - Law making in the USA has strictness of Love applied and various standards applied with it. // It is limited and confined. The words, "herein granted"; herein refers to inclusions & exclusions. Thus limited to that. Granted is that given from God. // It takes these following Beings (Spirits) to make Laws; they cannot work separately from each other; it is the condition: 1} Congress acceptance - "All legislative Powers herein granted shall be vested in a Congress of the US, which shall consist of a Senate and House of Representatives" ~(from CC). +To be an Officer in the USA GOV requires Christianity and not infidel nor false religion; because required by the Oath; 2} Must be in support of the CC (DOI & CON); 3} NOT in opposition to, rather IN support of the CC (DOI & CON); 4} Acceptance from the Executive Branch; 5} God is to be God of the Nation which is Christianity and His Laws, the Holy Bible; No opposition to, rather to His support as God; God is the Priority Being; 6} Citizen (Every Spiritual Moral Creature) Branch; 7} The Oath requires that Christians be in the Law Making Branches in all Offices that are directly connected to making the Laws. Otherwise any GOV Offices or Positions not directly connected to Law Making or in any GOV Branch Official not directly connected to Law Making, then an oath of agreement to support and not oppose the CC is required; in every public part. // Of these 7 conditions, the CC (DOI & CON) Rules over them all; it is the Covenant Contract; or Written Order under God for the Nation. // These DOC establish the operational foundation and operational application for every Branch; all Spiritual Moral Creatures are included as stated.

---T--- *<u>American citizens are to honor the CC (DOI &</u>* CON) as from GOD; which is included by requiring a pledge: // To become a Spiritual Citizen Creature is to contract with the DOI & CON; and with God~ the priority Being of the CC. Even if people do not decide to be a citizen, they nevertheless are under the authority of the DOI & CON; and God.

---T--- <u>The Agreement was made with God and the Spiritual Moral Creatures here on</u> Earth in the USA: // Now the Agreement should have the conditions done by such. God is always loyal to do His conditions.

---T--- <u>The DOI is a PRAYER to God</u>: // It states, "to the Supreme Judge of the World". It says, "appealing to the Supreme Judge of the world for the rectitude of our intentions ,,,for the support of this Declaration, with a firm reliance on the protection of Divine Providence".

---T--- <u>The DOI is actually a Prayer to</u> God; which is the form of, the start to form, the formation, of a Covenant Contract with God: // The words plainly say they are talking to God. It specifically says, "appealing to the Supreme Judge of the world for the rectitude of our intentions ,,,for the support of this Declaration, with a firm reliance on the protection of Divine Providence". +It also continues to state Principle Laws that are putting God as God over the Nation; that He is 1st priority; that He is where the Rights are coming from, etc.

+++

====== [CONCLUSION About AMENDMENTS]: DOI And CON And AMENDMENTS; AMENDMENTS ARE NOT FOR VOIDING, DELETING, TAKE AWAY, SUBTRACTION, RUINING, OR REPEALING; THE FFOG ESTABLISHED The FUNDAMENTAL TRUTHS; COMPARED To A BUILDING FOUNDATION WHICH ONLY DO BUILD UP And DO NOT DESTROY DOWN; ONLY TO ADD And NOT TO SUBTRACT:

---T--- No reversal of the Christian Doctrines stated in the DOI were ever made in the CON Constitutional Congress Meetings; rather they all supported it; supported it as the Ruling DOC over the CON.

---T--- The Principle Laws of the DOI were totally supported as the Identify of the start of the USA; that they are to be included as the Principle Laws of the USA; that which formed the Nation.

---T--- The DOI has repeatedly been used by the Judicial Branch in courts; including the USA Supreme Court: // as a DOC of the Law of the USA (Multitudes of cases and citations can be produced easily).

---T--- FFOG Thomas Jefferson, had difficulty in determining (discerning) how to apply the Laws and Principle Laws of the CC (DOI & CON). Not all the applications had been written down yet; are not yet today neither. Thus on some things we learn as we go; or it requires further study. However, Mr. Jefferson never removed, nor opposed them as truthfully explained and applied.

---T--- To Void or Reverse the CON is to make it a NO CON (CC) and a NO CON is a NO CON; and thus a Revolution. It is to state or say "NO" to the CON (CC) Ruling in any given area. In reality, The Basics were constructed as absolutes without provision for voiding or deleting.

---T--- The Amending Ability; the Ratification Allowance: // Ratification defined~ "added or passed or accepted". This is not subtracting or removing. Do your Basic Math.

---T--- AMENDMENTS & CHANGES of THE CON: // Reversed: CC Laws are not to be reversed. The Amendment Function excludes reversal from it's definition. // One EX: of such, is that of alcohol (recreational). // Amendments, which are additions, clarifications, or positive increasing adjustments to the CC~ are allowed. // Subtraction. Is to take away from; This is not legal. Because it ruins that which is, or deducts from the total, and leaves only the part; and is therefore stealing or removing that which already has been made as legal which the FFOG constructed. Amendment defined excludes subtraction. Subtraction is not part of the function of Amending. // Revolution would include reversal, or subtraction, or voiding. For this to occur, for EX: a part of the GOV, such as the Spiritual Creature Citizen Branch, must participate in a Revolution. However this has not occurred. // The CON states, "The Congress, whenever two thirds of both Houses shall deem it necessary, shall propose Amendments to this CON, or, on the Application of the Legislatures of two thirds of the several States, shall call a Convention for proposing Amendments, which, in either Case, shall be valid to all Intents and Purposes, as Part of this CON, when ratified by the Legislatures of three fourths of the several States, or by Conventions in three fourths thereof, as the one or the other Mode of Ratification may be proposed by the Congress; Provided that no Amendment which may be made prior to the Year One thousand eight hundred and eight shall in any Manner affect the first and fourth Clauses in the Ninth Section of the first Article; and that no State, without its Consent, shall be deprived of its equal Suffrage in the Senate." // See there that Amendment; in other words, The Amendment Function DOES NOT apply to the DOI. It Does Apply to the CON. // Definition of Amendment (1a): "1. improve or correct something: to make changes to something, especially a piece of text, in order to improve or correct it; 2. revise legislation: to revise or alter formally a motion, bill, or constitution; 3. behave better than before: to behave in a more acceptable way than in the past; 4. alteration to something: a change, correction, or improvement to something; 5. change to legal DOC: an addition or alteration to a motion, bill, or constitution; 6. process of altering something: the process of changing, correcting, or improving something". Webster's (1b), defines it as: "correct, improve, make better, change, revise, remove faults from; To correct; to supply a defect; to improve or make better, by some addition of what is wanted, as well as by expunging what is wrong, as to amend a bill before a legislature". // Therefore we perceive comprehension now. // As is stated, the DOI is Principle Laws; and is First Truths; is Self-Evident Truth Laws Written on Heart & Mind. These are not to be Amended; they are only to be added to; increased; etc. Same with the CON. The CON is the application of the Principle Laws, the First Truths, in the DOI. // The Amendment Function, as defined there above, is only an Adding. Although the definition of Amendment includes various functions, they are all categorized in that of Adding. None of them subtract. There are different methods of Adding. Adding by explaining or applying, or identifying more clearly, etc.

---T--- Expunging Function & Amendment Function: // Expunging includes in its definition~ to correct. +To expunge or correct a wrong requires the need~ that a Wrong exists. And in truth and etc., no wrong exists. +To correct, does not equal the voiding, or subtracting, or reversing. These are not allowed for any subject in the DOI & CON. It is limited to the subject of a WRONG. +Furthermore it is not for subtracting the total statement or principle; rather it is only a correction. Expunging is a corrective function, or to make right. To make right requires that a wrong exists with it. And no such exists. The subjects of the DOI, CON, Supporting DOCs, FFoG, the Common Law, God as placed or put in 1st priority given a position of God as God, are ALL the first priority in discerning a wrong. They are the Rule or Law of how to decide a wrong; they are the standard. Any spiritual conscience person can decide on any subject and claim a wrong or right on it. However that does not make it so!!! // FFoG Samuel Adams said, ",,,the Federal Constitution, according to the mode prescribed therein [Article V], has already undergone such amendments in several parts of it as from experience has been judged necessary" (171). // Basic Principle laws are stated. No subtractions were allowed for. They developed a system to build on, or to develop from, for positive progress; and desired to make statements to communicate that no wrongs are

37

included in these Basic Referential Principle Laws; none to be corrected; rather they are for positive progress; for adding to; not for subtracting from. // No wrongs exist, as also stated by FFOG George Washington warning about Judges or Branches usurping a Right to change the CC, saying: "If, in the opinion of the people, the distribution or the modification of the constitutional powers be in any particular wrong, let it be corrected by an amendment in the way which the Constitution designates. But let there be no change by usurpation, for „,is the „,weapon by which free governments are destroyed" (12b). See that he here warns that destroying the CC and such Branch function, (as the USA is attempting), will destroy the USA; it will not build them; will not help them; it will destroy. It is the work of demons to destroy, John10:10.

---T--- <u>REPEAL ACTION: //</u> The Repeal Action is the action that bans, or reverses, or voids, or subtracts. The Repeal Action is not applicable to the DOI & CON, ∼or CC. // Repeal Actions only can be done to Amendment Actions. Amendments are changes to the CON. An amendment can be repealed. It can be repealed by adding another one in connection to it; in other words, the amendment remains, but notation is added that another amendment repeals it; or applies to it. However as is stated, such actions as that are illegal to do to the DOI; and much to the CON. // Therefore as is proved, a Repeal is not an amendment, and an amendment is not a Repeal. No repeal opportunity is included in the Amendment Option. // However the DOI & CON cannot be changed on the Principle Law; and therefore God as that of Christianity, and the Religion of such, cannot ever be altered. // Amendments are sometimes called Articles.

---T--- <u>AMENDMENTS & REPEALs & the DOI & CON: //</u> Amendment or changing of the DOI is not legal. Those specific basic Principle Laws of the DOI are absolute in their making. Clarification of them, such as include enhancements, applications, and additions are stated as to be legal. // The Repeal action is not legal to the DOI & CON. Repeal includes∼ to deduce; to deduct; to take away; to subtract. These functions are not legal to the DOI & CON. Repeal is only applicable to an Amendment itself. Amendments may be Repealed. The Repeal function can be done to Amendments, but cannot be done to the DOI & CON. // Amendment does not include the definition of Repeal. // Amendments (from Index or table of Contents for Congress Meeting Notes used for the formation of the CON) says: "no Danger apprehended,„ 56 Mr. Lancaster--his Apprehensions for Constitutional Amendments „,212". +What they say here, is that they have made a function called, Amendment. And that they studied, researched, and discussed, if there were dangers, any possibilities, any way that such can be done, that of the Amendment function; as to if the Amendment function could ruin or decrease or subtract or remove the DOI & CON (CC). "Danger" would occur if decreases or subtractions were possible. They already constructed the CC to remain. Obviously the only "danger" of an any function would be to decrease or subtract from the construction of the CC. Hence, the Amendment function or process does not allow decrease or subtraction.

---T--- The FFOG stated the Basic Principle Laws. // No subtractions were allowed for. They developed a system to build on, or to develop from, for positive progress, and desired to state no wrongs to be corrected by progress.

---T--- <u>The Fundamental Principles Laws</u> were established and never to be voided, reversed, subtracted, nor deleted.

---T--- <u>Amendments are to only add or modify</u>; they are limited to that function; not to subtract, remove, or delete.

+++

====== [CONCLUSION]: THE DOI IS A GODLY CHRISTIAN DOCUMENT, THUS RELIGIOUS:

---T--- <u>The DOI is PRINCIPLE LAWS & They are First Tru</u>ths; & Self-Evident Truth Laws Written on the Heart & Mind: // In other words, they are Truths that other truths come from; if you reverse from truths, you end at these Truths; if you start, you start at these Truths, and then go forward or increase. EX: to learn of Who the First Cause is, you finally end at God. You may be the cause of a food meal that you eat; but you are not the First Cause. There are many causes that gave the effect of your meal, including seeds, dirt, rain, water, sunshine, cooking, your hands, etc. However the First Cause is the Cause that caused the sunshine, the rain, the creation of you, the plant seeds, etc. // Thus Principle Law is Laws that are General Laws. In other words, they apply to all parts of the subject that they state. They are not limited to one part. The Principle Laws in the DOI are First Truths, and Self-Evident Truth Laws Written on Heart & Mind. // Who wrote the Truth Laws Written on Heart & Mind ? Who wrote them there ? God did. // First Truths always Remain; they can only be added to, not subtracted; It is impossible to subtract a First Truth; the attempt to subtract a First Truth requires to use it (the 1st Truth) in the process of subtracting; therefore it cannot be removed; such is impossible.

---T--- <u>Principle Laws are Limited as Only To be Added to & Not Subtracted From:</u> // This is what is Truth of Principle Laws.

---T--- <u>The DOI is a PRAYER to God:</u> // It states, "to the Supreme Judge of the World". It says, "appealing to the Supreme Judge of the world for the rectitude of our intentions „,for the support of this Declaration, with a firm reliance on the protection of Divine Providence".

---T--- <u>The DOI is actually a Prayer to God;</u> which is the form of, the start to form, the formation, of a Covenant Contract with God: // The words plainly say they are talking to God. It specifically says, "appealing to the Supreme Judge of the world for the rectitude of our intentions „,for the support of this Declaration, with a firm reliance on the protection of Divine Providence". +It also continues to state Principle Laws that are putting God as God over the Nation; that He is 1st priority; that He is where the Rights are coming from, etc.

---T--- *"SUPREME Judge"; the SUPERIOR BEING~ GOD:* // The DOI states God as the Supreme Judge. Now this is His Position over the USA. // The USA GOV is to include and submit to God. Because God is the Supreme Judge, He is the Superior of ALL men; therefore He must be the Superior to the USA GOV; this is stated in the DOI, CON (CC) and all supporting DOCs.

---T--- "CREATOR" of the USA: // The DOI claims God as Creator of all. Now if God is the Creator of the Universe, then He is the Creator of this Earth; and if Creator of the Earth, then He is the Creator of the USA Land & Creatures. Therefore He OWNS the USA equally as any person owns their Clay Bowl that they eat their food with. // God has ownership Rights.

---T--- God is the "DIVINE PROVIDENCE": // Divine Providence is explaining by declaration (a formal statement) in the DOI, that God is the Controller, or the Manager, or the OverRuler; of all activities of all people of all material substance of all the world of all the Universe. Therefore the USA is to include Him as such.

---T--- GOD is GOD as DECLARED (Formal Statement) in the DOI: // Therefore God is God of the USA; to be included; not excluded. // Included as God, not included as a bug on the ground. Thus NO Idolatry.

---T--- "Rights" & Priority of GOD: //Some Rights are Not to be submitted to any form of GOV with men in position. This is one intention reason why the DOI and Independence was initiated; to tell England that we have "rights" from God which NO MAN NOR MAN GOV can take from us. Thus these Rights are priority to all men; and therefore GOD MUST BE THE RULER of the USA GOV.

---T--- DOI & CON Include the Subjects of Intending to Support Good & Oppose Evil as Defined Truthfully by Christianity; & to Include GOD; as a Check in the Checks & Balances System: // Sin Temptability; in other words, mankind exists in a place of good & evil with temptations to do evil, and possibility of doing evil, was agreed on by the DOI, CON, and FFOG Spiritual Moral Beings. // FFOG John Adams stated that humans are the same as, "since the Garden of Eden" and "no improvements in morals since the days of Jesus" (87); also stated in Federalist Paper 51~ "What is GOV itself but the greatest of all reflections on human nature". // FFOG Gouverneur Morris remarked that the USA CON would not work in France because the evil morals of the French people at that time about religious disrespect, violence proneness, promise breaking, and sexual immorality (9). // FFOG Rev. John Cotton warned of power abuse by GOV saying, "Let all the world learn to give mortal men no greater power than they are content they shall use ,,,unless they be better taught of God,,, they will certainly over-run those that give it, and those that receive it: there is a straine in a mans heart that will sometime or other runne out to excesse, unless the Lord restraine it ,,,Church power or other ,,,It is counted a matter of danger to the State to limit Prerogatives; but it is a further danger, not to have them limited ,,,It is therefore fit for every man to be studious of the bounds which the Lord hath set: and for the People ,,,Magistrates in the Commonwealth ,,,so Officers in Churches should desire to know the utmost bounds of their own power, and it is safe for both,,," (93).

---T--- FFOG Patrick Henry's Paper Near the Time of the DOI & RW prays to God:~ "Give Me Liberty or Give Me Death" states~: // "3/23, 1775 - (p) No man thinks more highly than I do of the patriotism, as well as abilities, of the very worthy gentlemen who have just addressed the house. But different men often see the same subject in different lights; and, therefore, I hope it will not be thought disrespectful to those gentlemen if, entertaining as I do opinions of a character very opposite to theirs, I shall speak forth my sentiments freely and without reserve. This is no time for ceremony. The question before the house is one of awful moment to this country. For my own part, I consider it as nothing less than a question of freedom or slavery; and in proportion to the magnitude of the subject ought to be the freedom of the debate. It is only in this way that we can hope to arrive at the truth, and fulfill the great responsibility which we hold to God and our country. Should I keep back my opinions at such a time, through fear of giving offense, I should consider myself as guilty of treason towards my country, *and of an act* of disloyalty toward the Majesty of Heaven, which I revere above all earthly kings. (p) Mr. President, it is natural to man to indulge in the illusions of hope. We are apt to shut our eyes against a painful truth, and listen to the song of that siren till she transforms us into beasts. Is this the part of wise men, engaged in a great and arduous struggle for liberty? Are we disposed to be of the numbers of those who, having eyes, see not, and, having ears, hear not, the things which so nearly concern their temporal salvation? For my part, whatever anguish of spirit it may cost, I am willing to know the whole truth, to know the worst, and to provide for it. (p) ,,,And judging by the past, I wish to know what there has been in the conduct of the British ministry for the last ten years to justify those hopes with which gentlemen have been pleased to solace themselves and the House. Is it that insidious smile with which our petition has been lately received? (p) Trust it not, sir; it will prove a snare to your feet. Suffer not yourselves to be betrayed with a kiss. Ask yourselves how this gracious reception of our petition comports with those warlike preparations which cover our waters and darken our land. Are fleets and armies necessary to a work of love and reconciliation? Have we shown ourselves so unwilling to be reconciled that force must be called in to win back our love? Let us not deceive ourselves, sir. These are the implements of war and subjugation; the last arguments to which kings resort. I ask gentlemen, sir, what means this martial array, if its purpose be not to force us to submission? Can gentlemen assign any other possible motive for it? Has Great Britain any enemy, in this quarter of the world, to call for all this accumulation of navies and armies? No, sir, she has none. They are meant for us: they can be meant for no other. They are sent over to bind and rivet upon us those chains which the British ministry have been so long forging. And what have we to oppose to them? Shall we try argument? Sir, we have been trying that for the last ten years. Have we anything new to offer upon the subject? Nothing. We have held the subject up in every light of which it is capable; but it has been all in vain. Shall we resort to entreaty and humble supplication? What terms shall we find which have not been already exhausted? Let us not, I beseech you, sir, deceive ourselves. Sir, we have done everything that could be done to avert the storm which is now coming on. We have petitioned; we have remonstrated; we have supplicated; we have prostrated ourselves before the throne, and have implored its interposition to arrest the tyrannical hands of the ministry and Parliament. Our petitions have been slighted; our remonstrance's have produced additional violence and insult; our supplications have been disregarded; and we have been spurned, with contempt, from the foot of the throne! In vain, after these things, may we indulge the fond hope of peace and reconciliation. (p) There is no longer any room for hope. If we wish to be free--if we mean to preserve inviolate those inestimable privileges for which we have been so long contending--if we mean not basely to abandon the noble struggle in which we have been so long engaged, and which we have pledged ourselves never to abandon until the glorious object of our contest shall be obtained--we must fight! I repeat it, sir, we must fight! An appeal to arms and to the God of hosts is all that is left us! They tell us, sir, that we are weak; unable to cope with so formidable an adversary. But when shall we be stronger? Will it be the next week, or the next year? Will it be when we are totally disarmed, and when a British guard shall be stationed in every house? Shall we gather strength but irresolution and inaction? Shall we acquire the means of effectual resistance by lying supinely on our backs and hugging the delusive phantom of hope, until our enemies shall have bound us hand and foot? Sir, we are not weak if we make a proper use of those means which the God of nature hath placed in our power. The millions of people, armed in the holy cause of liberty, and in such a country as that which we possess, are invincible by any force which our enemy can send against us. (p) Besides, sir, we shall not fight our battles alone. There is a just God who presides over the destinies of nations, and who will raise up friends to fight our battles for us. The battle, sir, is not to the strong alone; it is to the vigilant, the active, the brave. Besides, sir, we have no election. If we were base enough to desire it, it is now too late to retire from the contest. There is no retreat but in submission and slavery! Our chains are forged! Their clanking may be heard on the plains of Boston! The war is inevitable--and let it come! I repeat it, sir, let it come. (p) It is in vain, sir, to extenuate the matter. Gentlemen may cry, Peace, Peace - but there is no peace. The war is actually begun! The next gale that sweeps from the north will bring to our ears the clash of resounding arms! Our brethren are already in the field! Why stand we here idle? What is it that gentlemen wish? What would they have? Is life so dear, or peace so sweet, as to be purchased at the price of chains and slavery? Forbid it, ALMIGHTY GOD! I know not what course others may take; but as for me, give me liberty or give me death!".

---T--- At the AD 1787 Constitutional Convention in Philadelphia, Benjamin Franklin declared (as follows) that Christ and His Holy Bible were the Basis of the DOI & CON: // "methinks a melancholy proof of the imperfection of the Human Understanding. We indeed seem to feel our own want of political wisdom, since we have been running about in search of it,,, humbly applying to the Father of lights to illuminate our understanding? In the beginning of the contest with G. Britain, when we were sensible of danger we had daily prayer in this room for the divine protection. [[here is reference to the DOI]] Our prayer, sir, were heard, and they were graciously answered ,,,To that kind providence [[God is the Kind Providence]] we owe this happy opportunity of consulting in peace on the means of establishing our future nation felicity. And have we forgotten that powerful friend? [[God is that friend]] Or do we imagine we no longer need his assistance? I have lived, sir, a long time, and the longer I live, the more convincing, [[proof I see of this truth, that God governs in the affairs of men. And if a sparrow cannot fall to the ground without His notice, [[HSC]] is it probable that an empire can rise without His aid? ,,,We have been assured, Sir, in the Sacred Writings that except the Lord build the house, they labor in vain that build it. I firmly believe this; and I also believe that without His concurring aid, we shall succeed in this political building no better than the builders of Babel ,,,I therefore beg leave to move, that henceforth prayers imploring the assistance of Heaven, and its blessings on our deliberations, be held in the Assembly every morning before we proceed to business, and that one or more of the clergy of this city be requested to officiate in that service". // Roger Sherman seconded B. Franklins motion for prayer. // Jonathan Dayton recorded notes of the meeting which shares that experientially the words of Mr. Franklin "fell upon our ears with a right and authority, even greater than we may suppose an oracle to have had in a Roman senate".

---T--- Elias Boudinot in New Jersey First Provincial Congress stated that the FFOG~ +=were Christians for Christ, += doing Christian Activity, +=by Making the DOI: // "let us enter on this important business under the idea that we are Christians on whom the eyes of the world are now turned ,,,Let us earnestly call and beseech him for Christ's sake to preside in our councils" and "We can only depend on the all powerful influence of the Spirit of God, Whose Divine aid and assistance it becomes us as a Christian people most devoutly to implore. Therefore I move that some minister of the Gospel be requested to attend this Congress every morning ,,,in order to open the meeting with prayer" (189).

---T--- Revolution Peace Treaty with Britain Stated this Opening Remark: // "In the name of the most holy and undivided Trinity" (156).

---T--- Congress Repeatedly Proclaimed Days for Prayer to God: // Such as the Day (10/18, 1783) of prayer and thanksgiving for winning the RW that stated: "Whereas it hath pleased the Supreme Ruler of all human events ,,,a cessation of all hostilities by sea and land, and these US ,,,freedom, sovereignty and independence ,,,acknowledged ,,,the interposition of Divine Providence in our favor ,,,and the citizens ,,,have every reason for praise and gratitude to the God of their salvation ,,,and of our entire dependence on that Almighty Being ,,,the US in Congress assembled, do recommend it to the several States ,,,a day of public thanksgiving that all the people may ,,,assemble ,,,united voices the praises of their Supreme ,,,Benefactor for his numberless favors ,,,and above all that he hath been pleased to continue to us the light of the blessed Gospel and secured to us in the fullest extent the rights of conscience in faith and worship" (58). // Note the DOI & RW was with God as to be worshipped~ +in preparation, in start, and finished with such. And note he states the main intention/ purpose of the USA is~ The Gospel of Jesus Christ to the world !!!.

40

---T--- <u>The DOI is Christian & Godly as John Quincy Adams (FFOG) States:</u> // "The Declaration of Independence first organized the social compact on the foundation of the Redeemer's mission upon earth ,,,and laid the cornerstone of human GOV upon the first precepts of Christianity" and "The Declaration of Independence cast off all the shackles of this dependency"; and "The US of America were no longer Colonies. They were an independent nation of Christians" (184).

---T--- <u>The USA Courts include PRAYER:</u> // During DOI & CON Times (approx.), Prayers are recorded by Newspapers of various States as follows: // NH State~ ",,,the Throne of Grace was addressed by the Rev. Dr. Samuel Haven ,,,1791" (157). // RI State~ ",,,the Throne of Grace in prayer,,," (158). // Mass State~ ",,,The prayer was made,,," (159). // There are other similar newspaper records.

---T--- <u>Christ's Christianity is the Priority Subject of the USA Intention/ purpose</u>, both in Public & GOV; as one British Citizen & GOV Official said to Parliament in AD 1770: // "The people are Protestants; and of that kind which is the most adverse to all implicit submission of mind and opinion ,,,This is a persuasion not only favorable to Liberty but built upon it ,,,All Protestantism ,,,is a sort of dissent. But the religion ,,,in northern colonies ,,,is principle of resistance ,,,Protestant religion"(70).

---T--- <u>*SACRED Honor to God: "We pledge our ,,,SACRED Honor*"*:* // These are the words in the DOI. // The definition of "Sacred" is: "Make a compact; consecrated to or belonging to God; Holy; of or connected with religion or religious rites; regarded with the same respect and reverence accorded holy things" (1a). // This also proves again that the DOI & CON is a Covenant Compact or Contract; That it includes God & religion. // They decided not their words triflingly, but carefully. They intently/purposely put their life on the line, at risk of death; and all their material possessions. // Sacred is a word that includes God. Note that it says that they are making a sacred pledge. This is that which is consecrated to God. // Though the purpose/ intent was self-defense and based on having a "right" from God, it is, nevertheless, a terrible engagement to have to kill people in defensive war; especially when they knew it would send them in to eternity.

---T--- <u>Absence Law:</u> // There is absolutely no DOC, nor historical supporting DOC, nor life evidence from any FFOG, nor any promoting or allowance of, or encouragement to any other religion than Christianity; nor any God but Jesus Christ (Christianity); except Judaism (Christianity in it's earlier status); NOR any of these opposing or stopping Christianity; Nor any of these starting any system without Christianity.

---T--- <u>Inclusion/Exclusion Law:</u> // All other religions and false gods are specifically excluded and warned about; and in every instance of DOC and historical supporting DOC. Such includes Paganism, Heathenism, God Exclusion, etc.

---T--- <u>All the Meetings & DOC related to constructing</u> the DOI & CON are Christ's & Christianity related; as Intended/purposed: // +The First Continental Congress, 1774; +Second Continental Congress, 1775; +DOI meeting, 1776; +Articles of Confederation, 1777-1789; +Mount Vernon Conference, 1785; +Trade Conference at Annapolis, 1786. // ALL of these Christian DOCs; included Christian REP, Christian activity, and intented/purposed to be Christian.

---T--- <u>"Rights" & GOD as Ruler, Christ Jesus over All; Supreme Judge:</u> // The Rights are intended/ purposed not to be submitted to any form of GOV with men in position. This is another clear FACT or Truth that the USA GOV is to include and be submissive to "God, Creator, Supreme Judge, Divine Providence"; This is why (intention/purpose) the DOI & Independence was initiated; so as to tell England we have "rights" from "God, Creator, Supreme Judge, Divine Providence"; of which NO MAN, and NO MAN GOV can take from us. The Rights are from God and thus priority over all men. Therefore GOD MUST BE THE RULER of the USA GOV.

---T--- <u>The DOC titled the AOC</u> states Christ's Christian Truths: // About this DOC: +It is the former DOC of the CON; +It was applicable during the RW; +It applied the DOI before the CON was constructed to apply the DOI; +The CON refers to it often; +The CON was constructed with intention/ purpose to replace the AOC; +The CON is a continuation of the AOC but with more detail. // This is EV proving that Christianity is the CC.

---T--- <u>Christian Events for Christ were part of the</u> DOI: // "The Great Awakening" (the 1ˢᵗ); with its Events & Activities; was the work for Christ; such assisted the forming of the DOI & CON (CC).

---T--- <u>Christ's Christian Doctrines are Supported by FFOG & DOI & CON:</u> // Doctrines include: Sinfulness of man; Checks & Balances; Salvation by Christ Jesus; the Christian Holy Bible; Repentance; Right living; Conscience; Heart, spirit/Spirit; Atonement of Jesus; Resurrection Holiday (Easter); Christmas; Thanksgiving Holiday; Christian Churches; Devotion; Christian prayer; Right Christian living; Heart purity; The 10 commandments; etc.

---T--- <u>The Earlier Work of Spiritual Moral Creatures arriving to the USA</u> (Colonies etc,) was included in the writing of the DOI & CON; and was never Subtracted, or contradicted; Rather referred to as honorary and as a continuation of -- Establishment of the country as religious Christian to Christ; Adding to it, not subtracting from it; thus it continues to apply: // In AD 1137 Queen of Sweden sent colonies and set as priority "above all things shall the Governor consider and see to it that a time and due worship, becoming honesty, laud, and praise be paid to the most high God in all things ,,,Articles of the Christian faith". // Christopher Columbus was a Christian, who had intention/ purposes to preach the Gospel, raise money for the goal of recapturing Jerusalem from the Muslims; the Muslim's had, a few years earlier, attacked and murdered many in a take over of the city of Constantinople in AD 1453 destroying the Byzantine Empire (225). // Mayflower Compact AD 1620 - "establish this colony in God's name and for His glory and to advance the Christian faith". The ByLaws that applied this Covenant Compact, was called the Plymouth Constitution. It contained job descriptions for the governor, lieutenant governor, instructions about the General Court, how laws were to be made, and specific laws on life, liberty, and property. // Puritan's Covenants (there were more than one, and all Christian based); assisted in developing the DOI & CON as follows: +AD 1630 Puritan Covenant - had these intention/ purposes: Gospel spread to all the world, with the Great Commission

41

supported with Mat 28:19-20; to obey that Great Commission; enjoy liberty of Gospel with purity and peace; establish a Christian church; be a city of God in America. +AD 1639 Colony of Connecticut chose a set of laws for GOV that were according to the laws of God the Lord Jesus Christ. +AD 1677, the Quaker Trustees, (Christian DEN) of West Jersey (Pennsylvania as later) which provided freedom of Christian worship for all Christian DEN. // Puritans in totality were trying to establish a Theocracy GOV, and establish communities for assistance to Christianity; and to help provide a refuge for persecuted peoples from other lands, as stated by FFOG Roger Williams, John Winthrop, William Penn. // Also see (265).

---T--- All is under God: // The DOI states~ "One nation under God". This does not say, exclude, subtract, ignore, remove God. It says He is priority; top priority. // DOI states~ "laws of nature and of nature's God entitle them ,,,all men are created equal ,,,that they are endowed by their Creator with certain inalienable rights; that among these are life, liberty, and the pursuit of happiness.". // Notice the Rights come from God; and furthermore it is also self-evident that God is over man; and that he is created by God. // Laws of Nature are the Laws of Creation; those of the "Creator"; the "Creator" of "Nature"; "Creator" of All; God. +Laws of Nature include the Laws of Good & Evil and our Conscience, according to the Knowledge sources of the FFOG~ Holy Bible, W. Blackstone.

---T--- Christ's Christian religious Holy Bible is constantly referred to by the FFOG & DOI: // Pres. Andrew Jackson states that the Bible, "is the rock on which our republic rests". // Elias Boudinot writes his daughter Susan in the Congress notes, saying, "Oct. 17, 1774, of my important concerns, by taking from the Hours of the Night, endeavored to commit the Sermon to Writing for your careful perusal & Improvement. Read it with Attention - Consider it well - It is the TRUTH and the TRUTH will set you free. Be not deceived or discouraged. You are in Covenant with GOD by the Act of your Parents - I hope by your own private Acts. Be not afraid to go to him as you[r] Father - your Friend & your GOD. Remember that it is in the use of his own Appointed Means, that we are to expect the Blessing. And may the GOD of your Parents (for many Generations past) seal Instruction to your Soul and lead you to himself thro' the Blood of his too greatly despised Son, who notwithstanding, is still reclaiming the World to GOD thro' that Blood, not imputing to them their sins. To him be Glory forever. I have wrote this in Congress, amidst a Warm debate, to which I have been obliged to attend, at the same time, therefore, you must make the necessary corrections yourself. My kind Love to all who think it worth while to inquire after me. Am my Dearest Susan, Your very Afft. Father, Elias Boudinot". // WHAT was the FIRST BOOK PRINTED IN THE USA by the USA ?? The Holy Bible.

---T--- THEOCRACY: The USA GOV is a form of Theocracy; where God is the Ruler; Creator; etc.

---T--- The DOI declares that this nation is a form of Theocracy: // It states the Formation of a CC by the Formal Prayer stating this~ "to the Supreme Judge of the world,,, with a firm reliance on the protection of Divine Providence"; and Creator God and Rights from God; all putting God as God.

---T--- The DOI contracted by GOV on Aug 2, 1776 was Christian as FFOG Samuel Adams stated that God, the Holy Bible, and that all men should obey Him: // "We have this day restored the Sovereign to whom all men ought to be obedient. He reigns in heaven, and from the rising to the setting of the sun, let His kingdom come" (116).

---T--- God's Presence & Christianity is to be in the USA GOV Officials: // "Letters of Delegates to Congress: Volume 4 - 5/16, 1776 - 8/15, 1776 ,,,7/16. 1776. I congratulate you less upon the acct. of your late honourable Appointment than upon the declaration of the freedom & independance of the American colonies. ,,,Such inestimable blessings can not be too joyfully received, nor purchased at too high a price. They would be cheaply bought at the loss of all the towns & of every ,,,Have you not violated a fundamental principle of liberty in excluding the clergy [[clergy are to be included]] from your Legislatures ,,,I know their danger in a free GOV but I would rather see them excluded from civil power by custom than by law. They have property, wives & children, & of course are citizens of a community. Why therefore should they be Abridged of any one priviledge which Other citizens enjoy? Is it not a fact that by investing any men with more, or confining them to fewer priviledges than members of a community enjoy in general we render those men the enemies of that community Perhaps all the Mischief which the clergy have done in all countries has arisen from the first of the above causes. [[Here is the reasoning for the situation; reasoning includes intention/ purpose; such included was religious abuse; and too much power in one person, since they are already in clergy position; and also the abuse to the Christians, as in excluding them from GOV, which is what an ungodly GOV does]] Will not the clause in your Charter which excludes Clergymen from your Legislature hand down to posterity as well as hold up to the World an idea that you looked upon the CHRISTIAN RELIGION as well as its Ministers as unfriendly to good GOV? I wish our governments would treat RELIGION of all kinds, [[DEN favoritism was a subject]] & ministers of all DENS as if no such things or beings existed in the world. They mutually destroy each Other when any Attempts are made by either to support each other. When you have an idle minute it will give me pleasure to hear that you still remember your old friend, & humble Servant, B Rush [[Now what Mr. Rush here states is not a separation of Christianity from the USA GOV but contrarily, an inclusion of it; by having clergy as GOV Officials; Mr. Rush authored a personal Study Bible, was an Officer in a Bible society, and stated many times the support of Christianity as absolutely essential to the USA GOV; What he was referring to, as "destroy each Other" and as "no such things existed" are the divisions in Christianity, such as "religions of all kinds, & ministers of all DENs". Observe this statement that he made elsewhere that I have again stated here]]~ Benjamin Rush states, "I have always considered Christianity as the strong found of republicanism ,,,It is only necessary for republicanism to ally itself to the Christian religion to overturn all the corrupted political and religious institutions in the world" (97).

42

---T--- <u>Christianity of Christ & His Holy Bible, is the Basis of the DOI & RW:</u> // "Journals of the Continental Congress, 1774-1789 - Nov 1, 1777 -,,,The committee appointed to prepare a recommendation to these states, to set apart a day of thanksgiving, brought in a report; which was agreed to as follows: Forasmuch as it is the indispensable <u>duty of all men to adore the superintending providence of Almighty GOD; to acknowledge with gratitude their obligation to him for benefits received, and to implore such farther blessings as they stand in need of; and it having pleased him in his abundant mercy not only to continue to us the innumerable bounties of his common providence,</u> but also to smile upon us in the prosecution of a just and necessary war, for the defence and establishment of our unalienable rights and liberties [[note that the reason, intention/ purpose, of the GOV starting, the War, that is, which refers to the DOI, is on the basis of GOD]]; particularly in that he hath been pleased in so great a measure to prosper the means used for the support of our troops and to crown our arms with most signal success: It is therefore recommended to the legislative or executive powers of these US, to set apart Thursday, the eighteenth day of Dec. next, <u>for solemn thanksgiving and praise; that with one heart and one voice the good people may express the grateful feelings of their hearts, and consecrate themselves to the service of their DIVINE benefactor; and that together with their sincere acknowledgments and offerings, they may join the penitent confession of their manifold sins, whereby they had forfeited every favour, and their humble and earnest supplication that it may please GOD, through the merits of JESUS CHRIST,</u> [[Jesus Christ is God]] mercifully to forgive and blot them out of remembrance; <u>that it may please him graciously to afford his blessing on the governments of these states respectively, and prosper the public council of the whole; to inspire our commanders both by land and sea,</u> and all under them, with that wisdom and fortitude which may render them fit instruments, <u>under the providence of Almighty GOD, to secure for these US the greatest of all human blessings, independence and peace; that it may please him to prosper the trade and manufactures of the people and the labour of the husbandman, that our land may yet yield its increase; to take schools and seminaries of education, so necessary for cultivating the principles of TRUE liberty, virtue and piety, under his nurturing hand, and to prosper the means of RELIGION [[the religion here is Christianity]] for the promotion and enlargement of that kingdom which consisteth "in righteousness, peace and joy in the HOLY Ghost."</u> And it is further recommended, that servile labour, and such recreation as, though at other times innocent, may be unbecoming the purpose of this appointment, be omitted on so solemn an occasion.[Note 2: 2 This report, in the writing of Samuel Adams, is in the Papers of the Continental Congress, No. 24, folio 431.]".

---T--- <u>DOI Supports Christ & Christianity, Holy Bible, & Opposes Evil in the USA GOV:</u> // "Letter from Mr. Scudder to son: My Dear Son, York Town May 1. 1778 ,,,will prove advantageous to your own Education, and honorable to you in Point of Behavior among your Friends & Acquaintances. Carefully avoid the <u>Allurements of every Vice, and shun industriously the Temptations of youth.</u> [[Holy Bible terms]] <u>Tread diligently in the Paths of Virtue, & strive above all to obtain, through the Merits of your Redeemer,</u> [[Jesus]] <u>the inestimable Blessings of TRUE GODliness & undefiled RELIGION.</u> [[Christianity is the USA religion]]. A Seene is opening, my Dear Child, in this Country for the greatest imaginable Display of Talents and Education, and a Young Man with your <u>Capacity, Abilities and Learning can't fail under GOD,</u> if he sets out right, of making a Figure in public Life on the great Stage of this new World. Indeed I cannot help contemplating my Sons as shining in future in some of the most splendid Departments of this mighty rising American Empire, the Glory of the western World- and greatly eclipsing their Father in every civil Accomplishment. This is surely in their Power, since they now may improve themselves designedly for this Purpose; ,,,But how will it ring my Heart, if by any false Step, if by any fatal vicious Indulgence these my fond Hopes shall be disappointed ,,,Then indeed will my grey Hairs descend with Sorrow, & perhaps a speedy Pace, to the Grave. <u>O my Son, let it be your daily & nightly PRAYER to be delivered from every EVIL & every Temptation, and to be prepared for the whole will & Pleasure of GOD your Creator, Preserver and constant Benefactor.</u> Love & Respects to all, & am my Dear Son, your affectionate & Indulgent Father, Nathl Scudder."

---T--- <u>The Support of Jesus or Christ is Directly Stated by</u> the Signing of Almost Every GOV DOC, and in the text of the DOCs; the name of Jesus or Christ, as to His support, is stated hundreds of times in the AD 1700's - 1800's.

---T--- <u>DOI - The FFOG historically came & established</u> the USA for the Intention/ purpose of Christianity for Christ; & for such Religion to be Increased from here to the world, a mission center; & all occurring near the time of the DOI~ before, during , and after: // The charter of Carolina, in AD 1663 by Charles II, stated: "being excited with a laudable and pious zeal for the propagation of the Christian faith." // The charter granted to Rhode Island, in AD 1663, stated: "pursuing, with peaceable and loyal minds, their sober, serious and religious intentions, of godly edifying themselves and one another in the holy Christian faith and worship as they were persuaded; together with the gaining over and conversion of the poor, ignorant Indian natives, in these parts of America, to the sincere profession and obedience of the same faith and worship." // In the charter in AD 1701 by William Penn to Pennsylvania and territories thereunto belonging (Delaware thereafter), stated: "Because no people can be truly happy, though under the greatest enjoyment of civil liberties, if abridged of the freedom of their consciences as to their religious profession and worship; and Almighty God being the only Lord of Conscience, Father of Lights and Spirits, and the author as well as object of all divine knowledge, faith and worship, who only doth enlighten the minds and persuade and convince the understandings of the people, I do hereby grant and declare".

---T--- <u>The Continental-Confederation Congress, a legislative group</u> of Spiritual Moral Creatures that governed the USA from AD 1774 - 1789, and assisted in constructing the DOI, were all deeply Christian religious men for Christ: // Congress invested in encouraging the practice of the Christian religion in the new nation.

---T--- <u>Christian Activity; The FFOG desired & Requested Help from God</u>, in the times of the DOI, by actions of Public Devotion & Opposition to All Evil (anti-Christian activity): // "Journals of the Continental Congress, 1774-1789: Saturday, 3/16, 1776: Mr. W[illiam] Livingston, pursuant to leave granted, brought in a resolution for appointing a fast, which being taken into consideration was agreed to as follows: In times of impending calamity and distress; when the liberties of America are imminently endangered by the secret machinations and open assaults of an insidious and vindictive administration, it becomes the indispensable duty of these hitherto free and happy colonies, with TRUE penitence of heart, and the most REVERENT DEVOTION, PUBLICKLY to acknowledge the over ruling providence of GOD; to confess and deplore our offences against him [[anti-Christian - evil]]; and to supplicate his interposition for averting the threatened danger, and prospering our strenuous efforts in the cause of freedom, virtue [[rightness is encouraged]], and posterity. The Congress, therefore, considering the warlike preparations of the British Ministry to subvert our invaluable rights and priviledges, and to reduce us by fire and sword, by the savages of the wilderness, and our own domestics, to the most abject and ignominious bondage: Desirous, at the same time, to have people of all ranks and degrees duly impressed with a solemn sense of GOD's superintending providence, and of their duty [[duty to whom? To God, and to man, and to self]], devoutly to rely, in all their lawful enterprizes [[laws are considered here, and it is those of God]], on his aid and direction, Do earnestly recommend, that Friday, the Seventeenth day of May next, be observed by the said colonies as a day of humiliation, fasting, and PRAYER; that we may, with united hearts, confess and bewail our manifold SINS and transgressions [[any anti-Christian activity, which is evil]], and, by a sincere repentance and amendment of life [[stop all evil and do rightness]], appease his righteous displeasure and, through the merits and mediation of JESUS CHRIST [[identification of which God]], obtain his pardon and forgiveness; humbly imploring his assistance to frustrate the cruel purposes of our unnatural enemies; and by inclining their hearts to justice and benevolence, prevent the further effusion of kindred blood. But if, continuing deaf to the voice of reason and humanity, and inflexibly bent, on desolation and war, they constrain us to repel their hostile invasions by open resistance, that it may please the Lord of Hosts [[Biblical vs]], the GOD of Armies, to animate our officers and soldiers with invincible fortitude, to guard and protect them in the day of battle, and to crown the continental arms, by sea and land, with victory and success: Earnestly beseeching HIM to BLESS [["bless" is a Christian word]] our civil rulers, and the representatives of the people, in their several assemblies and conventions; to preserve and strengthen their union, to inspire them with an ardent, disinterested love of their country; to give wisdom and stability to their counsels; and direct them to the most efficacious measures for establishing the rights of America on the most honourable and permanent basis--That HE would be graciously pleased to BLESS all his people in these colonies with health and plenty, and grant that a SPIRIT [[these people were Spiritualist; that of the Good Spirit, the Holy Sprit]] of incorruptible patriotism, and of pure undefiled RELIGION [[the subject of religion that is pure and undefiled; this would reject non-Christian DEN as impure & defiled]] may universally prevail; and this continent be speedily restored to the blessings of peace and liberty, and enabled to transmit them inviolate to the latest posterity. And it is recommended to CHRISTIANs [[little Christ's]] of all DENS [[Only Christ related religions; that of various Christian DENs]], to assemble for PUBLIC WORSHIP, and abstain from servile labour on the said day."

---T--- <u>DOI & GOV support The Holy Bible, the Churches, & the Christian religion for Christ</u>: // "Letters of Delegates to Congress: Volume 5 - 8/16, 1776 - 12/31, 1776 - William Williams to Jonathan Trumbull, Sr. Hond & Dear Sir Philadel. 20th Sepr. 1776 ,,,This Event unhappy & distressing as it is has been foreseen & known ever since the quitting of Long Island, & had been determined by the Genl. & his Council; Congress had been made fully acquainted with & assented to it as absolutely necessary, & directed that it shod not be destroyed by us on leaving it. These Events however, & signal advantage gained by our oppressors, & the distress to which our army & Country are & must be subjected in consequence of them, are loud speaking testimonies of the displeasure & anger of almighty GOD against a SINful people, louder than sevenfold thunder. Is it possible that the most obdurate & stupid of the Children of America shod not hear & tremble? GOD has surely a controversie with this people, & He is most certainly able to manage it & He will accomplish his designs, & bring us to repentance & reformation, or destroy us. We must bend or break. The ways of his Providence are dark & deep but they are HOLY, wise, & just & altogether right, tho our feeble understandings comprehend them not, & tho his chastisements are severe & dreadful. They are dictated by unbounded wisdom & love. They have a meaning of awful & kind Import. Turn unto me for why will ye die O Sons of America. [[Bible vs]] We have thought GOD was for us & had given many & signal Instances of His power & mercy in our favor, & had greatly frowned upon & disappointed our enemies & verily it has been so, but have we repented & given Him the glory? Verily no. His hand seems to be turned & stretched out against us, & strong is his hand & high is his right hand. He can & will accomplish all his pleasure. It is GOD who has blunted the weapons of our warfare, that has turned the counsels of wise men into foolishness, [[Bible vs]] that has thus far ,,,I have always thot this was a just & righteous cause [[opposing all evil, anti-Christ activity]] in which we are engaged. I remain unshaken in that firm persuasion, & that GOD wod sooner or later vindicate & support it, I believe so still, but I believe this people must first be brot to know & acknowledge the righteousness of his judgment, & their own exceeding SINfulness & Guilt, & be deeply humbled under his mighty hand, & look & cry to & trust in Him for all their help & salvation but in the use & exertion of all the strength He has given us. Surely we have seen enough to convince us of all this, & then why are we not convinced, why is not every Soul humbled under the mighty hand of GOD, repenting & mourning for its SINS & putting away the EVIL of his doings, & looking to Him that smites us by humble, earnest & fervent PRAYER & Supplication day & night. Why are not the dear Children of GOD (surely there are many, tho the scorn & insult of our enemies) beseiging the Throne of Grace, sighing & crying for their own SINS & back slidings & for all the abominations that are done in the Land, & saying spare, spare thy people O Lord & give not thine heritage to reproach. Let not the vine which thy right hand has planted here be rooted up & destroyed, let not thy CHURCHes be wasted & devoured, let not virtue & the remains of RELIGION be torn down & trampled in the dust, let not thy Name be blasphemed, nor our insulting wicked foes say where is your GOD, nor the profane world that there is no GOD that rules the world & regardeth the right, that vindicateth the just & the righteous cause. I know that GOD can vindicate his own Name & honor without our help, & out of the stones raise up children to Abraham, & it is amazing folly & madness to cry the temple, the Temple of the Lord, & trust in that while we remain an incorrigible people. But such things are what GOD wod have us learn & practice while his judgments are abroad in the land, & with such like arguments fill our, mouths, & pour out our souls before Him. Are any? Are not all? in,,, England especially, who have any interest in HEAVEN, crying, beging & intreating for the out pouring of blessed SPIRIT of GOD upon the land, tis a most grievous & distressing consideration that GOD is pleased so to withhold the blessed influences & operations thereof, without which we shall remain stupid forever. Therefore with redoubled fervency of ardent PRAYER & Supplication, shod every soul that has one sparck of HEAVENly fire kindle it to a fervent Heat & expanded blaze. O New England, O my dear native land, how does my soul love thee. Be instructed therefore lest GODs Soul depart from thee, lest thou be like Corazin & Bethsaida in condemnation as thou hast been in privileges, lest He make thee as Admah & set thee as Zeboim. Are the ministers of the Gospel alive & awake & lifting up their voices like a trumpet & sounding the alarm of the Almightys anger & wrath ready to burst on the defenseless heads of a guilty people? Are they warning the wicked of their infinite danger, animating & arousing them to consideration? Are they with ardent zeal & fervour animating & enlivening the languid graces of the GODly, exciting & leading them to fervent PRAYER, sighing & crying for their own declensions & luke warmness in RELIGION & for the SINS & Iniquities of the Land, PRAYing, beging & intreating with unceasing & as it were resistless importunity for the copious effusions of the Blessed SPIRIT upon all orders & degrees of people & refusing to let GOD go, without an answer of peace, & in the midst of wrath to remember mercy, & not give up this his heritage to reproach nor blast the blooming hopes & prospects of this infant Country, the Asylum of Liberty & Religion? Strange that mankind shod need such alarming providences to produce such an effect. It is no more than to act like reasonable creatures, to possess a SPIRIT & temper that will add a thousand fold sweetness & pleasure to all the enjoyments of this world, to exchange the slavery of the DEVIL, that accursed enemy of our souls, for the service of GOD & the liberty of his children, to do justly, to love mercy & walk humbly with our GOD, to answer the sole end of our CREATION, to secure a peace here infinitely better than the world can give, & an ETERNITY of Peace & Happiness in the world to come. But still more strange if possible, & astonishing is it that they shod disregard the voice of the most high, remain thoughtless & stupid under the dreadful tokens of his anger & the awful judgments of his hand, by sickness & by the sword of our unnatural & enraged enemies threatening to depopulate the land & drench the plains with the blood of its inhabitants, leaving the weeping widows, helpless orphans & the all that survive the shocking carnage & subsequent masacre to drag out their lives in want, wretchedness & miserable bondage & all this aggravated with the certain prospect of leaving this dreadful curse intailed on all posterity. (p) A thorough repentance & reformation, without all peradventure will appease the Anger of a HOLY & just GOD, avert these amazing calamities, secure Liberty & Happiness to this & all succeeding Ages & ETERNAL felicity & glory to all the subjects of it. If such considerations & motives wont awaken a ,,,to serious thoughtfulness & attention, I know n[ot] what will, but the voice of the Arch Angel & the Trump[et] of GOD. I am hond & dear Sir most affectionately your dutiful Son & Servant. Wm Williams. P.S. You will not think proper to communicate this Letter to the Assembly. I am anxious beyond the power of language to describe, of contributing something to the Good & Salvation, temporal & ETERNAL, of my Countrymen. (Hope I have not been totally useless here.) If you shod think this may have any tendency, to awake our sleepy People & be of no disadvantage ,,,May GOD in great Mercy preserve your Health, & long continue your valuable & important Life,,,".

---T--- DOI is CHRISTIAN (Religious): // From the time of the DOI to very recent Congresses there have been following: +Enacted chaplains to the Militaries of the USA; +Prayers offered in the Congress; +Prayers offered in the Militaries.

---T--- The New England Primer, is An Educational Book for Learning; which is for Christ with Holy Bible SCs: // It was used in USA public schools with its many religious references for a long period of time before, during, and after the DOI & CON.

---T--- Christianity of Jesus & the Holy Bible was the Basis & part of the USA GOV for the DOI: // (Notice here, that THE RIGHT TO INDEPENDENCE WAS BASED ON "GOD, CREATOR, SUPREME JUDGE, DIVINE PROVIDENCE"): ~ "Journals of the Continental Congress, 1774-1789 - 10/30, 1778 - These US having been driven to hostilities by the oppressive and tyrannous measures of Great Britain; having been compelled to commit the essential rights of man to the decision of arms; and having been at length forced to shake off a yoke which had grown too burthensome to bear; they declared themselves free and independent. Confiding in the justice of their cause; confiding in Him, who disposes of human events; although weak and unprovoked, they set the power of their enemies at defiance. In this confidence they have continued through the various fortunes of three bloody campaigns, unawed by the power, unsubdued by the barbarity of their foes. Their virtuous citizens have borne, without repining, the loss of many things which make life desirable. Their brave troops have patiently endured the hardships and dangers of a situation fruitful in both, beyond former example. The Congress considering themselves bound to love their enemies, as children of that Being who is equally the Father of All; [[notice here that REP identify the God of the USA and the DOI as Christ and the Holy Bible]] and desirous, since they could not prevent, at least to alleviate the calamities of war, have studied to spare those who were in arms against them, and to lighten the chains of captivity. The conduct of those serving under the king of Great Britain hath, with some few exceptions, been diametrically opposite. They have laid waste the open country, burned the defenceless villages, and butchered the citizens of America. Their prisons have been the slaughter-houses of her soldiers, their ships of her seamen; and the severest injuries have been aggravated by the grossest insult. Foiled in their vain attempt to subjugate the unconquerable SPIRIT of freedom, they have meanly assailed the representatives of America with bribes, with deceit, and the servility of adulation. They have made a mock of humanity by the wanton destruction of men. They have made a mock of RELIGION by impious appeals to "GOD, CREATOR, SUPREME JUDGE, DIVINE PROVIDENCE", whilst in the violation of his SACRED commands: They have made a mock even of reason itself, by endeavouring to prove that the liberty and happiness of America could safely be entrusted to those who have sold their own, unawed by the sense of virtue or of shame. Treated with the contempt which such conduct deserved, they have applied to individuals. They have solicited them to break the bonds of allegiance, and imbue their souls with the blackest of crimes. But fearing that none could be found through these US equal to the wickedness of their purpose, to influence weak minds they have threatened more wide devastation. While the shadow of hope remained that our enemies could be taught by our EX:, to respect those laws which are held SACRED among civilized nations, and to comply with the dictates of a RELIGION which they pretend in common with us to believe and revere, they have been left to the influence of that RELIGION and that EX:. But since their incorrigible dispositions cannot be touched by kindness and compassion, it becomes our duty by other means to vindicate the rights of humanity. We, therefore, the Congress of the US of America, do solemnly declare and proclaim, that if our enemies presume to execute their threats, or persist in their present career of barbarity, we will take such exemplary vengeance, as shall deter others from a like conduct. We appeal to that GOD who searcheth the hearts of men, [[a Bible vs]] for the rectitude of our intentions: and in his HOLY presence we declare, [[a Holy Bible term]] that as we are not moved by any light and hasty suggestions of anger or revenge, so, through every possible change of fortune, we will adhere to this our determination."

---T--- The DOI is Christian for Christ & the GOV Supports Christian DENs of Christ: // "Journals of the Continental Congress, 1774-1789, 6/12, 1775 - The Congress met according to adjournment. The committee, appointed for preparing a resolve for a fast, brought in a report, which, being read, was agreed to as follows: As the great Governor of the World, [[notice congress states that God is the Absolute Governor over all man GOV systems]] by his supreme and universal Providence, not only conducts the course of nature [[the word nature used here, is in time, before the DOI; and with a definition about creation, mental states of men, and laws of existence]] with unerring wisdom and rectitude, but frequently influences the minds of men to serve the wise and gracious purposes of his providential government; and it being, at all times, our indispensible duty devoutly to acknowledge his superintending providence, especially in times of impending danger and public calamity, to reverence and adore his immutable justice as well as to implore his merciful interposition for our deliverance: This Congress, therefore, considering the present critical, alarming and calamitous state of these colonies, do earnestly recommend that Thursday, the 20th day of July next, be observed, by the inhabitants of all the English colonies on this continent, as a day of public humiliation, fasting and PRAYER; that we may, with united hearts and voices, unfeignedly confess and deplore our many SINS [[a Bible term]]; and offer up our joint supplications to the all-wise, omnipotent, and merciful Disposer of all events; humbly beseeching him to forgive our iniquities,[[Bible vs]] to remove our present calamities, to avert those desolating judgments, with which we are threatned, and to bless our rightful sovereign, King George the third, and [to] inspire him with wisdom to discern and pursue the true interest of all his subjects, that a speedy end may be put to the civil discord between Great Britain and the American colonies, without farther effusion of blood: And that the British nation may be influenced to regard the things that belong to her peace, before they are hid from her eyes: That these colonies may be ever under the care and protection of a kind Providence, and be prospered in all their interests; That the DIVINE BLESSING may descend and rest upon all our civil rulers, and upon the representatives of the people, in their several assemblies and conventions, that they may be directed to wise and effectual measures for preserving the union, and securing the just rights and priviledges of the colonies; That virtue and TRUE RELIGION may revive and flourish throughout our land; And that all America may soon behold a gracious interposition of HEAVEN, for the redress of her many grievances, the restoration of her invaded rights, a reconciliation with the parent state, on terms constitutional and honorable to both; And that her civil and RELIGIOUS priviledges may be secured to the latest posterity. And it is recommended to CHRISTIANs, of all DENS, [[here congress identifies Christianity as the God of the USA; in time, this is preceeding the DOI construction; and a variety of DENs existing; and no false religions supported]] to assemble for public worship, and to abstain from servile labour and recreations on said day. Ordered, That a copy of the above be signed by the president and attested by the Secy and published in the newspapers, and in hand bills.,,, Resolved ,,,and also the state of America."

---T--- The DOI reason (Intention/ purpose) is Religious Liberty, & which is Christ's Presence & Christianity: // "Letters of Delegates to Congress: Volume 10- 6/1, 1778 - 9/30, 1778; Gouverneur Morris to the Carlisle Commissioners - [6/20, 1778] ,,,Trusty and well-beloved servants of your SACRED master, in whom he is well pleased. As you are sent to America for the express purpose of treating with anybody and anything ,,,Should you therefore deign to read this address, your chaste ears will not be offended with the language of adulation, a language you despise. I have seen your most elegant and most excellent letter ,,,Members of the Congress." ,,,As that body have thought your propositions unworthy their particular regard, it may be some satisfaction to your curiosity, and tend to appease the offended SPIRIT of negotiation, if one out of the many individuals on this great Continent should speak to you the sentiments of America. Sentiments which your own good sense hath doubtless suggested, and which are repeated only to convince you that ,,,still a knowledge of our own rights, and attention to our own interests, and a SACRED respect for the dignity of human nature, have given us to understand the TRUE principles which ought, and which therefore shall, sway our conduct. You begin with the amiable expressions of humanity, the earnest desire of tranquility and peace. A better introduction to Americans could not be devised. For the sake of the latter, we once laid our liberties at the feet of your Prince, and even your armies have not eradicated the former from our bosoms. You tell us you have powers unprecedented in the annals of your history. And England, unhappy England, will remember with deep contrition, that these powers have been rendered of no avail by a conduct unprecedented in the annals of mankind. Had your royal master condescended to listen to the PRAYER of millions, he had not thus have sent you. Had moderation swayed what we were proud to call mother country, "her full-blown dignity would not have broken down under her." You tell us that "all parties may draw some degree of consolation, and even auspicious hope, from recollection." We wish this most sincerely for the sake of all parties. America, even in the moment of subjugation, would have been consoled by conscious virtue, and her hope was and is in the justice of her cause, and the justice of the ALMIGHTY. These are sources of hope and of consolation, which neither time nor chance can alter or take away. You mention "the mutual benefits and consideration of EVILs, that may naturally contribute to determine our resolutions." As to the former, you know too well that we could derive no benefit from an union with you, nor will I, by deducing the reasons to evince this, cast an insult upon your understandings. As to the latter, it were to be wished you had preserved a line of conduct equal to the delicacy of your feelings. You could not but know that men, who sincerely love freedom, disdain the consideration of all EVILs necessary to attain it. Had not your own hearts borne testimony to this TRUTH, you might have learnt it from the annals of your history. For in those annals instances of this kind at least are not unprecedented. But should those instances be insufficient, we PRAY you to read the unconquered mind of America. That the acts of Parliament you transmitted were passed with singular unanimity, we pretend not to doubt. You will pardon me, gentlemen, for observing, that the reasons of that unanimity are strongly marked in the report of a Committee of Congress, agreed to on the 22d of Apr. last ,,,and referred to in a late letter from Congress to Lord Viscount Howe and Sir Henry Clinton. ,,,You tell us you are willing "to consent to a cessation of hostilities, both by sea and land." It is difficult for rude Americans to determine whether you are serious in this proposition, or whether you mean to jest with their simplicity. Upon a supposition, however, that you have too much magnanimity to divert yourselves on an occasion of such importance to America, and perhaps not very trivial in the eyes of those who sent you, permit me to assure you, on the SACRED word of a gentleman, that if you shall transport your troops to England, where before long your Prince will certainly want their assistance, we never shall follow them thither. We are not so romantically fond of fighting, neither have we such regard for the city of London, as to commence a crusade for the possession of that HOLY land. Thus you may be certain that hostilities will cease by land. It would be doing singular injustice to your national character, to suppose you are desirous of a like cessation by sea. The course of the war ,,,You offer "to restore free intercourse, to revive mutual affection, and renew the common benefits of naturalization." Whenever your countrymen shall be taught wisdom by experience, and learn from past misfortunes to pursue their TRUE interests in future we shall readily admit every intercourse which is necessary for the purposes of commerce, and usual between different nations. To revive mutual affection is utterly impossible. We freely forgive you, but it is not in nature that you should forgive us. You have injured us too much. We might, on this occasion, give you some late instances of singular barbarity, committed as well by the forces of his Britannic Majesty, as by those of his generous and faithful allies, the Senecas, Onondagas and Tuscaroras. But we will not offend a courtly ear by the recital of those disgusting scenes. Besides this, it might give pain to that humanity which hath, as you observe, prompted your overtures to dwell upon the splendid victories obtained by a licentious soldiery over unarmed men in defenceless villages, their wanton devastations, their deliberate murders, or to inspect those scenes of carnage painted by the wild excesses of savage rage ,,,On the other hand, such of your subjects as shall be driven by the iron hand of Oppression to seek for refuge among those whom they now persecute, will certainly be admitted to the benefits of naturalization. We labour to rear an asylum for mankind, and regret that circumstances will not permit you, Gentlemen, to contribute to a design so very agreeable to your several tempers and dispositions. But further, your Excellencies say, "we will concur to extend every freedom to trade that our respective interests can require." Unfortunately there is a little difference in these interests, which you might not have found it very easy to reconcile, had the Congress been disposed to risque their heads by listening to terms, which I have the honour to assure you are treated with ineffable contempt by every honest Whig in America. ,,,they might extend the freedom of trade, or circumscribe it, at their pleasure, for what they might call our respective interests. But I trust it would not be to our mutual satisfaction. Your "earnest desire to stop the farther effusion of blood, and the calamities of war," will therefore lead you, on maturer reflection, to reprobate a plan teeming with discord, and which, in the space of twenty years, would produce another wild expedition across the Atlantic, and in a few years more some such commission as that "with which his Majesty hath been pleased to honour you." We cannot but admire the generosity of soul, which prompts you "to agree that no military force shall be kept up in the different States of North-America without the consent of the general Congress or particular Assemblies." ,,,You propose to us a devise to "perpetuate our union." It might not be amiss previously to establish this union, which may be done by your acceptance of the treaty of peace and commerce tendered to you by Congress. ,,,And such treaty, I can venture to say, would continue as long as your ministers could prevail upon themselves not to violate the faith of nations. You offer, to use your own language, the inaccuracy of which, considering the importance of the subject, is not to be wondered at, or at least may be excused, "in short to establish the powers of the respective legislatures in each particular State, to settle its revenue, its civil and military establishment, and to exercise a perfect freedom of legislation and internal government, so that the British States throughout North-America acting with us, in peace and war, under one common sovereign, may have the irrevokable enjoyment of every privilege that is short of a total separation of interests, or consistent with that union of force on which the safety of our common RELIGION and liberty depends." Let me assure you, gentlemen, that the power of the respective legislatures in each particular State is already most fully established, and on the most solid foundations. It is established on the perfect freedom of legislation and a vigorous administration of internal government.

47

,,,As the States of North-America mean to possess the irrevokable enjoyment of their privileges, it is absolutely necessary for them to decline all connection with a Parliament, who, even in the laws under which you act, reserve in express terms the power of revoking every proposition which you may agree to. We have a due sense of the kind offer you make, to grant us a share in your sovereign, but really, gentlemen ,,,You are solicitous to prevent a total separation of interests, and this, after all, seems ,,,Where this is not the case, your Excellencies have doubtless too much good sense as well as good nature to require it. We cannot perceive that our liberty does in the least depend upon any union of force with you; for we find that, after you have exercised your force against us for upwards of three years, we are now upon the point of establishing our liberties in direct opposition to it. Neither can we conceive, that, after the experiment you have made, any nation in Europe will embark in so unpromising a scheme as the subjugation of America. It is not necessary that everybody should play the Quixotte. One is enough to entertain a generation at least. Your Excellencies will, I hope, excuse me when I differ from you, as to our having a RELIGION in common with you: the RELIGION of America is the RELIGION of all mankind. [[note that only one religion is supported by Congress and FFOG, which is Christianity; and as the only true religion of all mankind]] Any person may worship in the manner he thinks most agreeable to the Deity; and if he behaves as a good citizen, no one concerns himself as to his faith or adorations, neither have we the least solicitude to exalt any one SECT or profession above another. I am extremely sorry to find in your letter some sentences, which reflect upon the character of his most Christian Majesty. It certainly is not kind, or consistent with the principles of philanthropy you profess, to traduce a gentleman's character without affording him an opportunity of defending himself: and that too a near neighbour, and not long since an intimate brother, who besides hath lately given you the most solid additional proofs of his pacific disposition, and with an unparalleled sincerity, which would do honour to other Princes, declared to your court, unasked, the nature and effect of a treaty he had just entered into with these States. ,,,Neither is it quite according to the rules of politeness to use such terms in addressing yourselves to Congress, when you well knew that he was their good and faithful ally. It is indeed TRUE, as you justly observe, that he hath at times been at enmity with his Britannic Majesty, by which we suffered some inconveniences: but these flowed rather from our connection with you than any ill-will towards us: At the same time it is a solemn TRUTH, worthy of your serious attention, that you did not commence the present war, a war in which we have suffered infinitely more than by any former contest, a fierce, a bloody, I am sorry to add, an unprovoked and cruel war. ,,,How then does the account stand between us. America, being at peace with all the world, was formerly drawn into a war with France, in consequence of her union with Great-Britain. At present America, being engaged in a war with Great Britain, will probably obtain the most honourable terms of peace, in consequence of her friendly connection with France. For the TRUTH of these positions I appeal, gentlemen, to your own knowledge. I know it is very hard for you to part with what you have accustomed yourselves, from your earliest infancy, to call your colonies. I pity your situation, and therefore I excuse the little abberations from TRUTH which your letter contains. At the same time it is possible that you may have been misinformed. For I will not suppose that your letter was intended to delude the people of these States. Such unmanly disingenuous artifices have of late been exerted with so little effect, that prudence, if not probity, would prevent a repetition. To undeceive you, therefore, I take the liberty of assuring your Excellencies ,,,to North-America," in other words the treaties of alliance and commerce between his most CHRISTIAN Majesty and these States, were not made in consequence of any plans of accommodation concerted in Great-Britain, nor with a view to prolong this destructive war. If you consider that these treaties were actually concluded before the draught of the bills under which you act was sent for America, and that much time must necessarily have been consumed in adjusting COMPACTS of such intricacy and importance, and further, if you consider the early notification of this treaty by the court of France ,,,and the assurance given that America had reserved a right of admitting even you to a similar treaty, you must be convinced of the TRUTH of my assertions. The fact is ,,,It seems to me, gentlemen, there is something (excuse the word) disingenuous in your procedure. I put the supposition that Congress had acceded to your propositions, and then I ask two questions. Had you full power from your commission to make these propositions? Possibly you did not think it worth while to consider your commission, but we Americans are apt to compare things together, and to reason. The second question I ask is, What security could you give that the British Parliament would ratify your COMPACTS? ,,,after you had filched from us our good name, and perswaded us to give to the common enemy of man the precious jewel of our liberties; after all this, I say, we should have been at the mercy of a Parliament, which, to say no more of it, has not treated us with too GREAT TENDERNESS. It is quite needless to add, that even if that Parliament had ratified the conditions you proposed, still poor America was to lie at the mercy of any future Parliament, or appeal to the sword, which certainly is not the most pleasant business men can be engaged in. For your use I subjoin the following creed of every good American. I believe that in every kingdom, state, or empire there must be, from the necessity of the thing, one supreme legislative power, with authority to bind every part in all cases, the proper object of human laws. I believe that to be bound by laws, to which he does not consent by himself or by his representative, is the direct definition of a slave. I do therefore believe, that a dependence on Great Britain, however the same may be limited or qualified, is utterly inconsistent with every idea of liberty, for the defence of which I have solemnly pledged my life and fortune to my countrymen; and this engagement I will SACREDly adhere to so long as I shall live. AMEN . Now if you will take the poor advice of one, who is really a friend to England and Englishmen, and who hath even some Scotch blood in his veins, away with your fleets and your armies, acknowledge the independence of America ,,,You have told the Congress, "If, after the time that may be necessary to consider this communication, and transmit your answer, the horrors and devastations of war should continue, we call GOD and the world to witness that the EVILs, which must follow, are not to be imputed to Great-Britain." I wish you had spared your protestation. Matters of this kind may appear to you in a trivial light, as meer ornamental flowers of rhetoric, but they are serious things registered in the high chancery of HEAVEN. Remember the awful abuse of words like these by General Burgoyne, and remember his fate. There is one above us ,,,You know that the cause of America is just. You know that she contends for that freedom, to which all men are entitled. That she contends against oppression, rapine, and more than savage barbarity. The blood of the innocent is upon your hands, and all the waters of the ocean will not wash it away. We again make our solemn appeal to the GOD of HEAVEN to decide between you and us. And we PRAY that in the doubtful scale of battle we may be successful, as we have justice on our side, and that the merciful SAVIOUR of the world may forgive our oppressors. [[again the identification of Jesus as the God of all and only religion to be supported]] ..I am, my Lords and Gentlemen, The friend of human nature, And one who glories in the title of, An AMERICAN ,,,Morris wrote to various members of the Carlisle commission as "An American."

---T--- The DOI & USA GOV is Christian of Christ; of His Holy Bible; & studied & based on: // "Letters of Delegates to Congress: Vol 1- AUG 1774 - AUG 1775 ,,,10/10/1774 Your Letter of 28th of last Month was very acceptable, your Observations relative to the Congress and the Town of Boston are just and with you I fear the Dispute must [be] decided by the Sword. The Acct. which You give me of the Pleasure you enjoy in your Aunts & Brother make my Absence less disagreable to me, the manner in which You speak of your Health & the Idea of its being entirely restored are vastly pleasing for though I have long been trying to view You & every Thing else dearest to Me through the Medium of RELIGION [&] Philosophy my fond Heart is sufficiently attached yet ,,,Tell her to remember that the SUPREME PARENT of the Universe IS A BEING OF INFINITE Goodness & Mercy that Judgment is his strange Work [[a Christian Bible vs; that God dislikes war]] and that He is Love & delights in the Communication of Happiness. Tell her to [PRAY] to him to pour out her whole Soul before him not ,,,earnest Desire for his DIVINE Direction & Blessing ,,,a firm Confidence in him, let her remember that whatsoever We ask in Faith We shall receive [[a Bible vs]] ,,,and surely to have our Souls filled with the knowledge & love of GOD with ardent desires to see & do his will and such a fixed determination chearfully to follow him as may enable us to present our bodies living sacrifices HOLY & acceptable unto GOD [[reference to Holy Bible Rom12:1-2]] must be at all Times fit & proper for Us. These are the great objects which her soul I doubt not is fixed upon,,,. We had an express from Boston giving an Acct. of the distressed & dangerous situation of the Town & Province. ,,,We have also wrote to the Comee. of Correspondence. Your PRAYERS for your native Country & her cruel Parent your reflections upon the endearment which absence creates in us & your reflection upon your blessed sisters & conclusion that our evening may be equally serene ,,,"

---T--- The DOI is Christian Christ Based as the Start of the USA; Nation existed before the CON was Constructed: // "Done in Congress, this 20th day of March, in the year of our Lord one thousand seven hundred and seventy-nine, and in the third year of our independence."; "Done in Congress ,,,the 20th day of October, one thousand seven hundred and seventy-nine, and in the 4th year of the independence of the US of America. Samuel Huntington, President."

---T--- DOI centers around Christ & Christianity; & in opposition to anti-Christianity: // "Letters of Delegates to Congress: Volume 5- 8/16, 1776 - 12/31, 1776 William Williams to Joseph Trumbull Dear Sir Philadel. 9/13 1776 ,,,you I trust that Congress will not give you up as ,,,for the northern Department. ,,,Many of them greatly resent the Conduct of the Gent. who has so interferd with you & there are appearances ,,,but things are not fully ripe yet nor can they possibly be attended to now. He had lately written a very long Epistle to inforce the necessity & expedience, the bestness & Cheapness &c of supplying the northern Army by a Contract with somebody there. It was hastily read thro in the House, & not the lest further notice taken of it. I presume he will not interpose in your departmt. again, tho I know He has paid but little attention to his orders in many things. ,,,Our Affairs are truly in a critical Situation, but far I hope from desperate. My trust & hope is in a merciful & just GOD, who with one Volition of his Will can change their appearance. I fear we shall be chastized for our SINS, but not forsaken I trust & firmly believe. But most certainly it becomes all to humble Themselves deeply before Him, repent of our SINS & most earnestly to supplicate his Favor. He will be known in the Judgements he executes. [[a Bible vs]] He has a Controversie with His People, & will certainly accomplish his Design in it. We must bend or break. No Means for our defence & Safety must be omitted & may GOD grant Our Officers & Soldiers, great Wisdom, understanding, Courage & Resolution. ,,,We have every thing to fight for, that is valuable & good. They have nothing but their pay & to establish the greatest of political & MORAL EVIL. They cannot, will not be always prospered. Every thing shod be done, & doubtless is, to inspire the Men with the greatest Intrepedity & by all acco They f'ot bravely on L. Island. ,,,Our Officers are far more acquainted with their movements & Intentions ,,,Are now ,,,in planing &c for forming a new & permanent Army. ,,,I am dear Sir with undissembled & strong Affection, your Friend & Bror, Wm. Williams [P.S.] I am grieved & confounded at the Conduct of some of our Militia ,,,Mr Huntington has several Times expresd his Wonder that you have wholly done writing him, that he continued a Correspondence with you whenever he had anything worth communicating. I really think it might be well, & that He is truly Friendly to You".

---T--- DOI is Christ & Christian based: // "Letters of Delegates to Congress: Volume 7 - 5/1, 1777 - 9/18, 1777 ,,,9/13th. 1777, Saturd. Eveng. In my last I hinted my & the common apprehention that Howe did not intend to fight till his Ships had got into the Delawar, but the event has shewd it otherwise. Thursday last was a day of most severe conflict, & it has pleased the HOLY GOD to suffer it end for that time to our great disadvantage. Between 8 & 9 oClock in the morning the enemy attempted to force a passage over ,,,heavy canonade which was returnd & brot on a prodigious fire ,,,Indeed tis hard for me to say whether the greater part will be well pleased with Howe's success. A flag is come to the Genl this day, it is said, with proposals to succur our wounded prisoners in their hands & with promise that the rest shall be treated as those of war &c. Some are disposed to make light of what has happened, & others to aggravate it to the highest degree. Most certainly it is a serious & important affair, to have such an Army so full of confidence & SPIRIT, so worsted, as to find it proper to retreat above 30 miles, & make their last stand, where such another encounter will certainly be fatal as to this City. It is an awful frown of DIVINE Providence, but we are not at all humbled under it, a sad sign that more dreadful EVILs await us. We are indeed at a most critical & tremendous crisis, a powerful army, flushed with victory & animated by the strongest motives, riches & glory before them, no hope of escape from shame & death but by conquest, pursuing & at the gates of this great City. Yet if we have a few days & the people turn out & behave as they ought on such an occasion, we might have yet great hope & to be sure, I am far from despairing, that GOD will yet save us. Yet we have reason to tremble. Our amazing SINS totally unrepented of to all appearance, is the burden of my perpetual fear, & apprehentions, but such language is most exceedingly ungrateful & unattended to here. What can we then expect but GOD's mercy is infinite & greater than our SINS. Yet does he usually save a people that wont be saved & fight against him Yet I must & cant but hope, but perhaps it is a false & illgrounded hope. I must however entertain, till I know it is so. The next news you receive from hence will be of vast importance, GOD grant in his infinite mercy, it may be happy. shod they succeed, tho the blow must be terrible & the wound deep ,,,GOD only knows. Congress are not disposed even to consider where we shod remove to ,,,We are in the hands of an infinitely wise & great Being, who orders all things well. O that every soul was joining with you in ardent supplications for the reformation of this people & for the deliverance & salvation of this Land ,,,With tender remembrance to my dear wife & other dear friends, I am most Affectionately your dutiful son & Servt -- W. Williams [P.S.],,,".

---T--- <u>DOI is Religious & Christian; all for Jesus; The GOV is concerned </u>that Citizen Branch of GOV maintain Christianity as the CC (DOI & CON) Declares; and about Opposing Evil: // "Letters of Delegates to Congress: Vol 7-- 5/1, 1777 - 9/18, 1777 - William Williams to Mary Williams - My dear Love Philadelphia 22d July 1777 ,,,It gave me not a little Satisfaction to hear of your Welfare, that of our dear Children & <u>Connections. GOD grant this may find you all in health &</u> safety. It was impossible for me to write you; my right arm which you know has been affected with the Rheumatism has been tenfold worse than ever, the pain at first fell suddenly into my wrist, sweld & became exceedingly painful, & after some Time returnd back to my Elbow & was worse than before & my whole arm was inexpressibly sore & painful from my Shoulder to my hand ,,,but by the mercy of GOD, & his blessing, it is much better but not perfectly well, & I fear it may return. Am able to write, tho have nothing very material to say ,,,The House swarms with ,,,we keep our Chambers pretty much & are Company for Selves, tho Mr Law is obligd to sleep in a lower bedroom, & at suppers. I have nothing to do & we dine by our Selves, abt 4 or 5 oClock. <u>The swearing & Wickedness that abounds in this City is truly shocking to chaste Ears & alarming in a MORAL View, the Judgments of GOD don't seem to have any Effect,</u> unless the most awful one, of rendering us worse. I tremble to think so, but I really fear it is TRUE, will he that made us, shew mercy to such a People <u>? His Mercy is boundless, & infinite. I will yet hope in it nor Limit the HOLY one of Israel. [[a Bible vs]] O, that Wickedness was confined to this City. Alass I fear 'tis as great in N. England & thro the Country. When I was here last Summer & heard of the Defeats at N York, the Northward &c I thot it was impossible but it shod alarm our Countrymen & awaken them to turn to him that smote Them but I found it far otherwise. Alass, the Chastisements of his Providence will have good</u> Effect without the inward <u>teaching of his SPIRIT, but GOD is pleased to withhold those Influences, [[a Bible vs of the Holy Spirit]] the most sore & distressing of all Calamities. O, that every Soul who has an Interest in HEAVEN wod cry day & night with ceaseless & unfailing ardor, that GOD wod pour out his blessed SPIRIT to awaken</u> & bring the Country to Repentance. Too few I fear think of the infinite importance of that Blessing even without any regard to our present Calamities. But what can I say or Do. GOD will work as pleaseth Him. Among the other SINS that prevail here extortion & oppression is not the least, & it is by the wicked Arts of our internal Enemys here brot to such a pass, tis hardly possible to tell the price of their Shop Goods. There are many Goods here & yet They keep the Prices at the most extravagent sums. I believe Linnens I used to sell at abt 2/ are 20/ & more, Tea £8, the pound, dirty base brown Sugar 5/ & more, Loaf 10/, rum 45/ the lowest the Gallon, Molasses, my drink with Water 6/ a quart, butter in market 5/ & 6/ the pound, beaf 2/6 & every thing in proportion & daily rising, & will rise, unless our affairs in infinite mercy shod take another turn. ,,,regret my absence & long to be with my dear Wife, Children & Friends, but there is no peace there, & I must stand in my Lot & wait the Will of GOD, & his appointed Time. If He shall ever bring me home again in Peace, I hope I shall not forget Jacobs Vow. May GOD be gracious to you & the dear Children, little do They know what I feel for Them. I wish to hear from you of every thing even the least Incidents. ,,,has better Intelligence. This is another sad Token of GODs anger but We dont lay it to heart. It is reported that a large reinforcement is arrived at N. York but we have not the certainty. (Afternoon) O sad, it this moment comes to my mind ,,,May GOD have mercy on & spare you & all my dear Friends, remember me tenderly to them all. With strong Affection I am tenderly yours,,,".

---T--- <u>DOI is Christ Based, Supports Religion, Christianity:</u> // "Letters of Delegates to Congress: Vol 4 -- 5/16, 1776 - 8/15, 1776 - John Adams to Benjamin Kent ,,,6/22. 1776 Your Letters of Apr. 24 and May 26 are before me ,,,both dated at Boston, a Circumstance which alone would have given Pleasure to a Man who has such an Attachment to that Town, and who has sufferd so much Anxiety for his Friends, in their Exile from it. We have not many of the fearfull, and still less of the Unbelieving among us, how slowly soever, you may think We proceed. Is it not a Want of Faith, or a Predominance of Fear, which makes some of you so impatient for Declarations in Words of what is every day manifested in Deeds of the most determined Nature and unequivocal Signification? *The only Question is, concerning the proper Time for making an explicit Declaration in Words. Some People must have Time to look around them, before, behind,* on the right hand, and on the left, then to think, and after all this to resolve. Others see at one intuitive Glance into the past and the future, and judge with Precision at once ,,,I am for the most liberal Toleration of all DENS of RELIGIONists but I hope that Congress will never meddle with RELIGION, [[here is supporting the allowance for all Christian DENs to have liberty and resolve themselves; but not that any specific DEN (religion) should have GOV favorism; respect; partiality]] further than to Say their own PRAYERS, and to fast and give Thanks, once a Year. Let every Colony have its own RELIGION, without Molestation. The Congress ,,,CHURCH to the ,,,"

---T--- <u>DOI & USA GOV is Christian; of Jesus Religion:</u> // "Journals of the Continental Congress, 1774-1789 - 3/19, 1782 - The Secretary at War, to whom was referred a memorial of Lieutenant Power, late of the regiment of artillery artificers, delivered in a report; Whereupon, Ordered ,,,commanding officer of the regiment that he did duty therein ,,,No. 149, I, folio 153.] On a report of a committee ,,,appointed to prepare a recommendation to the several states, to set apart a day of humiliation, fasting, and PRAYER Congress agreed to the following Proclamation: The goodness of the Supreme Being [[note the Being is the Supreme Judge as in the DOI]] to all his rational creatures, demands their acknowledgments of gratitude and love; his absolute government of this world dictates, that it is the interest of every nation and people ardently to supplicate his mercy favor and implore his protection. When the LUST OF DOMINION or LAWLESS AMBITION excites arbitrary power to INVADE THE RIGHTS, or endeavor to WRENCH WREST from a people their SACRED and UNALIENABLE INVALUABLE PRIVILEGES, and compels them, in DEFENCE of the same, to encounter all the horrors and calamities of a bloody and vindictive war; then is that people loudly called upon to fly unto that GOD for protection, who hears the <u>cries</u> of the distressed, and will not turn a deaf ear to the supplication of the OPPRESSED. Great Britain, hitherto left to infatuated councils, and to pursue measures repugnant to their her own interest, and distressing to this country, still persists in the chimerical idea design of subjugating these US; which will compel us into another active and perhaps bloody campaign. The US in Congress assembled, therefore, taking into consideration our present situation, our multiplied transgressions of the HOLY laws of our GOD, [[Bible words and reference to Jesus]] and his past acts of kindness and goodness exercised towards us, which we would ought to record with me the liveliest gratitude, think it their indispensable duty to call upon the different several states, to set apart the last Thursday in Apr. next, as a day of fasting, humiliation and PRAYER, that our joint supplications may then ascend to the throne of the RULER of the UNIVERSE, beseeching Him that he would to diffuse a SPIRIT of universal reformation among all ranks and degrees of our citizens; and make us a HOLY, that so we may be an HAPPY people; that it would please Him to impart wisdom, integrity and unanimity to our counsellors; to bless and prosper the REIGN of our illustrious ally, and give success to his arms employed in the DEFENCE of THE RIGHTS of human nature; that HE WOULD SMILE upon our military arrangements by land and sea; administer comfort and consolation to our prisoners in a cruel captivity; that he would protect the health and life of our Commander in Chief; give grant us victory over our enemies; establish peace in all our borders, and give happiness to all our inhabitants; that he would prosper the labor of the husbandman, making the earth yield its increase in abundance, and give a proper season for the in gathering of the fruits thereof; that He would grant success to all engaged in lawful trade and commerce, and take under his guardianship all schools and seminaries of learning, and make them nurseries of VIRTUE and PIETY; that He would incline the HEARTS of all men to peace, and fill them with universal charity and benevolence, and that the RELIGION of our DIVINE REDEEMER, [[Jesus referred to again]] with all its benign influences, may cover the earth,,, Done by the US in Congress assembled ,,,[Note 1: 1 This report, in the writing of a clerk ,,,No. 24, folio 467.]".

---T--- <u>DOI & USA GOV is Christ's Christianity Based:</u> // "Letters of Delegates to Congress: Volume 2- 9/1775 — 12/1775 - John Adams to Abigail Adams 10/23. 1775 ,,,. I rejoice in the happy Principles and the happy Temper, which apparently dictated them all. I feel myself much affected with the Breach upon the Family. But We can count a Mother, a Brother, an Aunt, and a Brothers Child among the slain by this cruel Pestilence. May GOD almighty put a stop to its Rage, and humble us under the Ravages already made by it. The sorrows of all our Friends on the Loss of your Mother are never out of my Mind. I PRAY GOD to spare my Parent whose Life has been prolonged by his Goodness hitherto, as well as yours that survives. The tremendous Calamities already felt of Fire, Sword and Pestilence, may be only Harbingers of greater still. We have no security against Calamities here-this Planet is its Region. The only Principle is to be prepared for the worst Events. If I could write as well as you, my sorrows would be as eloquent as yours, but upon my Word I cannot. The unaccountable Event which you allude to has reached this Place and occasioned a Fall. ,,,I would be glad however that the worst Construction might not be put. Let him have fair Play-tho I doubt. The Man who violates private Faith, cancells solemn Obligations, whom neither Honour nor CONSCIENCE holds ,,,Open barefaced IMMORALity ought not to be so countenanced. Tho I think, a Fatality attends us in some Instances, yet a DIVINE Protection and favour is visible in others, and let us be chearfull whatever happens. Chearfullness is not a SIN in any Times. I am afraid to hear again almost least some other should be sick in the House. Yet I hope better, and that you will reassume your wonted Chearfullness and write again upon News and Politics ,,RC,,,".

---T--- <u>DOI & USA GOV is Christian, supports</u> Christianity & all of its DENs to Magnify Jesus: // "Letters of Delegates to Congress: Volume 8 - 9/19, 1777 - 1/31, 1778 - ,,,10/25. 1777 This Town is a small one, not larger than Plymouth. There are in it, two German CHURCHes, the one Lutheran, the other Calvinistical. The CONGREGATIONs are pretty numerous, and their Attendance upon PUBLIC WORSHIP is decent. It is remarkable that the Germans, wherever they are found, are carefull to maintain the PUBLIC WORSHIP, which is more than can be said of the other DENS of CHRISTIANs, this Way. There is one CHURCH here erected by the joint Contributions of Episcopalians and Presbyterians, but the Minister, who is a Missionary, is confined for Toryism, so that they have had for a long Time no publick Worship. ,,,Congress have appointed two Chaplains, Mr. White and Mr. Duffield, the former of whom an Episcopalian is arrived and opens Congress with PRAYERS every Day. The latter is expected every Hour. Mr. Duche I am sorry to inform you has turned out an Apostate and a Traytor. Poor Man! I pitty his Weakness, and detest his WICKEDNESS. As to News, We are yet in a painful Suspense about Affairs at the Northward, but from Philadelphia, We have Accounts that are very pleasing. Commodore Hazelwood, with his Gallies, and Lt. Coll. Smith in the Garrison of Fort Mifflin, have behaved in a manner the most gallant and glorious. They have defended the River, and the Fort with a Firmness and Perseverance, which does Honour to human Nature. If the News from the Northward is TRUE ,,,I am wearied with the Life I lead, and long for the Joys of my Family. GOD grant I may enjoy it, in Peace. Peace is my dear Delight. War has no Charms for me. If I live much longer in Banishment I shall scarcely know my own Children. Tell my little ones, that if they will be very good, Pappa will come home. RC (MHi). Adams ,,,2:359-60."respondence (Butterfield), 1:311-12 ,,,Benjamin Church,,,".

---T--- <u>DOI & USA GOV is Christian for Jesus:</u> // "Letters of Delegates to Congress: Volume 18- 3/1, 1781 - 8/31, 1781 - Arthur Middleton to Aedanus Burke My dr. Sir Pa. 4/7/[1782] Your favr. of the 25 Jany. Came,,, The Strong Outlines you have drawn of the mellancholy real Situation of our Country in all points correspond exactly with what my anxious imagination had formed, whenever reason & reflexion led me to consider an Object allways uppermost in my mind; the picture is easily fill'd up, it is a melancholy one, & I fear with you that nothing but Time & skillfull management can restore that firm, orderly, & composed mode of proceeding so essential to establish the publick Happiness which is or ought to be the wish of all. I have much confidence in the Ability & Integrity of the men chosen to conduct affairs. I think I know the PURITY of THEIR INTENTIONS & I trust their Councills may yet lead us to prosperity. Upon mature Consideration of all Circumstances; of the unmerited Sufferings of so many, & of the resentments necessarily rous'd in a people whom I know to be naturally generous & Sensible, I rejoice that matters have been Conducted with so much moderation & Temper; tho' I could have wishd the Idea of Confiscation had been totally abolish'd, or at least put off till entire secure possession [of the] Country had restor'd Tranquillity, & the publick mind was free & open to the guidance of cool dispassionate reason. Your Sentiments upon the Subject are those of the Patriot & the friend of human Nature, & I wd. there had been more of your way of thinking-upon a thorough Investigation of this mode of Punishment, even in Cases of Treason, I have been & am principled against it; I cannot approve of the inhuman Sentence of visiting the SINS of the Fathers upon the guiltless women [and] Children, [[HOLY BIBLE quoted]] notwithstanding the SACRED Authority which may be quoted for it. It is a Doctrine suited only to the Climates of DESPOSTISM, & abhorrent to the dignified SPIRIT of pure & genuine republicanism. [[not Democracy, or mass rule against principle or right law; - because many Created people decide evil does not make it right]] In the Eye of reason the Individual shd. stand or fall by his own Actions, & those connected should be involved in the punishment no farther, than they have been partakers in the Crime. Banishment of the Individual, & a deprivation of the Benefits of Citizenship & property for life are surely sufficient both as a punishment & a prevention of Crimes, without reducing a whole family for the SIN of one to misery & destruction. Here my friend you have my Thoughts upon an Interesting Subject which concerns the good of mankind.,,,: "Next to the obedience due the Dictates of my own CONSCIENCE," Middleton continued, "it has ever lain nearest to my heart so to regulate my conduct as to wish your Approbation. I shall still be governed by the same motives, & trust I shall retain it to our Life's end-at parting with my Brother I entreated him to present my Duty to you, & to acquaint you that my mind was thoroughly at Ease with regard to my own fate; This I hoped would operate as a Balm to your affliction upon my Account. "To the many anxieties for my dearest Connections, the knowledge of your Ill health & Troubles have added grief indeed. ,,,how much I have felt for you. I am now anxious for my Brother -in short our day seems to be crowded with Troubles ".

---T--- <u>DOI is based on Christ's Christianity:</u> // "Letters of Delegates to Congress: Volume 10- 6/1, 1778 - 9/30, 1778 - Henry Marchant ,,,Dear Children, Philadelphia 7/20/1778 I recd. your endearing Letter of the 7th of July this Day and you can't conceive what a heartfelt Satisfaction it gave me; go on my dear Children and strive to excell in a<u>ll useful Knowledge, especially such as relates to GOD and that other World, where we are all to go.</u> [[priority and no idolatry is being taught here; seek God 1st]] To them that behave well in this World, the next will be a World of Happiness indeed-but to such as do ill here, it will be a world of EVERLASTING TORMENT. [[a Bible vs on heaven & hell]] GOD grant that when we have all left this World, we may not be parted from each other in the World to come; but that all, Father and Mother, Brother and Sisters, may meet together, never to part again, but live a whole <u>ETERNITY with GOD and CHRIST-with Abraham, Isaac & Jacob,</u> and all other good Men & Women and Children who have gone there before us. <u>Remember that GOD hates a Lye, and every thing that is dishonest-and that you must always be chearful and willing to do your Duty to GOD and Man, and to your Parents and to love one another and all good People,</u> and that you must try to perswade naughty Children to behave <u>better and to QUIT all their WICKED WORDS and WAYS, if they would ever expect to be happy</u> ,,,I rejoice that she does not forget her BIBLE-her Catechism & PRAYERS. I am glad to find Mr. Pemberton has been with and that he kindly advises you. I will agree with him, that you may not make a task of your grammar. Indeed my dear Child I know you love your book so well, that I think it needless you should task yourself with any book. I think a good and edifying book will never be a task to Miss Sally, I hope it will not with Miss Betsy. A little exercise in cyphering now and then I think is very well. I am also pleased that You take such notice of the business of the farm, and that you are able to give me so good an account of it. Your curiosity is excited to know the meaning of the tow upon some of the trees. I got some small twigs from trees of another sort of apples and pears and cut off a limb and stuck the small twiggs into it, to grow, and wrapt the tow & clay round to keep the rain out. Mr. Webster will explain it to you further if you ask him. Are you like to have a good many pears, peaches, and apples? ,,,currants? ,,,strawberries, huccleberries and blackberries? ,,,We have a Gentleman from France called a Plenipotentiary, that is, having full powers and authority from the King of France to join with us, his advice and to assist us against Our Enemies-And the King of France has also sent us a great many large Ships, to assist in taking the British Ships & People, and to drive them away from this good land which HEAVEN gave to Our

Fore-Fathers, and to us their children, and which the KING OF ENGLAND and his WICKED people have been endeavouring to take from us-And I hope by the Blessing of GOD that We shall by & by have peace thro' all this Country, and that you may live to grow up and enjoy it with thankfulness to GOD, and never forget what great things the LORD hath done for You. Was it not for this hope my Dear Children, I could never consent to leave you & your good Mamma so long year after year. Hoping we may soon meet & praise GOD for his great Goodness to Us all, I remain Your affectionate Father, Henry Marchant RC (RHi),,,".

---T--- DOI is Christian; Christ based: // The CON was constructed approx. same time as this following DOC that is signed by reference to the Lord Jesus Earthly coming~ Christmas: // "Journals of the Continental Congress, 1774-1789 - 10/16, 1787. Congress assembled. Present ,,,Accordingly Congress proceeded ,,,entered by Charles Thomson in Secret Journal, Foreign Affairs, Papers of the Continental Congress, No. 5, III, pp. 1674--1675.] Resolved Unanimously ,,,Chevalier John Paul Jones in commemoration of the valour and brilliant services of that Officer in the command of a squadron of french and American ships under the flag and commission of the US off the coast of England Great Britain in the late war; And ,,,Resolved2 That a letter be written to his Most CHRISTIAN Majesty informing him that the US in Congress Assembled ,,,convinced that he can no where else so well acquire that knowledge which may hereafter render him more extensively useful ,,,to reside at the court of his Most CHRISTIAN Majesty and do give you full power and authority there to represent us and to do and perform all such matters and things as to the said place or Office doth appertain or as may by our instructions be given unto you in Charge ,,,In testimony whereof we have caused the Seal of the US to be hereunto affixed. Witness his Excellency Arthur St Clair our president this twelfth day of October One thousand seven hundred and eighty seven and of our Sovereignty and independence the twelfth. [[date of DOI used as USA Start date]] The letter of Credence. Great and beloved friend We the US in Congress Assembled ,,,We PRAY GOD to keep your Majesty under his HOLY protection. Done at the city of New York the 12th day of Oct in the year of our Lord 1787 and of our sovereignty and independence the twelfth. ,,,hath prepared the following letter1 to his Most CHRISTIAN Majesty which having been duly signed and countersigned ,,,Papers of the Continental Congress, No. 81, III p. 21.] ,,,our sincere assurances that the various and important benefits for which we are endebted to your friendship will never cease to interest us in whatever may concern the happiness of your Majesty, your family and people. We PRAY GOD to keep you, our Great and beloved friend, under his HOLY protection. Done at the city of New York the 16 day of Octr. in the year of our Lord 1787 and of our Sovereignty and independence the twelfth,,,".

---T--- DOI & USA GOV is Christian, Based on Christ: // "The Revolutionary Diplomatic Correspondence of the US, Volume 5 - ,,,- The Hague, 7/5, 1782. Sir: Soon after my public reception by their high mightinesses ,,,to pay their respects to Congress and to me, as their representative with a very polite invitation to a public entertainment in their city, to be made upon the occasion ,,,me to transmit from them to Congress the enclosed compliment, which I promised to do. I was so much affected with the zeal and ardor of these worthy gentlemen and their constituents, which, with many other things of a similar kind, convinced me that there is in this nation a strong affection for America, and a kind of RELIGIOUS veneration for her just cause ,,,John Adams. ,,,the united provinces of the Netherlands had acknowledged the freedom and independency of the US of North America ,,,Congress of the said US. If ever any circumstances were capable of recalling to the minds of the people of these provinces the most lively remembrance of the cruel situation to which their forefathers found themselves once reduced, under the oppressive yoke of Spanish TYRANNY, it was, no doubt, that terrible and critical moment when the Colonies of North America, groaning under the intolerable weight of the chains with which the BOUNDLESS AMBITION of Great Britain had loaded them, were forced into a just and lawful war to recover the use and enjoyment of that liberty to which they were entitled by the SACRED and unalienable LAWS OF NATURE. If ever the citizens of this republic have had an occasion to remember, with sentiments of the liveliest gratitude, the visible assistance and protection of a Being who, after having constantly supported them during the course of a long, bloody war which cost their ancestors eighty years' hard struggles and painful labors, deigned by the strength of His powerful arm [[God was the God to whom they relied on during the DOI; Christ Jesus]] to break the odious fetters under which we had so long groaned, and who, from that happy era to the present time, has constantly maintained us in the possession of our precious liberties; if ever the citizens of these provinces have been bound to remember those unspeakable favors of the ALMIGHTY, it was no doubt at that moment when haughty Britain began to feel the effects of DIVINE indignation, and when the vengeance of HEAVEN defeated her sanguinary schemes; it was when treading under foot the SACRED ties of blood and nature, [[Bible vs often]] and meditating the destruction of her own offspring, her arms were everywhere baffled in the most terrible and exemplary manner, her troops defeated, and her armies led into captivity and at last that haughty power, humbled by that HEAVEN which she had provoked, saw the sceptre which she had usurped fall from her enfeebled hands; and America, shaking off the cruel yoke which an unnatural step-mother had endeavored to impose forever upon her, thanked bounteous HEAVEN for her happy deliverance. If ever the inhabitants of this country, and these of this city in particular, bare had a just cause for joy, and good grounds to conceive the highest hopes of prosperity and happiness, it was undoubtedly at that so much wished-for moment, when, with a unanimous voice, the fathers of the country declared the US of America to be free and independent, and acknowledged your excellency as minister plenipotentiary and envoy of the illustrious Congress. Impressed with the various sentiments of respect, joy, and gratitude, with which the unspeakable favors of the ALMIGHTY towards both countries must inspire every feeling and sensible mind ,,,American Congress, and to assure you, in the strongest terms, that if any event recorded in the annals of our country is capable of impressing us with the liveliest joy, and of opening to our minds the happiest prospect, it is that glorious and ever memorable day ,,,united provinces of the Netherlands, solemnly acknowledged the independence of the US of America; a step which, under the pleasure of GOD, must become the foundation of an unalterable

53

friendship, and the source of mutual prosperity to the two republics, whose union being cemented by interests henceforth common and inseparable, must forever subsist, and be constantly and RELIGIOUSly preserved by our latest posterity. Allow us, then, ye deliverers of America, ye generous defenders of her infant liberties ,,,wishes of the nation. Accept also of the fervent PRAYERS, which we address to HEAVEN, beseeching the ALMIGHTY to shower down His blessings on your republic and her allies. Permit us also to recommend to you, in the strongest manner, the interests of our country, and of this city in particular. Let those of our citizens who have been the most zealous in promoting the acknowledgment of your independence enjoy always a particular share of your affection. That among those who may follow our EX, no one may ever succeed in detracting from the good faith and integrity of Holland, or causing the sincerity of our efforts to advance our mutual interests to be suspected, which are founded on the unalterable principles of pure virtue, and a RELIGION common to both of us [[Christianity is the religion of the USA, not all religions; and proper definition of religion]],,,".

---T--- <u>DOI & USA GOV is Christian Based & </u>Christ centered: // "Journals of the Continental Congress, 1774-1789 - 11/17, 1779 - According to order ,,,Sr. Chevalier de la Luzerne, minister plenipotentiary of his most CHRISTIAN majesty, was introduced to an audience by Mr. [John] Mathews and Mr. [Gouverneur] Morris, the two members for that purpose appointed, and being seated in his chair, the secretary of the embassy delivered to the President a letter from his most CHRISTIAN majesty, directed on the out side " ,,,The bad state of health of the Sieur Gérard, our minister plenipotentiary to you ,,,We PRAY you to give full credit to all he shall say to you on our behalf, especially when he shall assure you of the sincerity of our wishes for your prosperity, as well as of the constancy of our affection and of our friendship for the US in general, and for each one of them in particular. We PRAY GOD to keep you, our very dear, great friends and allies, in his HOLY protection. Your good friend and ally, Louis. Done at Versailles, the 31 May, 1779. ,,,Gentlemen, <u>The wisdom and courage which have founded your republic; the prudence which presides over your deliberations; your firmness in execution; the skill and valor displayed by your generals and soldiers, during the course of the war, have attracted</u> the admiration and regard of the whole world. The King, my master, was the first to acknowledge a liberty acquired amidst so many perils and with so much glory. Since treaties dictated by moderation, have fixed upon a permanent base the union of France with the American republic, his majesty's whole conduct must have demonstrated how dearly he tenders your prosperity, and his firm resolution to maintain your independence by every means in his power. The events which have successively unfolded themselves, show the wisdom of those measures. A powerful ally hath acknowledged the justice of those motives which had compelled the King to take arms, and we may reasonably hope for the most solid success, from the operations of the united fleets. ,,,the desires of the French and the request of the Americans, which invited him to join his arms to those of your republic. Events have not completely answered his courage and his efforts, but his blood and that of my countrymen, shed in a cause so dear to us, hath cemented the base on which the alliance is founded, and impressed on it a character as indelible as are all those by which it is already consecrated. ,,,The relations ,,,between the subjects of the King ,,,inhabitants of the ,,,US continually, multiply; and we may already perceive in spite of those obstacles which embarrass the reciprocal communication, how natural it is, how advantageous it will be to the two ,,,nations and all who participate in it, and how much the monopolizing SPIRIT, the jealous attention and prohibitory edicts of the enemy to your freedom, have been prejudicial to your happiness ,,,I am certain of fulfilling my duty when I labour for your prosperity; and I felicitate myself upon being sent to a nation whose interests are so intimately blended with our own, that I can be useful ,,, To which the President returned the following answer: Sir, The early attention of our good friend and ally to these US is gratefully felt by all their virtuous citizens; and we should be unfaithful representatives if we did not warmly acknowledge every instance of his regard, and take every opportunity of expressing the attachment of our constituents to treaties formed upon the purest principles. His most CHRISTIAN Majesty, in rendering himself protector of the rights of mankind, [[here God, Christ Jesus is said]] became entitled to assistance from the friends of man. This title could not but be recognized by a monarch whose diadem is adorned with equity and TRUTH ,,,nor can we doubt that other powers will rejoice to see that haughty nation humbled, in proportion as they have been insulted by her presumptuous arrogance. We well know, and all the world must acknowledge, the moderation and friendship of the most CHRISTIAN King ,,,as in every other instance, we perceive his strict adherence to the principles of our defensive alliance ,,,A noble emulation which hath poured out the blood of the two nations, and mingled it together as a SACRED pledge of perpetual union! ,,,That they have not been still more beneficial, is to be attributed to those incidents which in the hand of OMNIPOTENCE determine all human events ,,,we are happy in his choice, and being thoroughly convinced of the intimate connexion between the interests and views of the allied nations ,,,and promote the welfare of your country ,,,to the citizens of America.1 [Note 1: 1 From this point Thomson resumed the entries.] ,,,dated in Congress, 11/17, 1779, and signed Samuel Huntington, President,,,".

---T--- <u>DOI Based on Christianity of Christ: // "Letters of </u>Delegates to Congress: Volume 6 -- 1/1, 1777 - 4/30, 1777 - John Adams to Abigail Adams - We long to hear of the Formation of a new Army. We shall loose the most happy opportunity of destroying the Enemy this Spring, if We do not exert ourselves instantly. We have from New Hampshire a Coll. Thornton ,,,The Fanatic soon began to examine the Dr. concerning the ARTICLES OF FAITH, and what he thought of original SIN ? Why, says the Dr., I satisfy myself about it in this manner. Either original SIN is divisible or indivisible. If it was divisible every descendant of Adam and Eve [[Holy Bible references; Genesis]] must have a Part, and the share which falls to each Individual at this Day, is so small a Particle, that I think it is not worth considering. If indivisible, then the whole Quantity must have descended in a right Line, and must now be possessed by one Person only, and the Chances are Millions and Millions and Millions to one that that Person is now in Asia or Africa and that I have nothing to do with it."

---T--- <u>DOI is for Christ, for Christianity, & USA GOV activities are</u> Christian: // "Journals of the Continental Congress, 1774-1789 - 6/2, 1788. - Congress assembled present ,,,chosen one of the Delegates to represent this State in the Congress of the US of America ,,,are hereby authorized and empowered to represent this State in the said Congress, during the Time aforesaid ,,,Given ,,,the Seal of the said State, this Seventh Day of May A. D. 1787, and in the Eleventh Year of (Seal) Independence. ,,,Secretary to the US for the department of foreign Affairs to whom were referred two letters from his Most CHRISTIAN Majesty dated the 30th Sept. 1787 - ,,,he has taken leave of us Manifests his attention to your dignity and interests, and affords Strong evidence of his attachment to the prosperity and happiness of these States. We PRAY GOD to have you, our great and beloved friend in his HOLY keeping. Written at New York the second day of June 1788. By your good friends the US of America in Congress Assembled. ,,,A Chas Thomson Secy . Great and beloved Friend and Ally -,,,to which the above is an Answer is as follows, [Note 1: 1 See Feb 5, 26 and 27, 1788.] Very Dear Great Friends and Allies ,,,The prudent and enlightened conduct which he constantly observed during the course of his Mission add to the proofs which he had before given of his zeal for our service ,,,to assure you in terms the most expressive of our Affection and of our sincere friendship for you. He cannot too strongly paint to you the lively interest which we take in the prosperity of the US in general, and in that of each of them in particular. On this we PRAY GOD that he will have you very dear great friends and Allies in his HOLY keeping. Done &ca. ,,,and Study to preserve and encrease the mutual attachment and intercourse which happily subsists between them. We receive with great pleasure the kind and explicit assurances of friendship contained in,,, We PRAY GOD to have you our great and beloved friend and Ally in his HOLY keeping. written at New York the second day of June 1788, By your good friends, the US of America in Congress ,,,[Note 2: 2 See May 30, 1788.]".

---T--- <u>DOI is Christian for Jesus; & Formation of the USA is based Christ's Holy Bible:</u> // "Letters of Delegates to Congress:Volume 23- 11/7, 1785 - 11/5, 1786 ,,,Nathaniel Gorham 338 6/7, 1786 to be pricked to the Heart; if silent solemnity, countenances bathed in tears, expressions of Compunction, & the closest Attention to the word, [[Holy Bible here noted]] may be deemed Evidences of it. In short it appeared [to m]any to be an awful place, & none other than the House of GOD, & ,,,Gate of HEAVEN. There is a great increase in the CHURCHes of the Plains, Mt. Bethel, Piscataway, as well as in New York, & its Vicinity. Cranberry, &c. The concern of Saul ,,,seems to have taken place in almost every family in several Neighbourhoods. Many of my Kinsmen according to the flesh are of the Number. Nine Ministers were there; & there appeared to be a remarkable Unction, as the French DIVINEs term it, afforded to most of them. "And THEY SHALL FEAR THE NAME OF THE LORD from the West &c." ,,,What think you of the Commencemt. or rather of the more compleat fulfilment of this Prophecy? Glorious things of old, were spoken of, & are now accomplishing in the City of GOD. I wish to ever have that PRAYER in my heart "THY KINGDOM COME." A wide field, on almost every hand, is opening for Labourers of the Baptist DEN, but they are comparatively few. Let us PRAY therefore &c. On the 29th Ult I recd Letters from home & all were well. Mrs. Manning spoke favourably of the Behaviour of the little Boy[s]. She sais they behave as well as she could reasonably expect & attend to their Learning. I wish Tasker had as great a taste for Books as George. Perhaps Age may alter this matter. Not long since I had Letters from all the little Boys to testify their regard to,,,, My Servant had often expressed to the Boys a desire to go to Virginia, it being a good place for a Taylor; and a Vessel sailed for Baltimore, from Providence, just about that time with a German & his wife who had resided some time in Providence. Any Attention which you may please to give in setting up the Advertizements, or inquiring relative to the premises, will be most kindly accepted by Your very unworthy friend, James Manning P.S. I shall endeavour to conduct the Boys living, &c for their highest Advantage, as far as I am competent to judge.RC (DLC: Robert Carter Papers). Addressed: "Honorable Robert Carter, Nomany Hall, Westmoreland County, Virginia."1 Robert Carter (1728--;1804) ,,,entered Manning's Baptist universe as a consequence of a remarkable conversion in 1778, which opened a new chapter in his quest for faith that lasted until about 1790 when he embraced the principles of Emanuel Swedenborg. For Carter's SPIRITual journey and RELIGIOUS activities during his Baptist years, see Louis Morton, Robert Carter of Nomini Hall, A 2 Apparently a reference to the conversion of Saul of Tarsus, whose dramatic experience on the road to Damascus is recorded in the New Testament book of Acts, 9:3--;18. 3 Isaiah 59:19. [[Holy Bible Vss]]".

---T--- <u>DOI is Christ & Christian with Different Branches of</u> GOV already early being designed before the CON: // "Letters of Delegates to Congress: Volume 8- 9/19, 1777 - 1/31, 1778 - Samuel Adams to James Warren - My dear sir York Town Pennsylva 10 ,,,1777 I sent you a few days ago an Account of the Success we ,,,the Enemy cannot get up with their Ships of War, Howe cannot long remain in the City. May Honor be given to whom Honor may be due. Congress have applyd with Diligence to Confederation. Most of the important Articles are agreed to. Each State retains its Sovereignty and Independence with every Power, Jurisdiction and Right which is not by the Confederation expressly delegated to the US in Congress assembled. Each State is to have one Vote in Congress; but there must be a Concurrence of Nine States in all Matters of Importance. ,,,The Representatives of Each State in Congress to be nominated, the contending States to strike off 13 Each and out of the remaining 13 not more than 9 nor less than 7 shall be drawn out by Lot, any five of them to hear & determine the Matter. I hope we shall finish the Confederation in a few days when I intend to renew my Request for the Leave of Absence, and return home. ,,,I am <u>determined by Gods Assistance never to forsake the great Cause in which my</u> Country is virtuously struggling; but there are others who have greater Abilities & more adequate to this important Service, than I have ,,,and I have the clear and full Testimony of my own Mind [[conscience & knowledge here referred to]] that I have at all Times endeavord to fill the Station ,,,I hope the Person to be elected in my Room will have understanding enough to know when the Arts of Flattery are playd upon him, and Fortitude of mind sufficient to resist & despise them. This I mention inter Nosmetipsos. <u>In this EVIL World there are oftentimes large Doses prepared</u> for those whose Stomacks will bear them. And it would be a disgrace to human Nature to affirm there are some who can take the fullest Cup without nauseating. I suppose you have by this time finishd a form of GOV. I hope the greatest Care will be taken in the Choice of a Governor. He, whether a wise Man or a Fool, will in a great Measure form the MORALS & Manners of the People. I beg Pardon for hinting the Possibility ,,,I believe my Country will fix their Eyes and their Choice on a Man of RELIGION and Piety; who will understand human Nature and the Nature and End of political Society- who will not by Corruption or Flattery be seducd to the betraying, even without being sensible of it himself, the SACRED Rights of his Country. We are told that the Prisoners taken at the Northward are sent into Massachusetts Bay ,,,I fear that inconsiderate Persons of Fashion and some significance will be inducd, under the Idea of Politeness ,,,dangerous to the Publick. There are other Reasons ,,,The Success of the present Campain hitherto has been great beyond our most sanguine Expectation. Let us ascribe Glory to GOD who has graciously vouchsafd to favor the Cause of America and of Mankind ,,,yet we must not slack our Hands. Every Nerve must be exerted in preparing ,,,Among the Train of EVILs it is likely to bring upon us, is the Destruction of MORALS ,,,JCC, 9:852."

---T--- DOI is a Christian DOC for Jesus: // "Journals of the Continental Congress, 1774-1789 - 3/19, 1782 - ,,,This report is in the Papers of the Continental Congress, No. 149, I, folio 153.] ,,,committee, consisting ,,,appointed to prepare a recommendation to the several states, to set apart a day of humiliation, fasting, and PRAYER Congress agreed to the following Proclamation: The goodness of the SUPREME BEING to all his rational creatures, demands their acknowledgments of gratitude and love; his ABSOLUTE GOVERNMENT OF THIS WORLD dictates, that it is the interest of every nation and people ardently to supplicate his mercy favor and implore his protection. When the LUST OF DOMINION or LAWLESS AMBITION excites arbitrary power to INVADE THE RIGHTS, or endeavor to WRENCH WREST from a people their SACRED and UNALIENABLE INVALUABLE PRIVILEGES, and compels them, in DEFENCE of the same, to encounter all the horrors and calamities of a bloody and vindictive war; then is that people loudly called upon to fly unto that GOD for protection, who hears the cries of the distressed, and will not turn a deaf ear to the supplication of the OPPRESSED. Great Britain, hitherto left to infatuated councils, and to pursue measures repugnant to their her own interest, and distressing to this country, still persists in the ,,,idea design of subjugating these US; which will compel us into another active and perhaps bloody campaign. The US in Congress assembled, therefore, taking into consideration our present situation, our multiplied transgressions of the HOLY laws of our GOD, and his past acts of kindness and goodness exercised towards us, which ,,,the liveliest gratitude, think it their indispensable duty to call upon the different several states, to set apart the last Thursday in Apr. next, as a day of fasting, humiliation and PRAYER, that our joint supplications may then ascend to the throne of the RULER of the UNIVERSE, beseeching Him that he would to diffuse a SPIRIT of universal reformation among all ranks and degrees of our citizens; and make us a HOLY, that so we may be an HAPPY people; that it would please Him to impart wisdom, integrity and unanimity to our counsellors; to bless and prosper the REIGN of our illustrious ally, and give success to his arms employed in the DEFENCE of THE RIGHTS of human nature; that HE WOULD SMILE upon our military arrangements by land and sea; administer comfort and consolation to our prisoners in a cruel captivity; that HE would protect the health and life of our Commander in Chief ,,,us victory over our enemies; establish peace in all our borders, and give happiness to all our inhabitants; that HE would prosper the labor of the husbandman, making the earth yield its increase in abundance, and give a proper season for the in gathering of the fruits thereof; that HE would grant success to all engaged in lawful trade and commerce, and take under his guardianship all schools and seminaries of learning, and make them nurseries of VIRTUE and PIETY; that He would incline the HEARTS of all men to peace, and fill them with universal charity and benevolence, and that the RELIGION of our DIVINE REDEEMER, with all its benign influences, may cover the earth as the waters cover the seas.,, [Note 1: 1 This report, in the writing of a clerk ,,,On a report of a committee, consisting of Mr. [Samuel] Livermore, Mr. [James] Madison, and Mr. [Abraham] Clark,,,".

---T--- The Executive Branch Inaugural Ceremony of the President includes God: // "so help me God"; and a Christian oath or appeal for his help. This has been done since the time of the first president~ George Washington.

---T--- The Gregorian Calendar was enacted by Congress, which is also known as the Christian calendar of Christ: // Because it is based on the birth of Jesus Christ as Lord of ALL; BC & AD (which BC is before His birth and AD is after His birth). The precise date of Christ's birth is unknown, and therefore an estimation was calculated.

---T--- DOI is Christian for Jesus & is the Basis of Formation of the USA GOV: // "Letters of Delegates to Congress: Volume 4- 5/16, 1776 - 8/15, 1776 - the North Carolina Council of Safety - Gentlemen Philadelphia Aug. 7 [i.e. 8] 1776 ,,,CHRISTIANITY the dear RELIGION of peace & Mercy should hold ,,,We ought not to forget the duties of the CHRISTIAN. Women and Children are ,,,worthy the American Arms-their weakness disarms rage. May their blood never sully our triumphs. But Mercy ,,,the Law of nations ,,,We have been large upon this Subject, as we have it much at heart to quiet the Apprehensions of our Frontiers ,,,We are Gentlemen, With great Respect, Your most Obedt Humble Servants, Wm Hooper Joseph Hewes John Penn RC (Nc-Ar). Written by 5:382-83."

---T--- DOI & USA GOV is Christian, enacting religious centered GOV activities for Christ: // During the total process and time periods, the activities included~ +the Congress appointed chaplains for itself and for the Militaries; and these supported the publication of a Holy Bible; and assisted Christian morality to the Militaries. +Public lands were granted to promote Christianity among the Indians. +National days (many of them) of thanksgiving and of "humiliation, fasting, and prayer" were proclaimed by Congress; at least twice a year throughout the Independence War.

---T--- Christianity, including Christian ministers were some of the REP, and involved with and supported by all of the REP sent to the congressional meetings for the DOI & CON. (63).

---T--- <u>DOI is Christ based with Christianity for Independence of</u> USA; & Christian men in Office with spiritual thoughts: // "Letters of Delegates to Congress: Volume 9- 2/1, 1778 - 5/31, 1778 - ,,,16th Apr. 1778 I sit down to let you know I am in this World tho in a very remote Part of it ,,,It would give me infinite Pleasure to hear of my Friends yourself in particular but since it is my Lott to know no more than the Burthen of General Report I must be contented. I receive great Pain from being informed that you are distressed on my Account. Be of good Chear I PRAY you. I have all that Happiness which flows from conscious Rectitude [[Rectitude defined as "being right morally and integrity - with God"]]. I am blest with as great a Portion of Health as usually belongs to the share of Mankind. Content with what I have and what I am I look forward serenely to the Course of Events confident that supreme Wisdom & Justice will provide for the Happiness of his Creatures [[here we reference the term happiness pertaining to Christ; used in the DOI]]. It gives me Pain that I am seperated from those I love but comparing this with what thousands suffer I dare not repine. Let me earnestly recommend to you so much of either RELIGION or Philosophy as to bear inevitable EVILs with Resignation [[here we have the opposition of evil, anti-Christ activity]]. I would that it were in my Power to solace and comfort your declining Age. The Duty I owe to a tender Parent demands this of me but a higher Duty hath bound me to the Service of my Fellow Creatures [[here is the putting of God as priority parent; opposes idolatry in the USA]]. The natural Indolence of my Disposition hath unfitted me for the Paths of Ambition and the early Possession of Power taught me how little it deserves to be prized. Whenever the present Storm subsides I shall rush with Eagerness into the Bosom of private Life but while it continues and while my Country calls for the Exertion of that little Share of Abilities which it hath pleased GOD to bestow on me I hold it my indispensible Duty to give myself to her. I know that for such Sentiments I am called a Rebel and that such Sentiments are not fashionable among the Folks you see. It is possible (tho I hope not) that your maternal Tenderness may lead you to wish that I would resign these Sentiments. ,,,PRAY remember me to him most affectionately and to my sister. She too has been much wounded. The Loss of her Infant must have distressed her greatly but perhaps her own Experience may have led her to prize Life at its just Value and if so it is a Blessing she may not think so estimable as to wish it for her Child. Remember me most tenderly to all her little Infants to Isaac particularly who I am told hath not forgotten me poor Child. I hope it may be in my Power to return his Attention by the Protection of a Parent. GOD forbid he should need it or any of them ,,,And now my Dear Madam let me again intreat you to make yourself happy. Discard the gloomy Ideas which are too apt to croud into the Mind in your Situation and Time of Life [[Christ the Comforter in experience is here noted]]. There is enough of Sorrow in this World without looking into Futurity for it. Hope the best. If it happens, well; if not, it is then Time enough to be afflicted and at any Rate the intermediate Space is well filled. Adieu. Yours most affectionately ,,,the American Revolution (Norman: University of Oklahoma Press, 1970), pp. 126 29 ,,,Morris wrote to his mother during his term of service in Congress,,,".

---T--- <u>DOI is involved & centered for Christ's Christianity;</u> & Based on His Holy Bible: // "Letters of Delegates to Congress: Volume: 3- 1/1, 1776 - 5/15, 1776 - ,,,10th Feby. 1776 I desired Mr. Greene,,,. You begin by observing that my letter was a pleasure and a disappointment, a TRUE picture this of life in general. The DIVINE wisdom has thought best (& I believe it is absolutely necessary) At the same time that we are surrounded with innumerable mercies and comforts to vary the scene with disappointm[ent], pain, sickness & other things which we call trouble. We are full fond of this world & too negligent of the next as <u>things now</u> stand. If there were no troubles, sickness or distress, but one continued state of health, ease & pleasure I believe they would be fatal to human nature. Let us then adore that all gracious Being whose goodness preserves, & whose mercies surround us & make life comfortable & who at the same time by the shortness & uncertainty of [. . .] and the various disappointments attending [...] shews us the Insufficiency of temporal enjoyment [and] kindly leads us to look for compleat happi[ness in] that World alone which is to come; May we all be prepared for it. [[preparing for eternal existence of Heaven or Hell; Christian truths]] I do not wonder that You [are] concerned at my constant application to business, I am amazed that I am so well, may this Instance of DIVINE goodness encrease my love & gratitude & induce Me to live more to his glory. Your dear Bror. Sammy ,,,him to his Maker. May you continue to have such a lively sense of the DIVINE wisdom & goodness as chearfully to resign yourself & every thing dear to you to his all wise direction and government. I am very glad your Bror. Charles has got a commission ,,,I hope with you that he may do his duty, do write to him as often as you can well and encourage him in the paths of RELIGION & Virtue ,,,& [I most] devoutly thank GOD that you are so [happy in] that nearest of all connections. May you [both have] wisdom to behave in such a manner as [that esteem,] regard & mutual affection may continue [&] encrease to your latest breath & ever ac[knowledge] that goodness which hath made You th[us]. I wrote Mr. Greene in great haste [when I] enclosed him the contracts to sign ,,,when [he returns] them to me I wish he would enclose a co[py of my] Letter to him that I may see whether [every thing] I wrote was as I would wish. We are very happy in the arrival of about 120 Tons of salt petre & 20 tons of powder & 1300 stand of Arms ,,,I hope every thing will [be] done to put your part of the Colony into a proper posture of defence. The Compy. I hope will make all proper ,,,RC (RHi)."

---T--- <u>The facts are that~ +</u>] Christian men wrote the DOI, +] then later the CON, +] wrote and proclaimed National Days & State Days for the country, public and GOV, to Give Thanks and Fast (self-denial) to Christ the God, +] such Days were before, during, and after the DOI, +] such Days were before, during, and after the CON. // This proves the CON did not make a change in religion; as some falsely say. One of many dated EX: Oct of 1789 (date near CON).

---T--- <u>Christianity was Included for Counsel & Prayers, including</u> Christian ministers & Christian Churches during the DOI & CON meetings.

---T--- <u>Christian Prayer to Christ was included at the Congressional</u> Meetings: // "Sept 6, 1774, Resolved that the Rev Mr Duche be desired to open the Congress tomorrow morning with prayers, at the Carpenter's Hall at 9:00 O'clock" (58). Every morning this occurred as a regular part of the meetings.

---T--- <u>National unity around Jesus & Christianity</u>: // June 1, 1774 the colonies proclaimed a Day of Fasting and Prayer. This is only 1 of thousands of such days proclaimed before, during, and after the DOI & CON construction.

---T--- <u>Reactions of the Towns to Samuel Adams & the</u> early Congress were reactions Christian's for God's Presence; & supported Christian Subjects: // EX: A reaction from Boston, says, "The Christian sympathy ,,,of our friends through the Continent cannot fail to inspire the inhabitants ,,,while we trust in the Supreme Ruler of the universe, that he will graciously hear our cries, and in his time free us from our present bondage and make us rejoice in his great salvation" (46a).

---T--- <u>DOI is a Christ Christian (Religious) DOC:</u> // Historian George Bancroft states that the Revolution and DOI was highly influenced by Christian ideas from the Christian Presbyterian DEN. (8).

---T--- <u>Christ's Holy Bible reading at the Congressional meeting:</u> // "Wed, Sept 7, 1774. Opened with prayer ,,,thanks of congress be given to Mr Duche ,,,for performing divine service, and for the excellent prayer ,,,the Bible was read,,, thirty-fifth Psalms ,,,it seemed as if heaven had ordained that Psalms to be read on that morning,,," (59).

---T--- <u>Massachusetts Congress in AD 1775 proclaimed~ +=Fasting &</u> Prayers for ALL the Created people, and, +=for churches of all DEN, and, +=quoted the Christian Bible in the meetings: // ",,,when His Children ask bread He will not give them a stone ,,,to the good people ,,,of all DENs ,,,be set apart as a day of public humiliation, fasting, and prayer ,,,to confess the sins, to implore the forgiveness of all our transgressions,,," (60).

---T--- <u>DOI & USA GOV Formation times & ac</u>tivities are Based on GOD Christ Jesus: // "Journal of the Senate of the US of America, 1789-1793 - 5/7, 1789. The Senate assembled ,,,part of the House of Representatives, to report ,,,The Committee appointed to prepare an answer to the President's speech, delivered to the Senate and House of Representatives of the US, reported as follows: Sir: We, the Senate of the US, return you our sincere thanks for your excellent speech delivered to both Houses of Congress; congratulate you on the complete organization of the federal government, and felicitate ourselves and our fellow citizens ,,,an office highly important by the powers constitutionally annexed to it, [[the GOV & GOV Officers based on the CC]] and extremely honorable from the manner in which the appointment is made. The unanimous suffrage ,,,favor is peculiarly expressive of the gratitude, confidence, and affection of the citizens of America ,,,We are sensible, sir, that nothing but the voice of your fellow citizens could have called you from a retreat, chosen with the loudest ,,,endeared by habit, and consecrated to the repose of declining years. We rejoice, and with us all America, that, in obedience to the call of our common country, you have returned once more to public life. In you all parties confide; in you all interests unite ,,,to avert the dangers to which we were exposed, to give stability to the present GOV, and dignity and splendor to that country, which your skill and valor, as a soldier, so eminently contributed to raise to independence and empire. When we contemplate the coincidence of circumstances, and wonderful combination of causes, which gradually prepared the people of this country for independence; when contemplate the rise, progress, and termination of the late war, which gave them a name among the nations of the earth, we are, with you, unavoidably led to <u>acknowledge and adore the great arbiter of the universe, by whom empires rise and fall</u>. [[a Holy Bible vs; and God stated]] A review of the many signal instances of DIVINE interposition in favor of this country, claims our most pious gratitude: and permit us, sir, to observe, that, among the great events which hard led to the formation and establishment of a federal GOV, we esteem your acceptance of the office of President as one of the most propitious and important. [[note that Congress and Citizens here put the Executive (President), Congress, and Citizens all under the Leadership of the Ruler~ Christ Jesus]] In the execution of the trust reposed in us, we shall endeavor to pursue that enlarged and liberal policy to which your speech so happily directs. We are conscious that the prosperity of each state is inseparably connected with the welfare of all, and that, in promoting the latter, we shall effectually advance the former. In full persuasion of this TRUTH, it shall be our invariable aim to divest ourselves of local prejudices and attachments, and to view the great assemblage of communities and interests committed to our charge with an equal eye. We feel, sir, the force, and acknowledge the justness of the observation, that the foundation of our national policy should be laid in private MORALity; if individuals be not influenced by MORAL principles, it is in vain to look for PUBLIC VIRTUE; it is, therefore, the duty of legislators to enforce, both by precept and EX:, the utility, as well as the necessity, of a strict adherence to the rules of distributive justice. We beg you to be assured that the Senate will, at all times, cheerfully co-operate in every measure which may strengthen the Union, [[<~ CC referenced as "Union" to the left; and to the right is the DOI ~>]] conduce to the happiness, or secure and perpetuate the liberties, of this great confederated republic. We commend you, sir, to the protection of Almighty GOD, earnestly beseeching him long to preserve a life so valuable and dear to the people of the US, and that your administration may be prosperous to the nation, and glorious to yourself. In Senate, May 16, 1789. Read and accepted; and Ordered".

---T--- <u>Definitions of DOI & CON & GOV</u> is to be CHRISTIAN for Christ: // By the People that designed and signed it.

---T--- <u>Benjamin Rush; signer of DOI, CON,</u> ratifying CON, served in Presidential administrations of John Adams, Thomas Jefferson, James Madison; also an educator, assisted in starting 5 schools, 3 remaining in existence; and part designer of the free public school system: // wrote in AD 1791 a report of educational policy including many reasons why the Holy Bible should always be in American schools. // also warned saying, "in contemplating the political institutions of the US, if we remove the Bible from schools, I lament that we waste so much time and money in punishing crimes and take so little pains to prevent them" (Benjamin Rush. Essays).

---T--- Noah Webster (a "schoolmaster to America", signed the DOI & CON, a soldier in the RW, a legislator, judge, participant in CON convention): // He States in a textbook for public schools, "All the miseries and evils which men suffer from vice, crime, ambition, injustice, oppression, slavery, and war, proceed from their despising or neglecting the precepts contained in the Bible" (Webster History, pgs 134-135).

---T--- God's Holy Bible & Christianity Supported in the GOV; & danger of power abuse: // Robert Winthrop, speaker in US House of Rep. of AD 1840 stated: "men, in a word, must necessarily be controlled either by a power within them or by a power without them, either by the word of God or by the strong arm of man, either by the Bible or by the baronet" (Robert Winthrop. Addresses and Speeches on Various Occasions. Boston: Little, Brown, and Co. 1852).

---T--- Christianity of Jesus is the Basis of the USA & DOI: // John Adams, writes to Thomas Jefferson, 6/18, 1813 states: "The general principles on which the fathers achieved independence were ,,,the general principles of Christianity" (21).

---T--- DOI is Christian for Christ: // Event, 6/12, 1775, the Continental Congress proclaimed a day of fasting and prayer and confession of sins throughout the country for God's blessings. (23). This is the time of DOI development. These are Holy Bible terms.

---T--- DOI & CON ~ USA made a Proclamation to Repeat that the DOI & CON is Christian- of the Holy Bible: // A Proclamation was made that the Year AD 1983 is to be called the USA Year of the Holy Bible (a Memorial): Signed by all Congress members and the President; includes the following statements: "Whereas Biblical teachings inspired concepts of civil GOV that are contained in our DOI and the CON of the US; Whereas this Nation now faces great challenges that will test this Nation as it has never been tested before; and Whereas that renewing our knowledge of and faith in God through Holy SC can strengthen us as a nation and a people,,,".

++

====== [CONCLUSION]: THE CON IS A GODLY CHRISTIAN DOCUMENT; THUS RELIGIOUS:

---T--- The DOI & CON Form One Document; Joint; Go Together: // This is proved in this chapter. Thus, this alone proves the conclusion; because The DOI is a Godly Christian DOC, and is the OverRuling DOC to the CON; therefore the CON is a sub-part of it and thus Godly also; The CON does not repeat the Fundamental Truths in the DOI; and therefore, the CON may appear at first sight as less godly than the DOI, or not as specifically stating the same truths clearly. However this is why, intention/ purpose, that knowledge of the construction of the Two Documents is needed; they are a Joint DOC; a CC; as One DOC; they go together; the CON is the application of the DOI; the CON does not remove the DOI; the CON is a continuation of the DOI.

---T--- The USA Courts include PRAYER: // During DOI & CON Times (approx.), Prayers are recorded by Newspapers of various States as follows: +NH State~ ",,,the Throne of Grace was addressed by the Rev. Dr. Samuel Haven ,,,1791" (157). +RI State~ ",,,the Throne of Grace in prayer,,," (158). +Mass State~ ",,,The prayer was made,,," (159). // There are other similar newspaper records.

---T--- The Wording Included in the CON is Godly: // It is true that the CON would ideally be better if it had more words included of various subjects such as God. However remember that the DOI is the controlling DOC, or overruling DOC of the CC; the two are a joined DOC; together they are one DOC. Thus it is very directly stated in the DOI. We have GOD, Creator, Supreme Ruler, Divine Providence as providing our Rights; etc. Now it is all seen as actually the other way~ CANNOT GET MUCH BETTER; IT IS VERY CLEAR. // In the CON we have subjects of: +The Holy Bible laws referenced; +Christian DEN; +The Christian Oath, or Oath to God; +Jesus Christ as the Signature and Authority of the DOC. // Supporting the godly intentions/ purposes includes all the supporting DOCs. // The CON needs the DOI to be reasonable and comprehensible. // The FFOG were trying to prevent the USA GOV from the following~ += false religions, += false Christianity, += controlling Christianity as in Europe, += having a USA Christian Church and not allowing for freedom of other Christian DEN, and += having a USA GOV control over the States Independency for Christian freedom and Christian DEN. // Thus because, in that they did not know how to word the situation in every instance, and had time constraints and mental struggles and such, they did as they did so. // No GOV REP nor Citizen REPs ever wanted the CON to state less than it did. This is proven by supporting DOC and etc. However there were FFOG and States that wanted more exacting language included. The subjects were always related to God. However the debates as to how to protect, prevent, and support all at the same time resulted in what we have now. // Now, today, Christians know what to say and how to include the words, and what intention/ purposes, if we would ever intend/purpose to do such. And we have our FFOG, the CC, and God to be thanked for our knowledge and ability. Let us bow our heads, and say~ Thank you.

---T--- Because that the CON Does Not Say the Same Things as the DOI is Not a Negative, Rather a Positive: // The FFOG did not have ink, time, and paper to use so easily as we do today. // It is further EV that they totally intended/ purposed to include the DOI. What sort of confusion is it to make a CON, such as they did, without including any Statements that would Declare the Starting Subjects of a Nation; those subjects that would be directly defining the starting of a Nation? Very confusing, that is how confusing. The Start of the Nation was the DOI, therefore that is the DOC that makes the Statements of the start of the Nation~ USA. The CON does include statements for the very start and formation of a Nation. // The FFOG did not use evil language; which is truly the attribute of right Personality Traits; or Character. Thus they stated Truths, and did not repeat them repeatedly nor loosely. // A DOC is not usually intended to repeat subjects; rather it is usually intended/ purposed to state Truths one time. At least, specific forms of documents; there are a variety of forms & formatting. // A DOC such as that of Outline Formats does not usually repeat to excessively on the same subject. Therefore the DOI & CON would not be expected to repeat excessively on the same subjects. // The CON needs the DOI to be reasonable and comprehensible. Without the DOI the CON does not really make sense. The way it is written proves that it is dependent on some other DOC, events, etc. // The CON refers to the DOI; By various ways.

---T--- <u>The CON has Lord Christ Christian Biblical Doctrines in it:</u> // Stealing, anti-idolatry, anti-evil, The Holy Bible, Christianity. // The Holy Bible Sabbath. The USA CON requires the President to approve all bills passed by Congress, or if he disapproves he returns it with his veto. And then specifically it is provided that if not returned by him within ten days, "Sundays excepted". Similar provisions are found in the Constitutions of most of the States; and there was in thirtysix of them the same expression, "Sundays excepted." This Sabbath is special to Christianity and is of no other religion (27). Based on the Holy Bible~ Exo 20; 1Cor 16:1-3.

---T--- <u>The Oath in the CON is a Christ's Presence subject:</u> // The Christian Oath, or oath before God. // It is a part of the Checks & Balances System. // It helps assure, and helps a responsibility of the testimony of a Testifier, to tell the truth. Bringing God in the function is the intention/ purpose. Bringing God to the words of the Testifier then made it more trustworthy. // 2 provisions are made with the Oath: Christianity was not forced for the internal Will of a person, and/or because secondary doctrines include that some Christian DEN people disagreed with Oaths thinking that the Holy Bible teaches against such Oathing to God; Thus a provision is allowed for an infidel or false religionist, or various DEN Christians, to make oaths ~BEFORE~ God, rather than ~TO~ God; as God is present watching and that God rewards or punishes accordingly. This was done by the word, "affirmation", as optional to the "oath".

---T--- <u>The CON is Signed with Reference to the Lord Jesus Christ:</u> // Every signer agreed to the Lord Jesus to be included. // It refers to the Lord Jesus Christ earthly coming in the flesh; Christmas. Mat1-2; Mar1; Luk1-2; Joh1; 1Joh1:7; 4:2-3. // This includes the Providential care of God. FFOG agreed to that statement that the Lord Jesus is the center of, and source of, and providential care of our time & activities. // Thus denying that Christ the Lord's name is not stated is thereby proven wrong. The closing statements & signature line states that the CON DOC is a Christian Godly DOC with the Lord Jesus as its authority. // The Lord referred to is the Lord of All; the Lord Jesus. This name is used repeatedly in the Holy Bible (600 times at least in the NT).

---T--- <u>Every REP was intending/ purpose to please God, Christ, in all parts of their life:</u> // Some may had failed at times in life and some may have later forsaken the Lord. However during the times of GOV construction the general consensus was Jesus and living for Him. Thus the GOV is part of such intention/ purpose, and action; part of, Not separate from~ Christianity. // EV that such was their life is provided in all the DOCs.

---T--- <u>The CON is intended/ purposed to accomplish and apply</u> the Christian Rights from Christ stated by the DOI. // The Rights come from God. // These Rights were also spoken of by the FFOG; and in the supporting DOC.

---T--- <u>The "Blessings" word, (used in the CON), is a Christian & godly word:</u> // This word is defined as~ "help that comes from God; divine favor".

---T--- <u>The Inaugural Ceremony of the Executive Branch is to God:</u> // This has included "so help me God"; and an oath to God, or in view of God; or an appeal for his help. Started with the first president George Washington, and continues to be done. It was done as part of the CON process.

---T--- <u>The Gregorian Calendar was</u> enacted by Congress, which is also known as the Christian calendar: // Because the Calendar is based on the birth of Jesus Christ as Lord of ALL. BC & AD is on the calendar; (BC is before Christ's birth & AD is after His birth; Christmas). // In reality, the exact date of Christ's birth is unknown; however, the Spiritually Reasoning Creatures who constructed the Calendar System, calculated an estimation. // Also, the Signatures on the CON refer to this Calendar.

---T--- <u>"Self - Evidence, GOD":</u> // Self-Evidence is a metaphysical law or internal truth; a spiritual; a witness that we are a spirit and laws govern our internal realm; a Christian term; a Christ-Presence.

---T--- <u>Activities of the FFOG & Society who made the CON & USA Mostly Christian:</u> // There was a serious mindset to rightness. Such included opposing evils such as vanity, pride of position, vain ambitions, evil worldliness by the Christian standard. // FFoG Samuel Adams stated his opposition to dances, balls, entertainment, expensive luxuries of GOV, immorality, etc.; and his support of the Great Awakenings, including George Whitefield, John Wesley, and their friends. // Religion of Christianity was supported here.

---T--- <u>CON Meetings acknowledged that~ +God is God, +Christ is God, and +opposed idolatry.</u>

---T--- <u>CON meetings involved God; Christ:</u> // "The Records of the Federal Convention of 1787 [Farrand's Records, Volume 3] CIV. Jonas Phillips to the President and Members of the Convention.1 [Note 1: 1 Documentary History of the CON, I, 281--283.] Sires With leave and submission I address myself To those in whome there is wisdom understanding and knowledge ,,,the honourable personages appointed and Made OVERSEERS of a part of the terrestrial globe of the Earth, Namely the 13 US of america in Convention <u>Assembled, the Lord preserve them amen. [[note here they Acknowledge God as God; and themselves only as overseers under Him; also opposes idolatry]]</u> I the subscriber being one of the people called Jews of the City of Philadelphia, a people scattered and despersed among all nations do behold with Concern that among the laws in the CON of Pennsylvania their is a Clause SECT. 10 to viz -- I do <u>believe in one GOD the Creator and governour of the universe the Rewarder</u> of the good and the punisher of the wicked -- and I do acknowledge the SCs of the old and New testament to be given by a devine inspiration [[Holy Bible supported]] -- to swear and believe that the new testament was given by devine inspiration is absolutly against the RELIGIOUS principle of a Jew. and is against his CONSCIENCE to take any such oath- -By the above law a Jew is deprived of holding any publick office or place of Government which is a Contridectory to the bill of Right SECT 2. Viz That all men have a natural and unalienable Right To worship almighty GOD according to the dectates of their own CONSCIENCE and understanding, and that no man aught or of Right can be Compelled to attend any Relegious Worship or Erect or support any place of worship or Maintain any minister contrary to or against his own free will and Consent nor Can any man who acknowledges the being of a GOD be Justly deprived or abridged of any Civil Right as a Citizen on account of his RELIGIOUS sentiments or peculiar mode of RELIGIOUS Worship, and that no authority Can or aught to be vested in or assumed by any power what ever that shall in any Case interfere or in any manner Controul the Right of CONSCIENCE in the free Exercise of RELIGIOUS Worship -- It is well known among all the Citizens of the 13 US that the Jews have been TRUE and faithful whigs, and during the late Contest with England they have been foremost in aiding and assisting the States with their lifes and fortunes, they have supported the Cause, have bravely faught and bleed for liberty which they Can not Enjoy -- Therefore if the honourable Convention shall in ther Wisdom think fit and alter the said oath and leave out the words to viz -- and I do acknoweledge the SC of the new testement to be given by devine inspiration then the Israeletes will think them self happy to live under a government where all Religious societys are on an Equal footing [[note here the DEN subject; and Christianity is the only religion of the USA]] -- I solecet this favour for my self my Children and posterity and for the benefit of all the Isrealetes through the 13 US of America My PRAYERS is unto the Lord. May the people of this States Rise up as a great and young lion, May they prevail against their Enemies, May the degrees of honour of his Excellencey the president of the Convention George Washington, be Extollet and Raise up. May Every one speak of his glorious Exploits. May GOD prolong his days among us in this land of Liberty -- May he lead the armies against his Enemys as he has done hereuntofore -- May GOD Extend peace unto the US -- May they get up to the highest Prosperetys -- May GOD Extend peace to them and their seed after them so long as the Sun and moon Endureth -- and may the almighty GOD of our father Abraham Isaac and Jacob endue this Noble Assembly with wisdom Judgement and unamity in their Councells, and may they have the Satisfaction to see that their present toil and labour for the wellfair of the US may be approved of, Through all the world and perticular by the US of america is the ardent PRAYER of Sires Your Most devoted obed Servant Jonas Phillips". +See here is not acceptance of false gods, nor any gods; but the true God; OT God = NT God; personal decisions are allowed, but not public advertisement & assembly of false gods; Religious societies are DEN or Christian Establishments.

---T--- Checks & Balances System is Intended/ Purposed to Include God & Oppose Evil: // The USA System developed a "Checks & Balances" system. Intention/purpose is what? Why? The following,,,. // Evil that is why. Because~ += this world is a place of good & evil; and += the exposure to evil; and += mankind is temptable to evil; and += people in "powerful" positions are potentially dangerous. Furthermore they had studied history and the current problems; those both had EV of the problem of evil. // God is the other reason why; the intention/ purpose to include God. Ideally they knew, as we know, that God, Christ Jesus, being perfect would be the perfect Ruler. However how God gets that done to mankind is the situation. Thus a "Checks & Balances" system. // The problem is that God, Christ Jesus, and Christianity, is the Check & Balance that Spirit Creatures are attempting to remove. Dear friend, do you not think it a form of insanity for the Creature to exclude their Creator ? // All the parts of the Checks & Balances System include parts of God & Christianity. The parts include the DOI & CON, which include~ God, Supreme Ruler, Creator, Divine Providence, Lord Jesus Christ, the Christian Oath, or Oath to God, and other Holy Biblical subjects and principles. // First priority is to be given to the Check of God; It may then enter in to idolatry, if not. Do you want to stand before some Spiritual Creature who is self-idolatry? Do you want to commune (fellowship) with them? They might exchange you for a piece of bread or 30 pieces of metal, (Pro6:26, Mat26:15). // These are all parts of God that are the Checks & Balances intended/ purposed against evil & for good.

---T--- Christ's Presence by Christian Oath required for USA GOV Officers as stated in CON: // "Journal of the Senate of the US of America, 1789-1793 -- 4/30, 1789. The Senate assembled: present as yesterday. The report of the Committee ,,,appointed to take order far conducting the ceremonial of the formal reception, &c. of the President of the US, having informed ,,,Senate ,,,the House of Representatives were notified that the Senate were ready to receive them in the Senate Chamber, to attend the President of the US while taking the OATH REQUIRED BY THE CONSTITUTION. Whereupon, the House of Representatives, preceded by their Speaker, came into the Senate Chamber ,,,introduced the President of the US ,,,when the Vice President informed him, that "the Senate and House of Representatives of the US were ready to attend him to take the OATH REQUIRED BY THE CONSTITUTION, and that it would be administered by the Chancellor of the state of New York." ,,,the OATH was administered. After which the Chancellor proclaimed, "Long live George Washington President of the US." ,,,in this first official act, my fervent supplications to that ALMIGHTY BEING who rules over the universe - who presides in the councils of nations --and whose providential aids can supply every human defect, that his benediction may consecrate to the liberties and happiness of the people of the US, a GOV instituted by themselves for these essential purposes: and may enable every instrument employed in its administration to execute with success, the functions allotted to his charge. In tendering this homage to the GREAT AUTHOR of every public and private good, I assure myself that it expresses your sentiments not less than my own; nor those of my fellow citizens at large, less than either. No people can be BOUND to acknowledge and adore the INVISIBLE HAND, which conducts the affairs of men, more than the people of the US [[USA, as a whole, bound to Christ]]. Every step by which they have advanced to the character of an independent nation, seems to have been distinguished by some token of providential agency; [[every part has included God, Christ; as here stated]] and in the important revolution just accomplished in the system of their united GOV the tranquil

61

deliberations and voluntary consent of so many distinct communities, from which the event has resulted, cannot be compared with the means by which most governments have been established, without some return of pious gratitude, along with an humble anticipation of the future blessings which the past seem to presage [[referencing the CON as a Christ centered action]]. These reflections, arising out of the present crisis, have forced themselves too strongly on my mind to be suppressed. You will join with me, I trust, in thinking, that there are none, under the influence of which, the proceedings of a new and free GOV can more auspiciously commence. ,,,honorable qualifications, I behold the surest pledges, that, as on one side, no local prejudices or attachments, no separate views, nor party animosities, will misdirect the comprehensive and equal eye which ought to watch over this great assemblage of communities and interests: so, on another, that the foundations of our national policy will be laid in the pure and immutable principles of private MORALity; and the pre-eminence of free GOV be exemplified by all the attributes which can win the affections of its citizens, and command the respect of the world ,,,since there is no TRUTH more thoroughly established, than that there exists in the economy and course of nature, an indissoluble union between virtue and happiness; between duty and advantage; between the genuine maxims of an honest and magnanimous policy, and the solid rewards of public prosperity and felicity: since we ought to be no less persuaded that the propitious smiles of HEAVEN can never be expected on a nation that disregards the ETERNAL rules of order and right, which HEAVEN itself has ordained: and since the preservation of the SACRED fire of liberty, and the destiny of the republican model of government, are justly considered as deeply, perhaps as finally staked, on the experiment entrusted to the hands of the American people. Besides the ordinary objects submitted to your care, it will remain with your judgment to decide, how far an exercise of the occasional power delegated by the fifth article of the CON, is rendered expedient at the present juncture, by the nature of objections which have been urged against the system, or by the degree of inquietude which has given birth to them [[reference again to the CON and all God centered; and the oath]]. Instead of undertaking particular recommendations on this subject, in which I could be guided by no lights derived from official opportunities, I shall again give way to my entire confidence in your discernment and pursuit of the public good: for, I assure myself, that whilst you carefully avoid every alteration which might endanger the benefits of an united and effective government, or which ought to await the future lessons of experience; a reverence for the characteristic rights of freemen, and a regard for the public harmony, will sufficiently influence your deliberations on the question, how far the former can be more impregnably fortified, or the latter be safely and advantageously promoted ,,,and must accordingly PRAY that the pecuniary estimates for the station in which I am placed, may, during my continuance in it, be limited to such actual expenditures as the public good may be thought to require. Having thus imparted to you my sentiments, as they have been awakened by the occasion which brings us together, I shall take my present leave; but not without resorting once more to the benign PARENT of the human race, in humble supplication that, since he has been pleased to favor the American people with opportunities for deliberating in perfect tranquility, and dispositions for deciding with unparalleled unanimity, on a form of GOV for the security of their union, and the advancement of their happiness; so his DIVINE blessing may be equally conspicuous in the enlarged views, the temperate consultations, and the wise measures, on which the success of this GOV must depend. Apr. 30. G. WASHINGTON. The President, the Vice President, the Senate, and House of Representatives, &c. then proceeded to St. Paul's Chapel, where DIVINE service was performed by the Chaplain of Congress, after which the President ,,,The Vice President and Senate returned to the Senate Chamber; and, Upon motion, unanimously agreed ,,,The House of Representatives also provided a copy of the same letter to their division - Journal of the House of Representatives of the US, 1789-1793 FRIDAY, MAY 1, 1789,,,".

---T--- CON is Christianity based; same as DOI; Appeal for Christ~ all during the SAME Times; God & Christianity included in various parts: // Christianity is the focus of this DOC as is signed by reference to the Lord Jesus Earthly coming; Christmas ~ "Journals of the Continental Congress, 1774-1789 - 10/16, 1787. Congress assembled. Present as yesterday. ,,,commission of the US off the coast of England Great Britain in the late war ,,,That a letter be written to his Most CHRISTIAN Majesty informing him that the US in Congress Assembled3 have bestowed ,,,it would be acceptable to Congress that his Majesty would be pleased to permit him to embark with his fleets of evolution; convinced that he can no where else so well acquire that knowledge which may hereafter render him more extensively useful ,,,at the court of his Most CHRISTIAN Majesty and do ,,,In testimony whereof we have caused the Seal of the US to be hereunto affixed. Witness his Excellency Arthur St Clair our president this twelfth day of Oct. One thousand seven hundred and eighty seven and of our Sovereignty and independence the twelfth. [[date of DOI, a Christian DOC, used as USA Nation formation start date]] ,,,assure you of the sincerity of our friendship. We PRAY GOD to keep your Majesty under his HOLY protection. Done at the city of New York the 12th day of Oct in the year of our Lord 1787 and of our sovereignty and independence the twelfth. ,,,prepared the following letter1 to his Most CHRISTIAN Majesty which having been duly signed and countersigned was delivered to the chevr. J. P. Jones ,,,Great and Beloved Friend We the US in Congress Assembled in ,,,for which we are endebted to your friendship will never cease to interest us in whatever may concern the happiness of your Majesty, your family and people. We PRAY GOD to keep you, our Great and beloved friend, under his HOLY protection. Done at the city of New York the 16 day of Octr. in the year of our Lord 1787 and of our Sovereignty and independence the twelfth.,,,".

---T--- CON is Christ Caring; Preparation times for CON has Christian Activity: // "Letters of Delegates to Congress: Volume 18- 3/1, 1781 - 8/31, 1781 - Arthur Middleton to Aedanus Burke My dr. Sir Pa. 4/7. [1782] ,,,I fear with you that nothing but Time & skillfull management can restore that firm, orderly, & composed mode of proceeding so essential to establish the publick Happiness which is or ought to be the wish of all,,,. I think I know the PURITY of THEIR INTENTIONS & I trust their Councills may yet lead us to prosperity. Upon mature Consideration of all Circumstances; of the unmerited Sufferings of so many, & of the resentments necessarily rous'd in a people whom I know to be naturally generous & Sensible, I rejoice that matters have been Conducted with so much moderation & Temper; tho' I could have wishd the Idea of Confiscation had been totally abolish'd, or at least put off till entire secure possession [of the] Country had restor'd Tranquillity, & the publick mind was free & open to the guidance of cool dispassionate reason. Your Sentiments upon the Subject are those of the Patriot & the friend of human Nature, & I wd. there had been more of your way of thinking-upon a thorough Investigation of this mode of Punishment, even in Cases of Treason, I have been & am principled against it; I cannot approve of the inhuman Sentence of visiting the SINS of the Fathers upon the guiltless women [and] Children, [[HOLY BIBLE quoted]] notwithstanding the SACRED Authority which may be quoted for it. It is a Doctrine suited only to the Climates of DESPOSTISM, & abhorrent to the dignified SPIRIT of pure & genuine republicanism. In the Eye of reason the Individual shd. stand or fall by his own Actions, & those connected should be involved in the punishment no farther, than they have been partakers in the Crime. Banishment of the Individual, & a deprivation of the Benefits of Citizenship & property for life are surely sufficient both as a punishment & a prevention of Crimes, without reducing a whole family for the SIN of one to misery & destruction. Here my friend you have my Thoughts upon an Interesting Subject which concerns the good of mankind ,,,Congress on Apr. 3.JCC, 22:161 ,,,"Testimony of my duty & gratitude," "Next to the obedience due the Dictates of my own CONSCIENCE ,,,I shall still be governed by the same motives, & trust I shall retain it to our Life's end-at parting with my Brother I entreated him to present my Duty to you, & to acquaint you that my mind was thoroughly at Ease with regard to my own fate; This I hoped would operate as a Balm to your affliction upon my Account. "To the many anxieties for my dearest Connections, the knowledge of your Ill health & Troubles have added grief indeed. Mr. R can tell how much I have felt for you. I am now anxious [for my?] Br[other]-in short our day seems to be crowded with Troubles & I flatter myself their Period is nearly closed....".

---T--- Christian Holidays were supported by the FFOG, society, and CON meetings.

---T--- Absence Law: // There is absolutely no DOC, nor historical supporting DOC, nor life EV from any FFOG, nor any promoting or allowance of, or encouragement to any other religion than Christianity; nor any God but Jesus Christ (Christianity); except Judaism (Christianity in it's earlier status); NOR any of these opposing or stopping Christianity; Nor any of these starting any system without Christianity.

---T--- Inclusion/Exclusion Law: // All other religions and false gods are specifically excluded and warned about; and in every instance of DOC and historical supporting DOC. Including Paganism, Heathenism, God Exclusion, etc.

---T--- The DOI & CON are a Covenant Contract with God & is Christian; as Stated in the Congress Meeting Notes of AD 1788: // "They Certainly have no authority to interfere in the establishment of any religion whatsoever; [["religion" as Christian DEN]] and I am astonished that any gentleman should conceive they have. Is there any power given to Congress in matters of religion? Can they pass a single act to impair our religious liberties? [[stating that no damage is ever to be done through a law or enactment from the USA GOV, towards Christ]] If they could, it would be a just cause of alarm. If they could, sir, no man would have more horror against it than myself. Happily, no sect here is superior to another. [[Christian DEN, with clarity, protected and the establishment clause pertain to this]] As long as this is the case, we shall be free from those persecutions and distractions with which other countries have been torn. If any future Congress should pass an act concerning the religion of the country, [[clearly identified that Christianity and no other, is this countries religion]] it would be an act which they are not authorized to pass, by the CON, and which the people would not obey. Every one would ask, "Who authorized the GOV to pass such an act? It is not warranted by the CON, and is barefaced usurpation." The power to make treaties can never be supposed to include a right to establish a foreign religion among ourselves, though it might authorize a toleration of others ,,,pagans,,, Mahometans ,,,". // Note what is identified: +Christianity; +Falsity religions; +having NO god (word "Pagan").

---T--- Christ Caring Events were part of the DOI & CON: // The 1st Great Awakening assisted the forming of the DOI. The event & activities were supported by the FFOG, and most of the population of the USA society of citizens. It was continuing during CON dates.

---T--- The DOI & CON did Include, & Did Not Ever Reject, the Work of the FFOG such as those arriving earlier to the USA (Colonies etc.); Because they cared affectionately for Christ: // Such is included in the writing of the DOI & CON. Such is always referred to as honorary; and that the same work is ONLY as a continuation of; a continuation of the same, not different, nor contrary. // The FFOG arriving earlier include the following: +In AD 1137 Queen of Sweden sent colonies and set as priority, saying, "above all things shall the Governor consider and see to it that a time and due worship, becoming honesty, laud, and praise be paid to the most high God in all things,,, Articles of the Christian faith. +Christopher Columbus was a Christian, who may have lacked, as some report, "administrative skills"; but he had intention/ purpose to preach the Gospel, raise money for the goal of recapturing Jerusalem from the Muslims; The Muslim's had recently, a few years earlier, attacked and murdered many in a take-over of the city of Constantinople in AD 1453 and destroyed the Byzantine Empire (225). +The Mayflower Compact AD 1620 states, "establish this colony in God's name and for His glory and to advance the Christian faith"; The ByLaws that applied this Covenant Compact, was called the Plymouth Constitution; such contained job descriptions for the governor, lieutenant governor, and the General Court, how laws were to be made, and specific laws on life, liberty, and property. +Puritan's Covenants assisted in developing the DOI & CON (2). +AD 1630 Puritan Covenant, had these intentions/ purposes as stated: "Gospel spread to all; enjoy liberty of Gospel with purity and peace; obey Mat 28:19-20 the Great commission to spread the Gospel; establish a Christian church; be a city of God in America. +AD 1639 Colony of Connecticut chose a set of laws for government that were according to the laws of God the Lord Jesus Christ. +AD 1677, the Quaker Trustees, (Christian DEN) of West Jersey

63

(Pennsylvania as called later), provided freedom of Christian worship for all Christian DEN. +Puritans in totality were trying to establish a Theocracy GOV. +Established communities for assistance to Christianity; resort for persecuted peoples from other lands as stated by FFOG Roger Williams, John Winthrop, William Penn. // Also see (265).

---T--- Christ's religious Holy Bible is constantly referred to by the FFOG, the DOI, & CON: // Andrew Jackson, (7th President of US) states that the Bible, "is the rock on which our republic rests".

---T--- Christ Christian Writings & Christian Activity Constantly Occurred & Supported the Process of the CON: // CON is a religious (Christ) DOC. Statements made in the Federalist Papers from Alexander Hamilton, James Madison, and John Jay are Christian in doctrine and reference; and pertain to the CON. They said one of the intention/ purposes of the CON was to put a limit on power abuse; and other statements as follows: "as there is a degree of depravity in man"; "our nation was not to be an oligarchy or judgeocracy"; "of the three powers above mentioned the judiciary is next to nothing". // FFOG John Adams says, "We have no GOV armed with power capable of contending with human passions unbridled by morality and religion. Avaridce, ambition, revenge or gallantry, would break the strongest of cords or our CON as a whale goes threw a net. Our CON was made only for a moral and religious people. It is wholly inadequate to the government of any other".

---T--- Christ Ceremony Events on CON Construction Day: // The same day that the CON was passed with the 1-A, the Congress enacted a day of thanksgiving and prayer~ on Sept 24, 1789.

---T--- Christ Activities & Events Based on Knowing that the DOI & CON were Christian & Religious: // Because of the DOI & CON, and starting at approx. the same time~ +There are Christian prayers at Congress meetings, Christian chaplains to the militaries, Christian prayers offered in the militaries. +Also FFOG James Madison enacted a national day of humility and prayer July 9, 1812; and they observed it with "religious solemnity". +and Congress in AD 1832 & 1833 approved land grants to Baptist and Jesuit schools. +and The 10 commandments are on the USA Supreme Court. +and The USA Supreme Court begins each session with the prayer saying, "God save the US and the honorable Court". +and The New England Primer was used in public schools with its many Christian religious references. // All these are because the DOI & CON were KNOWN to be based on the Christ Christianity Religion.

---T--- The 1st President Stated the DOI & CON were Christian for Christ: // George Washington states: "Whereas it is the duty of all nations to acknowledge the providence of Almighty God, to obey His will, to be grateful for His benefits, and humbly to implore His protection and favor ,,,for ,,,His providence ,,,in which we have been enabled to establish constitutions of GOV for our safety and happiness, and particularly the national one now lately instituted [[Notice here that he credits the constructing of the CON & DOI as intented/purposed for God & Lord, continues~]] for the civil and religious liberty ,,,prayers ,,,to the great Lord and Ruler of Nations, and beseech Him to pardon our national ,,,transgressions ,,,to promote the knowledge and practice of true religion and virtue".

---T--- FFOG in Congress meetings for the CON Construction intended/ purposed as a religious Christian DOC for Christ includes the following statements: // George Washington~ "It appears to me ,,,little short of a miracle ,,,in forming a system of N GOV". // James Madison~ "It is impossible for the man of pious reflection not to perceive in it a finger of that Almighty hand which has been so frequently and signally extended to our relief in the critical stages of the revolution"; and also "The Happy Union of these States is a wonder; their CON is a miracle". // Miracles~ are considered as assistance from God and as acknowledgement or recognition of Him.

---T--- Christianities Christ & the Holy Bible is the basis of the DOI & CON as stated by FFOG Benjamin Franklin: // In AD 1787, at the Constitutional Convention (CON preparation meetings) in Philadelphia~ "methinks a melancholy proof of the imperfection of the Human Understanding. We indeed seem to feel our own want of political wisdom, since we have been running about in search of it ,,,humbly applying to the Father of lights to illuminate our ,,,In the beginning of the contest with G. Britain , when we were sensible of danger we had daily prayer in this room for the divine protection. Our prayer, sir, were heard, and they were graciously answered ,,,To that kind providence we owe this happy opportunity of consulting in peace on the means of establishing our future nation felicity. And have we forgotten that powerful friend? Or do we imagine we no longer need his assistance? I have lived, sir, a long time, and the longer I live, the more convincing proof I see of this truth, that God governs in the affairs of men. And if a sparrow cannot fall to the ground without His notice, is it probable that an empire can rise without His aid? ,,,We have been assured, Sir, in the Sacred Writings that except the Lord build the house, they labor in vain that build it. I firmly believe this; and I also believe that without His concurring aid, we shall succeed in this political building no better than the builders of Babel ,,,I therefore beg leave to move, that henceforth prayers imploring the assistance of Heaven, and its blessings on our deliberations, be held in the Assembly every morning before we proceed to business, and that one or more of the clergy of this city be requested to officiate in that service". // Roger Sherman seconded B. Franklins motion for prayer to Christ in Congress meetings for the CON. // Jonathan Dayton records notes of this same meeting which share that experientially the words of Franklin~ "fell upon our ears with a right and authority, even greater than we may suppose an oracle to have had in a Roman senate".

---T--- Christian Prayers to Christ at every CON meeting.

---T--- FFOG stated Truths about the~ +=Christian Thoughts, Activities, & Events in construction of the CON: // Elias Boudinot in New Jersey First Provincial Congress stated, "let us enter on this important business under the idea that we are Christians on whom the eyes of the world are now turned ,,,Let us earnestly call and beseech him for Christ's sake to preside in our councils" and "We can only depend on the all powerful influence of the Spirit of God, Whose Divine aid and assistance it becomes us as a Christian people most devoutly to implore. Therefore I move that some minister of the Gospel be requested to attend this Congress every morning ,,,in order to open the meeting with prayer" (189). // John Adams, writes in defense of the CON and Christianity simultaneously, stating, "The moment the idea is admitted into society that property is not as sacred as the laws of God, and that there is not a force of law and public justice to protect it, anarchy and tyranny commence. If 'Thou shalt not covet,' and 'Thou shalt not steal," were not commandments of Heaven, they must be made inviolable precepts in every society, before it can be civilized or made free" (190). // Henry Laurens (President of Continental Congress; Delegate to Constitutional Convention) states, "I had the honor of being one among many who framed that CON ,,,In order effectually to accomplish these great ends, it is incumbent upon us to begin wisely and to proceed in the fear of God; and it is especially the duty of those who bear rule to promote and encourage piety (respect for God) and virtue and to discountenance every degree of vice and immorality [[2 words for evil or sin in Christianity]]" (194).

---T--- CON & DOI are Christ Christian DOC: // FFOG John Quincy Adams states: "The DOI first organized the social compact on the foundation of the Redeemer's mission upon earth ,,,and laid the cornerstone of human GOV upon the first precepts of Christianity"; and "The DOI cast off all the shackles of this dependency. The US of America were no longer Colonies. They were an independent nation of Christians" (184).

---T--- All the CON signers were Christ's Christian REP; & the Spiritual Creatures that sent them desired Christians: // 73 men were elected, by the colonies, to represent them in the CON convention meetings. Rhode Island opposed the Union and elected no one. 55 of them attended, which was not all of them, because there were situational and various difficulties to attend regularly; such as health, personal reasons, family, etc. This caused absences; leaving only 39 REP to sign the CON. All 73 were Christians.

---T--- Thanksgiving Day was Enacted for the Intention/ purpose to~ +=Thank God of the Holy Bible; and that += the USA exists to promote true Christian Religion worldwide for Christ: // Congress proclaimed a National Thanksgiving day. Christianity & the Holy Bible is the basis for such; statements include, ",,,recommend to the people of the US a day of public thanksgiving and prayer, to be observed by acknowledging, with grateful hearts, the many signal favors of Almighty God, especially by affording them an opportunity peaceably to establish a constitution of GOV for their safety and happiness" (14). +Pres. George Washington states that this Holiday~ ",,,it is the duty of all nations to acknowledge the providence of Almighty God, to obey His will, to be grateful for his benefits, and humbly to implore His protection ,,,I recommend and assign Thursday, the twenty-sixth day of Nov. next, to be devoted by the people of these US ,,,that we then may all unite unto him our sincere and humble thanks for His kind care and protection of the people of this country ,,,for the peaceable and rational manner in which we have been enabled to establish constitutions of GOV for our safety and happiness, and particularly the national one now lately instituted; for the civil and religious liberty with which we are blessed ,,,unite in most humbly offering prayers and supplications to the great Lord and Ruler of Nations, and beseech Him ,,,to promote the knowledge and practice of true religion and virtue ,,,A.D. 1789. " (14).

---T--- CON Meetings are Christian meetings of Christian men with Christian activity & support Christ: // The AOC construction was all Christian related; the CON is a reconstruction of this DOC. // The Congress meeting rules were as follows: +meeting agenda to be private at that time as the country was in such disarray that they felt it might turn mob, and to prevent rumors and falsity in reports; +guards were posted at the doors; +voting rules were made; +vote changing allowed, encouraging development and thoughtfulness and full participation; +speaking rules to allow an opportunity for all spiritual moral creatures; +attention from everyone was required in all activities; +they could dismiss themselves and re-enter to and from the convention meetings and revote; +wanted agreements from members not only a vote; +voting was not the way, rather it was to keep talking the subjects repeatedly until everyone felt satisfied; voting was to show that they agreed; however no subject was ended until everything that every person wanted to say on that subject was finished.

---T--- Plans were Christian Basis & Principles from Jesus: // Preliminary Plans for the Constitution were developed by including Christ. Such included States; those of the New Jersey Plan & the Virginia Plan. And FFOG Alexander Hamilton recommended that one of the British methods should be used, rather than trying ways unproved; such method is The Checks & Balances Method System. This would be applied to different sections of GOV.

---T--- All The meetings & DOCs related as the Basis of the DOI & CON are for Christ; included are the following: // +the First Continental Congress, AD 1774; +Second Continental Congress, AD 1775; +DOI meeting, AD 1776; +AOC, AD 1777-1789; +Mount Vernon Conference, AD 1785; +Trade Conference at Annapolis, AD 1786.

---T--- Another main source of writings, other than the Holy Bible, that was used to assist in the CON DOC, is that of Montesquieu "Spirit of Laws". This DOC is derived much from John Locke's writings. All these are based on the Holy Bible and history. (63).

---T--- Christian Sermons & Worship of Christ was part of Congress Meetings on July 4, 1787; & ordered as follows: // ",,,to partake of all the blessings of cultivated and Christian society" (36).

---T--- "God, Creator, Supreme Judge, Divine Providence, Lord Christ the Being, as a Spirit Presence, that was asked for by congress and observed by congress as among them (62).; God's Presence asked for by Prayer.

---T--- The CON is a Christ DOC & So are all other USA & State GOV DOCs as by the Closing Statements for the Signatures: // A Large quantity were signed with Christian time reference as a tool or DOC of the Lord Jesus; His coming in the flesh body (Christmas) & His name; and support for Him; EV that it was the Christian religion and doctrine of God & man that it is to support. // All the GOV DOCs included Christian principles. // This method was that of doing it in the name of God or the Lord Jesus; as His Ambassador or Representative. HSC~ 1Cor1:10; 5:4; Col3:17-"Now I beseech you, brethren, by the name of our Lord Jesus Christ, that you all speak the same thing; In the name of our Lord Jesus Christ, when you are gathered together; And whatsoever you do in word or deed, do all in the name of the Lord Jesus, giving thanks to God and the Father by him.". // The USA library of Congress has many of the DOCs there; Also copies are in various places worldwide. // DOCs include those of Congress, Executive, Judicial, and Supporting. // Thousands of DOCs. // EX: "Done in Convention by the Unanimous Consent of the States present the Seventeenth Day of September in the Year of our Lord one thousand seven hundred and Eighty seven and of the Independence of the US of America the Twelfth ,,,In witness whereof We have hereunto subscribed our Names". // EX: DOC From a congress meeting shortly after the DOI time~ "In witness whereof we have caused these presents to be given in Congress, at Philadelphia, the 29th day of December, in the year of our Lord, 1780, and in the 5th year of our independence. ,,,S. Huntington, President. Ch. Thomson, Sec'y.1 [Note 1: 1 This draft is in the Papers of the Continental Congress, No. 25, I, folio 277.] - Journals of the Continental Congress --FRIDAY, 12/29, 1780" (14a). // EX: DOC of the state of Pennsylvania agreeing and joining the National starting efforts~ "That the late province of Pensylvania, on the fourth day of July, in the year of our Lord one thousand seven hundred and seventy-six, did join with the other twelve, late provinces, now states, in the Declaration of Independence, and soon after established a CON and GOV founded on the authority of the people, which they continue still to exercise and enjoy; and they did also join in the Articles of Confederation of the US ,,,in the year of our Lord one thousand,,,- Journals of the Continental Congress" (14a). // EX: Statements on the DOI: "We, therefore, the representatives of the US of America in general Congress assembled, appealing to the Supreme Judge of the world for the rectitude of our intentions ,,,And for the support of this Declaration, with a firm reliance on the protection of Divine Providence, we mutually pleadge to each other our lives, our fortunes, and our sacred honor. The foregoing declaration was, by order of Congress, engrossed, and signed by the following members: See signatures." // The CON closes with the Lord Jesus Christ name & Christmas.

---T--- "Rights" & Priority of GOD; the Supreme Judge: //Some Rights are Not to be submitted to any form of GOV with men in position. This is one reason why the DOI & Independence was initiated; to tell England that we have "rights" from God which NO MAN NOR MAN GOV can take from us. Thus these Rights are priority to all men; and therefore GOD MUST BE THE RULER of the USA GOV.

---T--- Congress acknowledges that we are spirits & that God is a Spirit: // "a spirit of conciliation had been cultivated" reported as part of George Washington's observance of the meetings. (John4:24).

---T--- CON has Sabbath Laws, Sabbath Keeping, Christian Sabbath Laws~ +=before, during, and after the time of the DOI & CON; += for all Public & USA GOV; to Honor Christ: // "A day peculiar to that faith, and known to no other; It would be impossible within the limits of a lecture to point out all the ways in which that day is recognized" (27). // The US CON requires the President to approve all bills passed by Congress, or if he disapproves he returns it with his veto. And then specifically it is provided that if not returned by him within ten days, "Sundays excepted," after it shall have been presented to him it becomes a law. // Similar provisions of wording are found in the CONs of most of the States; thirtysix used the exact same expression, "Sundays excepted". // Louisiana had Sabbath statements in Four earlier CONs~ (AD 1812, 1845, 1852, 1864) as stating: "In law Sundays are generally excluded as days upon which the performance of any act demanded by the law is not required. They are held to be dies non juridical"; "And in the Christian world Sunday is regarded as the 'Lord's Day and a holiday, a day of cessation from labor."; "By statute, enacted as far back as 1838, this day is made in Louisiana one of 'public rest.'"; "This is the policy of the State of long standing and the framers of the CON are to be considered as intending to conform to the same." // It was a practice that studies are not pursued at any Branch of the military academies, on Sundays, while chaplains are required to hold religious services once at least on that day. // An English statute of Charles II tells no tradesman, artificer, workman, laborer, or other person was permitted to do or exercise any worldly labor, business or work of ordinary calling upon the Lord's Day, or any part thereof, works of necessity or charity only excepted. This statute, (with some varying), was enacted by most of the States (27). // Massachusetts & the USA Supreme Court had Sunday car driving laws of some sort, at one time. // The State of Georgia made a statute that illegalized freight trains operating on Sunday (a misdemeanor). // In many States, contracts made on Sunday are invalid. // No judicial proceedings can be held on Sunday. // All legislative bodies, municipal, state or national, abstain from work on that day. // South Carolina, City Council vs. Benjamin, "On that day we rest, and to us it is the Sabbath of the Lord - its decent observance in a Christian community is that which ought to be expected." // Pennsylvania Supreme Court: "It is not our business to discuss the obligations of Sunday any further than they enter into and are recognized by the law of the land. The common law adopted it, along with Christianity, of which it is one of the bulwarks." // In Arkansas Supreme Court, Shover vs. The State: "Sunday or the Sabbath is properly and emphatically called the Lord's Day, and is one amongst the first and most sacred institutions of the Christian religion. This system of religion is recognized as constituting a part and parcel of the common law, and as such all of the institutions growing out of it, or, in any way, connected with it, in case they shall not be found to interfere with the rights of conscience, are entitled to the most profound respect, and can rightfully claim the protection of the law-making power of the State." // The Supreme Court of Maryland, in Judefind vs. The State: "The Sabbath is emphatically the day of rest, and the day of rest here is the Lord's Day or Christian's Sunday. Ours is a Christian community, and a day set apart as the day of rest is the day consecrated by the resurrection of our Saviour, and embraces the twenty-four hours next ensuing the midnight of Saturday ,,,But it would scarcely be asked of a court, in what professes to be a Christian land, to declare a law unconstitutional because it requires rest from bodily labor on Sunday (except works of necessity and charity) and thereby promotes the cause of Christianity." // According to the Christian Advocate, Justice Morehauser of the New York

Supreme Court opposed legalizing Sunday Movies in Poughkeepsie, New York; while at a meeting of the American Legion luncheon. He said in part: "For myself, I am not for Sunday movies. I am for the American Sunday. And Sunday movies are one of the things that would help to break down our American Sunday. So I do not believe in them. I do not believe there is any great demand for them upon the part of our people. We do not need them. They will not ultimately benefit the average man. If you open the door to Sunday movies you will open the door to a lot of other things you do not want, banquets, races, ballets and farces, minstrels, wrestling, boxing, and many other things now prohibited by the Penal Code. Finally you will have the stores open on Sunday. And you will have Sunday at last a working day instead of a day of rest. And the working man will ultimately pay the price. I am for the poor man. I am for the working man, and have been all my life. But I tell you this agitation for a wide-open Sunday is not ultimately going to be for the benefit of the poor man or of the laboring man. It is going to result in tearing down our entire Sunday law, and that is going to be bad. I hope the clergy and the priesthood will take this matter up. I do not see why they do not start at once and not wait until some official action is taken that they might not approve of. We believe in God in this country. We have been brought up to respect His day ,,,in a belief that Sunday is a day of rest, for relaxation, for meditation and for church going, not a day to be commercialized. I do not know how you feel about it, but I think this belief of ours in God, this respect we in America have had for His day, has had a great deal to do with our success as a nation and with our prosperity. I hope the various civic organizations will take this matter up and give it the consideration they would any other public matter ,,,This matter is like every other important question in this country. You must be either for or against it. So far as I am concerned, I desire to record myself against Sunday movies and to do so with all the force and vigor of which I am capable." ~The churches followed up this lead by adopting strong resolutions of protest". (260). // The thought is that it is a religious day, consecrated by the Commandment, "Six days shalt thou labor, and do all thy work : but the seventh day is the Sabbath of the Lord thy God : in it thou shalt not do any work, thou, nor thy son, nor thy daughter, thy man servant, nor thy maid servant, nor thy cattle, nor the stranger that is within thy gates." Exo 20.

---T--- The Common Law System in the CON makes it Christ's Religious DOC of His Holy Bible: // Because The "Common Law" was the basis of the USA GOV for Law making, it is in the CON and written in words. It was a known system, and therefore no specific detailed writing of it is part of the CON. Neither was there enough time and knowledge and ability to make a total GOV system. Rather the system is identified and written two times in Amendment VII, as "common law". // The Common Law was a Holy Bible Based System that the Colonies used since coming and establishing in America. Please refer to Chapter 7 for the details of study regarding the Common Law.

---T--- The Laws in the CON come from The HOLY BIBLE: // Following is listed some: +The 10 Commandments; +Idolatry is both in the DOI & CON (in various forms); +Stealing (in various forms); +Covetousness (which is evil desires); +Dishonor to parents, posterity; +Securing freedom for rightness; +Freedom for the Gospel to be spoken; +Murder; +Dictatorship & Tyranny prevention; +Lying (with the oath & affirmation); +Marriage is supported, as the home & family is protected; +Adultery & fornication are opposed; stealing spouses & lying about marriage covenants; +Equal Rights to all creatures opposes evil desires of "race", gender, position of employment.

---T--- CON RIGHTS STATED is a surety to provide "rights" that support God, religion (Christianity), the Holy Bible, & against evil: // Rights are those that come from God, as supreme to man.

---T--- The CON supports God's true religion: // Not any or all "religion". God from the DOI and Truth and Religion words are to stay joined together.

---T--- The Continental-Confederation Congress, a legislative group of Spiritual Moral Beings that governed the USA from AD 1774 - 1789, and assisted in constructing the DOI, were all deeply Christian religious men affectionate for Christ: // Congress invested in encouraging the practice of the Christian religion in the new nation.

---T--- Congress~ += appointed Christian chaplains for itself & the militaries, +=sponsored the publication of a Holy Bible, +=encouraged and supported Christian morality in the militaries, += granted public lands to promote Christianity for the Indians, +=National days of thanksgiving and of "humiliation, fasting, and prayer" proclaimed at least twice a year throughout the RW.

---T--- Definitions of DOI & CON are Christ centered; and GOV is to be CHRISTIAN: // By the People that designed and signed it.

---T--- Benjamin Rush is a signer of DOI, CON, ratifying CON, served in Presidential administrations of John Adams, Thomas Jefferson, James Madison, an educator, assisted in starting 5 schools, 3 remaining in existence, and part designer of the free public school system: // He wrote in AD 1791 a report of educational policy including many reasons why the Bible should always be in American schools; and warned saying, "in contemplating the political institutions of the US, if we remove the Bible from schools, I lament that we waste so much time and money in punishing crimes and take so little pains to prevent them" (Benjamin Rush. Essays.).

---T--- Noah Webster, was "schoolmaster to America", signed the DOI & CON, soldier in the RW, legislator, judge, participant in CON convention: // In a textbook for public schools, he states: "All the miseries and evils which men suffer from vice, crime, ambition, injustice, oppression, slavery, and war, proceed from their despising or neglecting the precepts contained in the Bible" (Webster History, pgs 134-135).

---T--- God's Holy Bible & Christ Supported in the GOV; & danger of power abuse: // Robert Winthrop, speaker in USA House of Rep. of 1840 stated: "men, in a word, must necessarily be controlled either by a power within them or by a power without them, either by the word of God or by the strong arm of man, either by the Bible or by the baronet" (Robert Winthrop. Addresses and Speeches on Various Occasions. Boston: Little, Brown, and Co. 1852).

---T--- <u>FFOG John Adams writes to Thomas Jefferson, June 18, 1813 the following:</u> // "The general principles on which the fathers achieved independence were ,,,the general principles of Christianity" (21).

---T--- <u>The word "Conscience" is in most (by various forms) of the</u> Supporting DOCs & in the Previous DOCs which the CON was constructed from. // Furthermore the conscience is spoken of often in the Congressional meetings. It is also referred to in the CON often; of its actions and functions. The word's origin is from God, not man; and it is from Christianity, not any other religion or philosophy.

---T--- <u>Christian ministers were some</u> of the REP sent to the congressional meetings for the DOI & CON. (63).

---T--- <u>CON - Sin problem of man was agreed on by the DOI & CON & FFoG;</u> FFOG statements following: // John Adams stated that humanity was the same as, "since the Garden of Eden" and "no improvements in morals since the days of Jesus" (87). Also said in Federalist Paper 51 - "What is GOV itself but the greatest of all reflections on human nature". // Gouverneur Morris remarked that the USA CON would not work in France because evil morals of the French people at that time, such as religious disrespect, violence proneness, promise breaking, and sexual immorality (9). // Rev John Cotton warned of power abuse by GOV saying, "Let all the world learn to give mortall men no greater power than they are content they shall use ,,,unless they be better taught of God,,, they will certainly over-run those that give it, and those that receive it: there is a straine in a mans heart that will sometime or other runne out to excesse, unless the Lord restraine it ,,,Church power or other ,,,It is counted a matter of danger to the State to limit Prerogatives; but it is a further danger, not to have them limited ,,,It is therefore fit for every man to be studious of the bounds which the Lord hath set: and for the People ,,,Magistrates in the Commonwealth ,,,so Officers in Churches should desire to know the utmost bounds of their own power, and it is safe for both,,," (93).

---T--- <u>USA made a Proclamation</u> to make a Memorial by Repeating a Ceremony that the DOI & CON is for Christ & His Holy Bible: <u>// A Proclamation was made that the Year AD 1983 is to be called the USA Year of the Holy Bible: Signed by all Congress members and the President; includes the following statements: "Whereas Biblical teachings inspired concepts of civil GOV that are contained in our DOI and the CON of the US;</u> Whereas this Nation now faces great challenges that will test this Nation as it has never been tested before; and Whereas that renewing our knowledge of and faith in God through Holy SC can strengthen us as a nation and a people,,,".

---T--- <u>The first DOCs for the joining of the nation</u> are Christ's DOCs; They were the Articles of Association; & then following that was the AOC. // These are Christian Documents and these are what the CON was derived and constructed from; The CON is actually an enhancement of these. These are the previous DOCs of America before it was independent. These were not excluded or rejected, rather they were included and considered as good documents for the learning process. These are the DOCs which the CON is based on; they are NOT DOCs that the CON is NOT based on. Therefore Christian. And it was fully known that these were Christian DOCs; and that the CON was to be a Christian DOC and a continuation of these previous Documents. See next the AOC statements.

---T--- <u>Articles of Confederation (AOC), one of the main</u> Supporting DOCs for the CON: // The AOC was applicable for years 1777-1781. It was a DOC similar to the CON that we have today. It was a more detailed application of the DOI. It was part of the CC. The current CON we have now is more detailed than the AOC. // The AOC includes the following declarations: +It included God as First Place of Being; The term, or words used, are "And Whereas it hath pleased the Great Governor of the World,,,". +It included "spiritual" or "spirits" which is another word for the "Heart"; ",,,to incline the hearts of legislatures,,,". +It has the 10 Commandments of the Holy Bible, in it, in various applications. // The CON was intended/ purposed to be a continuation enhancement of this AOC.

---T--- <u>Self-Evidence tells to our Mind that the true Christian One God, not 2 or more; was the</u> Intention/ purpose of the FFOG: // Truth is the True God. // Self-evidence tells us~ +=not to trust various fairy tales about various gods of which is no truth; +=to trust evidence; +=not to trust different gods who differ from each other and all claiming to be god. Now what are we ?? // The FFOG trusted the true Religion of the True God of True Christianity.

---T--- <u>Congress Repeatedly Proclaimed Days for Prayer to God:</u> // Such as the Day (10/18, 1783) of prayer and thanksgiving for winning the RW that stated: "Whereas it hath pleased the Supreme Ruler of all human events ,,,a cessation of all hostilities by sea and land, and these US ,,,freedom, sovereignty and independence ,,,acknowledged ,,,the interposition of Divine Providence in our favor ,,,and the citizens ,,,have every reason for praise and gratitude to the God of their salvation ,,,and of our entire dependence on that Almighty Being ,,,the US in Congress assembled, do recommend it to the several States ,,,a day of public thanksgiving that all the people may ,,,assemble ,,,united voices the praises of their Supreme ,,,Benefactor for his numberless favors ,,,and above all that he hath been pleased to continue to us the light of the blessed Gospel and secured to us in the fullest extent the rights of conscience in faith and worship" (58).

++

====== [CONCLUSION]: THE DOI And CON ARE ONE DOCUMENT TOGETHER, A JOINT DOCUMENT, THEREFORE FORMING A TOTAL CONTRACT, A UNIT, EACH As A PART; ~And~ THE DOI Is THE RULING, (OVERRULING, Or MANAGING, Or CONTROLLING) DOCUMENT To

THE CON, THEREFORE TO THE USA; ~And~ THE CON Is A SUB-DOCUMENT Of THE DOI, NOT An OPPOSITION, NOR SUBTRACTION, NOR VOIDING DOCUMENT To THE DOI:

{Additionally, the other Chapters and Parts of this Book are to be known as applicable EV for proving these Conclusions; they are agreeable and related}:

---T--- Now the DOI & CON (CC) are mostly Principle Laws: // They are the Principle Laws Applied to a Subject. // Therefore, we do not have the problems that some Spiritual Moral Creatures are asserting. // Study is needed to comprehend it, as any subject needs study. Simply to do thinking and talking needs study; and they are basic activities we do; thus they are not simple to do. Language will need study because the English language has developed; and developed some in wrong ways; even though it has some very good positives about it.

---T--- The DOI is a group or set of Principle Laws & the CON is constructed to apply those Principle Laws. // And the CON has many Principle Laws in it.

---T--- The word "respecting" in the 1-A is very wrongly thought of: // This word is defined as "partiality or favorism". Hence confusion about a Nations Main Documents. And these Documents are the Referential Basis for this Nations Existence & Function.

---T--- The DOI & CON Do go together; & are as one sentence from start to end: // When a group or set of DOCs are constructed, they are constructed as an agreeable unit; no Spiritual Reasonable Moral person constructs a set of statements (DOCs) that have contradictions or disagreeable statements; such would mal-function. EX: If I told you that {1 + 1 = 2} and then I told you that {1 + 1 = 9}, then you would know that this is wrong. You would tell me that the statements disagree.

---T--- The DOI & CON are One Document together; they form one document; 2 pieces that make one; each a part to the total (whole): // Neither one can be separated from the other. The CON was specifically clearly designed and constructed with the intention/ purpose to apply the DOI; it applies the Principle Laws that are in the DOI.

---T--- The Great Seal Symbol of the USA was enacted by Congress & has the date of the DOI on it as the Start of the USA as a Nation; & as the Start of the Covenant Contract Date: // Thus this is EV of knowing that the CON is part of the DOI; and that the DOI is applicable; not excluded, removed, or deleted.

---T--- The CON accomplishes by various ways the Christian Rights that the FFOG stated as coming from God; stated such Rights in the DOI.

---T--- The CON is dated in reference to its controlling DOC date (DOI); proving that it is to be connected to the DOI: // This also proves the time of the Start of the USA; as a Nation. This CON statement says: "Done in Convention by the Unanimous Consent of the States present the Seventeenth Day of September in the Year of our Lord one thousand seven hundred and Eighty seven and of the Independence of the US of America the Twelfth". // The CON is signed using the Terms of the DOI. See the words~ INDEPENDENCE of the US.

---T--- The Congress Meeting Notes in constructing the CON in AD 1788 stated that the intention/ purpose of the CON is to support the "rights" stated in the DOI; to apply them: // States: "A CON ought to be understood by every one. The most humble and trifling characters in the country have a right to know what foundation they stand upon. I confess I do not see the end of the powers here proposed, nor the reasons for granting them. The principal end of a CON is to set forth what must be given up for the community at large, and to secure those rights which ought never to be infringed."

---T--- Here is reference to the DOI & CON as a Covenant Contract with God & as a Christian DOC in the Congress Meeting Notes of AD 1788: // "They Certainly have no authority to interfere in the establishment of any religion whatsoever; and I am astonished that any gentleman should conceive they have. Is there any power given to Congress in matters of religion? Can they pass a single act to impair our religious liberties? If they could, it would be a just cause of alarm. If they could, sir, no man would have more horror against it than myself. Happily, no sect here is superior to another. [[Christian DEN]] As long as this is the case, we shall be free from those persecutions and distractions with which other countries have been torn. If any future Congress should pass an act concerning the religion of the country, it would be an act which they are not authorized to pass, by the CON, and which the people would not obey. Every one would ask, "Who authorized the GOV to pass such an act? It is not warranted by the CON, and is barefaced usurpation." The power to make treaties can never be supposed to include a right to establish a foreign religion [[Christianity is the USA nations religion not foreign religions]] among ourselves, though it might authorize a toleration of others ,,,pagans ,,,Mahometans ,,,". // This is EV that the CON is~ +not opposing God in the DOI; +not opposing the Principle Laws in the DOI; +not contradicting that God should be included; +not removing, subtracting, or disagreeing with the inclusions of God in the DOI; +not EXCLUDING God from the USA; +Therefore it is EV proving that the CON & DOI are agreeable and ONE Document, a Covenant Contract, a Christian DOC.

---T--- The statement on the CON says: "to form a more perfect union" ~ with God: // This is identifying that a UNION has already been formed; referring to the DOI Union start. // It is also stating the following about the CON and its relation and connections to the DOI: +The CON is adding more parts to the DOI; +The CON is adding to make the Union (started by the DOI) more perfect; +The CON is part of the total Form (the DOI as part of the Form); +The CON is to be connected to the DOI; +The CON is to DO "more perfect"; +The CON is NOT TO DO actions of remove, subtract, oppose, disagree, or contradict that in the DOI.

---T--- "Blessings" word, Used in the CON, is a Christian word, a godly word: // Blessings is defined as "rewards that come from God; divine gifts". This is the same source of that the DOI states the rewards of happiness, and other Rights come from~ God is that source.

---T--- The CON states, "We the people of the US,,,". This is a present tense statement. Therefore it is declaring that the US is already existing as a Nation; that the US is in existence as the US: // The intention/ purpose is that the US~ +is in existence; +it is not non-existing; +it started to exist because of the DOI & at that time; +It Does Not say, "we now are forming the people of the US"; +And it Does Not say, "we are now hereby forming the US as a people". Therefore the CON & DOI are together and the DOI overrules the CON; and they form a CC.

---T--- The CC is proved by the EV of identifying God as Required to be included & that it is the true God: // The DOI states~ "God, Creator, Supreme Judge, Divine Providence". The CON is Signed stating~ "in the year of our Lord". The Lord is Jesus Christ the Lord; the time that the Lord is connected to is Christmas~ Christ Jesus earthly coming in the flesh body.

---T--- Before the CON the various Branches of GOV were already being established; some were already existing; the AOC Document was applicable and was attempting to apply the DOI. // EX: "Letters of Delegates to Congress: Volume 4- 5/16, 1776 -- 8/15, 1776". Note the word "Congress" there.

---T--- The CON Preamble States it is establishing the Rights of the DOI: "secure the blessings of liberty". // Liberty is one of the Rights stated in the DOI; as coming from God; not idolatry or no God.

---T--- The CON is the application of the Principles of God's DOI: // This is proved by the CON Preamble stating, "Secure the blessings of liberty". "Secure" is defined as~ to accomplish the stabilization, the security of". Thus intended/ purposed to accomplish the stabilization, the security, the finalizations, of the Liberty Right from the DOI; and the other Rights in the DOI. God has Rights also.

---T--- THE DOI is a National Holiday, Independence Day. Thus the CON references this date also; proving the starting of the Nation; that the CON is connected to the DOI.

---T--- DOI is Overruling DOC to CON: // The same DOI Principle Laws are stated in the Congress Meetings; and repeatedly: // For EX: "Journal of the Senate of the US of America, 1789-1793, 1/ 11, 1790, The Senate assembled: present as on Friday. ,,,Gentlemen of the Senate: ,,,to lay before you a copy of the adoption and ratification of the CON of the US ,,,and every exertion on our part shall be made to realize, and secure to our country, those blessings, which a gracious Providence has placed within her reach ,,,[[here are terms from the DOI]] ,,,the measures of GOV should, therefore, be calculated to strengthen the confidence that is due to that important TRUTH. [[See truth here; same as in the DOI]] ,,,the basis of the wealth and strength of our confederated Republic, must be the frequent subject of our deliberation, and shall be advanced by all proper means in our power ,,,Our cares and efforts shall be directed to the welfare of our country; and we have the most perfect dependence upon your co-operating with us, on all occasions, in such measures as will insure to our fellow citizens the blessings which they have a right to expect from a free, efficient, and equal, government". // See all those Principle Law words (Free, Equal); same as DOI. This is only 1 example of many Congress Meeting notes; Others do the same as this one.

---T--- Reasoning Attack: // The CON cannot be turned against the DOI. Such is the same activity of demons; the devil did this with Jesus the Lord by intentionally turning the Holy Bible against itself. (Mat4). Divide & conquer; To divide one part against another part. To attack the reasoning.

---T--- Absence Law: // There is absolutely no DOC, nor historical supporting DOC, nor life evidence from any FFOG, nor any promoting or allowance of, or encouragement to any other religion than Christianity; nor any God but Jesus Christ (Christianity); except Judaism (Christianity in it's earlier status); NOR any of these opposing or stopping Christianity; Nor any of these starting any system without Christianity.

---T--- Inclusion/Exclusion Law: // All other religions and false gods are specifically excluded and warned about; and in every instance of DOC and historical supporting DOC. Includes Paganism, Heathenism, God Exclusion, etc.

---T--- God's Laws are enacted by the CON; They are the same Laws of the Holy Bible; of Christ: // This is GOD of the DOI; the CON enacts the DOI by such; Includes the following: The Christian Bible, the Sabbath, the Oath, Stealing, Murder, Man-stealing, Assisting Religion, Opposing the partiality to Christian DEN, Prayer, Truth, Anti-dictatorship & tyranny, etc.

---T--- USA President states~ +] the DOI is the 1st Document of the CC; +] and that the DOI & CON are connected: // John Quincy Adams states: "The DOI first organized the social compact [[compact is defined as Covenant Contract]] on the foundation of the Redeemer's mission upon earth ,,,and laid the cornerstone of human GOV upon the first precepts of Christianity", and, "The Declaration of Independence cast off all the shackles of this dependency. The US of America were no longer Colonies. They were an independent nation of Christians" (184). This was written a long time after the CON was enacted.

---T--- DOI & CON Connected with DOI as the Overruling DOC to CON: // The DOI is Why we are a Nation and the CON is How to form a better ("more perfect" as stated in the CON) nation.

---T--- CITIZEN Branch Responsible to Keep CC with Christ: // This contract is to be kept by the Spiritual Moral Creatures, as responsibility of citizenry; as they are in the contract, as referred to in many ways. And it includes the basis that the Representatives which wrote up the contract were representing the Spiritual Moral creatures. // FFoG John Jay says: "Every member of the State ought diligently to read and to study the constitution of his country ,,,By knowing their rights, they will sooner perceive when they are violated and be the better prepared to defend and assert them" (6). // FFoG also state~ "The power under the Constitution will always be in the people. It is entrusted for certain defined purposes, and for a certain limited period to representation of their own choosing and whenever it is exercised contrary to their interest or not agreeably to their wishes, their servants can, and undoubtedly will be recalled". // Hence the Rights in the CC need to match with what the Officers are doing or the People need to reject the actions of the GOV.

---T--- <u>DOI & CON is Christ's Religious DOC; therefore the Religious 1-A & R-E & R~Est apply:</u> // It is none of these~ +Not neutral. +Not any religion. +Not all religions. +Not false religions. // It is all of these~ +to exist as a religious DOC, rather than to be a non-religious DOC. +to only be inclusive of the religion that the contract was referring to by intention/ purpose. // For those who signed the DOI it was a religious DOC. // The AOC was a preliminary to the CON; God is stated in it as the new GOV was to be under His domain~ "And Whereas it hath pleased the Great Governor of the World to incline the hearts of legislatures we respectively represent in Congress, to approve of, and to authorize us to ratify the said Articles of Confederation and perpetual union". ~The current CON is a ratification of the AOC; an enhancement of it; a continuation of it. // The CON is how to apply the DOI; the DOI Does not have an exact form of GOV in every detail; and the CON establishes the 5 Branches (Beings) of GOV under God~ Legislature, Executive, Judicial, Citizenship; also the operation and jurisdictions; with the 7 Parts of Operation~ of God, Laws (CC), Decisions with intention/ purpose, Citizens, Executive, Judicial, Congress. The DOI states some basic Branches of the Nation with citizens, congress, and God.

---T--- <u>DOI is OVERruling DOC to CON:</u> // Some of the different Branches of GOV were already early being designed BEFORE the CON. // The DOI was known and remained as the Nation establishment DOC. The AOC was the DOC that the CON replaced, which was also purposed as an application of the DOI. // Following is a Congress Meeting Letter stating these truths: "Letters of Delegates to Congress: Volume 8-- 9/19, 1777 - 1/31, 1778 - ,,,10 ,,,1777 ,,,I sent you a few days ago an Account of the Success we have had on the Delaware. The Honor of recovering Philadelphia seems to be intended for the brave Men who command there; for if the Enemy cannot get up with their Ships of War, Howe cannot long remain in the City. May Honor be given to whom Honor may be due. Congress have applyd with Diligence to Confederation. Most of the important Articles are agreed to. Each State retains its Sovereignty and Independence with every Power, Jurisdiction and Right which is not by the Confederation expressly delegated to the US in Congress assembled. Each State is to have one Vote in Congress; but there must be a Concurrence of Nine States in all Matters of Importance. The Proportion of the publick Expence to be paid by Each State to be ascertained by the Value of all the Lands granted to or surveyd for any Person, to be estimated according to such Mode as Congress shall from time to time direct. All Disputes about Boundaries are to be decided by Judges appointed in the following Mode: The Representatives of Each State in Congress to be nominated, the contending States to strike off 13 Each and out of the remaining 13 not more than 9 nor less than 7 shall be drawn out by Lot, any five of them to hear & determine the Matter. I hope we shall finish the Confederation in a few days when I intend to renew my Request for the Leave of Absence, and return home ,,,I am determined by Cods Assistance never to forsake the great Cause in which my Country is virtuously struggling; but there are others who have greater Abilities & more adequate to this important Service, than I have ,,,and I have the clear and full Testimony of my own Mind that I have at all Times endeavord to fill the Station they have thought fit to place me in to their Advantage. This will be deliverd to you by Mr. Hancock who has Leave of Absence till the first of ,,,next. ,,,I hope the Person to be elected in my Room will have understanding enough to know when the Arts of Flattery are playd upon him, and Fortitude of mind sufficient to resist & despise them. This I mention inter Nosmetipsos. In this EVIL World there are oftentimes large Doses prepared for those whose Stomacks will bear them. And it would be a disgrace to human Nature to affirm there are some who can take the fullest Cup without nauseating. I suppose you have by this time finishd a form of GOV. I hope the greatest Care will be taken in the Choice of a Governor. He, whether a wise Man or a Fool ,,,Choice on a Man of RELIGION and Piety; who will understand human Nature and the Nature and End of political Society-who will not by Corruption or Flattery be seducd to the betraying, even without being sensible of it himself, the SACRED Rights of his Country. We are told that the Prisoners taken at the Northward are sent into Massachusetts Bay. I hope Burgoyn will not be permitted to reside in Boston; for if he is, I fear that inconsiderate Persons of Fashion and some significance will be inducd, under the Idea of Politeness, to form Connexions with him, dangerous to the Publick. There are other Reasons which I should think would make his or any other officers being fixed in a populous Town uneligible. There are Prison ships I suppose provided for the Privates. The Success of the present Campain hitherto has been great beyond our most sanguine Expectation. Let us ascribe Glory to GOD who has graciously vouchsafd to favor the Cause of America and of Mankind ,,,Every Nerve must be exerted ,,,Among the Train of EVILs it is likely to bring upon us, is the Destruction of MORALS ,,,Adams ,,,7. JCC, 9:880. ,,,JCC, 9:852."

---T--- <u>God's DOI Rules CON:</u> // The Congress Meetings supported the DOI by celebrating the 4th of July, during the time period that the CON was being constructed; Such was done at a Christian Church with a Christian Assembly Worship Activity to Christ & The Holy Spirit.

---T--- <u>The preamble of the CON states that it</u> is intentioned to work out the DOI (of God): // The Preamble states~ "We the people of the United States, in order to form a more perfect Union, establish justice, insure domestic Tranquility, provide for the common defense, promote the General Welfare, and secure the Blessings of Liberty, to ourselves and our Posterity, do ordain and establish this CON for the United States of America." // "Blessings" is a word of Christianity; defined by Webster & Greek as "Divine Gifts from God". // The "rights" stated in the CON are the "rights" stated in the DOI. "Right" are identified as coming from God; superior to man. // The OT evil GOV, as was in Egypt with Pharoh, and the slavery of the Israelites, and protection of Christianity, was often referred to for the DOI & CON. It is a record from the Holy Bible (Genesis-Exodus). More EV is provided on this throughout this Book. // Furthermore the word, "ordain" is a Biblical Christian word; it relates to the priesthood of the OT.

71

Priests of the country and of personal homes was the thought for the word. The word "priest" includes in its definition the word concept~ "ordain"; It is a "ministerial function". FFOG Benjamin Franklin (in CON meetings) spoke such a message on the OT Christianity Priests, and exampled it for today; that which was in Israel, Egypt, and God from the Holy Bible. In the Holy Bible GOV Officials are stated to be "Ministers" for God (Romans 13). This was the Concept that was the Basis that the FFOG stated. +They did not desire evil demons, nor workers of iniquity; those things were part of what they were intending to separate from and resist by the actions of the DOI.

---T--- <u>The Checks & Balances System was based</u> on mankind tendency & temptation to do evil & problem of the carnal mind, that must be overcome; & the fact of the Fall of Eve & Adam in Christ's Holy Bible in Genesis: // This put us out of a perfect world in to a world of good & evil. // This System is intentional/ purpose to prevent abuses, assure rightness, protect mankind from GOV abuse, protect Christianity & spread it across the world, and secure our Rights as creatures of God Who is the total right Ruler. This fact is recorded repeatedly in Supporting DOCs to the DOI & CON. // Romans 8 of HSC.

---T--- <u>The CC as USA DOC are ANNOTATED; as is filed in various</u> Libraries of the GOV, and worldwide: // Annotated is defined as, including "to recognize these as what is written". // Includes the DOI under the title, "The Organic Laws of the US of America". // Also includes the DOC of the AOC, the CON, and the Northwest Ordinance. // The term, "The organic laws of the US of America" is defined as including, "as the structural laws".

---T--- <u>The CON is the Sub-DOC of the DOI</u> because of Constitutional Law~ the Definition of Constitution as follows (1a)(1b): // {A} "Political statement or DOC of fundamental laws: a written statement outlining the basic laws or principles by which a country or organization is governed"; {B} "A particular law, ordinance, or regulation, made by the authority of any superior, civil or ecclesiastical"; {C} "A system of fundamental principles for the government of rational and social beings". // This proves that the CON was furthering, or an application of some more specific laws to enhance the frame that was already established~ and what was it ?~ the DOI.

---T--- <u>The DOI is A DOC of the USA &</u> was never changed, repealed, reversed, or banned; It remains as a Memorial DOC; a Monument: // It is both a historical event & represents an historical event. // It was considered as the Overruling DOC of the USA & of CON. // The DOI~ +remains as included for the USA; +not Excluded of the USA; +It is intended/ purposed to be respected as part of the USA; +It is valued to be APPLIED to the USA; +It is known not to be contradicted, repealed, reversed, banned, opposed, changed. // It is rebellion and treason~ (to reject the DOI); against God, against the USA; To do so intentionally/ purposefully with knowledge.

---T--- <u>The formation of the USA was accomplished by the DOI</u>; No DOI, No USA: // Thus to deny the DOI denies the USA. The formation of the DOI forms the USA and the CON is an implementation of the DOI. // The term, USA, first appears in the DOI. The Name of this Country is started on the DOI. This is what brought the term and thus country in to name of existence as a formation separate from Britain. Before this they were called "United Colonies of North America" or "United Colonies" or "United Colonies of America" or "States". Thomas Paine wrote in AD 1776, "Free and independent States of America" (63).

---T--- <u>The "Declaration of Independence</u> established the principles which the CON made practical." (63).

---T--- <u>The CON in its Starting & Ending Salutations refers</u> to the DOI: // Starting~ "We the People of the United States, in Order to form a more perfect Union, establish justice, insure domestic tranquility, provide for the common defense, promote the general welfare, and secure the Blessings of Liberty to ourselves and our Posterity, do ordain and establish this Constitution for the United States of America". These statements are based on the DOI statements. // Ending Salutations on the CON refers to the DOI saying, "by the Unanimous Consent of the States present the Seventeenth Day of September in the Year of our Lord one thousand seven hundred and eighty seven and of the Independence of the United States of America the Twelfth". The DOI is referred to by the statement~ "Independence of the United States of America the Twelfth".

---T--- <u>The CON does not really make reasonable sense without the DOI.</u> // Many of the statements in the CON are based on the statements in the DOI.

---T--- <u>Formation of the USA was by the DOI with God:</u> // "They were originally nothing more than colonial corporations. On the Declaration of Independence, a GOV was to be formed. The small states, aware of the necessity of preventing anarchy, and taking advantage of the moment, extorted from the large ones an equality of votes. Standing now on that ground, they demand, under the new system, greater Rights, as men, than their fellow-citizens of the large states. The proper answer to them is, that the same necessity, of which they formerly took advantage, does not now exist; and that the large states are at liberty now to consider what is right, rather than what may be expedient" {Elliots Debates, July 7, 1787, (14a)}.

---T--- <u>The DOI was celebrated after CON</u>, in anniversary recognitions, as applicable to the USA from then continuously forward in time: // "Journals of the Continental Congress --WEDNESDAY, JUNE 28, 1786" (14a).

---T--- <u>The DOI was used as a legal</u> DOC to refer & base USA GOV decisions for the people of the USA from it's time of conception continuously forward in time: // For EX: "Journals of the Continental Congress -- FRIDAY, OCT ,,,1779" (14a).

---T--- +] <u>The DOI was the OverRuling DOC of the AOC;</u> +] The AOC was an application of the DOI; +] the CON replaced the AOC as a DOC under the DOI; +] The CON replaced the AOC as an application of the DOI. That was the Function Construction intended with the DOI & AOC and the same was intended/purposed with the DOI & CON: // Note as follows from (14a): +"Ordered, That the Board of Treasury be discharged from taking order respecting the account of F. Bailey; and that a warrant issue on Thomas Smith, commissioner of the continental loan office for Pensylvania, in favour of the committee lately appointed to publish the Declaration of Independence, the Articles of Confederation, &c., for the sum of eight hundred dollars new emission to enable them to pay for the publication of the said work." - Journals of the Continental Congress, 1774-1789, Saturday, May 26, 1781"; +"The committee appointed to collect and cause to be published two hundred copies of the Declaration of Independence, the articles of Confederation and perpetual union" - Journals of the Continental Congress --Friday, May 4, 1781"; +"That the late province of Pensylvania, on the fourth day of July, in the year of our Lord one thousand seven hundred and seventy-six, did join with the other twelve, late provinces, now states, in the Declaration of Independence, and soon after established a CON and GOV founded on the authority of the people, which they continue still to exercise and enjoy; and they did also join in the Articles of Confederation of the US" -- Journals of the Continental Congress --Friday, 22 Nov., 1782".

---T--- Michael Farris is a Constitution Attorney that has a book with some legal Truth in it; including this statement: "By basing our right to be a free nation upon God's law, we were also saying ,,,that we owed obedience to the law that allowed us to be ,,,a country ,,,By-laws must be interpreted to be in agreement with the Charter,,,---,,,the Declaration of Independence ,,,the CON of the US must be in agreement with the Declaration" (69).

---T--- The DOI is a Declaration of Congress whereas so is the CON an act of Congress, just the same: // "pursuant to the declaration of Congress" - Journals of the Continental Congress --TUESDAY, FEB. 23, 1779" (14a).

\+

====== [CONCLUSION]: GOD, LAWS Of GOD's NATURE, CREATOR, SUPREME RULER, DIVINE PROVIDENCE, LORD JESUS CHRIST Is To BE FIRST PRIORITY, WHICH IS PART Of BEING GOD, GIVEN SUPREME PLACE, The TRUTHFUL And FINAL AUTHORITY And RIGHT(s), And NO IDOLATRY:

-------------------------INTRODUCTIONS:

---T--- "Supreme Judge" is the Words of the DOI & Supporting DOC: // Supreme is defined as (1b): "Highest in authority; holding the highest place in government or power. In the universe, God only is the supreme ruler and judge. His commands are supreme, and binding on all his creatures; Highest, greatest or most excellent; as supreme love; supreme glory; supreme degree.". // Apply this love affection in intention and the USA Nation can commune with God. // Priority is not inferiority.

---T--- Theocracy, Idolatry, and God is what the CC Law Rules: // It is not in support of rules of life from infidels, atheists, false religionists, and anti-Christ's. Such is all written in the DOC of the USA. Thus God must be included in the USA GOV, including God's Religion (Doctrine, activity of God & man). This section will prove that: 1~ God is the Supreme Ruler of the USA; 2~ God is the only one and true God of Christianity; 3~ All other god's are forbidden as idolatry; 4~ The Christian religion is the religion of the USA.

---T--- The USA is NOT a Nation based on: // a} Every god; thus idolatry; thus every false religion included. b} Heathenry; thus no God. c} Anti-God; thus opposed or against God. d} Devil & demons. // And all Spiritual Moral Beings should be very glad that such is Not the basis for the USA. Such sorts of thinking & feeling are the cause of endless pain and Hell and problems.

~~~~~~~~~~~~~~~~~~~APPLICATION Of CONCLUSION BY ~~~~~~~~~~~~~~~~~~~~~
--------------------------------GOD Is TO BE FIRST PRIORITY, NO Idolatry, Over All ~ GOD Has 1st RIGHT As EXISTING AS GOD; And As BEING ALWAYS RIGHT & LOVING:

---T--- The DOI, CON, Supporting DOC, FFOG, all state that God is 1st priority. // The definition of God states such.
---T--- The 1-A of the CON, which is about Religion, is in 1st place as compared to the Intention to be 1st priority: // And it states that God's religion is to be priority with the GOV~ the Nation. // That it is not to be opposed, rather supported. // And the other amendments in the CON with it, about freedom of press and speech, are supportive for God to be spoke about in the USA and to the world; and as 1st priority. +Not unlimited freedom for evil talk, falsity gods, evil idolatry. Such evils as these, and rightnesses as said, are what caused the DOI to occur.
---T--- The CON includes the 10 commandments in various forms, such as lying, stealing, murder, dictatorship & tyranny, etc. Holy Bible of Christ Based.
---T--- The CON also includes The Common Law, which is based on the Holy Bible: // thus 10 commandments of Jesus Christ.
---T--- The name Jesus Christ on the CON, says He is Lord: // Lord is defined as being "sovereign and divine". These are the Lord's relation and connection to the universe and all that exists. This is saying He is God; Sovereign is the attribute of God; no Being is such except God. Divine is similar. This is continuing the DOI putting God as God over the nation. It says He is the Lord, not the creatures are the Lord. This was to prevent that which occurred in history and the application of the Holy SC~ "Rom 1:22, 24, 25 Professing themselves to be wise, they became fools,,,

Wherefore God also gave them up to uncleanness through the lusts of their own hearts, to dishonor their own bodies between themselves: Who changed the truth of God into a lie, and worshipped and served the creature more than the Creator, who is blessed for ever. Amen." He is Lord, not the people creatures.

---T--- GOV's First Priority is to put GOD first: // This is proven herein. EV by all work of the FFOG: by the Words of all the DOC; by the intent/ purpose authorizing the defensive war against Britain; by self-evidence; by the definition of God, etc. // God is named and stated to be 1st priority~ +Ruler or Supreme Ruler, Supreme Judge, of the Universe; God is God of the universe; +Creator makes Him owner of all that is created; of all parts of created life; +Divine Providence is the acknowledgement, recognition and identification that God is the Ruler over all activities and events of life.

---T--- The EV of the FFOG, DOCs, events, & activities of the USA prove God is priority; not idolatry.

---T--- The Creator, as stated in the DOI, has the Right to make the rules and be acknowledged as the Creator of all Spiritual Moral Creatures: // and all created material things and activities on the created Earth that the Creatures do. He is the property Owner, source, and Manager, the Time Beginning and End.

~~~~~~~~~~~~~~~~ APPLICATION Of CONCLUSION BY ~~~~~~~~~~~~~~~~~~~~~~~~~~~
--INCLUSION Of GOD In THE USA GOV:

---T--- Now to include God in the CC (DOI & CON) is defined as including Him. Now what is He? Basically a Spirit Being: // It makes no value as what He looks like in the form (except that He does not look like a monster). Anyway He is a Will, Decision, Supreme Conscience, Affection, Emotion, Thought, Reasoning, Desire, Intent/ purpose, Judgment. Now for the CC (DOI & CON) to make a CC with God and then Not include what He thinks is right & evil (Supreme Conscience) and what He feels, affections and emotions, and what His will is, and what He desires, intentions/ purposes, and what His reasons and thoughts are, is equal to excluding Him.

---T--- England (only the group of individuals supporting the evil in that Country, as contrarily there were many good Spiritual Moral Beings) was only including God, Christ Jesus, in name and not in Spirit or Heart: // Thus they only acted themselves under a cloak, or a falsity of appearance, sort of like a ship that has a white flag but the people on board have a black heart. Such evil is what the FFOG opposed. But saying is one thing, and body acts were not for Christ Abba Father.

---T--- To Include GOD in words written in the DOCs & then exclude God from applications is to add to that which is written; therefore lying; or to lie against that which is written.

---T--- To Include God in words written on the DOCs & Exclude God in activities, events, life, speeches of GOV~ is to lie: // If the words are in the Main Governmental DOCs, then how co/ God be excluded from GOV operations as those ???

---T--- Every State (in their CON preamble) in the USA included God as God, thus agreeing with anti-idolatry; & opposing False lies of separating Christ from the USA: // Quoted without the quotation marks are parts of those CON, as follows: +Alabama 1901, Preamble. We the people of the State of Alabama, invoking the favor and guidance of Almighty God, do ordain and establish the following CON. +Alaska 1956, Preamble. We, the people of Alaska, grateful to God and to those who founded our nation and pioneered this great land. +Arizona 1911, Preamble. We, the people of the State of Arizona, grateful to Almighty God for our liberties, do ordain this CON. +Arkansas 1874, Preamble. We, the people of the State of Arkansas, grateful to Almighty God for the privilege of choosing our own form of GOV. +California 1879, Preamble. We, the People of the State of California, grateful to Almighty God for our freedom. +Colorado 1876, Preamble. We, the people of Colorado, with profound reverence for the Supreme Ruler of Universe. +Connecticut 1818, Preamble. The People of Connecticut, acknowledging with gratitude the good Providence of God in permitting them to enjoy. +Delaware 1897, Preamble. Through Divine Goodness all men have, by nature, the rights of worshipping and serving their Creator according to the dictates of their consciences. +Florida 1885, Preamble. We, the people of the State of Florida, grateful to Almighty God for our constitutional liberty, establish this CON. +Georgia 1777, Preamble. We, the people of Georgia, relying upon protection and guidance of Almighty God, do ordain and establish this CON. +Hawaii 1959, Preamble. We, the people of Hawaii, Grateful for Divine Guidance ,,,establish this CON. +Idaho 1889, Preamble. We, the people of the State of Idaho, grateful to Almighty God for our freedom, to secure its blessings. +Illinois 1870, Preamble. We, the people of the State of Illinois, grateful to Almighty God for the civil, political and religious liberty which He hath so long permitted us to enjoy and looking to Him for a blessing on our endeavors. +Indiana 1851, Preamble. We, the People of the State of Indiana, grateful to Almighty God for the free exercise of the right to chose our form of GOV. +Iowa 1857, Preamble. We, the People of the State of Iowa, grateful to the Supreme Being for the blessings hitherto enjoyed, and feeling our dependence on Him for a continuation of these blessings ,,,establish this CON. +Kansas 1859, Preamble. We, the people of Kansas, grateful to Almighty God for our civil and religious privileges, establish this CON. +Kentucky 1891, Preamble. We, the people of the Commonwealth of Kentucky grateful to Almighty God for the civil, political and religious liberties. +Louisiana 1921, Preamble. We, the people of the State of Louisiana, grateful to Almighty God for the civil, political and religious liberties we enjoy. +Maine 1820, Preamble. We the People of Maine acknowledging with grateful hearts the goodness of the Sovereign Ruler of the Universe in affording us an opportunity ,,,and imploring His aid and direction. +Maryland 1776, Preamble. We, the people of the state of Maryland, grateful to Almighty God for our civil and religious liberty. +Massachusetts 1780, Preamble. We,,, the people of Massachusett's, acknowledging with grateful hearts, the goodness of the Great Legislator of the Universe in the course of His Providence, an opportunity and devoutly imploring His direction. +Michigan 1908, Preamble. We, the people of the State of Michigan, grateful to Almighty God for the blessings of freedom ,,,establish this CON. +Minnesota 1857, Preamble. We, the people of the State of Minnesota, grateful to God for our civil and religious liberty, and desiring to perpetuate its blessings. +Mississippi 1890, Preamble. We, the people of Mississippi in convention assembled, grateful to Almighty God, and invoking His blessing on our work. +Missouri 1845, Preamble. We, the people of Missouri, with profound reverence for the Supreme Ruler of the Universe, and grateful for His goodness, establish this CON. +Montana 1889, Preamble. We, the people of Montana, grateful to Almighty God for the blessings of liberty ,,,establish this CON. +Nebraska 1875, Preamble. We, the people, grateful to Almighty God for our freedom establish this CON. +Nevada 1864, Preamble. We the people of the State of Nevada, grateful to Almighty God for our freedom establish this CON. +New Hampshire 1792, Every individual has a natural and unalienable right to worship God according to the dictates of his own conscience. +New Jersey 1844, Preamble. We, the people of the State of New Jersey, grateful to Almighty God for civil and religious liberty which He hath so long permitted us to enjoy, and looking to Him for a blessing on our endeavors. +New Mexico 1911, Preamble. We, the People of New Mexico, grateful to Almighty God for the blessings of Liberty. +New York 1846, Preamble. We, the people of the State of New York, grateful to Almighty God for our freedom, in order to secure its blessings. +North Carolina 1868, Preamble. We the ,,,people of the State of North Carolina, grateful to Almighty God, the Sovereign Ruler of Nations, for our civil, political, and religious liberties, and acknowledging our dependence upon Him for the continuance of those. +North Dakota 1889, Preamble. We, the people of North Dakota, grateful to Almighty God for the blessings of civil and religious liberty, do ordain. +Ohio 1852, Preamble. We the people of the state of Ohio, grateful to Almighty God for our freedom, to secure its blessings and to promote our common. +Oklahoma 1907, Preamble. Invoking the guidance of Almighty God, in order to secure and perpetuate the blessings of liberty ,,,establish this. +Oregon 1857, Bill of Rights ,,,All men shall be secure in the Natural right, to worship Almighty God according to the dictates of their consciences. +Pennsylvania 1776, Preamble. We, the people of Pennsylvania, grateful to Almighty God for the blessings of civil and religious liberty, and humbly invoking His guidance. +Rhode Island 1842, Preamble. We the People of the State of Rhode Island grateful to Almighty God for the civil and religious liberty which He hath so long permitted us to enjoy, and looking to Him for a blessing. +South Carolina 1778, Preamble. We, the people of the State of South Carolina grateful to God for our liberties, do ordain and establish this CON. +South Dakota 1889, Preamble. We, the people of South Dakota, grateful to Almighty God for our civil and religious liberties ,,,establish this CON. +Tennessee 1796, That all men have a natural and indefensible right to worship Almighty God according to the dictates of their conscience. +Texas 1845, Preamble. We the People of the Republic of Texas, acknowledging, with gratitude, the grace and beneficence of God. +Utah 1896, Preamble. Grateful to Almighty God for life and liberty, we establish this CON. +Vermont 1777, Preamble. Whereas all GOV ought to ,,,enable the individuals who compose it to enjoy their natural rights, and other blessings which the Author of Existence has bestowed on man. +Virginia 1776, Bill of Rights,,, Religion, or the Duty which we owe our Creator, can be directed only by Reason, and that it is the mutual duty of all to practice Christian Forbearance, Love and Charity towards each other. +Washington 1889, Preamble. We the People of the State of Washington, grateful to the Supreme Ruler of the Universe for our liberties, do ordain this CON. +West Virginia 1872, Preamble. Since through Divine Providence we enjoy the blessings of civil, political and religious liberty, we, the people of West Virginia reaffirm our faith in and constant reliance upon God. +Wisconsin 1848, Preamble. We, the people of Wisconsin, grateful to Almighty God for our freedom, domestic tranquility. +Wyoming 1890, Preamble. We, the people of the State of Wyoming, grateful to God for our civil, political, and religious liberties ,,,establish this CON.

---T--- CC states Christian Nation for God: // Oklahoma Supreme Court reports rightly in AD 1959, saying, "It is well settled and understood that ours is a Christian Nation, holding the Almighty God in dutiful reverence. It is so noted in our DOI and in the constitution of every state of the Union. Since George Washington's first presidential proclamation of Thanksgiving Day, each such annual proclamation reiterates the principles that we are such a Christian Nation ,,,We consider the language used in our DOI, and in our national Constitution, and in our Constitution of Oklahoma, wherein those documents recognize the existence of God, and that we are a Christian nation and a Christian State" (252).

---T--- FFOG statements that God is Included in the USA as God: // All following is from (260h): +Patrick Henry said, "There is an insidious campaign of false propaganda being waged to the effect that our country is not a Christian nation, but a religious one,,, it cannot be emphasized too strongly or too often that this great nation was founded, not by religionist, but by Christians. Not on religion but by Jesus Christ." +Alexander Hamilton, member of the Constitution Convention, said, "Let a society be formed whose first duty shall be the preservation of Christianity". +The USA & Canada are desired all over the world because of their system of justice and fairness, and because our FFOG supported the dignity of a person. This came from the British system of jurisprudence which is based on the historical Decalogue (10 commandments) given to Moses from God and supported by Jesus Christ. This Judeo-Christian system is based on such solid Biblical code.

---T--- The CC Starts with God & Puts God in All the Parts & Ends with God: // The reason (intention/ purpose) for the dividing from England was "God, Creator, Supreme Judge, Divine Providence"; as the DOI states; That God is to be included as our King; God is the Being, as included; He tells us what is right & evil; He gives us Rights. That is the start of the CC. Thereafter, the CON is constructed with the intention/ purpose to apply the DOI; the DOI is for God, and thus God is applied to all parts of the USA National System. Now the end of the CC, which is the closing statements &

signature line on the CON, has Jesus Christ and reference to His time of Christmas; how He came in the flesh body & for Resurrection after the Atonement. Thank God for Christmas.

---T--- Pres. Thomas Jefferson wrote: // "The God who gave us life gave us liberty at the same time" and also asked, "Can the liberties of a nation be secure when we have removed a conviction that these liberties are of God?".

---T--- God is to be Included as OverRuling the States: // God is the reason for the States; where our Rights come from; the True God. Thus He is to be included in State GOV, not excluded. If He was not to be included then He would not be said as a subject. God, by definition of the word, is recognized as the TOP or Main authority and Being. And because truth is required for our legal system then the true God must be supported.

---T--- SACRED Honor: "We pledge our ,,,SACRED Honor" are the words in the DOI: // What is the definition of "Sacred"? "Make a compact; consecrated to or belonging to God; Holy; of or connected with religion or religious rites; regarded with the same respect and reverence accorded holy things". This proves again the establishment of a Covenant Compact or Contract; That it includes God & His religion. They chose not their words triflingly, but carefully. They purposely put their life at risk and all their material possessions. This is no light decision, or easy task. They engaged themselves in to position of killing other people in defensive war. Though their purpose and intent was self-defense, and based on having a "right" from God, it is, nevertheless, a terrible engagement to have to kill other people in war; Especially when they knew it would send them in to eternity.

---T--- "Rights" & Priority of GOD; the Supreme Judge: // Some Rights are Not to be submitted to any form of GOV with men in position. This is one reason why the DOI & Independence was initiated; intention/purpose~ to tell England that we have "rights" from God which NO MAN NOR MAN GOV can take from us. Thus these Rights are priority to all men; and therefore GOD MUST BE THE RULER of the USA GOV.

---T--- The CC was Intended/ purposed as a Christian National System for Christ, & with Laws Based on His Holy Bible; & with State & FED orderly arrangement: // Such was confirmed in the late AD 1800's by a Court Case; which states that the CC is to stay together, with the DOI as part of it. (261a). // The Common Law was also called the Moral Law. It was DIRECTLY included as part of the USA National System and the Law System while the States were yet joined with the Country of England (261b). // After Independence, such Law System was named Common Law and included in the States (261b). // The FED GOV system included the Common Law in the Bill of Rights, 7th Amendment. // Many FFOG in all Branches stated that the Constitution is based on the Common Law (261c). // The Common Law is based on God's Laws, and is stated by words "the laws of nature and of nature's God". These words are part of the, Religious, the Christian Systems; and the study of God's Principles thereof (261d). // Some quotes from cite (261d) are as follows: "But the abstract right of individuals to withdraw from the society of which they are members, is recognized by an uncommon coincidence of opinion ~ by every writer, ancient and modern; by the civilian, as well as by the common-law lawyer; by the philosopher, as well as the poet: It is the law of nature, and of nature's God, pointing to 'the wide world before us, where to chose our place of rest, and providence our guide"; "The common law is grounded upon the general customs of the realm; and includes in it the Law of Nature, the Law of God, and the Principles and Maxims of the Law: It is founded upon Reasons; and is said to be perfection of reason, acquired by long study, observation and experience, and refined by learned men in all ages"; "The law of nature is that which God at mans' creation infused into him, for his preservation and direction; and this is lex eterna and may not be changed: and no laws shall be made or kept, that are expressly against the Law of God, written in his Scripture; as to forbid what he commandeth"; "But this large division may be reduced to the common division; and all is founded on the law of nature and reason, and the revealed law of God, as all other laws ought to be". // Parts of the Judicial System is committing illegal acts against the USA citizens, CC, and God. +Thomas Jefferson (FFOG) said about judges, that "power [is] the more dangerous as they are in office for life and not responsible, as the other functionaries are, to the elective control."; also ,,, "[T]o consider the judges as the ultimate arbiters of all constitutional questions [is] a very dangerous doctrine indeed, and one which would place us under the despotism of an oligarchy ,,,The Constitution has erected no such single tribunal. The Constitution, on this hypothesis, is a mere thing of wax in the hands of the Judiciary which they may twist and shape into any form they please." (262 a & b). // Furthermore the CC includes a Christian Law System that is constructed for Limited GOV Rights of the Federal Level and of the State Level; Such identifying of such Relations of the Federal Level, which identification is enumerated with only seventeen Rights in which the FED GOV has to the States Independency (263). // Then it identifies by declaration that all other things are the Rights to be determined by the People and the States (the Ninth and Tenth Amendments). +Thomas Jefferson (FFOG) states the CC System~ "the States can best govern our home concerns and the general [federal] government our foreign ones. ,,,taking from the States the moral rule of their citizens and subordinating it to the general authority [federal government] ,,,would ,,,break up the foundations of the Union." (264). +Mr. Jefferson states that if the limits breakdown of the CC, there would be an illegal GOV in the FED, with excessive Rights and the Checks & Balances System would be dysfunctional (262c). // Note that the CC states, "The United States shall guarantee to every State in this Union a republican form of government" (Article IV, Section 4). // Thus illegalities are occurring against the State Independency existence, against the Rights of the State Independency, against the People and their votes, against the FED GOV Rights to the States which were identified and enumerated, and against the Christ's Christian Common Moral Law System, and against God and His Nature.

---T--- USA GOV Existence is for Christ's Christianity: // The CC & all DOC, including the supporting DOC clearly state that the USA GOV is based on God, Jesus Christ. To exclude Him is to end the USA GOV.

---T--- <u>Christianity for Christ Jesus the Lord</u> GOD is proclaimed as intention/ purpose of all GOV, public, & colonies: // Francis Hopkinson, DOI signer, Church Choir leader wrote a, "A Political Chatechism" which says, "What is the general object of an offensive war? For the most part, it is undertaken to gratify the ambition of a prince, who wishes to subject to his arbitrary will a people whom God created free, and to gain an uncontrolled dominion over their rights and property ,,,It is upon these principles that the people of America are resisting ,,,Great Britain, and opposing force with force ,,,Strictly so ,,,may Heaven prosper their virtuous undertaking!" (152). // John Hancock calls Mass. State to fasting and prayer to Christ in AD 1775: "In circumstances dark as these, it becomes us as men and Christians to ,,,reposed only on that God who rules in the armies of heaven and without whose blessing the best human councils are but foolishness and all created power vanity. It is the happiness of his church that when the powers of earth and hell combine against it ,,,then the throne of grace is of the easiest access ,,,when His children ask bread He will not give them a stone ,,,recommended to the good people of this colony ,,,as a day of public humiliation, fasting and prayer ,,,to confess the sins ,,,union of the American colonies in defence of their rights, for which, hitherto, we desire to thank Almighty God,,,". // Colonel Ethan Allen, and a group of unnamed soldiers, captured a British army and claimed to them, "In the name of the Great Jehovah and the Continental Congress" (153). // US Congress proclaims a godly day of fasting and prayer on 6/12/1775 which John Adams tells his wife, "Millions will be upon their knees ,,,before their great Creator ,,,his smiles on American councils and arms". // John Witherspoon speaks to Americans in AD 1775 that, "There is nothing more awful to think of than that those whose trade is war should be despisers of the name of the Lord of hosts and that they should expose themselves to the imminent danger of being immediately sent from cursing and cruelty on earth to the blaspheming rage and despairing horror of the infernal pit ,,,offer himself as a champion in his country's cause ,,,reverence the name and walk in the fear of the Prince of the kings of the earth ,,,issue God's protection,,," (154). // "Congress announces a congressional meeting "at 9 o'clock ,,, [[during USA formation time periods of DOI]] to attend Divine service at,,, Church; and that in the afternoon they meet ,,,and attend Divine service at ,,,church" (58). // Mass. State Legislature enacts army to be religious uniform in AD 1776, ",,,uniform ,,,and the colors be a white flag with a green pine tree and an inscription, "Appeal to Heaven" (155). // William Livingston and Congress pronounce a day of Christian fasting and prayer on 5/17/1776: "The Congress ,,,desirous ,,,to have people of all ranks and degrees duly impressed with a solemn sense of God's superintending providence, and of their duty devoutly to rely ,,,on His aid ,,,a day of humiliation, fasting, and prayer ,,,united hearts ,,,through the merits and mediation of Jesus Christ,,," (58). // Benjamin Rush shares that John Adams in the DOI meetings replied to him about winning against Britain stating, "Yes~ if we fear God and repent of our sins"; then continues, "This ,,,I hope, teach my boys that it is not necessary to disbelieve Christianity ,,,to arrive at the highest political usefulness,,," (97). // John Adams shares to his wife regarding the DOI: "This day will be ,,,memorable ,,,history of America ,,,celebrated by succeeding generations ,,,ought to be commemorated as the day of deliverance by solemn acts of devotion to God Almighty" and "It appears to me the eternal Son of God is operating powerfully against the British nation for their treating lightly serious things" (59). // Samuel Adams in AD 1780 states to US troops, "May every citizen in the army and in the country have a proper sense of the Deity upon his mind and an impression of the declaration recorded in the Bible, ("Him that honoreth me I will honor, but he that despiseth me shall be lightly esteemed" 1 Samuel 2:30)." // Congress regularly pronounced Christian Church worships assemblies; such as in AD 1781: "It was on the 19th of Oct. ,,,thanks to the Almighty ,,,recommended by George Washington to all the troops ,,,would assist at Divine service with a serious deportment and with that sensibility of heart,,, Providence" (156). And another one~ "That Congress will ,,,go in procession to the Dutch Lutheran Church and return thanks to Almighty God for the allied arms of the US and France with,,, surrender of,,, British Army,,," (58). // The word "God" referred to in the USA DOCs including DOI, CON, Notes of the DOCs meetings, State CONs, is referring to, "that Supreme Being spoken of in the Old and New Testaments and worshiped by Jew and Christian"(27). // Any who denied the Being of God was an automatic rejection and without a second thought, including acquiring positions in the GOV; (specific ones). // All State CONs have a preamble (or similar to) of: "Grateful to Almighty God." // The official oaths of Fed & State Office include: "So help me, God." // Courts have witnesses vow as to truth telling in testimony with God's name. // "Wills" commencement requires "in the name of God, Amen". // Foreigners make a separation form other allegiances to an allegiance to the USA with God as part of the ceremony. // David J. Brewer, an Associate Justice of the USA, shares that in every USA DOC there is absolutely no contrary evidence to any other God than the Christian God. There is no Buddha, no Judaism, no Mohammed, no Confucius, none, not one. Judaism is only recognized as a part Truth with its part of it as early Christianity (27).

---T--- <u>Creator God:</u> // FFOG John Quincy Adams says, "It is so obvious to every reasonable being,,, that the moment we begin to exercise the power of reflection, it seems impossible to escape the conviction that there is a Creator" and "It is in the Bible you must learn them, and from the Bible how to practice them" (178).

---T--- <u>USA is the Place for God & the Gospel:</u> // Mr. John Marrant, a black man, was a learned musician. One day walking, he came to a Christian assembly with Mr. George Whitefield and some other Christians. When George spoke Scripture and pointed his finger in the crowd, it seemed to point to Mr. Marrant, who was young in age; and he fell down under severe conviction. He laid down for about an half hour, and when he somewhat collected himself, got help from Mr. Whitefield, who discipled him for 3 days; then thereafter he submitted his life to Jesus and Christianity. John Marrant returned to his family to share Christ with them, and was rejected, and they forced him to leave. So he refuged in the forest where he met an indian, Cherokee, and made friends. They hunted, and various things for about 10 weeks, and then went to the Indian camp. However the Chief did not accept him, as he was different, and he was made prisoner. Mr. Marrant had learned the language from his friend and shared Christianity to them, and they were aware of conviction from God. The total tribe changed, and the Chiefs house became the house of God. Mr. Marrant shared the Gospel with other Indians also. Afterwards he shared the Gospel to some slaves on a plantation. Some of the slaves were badly treated for praying. John then was captured in the RW, but when the war was over, became a minister, officially ordained, and worked in England, Canada, and the USA for the Gospel of Jesus Christ (253).

---T--- Declared (Formal Statements) Said to Include, & Support the True God: // As a USA GOV we cannot INCLUDE & EXCLUDE God at the same time. We cannot oppose & support at the same time. We cannot work together & separate simultaneously. Furthermore this pertains to every decision of the laws and activities of physical matter that occurs on the USA Soil; of public advertisements & assemblies. The Spiritual or unseen is not to be controlled by the USA GOV. However the USA GOV & State GOV was not to promote or allow evil physical activity on the USA Soil. Evil includes false religion; false Christianity; any falsity that commits sin against the 10 commandments. The doctrines of Christianity, are not to be meddled or controlled by the USA GOV; but rather Christianity itself is to work it all to solution by itself. The USA GOV is Not to control Christianity in its activities; rather support Christianity. The USA GOV cannot include & exclude God at the same time on any decision of physical activity; assembly & advertisement. This also relates that the USA GOV cannot separate. To separate is defined as to what the USA GOV does & does not. USA GOV cannot exclude Christianity in everything; It actually must include Christianity in everything. If it excludes Christianity then it begins or initiates opposition. To oppose Christianity is to Breach and commit treason against the CC (DOI & CON). Physical activity is to be monitored with regards to whether it is Christian or not; business, etc. This is the only area where the USA GOV is to manage all areas. No anti-God or anti-Christ physical activity is to be promoted or allowed on USA Soil; Now what is allowed physical activity, is that which comes from the 10 commandments and the True God, Christ Jesus, including the Holy Bible; This is pertaining to public activity and/or activity that is some specific evils against the 10 Commandments.

---T--- GOV is to be Ministers of God not of demons Nor Evil: // Evil is what the CC was about. // "Rom13:6 ,,,for they are God's ministers, attending continually on this very thing". The Holy Bible states that they are to be Helpers, which is what a Minister is defined as; for positiveness of God. Now note the other Holy Scriptures with this: "Rom13:3-5 For rulers are not a terror to good works, but to the evil. ,,,do that which is good, and you shall have praise of the same: For he is the minister of God to you for good. But if you do that which is evil, be afraid,,, for he is the minister of God,,, Wherefore ,,,also for conscience sake". // The FFOG were intending/ purpose to establish a Priestly system. The word "ministers" is said 2 times in Romans 13. And its states that it was intended for the Good & Not the Evil; the word good is said at least 3 times; and evil is repeated. The word conscience is said, which is the discerner in our hearts between good & evil.

---T--- Word Laws; Word Definition Law: The CC Truthfully Defines GOD as Included: // Definitions following are from cite (1a). These are also the Definitions that the Supporting DOCs and FFOG used. +The word "God" is defined as: "Monotheistic Creator; ruler of the universe; eternal; infinite; all powerful; all-knowing; Supreme Being; Almighty; Deity; Magistrate; Supreme Divinity; Divine Father; Jesus Christ; Holy Trinity". +"Supreme Judge or Ruler" is defined as: "God; Jesus Christ; Holy Trinity; highest in Rank, authority; dominant; ultimate; final authority; God that Rules or GOVERNS; authoritative regulation for conduct or action; authority on regulations of a GOV and, or religion; Reign". +"DIVINE" is defined as: "Given or inspired by God, Sacred, Holy; Devoted; religious; theological; Jesus Christ; Holy Trinity". +"Providence" is defined as: "In theology, the care and superintendence which God exercises over his creatures. He that acknowledges a creation and denies a providence, involves himself in a palpable contradiction; for the same power which caused a thing to exist is necessary to continue its existence. Some persons admit a general providence, but deny a particular providence, not considering that a general providence consists of particulars. A belief in divine providence, is a source of great consolation to good men". +"Creator" is defined as: "The One Who Created All that exists; God". +"Lord" "Jesus Christ" is defined as: "Supreme Authority; God; Jehoshua; Messiah; Anointed".

~~~~~~~~~~~~~~~~~APPLICATION Of CONCLUSION BY ~~~~~~~~~~~~~~~~~~~~~~~~~
--CHRIST JESUS, CHRISTIANITY, Is The GOD:

---T--- Absence Law: // There is absolutely no DOC, nor historical supporting DOC, nor life evidence from any FFOG, nor any promoting or allowance of, or encouragement to any other religion than Christianity; nor any God but Jesus Christ (Christianity); except Judaism (Christianity in it's earlier status); NOR any of these opposing or stopping Christianity; Nor any of these starting any system without Christianity.

---T--- Inclusion/Exclusion Law: // All other religions & false gods are specifically excluded and warned about; and in every instance of DOC and historical supporting DOC. Including Paganism, Heathenism, God Exclusion, etc.

---T--- CC states the true USA God: // God, Laws of Nature's God, Creator, Supreme Judge, Divine Providence, Lord Jesus Christ. // Laws of Nature are the Laws of Creation.

---T--- Every reference to God in all history, supporting DOCs, CC, life EV, societal support, State CONs, pilgrims, activities, and events, and etc; all state clearly that Christianity and Christ Jesus are the God of the USA.

---T--- The fact that God is identified as God, limits Him to whomever that He is; if He is God, then He is God: // This then excludes any idols or false religions that are not actually God; Only the real God may qualify.

---T--- <u>Because the FFOG (every B</u>ranch) specifies that Truth is supported, then only the True God may be supported: // No false god or god that is not the true God may qualify.

---T--- <u>All religion, and the only</u> religion that was ever supported by the USA FFOG from the beginning to now, is Christ's Christianity, and the Churches thereof.

---T--- <u>God is One God. // They</u> did not say God's as plural; or many. It is a self-evidence Truth of responsibility for eternal judgment day, nevertheless; a SETLWHM.

---T--- <u>FFOG statements:</u> // From~ (260h): +Patrick Henry said, "There is an insidious campaign of false propaganda being waged to the effect that our country is not a Christian nation, but a religious one,,, it cannot be emphasized too strongly or too often that this great nation was founded, not by religionist, but by Christians. Not on religion but by Jesus Christ." +Alexander Hamilton, member of the Constitution Convention, said, "Let a society be formed whose first duty shall be the preservation of Christianity".

---T--- <u>The USA & Canada are desired all over the world because</u> of their system of justice & fairness; & because our FFOG supported the dignity of a person: // That system came from the British system of jurisprudence which is based on the historical Decalogue (10 commandments) given to Moses from God and supported by Jesus Christ.

~~~~~~~~~~~~~~~~~~APPLICATION Of CONCLUSION BY ~~~~~~~~~~~~~~~~~~~~~~
-----------------------------RIGHTS COME from, BASED on GOD, CHRIST JESUS, and NOT BASED or COMING From MAN Decisions Of Will & Words.   (Also Chptrs 5, 7, 8, 9):

---T--- <u>"Rights" & Priority of GOD:</u> // Some Rights are Not to be submitted to any form of GOV with men in position. HSC~"We ought to obey God rather than men". Act5:29. ~This applies in situations where God is opposite of men or when He is to be priority to the subject. This is one reason why the DOI & Independence was initiated; intention/ purpose; to tell England that we have "rights" from God which NO MAN NOR MAN GOV can take from us. Thus these Rights are priority to all men; and therefore GOD MUST BE THE RULER of the USA GOV.

---T--- <u>GOV abuse To God's Creatures:</u> // From CON Congress Meetings Notes, Table of Contents: "Defence of its Omission not satisfactory; Precaution in granting Powers ,,,167 - Sovereignty of the Federal GOV annihilates the States ,,,179 - Powers of Congress dangerous to State Laws ,,,180 - Proper and Right or justified authorization -,,,Convention not authorized to use the Expression 'We, the People' ,,,15,,,- Legislative Power controlled by Vice-President's Vote ,,,26"

---T--- <u>Rights are identified in DOCs as~</u> God, <u>Christianity,</u> Religion of Christianity, Christian DEN, Creation, Truth, Conscience; and that the USA is to support such.

---T--- <u>FFOG statements (260h):</u> // Patrick Henry said, "There is an insidious campaign of false propaganda being waged to the effect that our country is not a Christian nation, but a religious one,,, it cannot be emphasized too strongly or too often that this great nation was founded, not by religionist, but by Christians. Not on religion but by Jesus Christ." // Alexander Hamilton, member of the Constitution Convention, said, "Let a society be formed whose first duty shall be the preservation of Christianity".

---T--- <u>The USA & Canada are desired all over the</u> world because of their system of justice & fairness, & because our FFOG supported the dignity of a person: // This came from the British system of jurisprudence which is based on the historical Decalogue (10 commandments) given to Moses from God and supported by Jesus Christ. (260h).

---T--- <u>DOI & CON are CHRISTIAN based for Giving Christ Worship:</u> // Christian Holidays support the DOI & CON.

---T--- <u>Christian ministers, and only Christian</u> ministers, and only Christian related men were sent as the REP to the congressional meetings for the DOI & CON. (63).

---T--- <u>God & Christianity is the basis of our</u> Rights: // FFOG John Dickinson writes," Kings or parliaments could not give the rights essential to happiness ,,,We claim them from a higher source- from the King of kings, and Lord of all the earth. They are not annexed to us by parchments and seals. They are created in us by the decrees of Providence, which establish the laws of our nature. They are born with us; exist with us; and cannot be taken from us by any human power without taking our lives. In short, they are founded on the immutable maxims of reason and justice. It would be an insult on the Divine Majesty to say that he has given or allowed any man or body of men a right to make me miserable".

---T--- <u>Massachusetts proclaims a day to</u> God, Dec 11, 1783 Stating thankfulness for the RIGHTs & Purpose of the USA: // ~"divine providence; praise to God; to all citizens of State and US; dependence upon God; religiously observed as a day of thanksgiving and prayer; for all the people ,,,that all the people may then assemble to celebrate"; [[to celebrate that the USA purpose is to increase Christianity worldwide]] ",,,to celebrate that He hath been pleased to continue to us the light of the blessed Gospel ,,,that we also offer up fervent supplications ,,,to cause pure religion and virtue to flourish ,,,and to fill the world with His glory".

---T--- <u>The DOI & All DOC & Christianity Rights was on</u> Aug 2, 1776 stated by FFOG Samuel Adams: // ~"We have this day restored the Sovereign to whom all men ought to be obedient. He reigns in heaven, and from the rising to the setting of the sun, let His kingdom come" (116).

~~~~~~~~~~~~~~~~~~~~~APPLICATION Of CONCLUSION BY ~~~~~~~~~~~~~~~~~~~~~~~~~~~~
--LOVE GOD and PEOPLE:

---T--- Love is the law of God: // Love God, self, and others; we need God, the comforter, the teacher, protection, etc.

---T--- Love & Selfishness Or Self-Idolatry Or Self-Priority: // Parts of HSC in 1Cor13 include the opposition to Self-idolatry or self-priority or self-more Creature Beings. It includes: +Talking with unselfish Love intentions~ "though I speak ,,,and have not charity, I am become as sounding brass, or a tinkling cymbal". +Knowledge & trust in God with unselfish Love intentions~ "though I have the gift of prophecy, and understand all mysteries, and all knowledge; and though I have all faith ,,,and have not charity, I am nothing". +Giving or good deeds done with unselfish Love intentions~ "though I bestow all my goods to feed the poor, and though I give my body to be burned, and have not charity, it profiteth me nothing. // Love with non-self-1st priority includes Charity Does Not Seek It's Own by~ +"suffereth long; +is kind; +envieth not; +vaunteth not itself; +not puffed up; +not behave itself unseemly; +not easily provoked; +thinketh no evil; +Rejoiceth not in iniquity; +rejoiceth in the truth". These are Principle Law words. // True Love is Eternal & the Greatest~ "1Cor13:13 And now abideth faith, hope, charity, these three; but the greatest of these is charity". // "1Joh4:8 God is Love". // Charles Finney & the older times Oberlin College Group has some good studies on Benevolent Love & Selfishness.

~~~~~~~~~~~~~~~~~~~~~APPLICATION Of CONCLUSION BY ~~~~~~~~~~~~~~~~~~~~~~~~~~~~
-- LIBERTY Or FREEDOM:

---T--- These are what we have Freedom To Do: // Whenever there are freedoms in a World of Good & Evil, then such freedoms also Include that some things are Not allowed as Free To Do - Evil. For freedom to exist there must be a non-freedom that exists. Such is that evil cannot be allowed to be unlimited. Some specific evils are to be stopped; and some are limited.

---T--- Liberty: Christian based Liberty: // FFOG William Penn defines liberty as obedience to God, saying~ "Liberty without obedience is confusion and obedience without liberty is slavery". This is making a discernment of good & evil, God & idolatry.

---T--- This Liberty Freedom comes as a Right from God, Lord Jesus: // It is of conscience and for happiness potentiality. We are not slaves to man or dictatorships; we are to be free from GOV abuse; abuse from mankind.

---T--- Free for TRUE worship and religion, of the TRUE God, Lord Jesus Christ, the Supreme Ruler.

---T--- Free from evil that might come from mankind: // And the various forms of it are identified.

~~~~~~~~~~~~~~~~~~~~~APPLICATION Of CONCLUSION BY ~~~~~~~~~~~~~~~~~~~~~~~
-- INDIVIDUALISM:

---T--- Individualism: // The CC and God states such Law. A law of liberty, freedom, happiness, self evidence, and right from "God, Creator, Supreme Judge, Divine Providence, Lord Jesus Christ"; for property and respect from other Beings; and for existence; for life. This includes Personality freedom. For true Love, Existence, and Happiness; Assistance to the body and heart (spirit). // Peter seeing him saith to Jesus, Lord, and what shall this man do? Jesus saith to him, If I will that he tarry till I come, what is that to you? follow you me. ~Joh21:21-22. // The GOV has limitations put on it to meddle in Spiritual Moral Creatures. God is 1st priority; and evil is not permitted to do to citizens; No evil is to be done by calling it good; and no evil is to be done as a Right. HSC says not to call sin good; not to sin because to supposedly catch evil. That is not God's method nor expression. 1Tim5:13 opposes busybodies; Pro20:19 opposes spreading of evil communications & meddling in other Being's activities; Rom3:8~ "And not rather, (as we be slanderously reported, and as some affirm that we say,) Let us do evil, that good may come? whose damnation is just". Thus there are various activities that the FFOG were intending to prevent by including God in the CC.

~~~~~~~~~~~~~~~~~~~~~APPLICATION Of CONCLUSION BY ~~~~~~~~~~~~~~~~~~~~~~~
-- OATHS:

---T--- The Oath in the CON is a Christian subject for God: // The Christian Oath, or oath before God. // It is a part of the Checks & Balances System. // It helps assure, and helps a responsibility of the testimony of a Testifier, to tell the truth. Bringing God in the function is the intention/ purpose. Bringing God to the words of the Testifier then made it more trustworthy. // 2 provisions are made with the Oath: Christianity was not forced for the internal Will of a person, and/or because secondary doctrines include that some Christian DEN people disagreed with Oaths thinking that the Holy Bible teaches against such Oathing to God; Thus a provision is allowed for an infidel or false religionist, or various DEN Christians, to make oaths ~BEFORE~ God, rather than ~TO~ God; as God is present watching and that God rewards or punishes accordingly. This was done by the

80

word, "affirmation", as optional to the "oath". // This is part of the 10 commandments (the 9ᵗʰ); intentional/ purposed to protect against lying, support truth, and to include God in the procedure as "God of the GOV"; as overRuler of the courts; the Supreme Judge.

~~~~~~~~~~~~~~~~~APPLICATION Of CONCLUSION BY ~~~~~~~~~~~~~~~~~~~~
----------------------------------CREATOR And CREATION Of GOD:

---T--- CREATION: // Creation is to be supported; and comes with the acceptance and support of the True God.

---T--- Equality of Mankind is part of Creation: // The DOI states~ "all men are created equal ,,,endowed by their Creator". Which is of "race", gender, employment position, money status, etc.

---T--- Creation Supports that God is the Ruler of the USA. // Creation Rights are to be protected, not to be opposed. // Creation is to be taught & supported by the GOV.

---T--- "Earth is the Lord's and the Glory thereof" Psa24:1. The Earth is the Lord's property: // God has creation Rights. For Spiritual Moral Creatures to talk about receiving Rights from God and then to reject giving God His Rights of the Earth is a contradiction & unreasonable & not sane.

---T--- Laws of Nature is Creation ~&~ the God of Natures Law (Creator). "Nature's God". // This includes the conscience. // This includes the Laws of Nature, not the Wild Random 'anything goes' savagery of savages.

---T--- God as the Creator & Source of all that exists makes us responsible to Him for such; to acknowledge Him as a Being with a Will, affections, desires, intentions/ purposes, & His Decisions; & with all that does exist; & what to do with all that exists: // To deny this is to reject the CC (DOI & CON).

---T--- Thankfulness is required to the Creator for creating us, & all things that exist: // To be unthankful is an attribute not cared for. Thankfulness is one of the highest personality traits or character attributes that a Spiritual Moral Creature can have.

---T--- A Creator is an Owner: // And an Owner is NOT to be disrespected, scorned, rejected, opposed; but rather is to be affectionately cared for, respected, accepted, and supported.

~~~~~~~~~~~~~~~~~APPLICATION Of CONCLUSION BY ~~~~~~~~~~~~~~~~~~
----------------------------------EXISTENCE And PRESENCE Of GOD:

---T--- EVIDENCES To Help You Start Now to Commune with Jesus & Holy Trinity:
    =MIRACLES: Can you make a tree ? Can you make a foot ? No. Because you are not the Cause that is able to do such; that is, you cannot because you have not the ability. Therefore, those are Miracles. What is a Miracle ? An action that Spiritual Moral Creatures are not able to do. With your eye and mind you see and think about miracles constantly.
    =INVISIBILITY: Why does God remain invisible much of the time, that is unseen with the eye; Himself as a Being ? Because~ "Joh4:24 God is a Spirit: and they that worship him must worship him in spirit and in truth". Therefore if you are going to know God, you must apply yourself immediately; get at it; He is ONLY going to be known by knowing Him as A SPIRIT.
    =SHAPES: Can material substance by itself able, or have the ability to make shapes or forms ? For EX:~ if you have a bowl, and then you take the clay and shape it, then you are the cause of its shaping. The clay cannot think; it does not have any mind & Will to tell itself to turn this way or that, or make round or square, etc. God is the Shape or Form Maker: The world had no form until God as a Spirit formed it, Gen1:2; Jer4:23; He formed your hand, ear, & eye, Gen2:7; Psa94:9; 1Tim2:13; God forms babies in the womb, Isa44:2, 24; 49:5; Jer1:5; One intention/ purpose for Spiritual Moral Beings FORMATION is to Praise & thank GOD, Isa43:21, Psa100. DNA cannot do something without some Being giving it knowledge, in the form of programs, and giving it ability, in the form of energy.
    =KNOWLEDGE: Does material substance have knowledge? Is it able to think and make decisions and then apply some reasonings of some sort ?
    =FRIEND or ENEMY: What do you desire ? No better friend than God. He did the atonement on the Cross to prove that He will do anything for you; anything that is good; He cannot do evil.
    =SYSTEM of RULES or LAW: Whoever makes the Rules is God.
    =PRIORITIES: Will you put God 1st and start communing with Him constantly and more than any other subject ? Will you start including Him in all your subjects ?
    =GOOD & EVIL: You need to discern & decide.
    =REALITY: Reality is actually part of the definition of Truth. Now valuable parts of reality are~ +it is real & all other opposite is not real; +it will not change & all opposites will change; +it is eternal & all other is not, rather temporary. Reality relates to God because the truth is that God is unseen probably at the moment, yet He is MORE Real than everything other. Now this relates to you by whether you will activate

yourself to exist with that knowledge; start applying it. You start talking & listening & discerning what Spirit is communicating to you & start thinking & talking to Him as if He is standing with you or dwelling inside of you. Will you do it now ???

=GOD's PRESENCE & COMMUNION: Please commune with Him now. He loves You !!!

---T--- The Law Of God's Existence, and thus acknowledgement, acceptance, respect, honor, and involve Him in the affairs of the GOV.

---T--- "The Earth is the Lord's and the glory thereof" Psa24:1.

---T--- The Holy Bible states God's Existence & Presence: // The Holy Bible was agreed on; "laws of nature and of nature's God entitle them."~ as in the DOI. There is HSC in almost every DOC of the USA for the times of it's formation. // The Holy Bible is a Miracle Book; it's existence itself is a miracle and has records of miracles and the CC (DOI & CON) refer to it. // It is a Divine Book that has as it's most priority subject~ God's existence & Presence.

---T--- To deny God's existence is to deny the CC (DOI & CON) which declare God as existing and as "Divine Providence" which states He is present managing all activities of all Beings: // DOI states, that We the creatures of the "Creator".

---T--- The CON states, that Christ of the Christmas is present as Christ stated He was Lord of all; Immanuel~ God in the Flesh. Mat1:23. Lord Jesus Christ is EMMANUEL which is defined as God with us~ "Mat1:23 Behold, a virgin shall be with child, and shall bring forth a son, and they shall call his name Emmanuel, which being interpreted is, God with us".

---T--- We cannot deny God's existence anymore than we can deny our own existence: // To do so is to intently/ purposely be blind to the First Cause of all that is seen with the eye; to deny the conscience which records guilt for evil; and thus not responsible for such mental and heart condition.

---T--- "Life" as declared in the CC (DOI & CON) comes from The Creator.

---T--- Self evidence, SETLWHM, signals the realization of God's existence to our consciousness; this is Evidence to Self.

---T--- Life comes from life: // Nothing cannot make something or someone; and neither can a non-life thing make something or someone.

---T--- Life is a Right from God which we are to Commune (fellowship) with Him: // He is 1st priority for all Spiritual Beings. Therefore as is plain as anything can possibly be, is that to each individual God is more Real as existing and present than any other thing.

~~~~~~~~~~~~~~~~~APPLICATION Of CONCLUSION BY ~~~~~~~~~~~~~~~~~~~~~~~~
---------------------------------LAWS & RIGHTS --- LAWs (RULES or WHAT is RIGHT & WRONG) and GOD & RIGHTS {{These are What we have Freedom To Do; Whenever there are freedoms in a World of Good & Evil, then such freedoms also Include that some things are Not allowed as Free To Do - Evil. For freedom to exist there must be a non-freedom that exists. Such is that evil cannot be allowed to be unlimited.}}.
//////// The FFOG included Freedom from Evil not unlimited freedom to do evil: Holy Scriptures~ "1Cor8:9; Gal5:13; 1Pet2:16; 2Pet2:19 But take heed lest by any means this liberty of yours become a stumblingblock to them that are weak; For, brethren, you have been called to liberty; only use not liberty for an occasion to the flesh, but by love serve one another; As free, and not using your liberty for a cloke of maliciousness, but as the servants of God; While they promise them liberty, they themselves are the servants of corruption: for of whom a man is overcome, of the same is he brought in bondage"; The Liberty Bell states, "proclaim liberty throughout all the land unto all the inhabitants thereof" (Lev 25:10). ~Holy Scripture:

---T--- To say that we include God, as truly we do in the CC (DOI & CON), and yet to say that we do not have His laws, which is to say what He thinks is right & evil, is to not include God; and to remove Him: // Every Spiritual Moral Being has a definition of what is right & evil. And God being God, thus the priority authority, as a totally right Being, then knows best on the subject. // It is a lie to include God & exclude His care affections about what is right & evil. When we include another Being, then we include what makes them feel good & what makes them feel bad. // What rules they have of the household (laws). When we place ourself in some person's house to occupy, then we must affectionately care ourself with the house rules or we will lose our shelter; It is their house and to their rules (laws) must we intend and will to obey. We may think it is right to indulge the cookie jar a small amount more frequent than the House Authority might allow. // This is not to say that the House Authority is to be cruel, unkind, unloving, or hateful. But if such House Authority has stated that such is the Law (rule), as to good & evil, then we may appeal to the House Authority; but if the House Authority states the truth and the subject is Not to be changed, then there will not be further discussion on the subject; then to that we must obey, with Love.

---T--- To prevent evils, the GOV, or FFOG & Citizens put God as the Final Supreme Ruler: // This is a surety safeguard Check to Balance against evil; to limit it.

---T--- God is perfect, both in all His will, thoughts, reasonings, feelings, affections, emotions, judgment, intentions/purposes, desires, actions, and expressions; and to discernment of good & evil; never sins or does evil.

---T--- To exclude God's laws, which is what He thinks, wills, decides, loves, hates, desires, intention/ purpose, affections, yet to include God on the CC (DOI & CON) is to make void the USA DOCs: // This is a form of treason.

82

---T--- "Happiness" is to be a Right & laws for it: // The happiness which was legalized in the USA GOV was based on having God, Rightness with God, and no evil. It is stated clearly in all DOCs, including the CC (DOI & CON). TO be happy with evil or anti-Jesus is lie. If Spiritual Moral Beings are happy with evil, then it must be limited; and some evils are to be limited by laws.

---T--- "Life" is a Right & laws for it: // Life is full of laws. Each person has laws every day that they apply to all sorts of subjects. And thus laws are to be based on this fact.

---T--- Liberty" stated in the CC, & all DOC, comes from God: // Such Liberty is not to do unlimited evil. You yourself, are EV, a self-evidence, that unlimited evil cannot be the GOV system for society; you know such inside yourself. // Liberty to live for God; and for activities that are right. // God is the King and freedoms are based on Him, not man nor GOV.

---T--- FFOG stated Liberty with God not against God: // John Adams said, "Liberty is a moral right derived from the Legislator of the Universe". // Abraham Lincoln said, "Liberty is right because Christ said so, and Christ is God". // CON secures this Right as a Right from God; connected to the DOI. // The Liberty Bell states, "proclaim liberty throughout all the land unto all the inhabitants thereof" (Lev 25:10). ~Holy Scripture.

---T--- Laws that were evil is why the DOI occurred: // Such laws were not of the Holy Bible, nor God, nor right.

---T--- Liberty must be limited because of the existence of mankind is in a probationary status; in a world of good & evil: // There is temptation to evil; mankind is exposed to temptations to evil, and evil exists, and sometimes men decide to do evil, and history has EV that men sometimes decide evil, and etc.

---T--- Laws are Needed to protect from GOV abuse; dictatorship, tyranny, & evil: // The GOV system is to be under God and His laws; because God is perfect and God will not abuse us. Thus we are to make a law structure with God.

---T--- All of the Earth is Owned by Christ, The Supreme Governor & His Desire is that All Governments be Christian.

---T--- Responsibility: Obedience to Laws; Whose laws? Limited as To What Amount In Various Ways; To Much or Too Little: // FFOG John Ponet wrote in AD 1556, ",,,every commonwealth is kept and maintained in good order by obedience ,,,if obedience is too much or too little ,,,it causes much evil and disorder ,,,and the governor forgets their vocation and to usurp upon their subjects ,,,or ,,,breeds a licentious liberty, and makes the people to forget their duty ,,,and ,,,the commonwealth grows out of order and at length comes to havoc and utter destruction".

---T--- The relationship between each Spiritual Moral Creature as an individual & God: // was to be protected and encouraged and even required for specific Positions.

---T--- USA GOV should be Christian for Christ: // The CC, and all DOC clearly state that such be based on God, Jesus Christ; not exclude God.

---T--- Laws & Rights are for the Citizenry Branch, & also for Official Positions; which are actually Citizens also~ Restrictions: // Some FFOG would not agree & sign until specific subjects were included of what the GOV could or could not do; Some States would not agree to the CC unless such that the GOV was also included under laws.

---T--- Now if Spiritual Moral Creatures in employment positions are opposing the Laws of God, and His Nature Laws, and the Spiritual Moral Citizens are trying to live by God's laws, then how is a Nation to exist?

---T--- Leonard Bacon (history student in AD 1800's) said: // "O God, beneath thy guiding hand Our exiled fathers crossed the sea, And when they trod the wintry strand, with prayer and psalm they worshiped Thee. Thou heardst, well pleased, the song, the prayer - Thy blessing came; and still its power Shall onward through all ages bear The memory of that holy hour. Laws, freedom, truth, and faith in God, Came with those exiles o'er the waves, And where their pilgrim feet have trod, The God they trusted guards their graves. And here Thy name, O God of love, Their children's children shall adore, Till these eternal hills remove, And spring adorns the earth no more,,,". // About right laws.

---T--- GOD & Christian Laws to be the Basis: // "Journals of the Continental Congress, 1774-1789 - 3/19/1782 - ,,,appointed to prepare a recommendation to the several states, to set apart a day of humiliation, fasting, and PRAYER Congress agreed to the following Proclamation: The goodness of the Supreme Being to all his rational creatures, demands their acknowledgments of gratitude and love; his ABSOLUTE GOVERNMENT OF THIS WORLD dictates, that it is the interest of every nation and people ardently to supplicate his mercy favor and implore his protection. When the LUST OF DOMINION or LAWLESS AMBITION excites arbitrary power to INVADE THE RIGHTS, or endeavor to WRENCH WREST from a people their SACRED and UNALIENABLE INVALUABLE PRIVILEGES, and compels them, in DEFENCE of the same, to encounter all the horrors and calamities of a bloody and vindictive war; then is that people loudly called upon to fly unto that GOD for protection, who hears the cries of the distressed, and will not turn a deaf ear to the supplication of the OPPRESSED. Great Britain, hitherto left to infatuated councils, and to pursue measures repugnant to their her own interest, and distressing to this country ,,,The US in Congress assembled, therefore, taking into consideration our present situation, our multiplied transgressions of the HOLY LAWS of our GOD, and his past acts of kindness and goodness exercised towards us, which we would ought to record with me the liveliest gratitude, think it their indispensable duty to call upon the different several states, to set apart the last Thursday in Apr. next, as a day of fasting, humiliation and PRAYER, that our joint supplications may then ascend to the throne of the RULER of the UNIVERSE, beseeching Him that he would to diffuse a SPIRIT of universal reformation among all ranks and degrees of our citizens; and make us HOLY, that so we may be an HAPPY people; that it would please Him to impart wisdom, integrity and unanimity to our counsellors; to bless and prosper the REIGN of our illustrious ally, and give success to his arms employed in the DEFENCE of THE RIGHTS of human nature; that HE WOULD SMILE upon our military arrangements by land and sea; administer comfort and consolation to our prisoners in a cruel captivity; that he would protect the health and life of our Commander in Chief; give grant us victory over our enemies; establish peace in all our borders, and give happiness to all our inhabitants; that he would prosper the labor of the husbandman, making the earth yield its increase in abundance, and give a proper season for the in gathering of the fruits thereof; that He would grant success to all engaged in lawful trade and commerce, and take under his guardianship all schools and seminaries of learning, and make them nurseries of VIRTUE and PIETY; that He would incline the HEARTS of all men to peace, and fill them with universal charity and benevolence, and that the RELIGION of our DIVINE REDEEMER, with all its benign influences, may cover the earth,,, Done by the US in Congress assembled,,,".

---T--- <u>1-A, R-E, R~Est "prohibit free exercise":</u> // The USA cannot punish or disadvantage a Spiritual Moral Creature based on religious beliefs; that of True Religion. // This was reinstated as made applicable to the States by the 14th Amendment. // The 1-A protects speech, press, Rights of assembly and petition as pertaining to true religion; not for false religion. Religion Establishment includes DEN.

---T--- All Laws Based on the <u>TRUE GOD:</u> // The DOI states, "laws of nature and of nature's God entitle them"; "that they are endowed by their Creator with certain inalienable rights; that among these are life, liberty, and the pursuit of happiness." // These Laws of Nature, are the laws that are based on the God of Nature & the Creator God. // Laws are not for unlimited evil, rather for a life, for rightness, for the intention (pursuit) of happiness, not evilness; and for limited Liberty, not unlimited liberty, or unlimited freedom to do evil. If freedom, or liberty, was unlimited then evil would be unlimited. Freedom or liberty is limited to goodness and excludes evil. // Massachusetts Provincial Congress of AD 1774 stated: "Resistance to tyranny becomes the Christian and social duty of each individual ,,,continue steadfast, and with a proper sense of your dependence on God, nobly defend those rights which heaven gave, and no man ought to take from us".

---T--- <u>The CON was designed to protect,</u> to safeguard, against GOV evils: // Such as historically that had occurred worldwide and in particularly Europe, including England at the time; from tyranny and dictatorship.

---T--- <u>GOD, The TRUE GOD: Support of the True God:</u> // The DOI supports God. // Cite (8)(16) shares that: Presbyterian Elders of Mecklenberg, North Carolina drafted a declaration for their GOV in AD 1775; this was sent to US Continental Congress and used in the writing of our declaration - which said: "We do hereby dissolve the political bands which have connected us with the mother-country ,,,allegiance to the British crown ,,,declare ourselves a free and independent people; are, and of a right out to be, a sovereign and self-governing Association, under control of no power other than that of our God and the general GOV of Congress ["by Authority of the good People of these Colonies, solemnly Publish and Declare,,,] ,,,solemnly pledge to each other our mutual cooperation and our lives, our fortunes and our most sacred honor,,,". // Note the similarity to the DOI; Same concepts of God and His laws were desired and decided.

---T--- <u>Cooperation with the True God:</u> // Cooperation or working with God; "laws of nature and of nature's God entitle them"; Divine Providence, which is God, His Laws, and His Management of the World.

---T--- <u>Idolatry cannot be unlimitedly legal in the land:</u> // The USA GOV are not to deny the Right of God over the USA.

---T--- <u>The FFoG were in agreement with Isaac Newton</u> (Christian scientist & mathematician in England, in AD 1700's) whose studies assisted by providing more undeniable EV that the World was governed by God and His laws of nature.

---T--- <u>Providence (Divine) Doctrine in the DOI & DOC include God's Laws of Providential Management:</u> // Providence has the following definitions in the English language used then, which is about the same now. It is a Christian Bible Term and doctrine: // FFOG Samuel Johnson's AD 1755 Dictionary of the English Language defines it as: "foresight; timely care,,,; The care of God over created beings; divine superintendence". // FFOG Benjamin Franklin stated it in Congress meetings saying that God, "governs in the affairs of men". // FFOG Noah Webster's AD 1828 Dictionary (1b) defines it as: "In theology, the care and superintendence which God exercises over his creatures. He that acknowledges a creation and denies a providence, involves himself in a palpable contradiction; for the same power caused a thing to exist is necessary to continue its existence; a belief in divine providence, is a source of great consolation to good men. By divine providence is often understood God himself".

---T--- <u>The first prayer of Congress requested help from</u> God & was done in the name of Christ.

---T--- <u>They intentionally/ purposed religion, Christianity, God,</u> Creator, happiness, & serving the Nation was to include, & defined as including, God's Laws: // Samuel Johnson (signer of DOI) wrote to a graduating class of a GOV school, Columbia University, after the RW, saying, "you have the favor of Providence ,,,to qualify you the better to serve your Creator and your country ,,,Your first great duties, you are sensible, are those you owe to Heaven, to your Creator and Redeemer. Let these be ever present to your minds, and exemplified in your lives and conduct. (p) Imprint deep upon your minds the principles of piety towards God, and a reverence and fear of His holy name. The fear of God is the beginning of wisdom and its consummation is everlasting felicity. Possess yourselves of just and elevated notions of Divine Character, attributes, and administration, and of the end and dignity of your own immortal nature as it stands related to Him. (p) Reflect deeply and often upon these relations. Remember that it is in God you live and move and have your being ,,,and that you are the redeemed of the Lord that you are bought with a price, even the inestimable price of His precious blood of the Son of God. Adore Jehovah, therefore, is your God and your judge. Love, fear, and serve Him as your Creator, Redeemer, and Sanctifier. Acquaint yourselves with Him in His Word and holy ordinances ,,,And with respect to particular duties to Him, it is your HAPPINESS that you are well assured that he best serves his maker, who does most good to his country and to mankind."

---T--- <u>Orders from Christ RE the earth include</u> these given to Noah & all Spiritual Moral Beings thereafter, which have never been changed: // Gen9, "God blessed Noah and his sons, and said to them, Be fruitful, and multiply, and replenish the earth. And the fear of you and the dread of you shall be on every beast of the earth, and ,,,fowl of the air, on all that moveth on the earth, and ,,,fishes of the sea; into your hand are they delivered ,,,be you fruitful, and multiply; bring forth abundantly in the earth, and multiply". This is a working together with God in providence and Nature.

---T--- <u>Most of the FFoG Officials & </u>citizens, were trained educationally, either in college or home schooled or both: // Most Colleges required to know Greek and Latin and to have Christian learning; which often included ability to translate the 10 chapters of John from Greek into Latin; Furthermore the USA public citizenry was very literate and publishing many newspapers than any other country worldwide (89).

---T--- <u>Christ's Holy Bible is basis of nation as declared</u> by congress multiples of times; pertaining for enactment of activities; which activities were Christian.

---T--- <u>God (Christ) is to be the true ruler of the</u> USA GOV: // FFOG George Washington writes: "Let us unite ,,,imploring the Supreme Ruler of nations, to spread his holy protection over these US: to turn the machinations of the wicked to the confirming of our CON: to enable us at all times to root out internal sedition, and put invasion to flight: to perpetuate to out country that prosperity, which his goodness has already conferred, and to verify the anticipation of this GOV being a safeguard to human rights" (71). Now Mr. Washington is no fool to ask God to be the ruler and protector, then directly spit in Christ's face by not applying the commands in the Holy Bible and insisting that all Officers of the USA GOV do the same. The man would be a hypocrite and a deceiver if so. And what kind of protection could he depend on by praying to Christ and then insulting Him at the same time? +Mr. Washington also wrote: ",,,we may then unite in most humbly offering our prayers and supplications to the great Lord and Ruler of Nations and beseech him to pardon our national and other transgressions, to enable us all, whether in public or private stations, to perform our several and regular duties properly and punctually, to render our N GOV a blessing to all the People, by constantly being a government of wise, just and constitutional laws, discreetly and faithfully executed and obeyed, to protect and guide all Sovereigns and Nations (especially such as have shown kindness unto us) and to bless them with good GOV, peace, and concord. To promote the knowledge and practice of true religion and virtue, and the increase of science among them and us, and generally to grant unto all Mankind such a degree of temporal prosperity as he alone knows to be best."

~~~~~~~~~~~~~~~~~~APPLICATION Of CONCLUSION BY ~~~~~~~~~~~~~~~~~~~~~
------------------------------------PERFECTION Of GOD:

---T--- <u>God was put as the Supreme Ruler, because</u> God is perfect; does not do evil.

---T--- <u>God is perfect (totally right), both in all His will, thoughts</u>, reasonings, feelings, affections, emotions, intentions/purposes, judgment, desires, actions, and expressions. His discernment is always right; about the subjects of good & evil; never sins or does evil. He will never cause Unjust pain to any Spiritual Moral Creature; we His creation; children.

---T--- <u>Because the FFOG</u>, including all citizens, desired, intended/ purposed what was right, they put God as the Final Authority; so as to make the Check Point God.

---T--- <u>"Divine Providence" name of God asserts</u> God's perfect love, omnipotence, omnipresence, and omniscience to manage the World as Creator.

---T--- <u>The CC starts with God & ends with God:</u> // The reason, intention/ purpose, for the separation from England was God; everything was to be right. Thus God was prayed to by the CC for assistance; The CC is a form of Prayer; because God is totally right; He can be trusted; because He is totally right and always right and never evil.

~~~~~~~~~~~~~~~~~~APPLICATION Of CONCLUSION BY ~~~~~~~~~~~~~~~~~~~~~
----------------------------- CONSCIENCE And RESPONSIBILITY And GOD:

---T--- <u>Conscience activity, function, responsibility:</u> // "<u>Journals of the Continental Congress</u>, 1774-1789 - 3/19/1782 - ,,,Whereupon ,,,On a report of a committee ,,,appointed to prepare a recommendation to the several states, to set apart a day of humiliation, fasting, and PRAYER Congress agreed to the following Proclamation: The goodness of the Supreme Being to all his rational creatures, demands their acknowledgments of gratitude and love; his absolute government of this world dictates, that it is the interest of every nation and people ardently to supplicate his mercy favor and implore his protection. When the lust of dominion or lawless ambition excites arbitrary power to invade the rights, or endeavor to wrench wrest from a people their sacred and unalienable invaluable privileges ,,,".

---T--- <u>It is a self-evidence, a SETLWHM, and Conscience</u> situation with all Spiritual Conscience Creatures alive, that when we think of God, including Him, then we think and feel responsible: That God is the final authority; main authority. Thus in the CC (DOI & CON) God was put as such.

85

---T--- <u>Citizen Responsibility to support Christianity & God</u> as part of the GOV: // FFoG John Adams states, "We electors have an important constitutional power placed in our hands ,,,a check upon two branches of the legislature ,,,necessary to every subject (citizen) ,,,be in some degree a statesman and to examine and judge ,,,political principles and measures ,,,Let us examine them with a sober ,,,Christian spirit." (169a).

---T--- <u>CONSCIENCE~ USA GOV Supports It</u>: // Conscience is a Christian word for the moral consciousness of Christ; expesses God's Presence. // This agrees to encouragement for St Patrick's Day which day is a day of good & evil: "Letters of Delegates to Congress: Volume: 3- 1/ 1, 1776 - May 15, 1776 ,,,March 1776 ,,,On Sunday morning the 17th ,,,my attention from my Chamber window was Suddenly called to behold a mightly Cavalcade of Plebeians marching thro' the Street with drums beating and at every Small distance they halted & gave three Huzzas. I was apprehensive Some outrage was about to be Committed, but Soon perceived my mistaken apprehentions & that it was a RELIGIOUS exercise of the Sons of Saint Patrick, it being the anniversary of that Saint the morning Exercise was ushered in with the ceremony above describd. However Sir Should I leave you to Judge of the RELIGION of this City from the above Story only; it would not be Just, there are devout pious people in this City, a number of pious & Excellent preachers, & he who does not lead a virtuous & RELIGIOUS life here must accuse himself. Every man has Liberty to persue the dictates of his own CONSCIENCE. My Business is very arduous as well as Important. We commonly Set from Ten in the morning until between four & five in the afternoon Intent on business without any refreshment. It was very tedious at first but by usage is become Tolerable. I have by DIVINE blessing enjoyd a very good State of Health ever since my recovery from the Small Pox. I cannot forget my native Country; & prize Connecticutt higher than ever I did before. It is disagreable to be So long removed from my ,,,however I must cheerfully obey the calls & DICTATES OF PROVIDENCE with out refusing. I herewith send you a Resolve of Congress for a GENERAL FAST tho it may likely appear in the public papers. ,,,let me request an Interest in your PRAYERS that I may be enabled faithfully to perform the trust [[observe their conscience in operation]] reposed in me, & in due time be returnd to my family & native Land in peace. Am Sir with due respect, your Humble Servant ,,,A resolution of Mar. 16 recommended that May 17 be observed as a "day of humiliation, fasting, and PRAYER." JCC, 4:208-9.".

---T--- <u>The Conscience is referred to const</u>antly & in every area & Branch of the USA GOV.

---T--- <u>CONSCIENCE: That</u> Conscience be protected from N GOV.

---T--- <u>God being the Creator & Source of</u> all that exists makes us responsible to Him for such; to acknowledge what is His Will, decisions, intention/ purpose with all that does & does not exist; what to do with all that He created. To deny this is to reject the CC (DOI & CON).

---T--- <u>Conscience is to be cared for affectionately</u>: // Previous versions of the 1-A are as follows: +"Congress shall make no laws touching religion, or infringing the rights of conscience"; +"Congress shall not make any law infringing the rights of conscience, or establishing any sect or society"; +"Congress shall make no law establishing religion, or to prevent the free exercise thereof, or to infringe the rights of conscience"; +"Congress shall make no law establishing one religious sect or society in preference to others, or to infringe on the rights of conscience".

---T--- <u>Conscience of Christianity Frequently Included</u>: // Governing DOCs: ",,,liberty of conscience"~ is the statement, or thereto similar. Some DOC include both N GOV & State as follows (AD Years): 1640 Providence; 1649 Maryland; 1663 Rhode Island; 1664 Jersey; 1665 & 1669 Carolina; 1676 West Jersey; 1701 Delaware; 1776 Virginia; 1776 New Jersey; 1777 New York; 1782 Pennsylvania. There are many others, including an AD 1788 submission from 6 States to use the word "Conscience" in the Bill of Rights (163a).

---T--- <u>CONSCIENCE</u>: // Conscience is a part of the Self evidence; which "self-evidence" is in the DOI. // Conscience is a part of us as a spirit; a median by which God communes with us. // References in the CC made between the 5 Being's includes the conscience relationship. // Checks & Balances system is based partly on the conscience; a function of it. // Conscience was often referred and thus supports that God is the Ruler of the USA; and that is the Christian God.

---T--- <u>Study of our Spirit Being, the Conscience part</u>: // Conscience defined by various Dictionaries: +Easton's 1897 Bible Dictionary: "that faculty of the mind, or inborn sense of right and wrong, by which we judge of the moral character of human conduct. It is common to all men. Like all our other faculties, it has been perverted by the Fall (Joh16:2; Act26:9; Rom2:15). It is spoken of as "defiled" (Tit1:15), and "seared" (1Tim4:2). A "Conscience void of offence" is to be sought and cultivated (Act24:16; Rom9:1; 2Cor1:12; 1Tim1:5, 19; 1Pet3:21)." +Random House Dictionary, © Random House, Inc. 2010: Conscience defined: "1. the inner sense of what is right or wrong in one's conduct or motives, impelling one toward right action: to follow the dictates of conscience. 2. the complex of ethical and moral principles that controls or inhibits the actions or thoughts of an individual. 3. an inhibiting sense of what is prudent: I'd eat another piece of pie but my conscience would bother me. 4. conscientiousness." +Online Etymology Dictionary, © 2010 Douglas Harper: "knowledge within oneself, a moral sense; with-knowledge". ~Note here that it uses knowledge to discern between good & evil. +Nelson's Student Bible Dictionary, By Ronald F. Youngblood, Frederick Fyvie Bruce, R. K. Harrison: "A person's inner awareness of conforming to the will of God or departing from it, resulting in either a sense of approval or condemnation Rom2:14-15". // The Greek word is defined as: "co-perception; moral consciousness; to see completely; to understand, become aware, become conscious; informed; consider; perceive; comprehend; to know; the soul comprehending the difference between good & evil." (1c)(James Strong Concordance). // The OT saints knew in their heart (thoughts & feelings) and thus the ability was titled. Paul, in the Holy Bible, spoke of it immediately after having been saved from false Judaism and it appears that he learned the term from his previous studies. Adam was taught to categorize fairly soon. Co-perception is "co" with God, with right & evil, and with discerning what is right and the responsibility to such. The discerning ability and responsibility is the conscience; or the ability to know right from wrong; thus a responsibility comes with an ability, and of consciousness and understanding or knowing. // Truthfully, the word concept (at least) has existed from the beginning of mankind; and in the NT since Christ's time, AD 10. It may have had spelling changes or existed in various languages. But that does not tell us the word has not been in existence. EX: Discerning good & evil has been an activity starting with Eve & Adam; mankind has been responsible for good & evil starting from that time; therefore responsibility has been KN, ability therefore has been KN, and results of rewards & punishments has been KN, and Heaven & Hell has been KN, and etc. // Here are some related words used with conscience, that are in the spiritual realm: "Free will; Determinism; Metaphysics; Theology of Justification; Virtue; Ethics; Moral motivation or Intent; good & evil; judgment; discernment". // Word definition & Functioning of the Spiritual Sense or Faculty: The English word is derived from Latin, "with knowledge". This word describes internal awareness of a moral standard from God in the mind concerning the qualitative or rightness vivi wrongness of one's intents (motives) and actions, internally & externally. It works in conjunction with the consciousness to make aware and inform and provide knowledge which then requires the responsibility factor. It is often a feeling, a shameful feeling, a pressing, as distinguished from demonic activity which work on the thoughts & feelings. A "sense of guilt" about what ought to be, or should have been, done. Often it is not a product of the reasoning and judgment faculty, but a result of internal and/or external activity of ones own Being. // Dangers of deception or rejection of the Conscience: It can be reasoned and willed against. And Spiritual Conscience Beings can also reason themselves in to guilt; false guilt. Demonic activity can slander and accuse falsely; or for actual sins that are not resolved with God. Rev12:10. // It is influenced by training and cultural ideas of right & wrong. Thus it may not always be accurate. // Sensitivity should always be exercised with ones conscience because it is the voice of God and His Laws, frequently. Conscience is also a guide to us; An internal lamp or light to right & wrong. Pro6:23. The testimony of the experience and the truth of revelation (Holy Bible) clearly provide that through walking in God's light (Knowledge) morally, mystical senses, or spiritual senses, can be developed through daily contemplation, prayer, meditation, study, carefulness, selfless service to others, selfless reflection on Christ, which then encourages and receives sparks of insight or revelation (expressions) from God. Condemnation, guilt, inner light, inner darkness, conviction of right or wrong, or of duty demanded or offenses committed~ are all functions of the conscience. That God communicates Truth to the human mind or Conscience should be very well known as a fact of life. // The FFOG studied the conscience, for they were Christians and had studied the Lord Jesus and the faculties of the Spirit, our Being, and were familiar with this conscience part that influences us inside as a natural law of creation, and existence; and the Lord influences us through the conscience as well as through providence. // FFOG Joseph Butler cared about his conscience as God-given and to obey such; stating~ it is "intuitive"; is a "constitutional monarch"; the "universal moral faculty"; and learned that although it does not always direct our every action; that it is "authoritative"; that it assists a duality of regulating principles in human nature, one of "self-love" (seeking individual happiness) and the other, "benevolence" (compassion and seeking good for other Beings). // John Locke writing about the Law of Nature shares that human conscience is a fact; and this God-given faculty provided Rights of a citizen that relate to Moral Laws that exist; and that they may contradict that of GOV; And Holy SC testifies that we are to obey God first before an evil GOV. // FFOG Samuel Johnson shared that a deception is to use the conscience as a right to a cause of an unjust suffering to other Beings; that conscience is a conviction we feel regarding something to be done or avoided; or of issues of simple unperplexed morality; these are areas of its authority; that the conscience requires things to be completely known; and that we cannot dictate; and must be careful, in application to other Beings that which when we know not completely of them, which would then violate their Rights. // Various other Spiritual Moral Beings have realized the sensitivity and responsibility which is required of us by God, and assisted in directing their fellow citizens towards the value of conscience and carefulness with it, during times AD 1600's ~1700's, such as Spiritualists (Christian), Moravians, Wesley's, John Fletcher, Methodists, John Foxe, John Bunyan, Frederick Handel, Isaac Newton, Jacob Bohme, and William Law; all their friends. // Madame Guyon was persecuted from false Christians, or false religionists, and put in prison. She writes about the conscience, "On Faults Committed,,, we either wander among externals,,, we must instantly turn inwards; The business of those that are advanced to the degree ,,,is to lay their whole souls open before God, who will not fail to enlighten them, and enable them to see the peculiar nature of their faults. This examination, however, should be peaceful and tranquil; and we should depend on God for the discovery and knowledge of our sins, rather than on the diligence of our own scrutiny. When we examine with effort, we are easily deceived, and betrayed by self-love into error: We call the evil good, and the good evil,' (Isa5:20); but when we lie in full exposure before the Sun of Righteousness, his divine beams render the smallest atoms visible. We must, then, forsake self, and abandon our souls to God, as well in examination,,,". // The FFOG read studies from these Spiritual Moral Beings, and such like, and were encouraged in such truths. // God immediately causes our existence with the realization of our responsibility, requirement, and internal constitution construction of the conscience in our Being; Adam & Eve were instructed to do right and sin not, Genesis2-3. Sin includes a responsibility and the existence of the conscience. Conscience is as a law inside us; is the commandment of God. The wounding of it brings a pain, of which the "ancients" have stressed with poems and writings. It is a conscious experience that cannot be escaped. The reasoning faculty may try to minimize it by false reasoning, which Holy Scripture calls "searing" the conscience. However it cannot possibly be a pleasant experience to do so. Evil, whatever it does, even in its work to push away the presence of God (Holy Ghost) and the conscience, nevertheless cannot, as it is impossible. They cannot feel the feelings of the righteous, of a good conscience, and of the very affections of God; this is God inside. The conscience cannot be escaped from. It is with us forever; as the laws of God which we will carry with us forever; the little law book will be with us eternally, as the tabernacle of the OT was carried with the commandments contained. You cannot escape your conscience. We may damage it, try to reason, but no satisfaction will be resulted from either of those false remedies. It will exist in

Hell. // Historically some knowledge of the conscience was identified. One report shared that it was a doctrine that the Ancients thought on when there was less public activity involving political affairs. Attention should be to encourage us~ that~ when has the TV ever provided any wisdom? Pretend Acting is not a Christian profession, and the spreading of knowledge is better read and heard and shared than by some visual telecast which comes at random and subjects are mixed and cost is high and it is only a picture; The TV has caused so much hype, confusion, and distraction that Spiritual people have lost their discernment. Now this is not to deny technology or any usefulness. // International Standard Bible Encyclopedia, (paraphrased): shares that the Predictive Operation of the conscience, is "predictive" as providing an intuition or instinct of responsibility regarding death or after death. This is one of the strongest functions of it that exist in man. This act of the conscience provides death with its anticipation of something after death - of a judgment time with perfect justice according to the deeds. It is this which imparts to death its solemnity; "the anticipation of something after death"; "we instinctively know that we are going to our account." This natural and extremely strong instinct cannot be wrong. // Conscience should be educated carefully and rightly. Conscience must be experienced and exercised to learn God's presence and learn to exist rightly as a person of health and sensitivity. // For a person to be responsible to God and to man is EV that the person must know what they are to be responsible for; for this to occur there must be knowledge of what is right & evil; the 2 most primary ways to know what is right & evil is by God's revelation in the Holy Bible or by God Himself; He is a Spirit. We also learn from parents, society, and church about good & evil, what it is and various aspects about it. Thus this is the primary thought with the FFOG about the conscience. // We cannot be forced or mistreated by the GOV for they cannot judge in every instance; they are not God, and they are not micro-controllers of thoughts, worship, and devotions in the home, etc. Such is stated in the CC & written in Christ's Holy Bible. // The FFOG were very much concerned with the conscience and recorded and discussed it often; studied and lived and taught about the conscience. The word is often used in the States CON and is part of the definition of Self-Evidence by the FFOG. // The Holy Bible is full of SCs on the conscience. Act24:16 states~ "herein do I exercise myself, to have always a conscience void of offence toward God, and toward men". // FFOG Samuel Adams said, "Let divines and philosophers, statesmen and patriots, unite their endeavors ,,,by impressing the minds of men with the importance of educating their little boys and girls ,,,the fear and love of the Deity ,,,in subordination to these great principles ,,,the love of their country; of instructing them in the art of self-government, without which they never can act a wise part in the GOV of societies, great or small; in short, of leading them in the study and practice of the exalted virtues of the Christian system,,,". FFog Mr. Jefferson states, "Our rulers can have no authority over ,,,natural rights ,,,rights of conscience ,,,answerable ,,,to God,,,".

~~~~~~~~~~~~~~~~~~~APPLICATION Of CONCLUSION BY ~~~~~~~~~~~~~~~~~~~~~~~~
------------------------SELF-EVIDENCE ~ Defined As Including The Conscience, Heart, And Existence Of Truth:

---T--- Self-Evidence Law: The DOI states, "WE HOLD THESE TRUTHS TO BE SELF-EVIDENT". // This EV includes the conscience that is created in us, as Spiritual Moral Beings, helping to discern between Truth & Lie and Good & Evil. // Truth heart laws placed in us by God~ in our Being at creation. // The FFOG were establishing the truths including that~ +] God is the Supreme Ruler over us Spiritual Moral Beings; +] we are responsible to God 1st priority before men; +] This is self-evident in us. // Witho a basis of law we have no standard; no measure; no discernment. Who does not know this? We would be like a ship on sea in a storm without a sail, or compass, and no knowledge of what we are doing, where we are going, and where we came from. Thus Self-Evidence is EV inside of us to help us to discern, to know, to measure, a rule or law, to tell us that God, truth, the Holy Bible, Nature or Creation's God are the standards; these subjects we have as EV in our consciousness view. // It is better to obey God than man, when one is contrary to the other. Act5:29 of HSC. // Every thought and religion or idea of existence, and of God is not all truth or right. Anarchy, maniacism, lunaticism, foolishness is all around us. This is a place, or world, and existence of good & evil, which includes truth & falsities (lies). And we know it (self-evidence). Such self-evidence teaches us a Responsibility. // Self-evidence is in each person, and requires responsibility to God and His laws.

~~~~~~~~~~~~~~~~~~~APPLICATION Of CONCLUSION BY ~~~~~~~~~~~~~~~~~~~~~~~~
-----------------------------HEART Or SPIRIT And GOD And MANKIND:

---T--- SPIRIT ~ God is a Spirit & so are we~ SPIRIT: // The FFOG were Christian, conscience, self-evidence, aware of evil spirits, of God, used spiritual symbols such as the Eye of Providence over the Pyramid, the definition of providence in God's spiritual workings in the affairs of life, etc. This Spirituality includes society (citizen Branch), and it is of very much an encouragement to any Spiritual Moral Being's heart. If they would have been less spiritual we would not have such positive encouragements for truth, God, liberty, happiness, self-evidence, conscience, and rightness, and the true religion of Christianity. But at this time we may thank God almighty and His wondrous workings in providence for the benefits that have passed to us from this spirituality. // Joh4:24, Gen2.
---T--- GOD - CC, DOI & CON is Christian and Spiritual DOCs for Christ & the Holy Spirit.

---T--- <u>God's presence, Christianity, as a Spirit</u> asked for by congress and observed by congress as present among them (62). // They sensed God's presence. // They knew the Holy Bible that teaches that God the Holy Spirit helped write and that the Holy Spirit desires to dwell with each Spirit Creature constantly~ 1Cor6.

---T--- <u>SELF - EVIDENCE, GOD, SPIRITUAL</u>: CC, DOI & CON are SPIRITUAL DOCs: // Self-Evidence is a metaphysical law or internal truth; a spiritual subject; a witness that we are a spirit and that laws govern our internal realm~ Spirit.

---T--- <u>Conscience is part of our spirit (heart). Rom2:15.</u>

---T--- <u>*USA GOV required to be spiritual & heart related:*</u> // A Self~ Evidence (Self~E): // Self~E also includes conscience, and reasoning; these are parts of human Beings spirit. // Part of the GOV is to be spiritual; to abide by conscience. // 1Cor3:1, Mic3:8.

---T--- <u>Definition of Heart</u>: // *<u>Wikipedia Free Encyclopedia</u>*: ~ "Heart (symbol) - Traditional European heart symbol. [[This is the one we know of most commonly]]. The heart has long been used as a symbol to refer to the spiritual, emotional, moral, affections, and the intellectual center of a human being. As the heart was once widely believed to be the seat of the human mind, the word Heart continues to be used poetically to refer to the soul, and stylized depictions of hearts are used as prevalent symbols representing love. In religious texts the heart has historically been ascribed much mystical significance, either as a metaphor or as an organ genuinely believed to have spiritual or divine attributes". // The heart shape symbol used commonly today does generally simulate the physical heart shape. It is my estimation that this is its source. // The physical heart is a sort of pump, including 2 main parts; a part for the blood and a part for the oxygen. And it is red, or somewhat red. // *<u>The Free Dictionary</u>*, (freedictionary.com) Heart is defined as: ~ "Spiritual: ,,,The vital center and source of one's being, emotions, and sensibilities,,, The repository of one's deepest and sincerest feelings and belief,,, The seat of the intellect or imagination ,,,Emotional constitution, basic disposition, or character: 'a man after my own heart' [[1Sam13:14]] ,,,One's prevailing mood or current inclination,,, Capacity for sympathy or generosity; compassion ,,, Love; affection ,,,Courage; resolution; fortitude,,, The firmness of will or the callousness required to carry out an unpleasant task or responsibility ,,,The most important or essential part: get to the heart of the matter". // *<u>The American Heritage® Dictionary of the English Language, Fourth Edition copyright ©2000 by Houghton Mifflin Company. Updated in 2009. Published by Houghton Mifflin Company</u>*: ~ "heart - ,,,this organ considered as the seat of life and emotions, esp. love,,, emotional mood or disposition, a happy heart a change of heart,,, tenderness or pity, you have no heart ,,,a conventionalized representation of the heart, having two rounded lobes at the top meeting in a point at the bottom ,,,an archaic word for hearten". // *<u>Collins English Dictionary ~ Complete and Unabridged © HarperCollins Publishers 1991, 1994, 1998, 2000, 2003</u>*: ~ [[Bodily or Physical Heart]]: "heart (härt) 1. The hollow, muscular organ that pumps blood through the body of a vertebrate animal by contracting and relaxing. In humans and other mammals, it has four chambers, consisting of two atria and two ventricles. The right side of the heart collects blood with low oxygen levels from the veins and pumps it to the lungs. The left side receives blood with high oxygen levels from the lungs and pumps it into the aorta, which carries it to the arteries of the body. The heart in other vertebrates functions similarly but often has fewer chambers." // *<u>Similes Dictionary, 1st Edition. © 1988 The Gale Group, Inc.</u>* All rights reserved: ~ ",,,heart - ,,,of feelings and intuitions; in your heart you know it is true ,,,story would melt your ,,,intuition ,,,an inclination or tendency of a certain kind; he had a change of heart ,,,spirit disposition, temperament - your usual mood; he has a happy disposition ,,,a positive feeling of liking; he had trouble expressing the affection he felt; the warmness of his welcome made us feel right at home; affection, affectionateness, philia, warmness, warmheartedness, fondness, tenderness feeling - the experiencing of affective and emotional states; he had terrible feelings of guilt; soft spot - a sentimental affection". // *<u>Based on WordNet 3.0, Farlex clipart collection. © 2003-2008 Princeton University, Farlex Inc.</u>* ~ "heart,,, emotions, feelings, sentiments, love, affection ,,,nature, character, soul, constitution, essence, temperament, inclination, disposition ,,,tenderness, feeling(s), love, understanding, concern, sympathy, pity, humanity, affection, compassion, kindness, empathy, benevolence, concern for others; They are ruthless, formidable, without heart,,, courage, will, spirit, mind ,,,purpose, resolution, resolve ,,determination ,,,". // *<u>Collins Italian Dictionary 1st Edition © Harpercollins Publishers 1995</u>*: ~ "heart,,, the part of the body where one's feelings, especially of love, conscience etc. are imagined to arise,,, courage and enthusiasm ,,,kind-hearted; hard-hearted; broken-hearted,,, causing a person to feel pleasure; It was heart-warming to see the happiness of the children,,,". // *<u>Merriam Webster Online Free Dictionary</u>*: ~ "a : personality, disposition -a cold heart,,, intellect ,,,the emotional or moral as distinguished from the intellectual nature: as a : generous disposition : compassion ,,,love, affection ,,,courage, ardor -never lost heart,,, one's innermost character, feelings, or inclinations -knew it in his heart ~ a man after my own heart". ~ God said of David". // From God, The Holy Trinity & the Holy Bible: +Gen 6:5 tells thoughts are in the heart. +The heart is the same as the Spirit. +God is a Heart (Spirit). +Our spirit, or us, ourself, our personality, the person, is in the Holy Bible with the parts which include the conscience, will, thoughts, reasoning, judgment, affections, emotions, intents/purposes, and desires. This is the heart as God states it is. Also including the "Self". This is all you. // Some descriptions of the heart from some various peoples': +"The heart is like the sky, a part of heaven, but changes night and day too, like the sky" ~Lord Byron; +"Hearts ,,,mellow as well-tilled soil in which good seed flourishes" ~Valdimir G. Korolenko; +"Heart trembling a little like the door for Elijah the Prophet" ~Yehuda Amichai; +"A heart without affection is like a purse without money" ~Benjamin Mandelstamm; +"The human heart is like a millstone in a mill: when you put wheat under it, it turns and grinds and bruises the wheat to flour; if you put no wheat, it still grinds on, but then 'tis itself it grinds and wears away" ~Martin Luther.

---T--- <u>The most priority part of the Heart</u> or Spirit, although it is difficult to value one part of our Being more than others, is the Intention/ purpose & the Will/decisions. The intention to value God as 1st priority, only because He is a valuable Being to us and then decide to have this intention/ purpose; and then build all parts of our life with this 1st Priority Intention/ purpose. Have not self ulterior intentions, or any other subjects before this Intention/ purpose; love God as a Being & intend/ purpose Him as 1st priority. This makes a Person Good or Evil. Then do all the good you can to God & other Beings only because they are of value; not for other intentions of any other subject, rather only because the Beings are valuable to you in themselves. C. Finney has identified the Goodness Principle and the Love Principle very clearly; He did this to give more assistance to God's presence. Love includes all right Personality Traits or Attributes; and in balance; as a unit; working together. Goodness is what God does to all Beings. Goodness is a Principle Law word. It is to be part of the intention/ purpose. Such is to aim at a Being; not a rule or law, or material substance, etc. Although laws are part of it, the Being is to be valuable to us, because of themselves, without a selfish return receiving; is the subject. Although there is always a pleasure and receiving from doing right, it is not the priority; rather it is because of the Laws of Love, and rightness that such is part of it because it is that Love always effects for pleasure of heart or spirit. But pleasure is to be defined rightly. It can be a clear conscience, or having denied self for other Beings, etc. Nevertheless the 1st Priority is the Other Being themselves; as a value to us. // Mat22; 1Cor13; Heb4:12; Deu6; 18:19; Mar8:35.

++

---------------- RELIGION and GOD ------------------------

====== [CONCLUSIONS]: RELIGION: EVIDENCE For KNOWLEDGE ABOUT The RELIGIOUS CLAUSES; THE FIRST AMENDMENT:
These following conclusions will be proved: +] What religion is. +] What a Religion(ous) Establishment is. +] Religion is to be included as part of the USA GOV. +] Establishments of Religion are to be part of the USA GOV. +] This section attends with what dimensions, what limitations, what extensions, what protections, and what provisions are to be made about religion and Establishments of Religion. +] That no other religions are allowed to set up external activity in the USA (public assemblies or advertisements); nor to be supported by the USA GOV, and rather, only allowed as an internal belief (trust) in people; this is part of the evil that is opposed by the USA GOV. +] Separation; and What it is and Defined as. +] What is the Religious Test. +] Religious Clause (part 1) that states "Congress shall make no law respecting the establishment of religion". What is the explanation and definition of this. +] Religious Clause (part 2) that states "or prohibiting the free exercise thereof". What is the explanation and definition of this. +] Free Speech, part of the First Amendment Clause, or Religious Clause. This was part of the intention/ purpose for the existence and activity of the USA; a main subject~ God, 1st priority~ Christianity to the world; and also, the "round table", or open discussions and debating; "open-door" policy, for Truth. +] This Book is full of Evidence for these conclusions; General Evidences; Educational Evidences; Evidences of the Officers; Supporting DOC; FFoG lives; Events of the USA; Activities of the USA; CC; etc. +] The correct definition of the words "Religion" and of "Establishment" and of "Respecting" ~ in the Religious Clause, or 1st Amendment of the CON. +] Some activity that may be difficult to perceive, is not a support for anti-Christianity or falsity religion; rather it is a support for True Religion of Christianity. Regardless of paradoxical activity of such people as, James Madison and Thomas Jefferson, the DOI nevertheless states such as it does; And these men, as all those REP at that time were, Christians and supported the Christian religion. Any paradoxical activity was only intention/ purpose that the GOV people, as a group, would do right and not mix with evil and be preventative to evil with limitations to it; and also not make Christianity evil as in Europe. Two specific incidents that have been mostly used to do large wrong effects are that of Mr. Madison & Mr. Jefferson. These will be explained as proved rightly:

==== [Sub-Conclusion]: This Subject of the First Amendment is Formatted as part of the Conclusion, which Identifies the Intention/purpose of the First Amendment about Religion; this method of formatting gives you the Sub-parts about the Subject that are proved. It is divided in to 2 parts as sub-subjects to prove: The First, or 1st Amendment about Religion (1-A , R-E , R~Est) is a statement intended to prioritize God; as 1st priority; and to include God in the Checks & Balances System; His Being (& all the parts of His Being). The First Amendment in the CON reads~ "Congress shall make no law respecting an establishment of religion, or prohibiting the free exercise thereof". I repeat again, that this statement is studied as follows by dividing it in to 2 parts: //// Before starting the study of the 2 parts, we identify the Intentional/ Purpose of the 2 parts; which is the truthful interpretation and application of the 1-A , R-E , R~Est. Such is as follows: +) Prevent a national church, sect or DEN (as preferred or favoring status); which is made by a law; +) Protect the Right of freedom of conscience in Religious sects or DENs; +) Protect the States with making allowances for them to decide on religious establishments, and support to religious establishments (also titled as institutions or organizations or denominations or sects, etc.); +) Not prohibit national agreement and support of Christianity; but rather a joining of; including some carefulness about the relation; including no taxation for such (exacting dimensions not discussed at this time); +) Not separation of Christianity and N GOV; but rather a joining; and with carefulness (exacting dimensions not discussed at this moment; clarified in this book); +) No centralized control by the N GOV over Christianity and Churches; +) It is a assistance to application of the CC (DOI); +) Thereby with God as 1st

place priority, His Religion thereof is put in the order as He and Holy Scripture tells it to be; that the Nation is not in total control of it~ God & Christianity; rather the Church & DEN is in control of itself, and the Nation is secondary and supportive of such Religion & God; +) Religion is of the True Religion, which is the Doctrines of the True God & Man, and Basics thereof; and "establishments" are DEN; that is they are establishments of the True Religion, which includes organizations or institutions, secondary doctrines, and expressions.

/////////// ==[A]== [1ˢᵗ Part of 1-A, R-E, R~Est Studied; as Intended for Rightness]: 1ˢᵗ Amendment about Religion (1-A & R-E & R~Est) referring to the Part of the statement that states~ "Congress shall make No Law respecting an establishment of religion": // +} This amendment is an application to prevent Idolatry; for the Intention/ purpose that God can have 1ˢᵗ priority and the method/means includes His Religion (Christianity). This 1-A is a comparison; It compares with "You shall have no other gods before me" of the 10 Commandments; of the Holy Bible. This is to put God first in the USA; it is the application of the DOI~ to put God 1ˢᵗ priority. +} Thereby with God as 1ˢᵗ place priority, His Religion thereof is put in the order as He and Holy Scripture tells it to be; that the Nation is not in total control of it, rather the Church & DEN is in control of itself, and the Nation is secondary and supportive of such Religion and God. +} Religion is defined as the True Religion; which is the basic true doctrines of God & Man, and the true God, and mankind. +} Establishments are the denominations of the True Religion. Other names for establishments (in the various supporting DOC of the USA) include Sects, organizations, denominations, church, institutions, etc. Hence do not get confused from the studies herein (which shows the FFOG studies about various words to use in their DOCs) this Book. Establishments are mostly titled DEN in this Book. Establishments or DEN are made up of the true Religion (true God, true mankind, basic true doctrines of Christianity); and then Christian secondary doctrines, expressions, and organizations. // +"Congress"~ Who ?~ the REP of the Citizens. +"Make No Law"~ Do what ? Make No Law by this Law Making Branch. +"Establishments of Religion"~ About what subject ? About Establishments of Religion; that is Religion Establishments, or DEN, DEN of Christianity, or Christian Establishments. // "Respecting"~ Law that would do what to those Christian Establishments (DEN) ? A law that would "respect" or favor or be partial to one or two of such; the law would favor some Christian Establishment more than other Christian Establishments. +"Respecting": +} The 1-A, R-E, R~Est is a law. +} It is a law that disallows the USA to make any law that would equal~ "respecting" (or unequality). +} Respecting is defined as: to favor or be partial. Such respecting (partiality or favorism or unequality) then as is read by the statement, is directed to the subject of religion establishments (religious establishments or establishments of religion or establishments of the true religion). In other words, it is intended/ purposed Not to the Religion of Christianity itself, rather to the Establishments of Christianity (Religion or True Religion); Establishments of Christianity known in other words are as DEN. +} Thus no respecting (Partiality or Favorism or unequality) for a DEN. A DEN (Establishment of Christianity or True Religion) is defined as the secondary doctrines and expressions and organizations; those of Christianity. All Establishments (DEN of secondary doctrines, expressions, organizations) are to remain equal; without a law of partiality ("respecting") to any specific one. +To make a law "respecting", (partial or favoring)~ is to put one DEN, or only one secondary doctrine, or only one expression, or only one Christian organization as the Only one to receive legal support; to legalize such; which then illegalizes the other DEN. To do it by a law. +} To be "respecting" is not conceived rightly, often not at all, by our language today much. This is partly because we have multiplied (added) so many words to the English language; and also because we are using so many differing words for the same definition. These problems have caused the effects of confusing our minds about First Truths and SETLWHM; about conceiving words rightly; about thinking rightly. The word "respecting" is defined as, (both currently & historically) as: "to show honor or esteem for high regard; favor; favorism; partiality" (1a)(1b); thus inequality or unequal. +} Now the Holy Bible has been proved as the main source of knowledge used by the FFOG to construct the GOV systems. The KJV Holy Bible has the Older English that was being used at the same time. See here these Holy SCs that use the word "Respect(ing)" with this same definition. "Col3:24-25, Act10:34, Rom2:11, Eph6:9, 1Pet1:15-17 knowing of the Lord ye shall receive the reward ,,, [[or]] wrong [[punishment]] which he hath done: and there is no respect of persons; of a truth I perceive that God is no respecter of persons; for there is no respect of persons with God; neither is there respect of persons with Him; But as he which hath called you is holy, so be ye holy in all manner of conversation; Because it is written, Be ye holy; for I am holy. And if ye call on the Father, who without respect of persons judgeth according to every man's work". +} This all proves that no Christian DEN specific church, nor secondary doctrine, nor expression, should be managed with favorism or partiality ("respecting") by making a law; and then be made as a GOV institution by the USA GOV. +} To be "respecting" is conceived as to be partial or favorism; partiality or favorism given or expressed; or unequality expressed~ in the form of a law. The way "respecting" (Partiality or Favorism) would be given is to~ Make a law for that DEN or Christian Establishment, or True Religion of Christianity Establishment or organization; thus exclusive of other Christian Establishments. The 1-A says, rather, to NOT make a law, ("Make no law"). And it says "Make no law" to "respecting"~ that is to express Partiality or Favorism. And if a law was made then such would become part of GOV. That is not allowed. +} No Partiality or Favorism was to exist by a Law. That is not to be done; not to be given or expressed to a specific Christian DEN (Christian Establishment or True Religion Establishment). Again, Establishments of the True Religion includes secondary doctrines, expressions, and organizations. A law is not to be made about a specific one DEN as the only GOV DEN that receives favorism or partiality (respecting). Rather Christianity in general is to be supported; and all Christian DEN (secondary doctrines, expressions, organizations) allowed and supported. // Another Intention/ purpose reason No Church or DEN is said in the CON is that most of the States already had laws for State Christian Church Establishments. And they decided that this Statehood Right would remain with the States. And that the USA GOV would not have a Christian Church Establishment (DEN) for the National Structure. Because, for one thing, it would cause division since the States had various Christian DENs they were supporting; and because, for another thing, the USA GOV could not have all of the States Church Establishments as the States had different ones (9). This is a fact, well documented in history. The States would have problems joining the USA as each State, or most, had a different Christian Church Establishment (DEN or organization) as the State Church or Establishment. If the USA made a Law to favor (respect) only one Christian (True Religion) Establishment (DEN) then some of the States would not join the CON or Nation because they might have a different Establishment (DEN) of Christianity in their State. Some States had the Anglican Christian Church Establishment as a law in their State; other States had the Christian Church Establishment of the Congregational DEN as a law. Hence there was problems with the FFOG, in their knowledge, about how to have a Christian nation and systems. The States did not intend to favor (respect) DEN by making laws for the various Established Christian Churches (DEN) in their States; and often they did not express such. However they were trying to make a Christian system and thus made laws for Christian DEN (Establishments) in their State; which obviously appears as a Favorism or Partiality to that DEN (Establishment). // +} This does not say that the USA is to oppose Christianity or DEN (Establishments of the True Religion~ Christianity). Christianity & Establishments of Christianity (DEN) thereof are the Religion of the USA. +} This does not say that the USA GOV cannot give any support to any specific DEN (Christian Establishment). It can, and must, and needs to support Christian Establishments (DEN), in general; such is actually required by Law. And it can express or give attention to a specific DEN, as in one or more. That sort of attention or support does not make a law for that DEN; it does not make a law about that specific Christian Establishment; as the only one DEN (or more depending on the law made, if made) receiving some attention or expressions. // I have changed the word Establishment to Denomination, abbreviated as DEN, in this Book with the intention/ purpose to assist perception, conception, and comprehension that Establishment is defined as Denomination of Christianity. Now remember that the English Language is making different words for the same definition. Thus we are not changing the 1-A; rather simply using another word for the same definition to separate confusion for this study. Establishment EQUALS Denomination. Equal is equal. The Religion is already known to be the true religion~ Christianity; or the true God, true mankind, and the basic true doctrines of God & mankind. Establishments are only the application of the True Religion. By using DEN in place of, or as substitute for, Establishment, will assist our comprehension; to overcome problems caused by obscurity, by mixing of words and definitions with other words, by application of more current words known, by removal of unknown word problems, and by alerting of the awareness of right definitions. // The Word "establishment". What is its definition ? Webster (1a) says: "a thing established, as a business, military, organization; regarding as holding the chief measure of power and influence; the ruling inner circle of any nation, institution"; "establish" defined is: "make firm, settle; to set up; institute; to settle in a position; to make a Church the GOV institution". Webster of AD 1828 (1b) says: "Bring in that establishment by which all men should be contained in duty; That which is fixed or established; as a permanent military force, a fixed garrison, a local government, an agency, a factory, &c.". Websters (1a) defines the word "established church", as~ "a church officially recognized by the government and supported as a national institution; as was specifically the Church of England"; Websters (1a)(1b) defines "establishment" as: "a thing established as a business, military organization, household, etc; the Church of England; the Presbyterian Church of Scotland; the ruling inner circle of any nation, institution, etc.". and "establish" is defined as: "to make a state institution of (a church); to set up (a GOV, nation, business, etc.), permanently". Note this all proves that such refers to a DEN; and that DEN is expressions and secondary doctrines and organizations; because for EX: the Church of England is a specific DEN; Hence a Church DEN, secondary doctrine or expression of Christianity; as organized. Do you conceive this ? Establishment is DEN. That DEN is of the Religion; and that Religion is Christianity; True Religion; and True Religion is defined as~ The true God, the true mankind, and the true basic doctrines of God and mankind. // Now the God, the True God is already established; it is a Law; such is established by the CC~ the DOI & CON. It is the God of Christianity. Also the primary or main or basic Christian Doctrines are established by the CC. Such is done by Principle Laws; of which are the Principle Laws of the True God, true mankind, and the basic true doctrines of God and mankind which are~ eternity, truth, freedom of Will, liberty of life, Life, righteousness, Holy Bible, salvation, idolatry, murder, stealing, family structure, societal liberty, love, happiness, and limited or stopped evil (depending on which evil); are all included.

////////// ==[B]==[2nd Part of 1-A, R-E, R~Est Studied as Intended for Rightness]: 1st Amendment about Religion (1-A & R-E & R~Est) referring to the part of the statement that states~ "or prohibiting the free exercise thereof": // This part of the 1st Amendment is obviously another part of prevention of Idolatry continued, as it is the First (1st) Amendment, equally compared to the 1st 4 Commandments of the 10 Commandments (Holy Bible); continuing to allow God total freedom in the USA. This makes the USA GOV as an additional and ~LESSER~ entity; an entity made to support God's Freedom. // Prohibit not what ? That is the negative. Free exercise of What ? That is the positive. Hence Prohibit what; or do not stop nor decrease what ? Hence Free exercise what; or start or increase what ? ~~of Christ's Christianity (Religion) and its Establishments (DEN)~~ . // The statement actually reads~ 'No prohibiting the Free Exercise of Religion Establishments." Why does it read this way? Because that is Grammar Law, Statement Law, Sentence Law, and all of which are Language Laws. It has nouns that are not repeated. What Religion ?~ The True Religion of Christianity; which is the True God, true mankind, true basic doctrines of God and mankind. This is the correct or right reading of the words; the wording that the grammar and explanation of the statement in reality exists. // 'No Law is to be made prohibiting (against) Free Exercise of Establishments of Religion'. This includes every part of Christianity "Religion,,, Establishments"; this includes the Establishments of it, which are DEN. Or let us say it with only the last part and the 1st part of the sentence: +"Congress shall make No Law". +Now WHO ?? Congress~ The USA citizens and congress (Citizens REP; Congress is the Branch that is the Law Making Branch). +Do or Do Not what? Make No Law. +Make No Law About what subject? About ~ 1st part~ "respecting an establishment of religion" and about ~2nd part~ "or prohibiting the free exercise thereof". It is about the subject of Establishments of Religion. +Make No Law About the Subject of Establishments of Religion that would Do what to the Subject ? No "respecting" (which is favor or partiality) and no limiting or stopping free exercise. // Of what "religion" ? Now the conclusions about the CC already have Christianity as the Legal, the lawful, the True Religion of the USA. That is Law. God & Christianity are part of the USA GOV System; not to be excluded, rather included and applied. The 1-A or R-E or R~Est does not do anything with those directly. The 1-A & R-E & R~Est are doing to, or making applications of the Establishments of the Christian Religion. These are DEN. And DEN (Establishment) is defined as secondary doctrines, expressions, and organizations. Included in such are known through society as~ ceremonies, rituals, songs, hymns, meetings, Baptist, Presbyterian, Episcopalian, Lutheran, fellowships, prayer meetings, etc. // Now the 1-A sentence statement is talking about 5 subjects in total. The Subjects do not explain the interpretation, or definition of the statement; rather are only parts of the definition, explanation, and interpretation. The 5 subjects are as follows: 1} Congress; 2} Law Making; 3} Religion; 4} Respecting Establishments of Religion; 5} Prohibit free exercise of Establishments of Religion. // The word "thereof" is a referential word. In other words, it is referring to another subject not of itself. It is referring to "Establishment of Religion". The main subject of the 1-A , R-E , R~Est is God's Religion with the part of it as Establishment of Religion; or Religious Establishment; or DEN. Therefore it must be read as with the thought of the main subject and cannot be ended with a "thereof"; the "thereof" must be thought of with the word "Establishment of Religion"; or it is not a complete thought; it is confusion. And neither is it right grammar to exclude the first part of the sentence. Hence "No Law" must be included in the sentence. Therefore we word this 2nd part of the 1-A , R-E , R~Est for the study of it; such wording is "Congress shall make No Law of Prohibiting the Free Exercise of the Establishment of Religion". This is the part we are now studying. This part of the Amendment is the last part of the sentence, after the "Respecting" part above talked about (in the first division) in the study of the 1st Amendment. // Now this is Christianity Establishment parts, which is DEN, (secondary doctrines and expressions and organizations). The God is already known to be the Christian God; this is a truth. That is, Religion is the True God, true mankind, and the true basic doctrines of God & mankind. Thus the religious establishment thereof is DEN (secondary doctrines, expressions, organizations); because this is how religion functions on earth, and always has. The word, "establishment" is referring to Religious Organization or Institution; or DEN. Hence no Christian DEN can be prohibited by the USA in any way by making laws. // Make No law to favor (respecting) one DEN (as studied previously above), and Make No Laws to prohibit the free exercise of any DEN~ (DEN is an Establishment; Religion of Christianity). // Now where do Spiritual Moral people get the Right to Internally accept any god or false religion? By the fact that we have liberty in the DOI & CON of Free-will; that Christianity is not forced on Spiritual Moral folk; the CON does not say the USA GOV will force to accept Christianity. They may~ +internally decide on any false god or the true God; and +do the religion activities. However in application to such false gods and false religions, no Right is given for free exercise on USA Soil. It is limited; it has limited exercise; it is not to be Established; no organizations. It cannot have its denominations or organizations, or expressions actively expressed, or assembly buildings built on the USA soil in public; they may express it in public in personal ways (cloths, prayer, etc), but not advertisement nor public meetings, as such. Nor can it be part of the USA or State GOV. // All Christian DEN have freedom, "free exercise" to build buildings, organize, worship methods, prayer, holidays, etc. The 1-A continues with freedoms of Christianity and It's Establishments, by giving more Rights~ of Free Speech, of the Press to Print and Publicize, and of Assembly, or groups of Spiritual Moral Creatures to meet. These do not apply to evil. What Spiritual Creature, who is sane, will stand up and say that the FFOG were giving unlimited Rights to evil, and doing such at the time they were fighting for their lives against evil ??? Another Right is that the USA GOV is to have an "open-door" policy for hearing the citizens problems, or grievances; they are to be sensitive and submissive and listen; they are to desire to help problems of Spiritual Moral Creatures in the nation. // Now "prohibiting" is to stop or decrease in some way. Such is about the subject of Establishment of Religion; the True Religion~ Christianity. Establishment is DEN (secondary doctrines and expressions and organizations). So no Christian DEN can be prohibited by the USA in any way by any law making. // Repeated again is the fact that, the True God, Christianity Religion, primary doctrines, and expressions, are required as Legally already included in the CC (DOI & CON); and supporting DOC. This is proved continually in this Book, and especially in this Chptr 5. // All Christian Moral people and Christian denominations have unlimited freedom of exercising expressions internally and externally. // Freedom and freedom without prohibition is Not a Right given to false religions; rather it excludes freedom of exercise of false religions, as the CC (DOI & CON) state; with all the supporting DOCs. // All Publicity non-Christian activity on USA soil is illegal or limited; depending on what it is and what it does. NO LAW "respecting an establishment of religion" and "prohibiting free exercise thereof". Because this here makes a Law that states that the Establishments (DEN) of the Christianity Religion is not to be prohibited and to have freedom for exercising. Now if a nations activity is non-Christian, then it will oppose Christianity. Therefore such activity must be limited or illegal depending on what it is and what it does. // Individuals will have freedom of Christian religious expression. // The USA GOV and its agencies will not promote false religion. // The USA is to have God as God, Supreme Judge, Divine Providence, Lord Jesus Christ, Creator, etc.

/////////// Speech, Press, Publication, Assembly part of the AMENDMENTS of 1-A & R-E & R~Est; about Speech, Press, Assembly, etc; the Connecting Statements: These are a continuation of Freedoms, of Rights of Freedom, for the Priority intention/ purpose of Christianity; with the Rights~ for Free Speech, for the Press to Print and Publicize, and for assembly, or groups of Spiritual Moral Creatures meeting. Also the USA GOV is to have an "open-door" policy for hearing the citizens problems, or grievances; to be sensitive and submissive and listen; to desire to help problems of Spiritual Moral Creatures in the nation. // Now God was put in priority by the CC, all supporting DOC, FFOG lives, and etc. The communication of TRUTH is a basic need of Humanity; of Spiritual Moral Creatures. Truth is identified in the CC as a basic Right and Need. Communication of the Truth is a Right. It is a Freedom to talk truth. // This excludes the Freedom for Evil Speaking. To speak truth with evil intention/purpose is not a Right, neither. This is plainly obvious. In Holy Scripture there is a Principle Law that is written; that Evil Speaking is a Do Not; here are only a few of such HSCs~: Lev19:16; 2Sam19:27; Psa15:3; 50:20; 101:5; 140:11; Pro6:19; 10:18; 18:8; 25:23; 26:20; Jer6:28; 9:4; Rom1:29-30; 1Tim3:11; 5:13; 2Tim3:3; Tit2:3; 3:2; Jam4:11; 1Pet2:1; 2Pet2:10-11; Jud1:8-10; Rev12:10. This is NOT the liberty, or freedom, to speak evil. Such is clearly illegal by law, to do so publically. It is stated that no evil speaking against Christianity is to be done publically. It is the CC. This includes evil speaking for the supporting to increase publically subjects such as false religion, false Christianity, cursing or swearing, lying, Satanism, and criminal speaking as such. // The FFOG stated Principle Law by Freedom of Speech, Press, etc. These are General or Universal Laws~ Principle Laws. // The FFOG learned from history about the abuse that occurred in not allowing truth to increase by communication, including the Holy Bible; abuse from false Christian churches, false religions, and tyrannical governments. // Observe the connection of speech and press with the First Amendment, or that is part of it - "Congress shall make no law respecting an establishment of religion, or prohibiting the free exercise thereof; or abridging the freedom of speech, or of the press,,,". // The 1-A , R-E, R~Est including an Intention/ purpose, of many purposes, was as they said, so that the denominational issues of Christianity could assist each other, and take care of themselves; including that whereas the GOV had no Right to decide on such sacred things. Especially including because the GOV is not themselves trained and constantly working in the profession as clergy or special positions of special laymen in the churches. Additionally, this way Christianity could have freedom to increase in quantity and quality; that the USA could spread the Gospel freely without restriction; worldwide. This includes some of the other connecting intention/ purposes for "free speech", such as these: No Holy Bible burning as in Rome or others; no papist special confinement of the truth of the Holy Bible; no fear of GOV oppression for speaking the name of Jesus or God, etc.,; no GOV DEN controlling the others; no refusal of doctrinal debates, discussions, and round table meetings.

----------------------------- The format for the Conclusions above and below: // Arranged so that, Evidences (EV) of other chapters assist these conclusions. // Arranged so that EV of this chapter assists other chapters and conclusions therein. // The EVs are absolute and irrefutable; Truth. // Though the EV are not exactly ordered under each conclusion as is numbered, they are nevertheless, here provided; they are under each conclusion but they are only listed and not categorized any further to extreme sub-categories. Because all the sub-parts are connected together in thoughts and relations, I did not separate each statement or truth EV under each conclusion. Rather, all we must do, is to look and observe the evidential facts of truth, and the conclusions will be proved. // Now because the EVs, that are listed under each conclusion, are not exactly in a sub-category ordered, does not equal that it is unclear, nor that that conclusion is not true, nor not clarified. Rather all the EVs listed pertain to each conclusion they are under. The conclusions above and below are related, so that, if one is proved, then it very much proves the other conclusions. Hence, we only observe one EV and then observe how it proves each of the other conclusions elsewhere. Therefore the method is to, rather than sorting out each evidence under the conclusion, we are sorting the conclusions under the evidences. Because that, all the evidences provided here in this Chp, (and actually in the total Book), prove these conclusions herein this Chp. If each truth, that is EV, had to be sorted under each numbered conclusion then there would be much duplicity. So rather doing that, we simply read each EV and then observe how it does prove each conclusion, that it is listed under~ and if need, how it relates as EV to any other conclusion. This is also to state that an EV is to prove more than one {1} of the conclusions. // Why this method? Why does it function as such? Because Truth is a Unit; a Total; it cannot be divided; love is a unit; a total; it cannot be divided; rightness is a unit; it cannot be divided. And these are the same functions that Falsity, evil hatred, and evil have; they are units, a total, and cannot be divided. The parts function to the total conclusion, or main category; the main subject. The parts cannot contradict, be opposite, nor oppose the category total they are connected to, or under, or within. A pictorial comparison EX: a Circle or square has all the parts in it; but none of the parts are against it, nor oppose it, nor contradict it, nor opposite it, etc. Rather it is all within it, helps, supports, agrees, etc. // Every conclusion in this Book is proven with total proof (evidence). // They are the establishment of the USA GOV and any legality that does not agree, is conducting illegal activity; regardless of assertions. This is not saying that harshness be expressed to people, rather knowledge, alertness, awareness, and appeal to begin a correction revolution. The correctness has been stolen, corrupted, mis-interpreted, misconceived, mistaken, and illegal commissions.

++++++++++++++++++++++++++++++++++ EVIDENCES following:

---T--- <u>RELIGION to God is to be part of the USA:</u> // Everything the N GOV does is to~ +] include God as 1st priority; +] include the subjects of God, which is Christianity Religion, truth, right, not evil, Bible, creation, etc. // The CC states this.

---T--- <u>R-E, R~Est, or 1-A -- Religion & DEN & definition</u> of Religion & Religious Establishment (R~Est): // Religion & establishment is defined as DEN. // Other versions of the R-E , 1-A are as follows (31): +Sept 3, 1789, "Congress shall not make any law infringing the rights of conscience or establishing any religious sect or society". +"Congress shall make no law establishing any particular DEN of religion in preference to another, or prohibiting the free exercise thereof, nor shall the rights of conscience be infringed". +"Congress shall make no law establishing one religious society in preference to others, or to infringe on the rights of conscience". // Conscience is a Holy Biblical and creation term. // The FFOG did not want a nation to dictate a DEN as England was doing. // Religion was defined as DEN, which is secondary doctrines & expressions. And Christianity is the Religion, which is of the Holy Bible.

---T--- <u>The CON would be better if it had more words;</u> However the DOI Is the controlling or overRuling DOC of the two joined; making the CC. Thus it is very clear in the DOI: // Also remember that the FFOG intended/ purposed to prevent the USA GOV from: a= false religions, b= false Christianity, c= controlling Christianity as in Europe, d= having a USA Christian Church and not allowing for other Christian DEN, e= having USA GOV control over the States Independency for Christian freedom and Christian DEN.

---T--- <u>Conscience is to be Cared Affectionately for God's Presence:</u> // Previous versions of the 1-A are as follows: +"Congress shall make no laws touching religion, or infringing the rights of conscience". +"Congress shall not make any law infringing the rights of conscience, or establishing any sect or society". +"Congress shall make no law establishing religion, or to prevent the free exercise thereof, or to infringe the rights of conscience". +"Congress shall make no law establishing one religious sect or society in preference to others, or to infringe on the rights of conscience".

---T--- <u>SEPARATION of RELIGION to Christ & US GOV:</u> // The Congressional records & CON state the related official actions, activity, and words that occurred in congressional meetings. Following are records from early Congress Meetings dated from June 8 - Sep 25, 1789; which has these Truths stated: =t= NO (such) words, "separation of church and state" exist. =t= Religion is defined as: The prevention of what occurred in Britain, a legal establishment of a national single religious DEN in exclusion to all others; "respecting" is defined as "partiality, or favoring"; by making a law. =t= Remember this is why the pilgrims departed from England, and for that case Europe in general. =t= Other versions of the R-E, R~Est are as was stated by James Madison~ "nor shall any NATIONAL religion be established" (28). =t= In here we can find all the words and their definitions: The word religion & establishment is defined as "Christian DEN; which is defined as secondary doctrines, expressions, organizations". (see this as elsewhere in this Chp.). =t= Note these following other versions of the CON clause, R-E, R~Est, 1-A, recorded in the meetings: +The original first version was introduced Sep 3, 1789, stated: "Congress shall not make any law establishing any religious DEN". +The second version stated, "Congress shall make no law establishing any particular DEN". +The Third version stated, "Congress shall make no law establishing any particular DEN in preference to another". +The final version stated, "Congress shall make no law respecting the establishment of religion,,," (28). What we have here is religion establishment and DEN are the same definition hereby. =t= They expected no restriction to~ +Christ's Christian activities; +DEN; +conscience. Conscience is a Christian term about our Spiritual Moral Being and from the Holy Bible. // Fisher Ames (much involved in education) offered these things: +some of the final wording for the House version; +said this~ "Why then, if these (new) books for children must be retained - as they will be - should not the Bible regain the place it once held as a school book?" (28); +encouraged the Holy Bible while at the same time was assisting writing the CON. +taught that the Holy Bible is America's source of morals and should never be separated from the classroom (29). // James Madison wrote on June 12, 1788 to the Virginia Congress this: ",,,the people are decidedly against any exclusive establishment-- I believe it so in the other states ,,,general [[referring to national establishment of a DEN]] GOV to intermeddle with religion ,,,flagrant usurpation ,,,The US abound in such a variety of sects [[this word is usually defined as Christian DENs with their secondary doctrines, expressions]], that it is a strong security against religious persecution, and it is sufficient ,,,that no one sect will ever be able to outnumber or depress the rest" (49). // George Washington states: "Let us with caution indulge the supposition that morality can be maintained without religion, whatever may be conceded to the influence of refined education ,,,reason and experience both forbid us to expect that rational morality can prevail in exclusion of RELIGIOUS PRINCIPLE" (12a).

---T--- <u>RELIGION: For the GOV to abuse</u> Christ's Religion, is a major subject: // The FFoG knew history and were experiencing the abuse of a pretense in religion at the time; because England was a Christian Nation but their people in Government were not true Christians (many of them); rather only Christians by name, but not living by the commandments nor Holy Spirit of Christianity; rather evil doing. // These following are some Abuses of Christ & His Religion that the FFOG were desirous about: A~ unlimited allowance of false religion; A~ not practicing true religion; A~ not having true religion; A~ abusing those that have true religion. // And thus these abuses needed principles established in the GOV, or the GOV will be evil. And an evil GOV is a non-religious GOV. // These following thoughts of truth were constantly stated and applied by the FFOG; and they came from Holy Scriptures: "For the transgression of a land many are the princes thereof: but by a man of understanding and knowledge the state thereof shall be prolonged. A poor man that oppresseth the poor is like a sweeping rain which leaveth no food. They that forsake the law praise the wicked: but such as keep the law contend with them. Evil men understand not judgment: but they that seek the LORD understand all things. Better is the poor that walketh in his uprightness, than he that is perverse in his ways, though he be rich. Whoso keepeth the law is a wise son:

but he that is a companion of riotous men shameth his father. He that by usury and unjust gain increaseth his substance, he shall gather it for him that will pity the poor. He that turneth away his ear from hearing the law, even his prayer shall be abomination. Whoso causeth the righteous to go astray in an evil way, he shall fall himself into his own pit: but the upright shall have good things in possession. The rich man is wise in his own conceit; but the poor that hath understanding searcheth him out. When righteous men do rejoice, there is great glory: but when the wicked rise, a man is hidden. Happy is the man that feareth alway: but he that hardeneth his heart shall fall into mischief. As a roaring lion, and a ranging bear; so is a wicked ruler over the poor people. The prince that wanteth understanding is also a great oppressor: but he that hateth covetousness shall prolong his days. A man that doeth violence to the blood of any person shall flee to the pit; let no man stay him. Whoso walketh uprightly shall be saved: but he that is perverse in his ways shall fall at once. He that tilleth his land shall have plenty of bread: but he that followeth after vain persons shall have poverty enough. A faithful man shall abound with blessings: but he that maketh haste to be rich shall not be innocent. To have respect of persons is not good: for a piece of bread that man will transgress. He that hasteth to be rich hath an evil eye, and considereth not that poverty shall come upon him. Whoso robbeth his father or his mother, and saith, It is no transgression; the same is the companion of a destroyer. He that is of a proud heart stirreth up strife: but he that putteth his trust in the LORD shall be made fat. He that trusteth in his own heart is a fool: but whoso walketh wisely, he shall be delivered. He that giveth to the poor shall not lack: but he that hideth his eyes shall have many a curse.". {Pro28.}.

---T--- CC CON: The other areas of the CON are all based on the discerning and judging between good & evil. Such is activity of the conscience, affections, and intention/ purpose.

---T--- In FFOG meetings & discussions, these following are the wordings & concerning desires that were recorded & voiced to assist & prevent: // 1~ USA GOV would oppose religion~ Christ's Christianity and its laws and become main controller of it; 2~ USA GOV would select one sect or society, or secondary doctrine, also called DEN, over another, and make a law for it to be the USA GOV church and rule other DEN out or force others to follow it; 3~ National control would be gained over Christ's Christianity, and over Christianity in the states and their Churches by the word "national". 4~ USA GOV would not be able to assist Christ's Christian religion directly or indirectly without favoring DEN.

---T--- The 1-A makes all non-Christian activity against Christ on USA soil illegal or limited; depending on what it is & what it does: // Congress shall make~ NO LAW~ +"prohibiting free exercise thereof" ~ of~ "Establishment of Religion" ~ which is Christianity and its establishments~ or DEN~ which is the True God, true mankind, true basic doctrines of God & mankind; secondary doctrines, expressions, and organizations. Because this here makes a Law that states that Christianity is the Religion of the USA; and that it is not to be prohibited in freedom and exercising and establishing. Now if a nations activity is non-Christian then it will oppose Christ's Christianity. Therefore such activity must be limited or illegal depending on what it is and what it does.

---T--- To Say That Religion is Not Part of the GOV is to Take God Out of It; Thus this forms a lie: // The CC has made Laws~ +that include God, and, +that He is priority, and, +He is part of the Checks & Balances. The 1-A states that the GOV shall not oppose religion (True religion is to be promoted) ~ "prohibit the free exercise". This is a plain and factual statement that the GOV is to support it. There is not a neutral position. At any given point where the GOV & Religion contact there is either a support or opposition (forms of include~ denial, restriction, or refusal). Christ's Religion is not to be opposed or removed because it is disobedience to the 1-A.

---T--- Opposition: Forms of Opposition include Refusal, Denial, Rejection, Restriction, Disagreement.

---T--- False Religions opposed by God: // These following are illegal to be unlimited: Some false religions include the following. // Agnostics have doubts whether a God exists. // Atheists deny the existence of God. // Buddhists generally do not have the right concept of God. // Deists often have wrong concepts of God. Sometimes it includes an agreement that God exists, but do not agree that He is currently active in the universe with us His Spiritual creatures; that He does not commune with us; that God created the universe, wound it up, started it, departed, and has not been seen since. This is the one form of Deism, and not all the forms of it. // Hindus have a false god. // Wiccans generally acknowledge false deities, such as sometimes a God & a Goddess; and sometimes demons. // Some Zoroastrians believe in two deities: one all good and one all bad. // Freedom Rights & Evil Rights: All false religions & false Christianity has freedom to exist in the mind and free will of individuals. However, God opposes the USA to be used for establishing such religions in buildings for meeting places of groups; and public advertising. Spiritual Moral Beings may decide to it internally (their mind, free-will, decision, etc.) and practice it in their home; but they may not build religious buildings and print materials for the spreading of its acceptance; nor invite others to meet them in their home for religious meetings. // Some falsity religions are limited by not allowed in total, and others are limited to personal homes.

---T--- FFOG statements for Christ (260h): // Patrick Henry said, "There is an insidious campaign of false propaganda being waged to the effect that our country is not a Christian nation, but a religious one,,, it cannot be emphasized too strongly or too often that this great nation was founded, not by religionist, but by Christians. Not on religion but by Jesus Christ." // Alexander Hamilton, member of the Constitution Convention, said, "Let a society be formed whose first duty shall be the preservation of Christianity". // The USA & Canada are desired all over the world because of their system of justice & fairness, and because our FFOG supported the dignity of a person. This came from the British system of jurisprudence which is based on the historical Decalogue (10 commandments) given to Moses from God and supported by Jesus Christ.

---T--- <u>USA President George Washington cares for Christ by stating:</u> // "The blessed Religion revealed in the word of God,,,"~ regarding Christianity and the Holy Bible.

---T--- <u>Christ's R-E, 1-A, R~Est ~ of the CON:</u> // The text of the 1-A had some early draft versions to the religion section. And this proves that the word "religion" was defined and related as connected to to the word Establishment, Articles of Faith, mode of worship, etc.; which all are purposed to be Christian DEN~ secondary doctrines, expressions, organizations. Following are some of those versions: // Version of James Madison AD 1789~ "The Civil Rights of none shall be abridged on account of religious belief or worship, nor shall any national religion be established, nor shall the full and equal rights of conscience be in any manner, nor on any pretext infringed. No state shall violate the equal rights of conscience or the freedom of the press, or the trial by jury in criminal cases." // Version of House Select Committee, 7/28/89~ "No religion shall be established by law, nor shall the equal rights of conscience be infringed". // Version of Samuel Livermore, 8/15/89~ "Congress shall make no laws touching religion, or infringing the rights of conscience." // House version, 8/20/89~ "Congress shall make no law establishing religion, or to prevent the free exercise thereof, or to infringe the rights of conscience." // Initial Senate version~ "Congress shall make no law establishing religion, or prohibiting the free exercise thereof." // Final Senate version, 9/9/89~ "Congress shall make no law establishing articles of faith or a mode of worship, or prohibiting the free exercise of religion." // Version of Conference Committee~ "Congress shall make no law respecting an establishment of religion, or prohibiting the free exercise thereof." This version was approved as the Final Version by Congress House, 9/24/89; and by Congress Senate on 9/25/89; and ratified by the States in 1791.

---T--- <u>These are the intentions/ purposes desired & decided by the FFoG</u> & Public about the subject of God's Religion in the USA & GOV: // NO - to USA GOV control over all Christianity. // NO - to USA GOV selecting one Christian DEN (or a few) to give special partiality or favorism by making a law for it (or 2 or 3). // NO - to having false religions (any non-Christian) in the USA be allowed to exist without limitations. This is also part of the 2nd clause of the amendment, because false religions would prohibit true religions. // NO - to having the USA GOV force anyone to be a Christian. Internally (Will, decision, intention of people in the USA have the decision to not accept and follow Christianity, or false religions; however externally all people are to respect the Christian laws and religion, and abide and keep them, including no business on the Sabbath, etc.; and not public assembly nor advertising of false religion.) // NO - to USA GOV control over the sovereignty of the States in having a Christian Church (DEN 1 or 2) as a State Church. // YES - to having the USA GOV support Christianity in general and in some specific areas. // YES - to having the USA GOV be a Christian GOV. // These are the desires and intentions that were voiced and/or written. Not one EV is there that any REP wanted, or citizen Branch wanted, anything other than Christ with His Christianity; not one EV or statement that they wanted the USA GOV to be anything opposite of any of these - not one. Another way to say such as said, is that, there is total absence of any concern, intention/ purpose, or statement that any of the FFoG or DOC had~ +contrary or opposite of these; +or that they had a desire of not wanting the USA GOV to be Christian; +or that they did want other false religions in the USA. Such would be oppositional or contrary to that which they did. Yet none do exist. // As of now, the Citizen Branch has committed illegalities against the~ +USA CC (DOI & CON); +testimonies of the FFoG; +Public; +and all the other DOCs. So has the various USA GOV Officials & State GOV Officials. They do a breach of contract or covenant. (We know many people are unlearned, or untrained, or innocently deceived, and wrongly educated; that much is done unintentionally.).

---T--- <u>SPECIAL SUBJECT RELATED</u>, as follows, is part of this Religion sub-chapter; and then after this the chapter 5 continues as formatted.

~~~~~~~~~~~~~~~~~~~~,,,,,,,,,,,,,,,

---T--- <u>The SPECIAL SUBJECT is that of Separation of Church & State or GOV; and of Thomas Jefferson & James Madison; are studied for Rightness as follows:</u>

/////////// <u>Case of Danbury Baptist Church & Letter of Thomas Jefferson:</u> // In introduction of this subject, we desire you to meet USA President Thomas Jefferson; he wrote, "The God who gave us life gave us liberty at the same time" and, "Can the liberties of a nation be secure when we have removed a conviction that these liberties are of God?". // Separation of Church and State Case: +This case (situation not case) that Mr. Thomas Jefferson assisted with was ONLY an intended/ purposed that a DEN group's religious expression was protected by the "wall of separation" (a term loosely used in a letter; and this is the use of the term); for the free exercise of their DEN and that another DEN would not have favorism. +No such words were said~ "of Church and State (GOV) separation". Those words are added by people mis-interpreting or intently lying; or mistaken. A misinterpretation of Thomas Jefferson & the Danbury Baptist incident has thus made a lie. This was not a Separation of Church & State that has been explained by some people. Mr. Thomas Jefferson assisted with some people and their religious DEN. Words have been added to make this situation say what was never said, and to explain what was never intended/ purposed. No such words were said~ of Church and State separation. The situation was a protection of DENs, and by protecting this DEN, a Principle Law was established to protect all DENs. And actually it was not a law because the incident only occurred in a letter to the Church DEN; Congress was not included in the action; nor did the Executive President, Mr. Jefferson, make any decision to make a Law, or Law Formation. This was in the National Developmental Times. It was simply an appeal from a DEN to the President (Executive) Branch (T. Jefferson as Pres.) for assistance in discerning and helping with activity of Religion (the True Religion; Christianity). This action was Not the exclusion of religion from GOV, but the protection of it; the protection and allowance of such a DEN, as well as the other DENs, for equality of such DENs; and the free exercise of such a denominational worship and existence~ of the Danbury Baptist DEN. That was the total issue of the case. One Christian DEN was complaining that another Christian DEN was

97

receiving favors (respecting) while they themselves were abused, or might potentially be abused. +Yet now Spiritual Moral Beings have used this letter to exclude Religion of Christ's Christianity from GOV; which is a Falsity. +The court used, in AD 1947, this separation of church and state situation of Thomas Jefferson to remove religion. Whereas before it was protecting it and keeping it joined with the GOV. +If such a method, as this, that is if they can use such letters as this letter of Thomas Jefferson to the Danbury church, for the separation of church and State case mentioned (to make a judicial decision), then they can use it to reverse it (which would be to actually correct the 1947 case, to make it right); or make other cases which are Unconstitutional. Such a method is not designed in our system; it is Not a Right; and surely Not a Right from God. It is sometimes a pleasure to have exceptions to the Rule; surely all Moral Beings will agree to this. However this is an evil exception. Evil exceptions are not pleasurable, rather fearful. +This total situation (not a case) was not separating Religion & GOV, rather it was an application to support Christian DENs as equal with the GOV and not favor (respecting) one. It was actually a joining of religion & GOV. It was NOT a separating of Religion from GOV rather a Joining, an Inclusion of Religion with GOV. +The situation was a protection of DENs, and by protecting this DEN, a Principle Law was established to protect all DENs. +In Truth there is no such a Law of the USA that states separation of Church & GOV or State, nor Separation of Christian Religion & GOV. +This event and activity occurred with the Danbury Baptist Association and Thomas Jefferson. And the situation ONLY involved some written remarks in a letter. This event was a concern of the Danbury Baptist DEN because that the federal GOV would not make a law to favor a national DEN; and specifically that of the CO DEN. The intention/ purpose of Danbury Bap. Assoc. was that the Fed. GOV not exclude other DENs and only favor (Respecting) one DEN. Thus they wrote Pres. Jefferson about this desire. The statements that Jefferson used in communicating to them are NOT in the DOI, NOT in the CON, and NOT in the Notes of the Congressional Meetings. They are only in a letter to the Danbury Baptist DEN. This is the statement Mr. Jefferson made in the letter: "I contemplate with solemn reverence that act of the whole American people which declared that their legislature should "make no law respecting an establishment of religion, or prohibiting the free exercise thereof", thus building a wall of separation between Church and State" (40). Thus Mr. Jefferson was protecting their DEN; and the issue was DEN establishment of the GOV; a "respecting" or favorism. The situation was not Christianity & State mixing. +According to John Eidsmoe (9), Mr. Jefferson was using some words of a well known Baptist minister to assure them; the Baptist minister is Roger Williams, who said as follows: "When they have opened a gap in the hedge or wall of separation between the garden of the church and the wilderness of the world, God hath ever broke down the wall itself ,,,and ,,,to restore His garden ,,,it must of necessity be walled in ,,,unto Himself from the world,,,". Note that, "The wall" here is not GOV, but from "world" "wilderness"; that is, evil worldliness protection. "The wall" here of Jefferson, was only stated that the DEN was protected by the GOV; thus actually a statement of support by the GOV, of Christianity, and the DEN; and that GOV would not make a law to have favorite, or partiality, ("respecting") a national DEN. +Separation of Church and State is found Nowhere in the DOI & CON, Nor Any Supporting DOC. +This is an illegal enactment (AD 1947) by the Judicial branch; It is the Case of Everson vs. Board of Education. It involved bus transportation to a School proclaiming Christianity of some form. This situation with Thomas Jefferson's letter to the Danbury Baptist Assoc. is a decision made by the executive Branch in applying the CC. Such Event was used wrongly, and applied wrongly to the bus driving Case. +Thomas Jefferson wrote a statement conversing with the Danbury Baptist Assoc. +Thomas Jefferson closed his letter to Danbury Baptist Church with a prayer to Christ saying, "I reciprocate your kind prayers for the protection and blessing of the common Father and Creator of man". +The statement, repeated again as per above, of Thomas Jefferson said, "I contemplate with solemn reverence that act of the whole American people which declared that their legislature should "make no law respecting an establishment of religion, or prohibiting the free exercise thereof," thus building a wall of separation between church and state". Now note that he was answering to the Danbury Churches question that their DEN co/ exist and not be treated impartially by another Christian DEN; that the State would protect both of them (DEN) and not only one. This statement has nothing to pertain to a division or separation between the USA GOV or State GOV and Religion or Christianity. +This situation was not even a court case. It was only a letter from Thomas Jefferson to the Danbury Baptist Association. +The total situation regarding the event of the Danbury Baptist Church people was concerned that the GOV would force or support another Christian DEN with favor or partiality (respecting) them; and then decrease or stop their Christian DEN from existing or persecution. +This situation had nothing to do with a law of church and State separation. +Thomas Jefferson professed Christianity himself and supported it. +The Christian Danbury Baptists DEN feared that the Christian Congregationalist Church DEN would become the State sponsored religion. +No such purpose of separation of church and State occurred in this situation. No such words are used; none; zero. The subject was, rather, a limit on the abilities of the USA GOV by making a law ("respecting" or favorism) for one Christian DEN as a GOV Church. And that is all that this Case, (actually not a Case but a Situation of CC application) was about; nothing else. +T. Jefferson was not even a signer of the CON nor DOI, and not even a maker of the DOI. This situation, event, and letter has NOTHING to do with the CC (CON & DOI) etc. +On the day Thomas Jefferson sent his letter to the Church DEN he was making plans to attend Christian church assembly in the House of REP (2a). +T. Jefferson supported GOV having Christian activities in it. He signed a treaty in to law in AD 1803 that provided for a US GOV funded missionary to the Kaskaskia Indians. +Note the following supports to Christianity that Mr. Jefferson was part of: Virginia's CON in AD 1776 states, "That religion, or the duty which we owe to our Creator, and the manner of discharging it, can be directed only by reason and conviction, not by force or violence; and, therefore, that all men should enjoy the fullest toleration in the exercise of religion, according to the dictates of conscience, unpunished and unrestrained by the magistrate, unless under color of religion any man disturb the peace, the happiness, or safety of society, and that it is the mutual duty of all to practice Christian forbearance, love and charity toward each other". This makes a plain statement that, that State of Virginia, is a Christian GOV; and that that State requires duty that Christian attitudes be practiced; that such are owed to our Creator; there are not 2 Creators but only one; the main intention/ purpose is Christianity, as stated~ "moral duty of all to practice CHRISTIAN forbearance, love, and charity". Also, the statement therein is that DEN is included~ "the manner of discharging it". Now if Christ, the Creator, is the duty, then the manner thereof to discharge it, or apply the duty, is the DEN. The other Intentions/purposes of that Virginia CON include~ +did not want the GOV to control DEN; +did not want the State GOV to force Christianity, or to be the Ruler and make decisions for people; +wanted freedom for Christianity and DEN; +wanted Christianity and the Creator to be supported by the Virginia State GOV as the True Creator and religion. These sub-subjects here, all relate with the concerns at the start of this section on "Religion". +Now this is strange. Because all the letters that rightly define the 1-A, R-E, R~Est clause are rejected now, and yet these very people contradict themselves by doing such; because they use a little letter and make a big thing from it, which is also not rightly accurate, and then reject a big amount of letters and make them to be a little thing, or nothing. +Lastly, this situation was the following: +Was Only an application of the law. +Was Only by letters. +Was NOT by any enactment of congress. // R-E, 1-A, R~Est was part of Thomas Jefferson's statements for the Bill written in AD 1779, which are as follows, although the final version excluded the parenthesis content: "Well aware (that the opinions of men depend not on their own will, but follow involuntarily the evidence proposed to their minds) that Almighty God hath created the mind free,,, (that the opinions of men are not the object of civil GOV, nor under its jurisdiction) that to suffer the civil magistrate to intrude his powers into the field of opinion and to restrain the profession or propagation of principles, on supposition of their ill tendency is a dangerous fallacy which at once destroys all religious liberty ,,,that it is time enough for the rightful purpose of civil GOV for its officers to interfere when principles break out into overt acts against peace and good order ,,,We, the General Assembly, do enact, That no man shall be compelled to frequent or support any religious worship, place, or ministry whatsoever, nor shall be enforced, restrained, molested, or burdened in his body or goods, nor shall otherwise suffer, on account of his religious opinions or belief; but that all men shall be free to profess, and by agreement maintain, their opinion in matters of religion, and that the same shall in no wise diminish, enlarge, or affect their civil capacities" (50). +Note that Mr. Jefferson and this Congress discussed the subject of Heretics. The subject is the internal spirit condition that should not be forced to be a Christian. Neither is Heresy in HSC is to be reacted to with such an expression of killing. Christians are not to react by killing heretics; such is not a method or expression that is legal in HSC. Titus 3 is a HSC that tells to simply let them exist, but reject them, and tell them they are wrong. Thus T. Jefferson states that the GOV is not to control Christianity, nor force people to be Christians, nor control DEN. GOV is only to control the body actions, not personality or such, rather control by regulation of evil actions; as by a TO DO or NOT TO DO. +According to DOCs, John Locke was a valuable factor to T. Jefferson's concepts. Michael Malbin shared (51) that Mr. S. Gerald Sander submits a study proving John Locke's studies are in Mr. Jefferson's (99). A full comparison of Locke and Jefferson will not be submitted here, but here is some of Locke's writings: "civil interests" are "life, liberty, health and indolency of body; and the possessions of outward things, such as money, lands, houses, furniture, and the like"; and 'Civil authorities secure these things. But Church interests and such, is a free society that governs such ecclesiastical matters that civil is not to decide on. The Church is not to use physical power to force salvation on people' (99). Mr. Jefferson also says Christianity cannot be forced, and the civil authority cannot force internal belief, but only manage action, in preventing crimes against Christianity, which would also include forbidding allowance of false religions to practice outward actions (advertisements & assemblies) on USA soil though they may believe them internally. Mr. Jefferson states, "Our rulers can have no authority over ,,,natural rights ,,,rights of conscience ,,,answerable ,,,to God ,,,legitimate powers of government extend to such acts [[Acts here not internal beliefs, as he defines]] such as are injurious to others. But it does me no injury for my neighbor to say there are twenty gods, or no God [[notice he uses small letters for the word 'gods' showing he knows the person is believing in idolatry, and then uses a capital letter for the true God; and His existence, and not atheism]]. It neither picks my pocket nor breaks my leg,,," (51). +Mr. Jefferson & Mr. Locke agreed that atheism was wrong; that such religion cannot be allowed by GOV to set up its practice, must be limited; Also neither can any false religion, that is anti-Christian religion. However Mr. Locke also agreed that any verbal expression of atheism or anti-Christian religion should be managed by GOV, and penalized in some minor citation, as it is a threat to civil GOV and society. But Mr. Jefferson thought that the verbal expression of it was not to be GOV managed or penalized, but allow it, only in the private environment, but no public advertisement of it. Mr. Jefferson submitted Bills of Law to Virginia for speech crimes though, which included seditious (violence oriented) preaching, which is rebellion against civil GOV. Thus he had difficulties with how GOV and religion were to interact. Abuse potential could exist even in the GOV support of the Right.

/////////// Mr. James Madison; and various R-E, R~Est, 1-A Affectionate Concerns: // Mr. Madison constructed another version of 1-A as such. George Mason quoted Madison's version, and there were problems shared about it, because he thought the "toleration" word would give the interpretation to make the Rights coming from the GOV, when truly they are coming from God; as a free natural Right as created by God. Thus Mr. Mason made a version inserting a line, which reads as this~ "not of violence, or compulsion, all men are entitled to the full and free exercise of it according to the dictates of conscience; and therefore that no man or class of men ought on account of religion to be invested with particular emoluments or privileges, nor subjected to any penalties or disabilities, unless under color of religion the preservation of equal liberty, and the existence of the State be manifestly endangered" (75). Thus the only difference from Mason's and Madison's is the specification that the Rights come from God, and no GOV can usurp those Rights as they do not come from the GOV. Mr. Madison's version was rejected by Virginia congress as it provided too much allowance for GOV abuse on Christianity; All the remaining parts were kept but Mason's "free exercise" part was put in place

99

of "toleration", showing where the Rights come from, (GOD). // Other incidents occurred in Virginia between AD 1776 - 1785. Virginia's GOV penalized "dissenters" for expressing their religious opinions (which a dissenter was one who was non-Anglican), as the State GOV church was Anglican; it was an existing State Christian Church, the Anglican DEN. This proves that they intended for a Christian GOV, and protection of Christianity, and the exclusion of cults, or non-Christian; but that they did not know how to do the intention. They were now afraid that the GOV would gain excessive control as occurred in the history of Europe. Thus this penalty law on dissenters was eliminated. Also Dissenting ministers (non-Anglican) could not perform marriages unless they obtained a license, which said license, however, was not required of the State Church ministers. This law was removed in AD 1784. Also in a law that required the tithe collected go to the Anglican clergy (of the Episcopal Church) was eliminated. This law had GOV controlling the monies of the Church. Also there was a Bill of Law submitted to require "Establishing Support for teachers of the Christian Religion". But it failed as some thought GOV control of the Church excessive. However, the desires and intentions that GOV is to be Christian for Christ, support Christianity, that Christianity increase and be protected, and anti-Christian religions be refused, all existed. But there was much inability to word, apply, and design a GOV system to do these intention/ purposes; to do without abuse by GOV. The Bill mentioned, above, would have required all citizens to pay a tax for Christian workers in the teaching area. If Denominationalism was supported, then each person could specify which Christian church to give it to. The Law was planned to construct what essential doctrines made a Christian church. Thus, we see here the intention/ purpose was for~ +freedom of DENs in Christianity; and, +the avoidance of all non-Christian religions. Furthermore, at this same time, the congress voted to maintain the Episcopal Church as a GOV incorporation. What does this prove but a desire and intention that the GOV be Christian for Christ, and maintain Christianity (increase it and avoid oppositions- false religions). Hence, a reconvening meeting(s) during the next months occurred and members of other DEN spoke expressedly and the Bill of Law was removed. Mr. Madison's speech of Memorial and Remonstrance assisted to this intention~ in not favoring DENs. A general assessment on all Christian sects (DEN) could easily also be used for support of one sect also, so it was rejected. The reason Mr. Madison disagreed to GOV control of Christianity in the General Assessment Bill, was that some person(s) must have to decide on the essential and non-essential doctrines of Christianity; and, of the which doctrines, he listed out some of them in the report. And this "someone" to decide would be the GOV, and this he did not want. And inevitably the other congress members agreed; they did not want that either. This would open to that any disagreement on some area of Christian might then be called heresy, and then the GOV would gain control and even inflict punishments, which obviously removes religious liberty; and that is similar to what Europe did. The situation of Mr. Madison, is, that all the doctrines of Christianity are dependent on "light" as the Holy Bible says; That a man is not responsible to other men's "light" until he has it inside his mind and agrees with it. This is a heartily sensitivity affection. And the responsibility is to God. A non-essential doctrine (secondary doctrine) of Christianity, one that is not necessary to be right with God at the time, is (or are) not all learned all at once. Mr. Madison (in the letter, or Report, as named) said that many of the various doctrines of Christianity are~ "depending only on the evidence contemplated by their own minds, cannot follow the dictates of other men,,, is a duty towards the Creator ,,,and precedent both in order of time and degree of obligation,,,". Observe here he notes that "light" or the amount of Christian doctrines or knowledge is dependent on~ +God, +the man, +the timing of learning, +various circumstances of each individual, +the degree of such, or intensity or amount of learning, and +experience that each individual has with God. Some people may learn faster, others slower; some may be focused in one area more than others; some may be clergy others not; some may have had a Christian training or family, and others not; and so on, etc. // Some Moral Beings have asserted that Mr. Madison, in some of his ambiguous or difficult statements, was against USA GOV assistance to Christian religion. That is a lie. Observe all of his remarks and why he said them; for what intention reason, and what was the meetings about, and the terms and all of the other associated remarks he made. Plus he professed he was a Christian; and was a regular attendee of a Christian Church. He did reject Virginia tax benefits distributed to all churches, but this is a situation that the GOV being a funder of the church monetarily, a pass through, which was not agreed on. No opposition, rather support was promoted by Mr. Madison, for the USA GOV to assist Christian Churches financially in various efforts. By rejecting the GOV to control the Christian Churches is not a separation of State or GOV and Christ or His Christianity Religion, rather it is a support of the Rights & the Relations. GOV is to support God, Christianity, and the Religion thereof, not the other way around. If GOV controlled the Church finances then God and Christianity Religion would be supporting the GOV. Hence, rather then, though, not as a controlling of the monies to the Christian Church by going through the USA GOV first. Such, as these principles, is not opposition to the Christian Church, but a very obvious protection of the Christian Church from USA GOV abuse and control. No person desired the USA GOV to control, or be the taxman for the Christian Church. We know that they all, including Mr. Madison, intended/ purposed religion to flourish~ increase. +The Report (letter) of Memorial and Remonstrance by Mr. Madison is totally intended/ purposed of non-denominational favorism by the Virginia GOV; because they were voting to maintain the Episcopal Church as the GOV church and exclusion of other DENs. This Speech and Report was given in opposition to the General Assessment Bill. This is shown in the above congress meetings relayed and other notes in this section. +James Madison's statement has been misinterpreted. He was +a Christian, +supported Christianity, +attended a Christian Church, +supported Christian Chaplains to the Congress, and etc. Madison's statement of~ "Who does not see that the same authority which can establish Christianity, in exclusion of all other Religions, may establish with the same ease any particular sect [[DEN]] of Christians, in exclusions of all other Sects? [[DENs]] That the same authority which can force a citizen to contribute three pence only of his property for the support of any one establishment, may force him to conform to any other establishment in all cases whatsoever". What is the intention/ purpose of this statement? That~ +The power of the N GOV and its forcing peoples; +although Christianity is to be supported by N GOV, the power can be abused in requiring a DEN (Sect). So that is why they were so careful or confused or paradoxical on the wording; because they feared the N GOV would favor (partiality or "respecting") a DEN; that the same wording might be asserted if specific words were for excess positive or excess negative. The thought was essentially how do we give the N GOV power to support Christianity without the same tool (word) to be abused by GOV power to have a national church with partiality or favorism ("respecting") ? Mr. Madison was not saying to divide Christianity from N GOV, but rather on how to include it without it being abused. That is why he was asking the question, which says, I paraphrase, "yes we want Christianity, but remember how GOVs abused societies and DEN, and if we word it such and such a way, then, you all can notice, that the words might be used against the intention/ purpose for which we wrote them". Hence they continued to study on how to word the words to keep Christianity while preventing abuse by GOV. // The term "Religious establishment", used by James Madison, is defined as DEN (Christian); this is proved showing in his papers of "Memorial and Remonstrance": +The intention/ purpose of his paper and project was the Christian Church being supported by GOV in only one DEN. +Mr. Madison helped draft the 1-A which protects Christianity in general. +Following are some statements from Mr. Madison's paper Report of Memorial and Remonstrance, but not in exact order: ",,,the establishment proposed by this Bill is not the requisite for the support of the Christian Religion. [[The use of the word "religion" on the end of Christian, is referring to DEN of Christianity]]. To say that it is, is a contradiction to the Christian Religions itself; for every page of it disavows a dependence on the powers of this world ,,,this Religion both existed and flourished, not only without the support of human laws, but in spite of every opposition from them ,,,during the period of miraculous aid ,,,and the ordinary care of Providence ,,,Religion not invented by human policy ,,,preexisted and,,, supported ,,,before human policy ,,,Union of religious sentiments begets a surprising confidence, and Ecclesiastical Establishments [[Ecc. Esta. are words for Christian DEN]] tend to great ignorance and Corruption ,,, During almost fifteen centuries, has the legal establishment of Christianity been on trial,,, What has been its fruits? ,,,pride and indolence in the Clergy; bigotry and persecution. Enquire of the Teachers of Christianity for the ages in which it appeared in its greatest luster; those of every sect [[sect is DEN]], point to the ages prior to its incorporation with Civil policy ,,,Whilst we assert for ourselves a freedom to embrace, to profess, and to observe the Religion which we believe to be of divine origin, [[here he supports Christianity]] we cannot deny an equal freedom to those whose minds have not yielded to the evidence which has convinced us. If this freedom be abused, it is an offence against God, not against man: To God, therefore, not to man, must an account of it be rendered ,,,This right is in its nature an unalienable right ,,,It is the duty of every man to render to the Creator such homage, and such only, as he believes to be acceptable to him. This duty is precedent both in order of time and degree of obligation ,,,Before any man can be considered as a member of Civil Society, he must be considered as a subject of the Governor of the Universe ,,,much more must every man who becomes a member of any particular Civil Society, do it with a saving of his allegiance to the Universal Sovereign,,,". Note that he clearly states that "before" being an officer of GOV - "Civil Society" - "he must be a Subject", ~that is willing intention, "of the Governor of the Universe" ~ that is God. Thus the USA GOV (Law-making Branches) require Christian people in Office, but not of any specific DEN. Then Mr. Madison brought a paper with the Bill of Rights which showed some of the Christian denominational debates that were occurring; and said that Christianity in its activity about DEN will take care of itself; and that realm is out of GOV control. Some of the doctrines that the Christian DEN were discussing are in more of Mr. Madison's remarks in the Memorial & Remonstrance Paper Report; proving he was referring to Christian DENs and not Christianity in general; they are statements and in the form of questions. Following are some, which I paraphrase or shorten: +"Which Bible edition, Hebrew, Septuagint, Vulgate, copy, translation; Which canonical books, apocryphal, Lutheran, protestant"; + "Which method of inspired, viewed, dictated every letter by inspiration, essential parts only, matter in general words"; +"What doctrines are essential and what not; is it Trinitarianism, Arianism, Socinianism; salvation by faith or works also; by grace of free will"; +"What church system for workers to judge questions such as these; what is orthodoxy and heresy". Thus, as you read, all these are of the True God, of Christianity; and are only parts of it in the doctrinal, and expressions of assembly worship. The project of the Congress assembly here, with Mr. Madison and his Paper, was on discussing and making a Bill to provide tax~ "for the support of the Christian religion,,, church,,,". Mr. Madison was not opposing Christianity to be supported by the GOV in general, and in issues, but that the GOV does not become the money supporter and system that supplies the Church with money and makes the Church doctrine decisions. A system such as that was, by all, disagreed to. The Church finances, secondary doctrinal subjects, and worship expressions are to remain with the Church people, not the GOV; And to have the GOV receive taxes going through it before it goes to every Church DEN, or to some particular DEN, makes a very complex situation; and then the GOV would also become involved in deciding doctrinal issues. Mr. Madison explains the 1-A definition in a Congress meeting as this: ",,,Congress should not establish a religion and enforce the legal observation of it by law, nor compel men to worship God in any manner contrary to their conscience ,,,infringe the rights of conscience and establish a National Religion". The "conscience" word he used, is a Christian word and thus to offend this is an offense against God. Thus the 4 parts to the subject were such: 1} The GOV should not force people to believe Christianity or become Christians which is against free will; 2} GOV should not force any Christian DEN; 3} GOV should not be the financiers of all Christian churches; 4} GOV should not make a law for only one, or a few, particular Christian DEN. Mr. Madison did not say the GOV should not be for Christ, or Christian, or Christian supportive; because his life and statements reported already prove contrary. For EX here is a statement he made~ ",,,the belief in a God All powerful wise and good, is so essential to the moral order of the World and to the happiness of man,,,". At times, Mr. Madison, in his life, was undecided as to how to apply the laws, which shows that he was intending the GOV to remain Christian; but not let the GOV have ways to abuse Christianity in the future. Thus he supported the proclamation of national Christian holidays, for all who are "disposed" to worship God, but that the GOV would not force any to do so. Following is another statement he made which is intended that both the USA GOV is Christian but that GOV is not to force any Being to do such: "If the public homage of a people ,,,regard of the Holy and Omniscient Being ,,,guided ,,,by ,,,free choice, by the impulse of their hearts and the dictates of their consciences ,,,alone can be acceptable to Him whom no hypocrisy can deceive and no forced sacrifices propitiate".

/////////// CON Influence from Thomas Jefferson & James Madison: // Thomas Jefferson was not the only person, nor the largest effort on the CON, and surely not the DOI. He admits that he was not, as such, in a letter to Mr. Dry Joseph Priestly, June 1802, writing, "One passage in the paper you enclosed me must be corrected. It is the following, 'And all say it was yourself more than any other individual, that planned and established it', i.e., the CON. I was in Europe when the CON was planned and never saw it till after it was established." (30). In fact, TJ shares that he had little influence in reviewing the related CON meeting notes. // James Madison, in a letter to William Cogswell Mar. 10, 1834, states: "You give me a credit to which I have no claim in calling me 'the writer of the CON of the US'. This was not, like the fabled Goddess of Wisdom, the offspring of a single brain. It ought to be regarded as the work of many heads and many hands." (201). // Additionally, the fact is that, if any person would read some of any other person's of the FFOG's works, such as Samuel Adams or John Witherspoon or Elias Boudinot, they can easily see a much studied and influential terms from these people.

/////////// Courts and Various Officials have wrongly taken 1 or 2 statements from Mr. Jefferson & Mr. Madison; and misinterpreted them. Sadly it has occurred with other materials from our FFOG.

---T--- END of Mr. Madison & Mr. Jefferson Parts about the subject of Religion.

---T--- R-E is Intended/ purposed Not To Prohibit Religion of GOD~ +] in the USA, +] from the USA GOV: // Now if Religion is not prohibited in the USA then how co/ it be prohibited in the USA GOV? The 2 must agree or they will disagree. If they disagree then religion in the USA is open to prohibition: // Following is some of the Congress meetings that occurred about the subject. Peter Sylvester's speech to Congress on 8/15, 1789 shared RE subject of the language: "might be thought to have a tendency to abolish religion altogether". This statement is referring to the GOV preventing the explanation or interpretation that the USA is not to have any religion at all. Congress was in the process of the project of wording the CON of the CC. +Congress CON meetings continue that day as Mass. State REP Elbridge Gerry wants to arrange the phrase so that religion is not excluded in the USA GOV, but only non-DEN; thus he suggest using this statement: "no religious doctrine shall be established by law". This refers not to Christianity, but to the Secondary Doctrines of Christianity; these are what normally separates Christian DEN; also they are separated sometimes by practices, expressions in the assembly, or rituals or ceremonies, and some of these may be similar and different. // Then Mr. Sherman remarks RE that USA GOV have no authority to pass legislation RE religion. // Then James Madison spoke as follows as recorded by Lloyd: "Mr Madison said, he apprehended the meaning of the words to be, that Congress should not establish a religion and enforce the legal observation of it by law, nor compel men to worship God in any manner contrary to their conscience. Whether the words are necessary or not, he did not mean to say, but they had been required by some of the State Conventions, who seemed to entertain an opinion that under the clause of the CON, which gave power to Congress to make all laws necessary and proper to carry into execution the constitution, and the laws under, enabled them to make laws of such a nature as might infringe the rights of conscience and establish a national religion". Now you can see here that the DOI was being included in the CON construction; which again proves the CC; that God & His Religion is intended to be included. // Benjamin Huntington next shared the same as Sylvester's (per above) concern intended, saying, "that the words might be taken in such latitude as to be extremely hurtful to the cause of religion" and "hoped, therefore, the amendment would be made in such a way as to secure the rights of conscience, and a free exercise of the rights of religion, but not to patronize those who professed no religion at all". Hence he is saying a few sub-subjects of the main subject; identifying that~ a} GOV is to be supportive of Religion of Christ; b} GOV is not to be neutral about Religion of Christ; c} GOV is to protect from DEN partiality; d} GOV is to not force Christianity nor DEN on Folk; e} these are all Freedom Rights. // Mr. Madison next said if the word "national" was put in before "religion", as he previously had it, then that would solve the problems of Mr. Sylvester & Mr. Huntington. // Next then, Lloyd talks about Madison's words: "Madison believed that the people feared one sect [[Christian DEN]] might obtain a pre-eminence, or two combine together, and establish a religion to which they would compel others to conform. He thought that if the word national was introduced, it would point the amendment directly to the object it was intended to prevent". Thus here we see clearly and plainly that the R~Est clause is defined as Christian DEN, that one might gain pre-eminence, which is "respecting" (favorism), one or two even together, by a Law; and then excluded or force out all other Christian DEN; and even force that DEN on them and all the land; that it would require all people to only support one or two DEN. // Furthermore they intended/ purposed to only support Christianity, the main primary doctrines of God, man, and truth; Yet simultaneously not to support only one DEN, which is any secondary doctrines, expressions, or organizations. // Samuel Livermore, REP of New Hampshire, suggested the phrase be worded as "Congress shall not make any laws touching religion, or infringing the rights of conscience". // Next Elbridge Gerry stated that if the word "national" was inserted, then the Independency of the States might be threatened; because the word "national" would possibly provide people to excessive central GOV control (by N GOV). // Then Aug 20 meeting occurs with Fisher Ames, Rep of Mass., suggesting that a previous version be used as the clause language, which says, "Congress shall make no law establishing religion, or to prevent the free exercise thereof, or to infringe the rights of conscience". Now there seems to be no record of any further discussion provided for that day on this topic.

However there must have been discussion either not recorded, or out of the session meetings, because the subject went forward to the voting day of Sept 3. A similar version to Mr. Fisher Ames was presented for the final voting day; and this clause language reads: "Congress shall make no law establishing one religious sect or society in preference to others, or to infringe on the rights of conscience". This version dropped the free exercise clause which was concerned; Yet it proves again that Religion is DEN; that the intention was to support Christianity and not require a DEN. The Senate passed this version on the second round after a first defeat. They rejected a motion to eliminate the clause. They also rejected 2 other versions presented that day which read: "Congress shall not make any law infringing the rights of conscience, or establishing any religious sect or society" and "Congress shall make no law establishing any particular DEN of religion in preference to another, or prohibiting the free exercise thereof, nor shall the rights of conscience be infringed". That is only the Senate part of Congress, not the "House" part. Only the voting and versions is given for the meeting; not much open discussion recorded. // It may be the States were concerned over excessive central control. // The final version that passed then is this, "Congress shall make no law establishing religion, or prohibiting the free exercise thereof". Recorded at this time was the dissatisfaction of some senators who wanted more detail said about the exacting dimensions of the relationship of religion and GOV; of what was said to be "establishments". On Sept 9, a version was passed saying, "Congress shall make no law establishing articles of faith or a mode of worship, or prohibiting the free exercise of religion". Here we continue to observe the balance of freedom for Christianity and yet no DEN, of it, as such be given special GOV privileges of favorism; or made the N. GOV church. The House refused the version asking for conference. No record of discussion is given. The House sent this one up for vote: "Congress shall make no law respecting an establishment of religion, or prohibiting the free exercise thereof". It was passed by the House on Sept 24, and by the Senate on Sept 25.

---T--- <u>Congressional Meetings Discussions</u> Prove that the Christ's "religious establishment" is DEN: // Here in J. Elliot's record states: "That religion, or duty which we owe to our Creator, and the manner of discharging it, can be directed only by reason and conviction, not by force and violence; and therefore all men have an equal, natural and unalienable right to the free exercise of religion, according to the dictates of conscience, and that no particular religious sect or society ought opt be favored or established by law in preference to others" (98). // Note that~ +] the duty is to God, not any god; +] the word conscience is used, which is a Christian word relating to being good or wrong with God; +] no person will force any DEN on any other person, as Europe did; +] we do not force Christianity on any person, except that they abide by the Christian laws of the land; but interiorly they may agree with what they want; but they may not have public idolatry gods in the land; +] "respecting" is a "favoring" and that it refers to DEN; making a law for it; and Europe also had particular sects or societies, (DEN) as GOV supported; and then persecuted the other DEN or excluded them.

---T--- <u>God's R-E, 1-A is DEN Defined</u>: // Benjamin Rush, signer of the DOI, (also called the Father of American Medicine), says, "It would seem as if one of the designs of Providence in permitting the existence of so many sects of Christians ,,,some great truth ,,,be better preserved,,, Moravians ,,,Episcopal, Presbyterian, and Baptist ,,Quakers ,,,Holy Spirit ,,,Let the different sects of Christians not only bear with each other, but love each other,,," (244).

---T--- <u>No Enactments against Christ nor His Christianity;</u> & Principle Law was the Intentional/ Purpose Design of the System; & Religion includes DEN of Christianity: // "No purpose of action against religion can be imputed to any legislation, State, or national, because this is a religious people ,,,This is a Christian nation." US Supreme Court Case, Church of the Holy Trinity vs US. 1892. // FFoG John Adams states, "The general principles on which the fathers achieved independence were ,,,the general principles of Christianity ,,,those general principles of Christianity are as eternal and immutable as the existence and attributes of God" (21a). // FFOG Governor James Hammond of South Carolina, in AD 1844 encouraged the public by stating, ",,,I have always thought it a settled matter that I lived in a Christian land and that I was the temporary chief magistrate of a Christian people! That in such a country and among such a people I should be publicly called to an account, reprimanded, and required to make amends for acknowledging Jesus Christ as the Redeemer of the world,,," (255). // Most presidents of the USA have declared we are a Christian nation for Jesus Christ.

---T--- <u>In the USA, a Court Case, in AD 1985,</u> Supported that the 1-A had been previously interpreted & fully known to not promote false religions & anti-Christian religion & lifestyle; because the conscience needs freedom for Christ's presence; part of it states this: // "At one time it was thought that this right merely proscribed the preference of one Christian sect over another, but would not require equal respect for the conscience of the infidel, the atheist, or the adherent of a non-Christian faith such as Islam or Judaism. But when the underlying principle has been examined in the crucible of litigation, the Court has unambiguously concluded that the individual freedom of conscience protected by the First Amendment embraces the right to select any religious faith or none at all. This conclusion derives support not only from the interest in respecting the individual's freedom of conscience, but also from the conviction that religious beliefs worthy of respect are the product of free and voluntary choice by the faithful, and from recognition of the fact that the political interest in forestalling intolerance extends beyond intolerance among Christian sects-- or even intolerance among "religions"--to encompass intolerance of the disbeliever and the uncertain". // Now this is a promotion of good fairness, justice, and consideration for the poor infidel, sinner, and false religionist. However it Does Not provide a total study of the subject; which more specifically identified would be that the USA GOV opposes infidelity (which is sinning), and false religion. FFOG stated that Christianity internally was not forced to people; however they were not allowed to put in practice on USA soil various public activities; No, they were not forced to internally accept Christ, nor go to Church; but neither could they start a false religion on USA soil with public assemblies &

advertisements. The subject here is tolerance, conscience, freedom to decide a persons religion, whether true or untrue. However limitations are not discussed here; limitations on Islam, or infidelism, or atheism, DO exist; they are limited, etc.

---T--- Thomas Paine intentionally uses religion as Christian DEN, of Christ, in his "Common Sense" DOC to support America as independent: // "As to religion, I hold it to be the indispensable duty of all GOV, to protect all conscientious professors thereof, and I know of no other business which GOV hath to do therewith ,,,diversity of religious opinions among us: It affords a larger field for our Christian kindness. Were we all of one way of thinking, our religious dispositions would want matter for probation; and on this liberal principle, I look on the various DENs among us, to be like children of the same family, differing only, in what is called, their Christian names." This was stated approx. during DOI time.

---T--- The Inalienable Right from God: // For humankind there is a desire for purpose and towards societal community communion (fellowship). FFOG George Mason, as one of the authors of the Virginia Declaration of Rights, stated that our Being is best "directed only by reason and conviction, not by force or violence."

---T--- God's Religion can~ +] neither be separated, +] nor dis-involved, +] nor excluded: // God is God as was said in the DOI of the CC; includes God, not excludes Him. God tells (in HSC) that He intends to be included in these parts of life as not-idolatry, rather God~ "Abstain from all appearance of evil; touch not the unclean thing; whether you eat or drink or whatever you do, do all to the glory of God" 1The5:22; 1Cor10:31.

---T--- England, as all countries have, changed in areas, both as a Nation & with specific Spiritual Moral Agents who lived there: // One Spiritual Moral Being, who had others helping him, is King James, who was assistant to the Old English Bible~ the King James Version. They helped bring Christianity to America. The following are facts about King James I (260i): +Was a Christian. +Intended & Wanted the Holy Bible to all people. +Commissioned the Authorized King James Bible in AD 1611. +Fluent in Greek, Latin, French, English, Scots. Schooled in Italian & Spanish. +Wrote against the use of tobacco. +William Shakespeare was one of his subjects of study. +Learning & writing increased during the King's reign. +Formed the foundation for what is now known as the British Empire by uniting in AD 1603; First to call it Great Britain. +Reformation assistant, John Knox, read a sermon when he was crowned King. +King James was sickly, having crippling arthritis, weak limbs, abdominal colic, gout, and a number of other chronic illnesses; also physical handicaps effecting his legs & tongue; He required constant attention and care. +Opposed the Roman Catholic religion; Roman clerics tried to kill him more than once. +The King was born during the time of the Reformation. +In AD 1536, falsity religions burned William Tyndale to death for distributing the Holy Bible, and it was partly because of the King James' authorized Bible in English. +Roman Catholic Nicolo Molin, an ambassador, said that King James~ ",,,is a Protestant ,,,tries to extend his Protestant religion to the whole island. The King is a bitter enemy of our religion (Roman Catholic) ,,,frequently speaks of it in terms of contempt. He is all the harsher because of this last conspiracy (Gun Powder Plot) against his life,,, He understood that the Jesuits had a hand in it." +King James said this in Basilicon Doron: "I am no papist as I said before ,,Now faith ,,,is the free gift of God (as Paul sayeth). It must be nourished by prayer, which is nothing else but a friendly talking to God. Use oft to pray when ye are quiet, especially in your bed,,,". +He led a chaste life. Sir Henry Wotton (June 1602) said the following of King James: "There appears a certain natural goodness verging on modesty ,,,He wears short hair,,, among his good qualities none shines more brightly than the chasteness of his life, which he has preserved without stain down to the present time, contrary to the example of almost all his ancestors,,,." +F. A. Inderwick wrote in AD 1891: "James had a reputation for learning, for piety, for good nature, and for liberality." +In AD 1603, Sir Roger Wilbaham wrote: "The King is of sharpest wit and invention ,,,of the sweetest, most pleasant, and best nature that I ever knew, desiring nor affecting anything but true honor." +King James cared much for literature and wrote much, including the Basilicon Doron which contains instructions to his son on how to live, including this about rightness: "Keep your body clean and unpolluted while you give it to your wife whom to only it belongs, for how can you justly crave to be joined with a virgin if your body be polluted? Why should the one half be clean, and other defiled? And suppose I know, fornication is thought but a venial sin by the most part of the world, yet remember well what I said to you in my first book regarding conscience, and count every sin a breach of God's law, not according as the vain world esteems of it, but as God, Judge and Maker of the law, accounts of the same: hear God commanding by the mouth of Paul to abstain from fornication, declaring that the fornicator shall not inherit the kingdom of heaven, and by the mouth of John reckoning out fornication among other grievous sins that declares the committers among dogs and swine.". He continues with advice to his son on how to treat his wife: "your behavior to your wife, the Scripture can best give you counsel therein. Treat her as your own flesh, command her as her lord, cherish her as your helper, rule her as your pupil, please her in all things reasonable, but teach her not to be curious in things that belong not to her. You are the head, she is your body, it is your office to command and hers to obey, but yet with such a sweet harmony as she should be as ready to obey as you to command, as willing to follow as you to go before, your love being wholly knit unto her, and all her affections lovingly bent to follow your will." +King James loved his wife, Queen Anne, and wrote beautifully of her. They had nine children together. +King James is the founding Monarch of the United States. Under his reign, we have the first successful colonies planted on the American mainland: Virginia, Massachusetts, and Nova Scotia. King James ordered, wrote, and authorized this Evangelistic Grant Charter to settle the Colony of Virginia: "To make habitation,,, and to deduce a colony of sundry of our people into that part of America, commonly called Virginia ,,,in propagating of Christian religion to,,, people as yet live in darkness ,,,to bring a settled and quiet government."

---T--- The USA GOV exists with intentions/ purposes to~ a] secure Rights for Christ's Christians, b] protect Christ's Christian's consciences, c] not oppose Christ nor His Christianity, d] a-c is the duty of all Spiritual Moral Beings living withi, including GOV officials, +] be Christ religious, & that

104

DENs to be equal: // FFOG George Washington speaking at a yearly meeting of the Quaker Christians DEN states: "GOV ,,,among other purposes, instituted to protect the persons and consciences of men from oppression, it certainly is the duty of rulers ,,,themselves ,,,prevent it in others ,,,The liberty enjoyed by the people of these States, of worshipping Almighty God agreeably to their consciences, is ,,,their blessings ,,,their rights. While men perform their social duties faithfully, they do all that society or the state with propriety demand or expect; and remain responsible only to their Maker for the religion, or modes of faith, which they may prefer or profess" (100). He also states: "The blessed Religion revealed in the word of God,,,"~ regarding Christ & His Religion & His Holy Bible.

---T--- <u>FFOG Samuel Adams intended rightness to Christ by</u> defending to be independent from the fallen British GOV; as one reason because their religion was sure to be destroyed by 'Popery' or Episcopacy (104a). That is a DEN being favored ("respect") by the GOV.

---T--- <u>Christ's Christianity is Intended/ purposed to~ +] be supported as the GOV</u> religion; +] yet no special treatment for Christian DEN: // Such is proved by the Northwest Ordinance that was enacted in AD 1787 and reenacted in AD 1789. This states "Religion, morality, and knowledge, being necessary to good GOV and the happiness of mankind, schools and the means of learning shall forever be encouraged". This provided USA GOV lands and assistance for Christ & His Christian schools & Christian activities. The Enactment says "Should be FOREVER encouraged'. It Does Not say "NOT FOREVER" but "Forever"; thus continually and never discouraged.

---T--- <u>New York's State CON in AD 1783 Intended/ Purposed</u> to support Christ of Christianity & DEN: // "providing us in this State with,,, good ,,,a CON, for the securing our,,, rights and privileges. I do not say,, has not its imperfections, like all human institutions ,,,The rights of conscience, both in faith and worship, are fully secured to every DEN of Christians. Not one DEN in the State, or in any of the States, have it in their power to oppress another. They all stand upon the same common level, in point of religious privileges [[here note that DEN was the application of the word~ "religion; Judaism of the Jews, is an early Christian doctrine]] ,,,Nor is this confined to Christians only. The Jews also, which is their undoubted right, have the liberty of worshipping God ,,,no man is excluded from the rights of citizenship, on account of his religious profession, nor ought to be." [[the original words were slightly different in spelling due to older English spellings]] (46).

---T--- <u>Patrick Henry was a strong defend</u>er of the Intention/purpose to~ +] not have favor to one DEN, +] very much support that the USA GOV should be for Christ & Christianity. He worked very hard for both causes (9).

---T--- <u>Judge Story, a signer of the CON, said that</u> the Christ's religion term "religious establishment" is defined as including Christian DEN: // "It was under a solemn consciousness of the dangers from ecclesiastical ambition [[here is an attitude that can occur in clergy; a danger that the GOV tempts the clergy to compete against each other to be the GOV church; this is what causes DENs to sub-doctrines of Christianity; actually a whole multitude of temptations are presented to the clergy and Christian DENs when one is supported by the GOV and others not; rather they should attend to their conscience & communion with God's presence]], the bigotry of spiritual pride, and the intolerance of sects [[DENs is the definition of sects]], thus exemplified in our domestic as well as in foreign annals, that it was deemed advisable to exclude from the N GOV all power to act upon the subject (of religion and the 'things that are God's)". Now Mr. Judge Story was there in the room during the CON discussion, and he testifies that the definition of the word "religion" & "establishment" of the CON is Christ, Christian, & DEN.

---T--- <u>Another Intention/ purpose reason No Church or DEN is said</u> in the CON is that most of the States already had established State Christian Churches; and they decided that this statehood Right would remain with the States; and that the USA GOV would not establish a Christian Church religion (DEN); because for one it would cause division since the States had various Christian DENs they were supporting; and because the USA GOV could not have them all be established (9). This is a fact, well documented in history. If a DEN was named, then the States would think it was referring to them, and thus they would not join. Therefore they used the word R~Est in general without any DEN name; which includes the Priority Christian doctrines and all DEN~ all in one.

---T--- <u>"Religion" is the word for DEN</u>. R~Est is the word for DEN.

---T--- <u>Add these words together:</u> // God + Truth + Lord Jesus + Lifestyles + Christian DEN attendance + Activity + Holidays + Events + History + Religion, then Equals == Christianity —(less) idolatry —(less) falsities + (add) with Limitations of Contraries & Opposites.

---T--- <u>Alabama's CON of AD 1812 stated</u> Christ Care as this: // "There shall be no establishment of religion by law; no preference shall ever be given by law to any religious sect, society, DEN, or mode of worship; and no religious test shall ever be required as a qualification to any office or public trust under this state". Many of the States have in their CON that religion refers to DEN & Christianity.

---T--- <u>Testimony from Alexis de Tocqueville</u>, in paper of "Democracy in America" states: // "Religion in America ,,,must be regarded as the first of their political institutions ,,,I am certain that they hold it to be indispensable to the maintenance of their political institutions". GOV is under the "first"; and religion is part of the political institution; not excluded.

---T--- <u>1-A has intention/ purpose by statement that~</u> +] the USA GOV has no power to be god over Christ God, Christianity or true religion; states~ "not prohibit the free exercise of religion or religious establishments".

---T--- <u>Limits to evils against God's religion intended/ purposed:</u> // The FFOG studied nations with unlimited laws for false religions; they would abuse religions even on Holidays. An EX studied was of 2 nations as such having a war; that while they sung a hymn to God together as 2 opposing fighting armies, would then immediately thereafter the hymn, return to war fighting and killing each other.

---T--- <u>1-A makes Illegal all unlimited non-Christian</u> activity on USA Soil; by stating that the Lord JESUS CHRIST, God, is The Supreme Ruler of the USA; This includes the Holy Bible, which opposes all evil; also God is a total rightness Being, therefore.

---T--- <u>The Sept. 1774 meetings of Congress Prioritizing Prayer to Christ:</u> // Had a discussion about the worsening relationship with Britain. // Prayer was decided on to be done before the sessions. // John Jay & Edward Rutledge, {both professing Christians (2)(2a)(3); John Jay was President of the American Bible Society (2)}, proclaimed that there were various DENs present and how would this be thought of. // Samuel Adams said, "I am no bigot; I can hear a prayer from any man of piety and virtue, who is at the same time a friend to his country" (8). // John Adams recommended Rev Jacob Duche, an Episcopalian clergyman, to pray for the meetings; and it was agreed on. // Thus Religious DEN was a concern of the meetings. // All 55 congress REPs at the meeting were professing Christians, but of different DENs. 2 REPs had been involved with the deist DEN, at some time in their life. But both of these supported the Holy Bible as truth (9). // Those deists members changed later to more closer Christianity.

---T--- <u>According to all accurate historians & history students about DEN & 1-A:</u> // Sometimes the negatives are magnified; and to such degree that that it is difficult to know of any good at the time. This is not right interpretation to do. // There was an increase in the various increase of Christianity in the land in the form of DENs (Christian) starting. This is one sure EV as to the reason for the statements in the CON. Free exercise pertains to Christ's Christianity to be protected, but then they did not know what to do with all the sects or DENs. The CON was drafted in less than 100 days and these times were not easy; there were foreign threats, the Nation was un-established and without any stable GOV DOCs or tools to unify. So thus they proclaimed the Establishment Clause to~ +prevent any Christian DEN to gain control over the others, +to keep the States Free for State DEN Churches, +yet provide opportunity that the States would join the Nation, by the CON. // So what the historians tell us, and that which is even now occurring~ +Christianity increase in nation, +DENs starting, +various DENs dividing, +increase in technology and travel, making denominationalism easier to start, and more options exist and offer. Not that the Holy Bible is divided, but rather that~ +interpretation was inaccurate, as is now, +some people had little KN, especially on lesser Christian doctrines, +Holy Bibles were needed, +doctrines were remaining in debate and unsettled. So the DENs were increasing. We know of such a situation as that for this is how it is now. Thus it was sort of strifeful with the divisions, not physically, rather spiritually; and the FFOG knew there had been religious wars historically, even many themselves, their kin or friends had escaped it; and forefathers, even martyrs. So the way the FFOG reacted was to protect Christianity with the Free Exercise Clause (which we repeat, pertains to the Christian religion and none else); and then the Establishment Clause, to protect all the DENs so that none would get favored by a Law; as did the Church of England, which then abused the other ones, and become false Christianity. // Now to specify the denominationalism that was occurring, let me only name some of the churches that were arising and working in the areas: Moravians; Lutherans; Methodists; Catholics; Quakers; Anglicans; Dunkers; Episcopalians; Baptist of various divisions; Presbyterians; Congregationalist; Calvinist's of various divisions; Arminian's of various divisions. And we could name many more. // Denominationalism occurrence was less known in the AD 1700 ~1800's, than in our times currently; we know of it more.

---T--- <u>Continuing with this Subject of Christian Sects (DEN) Starting,</u> Disputing, & Dividing; & clarifying again that DENs is what the R-E, R~Est refers to in its definition: // During CC times, activities & events were occurring as follows: // The following situation put in double parenthesis is paraphrased from cite (73): {{A DEN with members, such as Isaac Backus with his family & mother Elizabeth, started a Christian sect (DEN) called The Separatist; which divided from involvement with the Congregationalist. They had opposition from other DENs, such as the Congregationalist & Baptists, about standards, activities, and taxes, etc. One subject at this time, was that some States were giving tax favor ("respecting") to some established Christian DENs and not to others; which Isaac Backus and some other small DENs contended with GOV about. These DEN disputes were taken to GOV courts and Isaac Backus got individuals on Congress involved, such as Samuel Adams. The situations were taken before State GOV Officials. These instances continued, as the Separatists Baptists, Quakers, "Old Baptists", etc., had open and GOV disputes, regarding favor with GOV, with taxes, with various subjects. The GOV was troubled. Situations were taken to the king of England by "address". Various DEN (Sects) went before the Continental Congress to present cases. John & Samuel Adams listened to presentations; Mr. Backus, a diligent note-taker and record keeper, noted that Mr. Adams said of the situation, that because the denomination was numerically so small, "a very slender one, hardly to be called an establishment"; referring to the DEN Isaac Backus was involved with; and that Charles Chauncy was against established Christian DENs, saying, "in principle against all civil establishments in religion".}}. // Thus note~ +all the denominational disputing, +concern how GOV & DEN co/ all relate to each other, +that the Nation was unorganized and undeveloped, +the Nation desired to be a Christian Nation. Note also that establishment and religion are the words and definitions pertaining to DENs. // The REP were in contemplation as to how to manage the situations. They could not take care of every problem of the world. They fully intended to Christ & Christianity be~ +supported, +Freedom Rights provided & protection, +in the USA GOV and Nation. That was already accomplished by the DOI; However further development was needed. The AOC were inadequate and the States, or Colony States were in disputes. Now the frequency and occurrence of many DEN disputes was occurring. // So what to do? US Congress tried to accomplish the Christian DEN to work together. // Following is from cite (73) paraphrased about Benjamin Franklin: Requested for a "public religion" which was to be Christian, but educate against superstition, and promote religious character and oppose moral depravity; wrote a paper on it saying the "public religion" would promote "the Excellency of the Christian religion above all others ancient or modern". // Pres. George Washington stated that the Christian DEN were living together more positively "than ever they have done in any former

106

age, or in any other nation." (73). // FFOG Thomas Jefferson noted in a notebook that, "Who are to be reputed good Christians? In Rome papists; in Geneva Calvinists; in north Germany, Lutherans; in London, none of the above"; also noting that Christian DEN were "one thing at one time and in one place,,, something else at another time, and in another place, or even in the same place" (73). // Many of the DEN decided to work together for the Revolution; Yet Some others did not agree with war, even defensive war. (73). // However many of them did not know how to work with other DEN; or what kind of relationship to have with other DEN (73). // Patrick Henry introduced a Bill titled the General Assessment Bill that named Christianity the established religion of Virginia. It provided a plan allowing each person to select a Christian Church of decision to share tax proceeds (73). // The USA GOV was not to have a law favoring a DEN, but the States could; because they were independently free in many areas.

---T--- There Is Not One Statement in the Structure of the USA that Declares or Asserts that the USA should be an "anything goes" nation. In other words~ +] it is a system to include in every place & in all activities of whether it is~ good or evil, truth or lie. +] It is not a system of~ 'every person to themselves, whenever, wherever, however, whatever': // That sort of system would eliminate the DOI with "truth" and "God" and "right"; and eliminate all the FFoG actions, activities, supporting DOCs, etc. If this was an 'anything and everything is allowed nation', then it would be a pagan nation. And this was clearly rejected in the Congress notes and in the CC.

---T--- The "Checks & Balances" system with God: // Such is said as part of the USA GOV often in the DOCs. // It is a system that~ +includes Christ's "religion"; +includes the congress notes, the DOI, and applies them. // Religion is part of the Checks & the Balances. // This is not a nation of evil religions or false religions but true religions. What Spiritual Moral Being will stand up and say that the FFOG said the USA should be Satanism, or paganism ?? // The Christian God & Religion is to~ +Check the GOV, +Check the Evil, +Balance the abusive potentials, +Check some evils by Stops, and Check other evils by limits.

---T--- Now what good or of what intention/ purpose, or use would a DOI & CON & supporting DOCs be for ?? What if not to apply ?? They are Not To be~ +rejected, +ignored, +excluded, +lied, +interpreted any way at any time.

---T--- From the First Meeting of Congress & continuing, the activity included was~ +] God, +] Christian Prayer to God, +] reading of Holy SC, +] pastor of a Christian Church. (8). // John Adams encourages that when future citizens of USA celebrate the DOI, they should have religious meetings and give thanks to God for it; states~ "by solemn acts of devotion to God almighty from one end of the continent to the other, from this time forward and forevermore" (8).

---T--- "Religion" had 2 definitions with our FFOG: // George Washington used "religion" as referring to: 1} True Right Religion & false wrong religion. 2} DEN. +He said the USA GOV is to be religious, and to support and promote the true Religion, not false religion. +He also used religion as referring to DENs as noted.

---T--- FFOG George Washington explains God's definition of the use of the word "religion" or "religious" or "Religious Establishment" as DENs: // "Every man conducting himself as a good citizen, and being accountable to God alone for his religious opinions, ought to be protected in worshipping the Deity ,,,If I could have entertained the slightest apprehension that the CON framed in the Convention, where I had the honor to preside, might possibly endanger the religious rights of any ecclesiastical Society, [[note this is a term used for Christian DEN]] certainly I would never have placed my signature to it; if I could conceive that the general GOV might ,,,render liberty of conscience insecure, I beg you will be persuaded that no one ,,,more zealous than myself to establish effectual barriers against the horrors of spiritual tyranny, [[which is false religions, no religion, abusive religion]] and every species of religious persecution ,,,Be assured, Gentlemen, that I entertain a proper sense of your fervent supplications to God for my temporal and eternal happiness" (49a). Note that "ecclesiastical Society" is DENs. Many words were used for DENs and not always the same term, such as "sect" and so on; The language was developing. Note also his teaching the citizens about Christ, Christianity, and the doctrine of eternity.

---T--- R~E, 1~A is Not Permission to Unlimited False Religions, or False gods; rather to God: // This would make the GOV the promoter of false religion. The CC promotes religion of the true God. False religion was what was intended to be protected against; limited. // Imagine some person going in to the civilization and congress meetings and declaring that we are going to set up devil religion. I do not wander if every hair on every head would be standing straight up; then immediately about that time, another war, called war of USA against USA, would probably have started.

---T--- God Is Christian God; one Only True God, NOT Multiple gods: // None of the FFoG and public agreed that there were multiple gods. Such is deceit (lie) & unreasonable. No activity promoted as agreed that there were many gods as the same god. There is NO statement that they agreed there was more than the one and only true God.

---T--- FFOG George Washington states, for God, the definition of DEN as the word "religion" or "religious establishment": // "May the same wonder-working Deity, who long since delivering the Hebrews from their Egyptian Oppressors ,,,whose providential agency has ,,,in establishing these US as an independent Nation-- still continue to water them ,,,and make the inhabitants of every DEN participate in the [[temporary]] and spiritual blessings of that people whose God is Jehovah". (49a).

---T--- Truth, rightness, and God require us to knowledge and discern what the 1-A does say & does not say.

---T--- R~E, 1~A has Religion & R~Est as~ +] only "religions" to the true God, +] not religions to any god, +] not religions to every god: // The CC section shows this. Additionally religion has to first have a God to then be established. Not any and every god was allowed to set up their government and false religions.

107

---T--- <u>Religion is about God:</u> // <u>It is the set,</u> or group of doctrines and applications of doctrines about God.

---T--- <u>The Treaty of Tripoli:</u> // This DOC & Incident has been proven a falsity. Furthermore, it has translation problems. Translations include by Dr. C. Snouck Hurgronje of Leiden. The DOC & incident actually highly support God. +The problem is that some of the people signing it did not know Arabic. Another problem is that some translations did not have any remarks about God in them; Whereas some other translations do have some remarks about God in them. +Other errors include inaccuracy about George Washington being President. +Even if this incident was true as misinterpreted, it is an extremely small amount of EV compared to a larger amount of EV, to make supposition that the USA GOV was in opposition to religion and GOD. However it is not True; thus the supposition is removed. And Contrarily the truth is, that this Treaty was in support of Christianity and rejecting Islamism.

---T--- <u>National Day of Prayer to GOD:</u> // The USA has proclaimed thousands of national days of prayers to God; Christ. // President Reagan & Congress made Prayer an annual holiday in AD 1983; some statements <u>from that Law: "In witness whereof, I have hereunto set ,,,in the year of our Lord nineteen hundred and eighty-three, and of the Independence of the US of American the</u> two hundred and seventh ,,,President of the US of America, do hereby proclaim Thursday, May 5 ,,,National Day of Prayer. I call upon every citizen ,,,to gather together ,,,in homes and places of worship to pray ,,,Prayer is the mainspring of the American spirit, a fundamental tenet of our people since before the Republic was founded. A year before the Declaration of Independence, in 1775, the Continental Congress proclaimed the first National Day of Prayer as the initial positive action they asked of every colonist ,,,in 1783 ,,,War ended ,,,which a National Day of Prayer had been proclaimed every spring for eight years ,,,the deepest expression of American belief -- our national dependence on the Providence of God ,,,Abraham Lincoln said ,,,"to pray to the God that made us" ,,,Revived as an annual observance by Congress in 1952, the National Day of Prayer ,,,expression of reverence ,,,bring renewed respect for God ,,,this Nation has fervently sought and received divine guidance ,,,to further recognize the source of our blessings, and to seek His help,,,". // Notice that the religion of the USA is identified again with the Calendar of Jesus the Christ; of the DOI which is Christianity.

---T--- <u>R-E, 1-A of CC (DOI & CON):</u> // Mr. Schaff shared a few similar Truths, that I have included. These Historical Statements are Provided in a Report, (from Revival Theology Resources. (revivaltheology.net). From a Book titled, <u>*"The American Idea of Religious Freedom; [Church and State in the US. 1888]"*</u> by Philip Schaff, Born in Coire, Switzerland, 1819: "What is the distinctive character of American Christianity in its organized social aspect and its relation to the national life, as compared with the Christianity of Europe? (p) It is a free church in a free state, or a self-supporting and self-governing Christianity in independent but friendly relation to the civil government. (p) This relationship of church and state marks an epoch. It is a new chapter in the history, of Christianity, and the most important one which America has so far contributed. It lies at the base of our religious institutions and operations, and they cannot be understood without it,,, (p) The relationship of church and state in the United States secures full liberty of religious thought, speech, and action, within the limits of the public peace and order. It makes persecution impossible. (p) Religion and liberty are inseparable. Religion is voluntary, and cannot and ought not to be forced. (p) This is a fundamental article of the American creed, without distinction of sect or party. Liberty, both civil and religious, is an American instinct. All natives suck it in with the mother's milk; all immigrants accept it as a happy boon, especially those who flee from oppression and persecution abroad. Even those who reject the modern theory of liberty enjoy the practice, and would defend it in their own interest against any attempt to overthrow it. (p) Such liberty is impossible on the basis of a union of church and state, where the one of necessity restricts or controls the other. It requires a friendly separation, where each power is entirely independent in its own sphere. The church, as such, has nothing to do with the state except to obey its laws and to strengthen its moral foundations; the state has nothing to do with the church except to protect her in her property and liberty; and the state must be equally just to all forms of belief and unbelief which do not endanger the public safety. (p) The family, the church, and the state are divine institutions demanding alike our obedience, in their proper sphere of jurisdiction. The family is the oldest institution, and the source of church and state. The patriarchs were priests and kings of their households. Church and state are equally necessary, and as inseparable as soul and body, and yet as distinct as soul and body. The church is instituted for the religious interests and eternal welfare of man; the state for his secular interests and temporal welfare. The one looks to heaven as the final home of immortal spirits, the other upon our mother earth. The church is the reign of love; the state is the reign of justice. The former is governed by the gospel, the latter by the law. The church exhorts, and uses moral suasion; the state commands, and enforces obedience. The church punishes by rebuke, suspension, and excommunication; the state by fines, imprisonment, and death. Both meet on questions of public morals, and both together constitute civilized human Society and ensure its prosperity. (p) The root of this theory we find in the New Testament. In the ancient world religion and politics were blended. Among the Jews religion ruled the state, which was a theocracy. Among the heathen the state ruled religion; the Roman emperor was the supreme pontiff (pontifex maximus), the gods were national, and the priests were servants of the state. Christianity had at first no official connection with the state,,, (p) For three hundred years the Christian church kept aloof from politics, and, while obeying the civil laws and paying tribute, maintained at the same time the higher law of conscience in refusing to comply with idolatrous customs and in professing the faith in the face of death. The early Apologists-Justin Martyr, Tertullian, Lactantius-boldly claimed the freedom of religion as a natural right. THE AMERICAN SYSTEM COMPARED WITH OTHER SYSTEMS. The American relationship of church and state differs from all previous relationships in Europe and in the colonial period of our history; and yet it rests upon them and reaps the benefit of them all. For history is an organic unit, and American history has its roots in Europe. 1. The American system differs from the ante-Nicene or pre-Constantinian separation of church and state, when the church was indeed, as with us, self-supporting and self-governing, and so far free within, but under persecution from without, being treated as a forbidden religion by the then heathen state. In America the government protects the church in her property and rights without interfering with her internal affairs. By the power of truth and the moral heroism of martyrdom the church converted the Roman Empire and became the mother of Christian states. 2. The American system differs from the hierarchical control of the church over the state, or from priest government, which prevailed in the Middle Ages down to the Reformation, and reached its culmination in the Papacy. It confines the church to her proper spiritual vocation, and leaves the state independent in all the temporal affairs of the nation. The hierarchical theory was suited to the times after the fall of the Roman Empire and the ancient civilization, when the state was a rude military despotism, when the church was the refuge of the people, when the Christian priesthood was in sole possession of learning and had to civilize as well as to evangelize the barbarians of northern and western Europe. By her influence over legislation the church abolished bad laws and customs, introduced benevolent institutions, and created a Christian state controlled by the spirit of justice and humanity, and fit for self-government. 3. The American system differs from the Erastian or Csaro-Papal control of the state over the church, which obtained in the old Byzantine Empire, and prevails in modern Russia, and in the Protestant states of Europe, where the civil government protects and supports the church, but at the expense of her dignity and independence, and deprives her of the power of self-government. The Erastian system was based on the assumption that all citizens are also Christians of one creed, but is abnormal in the mixed character of government and people in the modern state. In America, the state has no right whatever to interfere with the affairs of the church, her doctrine, discipline, and worship, and the appointment of ministers. It would be a great calamity if religion were to become subject to our ever-changing politics. 4. The American system differs from the system of toleration, which began in Germany with the Westphalia Treaty, 1648; in England with the Act of Toleration, 1689, and which now prevails over nearly all Europe; of late years, nominally at least, even in Roman Catholic countries, to the very gates of the Vatican, in spite of the protest of the Pope. Toleration exists where the government supports one or more churches, and permits other religious communities under the name of sects (as on the continent), or dissenters and nonconformists (as in England), under certain conditions. In America there are no such distinctions, but only churches or denominations on a footing of perfect equality before the law. To talk about any particular denomination as the church, or the American church, has no meaning, and betrays ignorance or conceit. Such exclusiveness is natural and logical in Romanism, but unnatural, illogical, and contemptible in any other church. The American laws know no such institution as "the church," but only separate and independent organizations. (p) Toleration is an important step from state-churchism to free-churchism. But it is only a step. There is a very great difference between toleration and liberty. Toleration is a concession, which may be withdrawn; it implies a preference for the ruling form of faith and worship, and a practical disapproval of all other forms. It may be coupled with many restrictions and disabilities. We tolerate what we dislike but cannot alter; we tolerate even a nuisance, if we must. Acts of toleration are wrung from a government by the force of circumstances and the power of a minority too influential to be disregarded. (p) In our country we ask no toleration for religion and its free exercise, but we claim it as an inalienable right. "It is not toleration," says Judge Cooley, "which is established in our system, but religious equality." Freedom of religion is one of the greatest gifts of God to man, without distinction of race and color. He is the author and lord of conscience, and no power on earth has a right to stand between God and the conscience. A violation of this divine law written in the heart is an assault upon the majesty of God and the image of God in man. Granting the freedom of conscience, we must, by logical necessity, also grant the freedom of its manifestation and exercise in public worship. To concede the first and to deny the second, after the manner of despotic governments, is to imprison the conscience. To be just, the state must either support all or none of the religions of its citizens. Our government supports none, but protects all. 5. Finally-and this we would emphasize as especially important in our time,-the American system differs radically and fundamentally from the infidel and red-republican theory of religious freedom. The word freedom is one of the most abused words in the vocabulary. True liberty, is a positive force, regulated by law; false liberty is a negative force, a release from restraint. True liberty is the moral power of self-government; the liberty of infidels and anarchists is carnal licentiousness. The American separation of church and state rests on respect for the church; the infidel separation, on indifference and hatred of the church, and of religion itself. (p) The infidel theory was tried and failed in the first Revolution of France. It began with toleration, and ended with the abolition of Christianity, and with the reign of terror, which in turn prepared the way for military despotism as the only means of saving society from anarchy and ruin. Our infidels and anarchists would [[redo]] this tragedy if they should ever get the power. They openly profess their hatred and contempt of our Sunday-laws, our Sabbaths, our churches, and all our religious institutions and societies. Let us beware of them! The American system grants freedom also to irreligion and infidelity, but only within the limits of the order and safety of society. The destruction of religion would be the destruction of morality and the ruin of the state. Civil liberty requires for its support religious liberty, and cannot prosper without it. Religious liberty is not an empty Sound, but an orderly exercise of religious duties and enjoyment of all its privileges. It is freedom in religion, not freedom from religion; as true civil liberty is freedom in law, and not freedom from law. Says Goethe: "In der Beschrnkung erst zeigt sich der Meister, Und das Gesetz nur kann dir Freiheit geben." (p) Republican institutions in the hands of a virtuous and God-fearing nation are the very best in the world, but in the hands of a corrupt and irreligious people they are the very worst, and the most effective weapons of destruction. An indignant people may rise in rebellion against a cruel tyrant; but who will rise against the tyranny of the people in possession of the ballot-box and the whole machinery of government? Here lies our great danger, and it is increasing every year. (p) Destroy our churches, close our Sunday-schools, abolish the Lord's Day, and our republic would become an empty shell, and our people would tend to heathenism and barbarism. Christianity is the most powerful factor in our society and the pillar of our institutions. It regulates the family; it enjoins private and public virtue; it builds up moral character; it teaches us to love God supremely, and our neighbor as ourselves; it makes good men and useful citizens; it denounces every vice; it encourages every virtue; it promotes and serves the public welfare; it upholds peace and order. Christianity is the only possible religion for the American people, and with Christianity are bound up all our hopes for the future. (p) This was strongly felt by Washington, the father of his country, first in war, first in peace, and first in the hearts of his countrymen; and no passage in his immortal Farewell Address is more truthful, wise, and worthy of constant remembrance by every American statesman and citizen than that in which he affirms the inseparable connection of religion with morality and national prosperity". It should be noted that Mr. Schaff did mis-interpret some areas, but also offered many helps. His falsity mis-interpretations are not because he intends to state evil, rather only deficiency of knowledge.

---T--- <u>Christ is the Being & Christianity is the Religion of the USA GOV in all Branches &</u> False religion Opposed: // FFOG George Washington has the following about him: +Main goal was the Holy Bible & Christianity as said, "true religion affords to GOV its surest support"; +accepted no pay for his services; +wrote his wife, "I rely confidently on that Providence which has hereto preserved and been bountiful to me"; +Some say he was a Deist, but not true, as he attended the Anglican Church regularly; +a committed attender to a Trinitarian Church; +kept a prayer journal; called the "daily sacrifice", found in AD 1890 which was full of devotionals and SC (9); +first order of the RW proved his Christianity by telling soldiers in the army to neither curse nor gamble; +ordered troops, on July 4, 1775, to not blasphemy, gambling, and drunkenness, and to a punctual attendance to Divine service (Christian); +a Quaker witnessed him praying, and told his wife about it at home, reporting he had morning & evening devotions (2); +told the Indians the most important thing to learn from the Americans is "to learn our ,,,above all, the religion of Jesus Christ ,,,Congress will do everything they can to assist you in this wise intention" (12); +said, "the propitious smiles of Heaven can never be expected on a nation that disregards the eternal rules of order and right which heaven itself has ordained" (13); +chose to be placed in to Presidential Office by dedication of himself to the Holy Bible with his hand on it (a ceremony also practiced today); and at the close of the inauguration he bowed down and kissed the Bible; then afterwards led congress across the street to St Paul's Cathedral for a 2 hr meeting of worship to Christ; the Christian Church worship assembly at St Paul's Cathedral had previously been an enactment of Congress in an Apr. 1789 resolution (14); +farewell address stated, "of all dispositions and habits which lead to political prosperity, religion and morality are indispensable supports. In vain would that man claim the tribute of patriotism who should labor to subtract these great pillars of human happiness ,,,and let us with caution indulge the supposition that morality can be maintained without religion" (15).

---T--- <u>Congress meetings (in forming the CON) in it's Table of Contents (Index) is EV of the FFOG USA GOV having Intention/ purpose to Prioritize Christ & Protect Christianity as the USA GOV religion:</u> // Such is as follows; it requires carefulness in interpreting as they are only summary statements, without a complete conclusion; sometimes only the subject of discussion is stated and are without the conclusions. Thus if it says "pagan in the US", it does not say that the Pagan religion is to be allowed to set up in the USA or GOV but is only a remark as to what subject was discussed: // "Henry Abbott-- RELIGION; opposed to an exclusive Establishment; no RELIGIOUS Test; PAGAN or Deist may obtain Office; OATH; by whom are we to swear? Jupiter ... 191" and ,,,"conduct of our rulers, and that, in a Christian country, it would be at least decent to hold out some distinction between the professors of Christianity and downright infidelity or paganism.". +"The seventh article declares, that the ratification of nine states shall be sufficient for the establishment of this CON, between the states ratifying the same ,,,making treaties, they might make a treaty engaging with foreign powers to adopt the Roman Catholic religion in the US, which would prevent the people from worshipping God according to their own consciences. The worthy member ,,,has in some measure satisfied ,,,mind on this subject. But others may be dissatisfied. Many wish to know what religion shall be established. I believe a majority of the community are Presbyterians. I am, for my part, against any exclusive establishment; but if there were any, I would prefer the Episcopal. The exclusion of religious tests is by many thought dangerous and impolitic. They suppose that if there be no religious test required, pagans, deists, and Mahometans might obtain offices among us, and that the senators and representatives might all be pagans. Every person employed by the general and state GOVs is to take an oath to support the former. Some are desirous to know how and by whom they are to swear, since no religious tests are required-- whether they are to swear by Jupiter, Juno, Minerva, Proserpine, or Pluto. We ought to be suspicious of our liberties. We have felt the effects of oppressive measures, and know the happy consequences of being jealous of our rights. I would be glad some gentleman would endeavor to obviate these objections, in order to satisfy the religious art of the society. Could I be convinced that the objections were well founded, I would then declare my opinion against the CON,,, [Mr. Abbot added several other observations." +Note here that they spoke concernedly of the intentions/ purposes that~ +there is disclarity in some of the general language phrases written; +Christianity be protected; +Christianity is the USA GOV religion, but there was wording problems on how to protect it without the wording being abused; +no total unlimited liberty is for evil or false religion; +no abusive GOV to Christianity, nor evil religion in GOV; +all the remarks of non-Christian are negative or disapproved, but allowed freedom for free will.

---T--- <u>About the Allowance of Religions that are Not Christian for Christ:</u> // Some religions say, "kill the infidel or heretic". This was known as a historical fact to the FFOG. Contrarily, this was to be protected against; with allowing them to live in the USA; but with limitations. They were provided the opportunity to live in the USA; and invited freely by free will to accept or reject Christ. The limitations are, however, that they~ +Cannot start their doctrine on USA soil with establishments such as public assemblies, +Cannot have GOV acceptance to promote infidelity, +Required to obey the Christian laws of the land, which include body actions and kind attitudes.

---T--- <u>Congress & DOI state God priority & Christianity is the USA GOV religion:</u> // Patrick Henry wrote, "bad men cannot make good citizens. It is impossible that a nation of infidels or idolaters would be a nation of freemen", and "I think of religion of infinitely higher importance than politics" (Patrick Henry, in a letter to his daughter, 1796); and in the same letter defended that he was a Christian. // Thus infidels & idolaters are 2 oppositional or contrary states of heart to Christianity; one being a rejecter (infidel) of God & the other a decider of other gods (idolater).

---T--- <u>GOV Enactment - The Old Deluder Act in AD 1642 & 1647 opposing demonology evils:</u> // This legal enactment was to keep Spiritual Moral Beings alert and aware of the battle in opposition of the Devil (& demons) and evil as sin. It was a Holy Biblical truth. It was intended/ purposed to keep demons from blinding people (mentally) with illiteracy and ignorance of the Holy Bible; which as had been done throughout history from false religions, evil GOV, and public evil.

---T--- <u>The New England Primer;</u> A catechism promoting Christ by FFOG for schools in the USA: // It included the following as lessons: "Play not with bad boys; ,,,be not a dunce; ,,,be wise to the Lord, good and evil; ,,,The Lord's prayer; ,,,Apostles creed; ,,,Hymns".

---T--- <u>FFOG statements with affection care to Christ & Christian Religion (260h):</u> // Patrick Henry said, "There is an insidious campaign of false propaganda being waged to the effect that our country is not a Christian nation, but a religious one,,, it cannot be emphasized too strongly or too often that this great nation was founded, not by religionist, but by Christians. Not on religion but by Jesus Christ." // Alexander Hamilton, member of the Constitution Convention, said, "Let a society be formed whose first duty shall be the preservation of Christianity". // The USA & Canada are desired all over the world because of their system of justice and fairness, and because our FFOG supported the dignity of a person; This came from the British system of jurisprudence which is based on the historical Decalogue (10 commandments) given to Moses from God and supported by Jesus Christ.

---T--- <u>USA GOV Congress, Executive, & Citizen enact, &</u> apply the Northwest Ordinance~ a USA DOC; which agrees & supports the statements of the DOI prioritizing God: // This enacted DOC states: "religion, morality, and knowledge being necessary to good GOV and the happiness of mankind, schools, and the means of education shall forever be encouraged". // This ordnance was to assist the USA GOV activities in pursuing advancement to the westward geographic parts of the country, and increase territory. Some dates of this DOC are after the DOI & CON. // Many States that participated in forming the CON and joining the USA supported this Ordinance. // Mississippi in AD 1817 stated, "religion, morality, and knowledge, being necessary to good GOV, the preservation of liberty and the happiness of mankind, schools and the means of education shall be forever encouraged in this state". This is similar to the NW Ordinance DOC.

---T--- <u>God's R-E, 1-A of CON has the following DOC that again proves</u> it's true & right definitions including these 5: 1~ Does not favor any particular Christian DEN by making a Law for it; 2~ Does not restrict Christian DENs from meeting & activity; 3~ The USA GOV does not control the Church in its doctrines & worship, thus control Christianity in general; 4~ The USA GOV is to assist the Christian Churches and doctrine; 5~ Only Christian Religion is true Religion and has support: // DOC: "GOV Bills and Resolutions, House of Representatives, 19th Congress, 1st Session: Read twice, and committed to a Committee of the whole House to-morrow. A Bill Authorizing the several RELIGIOUS Societies within the District of Columbia to incorporate certain persons for the management of property. Whereas it is reasonable and proper that all DENS of CHRISTIANs within the District of Columbia, whose members conduct ,,,Committee: Committee of the Whole House - 3/17, 1826 ,,,Read twice ,,,A Bill Authorizing the several RELIGIOUS Societies within the District of Columbia to incorporate certain persons for the management of property. Whereas it is reasonable and proper that all DENS of CHRISTIANs within the District of Columbia, whose members conduct themselves in a peaceable and orderly manner, should receive and enjoy equal right and privileges, without partiality, preference, or distinction, in all things concerning the temporalities and government of their CHURCHes, congregations, and societies: And whereas, also, it is necessary to their welfare ,,,they should be empowered to hold and acquire certain portions of property, in a corporate or congregational capacity, and enter into various engagements, of a civil or temporal nature, which can only be done by the assistance of the Congress of the US, which assistance may, nevertheless, be rightfully granted without disturbing private opinions, or affecting the rights of judgment in matters of RELIGION, or imposing an involuntary burden on any person whatsoever: And whereas it is most convenient to make provisions for their respective situations, by a general law, which shall reach their several exigencies in affairs of a temporal or civil nature, as far as a difference of circumstances will admit: The Congress of the US having, therefore, taken the premises into serious consideration, and conceiving themselves indispensably bound to secure and preserve the same equality of right, privileges, and advantages, to all quiet and inoffensive CHRISTIAN Societies in the District aforesaid, without any exception, whereby RELIGION may be encouraged and diffused, and peace, order, and universal tranquility prevail have agreed to enact,,,".

---T--- <u>Congress, Executive, Citizen Divisions of the USA GOV & State GOV</u> all have intentions/ purpose to support Lord Christ & Christianity as the center of activity; & oppose evils: // "The Debates in the Several State Conventions on the Adoption of the Federal CON [Elliot's Debates, Volume 2] ,,,"The migration or importation of such persons as any the states now existing shall think proper to admit, shall not be prohibited by Congress prior to the year 1808 ,,,The Hon. Mr. DOW, from We are, spoke very sensibly and feelingly against this paragraph. Several members, on the other side, spoke in favor of it ,,,Joshua Atherton, from Amherst, spoke as follows:-- Mr. President, I cannot be of the opinion of the honorable gentlemen who last spoke, that this paragraph is either so useful or so inoffensive as they seem to imagine, or that the objections to it are so totally void of foundation. The idea that strikes those, who are opposed to this clause, so disagreeably and so forcibly, is, hereby it is conceived (if we ratify the CON) that we become consenters to, and partakers in, the SIN and guilt of this abominable traffic, at least for a certain period,

111

without any positive stipulation that it should even then be brought to an end. We do not behold in it that valuable acquisition so much boasted of by the honorable member from Portsmouth, "that an end is then to be put to slavery." Congress may be as much, or more, puzzled to put a stop to it then, than we are now. The clause has not secured its abolition. We do not think ourselves under any obligation to perform works of supererogation in the reformation of mankind; we do not esteem ourselves under any necessity to go to Spain or Italy to suppress the inquisition of those countries; or of making a journey to the Carolinas to abolish the detestable custom of enslaving the Africans; [[opposing the slavery evil]] but, sir, we will not lend the aid of our ratification to this cruel and inhuman merchandise, not even for a day. There is a great distinction in not taking a part in the most barbarous violation of the SACRED laws of GOD and humanity, and our becoming guaranties for its exercise for a term of years. Yes, sir, it is our full purpose to wash our hands clear of it; and, however unconcerned spectators we may remain of such predatory infractions of the laws of our nature ,,,yet I cannot but believe, in justice to human nature, that, if we reserve the consideration, and bring this claimed power somewhat nearer to our own doors, we shall form a more equitable opinion of its claim to this ratification ,,,is too affecting."

---T--- <u>USA Congress, Executive, Citizens, & State GOV support Christ & His Christianity</u> with His Holy Bible during CON times: // Massachusetts proclaims a day to God 12/11, 1783: a thanksgiving to God: "divine providence; praise to God; to all citizens of State and US; dependence upon God; religiously observed as a day of thanksgiving and prayer; for all the people ,,,that all the people may then assemble ,,,to celebrate that He hath been pleased to continue to us the light of the blessed Gospel ,,,that we also offer up fervent supplications ,,,to cause pure religion and virtue to flourish ,,,and to fill the world with His glory". +USA existence is intended to shine the Gospel Light, Jesus, to the World. HSC~ 1Thes5:5.

---T--- <u>USA Citizens, DOI & activity, Congress, Executive, States, FFOG</u>, History Records, & the Starting of the USA are all Intending/ purpose of Christ's Christian supportive & Evil Oppositional: // "Letters of Delegates to Congress: Volume 10-- 6/1, 1778 - 9/30, 1778 - Henry Marchant to His Children - Dear Children, Philadelphia July 20th 1778 I recd. your endearing Letter of the 7th of July this Day and you can't conceive what a heartfelt satisfaction it gave me; go on my dear Children and strive to excell in all useful Knowledge, especially such as relates to GOD and that other World, where we are all to go. To them that behave well in this World, the next will be a world of happiness indeed-but to such as do ill here, it will be a world of EVERLASTING TORMENT. GOD grant that when we have all left this world, we may not be parted from each other in the world to come; but that all, father and mother, brother and sisters, may meet together, never to part again, but live a whole ETERNITY with GOD and CHRIST-with Abraham, Isaac & Jacob, and all other good men & women and children who have gone there before us. Remember that GOD hates a lye, and every thing that is dishonest- and that you must always be chearful and willing to do your duty to GOD and man, and to your parents and to love one another and all good people, and that you must try to perswade naughty children to behave better and to QUIT all their WICKED WORDS and WAYS, if they would ever expect to be happy. ,,,Sally has been very industrious to have read the books she mentions twice over. I rejoice that she does not forget her BIBLE-her Catechism & PRAYERS. I am glad to find Mr. Pemberton has been with and that he kindly advises you ,,,You take such notice of the business of the farm, and that you are able to give me so good an account of it. ,,, And the King of France has also sent us a great many large Ships, to assist in taking the British Ships & People, and to drive them away from this good land which HEAVEN gave to Our Fore-Fathers, and to us their children, and which the KING OF ENGLAND and his WICKED people have been endeavouring to take from us-And I hope by the Blessing of GOD that we shall by & by have peace thro' all this Country, and that you may live to grow up and enjoy it with thankfulness to GOD, and never forget what great things the LORD hath done for you. Was it not for this hope my Dear Children, I could never consent to leave you & your good Mamma so long year after year. Hoping we may soon meet & praise GOD for his great goodness to us all, I remain your affectionate Father, Henry Marchant RC (RHi) ,,,".

---T--- <u>Congress, Executive, Citizens, & States are</u> all Religious to Christ & opposed to Evil, anti-Christian: // "Journals of the Continental Congress, 1774-1789 - 8/3, 1784. The Committee of the States assembled: Present ,,,July 5, 1784, reported the draft of a letter to be signed ,,,It never was the idea of Congress that such Grant should be located or possession of the land taken till the general arrangements necessary for concluding a peace ,,,The cession of Virginia now relied on as a principal hope ,,,of the US, would prove an expence and disadvantage to the Union ,,,Ohio lands ,,,With perfect esteem and regard, I am Sir, Your Excellency's most obedt. and most hble. servt., Saml. Hardy. His Excellency B. H. The Govr. of the state of Virginia.1 [Note 1: 1 This report, in the writing of Jacob Read, is in the Papers of the Continental Congress ,,,"That a committee be appointed to prepare a proclamation for a day of solemn PRAYER and thanksgiving to Almighty GOD, to be observed <u>throughout the US of America,</u> on the exchange of the instruments of ratification of the Definitive Treaty of Peace, between the US of America and his Britannic Majesty; and the happy completion of the great work of Independency and peace to these US," reported the following form of a proclamation: [Note 1: 1 The words in parenthesis are in the report but not in the journal.] By the US of America, in the Committee of the States assembled, A Proclamation. WHEREAS IT HATH PLEASED THE SUPREME RULER OF THE UNIVERSE, OF HIS INFINITE GOODNESS AND MERCY, SO TO CALM THE MINDS AND DO AWAY THE RESENTMENTS OF THE POWERS LATELY ENGAGED IN A MOST BLOODY AND DESTRUCTIVE WAR, AND TO DISPOSE THEIR HEARTS TOWARDS AMITY AND FRIENDSHIP, THAT A GENERAL PACIFICATION HATH TAKEN PLACE, AND PARTICULARLY A DEFINITIVE TREATY OF PEACE BETWEEN THE SAID US OF AMERICA AND HIS BRITANNIC MAJESTY, WAS SIGNED AT PARIS, ON THE 3D DAY OF SEPTEMBER, *IN THE YEAR OF OUR LORD 1783;* THE INSTRUMENTS OF THE FINAL RATIFICATIONS OF WHICH WERE EXCHANGED AT PASSY, ON THE 12TH DAY OF MAY, *IN THE YEAR OF OUR LORD* 1784, WHEREBY A FINISHING HAND WAS PUT TO THE GREAT WORK OF PEACE, AND THE FREEDOM, SOVEREIGNTY AND INDEPENDENCE OF THESE STATES, FULLY AND COMPLEATELY established: And whereas in pursuit of the great work of freedom and independence, and the progress of the contest in which the US of America have been engaged, and on the success of which the dearest and most essential rights of human nature depended, the benign interposition of DIVINE Providence hath, on many occasions, been most miraculously and abundantly manifested; and the citizens of the US have the greatest reason to return their most hearty and sincere praises and thanksgiving to the GOD of their deliverance; whose name be praised: Deeply impressed therefore with the sense of the mercies manifested to these US, and of the blessings which it hath pleased GOD, to shower down on us, of our future dependance, at all times, on his power and mercy as the only source from which so great benefits can be derived; we, the US of America, in the Committee of the States assembled, do earnestly recommend to the supreme executives of the several states, to set apart Tuesday, the 19th day of Oct. next, as a day of public PRAYER and thanksgiving, that all the people of the US may then assemble in their respective CHURCHes and congregations, to celebrate with grateful hearts, and joyful and united voices, the mercies and praises of their all-bountiful CREATOR, most HOLY, and most righteous! for his innumerable favours and mercies vouchsafed unto them; more especially that HE hath been graciously pleased so to conduct us through the perils and dangers of the war, as finally to establish the US in freedom and independency, and to give them a name and place among the princes and nations of the earth; that HE hath raised up great captains and men of war from amongst us, to lead our armies, and in our greatest difficulties and distresses hath given us unanimity to adhere to and assert our just rights and privileges; and that HE hath been most graciously pleased also, to raise up a most powerful prince and magnanimous people, as allies, to assist us in effectually supporting and maintaining them; that he hath been pleased to prosper the labour of our husbandmen; that there is no famine or want seen throughout our land: And above all, that HE hath been pleased to continue to us the light of GOSPEL TRUTHS, and secured to us, in the fullest manner, the rights of CONSCIENCE in FAITH and WORSHIP. And while our hearts overflow with gratitude, and our lips pronounce the praises of our great and merciful CREATOR, that we may also offer up our joint and fervent supplications, that it may please HIM of his infinite goodness and mercy, to pardon all our SINS and offences; to inspire with wisdom and a TRUE sense of public good, all our public councils; to strengthen and cement the bonds of love and affection between all our citizens; to impress them with an earnest regard for the public good and national faith and honour, and to teach them to improve the days of peace by every good work; to PRAY that he will, in a more especial manner, shower down his blessings on Louis the Most CHRISTIAN King our ally, to prosper his house, that his son's sons may long sit on the throne of their ancestors, a blessing to the people entrusted to his charge; to bless all mankind, and inspire the princes and nations of the earth with the love of peace, that the sound of war may be heard of no more; that he may be pleased to smile upon us, and bless our husbandry, fishery, our commerce, and especially our schools and seminaries of learning; and to raise up from among our youth, men eminent for virtue, learning and piety, to his service in CHURCH and state; to cause virtue and TRUE RELIGION to flourish, to give to all nations amity, peace and concord, and to fill the world with HIS GLORY. DONE BY THE US, IN THE COMMITTEE OF THE STATES ASSEMBLED, WITNESS THE HONBL SAMUEL HARDY, CHAIRMAN, THIS-- DAY OF--, IN THE YEAR OF OUR LORD, &C. AND IN THE 9TH OF THE SOVEREIGNTY AND INDEPENDENCE OF THE US OF AMERICA.1 ,,,Papers of the Continental Congress, No. 32, folios 145--149.] ,,,".

---T--- USA GOV is Christian & Signs Many DOC with the Reference to the Lord Jesus & His Earthly coming. The intention/ purpose of such action is to state that~ +] the DOC is for the Being of Christ Jesus and His approval; seal of Approval; +] God & His presence is to be included as a Check; +] all connecting activity and relationships of the USA GOV is as a Christian Nation Ambassador and representation for the Being of Christ Jesus: // "Journals of the Continental Congress, 1774-1789 - 10/16, 1787. Congress assembled. Present as yesterday ,,,Papers of the Continental Congress ,,,writing of Mr Henry Lee. This motion and proceeding so far as relates to the Judges for the Western territory were entered by John Fisher ,,,Resolved That Congress proceed to the election of the judges for the western territory and the commissioners for settling the Accounts between the US and the individual States ,,,Resolved Unanimously ,,,off the coast of England Great Britain in the late war ,,,That a letter be written to his Most CHRISTIAN Majesty informing him that the US in Congress Assembled have bestowed ,,,of the Act of Congress of the 12 Oct ,,,The US of America in Congress Assembled ,,,constituted and appointed ,,,appoint you the said Thomas Jefferson our Minister plenipotentiary to reside at the court of his Most CHRISTIAN Majesty and do give you full power and authority there to represent us ,,,Charge ,,,In testimony whereof we have caused the Seal of the US to be hereunto affixed. Witness his Excellency Arthur St Clair our president this twelfth day of Oct. One thousand seven hundred and eighty seven and of our Sovereignty and independence the twelfth. [[date of DOI used as USA start date, when it became an individual Nation for God, Christ Jesus, as the Supreme Ruler]] The letter of Credence. Great and beloved friend We the US in Congress Assembled ,,,We PRAY GOD to keep your Majesty under his HOLY protection. Done at the city of New York the 12th day of Oct in the year of our Lord 1787 and of our sovereignty and independence the twelfth. The Secretary for foreign Affairs reports that agreeably to the Order of the 16 he hath prepared the following letter1 to his Most CHRISTIAN Majesty which having been duly signed and countersigned was delivered ,,,concern the happiness of your Majesty, your family and people. We PRAY GOD to keep you, our Great and beloved friend, under his HOLY protection. Done at the city of New York the 16 day of Octr. in the year of our Lord 1787 and of our Sovereignty and independence the twelfth ,,,":

---T--- USA GOV, Congress, Executive, DOI, Citizens representing themselves as~ +] Religious; religion defined as Christianity; +] Opposing GOV abuse & Evil, which is sin, anti-Christian, things against the Holy Bible; +] Relating to other Nations, or Foreign affairs as a Christian Nation Ambassador for Christ the Lord: // "The Revolutionary Diplomatic Correspondence of the US, Volume 5 ,,,July 5, 1782. Sir: Soon after my public reception by their high mightinesses, the body of merchants of the city of Schiedam ,,,to pay their respects to Congress and to me ,,,I was so much affected with the zeal and ardor of these worthy gentlemen and their constituents, which, with many other things of a similar kind, convinced me that there is in this nation a strong affection for America, and a kind of RELIGIOUS veneration for her just cause. I have the honor to be, &c., John Adams. ,,,united provinces of the Netherlands had acknowledged the freedom and independency of the US of North America, and admitted the said John Adams as minister plenipotentiary and envoy of the Congress of the said US. If ever any circumstances were capable of recalling to the minds of the people of these provinces the most lively remembrance of the cruel situation to which their forefathers found themselves once reduced, under the oppressive yoke of Spanish TYRANNY, it was, no doubt, that terrible and critical moment when the Colonies of North America, groaning under the intolerable weight of the chains with which the BOUNDLESS AMBITION of Great Britain had loaded them, were forced into a just and lawful war to recover the use and enjoyment of that liberty to which they were entitled by the SACRED and unalienable LAWS OF NATURE. If ever the citizens of this republic have had an occasion to remember, with sentiments of the liveliest gratitude, the visible assistance and protection of a BEING [[God]] who, after having constantly supported them during the course of a long, bloody war which cost their ancestors eighty years' hard struggles and painful labors, deigned by the strength of His powerful arm to break the odious fetters under which we had so long groaned, and who, from that happy era to the present time, has constantly maintained us in the possession of our precious liberties; if ever the citizens of these provinces have been bound to remember those unspeakable favors of the ALMIGHTY, it was no doubt at that moment when HAUGHTY Britain began to feel the effects of DIVINE indignation, and when the vengeance of HEAVEN defeated her sanguinary schemes; it was when treading under foot the sacred ties of blood and nature, and meditating the destruction of her own offspring, her arms were everywhere baffled in the most terrible and exemplary manner, her troops defeated, and her armies led into captivity and at last that haughty power, humbled by that HEAVEN which she had provoked, saw the sceptre which she had usurped fall from her enfeebled hands; and America, shaking off the cruel yoke which an unnatural step-mother had endeavored to impose forever upon her, thanked bounteous HEAVEN for her happy deliverance. If ever the inhabitants of this country, and these of this city in particular, ,,,just cause for joy, and good grounds to conceive the highest hopes of prosperity and happiness, it was undoubtedly at that so much wished ,,,when, with a unanimous voice, the fathers of the country declared the US of America to be free and independent, and acknowledged your excellency as minister plenipotentiary and envoy of the illustrious Congress. Impressed with the various sentiments of respect, joy, and gratitude, with which the unspeakable favors of the ALMIGHTY towards both countries must inspire every feeling and sensible mind ,,,general of the united provinces of the Netherlands, solemnly acknowledged the independence of the US of America; a step which, under the pleasure of GOD, must become the foundation of an unalterable friendship, and the source of mutual prosperity to the two republics, whose union being cemented by interests henceforth common and inseparable, must forever subsist, and be constantly and RELIGIOUSly preserved by our latest posterity. Allow us, then, ye deliverers of America, ye generous defenders of her infant liberties, to congratulate your illustrious envoy, and to express ,,,wishes of the nation. Accept also of the fervent PRAYERS, which we address to HEAVEN, beseeching the ALMIGHTY to shower down His blessings on your republic and her allies. Permit us also to recommend to you, in the strongest manner, the interests of our country, and of this city in particular. Let those of our citizens who have been the most zealous in promoting the acknowledgment of your independence enjoy always a particular share of your affection ,,,no one may ever succeed in detracting from the good faith and integrity of Holland, or causing the sincerity of our efforts to advance our mutual interests to be suspected, which are founded on the unalterable principles of pure virtue, and a RELIGION common to both of us ,,, [[Christianity was the religion common to both]]".

---T--- USA GOV of Congress, Executive, Citizens, all base relations & activities on Christ's Being with His Christianity & Laws: // "Journals of the Continental Congress, 1774-1789 -- 2/26, 1788. - [Note 1: 1 Charles Thomson resumes the entry.] Congress assembled. Present ,,,According to Order the Minister Plenipotentiary from most CHRISTIAN Majesty of France was introduced to a public Audience when he delivered a letter of Credence ,,,from his most CHRISTIAN Majesty of which the following is a translation ,,,Papers of the Continental Congress ,,,1788.] Very dear great friends and Allies Particular reasons relative to the good of our service have determined us to appoint a successor to the Chevalier de la Luzerne Our Minister plenipotentiary with you. We have chosen the count de Moustier to take his place in the same quality ,,,worthy of our good will. We PRAY You to give full faith to whatever he may say to You on our part, particularly when he shall assure You of the sincerity of our wishes for Your prosperity, as well as of the constant affection and friendship which we bear to the US in general, and to each of them in particular. We PRAY GOD that he will have You very dear great friends and Allies in his HOLY keeping. Written at Versailles the 30th . Sept. 1787. [Note 2: 2 Roger Alden takes up the entry.] Your good friend and Ally (signed) Louis Ct. de Montmorin. After which he addressed Congress in a speech of which the following is a translation. Gentlemen of the Congress, The relations of friendship and Affection which subsist between the King my Master and the US, have been established on a basis which cannot but daily acquire a new degree of solidity. It is satisfactory to be mutually convinced that an Alliance formed for obtaining a glorious peace, after efforts directed by the greatest wisdom, and sustained with admirable constancy, must always be conformable to the common Interests, and that it is a fruitful source of infinite advantages to both Nations, whose mutual confidence and intercourse will encrease in proportion as they become better known to each other. The King who was the first to connect himself with the US as a Sovereign Power, to second their efforts and favour their Interests, has never ceased since that memorable period, to turn his attention to the means of proving to them his Affection. This sentiment directs the vows which his Majesty forms for their prosperity. Their success will always interest him sensibly, and there is reason to hope for it from the wisdom of the measures which they will adopt. To this solemn Assurance of Interest and Attachment on the part of the King, to the Unanimous sentiment of the Nation, and to the fervent wishes of a great number of my countrymen ,,,the attention of the most considerable powers in Europe, and whose courage and patriotism have astonished all Nations. My happiness will be compleat, Gentlemen ,,,To which the President made the following reply. Sir ,,,It will always give us pleasure to acknowledge the friendship and important good offices which we have experienced from his Most CHRISTIAN Majesty and Your generous Nation; and we flatter ourselves that the same principles of magnanimity and regard to mutual convenience which dictated the connections between us, will continue to operate, and to render them still more extensive in their benefits to the two Countries ,,,We consider the Alliance as involving engagements highly interesting to both parties, and we are persuaded that they will be observed with entire and mutual good faith ,,,Sir,,,".

---T--- <u>USA Congress, Citizens, & States supporting Christ & His</u> Christianity; & Opposing Sin or evil; This situation is the self sin of idolatry; not having the true God; not as first priority in the USA: // "Letters of Delegates to Congress: Volume 13- 6/1, 1779 - 9/30, 1779 - ,,,Sepr. 22d. 1779 I thought ,,,your replicatory & defensive Letters have been in vain laid before Men willfully blind. But I hope better Things. I have Papers so arranged as to enlighten new Members and make the old SIN against conviction, if they do SIN,,,".

---T--- <u>USA GOV Congress, Relations, Relations with Other Nations, CON Meetings, Subjects of Desires, & GOV of States are ALL prioritizing Christ & Christianity:</u> // "Journals of the Continental Congress, 1774-1789 - 6/2, 1788. - Congress assembled present New hampshire, Massachusetts Rhode island New York, New Jersey Pensylvania, Delaware Virginia, North carolina South Carolina and Georgia and from New Jersey Mr [Abraham] Clarke.Mr Jonathan Hazard ,,,Rhode Island 1] - ,,,Papers of the Continental Congress, No. 179, I, p. 259.] ,,,and the Seal of the said State, this Seventh Day of May A. D. 1787, and in the Eleventh Year of (Seal) Independence ,,,,"That in their opinion it is expedient that the district of Kentucky be erected into an independent state and therefore they submit the following resolution, ,,,acts of the legislature of Virginia therein specified be referred to a committee consisting of a member from each state, to prepare ,,,for acceding to the independence of the said district of Kentucky and for receiving the same into the Union as a member thereof, in a ,,,the Articles of Confederation ,,,consistent with" in the original.] -,,,report ,,,of the Secretary to the US for the department of foreign Affairs to whom were referred two letters from his Most CHRISTIAN Majesty dated the 30th Sept. 1787 - [Note 5: 5 From this point to the end of the day the entries were made by John Fisher and attested by Charles Thomson, in Secret Journal Foreign, Papers of the Continental Congress, No. 6, III, pp. 415--418. They were also entered by Charles Thomson in Secret Journal, Foreign Affairs, Papers of the Continental Congress, No. 5, III, pp. 1682--1683.] ,,,Great and beloved friend and Ally ,,,We PRAY GOD to have you, our great and beloved friend in his HOLY keeping. Written at New York the second day of June 1788. By your good friends the US of America in Congress Assembled.A Chas Thomson Secy ,,,and 27, 1788.] ,,,The prudent and enlightened conduct which he constantly observed during the course of his Mission add to the proofs which he had before given of his zeal for our service. We are persuaded he will equally ,,,to assure you in terms the most expressive of our Affection and of our sincere friendship for you ,,,On this we PRAY GOD that he will have you very dear great friends and Allies in his HOLY keeping. Done &ca. ,,,interests of both Countries, and Study to preserve and encrease the mutual attachment and intercourse which happily subsists between them ,,,We PRAY GOD to have you our great and beloved friend and Ally in his HOLY keeping. written at New York the second day of June 1788, By your good friends, the US of America in Congress Assembled.B Chas Thomson Secy. B The translation of the letter1 ,,,[Note 2: 2 See May 30, 1788.]".

---T--- <u>Christ with His Christianity is the USA GOV Religion & All Others religions are</u> Opposed with Limitations: // All the following is From Congress Meeting Notes & Table of Contents of CONGRESS MEETING NOTES, AD 1788, in constructing the CON: "Senate responsible to State Legislatures; Federal CON favorable to Trial by Jury; RELIGION, no Power over it; an INFIDEL will never be chosen for Office; Amendments; exclusive Legislation; Liberty of the Press; Census; Requisitions done away ... 206, 210" // "RELIGIOUS Tests, Foundation of Persecution ... 200" // "Mr. WILSON — "wished Exclusion of Popish priests from Office ... 212" // "Mr. PATRICK CALHOUN--RELIGION; too great a Latitude allowed ... 312" // "Fallacy of the Opinion that the Pope, or a Foreigner, may be chosen President; RELIGION ... 198" // "RELIGION; Papists or MAHOMETANS may occupy the Chair; Disqualification in the States; would oppose Adoption ... 215" // "RELIGION; Tests; Persecutions; its Toleration in America; Sacrament in Great Britain; Office open to all RELIGIONS [[Christian DENs]]; Guaranty explained President must be a Native; Form of an Oath; governed by the RELIGION of the Person taking it; Case of an East Indian, a Gentoo, in Charles II.'s Time ... 197" [[note that the R-E is proved here as not to allow the external activity of false religions for public assemblies; that is those that are not Christian; not excessive allowance; only allowed in private personal homes]] // Congress Meeting Notes continue~ "I hope that I have in some degree satisfied the doubts of the gentleman. This article is calculated to secure universal religious liberty, by putting all sects on a level -- the only way to prevent persecution. I thought nobody would have objected to this clause, which deserves, in my opinion, the highest approbation. This country has already had the honor of setting an EX of civil freedom, and I trust it will likewise have the honor of teaching the rest of the world the way to religious freedom also. God grant both may be perpetuated to the end of time! (p) Mr. ABBOT, after expressing his obligations for the explanation which had been given, observed that no answer had been given to the question he put concerning the form of an oath. (p) Mr. IREDELL. Mr. Chairman ,,, (p) According to the modern definition of an oath, it is considered a "solemn appeal to the Supreme Being, for the truth of what is said, by a person who believes in the existence of Supreme Being and in a future state of rewards and punishments, according to that form which will bind his conscience most." [[Conscience is the true connection with the true GOD]] It was long held that no oath could be administered but upon the New Testament, except to a Jew, who was allowed to swear upon the Old. According to this notion, none but Jews and Christians could take an oath; and heathens were altogether excluded. At length, by the operation of principles of toleration, these narrow motions were done away. Men at length considered that there were many virtuous men in the world who had not had an opportunity of being instructed either in the Old or New

Testament, who yet very sincerely believed in a Supreme Being „,in a future state of rewards and punishments. It is well known that many nations entertain this belief who do not believe either in the Jewish or Christian religion. Indeed, there are few people so grossly ignorant or barbarous as to have no religion at all. And if none but Christians or Jews could be examined upon oath, many innocent persons might suffer for want of the testimony of others. In regard to the form of an oath, that ought to be governed by the religion of the person taking it. [[the concern here is not the oath for GOV Officials, rather that of including the oath as applied to areas of juries, courts, or various hiring of services to the GOV; and when the person is not a Christian; this is NOT a USA Right for permission or promoting of support to other false religions, (not Christian), nor to have non-Christians in specific Office; this is very clear by the facts of putting all of these remarks together; of that he states it is the oath in courts; of that he states he is a Christian and member of a Christian Church; of that he shares that the Christian religion is to be in promotion to the whole world, including "barbarians" and "grossly ignorant"]] I remember to have read an instance which happened in England, I believe in the time of Charles II. A man who was a material witness in a cause, refused to swear upon the book, and was admitted to swear with his uplifted hand. The jury had a difficulty in crediting him; but the chief justice told them, he had, in his opinion, taken as strong an oath as any of the other witnesses, though, had he been to swear himself, he should have kissed the book. A very remarkable instance also happened in England, about forty years ago, of a person who was admitted to take an oath according to the rites of his own country, though he was a heathen. He was an East Indian, who had a great suit in chancery, and his answer upon oath to a bill filed against him was absolutely necessary. Not believing either in the Old or New Testament, he could not be sworn in the accustomed manner, but was sworn according to the form of the Gentoo religion, which he professed, by touching the foot of a priest. It appeared that, according to the tenets of this religion, its members believed in a Supreme Being, and in a future state of rewards and punishments. It was accordingly held by the judges, upon great consideration, that the oath ought to be received; they considering that it was probable those of that religion were equally bound in conscience by an oath according to their form of swearing, as they themselves were by one of theirs; and that it would be a reproach to the justice of the country, if a man, merely because he was of a different religion from their own, should be denied redress of an injury he had sustained. Ever since this great case, it has been universally considered that, in administering an oath, it is only necessary to inquire if the person who is to take it, believes in a Supreme Being, and in a future state of rewards and punishments. If he does, the oath is to be administered according to that form which it is supposed will bind his conscience most. It is, however, necessary that such a belief should be entertained, because otherwise there would be nothing to bind his conscience that could be relied on; since there are many cases where the terror of punishment in this world for perjury could not be dreaded. I have endeavored to satisfy the committee. We may, I think, very safely leave religion to itself; and as to the form of the oath, I think this may well be trusted to the general GOV, to be applied on the principles I have mentioned. (p) Gov. JOHNSTON expressed great astonishment that the people were alarmed on the subject of religion. This, he said, must have arisen from the great pains which had been taken to prejudice men's minds against the CON. He begged leave to add the following few observations to what had been so ably said by the gentleman last up. (p) I read the CON over and over, but could not see one cause of apprehension or jealousy on this subject. [[favoring by making a law for one DEN & excluding all other DEN]] When I heard there were apprehensions that the pope of Rome could be the President of the US, I was greatly astonished. It might as well be said that the king of England or France, or the Grand Turk, could be chosen to that office. It would have been as good an argument. It appears to me that it would have been dangerous, if Congress could intermeddle with the subject of religion. True religion [[not false religion; note their discerning]] is derived from a much higher source than human laws, When any attempt is made, by any GOV, to restrain men's consciences, no good consequence can possibly follow. It is apprehended that Jews, Mahometans, pagans, &c., may be elected to high offices under the GOV of the US Those who are Mahometans, or any others who are not professors of the Christian religion, can never be elected to the office of President, or other high office, but in one of two cases. First, if the people of America lay aside the Christian religion altogether, it may happen. Should this unfortunately take place, the people will choose such men as think as they do themselves. Another case is, if any persons of such descriptions should, notwithstanding their religion, acquire the confidence and esteem of the people of America by their good conduct and practice of virtue, they may be chosen. I leave it to gentlemen's candor to judge what probability there is of the people's choosing men of different sentiments from themselves. (p) But great apprehensions have been raised as to the influence of the Eastern States. When you attend to circumstances, this will have no weight. I know but two or three states where there is the least chance of establishing any particular religion. The people of Massachusetts and Connecticut are mostly Presbyterians. In every other state, the people are divided into a great number of sects. [[note that Religion and establishing are easily known defined as DEN or SECT of Christianity]] are In Rhode Island, the tenets of the Baptists, I believe, prevail. In New York, they are divided very much: the most numerous are the Episcopalians and the Baptists. In New Jersey, they are as much divided as we are. In Pennsylvania, if any sect prevails more than others, it is that of the Quakers. In Maryland, the Episcopalians are most numerous, though there are other sects. In Virginia, there are many sects; you all know what their religious sentiments are. So in all the Southern States they differ; as also in New Hampshire. I hope, therefore, that gentlemen will see there is no cause of fear that any one religion shall be exclusively established. (p) Mr. CALDWELL thought that some danger might arise. He imagined it might be objected to in a political as well as in a religious view. In the first place, he said, there was an invitation for Jews and pagans of every kind to come among us. At some future period, said he, this might endanger the character of the US. Moreover, even those who do not regard religion, acknowledge that the Christian religion is best calculated, of all religions, to make good members of society, on account of its morality. I think, then, added he, that, in a political view, those gentlemen who formed this CON should not have given this invitation to Jews and heathens. All those who have any religion are against the emigration of those people from the eastern hemisphere (p) Mr. SPENCER was an advocate for securing every unalienable right, and that of worshipping God according to the dictates of conscience in particular. He therefore thought that no one particular religion should be established". // Now the subject is tests for all GOV Officials that are directly connected to making Laws & All others; for the intention/ purpose of the following: +"Religious tests, said he, have been the foundation of persecutions in all countries. Persons who are conscientious will not take the oath required by religious tests, and will therefore be excluded from offices, though equally capable of discharging them as any member of the society. It is feared, continued he, that persons of bad principles, deists, atheists, &c., may come into this country; and there is nothing to restrain them from being eligible to offices. He asked if it was reasonable to suppose that the people would choose men without regarding their characters. Mr, Spencer then continued thus: Gentlemen urge that the want of a test admits the most vicious characters to offices. I desire to know what test could bind them. If they were of such principles, it would not keep them from enjoying those offices. On the other hand, it would exclude from offices conscientious and truly religious people, though equally capable as others. Conscientious persons would not take such an oath, and would be therefore excluded. This would be a great cause of objection to a religious test. But in this case, as there is not a religious test required, it leaves religion on the solid foundation of its own inherent validity, without any connection with temporal authority; and no kind of oppression can take place; I confess it strikes me so. I am sorry to differ from the worthy gentleman. I cannot object to this part of the CON, I wish every other part was as good and proper. (p) Gov. JOHNSTON approved of the worthy member's candor. He admitted a possibility of Jews, pagans, &c., emigrating to the US; yet, he said, they could not be in proportion to the emigration of Christians who should come froth other countries; that, in all probability, the children even of such people would be Christians; and that this, with the rapid population of the US, their zeal for religion, and love of liberty, would, he trusted, add to the progress of the Christian religion among us. (p) The 7th article read without any objection against it. (p) Gov. JOHNSTON, after a short speech, which was not distinctly heard, made a motion to the following effect:-- That this committee, having fully deliberated on the CON proposed for the future GOV of the US of America, by the Federal Convention lately held at Philadelphia, on the 17th day of Sept. last, and having taken into their serious consideration the present critical situation of America, which induces them to be of opinion, that though certain amendments to the said CON may be wished for, yet that those amendments should be proposed subsequent to the ratification on the part of this state, and not previous to it,-- they therefore recommend that the Convention do ratify the CON, and at the Same time propose amendments, to take place in one of the modes prescribed by the CON. (p) Mr. LENOIR. Mr. Chairman, I conceive that I shall not be out of order to make some observations on this last part of the system, and take some retrospective view of some other parts of it. I think it not proper for our adoption, as I consider that it endangers our liberties. When we consider this system collectively, we must be surprised to think that any set of men, who were delegated to amend the Confederation, should propose to annihilate it; for that and this system are utterly different, and cannot exist together. It has been said that the fullest confidence should be put in those characters who formed this CON. We will admit them, in private and public transactions, to be good characters. But, sir, it appears to me, and every other member of this committee, that they exceeded their powers. Those gentlemen had no sort of power to form a new CON altogether; neither had the citizens of this country such an idea in their view. I cannot undertake to say what principles actuated them. I must conceive they were mistaken in their politics, and that this system does not secure the unalienable rights of freemen. It has some aristocratical and some monarchical features, and perhaps some of them intended the establishment of one of these governments. Whatever might be their intent, according to my views, it will lead to the most dangerous aristocracy that ever was thought of-- an aristocracy established on a constitutional bottom! I conceive (and I believe most of this committee will likewise) that this is so dangerous, that I should like as well to have no CON at all. Their powers are almost unlimited. (p) A CON ought to be understood by every one. The most humble and trifling characters in the country have a right to know what foundation they stand upon. I confess I do not see the end of the powers here proposed, nor the reasons for granting them. The principal end of a CON is to set forth what must be given up for the community at large, and to secure those rights which ought never to be infringed. The proposed plan secures no right; or, if it does, it is in so vague and undeterminate a manner, that we,,,, understand it. My constituents instructed me to oppose the adoption of this CON. The principal reasons are as follow: The right of representation is not fairly and explicitly preserved to the people, it being easy to evade that privilege as provided in this system, and the terms of election being too long. If our General Assembly be corrupt, at the end of the year we can make new men of them by sending others in their stead. It is not so here. If there be any reason to think that human nature is corrupt, and that there is a disposition in men to aspire to power, they may embrace an opportunity, during their long continuance in office, by means of their powers, to take away the rights of the people. The senators are chosen for six years, and two thirds of them, with the President, have most extensive powers. They may enter into a dangerous combination. And they may be continually ,,,The President may be as good a man as any in existence, but he is but a man. He may be corrupt. He has an opportunity of forming plans dangerous to the community at large. I shall not enter into ,,,system, but I conceive, whatever may have, been the intention of its framers, that it leads to a most dangerous aristocracy. It appears to me that, instead of securing the sovereignty of the states, it is calculated to melt them down into one solid empire. If the citizens of this state like a consolidated GOV, I hope they will have virtue enough to secure their rights. I am sorry to make use of the expression, but it appears to me to be a scheme to reduce this GOV to an aristocracy. It guaranties a republican form of GOV to the states; when all these powers are in Congress, it will only be a form. It will be past recovery, when Congress has the power of the purse and the sword. The power of the sword is in explicit terms given to it. The power

117

of direct taxation gives the purse. They may prohibit the trial by jury, which is a most sacred and valuable right. There is nothing contained in this CON to bar them from it. The federal courts have also appellate cognizance of law and fact; the sole cause of which is to deprive the people of that trial, which it is optional in them to grant or not. We find no provision against infringement on the rights of conscience. Ecclesiastical courts [[a concern that one Christian DEN is favored by making a law for it, then will abuse the other Christian DEN]] may be established which will be destructive to our citizens. They may make any establishment [[Christian DEN protection as is observed by the other statements]] they think proper. They have also an exclusive legislation in their ten miles square, to which may be added their power over the militia, who may be carried thither and kept there for life. Should any one grumble at their acts, he would be deemed a traitor, and perhaps taken up and carried to the exclusive legislation, and there tried without a jury. We are told there is no cause to fear. When we consider the great powers of Congress, there is great cause of alarm. They can disarm the militia. If they were armed, they would be a resource against great oppressions. The laws of a great empire are difficult to be executed. If the laws of the Union were oppressive, they could not carry them into effect, if the people were possessed of proper means of defence. (p) It was cried out that we were in a most desperate situation, and that Congress could not discharge any of their most sacred contracts. I believe it to be the case. But why give more power than is necessary? The men who went to the Federal Convention went for the express purpose of amending the GOV, by giving it such additional powers as were necessary. If we should accede to this system, it may be thought proper, by a few designing persons, to destroy it, in a future age, in the same manner that the old system is laid aside. The Confederation was binding on all the states. It could not be destroyed but with the consent of all the states. There was an express article to that purpose. The men who were deputed to the Convention, instead of amending the old, as they were solely empowered and directed to do, proposed a new system. If the best characters departed so far from their authority, what may not be apprehended from others, who may be agents in the new GOV? (p) It is natural for men to aspire to power- -it is the nature of mankind to be tyrannical; therefore it is necessary for us to secure our rights and liberties as far as we can. But it is asked why we should suspect men who are to be chosen by ourselves, while it is their interest to act justly, and while men have self-interest at heart. I think the reasons which I have given are sufficient to answer that question. We ought to consider the depravity of human nature, the predominant thirst of power which is in the breast of every one, the temptations our rulers may have, and the unlimited confidence placed in them by this system. These are the foundation of my fears, They would be so long in the general GOV that they would forget the grievances of the people of the states. (p) But it is said we shall be ruined if separated from the other states, which will be the case if we do not adopt. If so, I would put less confidence in those states. The states are all bound together by the Confederation, and the rest cannot break from us without violating the most solemn compact. If they break that, they will this. [[a concern that the Confederation Articles (AOC) not be ruined by the CON, whereas the AOC had more Christian words in it; but it was not detailed in other areas and did not include many areas]]".

---T--- <u>SACRED Honor to GOD</u>: "We pledge our ,,,SACRED Honor" are the words in the DOI. What is the definition of "Sacred"? It is this: "Make a compact; consecrated to or belonging to God; Holy; of or connected with religion or religious rites; regarded with the same respect and reverence accorded holy things": // This proves again, the intention/ purpose is the establishment of a Covenant Compact or Contract; that it includes God & religion. They decide not their words triflingly, but carefully. They purposely put their life at risk, and all their material possessions; this is no light thing, or easy task. They engaged themselves in to position of killing other people in war. Though there purpose and intent was self-defense and based on having a "right" from God, it is, nevertheless, a terrible engagement to have to kill people in defensive war. Especially when they knew it would send them in to eternity~ Heaven or Hell dwelling. This is a Religious Word and God's word; it is not a word without God, rather defined as including God, the true God.

---T--- <u>Christianity & Christ are the Religion & God Being of the USA GOV & all others are</u> NOT: // Congress Meetings, 1788 - "after a short exordium, which was not distinctly heard, proceeded thus ,,,Some are afraid, Mr. Chairman, that, should the CON be received, they would be deprived of the privilege of worshipping God according to their consciences, which would be taking from them a benefit they enjoy under the present CON, [[the AOC]] They wish to know if their religious and civil liberties be secured under this system, or whether the general GOV may not make laws infringing their religious liberties. [[That the DOI should nevertheless be the ruling DOC over the CON; that the CON is ONLY an application of the DOI]] ,,,The worthy member from Edenton mentioned sundry political reasons why treaties should be the supreme law of the land. It is feared, by some people, that, by the power of making treaties, they might make a treaty engaging with foreign powers to adopt the Roman Catholic religion in the US, which would prevent the people from worshipping God according to their own consciences". // Now subjects of intention/ purpose in this discussion is the protection of~ a+ Christianity, b+ the freedom of Christian DEN, c+ the freedom for Christian DEN to resolve themselves and their different thoughts of various Christian doctrines without GOV interference or rule, d+ no false religions be promoted by the USA GOV in their activities of public assemblies or advertisements in the USA, such as Roman Catholic in it's Strict or special form establishment, Pagans, or false Deists, or Mahometans, etc., e+ that USA GOV officials be under God's authority, Christians, as the Oath secures; or Christian supporting & evil opposing with limitations. // The congress meeting discussion continues~, "-- The worthy member. from Halifax has in some measure satisfied ,,,mind on this subject. But others may be dissatisfied. Many wish to know what religion shall be established. I believe a majority of the community are Presbyterians. I am, for my part, against any exclusive establishment; but if there were any, I would prefer the Episcopal. The exclusion of religious tests is by many thought dangerous and impolitic. They suppose that if there be no religious test required, pagans, deists, and Mahometans might obtain offices among us, and that the senators and representatives might all be pagans. Every person employed by the general and state GOVs is to take an oath to support the former. Some are desirous to know how and by whom they are to swear, since no religious tests are required-- whether they are to swear by Jupiter, Juno, Minerva, Proserpine, or Pluto. We ought to be suspicious of our liberties. We have felt the effects of oppressive measures, and know the happy consequences of being jealous of our rights. I would be glad some gentleman would endeavor to obviate these objections, in order to satisfy the religious art of the society. Could I be convinced that the objections were well founded, I would then declare my opinion against the CON. [Mr. Abbot added several other observations, but spoke too low to be heard.]". // Continuing the Congress meeting~ " --- Mr. Chairman, nothing is more desirable than to remove the scruples of any gentleman on this interesting subject. Those concerning religion are entitled to particular respect. I did not expect any objection to this particular regulation, which, in my opinion, is calculated to prevent evils of the most pernicious consequences to society. Every person in the least conversant in the history of mankind, knows what dreadful mischiefs have been committed by religious persecutions, Under the color of religious tests, the utmost cruelties have been exercised. Those in power have generally considered all wisdom centred in themselves; that they alone had a right to dictate to the rest of mankind; and that all opposition to their tenets was profane and impious. The consequence of this intolerant spirit had been, that each church has in turn set itself up against every other; and persecutions and wars of the most implacable and bloody nature have taken place in every part of the world. America has set an EX to mankind to think more modestly and reasonably --that a man may be of different religious sentiments from our own, without being a bad member of society. The principles of toleration, to the honor of this age, are doing away those errors and prejudices which have so long prevailed, even in the most intolerant countries. In the Roman Catholic countries, principles of moderation are adopted which would have been spurned at a century or two ago. I should be sorry to find, when examples of toleration are set even by arbitrary governments, that this country, so impressed with the highest sense of liberty, should adopt principles on this subject that were narrow and illiberal. (p) I consider the clause under consideration as one of the strongest proofs that could be adduced, that it was the intention of those who formed this system to establish a general religious liberty in America. Were we to judge from the examples of religious tests in other countries, we should be persuaded that they do not answer the purpose for which they are intended. What is the consequence of such in England? In that country no man can be a member in the House of Commons, or hold any office under the crown, without taking the sacrament according to the rites of the Church. This, in the first instance, must degrade and profane a rite which never ought to be taken but from a sincere principle of devotion. To a man of base principles, it is made a mere instrument of civil policy. The intention was, to exclude all persons from offices but the members of the Church of England. [[Christian DEN guarded so as all Various DEN allowed]] Yet it is notorious that dissenters qualify themselves for offices in this manner, though they never conform to the Church on any other occasion; and men of no religion at all have no scruple to make use of this qualification. It never was known that a man who had no principles of religion hesitated to perform any rite when it was convenient for his private interest. No test can bind such a one. I am therefore clearly of opinion that such a discrimination would neither be effectual for its own purposes, nor, if it could, ought it by any means to be made. Upon the principles I have stated, I confess the restriction on the power of Congress, in this particular, has my hearty approbation. [[concern that the Oath was not good enough to protect against evil or non-Christian men from lying, taking it insincerely]] (p) They Certainly have no authority to interfere in the establishment of any religion whatsoever; and I am astonished that any gentleman should conceive they have. Is there any power given to Congress in matters of religion? Can they pass a single act to impair our religious liberties? If they could, it would be a just cause of alarm. If they could, sir, no man would have more horror against it than myself. Happily, no sect here is superior to another. [[Christian DEN protected R-Est]] As long as this is the case, we shall be free from those persecutions and distractions with which other countries have been torn. If any future Congress should pass an act concerning the religion of the country, it would be an act which they are not authorized to pass, by the CON, and which the people would not obey. Every one would ask, "Who authorized the GOV to pass such an act? It is not warranted by the CON, and is barefaced usurpation." The power to make treaties can never be supposed to include a right to establish a foreign religion among ourselves, though it might authorize a toleration of others. (p) But it is objected that the people of America may, perhaps, choose representatives who have no religion at all, and that pagans and Mahometans may be admitted into offices. But how is it possible to exclude any set of men, without taking away that principle of religious freedom which we ourselves so warmly contend for? This is the foundation on which persecution has been raised in every part of the world. The people in power were always right, and every body else wrong. If you admit the least difference, the door to persecution is opened. [[thus the wording was the subject; as how to stop a GOV from supporting false religions, such as Mahometans & pagans from the USA GOV, and yet nevertheless protect the Christian religion from being abused or the GOV from falsely interpreting the words and bringing persecution. It was not intended to allow or support false religions as stated, but how to word the DOCs to protect against them, yet protect Christianity at the same time]]. Nor would it answer the purpose, for the worst part of the excluded sects would comply with the test, and the best men only be kept out of our counsels. But it is never to be supposed that the people of America will trust their dearest rights to persons who have no religion at all, or a religion materially different from their own. It would be happy for mankind if religion was permitted to take its own course, and maintain itself by the excellence of its own doctrines. The divine Author of our religion never wished for its support by worldly authority. Has he not said that the gates of hell shall not prevail against it? [[Holy Bible vs]]. The divine Author of our religion never wished for its support by worldly authority. Has he not said that the gates of hell shall not prevail against it? It made much greater progress for itself, than when supported by the greatest authority upon earth. (p) It has been asked by

119

that respectable gentleman (Mr. Abbot) what is the meaning of that part, where it is said that the US shall guaranty to every state in the Union a republican form of GOV, and why a guaranty of religious freedom was not included. The meaning of the guaranty provided was this: There being thirteen governments confederated upon a republican principle, it was essential to the existence and harmony of the confederacy that each should be a republican GOV, and that no state should have a right to establish an aristocracy or monarchy. That clause was therefore inserted to prevent any state from establishing any GOV but a republican one. Every one must be convinced of the mischief that would ensue, if any state had a right to change its GOV to a monarchy. If a monarchy was established in any one state, it would endeavor to subvert the freedom of the others, and would, probably, by degrees succeed in it. This must strike the mind of every person here, who recollects the history of Greece, when she had confederated governments. The king of Macedon, by his arts and intrigues, got himself admitted a member of the Amphictyonic council, which was the superintending government of the Grecian republics; and in a short time he became master of them all; It is, then, necessary that the members of a confederacy should have similar GOVs. But consistently with this restriction, the states may make what change in their own governments they think proper. Had Congress undertaken to guaranty religious freedom, or any particular species of it, they would then have had a pretence to interfere in a subject they have nothing to do with. Each state, so far as the clause in question does not interfere, must be left to the operation of its own principles. (p) There is a degree of jealousy which it is impossible to satisfy. Jealousy in a free GOV ought to be respected; but it may be carried to too great an extent. It is impracticable to guard against all possible danger of people's choosing their officers indiscreetly. If they have a right to choose, they may make a bad choice. (p) I met, by accident, with a pamphlet, this morning, in which the author states, as a very serious danger, that the pope of Rome might be elected President. I confess this never struck me before; and if the author had read all the qualifications of a President, perhaps his fears might have been quieted. No man but a native, or who has resided fourteen years in America, can be chosen President. I know not all the qualifications for pope, but I believe he must be taken from the college of cardinals; and probably there are many previous steps necessary before he arrives at this dignity. A native of America must have very singular good fortune, who, after residing fourteen years in his own country, should go to Europe, enter into Romish orders, obtain the promotion of cardinal, afterwards that of pope, and at length be so much in the confidence of his own country as to be elected President. It would be still more extraordinary if he should give up his popedom for our presidency. Sir, it is impossible to treat such idle fears with any degree of gravity. Why is it not objected, that there is no provision in the CON against electing one of the kings of Europe President? It would be a clause equally rational and judicious."

---T--- Absence Law: // There is absolutely~ +] No DOC, +] No historical supporting DOC, +] No life evidence from any FFOG, +] No promoting or allowance of, or encouragement to any other religion than Christianity, +] No God but Jesus Christ (Christianity); except Judaism (Christianity in it's earlier status), +] No opposing or stopping Christianity, +] No starting of any system without Christianity.

---T--- Inclusion/Exclusion Law: // All other religions and false gods are specifically excluded and warned about~ +] in every instance of DOC, and +] in every historical supporting DOC, and +] such Includes Paganism, Heathenism, God Exclusion, etc.

---T--- The Wording & More Words Included in the CON: // It is true that the CON would ideally be better if it had more words included of Christ Jesus. However, remember that~ +] the DOI is the controlling DOC; the overruling DOC to the CON of the joined CC; thus it is very clear in the DOI; +] the FFOG intended to prevent the USA GOV from: += false religions, += false Christianity, += controlling Christianity as in Europe, += having a USA Christian Church and not allowing for other Christian DEN, += having USA GOV control over the States Independency for Christian freedom and Christian DEN. // Hence because that they did not know how to word the thoughts in every instance, and because they were under time constraints, and mental struggles and such, they did as they did. // No GOV REP nor Citizen REPs ever intended/ purposed~ +the CON to state less than it did; this is proven by supporting DOC and etc.; +there were FFOG and States that wanted more exacting language included; including about Jesus Christ. // However the debates as to how to protect, prevent, and support all at the same time resulted in what we have now. At this time, Christians would be able to know what to say and how to format the words, if we would ever decide to do such. // Nevertheless once we comprehend that the DOI has function of the OverRuling DOC to the CON and is acutally part of Constitutional Law, and that they are One Document to be joined; and that they are a prayer to God; they are a CC; then we have knowledge of what they actually are and what to do with them.

---T--- Religion is for Christ's Christianity & Falsity Christianity Opposed: // Journal Of William Maclay includes records of Congress meetings and all Branch activity is discussed: "I have observed ever since we began to do business that a Jehu-like SPIRIT [[Biblical reference]] has prevailed with a number of gentlemen ,,,RELIGIOUS distinctions, coercive laws for taking the oaths, etc ,,,I have uniformly ,,,But be it so.' I have the TESTIMONY of MY OWN CONSCIENCE that I am right. High-handed measures are at no time justifiable ,,,We come here the servants ,,,The new GOV, instead of being a powerful machine ,,,From the hall there was a grand procession to SAINT Paul's CHURCH, where PRAYers were said by the BISHOP. The procession was well conducted and without accident, as far as I have heard. The militia were all under arms, lined the street near the CHURCH, made a good figure, and behaved well ,,,May 1st. Attended at the Hall at eleven. The PRAYers were over and the minutes reading. ,,,The abolishing of royalty, the extinguishment of patronage and dependencies attached to that form of GOV, were the exalted motives of many revolutionists, and these were the improvements meant by them to be made of the war which was forced on us by British aggression - in fine, the amelioration of government and bettering file condition of mankind. These ends and none other were publicly avowed, and all our CONs and public acts were formed in this SPIRIT ,,,They wished for the loaves and fishes of government, [[Biblical reference]] ,,,May 6th. No Senate this day; there was a commencement at SAINT Paul's CHURCH; the Senate were served with tickets. ,,,GOD forgive me for the vile thought, but I can not help thinking of a monkey just put into breeches when I saw him betray such evident marks of self-conceit. He made us a speech this day also, but, as I did not minute the heads of it when he spoke, I will not attempt to recollect it. ,,,May 26th. ,,,I made an apology to the Vice-President for the absence of our CHAPLAIN, Mr. Linn. There had been some conversation yesterday in the Senate about the style of the Bishop. ,,,The Vice-President revived the discourse ,,,as sure as GOD was in the firmament! ,,,July 4th. This is the anniversary of American Independence [[official recognition of the DOI as America's Overruling DOC]]. The day was celebrated ,,,The Cincinnati assembled at SAINT Paul's CHURCH, where an oration was pronounced by Colonel Hamilton ,,,The CHURCH was crowded. ,,,Excepting my attendance at SAINT Paul's CHURCH, I kept [the] house all day, as I find going out only hurts my knees, both of which are still affected by the rheumatism. ,,,If such a one errs it is the SIN of ignorance, and I think HEAVEN has pardons ready sealed for every one of them. "Behold, O GOD," ,,,faithfully have I played its powers. If the result has been error, intentional criminality was not with me." ,,,Wednesday, 16th. ,,,That people must be abandoned and forsaken by GOD who could speak of buying a judge as you would a horse. ,,,Many families in New England had concluded with a tremendous oath, "By GOD, I never will vote for the bill unless the proviso is thrown out!" ,,,. A resolution of the Representatives for appointing of a CHAPLAIN was concurred in, and the BISHOP appointed on the part of the Senate ,,,As the Scotchman said in his PRAYers, we were left to the freedom of our own will ",,,Circumstances may direct me to what is best. GOD has, however, given to every man his talent for the express purpose of making use of it; or, in other words, that he may conduct himself on the principles of right reason. May he enable me to keep my lamp trimmed always! [[Biblical reference]] ,,,He paused a little; got up rather hastily; said, "GOD bless you!" went out of the chamber ,,,The Speaker offered me his carriage, but then his servants were all gone to CHURCH. ,,,I went this afternoon to hear a negro preach. I can only say it would be in favor of RELIGION in general if PREACHERS manifested the same fervor and sincerity that were apparent in his manner. He declared himself untutored, but he seemed to have the BIBLE by heart. Tempora mutantur et nos mutamur in illis. ,,,I can with TRUTH,,,. From hence we went to St. Paul's, and heard the anniversary of independence pronounced by a Mr. B. Livingston. The CHURCH was crowded. I could not hear him well. Some said it was fine. I could not contradict them. ,,,But, be it so; so help me GOD, I mean not to alter one tittle! [[Biblical SC]] I am firmly determined to act without any regard to consequences of this kind,," I can answer with TRUTH, "I have tried the best in my power." ,,,If there is treason in the wish I retract it, but would to GOD this same General Washington were in HEAVEN! ,,,Dec. 17th. ,,,attended at the Board, having first heard PRAYers and sat a half hour at the Hall. ,,,Dec. 25th. This, being CHRISTmas-day, dined with Parson Ewing ,,,and may GOD grant peace in my day! ,,,We talk of corruption in Great Britain. I PRAY we may not have occasion for complaints of a similar nature here. ,,,whence both TRUTH and sincerity are banished ,,,nearer the TRUTH ,,,This man has abilities, but abilities without candor and integrity are characteristics of the DEVIL,,,".

---T--- Christ's Holy Bible & Christianity Religion is basis of USA GOV, DOI, Congress, States GOV, Citizens: // "Letters of Delegates to Congress:Volume 23- 11/7, 1785 - 11/5, 1786 ,,,June 7, 1786 to be pricked to the Heart; if silent solemnity, countenances bathed in tears, expressions of Compunction, & the closest Attention to the word, may be deemed Evidences of it. In short it appeared [to m]any to be an awful place, & none other than the House of GOD, & ,,,Gate of HEAVEN. There is a great increase in the CHURCHes of the Plains, Mt. Bethel, Piscataway, as well as in New York, & its Vicinity. Cranberry, &c. The concern of Saul seems to have taken place in almost every family in several Neighbourhoods. Many of my Kinsmen according to the flesh are of the Number. Nine Ministers were there; & there appeared to be a remarkable Unction, as the French DIVINEs term it, afforded to most of them. "And THEY SHALL FEAR THE NAME OF THE LORD from the West &c. ,,,What think you of the Commencemt. or rather of the more compleat fulfilment of this Prophecy? Glorious things of old, were spoken of, & are now accomplishing in the City of GOD. I wish to ever have that PRAYER in my heart "THY KINGDOM COME." A wide field, on almost every hand, is opening for Labourers of the Baptist DEN, but they are comparatively few. Let us PRAY therefore &c. On the 29th Ult I recd Letters from home & all were well. Mrs. Manning spoke favourably of the Behaviour of the little Boy[s]. ,,,they behave as well as she could reasonably expect & attend to their Learning. I wish Tasker had as great a taste for Books as George. Perhaps Age may alter this matter. ,,,the wealthy planter of Nomini Hall, had entered Manning's Baptist universe as a consequence of a remarkable conversion in 1778, which opened a new chapter in his quest for faith that lasted until about 1790 when he embraced the principles of Emanuel Swedenborg. For Carter's SPIRITual journey and RELIGIOUS activities during his Baptist years, see Louis Morton, Robert Carter of Nomini Hall, A 2 Apparently a reference to the conversion of Saul of Tarsus, whose dramatic experience on the road to Damascus is recorded in the New Testament book of ,," 'Acts 9:3--18:3 Isaiah 59:19'. <<< HOLY BIBLE vss.

---T--- GOV must have God first to conceive GOV rightly: // FFOG Thomas Paine said, "All the principles of science are of Divine origin. Man cannot make, or invent, or contrive principles; he can only discover them. And he ought to look through the discovery to the Author" (250).

---T--- Religion Affection to Christ & His Christianity is Required to be Supported by the USA GOV Officers; & States GOV: // "Letters of Delegates to Congress: Volume 8- 9/19, 1777 - 1/ 31, 1778 - ,,,Oct. ,,,1777 I sent you a few days ago an Account of the Success we have had on the Delaware. The Honor of recovering Philadelphia seems to be intended for the brave Men who command there; for if the Enemy cannot get up with their Ships of War, Howe cannot long remain in the City. May Honor be given to whom Honor may be due. [[Holy Bible vs]] Congress have applyd with Diligence to Confederation. Most of the important Articles are agreed to. Each State retains its Sovereignty and Independence with every Power, Jurisdiction and Right which is not by the Confederation expressly delegated to the US in Congress assembled. Each State is to have one Vote in Congress; but there must be a Concurrence of Nine States in all Matters of Importance. The Proportion of the publick Expence to be paid by Each

State to be ascertained by the Value of all the Lands granted to or surveyd for any Person, to be estimated according to such Mode as Congress shall from time to time direct. All Disputes about Boundaries are to be decided by Judges appointed in the following Mode: The Representatives of Each State in Congress to be nominated, the contending States to strike off 13 Each and out of the remaining 13 not more than 9 nor less than 7 shall be drawn out by Lot, any five of them to hear & determine the Matter. I hope we shall finish the Confederation in a few days when I intend to renew my Request for the Leave of Absence, and return home. ,,,I am determined by Cods Assistance never to forsake the great Cause in which my Country is virtuously struggling; but there are others who have greater Abilities & more adequate to this important Service, than I have. I hope therefore another will be appointed in my Room ,,,I have the clear and full Testimony of my own Mind that I have at all Times endeavord ,,,This will be deliverd to you by Mr. Hancock ,,,understanding enough to know when the Arts of Flattery are playd upon him, and Fortitude of mind sufficient to resist & despise them. ,,,In this EVIL World there are oftentimes large Doses prepared for those whose Stomacks will bear them. And it would be a disgrace to human Nature to affirm there are some who can take the fullest Cup without nauseating. I suppose you have by this time finishd a form of GOV. I hope the greatest Care will be taken in the Choice of a Governor. He, whether a wise Man or a Fool, will in a great Measure form the MORALS & Manners of the People ,,,But alas! Is there not such a Possibility! But I assure my self of better things. I believe my Country will fix their Eyes and their Choice on a Man of RELIGION and Piety; who will understand human Nature and the Nature and End of political Society-who will not by Corruption or Flattery be seducd to the betraying, even without being sensible of it himself, the SACRED Rights [[Rights coming from God]] of his Country ,,,I hope Burgoyn will not be permitted to reside in Boston; for if he is, I fear that inconsiderate Persons of Fashion and some significance will be inducd, under the Idea of Politeness, to form Connexions with him, dangerous to the Publick. There are other Reasons which I should think would make his or any other officers being fixed in a populous Town uneligible. There are Prison ships ,,,Let us ascribe Glory to GOD who has graciously vouchsafd to favor the Cause of America and of Mankind. We are impatiently waiting to hear from Rhode Island ,,,Every Nerve must be exerted in preparing for another Campain; for we may be attackd the next Spring with redoubled Vigor ,,,Among the Train of EVILs it is likely to bring upon us, is the Destruction of MORALS; for many will be ready to think Extortion and Injustice necessary and justifiable for their own Security. I am much pleasd to hear that the People of our State are loudly calling for & the Assembly,,,."

---T--- Religion & R~Est about God in the USA is defined as~ +] Christianity; +] Christian DEN, secondary doctrines, expressions; +] not any or every falsity religion: // "Letters of Delegates to Congress: Volume 1 AUG 1774 - AUG 1775 ,,,Octr. 9. 1774 I am wearied to Death with the Life I lead. The Business of the Congress is tedious, beyond Expression. This Assembly is like no other that ever existed. Every Man in it is a great Man-- an orator, a Critick, a statesman, and therefore every Man upon every Question must shew his oratory, -his criticism and his Political Abilities ,,,We should be entertained with Logick and Rhetorick, Law, History, Politicks and Mathematicks, concerning the Subject for two whole days, and then We should pass the Resolution unanimously in the Affirmative ,,,This Day I went to Dr. Allisons Meeting in the Forenoon and heard the Dr. -a good Discourse upon the Lords Supper. This is a Presbyterian Meeting. I confess I am not fond of the Presbyterian Meetings in this Town. I had rather go to CHURCH. We have better Sermons, better PRAYERS, better Speakers, softer, sweeter Musick, and genteeler Company. And I must confess, that the Episcopal CHURCH is quite as agreable to my Taste as the Presbyterian. They are both Slaves to the Domination of the Priesthood. I like the Congregational Way best--next to that the Independent. This afternoon, led by Curiosity and good Company I strolled away to Mother CHURCH, or rather Grandmother CHURCH, I mean the Romish Chappell. Heard a good, short, MORAL Essay upon the Duty of Parents to their Children, founded in Justice and Charity, to take care of their Interests temporal and SPIRITual. This Afternoons Entertainment was to me, most awfull and affecting. The poor Wretches, fingering their Beads, chanting Latin, not a Word of which they understood, their Pater Nosters and Ave Maria's. Their HOLY Water-their Crossing themselves perpetually-- their Bowing to the Name of JESUS, wherever they hear it-- their Bowings, and Kneelings, and Genuflections before the Altar. The Dress of the Priest was rich with Lace-- his Pulpit was Velvet and Gold. The Altar Piece was very rich--little Images and Crucifixes about-- Wax Candles lighted up. But how shall I describe the Picture of our Saviour in a Frame of Marble over the Altar at full Length upon the Cross, in the Agonies, and the Blood dropping and streaming from his Wounds. The Musick consisting of an organ, and a Choir of singers, went all the Afternoon, excepting sermon Time, and the Assembly chanted-- most sweetly and exquisitely. Here is every Thing which can lay hold of the Eye, Ear, and Imagination. Every Thing which can charm and beWITCH the simple and ignorant. I wonder how Luther ever broke the spell. Adieu. John Adams RC (MHi) . Adams, Family Correspondence (Butterfield), 1:166-67."

---T--- USA GOV is to have Officers that Support Jesus & Christianity & His Holy Bible: // "Letters of Delegates to Congress: Volume: 3- 1/1, 1776 - May 15, 1776 ,,,10th Feby. 1776 I desired Mr. Greene ,,,You begin by observing that my Letter was a pleasure and a disappointment, a TRUE picture this of life in general. The DIVINE Wisdom has thought best (& I believe it is absolutely necessary) At the same time that we are surrounded with innumerable mercies and comforts to vary the scene with disappointm[ent], Pain, Sickness & other things which we call trouble. We are full fond of this world & too negligent of the next as things now stand. If there were no troubles, wickedness or distress, but one continued State of health, ease & pleasure I believe they would be fatal to human nature. Let us then adore that all gracious Being whose Goodness preserves, & whose mercies surround us & make life comfortable & who at the same time by the shortness & uncertainty of [. . .] and the various disappointments attending [...] shews us the insufficiency of temporal enjoyment [and] kindly leads us to look for compleat happi[ness in] that World alone which is to come; May we all be prepared for it. I do not wonder that you [are] concerned at my constant application to business, I am amazed that I am so well, may this Instance of DIVINE goodness encrease my Love & Gratitude & induce me to live more to his glory. Your dear

122

Bror. Sammy, I am much pleased that you could in that beautiful sentiment of Popes so chearfully commit him to his Maker. May you continue to have such a lively sense of the DIVINE wisdom & goodness as chearfully to resign yourself & every thing dear to You to his all wise direction and government. I am very glad your Bror. Charles has got a Commission ,,,I hope with you that he may do his duty, do write to him as often as you can well and encourage him in the paths of RELIGION & Virtue. ,,,The Acct. which you give me of [Polly, Ray] and other relations is very acceptable & [I most] devoutly thank GOD that you are so [happy in] that nearest of all connections. May you [both have] wisdom to behave in such a manner as [that esteem,] regard & mutual affection may continue [&] encrease to your latest Breath & ever ac[knowledge] that goodness which hath made you th[us]. ,,,We are very happy in the Arrival of about 120 Tons of salt petre & 20 Tons of Powder & 1300 stand of Arms, we shall need them & much more for our enemies will do their utmost ,,,I hope every thing will [be] done to put your part of the Colony into a proper posture of defence. ,,,proper ,,,RC (RHi)."

---T--- <u>God of Christianity Agreed to the CC that the Spiritual</u> Moral Beings made with Him. This is proved because~ +] the Holy Bible states His Being; +] the Holy Bible states His Promises; +] the Holy Bible states the conditions of His Promises; +] the CC does the conditions for His Promises; +] victory was gained over evil; +] Christ's & the Holy Spirit's presence was increased; +] Christianity was increased. // Additionally, God will continue to honor the FFOG who made the CC and His promise to do His Part.

---T--- <u>False Religion is Opposed Equally as Any Falsity against God:</u> // For false religion or false gods must be opposed or set the DOI, CON, and supporting DOC's aside or make them turn against themselves; be contradicted. // Additionally it would be to oppose all the events, activities, and life styles of all the citizens & Officers of the GOV.

---T--- <u>CC Covenant is made with Jesus Christ Who is the real & true</u> God; thus His religion is to be the religion, not falsity religions: // The religion must be the same God, Jesus Christ, not other gods, which have a false god.

---T--- <u>Religion is not to be anti-God</u> or Non-god; rather God centered; God priority.

---T--- <u>Religion & Religious Establishment is defined,</u> by AD 1828 Webster's (1b): // Religion is to the TRUE God, not a FALSE god; religions to a false god are "false religions"; religion also includes specific applications of worship, as in DENs: "1. Religion, in its most comprehensive sense, includes a belief in the being and perfections of God [[not false god, but true GOD]], in the revelation of his will to man, in man's obligation to obey his commands, in a state of reward and punishment, and in man's accountableness to God; and also true godliness or piety of life, with the practice of all moral duties. It therefore comprehends theology, as a system of doctrines or principles, as well as practical piety; for <u>the practice of moral duties without a belief in a divine lawgiver, and without reference to his will or commands, is not religion.</u> 2. Religion, as distinct from theology, is godliness or real piety in practice, consisting in the performance of all known duties to God and our fellow men, in obedience to divine command, or from love to God and his law. Jam1. ,,,3. Religion, as distinct from virtue, or morality, consists in the performance of the duties we owe directly to God, from a principle of obedience to his will. Hence we often speak of religion and virtue, as different branches of one system, or the duties of the first and second tables of the law. 4. Any system of faith and worship. In this sense, religion comprehends the belief and worship of pagans and Mohammedans, as well as of Christians; any religion consisting in the belief of a superior power or powers governing the world, and in the worship of such power or powers. Thus we speak of the religion of the Turks, of the Hindoos ,,,as well as of the Christian religion. <u>We speak of false religion, as well as of true religion.</u> 5. The rites of religion; in the plural." // Noah Webster was a participant as FFOG in the USA DOC; he knows what he is talking about. // Religious Establishment is easily known to be defined as DEN.

---T--- <u>All the Events & Activities of the USA Nation was</u> in Support of Lord Jesus & Christianity.

---T--- <u>The USA as a Nation never had any Events or Activities</u> that ever supported any falsity religion in its construction ~ NEVER once.

---T--- <u>All supporting DOC provide EV in excess</u> that the only religion that is to be supported is TRUE RELIGION of Christianity that worships Christ of Christmas; NOT Falsity religion.

---T--- <u>The word Religion must be supportive of th</u>e TRUE God, the Lord Jesus because the CC & all DOC state limitations as to what it refers to. If such was UNLIMITED then ALL Evil would be able to be included. Now what Spiritual Conscience Being will say that it is unlimited ???

---T--- <u>God's Holy Bible & C</u>hristianity assisted developing the society of the USA & USA GOV: // Matthew Maury was an oceanographer, who was injured in an accident. Hence he was "bed-ridden". So he studied how to do something, of the which, while he was in bed, his family was reading Psa8:8. He asked them to read it repeatedly. The vs includes a part saying, "paths of the seas". He had a thought to study such therefore. Mr. Maury provided a chart of the "pathways of the seas", which increased advancement of KN in water travel. // Mr. Maury became desirous to learn more about, and from, Christ. He found a vs, Eccl1:6, which says, "Blowing toward the south, then turning toward the north, the wind continues swirling along; and on its circular courses the wind returns". He then learned that there are pathways in the air, circular flows, and which have rules, and can partially be predicted. The subject of Meteorology was increased with KN. Also jet-streams are what some of these air circular motions are called today, and this KN helps fly airplanes (251). // Mr. Maury was first assigned as a naval Officer by US Senator Sam Houston, in AD 1820's approx. Mr. Maury proclaimed God, Christianity, and the Holy Bible as his source of guidance saying, ",,,the Bible in confirmation of the doctrines of physical geography. ,,,The Bible is authority for everything it touches ,,,The Bible is true, and science is true ,,,They are both true; and when your men of science, with vain and hasty conceit, announce ,,,disagreement between them, rely upon it: the fault is not with the Witness of

His records, but with the "worm" [sinners]" (251). // Mr. Maury also assisted in developing the transatlantic telegraph cable, Nationally Observatory, National Weather Bureau, and the US Naval Academy. And all for love to God.

---T--- "The Bible of the Revolution"; This Book Divine is the Basis of the DOI, CON, USA: // The USA as a Nation printed a Holy Bible during the times of the DOI & CON. Such is EV they were supporting and spreading Christianity for Christ's Presence through the Land; the NGOV paid for it's printing and it's distribution to every citizen (of the Citizen Branch) of the USA. This was done in AD 1777 & 1782; and is called the "Bible of the Revolution".

---T--- The Symbols of the Great Seal of the USA, the pyramid with the eye, & its previous versions, are a Holy Bible based, symbol; for God: // See portions in this Chp on discussing them and the pictures included.

---T--- GOV Officer lives all supported Christ & Christianity in general & specific.

---T--- The Oath in the CON is a Christian subject for God: // The Checks & Balances system utilizes this for assuring responsibility of the testifier to tell the truth; Bringing God in the function is the intention/ purpose; bringing attention to God's presence to thought & words increases trustworthiness. // 2 provisions are made with the Oath: Christianity was not forced for the internal Will of a person, and/or because secondary doctrines include that some Christian DEN people disagreed with Oaths thinking that the Holy Bible teaches against such Oathing to God; Thus a provision is allowed for an infidel or false religionist, or various DEN Christians, to make oaths ~BEFORE~ God, rather than ~TO~ God; as God is present watching and that God rewards or punishes accordingly. This was done by the word, "affirmation", as optional to the "oath". The general name of the true God is used; by name in general, or such similarities (a similar conscience check). This is based on 9th commandment of the Great 10 commandments~ truth & lie. This puts God over the legal system.

---T--- God's Christian Oath required by the CON for USA GOV Officers: // "Journal of the Senate of the US of America, 1789-1793 - 4/30, 1789. The Senate assembled: present as yesterday. The report of the Committee ,,,postponed. Mr. Lee, in behalf of the committee appointed to take order far conducting the ceremonial of the formal reception, &c. of the President of the US, having informed ,,,Senate ,,,the House of Representatives were notified that the Senate were ready to receive them in the Senate Chamber, to attend the President of the US while taking the OATH REQUIRED BY THE CON. Whereupon, the House of Representatives, preceded by their Speaker, came into the Senate Chamber ,,,introduced the President of the US ,,,when the Vice President informed him, that "the Senate and House of Representatives of the US were ready to attend him to take the OATH REQUIRED BY THE CON, and that it would be administered by the Chancellor of the state of New York." ,,,the OATH was administered. After which the Chancellor proclaimed, "Long live George Washington President of the US." ,,,in this first official act, my fervent supplications to that ALMIGHTY BEING who rules over the universe--who presides in the councils of nations--and whose providential aids can supply every human defect, that his benediction may consecrate to the liberties and happiness of the people of the US, a GOV instituted by themselves for these essential purposes: and may enable every instrument employed in its administration to execute with success, the functions allotted to his charge. In tendering this homage to the GREAT AUTHOR of every public and private good, I assure myself that it expresses your sentiments not less than my own; nor those of my fellow citizens at large, less than either. No people can be BOUND to acknowledge and adore the INVISIBLE HAND, which conducts the affairs of men, more than the people of the US. Every step by which they have advanced to the character of an independent nation, seems to have been distinguished by some token of providential agency; and in the important revolution just accomplished in the system of their united government the tranquil deliberations and voluntary consent of so many distinct communities, from which the event has resulted, cannot be compared with the means by which most GOVs have been established, without some return of pious gratitude, along with an humble anticipation of the future blessings which the past seem to presage. These reflections, arising out of the present crisis, have forced themselves too strongly on my mind to be suppressed. You will join with me, I trust, in thinking, that there are none, under the influence of which, the proceedings of a new and free GOV can more auspiciously commence. ,,,honorable qualifications, I behold the surest pledges, that, as on one side, no local prejudices or attachments, no separate views, nor party animosities, will misdirect the comprehensive and equal eye which ought to watch over this great assemblage of communities and interests: so, on another, that the foundations of our national policy will be laid in the pure and immutable principles of private MORALity; and the pre-eminence of free GOV be exemplified by all the attributes which can win the affections of its citizens, and command the respect of the world. I dwell on this prospect with every satisfaction which an ardent love for my country can inspire: since there is no TRUTH more thoroughly established, than that there exists in the economy and course of nature, an indissoluble union between virtue and happiness; between duty and advantage; between the genuine maxims [[note Principle Law referenced; which is in the CC]] of an honest and magnanimous policy, and the solid rewards of public prosperity and felicity: since we ought to be no less persuaded that the propitious smiles of HEAVEN can never be expected on a nation that disregards the ETERNAL rules of order and right, which HEAVEN itself has ordained: and since the preservation of the SACRED fire of liberty, and the destiny of the republican model of GOV, are justly considered as deeply, perhaps as finally staked, on the experiment entrusted to the hands of the American people. Besides the ordinary objects submitted to your care, it will remain with your judgment to decide, how far an exercise of the occasional power delegated by the fifth article of the CON, is rendered expedient at the present juncture, by the nature of objections which have been urged against the system, or by the degree of inquietude which has given birth to them. Instead of undertaking particular recommendations on this subject, in which I could be guided by no lights derived from official opportunities, I shall again give way to my entire confidence in your discernment and pursuit of the public good: for, I assure myself, that whilst you carefully avoid every alteration which might endanger the benefits of an united and effective GOV, or which ought to await the future lessons of experience; a reverence for the characteristic rights of freemen, and a regard for the public harmony, will sufficiently influence your deliberations on the question, how far the former can be more impregnably fortified, or the latter be safely and advantageously promoted ,,,and must accordingly PRAY that the pecuniary estimates for the station in which I am placed, may, during my continuance in it, be limited to such actual expenditures as the public good may be thought to require. Having thus imparted to you my sentiments, as they have been awakened by the occasion which brings us together, I shall take my present leave; but not without resorting once more to the benign PARENT of the human race, in humble supplication that, since he has been pleased to favor the American people with opportunities for deliberating in perfect tranquility, and dispositions for deciding with unparalleled unanimity, on a form of GOV for the security of their union, and the advancement of their happiness; so his DIVINE blessing may be equally conspicuous in the enlarged views, the temperate consultations, and the wise measures, on which the success of this GOV must depend ,,,The President, the Vice President, the Senate, and House of Representatives, &c. then proceeded to St. Paul's Chapel, where DIVINE service was performed by the Chaplain of Congress, after which the President was reconducted to his house by the committee appointed for that purpose. The Vice President and Senate returned to the Senate Chamber; and, Upon motion, unanimously agreed ,,,House of Representatives of the US ,,,FRIDAY, MAY 1, 1789}".

---T--- USA GOV & All Branches Including Citizens Proclaimed~ +] a day to seek God with pray for help and protection, +] invited all Christian DENs, +] fully supporting Christian doctrines and Holy Bible: // "Letters of Delegates to Congress: Volume 1-- 8/1774 - 8/1775 [June 7-12, 1775] ,,,Resolved that it be and hereby it is recommended to the Inhabitants of the united Colonies in America of all DENS That Thursday the 20th day of July next be set apart as a day of public humiliation fasting and PRAYER, that a total Abstenence from Servile labor and recreastion be observed and all their RELIGIOUS Assemblies Solemnly Convened to humble themselves before GOD [[here referring to God, not any or every god]] under the heavy Judgments felt and threatened to confess our manifold SINS, to implore the forgiveness of HEAVEN, (that a sincere repentance reformation may influence our future Conduct) and that a Blessing may descend on the husbandry, Manufactures & other lawful Employments of this people and especially that the Union of these American Colonies in defence of their Just Rights & priviledges may be preserved, confirmed and prospered, that the Congresses may be inspired with Wisdom, that Great Britain and its Rulers may have their eyes opened to discern the things that shall make for the peace and Happiness of the Nation and all its Connections And that America may soon behold a Gracious interposition of HEAVEN for the redress of her many Grievances, the restoration of her invaded Liberties, a reconciliation with the parent State upon terms Constitutional and Honourable to them both and the Security of them to the latest posterity. MS (MHi). L On June 7, 1775, Congress resolved that the colonies should observe a day of fasting and PRAYER on the following July 20, and appointed John Adams, William Hooper, and Robert Treat Paine as a committee ,,,resolution adopted by Congress ,,,JCC, 2:81, 87-88."

---T--- *Checks & Balances with God: // The USA System developed* a "Checks & Balances" system because of the sin problem (sometimes called), or tendency to evil, or at least the potential of each person to do evil; or that mankind is temptable to evil; that people in "powerful" positions are potentially dangerous; that we live in a world of good & evil. // Ideally they knew, as we know, that God, Christ Jesus, being perfect would be the perfect Ruler. However how God and we get that done to mankind is an issue. Thus a "Checks & Balances" system. // Here is the current problem: The God, Christ Jesus and Christianity, is the Check that evil is attempting to remove and oppose. Both the N GOV & many States are attempting such. // THE DOI & CON, which include~ God, Supreme Ruler, Creator, Divine Providence, Lord Jesus Christ, the Christian Oath, or Oath to God, and other Holy Biblical subjects, such as religion, is to be put as first; NOT IDOLATRY, in the USA and STATE GOV Decisions and activities.

---T--- USA GOV Including All Branches, Which God is One Branch~ +] Do Not Support False Religions; not heathen, not savage, not infidel, not idolatry; +] Do Support Christianity: // "Letters of Delegates to Congress: Volume 23-- 11/7, 1785 ~ 11/5, 1786 ,,,Aug. 26. 1786 Upon receiving your letter of the 1st I did myself the honor of immediately communicating it to the US in Congress assembled, who have thereupon been pleased to pass a resolution respecting the Indian Congregation, a copy of which is herewith enclosed. ,,,I most heartily join you in PRAYER to GOD that He "may grant these poor sufferers a time of peace & rest after so many tribulations that other HEATHEN may see the great difference of a civilised CHRISTIAN life and the life of SAVAGES." Please to convey to the revd. D. Zeisberger my sincere respects and the esteem I have for his zeal & perseverance in the good work in which he has been so long engaged. I hope he will continue to the end & that his labours will be crowned with success. With great respect, I am, Revd & Dear Sir, Your obedt humble Servt, Cha Thomson P.S. ,,,1. Ettwein's August I letter PRAYing for the relief of about 100 displaced Moravian Indians seeing to return to their homes on the Muskingum River was referred Aug. 8 to a committee which reported Aug. 17. The committee's recommendation that they be permitted to return to their former settlement and be provided axes, hoes, blankets, and up to 500 bushels of corn for the ensuing winter from the public stores at Fort McIntosh was adopted by Congress Aug. 24. See JCC, 31:505n, 526, 562-63. Ettwein's letter ,,,PCC. 2. See Thomson to Butler, Aug. 15,,,".

---T--- USA GOV intends/purposes the~ +] DOI as Religious & Christian for Christ; +] Citizen Branch to maintain Christ's Christianity as the CC (DOI & CON) Proclaim: // "Letters of Delegates to Congress: Volume 7- 5/1, 1777 ~ 9/18, 1777 - ,,,22d July 1777, in the morning I received yours of the 26 June by Brown. It gave me not a little Satisfaction to hear of your Welfare, that of our dear Children & Connections. GOD grant this may find you all in health & safety. It was impossible for me to write you; my right arm which you know has been affected with the Rheumatism has been tenfold worse than ever, the pain at first fell suddenly into my wrist, sweld & became exceedingly painful, & after some Time returnd back to my Elbow & was worse than before & my whole arm was inexpressibly sore & painful from my Shoulder to my hand so that I cod not dress, undress nor sleep for some time, but by the mercy of GOD, & his blessing, it is much better but not perfectly well, & I fear it may return. Am able to write, tho have nothing very material to say ,,,The House swarms with French men, part of the seventy odd Mr Dean has sent over &c tho we have very little to do with them save at Breakfast Time,,, Mr Law is obligd to sleep in a lower bedroom, & at suppers. I have nothing to do & we dine by our Selves, abt 4 or 5 oClock. The swearing & Wickedness that abounds in this City is truly shocking to chaste Ears & alarming in a MORAL View, the Judgments of GOD don't seem to have any Effect, unless the most awful one, of rendering us worse. I tremble to think so, but I really fear it is TRUE, will he that made us, shew mercy to such a People ? His Mercy is boundless, & infinite. I will yet hope in it nor Limit the HOLY one of Israel. [[Christianity is the Religion]] O, that Wickedness was confined to this City. Alass I fear 'tis as great in N. England & thro the Country. ,,,Alass, the Chastisements of his Providence will have good Effect without the inward teaching of his SPIRIT, but GOD is pleased to withhold those Influences, the most sore & distressing of all Calamities. O, that every Soul who has an Interest in HEAVEN wod cry day & night with ceaseless & unfailing ardor, that GOD wod pour out his blessed SPIRIT to awaken & bring the Country to Repentance. Too few I fear think of the infinite importance of that Blessing even without any regard to our present Calamities. But what can I say or Do. GOD will work as pleaseth Him. Among the other SINS that prevail here extortion & oppression is not the least, & it is by the wicked Arts of our internal Enemys here brot to such a pass ,,,butter in market ,,beaf 2/6 & every thing in proportion & daily rising, & will rise, unless our affairs in infinite mercy shod take another turn. ,,,I regret my absence & long to be with my dear Wife, Children & Friends ,,,wait the Will of GOD, & his appointed Time. If He shall ever bring me home again in Peace, I hope I shall not forget Jacobs Vow. May GOD be gracious to you & the dear Children, little do They know what I feel for Them. ,,,If They shod I hope We shall find a place of Safety, & that it will prove a trap & Snare to them & trust it will ,,,I dare say your Father ,,,has better Intelligence. This is another sad Token of GODs anger but We dont lay it to heart. It is reported that a large reinforcement is arrived at N. York but we have not the certainty. (Afternoon) O sad, it this moment comes to my mind ,,,May GOD have mercy on & spare you & all my dear Friends, remember me tenderly to them all. With strong Affection I am tenderly yours, W. Williams RC (CSmH) . 1 Gov. Jonathan Trumbull."

---T--- <u>Jesus Christ is Worshipped by the USA GOV all Branches expressing~ +] Opposition to</u> GOV abuse, which is defined as that of anti-Christian evils, +] Supporting Christianity with the religion thereof: // "Journals of the Continental Congress, 1774-1789 - MAR 19, 1782 - ,,,Whereupon, Ordered ,,,regiment of artillery artificers ,,,On a report of a committee, consisting of Mr. [Joseph] Montgomery, Mr. [Oliver] Wolcott, and Mr. [John Morin] Scott, appointed to prepare a recommendation to the several states, to set apart a day of humiliation, fasting, and PRAYER Congress agreed to the following Proclamation: The goodness of the SUPREME BEING to ALL HIS RATIONAL CREATURES, [[all people in world esp. USA Citizens]] demands their acknowledgments of gratitude and love; his absolute government of this world dictates, that it is the interest of every nation and people ardently to supplicate his mercy favor and implore his protection. When the LUST OF DOMINION or LAWLESS AMBITION excites arbitrary power to INVADE THE RIGHTS, or endeavor to WRENCH WREST from a people their SACRED and UNALIENABLE INVALUABLE PRIVILEGES, and compels them, in DEFENCE of the same, to encounter all the horrors and calamities of a bloody and vindictive war; then is that people loudly called upon to fly unto that GOD for protection, who hears the cries of the distressed, and will not turn a deaf ear to the supplication of the OPPRESSED. Great Britain, hitherto left to infatuated councils, and to pursue measures repugnant to their her own interest, and distressing to this country, still persists in the chimerical idea design of subjugating these US; which will compel us into another active and perhaps bloody campaign. The US in Congress assembled, therefore, taking into consideration our present situation, our multiplied transgressions of the HOLY laws of our GOD, and his past acts of kindness and goodness exercised towards us, which we would ought to record with me the liveliest gratitude, think it their indispensable duty to call upon the different several states, to set apart the last Thursday in April next, as a day of fasting, humiliation and PRAYER, that our joint supplications may then ascend to the throne of the RULER of the UNIVERSE, beseeching Him that he would to diffuse a SPIRIT of universal reformation among all ranks and degrees of our citizens; and make us a HOLY, that so we may be an HAPPY people; that it would please Him to impart wisdom, integrity and unanimity to our counsellors; to bless and prosper the REIGN of our illustrious ally, and give success to his arms employed in the DEFENCE of THE RIGHTS of human nature; that HE WOULD SMILE upon our military arrangements by land and sea; administer comfort and consolation to our prisoners in a cruel captivity; that he would protect the health and life of our Commander in Chief; give grant us victory over our enemies; establish peace in all our borders, and give happiness to all our inhabitants; that he would prosper the labor of the husbandman, making the earth yield its increase in abundance, and give a proper season for the in gathering of the fruits thereof; that He would grant success to all engaged in lawful trade and commerce, and take under his guardianship all schools and seminaries of learning, and make them nurseries of VIRTUE and PIETY; that He would incline the HEARTS [[the heart is the Spirit technically]] of all men to peace, and fill them with universal charity and benevolence, and that the RELIGION of our DIVINE REDEEMER, [[Christ Jesus]] with all its benign influences, may cover the earth [[the USA is the ambassador of Christ to spread the Gospel of Jesus to how much of the Earth???]] ,,,Done by the US in Congress assembled, &c. &c.?1 [Note 1: 1 This report, in the writing of a clerk, is in the Papers of the Continental Congress, No. 24, folio 467.] ,,,".

---T--- <u>God's 1-A & R-E & R~Est~ +] Does Not Pertain</u> to all religions; +] Does Pertain Only to Christianity & of different DENs of Christianity: // "Letters of Delegates to Congress: Volume 4-- 5/16, 1776 - 8/15, 1776 - ,,,6/22. 1776 Your Letters ,,,before me ,,both dated at Boston, a Circumstance which alone ,,,sufferd so much anxiety for his friends, in their exile from it. We have not many of the fearfull, and still less of the unbelieving among us, how slowly soever, you may think we proceed. Is it not a want of faith, or a predominance of fear, which makes some of

126

you so impatient for declarations in words of what is every day manifested in deeds of the most determined nature and unequivocal signification? ,,,I am for the most liberal toleration of all DENS of RELIGIONists but I hope that Congress will never meddle with RELIGION, further than to say their own PRAYERS, and to fast and give thanks, once a year. Let every colony have its own RELIGION, without molestation. The Congress ordered CHURCH to the Massachusetts Council,,,".

---T--- <u>USA GOV is for Christ and~ +] CHRISTIAN, +] Religious thereof, +] with Christian Chaplains, +] Constantly using Christian Holy Bible words, +] with Christian Oath as part of USA Officials:</u> // "Letters of Delegates to Congress: Volume 7 - 5/1/1777 - 9/18/1777 John Adams to Nathanael ,,,Dear Sir. ,,,6/2d. 1777 Yours of the 28 Ult. is before me. ,,,It is certain that RELIGION and MORALity have no less obligations upon Armies, than upon Cities and contribute no less to the Happiness of Soldiers than of Citizens. There is one Principle of RELIGION which has contributed vastly to the Excellence of Armies, who had very little else of RELIGION or MORALity, the Principle I mean is the SACRED obligation of oaths, which among both Romans and Britans, who seem to have placed the whole of RELIGION and MORALity in the punctual observance of them, have done Wonders. It is this alone which prevents Desertions from your Enemies. I think our CHAPLAINS ought to make the SOLEMN Nature and the SACRED obligation of oaths the favourite Subject of their SERMONS to the Soldiery. Odd as it may seem I cannot help considering a serious sense of the Solemnity of an oath as the corner Stone of Discipline, and that it might be made to contribute more, to the order of the Army, than any or all of the Instruments of Punishment. ,,,What that will be Time must discover. It is, in my humble opinion, utterly improper that this Gentn. should hold a seat in Congress, and a Command in the Army, and I took the first opportunity to express my opinion of the Inconsistency and Danger of it. ,,,be respectable.,,,".

---T--- <u>Falsity Religions Not to be Supported by God's USA GOV:</u> // From Congress Meeting Notes of 1778, Table of Contents: "Mr. WILSON -- wished Exclusion of Popish priests from Office, ... 212". The intention here is that religious abuse does not occur as it did in Europe, as from both doctrine and expressions. The falsities of Catholicism of that the situation referred to was also inclusive that this denomination refused freedom to other DENs.

---T--- <u>Limitations Required by God for~ +] False Christianity & False Religions & Religious Abuse; ~AND~ +] Freedom of Exercise for Christianity & DEN as R~Est is defined as DENs of Christianity:</u> // "The Debates in the Several State Conventions on the Adoption of the Federal Constitution [Elliot's Debates, Volume 1] MARYLAND. The province of Maryland was included originally in the patent ,,,The territory was bounded by a right line, drawn from Watkins's Point, on Chesapeake Bay, to the ocean, on the east ,,,The first emigration made under the auspices of Lord Baltimore was in 1632, and consisted of about 200 gentlemen of considerable fortune and rank, and their adherents, being chiefly Roman Catholics. "He laid the foundation of this province (says Chalmers) upon the broad basis of security to property and of freedom of RELIGION, granting, in absolute fee, fifty acres of land to every emigrant; establishing CHRISTIANITY agreeably to the old common law, of which it is a part, without allowing preeminence to any particular SECT [[Christian DEN]]. The wisdom of his choice soon converted a dreary wilderness into a prosperous colony." The first legislative assembly of Maryland, held by the freemen at large, was in 1634--1635; but little of their proceedings is known. No acts appear to have been adopted until 1638--1639, when provision was made, in consequence of an increase of the colonists, for a representative assembly, called the House of Assembly, chosen by the freemen; and the laws passed by the Assembly, and approved by the proprietary, or his lieutenant, were to be of full force. At the same session, an act, which may be considered as in some sort a Magna Charta, was passed, declaring, among other things, that "HOLY CHURCH, within this province, shall have all her rights and liberties; that the inhabitants shall have all their rights and liberties according to the great charter of England;" ,,,In 1649, an act was passed punishing blasphemy, or denying the HOLY Trinity, with death, and confiscation of goods and lands. Under the protectorate of Cromwell, roman Catholics were expressly denied any protection in the province; and all others, "who profess faith in GOD by JESUS CHRIST, though differing in judgment from the doctrine, worship, or discipline, publicly held forth," were not to be restrained from the exercise of their RELIGION. In 1696, the CHURCH of England was established in the province; and in 1702, the liturgy, and rites, and ceremonies, of the CHURCH of England, were required to be pursued in all the CHURCHes-- with such toleration for dissenters, however, as was provided for in the act of William and Mary. And the introduction of the test and abjuration acts, in 1716, excluded all Roman Catholics from office. It appears to have been a policy, adopted at no great distance of time after the settlement of the colony ,,,country. In that year an act passed which made the estate partible among all the children; and the system thus introduced has, in its substance, never since been departed from. ,,,Upon the revolution of 1688, the GOV of Maryland was seized into the hands of the crown, and was not again restored to the proprietary until 1716. From that period no interruption occurred until the American Revolution,,,".

---T--- <u>Jesus Resists stating No Evil or Anti-Christian has a Right Nor Unlimited with</u> the USA GOV: // FFOG John Adams was shocked by evil, such as that in France, and stated that the condition of a nation can be measured by the observation of the women, families, fathers: "From all,,, I,,, read of History of GOV, of human life and manners, I had drawn the Conclusion, that the manner of Women ,,,infallible Barometer, to ascertain the degree of Morality and Virtue in a Nation. All that I have since read and all the observations I have made in different Nations, have confirmed me in this opinion. The Manners of Women, are the surest Criterion by which to determine whether a Republican GOV is practicable in a Nation or not. The Jews, the Greeks, the Romans, the Swiss, the Dutch, all lost their public Spirit, their Republican Principles and habits, and their Republican Forms of GOV, when they lost the Modesty and Domestic Virtues of their Women ,,,The foundations of national Morality must be laid in private Families. In vain are Schools,,, universities instituted, if loose Principles and licentious habits are impressed upon Children in their earliest years.

The Mothers are the earliest and most important Instructors of youth ,,,The Vices and Examples of the Parents cannot be concealed from the Children. How is it possible that Children can have any just Sense of the sacred Obligations of Morality or Religion if, from their earliest Infancy, they learn that their Mothers live in habitual Infidelity to their fathers, and their fathers in as constant infidelity to their Mothers." +Also stated, ",,,Contract of marriage is not only a civil and moral Engagement, but a Sacrament, one of the most Solemn Vows and Oaths of Religious devotion. Can they then believe Religion and Morality too any thing more than a Veil, a Cloak, an hypocritical Pretext, for political purposes of decency and Conveniency." (117).

---T--- <u>Religion, 1-A & R-E Section Includes that the USA GOV Supports that</u>~ +] God be 1st Priority, +] no idolatry existing against such, +] the USA GOV is not the GOD, nor to usurp authority over God, but to be a servant of God, +] Christianity & religion thereof, +] not all religions: // The 1-A & R-E & R~Est refers to the 1st 4 Commandments of the Ten Commandments (Holy Bible)~ You shall have no other gods before me == Congress shall make no law ,,,prohibiting the free exercise thereof (of religion); and no establishment of religion. This is the very 1st Article in the Bill of Rights. // This prevents and protects Spiritual Conscience Folk to NOT bow down to the GOV.

---T--- <u>The 1-A & R-E & R~Est includes that</u>~ They forbid or "exclude from the N GOV all power to act upon the subject (religion and the 'things that are God's')": // Free exercise is for DEN secondary doctrines and expressions for GOD. // Christ limits any anti-Christ religion on USA soil. // Christ's religion is to follow Him by application of His Holy Bible, conscience, and the Holy Spirit, or God's Presence. He says be a doer of the Word~ "Jam1:21-22 Wherefore lay apart all filthiness and superfluity of naughtiness, and receive with meekness the engrafted word, which is able to save your souls. But be you doers of the word, and not hearers only, deceiving your own selves". // Freedom of speech and press was intended/ purposed to communicate to the world from the USA about the Gospel Good News of knowing that Christ Jesus says to "know the truth, and the truth shall set you free; Go you into all the world and preach the Gospel", Joh8, Mat28. TRUTH is included in the CC with GOD & CHRIST the LORD.

---T--- <u>Citizen Responsibility to support the Christ Creator & His Christianity to be included in GOV</u>: // FFOG John Adams, "We electors have an important constitutional power placed in our hands: ,,,a check upon two branches of the legislature ,,,necessary to every subject (citizen) ,,,be in some degree a statesman and to examine and judge ,,,political principles and measures ,,,Let us examine them with a sober,,, Christian spirit." (169a). The "elector" and "subject" is the citizen.

---T--- <u>All Branches of USA GOV Declare that</u>~ +] the USA starts itself as a Nation that has "God, Creator, Supreme Judge, Divine Providence; as their Supreme Ruler, +] identifies the true God as including Christ Jesus, +] the USA GOV is for continual use of Christian Religion, of Christian Words both in person communication and writings, and of Christian Activity, +] GOV abuse to Christ & Christian religion was a desire to oppose: // "Journal of the House of Representatives of the US, 1789-1793, July 22, 1789: A petition of Richard Phillips was presented to the House, and read, PRAYing relief in consideration of indigence occasioned by military services rendered during the late war. "Journals of the Continental Congress, 1774-1789 - Oct 30, 1778 - These US having been driven to hostilities by the oppressive and tyrannous measures of Great Britain; having been compelled to commit the essential rights of man to the decision of arms; and having been at length forced to shake off a yoke which had grown too burthensome to bear; they declared themselves free and independent. Confiding in the justice of their cause; confiding in HIM, [[God is the intention/ purpose]] who disposes of human events; although weak and unprovoked, they set the power of their enemies at defiance. In this confidence they have continued through the various fortunes of three bloody campaigns, unawed by the power, unsubdued by the barbarity of their foes. Their virtuous citizens have borne, without repining, the loss of many things which make life desirable. Their brave troops have patiently endured the hardships and dangers of a situation fruitful in both, beyond former EX. The Congress considering themselves bound to love their enemies, as children of that Being [[God]] who is equally the Father of All; and desirous, since they could not prevent, at least to alleviate the calamities of war, have studied to spare those who were in arms against them, and to lighten the chains of captivity. The conduct of those serving under the king of Great Britain hath, with some few exceptions ,,,the severest injuries have been aggravated by the grossest insult. Foiled in their vain attempt to subjugate the unconquerable SPIRIT of freedom, they have meanly assailed the representatives of America with bribes, with deceit, and the servility of adulation. They have made a mock of humanity by the wanton destruction of men. They have made a mock of RELIGION by impious appeals to GOD, whilst in the violation of his SACRED commands: They have made a mock even of reason itself, by endeavouring to prove that the liberty and happiness of America could safely be entrusted to those who have sold their own, unawed by the sense of virtue or of shame. [[good & evil]] Treated with the contempt which such conduct deserved, they have applied to individuals ,,,break the bonds of allegiance, and imbue their souls with the blackest of crimes. But fearing that none could be found through these US equal to the wickedness of their purpose, to influence weak minds they have threatened more wide devastation. While the shadow of hope remained that our enemies could be taught by our EX, to respect those laws which are held SACRED among civilized nations, and to comply with the dictates of a RELIGION which they pretend in common with us to believe and revere, they have been left to the influence of that RELIGION and that EX. [[Identified here are +} falsity of intentions/purposes; +} Christ & Christianity as USA GOV; c} England's religion was also Christianity; however England's GOV had decided not to apply it in all actions, but rather only in name, making a form of false Christianity]] But since their incorrigible dispositions cannot be touched by kindness and compassion, it becomes our duty by other means to vindicate the rights of humanity. We, therefore, the Congress of the US of America, do solemnly declare and proclaim, that if our enemies presume to execute their threats, or persist in their present career of barbarity, we will take such exemplary vengeance, as shall deter others from a like conduct. We appeal to that GOD who searcheth the hearts of men, for the rectitude of our intentions: and in his HOLY presence we declare, that as we are not moved by any light and hasty suggestions of anger or revenge, so, through every possible change of fortune, we will adhere to this our determination,,,".

---T--- <u>The Function or Operation of Governmental System was for Jesus as following:</u> // The States already made the requirement that only Christians serve in their States, and that they were Christian states, and supportive of such, but not denominational. // Thus the Fed was not to interfere with this, but support it; so the Fed was to be Christian, but not be dictatorship over DEN. // If the States were Christian servants, having declared such including that Christian doctrines are in their CONs with the Holy Bible required, then why would they put in anti-Christian in Fed? They would not, nor did not intend such. // The Fed CON did not and was not to change the states CON, but support it, which were Christian; The Fed CON did not change the states CON rather agreed on the Principle Laws, including God as God of the USA & Christian religion.

---T--- <u>God's USA States~ +] were Christian; +] required Officers to support Christ & Christianity & the Holy Bible; +] allowed no anti-Christian REP:</u> // The States required a verbal declaration Oath or Affirmation to God that the REP had to intend/ purpose and decide to get in office.

---T--- <u>USA GOV to prioritize Christ & Christianity & have His Holy Bible as Basis of Law:</u> // FFoG John Adams said the following: +"Suppose some nation in some distant Region, should take the Bible for their only law Book, and every member should regulate his conduct by the precepts there exhibited. Every member would be obliged in Conscience to temperance and frugality and industry, to justice and kindness and Charity towards his fellow men, and to Piety and Love, and reverence towards almighty God. In this Commonwealth, no man would impart his health by Gluttony, drunkenness, or Lust- no man would sacrifice his most precious time to cards, or any other trifling and mean amusement --no man would steal or lie or any way defraud his neighbour, but would live in peace and good will with all men-- no man would blaspheme his maker or profane his worship, but a rational and manly, a sincere and unaffected Piety and devotion, would reign in all hearts. What a Eutopa, what a Paradise would this region be,,,." (97a). Also, "Christianity has No other institution for education, no kind of political discipline, coud diffuse this kind of necessary Information, so universally among all ranks and descriptions of citizens. The duties and Rights of the man and the citizens are thus taught from early Infancy to every creature." (97a). +Also, ",,,the duties of religion and morality comprehends a very extensive connection with society at large and the great interests of the public" (117).

---T--- <u>Civilization or Right Social Order needs Christ's Presence:</u> // The most civilized countries are the most Christian countries in the world and thus the USA has advantaged because of such Christian civilization.

---T--- <u>R-E or R~Est~ This intention/ purpose was affectionately cared for with</u> attitudes to Christ & that His Christianity is not abused; & that the different DENs are encouraged.

---T--- <u>Christ's R-E, 1-A ~ has Religion intended/ purposed to define that~ +] NOT false Religion NOR Evil Religion; +] Rather it IS True, Good, Right Religion:</u> // How co/ any Creature Conscience Person stand up in the USA and proclaim that the 1-A includes evil religion or false religion ?? Such is folly & falsity. Such a concept is so far from the FFoG intention/ purpose construction that it makes the south go very far from the north so as to be unseen at the start of the south. // The word "Religion" & "Religious Establishment" defined herein~ +is Christian denomination. +is a relationship with God; a communion (fellowship). +The total intention/ purpose of the CC (DOI & CON) & RW was to be Right with God and depart from evil in every area.

---T--- <u>What & How is Religion to be applied in Difficult Situations:</u> // Including the teaching from Communion with God; our minds need Him~ Jam 1 says He fellowships (communes) liberally". // Constitutional Law {CC of DOI + CON} is the Inclusion of Principle Laws. Principle Laws can be applied: +universally or generally; +not limited to single situations; +have exceptions to the Rules or Laws; +include Love & it's parts; +EX of some are ~without dictatorship ~with liberty or freedom ~limits to evil ~discernment principles between good & evil; +Principle Laws do not list every application but have the Universal or General Rule or Law which fits to all or most applications (situations).

---T--- <u>Christianity to Christ is supported by the USA GOV</u> and the evils of the British GOV at the time were against Christianity.

---T--- <u>God's R-E, 1-A is The Intention/ purpose of~ a] the part that states The Free Exercise, or not Prohibiting is that Religion & R~Est is defined as Christian DEN (Secondary Doctrines & Expressions); And such should Not be limited by the USA GOV; and, b] the part that states The No Making a Law for Any Establishment of Religion is that No Law should be made to limit the USA GOV to only 1 or 2 DEN; because to make such a Law expresses partiality favorism (respecting) to that DEN Religious establishment.</u> +Now that this is straightened Rightly, we realize why the following required freedom for Christian Devotions and Prayer as enacted by All Branches of the USA GOV & All State GOV as follows: // "Journals of the Continental Congress, 1774-1789, 6/12, 1775 - The Congress met according to adjournment. The committee, appointed for preparing a resolve for a fast, brought in a report, which, being read, was agreed to as follows: As the great Governor of the World, [[<<< who here is said to be the most High Political Governor Ruler of the USA?? >>>]] by his supreme and universal Providence, not only conducts the course of nature with unerring wisdom and rectitude, but frequently influences the minds of men to serve the wise and gracious purposes of his providential government; and it being, at all times, our indispensible duty devoutly to acknowledge his superintending providence, especially in times of impending danger and public calamity, to reverence and adore his immutable justice as well as to implore his merciful interposition for our deliverance: This Congress, therefore, considering the present critical, alarming and calamitous state of these colonies, do earnestly recommend that Thursday, the 20th day of July next, be observed, by the inhabitants of all the English colonies on this continent, as a day of public

129

humiliation, fasting and PRAYER; that we may, with united hearts and voices, unfeignedly confess and deplore our many SINS; and offer up our joint supplications to the all-wise, omnipotent, and merciful Disposer of all events; humbly beseeching him to forgive our iniquities, to remove our present calamities, to avert those desolating judgments, with which we are threatned, and to bless our rightful sovereign, King George the third, and [to] inspire him with wisdom to discern and pursue the TRUE interest of all his subjects, that a speedy end may be put to the civil discord between Great Britain and the American colonies, without farther effusion of blood: And that the British nation may be influenced to regard the things that belong to her peace, before they are hid from her eyes: That these colonies may be ever under the care and protection of a kind Providence, and be prospered in all their interests; That the DIVINE blessing may descend and rest upon all our civil rulers, and upon the representatives of the people, in their several assemblies and conventions, that they may be directed to wise and effectual measures for preserving the union, and securing the just rights and priviledges of the colonies; That virtue and TRUE RELIGION may revive and flourish throughout our land; And that all America may soon behold a gracious interposition of HEAVEN, for the redress of her many grievances, the restoration of her invaded rights, a reconcilation with the parent state, on terms constitutional and honorable to both; And that her civil and RELIGIOUS priviledges may be secured to the latest posterity. And it is recommended to CHRISTIANs, of all DENOMINATIONS, to assemble for public worship, and to abstain from servile labour and recreations on said day. Ordered, That a copy of the above be signed by the president and attested by the Secy and published in the newspapers, and in hand bills.1 [Note 1: 1 It was printed in the Pennsylvania Packet, 19 June, 1775. A portion of one of the original broadside issues is in the Papers of the Continental Congress ,,,and also the state of America."

---T--- All USA Activity expressed ONLY the Intention/ purpose Support of Only the Holy Spirit's Christianity including the various DEN of Christianity to the Holy Spirit, including Messiahward, which is Judaism Proper if it be kind and caring to the NT; without violence; and which is Early Christianity (Messiahward). // Simeon & Anna knew the Holy Spirit and were communing with Him when the Messiah came in the Flesh~ Emmanuel of Christmas; the affectionate One. Luk2.

---T--- R-E: Intention/ purpose Reason about the Holy Spirit's Presence & His Religious Establishment part was~ +] Not to Support All Religions of True & False; +] It Is Not To favor (respecting) to any Christian DEN by making a law for that DEN & excluding other DEN: // The following proves the FFOG studied the history of religious abuse, including false Christianity; and because it is a danger, a Check of God was put on it: "The Debates in the Several State Conventions on the Adoption of the Federal CON [Elliot's Debates, Volume 1] NORTH AND SOUTH CAROLINA. In Mar, 1662, (Apr, 1663) Charles II. made a grant, to Lord Clarendon and others, of the territory lying on the Atlantic Ocean ,,,within 36 degrees of north latitude ,,,and within 31 degrees of north latitude ,,,into a province, by the name of Carolina ,,,The grantees were created absolute lords proprietaries, saving the faith, allegiance, and supreme dominion of the crown, and invested with as ample rights and jurisdictions as the Bishop of Durham possessed in his palatine diocese. The charter seems to have been copied from that of Maryland, and resembles it in many of its provisions. It further required that all laws should "be consonant to reason, and, as near as may be conveniently, agreeable to the laws and customs of this our kingdom of England." And it declared that the inhabitants and their children, born in the province, should be denizens of England, and entitled to all the privileges and immunities of British-born subjects. In 1665 ,,,Several detached settlements were made in Carolina, which were at first placed under distinct temporary governments ,,,Thus various independent and separate colonies were established, each of which had its own Assembly, its own customs, and its own laws --a policy which the proprietaries had afterwards occasion to regret, from its tendency to enfeeble and distract the province. In the year 1669, the proprietaries, dissatisfied with the systems already established within the province, signed a fundamental CON for the government thereof, the object of which is declared to be, "that we may establish a GOV agreeable to the monarchy, of which Carolina is a part, that we may avoid making too numerous a democracy." This CON was drawn up by the celebrated John Locke. It provided that the oldest proprietary should be the palatine, and the next oldest should succeed him. Each ,,,proprietaries ,,,hold ,,,office ,,,and to consist of the proprietaries or their deputies, of the nobility, and of representatives of the freeholders chosen in districts. They were all to meet in one apartment, (like the ancient Scottish Parliament,) and enjoy an equal vote. No business, however, was to be proposed, until it had been debated, in the grand council, (which was to consist of the proprietaries and forty-two counsellors,) whose duty it was to prepare bills. No act was of force longer than until the next biennial meeting of the Parliament, unless ratified by the palatine and a quorum of the proprietaries. All the laws were to become void at the end of a century, without any formal repeal. The CHURCH of England (which was declared to be the only TRUE and orthodox RELIGION) was alone to be allowed a public maintenance by Parliament; but every congregation might tax its own members for the support of its own minister. Every man of seventeen years of age was to declare himself of some CHURCH or RELIGIOUS profession, and to be recorded as such; otherwise he was not to have any benefit of the laws. And no man was to be permitted to be a freeman of Carolina, or have any estate or habitation, who did not acknowledge a GOD, and that GOD is to be publicly worshipped. In other respects there was a guaranty of RELIGIOUS freedom. There was to be a public registry of all deeds and conveyances of lands, and of marriages and births.,,, With a view to prevent unnecessary litigation ,,,provided that "it shall be a base and vile thing to plead for money or reward;" and that, "since multiplicity of comments, as well as of laws, have great inconveniences, and serve only to obscure and perplex, all manner of comments and expositions on any part of these fundamental constitutions, or on any part of the common or statute law of Carolina, are absolutely prohibited." After a few years' experience of its ill arrangements, and its mischievous tendency, the proprietaries, upon the application of the people, (in 1693,) abrogated the CON, and restored the ancient form of GOV. Thus perished the labors of Mr. Locke; and thus perished a system, under the administration of which,

130

it has been remarked, the Carolinians had not known one day of real enjoyment, and that introduced EVILs and disorders which ended only with the dissolution of the proprietary GOV!" // The problems here was no freedom of starting other Christian DEN. And the proprietaries were excessively monarchy and became dictatorship.

---T--- Religion is Intended/ purposed that the USA GOV Puts God 1st by~ +] be Christian Nation; +] Not be False Religion; +] Not be False Christianity; +] Spiritual Moral Folk are invited to live in the USA; +] Not to set up a false religion by public assemblies or activity; +] Not infidels, Nor Pagans in Employment Office directly connected to making Laws; +] USA GOV Not abuse the Citizen Branch & Christian Religion; +] Affection care frequently for Christian Religion be expressed: // Words in Capital Letters are specific proofs in the following DOC from the Congress Meeting Notes during formation of the CON, The INDEX portion (Table of Contents); it has only a brief mention of the subject, of which full conclusion cannot be made, in every mention, either in support or against the subject as it only mentions the subject; also showing a Checks & Balances System: "The Debates in the Several State Conventions on the Adoption of the Federal CON [Elliot's Debates, Volume 4] INDEX. By Speakers' Names. ,,,ORGANIZATION of the Convention ,,,1 RULES for the Government of the Convention, Electors, &c, ... 2 HENRY ABBOTT-- RELIGION; opposed to an exclusive ESTABLISHMENT; no RELIGIOUS Test; PAGAN or Deist may obtain Office; OATH; BY WHOM ARE WE TO SWEAR? Jupiter, &c ... 191 Mr. BLOODWORTH-- opposed to Congressional Control over Elections ,,, 67 Defence of its Omission not satisfactory; Precaution in granting Powers, 167. ,,,Sovereignty of the Federal GOV annihilates the States ... 179 Powers of Congress dangerous to State Laws, ... 180 ,,,Mr. CALDWELL -- MAXIMS, FUNDAMENTAL PRINCIPLES ... 9 ,,,Elections liable to Abuse, ... 62 Abuse of Parliamentary Power, ... 65 SWEEPING CLAUSE, NOT PLAIN; "PURSUANCE" EQUIVOCAL AND AMBIGUOUS ... 187 RELIGION; conceived that Jews, MAHOMETANS, and PAGANs, are invited to the US, ... 199 Mr. WILLIAM R. DAVIE (a Member of the Federal Convention)--for investigating the Subject, and discussing Clause by Clause, ... 8 Confederacies; Amphictyonic; European, ... 59 (history studied) ,,,Principle on which the CON was formed, ... 102 ,,,Separation of Powers, 120 ,,,thirteen Councillors would destroy Presidential Responsibility, 122. State Sovereignty represented in the Senate; ,,,Laws, their Execution; Judiciary ,,,Federal Laws conflicting with those of the States; Legislation on Individuals instead of States ,,,Powers of Congress; Tendency to destroy the State Governments ... 93 ,,,Mr. IREDELL--Full and fair Discussion necessary, ... 4 ,,,Obedience to two Governments,. ... 35 ,,,Reference to British GOV, ... 38 Elections; Control by general GOV; executive, legislative, and judicial, separate, an Improvement, ... 73 ,,,Commons an Overmatch for King and Lords, ... 132 ,,,Senate's Power ought to counteract that of the House, to preserve State Sovereignty, 133 ,,,Laws CONSISTENT WITH THE CONSTITUTION BINDING ON THE PEOPLE; POWERS usurped; Powers intended to be given, legal without new Authority, &c., ... 179 ,,,Abuse of Power ,,,RELIGION; Tests; Persecutions; its Toleration in America; Sacrament in Great Britain; Office open to all RELIGIONS [[Christian DENs]]; Guaranty explained [[Christian DENs]] ,,,Form of an Oath; governed by the RELIGION of the Person taking it; Case of an East Indian, a Gentoo, in Charles II.'s Time, ... 197 State Officers amenable to the Courts CONSTITUTION MUST BE THE SUPREME LAW, ... 150 ,,,Fallacy of the Opinion that the Pope, or a Foreigner, may be chosen President; RELIGION, ... 198 ,,,. RELIGION; Papists or MAHOMETANS may occupy the Chair; Disqualification in the States; would oppose Adoption, ... 215 ,,,Distinction between a Monarchy and Republic, ... 10 ,,,Congress, its Powers limited and enumerated, ... 140 ,,,RELIGION, no Power over it; an INFIDEL will never be chosen for Office ,,,Objections to the new Form of GOV, ... 50 ,,,should be guarded against ,,,RELIGIOUS Tests, Foundation of Persecution, ... 200 ,,,Mr. WILSON -- wished Exclusion of Popish priests from Office, ... 212 ,,,Mr. PATRICK CALHOUN--RELIGION; too great a Latitude allowed, ... 312".

---T--- USA GOV is Officers Supporting Christ, Christianity, & the Holy Bible; Existence Purpose: // "Letters of Delegates to Congress: Volume 1- 8/1774 - 8/1775 Samuel Ward to Mary Ward? My dearest Philadelphia Octr. 10th. 1774 ,,,your observations relative to the Congress and the Town of Boston are just and with you I fear the dispute must [be] decided by the sword. The Acct. which you give me of the pleasure you enjoy in your Aunts & Brother make my absence less disagreable to me, the manner in which You speak of your health & the idea of its being entirely restored are vastly pleasing for though I have long been trying to view you & every thing else dearest to Me through the Medium of RELIGION [&] Philosophy my fond Heart is sufficiently attached yet ,,,Tell her to remember that the supreme Parent of the Universe is a Being of infinite goodness & mercy that judgment is his strange Work [[Holy SC]] and that He is love & delights in the communication of happiness. Tell her to [PRAY] to him to pour out her whole Soul before him not [,,,] earnest desire for his DIVINE Direction & Blessing [,,,] a firm confidence in him, let her remember that whatsoever We ask in faith we shall receive (if it be best for us) and surely to have [[Holy Bible SC]] our souls filled with the Knowledge & Love of GOD with ardent desires to see & do his Will and such a fixed Determination chearfully to follow him as may enable us to present our bodies living sacrifices HOLY & acceptable unto GOD [[reference to Holy Bible Rom12.1-2]] must be at all times fit & proper for us. These are the great objects which her soul I doubt not is fixed upon, if they were in my power she knows I should bestow them in a moment. How much more may she expect every thing from a parent whose goodness endureth for ever & as much exceeds mine as the light of the meridian Sun does that of the poorest candle & much more. We had an express from Boston giving an Acct. of the distressed & dangerous situation of the Town & Province ,,,Correspondence. Your PRAYERS for your native Country & her cruel parent your reflections upon the endearment which absence creates in us & your reflection upon your blessed sisters & conclusion that our evening may be equally serene gave me the highest pleasure. ,,,Tell Debby that Israel came well until I got within fifteen miles of New York & there I left her,,,".

---T--- <u>The CC (DOI & CON) with God is the basis of the Laws</u> of the USA: // "This CON, and the Laws of the US which shall be made in Pursuance thereof ,,,or which shall be made, under the Authority of the US, shall be the supreme Law of the Land." THIS STATEMENT is written 2 (Two) Times in the CON. The CON is the application of the DOI.

---T--- <u>RELIGION of Christian duty is the Intention/ purpose assigned that Christ is to~ +]</u> the USA GOV; +] All Branches including Citizens; +] Soldiers; +] expressed by having Christian chaplains; +] expressed by Christian sermons to the soldiers; +] expressed by Not separating it from, rather including it in Activities & Events: // "Letters of Delegates to Congress: Volume 7- 5/1, 1777 - 9/18, 1777 - John Adams to Nathanael Greene - Dear Sir. Phyladelphia 6/2, 1777 Yours of the 28 Ult. is before me. ,,,It is certain that RELIGION and MORALity have no less obligations upon Armies, than upon Cities and contribute no less to the Happiness of Soldiers than of Citizens. There is one Principle of RELIGION which has contributed vastly to the Excellence of Armies, who had very little else of RELIGION or MORALity, the Principle I mean is the SACRED obligation of oaths, which among both Romans and Britans, who seem to have placed the whole of RELIGION and MORALity in the punctual observance of them, have done Wonders. It is this alone which prevents Desertions from your Enemies. I think our Chaplains ought to make the Solemn Nature and the SACRED obligation of oaths the favourite Subject of their Sermons to the Soldiery. Odd as it may seem I cannot help considering a serious sense of the Solemnity of an oath as the corner Stone of Discipline, and that it might be made to contribute more, to the order of the Army, than any or all of the Instruments of Punishment.".

---T--- <u>USA Officials & GOV prioritizes Christ & His Christianity</u> Religion: // "Letters of Delegates to Congress: Volume 7- 5/1, 1777 - 9/18, 1777 - John Witherspoon to David Witherspoon - Dear David, Philadelphia, 6/11, 1777. ,,,I hope, my dear boy, if you continue to keep the path which I have chalked out to you, you will be useful, happy, and successful in life. Give great application to your studies, but above all be attentive to your MORAL conduct. It is my earnest desire that you should, as soon as possible, renew your baptismal engagements, agreeably to the conversation I had with you here. Remember, my beloved child, that those who have been trained up in the fear of GOD, cannot SIN at so cheap a rate as others, and that the great advantages which you have had, and do still enjoy, must be accounted for. I wish your accomplishment in every respect, and therefore bear with me while I put you in mind to prevent at any rate a habit of holding down your head, or keeping it on one side, or any other ungraceful habit. Let there be decency in your outward carriage, reserve and modesty in your conversation, and humility in your heart ,,,I am, dear David, Your affectionate father, Jno. Witherspoon. P.S. If the enemy leave New Jersey, as there is some prospect at present, you shall have notice immediately.. MS not found; reprinted from CHRISTIAN Advocate 2 (Oct., 1824): 445."

---T--- <u>USA GOV is for God by~ +] Christianity, +] Supports Christian Activity, +]</u> Opposes evil (sin and anti-Christian) Activity: // "Letters of Delegates to Congress: Vol 13 - 6/1, 1779 - 9/30, 1779 Thomas Burke's "Epistle" [July 16? 1779] An EPISTLE Hail, mighty Thomas! ,,,Whose splendid periods flash for Lees defence, Replete with every thing but common sense. You by whose labors no man e'er was wiser, You of invective, great monopolizer; You who, unfeeling as a Jew or Turk, Attack a ,,,You who, in fervor of satiric vein, Maul and abuse the mild and meek ,,,And eager to traduce the worthiest men, Despise the energy of Drayton's pen.O say, what name shall dignify the lays, Which now I consecrate to sing thy praise; In pity tell, by what exalted name Thou would'st be damn'd to an ETERNAL flame. Shall Common Sense, or Comus greet thine ear, A piddling poet, or puft pamphleteer; Behold around thee, how thy triumphs lie, Of reputations hosts before thee die; On envy's altars hecatombs expire, And Faction fondly lights her pupil's fire.That pupil most devoted to her will, Who for the worthless wags his quibbling quill; And with a TRUE democracy of SPIRIT Bravely attacks the most exalted merit.Thou pupil worthy her attentive care, By Satan granted to her earnest PRAYER; When on the brink of fate smooth Adams stood, And saw his Arthur flound'ring in the flood. While plausive Richard, in whose gloomy breast Revenge and terror stood by turns confest; Doubtful his brothers measures to defend, With Berkenhout their confidant and friend; Or breaking thro' the weak fraternal ties,To save himself the doctor sacrifice. 'Twas in that desperate, the important hour, When Faction, trembling for her tott'ring pow'r, Thus pour'd her vows- "Author of ev'ry crime! Whose pangs shall last beyond the reach of time; By all those crimes, and all those pangs, give ear, And if, O sire, thy daughter e'er was dear; If e'er obedient to her father's call, The crowds of Faction fill'd his spacious hall; If e'er the populace by her possest, Have plung'd their daggers in a patriot breast; And forc'd humanity herself to fly, with banish'd Justice to yon azure sky; Attend, attend, attend, my fav'rites see, Their hopeless eyes are fix'd alone on thee; Oh help them, save them, or my sway is o'er, Opprest like thee, like thee to rise no more." The PRAYER was heard, the dreadful monarch spoke. While HELL convuls'd e'en to her center shook: "since on mankind to fix my iron reign, Nor SIN, nor death suffice, I give them Payne. "Say, mighty Thomas, on what awful day You first beheld the morn's resplendent ray; That day to envy shall most SACRED be, And all her squinting sons shall wait on thee. But sure no mortal mother did thee bear, Rather a cholic in the prince of air, On dusky pinions borne o'er Ether's plain, Expell'd thee from him with a griping pain. For as Minerva, queen of sense uncommon, Owed not her birth to goddess or to woman; But softly crept from out her father's scull, At a small crack in't when the moon was full; So you, great Common Sense, did surely come From out the crack in grisly Pluto's bum. Such as thy origin such be thy fate, To war 'gainst virtue with a deadly hate; By daily slanders earn thy daily food, Exalt the wicked, and depress the good; And having spent a lengthy life in EVIL, Return again unto thy parent DEVIL.".

---T--- <u>USA GOV Intended/ Purposed to Be God's & Christian & Religion thereof as proved by</u> the Supports to Christianity as of~ +assisting & promoting it in society; +assisting the Christian DEN of the Moravian Movement, which involved Mr. Zinzendorf at some times; +assisting land use for Christian society in public businesses; +not supporting false religions, nor infidel, nor heathen society, nor idolatry: // "Letters of

Delegates to Congress:Volume 23 - 11/7, 1785 - 11/5, 1786 Charles Thomson to John Ettwein Revd. Sir, Office of Secretary of Congress, 8/26. 1786 Upon receiving your letter of the 1st I did myself the honor of immediately communicating it to the US in Congress assembled, who have thereupon been pleased to pass a resolution respecting the Indian Congregation, a copy of which is herewith enclosed. ,,,I most heartily join you in PRAYER to GOD that He "may grant these poor sufferers a time of peace & rest after so many tribulations that other HEATHEN may see the great difference of a civilised CHRISTIAN life,,, Please to convey to the revd. D. Zeisberger my sincere respects and the esteem I have for his zeal & perseverance in the good work in which he has been so long engaged. I hope he will continue to the end & that his labours will be crowned with success. With great respect, I am, Revd & Dear Sir, Your obedt humble Servt, Cha Thomson P.S. Enclosed I also send you An Ordinance passed by Congress for the regulation of Indian Affairs ,,,Ettwein's August I letter PRAYING for the relief of about 100 displaced Moravian Indians seeing to return to their homes on the Muskingum River was referred Aug. 8 to a committee which reported Aug. 17. The committee's recommendation that they be permitted to return to their former settlement and be provided axes, hoes, blankets, and up to 500 bushels of corn for the ensuing winter from the public stores at Fort McIntosh was adopted by Congress Aug. 24. See JCC, 31:505n, 526, 562-63".

---T--- Religion To God of the USA GOV Intended/ purposed includes~ +] Christian teaching about Christ, +] Holy Bible training, +] Truth Based, +] Church Assembly attended by USA GOV Officials, +] Subjects of Public Support are Christian Truths of Heaven & Hell, & Spirit of God: // "Letters of Delegates to Congress: Volume 19 - 8/1, 1782 - 3/11, 1783 --Elias Boudinot to Susan Boudinot - My dearest Susan. ,,,Philadelphia Octr. 30th. 1782 ,,,I propose this Letter as a serious one-- I have for some time past been led by Circumstances, to reflect more seriously on the prospect of you launching into life, and leaving your Fathers Roof, as well as his immediate Protection & Guardianship. I have reflected how far, I have done my Duty in executing the Trust committed to me, by the great Governor of the Universe in your Education--in a proper Provision for you in Life, in preparing you for usefulness in whatever Station it may please GOD to call you-- and laying a rational foundation, by the aid of DIVINE Grace, for your enjoyment of a glorious & happy Immortality in the life to Come. Through the unmerited Blessing of a kind Providence, I cannot blame myself greatly, for any deficiency in your Education and Provision for Life--Nature wants but little and not that little long. I have confidence in you, that if you make good use of and continue improving those Abilities & that knowledge you now possess, your usefulness in this Life under GOD, may be of some Importance to your Fellow Creatures. But my dear Child, all these are but secondary Objects. How stands it as to your preparation for and hope in the prospects of a joyfull Immortality--I can assure you in all the sincerity of TRUTH, that you have been from your first Conception, dedicated to GOD, as his peculiar Property. At your Birth (which was a Miracle of Mercy, and deserves your whole Soul, as a living Monument thereof) you was repeatedly, by the most solemn Acts of RELIGIOUS Worship in the fear of GOD, given up to him. Your Baptism in the Face of the CHURCH of CHRIST, was an Express Covenant with GOD in CHRIST on your Behalf, by which you Altogether became the Lord's --Your Parents became bound on your Part, and I devoutly trust that the Contract stands ratified in HEAVEN. You have been instructed from your Childhood in the knowledge of your Lost State by Nature --the absolute necessity of a Change of Heart, and an entire renovation of Soul, to the Image of JESUS CHRIST --of Salvation, thro' his meritorious Righteousness only --and the indispensable necessity of personal holiness without which no man shall see the lord. [[SC of Holy Bible]] You are well acquainted that the most perfect & consummate Doctrinal Knowledge, is of no avail, without it operates on & sincerely affects the Heart -Changes the Practice-- and totally influences the Will--and that without the almighty Power of the SPIRIT of GOD, enlightening your Mind, subduing your Will, and continually drawing you to himself-- you can do nothing. Altho' at the same Time, your own Constant unwearied Endeavours after Holiness and perpetual Applications to a MERCIFUL SAVIOUR for this Aid, are as necessary as if you could accomplish your own Salvation by your own Works. Blessed be GOD, this has been your happy Lot, but my dearest Susan, all our Tears, PRAYERS, Dedications, Instructions, Example, & Admonitions will not accomplish the Event so devoutly to be wished. What have You done, in your own Person, since you have come to the Age of discretion? Have you confirmed the all gracious Covenant. Have you justified your Parents, in the multiplied Acts of devoting you to GOD? They have travailed in Birth a second time with you, till you should be born again to newness of Life. Your baptismal Covenant was the Act of your Parents, in your Name & Behalf, but it is high Time, that this Act of your Parents should be acknowledged & renewed by you, in the solemn dedication of yourself in the LORDS SUPPER. This is an Ordinance designed as a solemn Seal of the same Covenant, as if designed by your Baptism. They are both Seals of the same Covenant, and a worthy Subject, of one is a worthy subject of the other. I have a most earnest desire, that this important Event in your Life, should take place before you launch into the world, and leave your Father's assiduous care, that he may be blessed, with seeing the work completed, as far as human endeavours can go. That you may go forth under the protection of the GOD of HEAVEN, as his peculiar inheritance by your own Act, in Compliance with his positive Command "Do this in remembrance of me." I was led to this train of reflection by a Sermon I lately heard on this Subject-- the only one I remember that fully came up to my Sentiments and which I verily believe is founded on the TRUTH,,,. My Anxiety for your accomplishing (and that without delay) your whole Duty, made me wish most heartily, you could have heard it delivered, because it might have removed all scruples, which too often injure young & tender minds. To shew you my warmest desires for your SPIRITual Growth in Grace and that you may go from under my immediate Care, the Subject of the DIVINE SPECIAL GRACE & GOVERNMENT, I have amidst all the Variety".

---T--- The First National GOV {Citizens & Pilgrims} had Intentions/purposes of to Christ by~ +] Establishing Christianity as the Religion, +] Opposing false (non-Christian) religions: // Christopher Columbus was a Christian and purposed to preach the Gospel, raise money for this goal of recapturing Jerusalem from the Muslims. The Muslim's had a few years earlier attacked and murdered many in a take over of the city of

133

Constantinople in AD 1453 and destroyed the Byzantine Empire (225). // Mayflower Compact AD 1620 states~ "establish this colony in God's name and for His glory and to advance the Christian faith". The ByLaws that applied this Covenant Compact, was called the Plymouth Constitution. It contained job descriptions for the governor, lieutenant governor, and rules of the General Court, how laws were to be made, and specific laws on life, liberty, and property. // Also see cite (265).

---T--- <u>USA GOV Constantly Intending/ purposing God's Presence with</u> Christianity Religion by stating with expressions~ +] Christian terms or words, +] Christian Activity in all its relations; +] Foreign relations as representing the USA as a Christian Nation for Christ: // "Journal of the executive proceedings of the Senate of the US of America, 1789-1805 - ,1/ 17, 1791 ,,,of file US, by Mr. Lear, his Secretary, who communicated to the Senate a letter from his most CHRISTIAN Majesty to the President and members of Congress; and ,,,US,1/ 17th, 1791 ,,,I lay before you a letter from his most CHRISTIAN Majesty ,,,Go. WASHINGTON. The letter referred to in the message, is as follows: To our very dear friends and allies ,,,US of North America. Very Dear Great Friends and Allies We have received the letter by which you inform us of the new mark of confidence that you have shown to Mr. Jefferson, and which puts a period to his appointment of Minister Plenipotentiary at our Court ,,,It is with the most Sincere pleasure that we embrace this opportunity of renewing these assurances of regard and friendship, which we feel for the US in general, and for each of them in particular; under their influence, we PRAY GOD that he will keep you, very dear friends and allies, under his HOLY and beneficent protection. Done at Paris, this 11th of Sept, 1790. Your good friend and ally, Louis. Montmorin, [SEAL.] The US of North America."

---T--- <u>Christianity as the Religion of Truth & the Holy Bible</u> is Intended/ Purposed for God by FFOG & All USA GOV Branches & State GOV as proved by expressions of~ +] Supported such; +] opposed false religion, +] opposed evil: // "Journals of the Continental Congress, 1774-1789 - 3/20, 1779 A letter from J. Clark and ,,,Johnston, auditors in the army, was read ,,,Ordered ,,,A petition of,,, a soldier in Captain Spaulding's independent company, was read, PRAYing, for sundry reasons ,,,[Note 2: 2 The petition of Lawrence, dated Feb. 20, is in the Papers of the Continental Congress, No. 42, IV, folio 184.] Ordered, That the PRAYER of his petition be granted. The committee appointed to prepare a recommendation to the several states to set apart a day of fasting humiliation and PRAYER, brought in a draught, which was taken into consideration, and agreed to as follows: Whereas, in just punishment of our manifold transgressions, it hath pleased the SUPREME DISPOSER OF ALL EVENTS to visit these US with a destructive calamitous war, through which His DIVINE Providence hath, hitherto, in a wonderful manner, conducted us, so that we might acknowledge that the race is not to the swift, nor the battle to the strong: and whereas, there is but too much Reason to fear that notwithstanding the chastisements received and benefits bestowed, [[SC from Holy Bible]] too few have been sufficiently awakened to a sense of their guilt, or warmed our Bosoms with gratitude, OR TAUGHT TO AMEND THEIR LIVES AND TURN FROM THEIR SINS, that so He might turn from His wrath. And whereas, from a consciousness of what we have merited at His hands, and an apprehension that the malevolence of our disappointed enemies, like the incredulity of PHARAOH, may be used as the scourge of Omnipotence to vindicate his slighted Majesty, there is reason to fear that he may permit much of our land to become the prey of the spoiler, and the Blood of the innocent be poured out that our borders to be ravaged, and our habitations destroyed: Resolved, That it be recommended to the several states to appoint the first Thursday in May next, to be a day of fasting, Thanksgiving humiliation and PRAYER to Almighty GOD, that he will be pleased to avert those impending calamities which we have but too well deserved: that he will GRANT US HIS GRACE TO REPENT OF OUR SINS, AND AMEND OUR LIVES, ACCORDING TO HIS HOLY WORD: that HE will continue that wonderful protection which hath led us through the paths of danger and distress: that HE will be a husband to the widow and a father to the fatherless children, [[SC of Holy Bible]] who weep over the barbarities of a savage enemy: that he will grant us patience in suffering, and fortitude in adversity: that he will inspire us with humility and moderation, and gratitude in prosperous circumstances: that HE will give wisdom to our councils, firmness to our resolutions, and victory to our arms That HE will have Mercy on our Foes, and graciously forgive them, and turn their Hearts from Enmity to Love. That HE will bless the labours of the husbandman, and pour forth abundance, so that we may enjoy the fruits of the earth in due season. [That HE will cause union, harmony, and mutual confidence to prevail throughout these states: that HE will bestow on our great ally all those blessings which may enable him to be gloriously instrumental in protecting the rights of mankind, and promoting the happiness of his subjects and advancing the Peace and Liberty of Nations. That HE will give to both Parties to this Alliance, Grace to perform with Honor and Fidelity their National Engagements].1 That HE will bountifully continue his paternal care to the commander in chief, and the officers and soldiers of the US: that HE will grant the blessings of peace to all contending nations, freedom to those who are in bondage, and comfort to the afflicted: that HE will diffuse useful knowledge, extend the influence of TRUE RELIGION, and give us that peace of mind, which the world cannot give: that HE will be our shield in the day of battle, our COMFORTER in the hour of death, and our kind parent and MERCIFUL JUDGE through time and through ETERNITY. [Note 1: 1 Words in brackets are in writing of John Jay.]".

---T--- <u>US GOV Intended/ purposed to~</u> +] be Christian; +] be Religious to Christ of Christianity; +] pay Christian Chaplains; +] Require Christian Oaths or an Oath Agreeing to God's presence; +] Support the Holy Bible Words: // "Letters of Delegates to Congress: Volume 7 - 5/1, 1777 - 9/18, 1777 John Adams to Nathanael Greene Dear Sir. Phyladelphia June 2d. 1777 Yours of the 28 Ult. is before me. ,,,It is certain that RELIGION and MORALity have no less obligations upon Armies, than upon Cities and contribute no less to the Happiness of Soldiers than of Citizens. There is one Principle of RELIGION which has contributed vastly to the Excellence of Armies, who had very little else of RELIGION or MORALity, the Principle I mean is the SACRED obligation of oaths, which among both Romans and Britans, who seem to have placed the whole of RELIGION and MORALity in the punctual observance of them, have done Wonders. It is this alone which prevents Desertions from your Enemies. I think our CHAPLAINS ought to make the SOLEMN Nature and the SACRED obligation of oaths the favourite Subject of their SERMONS to the Soldiery. Odd as it may seem I cannot help considering a serious sense of the Solemnity of an oath as the corner Stone of Discipline, and that it might be made to contribute more, to the order of the Army, than any or all of the Instruments of Punishment ,,,What the success of such a Motion will be, I know not, but I (will certainly discharge my Duty to myself and my Constituents and Posterity) believe such a Motion will be made. I agree entirely in your sentiments concerning the Danger of entrusting so many important Commands to foreigners. Mr Deane I fear has exceeded his Powers. Mr Du Coudray shall never have my Consent to be at the Head of the Artillery. ,,,PRAY what is your opinion of General Conway ,,,We are anxious to ,,,LB (MHi). 1 General Greene's May 28 letter to Adams ,,,Schuylkill River on 9/15, 1777 ,,,Am. Archives, 5th ser. 2:283; John Adams' Diary, 9/18, 1777; and Edmund C. Burnett, The Continental Congress (New York: Macmillan Co., 1941) ,,,also John Adams to Nathanael Greene, 7/7, 1777."

---T--- <u>USA GOV is Intended/ Purposed to~ +] be Christian for Christ; +] Support Christian</u> Missionary Activity; +] Support Christian Employments to Peoples who are not Christian; +] All Branches of USA GOV & STATE GOV to participate in these intentions; +] Signs DOCs as a Representative Ambassador Nation for Jesus Christ: // "Journals of the Continental Congress, 1774-1789 - 5/27, 1785. - Congress assembled. Present, New Hampshire, Massachusetts, Rhode Island, Connecticut, New Jersey, Pennsylvania, Maryland, Virginia and South Carolina; and from the state of New York, Mr. [Melancton] Smith; from North Carolina, Mr. [Richard Dobbs] Spaight, and from Georgia, Mr. [William] Houstoun. - Mr. Charles Pettit, a delegate for the state of Pennsylvania, attended, and produced credentials; by which it appears, that on the seventh day of Apr., 1785, he was appointed a delegate of that State for the present year. Pennsylvania, SS. [SEAL] John Dickinson. In the Name and by the authority of the Freemen of the Commonwealth of Pennsylvania.--The Supreme Executive Council of the Commonwealth - To the Honorable Charles Pettit Esquire. Whereas on the seventh day of this Month You was by the General Assembly of this Commonwealth appointed a Delegate: You are therefore hereby Commissioned a Delegate to represent this State in Congress for the present Year. Given in Council under the hand of His Excellency John Dickinson Esquire, President, and the Seal of the State at Philadelphia <u>this eighteenth day of April in the YEAR OF OUR LORD one thousand seven hundred and eighty five. Attest</u>: John Armstrong, Jr. Sy.1 [Note 1: 1 ,,,On motion of Mr. [Charles] Pinckney, seconded by Mr. [William] Grayson, Resolved, That the geographer of the US be continued in Office for a term not exceeding three years ,,,According to order, Congress ,,,a Surveyor from each State, in conformity to the "Ordinance for ascertaining the mode of disposing of lands in the western territory," and, the ballots being taken, Mr. Nathaniel Adams was elected from the State of New Hampshire; Mr. Rufus Putnam from Massachusetts; Mr. Caleb Harris from Rhode Island and Providence plantations; Mr. William Morris from New York; Mr. Adam Hoops from Pennsylvania; Mr. James Simpson from Maryland; Mr. Alexander Parker from The Committee [consisting of Mr. David Ramsay, Mr. William Samuel Johnson and Mr. Samuel Dick] to which was referred the petition of Jacob Fowler PRAYing for the assistance of Congress to enable him to instruct the Indians of the Montauk tribe in reading, writing, and the principles of the CHRISTIAN RELIGION, report that they have conversed with and enquired the character of the said Petitioner and find him a person suitable to be employed in the business which he PRAYs the assistance of Congress to enable him to perform. They also are of opinion that not only the principles of RELIGION but sound policy requires that the benevolent intentions of the said Jacob Fowler meet with the encouragement of Congress. Your Committee therefore recommend the following resolution. Resolved, That the Board of Treasury advance to Jacob Fowler the sum of one hundred dollars to encourage him to instruct the Indians in reading, writing and the principles of CHRISTIAN RELIGION and that he be recommended to the Legislature of New York and to all charitable well disposed individuals as a person deserving encouragement and their charitable aid to enable him to prosecute his laudable intention with respect to the Indians ,,,".

---T--- <u>USA GOV, Congress, Executive, Citizens, States GOV</u> Intended/ purposed to~ +] Support God's presence, Christianity, it's Religion, & Christian activities; +] Oppose false Christianity, Devil & Demons, & evil: // "Letters of Delegates to Congress: Volume 6- 1/1, 1777 - 4/30, 1777 - John Adams to Abigail Adams - Philadelphia Mar. 14. 1777 Congress has been sitting several Days and proceeding upon Business. I have been in Town above a Week and have spent much of my Time, in making Inquiries after the cheapest Places in Town for Board and stabling. I have at last removed my Horses from a stable at six and six Pence a Night, to another at three dollars a Week each. ,,,I am this day to remove my Quarters, from three Pounds a Week for myself and thirty shillings for my servant, to another Place where they vouchsafe to keep me for forty seven and six Pence, and my servant for twenty shillings. ,,,I shall then live at the cheapest Lay. ,,,Cheap indeed! What will become of you, I know not. How you will be able to live is past my Comprehension, but I hope the Regulation of Prices, will be of Service to you. ,,,I wish to hear often from you. Believe the Post may be now trusted. Believe me to be more yours, and more anxious for your Welfare than any Words can express. The GOV of Pensilvania is taking Root downwards, and bearing Fruit upwards, notwithstanding the Squibbs in the News Papers. They are making Treason Laws and Militia Laws, &c. The Jersey GOV is making a Militia Law too. The PEOPLE of that State will be all soldiers ,,,The Quakers too are inflamed with Resentment. They say, that they were used worse, than any other People. In a Time ,,,especially a War like this, one may see the Necessity and Utility, of the DIVINE Prohibitions of Revenge, and the Injunctions of forgiveness of Injuries and love of Enemies, which We find in the CHRISTIAN RELIGION. Unrestrained, in some degree by these benevolent Laws, Men would be DEVILS, at such a Time as this,,, Prattle for me to my little Friends. Give them my best Wishes, Blessings and PRAYERS ,,,1 Adams lodged at Mrs. Sarah Yard's until Mar. 14 ,,,2:257n.7,,,".

---T--- <u>God's USA GOV, Congress, Citizens, Churches (Christian), Executive~ +] all opposed</u> to false religion, +] all support Christian religion to other people of false religions, +] provides land for Christian use: // "Date: 3/3, 1823 - Where or how concluded: Act of Congress. - Reference:

Statutes at Large, Volume III, page 749. Tribe: Moravian or CHRISTIAN Indians. Description of cession or reservation: Congress, by the provisions of this act, appropriated $1,000 with which ,,,An ordinance of Congress of Sept. 3, 1788, set apart three tracts of 4,000 acres each at Shoenbrun, Gnadenhutten, and Salem, on Muskingum river, for the Society of United Brethren, to be used in propagating the gospel among the HEATHEN. By act of Congress approved June 1, 1796, provision was made for surveying and patenting these tracts to the society in question, in trust for the benefit of the CHRISTIAN Indians. Under the provisions of the act of Mar. 3, 1823, Lewis Cass was appointed to negotiate for the relinquishment of the title to the U. S. This he secured and transmitted the relinquishment of both the society and the Indians ,,,Congress made provision for the disposition of the lands. Indian Land Cessions in the US, 1784 to 1894."

---T--- Christianity is the Basis for the Formation of the USA Nation & it is done in the name of Jesus Christ: // "Journals of the Continental Congress, 1774-1789 - 11/29, 1781 - ,,,letter to his Most CHRISTIAN Majesty, being reported, and sundry amendments being made, was passed. The secretary of foreign affairs ,,,to his Most CHRISTIAN Majesty; which, being amended, was agreed to as follows: The US in Congress assembled, to their great, faithful and beloved friend and ally, Lewis the sixteenth, king of France and Navarre. Great, Faithful and Beloved Friend and Ally, At a period so glorious to the arms of France, both by sea and land, and so favourable to the fortunes of America, it is with peculiar satisfaction that we congratulate the monarch, whose wise counsels and generous support have so largely contributed to events illustrious in themselves, and promising consequences truly important. We wish to convey to your Majesty our sense of the victory obtained by the Count de Grasse over the enemy's fleet on our coast, and the subsequent reduction of the British armament in Virginia; and we repeat our grateful acknowledgments for the various aids so seasonably extended to us. From the benevolence and magnanimity which have hitherto interested your Majesty in the welfare of these states, we are convinced that you will on this occasion feel an equal pleasure with ourselves, whose immediate advantage is the result of such fortunate exertions ,,,harmony and affection which have subsisted between the troops of the two nations. The distress occasioned to the common enemy by combined operations, will, we trust, point out to both nations the utility of similar measures in future ,,,will urge the US to every effort which their particular interests, added to their desire of seconding your Majesty's views, can call forth to ensure the complete success of attacks upon the enemy's strongholds. It is with great pleasure that the US continue to number some of your Majesty's subjects amongst their most able, SPIRITed and faithful officers. ,,,Major General ,,,enlightened ,,,We PRAY GOD, great, faithful and beloved friend and ally, always to keep your Majesty in his HOLY protection. Done at Philadelphia, THE TWENTY-NINTH DAY OF NOVEMBER, IN THE YEAR OF OUR LORD 1781, and in the sixth year of our independence. By the US in Congress assembled. Your faithful friends and allies. (Signed) John Hanson, President.1".

---T--- Christianity & It's Laws is the US GOV Religion as Declared by God, Congress, History, States, Cities, Citizens: // "Letters of Delegates to Congress: Volume 1- 8/1774 - 8/1775 ,,,24th Septr. 1774 The Letters which I first received from Nancy & Sammy gave Me great Pleasure, to find that you bore the Shock which the News from Boston must give you so well and that such a SPIRIT prevailed in the Town and in my own Family in particular gave Me the highest Satisfaction. A noble Ardor prevailed here. We proposed turning the Congress into a Council of War ,,,in this fleeting World of that blessed Child whom infinite Goodness hath re moved from Pain & Sickness to a Country where all sighing & Sorrow are excluded effected Me much. ,,,Though daily thought of and ex- pected I could have been glad to have been present & enjoyed the di- vine Instructions Given to all around her. May they sink deep into every Heart, may those who are not yet prepared for the last Change be sensible that youth is no Security against Death ,,,I was going to say only important Business of this Life, a due Preparation for Death and may you all learn that in that happy Situation Death though sometimes a painful is a kind & most desirable Messenger to introduce You to real and ETERNAL Life and Bliss. I wuld have been glad to have performed the last offices to that dear Saint but some other had the melancholy Pleasure of closing her Eyes and it is enough that She is happy. May We all (as She desired) Give Glory to GOD ,,,What has been done in Congress relative to the Massachusetts You'l have in the Paper probably before this reaches you. I long to write to your Aunts & to each of you but go into Congress about 9 o'Clock A.M. sitt until 3 or after, dine at 4 or after that. The Remainder of the Day is necessary for Relaxation & my Eyes are such I dont think it prudent to write by Candle Light. I fear my Friends will take it unkindly & how to help it I know not but shall comply with their Expectations as much as possible. Give my most affectionate Regards to your Aunts and to all my immediate Connections. ,,,May GOD of his infinite Mercy preserve You from all EVIL and lead You in the Way everlasting. Your most affectionate Father Sam: Ward [P.S.] I say nothing about my own Business because of the SABBATH. ,,,RC (RHi). Addressed: "To Mr. Samuel Ward Junr. In (Rhode Island) ,,,Congress had publicly announced "the means to be taken for the preservation of the liberties of America." ,,,JCC, 1:42. 3 Ward was a Sabbatarian Baptist who observed the SABBATH on Saturday. Ward, Correspondence (Knollenberg), p. 20; Frank S. Mead, Handbook of DENOMINATIONS in the US, 2d ed. rev. (New York: Abingdon Press, 1961), pp. 50-51."

---T--- USA GOV has~ +] Christian Officers, +] Christian Activity, +] God & Christianity as the basis of CC DOI: // "Letters of Delegates to Congress: Volume 7- 5/1, 1777 - 9/18, 1777; ,,,9/10, 1777 Yours of the 22d of August ,,,I shall at all Times make it my Pleasure & Happiness to oblige you, and am your very humble Servt. ,,,2 The preceding day Marchant wrote the following letter to his daughter Sarah. "It is no small Pleasure to find a growing and improving Correspondent in my Daughter Sally. Go on my Dear thus improving, and add daily one Virtue to another. And may GOD grant that his Grace may really affect your Heart with suitable Impressions of His Goodness. Remember that GOD made You, that GOD keeps you alive, and preserves you from all Harm, and gives You all the Powers and the Capacity whereby you are able to read of Him, and of JESUS CHRIST your Saviour and Redeemer, and to do every other needful Business of Life. And while you look around you and see the great Priveleges and Advantages you have above what other Children have, of learning to read and write, of being taught the meaning of the Great TRUTHS of the BIBLE, you must remember not to be proud on that Account, but to bless GOD, and be thankful and endeavour in your turn to assist others with the knowledge you may gain. And be kind and good to all poor People, and poor Children that have not your Opportunity, especially in a kind and tender Manner assist your Sister and Brother. And at all Times remember the great Obligations you are under to your Parents for their Care of you, especially think from Day to Day how kind a Mama You have, how when you are sick she Nurses and provides for you. ,,,for the Information You give me of the farming Business. Let us all be thankful to GOD for giving us such a Plenty of the Fruits of the Earth." Marchant Papers, RHi.".

---T--- <u>Christianity is the Religion to Jesus Christ of the USA GOV, Congress,</u> Executive, Citizens, States GOV, Churches, CC (DOI & CON), FFoG, & all; & was such from the start: // "Letters of Delegates to Congress: Volume 12- 2/1, 1779 - 5/31, 1779 - ,,,[Apr.] 13th [1779] Commercial Committee. Congress ,,,Reports of Committees ,,,for me, but a full approbation of my conduct in the exertions I have made in the great cause of my country; and you may be assured, if I had nothing further in view than what respects me personally, I should immediately return to private life; But I consider myself called upon to Act, not ownly, for the present generation, but for ought I know, millions yet unborn. Since I have been in the southern states, I have had opportunity of being acquainted with many of the principal people and have made myself somewhat acquainted with the constitutions & Laws under which they have lived; And I'm fully convinced that it is owing under providence to the care our fore-fathers took in New England, ,,,in enacting such a good code of Laws, both to preserve our civil & RELIGIOUS liberties, that the people in this land are not now in a state of abject slavery. I have ever considered this War as a judgment of HEAVEN upon us, for our SINS, as a people, and I'm very sure if their was a general reformation, we should soon see our difficulties removed; But the growing vices of the times, gives me great concern. As I have the pleasure of corresponding with a number of the clergy in New England, they all give me the following account, that they apprehend their is great danger of a general failure of the support of the gospel; But I can't yet bring my self to believe that my countrymen in New England, are so far degenerated; But if such an event should take place, and our CHURCHes be dispersed, I fear, we shall be a ruined people indeed; you may suppose it gives me real concern for the CHURCH of which I have the honor of being a member; and permit me, sir, to ask, whither you think our Revd. & worthy friend Mr. Wadsworth ,,,is encouraged & supported in the great work of the ministry as he ought to be? I do not pretend to know, for tho' I correspond with him, I take it, he has too tender a regard for his people to make complaints against them, but from my knowledge of you as a supporter of the CHURCH, are the reasons of my writing thus freely. ,,,His most CHRISTIAN Majesty, guarantees to us, sovereignty, independence &c. We are a young republican state, and are growing into importance with the nations of the earth; I wish we may be able to keep up to the TRUE republican principles, and not copy too much after monarchical GOV. It would give me pleasure to communicate some great affairs of state, but I'm not at liberty to add, at present. Please to give my kind regards to Mrs. Putnam, and respectful compliments to your worthy brothers, Capt. Putnam & Dr Putnam, and inform ,,,I am, my dear sir, with ,,,& sincerity, your most obedt. humble servant; S. Holten RC (MiDhEI). 1 Edmund Putnam (1734-1810) was a deacon in the First Congregational Parish in Danvers ,,,Rev Benjamin Wadsworth (1750- 1826), a graduate of Harvard College, was the minister of the First Congregational Parish in Danvers. Ibid., pp. 454-55."

---T--- <u>US GOV Congress, Citizens, State GOV all Support Christ by~ +]</u> Christian Educational (Schools) Institutions; +] Christianity: // "Letters of Delegates to Congress: Volume 2- 9/1775 - 12/1775 ,,,I cannot exclude from my Mind your melancholly Situation. The Griefs of your Father and Sisters, your Uncles and Aunts, as well as the remoter Connections, often croud in upon me, when my whole Attention ought to be directed to other Subjects. Your Uncle Quincy, my Friend as well as Uncle, must regret the loss of a beloved Sister, Dr. Tufts my other Friend I know bewails the loss of a Friend, as well as an Aunt and a sister, Mr. Cranch the Friend of my youth as well as of my riper Years, whose tender Heart sympathizes with his fellow Creatures in every Affliction and Distress, in this Case feels the Loss of a Friend, a fellow CHRISTIAN, and a Mother. But alas what avail these mournfull Reflections. The best Thing We can do, the greatest Respect We can show to the Memory of our departed Friend, is to copy into Our own Lives, those Virtues which in her Lifetime rendered her the Object of our Esteem, Love and Admiration. ,,,Above all Things my dear, let us inculcate these great Virtues and bright Excellencies upon our Children. ,,,Your Mother had a clear, and penetrating Understanding and a profound Judgment, as well as an honest and a friendly and a charitable Heart. ,,,My Opinion of the Duties of RELIGION and MORALity, comprehends a very extensive Connection with society at large, and the great Interest of the public. Does not natural MORALity, and much more CHRISTIAN Benevolence, make it our indispensible Duty to lay ourselves out, to serve our fellow Creatures to the Utmost of our Power, in promoting and supporting those great Political systems, and general Regulations upon which the Happiness of Multitudes depends. The Benevolence, Charity, Capacity and Industry which ex- erted in private Life, would make a family, a Parish or a Town Hap- py, employed upon a larger Scale, in Support of the great Principles of Virtue and Freedom of political Regulations might secure whole Nations and Generations from Misery, Want and Contempt. Public Virtues, and political Qualities therefore should be incessantly cherished in our Children. RC (MHi) . Adams, Family Correspondence (Butterfield), 1: 316-17. 1 In another letter to Abigail this day, Adams dilated upon the capabilities of human nature and "the virtues and powers to which men may be trained, by early education and constant discipline." "It should be your care, therefore," he urged, "and mine, to elevate the minds of our children and exalt their courage; to accelerate and animate their industry and activity; to excite in them an habitual contempt of meanness, abhorrence of injustice and inhumanity, and an ambition to excel in every capacity, faculty, and virtue." " (Butterfield), 1:317-18. John Adams to Abigail Adams Octr ,,,1775 There is, in the human Breast, a social Affection, which extends to our whole

Species. Faintly indeed; but in some degree. The Nation, Kingdom, or Community to which We belong is embraced by it more vigorously. It is stronger still towards the Province to which we belong, and in which We had our Birth. It is stronger and stronger, as We descend to the County, Town, Parish, Neighbourhood, and Family, which We call our own. And here We find it often so powerfull as to become partial, to blind our Eyes, to darken our Understandings and pervert our Wills. It is to this Infirmity, in my own Heart, that I must perhaps attribute that local Attachment, that partial Fondness, that overweening Prejudice in favour of New England, which I feel very often and which I fear sometimes, leads me to expose myself to just Ridicule. New England has in many Respects the Advantage of every other Colony in America, and indeed of every other Part of the World, that I know any Thing of. ,,,The Institutions in New England for the Support of RELIGION, MORALS and Decency, exceed any other, obliging every Parish to have a Minister, and every Person to go to Meeting &c. ,,,The public Institutions in New England for the Education of Youth, supporting Colledges at the public Expence and obliging Towns to maintain Grammar schools, is not equalled and never was in any Part of the World. 4. The Division of our Territory, that is our Counties into Townships, empowering Towns to assemble, choose officers, make Laws, mend roads, and twenty other Things, gives every Man an opportunity of shewing and improving that Education which he received at Colledge or at school, and makes Knowledge and Dexterity at public Business common. 5. Our Laws for the Distribution of Intestate Estates occasions a frequent Division of landed Property and prevents Monopolies, of Land. But in opposition to these We have laboured under many Disadvantages. The exorbitant Prerogatives of our Governors &c. which would have overborn our Liberties, if it had not been opposed by the five preceding Particulars. RC (MHi) . Adams, Family Correspondensc (Butterfield), 1:318-19."

---T--- R-E & 1-A has~ +] Religion & Religious Establishment as Rightly Defined to be Christian DEN (which is Christian Secondary Doctrines and Expressions); AND +] These have Free Exercise without prohibition; AND +] the Establishment of Religion was not to favor (partial or respecting) any Specific Christian DEN by making it the USA GOV Church; AND +] USA GOV is Required To Be Religious; AND +] The CC (DOI & CON) have happiness in them, of the which that happiness is based on God; AND +] the religion of the US GOV is the Christianity Religion: // "Letters of Delegates to Congress: Volume 9- 2/1, 1778 - 5/31, 1778 - Gouverneur Morris to Anthony Wayne Dr Wayne. York Town 21st May 1778. ,,,I am sorry the business of the Army hath been so long delayed. For your Comfort I have to assure you that it goes on tho not with the Rapidity You and I and every Body else wish ,,,Sincere Pleasure as it hath long been my fixed Opinion that VIRTUE AND RELIGION ARE THE GREAT SOURCES OF HUMAN HAPPINESS. [[Note the happiness comes from rightness & Christ; not from sin & evil]] More especially is it necessary in your Profession firmly to rely upon the GOD of Battles, for his Guardianship and Protection in the dreadful Hour of Trial. But of all these Things you will and I hope in the MERCIFUL LORD [[this is Jesus]] ,,,PRAY believe me with great sincerity, yours, Gouvr Morris RC (PHi) ,,,See JCC, 11:525 ,,,May 11, 1778".

---T--- R-E & R~Est & 1-A Explains that the USA GOV States~ +] Only Support for the Christ's Christian Religion; +] all other Religions are false; Not to be Supported; rather to be warned against; +] the Holy Bible is the basis of laws; +] Idolatry is opposed; +] No gods from other nations are supported; +] Evil activity; sin is opposed: // "Letters of Delegates to Congress: Volume 11- 10/1, 1778 - 1/31, 1779 Samuel Adams ,,,I am much pleasd with the Respect lately shown to the Count D'Estaing and his Officers,,,. but not with the Etiquet of your publick Entertainment. ,,,The Arrangement of the Toasts was not perfectly agreable to my Idea of Propriety. This may be thought unworthy of Notice. But there is no Appearance made by the Publick but, like that of a private Individual, adds more or less to its Honor or Disgrace. Besides, Things which detatchd & by themselves are justly considered as Trifles light as Air, when they are connected with and made Parts of a great Machine, become important and do good or Hurt. ,,,It must be confessd it is grounded on Principles truly and altogether Republican. Yet the old fashioned Whiggs murmur at it; and with a Mixture of Pleasure and Indignation contrast the present with past Times when it was made a Capital Point, to keep the former under the Controul of the latter. Men are prone to Idolatry; and some who seem to scorn the worshiping GODs of other Nations will bow down to graven Images of Gold & Silver, and, strange Infatuation! of Wood in the Form of an Ass, an Ape or a Calf, no matter what, if it be the Work of their own Hands. In TRUTH, my Friend, the Congress appears to be in an awkard Situation. While they are exerting their utmost Influence, on all proper Occasions, to support the civil Authority of the several States over the military, there are some Men, even in that State which my Partiality had almost led me to pronounce the most respectable in the Union who would have less Respect shown to them than to the Creatures which they have made. Tyrants have been the Scourges and Plagues of Mankind, and Armies their Instruments. These have been said by ignorant Flatterers & Sycophants to be the Vicegerents of the Almighty to punish Men for their SINS, and therefore not to be resisted or contrould. [[Note the application of idolatry by the USA Congress & all USA & State GOV Branches; that idolatry is a sin & should be avoided]]. The Time may come when the SINS of America may be punishd by a standing Army; and that Time will surely come when the Body of the People, shall be so lost to the Exercise of common Understanding and Caution, as to suffer the Civil to stoop to the Military Power. ,,,was made to Congress by the Chief Justice who well understands his Duty and is a Gentleman of SPIRIT ,,,acted upon the Principle of Honor ,,,3) RC (MHi: Warren-Adams Papers). 979-80 ,,,to Congress ,,,Dec. 8, 1778 ,,,Nov 9, 1778."

---T--- Christianity DEN is the religion of the all Branches of the USA GOV~ because the God of it is the only Being with Ability & therefore has instructed us to apply that Religion with intentions/purposes~ +] to support it; +] to not oppose; +] to dwell together peaceably: // "The Revolutionary Diplomatic Correspondence of the US, Volume 4 J. Adams to the President of Congress.*,,, 12/21, 1780.Sir: The sentiments and affections of a people may be learned from many little circumstances which few persons attend to. The poets and orators are generally considered as the surest repositaries of popular ideas both in ancient and modern nations. The clergy may be classed among the latter, and it is very certain that most public preachers accommodate both their sermons and their PRAYERS in some degree to the general taste of their hearers, and avoid everything which will unnecessarily give them offense. At Rotterdam there are several English CHURCHes. The Presbyterian CHURCH, which would be the least likely, one should think, to be bigoted to England, I attended. The parson, after petitioning HEAVEN in his PRAYER for the States of Holland and West Friesland, the States-General ,,,added a petition for England, for the king, queen, and royal family, for their health, long life, and prosperity, and added, with peculiar emphasis, that he might triumph over all his enemies in the four quarters of the globe. At Amsterdam I have attended both the Episcopal and Presbyterian CHURCHes, and heard similar supplications to HEAVEN in both. At Utrecht I attended the Presbyterian CHURCH, and there heard a PRAYER for the English with more fervor still and in greater detail. The parson was quite transported with his zeal, and PRAYed that the rebellion which has so long prevailed might be suppressed and hide its head in shame. At Leyden there is another English CHURCH. The parson, I am told, is a tory, but prudently omits such kind of PRAYERS. This is a work of supererogation in these reverend zealots, and is, therefore, a stronger proof that such sentiments are popular. The English, who are numerous in all these cities, are universally in favor of the British ministry. But there are so many Dutch families who understanding the English language, worship in these CHURCHes, that the clergy would not give them offense if such PRAYERS were offensive. This is the more remarkable, as the RELIGION of North America is much more like that of this republic than like that of England. But such PRAYERS recommend the parsons to the Prince of Orange and the English party, and no other party or person has influence or courage enough to take offense at them. I have the honor to be, etc., John Adams."

---T--- <u>US GOV is CHRISTIAN for Jesus Christ: they established an ally with France</u> because the GOV of France was Christian: // "Journals of the Continental Congress, 1774-1789 - 5/13, 1782 According to order ,,,of which the following is a translation: Gentlemen of the Congress: since the alliance so happily concluded between the King my master and the US, you have taken too intimate a part in every event which interested his glory and happiness, not to learn with sincere joy, that Providence has granted a dauphin to the wishes of the king your ally, and to those of France ,,,The connexions which unite the two nations, connexions formed in justice and humanity, and strengthened by mutual interests, will be as durable as they are natural ,,,the supporter of your children, and the guarantee of their freedom. The letter from his Most CHRISTIAN Majesty was then delivered and read, of which the following is a translation: Very dear great friends and allies: Satisfied with the interest you take in every event which affects us, we are anxious to inform you of tile precious mark which DIVINE Providence has just given us of his goodness, and of the protection he has granted to our kingdom. ,,,You will easily be convinced of the pleasure with which we shall receive every proof that you may give of your sensibility upon this occasion. We cannot renew, at a period more affecting to us, the assurance of our affection and of our constant friendship for you. Upon which we PRAY GOD that he would have you, very dear great friends and allies, in his HOLY keeping."

---T--- <u>Christian Attitudes, Activities, Holy Bible, & DEN</u> promoted as the priority intention/ purpose for God by all Branches of the USA GOV: // "The Revolutionary Diplomatic Correspondence of the US, Volume 6 ,,,Passy, 10/16, 1783. My Dear Friend: I have nothing material to write to you respecting public affairs, but I can not let Mr. Adams, who will see you, go without a line to inquire after your welfare, to inform you of mine, and assure you of my constant respect and attachment. I think with you that your Quaker article [[Christian DEN]] is a good one, and that men will in time have sense enough to adopt it, but I fear that time is not yet come. What would you think of a proposition, if I should make it, of a compact between England, France, and America? ,,,You do not want to conquer and govern one another. ,,,How many excellent things might have been done to promote the internal welfare of each country; what bridges, roads, canals, and other useful public works and institutions, tending to the common felicity, might have been made and established with the money and men foolishly spent during the last seven centuries by our mad wars in doing one another mischief! You are near neighbors, and each have very respectable qualities. Learn to be quiet and to respect each other's rights. You are all CHRISTIANs. [[here Congress identifies the US, England & France as all Christian Nations; though parts of the populations were not Christians sometimes]] ,,,One is The Most CHRISTIAN King, and the other Defender of the Faith. Manifest the propriety of these titles by your future conduct. "By this," says CHRIST, "shall all men know that ye are my disciples, if ye love one another." Seek peace and insure it. Adieu, yours, &c., B. Franklin."

---T--- <u>US GOV supporting God & Christianity religion</u> ~ the term religion(ous) here is used in place of Christianity: // "Journals of the Continental Congress, 1774-1789 - 4/23, 1785. - Congress assembled. Present ,,,That the Oaths required by the Secretary at War, may be taken before any executive officer one of the Judges of the Supreme Court in the State of New York duly qualified to administer oaths any thing in an Ordinance passed on the 27th day of 1/, 1785, notwithstanding ,,,Congress resumed the consideration of the Ordinance under debate yesterday: The following part of the Ordinance being under debate: "Provided that none of the lands within the said Territory, be sold under the price of one dollar the Acre, to be paid in specie ,,,The following paragraph in the Ordinance being under debate: "There shall be reserved the central section of every Township, for the maintenance of public Schools; and the section immediately adjoining the same to the northward, for the support of RELIGION. [[defined as Christian Churches; or buildings & ministries of Christian use]] ,,,A motion was made by Mr. [Charles] Pinckney, seconded by Mr. [William] Grayson, to amend the paragraph by striking out these words, "for the support of RELIGION;" and in their place to insert, "for RELIGIOUS and charitable uses." On which it was moved by Mr. [William] Ellery, seconded by Mr. [Melancton] Smith, to amend the amendment by striking out the words "RELIGIOUS and," so that it read "for charitable uses."1 [Note 1: 1 A record of this proceeding on the Pinckney amendment, in the writing of Hugh Williamson, is in the Papers of the Continental Congress, No. 36, III, folio 33.] And on the question, shall the words moved to be struck out of the amendment, stand? the yeas and nays being required by Mr. [Charles] Pinckney, [Note 1: 1 The vote is also in the Papers of the Continental Congress, No. 36, III, folio 39.] So the question was lost, and the words were struck out. And thereupon, the motion of Mr. [Charles] Pinckney for the amendment was withdrawn. A motion was then made by Mr. [William] Ellery, seconded by Mr. [Melancton] Smith, to strike out the following words in the foregoing paragraph: "and the section immediately adjoining the same to the northward, for the support of RELIGION ,,,A division of the motion was called for by Mr. [Rufus] King: And on the question, shall the former part stand? namely, "and the section immediately adjoining the same to the northward, for the support of RELIGION.",,,". The difficulty here was how to simultaneously not to express favorism to one Christian DEN yet support the Christian religion.

---T--- <u>Attention to God's Presence with the Christianity Religion was</u> a Constant Intention/ Purpose Affectionate Concern in Every Activity of the USA GOV: // "Letters of Delegates to Congress: Volume 19- 8/1, 1782 - 3/11, 1783 to the Chevalier de La Luzerne Sir, Philadelphia, Aug. 14, 1782 ,,,We observe with the utmost satisfaction, that the General Assemblies of almost every State in the union, have been pleased to assure you, and through you to assure his Most CHRISTIAN Majesty, of the sincere pleasure they have received ,,,of gratitude or affection for his Most CHRISTIAN Majesty ,,,--it was universally believed; and we beg leave to assure you from our own knowledge, for we attended during the whole sitting of the Assembly, that the pleasing report ,,,the citizens of North-Carolina; it filled every countenance with joy, and every heart with gladness: Every man found himself personally concerned in an event which contributes so much to the happiness of a people they esteem ,,,We request you would do us the justice to believe, that the citizens of North-Carolina will not fail to PRAY, that the SUPREME RULER OF THE UNIVERSE may prosper and preserve the Dauphin and his royal parents; for we are fully convinced, that under GOD we are indebted for our early deliverance, the preservation of our liberties and establishment of our independence, to the generous interposition of his Most CHRISTIAN Majesty, and the persevering valour of the French nation. We have the honor to be, with the utmost consideration and esteem, Your most obedient, and very humble servants. Hugh Williamson, William Blount, Delegates in Congress from the State of North-Carolina."

---T--- <u>Intentions/purposes of the USA GOV was to constantly support~</u> +] Jesus Christ's Being, +] Christianity, +] the Religion thereof, +] the Morality thereof, +] the Opposition of False Religion: // "Letters of Delegates to Congress: Volume 2 Sept. 1775 - Dec. 1775 - John Adams to Abigail Adams - Nov. 18. 1775. ,,,Your kind Letter of the 5th. Inst. came to Hand yesterday by Captain McPherson. I admire your skill in Phisiognomy ,,,I agree with you in your sentiments that there is reason to be diffident of a ,,,who grossly violates the Principles of MORALS, in any one particular habitually. ,,,This sentiment was conveyed to us in one of the paradoxes of the ancient stoicks, that "all SINS were equal," and the same Idea is suggested from higher authority, he that violates the Law in any one instance is guilty of all ,,,exact in his MORALS. And you know that I look upon RELIGION as the most perfect system, and the most awfull sanction of MORALity. Your goodness of heart, as well as your sound judgment will applaud me for using the utmost caution in my Letters. But if you could see me, and observe how I am employed you would wonder that I find time to write to any body. I am very busy and so is every body else here. I hope to be with you at CHRISTmas, and then to be excused from coming here again, at least until others have taken their turns. The late appointment you mention gives me many very serious thoughts. ,,,It is an Office of high trust, and of vast Importance at any time: But of greater at this, than any other. The confusions and distractions of the times, will encumber that Office with embarrassments, expose it to dangers and slanders, which it never knew before. Besides I am apprehensive of other difficulties. Mr. [William] Cushing has been on that bench, and was my senior at the Bar. Will he accept under another? Mr. Paine too has taken an odd turn in his head of late, and is so peevish, passionate and violent that he will make the place disagreable, if he does not think better of it. Mr. Cushing, Mr. Serjeant [Sargeant] and Mr. Read are very able Men, and Mr. Paine might be so if he was undisturbed in his mind. But the unhappy affair in his Family, his CHURCH and Town, appears to me to have affected his mind too much. It is a melancholly thought to me, because I have ever had a friendship for him ,,. That ambition and avarice reign every where as you observe, is most TRUE. ,,,Remember me to all. ,,,Congress did not meet on Nov. 18, the only Saturday it failed to sit while in session before Feb. 3, 1776. JCC, 3:359 ,,,Dr. Benjamin CHURCH's apostasy stimulated Adams to several discussions on this subject."

---T--- <u>USA GOV is to have God by~</u> +] Christian Activity; +] Christian Officers required; +] The Responsibility of Citizens to Select Christian GOV Officers: // Following states~ "God's Anointee people". The following congress meeting notes have subject matter revolving around~ +] God; +] no idolatry; +] opposing evil by limiting it, which include any infidelity or idolater or anti-Christian; +] because God desires to protect us; +] to have Spiritual Moral Beings in Office; that is should be a "religious men" and those who will not make a "mock of religion" and those who hold religion in "serious nature": // "Letters of Delegates to Congress: Volume 16- 9/1, 1780 - 2/28, 1781, Artemas Ward to Unknown - Sir Philadelphia Decr. 14 1780 ,,,I am much obliged to you for the same, & am rejoiced to hear of your welfare, & that of your family. You are pleased to mention with a note of admiration the merciful Interposition of DIVINE Providence, in the detection of Arnolds Traitrous Conspiracy. It is really a very great mercy & I sincerely wish we may all be truly thankful therefor, not only in word, but in deed; & not only for that particular favour, but for the many undeserved interpositions of DIVINE Providence in our behalf, through the whole course of the present war. May we not truly say that, this war has been attended with as signal favours almost, as attended GODs anoint[ed] people? If we take an impartial retrospective view Thereof, shall we not have TRUE reason to be astonished at the many remarkable deli[verances] which have been wrought out for us? I have observed from the beginning of the war to the present Period, that when we were weakest & the most exposed the greatest things have been accomplished, and when we have to the human eye appeared, to be in the best Situation, and the fairest prospect before us, the least has been done. And those men & things in which we have placed great confidence, have rendered us but little Service. I readily concur with you in Opinion, that it is of importance that men in power and high places of trust should be watched. I am also of opinion it is of the highest importance that those who have a right to elect into office or places of trust, should be more careful to make choice of honest, sensible, RELIGIOUS men than they commonly are. They ought to avoid that man who will not shake his hands from holding of bribes, as they would their greatest adversary. And that man who makes a mock of all RELIGION & ridacules every thing of a Serious nature is one in my opinion who ought to be carefully shuned & avoided. Towns and Counties making a bad choice of Representatives, will be a means of bad delegates in Congress being chosen, & bad delegates in Congress will also make bad appointments of men to the offices that they have a right to fill with officers! From hence appears that each town or County has a share in every appointment, immediately from the highest to the lowest officer, &, that a bad choice of Representatives leads to a bad choice of a General officer. From this view of the matter also appears the importance of towns and Societys being well instructed in their duty in this respect."

---T--- <u>Christ & Christianity Centered Attention of the USA GOV in Relations</u> & Activities: // "Letters of Delegates to Congress: Volume 18- 3/1, 1781 - 8/31, 1781 -Congress to the King of France [Nov 23 ? 1781] ,,,The US in Congress Assembled to their Great, faithful & beloved freind & Ally Lewis the 16th. King of France & Navarre ,,,ours that your majesty will feel yourself equally affected by it while you continue to possess that benevolent attachment to us which has hitherto interested you in our affairs. The distress which the common enemy have experienced from these combined operations will we presume point out to both nations the utility of similar measures in future, and while on the one hand it prompts your majesty to supply that naval force which the situation of our country renders necessary to offensive operations, it urges on the other the US to every exertion which their particular interests & their desire of seconding your majestys views can call forth. It is with peculiar pleasure that the US continue to number some of your majesty's subjects among their most able, SPIRITed & faithful servants. It affords to the world a striking proof of the intimate connection between the Allied nations & at the same time serves to cement the union which it manifests ,,,one of the most important States in the union,,,. We PRAY GOD Great, faithful & beloved freind & Ally, to keep you in his HOLY protection. Done at Philadelphia the 22n. ,,,day of Novr IN THE YEAR OF OUR LORD 1781 & in the fifth ,,,year of our independence. By the US (your Majestys faithful freinds & allies) in Congress assembled. ,,Congress. Repd. 25th Novr 1781." FC (DNA: PCC, item 79) ,,,Humbly submitted to Congress by the Secretary for Foreign affairs ,,,Endorsed by Charles Thomson ,,,"report a letter to his Most CHRISTIAN Majesty, to be sent by the Marquis de la Fayette," for which see JCC, 21:1136,,,".

---T--- <u>US GOV is Intended/ purposed to~ +] be Christian; +]</u> Establish Christ & Christianity to the World; +] Oppose false religions (anti-Christian): // "Journals of the Continental Congress, 1774-1789 - 10/18, 1780, A report from the Board of War was read; Whereupon, Ordered ,,,That on the Act of Congress of the 18th. of Mar. last ,,,to enable the said Commissioners to proceed on the execution of their duties of office and for which ,,,Edwd Chinn and John Wells are to be accountable ,,,That if a truce be proposed for so long a period, or for an indefinite period, requiring so long notice previous to a renewal of hostilities as to evince that it is, on the part of Great Britain, a virtual relinquishment of the object of the war, and an expedient only to avoid the mortification of an express acknowledgment of the independence and sovereignty of these US, the said minister be at liberty, with the concurrence of our ally, to accede thereto; provided, the removal of the British land and naval armaments from the US be a condition of it. That in case a truce shall be agreed on by the belligerent parties, Congress rely on his attention and prudence to hold up the US to the world in a style and title not derogatory to the character of an independent and sovereign people. That with respect to those persons who have either abandoned or been banished from any of the US, since the commencement of the war, ,,,that Great Britain will make full compensation for all the wanton destruction which the subjects of that nation have committed on the property of the citizens of the US. That, in a treaty of peace, it is the wish of Congress not to be bound by any publick engagement to admit British subjects to any of the rights or privileges of citizens of the US; but at all times to be at liberty to grant or refuse such favours, according as the publick interest and honour may dictate; and that it is their determination not to admit them to a equality in this respect with the subjects of his Most CHRISTIAN Majesty, unless such a concession should be deemed by the said minister preferable to a continuance of the war on that account ,,,Diplomatic Correspondence of the American Revolution (Wharton), IV, 100.] Congress took into consideration the resolution reported for setting apart a day of thanksgiving and PRAYER, and agreed to the following draught: Whereas ,,,it hath pleased Almighty GOD, the Father of all mercies, amidst the vicissitudes and calamities of war, to bestow blessings on the people of these states, which call for their devout and thankful acknowledgments, more especially in the late remarkable interposition of his watchful providence, in rescuing the person of our Commander in Chief and the army from imminent dangers, at the moment when treason was ripened for execution; in prospering the labours of the husbandmen, and causing the earth to yield its increase in plentiful harvests; and, above all, in continuing to us the enjoyment of the GOSPEL of PEACE; [Note 2: 2 From this point the entries are by Thomas Edison.] It is therefore recommended to the several states to set apart Thursday, the seventh day [of Dec. next, to be observed as a day of public thanksgiving and PRAYER; that all the people may assemble on that day to celebrate the praises of our DIVINE Benefactor; to confess our unworthiness of the least of his favours, and to offer our fervent supplications to the GOD of all grace; that it may please him to pardon our heinous transgressions and incline our hearts for the future to keep all his laws that it may please him still to afford us the blessing of health; to comfort and relieve our brethren who are any wise afflicted or distressed; to smile upon our husbandry and trade and establish the work of our hands; to direct our publick councils, and lead our forces, by land and sea, to victory; to take our illustrious ally under his special protection, and favor our joint councils and exertions for the establishment of speedy and permanent peace; to cherish all schools and seminaries of education, BUILD UP HIS CHURCHES IN THEIR MOST HOLY FAITH AND TO CAUSE THE KNOWLEDGE OF CHRISTIANITY TO SPREAD OVER ALL THE EARTH. Done in Congress, the lath day of Oct., 1780, and in the fifth year of the independence of the US of America.,,,".

---T--- <u>Christian words, activity, & relations for Christ was the</u> constant occurrence in the USA GOV: // "Written at Versailles, the 22 of Oct., 1781. Your good friend and ally, (Signed) Louis. (Underneath,) Gravier de Vergennes. The President then addressed the minister as follows: Sir: The repeated instances of friendship which the US of America have received from his Most CHRISTIAN Majesty, give him too just a title to their affections to permit them to be indifferent to any event which interests his happiness. Be assured, sir, that Congress learn with the most lively satisfaction, that it has pleased the DIVINE Giver of all good gifts, to bless their august ally with an heir to his throne. Our earnest PRAYER is, that he may with it inherit the virtues which have acquired to his Majesty so much glory, and to his dominions so much prosperity, and which will be the means of cementing and strengthening the union so happily established between the two nations; an union the mutual advantages,,,".

---T--- <u>US GOV is Christian as they~ +] Represented themselves as</u> Christ's Ambassador in Relations with a friendship (alliance) with France, +] Allied & befriended the GOV of France because it was Christian, +] the US GOV was praying with France to the Christian God, as the mutual God: // "Journals of the Continental Congress, 1774-1789- 5/13, 1782 According to order ,,,public audience, addressed Congress in a speech, of which the following is a translation: Gentlemen of the Congress: since the alliance so happily concluded between the King ,,,and the US, you have taken too intimate a part in every event which interested his glory and happiness, not to learn with sincere joy, that Providence has granted a dauphin to the wishes of the king your ally, and to those of France. His Majesty imparts this event, gentlemen, in the letter which I am directed to have the honor of delivering. The connexions which unite the two nations, connexions formed in justice and humanity, and strengthened by mutual interests, will be as durable as they are natural. The prince who is just born will one day be the friend and ally of the US. He will, in his turn, support them with all his power, and ,,,be the father and protector of his people ,,,supporter of your children, and the guarantee of their freedom. The letter from his Most CHRISTIAN Majesty was then delivered and read, of which the following is a translation: Very dear great friends and allies: Satisfied with the interest you take in every event which affects us, we are anxious to inform you of tile precious mark which DIVINE Providence has just given us of his goodness, and of the protection he has granted to our kingdom. ,,,You will easily be convinced of the pleasure with which we shall receive every proof that you may give of your sensibility upon this occasion. We cannot renew, at a period more affecting to us, the assurance of our affection and of our constant friendship for you. Upon which we PRAY GOD [[referring to the Christian God as they noted Christian Majesty]] that he would have you, very dear great friends and allies, in his HOLY keeping."

---T--- <u>USA GOV with a Continuous Intention for Jesus & His Christianity & His Holy Bible to</u> be in all homes of the USA: // "Letters of Delegates to Congress: Volume 19- 8/1, 1782 - 3/11, 1783 - George Duffield and William White ,,,Addressed: "Reverend Dr. White & reverend Mr. Duffield Chaplains of the US in Congress assemd." In the hand of James Duane. 1 The Philadelphia printer Robert Aitken had petitioned Congress on 1/ 21, 1781, to secure authorization for an American edition of the BIBLE he had undertaken but was fearful of completing "without the sanction of Congress." The scarcity of BIBLEs had long been of concern, for Congress had been urged to import several thousand from abroad in 1777, and a committee consisting of James Duane, Thomas McKean, and James McLene had been appointed in Oct. 1780 to consider a recommendation for urging the states to regulate the printing of "correct editions of the old and new testament." Aitken's memorial had been referred on 1/ 26, 1781, to this committee (to which John Witherspoon had been added in the place of McLene), which had apparently been consulting with the printer as he proceeded, although no record of its work prior to the writing of this letter has been found. Aitken was obviously now nearing completion of the publication and the committee decided to consult the congressional chaplains before reporting to Congress, which resolved on Sept. 12 to "recommend this edition of the BIBLE to the inhabitants of the US" and authorize Aitken "to publish this recommendation in the manner he shall think proper."

---T--- <u>DOI & USA GOV is~ +] Christian; +] Religious; +] Supporting the Conscience,</u> known by the USA GOV to be a Christian word for the Presence of God, the Moral Consciousness of Christ: // "Letters of Delegates to Congress: Vol ,,,3- 1/ 1, 1776 - 5/15, 1776 Samuel Huntington to James Cogswell Honrd Sir, Philadelphia 30th Mar. 1776 I take this Opportunity to pay my respects to you ,,,altho have nothing of news to communicate relative to public affairs more than you will receive in the public prints. On Sunday morning the 17th Inst my attention from my Chamber window was Suddenly called to behold a mightly Cavalcade of Plebeians marching thro' the Street with drums beating and at every Small distance they halted & gave three Huzzas. I was apprehensive Some outrage was about to be Committed, but Soon perceived my mistaken apprehensions & that it was a RELIGIOUS exercise of the Sons of Saint Patrick, it being the anniversary of that Saint the morning Exercise was ushered in with the ceremony above describd. However Sir Should I leave you to Judge of the RELIGION of this City from the above Story only; it would not be Just, there are devout pious people in this City, a number of pious & Excellent preachers, & he who does not lead a virtuous & RELIGIOUS life here must accuse himself. Every man has Liberty to persue the dictates of his own CONSCIENCE. My Business is very arduous as well as Important. We commonly Set from Ten in the morning until between four & five in the afternoon Intent on business without any refreshment. It was very tedious at first but by usage is become Tolerable. I have by DIVINE blessing enjoyd a very good State of Health ever since my recovery from the Small Pox. I cannot forget my native Country; & prize Connecticutt higher than ever I did before. It is disagreable to be So long removed from my [[family & friends]] however I must cheerfully obey the calls & dictates of Providence with out refusing. I herewith send you a Resolve of Congress for a general Fast tho it may likely appear in the public papers. ,,,Please to present my Duty to Madam, my kind

Respects to Mr Justice Devotion; & let me request an Interest in your PRAYERS that I may be enabled faithfully to perform the Trust reposed in me, & in due time be returnd to my [[family]] & native Land in peace. Am Sir with due respect, your Humble Servant, Saml Huntington RC (PHi) I James Cogswell (1720-1807), minister of Windham, Conn. Franklin B. Dexter ,,,2 A resolution of Mar. 16 recommended that May 17 be observed as a "day of humiliation, fasting, and PRAYER." JCC, 4:208-9.".

---T--- <u>The USA DOI Supports Religion of Christianity</u> by making The 1-A, R~Est, R-E which is intended/ purposed to be~ +] a Religious Section of the USA, +] as not including all religions, +] as including only that of Christianity with all the different DENs of it: // "Letters of Delegates to Congress: Volume 4- 5/16, 1776 - 8/15, 1776 - John Adams to Benjamin Kent - Sir Philadelphia 6/22. 1776 Your Letters of Apr. 24 and May 26 are before me ,,,We have not many of the fearfull, and still less of the unbelieving among us, how slowly soever, you may think We proceed. Is it not a want of faith, or a predominance of fear, which makes some of you so impatient for declarations in words of what is every day manifested in deeds of the most determined nature and unequivocal signification? That we are divorced, a Vinculo as well as from Bed and Board, is to me, very clear. The only question is, concerning the proper time for making an explicit declaration in words. Some people must have time to look around them, before, behind, on the right hand, and on the left, then to think, and after all this to resolve. Others see at one intuitive glance into the past and the future, and judge with precision at once. But remember you cant make thirteen clocks strike precisely alike, at the same second. I am for the most liberal toleration of all DENOMINATIONS of RELIGIONists but I hope that Congress will never meddle with RELIGION, further than to say their own PRAYERS, and to fast and give Thanks, once a year. Let every Colony have its own RELIGION, without molestation. The Congress ordered CHURCH to the Massachusetts Council,,,".

---T--- <u>DOI & US GOV is Christian with Christ's Religion:</u> // "Journals of the Continental Congress, 1774-1789 - 3/19, 1782 - ,,,Whereupon, Ordered ,,,of artillery artificers ,,,committee, consisting of ,,,appointed to prepare a recommendation to the several states, to set apart a day of humiliation, fasting, and PRAYER Congress agreed to the following Proclamation: The goodness of the SUPREME BEING TO ALL HIS RATIONAL CREATURES, demands their acknowledgments of gratitude and love; his absolute government of this world dictates, that it is the interest of every nation and people ardently to supplicate his mercy favor and implore his protection. When the LUST OF DOMINION or LAWLESS AMBITION excites arbitrary power to INVADE THE RIGHTS, or endeavor to WRENCH WREST from a people their SACRED and UNALIENABLE INVALUABLE PRIVILEGES, and compels them, in DEFENCE of the same, to encounter all the horrors and calamities of a bloody and vindictive war; then is that people loudly called upon to fly unto that GOD for protection, who hears the <u>cries</u> of the distressed, and will not turn a deaf ear to the supplication of the OPPRESSED. Great Britain, hitherto left to infatuated councils, and to pursue measures repugnant to their her own interest, and distressing to this country, still persists ,,,which will compel us into another active and perhaps bloody campaign. The US in Congress assembled, therefore, taking into consideration our present situation, our multiplied transgressions of the HOLY laws of our GOD, and his past acts of kindness and goodness exercised towards us, which we would ought to record with me the liveliest gratitude, think it their indispensable duty to call upon the different several states, to set apart the last Thursday in April next, as a day of fasting, humiliation and PRAYER, that our joint supplications may then ascend to the throne of the RULER of the UNIVERSE, beseeching Him that he would to diffuse a SPIRIT of universal reformation among all ranks and degrees of our citizens; and make us a HOLY, that so we may be an HAPPY people; that it would please Him to impart wisdom, integrity and unanimity to our counsellors; to bless and prosper the REIGN of our illustrious ally, and give success to his arms employed in the DEFENCE of THE RIGHTS of human nature; that HE WOULD SMILE upon our military arrangements by land and sea; administer comfort and consolation to our prisoners in a cruel captivity; that he would protect the health and life of our Commander in Chief; ,,,grant us victory over our enemies; establish peace in all our borders, and give happiness to all our inhabitants; that he would prosper the labor of the husbandman, making the earth yield its increase in abundance, and give a proper season for the in gathering of the fruits thereof; that He would grant success to all engaged in lawful trade and commerce, and take under his guardianship all schools and seminaries of learning, and make them nurseries of VIRTUE and PIETY; that He would incline the HEARTS of all men to peace, and fill them with universal charity and benevolence, and that the RELIGION of our DIVINE REDEEMER, with all its benign influences, may cover the earth as the waters cover the seas. ?Done by the US in Congress assembled ,,,Mr. [Samuel] Livermore, Mr. [James] Madison, and Mr. [Abraham] Clark ,,,supplies furnished and services rendered to the said states,,,".

---T--- <u>Every Part of this Book proves that</u> Christianity to Christ; thus the religion thereof is to be part of the USA GOV; as the Priority Intention/ purpose reason for the USA Existence.

---T--- <u>DOI, Congress, Citizens are all Christ Caring & Christian based:</u> // "Letters of Delegates to Congress: Volume 2- 9/1775 - 12/1775 - John Adams to Abigail Adams Octr. 23. 1775 ,,,Your Letters ,,,I rejoice in <u>the happy Principles and</u> the happy Temper, which apparently dictated them all. I feel myself much affected with the Breach upon the Family. But We can count a Mother, a Brother, an Aunt, and a Brothers Child among the slain by this cruel Pestilence. May GOD almighty put a stop to its Rage, and humble us under the Ravages already made by it. The sorrows of all our Friends on the Loss of your Mother are never out of my Mind. I PRAY GOD to spare my Parent whose Life has been prolonged by his Goodness hitherto, as well as yours that survives. The tremendous Calamities already felt of Fire, Sword and Pestilence, may be only Harbingers of greater still. We have no security against Calamities here-this Planet is its Region. The only Principle is to be prepared for the worst Events. If I could write as well as you, my sorrows would be as eloquent as yours, but upon my Word I cannot. The unaccountable Event which you allude to has reached this Place and occasioned a Fall. ,,,I would be glad however that the worst Construction might not be put ,,,violates private Faith, cancells solemn Obligations, whom neither Honour nor CONSCIENCE holds [[the use of Christian values, terms, and attitudes of spirit are in common]] ,,,Open barefaced IMMORALity ought not to be so countenanced. Tho I think, a Fatality attends us in some Instances, yet a DIVINE Protection and favour is visible in others, and let us be chearfull whatever happens. Chearfullness is not a SIN in any Times. I am afraid to hear again almost least some other should be sick in the House. Yet I hope better, and that you will reassume your wonted Chearfullness and write again upon News and Politics. Send your Letters to Warren for Conveyance ,,,RC (MHi) ,,,1:311-12 ,,,Oct. 10, 1775, note.".

---T--- Christ & Christianity & DEN is Supported by the DOI, Congress, citizens, activity of citizens; & All these oppose anti-Christian activity, calling it apostasy & traitor: // "Letters of Delegates to Congress: Volume 8- 9/19, 1777 - 1/31, 1778 - John Adams to Abigail Adams - My best Friend York Town Octr. 25. 1777 This Town is a small one, not larger than Plymouth. There are in it, two German CHURCHes, the one Lutheran, the other Calvinistical. The CONGREGATIONS are pretty numerous, and their Attendance upon PUBLIC WORSHIP is decent. It is remarkable that the Germans, wherever they are found, are carefull to maintain the PUBLIC WORSHIP, which is more than can be said of the other DENOMINATIONS of CHRISTIANs, this Way. There is one CHURCH here erected by the joint Contributions of Episcopalians and Presbyterians, but the Minister, who is a Missionary, is confined for Toryism, so that they have had for a long Time no publick Worship. ,,,Congress have appointed two Chaplains, Mr. White and Mr. Duffield, the former of whom an Episcopalian is arrived and opens Congress with PRAYERS every Day. The latter is expected every Hour. Mr. Duche I am sorry to inform you has turned out an Apostate and a Traytor. Poor Man! I pitty his Weakness, and detest his WICKEDNESS. ,,,Commodore Hazelwood, with his Gallies, and Lt. Coll. Smith in the Garrison of Fort Mifflin, have behaved in a manner the most gallant and glorious. They have defended the River, and the Fort with a Firmness and Perseverance, which does Honour to human Nature. If the News from the Northward is TRUE, Mr. Howe will scarcely venture upon Winter Quarters in Philadelphia. We are waiting, for News, from Rhode Island. I am wearied with the Life I lead, and long for the Joys of my Family. GOD grant I may enjoy it, in Peace. Peace is my dear Delight. War has no Charms for me. If I live much longer in Banishment I shall scarcely know my own Children. Tell my little ones, that if they will be very good, Pappa will come home. RC (MHi). Adams, Family Correspondence (Butterfield), 2:359-60.".

---T--- Congress, Citizens, & Activity are all Christian for Christ & oppose evil or anti-Christian activity: // "Letters of Delegates to Congress: Volume 18- Mar 1, 1781 - Aug 31, 1781 - Arthur Middleton to Aedanus Burke My dr. Sir Pa. Apr. 7th. [1782] Your favr. of the 25 Jany. came safe to hand ,,,& I take advantage of the return of Col. Motte to present you my Acknowledgts. ,,,for yr. kind remembrance of me. The Strong Outlines you have drawn of the mellancholy real Situation of our Country in all points correspond exactly with what my anxious imagination had formed, whenever reason & reflexion led me to consider an Object allways uppermost in my mind; ,,,nothing but Time & skillfull management can restore that firm, orderly, & composed mode of proceeding so essential to establish the publick Happiness [[DOI terms in use after the DOI]] which is or ought to be the wish of all. I have much confidence in the Ability & Integrity of the men chosen to conduct affairs. I think I know the PURITY of THEIR INTENTIONS & I trust their Councills may yet lead us to prosperity. Upon mature Consideration of all Circumstances; of the unmerited Sufferings of so many, & of the resentments necessarily rous'd in a people whom I know to be naturally generous & Sensible, I rejoice that matters have been Conducted with so much moderation & Temper; tho' I could have wishd the Idea of Confiscation had been totally abolish'd, or at least put off till entire secure possession [of the] Country had restor'd Tranquillity, & the publick mind was free & open to the guidance of cool dispassionate reason. Your Sentiments upon the Subject are those of the Patriot & the friend of human Nature, & I wd. ,,,I have been & am principled against it; I cannot approve of the inhuman Sentence of visiting the SINS of the Fathers upon the guiltless women [and] Children, [[HOLY BIBLE quoted]] notwithstanding the SACRED Authority [[God here]] which may be quoted for it. It is a Doctrine suited only to the Climates of DESPOSTISM, & abhorrent to the dignified SPIRIT of pure & genuine republicanism. In the Eye of reason the Individual shd. stand or fall by his own Actions, & those connected should be involved in the punishment no farther, than they have been partakers in the Crime. Banishment of the Individual, & a deprivation of the Benefits of Citizenship & property for life are surely sufficient both as a punishment & a prevention of Crimes, without reducing a whole family for the SIN of one to misery & destruction. Here my friend you have my Thoughts upon an Interesting Subject which concerns the good of mankind. ,,,FC (ScHi: Middleton Papers). Congress on Apr. 3.JCC, 22:161. ,,,"Next to the obedience due the Dictates of my own CONSCIENCE," Middleton continued, "it has ever lain nearest to my heart so to regulate my conduct as to wish your Approbation. I shall still be governed by the same motives, & trust I shall retain it to our Life's end-at parting with my Brother I entreated him to present my Duty to you, & to acquaint you that my mind was thoroughly at Ease with regard to my own fate; This I hoped would operate as a Balm to your affliction upon my Account. "To the many anxieties for my dearest Connections, the knowledge of your Ill health & Troubles have added grief indeed.,,,".

---T--- The USA intended/ purposed CHRIST & Christianity with their~ +] words, +] activity, +] relations with other Spiritual Moral Beings & Nations, +] was a constant, not changing, occurrence: // "Written at Versailles, the 22 of Oct, 1781. Your good friend and ally, (Signed) Louis. (Underneath,) Gravier de Vergennes. The President then addressed the minister as follows: Sir: The repeated instances of friendship which the US of America have received from his Most CHRISTIAN Majesty, give him too just a title to their affections to permit them to be indifferent to any event which interests his happiness. Be assured, sir, that Congress learn with the most lively satisfaction, that it has pleased the DIVINE Giver of all good gifts, to bless their august ally with an heir to his throne. Our earnest PRAYER is, that he may with it inherit the virtues which have acquired to his Majesty so much glory, and to his dominions so much prosperity, and which will be the means of cementing and strengthening the union so happily established between the two nations; an union the mutual advantages,,,".

---T--- <u>The USA GOV is Supportive of God & Christian</u> Religion & Enacts Christian holidays as USA GOV Laws for all Branches: // "Journals of the Continental Congress, 1774-1789 — 10/20, 1779 - A letter, of 8, from James Avery was read, enclosing a letter, of Sept. 10, from Colonel J. Allan, at Machias, to the council of Massachusetts bay: An appeal ,,,The committee appointed to prepare a recommendation to the several states, for setting apart the second Thursday in Dec. next, as a day of general thanksgiving, brought in a draught, which was agreed to as follows: Whereas it becomes us humbly to approach the throne of Almighty GOD, with gratitude and praise for the wonders which his goodness has wrought in conducting our fore-fathers to this western world; for his protection to them and to their posterity amid difficulties and dangers; for raising us, their children, from deep distress to be numbered among the nations of the earth ,,,and especially for that he hath been pleased to grant us the enjoyment of health, and so to order the revolving seasons, that the earth hath produced her increase in abundance, blessing the labors of the husbandmen, and spreading plenty through the land; that he hath prospered our arms and those of our ally; been a shield to our troops in the hour of danger, pointed their swords to victory and led them in triumph over the bulwarks of the foe; that he hath gone with those who went out into the wilderness against the savage tribes ,,,and above all, that he hath diffused the glorious light of the gospel, whereby, through the merits of our gracious REDEEMER, we may become the heirs of his ETERNAL glory: therefore, Resolved, That it be recommended to the several states, to appoint Thursday, the 9th of Dec. next, to be a day of public and solemn thanksgiving to Almighty GOD for his mercies, and of PRAYER for the continuance of his favor and protection to these US; to beseech HIM that HE would be graciously pleased to influence our public councils, and bless them with wisdom from on high, with unanimity, firmness, and success; that HE would go forth with our hosts and crown our arms with victory; that he would grant to his CHURCH the plentiful effusions of DIVINE grace, and pour out his HOLY SPIRIT on all ministers of the gospel; that he would bless and prosper the means of education, and spread the light of CHRISTIAN knowledge through the remotest corners of the earth; that he would smile upon the labours of HIS people and cause the earth to bring forth her fruits in abundance; that we may with gratitude and gladness enjoy them; that HE would take into his HOLY protection our illustrious ally, give him victory over his enemies, and render him signally great, as the father of his people and the protector of the rights of mankind; that he would graciously be pleased to turn the hearts of our enemies, and to dispense the blessings of peace to contending nations; that he would in mercy look down upon us, pardon our SINS and receive us into his favor, and finally, that HE would establish the independence of these US upon the basis of RELIGION and virtue, and support and protect them in the enjoyment of peace, liberty and safety ,,,as the sun and moon shall endure, until time shall be no more."

---T--- <u>RELIGION Includes~ +] Only One God, +] the Christian Religion</u> Supported, +] False religions opposed, +] religious persecution opposed with protection against it supported: // "Letters of Delegates to Congress: Volume 1- 8/1774 — 8/1775 - John Sullivan to John Langdon - Sir, Philadelphia, Septem'r [i.e. Oct.] 5th, 1774.- ,,,I should gladly give you an account of our proceedings ,,,Repeal of or forever restrain our trade from Great Britain, Ireland & the West Indies; among which Acts is the Canada Bill ,,,in my opinion the most dangerous to American Liberties among the whole train; for when we reflect on the dangerous situation the Colonies were in at the commencement of the Late War with a number of those Canadians on their backs who were assisted by Powerful Indian Nations determined to extirpate the Race of Protestants from America to make way for their own Cursed RELIGION so Dangerous [[all religions are not supported only because they say they have a god]] to the State & favorable to Despotism, & contemplate that by the late Act their Territory is so far extended as to include by far the greater part of North America ,,,Great Britain & assisted by the same Indian Nations, we must suppose our Situation to be Infinitely more Dangerous now than it was then, for while we are engaged with the Canadians on our Frontiers our Seaports must yield to the Ministerial fleet & army & if they once prevail no man must expect safety until he professes that HOLY RELIGION [[this is the Christian religion]] which our Sovereign has been pleased to establish [[not separated but included as established; not as one DEN favored, rather Christianity]] ,,,I am certain that two GODs may as well exist in the universe as those two RELIGIONS where the Papists have power to extirpate the professors of the other. We can easily discover the designs of the Act & are determined to Counteract it at all events. I hope to have the pleasure of seeing you in a few days after this Letter comes to hand & give you a particular account of our proceedings: in the interim I am yours respectfully, Jno Sullivan".

---T--- <u>Some of the FFOG did stumble,</u> wander, and study about various doctrines & false religions, such as Masons & Deism; yet the doctrines & expressions of those 2 false religions were different then, seemingly more closer to Christ's Christianity: // However, they Did Not in their public papers, and private supporting papers (DOC), support any other religion than Christianity; AND they Did make SUCH plain in all their papers (DOC), both private and public. The fact that God, Creator, Divine Providence, Supreme Judge, Lord Jesus is the basis of the CC provides the controlling DOC for the USA. Not some wanderings, searchings, and studies that did, or may have occurred.

---T--- <u>Christianity, Religion thereof, Christian Churches, & the Holy Bible</u> are the Basis for the CC DOI; To Increase God's Presence; & supported by the US GOV. Also, there are many SC vses herein following: // "Letters of Delegates to Congress: Volume 5- 8/16, 1776 — 12/31, 1776 - William Williams to Jonathan Trumbull, Sr. Hond & Dear Sir Philadel. 20th Sepr. 1776 ,,,Evacuation of N York by our army on Sab. Day the 15th, of most of our heavy cannon falling into the hands of our Enemies ,,,This event unhappy & distressing as it is has been foreseen & known ever since the quitting of long Island, & had been determined by the Genl. & his Council; Congress had been made fully accquainted with & assented to it as absolutely necessary, & directed that it shod not be destroyed by us on leaving it. These events ,,,gained by our oppressors, & the distress to which our Army & Country are & must be subjected in consequence of them, are loud speaking testimonies of the displeasure & anger of almighty GOD against a SINful people, louder than sevenfold thunder. Is it possible that the most obdurate & stupid of the Children of America shod not hear & tremble? GOD has surely a controversie with this people, & He is most certainly able to manage it & He will accomplish his designs, & bring us to repentance & reformation, or destroy us. We must bend or break. The ways of his providence are dark & deep but they are holy, wise, & just & altogether right, tho our feeble understandings comprehend them not, & tho his chastisements are severe & dreadful, they are dictated by unbounded wisdom & love. They have a meaning of awful & kind import. Turn unto me for why will ye die O Sons of America. We have thought GOD was for us & had given many & signal instances of His power & mercy in our favor, & had greatly frowned upon & disappointed our enemies & verily it has been so, but have we repented & given HIM the glory? Verily no. His hand seems to be turned & stretched out against us, & strong is his hand & high is his right hand. He can & will accomplish all his pleasure. It is GOD who has blunted the weapons of our warfare, that has turned the counsels of wise men into foolishness, that has thus far blasted & disappointed our hopes, & made us flee before our enemies, & given them possession of our strong Holds. Trouble does not spring out of the dust nor rise out of the Ground. I have always thot this was a just & righteous cause in which we are engaged. I remain unshaken in that firm persuasion, & that GOD wod sooner or later vindicate & support it, I believe so still, but I believe this people must first be brot to know & acknowledge the righteousness of his judgment, & their own exceeding SINfulness & Guilt, & be deeply humbled under his mighty hand, & look & cry to & trust in Him for all their help & salvation but in the use & exertion of all the strength He has given us. Surely we have seen enough to convince us of all this, & then why are we not convinced, why is not every soul humbled under the mighty hand of GOD, repenting & mourning for its SINS & putting away the EVIL of his doings, & looking to Him that smites us by humble, earnest & fervent PRAYER & Supplication day & night. Why are not the dear Children of GOD (surely there are many, tho the scorn & insult of our enemies) beseiging the Throne of Grace, sighing & crying for their own SINS & back slidings & for all the abominations that are done in the land, & saying spare, spare thy People O Lord & give not thine Heritage to reproach. Let not the vine which thy right Hand has planted here be rooted up & destroyed, let not thy CHURCHes be wasted & devoured, let not virtue & the remains of RELIGION be torn down & trampled in the dust, Let not thy Name be blasphemed, nor our insulting wicked Foes say where is your GOD, nor the profane world that there is no GOD that rules the world & regardeth the Right, that vindicateth the just & the righteous cause. I know that GOD can vindicate his own Name & Honor without our help, & out of the Stones raise up Children to Abraham, & it is amazing folly & madness to cry the temple, the Temple of the Lord, & trust in that while We remain an incorrigible people. But such things are what GOD wod have us learn & practice while his judgments are abroad in the land, & with such like arguments fill our mouths, & pour out our souls before Him. Are any? Are not all? in N England especially, who have any Interest in HEAVEN, crying, beging & intreating for the out pouring of blessed SPIRIT of GOD upon the land, tis a most grievous & distressing consideration that GOD is pleased so to withhold the blessed influences & operations thereof, without which we shall remain stupid forever. Therefore with redoubled fervency of ardent PRAYER & supplication, shod every soul that has one sparck of HEAVENly fire kindle it to a fervent heat & expanded blaze. O New England, O my dear native land, how does my soul love thee. Be instructed therefore lest GODs Soul depart from thee, lest thou be like Corazin & Bethsaida in condemnation as thou hast been in privileges, lest He make thee as Admah & set thee as Zeboim. Are the ministers of the Gospel alive & awake & lifting up their voices like a trumpet & sounding the Alarm of the Almightys anger & wrath ready to burst on the defenseless Heads of a guilty people? Are they warning the wicked of their infinite danger, animating & arousing them to consideration? <u>Are they with ardent Zeal & Fervour animating & enlivening the languid graces of the GODly, exciting & leading them to fervent PRAYER, sighing & crying for their own declensions & luke warmness in RELIGION & for the SINS & Iniquities of the land, PRAYing, beging & intreating with unceasing & as it were resistless importunity for the copious effusions of the Blessed SPIRIT upon all orders & degrees of people & refusing to let GOD go</u>, without an answer of peace, & in the midst of wrath to remember mercy, & not give up this his heritage to reproach nor blast the blooming hopes & Prospects of this infant Country, the Asylum of Liberty & <u>Religion</u>? Strange that mankind shod need such alarming Providences to produce such an effect. It is no more than to act like reasonable creatures, to possess a SPIRIT & temper that will add a thousand fold sweetness & pleasure to all the enjoyments of this world, to exchange the slavery of the DEVIL, that accursed enemy of our souls, for the service of GOD & the Liberty of his Children, to do justly, to love mercy & walk humbly with our GOD, to answer the sole end of our CREATION, to secure a peace here infinitely better than the world can give, & an ETERNITY of peace & happiness in the world to come. But still more strange if possible, & astonishing is it that they shod disregard the voice of the most high, remain thoughtless & stupid under the dreadful tokens of his anger & the awful Judgments of his hand, by sickness & by the sword of our unnatural & enraged enemies threatening to depopulate the land & drench the plains with the blood of its inhabitants, leaving the weeping widows, helpless orphans & the all that survive the shocking Carnage & subsequent masacre to drag out their Lives in Want, wretchedness & miserable bondage & all this aggravated with the certain prospect of leaving this dreadful curse intailed on all Posterity. A thorough repentance & reformation, without all peradventure will appease the anger of a HOLY & just GOD, avert these amazing Calamities, secure Liberty & Happiness to this & all succeeding Ages & ETERNAL felicity & glory to all the subjects of it. If such considerations & motives wont awaken a ,,,to serious thoughtfulness & attention, I know n[ot] what will, but the voice of the Arch Angel & the Trump[et] of GOD. I am hond & dear Sir most affectionately your dutiful Son & Servant. Wm Williams P.S. You will not think proper to communicate this letter to the Assembly. I am anxious beyond the power of language to describe, of contributing something to the good & salvation, temporal & ETERNAL, of my Countrymen. (Hope I have not been totally useless here.) If you shod think this may have any tendency, to awake our sleepy people ,,,May GOD in great mercy preserve your Health, & long continue your valuable & important life. With kindest remembrance to my dear Wife & Friends. W W".

---T--- <u>RELIGION to Christ & His Holy Bible was</u> Enacted by Congress as the Duty of the USA GOV as they Supplied Provisions for the Aitken Holy Bible to be Printed & Distributed to all of the USA Citizens: // "Letters of Delegates to Congress: Volume 7- 5/1, 1777 - 9/18, 1777 [ca. Jul 7, 1777] ,,,The Congress desire to have a BIBLE printed under their care & by their encouragement, & request you to inform them 1. How many thousand pounds of Types would be sufficient to set, or Compose a whole BIBLE of the common sort; and what they would cost ? 1 Three Philadelphia Presbyterian clergymen-Francis Alison, John Ewing, and William Marshall-this day submitted a petition to Congress PRAYing that "unless timely care be used to prevent it we shall not have BIBLEs for our Schools, & families, & for the publick Worship of GOD in our CHURCHes." "<u>We therefore," they continued, "think it our Duty to our Country & to the CHURCHes of CHRIST to lay this design before this honourable house, humbly requesting that under your care, & by your encouragement, a Copy of the HOLY BIBLE may be printed,</u> so as to be sold nearly as cheap as the Common BIBLEs, formerly imported from Britain & Ireland, were sold." See JCC, 8:536, and PCC, item 42, 1:35 ,,,committee consisting of ,,,For the printers' responses, one of which is dated July 10, 1777, see PCC, item 46, 1: 155-73."

---T--- <u>R-E, R~Est, 1-A -- Here is~ a] a correction of abuses by</u> one part of the US GOV to another part of the same, to including the citizens; to Religion or Christianity; b] the US using the Holy Bible to define it's activities; c] the US Opposing~ +"worldliness" (evil sort), +Sins, +evil "party life", +"vices", +the "excessive expensive", +any excess riches to GOV Officers, +Fashion, +Entertainment, +Evil Worldly trends, +Dancing, +Vanity, +etc: // "Letters of Delegates to Congress: Volume 16- 9/1, 1780 – 2/28, 1781 - Samuel Adams to John Scollay - My dear Sir Philade 12/30/1780 ,,,Our Government, I perceive, is organizd on the Basis of the new CON. I am afraid there is more Pomp & Parade than is consistent with those sober Republican Principles, upon which the Framers of it thought they had founded it. Why should this ,,,Era be introducd with Entertainments expensive & tending to dissipate the Minds of the People? Does it become us to lead the People to such publick diversions as promote superfluity of dress & ornament, when it is as much as they can bear to support the expense of cloathing a naked army? Will vanity & levity ever be the stability of GOV, either in states, in cities, or what, let me hint to you is of the last importance, in families? Of what kind are those manners, by which, as we are truly informd in a late speech, "not only the freedom but the very existence of republicks is greatly affected?" How fruitless is it, to recommend "the adapting the Laws in the most perfect manner possible, to the suppression of idleness, dissipation & extravagancy, " if such recommendations are counteracted by the example of men of RELIGION ,,,& publick station? I meant to consider this subject in the view of the mere citizen. But I have mentiond the SACRED Word RELIGION. I confess, I am surprizd to hear, that some particular persons have been so unguarded as to give their countenance to such kind of amusements. I wish Mr ,,,would recollect his former ideas when his friend Whitefield thunderd in the Pulpit against assemblies & balls. I think he has disclaimd diversions, in some instances, which to me have always appeard innocent. Has he changd his opinions, or has the tendency of things alterd? Do certain manners tend to quench the SPIRIT of RELIGION at one time & are they harmless at another? Are MORALS so vague as to be sanctified or dispens'd with by the authority of different men? He does not beleive this-but I will not be severe, for I love my friend. RELIGION out of the question for the present. It was asked in the Reign of Charles the 2d of England, How shall we turn the minds of the people from an attention to their liberties? The answer was, by making them extravagant, luxurious, effeminate. Hutchinson advisd the abridgment of what our people called English Liberties, by the same means. We shall never subdue them, said Bernard, but by eradicating their manners & the principles of their education. Will the judicious citizens of Boston be now caught in the snare, which their artful insidious Enemies, a few years ago laid for them in vain? Shall we ruin ourselves by the very means, which they pointed out in their Confidential Letters, tho even they did not dare openly to avow them? Pownal, who was indeed a mere Fribble, venturd to have his riots & routs at his own house, to please a few boys & girls. Sober people were disgusted at it, & his privy Councellors never thought it prudent to venture so far as expensive balls. Our Bradfords, Winslows & Winthrops would have revolted at the idea of opening scenes of dissipation & folly; knowing them to be inconsistent with their great Design, in transplanting themselves into what they called this "Outside of the World. " But I fear I shall say too much. I love the People of Boston. I once thought, that City would be the CHRISTIAN Sparta. But Alass! Will men never be free! They will be free no longer than while they remain virtuous. Sidney tells us, there are times when people are not worth saving. Meaning, when they have lost their virtue. I PRAY GOD, this may never be truly said of my beloved Town. Adieu-My Respects to Mrs. Scollay & Family & beleive me to be sincerely, Your Friend, SA [P.S.] If Mr B A ,,,thinks a question from me worth his answering, ask him whether he has lost some valueable books which I have seen in his library, the works of our illustrious Forefathers."

---T--- <u>The Intention/ Purpose of the USA GOV about RELIGION To God, is to Support it,</u> Including~ +Churches, +Holy Bible, +Salvation, +Altar devotions, +Religion of Christianity; +and all these to increase in amount of peoples, of activities, and in the land, +as priority: // "Letters of Delegates to Congress:Volume 23- 11/7, 1785 - 11/5, 1786 - ,,,I rejoice to hear of yours, & the welfare of your family. I rejoice that the RELIGION of JESUS prevails in your Parts; I can tell you the same agreeable News from this quarter. Yesterday I returned from Piscataway in East Jersey, where was held a Baptist annual Meeting, I think the largest I ever saw, but much more remarkable still for the DIVINE Influences which GOD was pleased to Grant. Fifteen were baptized; a number, during the three Days, professed to experience a change of Heart. CHRISTIANs were remarkably quickned; Multitudes appeared, with Peter's hearers,,,".

---T--- <u>R-E, R~Est, 1-A</u> ~ Following proves what such is intended for as various versions & discussions about God's Religion & words to be used: // Before it is quoted, here are some prepatory intentions/purposes they had: A] NOT want USA GOV (Federal) to make a control system of all Christianity; This is seen as it states that they shall not "prohibit free exercise"; and, B] NOT one Christian DEN to be the GOV DEN so that all other

DEN cannot exist; or that all people must support only the one DEN; This is clearly stated below in the ending discussions on the Church of England; and also the statement, "make No Law for any establishment of religion" (DEN is establishment of Religion~ secondary doctrine and expressions). // There is only 2 sub-subjects here related to religion & R~Est in Principle Law: 1} The subject of conscience; a person may not have light (knowledge) enough to match another person's light. And thus, for GOV to control that, is to control Christianity, which is related to the "A]" mentioned above. AND, 2} DENs are related to conscience also, because one man's convictions or conscience concerns on specific secondary doctrines & expressions is not the same of another man's. Yes, only Christianity is supported as proved. But there are doctrines & expressions within Christianity that were disagreed with, unknown, have variety, etc.,~ such as Church ceremonies, Gifts of the Spirit, order of the Church, the second coming of Christ, and so on. A Christian may rightly by conscience vary on these and yet have a good conscience. It is not GOV decision to dictate what a man is to know and be convicted of; They are Not God Nor the Church: // "Journal of the Senate of the US of America, 1789-1793, 9/3, 1789 - The Senate assembled: present as yesterday, And resumed the consideration of the resolve of the House of Representatives, of the 24th of August, upon the proposed amendments to the CON of the US ,,,[[here following are discussions on how to word the part of the religious clause]] - On motion to amend article third, and to strike out these words: 'RELIGION, or prohibiting the free exercise thereof,' and insert 'one RELIGIOUS SECT or society in preference to others:' It passed in the negative. On motion for reconsideration: It passed in the affirmative. On motion that article the third be stricken out: It passed in the negative. On motion to adopt the following, in lieu of the third article: 'Congress shall not make any law infringing the rights of CONSCIENCE, or establishing any RELIGIOUS SECT or society:' It passed in the negative. On motion to amend the third article, to read thus: 'Congress shall make no law establishing any particular DENOMINATION of RELIGION in preference to another, or prohibiting the free exercise thereof, nor shall the rights of CONSCIENCE be infringed:" It passed in the negative. On the question upon the third article as it came from the House of Representatives: It passed in the negative. On motion to adopt the third article proposed in the resolve of the House of Representatives, amended by striking out these words, 'nor shall the rights of CONSCIENCE be infringed:' It passed in the affirmative."

---T--- RELIGION & R~Est includes~ Jesus's Christian terms, activity, events, & desires constantly the intention/ purpose of the Congress, Executive, & CC (DOI & CON): // "Journal of the executive proceedings of the Senate of the US of America, 1789-1805 ,1/ 17, 1791. A message from the President of file US, by Mr. Lear, his Secretary ,,,CHRISTIAN Majesty to the President and members of Congress; and he withdrew. US, 1/ 17th, 1791. Gentlemen of the Senate: I lay before you a letter from his most CHRISTIAN Majesty, addressed to the President and members of Congress of the US of America. Go. WASHINGTON. To our very dear friends and allies, the President and members of the general Congress of the US of North America. Very Dear Great Friends and Allies: We have received the letter ,,,It is with the most sincere pleasure that we embrace this opportunity of renewing these assurances of regard and friendship, which we feel for the US in general, and for each of them in particular; under their influence, we PRAY GOD that he will keep you, very dear friends and allies, under his HOLY and beneficent protection. Done at Paris, this 11th Sept., 1790. Your good friend and ally, LOUIS. MONTMORIN, [SEAL.] The US ,,,Ordered".

---T--- R-E ~ Observation of EV that the FFOG desires, attitudes, & intention/ purpose that~ +] Christ be priority; AND, +] Christianity is not abused; AND, +] All different Christian DEN are encouraged by the USA GOV; AND, +] Christianity is supported by the USA GOV; AND, +] Religion is to be true not false; AND, +] Religion & R~Est is de= as Christian DEN; AND, +] The evils of the British GOV at the time were against Christianity: // Times of Christian devotion and prayer is again enacted by USA GOV~ "Journals of the Continental Congress, 1774-1789, 6/12, 1775 - The Congress met according to adjournment. The committee, appointed for preparing a resolve for a fast, brought in a report, which, being read, was agreed to as follows: As the great GOVERNOR of the World, by HIS supreme and universal Providence, not only conducts the course of nature with unerring wisdom and rectitude, but frequently influences the minds of men to serve the wise and gracious purposes of HIS providential government; and it being, at all times, our indispensible duty devoutly to acknowledge his superintending providence, especially in times of impending danger and public calamity, to reverence and adore his immutable justice as well as to implore his merciful interposition for our deliverance: This Congress, therefore, considering the present critical, alarming and calamitous state of these colonies, do earnestly recommend that Thursday, the 20th day of July next, be observed, by the inhabitants of all the English colonies on this continent, as a day of public humiliation, fasting and PRAYER; that we may, with united hearts and voices, unfeignedly confess and deplore our many SINS; and offer up our joint supplications to the all-wise, omnipotent, and merciful Disposer of all events; humbly beseeching HIM to forgive our iniquities, to remove our present calamities, to avert those desolating judgments, with which we are threatned, and to bless our rightful sovereign, King George the third, and [to] inspire him with wisdom to discern and pursue the TRUE interest of all his subjects, that a speedy end may be put to the civil discord between Great Britain and the American colonies, without farther effusion of blood: And that the British nation may be influenced to regard the things that belong to her peace, before they are hid from her eyes: That these colonies may be ever under the care and protection of a kind Providence, and be prospered in all their interests; That the DIVINE blessing may descend and rest upon all our civil rulers, and upon the representatives of the people, in their several assemblies and conventions, that they may be directed to wise and effectual measures for preserving the union, and securing the just rights and priviledges of the colonies; That virtue and TRUE RELIGION may revive and flourish throughout our land; And that all America may soon behold a gracious interposition of HEAVEN, for the redress of her many grievances, the restoration of her invaded rights, a reconcilation with the parent state, on terms constitutional and honorable to both; And that her civil and

RELIGIOUS priviledges may be secured to the latest posterity. And it is recommended to CHRISTIANs, of all DENOMINATIONS, to assemble for public worship, and to abstain from servile labour and recreations on said day. Ordered, That a copy of the above be signed by the president and attested by the Secy and published in the newspapers, and in hand bills.1 [Note 1: 1 It was printed in the Pennsylvania Packet, 19 June, 1775 ,,,Papers of the Continental Congress, No. 23, folio 5. ,,,On motion ordered that the letter to the Inhabitants of Canada be published in English. ,,,Resolved that the Congress ,,,to take into consideration the ways and means of raising money, and also the state of America."

---T--- <u>Religion in the USA is Christian to Jesus & the R~Est</u> Pertains to Christian DENs, not any or every religion allowed: // Congress Meeting Note on forming the CON, 1788: "Mr. Chairman, I am one of those who formed this CON. The gentleman says, we exceeded our powers. I deny the charge. We were sent with a full power to amend the existing system. This involved every power to make every alteration necessary to meliorate and render it perfect. It cannot be said that we arrogated powers altogether inconsistent with the object of our delegation. There is a clause which expressly provides for future amendments, and it is still in your power. What the Convention has done is a mere proposal. It was found impossible to improve the old system without changing its very form; for by that system the three great branches of GOV are blended together. All will agree that the concession of a power to a GOV so constructed is dangerous. The proposing a new system, to be established by the assent and ratification of nine states, arose from the necessity of the case. It was thought extremely hard that one state, or even three or four states, should be able to prevent necessary alterations. ,,,the general welfare in the power of a few members of the Union. It was, therefore, thought by the Convention, that, if so great a majority as nine states should adopt it, it would be right to establish it. It was recommended by Congress to the state legislatures to refer it to the people of their different states. Our Assembly has confirmed what they have done, by proposing it to the consideration of the people. It was there, and not here, that the objection should have been made. This Convention is therefore to consider the CON, and whether it be proper for the GOV of the people of America; and had it been proposed by any one individual, under these circumstances, it would be right to consider whether it be good or bad. The gentleman has insinuated that this CON, instead of securing our liberties, is a scheme to enslave us. He has produced no proof, but rests it on his bare assertion-- an assertion which I am astonished to hear, after the ability with which every objection has been fully and dearly refuted in the course of our debates. I am, for my part, conscious of having had nothing in view but the liberty and happiness of my country; and I believe every member of that Convention was actuated by motives equally sincere and patriotic. (p) He says that it will tend to aristocracy. Where is the aristocratical part of it? It is ideal. I always thought that an aristocracy was that GOV where the few governed the many, or where the rulers were hereditary [[Christian]]. This is a very different GOV from that. I never read of such an aristocracy. The first branch are representatives chosen freely by the people at large. This must be allowed upon all hands to be democratical. The next is the Senate, chosen by the people, in a secondary manner, through the medium of their delegates in the legislature, This cannot be aristocratical. They are chosen for six years, but one third of them go out every second year, and are responsible to the state legislatures. The President is elected for four years. By whom? By those who are elected in such manner as the state legislatures think proper. I hope the gentleman will not pretend to call this an aristocratical feature. The privilege of representation is secured in the most positive and unequivocal terms, and cannot be evaded. The gentleman has again brought on the trial by jury. The Federal Convention, sir, had no wish to destroy the trial by jury. It was three or four days before them. There were a variety of objections to any one mode. It was thought impossible to fall upon any one mode but what would produce some inconveniences. I cannot now recollect all the reasons given. Most of them have been amply detailed by other gentlemen here. I should suppose that, if the representatives of twelve states, with many able lawyers among them, could not form any unexceptionable mode, this Convention could hardly be able to do it. As to the subject of RELIGION, I thought what had been said would fully satisfy that gentleman and every other. No power is given to the general GOV to interfere with it at all. Any act of Congress on this subject would be a usurpation. (p) NO SECT IS PREFERRED TO ANOTHER. [[sect is de= as Christian DEN]] Every man has a right to worship the Supreme Being [[The true only God; not false gods; "worship in the manner he thinks proper" is Christian DEN; but DEN have various expressions and secondary doctrines~ these 2 subjects are the "worship in the manner"]] in the manner he thinks proper. No test is required. All men of equal capacity and integrity, are equally eligible to offices. Temporal violence might make mankind wicked, but never religious. A test would enable the prevailing sect to persecute the rest. [[here the oath is Christian, intended to~ +require the inclusion of God; +and not to require any one specific Christian DEN, sect, not limited; rather all are allowed]] I do not suppose an INFIDEL, [[Unbeliever is infidel to Christianity]] or any such person, will ever be chosen to any office, unless the people themselves be of the same opinion. He says that Congress may establish ecclesiastical [[de= of this word is to have courts in the Church]] courts. I do not know what part of the CON warrants that assertion. It is impossible. No such power is given them. The gentleman advises such amendments as would satisfy him, and proposes a mode of amending before ratifying. If we do not adopt first, we are no more a part of the Union than any foreign power. It will be also throwing away the influence of our state to propose amendments as the condition of our ratification. If we adopt first, our representatives will have a proportionable weight in bringing about amendments, which will not be the case if we do not adopt. It is adopted by ten states already. The question, then, is, not whether the CON be good, but whether we will or will not confederate with the other states. The gentleman supposes that the liberty of the press is not secured. The CON does not take it away. It says nothing of it, and can do nothing to injure it. But it is secured by the CON of every state in the Union in the most ample manner."

---T--- <u>EV proves that Religion & Religious Test & CON are Intended/ purposed by</u> Executive, Citizens, Congress, Churches to~ +] support ONLY Christ's Christian Religion including the various DEN; +] including Judaism Proper; +] The NT is a priority subject of positive inclusion by the FFOG;

+] because only Christianity is to be supported then only godly men, supporting the CC, can be in Office; Positions directly Making Laws; +] the OATH, CON, & CC, & Meetings acknowledging Christ as God; +] oppose idolatry: // "The Records of the Federal Convention of 1787 [Farrand's Records, Volume 3] CIV. Jonas Phillips to the President and Members of the Convention.1 [Note 1: 1 Documentary History of the CON, I, 281--283.] Sires With leave and submission I address myself To those in whome there is wisdom understanding and knowledge ,,,are the honourable personages appointed and made overseers of a part of the terrestrial globe of the Earth, Namely the 13 US of america in Convention Assembled, the Lord [[Jesus here]] preserve them amen -- [[note here that, +God is acknowledged as God with Priority, +themselves are only overseers for God, +idolatry is opposed]]. I the subscriber being one of the people called Jews of the City of Philadelphia, a people scattered and despersed among all nations do behold with Concern that among the laws in the CON of Pennsylvania their is a Clause". // "SECT. 10 to viz -- I do believe in one GOD the Creature and governour of the universe the Rewarder of the good and the punisher of the wicked -- and I do acknowledge the SCs of the old and New testament to be given by a devine inspiration -- to swear and believe that the new testament was given by devine inspiration is absolutly against the RELIGIOUS principle of a Jew, and is against his CONSCIENCE to take any such oath-- By the above law a Jew is deprived of holding any publick office or place of Government which is a Contridectory to the bill of Right SECT 2. Viz That all men have a natural and unalienable Right To worship almighty GOD according to the dectates of their own CONSCIENCE and understanding, and that no man aught or of Right can be Compelled to attend any Religious Worship or Erect or support any place of worship or Maintain any minister contrary to or against his own free will and Consent nor Can any man who acknowledges the being of a GOD be Justly deprived or abridged of any Civil Right as a Citizen on account of his RELIGIOUS sentiments or peculiar mode of RELIGIOUS Worship, [[DEN referenced and not any religion of falsity, but Christianity]] and that no authority Can or aught to be vested in or assumed by any power what ever that shall in any Case interfere or in any manner Control the Right of CONSCIENCE in the free Exercise of RELIGIOUS Worship -- It is well known among all the Citizens of the 13 US that the Jews have been TRUE and faithful whigs, and during the late Contest with England they have been foremost in aiding and assisting the States with their lifes and fortunes, they have supported the Cause, have bravely faught and bleed for liberty which they can not enjoy -- Therefore if the honourable Convention shall in ther Wisdom think fit and alter the said oath and leave out the words to viz -- and I do acknoweledge the SC of the new testament to be given by devine inspiration then the Israeletes will think them self happy to live under a government where all Religious societys are on an Equal footing [[note Christian DEN not falsity religions is religious societies; NT related]] -- I solecet this favour for my self my Children and posterity and for the benefit of all the Isrealetes through the 13 US of America My PRAYERS is unto the Lord. May the people of this States Rise up as a great and young lion, May they prevail against their Enemies, May the degrees of honour of his Excellencey the president of the Convention George Washington, be Extollet and Raise up. May every one speak of his glorious exploits. May GOD prolong his days among us in this land of liberty -- May he lead the armies against his enemys as he has done hereuntofore -- May GOD Extend peace unto the US -- May they get up to the highest prosperetys -- May GOD Extend peace to them and their seed after them so long as the sun and moon endureth -- and may the almighty GOD of our father Abraham Isaac and Jacob endue this Noble Assembly with wisdom judgement and unamity in their councells, and may they have the satisfaction to see that their present toil and labour for the wellfair of the US may be approved of, through all the world and perticular by the US of america is the ardent PRAYER of Sires Your Most devoted obed Servant Jonas Phillips".

---T--- R-E, R~Est, 1-A Intention/ Purposes of the FFOG, Congress, Citizens proved by Expressed Support to God's~ +] Christianity, +] Religion Thereof, +] Truth, +] Discerning how to think Right about the various Christian DENs: // "Letters of Delegates to Congress: Volume 25- 3/1, 1788- 12/31, 1789 - Thomas Tudor Tucker to St. George Tucker - New York Apl. 17th. 1788. I am now, my dear St George, at liberty to write to you on a Subject which for some time past has given me much Disturbance & Perplexity of Mind. For HEAVEN's sake, what do you make of the Letters of our dear ,,,In Sept. last I received a long one from him containing such Matter as fill'd me with Astonishment & Anxiety. Agitated betwixt Wonder & Uneasiness I scann'd it as well as my Understanding wou'd enable me & found a perfect Connexion of Ideas throughout the whole, which gave me some Relief. ,,,but nothing occurr'd that afforded me any Light on the Subject. In this State of anxious Uncertainty, I wrote to him in the most pressing Terms to releive me from my Suspence by writing to me immediately the fullest Explanation he felt himself at liberty to give of these wonderful Discoveries, with the Source from whence they were derived. But I cou'd not venture to express a Doubt of the reality of every thing he asserted. In all my sober Moments I acknowledge the Superintendance of a DIVINE Power [[here is the conscious awareness of God as a Spirit and of His laws in creation]], & suppose that he acts by general Laws contrived to effect the Happiness of all sentient Beings. How far these general Laws may in the MORAL as in the physical World produce Phoenomena that to our Understandings seem irregular & not resulting from the general principle, & therefore often term'd miraculous, I am not qualified to determine. A general propensity to RELIGION in Mankind, I have consider'd as Evidence of the Deity's Existence. The Tenets of all the different SECTS [[here is the study to discern as to what to do with the various Christian DENs]] appear to me to abound with Absurdities, as far as I have Knowledge of them. Not because I cannot explain every thing, but because many things seem to be contradictory to that Reason which has been given by GOD for our Guide. He cou'd not give us Reason & then take pains (if I may so express myself) to confound it's Operation. June 13th. I know not how I have been prevented from continuing the Subject. I was going to add many other Observations, but shall rather proceed to Facts. I reced a very long Letter from N. in Answer, with a full Account of what had happen'd to him, & accompanied with several of Swedenborg's Books which I have not been able yet to read with Attention. I find he has sent them also to you & to our Friends in Bermuda. Our dear Sister B. sent them also to me by Mr. D. Tucker, without many remarks upon them, but N. says she reads them with Intelligence & Conviction. He is impatient to hear from you, & is also so earnest with me that I am perfectly at a loss how to write to him. PRAY, help me out, if you can. Perhaps you have read those Books, & can form a better Judgment of them than I can. I shou'd be glad to have your Sentiments as fully as possible upon this very extraordinary Change. I must confess I was for some time even afraid to enquire about him, but am now happy to find that he goes on with his Business, & with rather better Prospects than formerly. HEAVEN bless you, my dear St. George. Yrs. most truly & sincerely, Thos. Tud. Tucker - RC (ViW: Tucker-Coleman Papers).   1 That is, their brother Nathaniel, a Charleston physician, who was exploring the theological writings of Emanuel Swedenborg (1688--;1772), a proponent of a "new CHRISTIANITY" of gradual redemption through the personal regulation of SPIRITual states."

---T--- Intention/ Purposes as Reasons for the USA Existence include~ a] Religious Liberty; that of Christianity; b] R-E & E~Est & 1-A to state that one Christian DEN is not to be favored more than another by making a Law for that DEN in the USA GOV; c] the Holy Bible & Truth continually used: // "Letters of Delegates to Congress: Volume 10- 6/1, 1778 - 9/30, 1778,,,- [June 20, 1778] ,,,Trusty and well-beloved servants of your SACRED master, in whom he is well pleased.   As you are sent to America for the express purpose of treating with anybody and anything, you will pardon an address from one who disdains to flatter those whom he loves. Should you therefore deign to read this address, your chaste ears will not be offended with the language of adulation, a language you despise. I have seen your most elegant and most excellent letter "to his Excellency Henry Laurens, the President, and other Members of the Congress." ,,,As that body have thought your propositions unworthy their particular regard, it may be some satisfaction to your curiosity, and tend to appease the offended SPIRIT of negotiation, if one out of the many individuals on this great Continent should speak to you the sentiments of America. Sentiments which your own good sense hath doubtless suggested, and which are repeated only to convince you that, notwithstanding the narrow ground of private information on which we stand in this distant region, still a knowledge of our own rights, and attention to our own interests, and a SACRED respect for the dignity of human nature, have given us to understand the TRUE principles which ought, and which therefore shall, sway our conduct. You begin with the amiable expressions of humanity, the earnest desire of tranquility and peace. A better introduction to Americans could not be devised. For the sake of the latter, we once laid our liberties at the feet of your Prince, and even your armies have not eradicated the former from our bosoms. You tell us you have powers unprecedented in the annals of your history. And England, unhappy England, will remember with deep contrition, that these powers have been rendered of no avail by a conduct unprecedented in the annals of mankind. Had your royal master condescended to listen to the PRAYER of millions, he had not thus have sent you. Had moderation swayed what we were proud to call mother country, "her full-blown dignity would not have broken down under her." You tell us that "all parties may draw some degree of consolation, and even auspicious hope, from recollection." We wish this most sincerely for the sake of all parties. America, even in the moment of subjugation, would have been consoled by conscious virtue, and her hope was and is in the justice of her cause, and the JUSTICE OF THE ALMIGHTY. These are sources of hope and of consolation, which neither time nor chance can alter or take away. You mention "the mutual benefits and consideration of EVILs, that may naturally contribute to determine our resolutions." As to the former, you know too well that we could derive no benefit from an union with you, nor will I, by deducing the reasons to evince this, cast an insult upon your understandings. As to the latter, it were to be wished you had preserved a line of conduct equal to the delicacy of your feelings. You could not but know that men, who sincerely love freedom, disdain the consideration of all EVILs necessary to attain it. Had not your own hearts borne testimony to this TRUTH, you might have learnt it from the annals of your history. For in those annals instances of this kind at least are not unprecedented. But should those instances be insufficient, we PRAY you to read the unconquered mind of America. That the acts of Parliament you transmitted were passed with singular unanimity, we pretend not to doubt. You will pardon me, gentlemen, for observing, that the reasons of that unanimity are strongly marked in the report of a Committee of Congress, agreed to on the 22d of Apr. last ,,,and referred to in a late letter from Congress to Lord Viscount Howe and Sir Henry Clinton. ,,,You tell us you are willing "to consent to a cessation of hostilities, both by sea and land." It is difficult for rude Americans to determine whether you are serious in this proposition, or whether you mean to jest with their simplicity. Upon a supposition, however, that you have too much magnanimity to divert yourselves on an occasion of such importance to America, and perhaps not very trivial in the eyes of those who sent you, permit me to assure you, on the SACRED word of a gentleman, that if you shall transport your troops to England, where before long your Prince will certainly want their assistance, we never shall follow them thither. We are not so romantically fond of fighting, neither have we such regard for the city of London, as to commence a crusade for the possession of that HOLY land. Thus you may be certain that hostilities will cease by land. It would be doing singular injustice to your national character, to suppose you are desirous of a like cessation by sea. The course of the war, and the very flourishing state of your commerce, notwithstanding our weak efforts to interrupt it, clearly shew that you can exclude us from the sea. The sea your kingdom. You offer "to restore free intercourse, to revive mutual affection, and renew the common benefits of naturalization." Whenever your countrymen shall be taught wisdom by experience, and learn from past misfortunes to pursue their TRUE interests in future we shall readily admit every intercourse which is necessary for the purposes of commerce, and usual between different nations. To revive mutual affection is utterly impossible. We freely forgive you, but it is not in nature that you should forgive us. You have injured us too much. We might, on this occasion, give you some late instances of singular barbarity, committed as well by the forces of his Britannic Majesty, as by those of his generous and faithful allies, the Senecas, Onondagas and Tuscaroras. But we will not offend a courtly ear by the recital of those disgusting scenes. Besides this, it might give pain to that humanity which hath, as you observe, prompted your overtures to dwell upon the splendid victories obtained by a LICENTIOUS soldiery over unarmed men in defenceless villages, their WANTON devastations, THEIR DELIBERATE MURDERS, or to inspect those scenes of carnage painted by the wild excesses of savage rage. These amiable traits of national conduct cannot but revive in our bosoms that partial AFFECTION we once felt for everything which bore the name of Englishman. As to the common benefits of naturalization, it is a matter we conceive to be of the most sovereign indifference,,,,. These will hardly claim naturalization in either of those places as a benefit. On the other hand, such of your subjects as shall be driven by the iron hand of Oppression to seek for refuge among those whom they now persecute, will certainly be admitted to the benefits of naturalization. We labour to rear an asylum for mankind, and regret that circumstances will not permit you, Gentlemen, to contribute to a design so very agreeable to your several tempers and dispositions. But further, your Excellencies say, "we will concur to extend every freedom to trade that our respective interests can require." Unfortunately there is a little difference in these interests, which you might not have found it very easy to reconcile, had the Congress been disposed to risque their heads by listening to terms, which I have the honour to assure you are treated with ineffable contempt by every honest Whig in America. ,,,they might extend the freedom of trade, or circumscribe it, at their pleasure, for what they might call our respective interests. But I trust it would not be to our mutual satisfaction. Your "earnest desire to stop the farther effusion of blood, and the calamities of war," will therefore lead you, on maturer reflection, to reprobate a plan teeming with discord, and which, in the space of twenty years, would produce another wild expedition across the Atlantic, and in a few years more some such commission as that "with which his Majesty hath been pleased to honour you." ,,,It might not be amiss previously to establish this union, which may be done by your acceptance of the treaty of peace and commerce tendered to you by Congress ,,,And such treaty, I can venture to say, would continue as long as your ministers could prevail upon themselves not to violate the faith of nations. You offer, to use your own language, the inaccuracy of which, considering the importance of the subject, is not to be wondered at, or at least may be excused, "in short to establish the powers of the respective legislatures in each particular State, to settle its revenue, its civil and military establishment, and to exercise a perfect freedom of legislation and internal government, so that the British States throughout North-America acting with us, in peace and war, under one common sovereign, may have the irrevokable enjoyment of every privilege that is short of a total separation of interests, or consistent with that union of force on which the safety of our common RELIGION and liberty depends." Let me assure you, gentlemen, that the power of the respective legislatures in each particular State is already most fully established, and on the most solid foundations. It is established on the perfect freedom of legislation and a vigorous administration of internal government ,,,As the States of North-America mean to possess the irrevokable enjoyment of their privileges, it is absolutely necessary for them to decline all connection with a Parliament, who, even in the laws under which you act, reserve in express terms the power of revoking every proposition which you may agree to. We have a due sense of the kind offer you make, to grant us a share in your sovereign, but really, gentlemen, we have not the least inclination to accept of it ,,,You are solicitous to prevent a total separation of interests ,,,We cannot perceive that our liberty does in the least depend upon any union of force with you; for we find that, after you have exercised your force against us for upwards of three years, we are now upon the point of establishing our liberties in direct opposition to it. ,,,One is enough to entertain a generation at least ,,,excuse me when I differ from you, as to our having a RELIGION in common with you: the RELIGION of America is the RELIGION of all mankind. Any person may worship in the manner he thinks most agreeable to the Deity; and if he behaves as a good citizen, no one concerns himself as to his faith or adorations, neither have we the least solicitude to exalt any one SECT or profession above another. I am extremely sorry to find in your letter some sentences, which reflect upon the character of his most CHRISTIAN Majesty. It certainly is not kind, or consistent with the principles of philanthropy you profess, to traduce a gentleman's character without affording him an opportunity of defending himself: and that too a near neighbour, and not long since an intimate brother ,,,in addressing yourselves to Congress, when you well knew that he was their good and faithful ally. It is indeed TRUE, as you justly observe, that he hath at times been at enmity with his Britannic Majesty, by which we suffered some inconveniences: but these flowed rather from our connection with you than any ill-will towards us: At the same time it is a solemn TRUTH, worthy of your serious attention, that you did not commence the present war, a war in which we have suffered infinitely more than by any former contest, a fierce, a bloody, I am sorry to add, an unprovoked and cruel war. ,,,America, being at peace with all the world, was formerly drawn into a war with France, in consequence of her union with Great-Britain ,,,For the TRUTH of these positions I appeal, gentlemen, to your own knowledge. I know it is very hard for you to part with what you have accustomed yourselves, from your earliest infancy, to call your colonies. I pity your situation, and therefore I excuse the little abberations from TRUTH which your letter contains. At the same time it is possible that you may have been misinformed. For I will not suppose that your letter was intended to delude the people of these States. Such unmanly disingenuous artifices have of late been exerted with so little effect, that prudence, if not probity, would prevent a repetition. To undeceive you, therefore, I take the liberty of assuring your Excellencies ,,,in other words the treaties of alliance and commerce between his most CHRISTIAN Majesty and these States, were not made in consequence of any plans of accommodation concerted in Great-Britain, nor with a view to prolong this destructive war. If you consider that these treaties were actually concluded before the draught of the bills under which you act was sent for America, and that much time must necessarily have been consumed in adjusting compacts of such intricacy and importance, and further ,,,you must be convinced of the TRUTH of my assertions. The fact is ,,,It seems to me, gentlemen, that there is something (excuse the word) disingenuous in your procedure. I put the supposition that Congress had acceded to your propositions, and then I ask two questions. Had you full power from your commission to make these propositions? Possibly you did not think it worth while to consider your commission, but we Americans are apt to compare things together, and to reason. The second question I ask is, What security could you give that the British Parliament would ratify your

152

compacts? You can give no such security, and therefore we should, after forfeiting our reputation as a people, after you had filched from us our good name, and perswaded us to give to the common enemy of man the precious jewel of our liberties; after all this, I say, we should have been at the mercy of a Parliament, which, to say no more of it, has not treated us with too great tenderness. ,,,For your use I subjoin the following creed of every good American. I believe that in every kingdom, state, or empire there must be, from the necessity of the thing, one supreme legislative power, with authority to bind every part in all cases, the proper object of human laws. I believe that to be bound by laws, to which he does not consent by himself or by his representative, is the direct definition of a slave. ,,,Amen . Now if you will take the poor advice of one, who is really a friend to England and Englishmen, and who hath even some Scotch blood in his veins, away with your fleets and your armies, acknowledge the independence of America ,,,Your nation totters on the brink of a stupendous precipice, and even delay will ruin her. You have told the Congress, "If, after the time that may be necessary to consider this communication, and transmit your answer, the horrors and devastations of war should continue, we call GOD and the world to witness that the EVILs, which must follow, are not to be imputed to Great-Britain." I wish you had spared your protestation. Matters of this kind may appear to you in a trivial light, as meer ornamental flowers of rhetoric, but they are serious things registered in the high chancery of HEAVEN. Remember the awful abuse of words like these by General Burgoyne, and remember his fate. There is one above us, who will take exemplary vengeance for every insult upon his Majesty. You know that the cause of America is just. You know that she contends for that freedom, to which all men are entitled. That she contends against oppression, rapine, and more than savage barbarity. The blood of the innocent is upon your hands, and all the waters of the ocean will not wash it away. We again make our solemn appeal to the GOD of HEAVEN to decide between you and us. And we PRAY that in the doubtful scale of battle we may be successful, as we have justice on our side, and that the merciful SAVIOUR of the world may forgive our oppressors. I am, my Lords and Gentlemen, The friend of human nature, And one who glories in the title of, An AMERICAN ,,,reprinted from the Pennsylvania Gazette, June 20, 1778 ,,,July 21, Sept. 19,,,".
---T--- R-E , 1-A is proved because~ +] Jesus & Christianity is the True Religion ~&~ +] Christian DEN is Religion & R~Est Defined ~&~ +] Opposed to True Religion being Abused by False Religion (that of non-Christian): // "The Revolutionary Diplomatic Correspondence of the US, Volume 3 ,,,May 17, 1780. Sir: General Conway, in his speech in the House of Commons on the 6th of May ,,,In order to determine it, one should consider what is meant by a natural alliance; and I know of no better rule than this: When two nations have the same interests in general they are natural allies; when they have opposite interests they are natural enemies ,,,The general will not pretend that nature, in the constitution of American minds or bodies, has laid any foundation for friendship or enmity towards one nation more than another. The general observes, further, that habit has raised another barrier between France and America. But he should have considered that the habits of affection or enmity between nations are easily changed, as circumstances vary and as essential interests alter. ,,,and it is now much to be doubted whether any nation of Europe is so universally and heartily detested by them. On the contrary, most of the other nations of Europe have treated them with civility, and France and Spain with esteem, confidence, and affection, which has greatly changed the habits of the Americans in this respect ,,,RELIGION is the fourth part of the barrier. But let it be considered, first, that there is not enough of RELIGION of any kind among the people in power in England to make the Americans very fond of them. Secondly, that what RELIGION there is in England is as far from being the RELIGION of America as that of France. [[Religion of America as a Total; supported Christianity]] The hierarchy of England is quite as disagreeable to America as that of any other country ,,,Americans know very well that the SPIRIT of propagating any RELIGION by conquest and of making proselytes by force or by intrigue is fled from all other countries of the world in a great measure, and that there is more of this SPIRIT remaining in England than anywhere else. And the Americans had, and have still, more reason to gear the introduction of a RELIGION that is disagreeable to them, at least as far as bishops and hierarchy go, from a connection with England than with any other nation of Europe. The alliance with France has no article respecting RELIGION. France neither claims nor desires any authority or influence over America in this respect; whereas England claimed and intended to exercise authority and force over the Americans, at least so far as to introduce bishops; and the English society for propagating RELIGION in foreign parts has, in fact, for a century sent large sums of money to America to support their RELIGION there, which really operated as a bribe upon many minds and was the principal source of toryism. So that upon the whole the alliance with France is in fact more natural, as far as RELIGION is concerned, than the former connection with Great Britain, or any other connection that can be found. Indeed, whoever considers attentively this subject will see that these three circumstances of habit, language, and RELIGION will for the future operate as natural causes of animosity between England and America, because they will facilitate migration. The loss of liberty, the decay of RELIGION ,,,which can not but take place in England, will tempt numbers of their best people to emigrate to America; and to this fashion, language, and RELIGION will contribute. ,,,Nature has already sufficiently discovered itself, and all the world sees that the British GOV have for many years not only indulged in themselves the most unsocial and bitter passions against Americans, but have systematically encouraged them in the people. After all, the circumstances of modes, language, and RELIGION have much less influence in determining the friendship and enmity of nations than other more essential interests. Commerce is more than all these and many more such circumstances, Now, it is easy to see that the commercial interests of England and America will forever hereafter be incompatible. ,,,The boundaries of territory will also be another constant source of disputes. If a peace should unhappily be made leaving England in possession of Canada, Nova Scotia, the Floridas, or any one spot of ground in America, they will be perpetually encroaching upon the States of America; whereas France having renounced all territorial jurisdiction in America, will have no room for controversy ,,,America became the natural friend of France and she the natural friend of the US--powers naturally united against a common enemy, whose interests will

long continue to be reciprocally secured and promoted by mutual friendship. It is very strange that the English should thus dogmatically judge of the interests of all other nations. ,,,."

---T--- <u>USA GOV is Acting as an Ambassador for Jesus Christ the</u> Lord in Relations with Christian Allies & with Christian Purposes of Holy Keeping: // "The Revolutionary Diplomatic Correspondence of the US, Volume 4 Congress-- Instructions to Laurens.* [Note *: * MSS. Dep. of State; 5 Sparks' Dip. Rev. Corr., 145.] In Congress, 12/23, 1780. Sir: You will herewith receive a commission appointing you our minister at the court of Versailles; in pursuing the objects of which you will conform to the following instructions: Upon your arrival you will communicate fully to our minister plenipotentiary at that court the business on which you are sent, and avail yourself of his information and influence for obtaining the aids mentioned in the estimate delivered to you. Instructions to him for that purpose are herewith transmitted, which you will deliver immediately on your arrival. You will convey to his most CHRISTIAN majesty the grateful sense Congress have of the noble and generous part he has taken with regard to the US, and use every possible means to impress him with the urgent and critical state of our affairs at present, which induced the appointment of a special minister to solicit his effectual aid. You will, in particular, give him full information of the present state of our military affairs, and the measures taken for providing a respectable force for the ensuing campaign ,,,You are to use every effort in your power to enforce the necessity of maintaining a naval superiority in the American seas. You will assure his most CHRISTIAN majesty on our part that, if he will please to communicate to us his intentions respecting the next campaign in America, we will use every effort in our power for an effectual co-operation. ,,,the commanders-in-chief of his most CHRISTIAN majesty's fleet and army at Rhode Island, the Marquis de la Fayette ,,,You will embrace every opportunity of informing us of the success of your negotiations, and receive and obey such instructions as you may from time to time receive from Congress. When the purpose of your mission shall be as fully effected as you may deem practicable you are to return and report your success to Congress without delay, unless you shall previously receive other orders.* [Note *: * ,,,We PRAY GOD to further you with His goodness in the several objects hereby recommended, and that He will have you in His HOLY keeping. Samuel Huntington, President."

============== Educational Institutions, SCHOOLS, are to Include God & CHRISTIANity ==== After This Subject is More Specifically Studied Below, The Chapter then Continues with Additional Evidences as it was above About Religion In General =======================

---T--- <u>Educational Institution Evidence with Documents</u> includes the following proving that the USA started & funded schools centered in & for Christianity (God, Truth, Holy Bible, Creation): // Harvard~ Educational Institution: One of America's first Gov't college (2). Named after reverend John Harvard, 1607-1638; died of tuberculosis early in life. Rules of the school included: "let every student be plainly and earnestly pressed to consider well the main end of his life and studies is to know God and Jesus Christ which is eternal life (John17:3)". It was a Christian Institution for 2 centuries. The Presidents were Christians. Other requirements included: ",,,the Lord only giveth wisdom ,,,seriously set ,,,by prayer in secret to seek it of him"; "Every one shall so exercise himself in reading the SCs twice a day, that he shall ,,,give ,,,account of his proficiency therein" (43). A memorial of stone at Harvard says: "After God had carried us safe to New England and we had built our houses, provided necessaries for our livelihood, reared convenient places for God's worship, and settled the civil GOV, one of the next things we longed for and looked after was to advance learning and perpetuate it to posterity; dreading to leave an illiterate ministry to the Churches, when our present ministers shall lie in the dust". // According to studies of Dr. D. James Kennedy and Jerry Newcombe~ "almost every one of the first 123 colleges and universities in the USA has a Christian origin". // Ivy League Schools proclaimed Christianity. // William and Mary University: Declared it's purpose as, ",,,,that the Christian faith may be propagated,,,". // Yale College: Regulations at this school include: "all scholars shall live religious, godly, and blameless lives according to the rules of God's Word, diligently reading the Holy SC, the fountain of light and truth; and constantly attend upon all the duties of religion, both in public and secret"; "If any scholar shall deny the Holy SC or any part of them to be the Word of God, or be guilty of heresy or any error directly tending to subvert the fundamentals of Christianity, and continuing obstinate therein after the first and second admonition, he shall be expelled"; ",,,every scholar, besides private ,,,prayer ,,,shall be present morning and evening at public prayer,,,"; "The SCs ,,,morning and evening to be read by the Students ,,,to promote the power and Purity of Religion" (44). // Columbia University: Formed in AD 1754. Advertised their institution as, "the chief thing that is aimed at in this college is to teach and engage children to know God in Jesus Christ." // Princeton College: Founded in AD 1746; Christian much of it's existence; public statement was "Under God's Power She Flourishes". Rev John Witherspoon was president of the college and a signer of the DOI. // Rutgers University: Began in AD 1766. Assisted by Rev Theodore Frelinghuysen. Motto: "Son of Righteousness, Shine upon the West also".

---T--- <u>The American public school system was developed</u> in 17th century and began in Massachusetts in order for children to learn to read Holy SC (2).

---T--- <u>2 other intentions/purposes of the GOV in starting</u> or funding GOV Schools was for Christ's Presence & Christianity & to educate the Indian people with Christianity; & to provide the Churches with ministers (2). +This agrees with the CC (DOI) Intentions/purposes and is therefore legal.

---T--- <u>Alexis de Tocqueville, French observer in</u> (Democracy in America: London's Saunders & Otley, 1838) reports that: "There is no country in the whole world in which the Christian religion retains a greater influence over the souls of men as that in America,,,".

154

---T--- <u>The USA GOV Officials that made the CC (DOI & CON) were all Christian;</u> also those sent by the State GOV: // Delaware CON states: "Every person who shall be chosen a member of either house, or appointed to any office or place of trust ,,,shall ,,,make and subscribe the following declaration, to wit: I _____, do profess faith in God the Father, and in Jesus Christ His only son and in the Holy Ghost, one God, blessed for evermore, and I do acknowledge the Holy SCs of the old and new Testament to be given by divine inspiration"(32). // Pennsylvania CON: "Frame of GOV ,,,And each member of the legislature, before he takes his seat, should make and subscribe the following declaration, viz: I do believe in one God, the Creator and Governor of the universe, the rewarder of the good and the punisher of the wicked, and I do acknowledge the SCs of the Old and New Testament to be given by Divine Inspiration" (31). Observe here that the REP from PA all attended Church, which included Benjamin Franklin who wrote much stating that he attended various Christian Churches regularly (33); he then here made this declaration to be a REP for PA professing himself to be Christian, to believe the Bible, and believe the trinity. // Massachusetts CON: "All persons elected to state office or to the legislature must make and subscribe the following declaration, viz. I, _____, do declare that I believe the Christian RELIGION, and have firm persuassion of its truth" (32). // North Carolina CON: "No person, who shall deny the being of God, or the truth of the protestant religion, or the divine authority either of the old or new testaments, or who shall hold religious principles incompatible with the freedom and safety of the state, shall be capable of holding any office, or place of trust or profit in the civil department, within this state" (32). // Maryland CON (early, AD 1851, 1864): "That no other test or qualification ought to be required ,,,than such oath of support and fidelity to this state ,,,and a declaration of a belief in the Christian religion"; "no other test or qualification for admission to any office of trust or profit shall be required than the official oath and a declaration of belief in the Christian religion; and if the party shall profess to be a Jew the declaration shall be of his belief in a future state of rewards and punishments."; "a declaration of belief in the Christian religion, or of the existence of God, and in a future state of rewards and punishments." (27)(32). // Tennessee CON of AD 1796 defines religious test: "No person who denies the Being of God or a future state of rewards and punishments shall hold any office in the civil department of this state,,, That no religious test shall ever be required as a qualification to any office or public trust under this state" (32). // Vermont CON in AD 1777-1786 was approx. as follows: "Frame of GOV,,, And each member [of the legislature], before he takes his seat, shall make and subscribe the following declaration, vis: I do believe in one God, the Creator and Governor of the universe, the rewarder of the good and punisher of the wicked. And I do acknowledge the SCs of the old and new testament to be given by divine inspiration, and own and profess the [Christian] religion ,,,And no further or other religious test shall ever, hereafter, be required of any civil officer or magistrate in this State" (37)(38)(32). // Carolinas CON declared: "No man shall be permitted to be a freeman of Carolina, or to have any estate or habitation within it that doth not acknowledge a God, and that God is publicly and solemnly to be worshiped". // New Hampshire CON of AD 1784 & 1792, required that senators and representatives should be of the "Protestant, religion," and this provision remained until 1877. // North Carolina CON of AD 1776: "That no person who shall deny the being of God or the truth of the Protestant religion, or the divine authority either of the Old or New Testaments, or who shall hold religious principles incompatible with the freedom and safety of the State, shall be capable of holding any office or place of trust or profit in the civil department within this State." This remained until 1835, when it was amended by changing the word "Protestant" to "Christian," and as such remained until the CON of 1868. And in that Constitution, among the persons disqualified for office were "all persons who shall deny the being of Almighty God." // New Jersey CON of AD 1776 declares: "that no Protestant inhabitant of this colony shall be denied the enjoyment of any civil right merely on account of his religious principles, but that all persons professing a belief in the faith of any Protestant sect, who shall demean themselves peaceably under the government as hereby established, shall be capable of being elected into any office of profit or trust, or being a member of either branch of the legislature." // South Carolina CON of AD 1776 required that no person should be eligible for REP "unless he be of the Protestant religion". // Connecticut Fundamental Orders required the governor to take an oath to~ "further the execution of justice according to the rule of God's word; so help me God, in the name of the Lord Jesus Christ". // Mississippi CON of AD 1817 states: "no person who denies the being of God or a future state of rewards and punishments shall hold any office in the civil department of the State". // Other states have similar declarations. // Denominational requirements were not included.

---T--- <u>CON Statements in All 50 States have the intention/ purpose of positive prioritizing</u> the inclusion of God, & other Christian terms. Examples follow with added explanations: // The original words were slightly different in spelling because of older English spellings for this New York CON of AD 1783 stating~ "providing us in this State with ,,,good a CON, for the securing our,,, rights and privileges. I do not say,, has not its imperfections, like all human institutions ,,,The rights of conscience, both in faith and worship, are fully secured to every DEN of Christians. Not one DEN in the State, or in any of the States, have it in their power to oppress another. They all stand upon the same common level, in point of religious privileges ,,,Nor is this confined to Christians only. The Jews also, which is their undoubted right, have the liberty of worshipping God ,,,no man is excluded from the rights of citizenship, on account of his religious affiliation, nor ought to be." See there that DEN was the application of religion or R~Est word; then the word religion was used to include Jews, which is Judaism as an early Christian doctrine. That gives the Jews opportunity to develop their interior heart to the Messiah, and whereby to express thankfulness for the Jewish people for having brought us Christianity to some extent. +CON of AD 1846: "We the people of the State of New York, grateful to Almighty God four our freedom: in order to secure its blessings, do establish this CON". // John Rodgers states~ "The Divine Goodness Displayed in the American Revolution" (46). // New Jersey, AD 1844: "We. The people of the State of New Jersey, grateful to Almighty God for the civil and religious liberty which He hath so long permitted us to enjoy, and looking to Him for a blessing upon our endeavors to secure and transmit the same unimpaired to succeeding

155

generations, do ordain and establish this CON". // Rhode Island, AD 1842: "We, the people of the State of Rhode Island,,, grateful to Almighty God for the civil and religious liberty ,,,looking to Him ,,,do ordain and establish this CON of GOV". // North Carolina, AD 1868: "We the people of the State of North Carolina, grateful to Almighty God, the sovereign ruler of nations, for the preservation of the American Unions, and the existence of our civil, political, and religious liberties, and acknowledge our dependence upon Him for the continuance of those blessings ,,,and for the better GOV of this State, ordain and establish this CON". // Louisiana (at one point in time): "We, the people of Louisiana, grateful to Almighty God for the civil, political, economic, and religious liberties we enjoy, and desiring to protect individual rights to life, liberty, and property; afford opportunity for the fullest development of the individual; assure equality of rights; promote the health, safety, education, and welfare of the people; maintain a representative and orderly government; ensure domestic tranquility; provide for the common defense; and secure the blessings of freedom and justice to ourselves and our posterity, do ordain and establish this CON". // Alabama, AD 1819: "We, the people of the Alabama Territory, having the right of admission into the General Government, as a member of the Union, consistent with the CON and laws of the US ,,,Congress, entitled in order to establish justice, insure tranquility, provide for the common defence, promote the general welfare, and secure to ourselves and our posterity the rights of life, liberty, and property, do ordain and establish the following CON,,,". +CON of AD 1861: "We the People of the State of Alabama, ,,,the US of America, and being now by our representatives in Convention assembled, and acting in our sovereign and independent character; in order to establish justice, insure domestic tranquillity, and secure the blessings of liberty to ourselves and our posterity - invoking the favor and guidance of Almighty God - do ordain and establish the following CON,,,". +Alabama had these following rights in the AD 1800's at one point in time: "SEC. 3. No person within this state shall, upon, any pretence, be deprived of the inestimable privilege of worshipping God in the manner most agreeable to his own conscience; nor be compelled to attend any place of worship, nor shall any one ever be obliged to pay any tythes, taxes, or other rate, for the building or repairing any place of worship, or for the maintenance of any minister or ministry. SEC. 4. No human authority ought, in any case whatever, to control or interfere with the rights of conscience. SEC. 5. No person shall be hurt, molested, or restrained in his religious profession, sentiments, or persuasion, provided he does not disturb others in their religious worship. SEC. 6. The civil rights, privileges, or capacities of any citizen, shall in no way be diminished, or enlarged, on account of his religious principles". +Alabama's Oath for office at one point in time included: "so help me God." +Alabama at one point in time had the Ordinance DOC of their CON state this: "Done in Convention, at Huntsville, this second day of August, in the year of our Lord one thousand eight hundred and nineteen, and of American Independence the forty-fourth". Thus making it a Christian DOC. // Every State of the USA, in their State CON, mostly in the preamble, makes a statement that God is intended/ purposed to be included as priority of the state. Thus~ +no idolatry; +He is the reason for the state; +our Rights come from the only true God; +He is not to be excluded. If God was not to be included then He would not be included. And if He was not God, and to be applied as God, then it would not say He was God. God, by definition of the word, is referred to. And because Truth is required for our legal system then the true God must be supported. Also the words "religion" and R~Est was used, protected, and given liberty; and defined as Christian DEN. Also the word "conscience" is included; which is a Christian word.

---T--- Religion & R~Est was Intended/ Purposed as~ +] God caring; +] Christian DEN; +] Christianity supportive: // Ohio's CON of AD 1789 states: "Religion, morality, and knowledge, being essentially necessary to the good government and the happiness of mankind, schools and the means of instruction shall forever be encouraged by legislative provision" (32).

---T--- States CON's were~ +] God's Being prioritive, +] Christian, +] of the Christian Religion, +] Christianity Required by the States. Following are EX of only a few representing the many: // Indiana CON, AD 1816: "Religion, morality, and knowledge, being essentially necessary to the good GOV and the happiness of mankind, schools and the means of instruction shall forever be encouraged by legislative provision" (32). // Mississippi CON of AD 1817: "Religion, morality, and knowledge, being necessary to good GOV, the preservation of liberty and the happiness of mankind, schools and the means of education shall be forever encouraged in this state" (32). // Alabama & Illinois both had CON very similar as this in the AD 1800's: "religion, morality, and knowledge being necessary to good GOV and the happiness of mankind, schools, and the means of education shall forever be encouraged". // Nebraska CON of AD 1875: "Religion, morality, and knowledge, however, being essential to good GOV, it shall be the duty of the legislature to pass suitable laws ,,,to encourage schools and the means of instruction".

---T--- All the REP~ +] attended assemblies to Worship Christ at a Christian Church, +] were from various DEN. (the abbreviation for the DEN is included with some following); as has also been mentioned elsewhere in this Book: // For EX REP: Gunning Bedford-PB; Jacob Broom-LU; John Dickinson-QU/EP; George Read-EP; Richard Bassett-ME; James Wilson-EP/ND/D; Gouverneur Morris-EP; Thomas Mifflin-QU/LU; George Clymer-QU/EP; Thomas FitzSimmons-CT; Benjamin Franklin-ND/D; Robert Morris-EP; Jared Ingersoll-PB, (33). // Thus no more lies stating they were not supporting "religion" and not supporting Christianity and not in full support of God, and the Holy Bible. // AND the FFOG following participated in Christian organizations; as officers in GOV they had various Christian Bible ministry positions or involvement: +American Bible Society (from ABS various DOCs): John Quincy Adams, Elias Boudinot, James Brown, DeWitt Clinton, Jonas Galusha, William Gaston, Charles Goldsborough, William Gray, Felix Grundy, John Jay, William Jones, Francis Scott Key, Rufus King, Andrew Kirkpatrick, John Langdon, George Madison, John Marshall, David Lawrence Morril, Joseph Nourse, William Phillips, Charles Cotesworth Pinckney, Thomas Posey, Isaac Shelby, John Cotton Smith (168), Caleb Strong, William Tilghman, Smith Thompson, Daniel Tompkins, Robert Troup, Peter Vroom, Bushrod Washington, William Wirt, Thomas Worthington. +Chaplains or Clergymen: Abraham Baldwin, Joel Barlow, Lyman Hall, Robert Treat Paine (165), John Witherspoon. +New Jersey Bible Society (from NJBS various DOCs): Joseph Bloomfield, Elias Boudinot, John Hamilton, Andrew Kirkpatrick. +Massachusetts Society for Promoting Christian Knowledge (from this organizations various DOCs): Elias Boudinot. +Middlesex County Bible Society (from this organizations various DOCs): John Brooks. +Providence Auxiliary Bible Society (from this organizations DOCs): James Burrill, Jr. +Society for Propagating the Gospel Among the Indians and Others (from this organizations DOCs): Elias Boudinot, Francis Dana, Samuel Dexter, Benjamin Lincoln, John Lowell, William Phillips, James Sullivan. +Missionary Society of Connecticut (from this organizations various DOCs): John Davenport, John Treadwell. +Proposal to start The Christian Constitutional Society to Spread Christian GOV to Other Nations: Alexander Hamilton. +American Sunday School Union (from this organizations various DOCs): Francis Scott Key, Marquis De Lafayette, John Marshall, David Lawrence Morril, Albion Parris, Bushrod Washington, William Wirt. +Baltimore Bible Society (from this organizations various DOCs): James McHenry. +Massachusetts Bible Society (from this organizations various DOCs): William Phillips. +American Society for Educating Pious Youth for the Gospel Ministry: William Phillips (166). +Ohio Bible Society (from their DOCs): Rufus Putnam. +Philadelphia Bible Society (from their DOCs): Benjamin Rush. +Connecticut Bible Society (from their DOCs): John Cotton Smith. +Litchfield County Foreign Missionary Society (167): John Cotton Smith.

---T--- <u>RELIGION ~ False Religion (any</u> religion other than Christian to Jesus, because it is without the true God).

---T--- <u>USA & USA GOV FFOG prioritize God by~</u> +] Opposing Infidelity, +] Opposing Unlimited Support of Sinner Systems, +] Supporting Christianity Systems: // John Adams states, "The idea of infidelity cannot be treated with too much resentment or too much horror. The man who can think of it with patience is a traitor in his heart and ought to be execrated as one who adds the deepest hypocrisy to the blackest treason" (169). // Benjamin Rush states, "I anticipate nothing but suffering to the human race while the present systems of paganism, deism, and atheism prevail in the world" (97). // Alexander Hamilton states, "The attempt by the rulers of a nation to destroy all religious opinion and to pervert a whole people to atheism is a phenomenon of profligacy ,,,To establish atheism on the ruins of Christianity to deprive mankind of its best consolations and most animating hopes and to make gloomy desert of the universe" (170). // John Jay states, "I do not recollect to have had more than two conversations with atheists ,,,was at a large party, of which were several of that description [[referring to France]]. They spoke freely and contemptuously of religion ,,,one of them asked me if I believed in Christ? I answered that I did, and that I thanked God I did ,,,English physician who had resided many years at Paris ,,,he is an atheist ,,,I very concisely remarked that if there was no God there could be no moral obligations, and I did not see how society could subsist without them,,," (105a). // Samuel Adams states, "I have a thorough contempt for all men,,, who appear to be the irreclaimable enemies of religion" (171). // Gouverneur Morris states, "The most important of all lessons (from the SCs) is the denunciation of ruin to every State that rejects the precepts of religion" (172). // John Witherspoon states, "Shun, as a contagious pestilence ,,,those especially whom you perceive to be infected with the principles of infidelity or who are enemies to the power of religion" and "Whoever is an avowed enemy of God ,,,call him an enemy to his country" (154).

---T--- <u>The USA, USA GOV, & FFOG Exist to teach</u> God's Presence & Christianity, which includes the schools: // Daniel Tompkins states~ ",,,instruction for the rising generation ,,,inculcate correct principles and habits of morality and religion, and thus render them useful citizens,,," (174). // Daniel Webster~ "A profound religious feeling is to be instilled and pure morality inculcated under all circumstances. All this is comprised in education." (147a). // Noah Webster~ ",,,Christian religion is the most important and one of the first things in which all children, under a free GOV, ought to be instructed,,," (175). // Joseph Story~ "Why may not the Bible ,,,be read and taught as Divine revelation in the college ,,,its general precepts expounded, its evidences explained and its glorious principles of morality inculcated? ,,,Where can the purest principles of morality be learned so clearly or so perfectly as from the New Testament?" {US Legal case AD 1800's}. // William Samuel Johnson~ ",,,a public education, the purpose ,,,to qualify you the better to serve your Creator and your country ,,,Your first great duties ,,,those you owe to Heaven, to your Creator and Redeemer." (173). // Benjamin Rush~ "The only foundation for a useful education in a republic is to be laid in religion. Without this there can be no virtue, and without virtue there can be no liberty,,,. Without religion ,,,learning does real mischief to the morals and principles of mankind." and ",,,never invented a more effectual means of extirpating Christianity from the world than by persuading mankind that it was improper to read the Bible at schools,,," (145). Also about the Holy Bible says~ ",,,it should be read in our schools in preference to all other books,,, produce private and public happiness" (97). // Fisher Ames~ "Why should not the Bible regain the place it once held as a school book? Its morals are pure ,,,The reverence for the Sacred Book ,,,early impressed lasts long,,," (29). // Samuel Adams to the Legislature of Massachusetts~ ",,,encouraging our University, town schools, and other seminaries of education, that our children and youth ,,,may have their minds impressed with a strong sense of the duties they owe to their God" and "assured by the enacting and executing ,,,and by establishing such modes of education as tend to inculcate in the minds of youth the feelings and habits of piety, religion, and morality" (171). Also, "Education ,,,leads the youth ,,,with a profound reverence of the Deity ,,,It will excite in them a just regard to Divine revelation" (116).

---T--- <u>FFOG stated that the USA is to be~</u> +] Christ affectionate, +] Christian Religion, +] Holy Bible centered: // John Quincy Adams states, ",,,it is not so much praiseworthy to be acquainted with as it is shameful to be ignorant of it" (178). // Gouverneur Morris, ",,,holy writings not only as the most authentic and instructive in themselves, but as the clue to all other history. ,,,All of private and public life is there displayed,,," (172). // Patrick Henry, "The Bible is a book worth more than all the other books that were ever printed" (179). // Daniel Webster, ",,,the Bible ,,,indebted for right views of civil liberty. The Bible ,,,teaches man ,,,responsibility ,,,dignity, and his equality with his fellow man" (180). // John Jay, "The Bible is the best of all books, for it is the word of God and teaches us the way to be happy in this world and the next. Continue therefore to read it and to regulate your life by its precepts" (181). Also, "We know that a great proportion of mankind are ignorant of the revealed will of God ,,,by conveying the Bible to people thus circumstanced, we certainly do them a most interesting act of kindness. We thereby enable them to learn that man was originally created and placed in a state of happiness, and becoming disobedient, was subjected to the degradation and evils which he and his posterity have since experienced. The Bible will also inform them that our gracious Creator has provided for us a Redeemer, in Whom all the nations of the earth should be blessed, that this Redeemer has made atonement,,," (6). John Jay was president of the American Bible Society. // Noah Webster, "The Bible is the chief moral cause of all that is good ,,,best corrector of all that is evil in human society; the best book for regulating the temporal concerns of men" (182).

---T--- USA GOV based on Christ's Christian religion: // FFOG Noah Webster proclaims, "No truth is more evident to my mind than that the Christian religion must be the basis of any GOV intended to secure the rights and privileges of a free people" (175).

---T--- God's R-E, R~Est, 1-A, Religion - defined - proved by Patrick Henry~ stating that the USA Nation is~ +Christian, +but not denominational: // Statement Law applies. // Unit Law applies. There is a group which is the Total of Christians in the USA; This is a unit. Now within that group are various "Faiths" (which is the word Mr. Henry uses for DEN). // The word Religion(ists) used here by Mr. Henry includes True & False Religions. // Statement Law and Reference (or Context Law) proves that he is referring to the persecution that was experienced in Europe, with the GOV tyranny to limit the Church to one DEN, for which is why the pilgrims came. Here is Mr. Henry's Statement~ "It cannot be emphasized too strongly or too often that this great nation was founded, not by religionists, but by Christians, not on religions, but on the gospel of Jesus Christ! For this very reason peoples of other faiths have been afforded asylum, prosperity, and freedom of worship here" (34).

---T--- USA FFOG, Early Officials, CON authors~ were Christ Caring Christians: // George Washington~ 1st President, was a devoted Christian as evidenced by his prayers as follows: +Prayer ending with the words, "Almighty God, and most merciful Father ,,,bless my family, kindred, friends and country; be our God and Guide this day and forever, for His sake who lay down in the grave and rose again for us, Jesus Christ our Lord. Amen". +Ended Inaugural Prayer with, ",,,grant our supplication, we beseech Thee, through Jesus Christ our Lord, Amen". +Prayer~ "No people can be bound to acknowledge and adore the invisible hand which conducts the affairs of men more than the people of the US. Every step by which they have advanced to the character of an independent nation seems to have been distinguished by some token of providential agency.". // Patrick Henry says, "It cannot be emphasized too strongly or too often that this great nation was founded, not by religionists, but by Christians; not on religion, but on the gospel of Jesus Christ. For this very reason peoples of other faiths have been afforded asylum, prosperity, and freedom of worship here." (34). // John Adams (2nd President) says, "The general principles on which the fathers achieved independence were ,,,the general principles of Christianity." // Thomas Jefferson (3rd Pres.), in AD 1805 stated a national prayer, "Almighty God, Who has given us this good land for our heritage: we humbly beseech Thee that we may always prove ourselves a people mindful of Thy favor and glad to do Thy will. Bless our land with honorable ministry, sound learning, and pure manners. Save us from violence, discord, and confusion, from pride and arrogance, and from every evil way. Defend our liberties, and fashion into one united people the multitude brought hither out of many kindreds and tongues. Endow with Thy spirit of wisdom those to whom in Thy Name we entrust the authority of GOV, that there may be justice and peace at home, and that through obedience to Thy law, we may show forth Thy praise among the nations of the earth. In time of prosperity fill our hearts with thankfulness, and in the day of trouble, suffer not our trust in Thee to fail; all of which we ask through Jesus Christ our Lord, Amen.". // James Madison (4th Pres.), in AD 1787 stated, "We have staked the whole future of American civilization, not upon the power of government, far from it. We have staked the future ,,,upon the capacity of each and all of us to govern ourselves, to sustain ourselves, according to the Ten Commandments of God.". See That? That is the CC & Conscience. // John Quincy Adams (6th Pres.), on July 4, 1821 stated, "The highest glory of the American Revolution was this: it connected, in one indissoluble bond, the principles of civil GOV with the principles of Christianity. From the day of the Declaration ,,,they (the American people) were bound by the laws of God, which they all, and by the laws of The Gospel, which they nearly all, acknowledged as the rules of their conduct.". CC & Conscience. // John Jay (1st US Supreme Court Chief Justice), states, "Providence has given to our people the choice of their rulers, and it is the duty, as well as the privilege and interest, of our Christian nation, to select and prefer Christians for their rulers.". // Noah Webster, worked as author on the first dictionary of the USA, states in AD 1833, "The religion which has introduced civil liberty is the religion of Christ and His Apostles ,,,this is genuine Christianity, and to this we owe our free constitutions of government ,,,the moral principles and precepts contained in the SC ought to form the basis of all our civil constitutions and laws.".

---T--- USA & USA GOV to be Religious for Christ & Moral: // FFOG George Washington states in Farewell speech: "Of all the dispositions and habits which lead to political prosperity, religion and morality are indispensable supports. In vain would ,,,man claim ,,,patriotism, who ,,,subvert these great pillars of human happiness ,,,The mere politician ,,,ought to respect and to cherish them. A volume could not trace all their connections with private and public felicity ,,,where is the security for property, for reputation, for life, if the sense of religious obligation desert ,,,caution indulge the supposition that morality can be maintained without religion ,,,forbid us to expect that national morality can prevail, in exclusion of religious principle" (15).

---T--- USA Nation & GOV are to teach God & His Christian Religion & It's Laws to~ +] the Citizens, +] the children: // FFOG Samuel Adams writes, "A general dissolution of principles and manners will more surely overthrow the liberties of America than the whole force -- Of the common enemy. [[here is immoral or non Christian conduct law breaking within the country; worse than non-Christian enemies from without]]. When the

158

people are virtuous they cannot be subdued; but when once they lose their virtue they will be ready to surrender their liberties to the first external or internal invader ,,,[[FFOG studied the OT with the Israelites & evil Egyptian GOV; the spiritual laws]]. If virtue and knowledge diffused ,,,they will never be enslaved. This will be their great security" (134). +Also states, "Let divines and philosophers, statesmen and patriots, unite their endeavors to renovate the age, by impressing the minds of men with the importance of educating their little boys and girls, of inculcating in the minds of youth the fear and love of the Deity ,,,and, in subordination to these great principles, the love of their country ,,,In short, of leading them in the study and practice of the exalted virtues of the Christian system." (46a). +And, John Adams told Samuel, ",,,I agree" (116).

---T--- <u>The USA Required to~ +] Put the Lord Jesus God as Priority Ruler</u> over the property that has been so kindly and graciously delegated from God to the USA; so as to be a Christian nation with our "Christian Rights" (property) coming from God; as our FFoG plainly stated in the CC & DOC & lives.

---T--- <u>US GOV CON signers, FFOG Officials, Citizens, and</u> etc., All State that~ +] Christ is the God Ruler of the USA, +] the Holy Bible is the USA GOD book: // George Mason states: "My soul I resign into the hands of my Almighty Creator ,,,I willingly ,,,submit, humbly hoping ,,,through the merits of my blessed Savior, a remission of my sins.". // John Jay: "Unto Him who is the author and giver of all good, I render sincere and humble thanks ,,,especially for our redemption and salvation by His beloved Son". // John Dickinson: "Rendering thanks to my Creator for my existence ,,,for my birth in a country enlightened by the Gospel and enjoying freedom ,,,to Him I resign myself, humbly confiding in His goodness ,,,mercy through Jesus Christ for the events of eternity". // Robert Treat Paine: "I Believe the Bible to be the written word of God & to Contain in it the whole Rule of Faith & manners; I consent to the Assemblys Shorter Chatachism as being Agreeable to the Reveal'd Will of God & to contain in it the Doctrines that are According to Godliness. I have for some time had a desire to attend upon the Lords Supper and to Come to that divine Institution of a Dying Redeemer, and I trust I'm now convinced that it is my Duty Openly to profess him lest he be ashamed to own me another day; I humbly therefore desire that you would receive me into your Communion & Fellowship & I beg your Prayers for me that Grace may be carried on in my soul to Perfection, & that I may live answerable to the Profession I now make which (God Assisting) I purpose to be the main End of all my Actions." (from a letter in AD 1749).

---T--- <u>Discussion about God & His 1-A, R-E, R~Est in Congress Meetings proves</u> the Conclusion of this Chapter: // Aug. 15, 1789. "Mr. [Peter] Sylvester [of New York] had some doubts ,,,He feared it [the First Amendment] might be thought to have a tendency to abolish religion altogether ,,,Mr. [Elbridge] Gerry [of Massachusetts] said it would read better if it was that "no religious doctrine shall be established by law.",,,Mr. [James] Madison [of Virginia] said he apprehended the meaning of the words to be, that "Congress should not establish a religion, and enforce the legal observation of it by law.",,,[The State's] ,,,seemed to entertain an opinion that under the clause of the CON ,,,it enabled them [Congress] to make laws of such a nature as might ,,,establish a national religion; to prevent these effects he presumed the amendment was intended ,,,Mr. Madison thought if the word "national" was inserted before religion, it would satisfy the minds of honorable gentlemen ,,,He thought if the word "national" was introduced, it would point the amendment directly to the object it was intended to prevent" (28). See here there are 2 or 3 desires intended/ purposed about the R-E and the definition of "religion" & R~Est. // Then Governor Johnston's comments in NC ratification of the US CON meetings state: "I know but two or three States where there is the least chance of establishing any particular religion. The people of Massachusetts and Connecticut are mostly Presbyterians. In every other State, the people are divided into a great number of sects [[DEN]]. In Rhode Island, the tenets of the Baptist, I believe, prevail. In New York, they are divided very much: the most numerous are the Episcopalians and the Baptists. In New Jersey, they are as much divided as we are. In Pennsylvania, if any sect [[DEN]] prevails more than others, it is that of the Quakers. In Maryland, the Episcopalians are most numerous, though there are other sects. In Virginia, there are many sects; you all know what their religious sentiments are. So in all the Southern States they differ; as also in New Hampshire. I hope, therefore, that gentlemen will see there is no cause of fear that any one religion [[DEN]] shall be exclusively established." (138). See those thoughts, very plainly here, that the concern is regarding the establishment statement of the R~Est; that religion is defined as Christian DEN (secondary doctrines and expressions); and that all the States were Christian centered; and to prevent the US GOV from making a law for (respecting or partiality) to only 1 or 2 Christian DEN, which would offend the other citizens of other Christian DEN; and also "subdue" the States sovereignty to have a Christian DEN of some sort. // In that same meeting in NC, Henry Abbot continues: "Many wish to know what religion shall be established. [[DEN]] I believe a majority of the community are Presbyterians. I am, for my part, against any exclusive establishment; but if there were any, I would prefer the Episcopal" (138). // Joseph Story, CON Signer states, ",,,the whole power over the subject of religion is left exclusively to the State GOVs to be acted upon according to their own sense of justice and the State CONs" (52). // Thomas Jefferson states, "I consider the GOV of the US [the federal GOV] as interdicted by the CON from intermeddling with religious institutions, their doctrines, discipline, or exercises [[DEN is referred to as they are institutional, having doctrines, disciplinary training and tasks, and expressions~ "exercises"]]. This results not only from the provision that no law shall be made respecting (partiality) the establishment or free exercise of religion [the First Amendment], but from that also which reserves to the States the powers not delegated to the US [the Tenth Amendment] ,,,It must then rest with the States." (111). See & Observe here the 3 definitions that the USA GOV had of Religion & R~Est~ 1} that the USA GOV is not to make the decisions to control Christianity, 2} the States have the Sovereignty for Christianity; if the USA GOV had Rights over Religion, then they could dictate to the States to not be Christian, and this they did not want. 3} that religion & R~Est is Christian DEN; because at this time most of the States had a Christian DEN as a State sponsored Church. Thus, Mr. Jefferson here knew this, and was here defending their Right for that Religious freedom, proving again that R~Est refers to Christian DEN.

---T--- <u>God was Magnified by</u> <u>The State GOV stating they~ +]</u> were Christian, +] Protected From Religious Abuse by Establishing True Christianity for Systems, +] States Independency Intended for Supporting Christianity, including monetarily & a variety of ways ~&~ by The USA GOV stating they~ +] are of the Christian Religion, +] Not any or every religion: // Massachusetts State CON in AD 1780: "As the happiness of a people and the good order of preservation of civil GOV essentially depend upon piety, religion and morality; and as these cannot be generally diffused through a community but by the institution of the public worship of God and of public instructions in piety, religion and morality: Therefore to promote their happiness and to secure the good order and preservation of their GOV, the People of this Commonwealth have a right to invest their Legislature with power to authorize and require ,,,the several towns, parishes, precincts, and other bodies politic or religious societies, to make suitable provision at their own expense for the institution of public worship of God and for the support and maintenance of public Protestant teachers of piety, religion, and morality" (140). // New Hampshire, AD 1783: "As morality and piety rightly grounded on evangelical principles will give the best and greatest security to government and will lay in the hearts of men the strongest obligations to due subjection; and as the knowledge of these is most likely to be propagated through a society by the institution of the public worship of the Deity and of public instruction in morality and religion; therefore, to promote these important purposes, the people of this State have a right to empower, and do hereby fully empower, the legislature to authorize, from time to time, the several towns, parishes, bodies corporate, or religious societies within this State to make adequate provision at their own expense for the support and maintenance of public Protestant teachers of piety, religion, and morality" (139). // Josiah Bartlett with people of New Hampshire state, ",,,to confess before God their aggravated transgressions and to implore His pardon and forgiveness through the merits and mediation of Jesus Christ,,, that the knowledge of the Gospel of Jesus Christ may be made known to all nations, pure and undefiled religion universally prevail, and the earth ,,, with the glory of the Lord." (149). // Joseph Story stated, "If men quarrel with the ecclesiastical establishment, the civil magistrate has nothing to do with it unless their tenets and practice are such as threaten ruin or disturbance to the state." (52). See there the definition of "ecclesiastical" is "Christian church or clergy" not any religion; and the fact of establishment being used in connection to Christian DEN (ecclesiastical). // There are falsities that claim a negative against the State Christian Churches; they such were abusing the other Christian DEN; and of favoring only 1 or 2 Christian DEN. However they were developing and did not know how to keep Christ & Christianity and not express favorism; thus it is a falsity. The situation was solved by fellowshipping communion through to solutions: +Many States had CON to protect all Christian DEN: +State of NH says: "And every DEN of Christians ,,,shall be equally under the protection of law; and no subordination of any one sect or DEN to another shall ever be established by law" (139). +State of Conn. says: "And each and every society or DEN of Christians in this State shall have and enjoy the same and equal powers, rights, and privileges" (139). +NC State says: "There shall be no establishment of any one religious church or DEN in this State in preference to any other" (139). +NJ State says: "There shall be no establishment of any one religious sect ,,,in preference to another" (139). // Christian DEN existence freedom was the intention/ purpose reason for the DOI: Charles Carroll, DOI Signer, states, "To obtain religious as well as civil liberty I entered jealously into the Revolution, and observing the Christian religion divided into many sects, I founded the hope that no one would be so predominant as to become the religion of the State. That hope was thus early entertained, because all of them joined in the same cause, with few exceptions of individuals" (142).

---T--- <u>The 1-A included the Intentions/purposes</u> of Expressing to God that~ a] Oppose religious abuse of Christian DEN; where one Christian DEN controls all the others; b] Oppose having falsity Religions; c] To be A Christian Religious Nation: // Reports in Congress Meetings Notes during AD 1800's: "They (the Founders) intended, by this Amendment, to prohibit "an establishment of religion" such as the English Church presented, or any thing like it. But they had no fear or jealousy of religion itself, nor did they wish to see us an irreligious people" (144).

---T--- <u>R-E, R~Est, 1-A~ states Priority of Love to Christ be Expressed by~</u> +] that Christianity is the USA GOV Religion as the True Doctrine of God & of man; +] that Christianity was not to be managed with Indifference or Neutrality; +] that Christianity be managed with special Regards & Care Affection; +] that State Independency was free from USA GOV control; +] that the 1-A, R~Est was to avoid any Christian DEN receiving excess partiality by making law for a special DEN; +] that the Free Exercise of religion was to prevent USA GOV control of Christianity; +] that No Force is to be applied to the Will & Decisions & conscience of people; +] that Christianity of all DEN may be supported Fully for freedom in organizing & expressions: // Joseph Story, Judge of Supreme Court, with FFOG states that~ "We are not to attribute this First Amendment prohibition of a national religious establishment to an indifference to religion in general, indifference defined as which means either in support or opposition to any particular "religion", and especially to Christianity (which none could hold in more reverence, than the framers of the CON) [[see here that the USA GOV Officials were Christian with Christian purposes]] ,,,Probably, at the time of the adoption of the CON, and of the Amendment to it now under consideration, the general, if not the universal, sentiment in America was that Christianity ought to receive encouragement from the State ,,,An attempt to level all religions and to make it a matter of state policy to hold all in utter indifference would have created universal disapprobation [[disapproval]] if not universal indignation [[anger]]" (52). See here~ +not to be indifferent to; +in other words, not to be neutral; +not to be not desirous to the subject to where it is as if the subject was not valuable as needing to be included in the GOV. Then Mr Story continued saying (as paraphrased), that the USA GOV including citizen Branch were all in defense of Christ's Christianity and in opposition of any other religions establishing on USA soil. Mr. J. Story also states~ "The real object of the First Amendment was not to countenance, much less to advance, Mahometanism, or Judaism, or infidelity, by prostrating Christianity; but to exclude all rivalry among Christian sects." (52). See there that DEN was the intention/ purpose for the 1-A, , R~Est. And that Christianity was already established without question; as truth. // A Congress Judiciary Committee shared in AD 1853 & 1854 that~ "Had the people, during the Revolution, had a suspicion of any attempt to war against Christianity, that Revolution would have been strangled in its cradle. At the time of the adoption of the CON and the amendments, the universal [[note "universal" refers to all the Nation]] sentiment was that Christianity should be encouraged, not any one sect [[DEN]]. Any attempt to level and discard all religion would have been viewed with universal indignation ,,,It [[religion]] must be considered as the foundation on which the whole structure rests ,,,In this age there can be no substitute for Christianity; that in its general principles, is the great conservative element on which we must rely for the purity and permanence of free institutions. That was the religion of the founders of the republic, and they expected it to remain the religion of their descendents" (143). // Benjamin Rush states: "But the religion I mean to recommend in this place is that of the New Testament ,,,All its doctrines and precepts are calculated to promote the happiness of society and the safety and well being of civil government" (145). // FFOG John Witherspoon said, as paraphrased, that it is absurd to vote people in Office without thinking of their Faith.

---T--- The USA FFoG prioritized God by~ +] studing discernment between True & False Religions; +] Only Supported Christianity Religion: // Benjamin Rush states: "I had rather see the opinions of Confucius or Mohamed inculcated upon our youth than see the grow up wholly devoid of a system of religious principles. But the religion I mean to recommend in this place is that of the New Testament ,,,All its doctrines,,," (145). // John Adams writes to Thomas Jefferson: "The general principles on which the fathers achieved independence were ,,,the general principles of Christianity ,,,Now I will avow that I then believed, and now believe, that those general principles of Christianity are as eternal and immutable as the existence and attributes of God ,,,they would never make discoveries in contradiction to these general principles" (21). // Zephaniah Swift (first law book text writer after USA DOI) states: "Indeed moral virtue ,,,by the precepts of Christianity ,,,Christian doctrines ,,,purity of heart and holiness of life ,,,contemplate it ,,,evidence of its superiority over all the systems of pagan philosophy,,," (141). // Toleration of non-Christian religions was~ +allowed to be existent in the USA; +However not unlimited, rather limited; +they may Not set up public assembly and advertisements; +they may only internally agree with the false religion; and practice in private life at home. Such tolerance as this, in the USA, is Not because we are Not a Christian nation; Rather it is because we Are a Christian Nation; Christianity allows freedom of Will; Such tolerance is only known by such as Christianity; which is love provision of Free-Will.

---T--- God's Religion Religious Test~ for Official Candidates included the intention/ purpose to~ +] Prohibit the USA GOV to make decisions for Spiritual Conscience Beings Personal choice of Christian DEN; +] yet let the States have Freedom for the existence of Christian DEN: // North Carolina ratifying conventions for the USA CON had discussions where a remark was made about what States had dangers of false religion; for citizens to forsake Christianity is to break the CC (DOI & CON) with God. This is the statement: "It is apprehended that Jews, Mahometans, pagans, &c., may be elected to high offices ,,,but in two cases. First, if the people of America lay aside the Christian religion altogether ,,,if acquire the confidence and esteem of the people of America,,," (138). // Richard Dobbs Spaight in CON Meetings regarding the CON formation: "As to the subject of religion ,,,no power is given to the general GOV to interfere with it at all,,, No sect [[DEN]] is preferred to another. Every man has a right to worship the Supreme Being in the manner he thinks proper. No test is required. All men of equal capacity and integrity are equally eligible to offices ,,,I do not suppose an infidel, or any such person, will ever be chosen to any office unless the people themselves be of the same opinion" (138). // Justice James Iredell shares: ",,,pagans and Mahometans may be admitted into offices ,,,But it is never to be supposed that the people of America will trust their dearest rights to persons who have no religion at all, or a religion ,,,different from their own" (138). // Tennessee AD 1796 CON required a belief in "the being of God", but no "religious test" proving the intention/ purpose that God is required, but any specific Christian DEN is not required.

---T--- God's Being & Christianity is the basis of law in the USA GOV: // FFOG Rufus King says: "In our laws ,,,by the oath which they prescribe, we appeal to the Supreme Being so to deal with us hereafter as we observe the obligation of our oaths. The Pagan world ,,,are without the might influence of this principle which is proclaimed in the Christian system -- their morals were destitute ,,,which Christianity inspires" (146). // A Congress Judiciary Committee stated: "Laws will not have permanence or power without the sanction of religious sentiment -- without a firm belief that there is a Power above us that will reward our virtues and punish our vices" (143).

---T--- God's Oath Doctrine: It is Required that the USA GOV is Christian (citizens included) or Christian Supporting; and of the Christian Doctrine of Truth of God Religion: // OATH by definition: +"a solemn promise made on the basis of God". +No one but God is referred to in "oath". +No man is referred to, nor was referred to by the FFOG in establishing the Oath. +An oath recognizes God's existence, and gives (submits) themselves to His observation of whether they tell the truth or not; attends that God is present; +and that God has punishments or rewards as a result. // FFOG Daniel Webster says: "What is an oath? ,,,It is founded on a degree of consciousness that there is a Power above us that will reward our virtues or punish our vices ,,,Our system of oaths ,,,by which we hold liberty and property and all our rights, are founded on or rest on Christianity and a religious belief" (147). // FFOG Justice Joseph Story was cited in a newspaper, New York Spectator, Aug 23, 1831: ",,,rejected a witness who declared his disbelief in the existence of God. The presiding judge remarked that he ,,,not ,,,aware that ,,,a man ,,,who did not believe in the existence of God; that this belief constituted the sanction of all testimony in court of justice ,,,knew of no cause in a Christian country where a witness had been permitted to testify without such belief". // AD 1834 Tennessee legal guide requirement for Judges to hold position is this: "Judges, justices of the peace, and all other persons who are or shall be empowered to administer oaths, shall ,,,require the party to be sworn to lay his hand upon the holy evangelists of Almighty God in token of his engagement to speak the truth ,,,repeating the words, 'So help me God', shall kiss the holy gospels as a scale of confirmation to said engagement" (148). // What about Spiritual Moral Beings who had Christian doctrinal problems with oaths ?? A provision was available where they could~ +stand, +raise their hand, +solemnly appeal before God, attending that He is present, rather than to God, +attending that God has punishments & rewards, +agreeing to tell the truth. // John Witherspoon, signer of DOI, said the oath was "an appeal to God, the Searcher of hearts, for the truth,,,".

---T--- <u>False Religion ~ Parts of Catholicism</u>: // The problem with the Catholic system is that it has had parts that are seriously wrong in past history and had some parts that were wrong at that time. It was not that the FFOG wanted to hurt any Catholic. The word Catholic has a good definition. Catholics have done many good deeds. Catholicism has changed vastly, and at times. Rather there was some doctrinal disagreements on truth & Spirit which are of such seriousity that potentiality for causing evil existed. There was history where some of the Catholic church abused other Christian DEN; and the fact that the Catholic system of organization allows to much authority in one person, the Papal, without Checks, and this is dangerous; and that Catholic members dedicated themselves to Papal authorities in other countries (while residing as a citizen in a different country) which would then cause them to be disloyal to the US or a State~ as citizens. There were Catholic Beings that assisted the USA GOV in various ways, to which we are thankful. This recognizes some were true Christians in heart, and they may or may not have supported various doctrines; and had differing degrees of KN.

---T--- <u>R-E, 1-A, R~Est ~ states that Christianity is the USA Religion~ or doctrine of God & man</u>: // R-E clause does not support all religions, True & False, but only Christian. // Even false Christianity was to be refused. Sometimes Catholics were refused, because they supported various doctrines that would refuse other DEN; or because of the loyalty to the Papal system in a foreign country, and the allowance of too much power in one Papal. // Mass. State CON of AD 1780's: "We ,,,exclusion of these from offices who will not disclaim these principles of spiritual jurisdiction which Roman Catholics in some centuries have held and which are subversive of a free GOV established by the people" (140). // Other States had CON that prevented people who were dedicated to "religious principles incompatible with the freedom and safety of the State". // FFOG Joseph Story stated, "If men quarrel with the ecclesiastical establishment, the civil magistrate has nothing to do with it unless their tenets and practice are such as threaten ruin or disturbance to the state. He is bound, indeed, to protect ,,,papists [Roman Catholics] ,,,But while they acknowledge a foreign power superior to the sovereignty of the kingdom, they cannot complain if the laws of that kingdom will not treat them upon the footing of good subjects" (52). The definition of "ecclesiastical" refers not to supporting all or any religion, but rather only one religion, the Christian Religion; as the Right to be supported by the USA GOV. // FFOG Zephaniah Swift (writer of the first law textbook in America after the DOI), stated that ONLY the Christian religion is the religion of intention, full protection, and full allowance of Rights: "Christians of different DENs ought to consider that the law knows no distinction among them; that they are all established upon the broad basis of equal liberty, that they have a right to think, speak, and worship as they please, and that no sect [[DEN]] has power to injure and oppress another. When they reflect that they are equally under the protection of the law, all will revere and love the constitution, and feel interested in the support of the GOV. No DEN can pride themselves in the enjoyment of superior and exclusive powers and immunities". (141). See here that he limits the R~Est or 1-A to the Christian religion; not every, or all religions.

---T--- <u>US Soil Exists for the Promotion~ +] Not of false religion or anti-Christ; +] to Only Christ's Christianity Religion thereof; +] such is to be part of the US GOV</u>: // One may trust, or agree with a false religion, only internally in their Being. Any person should not be coerced, or forced to agree with Christ internally. However, no allowance is Righted for using US Soil for building public buildings, doing or establishing activities in GOV, public assemblies, public advertisements for false religions or infidel support. // Following is Thomas Paine's anti-Christ religion books that defended infidelity and tried to increase it in the US; and the reaction from the US GOV: +T. Paine's anti-Christian activities included wanting to bring some of his disciples to the US from Germany; and John Adams replies this: "The Christian religion is, above all the religions that ever prevailed or existed in ancient or modern times, the religion of wisdom, virtue, equity, and humanity, let the Blackguard (scoundrel, rogue) Paine say what he will"; and then said to the German disciples, "The German letter proposing to introduce into this country a company of schoolmasters, painter, poets, &c., all of them disciples of Mr. Thomas Paine, will require no answer. I had rather countenance [[allow]] the introduction of Ariel and Caliban [[two evil spirits in Shakespearean writings]] with a troop of spirits" (21). +Benjamin Franklin responds to T. Paine, "I will not enter into any discussion of your principles, though you seem to desire it ,,,the consequence of this ,,,will be a great deal of odium [[hate]] drawn upon yourself, mischief to you, and no benefit to others. He that spits in the wind, spits in his own face. Think how great a portion of mankind consists of weak ,,,ignorant men and women ,,,inexperienced, inconsiderate youth ,,,who ,,,need ,,,religion ,,,vice ,,,virtue ,,,I would advise you ,,,to burn this piece before it is seen by any other person,,," (222). +Samuel Adams to T. Paine: "When I heard you had turned your mind to a defense of infidelity, I felt myself much astonished and more grieved that you had attempted a measure so injurious to the feelings and so repugnant to the true interest of so great a part of the citizens of the US ,,,Do you think that your pen, or the pen of any other man, can unchristian-ize the mass of our citizens, or,,, hope,,, them to assist you in so bad a cause?" (116). +Benjamin Rush said T. Paine's work was "absurd and impious" (97). +Elias Boudinot, Congress REP, wrote a paper in defense of Christianity ("Age of Revelation") to oppose T. Paine's anti-Christ work. +William Paterson states of T. Paine's work, "Infatuated Americans, why renounce your country, your religion, and your God? Oh shame, where is thy blush? Is this the way to continue independent, and to render the 4th of July immortal in memory and song?"(162). +Zephaniah Swift states of T. Paine's writings, "We cannot sufficiently reprobate the beliefs of Thomas Paine in his attack on Christianity by publishing his 'Age of Reason' ,,,He has the impudence and effrontery ,,,to address to the citizens of the US ,,,which is intended to shake their faith in the religion of their fathers ,,,No language can describe the wickedness of the man who will attempt to subvert a religion which is a source of comfort and consolation of its votaries [[devout worshipers]],,," (141a). +John Witherspoon said T. Paine was ",,,an enemy of the Christian faith" (154). +John Quincy Adams said T. Paine ",,,departed from the fundamental principles that produced strong representative government" (163). +Patrick Henry opposed T. Paine (164). +There are multiple other DOCs of the FFOG that opposed T. Paine's work and defended the Christian religion. // We hope that T. Paine changed his heart status eventually.

---T--- The Feelings of the USA GOV, Congress, Citizens, Executive, DOI, CON are all for Christ & His~ +] Christianity; +] True Religion; +] Rejection of False Religion: // We are all sentimental Beings; that is Beings with feelings, sensitive Beings, able or able to feel; everything we do includes a feeling. FFOG share the following feelings~ // William Paterson feels, "Infatuated Americans, why renounce your country, your religion, and your God? Oh shame, where is thy blush? Is this the way to continue independent, and to render the 4th of July immortal in memory and song?" (162). // Patrick Henry feels, "The great pillars of all government and of social life [are] virtue, morality, and religion. This is the armor, my friend, and this alone, that renders us invincible". // Daniel Tompkins feels, "As guardians of the prosperity, liberty, and morals of the State, we are therefore bound by every injunction of patriotism and wisdom ,,,to patronize public improvements and to cherish all institutions for the diffusion of religious knowledge and for the promotion of virtue and piety" (174). // Charles Carrol feels, "Without morals a republic cannot subsist any length of time; they ,,,who are decrying the Christian religion, whose morality is so sublime and pure ,,,are undermining the solid foundation of morals, the best security for the duration of free governments" (186). // William Ellery, DOI signer, feels, "However gradual may be the growth of Christian knowledge and moral reformation, yet unless it begun, unless the seeds are planted, there can be no tree of knowledge and, of course, no fruit. The attempt to Christianize the heathen world and to produce peace on earth and goodwill towards men is humane, Christian, and sublime" (187). // John Jay (US Judge) feels, "Only one adequate plan has ever appeared in the world, and that is the Christian dispensation" (6); and "It is the duty of all wise, free, and virtuous governments to countenance and encourage virtue and religion" (174). // John Witherspoon feels, "The Christian religion is superior to every other ,,,not only an excellence in the Christian morals, but a manifest superiority in them to those which are derived from any other source" (154). // Noah Webster feels, "The Christian religion, in its purity, is the basis, or rather the source of all genuine freedom in GOV ,,,no civil GOV of a republican form can exist and be durable in which the principles of that religion have not a controlling influence" (188). // Abraham Baldwin feels, "When the minds of the people in general are viciously disposed and unprincipled, and their conduct disorderly, a free GOV will be attended with greater confusions and evils more horrid than the wild, uncultivated state of nature. It can only be happy ,,,when the public principle and opinions are properly directed and their manners regulated. This is an influence beyond the reach of laws and punishments and can be claimed only by religion and education." (192). // John Hancock feels, "Sensible of the importance of Christian piety and virtue to the order and happiness of a state, I cannot but earnestly commend to you every measure for their support and encouragement ,,,The very existence of the republics ,,,depend much upon the public institutions of religion" (193). // Oliver Ellsworth feels, "The primary objects of GOV, are peace, order, and prosperity of society ,,,To the promotion of these objects, particularly in a republican GOV, good morals are essential. Institutions for the promotion of good morals are therefore objects of legislative provision and support and among these ,,,religious institutions are eminently useful and important" (195).

---T--- The Religion of the R-E or 1-A or R~Est states there exist NO separation of USA & Christ's Christian Religion: // A US Supreme Justice and Judicial History Scholar, William Rehnquist, studied the "separation of church and state"; and provides clarity in reporting this as follows: "There is simply no historical foundation for the proposition that the Framers intended to build the 'wall of separation' ,,,in 'Everson,,, ' [[Case]] ,,,But the greatest injury of the 'wall' notion is its mischievous diversion of judges from the actual intentions of the drafters of the Bill of Rights ,,,No amount of repetition of historical errors in judicial opinions can make the errors true. The 'wall of separation between church and State' is a metaphor based on bad history ,,,It should be frankly and explicitly abandoned ,,,Our perception has been clouded not by the Constitution, but by the mists of an unnecessary metaphor." {Also see~ US Law Case - Wallace vs. Jaffree}. And Mr. Rehnquist states that the Judicial Branch has and is committing illegal actions and enactments, and that they have established an illegal law basis system on accepting past decisions to apply to the present. He continues saying: "The Court's opinion in 'Everson - while correct in bracketing Madison and Jefferson together in their exertions in their home State leading to the enactment of the Virginia Statue of Religious Liberty -- is totally incorrect in suggesting that Madison carried these views onto the floor of the US House of Representatives when he proposed the language which would ultimately become the Bill of Rights. The repetition of this error in the Court's opinion in 'Illinois ex rel. McCollum vs. Board of Education,,, and inter alia, Engel vs. Vitale,,, does not make it any sounder historically. Finally, in 'Abington School District vs. Schempp,,, the Court,,, [[claimed that]] views of Madison and Jefferson, preceded by Roger Williams, came to be incorporated ,,,in the Federal CON ,,,likewise in those of most of our States. On the basis of what evidence we have,,, is demonstrably incorrect as a matter of history. And its repetition in varying forms in succeeding opinions of the Court can give it no more authority than it possesses as a matter of fact; stare decisis [the reliance on previous precedent] may bind courts as to matters of law, but it cannot bind them as to matters of history" {US Law Case - Wallace vs. Jaffree}. ALSO Justice Rehnquist states during a trial~ "It would come as much of a shock to those who drafted the Bill of Rights, as it will to a large number of thoughtful Americans today, to learn that the CON, as construed by the majority, prohibits the Alabama Legislature from "endorsing" prayer. George Washington himself, at the request of the very Congress which passed the Bill of Rights, proclaimed a day of "public thanksgiving and prayer, to be observed by acknowledging with grateful hearts the many and signal favors of Almighty God". History must judge whether it was the Father of his Country in 1789, or a majority of the Court today, which has strayed from the meaning of the Establishment Clause".

---T--- <u>FFOG, Congress, & Executive state the USA GOV</u> & USA exists to be for God & His~ +] Christianity, +] Holy Bible, +] Religious of Such: // John Adams: "The general principles on which the fathers achieved independence were the general principles of Christianity. I will avow that I then believed, and now believe, that those general principles of Christianity are as eternal and immutable as the existence and attributes of God"~and~ "The Holy Ghost carries on the whole Christian system in this earth. Not a baptism, not a marriage, not a sacrament can be administered but by the Holy Ghost ,,,There is no authority, civil or religious ~ there can be no legitimate GOV but what is administered by this Holy Ghost. There can be no salvation without it. All without it is rebellion and perdition, or in more orthodox words damnation." (237). Also, "Without religion, this world would be something not fit to be mentioned in polite company: I mean hell." ,,,and, "The Christian religion is, above all the religions that ever prevailed or existed in ancient or modern times, the religion of wisdom, virtue, equity and humanity." ,,,and, "Suppose a nation in some distant region should take the Bible for their only law book and every member should regulate his conduct by the precepts there exhibited ,,,What a Eutopia~ what a Paradise would this region be!", and, "I have examined all religions, and the result is that the Bible is the best book in the world." (21a). // John Quincy Adams: "My hopes of a future life are all founded upon the Gospel of Christ and I cannot cavil or quibble away ,,,the whole tenor of His conduct by which He sometimes positively asserted and ,,,His disciples in asserting that He was God." (238). Also, "The hope of a Christian is inseparable from his faith. Whoever believes in the Divine inspiration of the Holy SCs must hope that the religion of Jesus shall prevail throughout the earth. Never since the foundation of the world have the prospects of mankind been more encouraging to that hope than they appear to be at the present time. And may the associated distribution of the Bible proceed and prosper till the Lord shall have made "bare His holy arm in the eyes of all the nations, and all the ends of the earth shall see the salvation of our God [Isaiah 52:10]." (239). Also, "In the chain of human events, the birthday of the nation is indissolubly linked with the birthday of the Savior. The Declaration of Independence laid the cornerstone of human GOV upon the first precepts of Christianity." (184). // Samuel Adams: "I ,,,[rely] upon the merits of Jesus Christ for a pardon of all my sins." (116). Also, "The name of the Lord (says the SC) is a strong tower; thither the righteous flee and are safe [Proverbs 18:10]. Let us secure His favor and He will lead us through the journey of this life and at length receive us to a better" (228). Also, "I conceive we cannot better express ourselves than by humbly supplicating the Supreme Ruler of the world ,,,that the confusions that are and have been among the nations may be overruled by the promoting and speedily bringing in the holy and happy period when the kingdoms of our Lord and Savior Jesus Christ may be everywhere established, and the people willingly bow to the scepter of Him who is the Prince of Peace" ,,,and requested Massachusetts to pray to God for, "peaceful and glorious reign of our Divine Redeemer may be known and enjoyed throughout the whole family of mankind." ,,,and "we may with one heart and voice humbly implore His gracious and free pardon through Jesus Christ, supplicating His Divine aid ,,,[and] above all to cause the religion of Jesus Christ, in its true spirit, to spread far and wide till the whole earth shall be filled with His glory." (171). // Gunning Bedford: "To the triune God - the Father, the Son, and the Holy Ghost - be ascribed all honor and dominion, forevermore - Amen." (229). // Elias Boudinot: "Let us enter on this important business under the idea that we are Christians on whom the eyes of the world are now turned ,,,[Let us earnestly call and beseech Him, for Christ's sake, to preside in our councils]" (189). Mr. Bedford writes a letter to his daughter: "You have been instructed from your childhood in the knowledge of your lost state by nature~ the absolute necessity of a change of heart and an entire renovation of soul to the image of Jesus Christ ~ of salvation through His meritorious righteousness only ~ and the indispensable necessity of personal holiness without which no man shall see the Lord [Hebrews 12:14]. You are well acquainted that the most perfect and consummate doctrinal knowledge is of no avail without it operates on and sincerely affects the heart, changes the practice, and totally influences the will ~ and that without the almighty power of the Spirit of God enlightening your mind, subduing your will, and continually drawing you to Himself, you can do nothing ,,,may the God of your parents (for many generations past) seal instruction to your soul and lead you to Himself through the blood of His too greatly despised Son, Who notwithstanding, is still reclaiming the world to God through that blood, not imputing to them their sins. To Him be glory forever!" (189)(228)(240). Also, "For nearly half a century have I anxiously and critically studied that invaluable treasure [the Bible]",,,and, "I still scarcely ever take it up that I do not find something new~ that I do not receive some valuable addition to my stock of knowledge or perceive some instructive fact never observed before. In short, were you to ask me to recommend the most valuable book in the world, I should fix on the Bible as the most instructive both to the wise and ignorant. Were you to ask me for one affording the most rational and pleasing entertainment to the inquiring mind, I should repeat, it is the Bible", and, "should you renew the inquiry for the best philosophy or the most interesting history, I should still urge you to look into your Bible. I would make it, in short, the Alpha and Omega of knowledge." (189)(228)(240). // Jacob Broom: Wrote his son, James, as attending Princeton University: "I flatter myself you will be what I wish, but don't be so much flatterer as to relax of your application - don't forget to be a Christian. I have said much to you on this head, and I hope an indelible impression is made." (241). // Charles Carroll: "Grateful to Almighty God for the blessings which, through Jesus Christ Our Lord, He had conferred

164

on my beloved country in her emancipation and on myself in permitting me, under circumstances of mercy, to live to the age of 89 years, and to survive the fiftieth year of independence, adopted by Congress on the 4th of July 1776, which I originally subscribed on the 2d day of August of the same year and of which I am now the last surviving signer." (242). Also, "I, Charles Carroll ,,,give and bequeath my soul to God who gave it, my body to the earth, hoping that through and by the merits, sufferings, and mediation of my only Savior and Jesus Christ, I may be admitted into the Kingdom prepared by God for those who love, fear and truly serve Him." (142). // Gabriel Duvall: "I resign my soul into the hands of the Almighty Who gave it, in humble hopes of His mercy through our Savior Jesus Christ" (Will and Testament, Sept 21, 1840). // Benjamin Franklin: "As to Jesus of Nazareth, my opinion of whom you particularly desire, I think the system of morals and His religion as He left them to us, the best the world ever saw or is likely to see" (243). // Elbridge Gerry: Gerry declared a Proclamation Day of Thanksgiving and Praise, Oct 24, 1810, for Massachusetts which stated, ",,,with one heart and voice we may prostrate ourselves at the throne of heavenly grace and present to our Great Benefactor sincere and unfeigned thanks for His infinite goodness and mercy towards us from our birth to the present moment for having above all things illuminated us by the Gospel of Jesus Christ, presenting to our view the happy prospect of a blessed immortality"; then he made 2 Proclamation Days for Fasting and Prayer, AD 1811 & 1812, stating this, "And for our unparalleled ingratitude to that Adorable Being Who has seated us in a land irradiated by the cheering beams of the Gospel of Jesus Christ,,," and "deeply impressed with a scene of our unparalleled ingratitude, let us contemplate the blessings which have flowed from the unlimited grave and favor of offended Deity, that we are still permitted to enjoy the first of Heaven's blessings: the Gospel of Jesus Christ". // Alexander Hamilton: started The Christian Constitutional Society, and listed two goals for its formation~ first, the support of the Christian religion; and second, the support of the USA CON. This organization was to have numerous clubs throughout each State which would meet regularly and work to elect to Office those who reflected the goals of the Christian Constitutional Society. // John Hancock: "Sensible of the importance of Christian piety and virtue to the order and happiness of a state, I cannot but earnestly commend to you every measure for their support and encouragement." (211). John Proclaimed many days of Prayer, fastings, thanksgiving, and humiliation to God, The Christ, during his service in government: Some here from AD 1784, 1788, 1790, 1793: "all nations may bow to the scepter of our Lord and Savior Jesus Christ and that the whole earth may be filled with his glory"; and "that the spiritual kingdom of our Lord and Savior Jesus Christ may be continually increasing until the whole earth shall be filled with His glory"; and "to cause the benign religion of our Lord and Savior Jesus Christ to be known, understood, and practiced among all the inhabitants of the earth."; and "that the kingdom of our Lord and Savior Jesus Christ may be established in peace and righteousness among all the nations of the earth"; and "that with true contrition of heart we may confess our sins, resolve to forsake them, and implore the Divine forgiveness, through the merits and mediation of Jesus Christ, our Savior,,, finally to overrule all the commotions in the world to the spreading the true religion of our Lord Jesus Christ in its purity and power among all the people of the earth". // John Hart-- (Will and Testament, attested Apr 16, 1779): "Thanks be given unto Almighty God therefore, and knowing that it is appointed for all men once to die and after that the judgment [Hebrews 9:27],,, principally, I give and recommend my soul into the hands of Almighty God who gave it and my body to the earth to be buried in a decent and Christian like manner ,,,to receive the same again at the general resurrection by the mighty power of God". // Patrick Henry: In his Will (Funeral) stated, "The religion of Christ can give them one which will make them rich indeed."; "The Bible ,,,is a book worth more than all the other books that were ever printed."; and "Righteousness alone can exalt America as a nation. Whoever thou art, remember this; and in thy sphere practice virtue thyself, and encourage it in others." (120). Also, "Being a Christian ,,,is a character which I prize far above all this world has or can boast." (164). // Samuel Huntington: A Proclamation for thanksgiving, humility, and prayer day on Mar 9, 1791, which stated, "It becomes a people publicly to acknowledge the,,, Divine Providence and,,, dependence upon the Supreme Being as their Creator and ,,,humility and ,,,mediation of our Lord and Savior Jesus Christ". // James Iredell: "merciful Father ,,,thanksgivings ,,,for the sake of Jesus Christ" (226). // John Jay: "Condescend, merciful Father! to grant as far as proper these imperfect petitions, to accept these inadequate thanksgivings, and to pardon whatever sin hath mingled in them for the sake of Jesus Christ, our blessed Lord and Savior; unto Whom, with Thee, and the blessed Spirit, ever one God, be rendered all honor and glory, now and forever" and "Mercy and grace and favor did come by Jesus Christ, and also that truth which verified the promises and predictions concerning Him and which exposed and corrected the various errors which had been imbibed respecting the Supreme Being, His attributes, laws, and dispensations" and "I recommend a general and public return of praise and thanksgiving to Him from whose goodness these blessings descend. The most effectual means of securing the continuance of our civil and religious liberties is always to remember with reverence and gratitude the source from which they flow" and "The Bible is the best of all books, for it is the word of God and teaches us the way to be happy in this world and in the next. Continue therefore to read it and to regulate your life by its precepts" (105a). Also~ "By conveying the Bible to people ,,,we certainly do them a most interesting act of kindness. We thereby enable them to learn that man was originally created and placed in a state of happiness, but, becoming disobedient, was subjected to the degradation and evils which he and his posterity have since experienced. The Bible will also inform them that our gracious Creator has provided for us a Redeemer in whom all the nations of the earth should be blessed — that this Redeemer has made atonement 'for the sins of the whole world,,, The Bible will also [encourage] them with many explicit and consoling assurances of the Divine mercy to our fallen race, and with repeated invitations to accept the offers of pardon and reconciliation" (6). // Thomas Jefferson: "I am a real Christian~ that is to say, a disciple of the doctrines of Jesus Christ" and "The doctrines of Jesus are simple, and tend all to the happiness of man."; and "The practice of morality being necessary for the well being of society, He [God] has taken care to impress its

165

precepts so indelibly on our hearts that they shall not be effaced by the subtleties of our brain. We all agree in the obligation of the moral principles of Jesus and nowhere will they be found delivered in greater purity than in His discourses" (30). Also, "I am a Christian in the only sense in which He wished anyone to be: sincerely attached to His doctrines in preference to all others." (111). // William Samuel Johnson: "I am ,,,endeavoring ,,,to attend to my own duty only as a Christian ,,,let us take care that our Christianity, though put to the test ,,,be not shaken, and that our love for things really good wax not cold." (173). // James Kent: "My children, I wish to talk to you. During my early and middle life I was, perhaps, rather skeptical with regard to some of the truths of Christianity. Not that I did not have the utmost respect for religion and always read my Bible, but the doctrine of the atonement was one I never could understand, and I felt inclined to consider as impossible to be received in the way Divines taught it. I believe I was rather inclined to Unitarianism; but of late years my views have altered. I believe in the doctrines of the prayer books as I understand them, and hope to be saved through the merits of Jesus Christ ,,,My object in telling you this is that if anything happens to me, you might know, and perhaps it would console you to remember, that on this point my mind is clear: I rest my hopes of salvation on the Lord Jesus Christ" (227). // Francis Scott Key: "May I always hear that you are following the guidance of that blessed Spirit that will lead you into all truth, leaning on that Almighty arm that has been extended to deliver you, trusting only in the only Savior, and going on in your way to Him rejoicing." (233). // James Madison: "A watchful eye must be kept on ourselves lest, while we are building ideal monuments of renown and bliss here, we neglect to have our names enrolled in the Annals of Heaven." (201). Also, "I have sometimes thought there could not be a stronger testimony in favor of religion or against temporal enjoyments, even the most rational and manly, than for men who occupy the most honorable and gainful departments and [who] are rising in reputation and wealth, publicly to declare their satisfactoriness by becoming fervent advocates in the cause of Christ; and I wish you may give in your evidence in this way." (77). // James Manning: "I rejoice that the religion of Jesus prevails in your parts; I can tell you the same agreeable news from this quarter. Yesterday I returned from Piscataway in East Jersey, where was held a Baptist annual meeting (I think the largest I ever saw) but much more remarkable still for the Divine influences which God was pleased to grant. Fifteen were baptized; a number during the three days professed to experience a change of heart. Christians were remarkably quickened; multitudes appeared" (228). // Henry Marchant: taught his daughter, "And may God grant that His grace may really affect your heart with suitable impressions of His goodness. Remember that God made you, that God keeps you alive and preserves you from all harm, and gives you all the powers and the capacity whereby you are able to read of Him and of Jesus Christ, your Savior and Redeemer, and to do every other needful business of life. And while you look around you and see the great privileges and advantages you have above what other children have (of learning to read and write, of being taught the meaning of the great truths of the Bible), you must remember not to be proud on that account but to bless God and be thankful and endeavor in your turn to assist others with the knowledge you may gain" (228). // George Mason: George has stated many other similar remarks as this one in his (funeral) Will: "My soul I resign into the hands of my Almighty Creator, Whose tender mercies are all over His works,,, humbly hoping from His unbounded mercy and benevolence, through the merits of my blessed Savior, a remission of my sins.". // James McHenry: "Public utility pleads most forcibly for the general distribution of the Holy SCs. Without the Bible, in vain do we increase penal laws and draw entrenchments around our institutions" and "Bibles are strong protections. Where they abound, men cannot pursue wicked courses and at the same time enjoy quiet conscience." (127). // Thomas McKean: As a Judge he concluded a Mr. Roberts as guilty for treason with a sentence of death, and encouraged him the following: "You will probably have but a short time to live. Before you launch into eternity, it behooves you to improve the time that may be allowed you in this world: it behooves you most seriously to reflect upon your past conduct; to repent of your evil deeds; to be incessant in prayers to the great and merciful God to forgive your manifold transgressions and sins; to teach you to rely upon the merit and passion of a dear Redeemer, and thereby to avoid those regions of sorrow~ those doleful shades where peace and rest can never dwell, where even hope cannot enter. It behooves you to seek the [fellowship], advice, and prayers of pious and good men; to be [persistent] at the Throne of Grace, and to learn the way that leadeth to happiness. May you, reflecting upon these things, and pursuing the will of the great Father of light and life, be received into (the) company and society of angels and archangels and the spirits of just men made perfect; and may you be qualified to enter into the joys of Heaven~ joys unspeakable and full of glory!" (A Pennsylvania court case, Republica vs. John Roberts). // Gouverneur Morris: "Your good morals in the army give me sincere pleasure as it hath long been my fixed opinion that virtue and religion are the great sources of human happiness. More especially is it necessary in your profession firmly to rely upon the God of Battles for His guardianship and protection in the dreadful hour of trial. But of all these things you will and I hope in the merciful Lord." (228). Also, "There must be religion. When that ligament is torn, society is disjointed and its members perish,,, [The most important of all lessons is the denunciation of ruin to every state that rejects the precepts of religion]" (172). // Jedidiah Morse: "To the kindly influence of Christianity we owe that degree of civil freedom and political and social happiness which mankind now enjoys. All efforts made to destroy the foundations of our Holy Religion ultimately tend to the subversion also of our political freedom and happiness. In proportion as the genuine effects of Christianity are diminished in any nation ,,,in the same proportion will the people of that nation recede from the blessings of genuine freedom,,, Whenever the pillars of Christianity shall be overthrown, our present republican forms of GOV~ and all the blessings which flow from them~ must fall with them." (209). // John Morton: "With an awful reverence to the Great Almighty God, Creator of all mankind, being sick and weak in body but of sound mind and memory, thanks be given to Almighty God for the same. (Will and testament, attested 1/ 28, 1777). // James Otis: "Has (government) any solid foundation? Any chief cornerstone? ,,,I think it has an everlasting foundation in the unchangeable will of God ,,,The sum of my argument is that civil government is of God" (197). // Robert Treat Paine: "I am constrained to express my adoration of the Supreme Being, the Author of my existence, in full belief of His Providential goodness and His forgiving mercy revealed to the world through Jesus Christ, through whom I hope for never ending happiness in a future state" (Will & Testament of Robert Treat Paine, May 11, 1814). Also, "I desire to bless and praise the name of God most high for appointing me my birth in a land of Gospel Light where the glorious tidings of a Savior and of pardon and salvation through Him have been continually sounding in mine ears ,,,I believe the Bible to be the written word of God and to contain in it the whole rule of faith and manners" (165). // William Paterson: Attended Christian schools in youth; and said, "Religion and morality ,,,are necessary to good GOV, good order, and good laws, for 'when the righteous are in authority, the people rejoice'" (203)(215). Also proclaimed Christian prayer days and used SC in court. // Timothy Pickering: "Pardon, we beseech Thee, all our offences of omission and commission; and grant that in all our thoughts, words, and actions, we may conform to Thy known will manifested in our consciences and in the revelations of Jesus Christ, our Savior" (230). Also, "We do not grieve as those who have no,,, resurrection to a life immortal. Here the believers in Christianity manifest their superior advantages, for life and immortality were brought to light by the gospel of Jesus Christ [II Timothy 1:10]. Prior to that revelation even the wisest and best of mankind were involved in doubt and they hoped, rather than believed, that the soul was immortal" (231). // John Randolph of Roanoke: "I have thrown myself, reeking with sin, on the mercy of God, through Jesus Christ His blessed Son and our (yes, my friend, our) precious Redeemer; and I have assurances as strong as that I now owe nothing to your rank that the debt is paid and now I love God~ and with reason. I once hated him~ and with reason, too, for I knew not Christ. The only cause why I should love God is His goodness and mercy to me through Christ" (232). Also, "I am at last reconciled to my God and have assurance of His pardon through faith in Christ, against which the very gates of hell cannot prevail. Fear hath been driven out by perfect love,,," and "I have looked to the Lord Jesus Christ, and hope I have obtained pardon" and "I still cling to the cross of my Redeemer, and with God's aid firmly resolve to lead a life less unworthy of one who calls himself the humble follower of Jesus Christ" (233). // Benjamin Rush: "The greatest discoveries in science have been made by Christian philosophers ,,,there is the most knowledge in those countries where there is the most Christianity."; and "The only means of establishing and perpetuating our republican forms of GOV is the universal education of our youth in the principles of Christianity by means of the Bible" (145). Also, "The Gospel of Jesus Christ prescribes the wisest rules for just conduct in every situation of life. Happy they who are enabled to obey them in all situations! ,,,Nothing but His blood will wash away my sins [Acts 22:16] ,,,Come, Lord Jesus! Come quickly! [Revelation 22:20]" (244). Also, "I do not believe that the CON was the offspring of inspiration, but I am as satisfied that it is as much the work of a Divine Providence as any of the miracles recorded in the Old and New Testament."; and "By renouncing the Bible, philosophers swing from their moorings upon all moral subjects ,,,It is the only correct map of the human heart that ever has been published."; and "The great enemy of the salvation of man, in my opinion, never invented a more effective means of limiting Christianity from the world than by persuading mankind that it was improper to read the Bible at schools."; and "Christianity is the only true and perfect religion ,,,in proportion as mankind adopt its principles and obey its precepts, they will be wise and happy."; and "The Bible contains more knowledge necessary to man in his present state than any other book in the world."; and "The Bible ,,,should be read ,,,in preference to all other books because it contains the greatest,,, knowledge which is calculated to produce private and public happiness." (97). // Roger Sherman: Stated~ "I believe that there is one only living and true God, existing in three persons, the Father, the Son, and the Holy Ghost ,,,That the SCs of the Old and New Testaments are a revelation from God, and a complete rule to direct us how we may glorify and enjoy Him ,,,That He made man at first perfectly holy; that the first man sinned, and as he was the public head of his posterity, they all became sinners in consequence of his first transgression ,,,the pains of hell forever ,,,the offer of pardon and salvation to all mankind ,,,who are willing to accept the Gospel offer ,,,a visible church to be a congregation of those who make a credible profession of their faith in Christ, and obedience to Him,,," (81). It was a practice of Roger to purchase a Bible after every congress session and give it to his children (81). // Richard Stockton: (Will of Richard Stockton, May 20, 1780), "As my children will have frequent occasion of perusing this instrument, and may probably be particularly impressed with the last words of their father, I think it proper here not only to subscribe to the entire belief of the great and leading doctrines of the Christian religion, such as the being of God; the universal defection and depravity of human nature; the Divinity of the person and the completeness of the redemption purchased by the blessed Savior; the necessity of the operations of the Divine Spirit; of Divine faith accompanied with an habitual virtuous life; and the universality of the Divine Providence: but also, in the bowels of a father's affection, to exhort and charge [my children] that the fear of God is the beginning of wisdom, that the way of life held up in the Christian system is calculated for the most complete happiness that can be enjoyed in this mortal state, [and] that all occasions of vice and immorality is injurious either immediately or consequentially~ even in this life". // Thomas Stone: "Shun all giddy, loose, and wicked company; they will corrupt and lead you into vice and bring you to ruin. Seek the company of sober, virtuous and good people,,, which will lead [you] to solid happiness" (218). // Joseph Story: "Why may not the Bible ,,,be read and taught as Divine revelation in the college ,,,its general precepts expounded, its evidences explained and its glorious principles of morality inculcated? ,,,Where can the purest principles of morality be learned so clearly or so perfectly as from the New Testament?" (US Legal case AD 1800's). // Caleb Strong: Proclamation of Fasting, prayer, and humiliation on Feb 13, 1813 to Massachusetts, that ",,,all nations may know and be obedient to that grace and truth which came by Jesus Christ". // Zephaniah Swift: "Jesus Christ has in the clearest manner inculcated those duties which are productive of the highest moral felicity and consistent with all the innocent enjoyments, to which we are impelled by the dictates of nature. Religion, when fairly considered in its genuine simplicity and uncorrupted state, is the source of endless rapture and delight" (141). // Charles Thomson: "I am a

Christian. I believe only in the SCs, and in Jesus Christ my Savior". // Jonathan Trumbull: "The examples of holy men teach us that we should seek Him with fasting and prayer, with penitent confession of our sins, and hope in His mercy through Jesus Christ the Great Redeemer" (234). Also, "Principally and first of all, I bequeath my soul to God the Creator and giver thereof, and my body to the earth to be buried in a decent Christian burial, in firm belief that I shall receive the same again at the general resurrection through the power of Almighty God, and hope of eternal life and happiness through the merits of my dear Redeemer Jesus Christ" (235). Also requested Connecticut State to pray that~ "God would graciously pour out His Spirit upon us and make the blessed Gospel in His hand effectual to a thorough reformation and general revival of the holy and peaceful religion of Jesus Christ" (236). // George Washington: "You do well to wish to learn ,,,above all, the religion of Jesus Christ. These will make you a greater and happier people than you are." (12). // Daniel Webster: "The Christian religion~ its general principles~ must ever be regarded among us as the foundation of civil society." (147). // Noah Webster: "The religion which has introduced civil liberty is the religion of Christ and His apostles ,,,This is genuine Christianity and to this we owe our free constitutions of GOV."; and "Our citizens should early understand that the genuine source of correct republican principles is the Bible, particularly the New Testament, or the Christian religion". (176). Also, "The Bible is the chief moral cause of all that is good and the best corrector of all that is evil in human society~ the best book for regulating the temporal concerns of men." (175). // John Witherspoon: "There is no salvation in any other than in Jesus Christ of Nazareth." and "It is very evident that both the prophets in the Old Testament and the apostles in the New are at great pains to give us a view of the glory and dignity of the person of Christ. With what magnificent titles is He adorned! What glorious attributes are ascribed to him! ,,,that He is truly and properly God~ God over all, blessed forever!" // Oliver Wolcott: "Through various scenes of life, God has sustained me ,,,may my heart with gratitude acknowledge His goodness; and may my desires be to Him and to the remembrance of His name ,,,May we then turn our eyes to the bright objects above, and may God give us strength to travel the upward road. May the Divine Redeemer conduct us to that seat of bliss which He himself has prepared for His friends ,,,our pleasures never be dampened by the fear of future separation ,,,God's Providence ,,,May a happiness be granted to those I most tenderly love, which shall continue and increase through an endless existence. Your cares and burdens must be many and great, but put your trust in that God Who has hitherto supported you and me; He will not fail to take care of those who put their trust in Him ,,,It is most evident that this land is under the protection of the Almighty, and that we shall be saved not by our wisdom nor by our might, but by the Lord of Host Who is wonderful in counsel and Almighty in all His operations." (228).

---T--- Congress (FFoG) states the Holy Spirit & Christ with Their~ +] Christianity Religion, +] Holy Bible, +] are the Religion & Law Making Basis of GOV: // Noah Webster states, "The moral principle and precepts contained in the SCs ought to form the basis of all our civil constitutions and laws" and "All the miseries and evils which men suffer from vice, crime, ambition, injustice, oppression, slavery and war, proceed from their despising or neglecting the precepts contained in the Bible" (176). // Joseph Story, "One of the beautiful boasts of our municipal jurisprudence is that Christianity is a part of the Common Law. There never has been a period in which the Common Law did not recognize Christianity as lying at its foundations. I verily believe Christianity necessary to the support of civil society" (183). // Daniel Webster states, "The Christian religion~ its general principles~ must ever be regarded among us as the foundation of civil society" and "We seek to prevent in some measure the extension of the penal code by inspiring a salutary and conservative principle of virtue and of knowledge in an early age ,,,By general instruction we seek, as far as possible, to purify the whole moral atmosphere ,,,and to turn the strong current of feeling and opinion , as well as the censures of the law and the denunciations of religion, against immorality and crime" (147). // John Adams, "The study and practice of law,,, does not dissolve the obligations of morality and religion" (21). // Benjamin Rush, "I have always considered Christianity as the strong found of republicanism ,,,It is only necessary for republicanism to ally itself to the Christian religion to overturn all the corrupted political and religious institutions in the world" (97). // DeWitt Clinton, "The ethics, doctrines, and examples furnished by Christianity exhibit the best models for the laws." and "The sanctions of the Divine law ,,,cover the whole ,,,human action ,,,The laws which regulate our conduct are the laws of man and the laws of God" (177). // John Adams, "The moment the idea is admitted into society that property is not as sacred as the laws of God, and that there is not a force of law and public justice to protect it, anarchy and tyranny commence. If 'Thou shalt not covet,' and 'Thou shalt not steal," were not commandments of Heaven, they must be made inviolable precepts in every society, before it can be civilized or made free" (190). // John Quincy Adams, "The law given from Sinai was a civil and municipal as well as a moral and religious code ,,,laws essential to the existence of men in society and most of which have been enacted by every nation which every professed any code of laws. Vain indeed would be the search among the writings of profane antiquity ,,,to find so broad, so complete and so solid a basis for morality as this Decalogue (Ten Commandments) lays down." and "Human legislators can undertake only to prescribe the actions of men,; they acknowledge their inability to govern and direct the sentiments of the heart ,,,It is one of the greatest marks of Divine favor bestowed upon the children of Israel that the legislator (God) gave them rules not only of action, but for the government of the heart" (175). // William Findley, RW Soldier & US Congressman, states, "It pleased God to deliver, on Mount Sinai, a compendium of this holy law and to write it with His own hand on durable tables of stone. This law, which is commonly called the Ten Commandments or Decalogue ,,,was incorporated in the judicial law" (191). // Noah Webster states, "The opinion that human reason left without the constant control of Divine laws and commands will ,,,give duration to a popular government is as chimerical as the most extravagant of ideas that enter the head of a maniac ,,,Where will you find any code of laws among civilized men in which the commands and prohibitions are not founded on Christian principles? I need not specify the prohibition of murder, robbery, theft, and trespass" (175). // John Witherspoon, "The

Ten Commandments „,are the sum of the moral law" and "To PROMOTE true religion is the best and most effectual way of making a virtuous and regular people. Love to God and love to man is the substance of religion; when these prevail, civil laws will have little to do „,The Magistrate (or ruling part of any society) ought to encourage piety „,and make it„, object of public esteem." and "Those who are vested with civil authority ought „,to promote religion and good morals among all under their government" (154). Also, "The first point of justice „,consists in piety; nothing certainly being so great a debt upon us as to render to the Creator and Preserver those acknowledges which are due to Him,„," (171).

---T--- <u>FFOG Congress & Executive Officials state the USA GOV is~</u> +] Desirous of Judaism, with positive care affection, +] Religious, +] of Christ's Christianity, +] opposes other religions as false: // Benjamin Rush states, "I have always considered Christianity as the strong found of republicanism „,It is only necessary for republicanism to ally itself to the Christian religion to overturn all the corrupted political and religious institutions in the world" (97). // George Washington accepted Judaism because it is actually Christianity in earlier time periods, except those who support it and reject Christ, are not totally accepted; he writes to a Hebrew congregation of Savannah: "May the same wonderworking Deity, who long since delivered the Hebrews from their Egyptian oppressors and planted them in the promised land, whose Providential agency has lately been conspicuous in establishing the US as an independent nation, still continue to water them with the dews of Heaven and to make the inhabitants of every DEN participated in the temporal and spiritual blessings of that people whose God is Jehovah" (12). // „,And John Adams shares the same, "I will insist that the Hebrews have done more to civilize men than any nation „,They preserve and propagate to all mankind the doctrine of a supreme, intelligent, wise, almighty Sovereign of the Universe „,the great principle of all morality, and consequently of all civilization" (21). // John Witherspoon, "To the Jews were first committed the care of the Sacred Writings „,Yet was the providence of God particular manifest in their preservation and purity. The Jews were so faithful in their important trust." (154b). // Elias Boudinot served as President of the "Society for Ameliorating the State of the Jews" to assist persecuted Jews in coming to the USA for asylum and to have invitation to their Messiah Christ. (185).

---T--- <u>Congress & GOV Officials state USA GOV is for CHRIST and~</u> +] opposed to false religion which is anti-Christian, AND +] not all religions are to be supported: // John Witherspoon states, "Christ Jesus — the promise of old made unto the fathers, the hope of Israel [Acts 28:20], the light of the world [John 8:12], and the end of the law for righteousness to every one that believeth [Romans 10:4] — is the only Savior of sinners, in opposition to all false religions and every uninstituted rite; as He Himself says (John 14:6): 'I am the way, and the truth, and the life: no man cometh unto the Father but by Me.'" (137).

---T--- <u>FFOG state USA GOV is to be CHRIST CENTERED, CHRISTIAN, & RELIGIOUS:</u> // DeWitt Clinton states, "The sanctions of religion compose the foundations of good GOV" (177). // Benjamin Rush proclaims the work of and for Christ, "I do not believe that the CON was the offspring of inspiration, but I am as satisfied that it is as much the work of a Divine Providence as any of the miracles recorded in the Old and New Testament" (97). // John Witherspoon states, "God grant that in America true religion and civil liberty may be inseparable and that the unjust attempts to destroy the one may in the issue, tend to the support and establishment of both" (154a). Note he says~ +"true religion" is different from false religion; +religion and GOV are inseparable in there relation; and surely not in an abusive relation. The CC had the same intentions/purposes. // Jedidiah Morse (Geography Teacher and writer, AD 1780's), "To the kindly influence of Christianity we owe that degree of civil freedom, and political and social happiness „,In proportion as the genuine effects of Christianity are diminished in any nation „,in the same proportion will the people of that nation recede from the blessings „,All efforts to destroy the foundation of our holy religion tend to the subversion also of our political freedom „,Whenever the pillars of Christianity „,overthrown, our present republican forms of GOV „,must fall" (209). // A Musical song was a national favorite many years before it was enacted by Congress in AD 1931 as a National Anthem. In it are the words, "And this be our motto, 'In God is our trust'". // Our Pledge of Allegiance to the Flag states, "one Nation under God, indivisible, with liberty and justice for all". // James Otis states, "Has (government) any solid foundation? Any chief cornerstone? „,I think it has an everlasting foundation in the unchangeable will of God „,The sum of my argument is that civil GOV is of God" (197). // John Hart states, "We will look for the permanency and stability of our new GOV to Him who bringeth princes to nothing and teacheth senators wisdom" (196). Also, "Thanks be given unto Almighty God therefore, and knowing that it is appointed for all men once to die and after that the judgment [Hebrews 9:27] „,principally, I give and recommend my soul into the hands of Almighty God who gave it and my body to the earth to be buried in a decent and Christian like manner „,to receive the same again at the general resurrection by the mighty power of God." (from his Will, Apr. 16, 1779). // James Madison states, "No people ought to feel greater obligations to celebrate the goodness of the Great Disposer of Events and of the Destiny of Nations than the people of the US „,And to the same Divine Author of every good and perfect gift we are indebted for all those privileges and advantages, religious as well as civil, which enjoyed in this favored land" (198). // During Samuel Adams time, the FFOG made this statement: "The Supreme Ruler of the Universe, having been pleased in the course of His providence to establish the independence of the US of America „,we ought to be led by religious feelings of gratitude and to walk before Him in all humility according to His most holy law „,implore the forgiveness of sins through the merits of Jesus Christ and humbly supplicate our heavenly Father" (199). // Noah Webster's dictionary is full of quotes of Bible vss for the American Language; one of the first, if not the first, dictionaries for Independent America.

---T--- <u>US GOV is CHRISTIAN & Religious to God as stated by FFOG:</u> // Jonathon Trumbull, "And I do hereby call upon the people „,to offer to our Almighty and all-gracious God, through our Great Mediator, our sincere and solemn prayers for his Divine assistance and the influences of His Holy

Spirit" (200). // George Clinton, 'We live in a republic highly favored of heaven, and under a social compact ,,,all to inspire us with becoming gratitude to the great ruler of nations, on whose favor all our happiness depends" (174).

---T--- <u>Christian Prayer to God has Continually Been</u> Part of the USA: // US Justice Antonin Scalia spoke for Justices William Rehnquist, Byron White, Clarence Thomas, this fact: "From our Nation's origin, prayer has been a prominent part of governmental ceremonies and proclamations. The DOI, the DOC marking our birth,,, "appealed to the Supreme Judge of the world for the rectitude ,,,intentions" and avowed "a firm reliance on the protection of divine Providence". In his first inaugural address, after swearing his oath of office on a Bible, George Washington deliberately made a prayer a part of his first official act as President ,,,Such applications have been a characteristic feature of inaugural addresses ever since. Thomas Jefferson, for EX, prayed in his first inaugural address ,,,In his second inaugural address ,,,acknowledged his need for divine guidance and invited his audience to join his prayer ,,,Similarly, James Madison, in his first inaugural address, placed his confidence "in the guardianship and guidance of that Almighty Being ,,,with fervent supplications and best hopes for the future" ,,,The other two branches of the Federal GOV also have a long-established practice of prayer at public events,,," {US Legal case - Lee vs. Weisman}.

---T--- <u>US GOV is to be Christian for Christ Caring Religion as stated by FFOG:</u> // John Adams states, ",,,religion and morality alone ,,,establish the principles ,,,which freedom ,,,Religion and virtue are the only foundations ,,,of republicanism and of all free governments" (21). Also, "Such compliances (compromises) ,,,of my honor, my conscience, my friends, my country, my God, as the SCs inform us must be punished with nothing less than hell-fire, eternal torment; and this is so unequal a price to pay for the honors and emoluments (profits from government) ,,,that I cannot prevail upon myself to think of it (compromise). The duration of future punishment terrifies me." (21a). // History of US per (34): "It cannot be emphasized too strongly or too often that this ,,,nation was founded, not by religionists, but by Christians; not on religions, but on the gospel of Jesus Christ!". // John Quincy Adams, ",,,the foundation of all morality ,,,is ,,,existence of God ,,,immortality of the ,,,soul ,,,future state of rewards ,,,and punishments ,,,disbelieve either of these ,,,that man will have no conscience ,,,have no other law than that of the tiger or shark; the laws of man may bind him in chains or may put him to death, but ,,,never make him wise, virtuous, or happy" (178). // Samuel Adams, "Religion and good morals are the only solid foundations of public liberty and happiness. Neither the wisest CON nor the wisest laws will secure the liberty and happiness of a people ,,,corrupt" (171). // Fisher Ames, "GOV ,,,is a firm compact sanctified from violation of,,, morality, and religion" (29)(211). // Abraham Baldwin, "A free GOV ,,,can only be happy when the public principles ,,,are ,,,directed ,,,by religion,,," (74). // Nathanael Greene, "Truth ,,,and religion are the only foundation to build human happiness upon." (212). // John Hancock, ",,,importance of Christian piety and virtue to the order and happiness of a state,,," (193). // George Mason, "We are now ,,,among the nations,,, whether our Independence shall prove a blessing or a curse ,,,depend upon ,,,wisdom or folly, virtue or wickedness,,,". // Richard Henry Lee, ",,,true that a popular government cannot flourish without ,,,virtue,,," (213). // Gouverneur Morris, ",,,religion is the only solid base of morals and that morals are the only possibly support of free governments." (11a)(214). // William Paterson, "Religion and morality ,,,are necessary to good GOV, good order, and good laws, for "when the righteous are in authority, the people rejoice"" (203)(215). // David Ramsay, "Remember that there can be no political happiness without liberty ,,,no liberty without morality ,,,no morality without religion." (216). // Benjamin Rush, ",,,governments ,,,without ,,,religion and social worship, men become savages" (145). // Jeremiah Smith, "Cherish and promote ,,,virtue and religion. They are indispensable to ,,,free GOV ,,,Let it never be forgotten,,," (217). // Joseph Story, ",,,it is impossible for those who believe in the truth of Christianity as a divine revelation, to doubt that it is the especial duty of GOV to foster and encourage it among all the citizens and subjects ,,,problem ,,,free GOV can be permanent where the public worship of God and the support of religion constitute no part of the policy or duty of the state in any assignable shape" (52). // Thomas Stone, "Shun all giddy, loose and wicked company; they will corrupt and lead you into vice and bring you to ruin." (218). // James Wilson, ",,,religion and law are twin sisters,,," (206). // Daniel Webster, ",,,religious sentiment ,,,inspires respect for law and order, gives strength to the whole social fabric. Moral habits ,,,cannot ,,,be ,,,on any other foundation than religious principle nor any GOV ,,,Whatever makes men Christian, makes them good citizens." (147a).

---T--- <u>GOD's RELIGION & RELIGIOUS TEST --</u> Christianity for Officials; as stated by FFOG: // John Adams states, "We electors have an important constitutional power placed in our hands ,,,a check upon two branches of the legislature ,,,necessary to every subject (citizen) ,,,be in some degree a statesman and to examine and judge ,,,political principles and measures ,,,Let us examine them with a sober,,, Christian spirit." (169a). // Noah Webster, "In selecting men for office ,,,Regard not the particular sect [[DEN]] of the candidate ,,,But the SCs teach a different doctrine. They direct that rulers should be men "who rule in the fear of God, able men, such as fear God, men of truth, hating covetousness" {Exodus 18:21} ,,,It is to the neglect of this rule ,,,in our citizens ,,,which disgrace a republican GOV". This was stated about the Subject of the Religious Test & Oaths. // Chandler Robbins said, ",,,rulers be "just men -- fearers of God -- haters of covetousness" ,,,they "shake their hands from holding bribes". // Samuel Adams, Matthias Burnet, Gouverneur Morris, John Witherspoon, Daniel Webster, Noah Webster, George Washington, and others shared the same truths. // John Jay, ",,,it is the duty, as well as the privilege and interest of our Christian nation, to select and prefer Christians for their rulers" (105a). // John Witherspoon, "It is in the man of piety and inward principle ,,,we may find ,,,uncorrupted patriot ,,,useful citizen ,,,invincible soldier. -- God grant that in America religion and civil ,,,inseparable" (154a). // Roger Sherman, ",,,all civil rights and the right to hold office were extended to persons of any Christian DEN." (39).

---T--- <u>Religion & R~Est & 1-A is Christ's Christian DEN:</u> // Roger Sherman stated, ",,,all civil rights and the right to hold office were extended to persons of any Christian DEN." (39).

---T--- <u>USA GOV is to be Religious for God:</u> // In AD 1892, a US Supreme Court stated, "happiness of a people and the good order and preservation of civil GOV ,,,depend upon piety, religion and morality"; and "Religion, morality, and knowledge are necessary to good GOV".

---T--- <u>USA GOV is Christ based with His Holy Bible as It's Book:</u> // FFOG quoted the Holy Bible more than any other source of knowledge that they referenced for GOV basis.

---T--- <u>Religion & GOV Need to Relate as Part of GOD's CC:</u> // FFOG James Madison shared many things on religion, and all of his statements must be studied, not some. Because by reading only a few small statements will make disclarity. // The danger of the relationship of GOV & Religion is where falsities are applied as a way to prevent abuse to each other from each other. Falsities Do Not help.

---T--- <u>R-E , 1-A , R~Est Includes Supports to Christ & His Christianity Religion by Some</u> Connecting Statements: // Freedom of Press. // Petition the GOV. // Such are Round-table discussions and "Open-door" policies. // Truth~ "We hold these truths". This is contrary to pluralism.   Contrary doctrines cannot be of God; that is contrary gods. They cannot all be the same God or God Himself.   One must be right and the others wrong; or all wrong; or all right.

---T--- <u>The 1-A, R-E, R~Est is 2 Parts of the Same Subject~ God:</u> // The doctrine of God and of man is one part of it; one truth of it. And the other part is about another truth of it; Christian DEN.

---T--- <u>Study about God can include making a list of the desires Intended/ purposed</u> by the FFoG; then put those on one side of a piece of paper; then take the words from the 1-A, R-E or R~Est and put it on the other side of the paper. Then study it to learn more of what the definition of the amendment is: // One problem, actually not a problem but help, is that they were knowledgeable of Principle Law, to some extent. And they presumed that other Spiritual Moral Beings were nearly as knowledgeable as themselves in some areas. // It is a 3 or 4 definition situation. // Pluralism was not supported, nor agreed on, as the right doctrine of God and man. Such is Not in the DOI or CON. // Freedom is not freedom FROM religion for they all said religion is necessary. What sort of mind would think that the FFOG were saying freedom from religion when they all worshipped Christ in Christian Churches. A society that opposes itself will self-destruct. They knew that. // Infidelity and Atheism is "no God"; and thus these are immediately discerned as illegal because the CC is with God; and with GOV; which GOV includes the people (citizens). // They said the USA GOV cannot be allowed to decide on secondary doctrines of Christianity, (part of DEN) because it is not their jurisdiction. // "Free Exercise of religion", is defined as what?? NOT~ +false religion; +any religion; +all religions; +forced Will to agree to be a Christian; +allowed to set up public religious activity and buildings of any religion; or all religions. To the following it is YES~ +The free will to accept or reject the Christian religion; +The Free Exercise to attend to any Christian DEN; +The Free Exercise to public activity of any Christian DEN; which is secondary doctrines and expressions. // Free Speech clause is part of the R-E intended as priority for the promotion of the Gospel to the nation and world. To deny this is to deny that they had God as God; it is to accuse them of idolatry. The intention/ purpose of DOC & CC is to make an agreement with God; with Him as 1ˢᵗ priority. // It is true that every secondary doctrine has only one definition but people do not learn at the same rate. // All Expressions, such as practices or ceremonies, are not exactly the same; there are different ceremonies that are all right in the Holy Bible, but not told how often and how long and how exactly. // Neutrality of the CON is a Falsity~ a "false theory and a falsehood in practice" (136). Neutrality is said nowhere and it is a "DO NOT". // It is a lie that the DOI & CON support every religion. The total intention/ purpose of them was based on the true God; and of opposing false religion of some Europeans. // Caution must be used in the relation of GOV & religion. // Those denying religion & GOV to be mixed, are, whether intentionally or not, trashing the USA society in to irreligiousness; and thereby sinking us in to Hell. As Eternal Spiritual Moral Beings, it is the intention/ purpose, for the goodness of each, to climb the ladder to Heaven; and to avoid the demons attempts to pull us off the ladder and throw us in to the pit of Hell. This life is an extreme place of need; and this is easily noticed if distractions and bad desires are removed; burdens with decisions, spiritual & physical, troubles, trials, temptations on every side. Then "filthy dreamers" (Jud1:8) come and think they are "free" of religion; but in essence deceivers, putting up nothing but illusion, moral relativism, unreal, non-truth, empty, purposelessness, and ends in futility (Vanity); 2Pet2:19~"While they promise them liberty, they themselves are the servants of corruption: for of whom a man is overcome, of the same is he brought in bondage".

---T--- <u>GOD & RELIGION & USA GOV</u> ~ No Separation Rather Covenant Contract of Joining or Union: // To say not religion is to say not God; and to say not God is to say no religion. To say no God is to deny the CC (DOI & CON). Therefore it is truthful to state that the FFOG cannot be saying no religion is to be included as part of GOV.

---T--- <u>Theology, known as the Study for KN of God, Supported:</u> // Christian Theology was Supported in the Majority of GOV Activities. Following are some subjects that were constantly agreed and applied: +The Sabbath; +Christian Church existence; +Christian Church attendance; +Prayer; +Providence; +No idolatry; +No alcohol (recreational); +No slavery; +No murder; +No stealing; +No public bad language; +Protection of life; +Happiness of people in righteousness; +Truth; +Love; +Justice; +Mercy; +The Holy Bible; +No dictatorship; +Freedom of Christian DEN; +The Holy Trinity; +Christmas; +Thankfulness; +"fasting" or self-denial; +Knowledge; +No illicity Fornication Activity with pornographic; +No evil hate; +Education to the young; +The family; +No homosexuality license; +Assistance to the poor, bodily & spiritually ill; +No abortion; +No false religion. +Etc.

171

---T--- <u>R-E , R~Est -- God Religion</u>: // Religious Spiritual Moral Beings can be abusive. // Religious people can be unreasonable. // Therefore Truth, Love, Kindness, Checks & Balances, Holy Bible, etc. were included; to get help from God.

---T--- <u>RELIGION WORD USED & with Word ESTABLISHMENT to Increase God's Presence:</u> // Defined with 2 different definitions, with one instance for All Religions (Doctrines of God, god, and man; True & False) in the world; and the other instance for Christian DEN: // "Journal of the House of Representatives of the US, 1789-1793. Wednesday, July 22, 1789: Also, a petition of Hannah Adams, PRAYing that an exclusive privilege may be granted her for a limited time, to publish and vend a work which she has compiled, entitled "An Alphabetical Compendium of the Various SECTS Which Have Appeared in the World From the Beginning of the CHRISTIAN Era, to the Present Day, with an Appendix, Containing a Brief Account of the Different Schemes of RELIGION now Embraced Among Mankind." That refers to a book title of Hannah's, who was a Christian author which, in the book, included a list of all, or most, of the religions in the world. The book specifically and very plainly uses 2 words for religion~ 1~ One use of the word included all religions of the world, both true and false. 2~ The other use of the word in the book was for religions as specifically, "Christian religious denominations"; that is Christian denominations. The Book was changed in its title later to be, "Dictionary of All Religions and of Religious Denominations". As you see, that is more clearly proving Hannah's 2 uses of, or definitions of the word "religion". The book was also a book on the defense of the Christian religion. It had a chapter on all the religions in the world, and also a chapter titled as, "truth and excellency of the Christian religion"; and also a chapter called, "A Brief Account of Paganism, Mohammedanism, Judaism, and Deism". Thus Hannah was aware that Christianity was the US GOV religion, and discussed the falsities of false religions. She was one of the first women authors of the US (US independent from Britain). She also wrote papers on the 4 Christian Gospels and a book on the Evidences of Christianity.

---T--- <u>Charles Finney & His Co-Workers, (friends) assisted</u> in One of the Great Awakening Events & Activities; & Opposed Slavery; & supported that GOV & Religion must be Joined: // Following is stated, in Finney's, "Lectures on Revivals of Religion" AD 1835: "God cannot sustain this free and blessed country, which we love and pray for, unless the church will take right ground. Politics are a part of religion in such a country as this, and Christians must do their duty to the country as a part of their duty to God. It seems sometimes as if the foundations of the nation were becoming rotten, and Christians seem to act as if they thought God did not see what they do in politics. But I tell you, he does see it, and he will bless or curse this nation, according to the course they take."

---T--- <u>USA GOV has Limitations to Any religion that</u> is not Christ's Christianity, including false religions, such as Muslim or Islam: // "The Revolutionary Diplomatic Correspondence of the US, Volume 2 A. Lee to Committee on Foreign Affairs.* [Note *: * MSS. Dep. of State; 1 Sparks' Rev. Dip. Corr., 440.] Paris, July 29, 1777. Gentlemen: ,,,On my first interview with his excellency the Baron de Schulenburg, he informed me that, upon receiving information of my intending to come to Berlin, he had written to signify the King's resolution not to receive me as a public minister, but that he should be glad to receive any information relative to the proposal of carrying on trade with us. I urged the EX of civil wars both in England and Holland, during which public ministers were received from them by neutral powers, without its being deemed as an infringement of their neutrality, with many other similar instances of great authority. He answered that his majesty had pledged his honor to the King of Great Britain not to interfere in this dispute; he therefore wished that I would confine myself entirely to the subject of trade, as he could not hear any further propositions.* [Note *: * The distinction between recognition of independency and recognition of belligerency is well settled. ,,,The situation of the Empress of Russia is not more favorable; she is under a constant alarm for the internal quiet of her kingdom, in which there are everywhere the seeds of great and dangerous discontent. A considerable force is required to preserve the acquisitions she has made in Poland. The peace with the Porte is an armed truce, which threatens to break out into action every moment. The first and most sacred principle of the MAHOMETAN RELIGION is the union of all Mussulmans; the dividing the Crimea from them is, for this reason, a mortal wound to their religious principles, and renders the late peace universally odious, Perpetual obstacles are therefore raised to the execution of it; and the Turks are openly preparing to avenge their late defeats. So circumstanced, it is certain the Empress is herself in great need of assistance, instead of being in a condition to give it; which, were she able, it is conceived she would never stoop to do as a subsidiary of Great Britain in such a contest, and in such company as the little German princes. ,,,Every day confirms me more and more in the opinion that our enemies can not continue the war another campaign with any effect, and that the acknowledgment of your independency will be a serious subject of deliberation among the powers of Europe the ensuing winter. Yours, etc., Arthur Lee". // Also (265).

---T--- <u>USA GOV states itself as an Ambassador Nation for Christ's Christianity</u> to other Nations & World as In AD 1904 when the Panama Canal Geographical area was purchased by the USA. // President William H. Taft states in a congressional message: "Our defense of the Panama Canal ,,,require us to recognize our position as one of the foremost in the family of nations, and to clothe ourselves with sufficient naval power to give force to our reasonable demands, and to give weight to our influence in those directions of progress that a powerful Christian nation should advocate."

---T--- <u>God's 1-A ~ Establishment</u> Section, R~Est ~ is Christian DEN Subject related: // Now here are the intention/ purpose related desires that were occurring inside the Spiritual Moral Beings known as the FFOG, Congress, Citizens~ about the various DENs. The situation was, not whether to be a Christian GOV because that was already accomplished with start of the CC part DOI; and with many other proofs; such was not disagreed. // However there were DEN differences that existed. // Richard Henry encourages Congress to construct a US GOV not to be exclusive ("respecting" or partial) of some Christian DENs and inclusive of others: "Letters of Delegates to Congress: Volume 22- 11/1, 1784 — 11/6, 1785 - Richard Henry Lee

172

to John Adams - Dear Sir, Having yesterday written a long letter to you, I have now only to request your attention to the following business, which is of very great importance to those whom it concerns, and who form a considerable portion of the Citizens of these States. The representation of those professing the CHURCH of England system of RELIGION, having been lately assembled at Philadelphia where Lay & Clerical deputies from seven States were convened in General Convention for the purpose, among other things, of preserving and maintaining a succession of DIVINEs in their CHURCH, in a manner which they judge consonant to the gospel, and no way interfering with the RELIGIOUS or civil rights of others ,,,have sent an address to the Archbishops and Bishops of England, ,,,proposing a plan for the consecration of American Bishops. It is imagined, that before anything is done in this business by the Bishops of England, that they will consult the King and Ministry; who, it is apprehended may now, as heretofore, suppose that any step of the kind being taken in England might be considered here as an officious intermeddling with our affairs that would give offence on this side the water. Should this be the case, the CHURCH of England Members in Congress have the greatest reliance on your liberal regard for the RELIGIOUS rights of all men, that you will remove mistaken scruples from the mind of administration, by representing how perfectly consonant it is with our revolution principles professed thro- out all the States, that every DEN of CHRISTIANs has a right to pursue its own RELIGIOUS modes, interfering not with others. That instead of giving offence, it must give content, by evidencing a friendly disposition to accommodate the people here who are members of the CHURCH in question. In proof of this, Congress did lately shew their attention to the accommodation of this Class of CHRISTIANs, by communicating to the different Executives your information from the Danish Minister ,,,".

---T---   1-A ~ Both parts of the Amendment are about God. The R-E or R~Est is defined as~ +] pertaining to the Freedom of Christian DENs (secondary doctrines & expressions & organizations usually called establishments); and +] NOT the separation of US GOV from religion; and +] the Religion of the US is Christian; and +] the US is Not of Infidelity: // Such is all stated by the FFOG following in a report on negative criticism received from Britain about US freedom for all Christian DEN; Note also that the word Religion is defined as Christian DEN. This report has a variety of quotation marks in it: "The Revolutionary Diplomatic Correspondence of the US, Volume 3 - J. Adams to the President of Congress.* - [Note *: * MSS. Dep. of State; 3 Sparks' Dip. Rev. Corr., 144 ,,,Paris, June 17, 1780. Sir: The refugees in England are so great an obstacle to peace, that it seems not improper for me to take notice of them to Congress. Governor Hutchinson is dead ,,,He was born to be the cause and the victim of popular fury, outrage, and conflagrations. Descended from an ancient and honorable family; born and educated in America, professing all the zeal of the Congregational RELIGION; affecting to honor the characters of the first planters of the New World, and to vindicate the character of America, and especially of New England; early initiated into public business; industrious and indefatigable in it; beloved and esteemed by the people ,,,minutely informed in the history of his country; author of an history of it which was extensively read in Europe; engaged in extensive correspondence in Europe as well as in America; favored with the crown of Great Britain ,,,controversy between Great Britain and America in the manner and at the time it was done, and involved the two countries in an enmity which must end in their everlasting separation ,,,I think I see visible traces of his councils in a number of pamphlets not long since published in London, and ascribed to Mr. Galloway. It is most probable that they were concerted between the ministry and the refugees in general, and that Mr. Galloway was to be given out as the ostensible, as he probably was the principal, author. "The Cool Thoughts on the Consequences of American Independence," although calculated to inflame a hasty, warlike nation to pursue the conquest of America, are sober reasons for defending our independence and our alliances, and therefore proper for me to lay before my countrymen. The pamphlet says: "It has been often asserted that Great Britain has expended in settling and defending America more than she will ever be able to repay, and that it will be more to the profit of this kingdom to give her independence ,,,He concludes: "That posterity will feel that America was not only worth all that was spent upon her, but that a just, firm, and constitutional subordination of the Colonies was absolutely necessary to the independence and existence of Great Britain." Here I think I see the traces of Mr. Hutchinson. Another argument, he says, much relied on by the advocates for American independence is, "that a similarity of laws, RELIGION, and manners has formed an attachment between the people of Great Britain and America which will insure to Great Britain a preference in the commerce of America." He agrees "that a uniformity of laws and RELIGION, [[the religion of Great Britain was most always Christianity and even became the GOV religion of it]] united with a subordination to the same supreme authority, in a great measure forms and fixes the national attachment. But when the laws and the supreme authority are abolished, the manners, habits, and customs derived from them will soon be effaced. When different systems of laws and governments shall be established, other habits and manners must take place. The fact is that the Americans have already instituted GOVs as opposite to the principles upon which the British GOV is established as human invention could possibly devise. New laws are made, and will be made, in conformity to and in support of their new political systems, and, of course, destructive to this national attachment. Their new States being altogether popular, their essential laws do already and will continue to bear a greater resemblance to those of the democratical cantons of Switzerland than to the laws and policy of Great Britain. Thus we find in their first acts the strongest of all proofs of an aversion in their rulers to our national policy, and a sure foundation laid to obliterate all affection and attach-merit to this country among the people. How long, then, can we expect that their attachment, arising from a similarity of laws, habits, and manners, if any such should remain, will continue? No longer than between the United Provinces and Spain, or the Corsicans and the Genoese, which was changed, from the moment of their separation, into an enmity, which is not worn out to this day." How it is possible for these rulers,,, unite in reducing the powers of those rulers as this author asserts, I know not. I leave him to reconcile it. If he had been candid and confessed that the attachment in American minds in general is not very strong to the laws and GOV of England, and that they rather prefer a different form of GOV, I should have agreed with him, as I certainly shall agree that no attachment between nations arising merely from a similarity of laws and government is ever very strong, or sufficient to bind nations together who have opposite or even different interests. "As to the attachments" says he, "arising from a similarity of RELIGION, they will appear still more groundless and ridiculous. America has no predominant RELIGION. [[now he clarifies the definition of the word Religion as Christian DEN]] There is not a RELIGIOUS society in Europe which is not to be found in America. If we wish to visit the CHURCHes of England, or the meetings of the Lutherans, Methodists, Calvinists, Presbyterians, Moravians, Menonists, Swinfielders, Dumplers, or Roman Catholics, we shall find them all in America. "What a motley, or rather how many different and opposite attachments will this jumble of RELIGIOUS make! "Should there be any remains of this kind of national attachment, we may conclude that the Lutherans, Calvinists, Menonists, Swinfielders, Dumplers, and Moravians will be attached to Germany, the country from whence they emigrated and where their RELIGIOUS are best tolerated; the Presbyterians and Puritans to Ireland; and the Roman Catholics to France, Spain, and the pope, and the small number of the CHURCH of England to Great Britain. "Do we not daily see monarchies at war with monarchies, INFIDELs with INFIDELs, CHRISTIANs with CHRISTIANS, Catholics with Catholics, and dissenters with dissenters? What stress then, can be justly laid on an attachment arising from a similarity of laws, government, or RELIGION? "It has also been asserted that ,,,merits will be led from motives of interest to give the preference in trade to this country, because we can supply her with manufactures cheaper than she can raise them or purchase them from others. ,,,When she shall have a separate and distinct interest of her own to pursue, her views will be enlarged, her policy exerted to her own benefit, and her interest, instead of being united with, will become not only different from, but opposite to, that of Great Britain ,,,The nature of commerce is roving; she has been at different periods in possession of the Phoenicians, Carthagenians, and the Venetians; Germany and France lately enjoyed her, and supplied Great Britain with their manufactures. Great Britain at present folds her in her arms." Surely it was never intended that any American should read this pamphlet, it contains so many arguments and motives for perseverance in our righteous and glorious cause. It is astonishing, however, that instead of stimulating England to pursue their unjust and inglorious enterprise, it does not convince all of the impracticability of it, and induce them to make peace. I have the honor to be, etc., John Adams."

---T--- The 1-A, R~E, R~Est includes the Means or Particular Subjects which apply to Christianity Increasing Christ's Presence: // Such includes freedom~ of speech, of the "press", of peaceable assemblies of people (Christian DENs), and of Petitions of Grievances. This is assistance to Christianity to increase and allow no decrease.

---T--- 1-A, R~Est Section Conceived Rightly includes that~ +] FFOG affectionately cared for Christ, were Christians, & Christianity Supportive; +] US GOV is to be affectionate for Christ, & Christianity Supportive; +] Enactment of Christian Laws, such as including the Sabbath: // "Journal of the Congress of the Confederate States of America, 1861-1865 [Volume 5], Apr 9, 1862 The House met pursuant to adjournment, and was opened with PRAYER by the Rev. Mr. Pettigrew. The Chair announced the following appointments on committees, viz: Mr. Chilton, from the same committee, to whom was referred sundry petitions on the subject of Sunday mails, made a report; which is as follows, to wit: SUNDAY MAIL. Report of the Committee on Post-offices and Post-Roads. The Committee on Post-Offices and Post-Roads, to whom sundry memorials were referred against the transportation and opening of the mails on Sundays, report: That the subject-matter of the memorials was several times before the Congress of the US, and several elaborate reports were made thereon. These reports, which were adverse to the PRAYER of the petitioners, your committee have examined with care, especially that made by the Hon. Richard M. Johnson, on the 4th of Mar., 1830, which was regarded as an able exposition of the matter, and received very generally with favor, but which, when closely analyzed, will be found sophistical and unsatisfactory in its reasoning and conclusion, while much is contained in it to admire and applaud. We heartily assent to the great fundamental TRUTH, that no free GOV should ever interfere in matters of RELIGION to control the RELIGIOUS faith and CONSCIENCEs of men. Our excellent CON provides that "Congress shall make no law respecting an ESTABLISHMENT of RELIGION, or prohibiting the free exercise thereof," and every effort tending, however remotely, to obtain legislative interference in the ESTABLISHMENT of RELIGIOUS creeds [[Christian DEN is said by the word here as "Creeds"]] should the indignantly rejected as a stab upon RELIGION itself, the liberty of CONSCIENCE, and the freedom of thought. It does not follow, however, from what we have said, that Congress should, by its legislation, ignore the existence and overruling Providence of the Supreme Being, or enact laws in contravention of His known will. No sane mind would for a moment conceive that the framers of our CON, in the very outset of our GOV, in view of the trials and difficulties which awaited us, in view of the fact that in all probability we should soon be required "To bathe our infant liberties In the baptism of our blood" intended to give any sanction to the ESTABLISHMENT of RELIGION by law, or to interpose in behalf of any RELIGIOUS creed [[see that the R-E or R~Est pertains to Christian DEN]], when "invoking the favor and guidance of Almighty GOD," they ordained and established our fundamental law. No one would suppose that the opening of our sessions by solemn invocations offered up by pious ministers to Almighty GOD for wisdom to direct and strength to support us in the faithful discharge of our duties, was an unconstitutional interference in matters of RELIGION: Neither has it been deemed unconstitutional to appoint chaplains in the Army, that they may minister to the intellectual, MORAL, and RELIGIOUS culture of our troops; that they may come round the bed of the sick or wounded soldier, and by "pointing the way" wreath the haggard countenance of death with the smiles of joy as the hope of a happy immortality becomes the sunlight of the soul. The memorialists do not propose that Congress should, by law, declare that any day, or any portion of time, has been set apart by the Almighty for RELIGIOUS exercises. Congress has no such power. Its sphere of legitimate legislation is quite limited, being bounded by the express grant of

174

powers contained in the CON. They merely ask that Congress shall not by affirmative legislation do violence to RELIGION and the MORAL sense of the community, by requiring the mail to be carried, opened, or distributed and delivered on the CHRISTIAN SABBATH. [[see here the Christian religion supported by the FFOG]] And is it unconstitutional for Congress to decline the violation of the SABBATH day? Such was the conclusion at which the committee arrived in the celebrated report of Mr. Johnson. Then it follows that it is unconstitutional for Congress to decline holding sessions on the SABBATH day. By parity of reasoning it should require all its agents in every department of the GOV to continue their usual routine of duties and labors on the SABBATH. If it be necessary to have the mail carried and opened on the SABBATH, as a matter of public convenience, it is equally necessary that the judicial courts should be kept open on the SABBATH, the CON providing for a speedy trial. Why are they not kept open? Out of respect for the CHRISTIAN SABBATH. Why are the doors of this hall closed on the SABBATH? It is because of our reverence for RELIGION, and from a decent respect for the CHRISTIAN constituency who send us here, whose MORAL sense would be shocked by a desecration of the day, in devoting it to the usual purposes of legislation. In the old GOV, such petitions as those before us, were regarded as covert attempts to obtain the recognition, by law, of one RELIGIOUS dogma as a pretext for another and another still, until some SECTS should become established, and, panoplied with the power of the State, should triumph over its opposers and introduce all the horrors of "the HOLY inquisition." We were exhorted to remember "that Cataline, a professed patriot, was a traitor to Rome; Arnold, a professed Whig, a traitor to America; and Judas, a professed disciple, was a traitor to his DIVINE Master." While the committee ,,,that while the Confederate States Government in its fundamental law professes to "invoke the favor and guidance of Almighty GOD," it should not be guilty of treason by trampling His statutes under foot, and setting His authority at defiance. Your committee will not go into an examination as to the foundation of the obligation to observe the SABBATH as a day of rest, of worship, and for MORAL and RELIGIOUS improvement. [[note that they are acknowledging God as 1st priority to the nation; preventing idolatry]] Whether it be deducible from the nature of our Constitution as essential to our physical, as well as MORAL and SPIRITual development, or from the decalogue, as a positive institution, or from the practice and EX of the Apostles and CHRISTIANs from their day to the present, it is certain that the CHRISTIAN people composing the States of this Confederacy, esteem its day set apart by DIVINE appointment for rest from secular employment, and to be dedicated to worship and MORAL culture. It is equally certain that they concur in the opinion that its desecration is a SIN, and the sole question is, shall the GOV continue unnecessarily to desecrate it. Shall it, in the absence of some overruling necessity, deny to a large number of its employees the privileges of the sanctuary, and the means it affords for MORAL and RELIGIOUS improvement? Your committee believe that this should not be done. The stoppage of the mail one day in seven would not materially interfere with the revenues of the Post-Office Department, while it would considerably lessen the cost of transportation. It will be remembered that under the CON the Department must be self-sustaining by the 1st day of Mar., 1863, and this will contribute to produce that result. Besides, by curtailing the service on the main routes and thus lessening the expense, greater facilities can be afforded for sending the mails into the interior and poorer Sections, where the revenue might not equal the expense. ,,,This, however, is remedied by the modern invention of the telegraph, and the erection of numerous railroads and introduction of express companies; so that none of the EVILs then anticipated would be experienced now. The star-bid system on which contracts are now let out, has, in a great measure, dispensed with coaches as a means of carrying the mails; and your committee believe that very little inconvenience would result from ceasing to transmit them on SUNDAY. It may, however, be said, we are in the midst of a great revolution, and that while it lasts it is important the mail service should not be curtailed. Your committee believe that the public interest will not suffer by it. The accounts of interesting events, battles, etc., are either sent by telegraph, or private persons, or express. They rarely go at the earliest moment by the mails, which delay at distributing offices for distribution. Besides, if one-seventh of the employees engaged in the mail service were transferred to the Army, it would constitute no inconsiderable addition; and if the rolling stock required for the mail on Sunday should be allowed to remain unemployed one-seventh of the time, some compensation might result, should the war be protracted, in its fitness to aid the Government in necessary transportation for a much longer period than it otherwise would. The fact, therefore, that we are engaged in a war furnishes an additional reason why we should postpone the mail service on the SABBATH. Superadded to all this, the fact that our GOV in the commencement of its career, in the midst of the most bloody struggle for the maintenance of our rights, had paused to pay a tribute to virtue and RELIGION, would present a spectacle of the MORALly sublime that would stand forth as a beacon light to the CHRISTIAN nations of the earth; would show that as a nation "we honor not GOD with our lips, when our hearts are far from Him;" would furnish proof of the Sincerity of our profession of reliance upon the favor and guidance of Him who "holds the destinies of all nations in His hands," and who "honors them that honor Him." Whatever, therefore, may be the action of the House as to its concurrence in the views of the committee, they feel that in thus plainly and frankly laying them before the representatives of the people they have discharged their duty to themselves, their country, and their GOD. Their adoption or rejection is with the Congress. The opposite of these views have hitherto obtained ascendency in the old GOV, and, whether as a sequence or not, is a question which we may not decide; the finger of the Almighty has inscribed upon its walls "Mene, Mene, Tekel, Upharsin." May the Confederate States profit by the EX, and while eschewing all bigotry, whether political or RELIGIOUS, and all attempts to violate the rights of CONSCIENCE, early learn that the only sure basis of national prosperity and happiness are the great principles of justice, MORALity, and RELIGION, as taught in the revealed will of GOD, and that the Great Lawgiver will not suffer these principles to be violated with impunity. The fears expressed in reports upon this subject heretofore submitted to the old Congress, that should the GOV repeal a law requiring a large number of its citizens to violate the CHRISTIAN SABBATH, it would be the beginning of a series of acts which would end in the union of

CHURCH and state, and entail upon the people all the persecution and horrors of the Spanish Inquisition, are utterly groundless and unworthy of patriots and CHRISTIAN statesmen. The several States not only decline to pass laws requiring the violation of the SABBATH, but many, if not all of them, have penal enactments against its violation, and these have been enforced for many years. Why have not RELIGIOUS persecution, the "HOLY inquisition," and the "auto da fé" found a place in some of them? The common law, which is said to be "the perfection of reason," has always deferred to the CHRISTIAN SABBATH, and sternly declares all contracts made on Sunday absolutely void. Why has not persecution followed its behest? No! Such enormities and cruelties result "to nations that forget GOD." They spring up when frenzied fanaticism has supplanted vital piety, and when "bigotry has murdered RELIGION to frighten fools with her ghost." It is to forestall and prevent such results that your committee would urge upon Congress, thus early in the eventful history of our Republic, to blot out the laws of the old GOV requiring the SABBATH to be violated. The EX thus furnished of respect to piety and RELIGION would permeate society and stimulate individuals to more orderly and virtuous lives. It is impossible to estimate the beneficent effects of such a MORAL reform upon the masses of our population. One of the wisest and best of men* was wont to say: [Note *: * Sir Mathew Hale] "A SABBATH well spent brings a week of content, And a health for the toils of the morrow: While a SABBATH profaned, what e'er may be gained, Is a certain forerunner of sorrow." However this may be, its needless profanation by the GOV in the transmission and delivery and opening of the mails interferes with the worship of GOD, withdraws many from RELIGIOUS contemplation, deprives others of MORAL and RELIGIOUS culture, and furnishes an EX of impiety which tends to deMORALize our people. The right minded will readily distinguish between the usual mail service which may be stopped one day in seven without maternal detriment to any one, and those works of necessity and charity which may and ought to be done under the DIVINE license. "It is lawful to do good on the SABBATH day." In conclusion the committee recommend the following bill for the adoption of the Congress: A bill to repeal so much of the existing law as requires the mails to be carried, delivered, or opened on Sunday; which was read first and second times and, together with the report, ordered to be printed and placed on the Calendar. ,,,The bill was placed on the Calendar. Mr. Clark, from the same committee, to whom was referred a memorial of sundry citizens of North Carolina and Virginia in relation to a stage line from Wytheville to independence, reported ,,,Mr. Chilton, from the same committee, to whom was referred sundry petitions for the establishment of post routes, reported ,,,from the same committee,,,".

---T--- R-E ~ Establishment Section (R~Est) is Defined as~ +] Christ's Christianity is the USA Religion, +] Different DENs are acceptable, +] DEN is of Christianity, but different on secondary doctrines & different expressions, +] Not any one Christian DEN allowed to have a law making it as the USA GOV religion, +] False Christianity is Excluded. The following report also proves concerns about~ +Religious persecution, +truth in Christianity, +and that Roman Catholicism was in observation and so they put a "Check" on it, because it was at the time a mix of false Christianity and had become abusive historically: // "The Debates in the Several State Conventions on the Adoption of the Federal CON [Elliot's Debates, Volume 1] MARYLAND. The first emigration made under the auspices of Lord Baltimore was in 1632, and consisted of about 200 gentlemen of considerable fortune and rank, and their adherents, being chiefly Roman Catholics. "He laid the foundation of this province (says Chalmers) upon the broad basis of security to property and of freedom of RELIGION, granting, in absolute fee, fifty acres of land to every emigrant; establishing CHRISTIANITY agreeably to the old common law, of which it is a part, without allowing preeminence to any particular SECT [[DEN]]. The wisdom of his choice soon converted a dreary wilderness into a prosperous colony." The first legislative assembly of Maryland, held by the freemen at large, was in 1634--1635; but little of their proceedings is known. No acts appear to have been adopted until 1638--1639, when provision was made, in consequence of an increase of the colonists, for a representative assembly, called the House of Assembly, chosen by the freemen; and the laws passed by the Assembly, and approved by the proprietary, or his lieutenant, were to be of full force. At the same session, an act, which may be considered as in some sort a Magna Charta, was passed, declaring, among other things, that "HOLY CHURCH, within this province, shall have all her rights and liberties; that the inhabitants shall have all their rights and liberties according to the great charter of England;" ,,,In 1649, an act was passed punishing blasphemy, or denying the HOLY Trinity, with death, and confiscation of goods and lands. Under the protectorate of Cromwell, roman Catholics were expressly denied any protection in the province; and all others, "who profess faith in GOD by JESUS CHRIST, though differing in judgment from the doctrine, worship, or discipline, publicly held forth," were not to be restrained from the exercise of their RELIGION. In 1696, the CHURCH of England was established in the province; and in 1702, the liturgy, and rites, and ceremonies, of the CHURCH of England, were required to be pursued in all the CHURCHes --with such toleration for dissenters, however, as was provided for in the act of William and Mary. And the introduction of the test and abjuration acts, in 1716, excluded all Roman Catholics from office. ,,,Upon the revolution of 1688, the GOV of Maryland was seized into the hands of the crown, and was not again restored to the proprietary until 1716. From that period no interruption occurred until the American Revolution."

---T--- USA Nation has a Responsibility to Include God stated by FFOG: // Abraham Lincoln states, "It is the duty of Nations ,,,to recognize the sublime truth ,,,in the Holy Scriptures and proven by all history that those nations only are blessed whose God is the Lord [Psalms 33:12]". // George Washington, "It is the duty of all Nations to acknowledge the providence of Almighty God, to obey His will, to be grateful for His benefits, and humbly to implore His protection and favor" (71). // Thomas Jefferson states, "necessary to make us a happy and a prosperous people ,,,acknowledging and adoring an overruling Providence" (111). // John Adams, "The safety and prosperity of Nations ultimately and essentially depend on the protection and the blessing of Almighty God, and the National acknowledgement of this truth is ,,,and indispensable duty which the people owe to Him" (21a). // James Otis, "The sum of my argument is that civil government is of God" (197).

---T--- <u>Religious Test is Rightly Defined</u>: +] Attend to God's presence, +] It did Require Christianity, +] One intention/ purpose reason for the "religious" word in the R-E & R~Est was so that all DENs of Christianity would be protected: // And in application of such then, Officers needed some Christianity requirement. But this was not to require a specific secondary doctrine or DEN. That was the "religious test" not required; that no DEN; DEN are secondary Christian doctrines or expressions. However what was required was, the Oath and affirmation to God. An allowance was provided as applicable to Spiritual Moral Beings who do not know Jesus the True God; or who has a false god; it is a special oath and affirmation; it required a promise to tell the truth, obviously; yet it also required them to agree that God was present watching; it required them to agree that they are promising before God's presence and that God rewards & punishes accordingly; called an affirmation. // "The Records of the Federal Convention of 1787 [Farrand's Records, Volume 3] CCVIII. ,,,Robertson, Debates of the Convention of Virginia, 1788 (2d edit., 1805), pp. 151--152] June 10. 1788. Freedom of RELIGION is said to be in danger. I will candidly say, I once thought that it was, and felt great repugnance to the constitution for that reason. I am willing to acknowledge my apprehensions removed -- and I will inform you by what process of reasoning I did remove them. The CON provides, that "the senators "and representatives before mentioned, and the members of the "several state legislatures, and all executive and judicial officers, "both of the US and of the several states, shall be bound "by oath, or affirmation, to support this CON; but no religious test shall ever be required as a qualification to any office "or public trust under the US." It has been said, that if the exclusion of the RELIGIOUS test were an exception from the general power of congress, the power over RELIGION would remain. I inform those who are of this opinion, that no power is given expressly to congress over RELIGION. The senators and representatives, members of the state legislatures, and executive and judicial officers, are bound by oath, or affirmation, to support this CON. This only binds them to support it in the exercise of the powers constitutionally given it. The exclusion of RELIGIOUS tests is an exception from this general provision, with respect to oaths, or affirmations. Although officers, &c. are to swear that they will support this CON, YET THEY ARE NOT BOUND TO SUPPORT ONE MODE OF WORSHIP, OR TO ADHERE TO ONE PARTICULAR SECT. It puts all SECTS on the same footing. A man of abilities and character, of any SECT whatever, may be admitted to any office or public trust under the US. I am a friend to a variety of SECTS, because they keep one another in order. How many different SECTS are we composed of throughout the US? How many different SECTS will be in congress? We cannot enumerate the SECTS that may be in congress. And there are so many now in the US that they will prevent the ESTABLISHMENT of any one SECT in prejudice to the rest, [[see here the referring to the Establishment clause of religion as defined as DEN (secondary doctrines, expressions); not of all gods or a false god with false religion]] and will forever oppose all attempts to infringe RELIGIOUS liberty. If such an attempt be made, will not the alarm be sounded throughout America? If congress be as wicked as we are foretold they will, they would not run the risk of exciting the resentment of all, or most of the RELIGIOUS SECTS in America. The judiciary is drawn up in terror -- here I have an objection of a different nature. I object to the appellate jurisdiction as the greatest EVIL in it. Bills and Resolutions, House of Representatives, 19th Congress, 1st Session: Read twice, and committed to a Committee of the whole House to-morrow. A Bill Authorizing the several RELIGIOUS Societies within the District of Columbia to incorporate certain persons for the management of property. Whereas it is reasonable and proper that all DENOMINATIONS of CHRISTIANs within the District of Columbia, whose members conduct ,,,". //~See there the concern that the wording of the CON endangered religion; and then his concern was removed because, the CON requires an oath or affirmation made by all Branches which have employees; to support the CON (which includes the CC DOI); and also it includes a No Religious Rest~ which is that No one specific Christian DEN is required, rather people from any Christian DEN, may be hired for public service as USA GOV Officer; this was so as to protect different sects (DENs) of Christianity.

---T--- <u>OATH, an Attending to Christ's Presence by a Christian Oath or Affirmation, required to</u> be USA GOV Officer: // The oath was thought unbiblical by some Spiritual Moral Beings; because it is a debatable Christian doctrine~ secondary doctrine. Some Spiritual Moral Beings thought the Holy Bible taught not to oath to God; so an affirmation acknowledging God's presence was provided, as an alternative. The respect to God was a requirement, that the FFOG made. Oaths & affirmations were intentional/ purposed as a method to put God first; and assist the honesty of testimonies or employment work duties. And this is in the CON. Thus making the Christian Religion a necessity, to some degree, to be a USA GOV Officer: // "The Records of the Federal Convention of 1787 [Farrand's Records, Volume 3] CCVIII. Edmund Randolph in the Virginia Convention.1 ,,,pp. 151--152] June 10. 1788. Freedom of RELIGION is said to be in danger. I will candidly say, I once thought that it was, and felt great repugnance to the CON for that reason. I am willing to acknowledge my apprehensions removed -- and I will inform you by what process of reasoning I did remove them. The CON provides, that "the senators "and representatives before mentioned, and the members of the "several state legislatures, and all executive and judicial officers, "both of the US and of the several states, shall be bound "by oath, or affirmation, to support this CON; but no religious test shall ever be required as a qualification to any office "or public trust under the US." It has been said, that if the exclusion of the RELIGIOUS test were an exception from the general power of congress, the power over RELIGION would remain. I inform those who are of this opinion, that no power is given expressly to congress over RELIGION. The senators and representatives, members of the state legislatures, and executive and judicial officers, are bound by oath, or affirmation, to support this CON. This only binds them to support it in the exercise of the powers constitutionally given it. The exclusion of RELIGIOUS tests is an exception from this general provision, with respect to oaths, or affirmations. Although officers, &c. <u>are to swear that they will support this CON, yet they are not bound to support one mode of worship, or to adhere to one particular SECT [[DEN]]</u>. It puts all SECTS on the same footing. A man of abilities and character, of any SECT whatever, may be admitted to any office or public trust under the US. I am a friend to a variety of SECTS, because they keep one another in order. How many different SECTS are we composed of throughout the US? How many different SECTS will be in congress? We cannot enumerate the SECTS that may be in congress. And there are so many now in the US that they will prevent the ESTABLISHMENT of any one SECT in prejudice to the rest, and will forever oppose all attempts to infringe RELIGIOUS liberty. If such an attempt be made, will not the alarm be sounded throughout America? If congress be as wicked as we are foretold they will, they would not run the risk of exciting the resentment of all, or most of the RELIGIOUS SECTS in America. The judiciary is drawn up in terror -- here I have an objection of a different nature. I object to the appellate jurisdiction as the greatest EVIL in it. Bills and Resolutions, House of Representatives, 19th Congress, 1st Session: Read twice, and committed to a Committee of the whole House to-morrow. A Bill Authorizing the several RELIGIOUS Societies within the District of Columbia to incorporate certain persons for the management of property. Whereas it is reasonable and proper that all DENOMINATIONS of CHRISTIANs within the District of Columbia, whose members conduct ...".

---T--- R-E or R~Est "Establishment of Religion" Words Defined as, Christianity in its various DENs; DEN are defined as secondary doctrines & expressions & organizations or establishments; & all for God: // Thus this clearly proves that the definition and application of the R-E or R~Est was to protect the USA GOV control of favoring (respecting) one Christian DEN. AND that an oath or affirmation to God, which is Christianity, but no one DEN, was required; thus this is further protection of Christianity. Note following how they use the word "establishment" and "religion", as that of the USA GOV favoring one Christian DEN (sect) over another. This does not say that GOV is separate from Christianity, or that "religious" or "religious establishment" was to allow all doctrines of God and man. Note also the protection against a "wicked" government; wicked as a word of the Holy Bible & Christianity: // "The Records of the Federal Convention of 1787 [Farrand's Records, Volume 3] CCVIII. ,,,[Note 1: 1 Robertson, Debates of the Convention of Virginia, 1788 (2d edit., 1805), pp. 151--152] June 10. 1788. Freedom of RELIGION is said to be in danger. I will candidly say, I once thought that it was, and felt great repugnance to the CON for that reason. I am willing to acknowledge my apprehensions removed -- and I will inform you by what process of reasoning I did remove them. The CON provides, that "the senators "and representatives before mentioned, and the members of the ,,,several state legislatures, and all executive and judicial officers ,,,both of the US and of the several states, shall be bound ,,,by oath, or affirmation, to support this CON; but no religious test shall ever be required as a qualification to any office ,,,or public trust under the US,,, It has been said, that if the exclusion of the RELIGIOUS test were an exception from the general power of congress, the power over RELIGION would remain. I inform those who are of this opinion, that no power is given expressly to congress over RELIGION. The senators and representatives, members of the state legislatures, and executive and judicial officers, are bound by oath, or affirmation, to support this CON. This only binds them to support it in the exercise of the powers constitutionally given it. The exclusion of RELIGIOUS tests is an exception from this general provision, with respect to oaths, or affirmations. Although officers, &c. are to swear that they will support this CON, yet they are not bound to support one mode of worship, or to adhere to one particular SECT [[DEN]]. It puts all SECTS on the same footing. A man of abilities and character, of any SECT whatever, may be admitted to any office or public trust under the US. I am a friend to a variety of SECTS, because they keep one another in order. How many different SECTS are we composed of throughout the US? How many different SECTS will be in congress? We cannot enumerate the SECTS that may be in congress. And there are so many now in the US that they will prevent the ESTABLISHMENT of any one SECT in prejudice to the rest, and will forever oppose all attempts to infringe RELIGIOUS liberty. If such an attempt be made, will not the alarm be sounded throughout America? IF CONGRESS BE AS WICKED AS WE ARE foretold they will, they would not run the risk of exciting the resentment of all, or most of the RELIGIOUS SECTS in America. The judiciary is drawn up in terror -- here I have an objection of a different nature. I object to the appellate jurisdiction as the greatest EVIL in it. Bills and Resolutions, House of Representatives, 19th Congress, 1st Session: Read twice, and committed to a Committee of the whole House to-morrow. A Bill Authorizing the several RELIGIOUS Societies within the District of Columbia to incorporate certain persons for the management of property. Whereas it is reasonable and proper that all DENOMINATIONS of CHRISTIANs within the District of Columbia, whose members conduct ...". +This was the general comprehension and agreement of all the FFOG spiritual moral Beings.

---T--- R-E , R~Est has following EV of a Desire That~ +] only the Holy Spirit's Christianity Religion be acceptable, AND, +] all Christian DENs be accepted, as legal in the USA: // "Committee of the Whole House Mar. 17, 1826 Read twice, and committed to a Committee of the whole House to-morrow. A Bill Authorizing the several RELIGIOUS Societies within the District of Columbia to incorporate certain persons for the management of property. Whereas it is reasonable and proper that all DENOMINATIONS of CHRISTIANs within the District of Columbia, whose members conduct themselves in a peaceable and orderly manner, should receive and enjoy equal right and privileges, without partiality, preference, or distinction, in all things concerning the temporalities and government of their CHURCHes, congregations, and societies: And whereas, also, it is necessary to their welfare ,,,that they should be empowered to hold and acquire certain portions of property, in a corporate or congregational capacity, and enter into various engagements, of a civil or temporal nature, which can only be done by the assistance of the Congress of the US, which assistance may, nevertheless, be rightfully granted without disturbing private opinions, or affecting the rights of judgment in matters of RELIGION, or imposing an involuntary burthen on any person whatsoever: And whereas it is most convenient to make provisions for their respective situations, by a general law, which shall reach their several exigencies in affairs of a temporal or civil nature, as far as a difference of circumstances will admit: The Congress of the US having, therefore, taken the premises into serious consideration, and conceiving themselves indispensably bound to secure and preserve the same equality of right, privileges, and advantages, to all quiet and inoffensive CHRISTIAN

178

Societies in the District aforesaid, without any exception, whereby RELIGION may be encouraged and diffused, and peace, order, and universal tranquility prevail have agreed to enact,,,".

---T--- R-E, 1-A & 14ᵗʰ Amendment: // This clause part was made applicable to the States by the 14th Amendment as pertaining to a case~ in AD 1940, Cantwell vs. Connecticut. The Degrees of this situation is not discussed as of now; Only awareness of it. IT IS A Wrong Application & Interpretation.

---T--- Virginia's Declaration of Rights, AD 1776, with Affections to Jesus, was an Effect on the USA 1-A: // It states~ ",,,all men are equally entitled to the free exercise of religion, according to the dictates of conscience; and that it is the mutual duty of all to practise Christian forbearance, love, and charity toward each other". This Declaration of Rights also protects speech, press, Rights of assembly and petition as pertaining to religion. Thus but not for false religion. // Pennsylvannia State had some similar statements as this of Virginia.

---T--- Christianity & Religion: // The grammar or words used by the FFOG was constantly inclusive with Holy Bible vses and statements from it.

---T--- Religion & FREE WILL: // John Locke was studied, referenced, utilized as a knowledge source of the FFOG. Mr. Locke Systems Included~ +that Christianity & GOV be together, +that were used and applied to many States, +that all men were in the world to work out their own salvation and that GOV is not to hinder or dictate that area or coerce the decision making of the individual.

---T--- The English Bill of Rights AD 1689 was an effect on the USA Formation: // This protected citizens Right to assemble and petition GOV.

---T--- USA GOV & USA is CHRISTIAN: // The fact that they all were Christians, and only Christians, and all intentionally/ purposed only Christ's Christian doctrines, is a fact too difficult to deny, ignore, or deceitfully change.

---T--- 12 of the 13 Colony States had a GOV Christian Church for Christ Worship.

---T--- RELIGIOUS TEST: The Test of Religion is of DEN: // Maryland State, in AD 1776, (which is after the USA DOI date), enacted a Declaration of Rights; which assists in helping us comprehend the right definition of the No Religious Test of the USA CON. The Test is referring to Christian DEN. It states, "That no other test or qualification ought to be required, on admission to any office of trust or profit, than such oath of support and fidelity to this State ,,,and a declaration of a belief in the Christian religion ,,,That the manner of administering an oath to any person, ought to be such, as those of the religious persuasion, profession, or DEN, of which such person is one, generally esteem the most effectual confirmation, by the attestation of the Divine Being" (14a). // The DOI states one must be religious, God, conscience, truth, creation, etc., And the Charter DOCs, such as the AOC, (which was what the CON was constructed from) reads, ",,,and Almighty God being the only Lord of Conscience, Father of Lights and Spirits; and the Author as well as Object of all divine knowledge, Faith and Worship,,,". It concludes, ",,,And that all persons who also profess to believe in Jesus Christ, the Savior of the World, shall be capable to serve this GOV in any capacity, both legislatively and executively,,,".

---T--- The USA GOV & Citizens are to be a Jesus Christian Religion Not false religion: // FFOG John Adams visited France and stated about false religion including false Christianity: "This afternoon, led by Curiosity and good Company I strolled away to ,,,Church ,,,most awful and affecting. The poor wretches fingering their Beads, chanting Latin, not a Word of which they understood ,,,water~ their Crossing ,,,perpetually,,,".

---T--- Christian Activities for Christ of USA GOV Congress; include the following list of only a few of many; many more not included here are all similar: // Proclamations, Letters, Speeches, etc: {Dates between AD 1700's - 1900's; mostly earlier}: +Thanksgiving Day, A national Thanksgiving Proclamation reinstated, issued by US Pres. Franklin Roosevelt. +Lincoln Day~ Massachusetts; A statewide Lincoln Day issued by Calvin Coolidge (Governor). +Support Speech for Christianity: by USA Pres. Woodrow Wilson related to the Christian Men's Association. +A national Thanksgiving Day. +US Pres. Ulysses S. Grant~ A National Thanksgiving. +Pres. Abraham Lincoln~ A National Thanksgiving Day. +General Order Respecting the Observance of the Sabbath by Abraham Lincoln who, during the Civil War, quoted from two separate General Orders of George Washington. +By James Buchanan~ A National Humiliation, Fasting and Prayer. +Letter of US Pres. James Garfield recounting the results of a Christian Revival. +American Bible Society Certificate Signed by First Chief Justice John Jay enlisting to be a member as President. +A Letter by Charles Carroll (a Signer of the DOI), which expresses his strong faith in the redeeming power of Christ. +Thanksgiving Day- By Governor of Massachusetts. +US Pres. James Madison~ A National day of Humiliation and Prayer; Also 4 Hymns were part of this ceremony. +Thanksgiving Day- Massachusetts~ By Mr. Elbridge Gerry. +Letter from John Adams to Benjamin Rush in response to his letter where Christian affections were expressed. +DOC with Thomas Jefferson's signature that includes "in the year of our Lord Christ, 1807." +Connecticut State, by Governor Jonathan Trumbull~ A statewide Fasting, Humiliation and Prayer. +New Hampshire, by Gov. John Langdon, A Thanksgiving Day. +US Pres. John Adams issued a national fasting and prayer day. +Massachusetts, by Gov. Samuel Adams, A Thanksgiving Day. +Massachusetts, by Gov. Samuel Adams~ A statewide Fasting, Humiliation and Prayer. +By Pres. George Washington~ A Thanksgiving. +Letter by Jacob Broom, (Signer of the CON), reminding his son 'to be a Christian. +DOC with Samuel Chase (a signer of the DOI), verifying that a person takes an oath declaring a belief in the Christian religion. +New Hampshire, by Gov. Josiah Bartlett, A Thanksgiving Day. +New Jersey, by William Paterson~ A Thanksgiving Day. +Massachusetts, By Gov John Hancock~ A Thanksgiving Day. +Election Sermon by Daniel Foster~ an Election Day Sermon preached before John Hancock and Samuel Adams. +By Pres. George Washington~ A National Thanksgiving. +Connecticut State, by Samuel Huntington, A Thanksgiving Day. +By John Hanson, Pres. of Continental Congress~ A Day of Thanksgiving. +By Thomas McKean, Pres of Congress~ A Thanksgiving. +By Continental Congress~ A National Thanksgiving Day. +Holy Bible by USA GOV to all USA Citizens: Date (approx. 1700's)~ Benjamin Rush's Personal Bible Study, (Signer of the DOI), made available to citizens and supported by US GOV.

---T--- <u>R-E, 1-A ~ "Wall of Separation"; or "Separation of Church & State"</u>: // A falsity has been done, as interpreted by some Branches of GOV; saying that a wall of separation be maintained between the GOV and religion; or as also expressed, separation between church and state. // However that is contrary, specifically, to the 1-A which states that: +} Spiritual Moral Beings will have freedom of Christian religious expression; +} The USA GOV and its agencies will not recognize with favor by making a law for one Christian DEN more than any other; +} The USA GOV and its agencies will not promote false religion; +} The USA is to have God as God, Supreme Judge, Divine Providence, Lord Jesus Christ, Creator, (per CC), etc. // The statement of separating Church & State or GOV & Religion has never occurred. Rather it is a falsity wrongly inserted from Thomas Jefferson & James Madisons activities.

---T--- <u>Religious Christian Ceremonies Worshipping Christ by the USA GOV</u> supported & INCLUDED: // George Washington's Presidential Inauguration was a Christian ceremony; Included God's name, His Care, His respect, prayer to Him, stated as an "act of devotion", a recognition of spirits, the Christian God Who is a Spirit, and the Holy Bible doctrines. +Congress enacted a Christian Worship Assembly meeting at St Paul's Chapel afterwards (14).

---T--- <u>Christian Religion to God INCLUDED in USA GOV</u>: // Letter from Pres. George Washington to Dutch Reformed Christian Church states that the USA GOV is to be based on Christianity: "While just government protects all their religious rights, true religion affords to GOV its surest support ,,,It is impossible to rightly govern ,,,without God and the Bible".

---T--- <u>1-A , R~Est: RELIGION & Religious Establishment are defined</u> as Christ's Christian DEN: The States had definitions of Religion, or Religious Establishments, as Christian DEN in their CON; & supported Christianity & the Holy Bible: // Massachusetts CON of AD 1780: "It is the right, as well as the duty, of all men in society, publicly, and at stated seasons, to worship the Supreme Being, the Great Creator and Preserver of the <u>univers.</u> And no subject shall be hurt, molested, or restrained, in his person, liberty, or estate, for worshipping God in the manner and seasons, most agreeable to the dictates of his own conscience. Article III. And every DEN of Christians, demeaning themselves peaceabley, and as good subjects of the commonwealth, shall be equally under the <u>protection</u> of the law: and no subordination of any sect or DEN to another shall ever be established by law" (32). // New Hampshire AD 1784, 1792: "Every individual has a natural and unalienable right to worship God according to the dictates of his own conscience, and reason ,,,And every DEN of Christian demeaning themselves quietly, and as good citizens of the state, shall be equally under the protection of the laws. And no subordination of any one sect or DEN to another shall ever be established by law" (32). // South Carolina AD 1778: "That all persons and religious societies who acknowledge that there is one God, and a future state of rewards and punishments, and that God is publicly to be worshiped, shall be freely tolerated,,,. That all DENs of Christians ,,,in this State, demeaning themselves peaceably and faithfully, shall enjoy equal religious and civil privileges" (35). // Many other states had similar CON. Citations (31)(32)(35) and others have more of them. // The wording here protects the worship of God; that the worship of God be restricted to Christianity; not supported outside of that. No freedom was unlimited outside of Christian DENs; rather limitations.

---T--- <u>R-E, R~Est, 1-A, Religion & DEN & definitions</u>: "established religion" is defined as DEN, which is secondary doctrines & expressions for the Holy Spirit: // Congressional report in the Senate of the US, made 1/, 19, 1853 by Mr. Badger: "The [First Ammendment] clause speaks of,,, [[an establishment of religion]]. What is meant by that expression? It referred, without doubt, to that establishment which existd in the mother-country ,,,endowment at the public expense, peculiar privileges to its members, or disadvantages or penalties upon those who should reject its doctrines or belong to other communions,-- such law would be a,,, [[~"law respecting an establishment of religion"~]] ,,,They intended, by this amendment, to prohibit,,, such as the English Church presented, or any thing like it. But they had no fear or jealousy of religion itself, nor did they wish to see us an irreligious people ,,,they did not intend to spread over all the public authorities and the whole public action of the nation the dead and revolting spectable of atheistic apathy. Not so had the battles of the Revolution been fought and deliberations of the Revolutionary Congress been conducted" (36). // Mar 27, 1854. US Congressional report from the House Committee on the Judiciary: "What is an establishment of religion? It must have a creed defining what a man must believe; it must have rites and ordinances, which believers must observe; it must have ministers of defined qualifications, to teach the doctrines and administer the rites; it must have tests for the submissive and penalites for the non-conformist. There never was an established religion without all these ,,,(p) Had the people, during the Revolution had a suspiciaon of any attempt to war against Christianity, that Revolution would have been strangled in its cradle. At the time of the adoption of the CON and the amendments, the universal sentiment was that Christianity should be encouraged, not any one sect [[DEN]]. Any attempt to level and discard all religion would have been viewed with universal indignation" (36). // Notice Established Religion is defined as creeds, ordinances for believers, official ministers, and penalties for non-conformists. They did not want US GOV dictating secondary doctrines, such as physical healing, or how to manage children exactly, or various such freedoms, which many are based on personality and God's guidance to an individual.

---T--- <u>FFOG in Constructing the CC & 1-A intended to assist God by preventing</u> the USA GOV from dictating secondary doctrines of Christianity, such as physical healing, or how to manage children exactly, or various such freedoms, which many are based on personality and God's guidance to an individual.

---T--- <u>Religion Defined ~&~ R-E, R~Est, 1-A Clauses</u>: // 3 points: 1} Religious Establishment and Religion is defined as DEN, AND, 2} The operation of the GOV was that the States were given liberty to have a Christian DEN, but the USA GOV was not allowed to make a law to have one DEN favored, AND, 3} The USA GOV was not to restrict the States freedom exercise of DEN; which included having a State DEN(s): // FFOG Thomas

Jefferson, as an Officer of the GOV in AD 1808, wrote in a letter to Samuel Adams: "I consider the GOV of the US as interdicted [prohibited] by the CON from intermeddling with religious institutions, their doctrines, discipline, or exercises. This results not only from the provisions that no law shall be made respecting the establishment or free exercise of religion, but from that also which reserves to the States the powers not delegated to the US [10th Amendment]. Certainly, no power to prescribe any religious exercise, or to assume authority in religious discipline, has been delegated to the General GOV. It must then rest with the States, as far as it can be in any human authority" (30).

---T--- <u>Religion & DEN & God's definition of religion & R~Est</u>: // FFOG Alexis de Tocqueville in his paper titled, "The Republic of the US of America and its Political Institutions, Reviewed and Examined" (AD 1800's) states that denominationalism was discouraged, but Christianity was encouraged: "In the US, if a political character attacks a sect" [[DEN]] ,,,[[unquote but paraphrase - he may yet get some support]] ,,,"but if he attacks all the sects [[DEN]] together [[of Christianity]] ,,,every one abandons him and he remains alone".

---T--- <u>Religion & definition of Religion & R~Est includes</u> PROTECTION of these as follows: // One Dictionary used was Noah Webster's of 1828, as claimed by David Barton's history study (4). // In that dictionary, the definition has 5 requirements to be a Religion: 1} belief in God; 2} belief that God reveals His will to man; 3) belief in man's duty to obey God's commands; 4) belief in man's responsibility to God including rewards and punishment; 5) belief in godliness, piety, and practicing righteousness in life. Thus to omit (remove) any of these is not protected without limitations; And removing any of these is not supported by the USA GOV as a religion, because it is not believing in God, nor His revealed will (Holy Bible). The True God, truth, and True Religion, in other words.

---T--- <u>RELIGION: Other EVs Proving GOV Was</u> To Be for Christ & Support Of Such True Religion Thereof: // FFOG Thomas Jefferson wrote the following statement using notes from studies of Mr. Locke & Mr. Shaftesbury: "no man has the right to abandon the care of his salvation to another" (24). // The New Haven Colony Charter of AD 1644 states: "The Judicial laws of God, as they were delivered by Moses ,,,are to be a rule to all the courts in this jurisdiction"(25). // Pres. George Washington kept a Prayer journal, of which one said: "I have called on Thee for pardon and forgiveness of sins,,, accept and answer for the sake of Thy dear Son, Jesus Christ our Lord, Amen". Also, in a Thanksgiving proclamation of AD 1789, he said, "It is the duty of all nations to acknowledge the Providence of the Almighty God, to obey His will, to be grateful for His benefits, and humbly to implore his protection and favor". // Here we see in the same year as the CC & DOI~ +statements supportive of the Federal DOI, +statements that Christianity is its GOV, +only Christianity Religion not others, +they would not support a war, nor send representatives to the Federal GOV, who would oppose such that they simultaneously agreed & supported; the Law of Contradiction, Law of Confusion, a Falsity, and impossibility. // In AD 1776, in Ashfield, Massachusetts, an enactment passed in a meeting that states: "We do not count any GOV but the Governor of the Universe and under Him a state General to consult with the rest of the US for the good of the whole" (26). // A rally cry of the Americans & GOV during the DOI RW was, "We have no king but Jesus" (2). // The USA Schools taught: +Christ & Holy Bible; +supported by John Adams & John Hancock; +A book called The New England Primer, which states, "There is a dreadful fiery hell, where wicked ones must always dwell; there is a heaven full of joy, where goodly ones must always stay; to one of these my soul must fly, as in a moment, when I die ,,,thou hast thy God offended so, thy soul and body I'll divide: thy body in the grave I'll hide, and thy dear soul in Hell must lie with Devils to Eternity ,,,thus end the days of woeful youth, who won't obey or mind the truth; nor hearken to what preachers say, but do their parents disobey: they in their youth go down to Hell, under eternal wrath to dwell. Many don't live out half their days, for cleaving unto sinful ways" (117). // Puritan Covenants state: "We ,,,submit our persons, lives, and estates unto our Lord Jesus Christ, the king of kings and Lord of Lords and to all those perfect and most absolute laws in his holy word" (27). // The Colonists considered the land of the US as Gods land. So did William Livingston, a New Jersey Delegate, a rep. to the Constitutional Convention, stating: "The land we possess is the gift of heaven to our fathers and Divine Providence seems to have decreed it to our latest posterity" (23).

---T--- <u>Intention/ Purpose In Starting The USA Is Christ Religious</u>: // Christopher Columbus stated his mission and purpose in coming to the US was~ "to bear the light of Christ west to the heathen undiscovered lands" (23).

---T--- <u>Christ RELIGION & the RELIGIOUS TEST</u>; The CON statement says, "no religious test shall ever be required as a qualification to any office or public trust under the US": // This does not say nor define that Christianity or God is not required. Rather the DOI states that those are required. // God, truth, Bible, Creation, providence are all in the DOI. Hence it does not define that. // It is referring to Christian DEN as what is not required. Freedom to have DEN is provided, which includes expressions thereof and secondary doctrines. // Tennessee CON of AD 1796 defines religious test. "No person who denies the Being of God or a future state of rewards and punishments shall hold any office in the civil department of this state. ,,,That no religious test shall ever be required as a qualification to any office or public trust under this state"(32). +God and the Bible were not religious tests as is seen here; but religion is DEN. This article must be taken together. Furthermore the definition of Religious used here is not GOD Himself as a Being, nor Christianity; rather secondary doctrines of, expressions of, or organizational structures of Christianity. A DEN test is a religious test, as they knew it at such time. They did not require that a person be a PB or ME or LU, for Example. // Maryland CON: "That no other test or qualification ought to be required ,,,than such oath of support and fidelity to this state ,,,and a declaration of a belief in the Christian religion" (32). Thus we see here that religious test is not referring to Christianity or the Holy Bible, but to go beyond that, as in "no other". Because they DO REQUIRE a belief in God and the Christian religion. "No other" in that statement refers Christian secondary doctrines, or expressions, or establishments of organization; which are all DEN. // Vermont CON in AD 1786: "Frame of GOV ,,,And each member [of the

181

legislature], before he takes his seat, shall make and subscribe the following declaration, vis: I do believe in one God, the Creator and Governor of the universe, the rewarder of the good and punisher of the wicked. And I do acknowledge the SCs of the old and new testament to be given by divine inspiration, and own and profess the [Christian] religion ,,,And no further or other religious test shall ever, hereafter, be required of any civil officer or magistrate in this State". Here it is stated that "other religious" is DEN. However note that the Religion of Christianity, the Bible, and such was required. Note that the one part is to not be required, and the other part is to be required.

---T--- Religion, 14th Amendment: // The 14th Amendment is partly illegal. The Case of "Everson", AD 1947, was applied together with the 1st Amendment. And these 2 were applied to make religious activity illegal in public schools and public institutions, etc. And it was done by a court; Judicial Branch; did such without a Right to make such laws. This is the way it is illegal~ +The 14th Amendment was ratified (AD 1868) as to provide that the slaves who had been freed during the Civil War would have civil rights in every state. Now you, dear reader, ask me how that relates to the 1st Amendment in application to make religion illegal in public schools and public institutions, etc. ?? It Does Not. A court in AD 1970, "Walz", said that the court in AD 1947 made a change to the USA GOV system, that was "revolutionary". Hence illegal.

---T--- R~Est adoration to Christ God: // FFOG William Penn in "The London" of AD 1819 gave a Biographical saying: "It was his wish that every man who believed in God should partake of the rights of a citizen and that every man who adored him as a Christian, of whatever sect he might be should be partaker in authority."

---T--- Christianity IS EXPECTED or REQUIRED to Magnify Christ & DEN is the definition of the Religion word in the R-E, R~Est, 1-A: // FFOG Roger Sherman worked with the Congress of DOI, AOC, CON, and spoke much. These instructions were written by a GOV committee, which included Sherman for establishing an embassy in Canada: "You are further to declare that we hold sacred the rights of conscience, and may promise to the whole people, solemnly in our name, the free and undisturbed exercise of their religion ,,,And ,,,that all civil rights and the right to hold office were to be extended to persons of any Christian DEN" (39).

---T--- R-E: has God's Religion & R~Est defined as DEN as stated by FFOG: // John Jay wrote: "Providence has given to our people the choice of their rulers, and it is the duty as well as the privilege and interest of our Christian nation to select and prefer Christians for their rulers" (6). As a congress member, he disagreed with England's Parliament which appointed an Episcopal bishop over the USA. He did not disagree because of the Christianity religion, but rather because of England's abuse towards other DENs, and using GOV to demand only 1 Christian DEN; and also to rule all religion. // Mr. Sherman made these remarks of conditional considerations that if such a bishop were appointed, "divested of the power annexed to that office by the common law of England ,,,then we shall be more easy about this ,,,if such bishop had no power over the civil or religious interests of other DEN".

---T--- Christ Centered & Christian Supporting GOV Officers & Citizens required: // Activity in the election for the 2nd Presidency was between John Adams & Thomas Jefferson. The public citizens concern was whether Thomas Jefferson was really a Christian or not. John Adams was more orthodoxy and obviously a Christian. Preachers warned whether Mr. Jefferson went to Church or kept the NT Sabbath. Abigail Adams, an active participant in politics and wife of John Adams, appealed that possibly Thomas Jefferson was not supporting Christianity to its fullest extent, and that he was maybe a deist. Spiritual Moral Citizens began testifying for Jefferson that he was a Christian; such included Tunis Wortman and Dewitt Clinton. Not one person contended the fact that Christianity was not required; Rather Christianity was required; and the citizens intention was that Mr. Jefferson meet such requirements (9).

---T--- R-E, R~Est, 1-A: +] Includes prevention of a national Christian DEN; which would occur by making a law for it to receive partiality ("respecting"). +] It Is Not a statement to accept all religions.

---T--- R-E, R~Est was intended/ purposed for Christ where one part is that~ a] Religion & Establishment of Religion~ to be defined as DEN, and, b] Christianity Supported: // The word Religion was used with the word "establishment" to state that it was religion establishment, or Religious Establishment, or Religious Organization; that is referred to. +FFOG Roger Sherman in CON meetings notes states: ",,,Congress had no authority ,,,by the Constitution to make religious establishments,,,". +FFOG James Madison states: ",,,he apprehended the meaning of the words to be, that Congress should not establish a religion, and enforce the legal observation of it by law, nor compel men to worship God in any manner contrary to their conscience [[conscience is a Christian & Holy Bible word]] ,,,establish a national religion,,," (14).

---T--- USA GOV is for Christ by being~ +] CHRISTIAN; +] Submissive to God's LAWs: // Following is from FFOG George Washington: +Farewell address states: "Of all the dispositions and habits which lead to political prosperity, Religion and Morality are indispensable supports. In vain would man claim ,,,Patriotism, who ,,,subvert these pillars of human happiness, these firmest props of the duties of Men and Citizens. The mere Politician, equally with the pious man, out to respect and cherish them ,,,where is the security for property, for reputation, for life, if the sense of religious obligation desert the oaths which the instrument of investigation in Courts of Justice? ,,,forbid us to expect that national morality can prevail in exclusion of religious principle. It is substantially true that virtue or morality is a necessary spring of popular government." ~Thus here he notes that Good GOV requires Religion~ True Religion. +Professed Christianity as the US President. +Spoke frequently at religious gatherings supporting Christian work and doctrines; thanked them for their contributions to the nation; asked for their prayers; committed himself to pray for them; known to care for, and friendly with clergy. +To Church assemblies said this: "Throne of Grace; pure spirit of Christianity; that Government ,,,approved by Heaven which promotes peace and secures protection to its Citizens". +Said to the Society of the United Brethren

182

(Moravian) that the USA GOV was in support and working with them for a common Christian purpose of assisting people who are not Christian, as follows: "co-operate, as far as the circumstances may conveniently admit, with the disinterested endeavors of your Society to civilize and Christianize the Savages of the Wilderness" (100). And the USA GOV did assist financially and with land. +Mason Locke Weems, in a book, "The Life of George Washington,,,", reports him as giving much support of Christianity.

---T--- <u>Christianity of Jesus is~ +] Required for Citizenship;</u> or at least to support & abide by Christian laws: // Judicial court case in AD 1799 of Supreme Court of Maryland, John M'Creery's Lessee vs. Allender: The case involves that the Will of someone who died and their citizenship was in question, since they immigrated from Ireland. They submitted the documentation of the citizenship. Following are some naturalization statements required to and made by Mr. M'Greery: ",,,subscribe a declaration of his belief in the Christian Religion, and take the oath required by the Act of Assembly of this State, entitled, 'An Act for Naturalization'".

---T--- <u>USA is a Christian Nation for God:</u> // Judicial court case in AD 1931, US Supreme Court, US vs. Macintosh: A Canadian applied for naturalization to the US and the court stated: "We are a Christian people ,,,according ,,,the equal right of religious freedom, and acknowledging with reverence the duty of obedience to the will of God".

---T--- <u>Christian Officers to Support Christ as part of Work in the GOV:</u> // John Jay, AD 1800's, a US Judge, said, ",,,it is the duty as well as the privilege and interest of our Christian nation to select and prefer Christians for their rulers". // Duty not only privilege. // All Officers directly connected with making laws requires Christian; any other GOV positions must support Christianity in Public activities and laws.

---T--- <u>Christianity of Lord Jesus is the USA Religion, & All Other religions</u> are Not; & the proper definitions of the "religion" & "establishment" statements in the CON are DEN: // FFOG Justice Joseph Story with a commentation about the CON & DOI states: "The real difficulty lies in ascertaining the limits to which GOV may rightfully go in fostering and encouraging religions,,,"; "The real object of the First Amendment was not to ,,,advance, Mahometanism, or Judaism, of infidelity, by prostrating Christianity; but to exclude all rivalry among Christian sects, and to prevent any national ecclesiastical establishment which should give to a hierarchy (a denominational council) the exclusive patronage of the N GOV ,,,thus cut off the means of religious persecution ,,,of former ages ,,,rights of conscience in matters of religion which had been trampled upon ,,,from the days of the Apostles to the present age,,,"; "intolerance of sects ,,,exclude N GOV all power to act upon the subject ,,,thus the whole power over the subject of religion is left exclusively to the State GOVs"; "We are not to attribute this prohibition of a national religious establishment [in the First Amendment] to an indifference to religion in general, and especially to Christianity, (which none could hold in more reverence than the framers of the CON) ,,,at the time of ,,,the CON, and ,,,Amendments to it ,,,America was ,,,Christianity ought to receive encouragement from the State ,,,An attempt to level all religions, and to make it a matter of state policy to hold all in utter indifference, would have created universal disapprobation, if not universal indignation. (p) It remains to be seen ,,,whether any free GOV can be permanent, where the public worship of God, and the support of religion, constitute no part of the policy or duty of the state in any assignable shape" (52). // Thomas McIntyre Cooley, a commentator on the CON stated: ",,,the American constitutions contain no provisions which prohibit the authorities from such solemn recognition of a superintending Providence in public transactions and exercises as the general religious sentiment of mankind inspires, and as seems meet in finite and dependent beings ,,,all must acknowledge ,,,in ,,,human affairs ,,,care and control of the Great Governor of the Universe ,,,with thanksgiving ,,,contrition ,,,with penalties of His broken laws. No principle of Constitutional law is violated when thanksgiving or fast days are appointed; when chaplains ,,,for the army ,,,legislative sessions are opened with prayer or the reading of the SCs, or when religious teaching is encouraged by exempting ,,,religious worship from taxation ,,,care be taken to avoid discrimination in favor of any one DEN or sect,,," (53).

---T--- <u>Religion is defined as~ +] inclusive of DEN & methods</u> of Worship, (expressions); +] but the God, of Christianity, is the Same: // Daniel Webster, in AD 1800's, reports to the US Supreme Court saying, "At the meeting of the first Congress, there was a doubt in the minds of many about the propriety of opening the session with prayer; and the reason assigned was, as here, the great diversity of opinion and religious belief ,,,Mr. Samuel Adams ,,,rose in that assembly, and with the air of a perfect Puritan said it did not become men professing to be Christian men [[note they were all Christians]] who had come together for solemn deliberation ,,,to say that there was so wide a difference in their religious belief that they could not, as one man, bow the knee in prayer to the Almighty, Whose advice and assistance they hoped to obtain ,,,that where there is a spirit of Christianity, there is a spirit which rises above form, above ceremonies, independent of sect, or creed, and the controversies of clashing doctrines" (147). This was agreed by the Congress meeting and they prayed.

---T--- <u>Some of the First National Holy Bible Societies were started</u> by US Congress Members, DOI signers; and similarly other Bible societies, as provided by (249). // Benjamin Rush assisted in starting the Philadelphia Bible Society; which had intentional purposes to get the Bible to all people and stimulate other Bible societies to start in other cities. // Elias Boudinot started the American Bible Society, which was a National Bible society; this was intented/purposed to send Bibles worldwide, not only nationwide. // These other following FFOG assisted in various Holy Bible societies: Charles Cotesworth Pickney, John Langdon, James McHenry, Rufus King, Thomas Jefferson, John Brooks, John Hamilton, Rufus Putnam, Matthew Clarkson, John Marshall, Bushrod Washington, Smith Thompson, William Wirt, Felix Grundy, Robert Troup, Joseph Nourse, John Quincy Adams, Daniel Thompkins, William Tilghman, Andrew Kirkpatarick, William Gaston, James Burrill Jr., Peter Vroom, John Cotton Smith, George Madison, David Morrill, William Jones, Charles Goldsborough, Jonas Galusha, Joseph Bloomfield, DeWitt Clinton, Thomas Worthington, Isaac Shelby, Thomas

Posey. ~These people were DOI & CON signers, RW Generals, US Supreme Court Judges, Attorney Generals, US Secretaries, Presidents, Vice Presidents, State Supreme Court Judges, State Governors of the US. And do not forget their wives, children, and relatives which assisted.

---T--- <u>USA Started by Christians for Christ & for Christianity</u> reasons of intention/ purpose: // Christopher Columbus said: "Our Lord opened ,,,my understanding; I could feel his hand upon me; so it became clear to me that it was feasible to navigate from here to there ,,,through the holy and sacred SCs ,,,in the name of our Savior ,,,is the preaching the Gospel recently in so many lands".

---T--- <u>America's First Colonies prioritized Christ by these</u> Statements in their DOCs: // =t= ",,,in propagating of Christian religion ,,,to bring a settled and quiet government"; =t= "The principal effect which we can desire ,,,the Christian religion"; =t= "Having undertaken for the glory of God, and advancement of the Christian faith ,,,voyage ,,,combine ourselves together into a civil body politick"; =t= "our said people ,,,may be ,,,religiously, peaceable, and civilly governed ,,,the Christian faith, which in our royal intention is ,,,the principal end of this plantation"; =t= "We are ,,,professing ourselves fellow members of Christ ,,,entered into Covenant with him for this work"; =t= "be as a city upon a hill,,, pious zeal for extending the Christian religion ,,,having no knowledge of the Divine Being,,,"; =t= "a great cross ,,,to the appointed place with the assistance of the Governor and his associates ,,,we erected a trophy to Christ the Savior"; =t= "They cherished ,,,for the propagation and advance of the Gospel of the kingdom of Christ in the remote parts of the world"; =t= "Excited with ,,,pious zeal for the propagation of the Christian faith ,,,in the parts of America"; =t= "pursuing, with peaceable and loyal minds, sober, serious and religious intentions ,,,in the holy Christian faith ,,,a most flourishing civil state ,,,grounded upon gospel principles"; =t= "when they touched shore they kneeled in thanks to God ,,,a religious colony ,,,invited John and Charles Wesley ,,,to serve as chaplains".

---T--- <u>State GOV Supported Christ & Christian</u> Religion & INCLUDED such: // About the Connecticut CON: "Fundamental Orders of Connecticut"; written mostly by minister Thomas Hooker; an Historian reports that our USA CON is similar to this CON more than any of the 13 colonies (25). The purpose ordered to the committee was to make the laws, "as near the law of God as they can be" (41). It was enacted in AD 1639 with the following preamble, "when a people are gathered together the word of God required that to maintain the peace and union of such a people, there should be an orderly and decent GOV established according to God". // New Hampshire CON: "Considering with ourselves the holy will of God ,,,that we should not live without wholesome laws and civil GOV among us ,,,do in the name of Christ and in the sight of God, combine ourselves together to erect and set up ,,,such government, to our best discerning agreeable to the will of God". // The New England Confederation was formed with the States of Massachusetts, New Plymouth, New Haven, Connecticut in AD 1643, and stated: "We all came into these parts of America, with one and the same end ,,,the kingdom of our Lord Jesus Christ". // New Haven Colony in AD 1644 had these laws for their courts: "The judicial laws of God as they were delivered by Moses ,,,are to be a rule to all the courts" (42). // Carolina's CON in AD 1669 required that people believe in God's existence; the courtroom is to acknowledge Divinity, justice, and human responsibility; church membership. // New York Congress enacted in AD 1665 states~ "the public worship of God" and teach "people in the true religion". // Pennsylvania had Quaker William Penn write their GOV plan in AD 1682 stating, "Make and establish such laws as shall best preserve true Christian and civil liberty in all opposition to all unchristian ,,,practices". Their laws were simplified by stating whatever was Christian was legal and whatever was not Christian was illegal.

---T--- <u>Right to Life is in the 7th Amendment</u> & it is acknowledged as part of the DOI; coming from God; opposes abortion: // Virginia State in AD 1810 had laws declaring children in the womb are not to be killed. // Abortion is not right according to the Holy Bible; in Exo21; Deu19; 1Sam19; Job31; Psa51; 94; 139; Prov6; Isa44; 49; 59; Jer1; Luk1. // James Wilson: Was a Judge put on the US Supreme Court by Pres. George Washington. He started America's first organized legal training teaching students that, ",,,beautiful and undeviating, human life, from its commencement to its close, is protected by the Common Law. In the contemplations of law, life begins when the infant is first able to stir in the womb. By the law, life is protected" (206). // Right to life is the purpose of GOVs. John Quincy Adams says, "Ask the DOI and that will tell you that its authors hold for self-evident Truth that the right to life is the first of the unalienable rights of man ,,,to secure and not to destroy,,, governments are instituted among men" (184). // John Witherspoon says, "Some nations have given parents the power of life and death over their children ,,,we have denied the power of life and death to parents" (154).

---T--- <u>Religion Includes Only DEN of Lord Christ</u>: // FFOG William Penn was a Quaker, a Christian, and stated this: "Established" an absolute toleration; It was his wish that "every man who believed in God should partake of the rights of a citizen; and that every man who adored him as a Christian, of whatever sect he might be, should be partaker in authority". Notice he says a person is required to be a Christian for civil rights; but it is not a requirement of any specific DEN; thus if any Spiritual Moral Being does not decide to be a Christian, then they must support & abide by Christian Laws, and Not start any public activities opposite of Christianity; which is pledging to keep the CC as required to be a citizen.

---T--- <u>Education was Christian for Christ</u>: // In AD 1642 & 1647 Laws required students to read the Holy Bible.

---T--- <u>The Intention/ PURPOSE of the Plans for the</u> Revolution & Start of the USA as a New Nation was~ +] for Christ & Christianity; +] to have a GOV that is Christian with the True Religion: // Plan making before the RW had Groups called Committees of Correspondence. These were there intentions/purposes: +Specify their Rights as people, as Christians, and as subjects of Britain; +Specify how these Rights were violated; +Publicize this information. In Boston they stated~ "The Christian sympathy ,,,free us from our present bondage,,," (46). // Days of prayer and fasting were set up for America (9). // Samuel Adams, from these meetings, published a DOC titled, "The Rights of the Colonists" in AD 1772; it specified their Rights as Christians stating: "These may be best understood by reading and carefully studying the institutes of the great Law Giver and Head of the Christian Church, which are to be found clearly written ,,,in the New Testament" (45). // The intention reason for the RW was to defend Christian Rights, as George Washington states to troops in AD 1776, "Every officer ,,,to live ,,,as becomes a Christian Soldier defending the dearest rights and liberties of his country"; and in AD 1778, ",,,it should be our highest glory to add,,, character of Christian"; and in AD 1783, in a letter to all the State Governors, "I now make it my earnest prayer, that God would have you, and the State over which you preside, in his holy protection ,,,the Divine Author of our blessed religion ,,,happy nation" (12). // The Boston Tea Party involved with the DOI included activities of prayer, fasting, and congress meetings (4). // A USA motto was~ "No King but King Jesus!".

---T--- <u>Religion is defined as DEN</u> & God is supported: // FFOG Benjamin Franklin wrote to the French: ",,,religion, under its various DENs, is not only tolerated, but respected and practiced. Atheism is unknown,,, infidelity rare and secret,,," (47).

---T--- <u>GOV Bell proclaims God</u> & Holy Bible: // The Liberty Bell was sounded with the DOI in AD 1776; and has this engraved on it: "Proclaim liberty throughout the land unto all the inhabitants thereof. LEVITICUS 25:10".

---T--- <u>Religion is not the banning</u> of God's Religion from the GOV, rather a Religious DEN: // FFOG did not intend the FED GOV to make a law for only one DEN, and exclude other DENs. (51).

---T--- <u>History, DOCs from the</u> immigrant colonies, public of the US, & the GOV of the US, all have EV that prove that all Spiritual Moral Folk were aware of, conscious of, and wrote that they were Christian religionists for Christ; and departed from Europe because of false religions.

---T--- <u>History, DOCs from the immigrant colonies</u>, public of the US, & the GOV of the US, prove with EV that These Spiritual Moral Folk were all were aware of, conscious of, and wrote that they were Christian religionists for Christ; and DID NOT DESIRE, infidelism, nor atheism, nor false gods. However they did desire to have a limited tolerance to infidels, atheism, or non-Christians. Such is what Europe and the false religionists there did not have; that is no tolerance for specific subjects and evil violence about it.

---T--- <u>Actions of the USA GOV, immigrant</u> colonies, and public prove they were Christ Caring Religionists.

---T--- <u>Christianity religion for Christ IS REQUIRED to be part</u> of the USA GOV, Except a Specific Religious DEN IS NOT REQUIRED: // The DOI was never dismissed, or stated as changed or rejected or altered or removed in any way as the Ruling or Presiding DOC over the CON when the CON was done. The DOI was and is to be the Ruling DOC over the CON.

---T--- <u>Christianity Religion of Jesus Required to be Part of the USA</u> GOV & All Religious DEN Supported: // The Northwest Ordinance was enacted in AD 1700's stating the US GOV purposes as: "religion, morality, and knowledge being necessary to good GOV and the happiness of mankind, schools, and the means of education shall forever be encouraged". NOTE: It was reenacted after the CON was constructed; this proves the continued purpose of the US GOV was the same. Part of the purpose of this was GOV ventures and explorations to the west territory. And what does it state again? That the US GOV is to spread Christianity to the west part of its new territory.

---T--- <u>The N GOV was Not to Make a Law to Favor a DEN Christian</u> Church; but the States had Laws for DEN (Established Christian Churches); and the continued freedom to do such; such liberty remained to the States. These Churches were DENs, and there could be more than one DEN. The States stopped their participation of limiting to only specific DENs eventually in the AD 1800's. However they did not depart from Christianity; because this was the total intention/ purpose reason of the States & USA Existence. Rather the States formed a denominational free structure. In the AD 1700's - 1800's the CON of at least 9 of the 13 colonies had State churches (established DENs), which includes Georgia, New York, Massachusetts, Connecticut, North and South Carolina, New Hampshire, Maryland, and Virginia. Some of those DEN were the Christian churches of Anglican and Congregational (48).

---T--- <u>Concern - no national DEN established</u>: // But they allowed and supported State DENs at the time.

---T--- <u>Concern - that the Nation be a Christian</u> nation and Christian GOV for Christ.

---T--- <u>Religion & R~Est is defined as inclusive of</u> DEN, secondary doctrine, expression: // The religion is part of Christianity. The word "respecting" is defined as, "to show honor or esteem for high regard" (1a); "favor or partiality". ~(same definition by FFOG & DOC). Thus respect (favor, partiality, or higher regard) was towards an "establishment" of religion, and which refers to DEN. No specific DEN of Christianity should be established, but Christianity is already established.

---T--- <u>Forcing People to be Christian's internally is</u> prohibited by N GOV, but Christianity is supported nevertheless: // FFOG James Madison states: "Whilst we assert for ourselves a freedom to embrace, to profess and to observe the Religion which we believe to be of divine origin, we cannot deny an equal freedom to those whose minds have not yet yielded to evidence which has convinced us. If this freedom be abused, it is an offense against God, not against man: To God, therefore, not to man, must an account of it be rendered" (49). Thus God is supported here but not forcing people to internally "believe" the Lord; however the laws of the land do require physical obedience, as, Not stealing, No Business on the Sabbath, etc.; And disallowance of public buildings & public assemblies & public advertisements for falsity religions or gods.

---T--- <u>History, as occurred in Europe & Asia, included</u>~ +GOV abuse, +religious persecution, +false religion, +and false Christianity. These were all subjects that the FFOG, including the citizens, studied for the construction of the CC (DOI & CON). This proves that the DOCs and GOV was intending/ purpose to do what is right, and protect from evils of the past; by study of the past history. Thus rightful study and inclusive statements and definitions must be considered in interpretations. Congress meetings were recorded by note taking, and they are available. For EX on the subject of Thanksgiving Days, the situation was that God should be thanked, and for various reasons. // However some REP did not appreciate the abuse of Holidays. This is remarks by Mr. Burke & Mr Boudinot: "Mr Burke did not like this mimicking of European customs, where they made a mere mockery of thanksgivings. Two armies had a war. And during a battle they sung a song called, "Te Deum" for the same event, though to one it was a victory, and to the other a defeat (death included). Mr Boudinot was sorry to hear arguments drawn from the abuse of a good thing against the use of it. He hoped no gentleman would make a serious opposition to a measure both prudent and just". Evidently Te Deum is a song maybe to God giving thanks.

---T--- <u>Religion is referring to DENs (Secondary doctrines & expressions), all of Christ</u>: // FFoG J. Madison stated in the congressional meeting notes about the sects or DENs on the Chaplain subject: ",,,to say nothing of the other sects ,,,Roman Catholics & Quakers,,,".

---T--- <u>Christ is the Being of USA GOV Religion; but exactly how to support Him without forcing other Spiritual Moral people was a Care at times by GOV; including the abuses of history; & religion & R~Est is defined as including DEN (sect)</u> (DEN are Christian secondary doctrines & Christian expressions): // FFOG Mr. Madison wrote to Mr. Livingston in AD 1822 about making the 4 godly thanksgiving days a subject of law by the N GOV: ",,,I was ,,,careful to make the Proclamations ,,,indiscriminate, and merely recommendatory; or rather mere designations of a day, on which all who thought proper might unite ,,,religious purposes ,,,I presume your reserve to the Govt a right to appoint particular days for religious worship throughout the State, without any penal sanction enforcing the worship. (p) ,,Catholic portion of the people ,,,sect in the U.S ,,,the general progress made within the two last centuries in favor of this branch of liberty ,,,there remains in others a strong bias towards the old error, that without some sort of alliance or coalition between Govt & Religion neither can be duty supported ,,,the danger cannot be too carefully guarded agst. (p) It was the belief of all sects at one time that the establishment of Religion by law, was right & necessary; that the true religion ought to be established in exclusion of every other; and that the only question to be decided was which was the true religion. The EX of Holland proved that at toleration of sects, dissenting from the established sect, was safe & even useful. The EX of the Colonies, now States, which rejected religious establishments ,,,proved that all Sects might be safely ,,,put on a equal & entire freedom ,,,We are teaching the world the great truth that Govts do better without Kings & Nobles than with them. The merit will be doubled by the other lesson that Religion flourishes in greater purity, without than with the aid of Govt" (49). Thus observe that Christianity is the USA GOV religion but not sects (DEN). Religion in the CON of the CC is True Religion, not False. The situation in Holland was to allow all DEN of Christianity without partiality ("respecting") to one DEN. But how to practice and exact dimensions and applications were difficult at times. // An attempt to establish, by incorporation, the Episcopal Church in Alexandria, Washington D.C. was vetoed by Madison in AD 1811.

---T--- <u>Christianity of Christ is~ +] the Religion of & Supported by the USA GOV</u>: // Thomas Jefferson supported federal money given to start Christian ministries and churches to the Indians. Even after the CON, the Fed GOV supported and provided monies for Christian activity & ministry to the Indians (54)(55).

---T--- <u>The USA & GOV has Christ's Religion of Christianity: //</u> The USA GOV enacted and spent money to set up Church schools, Christian religion, missionary teachers for the Indians in the AD 1800's (including later 1800's); such included the DEN of Moravians (United Brethren), Missionary Society of New York, Baptist, David Brainard, Rev. Mr Steiner (56)(57).

---T--- <u>Prayer of Humiliation & self-denial</u> (fasting) was continuously proclaimed by the USA GOV: Thousands of times, including the States and USA.

---T--- <u>Holy Bible Study</u>: // All FFOG owned and read Holy Bibles. John Quincy Adams read the Bible completely every year from a young age.

---T--- <u>The States & CONs were~ +] Christian including Applying Christ's Holy</u> Bible, +] Provided Freedom of Christian Denomination, which is secondary doctrines & expressions: // Vermont CON of AD 1777, supported the free exercise of Christian DEN worship, stating: "Nevertheless, every sect or DEN of people ought to observe the Sabbath, or the Lord's Day, and keep up and support some sort of religious worship, which to them shall seem most agreeable to the revealed will of God.". This was repeated in the AD 1786 CON. // South Carolina CON of AD 1778 declared, "the Christian Protestant religion shall be deemed and is hereby constituted and declared to be the established religion of this State." They also rejected pretense of religion; and rejected any DEN to be the established religion of the State without agreeing and subscribing to including this~ "that the Christian religion is the true religion ; that the holy SCs of the Old and New Testament are of divine inspiration, and are the rule of faith and practice." // Some colonies, including New England, required that the support of the Christian church was of public duty. // Massachusetts CON, of AD 1780 stated~ "the legislature shall, from time to time, authorize and require, the several towns, parishes, precincts, and other bodies politic or religious societies to make suitable provision at their own expense for the institution of the public worship of God and for the support and maintenance of Protestant teachers of piety, religion and morality in all cases where such provision shall not be made voluntarily." // New Hampshire CON of AD 1784, Article 6 of the Bill of Rights, and repeated in the CON of AD 1792, stated, "the legislature to authorize from time to time, the several towns, parishes, bodies corporate, or religious societies within this State, to make adequate provision at their own expense for the support and maintenance of public Protestant teachers of piety, religion and morality." // Carolinas Fundamental CON of AD 1769, prepared by John Locke, Article 96 reads : "As the country comes to be sufficiently planted and distributed into fit divisions, it shall belong to the parliament to take care for the building of churches, and the public maintenance of divines to be employed in the exercise of religion according to the Church of England, which being the only true and orthodox and the national religion of all the king's dominions, is so also of Carolina, and, therefore, it alone shall be allowed to receive public maintenance by grant of parliament." // Maryland CON of AD 1776, provided "the legislature may, in their discretion, lay a general and equal tax, for 'the support of the Christian religion."

---T--- <u>USA GOV to be Christ Prioritizing & NOT idolatrous gods</u>: // John Jay as US Supreme Court Judge, signer of CON, and Governor of New York said these things: +That USA should be true to Christ ~ "Even the Jews ,,,of Heaven, met with frowns, when they forgot the smiles of the benevolent Creator. By tyrants of Egypt, of Babylon, of Syria, and of Rome, they were severely chastised; and those tyrants themselves, when they had executed the vengeance of Almighty God, their own crimes bursting on their own heads, received justly due to their violation of the sacred rights of mankind. You were born equally free with the Jews,,,"; +Declared that US turn from all evil and trust Christ~ "Let a general reformation of manners take place ,,,universal charity, public spirit, and private virtue be inculcated, encouraged, and practiced. Unite in ,,,vigorous defense of your country ,,,rely upon ,,,Providence of Almighty God,,,"; +declared in GOV public declarations for Christ's Gospel~ "The holy gospels are yet to be preached to these western regions,,,"; +wrote in his Will regarding Christ: "Unto Him who is the author and giver of all good, I render sincere and humble thanks ,,,especially for our redemption and salvation by his beloved Son,,,"; +said to his children, "My children, read the Bible and believe it". (105); +as President of the American Bible Society wrote: "Our Redeemer commanded his apostles to preach the Gospel to every creature: The Old Testament ,,,prophecies respecting the Messiah ,,,apostles guided by the Holy Spirit ,,,The Bible contains ,,,Divine revelations ,,,making known the Holy SCs, and inculcating the will of their Divine and merciful Author, throughout the world,,, The Bible informs us ,,,that our gracious Creator has provided for us a Redeemer, in whom all the nations of the earth should be blessed" (106); +tells the clergy to dutifully insist that the US GOV abide in moral and religious obedience, ",,,it is the right and duty of our pastors to press the observance of all moral and religious duties, and ,,,on every course of conduct which may be repugnant to them,,," (106); +states that the US GOV and Citizens religion is Christian and no infidels allowed, "whether our religion permits Christians to vote for infidel rulers ,,,what the prophet said to Jehoshaphat about his attachment to Ahab ,,,(2Chr 19:2: "Shouldest thou help the ungodly, and love them that hate the Lord?")",~ telling that this SC helps answer whether infidels should be voted in the USA (106).

---T--- <u>FFOG & CC times include no rebuke</u> or negative against Lord Jesus & His Christianity; rather reference to it is always solemn and respectable.

---T--- <u>Chaplains appointed by the</u> USA GOV were only from Christ's DENs.

---T--- <u>Judicial Branch acknowledges Christianity of Christ is the USA Basis</u>: // Court decisions as follow: // in The People vs. Ruggles with Chief Justice of the Supreme Court of New York, Mr. Kent, states, "The people of this State, in common with the people of this country, profess the general doctrines of Christianity, as the rule of their faith and practice." // New York Supreme Court, in Lindenmuller vs. The People, stated, "Christianity is not the legal religion of the State, as established by law. If it were, it would be a civil or political institution, which it is not; but this is not inconsistent with the idea that it is in fact, and ever has been, the religion of the people. This fact is everywhere prominent in all our civil and political history and has been, from the first, recognized and acted upon by the people, as well as by constitutional conventions, by legislatures and by courts of justice." +Now this case has a mix of truth & falsity: 1} There is a confusion of words; the ending statements say that Christianity is "everywhere prominent in all our civil and political history and has been, from the first ,,,as well as by constitutional conventions, by legislatures and by courts of justice"; yet the court says a few sentences before that, "Christianity is not the legal religion of the State, as established by law". 2} "Prominence" is defined as priority and law; this contradicts saying "Christianity is not,,, law". 3} The Case states, 'If Christianity was the legal religion of the State, then it would be a civil or political institution, which it is not'. Yet later states, "Christianity is everywhere prominent [[law & priority]] in all our civil and political history and has been, from the first,,, by constitutional conventions, by legislatures and by courts of justice". How many parts of the USA is said ? "ALL". And "By" how is said to be, "constitutional conventions, legislature, courts of justice", which are all law making and applying Branches. 4} Being the "legal religion" does not equal to be a "civil or political institution". The DOI & CON already made Christianity the legal religion of the USA. Therefore the judge & jury are wrong; errored. Now because Christianity is the legal religion does not equal that the US GOV, or civil or political groups or people, then are to manage the Church and Christianity in every detail; as an institution. So the Court case errors in words and thoughts here.

---T--- <u>Christ Christian religion is the legal religion in the USA but DEN</u> is not; nor is secondary doctrines nor expressions.

---T--- <u>Basis of law is that Glorious Spiritual Moral Being~ Christ of Christianity</u>: // Law Case of South Carolina, City Council vs. Benjamin stated, "It is not perhaps necessary for the purposes of this case to rule and hold that the Christian religion is part of the common law of South Carolina. Still it may be useful to show that it lies at the foundation of even the article of the CON under consideration, and that upon it rest many of the principles and usages, constantly acknowledged and enforced, in the courts of justice.". // The Pennsylvania Supreme Court, in Updegraph vs. The Commonwealth, declared: "Christianity, general Christianity, is, and always has been, a part of the common law of Pennsylvania; Christianity, without the spiritual artillery of European countries; for this Christianity was one of the considerations of the royal charter, and the very basis of its great founder, William Penn; not Christianity founded on any particular religious tenets; not Christianity with an established church, and tithes, and spiritual courts; but Christianity with liberty of conscience to all men."

---T--- <u>Everything is about Christ's Christianity for the Construction of the USA</u>: // The intention reasons for coming to the land, the Spiritual people that came, the falsities that were departed from, the colleges, the DOCs, the REP in GOV, the State GOV CON, the DOI, the intention reasons for the RW, the Christian prayer before meetings, the sources constantly used and referenced, the ministers, the reasons for expanding USA territory, etc.

187

---T--- <u>At various times in the past of</u> the USA the majority population was studied and found professing Christianity & Jesus as the truth; and always somehow related to some Christian DEN~ 70% and upwards.

---T--- <u>No other religion has ever had any</u> major population of the number of US citizens involved in it, as God's True Religion of Christianity.

---T--- <u>The Holy Bible:</u> // This book was the most popular book in the USA in CC times. An EX, is that of a Bible Publisher, in their business existence, published and circulated 450 million copies.

---T--- <u>All the evidence herein is facts &</u> proved; thus Truth.

---T--- <u>Christian Churches</u> are built in the land in multiples; All for Jesus.

---T--- <u>Holidays include Christmas & Resurrection</u> Day (Easter); & Thanksgiving (to God) Day.

---T--- <u>Social Truths in the US Nation are All Christian to Jesus;</u> including the activity, church activity, Christian Sabbath, Holy Bible, Laws, supporting of God, and the Holidays, etc.,~ all EV that this is a Christ centered nation.

---T--- <u>There was intended/ purpose to be no contention or disagreement</u> between GOV & God's Christianity in the USA.

---T--- <u>Truly Christian professors can be hypocrites</u>, or false, or evil, or make mistakes, or support falsity or such, but this does not make Christianity wrong, but them wrong.

---T--- <u>Christianity Religion is open to criticism;</u> it is not beyond common inspection; God is God.

---T--- <u>The Devil/ demons intend</u> & want to ruin our nation by making it non-Christian against Lord Jesus.

---T--- <u>American Citizens have a Duty to Christ with Christianity Religion:</u> // To respect, thankful, attitude of desire, care affection; because it was the intention/ purpose of the CC, the pilgrims, and all GOV establishments of the USA historically; because God is God, their Creator. The Religion of Christianity is not a non-existing part of it, rather an inseparable existing part of it.

---T--- <u>USA GOV Intended to be CHRIST Centered:</u> // FFOG Alexander Hamilton was planning and working on a project intended/ purposed for uniting the Christian DEN together: A National organization with State & Local Chapters to distribute literature, perform charity deeds in various areas, promote the Christian religion, and rule of law under the CON; for which he claimed are the necessary elements in American society. (102).

---T--- <u>"Love, joy, peace, long-suffering, gentleness, goodness, faith,</u> meekness, temperance; against such there is no law." Holy Bible. // Our country has attempted to put these Personality Traits (attributes) in its GOV DOCs and is thus Christian for the Holy Spirit.

---T--- <u>USA GOV & CITIZENS to BE Christ Religious Christians:</u> // FFOG John Adams on Nov 23, 1797 assessed the US and said to congress that this is not right and needs changing, as the Country was turning from good to evil; thus stated: "The state of society has so long been disturbed, the sense of moral and religious obligations so much weakened, public faith and national honor have been ,,,impaired ,,,the law of nations ,,,lost ,,,while price, ambition, avarice, and violence, have been so long unrestrained, there remains no reasonable ground on which to raise an expectation ,,,not be plundered". Hence on Mar. 6, 1799 they proclaimed for Apr. 25 as a "day of solemn humiliation, fasting, and prayer" to be devoted "to the sacred duties of religion in public and private" to repentance, thanksgiving, and the prayer for the Lord to protect the US from "unreasonable discontent,,, disunion, faction, sedition, and insurrection; that He would preserve our country from the desolating sword" (117). // Wife Abigail & John Adams absolutely rejected that the US be ruled by non-Christians; and Abigail expressed it in a letter, "What is the difference of Character between a Prince of Wales, & a Burr? Have we any claim to the favour of protection of Providence, when we have against warning admonition and advise Chosen as our chief Majestrate a man who makes not pretentions to the belief of an all wise and supreme Governour of the World, ordering or directing or overruling the events which take place in it? ,,,he is not a believer in the Christian system,,," (118).

---T--- <u>USA GOV Officials should be Christian for Christ; connected directly to law making:</u> // Thomas Jefferson, at times in his life, professed & practiced Christianity, including church attendance; and professed Christianity in the CON meetings. Not much EV exists that he was not a Christian except a couple of strange decisions on how to relate Christianity and the USA GOV in specific applications; neither of which was anti-Christ. +Gouverneur Morris professes himself to be a Christian, and defended that T. Jefferson was a Christian when there were doubts about it; and that USA GOV officials should be Christian, stating, ",,,those who discontented creatures ,,,say that ,,,Jefferson is not a Christian; yet they must acknowledge that, in true Christian meekness, when smitten on one cheek he turns the other, and by his late appointment of Monroe has taken especial care that a stone which the builders rejected should become the first of the corner [[Bible vs.]]. These are his works; and for his faith, it is not a grain of mustard; but the full size of a pumpkin,,," (107).

---T--- <u>Congress meetings ordered to</u> start with Christian prayer to God (62).

---T--- <u>Congress meetings of July 4, 1787 at a Christian</u> Church with a Christian sermon to be listened to (62).

---T--- <u>Christianity of Jesus promoted by USA GOV:</u> // Pres. George Washington's Farewell Address to the People of the USA: It supports we are a spirit, as taught by Christian Bible, and that God is a Spirit: "The Spirit, unfortunately, is inseparable from our nature, having its root in the strongest passions of the human mind." Then he continues with the sinful state of man & world: "A just estimate of that love of power, and proneness to abuse it, which predominates in the human heart, is sufficient to satisfy us of the truth of this position. -the necessity of reciprocal checks in the exercise of political power; by dividing and distributing it into different depositories, & constituting each the Guardian of the Public Weal against invasions by the others, has been evinced by experiments ancient & modern; -some of them in our country & under our own eyes. - To preserve them must be as necessary as to institute them,,,". Then about GOV, says it is to be Christian: "Tis ,,,true, that virtue or morality is a necessary spring of popular government. -the rule ,,,of Free GOV. -Who ,,,is a sincere friend to it, can look with indifference upon attempts to shake the foundation of the fabric". Then a recommendation to the Christian religion: "Cultivate peace and harmony with all -Religion and morality enjoin this conduct,,,". His life was in support of Christianity.

---T--- <u>Religion of USA GOV is God's Christianity:</u> // FFOG Benjamin Franklin, a Christian, who was non-denominational, in that he attends all sorts of Christian Churches, including the orthodox, quotes the Holy Bible as it is God's word, lives his life by the Holy Bible, prays to Christ, says Christ is God, encourages others to pray to Christ (including the congress), states trust in Christ, and even includes Deism as a Christian DEN, and contributed money to various orthodox Christian DENs. He was non-denominational so much, that he evidently did not become a member of any DEN. Rather he may have considered that is what Deist meant; he surely proclaimed that God becomes involved with man in providence. He was not a Deist for a long time. Though not a member of any DEN, he regularly attended as a member, and supported the doctrines and churches as a member. He started the first hospital in the USA which he based on HSC spoke from his own mouth for the cause of it.

---T--- <u>Deism:</u> // <u>This word or</u> system was utilized as an alternative at least by 1 or 2 of the FFoG, including Benjamin Franklin in early years. But the Deism then is not the same as now. The doctrines of Deism then, had many actually similar doctrines to Christianity, and made it a sort of Christian DEN. Generally Deist is often defined as "a belief in the existence of God but deny direct intervention of God in a persons life or natural order"; in other words, He is Creator but set things with laws in order, and stands apart, letting things occur as activity occurs by natural laws. Deism never was very common in America and was forbidden by most States at the time of the Constitutional Convention. But many of Deisms doctrines at the time of the DOI in America were similar to Christian.

---T--- <u>USA GOV is Christian & Religious for Lord Jesus:</u> // FFOG Christopher Columbus requested assistance from England King Henry VII for travels to parts of the world; but was denied. Later in AD 1496, the King re- considered again, and appointed John Cabot to go and search the lands for England; Cabot made 2 trips; and claimed the coast (pre-America) for England. The Natives were unorganized, considered as heathens, and did not have any known claims to the land. Europeans disagreed on the Rights and boundaries and some war and treaties were experienced; but the lands in the 13 colonies (later States) were vested as Britain's. In the AD 1600's British immigrants outnumbered other immigrants [[and thus Britain was more active, more working for such]]. This gave Right for Christian laws; law and laws were set up, and a GOV, with the use of the English Law known as the Common Law, including the Magna Carta, and the English Bill of Rights; all are based on Christianity (63).

---T--- <u>Religion & 13th Amendment ~ is the</u> following from the 1-A; Assembly for Christians & to have communication & relations with the GOV; to attend to Christ: // Assemble: "Congress shall make no law ,,,abridging ,,,the right of the people peaceably to assemble, and to petition the GOV for a redress of grievances".

---T--- <u>Enlightenment From Christ Expressions for Christianity Support:</u> // Enlightenment is a Christian term and experience, all of which the FFOG were seeking and testified about. History has record of this term. It is a term used that explains a receiving of mental and heart wisdom from the Father of Lights as stated in the Holy Bible (Jesus is the Light). False religions know nothing of this term or experience. (Jam3-4; 1Joh1; Joh4).

---T--- <u>The System & Operation of the GOV, National & State,</u> is to be for Lord Jesus: // Every State wanted independence in DEN Christian subjects, which is secondary doctrines and expressions. And every Colony {13 of them} State had as a requirement, in any GOV position, to be a Christian (these DOC's are shown in State CON's). Thus the N GOV was to be Christian for where does N GOV (congress) come from? From the States. The President was the only position that might not come from the States, as this person may be any person in the US; but if the States required only Christians in Office in their States, then obviously they intended/ purposed for a Christian to be in office of PRE. // Furthermore if the Congress (Legislature) is the one who makes the Laws, (which can also be made by public vote and the CC), and all the States required Christians only to be in Congress; then all the US Congress is to be Christians, and all the laws are to be Christian.

---T--- <u>RELIGION</u>: Principle Law: // The Intentions of the FFoG is not difficult, as those who are in the bewilderment of evil thinking and unclarified principles. The EV is actually extremely much. All the FFOG were professing Christians, all from States that had laws requiring that all REP be Christians. All the States stated that they did not want the N GOV to control the States, nor provide language that could by abuse, control DEN as England and Europe did; nor control Christianity in general. Thus the tools they devised to do such, was to maintain the States Right to have the Christian requirements for REP, have the N GOV support Christianity, "rights, God, Divine Providence, free exercise,,,", except not let them have those other controls. Thus they are to support Christianity in general, have Christian Officers, have Christian laws, not support only 1 DEN, freedom of secondary doctrines, freedom of expressions of Christianity, and not control all Christianity in general, do not support other non-Christian religions, and never oppose Christianity. This was all difficult to put in words. They stated this~ that it was difficult. And they stated there was difficulty in applying it; that is to support and not support differing subjects, and simultaneously. Because they had not written specific applicational laws or rules, they instead wrote Principle Law. Thus principles are difficult, sometimes, to apply, to know how much, and to what subjects.

---T--- <u>Relationship of GOV & Religion as to Total & Particular Subjects; God & DEN:</u> // Religion should be in the schools and in the GOV. But the GOV must not control religion. // FFOG Gouverneur Morris declares that Religion is the only solid basis of good morals, stating, "therefore education should teach the precepts of religion, and the duties of man toward God [[now if schools should, what should the GOV be standing for?]] These duties are, internally, love and adoration; externally, devotion and obedience; therefore provision should be made for maintaining divine worship as well as education. But each one has a right to entire liberty as to religious opinions, for religion is the relation between God and man; therefore it is not within the reach of human authority" (11a).

---T--- <u>FFoG used the terms, "religion of America"</u> which was Christian (66).

---T--- <u>The FFoG were for Christ & Christian & expected the N GOV</u> to~ a) be Christian, b) be Christian supporting, c) support the Holy Bible, d) be opposite of evil, or sin in society: // Thomas Jefferson with Virginia Bill for Religious Liberty proclaimed that "to compel a man to furnish contributions of money for the propagation of opinions which he disbelieves, is sinful and tyrannical" (64). Notice his support of Christian doctrinal, TRUTH, and the words, "sinful" and "tyrannical". These are Christian words. He does not want N GOV or State GOV to support evil or anti-Christ practices, laws, or actions.

---T--- <u>God, Christ Jesus, the Holy Bible,</u> & their Religion was to be an Agreement with by the N GOV; that was the intention/ purpose: // Pres. George Washington & Congress included the priority for a Holy Bible at his presidential inauguration meeting. // The Congress meetings agreed to Mr. Washington's closing remark: "We have raised a standard to which the good and wise can repair; the event is in the hands of God" (67).

---T--- <u>Religion for God & GOV to Agree & Work together:</u> // A US Supreme Court Judge, (as an infidel), could not deny the truth; and testifies that the US must not do what they are doing in opposing Christianity, because this is a Christian nation and requires a specific good relation with Christianity. Such is, William O. Douglas: he states in Zorach vs. Clausen, US case that~ "The First Amendment ,,,does not say that in every and all respects there shall be a separation of Church and State. Rather it studiously defines the manner, the specific ways, in which there shall be no concert or union,,, That is the common sense of the matter. Otherwise the state and religion would be aliends to each other ~ hostile, suspicious, and even unfriendly ,,,Prayers in our legislative ,,,appeals to the Almighty ,,,of the Chief Executive ,,,Thanksgiving Day a holiday; 'so help me God' in our courtroom oaths ,,,all ,,,references to the Almighty that run through our laws, our public rituals, our ceremonies ,,,the Court opens each sessions: 'God save the US and this Honorable Court'" (68).

---T--- <u>Martin Luther was a known Christian forefather</u>, and a counselor of the USA GOV REP, since they read, studied, and knew of the Christian reformations; and of the subjects warning of mans sin potentiality and need for restraints. Mr Luther stated: ",,,the world and the masses are and always will be unchristian, although they are all baptized and are nominally Christian. Christians, however, are few and far between, as the saying is ,,,since the wicked always outnumber the good ,,,to govern an entire country ,,,with the Gospel would be alike a shepherd ,,,in one fold wolves, lions, eagles ,,,any beast keep from molesting,,," (90). // Now this statement is sort of generalistic. This is not a statement that should be used to support evil, rather oppose it. The majority are not always non-Christian, rather sometimes. Nevertheless arise to alertness with KN and application of prevention.

---T--- <u>Historian's research & testimony states we are Christian Nation:</u> // A. James Reichley in writing titled, "Religion in American Public Life", says, "The single most influential cultural force at work in the new nation was the combination of religious beliefs and social attitudes known as Puritanism,,,"; and continues, that 87.5 % of the US Citizens at the time of the Revolution were Christians.

---T--- <u>USA GOV is to be for Jesus & Christianity</u> Religious: // FFOG John Adams said government was a "divine science" (66).

---T--- <u>R~Est was defined as Christian DENs:</u> // FFOG George Washington was a lifetime member of the Anglican Christian Church, and expressed favor for all Christian DENs; he influenced protection of the dissident sects (70). Sects is another word that was used for DEN's.

---T--- <u>FFOG supported</u> <u>the Christian Doctrine that there exists temptation</u> to evil, or sin, and the potentiality of man to sin, & evils of GOV. They constructed a Checks & Balances system, which includes the CC with God & Holy Bible, to assist in this Christian Religion Doctrine: // Patrick Henry in CON congress meetings stated, "Where are your checks in this GOV? Your strong holds will be in the nabs of your enemies: it is on a supposition that our American governors shall be honest, that all the good qualities of this GOV are founded: But its defective, and imperfect construction, puts it in their power to perpetrate the worst of mischief's, should they be bad men: And, Sir, would not all the world, from the Eastern to the Western hemisphere, blame our distracted folly in resting our rights upon the contingency of our rulers being good or bad. Shew me that age and country where the rights and liberties of the people were placed on the sole chance of their rulers being good men, without a consequent loss of liberty?" (86).

---T--- <u>Religion defined as Christianity is a Necessary</u> Part for God of the USA GOV: // FFOG George Washington states: "IT IS IMPOSSIBLE TO GOVERN THE UNIVERSE WITHOUT THE AID OF A SUPREME BEING. It is impossible to reason without arriving at a Supreme Being. Religion is as necessary to reason, as reason is to religion. The one cannot exist without the other. A reasoning being would lose his reason, in attempting to account for the great phenomena of nature, had he not a Supreme Being to refer to,,,", and ",,,Sovereign Arbiter of Nations, that his Providential care may still be extended to the US; that the virtue and happiness of the People, may be preserved,,," (71).

---T--- <u>The FFoG studied Spiritual Moral Beings & National & GOV Systems</u>; & used mostly Christ's Holy Bible; & the other Sources are Christian: // With intentions/purposes to learn about GOV system's, the knowledge was all received from Christian Sources; the 1st priority source was the Holy Bible. The FFOG recorded the sources as follows: // Charles Montesquieu: taught that mans physical Being and the Natural World are both governed by laws of God; all law is from God; opposed the Mohammedan religion (Islam). // William Blackstone: wrote about the "Law of Nature" as that which is "dictated by God Himself". // John Locke: wrote papers on natural law and natural rights, including this~ "Human laws, must be made according to the general Laws of Nature, and without contradiction to any positive Law of SC, otherwise they are ill made"; also said that the natural rights of man are "life, liberty, and property". // Grotius: wrote "any order that is contrary to the law of nature or to the commandments of God, the order should not be carried out. For when the Apostles said that ,,,[[Act5:29]]"; also wrote papers titled, "The Rights of War and Peace", and "The Truth of the Christian Religion" (94). // Samuel de Pufendorf: writing titled, The Law of Nature and Nations. // Algernon Sidney: wrote a paper titled, "Discourse on Government", which taught the God-given right of free men opposes governmental oppression. He himself was beheaded for alleged plotting against pro-Catholic King Charles II (9). // Sir Edward Coke: was a Predecessor of William Blackstone; very seriously opposed illegal exercise of governmental authority. Wrote good studies which assisted right GOV in England. // John Milton: provided good EX and instructions against governmental tyranny and individual Rights. // The Principles of Truth that the FFoG learned from these sources include: +Realization of God's existence, presence, and providence by which He guides and controls the universe and affairs of men; +Respect for religion with God; +Respect for Holy SC; +Human reason is from God and used to apprehend truth but does not take priority over revelation; +Man is not a perfect Being; +God ordains human government because of sin potentiality & the world of good & evil; +Physical Laws over physical things and Moral Laws over Moral things are from God; +Holy SCs reveal Moral Law and Law of Nature which include the conscience in man; +Human law must be in order with divine law of SC and Law of Nature (conscience); +Divine Law & Law of Nature from God are the basis of national law; These laws are also the basis for resistance to tyranny or evil; +These laws are basis of Rights from God, life, liberty, happiness; +Governments can be abusive; +Separate National powers to prevent abuse; +Freedom of Rights provides incentives (9). // Also (265).

---T--- <u>The FFoG Included Christ, Christianity, the Holy Bible</u>, Righteousness, Affectionate Heart & Body Actions & Love: // John Adams says, "Christian benevolence makes it our indispensable duty to lay ourselves out to serve our fellow creatures to the utmost of our power" (59). // John Quincy Adams states, "The doctrines promulgated by Jesus and His apostles,,, lessons of peace, benevolence, meekness, brotherly love, charity" (184). // Richard Henry Lee says, "Christian philosophy in its tenderness for human infirmities, strongly inculcates principles ,,,benevolence" (213). // James Kent says, "Christianity ,,,taught the duty of benevolence to strangers" (204). // Similar statements were made by many others. Christian love is the basis of the US, and such love assists people and opposes evil.

---T--- <u>Noah Webster's books were distributed</u> through the US as school resources; they included a "Moral Catechism" which said~ "God's word, contained in the Bible has furnished all necessary rules to direct our conduct", and had a section~ "Federal Catechism". Thus God's religion was always part of GOV.

---T--- <u>The USA CON is to~</u> +] be Christian; +] have Christ as the Ruler; +] receive expressions of honor from Christ if He is honored; +] oppose false religion: // FFOG George Washington writes: "Let us unite,,, imploring the Supreme Ruler of nations, to <u>spread his holy protection over these</u> <u>US: to turn the machinations of the wicked to the confirming of our CON</u>: to enable us at all times to root out internal sedition, and put invasion to flight: to perpetuate ,,,country that prosperity, which his goodness has already conferred, and to verify the <u>anticipation of this government being a</u> <u>safeguard to human rights</u>" (71). +The word "constitution" is used in this that He wrote~ ",,,we may then unite in most humbly offering our prayers and supplications to the great Lord and Ruler of Nations and beseech him to pardon our national and other transgressions, to enable us all, whether in public or private stations, to perform our several and regular duties properly and punctually, to render our N GOV a blessing to all the People, by constantly being a government of wise, just and constitutional laws, discreetly and faithfully executed and obeyed, to protect and guide all Sovereigns and Nations (especially such as have shown kindness unto us) and to bless them with good GOV, peace, and concord. <u>To</u> <u>promote the knowledge and practice of true religion and virtue</u>, and the increase of science among them and us, and generally to grant unto all Mankind such a degree of temporal prosperity as he alone knows to be best." (71). Notice the USA GOV is to be a promoter of the Christian religion as the true religion; thus there are false religions of the which are not true. // Now George is no fool to ask God to be the Ruler and Protector, which is Christ, as this was his whole doctrine, then directly reject Christ by not applying the commands of Christ in the Holy Bible; and then also encourage all citizens and Officers do the same. The man would be a hypocrite and a deceiver if so. And what protection could he trust for by praying to Christ and then insulting Him at the same time?

---T--- <u>Definition of Religion & R~Est includes the following~</u> +] Religion as rightly defined had 2 definitions by the FFoG, one of which was DEN; & the other as of true vs. false system of God & man. +] Religion true is of God & part of the USA GOV, whereas false religions are not so. +] Not every religion is to be promoted & have unlimited Rights by the USA GOV. +] Religion true, Christianity, is to be part of the USA GOV: // FFOG George Washington wrote: ",,,we may then unite in most humbly offering our prayers and supplications to the great Lord and Ruler of Nations ,,,to render our N GOV a blessing to all the People, by constantly being a GOV of wise, just and constitutional laws, discreetly and faithfully executed and obeyed, to protect and guide all Sovereigns and Nations ,,,to bless them with good GOV ,,,To promote the knowledge and practice of true religion and virtue ,,,and generally to grant unto all Mankind such a degree of temporal prosperity as he alone knows to be best.", continuing, " Let us with caution indulge the supposition, that morality can be maintained without religion ,,,reason and experience both forbid us to expect that National morality can prevail in exclusion of religious principle", continuing, "It is the duty of all Nations to acknowledge the providence of Almighty God, TO OBEY HIS WILL, to be grateful for his benefits, and humbly to implore his protection and favor" (71). +Mr. Washington also writes, "Of all the dispositions and habits which lead to political prosperity [[note political related]], Religion and morality are indispensable supports. [[note that religion to politics is the most needed to cause it to succeed]] In vain would that man claim the tribute of Patriotism, who should labour to subvert these great Pillars of human happiness, these firmest props of the duties of Men and citizens. [[note that happiness of

191

the DOI is related to true religion as necessary; that Patriotism is vain to claim unless true religion is its basis]]. The mere Politician, equally with the pious man ought to respect and to cherish them ,,,Let it simply be asked where is the security for property, for reputation, for life, if the sense of religious obligation desert the oaths, which are the instruments of investigation in Courts of Justice? ,,,It would improper to omit in this official Act, my fervent supplications to that Almighty Being who rules over the Universe, who presides in the Councils of Nations, and whose <u>providential aids can supply every human defect, that his benediction may consecrate to the liberties and happiness of the People of the US, a GOV instituted by themselves for these essential purposes</u>; and may enable every instrument employed in its administration to execute ,,,the functions allotted to his charge. [[note here that the whole of the USA GOV is purposed for Christ & religion]]. In tendering this homage to the Great Author of every public an private good,,,. No people can be bound to acknowledge and adore the invisible hand, which conducts the Affairs of men more than the People of the US. Every step, by which they have advanced to the character of an independent nation, seems to have been distinguished by some token of providential agency. [[note here that God is to be included in GOV]]. ,,,The General hopes and trusts, that every officer and man will endeavor so to live, and act, as becomes a Christian Soldier defending the dearest Rights and Liberties of his country [[note that Officers are to be Christian]]. ,,,It shall be my endeavor ,,,whatever may be in my power ,,,the preservation of the civil and religious liberties of the American People. ,,,The liberty enjoyed by the People of these States of worshipping Almighty God agreeable to their consciences is not only among the choicest of their blessings but also of their right. ,,,While men perform their social duties faithfully, they do all ,,,society or the state can demand or expect ,,,remain responsible only to their Maker for the religion, or modes of faith ,,,[[note that the US GOV is only supportive of public Christianity, with its various DENs, and all else is a violation for public activities]] ,,,abundant reason to rejoice that in this Land the light of truth and reason [[the US GOV is to be a guard of truth; not promoter of falsities]] has triumphed over the power of bigotry and superstition, and that every person may here worship God according to the dictates of his own heart. [[Note a primary reason of the FFoG is the worship of God; the true God, not any god or multiple gods]] In this enlightened Age ,,,a man's religious tenets will not forfeit the protection of the Laws, nor deprive him of the right of attaining ,,,offices ,,,in the US" (71). Note it refers to history of Europe that had enacted GOV control of religion and dictated what DEN of Christianity. Also note that "religious" is used with "tenets" which is defined as "doctrines", which is what DENs include~ secondary doctrines & expressions.

---T--- <u>Lord Christ's Holy Bible is the Book of the USA; & the Holy Spirit is our Priority Being:</u> // US Pres. Ronald Reagan and Congress proclaimed 1983 as the US year of the Holy Bible; declared & enacted as public law~ Oct 4, 1982. Statements in the Law are as follows: "Our DOI as well as the CON of the US embraced concepts of civil GOV that were inspired by Holy SCs ,,,we are at a unique point in our spiritual development as a nation ,,,among them, Presidents Washington, Jackson, Lincoln, and Wilson ,,,paid tribute to the surpassing influence that the Bible is ,,,words of ,,,Jackson, "the rock on which our Republic rests" ,,,third century as a nation dedicated to the proposition that all men are created equal and that they are endowed by their Creator with certain inalienable rights ,,,challenge ,,,preservation of religious freedom ,,,were met in whole or in part by the Providence of God, and our faith and trust in Him ,,,the challenges of the 1980's ,,,can be met if we follow the EX of our forefathers and renew our knowledge of and faith in God through study and application of teachings of the Holy SCs ,,,1983 can be a year of spiritual renewal as a nation ,,,That is why I and 29 Senators are introducing a joint resolution today that, once passed, authorizes and requests the President to declare 1983 as year of the Bible ,,,Our joint resolution ,,,is straight forward ,,,notes the surpassing influence the Bible has had in the formation of this Nation, and its roots in our early settlement and our form of civil GOV. This joint resolution requests the President to designate 1983 as the Year of the Bible ,,,in recognition of the formative influence of the Bible has been for our Nation, and of our national need to study and apply the teachings of the Holy SCs,,, Already plans are underway to use 1983 as a year to foster biblical teaching and study ,,,Whereas the Bible, the Word of God, has made a unique contribution in shaping the US as a distinctive and blessed nation and people; Whereas deeply held religious convictions springing up from the Holy SCs led to the early settlement of our Nation; Whereas Biblical teachings inspired concepts of civil GOV that are contained in our DOI and the CON of the US ,,,Whereas the history of our Nation clearly illustrates the value of voluntarily applying the teachings of the SCs in the lives of individuals, families, and societies ,,,Whereas that renewing our knowledge of and faith in God through Holy SC can strengthen us as a nation and a people: Now, therefore, be it Resolved by the Senate and House of Representatives of the US of America in Congress assembled, That the President is authorized and requested to designate 1983 as a national "Year of the Bible" in recognition of both the formative influence the Bible has been for our Nation, and our national need to study and apply the teachings of the Holy SCs". +See there that these Spiritual Moral Beings state that the Holy Bible is the source of the "concepts ,,,contained in our DOI and the CON of the US".

---T--- <u>USA Formation Based on God's Holy Bible as quotes taken from cite (249):</u> // Pres. Franklin Roosevelt stated, "In the formative days of the Republic, the directing influence the Bible exercised upon the Fathers of the Nation is conspicuously evident ,,,we cannot read the history of our rise and development as a Nation without reckoning with the place the Bible has occupied in shaping the advances of the republic ,,,I suggest a nationwide reading of the Holy Scriptures". // Pres. Woodrow Wilson stated, "America was born to exemplify that devotion to the elements of righteousness which are derived from the revelations of Holy Scripture". // Pres. Teddy Roosevelt said, "The teachings of the Bible are so interwoven and intertwined with our whole civic and social life that it would be literally ,,,impossible for us ,,,life ,,,if these teachings were removed". // Pres. Andrew Jackson said, "It [the Bible] is the rock on which our Republic rests".

---T--- <u>God's Holy Bible is a Priority Part of the USA GOV as declared by FFOG; Cited from (249):</u> // Benjamin Rush says, "The Bible ,,,is the only correct map of the human heart,,,". John Jay says, "The Bible is the best of all books, for it is the Word of God,,,". John Quincy Adams says, ",,,universal recommendation is the Bible". Robert Treat Paine says, ",,,the Bible ,,,the written Word of God". William Samuel Johnson says, ",,,Acquaint yourselves with Him in His word and holy ordinances". James Wilson says, "directly from Himself ,,,revelation ,,,the Holy Scriptures".

---T--- <u>The USA GOV is for Christ, Christian, Religious, & with Christian Officers:</u> // FFOG George Washington's prayers: "Almighty God, and most merciful Father, who didst command the children of Israel to offer a daily sacrifice to Thee [[from the Holy Bible]] ,,,my sins, remove them from Thy presence, as far as the east is from the west, and accept of me for the merits of Thy Son, Jesus Christ ,,,to the saving of my soul in the day of the Lord Jesus ,,,O most Glorious God, in Jesus Christ my merciful and loving Father ,,,Thy holy word [[the Holy Bible]] ,,,faith and repentance, increase my faith, and direct me to the true object, Jesus Christ the Way, the Truth, and the Life, bless ,,,the people of this land ,,,those Thou hast appointed to rule over us in church & state [[note pertaining to people hired]] ,,,for the sake of,,, Dear Son, Jesus Christ our Lord ,,,likeness of,,, Son, Jesus Christ ,,,attain resurrection of the just unto eternal life ,,,unite us all in praising and glorifying Thee in all our works [[note the purpose of the US is unity of the people for to worship Jesus Christ]] ,,,Bless O Lord the whole race of mankind, and let the world be filled with the knowledge of Thee and Thy Son, Jesus Christ ,,,defend me ,,,from all evil ,,,for Jesus Christ sake ,,,[[evil is that which is opposed to Jesus & by USA GOV]] ,,,I thine ,,,creature and servant ,,,the Lord Jesus Christ ,,,Bless the people of this land ,,,be our guide [[Jesus is guide of the USA GOV]] ,,,receive me unto the bosom of Thy love ,,,safely rest under Thy protection ,,,in the name of ,,,Jesus Christ ,,,Bless all in authority over us ,,,Almighty and eternal Lord God, the great Creator of heaven and earth, and the God and Father of our Lord Jesus Christ [[note the DOI Creator & laws are referring to Jesus]]" (72).

---T--- <u>The USA GOV is to constantly be careful to desire, encourage, & support</u> what is right; including Christian activity for God: // FFOG George Washington states about "conscientious scruples" (a word that is the internal state of a person who is anxious or disturbed or uneasy in that they are trying to determine what is right in a specific area): "In my opinion the conscientious scruples of all men should be treated with great delicacy and tenderness,,," (71).

---T--- <u>God's USA GOV is Not to Support Evil</u> Nor anti-Christ Activities: // FFOG George Washington states: ",,,contempt of the religion of a country by ridiculing any of its ceremonies, or affronting its ministers or votaries, has ever been deeply resented ,,,you are to be particularly careful to restrain every officer and soldier from such imprudence and folly, and to punish every instance of it ,,,as far as lies in your power ,,,protect and support the free exercise of religion of the country ,,,rights of conscience in religious matters" (49a). Note conscience is a divine word from Christianity and part of the self-evidence; and connected to religion.

---T--- <u>The Christian Revivals of history,</u> are Fact (Truth or Reality); they Increased God's Presence; they are titled in historical DOCs, including Encyclopedias, as "Great Awakenings". Some of these occurred in Europe and the USA in AD 1700's & 1800's. They greatly effected the USA & GOV with citizenry to increase Christianity to Spiritual Moral Beings & activities, both in quantity & quality; although Christianity was already part of the USA. Following are only a few of many Revivals: // This is recorded by Spiritual people in the USA, such as noted by Charles Finney, Asa Mahan, of whom were involved in the 2nd Great Awakening. However this is their notes about the 1st Great Awakening which occurred before they were alive; and it was actually written by the Spiritual moral folks involved: From Charles Finney's notes~ "prayer prevailed at Cambuslang, AD 1741-2, in the revival under William McCulloch and Whitefield. When Whitefield reached Cambuslang he immediately preached, on the braeside, to a vast congregation (on a Tuesday at noon). At six o'clock he preached again, and a third time at nine. Then McCulloch took up the parable and preached till one in the morning, and still the people were unwilling to leave. So many were convicted, crying to God for mercy, that Whitefield described the scene as "a very field of battle." On the ensuing Communion Sunday, Whitefield preached to twenty thousand people; and again on the Monday, when, he said: "You might have seen thousands bathed in tears, some at the same time wringing their hands, others almost swooning, and others crying out and mourning over a pierced Savior. It was like the Passover in Josiah's time." On the voyage from London to Scotland, prior to this campaign, Whitefield had "spent most of his time on board ship in secret prayer." (See Gledstone's "George Whitefield, M.A., Field Preacher.")".

---T--- <u>Christian Revivals were increased in the USA by the</u> ministries of the Christian DEN called the Salvation Army: // This organization established their Christian assemblies in many places in the USA. A devoted Christian Salvation Army Woman was one of the first to start the Salvation Army ministry works in the USA. The Salvation Army is part of the Holiness Movement. Their work went worldwide for evangelizing Spiritual Moral Beings for Christianity. They had good~ +} clothing standards, +} bodily health standards, +} doctrinal standards, +} help to poor & needy people standards, +} Love & the Holy Spirit in their Hearts, +} rightness in their words, +} opposed recreational alcohol in the USA, +} praised and thanked the true & living God; intending for His presence. This organization was part of the 2nd Great Awakening for Christianity in the USA & Europe.

---T--- <u>Virginia & Pennsylvania States Congress & Citizens had</u> a similar Bill of Rights; as that of the USA. Virginia State was a sample that was used by the USA GOV Congress; It has very many similarities in parts, and it was first, before the USA CON, in time. The Virginia Declaration of Rights is as it is titled. It was approved by the Virginia Constitutional Convention on June 12, 1776. It is as follows: // "A DECLARATION OF RIGHTS made by the representatives of the good people of Virginia, assembled in full and free convention which rights do pertain to them and their posterity, as the basis and foundation of GOV. Section 1. That all men are by nature equally free and independent and have certain inherent rights, of which, when they enter into a state of society, they cannot, by any compact, deprive or divest their posterity; namely, the enjoyment of life and liberty, with the means of acquiring and possessing property, and pursuing and obtaining happiness and safety. Section 2. That all power is vested in, and consequently derived from, the people; that magistrates are their trustees and servants and at all times amenable to them. Section 3. That GOV is, or ought to be, instituted for the common benefit, protection, and security of the people, nation, or community; of all the various modes and forms of GOV, that is best which is capable of producing the greatest degree of happiness and safety and is most effectually secured against the danger of maladministration. And that, when any government shall be found inadequate or contrary to these purposes, a majority of the community has an indubitable, inalienable, and indefeasible right to reform, alter, or abolish it, in such manner as shall be judged most conducive to the public weal. Section 4. That no man, or set of men, is entitled to exclusive or separate emoluments or privileges from the community, but in consideration of public services; which, nor being descendible, neither ought the offices of magistrate, legislator, or judge to be hereditary. Section 5. That the legislative and executive powers of the state should be separate and distinct from the judiciary; and that the members of the two first may be restrained from oppression, by feeling and participating the burdens of the people, they should, at fixed periods, be reduced to a private station, return into that body from which they were originally taken, and the vacancies be supplied by frequent, certain, and regular elections, in which all, or any part, of the former members, to be again eligible, or ineligible, as the laws shall direct ,,,Section 12. That the freedom of the press is one of the great bulwarks of liberty, and can never be restrained but by despotic governments ,,,Section 15. That no free GOV, or the blessings of liberty, can be preserved to any people but by a firm adherence to justice, moderation, temperance, frugality, and virtue and by frequent recurrence to fundamental principles. <u>Section 16. That religion, or the duty which we owe to our Creator, and the manner of discharging it, can be directed only by reason and conviction, not by force or violence; and therefore all men are equally entitled to the free exercise of religion, according to the dictates of conscience; and that it is the mutual duty of all to practice Christian forbearance, love, and charity toward each other."</u> (14a). // Now note religion is DEN, which includes secondary doctrines of Christianity, expressions (ceremonies included), and organizations. Christian laws were to be kept, and acknowledged as the true God.

---T--- <u>States GOV & Citizens</u> Support GOV & Religion for God as Together: // Virginia States Congress resolutions of AD 1798 with James Madison states. "The Virginia Resolution, Dec. 24, 1798 RESOLVED, That the General Assembly of Virginia, doth unequivocally express a firm resolution to maintain and defend the CON of the US, and the CON of this State, against every aggression either foreign or domestic, and that they will support the GOV of the US in all measures warranted by the former. (p) That this assembly most solemnly [[solemnly is a Christian word, a sacred word]] declares a warm attachment [[righteous affections here expressed]] to the Union of the States, to maintain which it pledges all its powers; and that for this end, it is their duty to watch over and oppose every infraction of those principles which constitute the only basis of that Union, because a faithful observance of them, can alone secure it's existence and the public happiness. (p) That this Assembly doth explicitly and peremptorily declare, that it views the powers of the federal GOV, as resulting from the compact, to which the states are parties; as limited by the plain sense and intention of the instrument constituting the compact; as no further valid that they are authorized by the grants enumerated in that compact; and that in case of a deliberate, palpable, and dangerous exercise of other powers, not granted by the said compact, the states who are parties thereto, have the right, and are in duty bound, to interpose for arresting the progress of the evil, [[evil is a Christian word, which is includes wrongs against God]] and for maintaining within their respective limits, the authorities, rights and liberties appertaining to them. (p) That the General Assembly doth also express its deep regret, that a spirit has in sundry instances, been manifested by the federal GOV, to enlarge its powers by forced constructions of the constitutional charter which defines them; and that implications have appeared of a design to expound certain general phrases (which having been copied from the very limited grant of power, in the former articles of confederation were the less liable to be misconstrued) [[this supports the AOC (a Christian DOC)]] so as to destroy the meaning and effect, of the particular enumeration which necessarily explains and limits the general phrases; and so as to consolidate the states by degrees, into one sovereignty, the obvious tendency and inevitable consequence of which would be, to transform the present republican system of the US, into an absolute, or at best a mixed monarchy. (p) That the General Assembly doth particularly protest against the palpable and alarming infractions of the CON, in the two late cases of the "Alien and Sedition Acts" passed at the last session of Congress; the first of which exercises a power no where delegated to the federal GOV, and which by uniting legislative and judicial powers to those of executive, subverts the general principles of free GOV; as well as the particular organization, and positive provisions of the federal constitution; and the other of which acts, exercises in like manner, a power not delegated by the CON, but on the contrary, expressly and positively forbidden by one of the amendments thereto; a power, which more than any other, ought to produce universal alarm, because it is leveled against that right of freely examining public characters and measures, and of free communication among the people thereon, [[The CC supported]] which has ever been justly deemed, the only effectual guardian of every other right. (p) That this state having by its Convention, which ratified the federal CON, expressly declared, that among other essential rights, "the Liberty of Conscience and of the Press cannot be cancelled, abridged, restrained, or modified by any authority of the US,,, [[Conscience is a Christian word exclusively]] and from its extreme anxiety to guard these rights from every possible attack of sophistry or ambition, [[evil desires]] having with other states, recommended an amendment for that purpose, which amendment was, in due time, annexed to the CON; it would mark a reproachable inconsistency, and criminal degeneracy, if an indifference were now shewn, to the most palpable violation of one of the Rights, [[Rights from God]] thus declared and secured; and to the establishment of a precedent which may be fatal to the other. (p) That the good people of this commonwealth, having ever felt, and continuing to feel, the most sincere affection for their brethren of the other states; the truest anxiety for establishing and perpetuating the union of all; and the most scrupulous fidelity to that CON, which is the pledge of mutual friendship, and the instrument of mutual happiness; the General Assembly doth solemnly appeal to the like dispositions of the other states, in confidence that they will concur with this commonwealth in declaring, as it does hereby declare, that the acts aforesaid, are unconstitutional; and that the necessary and proper measures will be taken by each, for co-operating with this state, in maintaining the Authorities, Rights, and Liberties, referred to the States respectively, or to the people. (p) That the Governor be desired, to transmit a copy of the foregoing Resolutions to the executive authority of each of the other states, with a request that the same may be communicated to the Legislature thereof; and that a copy be furnished to each of the Senators and Representatives representing this state in the Congress of the US. Agreed to by the Senate, Dec. 24, 1798." // This system is intending for a Checks & Balance System to prevent evil & promote Christianity.

---T--- <u>Kentucky State CON supports that </u>the USA GOV is supporting, not opposing, the CC; which includes Jesus & His Christianity. // Resolution of Congress with Thomas Jefferson in AD 1799 states ~ "RESOLUTIONS IN GENERAL ASSEMBLY -- (p) THE representatives of the good people of this commonwealth in general assembly convened, having maturely considered the answers of sundry states in the Union, to their resolutions passed at the last session, respecting certain unconstitutional laws of Congress, commonly called the alien and sedition laws, would be faithless indeed to themselves, and to those they represent, were they silently to acquiesce in principles and doctrines attempted to be maintained in all those answers, that of Virginia only excepted. To again enter the field of argument, and attempt more fully or forcibly to expose the unconstitutionality of those obnoxious laws, would, it is apprehended be as unnecessary as unavailing. (p) We cannot however but lament, that in the discussion of those interesting subjects, by sundry of the legislatures of our sister states, unfounded suggestions, and uncandid insinuations, derogatory of the true character and principles of the good people of this commonwealth, have been substituted in place of fair reasoning and sound argument. Our opinions of those alarming measures of the general GOV, together with our reasons for those opinions, were detailed with decency and with temper, and submitted to the discussion and judgment of our fellow citizens throughout the Union. Whether the decency and temper have been observed in the answers of most of those states who have denied or attempted to obviate the great truths [[Truth]] contained in those resolutions, we have now only to submit to a candid world. Faithful to the true principles [[Truth & Principles supported]] of the federal union, unconscious of any designs to disturb the harmony of that Union, and anxious only to escape the fangs of despotism, [[word defined as unlimited power without constitution or Spiritual Moral Beings to Check it]] the good people of this commonwealth are regardless of censure or calumniation. (p) Least however the silence of this commonwealth should be construed into an acquiescence in the doctrines and principles advanced and attempted to be maintained by the said answers, or least those of our fellow citizens throughout the Union, who so widely differ from us on those important subjects, should be deluded by the expectation, that we shall be deterred from what we conceive our duty; or shrink from the principles contained in those resolutions: therefore. (p) RESOLVED, That this commonwealth considers the federal union, upon the terms and for the purposes specified in the late compact, [[CC supported]] as conducive to the liberty and happiness [[DOI terms referred to]] of the several states: That it does now unequivocally declare its attachment to the Union, and to that compact, agreeable to its obvious and real intention, and will be among the last to seek its dissolution: That if those who administer the general GOV be permitted to transgress the limits fixed by that compact, by a total disregard to the special delegations of power therein contained, annihilation of the state GOVs, and the erection upon their ruins, of a general consolidated government, will be the inevitable consequence: That the principle and construction contended for by sundry of the state legislatures, that the general GOV is the exclusive judge of the extent of the powers delegated to it, stop nothing short of despotism; since the discretion of those who administer the government, and not the CON, would be the measure of their powers: That the several states who formed that instrument, being sovereign and independent, have the unquestionable right to judge of its infraction; and that a nullification, by those sovereignties, of all unauthorized acts done under colour of that instrument, is the rightful remedy: That this commonwealth does upon the most deliberate reconsideration declare, that the said alien and sedition laws, are in their opinion, palpable violations of the said CON; and however cheerfully it may be disposed to surrender its opinion to a majority of its sister states in matters of ordinary or doubtful policy; yet, in momentous regulations like the present, which so vitally wound the best rights of the citizen, it would consider a silent acquiescence as highly criminal: That although this commonwealth as a party to <u>the federal compact</u>; will bow to the laws of the Union, yet it does at the same time declare, that it will not now, nor ever hereafter, cease to oppose in a constitutional manner, every attempt from what quarter soever offered, to violate that compact: (p) AND FINALLY, in order that no pretexts or arguments may be drawn from a supposed acquiescence on the part of this commonwealth in the constitutionality of those laws, and be thereby used as precedents for similar future <u>violations of federal compact</u>; this commonwealth does now enter against them, its SOLEMN PROTEST. Approved Dec. 3rd, 1799." // This State has a CON that requires Christianity for holding office, and here also promotes the DOI & CC, and Christian Rights from God.

---T--- <u>What it Does Not Say or Define:</u> // It cannot be defined as saying we are not supportive of God, because we are supportive of the true God & Religion. // Nor does it define that we are not limited about the True God, because we are limited to the True God. And because we are limited to the True God, we are limited to the True Christian Church, Holy Bible, Truth, and anti-sin (evil). Because if not, it would break the Law of Contradiction to the Statements in the CC DOI; would also break the Law of Making the Statements True~ that the statements in the DOI are True

195

and must remain true and must not be made false; would also break the Law of Application~ that the statements in the DOI do not apply to what they say they apply to; whichas in reality they must apply to what they say they apply to; if they do not, they are as nothing, zero.

---T--- <u>LAW of AGREEMENT or DISAGREEMENT</u>: God Positive or negative; Law of Support or Opposition; FOR or AGAINST; AIDE or FIGHT AGAINST; Help or Hinder; There EXISTS NO NEUTRALITY -- AGREEMENT or DISAGREEMENT: // "Neutrality" concept must be according to truth. We cannot take the word and start to claim it defines this or that, or such, etc. +Neutrality does exist in specific subjects, IF we apply this word as it really is defined by truth. +Neutrality exists when a person is undecided on a subject; then they are neutral, for the moment. And as long of time that they are undecided on the subject, then for that amount of time they are neutral. +Spiritual Moral Beings are neutral on subjects that do not contradict or oppose, or are different than each other; because they are generally not subjects of right & wrong (in these subjects it is actually right OR wrong); such as subjects of main doctrine. For EX, if a person has decided to grow corn and both methods of planting do not make a difference, then neutrality is proper in deciding either way. +However on subjects, (that need decisions or include a decision), that contradict, or oppose, or are different than each other in such ways as right OR wrong, or on subjects of doctrine, which is in essence truth or lie (falsities), neutrality cannot exist. +Now in a world of good & evil and existing as Beings of Free-Will, then we must not ignore or deny that 2 sides are given to a truth or a rightness; that is one is either truth ~OR~ lie, right ~OR~ wrong. +Christ has surely and plainly instructed this truth to prevent us from deceit, assist our comprehension, avoid confusion, triumph over wiles of demons, and give us light from His wonderful countenance; and teach His loved children. What did He say? He said it multiple many times by direct statement and by EX in life: "How can 2 walk together except they agree? A house divided shall not stand; He who is not against me is for me; if they are not against me they are for me; put you a difference between that which is holy & unholy; be all of one mind; the world does not believe for they are not one"~ [[all Holy Scriptures]]. Hence we must agree or there is division. Agree OR disagree. There is no neutral area. If we do not agree then we will train others to agree with our position and then there will be 2 groups of Spiritual Moral people in the land that disagree; and it cannot be done and have unity or maintain existence. // In the subjects that must be agreed on, there cannot be any laws against or "neutral" (which actually oppose). An EX of such subject is the Religion of Christianity; because this is what was intended by the CC; inclusive of DEN freedom. // Some specific subjects require agreement and some specific subjects do not; Some are limited to agreement and others are allowed for freedom, or variation. How much freedom is given to each subject is another part of agreement; this is the putting of limits on the subject. If a group of Spiritual Moral people want to have a righteous land (as our FFoG did) and free from evil, then they must have agreement. Agreement in some specific subjects & disagreement in other subjects. This includes legalizing business to occur. Someone has to say what the rule is. Otherwise there is disagreement and this is a form of war or strife. // For EX let us take the subject of the Sabbath (SB) day. If one spiritual moral Being says 'yes', and another 'no', and they reside next to each other, they begin to have a society in which a habitual living is done; they that are disagreeing with the Sabbath tells others the same, because of wants for business to sell goods and/or services on the SB; thus the 2 opposing sides on the SB begin to multiply in number of people and activities; Thus now they cannot agree to have 2 societies that oppose each other; For one will have groups working on the SB and telling the other one that the other one is wrong, and the same with the other group; thus division and disagreement. One group will eventually multiply insisting the other work or do the same on the subject of the SB; There is a constant disagreement, the one against the other. It could even accelerate to such an increase in anti-Christ people that the Christian could not get a job without working on Sunday. Now get a number of doctrines, or subjects such as this, and you have anarchy. Deny, ignore, deceive as you want, but the fact is, one group wants as many SB activity to support them, and the Christians want as many the other way; one group says "YES", the other "NO"; one says "STOP", the other "START". // Another EX is recreational alcohol. Drunkenness influence by selling this "liquid demon" and tempting those who disagree with it; drunkards also tempt the disagreeing people family members; then alcohol business sets up increasingly, and the opposing group is efforting to stop it more and more; and there exists 2 opposing forces in the land. Then effects start occurring from alcohol; such are dangerous. // Christianity is the support of the persuasion of our neighbors; thus attempting to persuade others from a life of sin. // Ways the GOV is enacting laws are deceptions in the form of "neutrality" when they refuse to support Christ & His Christianity in Office and set up freedoms for evil, licenses for evil, support for evil, encouragements for evil, and do not oppose it; and falsely claim neutrality. It is a cloak, a covering for evil, and claiming it is a freedom and care and right concept, when it is not. The Following are some ways some Spiritual Moral Beings have tried to abide by the 1-A Law by non-Christianity: +Observe the Libraries of the land that are filled with evils of every sort; witchcraft, pornography, anti-Christian, all sorts of opposition to our GOV form, and etc. +Deliberate Disadvantage Principle (A Law used today): GOV action that intentionally prejudices people who have or have not a specific religious doctrine is a violation of the Free Exercise Clause unless the GOV proves that a rule on the religious doctrine is of interest (65). This whole law of the courts is untruthful & unreasonable. Whose interest? A sinner? An anti-Christian group? A judge? A society of multitude? There is no Free Exercise Neutrality here, nor protection, but such opening for the mind to fall out the other side. +Burdensome Effect Principle: If GOV rules (laws) for secular/neutral purposes (without intent to provide advantage to religious doctrines or discourage people against their religious doctrine) then arises conflicts with the action or inaction of the religious doctrine; then the Free Exercise Clause requires exemptions under these conditions: 1~ Cognizable injury suffered by the claimant; 2~ Exemption does not violate the Establishment Clause; 3~ Exemption does not require GOV to have no regulation program; 4~ Religious doctrines of the person is sincerely upheld; 5~ Violation of the religious doctrines includes extra-temporal consequences; 6~ Selection of the best option so as to cause the least burden upon the person and the practice of their religious doctrine; 7~ GOV cannot prove that the rule is necessary to some interest (65). Those will not work, because it is the establishment of anti-religion in the land. It is a lie in the form of a colorful snake wrapped up to appear as a butterfly. +Intentional Advantage Principle (A law used today): GOV rules that intentionally either~ 1~ Support religious doctrines; or 2~ Does not apply the GOV rules to these people with the religious doctrines; or 3~ The rules action presents a significant threat to religious liberty; or 4~ If the rules action is discriminatory, then they violate the Establishment Clause (65). +Independent Impact Principle (A Law used today): GOV rules (laws) violate the Establishment Clause if: 1~ Benefits religious doctrines, and 2~ Has no independent secular impact, and 3~ Even if the purpose of the rule is non-religious OR 4~ Even if the GOV rule has general applicability and 5~ If the GOV rules action endangers religious liberty (65). // Many parts of the GOV have become so deceitful as to make laws against Christianity and then define it as Neutral or innocent. // Some GOV wants to make laws but they also want to deny laws that the FFoG established, and then tell everyone they are abiding by those laws that the FFoG established for the GOV. // Denial; there will be a constant pull and tension. We see and observe it everywhere we look today; in politics, in business, in activities right & left; in lobbying, in so many and so much it is overwhelming, and a terrible weight on the mind. // We cannot deny the fact of evil spirits; if we build a society against God's laws then we are inviting the evil spirits in the land. // Now some Spiritual Moral Beings may not value their eternal dwelling place of Heaven or Hell. Nevertheless there is NO neutrality here. It is eternal; it is a serious subject; it is good or evil. // Now as to a person's internal Will, it must not be forced. But as to activities of the land & Law making, some form of GOV must exist to have agreement. // Now all FFOG DISAGREED with false religion, religious abuse, and false "Christianity"; and thus now why would they then simultaneously also AGREE to construct a structure for the existence of it wherein they AGREED that would result in the same Problems as that which they had previously studied and DISAGREED with and were efforting to stop? They did not agree that all disagreements co/ exist in one place simultaneously; for this would DISAGREE with the CC (DOI & CON) statements, all the supporting DOC, all the work reported, and all the intentions/purposes of the USA. // Subjects of Disagreement & Agreement must be known. // Subjects that the FFoG stated we are to be in Agreement on in this country are God (Christianity), Truth, the Holy Bible, Self-Evidence of Christ and truth, Creation, Rights of people coming from God; the GOV being an assistance to the Rights and protector and guarantee of those Rights coming from God, such as life, liberty, and happiness and that which is associated; no unlimited evil (sin) supported by the GOV in the land; no opposition to Christianity and its doctrines; Christian people in GOV positions; freedom of DENs; no GOV supreme control of Christianity; the CC; limitations about evil. This applies to Law Making and Public Activities. // Thus the GOV must either oppose or support Laws of Christ; every decision, thought, will, affection, intention/ purpose, and action is either on one side or the other. If any Christian commandment that prohibits something is made legal, and the GOV allows or accepts or promotes it, then it is anti-Christ at that point; and is the development of an anti-God GOV and society which is plainly illegal in the USA CC (DOI & CON).

---T--- <u>USA GOV, Congress, Executive, Historians</u> all state that Christ's Religion of Christianity is to be Part of USA GOV: // James Madison expressed it in his Memorial and Remonstrance, "The Religion then of every man must be left to the conviction and conscience of every man; and it is the right of every man to exercise it as these may dictate. This right is in its nature an unalienable right.". // George Mason in AD 1776 states, "No free GOV, or the blessings of liberty can be preserved to any people, but by a firm adherence to justice, moderation, temperance, frugality, and virtue, and by frequent recurrence to fundamental principles.". // Tocqueville stated, "the first of their political institutions" ,,,[[paraphrased]]~ 'was the Americans religion of Christianity and the various DENs of it'.

---T--- <u>Williamsburg Charter states:</u> // "<u>Religious liberty</u> finally depends on neither the favors of the state and its officials nor the vagaries of tyrants or majorities. The Religious Liberty clauses are a brilliant construct in which both No establishment and Free exercise serve the ends of religious liberty and freedom of conscience. No longer can sword, purse and sacred mantle be equated. Now, the GOV is barred from using religion's mantle to become a confessional State, and from allowing religion to use the government's sword and purse to become a coercing Church".

---T--- <u>God's Religion is the Cause of the Effect of GOV.</u> // These FFOG knew and applied such Religion stating: +George Washington, "political prosperity ,,,religion and morality are indispensable supports". +John Adams (21), "religion and morality alone, which can establish the principles upon which freedom can securely stand". +Noah Webster (46a), "The principles of all genuine liberty, and of wise laws and administrations are to be drawn from the Bible and sustained by its authority". +Abraham Lincoln (134a), "The only assurance of our nation's safety is to lay our foundation in morality and religion". +John Witherspoon (154a), "God grant that in America true religion and civil liberty may be inseparable and that the unjust attempts to destroy the one, may in the issue tend to the support and establishment of both". +James Madison (62a), "We have staked the whole future of American civilization not upon the power of government, far from it. We have staked the future of all of our political institutions ,,,upon the capacity of each and all of us to govern ourselves, to control ourselves, to sustain ourselves according to the ten commandments of God.". +B. F. Morris (36), "The state must rest upon the basis of religion, and it must preserve this basis, or itself must fall". +Thomas Jefferson (30), "the liberties of a nation ,,,secure ,,,when we have removed the only firm basis, a conviction in the minds of the people that these liberties are the gift of God". +Timothy Dwight (247), "Where there is no religion, there is no morality ,,,security of life, liberty ,,,buried in the ruins". +Abigail Adams (97a), "A patriot without religion ,,,is as great a paradox, as an honest man without the fear of God ,,,The Scriptures tell us righteousness exalteth a Nation".

---T--- <u>The USA GOV is NOT to Be NO RELIGION</u>; Rather to HAVE RELIGION: // Infidelity was specifically, clearly, and obviously opposed. The word was used. Infidel thinking, is that the person desires no religion, or actually also is defined as anti-Christ; because the infidel rejects and disagrees with Christ. So infidelity was discouraged and not agreed with.

---T--- <u>USA GOV to God Centered & CHRISTIAN and RELIGIOUS,</u> NOT False Religion, NOT false Christianity, NOT Infidel (NO Religion): // FFOG John Adams said, "Our CON was made ONLY for a moral and religious people. It is wholly inadequate for the government of any other"; and not for "a republic of thirty million atheists". // Religious Abuse: Cloaks or false Christians or false religion is historically true. So what of it? Who does not know we are in a world of good & evil, and falsities can take many forms including counterfeit? The false Christians or false Judaism also existed in Christ's Fleshly Body times. // FFOG Samuel Adams wrote to Thomas Paine declaring that US GOV, US Citizens, and such are to be Christian: "When I heard you had turned your mind to a defense of infidelity, I felt myself much astounded and more grieved, that you had attempted a measure so injurious to the feelings and so repugnant to the true interest of so great a part of the citizens of the US. The people of New England, if you will allow me to use a SC phrase, are fast returning to their first love,,," (116). // John Adams, Pres., said these thoughts of Paine as an "insolent Blasphemer of things sacred and a transcendent Libeller of all that is good" and "It is indeed a disgrace to the moral character and the understanding of this Age, that this worthless fellow should be believed in any thing. But impudence and malice will always find admirers" (97a). // Why did they take such oppositions to Mr. Paine? Because some positions of GOV in Office of Legalities require to be a Christian. And Mr. Paine was attempting to oppose Christianity in the GOV and had gotten in position. // False religion or false OT Christians killed Christ. The Israelites turned and started false religion, such as Baal, which mixed Judaism with lies.

---T--- <u>WHAT ATTITUDES of HEART & BODY</u> ACTIONS TOWARDS God & RELIGION: // +Religion must be respected & affectionately cared for; to be related to with a special regard and desire for it. +For protection. +It must be defined. +It is not anti-God as the DOI states. Religion here is not to anti-Christ; all the States required only Christians to be an Officer for Law making; and they were all Christians. +It must be related as Truth; the DOI respects truth and the truth they all intended, lived, and said was that of God, or Christ; Christ was in all the lives of the pilgrims, colonies, GOV, GOV Officers, GOV establishments, systems, public, and GOV schools. +Thus religion must be managed with special relations. +It was not to be excluded as some illegal GOV Officials today are doing. +It is not to be confused and made that all religions are equal, as Islam, Buddha, etc. as with Christian; they declared it; fully knew history and rejected these falsity religions; refusing them to exist without limits, or unlimited Freedom Rights as legal basis in the US. +Privately the person has the Right to believe in falsity religions, but in the GOV, both State and NAT, and with public regulations and licenses, they were to not be given any such permission to own land with intention to start their false belief in a building or place of assembly meetings, nor public advertisements. // Thus guidelines must be set forth, now more than ever, to further clarify the definitions of the terms that the FFoG & US DOCs stated. Especially because the operation of the States & N GOV has become more complex. All State CON had Christianity supported and Christianity required to acquire an Office. Now many States have removed those and therefore the basis which the USA N GOV relied on has now been changed, and is NOT operative as was planned & designed. So the terms used then are not familiar with us today, and the operations are also unfamiliar. So guidelines on what "religion" is accepted, and definition of "religion" & R~Est words used in the USA CON; and then what the N GOV may do, and may not do, needs to be declared. Stop continued confusion and lies to enter in. We are Not a System of anti-religion, nor anti-Christ, nor polytheism, nor pluralistic society. These paganistic, heathenistic, demonic, folly, vanity, and crazy systems of existence are all falsities that are causes of PAIN. These are not designed, intended, said, or lived; they are actually opposed by FFoG and the CC. // Also see (265).

---T--- <u>CHRISTIANITY of Lord Jesus to be in GOV Officials</u> & Citizens; FFOG State following: // John Adams, "Our CON was made only for a moral and religious people. It is wholly inadequate to the government of any other". // Benjamin Franklin, "Only a virtuous people are capable of freedom. As nations become corrupt and vicious, they have more need of masters". // Samuel Adams, "Neither the wisest CON nor the wisest laws will secure the liberty and happiness of a people whose manners are universally corrupt".

---T--- <u>RELIGIOUS WEEK ENACTMENT in DEC 2007</u>: // This Congress (US Congress, Dec 18, 2007) proclamation was made to recognize a "national religious week". +In many parts it is illegal; because parts of it are anti-Christian and against the FFOG and CC (DOI & CON). Many times demons like to do bad by appearing good; this is witchcraft. Now on religious diversity, does it include Wiccans? Sorcery? Satanism? Demons? Devilry? Islam? Buddha? NO. And what of all the evil music groups & evil TV? What in the world is this devilry doing on USA Soil? It is barbaric, satanic, and evil. Does it include establishing infidel laws which oppose Christian laws? NO. Observe that every historical evidence that the Congress stated in the enactment is Christian. Not one is any "religion" but Christian. What a minute!!! What was that??? That is right!!! Every DOC says only Christian, and always if referring to other false religions speaks rejection of them. // Now the wording of this Enactment is noted that, for the truth of such it is herein included; however for the falsity of such, it is herein warned as to the inclusion of such illegality against the US. AND as you will read, every Religious Reference herein is Christian; thus the Religion they are enacting must be Christian; there are easily 100 Christian Evidences herein in the form of Holidays, events, activities, Officials, REPs, DOCs, enactments, etc., including multiples of Holy Scriptures; and it states 200 years of the USA and it is all Christian Activity. There is no other religion herein, no false religion. Following is the Enactment wording: "Affirming the rich spiritual and religious history of our Nation's founding and subsequent history and expressing support for designation of the first week in May as `American Religious History Week' for the appreciation of and education on America's history of religious faith. In The House of Representatives Dec. 18, 2007 ,,,submitted the following resolution; which was referred to the Committee on Oversight and Government Reform RESOLUTION Affirming the rich spiritual and religious history of our Nation's founding and subsequent history and expressing support for designation of the first week in May as `American Religious History Week' for the appreciation of and education on America's history of religious faith. Whereas religious faith was not only important in official American life during the periods of discovery, exploration, colonization, and growth but has also been acknowledged and incorporated into all 3 branches of American Federal GOV from their very beginning; Whereas the Supreme Court of the US affirmed this self-evident fact in a unanimous ruling declaring `This is a religious people ,,,From the discovery of this continent to the present hour, there is a single voice making this affirmation'; Whereas political scientists have documented that the most frequently-cited source in the political period known as The Founding Era was the Bible; Whereas the first act of America's first Congress in 1774 was to ask a minister to open with prayer and to lead Congress in the reading of 4 chapters of the Bible; Whereas Congress regularly attended church and Divine service together en masse; Whereas throughout the American Founding, Congress frequently appropriated money for missionaries and for religious instruction, a practice that Congress repeated for decades after the passage of the CON and the First Amendment; Whereas in 1776, Congress approved the DOI with its 4 direct religious acknowledgments referring to God as the Creator (`All people are endowed by their Creator with certain unalienable rights, that among these are life, liberty and the pursuit of happiness'), the Lawgiver (`the laws of nature and nature's God'), the Judge (`appealing to the Supreme Judge of the world'), and the Protector (`with a firm reliance on the protection of Divine Providence'); Whereas upon approving the DOI, John Adams declared that the Fourth of July `ought to be commemorated as the day of deliverance by solemn acts of devotion to God Almighty'; Whereas 4 days after approving the Declaration, the Liberty Bell was rung; Whereas the Liberty Bell was named for the Biblical inscription from Leviticus 25:10 emblazoned around it: `Proclaim liberty throughout the land, to all the inhabitants thereof'; Whereas in 1777, Congress, facing a National shortage of `Bibles for our schools, and families, and for the public worship of God in our churches,' announced that they `desired to have a Bible printed under their care & by their encouragement' and therefore ordered 20,000 copies of the Bible to be imported `into the different ports of the States of the Union'; Whereas in 1782, Congress pursued a plan to print a Bible that would be `a neat edition of the Holy SCs for the use of schools' and therefore approved the production of the first English language Bible printed in America that contained the congressional endorsement that `the US in Congress assembled ... recommend this edition of the Bible to the inhabitants of the US'; Whereas in 1782, Congress adopted (and has reaffirmed on numerous subsequent occasions) the National Seal with its Latin motto `Annuit Coeptis,' meaning `God has favored our undertakings,' along with the eye of Providence in a triangle over a pyramid, the eye and the motto `allude to the many signal interpositions of Providence in favor of the American cause'; Whereas the 1783 Treaty of Paris that officially ended the Revolution and established America as ,,,independent begins with the appellation `In the name of the most holy and undivided Trinity'; Whereas the delegates to the Constitutional Convention concluded their work by in effect placing a religious punctuation mark at the end of the CON in the Attestation Clause, noting not only that they had completed the work with `the unanimous consent of the States present' but they had done so `in the Year of our Lord one thousand seven hundred and eighty seven'; Whereas James Madison declared that he saw the finished CON as a product of `the finger of that Almighty Hand which has been so frequently and signally extended to our relief in the critical stages of the Revolution,' and George Washington viewed it as `little short of a miracle,' and Benjamin Franklin believed that its writing had been `influenced, guided, and governed by that omnipotent, omnipresent, and beneficent Ruler, in Whom all inferior spirits live, and move, and have their being'; Whereas from 1787 to 1788, State conventions to ratify the US CON not only began with prayer but even met in church buildings; Whereas in 1795 during construction of the Capitol, a practice was instituted whereby `public worship is now regularly administered at the Capitol, every Sunday morning, at 11 o'clock'; Whereas in 1789, the first Federal Congress, the Congress that framed the Bill of Rights, including the First Amendment, appropriated Federal funds to pay chaplains to pray at the opening of all sessions, a practice that has continued to this day, with Congress not only funding its congressional chaplains but also the salaries and operations of more than 4,500 military chaplains; Whereas in 1789, Congress, in the midst of framing the Bill of Rights and the First Amendment, passed the first Federal law touching education, declaring that `Religion, morality, and knowledge, being necessary to good government and the happiness of mankind, schools and the means of education shall forever be encouraged'; Whereas in 1789, on the same day that Congress finished drafting the First Amendment, it requested President Washington to declare a National day of prayer and thanksgiving, resulting in the first Federal official Thanksgiving proclamation that declared `it is the duty of all nations to acknowledge the providence of Almighty God, to obey His will, to be grateful for His benefits, and humbly to implore His protection and favor'; Whereas in 1800, Congress enacted naval regulations requiring that Divine service be performed twice every day aboard `all ships and vessels in the navy,' with a sermon preached each Sunday; Whereas in 1800, Congress approved the use of the just-completed Capitol structure as a church building, with Divine services to be held each Sunday in the Hall of the House, alternately administered by the House and Senate chaplains; Whereas in 1853 Congress declared that congressional chaplains have a `duty ... to conduct religious services weekly in the Hall of the House of Representatives'; Whereas by 1867, the church at the Capitol was the largest church in Washington, DC, with up to 2,000 people a week attending Sunday service in the Hall of the House; Whereas by 1815, over 2,000 official governmental calls to prayer had been issued at both the State and the Federal levels, with thousands more issued since 1815; Whereas in 1853 the US Senate declared that the Founding Fathers `had no fear or jealousy of religion itself, nor did they wish to see us an irreligious people ,,,they did not intend to spread over all the public authorities and the whole public action of the nation the dead and revolting spectacle of atheistically apathy'; Whereas in 1854 the US House of

Representatives declared `It [religion] must be considered as the foundation on which the whole structure rests „,Christianity; in its general principles, is the great conservative element on which we must rely for the purity and permanence of free institutions'; Whereas, in 1864, by law Congress added `In God We Trust' to American coinage; Whereas in 1864, Congress passed an act authorizing each State to display statues of 2 of its heroes in the US Capitol, resulting in numerous statues of noted Christian clergymen and leaders at the Capitol, including Gospel ministers such as the Revs. James A. Garfield, John Peter Muhlenberg, Jonathan Trumbull, Roger Williams, Jason Lee, Marcus Whitman, and Martin Luther King Jr.; Gospel theologians such as Roger Sherman; Catholic priests such as Father Damien, Jacques Marquette, Eusebio Kino, and Junipero Serra; Catholic nuns such as Mother Joseph; and numerous other religious leaders; Whereas in 1870, the Federal GOV made Christmas (a recognition of the birth of Christ, an event described by the U.S. Supreme Court as `acknowledged in the Western World for 20 centuries, and in this country by the people, the Executive Branch, Congress, and the courts for 2 centuries') and Thanksgiving as official holidays; Whereas beginning in 1904 and continuing for the next half-century, the Federal GOV printed and distributed The Life and Morals of Jesus of Nazareth for the use of Members of Congress because of the important teachings it contained; Whereas in 1931, Congress by law adopted the Star-Spangled Banner as the official National Anthem, with its phrases such as `may the Heav'n-rescued land Praise the Power that hath made and preserved us a nation,' and `this be our motto, `In God is our trust!'; Whereas in 1954, Congress by law added the phrase `one nation under God' to the Pledge of Allegiance; Whereas in 1954 a special Congressional Prayer Room was added to the Capitol with a kneeling bench, an altar, an open Bible, an inspiring stained-glass window with George Washington kneeling in prayer, the declaration of Psalm 16:1: `Preserve me, O God, for in Thee do I put my trust,' and the phrase `This Nation Under God' displayed above the kneeling, prayerful Washington; Whereas in 1956, Congress by law made `In God We Trust' the National Motto, and added the phrase to American currency; Whereas the CONs of each of the 50 states, either in the preamble or body, explicitly recognize or express gratitude to God; Whereas America's first Presidential Inauguration incorporated 7 specific religious activities, including——(1) the use of the Bible to administer the oath; (2) affirming the religious nature of the oath by the adding the prayer `So help me God!' to the oath; (3) inaugural prayers offered by the President; (4) religious content in the inaugural address; (5) civil leaders calling the people to prayer or acknowledgement of God; (6) inaugural worship services attended en masse by Congress as an official part of congressional activities; and (7) clergy-led inaugural prayers, activities which have been replicated in whole or part by every subsequent President; Whereas President George Washington declared `Of all the dispositions and habits which lead to political prosperity, religion and morality are indispensable supports'; Whereas President John Adams, one of only 2 signers of the Bill of Rights and First Amendment, declared `As the safety and prosperity of nations ultimately and essentially depend on the protection and the blessing of Almighty God, and the national acknowledgment of this truth is not only an indispensable duty which the people owe to Him'; Whereas President Jefferson not only attended Divine services at the Capitol throughout his presidency and had the Marine Band play at the services, but during his administration church services were also begun in the War Department and the Treasury Department, thus allowing worshippers on any given Sunday the choice to attend church at either the US Capitol, the War Department, or the Treasury Department if they so desired; Whereas Thomas Jefferson urged local governments to make land available specifically for Christian purposes, provided Federal funding for missionary work among Indian tribes, and declared that religious schools would receive `the patronage of the government'; Whereas President Andrew Jackson declared that the Bible `is the rock on which our Republic rests'; Whereas President Abraham Lincoln declared that the Bible `is the best gift God has given to men „,But for it, we could not know right from wrong' Whereas President William McKinley declared that `Our faith teaches us that there is no safer reliance than upon the God of our fathers, Who has so singularly favored the American people in every national trial and Who will not forsake us so long as we obey His commandments and walk humbly in His footsteps'; Whereas President Teddy Roosevelt declared `The Decalogue and the Golden Rule must stand as the foundation of every successful effort to better either our social or our political life'; Whereas President Woodrow Wilson declared that `America was born to exemplify that devotion to the elements of righteousness which are derived from the revelations of Holy SC'; Whereas President Herbert Hoover declared that `American life is builded, and can alone survive, upon „,[the] fundamental philosophy announced by the Savior nineteen centuries ago'; Whereas President Franklin D. Roosevelt not only led the Nation in a 6 minute prayer during D-Day on June 6, 1944, but he also declared that `If we will not prepare to give all that we have and all that we are to preserve Christian civilization in our land, we shall go to destruction'; Whereas President Harry S. Truman declared that `The fundamental basis of this Nation's law was given to Moses on the Mount. The fundamental basis of our Bill of Rights comes from the teachings which we get from Exodus and St. Matthew, from Isaiah and St. Paul'; Whereas President Harry S. Truman told a group touring Washington, DC, that `You will see, as you make your rounds, that this Nation was established by men who believed in God. „,You will see the evidence of this deep religious faith on every hand'; Whereas President Dwight D. Eisenhower declared that `Without God there could be no American form of GOV, nor an American way of life. Recognition of the Supreme Being is the first, the most basic, expression of Americanism. Thus, the founding fathers of America saw it, and thus with God's help, it will continue to be' in a declaration later repeated with approval by President Gerald Ford; Whereas President John F. Kennedy declared that `The rights of man come not from the generosity of the state but from the hand of God'; Whereas President Ronald Reagan, after noting `The Congress of the US, in recognition of the unique contribution of the Bible in shaping the history and character of this Nation and so many of its citizens, has ... requested the President to designate the year 1983 as the `Year of the Bible',' officially declared 1983 as `The Year of the Bible'; Whereas every other President has similarly recognized the role of God and religious faith in the public life of America; Whereas all sessions of the US Supreme Court begin with the

200

Court's Marshal announcing, `God save the US and this honorable court'; Whereas a regular and integral part of official activities in the Federal courts, including the US Supreme Court, was the inclusion of prayer by a minister of the Gospel; Whereas the US Supreme Court has declared throughout the course of our Nation's history that the US is `a Christian country', `a Christian nation', `a Christian people', `a religious people whose institutions presuppose a Supreme Being', and that `we cannot read into the Bill of Rights a philosophy of hostility to religion'; Whereas Justice John Jay, an author of the Federalist Papers and original Justice of the US Supreme Court, urged `The most effectual means of securing the continuance of our civil and religious liberties is always to remember with reverence and gratitude the Source from which they flow'; Whereas Justice James Wilson, a signer of the CON, declared that `Human law must rest its authority ultimately upon the authority of that law which is Divine ... Far from being rivals or enemies, religion and law are twin sisters, friends, and mutual assistants'; Whereas Justice William Paterson, a signer of the CON, declared that `Religion and morality ... [are] necessary to good GOV, good order, and good laws'; Whereas President George Washington, who passed into law the first legal acts organizing the Federal judiciary, asked, `where is the security for property, for reputation, for life, if the sense of religious obligation desert the oaths in the courts of justice?'; Whereas some of the most important monuments, buildings, and landmarks in Washington, DC, include religious words, symbols, and imagery; Whereas in the US Capitol the declaration `In God We Trust' is prominently displayed in both the US House and Senate Chambers; Whereas around the top of the walls in the House Chamber appear images of 23 great lawgivers from across the centuries, but Moses (the lawgiver, who --according to the Bible --originally received the law from God,) is the only lawgiver honored with a full face view, looking down on the proceedings of the House; Whereas religious artwork is found throughout the US Capitol, including in the Rotunda where the prayer service of Christopher Columbus, the Baptism of Pocahontas, and the prayer and Bible study of the Pilgrims are all prominently displayed; in the Cox Corridor of the Capitol where the words `America! God shed His grace on thee' are inscribed; at the east Senate entrance with the words `Annuit Coeptis' which is Latin for `God has favored our undertakings'; and in numerous other locations; Whereas images of the Ten Commandments are found in many Federal buildings across Washington, DC, including in bronze in the floor of the National Archives; in a bronze statue of Moses in the Main Reading Room of the Library of Congress; in numerous locations at the U.S. Supreme Court, including in the frieze above the Justices, the oak door at the rear of the Chamber, the gable apex, and in dozens of locations on the bronze latticework surrounding the Supreme Court Bar seating; Whereas in the Washington Monument not only are numerous Bible vss and religious acknowledgements carved on memorial blocks in the walls, including the phrases: `Holiness to the Lord' (Exodus 28:26, 30:30, Isaiah 23:18, Zechariah 14:20), `Search the SCs' (John 5:39), `The memory of the just is blessed' (Proverbs 10:7), `May Heaven to this Union continue its beneficence', and `In God We Trust', but the Latin inscription Laus Deo meaning `Praise be to God' is engraved on the monument's capstone; Whereas of the 5 areas inside the Jefferson Memorial into which Jefferson's words have been carved, 4 are God-centered, including Jefferson's declaration that `God who gave us life gave us liberty. Can the liberties of a nation be secure when we have removed a conviction that these liberties are the gift of God? Indeed I tremble for my country when I reflect that God is just, that His justice cannot sleep forever'; Whereas the Lincoln Memorial contains numerous acknowledgments of God and citations of Bible vss, including the declarations that `we here highly resolve that ... this nation under God ... shall not perish from the earth'; `The Almighty has His own purposes. `Woe unto the world because of offenses; for it must needs be that offenses come, but woe to that man by whom the offense cometh' (Matthew 18:7); `as was said three thousand years ago, so still it must be said `the judgments of the Lord are true and righteous altogether' (Psalms 19:9); `one day every valley shall be exalted and every hill and mountain shall be made low, the rough places will be made plain, and the crooked places will be made straight and the glory of the Lord shall be revealed and all flesh see it together (Dr. Martin Luther King's speech, based on Isaiah 40:4-5); Whereas in the Library of Congress, The Giant Bible of Mainz, and The Gutenberg Bible are on prominent permanent display and etched on the walls are Bible vss, including: `The light shineth in darkness, and the darkness comprehendeth it not' (John 1:5); `Wisdom is the principal thing; therefore, get wisdom and with all thy getting, get understanding' (Proverbs 4:7); `What doth the Lord require of thee, but to do justly, and to love mercy, and to walk humbly with thy God' (Micah 6:8); and `The heavens declare the Glory of God, and the firmament showeth His handiwork' (Psalm 19:1); Whereas numerous other of the most important American GOV leaders, institutions, monuments, buildings, and landmarks both openly acknowledge and incorporate religious words, symbols, and imagery into official venues; Whereas such acknowledgments are even more frequent at the State and local level than at the Federal level, where thousands of such acknowledgments exist; and Whereas the first week in May each year would be an appropriate week to designate as `American Religious History Week': Now, therefore, be it Resolved, That the US House of Representatives -- (1) affirms the rich spiritual and diverse religious history of our Nation's founding and subsequent history, including up to the current day; (2) recognizes that the religious foundations of faith on which America was built are critical underpinnings of our Nation's most valuable institutions and form the inseparable foundation for America's representative processes, legal systems, and societal structures; (3) rejects, in the strongest possible terms, any effort to remove, obscure, or purposely omit such history from our Nation's public buildings and educational resources; and (4) expresses support for designation of a `American Religious History Week' every year for the appreciation of and education on America's history of religious faith."

---T--- <u>Unitarian & Universalists Beliefs</u> at that time varied; & included differences than today, and are not the same. Thus remarks about the words and beliefs of "Unitarians" & "Universalists" then cannot be said they are like today.

---T--- <u>R-E & R~Est ~~</u> State CON's Support the Truth & Sources of the USA CON: // R-E & R~Est is not anti-Christian; rather supports Christianity; supports DENs (secondary doctrines & expressions & organizations or otherwise known as establishments); that the USA GOV is not to favor a DEN with extra support over other DEN, by making a law for it. // Following is a draft (that Thomas Jefferson assisted in writing) of a "Bill for Religious Freedom" made in AD 1777. The actual Bill was passed by Virginia State Congress. The Draft was supported for years before it finally passed State Congress. At the time of the draft, the Anglican Church was officially recognized as the State religion DEN. This draft and eventual law, was intended/ purposed partly to disestablish that DEN (Anglican Church), and provide allowance of equal protection or support of all Christian DENs. There was another proposal that was submitted which was to make many Christian DENs recognized, by listing them. But that was rejected. The Law is very respective and inclusive of God (the Christian True God), and nevertheless protects all Christian DENs. This Bill is often called "the precursor to the Religion Clauses of the First Amendment" of the USA CON. It is this Amendment that guarantees religious freedom for individuals and for Christian DENs. +The concerns and thoughts at the time, was that Virginia State had been, approx. the times of the Revolutionary Independence, excessively controlled by the Church of England; which was increasingly gaining abusive control over Christianity and GOV, and abusing other Christian DENs. Also, 9 of the 13 colonies had an established "official" State religion. And the concerns here was to safeguard religious intolerance, and safeguard bloodshed and wars that occurred in history of many European countries from false religiousness. In AD 1777, Thomas Jefferson became Governor and introduced this draft into the legislature. Patrick Henry submitted another idea as an alternative Bill. It proposed that Christianity become the established religion of the State and that all DENs be given equal privileges. Mr.Jefferson's Bill gradually collected support from Baptists, Presbyterians, Jews, a few Anglicans, and various people wearied of religious conflict. Also occurring in the approximate times, was the speech by James Madison to the Virginia General Assembly called A Memorial and Remonstrance. Now, however, it would probably have been a better thing to establish closer connections of GOV and Christianity; which would have been accomplished by Henry's Bill. However the Bill of Henry's was rejected. Why? Because they did not want GOV to control the decisions of Christianity and doctrines. Even though Christianity was desired to be the basis for it all, they did not know how to make the system work in one area without inserting a problem in another area; such as a problem of potential GOV abuse to Christians. So T. Jefferson's Bill was passed. // Here is the Draft of the AD 1777 version: "A BILL FOR ESTABLISHING RELIGIOUS FREEDOM SECTION I. Well aware that the opinions and belief of men depend not on their own will, but follow involuntarily the evidence proposed to their minds; that Almighty God hath created the mind free, and manifested his supreme will that free it shall remain by making it altogether insusceptible of restraint; that all attempts to influence it by temporal punishments, or burthens, or by civil incapacitations, tend only to beget habits of hypocrisy and meanness, and are a departure from the plan of the holy author of our religion, who being lord both of body and mind, yet chose not to propagate it by coercions on either, as was in his Almighty power to do, but to extend it by its influence on reason alone; that the impious presumption of legislators and rulers, civil as well as ecclesiastical, who, being themselves but fallible and uninspired men, have assumed dominion over the faith of others, setting up their own opinions and modes of thinking as the only true and infallible, and as such endeavoring to impose them on others, hath established and maintained false religions over the greatest part of the world and through all time: That to compel a man to furnish contributions of money for the propagation of opinions which he disbelieves and abhors, is sinful and tyrannical; that even the forcing him to support this or that teacher of his own religious persuasion, is depriving him of the comfortable liberty of giving his contributions to the particular pastor whose morals he would make his pattern, and whose powers he feels most persuasive to righteousness; and is withdrawing from the ministry those temporary rewards, which proceeding from an approbation of their personal conduct, are an additional incitement to earnest and unremitting labours for the instruction of mankind; that our civil rights have no dependence on our religious opinions, any more than our opinions in physics or geometry; that therefore the proscribing any citizen as unworthy the public confidence by laying upon him an incapacity of being called to offices of trust and emolument, unless he profess or renounce this or that religious opinion, is depriving him injuriously of those privileges and advantages to which, in common with his fellow citizens, he has a natural right; that it tends also to corrupt the principles of that very religion it is meant to encourage, by bribing, with a monopoly of worldly honors and emoluments, those who will externally profess and conform to it; that though indeed these are criminal who do not withstand such temptation, yet neither are those innocent who lay the bait in their way; that the opinions of men are not the object of civil GOV, nor under its jurisdiction; that to suffer the civil magistrate to intrude his powers into the field of opinion and to restrain the profession or propagation of principles on supposition of their ill tendency is a dangerous fallacy, which at once destroys all religious liberty, because he being of course judge of that tendency will make his opinions the rule of judgment, and approve or condemn the sentiments of others only as they shall square with or differ from his own; that it is time enough for the rightful purposes of civil GOV for its officers to interfere when principles break out into overt acts against peace and good order; and finally, that truth is great and will prevail if left to herself; that she is the proper and sufficient antagonist to error, and has nothing to fear from the conflict unless by human interposition disarmed of her natural weapons, free argument and debate; errors ceasing to be dangerous when it is permitted freely to contradict them. SECT. II. WE, the General Assembly of Virginia, do enact that no man shall be compelled to frequent or support any religious worship, place, or ministry whatsoever, nor shall be enforced, restrained, molested, or burthened in his body or goods, nor shall otherwise suffer, on account of his religious opinions or belief; but that all men shall be free to profess, and by argument to maintain, their opinions in matters of religion, and that the same shall in no wise diminish, enlarge, or affect their civil capacities. SECT. III. AND though we well know that this Assembly, elected by the people for the ordinary purposes of legislation only, have no power to restrain the acts of succeeding Assemblies, constituted with powers equal to our own, and that therefore to declare this act irrevocable would be of no effect in law; yet we are free to declare, and do declare, that the rights hereby asserted are of the natural rights of mankind, and that if any act shall be hereafter passed to repeal the present or to narrow its operation, such act will be an infringement of natural right." END of Draft. // Now some parts of the actual Bill passed by Congress is as follows: "Section II reads: Be it enacted by the General Assembly, That no man shall be compelled to frequent or support any religious worship, place or ministry whatsoever, nor shall be enforced, restrained, molested or burdened in his body or goods, nor shall otherwise suffer on account of his religious opinions or belief; but that all men shall be free to profess, and by argument to maintain, their opinion in matters of religion, and that the same shall in no wise diminish, enlarge, or affect their civil capacities ,,,To compel a man to furnish contributions of money for the propagation of opinions which he disbelieves and abhors, is sinful and tyrannical... And: ...our civil rights have no dependence on our religious opinions ...". Religion here is defined as~ Christian DEN (secondary doctrines & expressions).

---T--- *Free Speech Clause, as part of the 1-A &* R-E & R~Est is intended/ purposed for the Increase of Christianity to the Earth. That intention/ purpose is the reason that the USA exists: // The Mission of the USA as proved by the CC and the following supporting DOC: and also the freedom of Spiritual Moral Beings includes the Right to talk (expression) as a natural Right from God: // Mr. Dan Gilbert shares (95), as paraphrased, that it is Christ's Law that Truth sets free and that all men should know the truth; Thus the Right of Freedom of Speech and press assists to increase the knowledge of truth by word and means; It is the Right of every man to have such. Communication is Sacred. // The FFOG learned from history about the abuse that occurred in not allowing truth to increase by communication, including the Holy Bible; abuse from false Christian churches, false religions, and tyrannical governments. // Observe the connection of speech and press with the 1-A; or that is part of it - "Congress shall make no law respecting an establishment of religion, or prohibiting the free exercise thereof; or abridging the freedom of speech, or of the press,,,". The True Religion is connected to Speech & Press. This is not intended/ purposed for demons to have unlimited freedom to talk, and all forms of evil talk. // The 1-A , R-E , R~Est are Intended/ purposed as including for denominational subjects of Christianity; thus they could assist each other, and take care of themselves; including that whereas the GOV had no Right to decide on such sacred things. The GOV is limited to its actions to the Church or Christianity, not unlimited. Especially because the GOV is not themselves trained and constantly working in the profession as clergy or special positions of special laymen in the churches. Additionally, this way Christianity could have freedom to increase in quantity & quality; that the USA could spread the Gospel freely without restriction. This includes some of the other connecting intention/ purposes for "free speech", such as these: No Bible burning as Rome or others; no papist special confinement of truth of Bible; no fear of GOV oppression for speaking the name of Jesus; no GOV DEN controlling the others; no refusal of doctrinal debates, discussions, and round table meetings. // This is NOT the liberty, or freedom, to speak evil. Such is clearly illegal by law, to do so publically. It is stated that no evil speaking against Christianity is to be done publically. It is the CC & all citizens get their citizenship Rights from the God of the CC & the CC; to which they must agree to support. This includes evil speaking~ publically subjects such as false religion, false Christianity, cursing or swearing, lying, Satanism, and criminal speaking as such.

---T--- Statements made by every Branch of USA GOV, including the Citizen, Congress, Executive, Judicial, State GOVs & Officers, and every Spiritual Moral Being in the first 20 yrs before & 20 yrs after the CC do this~ they Support Religion of Christianity, Jesus Christ, all DEN allowance, The Holy Bible, the USA is Christian, and the USA GOV to be Christian.

---T--- The 1-A was placed in first position, "First Amendment" as number one; as it is the most priority and fundamental for society and existence (70).

-------------------------------- *CONTINUING of the RELIGION Section, but this here is MAKING a SPECIAL SUB-Section FOR the OFFICIALS of the USA GOV in the time frame of 40 yrs (plus) which is the time of the DOI & CON (CC); They are All Christians and Supporting of Christianity*

---T--- LIST of FFOG (Most of the Officers are here who established the USA GOV for the 1ˢᵗ 40 yrs); and a general brief description of them: // The USA GOV was Christian AND was REQUIRED to HAVE Christian Spiritual Moral Beings in Offices of Law making functions; AND to operate by Christian laws. And all the Spiritual Moral Beings were Christians of the Congress, Executive, Judicial Branches; Official positions directly connected to Law making. The system required them to support the CC (DOI & CON) to say the least; and to oppose it in no part.

---T--- Many of the REPS & Various Officials for the First 40 year Time Frame of the USA: // Now about these Spiritual Moral Beings and this report, and any negative subject about their actions in life was not included, although there are a few that had some. The intention/ purpose here is not to distort or deceive or ignore or interpret wrongly. Rather it is because~ +there was usually some good deeds offered by them; +they are dead and I do not take pleasure in repeating such about them that have passed to eternity; +it is Evil Speaking (HSC) to repeat sins of other Spiritual people when they have repented; +studies of such subjects are not for this place and time; +some of it is not clear as to what happened. // CON meetings included some participation. There were meetings to sign the CON, and there were some REPs who could not attend because of various causes, including bad health, or family member ill, or circumstances. Hence, there were 73 REP assigned to participate; and some of the others did participate through various other methods. // Of the group of REPs that were CON Signers, most were members of an orthodox Christian Church.

Only 4 of these members expressed struggles about orthodox Christianity; yet they remained in support of most Christian doctrines and lived as Christians; and professed Christianity in some form. These 4 expressed some enigmas or difficulties pertaining to some of the Christian doctrines, which include the trinity, and the denominationalism, and such; however they continued to profess Christianity in their personal life, to live in opposition to sin, to support most of the Christian doctrines, and attend Christian assemblies. Those 4 are Benjamin Franklin, Thomas Jefferson, James Madison, and Gouverneur Morris. Sometimes John Adams is included, but reports prove very differently. // According to a report by James Hutchinson Smylie (9), 44 men who served on the Congress for the CON were clergymen. // Most of these made statements regarding their Christianity as a condition to be a REP (70). // All attended Congressional Church and prayer meetings while attending Congress meetings. // It is part of the Christian doctrine that there is only one and true God, God the Father, Jesus, and Holy Spirit, the Trinity, and no other way to live and go to heaven but this way of Jesus; and that is the only true and one religion. All of them supported this doctrine (teaching); thus they would not agree to other members, if the members attempted to initiate anti-Christian GOV. // John Adams: died on the 50th anniversary of the US, July 4, 1826; raised as a puritan and maintained through life; may have questioned some of the doctrines of Christianity at a small point of time in life, but however remained faithful to it. Instructed his son to read 5 Bible chapters per day; considered GOV to be a "divine science" (66). Wrote a government book, "A Defense of the Constitutions of Government of the USA", which defends Christian GOV subjects; wrote a letter to John Quincy Adams, his son, declaring, "My custom is, to read four to five chapters every morning immediately after rising from my bed ,,,It is essential, my son, in order that you may go through life with comfort ,,,and usefulness to your fellow-creatures ,,,your own conduct and temper ,,,it is in the Bible, you must learn them, and from the Bible how to practice them. Those duties are to God, to your fellow -creatures, and to your self. "Thou shalt love the Lord thy God, with all thy heart, and with all thy soul, and with all thy mind, and with all thy strength, and thy neighbour as thyself", ON these two commandments, Jesus Christ expressly says, "hang all the law and the prophets; that is to say, the whole purpose of Divine Revelation,,," (66). Accusations of John saying "no religion in it" is referring to contextual definition of religion; and a special sense of it; and a special application of it; because he in the same discussion said, "Without religion this world would be something not fit to be mentioned in polite company, I mean hell". His father was a Church deacon, coming from a family of a strong puritan part of England; and his father taught him to read before entering school. John warned against sin as defined in the Bible, and of which was occurring in France (97a)(117). John defended orthodox Christianity with full persuasion and enjoyed the Great Awakening (117). He wrote, that he was aware of the doctrinal debates between Calvinists and Arminians and was planning on being in the clergy; made a resolution in college to "rise with the sun and to study the Scriptures, on Thursday, Friday, Saturday, and Sunday mornings, and to study some Latin author the other 3 mornings"; Had learned Greek and Latin when young; married Abigail Smith, the daughter of a minister, and herself a very devout Christian, who seriously gave attention to the presence of God in providence, realizing the spiritual activities in the unseen, such as HSC of Nehemiah's building of the walls (97a). John supported that law should have a basis on the Holy Bible. Supported revealed religion or experiences with God as a Spirit; that the Bible is the Word of God's truth; that many people had corrupted Christianity historically and doctrines of the Bible; about Natural Rights, said that, "The great and almighty Author of nature, who at first established those rules which regulate the world, can as easily suspend those laws whenever his providence see sufficient reason ,,,no objection to the miracles of Jesus" (97a). // John Jay: Worked as Judge of US Supreme Court; Governor of New York 1795-1801; tried to abolish slavery; enacted a law to "prevent the profanation of the Sabbath"; born of French Huguenots; it is said about his parents that~, ",,,parents ,,,so loved and reverenced ,,,fervent piety ,,,strong masculine sense ,,,shrewd observer and admirable judge of men; resolute, preserving, and prudent; and affectionate father, a kind master ,,,governing all under his control with absolute sway. His mother had a cultivated mind and fine imagination; mild and affectionate in her temper and manners ,,,took delight in the duties as well as the pleasure of domestic life; while a cheerful resignation to the will of Providence ,,,bore witness ,,,of religious faith,,,". His schooling included Episcopal minister Rev Mr. Stoope; attended Episcopal Christian church, mostly attended by French Huguenots; attended Christian college, Kings College. // John Dickinson: Quaker/Episcopalian Christian Church member; Christian family life; contributed to the Quaker Christian Church (70). From a letter titled, "Letters from a Farmer in Pennsylvania"~ ",,,while Divine Providence, that gave me existence in a land of freedom, permits my head to think, my lips to speak, and my hand to move ,,,wherewith heaven itself, hath made us free [[a Christian Bible vs.]] ,,,I pray God that he may be pleased to inspire you ,,,with a spirit of ,,,shall guide you ,,,to determine ,,,America's character is ,,,for his ,,,Sovereign ,,,let us implore the protection of the infinitely good and gracious being {Proverbs 8:15}, by whom kings reign, and princes decree justice ,,,beautiful ,,,language of the sacred SCs {Micah 4:4} that they should sit every man under his vine, and under his fig-tree, and none should make them afraid" (89). Said, "Rendering thanks to my Creator for my existence and station among His works, for my birth in a country enlightened by the Gospel and enjoying freedom, and for all His other kindnesses, to Him I resign myself, humbly confiding in His goodness and in His mercy through Jesus Christ for the events of eternity and [Governments] could not give the rights essential to happiness ,,,We claim them from a higher source: from the King of kings, and Lord of all the earth" (150). // William Samuel Johnson: Member of Christian Anglican Church; lay preacher; well studied in the Bible and theology; served as President of King's College, a Christian College; asserted the following to students at King's College, ",,,You have, by the favor of Providence ,,,to qualify you ,,,to serve you Creator and your country ,,,Your first duties ,,,are those you owe to Heaven, to your Creator and Redeemer [[names for Jesus]] ,,,Let these ever be present in your minds, and exemplified in your lives and conduct. Imprint deep upon your minds the principles of piety towards God, and a reverence and fear of His holy name. The fear of God is the beginning of wisdom [[a Christian Bible vs.]] ,,,Possess yourselves of ,,,notions of the Divine character, attributes ,,,of your immortal nature as it stands related to Him,,, Remember that it is in God you live and move and have your being [[Bible vs.]] ,,,of the precious blood of the Son of God. Adore Jehovah,,, God and your Judge,,, Acquaint yourselves with Him in His word and holy ordinances ,,,who does most good to his country and to mankind". // Nicholas Gilman: Soldier in RW; Senator; signer of CON; member of Congregational Christian Church; never married; public servant until his death, when he was senator; spoke little; friend of John Langdon religiously (70). Obituary reads, ",,,in every situation in which he has been placed, he has conducted with honor ,,,friend of the widow and fatherless, and the hearts of the poor were made glad ,,,Those who knew him can well appreciate his virtues ,,,as a brother he was amiable, affectionate, and kind ,,,The loss to this town, and the religious society to which he belonged is very grieved. He was ready to contribute liberally to the support to all public expenses and particularly to the support of religious worship" (33). // Some FFoG did not sign the CON due to personal health or circumstances, or such, but worked at the meetings at some time. // Robert Yates: US Justice; parents of Dutch Reformed Christian Church and continued with it; studied law taught by William Livingston; assisted in New York CON; assisted in USA CON meetings; defender of US citizen Rights and State sovereignty (33). // Caleb Strong: member of Congregational Christian Church; Senator; assisted in writing a Puritan State CON for Massachusetts and very religious and assisted making the GOV State Christian church (70); graduate of Harvard, Christian school at the time; Christian parents; Governor of Mass. (33). Wrote religious article in State of Mass. CON. // William Pierce: soldier; Member of Episcopal Christian Church; well educated; had to leave meetings for State GOV business and thus unable to sign US CON; made character sketches of the Congress members; weak in physical health, died early (70). // George Wythe: lawyer and judge; DOI signer; Episcopal Christian Church member; William Pierce stated GW as "One of the most learned legal characters of the present age ,,,exemplary life ,,,good principles. No man,,, understands the history of government better ,,,able writer"(66). // James McClung: State GOV officer; physician; graduate of Christian College, William and Mary College; nothing else is known of his religion; replacement member for others not yet approving of the meetings as selected by George Washington; departed meetings early (70). // Edmund Jennings Randolph: State Attorney General, Secretary of State, First US Attorney General; member of Episcopal Christian Church; graduated from William and Mary College, a Christian school; contributed good GOV organizational ideas, defender of citizen Rights, opposed GOV abuse, supported Checks & Balances on GOV (33). // John Francis Mercer: soldier, lawyer, US House Rep; State Governor; Episcopal Christian Church member; aggressive speaker; opposed US CON because the formation was potential GOV abuse to rights of citizens; stating "it would never work" (33). // William Richardson Davie: soldier in RW; graduate of Princeton Christian school; wounded in war; Christian parents; Governor; member of Presbyterian Christian Church; enjoyable friendly and hospitable personality (85). Opposed false religions, such as Jacobins, and rebuked the French for the "moral principle" (33). // Luther Martin: Attorney General; teacher; lawyer; member of Episcopal Christian Church; devout Christian parents (33). Very good law worker; supported Independency of State (33). Aggressive speaker; dedicated to as stated, "the sacred truths of the Christian Religion" (33). Proposed the electoral college system for selection of President (33). // Oliver Ellsworth: US Judge, senator, State judge, legislator, lifetime faithful member of Congregationalist Christian Church; opposed the French anti-Christian condition; attended Christian college, Princeton; trained by Minister Joseph Bellamy; Christian parents who wanted him to be a clergy; active speaker in US CON meetings; supported State independency rights. Made these statements, "the people of the states are strongly attached to their own constitutions [[which were very much Christian in laws and support; as shown in this book and cited]]. If you hold up a system of government destructive of their constitutional rights, they will oppose it ,,,the US ,,,on their side ,,,line dividing jurisdictions - the states on the other - with both having power to defend their respective sovereignties" (33). Supporter of State GOV Christian Church establishment, supported US GOV enactments against evil, as said, "evil amusements" which included, "play going, gaming ,,,horse races" (33). William Pierce describes him as "gentleman ,,,deep, and copious understanding ,,,always attentive to his duty,,, respected for his integrity,,," (66). // Alexander Martin: senator, Governor, politician for 35 yrs, lawyer, soldier; graduate of Christian college, Princeton; no reports of speaking at US CON meetings; dedicated Christian and member of Episcopalian Christian Church; Christian parents with his father as a clergy of a Presbyterian Church (70). // Eldridge Gerry: Governor, Vice President of the US; signer of DOI & AOC; educated at Harvard by Christian clergy; close friends to Samuel and John Adams in religion (70). Assisted his family in business of shipping dried fish to Europe and West Indies; humble supporter of Checks & Balances; dedicated Christian who promoted the US to be a Christian country to the world (70). Episcopal Christian Church member; much assisted US CON formation, aggressive speaker and participant (33). Opposed a total democracy for it tends to anarchy (33). // John Lansing: US Justice, lawyer, legislator; desired the Bill of Rights and opposed US CON because of potential threat to civil rights (70). Spoke little at CON meetings (33). Defended State independency by saying that "all reasoning on systems unaided by experience has generally been productive of false inferences." (33). Member of Dutch Reformed Christian Church. // William Churchhill Houston: lawyer; of bad physical health (Tuberculosis) (33). Teacher of math and natural philosophy at Princeton college (Christian college); very dedicated Christian and member of Presbyterian Christian Church; educated by Poplar Tent Academy by Presbyterian clergy (33). // William Houston: lawyer; legislator; reported to have "good and honorable principles" (66). Episcopalian Christian Church member; Christian parents; supported the US CON. // John Randolph of Roanok: REP during John Adams, Thomas Jefferson, James Madison, John Quincy Adams, Andrew Jackson Presidencies; said, "I still cling to the cross of my Redeemer, and with God's aid firmly resolve to lead a life less unworthy of one who calls himself the humble follower of Jesus Christ". // Richard Stockton: Judge; DOI Signer; said, "As my children will have frequent occasion of perusing this instrument, and may probably be particularly impressed with the last words of their father, I think it proper here not only to subscribe to the entire belief of the great and leading doctrines of the Christian religion, such as the being of God; the universal defection and depravity of human nature; the Divinity of the person and the completeness of the redemption purchased by the blessed Savior; the necessity of the operations of the Divine Spirit; of Divine faith accompanied with an habitual virtuous life; and the universality of the Divine Providence: but also, in the bowels of a father's affection, to exhort and charge [my children] that the fear of God is the beginning of wisdom, that the way of life held up in the Christian system is calculated for the most complete happiness that can be enjoyed in this mortal state, [and] that all occasions of vice and immorality is injurious either immediately or consequentially~ even in this life" (Will of Richard Stockton, May 20, 1780). // Nathaniel Gorham: Samuel Adams recommended him; legislator; member of Congregational Christian Church; wrote Mass. State CON (33). Gave oath to the State CON to be State Officer which required Christianity profession. // James Wilson: US Associate Justice (33). Died young of a fever (33). Spoke often at US CON meetings; supported the CON (33). JW stated in congress meetings that US law must be based on Divine law~ and used England as EX: saying, "Parliament may, unquestionably, be controlled by natural or revealed law, proceeding from divine authority", which is to say that God's laws are over and above GOV or any laws therefrom. // Jared Ingersoll, Jr: lawyer; spoke little at CON meetings; graduate of Christian college, Yale; Presbyterian Christian Church member (131). // Richard Dobbs Spaight: Governor, legislator, soldier; Episcopalian in church affiliation but not much record of his religious life; died in a duel with pistols, because another person was insisting him to resolve charges against him. He died in the duel. Had poor physical health for extended time (70). Attended the meetings on every occasion and defended state independency (33). // Daniel Jenifer: Episcopal, not many other records about him; State politician (33). // James Otis: Leader of the Sons of Liberty; Attorney & Jurist; Mentor of Samuel Adams and John Hancock; said, "Has it (government) any solid foundation? Any chief cornerstone? ,,,I think it has an everlasting foundation in the unchangeable will of God ,,,The sum of my argument is that civil GOV is of God" (197). // John Hart: Signer of DOI, said, "We will look for the permanency ,,,of our new GOV to Him who bringeth princes to nothing and teaches senators wisdom" (196). // John Rutledge: Episcopalian Christian Church member continued for life; home schooled by his mother and by Christian clergy (33). Educated in Britain in law and practiced while there (33). Lawyer; Governor; State Justice; US Justice; dedicated to the Holy Bible & God & that religion was necessary for the country (70). // Thomas Mifflin: soldier in RW; Governor; legislator; Christian parents (132). // Charles Pinckney III: very knowledgeable on government, history, philosophy, and law (66). Senator; soldier; lawyer; relative of Charles Cotesworth Pinckney; Episcopal Christian Church affiliations. // Robert Morris: signer of DOI, AOC, & CON; very helpful financier of the RW; Episcopal Christian Church member; father died while he was young; hard worker for the country; evidently some physical problems. Congressman during his assisting days (33). // James McHenry; importing business; born in Ireland; physician; member of Presbyterian Christian Church; soldier; Legislator; assisted in establishing West Point University; Fort McHenry is named after him; talked little in CON meetings; very devout Christian and church member; assisted the Bible society which goal is to get Bibles in every home, and wrote this article for them: "Neither, in considering this subject, let it be overlooked, that public utility pleads most forcibly for the general distribution of the Holy SCs. The doctrine they preach, the obligations they impose, the punishment they threaten, the rewards they promise, the stamp and image of divinity they bear, which produces a conviction of their truths, can alone secure to society, order and peace, and to our courts of justice and constitutions of government, purity, stability and usefulness. In vain, without the Bible, we increase penal laws and draw intrenchments around our institutions. Bibles are strong intrenchments. Where they abound, men cannot purse wicked courses, and at the same time enjoy quiet conscience." (127). // Jonathan Dayton: Senator, CON signer; Episcopal Christian Church member; represented his father for CON meetings; the youngest of the CON signers; soldier and prisoner of war, but released as exchange (33). Close friends with Livingston and Paterson (33). Claimed Christianity to be selected Official; Dayton Ohio named after him (33). // Abraham Baldwin: Congregationalist Christian Church member; Clergyman; Army Chaplain; intense religious parents who provided a Puritan training; attended Christian school, Yale Univ. and schooled for Christian ministry; invited to join staff at Yale for his superb study in ministry, and accepted; a Congregational minister (70). Was called the "Puritan of Georgia" by peers (70). Started College of Georgia, a Christian religious college, which had part of it's Charter written by him as stated~ "As it is the distinguishing happiness of free governments that civil order ,,,the public prosperity ,,,even existence ,,,depend upon suitably forming the minds and morals of their citizens ,,,When ,,,unprincipled ,,,disorderly ,,,confusions and evils more horrid than the wild ,,,happy when the public principles and opinions are properly directed,,,"; very punctual, good thinker (33). // James Madison: Episcopalian Church member and attendee; author of 29 of Federalist Papers; said, "If men were angels no government would be necessary" and "Religion, or the duty we owe to our Creator, and the manner of discharging it, can be directed only by reason and conviction, not by force or violence; and, the influence ,,,claimed only by religion and education. It should therefore be among the first objects of those who wish well ,,,the national prosperity to encourage and support the principles of religion and morality ,,,love of virtue and good order,,," (74). // George Clymer: Signer of DOI; was both Episcopal Christian Church member with sometime as Quaker Christian (33). Very gentleman character, careful mannered, "shunned applause" ,,,; said, "that all men should enjoy the fullest toleration in the exercise of religion according to the dictates of conscience, unpunished and unrestrained by the magistrate, unless under color of religion any man disturb the peace, the happiness, or safety of society, and that it is the mutual duty of all to practice Christianity forbearance [[note he says that the USA GOV encourages the "duty of ALL to practice Christianity"]] (70). His parents were members of Episcopalian Christian Church, the State church at that time (70). Home-schooled including a Christian teacher, Episcopalian minister, and then attended Princeton in preparation for Christian ministry (70). Close lifetime Christian friends of Rev. John Witherspoon, William Bradford, and Rev Samuel Stanhope Smith (70). Studied theology in his personal time (70). Said, "love, and charity toward each other". Wrote William Bradford on June 10, 1773 this,

206

",,,I hope the fortitude & zeal with which they enter on the ministerial duties will procure them ,,,success ,,,Nevertheless it ought to be ,,,that spiritual events are not limited or proportioned always to human means,,, dependence upon Providence" and then again Sept 25, 1773 saying, ",,,I can only condole with the Church on the loss of a fine Genius and persuasive Orator ,,,keep the Ministry ,,,in view whatever your profession be ,,,becoming fervent Advocates in the cause of Christ, & I wish you may give in your evidence in this way,,," (77)(70). // Daniel Carroll: Legislator; Catholic; support of central GOV; supported religious freedom; reported as very devout religious of high character (70). // William Few: self-taught lawyer; soldier, senator, signer of CON; member of Methodist Christian Church; reported that as a youth he read every book in his father's library, including the Holy Bible, and as very religious and giving what he could to charity (82). // Timothy Pickering: General in RW; CON ratifier; US Postmaster while Pres. George Washington; Secretary of War with Pres. G. Washington & John Adams; said, "Pardon, we beseech Thee, all our offences of omission and commission; and grant that in all our thoughts, words, and actions, we may conform to Thy known will manifested in our consciences and in the revelations of Jesus Christ, our Savior" (230). // William Paterson: State Attorney, Senator, Supreme Court Justice; Governor of New Jersey; born in Ireland; attended Christian schools; Rep Pierce shared that he was a "kind of men whose power ,,,upon you and create wonder and astonishment ,,,never speaks but when he understands his subject well" (66). While young, he took a trip to West Indies and shares this in his journal, ",,,in the West Indies ,,,year 1776, a new scene opened to me for which I was little prepared, for I had previously lived with religious people, and my new acquaintances, and those with whom I was to transact business were the reverse of this. No one went there to settle for life; all were in quest of fortune, to retire and spend it elsewhere; character was little thought of. Of course it required the utmost circumspection and caution to steer clear of difficulties. A kind superintending Providence, in this, as in my other concerns of my life, enabled me, however, to surmount every difficulty, young and inexperienced as I then was" (128). // Thomas Fitzsimons: Congressman; militia soldier; Catholic; born in Ireland; gave financially for the RW; high character catholic (33). // John Witherspoon: Senator; Reverend; signer of DOI; President of Princeton (College of New Jersey) a Christian GOV College; Pastor of Presbyterian Christian Church; strong influence in the development of the DOI & CON & GOV systems & Checks & Balance system towards Christian doctrines (9). A supporter of "covenanting" doctrine between GOV & people; and that of "natural rights" (which Roger Schultz, in his book "Covenanting in America" linked Witherspoon's studies to John Locke; thus proving Christianity for USA GOV). // Patrick Henry: serious encourager for religious freedom; volunteered as legal defender of the "dissident sects" which he said their only crime was "preaching the Gospel of the Son of God" (70). Was a private man later in life; an historian wrote that he was a Holy Bible student and respecter of truth, stating: "After the manner of the Bereans he seems to have searched the SCs daily and diligently ,,,history and evidences of Christianity on every side ,,,No one not a professed theologian, and but few ,,,of those who are ,,,more laborious and extensive inquiries to arrive at the truth" (70). In 1779 introduced the General Assessment Bill that named Christianity the established faith of Virginia (73). These are notes in his Bible~ "Believers who are in a State of Grace, have need of the word of God,,, therefore implies a possibility of falling ,,,Grace ,,,to neglect the means for our own preservation is to tempt God: and to trust to them is to neglect him ,,,Humility, the better any man is, the lower thoughts he has of himself ,,,Ministers to take heed to themselves & their flock ,,,The apostles did greater miracles than Christ, in the matter, not manner, of them"; and wrote a letter to William Bradford in 1772 saying, "A watchful eye must be kept on ourselves lest while we are building ideal monuments of Renown and Bliss here we neglect to have our names enrolled in the Annals of Heaven. {Bad health has} intimated to me not to expect a long or healthy life ,,,have little spirit and alacrity to set about any thing that is difficult in acquiring and useless in possessing after one has exchanged Time for Eternity" (70). He also wrote, "The belief in a God All Powerful, wise and good, is so essential to the moral order of the world and ,,,happiness of man,,,"; and believed in the Christian God as having spiritual experiences with Him, "capacities to be impressed with it" (78). In AD 1809 at inaugural address said, "guardianship and guidance of that Almighty Being, whose power regulates the destiny of nations" (79). Home-schooled much of the time, learned Greek, Latin, and good in mathematics, interested in history, well studied, studied law, a very good lawyer (9). A questionable law case that has caused doubts of His consistent Christian profession, the "Parson's Cause" case, was actually done to defend against worldly and wrong clergy in the Church and in defense of Dissenters (9). Some accused him of non-Christianity and he replied, ",,,some good people think I am no Christian. This thought gives me much more pain than the appellation of Tory; because I think religion of infinitely higher importance than politics; and I find much cause to reproach myself that I have lived so long, and have given no decided and public proofs of my being a Christian. But, indeed ,,,this is a character which I prize far above all this world has, or can boast" (120). Was very concerned that one Christian DEN not be favored over the others; opposed GOV that were not Christian, such as in France (120). Wrote to his sister, ",,,Perhaps I may never see you in this world. O may we meet in heaven, to which the merits of Jesus will carry those who love and serve him." (120). // William Blount: soldier; legislator; member of Presbyterian Christian Church; Episcopal parents; political; died young at age 50; reports prove he promoted religion and morality for society and opposed false teaching as French Jacobins; had to be a Christian to hold Office. // John Langdon: Congregationalist Christian Church member; US Senator; risked all his belongings to the RW (70). As State GOV Official he proclaimed a day of prayer and fasting in AD 1786, which stated this, "Vain is the acknowledgement of a Supreme Ruler of the Universe, unless such acknowledgements influence our practice, and call forth those expressions of homage and adoration that are due to his character and providential government, agreeably to the light of nature, enforced by revelation, and countenanced by the practice of civilized nations, in humble and fervent application to the throne ,,,It having been the laudable practice of this State, at the opening of the Spring, to set apart a day for such ,,,to assemble together ,,,places of worship; that the citizens of this State may, with one heart and voice, penitently confess their manifold sins

207

,,,implore the divine benediction, that a true spirit of repentance and humiliation ,,,that He would be pleased to bless the great Council of the United-States of America ,,,to keep this State under his most holy protection: that all in the legislature, executive and judicial departments, may be guided ,,,all ,,,lives, in all godliness and honesty ,,,revive religion, and spread abroad the knowledge of the true GOD, the Savior of man, throughout the world. And all servile labor and recreations are forbidden on said day ,,,this twenty-first day of February, in the year of our LORD, one thousand seven hundred and eighty-six, and in the tenth year of the Sovereignty and Independence of the US of America"; and as GOV Official of the same State proclaimed a General Thanksgiving Day to the Lord Jesus which is the same as our Thanksgiving day today; opposed evil or anti-Christian activity in the USA and GOV as stating, "there was evidence in New Hampshire of an infidel age in which the indolent, extravagant and wicked may divide the blessings of life with the industrious, the prudent and the virtuous" (33). Attended various Christian DEN; when his brother died he changed to more dedication to Christ and then assisted establishing the Bible Society in New Hampshire which goals to put the Bible in every home of New Hampshire (42). Governor of New Hampshire; hosted US president Monroe to his Christian Church; soldier in RW; ship builder for American Navy. // Gunning Bedford: active member of Presbyterian church and buried there (70). Military officer; continental congress member; CON signer; Federal judge. // Richard Bassett: Methodist Christian Church member; reported by REP William Pierce as "a religious enthusiast, lately turned Methodist, who serves his country ,,,man of plain sense, and has modesty enough to hold his tongue. He is a gentlemanly man, and is in high estimation among the Methodists" (66). An historian wrote, ",,,converted to Christian Methodism during the Revolution,,, close personal friend of Bishop Francis Asbury, who held meetings on his plantation. Bassett freed his slaves and then employed them as hired labor ,,,He is best remembered for his contributions to the life of his chosen church, his generosity toward what he saw as the work of God" (33). He was adopted and raised in a Christian home; large influence in Delaware ratifying the new CON. // James McClurg: Physician; banker; speculator. // Gouverneur Morris: Episcopalian Christian Church member; wrote and spoke of His Bible knowledge; at life's end, wrote, "descend towards the grave full of gratitude to the Giver of all good"; credited to him is this expression~ "We the people of the US" (70). Very well learned of the "Christian consensus" (33). Lost leg and replaced with wooden leg; said of slavery, "it is the curse of heaven"; detested the moral status in France; said statements: "Providence has kindly interfered so far for our preservation" and "confident that the Fountain of supreme wisdom and virtue will provide for the happiness of his creatures ,,,little share of my abilities, which it has pleased God to bestow on me, I hold it my indispensable duty to give myself,,,", and "I hope in God" and "His bounty is as unbounded as His power ,,,surrender with respectful obedience what He shall think proper ,,,O God! Thy will be done" and ",,,demand our thanks to Almighty God, by whose Providence they are ordered", and ",,,hope in the kindness of that Being ,,,O God! It is thy wisdom ,,,impressed in the heart of each individual, the same conviction of His existence, and the existence of God ,,,the principles of the religion we profess" and "The Almighty will work out his wise ends by the means of human folly" and ",,,truth alone ,,,virtue ,,,justice, the love of humanity ,,,The idea of a Deity is always present, the habit of contemplating him in his works, of imitating his goodness, of submitting to his will ,,,calm resignation which arises from a belief that God can will nothing but what is good", referring to Christ, "It is he who commands us that we abstain from wrong ,,,who tells you, "do unto others as ye would that they should do unto you"" (11a). Wrote in defense of Thomas Jefferson being a Christian and supporting Christianity. // John Blair: Episcopalian Christian Church member and remained active in it and buried at a Church (70). Wrote a letter to his sister when her husband died saying Christian vss and truths, ",,,my own and real sympathy for yours ,,,it being appointed for all men once to die ,,,Let us seek for comfort where alone it may be found ,,,from the Great Being from whom we ourselves proceeded and who being the Sole Author of all our enjoyments ,,,in His general Providence ,,,School of Adversity if we will but make a proper use of its Sacred Lessons. If in this life only we had hope ,,,But now as our Holy Religion teaches we may contemplate him translated to a better Life ,,,of Bliss which eye hath not seen nor ear heard nor the heart conceived [[multiple Bible vses here.]]. May the Celestial vision,,," (80). // Pierce Butler: soldier, Senator, Episcopalian Christian Church member; British soldier at age 12; born in Ireland; requested for more specific language in the GOV papers to prevent GOV abuse and need of Checks & Balances; promoted State independency (33). // Roger Sherman: Congregationalist Christian Church member, joining in AD 1742, Lay Theologian, deacon, clerk, treasurer of the Church (70). Born in poverty, raised in the Congregational Church, Sabbath faithfully observed by his parents and home, and learned to read with the Holy Bible and the Westminster catechism (121). A shoemaker; reported by REP John Adams as, ",,,an old Puritan, as honest as an angel,,," (59). Tombstone inscription, "In Memory of the Hon. Roger Sherman ,,,He ever adorned the profession of Christianity which he made in youth; and, distinguished through life for public usefulness, died in the prospect of a blessed immortality" (70). His pastor, Rev Jonathon Edwards, the second, said, "I esteem him one of the best preachers that I am acquainted with, sound in faith,,," (81). RS wrote a sermon in AD 1789 titled, "A Short Sermon on the Duty of Self-Examination Preparatory to Receiving the Lord's Supper" due to the neglect of many, which included Jesus, salvation, repentance, faith, confession of sins, renewed surrender, request to God for strength to love and live more to God not self (39). The 1788 creed of the White Haven Church is clearly RS handwriting and includes the Trinity, Holy Bible as God's word, sin nature, eternal heaven or hell, salvation, sacraments, final judgment, visible church, which is quoted below (121). Taught his children the Holy Bible; quoted to his daughter, "Psa 90:12, so teach us to number our days, that we may get us a heart of wisdom"; and before his son died, his daughter reported to RS that he "expressed penitence for sins and his belief of a necessity of the atonement of Christ,,," (121). RS loved religion and wanted all to have it, ",,,I hope all well wishers to pure religion will use their influence to preserve Peace ,,,Perhaps there is nothing more pleasing to the adversary of mankind than discord among Christian brethren" (121). It is reported that he had religious writings and they displayed, ",,,great familiarity with the Bible, of

208

which he was a constant student. It was his custom to purchase a Bible at the commencement of every session of Congress, to peruse it daily, and to present it to one of his children on his return home" (81). Wrote this confession of faith: "I believe that there is one only living and true God, existing in three persons, the Father, the Son, and the Holy Ghost ,,,That the SCs of the old and new testaments are a revelation from God, and a complete rule to direct us,,, so as he is not the author or approver of sin,,, That he creates all things and preserves and governs ,,,with the freedom of will in moral agents ,,,That he made man at first perfectly holy, that the first man sinned ,,,inclined to evil,,, liable ,,,to the pains of hell,,, send his own son to become man ,,,offer of pardon and salvation to all mankind ,,,saved ,,,willing to accept the gospel offer ,,,persevere in holiness ,,,repentance and faith ,,,visible church to be a congregation of those who make ,,,profession of their faith in Christ, and obedience to him, joined by the bond of the covenant ,,,at ,,,death ,,,final judgment of all mankind ,,by Christ the judge,,," (81). Encouraged Pres. G. Washington for a national holiday of Thanksgiving Day (70). Supported the USA GOV law system requires based on Holy SC, God and His Laws of Revelation and Creation~ as in congress meeting, shared on a war committee Deu 25:3 as a rule, and insisted the Rights of individual doctrine (DOI); and Rights based on God, include life, property, wife, and children and these are not to be taken away except by some specific rule of God (39). RS was the only FFoG that served & signed with congress for DOI & CON; he clearly stated that the US GOV is to be Christian; made strict reference that USA GOV is for truth and God, not idolatry god or untrue god, rather the true God & true religion; ~as congress member he wrote instructions for an embassy to Canada that the USA should "further to declare that we hold sacred the rights of conscience, and may promise to the whole people, solemnly in our name, the free and undisturbed exercise of their religion" and ~clarified it that the civil rights (citizenship full liberty) and to hold any civil office was extended to person of any Christian DEN~ thus the definition of religion in the R-E includes Christian DEN; in AD 1758, as judge in New Milford, he legally fined an individual for breaking the Sabbath; reports that RS was the one who ideologically stated that each State is represented by vote according to population (39). Advocate of States Rights; opposed excessive power vested in the Presidency, executive, and suggested a Check be put on it by congress; one of congress members who spoke the most in CON meetings. // Hugh Williamson: member of Presbyterian Christian Church, clergyman, physician, scientist, US House Rep.; Christian parents; studied hard, good moral and religious conduct, a clergyman, visited and prayed with the sick in the neighborhood (130). Frail health and chronic lung problems hindered him (130). Very good writer and included Christianity; in one article spoke of the accuracy of the Holy Bible, Noah flood account, and Moses (70). Good in math, taught his way through medical school (70). // David Brearly: Episcopalian Christian Church member, was a "warden of St Michael's Church", "complier of the Protestant Episcopal prayer book and a delegate to the Episcopal General Convention in 1786" (82). A participative Christian layman. // George Read: DOI signer, Senator, lawyer, judge; Episcopalian Christian Church member; assisted in writing the Laws and CON of Delaware, which required every GOV officer take oath, ",,,faith in God the Father ,,,Jesus Christ,,, Holy Ghost, one God blessed ,,,acknowledge the Holy SCs of the Old and New Testament to be given by divine Inspiration" (32)(85). Devoted church member; Christian devoted wife; studied well in college. // William Livingston: Lawyer and legislator in New York; general in RW; youth spent with mother and more with grandmother in Christian home; attended a Christian college, Yale; wrote articles for newspapers in defense of Christianity against the falsities from various groups, including potential control by one Christian DEN, such as the Episcopalian, (hence the relation of the R-E , R~Est clause) as the GOV church (125). Governor of New Jersey, CON signer, Member of Presbyterian Christian Church, also the Dutch Reformed Christian Church; invited often in religious and GOV issues (126). Assisted funding Alexander Hamilton's education (125). // Charles Cotesworth Pinckney: General in the RW, signer of CON, Diplomat and Legislator, prisoner of RW; father was legislator and both parents devoted Anglican Christian Church members and supported dissenters (other Christian DEN) (122). Wrote, "To the eternal and only true God be all honor and glory, now and forever. Amen!" in his Will of Death; youth training included, listening to sermons to learn the Holy Bible text, study it at home, and memorize it on the Sabbath day, which taught him to always exert to love Christ and the Church (122). Very academically trained, learning to spell before age 2 yrs, sent to England for schooling; at age 13 his father died of a fever, and mother wrote him and his brother of it, "He has set you a great and good EX, may the Lord enable you both to follow it, and may God almighty fulfill all your pious father's prayers upon both of your heads; they were almost incessant for blessings both spiritual and temporal upon you both ,,,His affection for you was as great as ever was upon Earth, and you were good children and deserved it; he thought you so, he blessed and thanked God for you and had most comfortable hopes of you,,, God Almighty bless guide and protect you, make you his own children and worth such a father as yours was,,," (122). His fathers Will stated, ",,,that my beloved son Charles ,,,may ,,,that he will employ all his future abilities in the service of God and his country, in the cause of virtuous liberty, as well religious as civil, and in support of private right and justice between man and man" who himself was a lawyer and judge in the USA (122). Learned Greek, Latin, taught to translate Psalms at Westminster in England, and learned strict courses 8 to 9 hours every day, except 2 days (122). Taught by William Blackstone (orthodox Christian whom believed natural law was dictated by God), taking 4 volumes of notes from (122). Studied at Oxford in AD 1764 onward for a few years, reading, attending Parliament and courtroom trials, and had to be cautioned of so much study and to take care of his health by his mother (122). Studied military science (9). Returned to America and elected to South Carolina Commons House of Assembly; served as a church vestryman and 2 yrs as church warden; supported the Christian religion, it's orthodoxy doctrines, and opposed changing the truth and doctrine any at all. Concern for all Christian DEN, inviting ministers of other DEN to his house regularly as his father also desired (122). Wrote Baptist Rev. Furman, "Religion is always venerable, always necessary; and when she is delineated with the beauty and eloquence she was today in the (Baptist) church, we are enraptured with her portrait and sensibly feel that all her ways are ways of pleasantness and all her paths are paths of peace" (122) [[note he said "religion is ALWAYS ,,,NECESSARY"]]. Letter from Rev Furman said, "God has been pleased, dear General ,,,The Voice of the Community declares ,,,May you continue to live long ,,,To be the supporter of pious and benevolent Institutions ,,,exhibit ,,,the Christian ,,,Character,,,"; and a headmaster at Westminster confirmed that CPC ",,,strictness of your principles, and your attachment to truth,,,"; and known for his kindness (122). Rev Gadsen reported that CCP, ",,,In the day of trouble you would have found him, had you entered the private circle, meek, quiet, patient, and practicing a Christian resignation. You met him in this holy temple, and kneeled with him, and those most dear to him at that altar of the Savior,,," (129). Helped establish the Bible Society in South Carolina which eventually joined the American Bible society; served as member (122). Supported GOV operation of senators not to have long term, and no money for their time as legislators, thinking it a bad motive of evil desire to politicians; and distrusted GOV powers, thus helping set up Checks & Balances, and that GOV Officials is only for Christians (33). Buried in St Michael's churchyard with a plaque on the church wall including these remarks, "To the memory of General Charles Cotesworth Pinckney one of the founders of the American Republic ,,,He combined the virtues of the Patriot and the Piety of the Christian,,," (122). // Alexander Hamilton: Episcopalian Christian Church member (70). Attended a Christian college, Kings College (33). Reported about him, that "He believed in the moral decay of the US ~ the loss of religious principle in consequence of the teachings of Paine ,,,who ,,,unsettle the simple faith of the early patriots [[note here that the FFoG did not want anti-Christian religions to occur in the USA]] ,,,Bishop Moore's account of his death ,,,shows that he was a man of earnest, simple faith ,,,his belief was very strong ,,,wanted and encouraged an organization to start and be called 'The Christian Constitutional Society'" (83). Wrote, ",,,the present CON is the standard to which we are to cling ,,,I now offer you the outline of the plan they have suggested. Let an association be formed to be denominated 'The Christian Constitutional Society', its object to be 1st: The support of the Christian religion. 2d: The support of the US" (83). Said that a democracy is a form of GOV that is anti-Christian and "incompatible" with Christianity (33). Was a dedicated Christian in life and at death. Born on Island in West Indies, mother died early, raised in adoption some; wrote in a letter, re: the death of his son, to Gouverneur Morris, ",,,It was the will of heaven, and he is now out of reach of the seductions and calamities of a world full of folly, full of vice ,,,I firmly trust ,,,he has safely reached the haven (of eternal repose),,," (101). He died in a Dueling, but did not want to do it, yet for some reason felt to indicate his sincerity to this other fellow by it, or his innocency; and never intended to shoot the gun (101). Dueling was a legal allowance, at the time, as evidently some sort of way to solve disputes of right & wrong (101). RE: his death and Duel, he says, "I was certainly desirous of avoiding this interview (term used for duel) for the most cogent of reasons: ,,,My religious and moral principles are strongly opposed to the practice of dueling ,,,I am conscious of no ill will to Col. Burr, distinct from political opposition, which, as I trust, has proceeded from pure an upright motives ,,,it pleases God to give me the opportunity, to reserve and throw away my first fire ,,,and thus giving a double opportunity to Col. Burr to pause and reflect,,," (49b). Continuing, "Any man of ordinary understanding ,,,owed it to his family and the rights of self-defense to fire at his antagonist,,," (104). Continuing AH says, "Unless I shall first have terminated my earthly career, to begin, as I humbly hope, from redeeming grace and divine mercy, a happy immortality. If it had been possible for me to have avoided the interview [[dueling term]], my love for you and my precious children would have been alone a decisive motive ,,,Fly to the bosom of your God, and be comforted ,,,The scruples of a Christian determined me to expose my own life to extent, rather than subject myself to the guilt of taking another ,,,I charge you to remember that you are a Christian. God's will be done! The will of a merciful God,,," (49b). The Dueling did occur with Burr firing immediately, striking Hamilton on the right side fracturing a rib, and with Hamilton's pistol accidentally firing as he said, "Pendleton knows ,,,I did not intend to fire at him" (103). 2 Ministers visited him on his deathbed (fatally wounded), Episcopal Bishop Benjamin Moore and Dutch Reformed Church Bishop Dr Mason. AH requested communion. There was discussions that Dueling was a sin, for which AH confessed, "It was always against my principles. I used every expedient to avoid the interview [[Dueling term]]; but I have found, for some time past, that my life must be exposed to that man. I went to the field determined not to take his life" and then put his hands towards heaven and stated emphatically, "I have a tender reliance on the mercy of the Almighty, through the merits of the Lord Jesus Christ". (102). // James Kent: Law Teacher; Judge; "Father of American Jurisprudence"; said, "My children, I wish to talk to you. During my early and middle life I was, perhaps, rather skeptical with regard to some of the truths of Christianity. Not that I did not have the utmost respect for religion and always read my Bible, but the doctrine of the atonement was one I never could understand, and I felt inclined to consider as impossible to be received in the way Divines taught it. I believe I was rather inclined to Unitarianism; but of late years my views have altered. I believe in the doctrines of the prayer books as I understand them, and hope to be saved through the merits of Jesus Christ ,,,My object in telling you this is that if anything happens to me, you might know, and perhaps it would console you to remember, that on this point my mind is clear: I rest my hopes of salvation on the Lord Jesus Christ" (227). // Henry Marchant: US Continental Congress REP; Rhode Island Attorney General; US Judge appointed by George Washington. Said, "Remember that God made you, that God keeps you alive and preserves you from all harm, and gives you all the powers and the capacity whereby you are able to read of Him and of Jesus Christ, your Savior and Redeemer, and to do every other needful business of life. And while you look around you and see the great privileges and advantages you have above what other children have (of learning to read and write, of being taught the meaning of the great truths of the Bible)" (228). // James Manning: member of Continental Congress; said, "I rejoice that the religion of Jesus prevails in your parts" (228). [[see here Religion is Christianity]]. // Thomas McKean: Congress REP DOI signer; Chief Justice of Supreme Court of Pennsylvania; Governor of Pennsylvania and Delaware. Said, "You will probably have but a short time to live. Before you launch into eternity, it behooves you to improve the time that may be allowed you in this world: it behooves you most seriously to reflect upon your past conduct; to repent of your evil deeds; to

210

be incessant in prayers to the great and merciful God to forgive your manifold transgressions and sins; to teach you to rely upon the merit and passion of a dear Redeemer, and thereby to avoid those regions of sorrow ,,,where even hope cannot enter,,, Throne of Grace ,,, May you, reflecting upon these things ,,,the Father of light and life ,,,angels and archangels and the spirits of just men made perfect; and ,,,into the joys of Heaven ,,,unspeakable and full of glory" (case Republica vs. John Roberts). // Jedidiah Morse: Historian of the American Revolution; lived during the US early years. Said, "To the kindly influence of Christianity we owe that degree of civil freedom and political and social happiness which mankind now enjoys. All efforts made to destroy the foundations of our Holy Religion ultimately tend to the subversion also of our political freedom,,," (209). // John Morton: REP; Judge; DOI signer. Said, "With an awful reverence to the Great Almighty God, Creator of all mankind, being sick and weak in body but of sound mind and memory, thanks be given to Almighty God for the same" (Will and testament, attested 1/ 28, 1777). // Robert Treat Paine: Chaplain; DOI Signer; Attorney General of Massachusetts. Said, "I desire to bless and praise the name of God most high for appointing me my birth in a land of Gospel Light where the glorious tidings of a Savior and of pardon and salvation through Him have been continually sounding in mine ears" (165). // Thomas Stone: DOI Signer; delegate to USA CON Convention; Said, "Shun all giddy, loose and wicked company; they will corrupt and lead you into vice and bring you to ruin." (218). // Zephaniah Swift: US Congress REP; Judge; Writer of America's first Legal Textbook. Said, "Jesus Christ has in the clearest manner ,,,Religion ,,,delight" (141). // Oliver Wolcott: DOI signer; General In Army; Connecticut Governor. Said, "May we then turn our eyes to the bright objects above, and may God give us strength to travel the upward road. May the Divine Redeemer conduct us to that seat of bliss which He himself has prepared for His friends; at the approach of which every sorrow shall vanish from the human heart" (228). // Charles Thomson: Secretary of the Continental Congress; designer of some versions of the Great Seal of the US. Signer of the initial DOI Draft from Congress. Translator of the Holy Bible. Latin teacher and scholar. Said, "I am a Christian. I believe only in the SCs, and in Jesus Christ my Savior". // Jonathon Trumbull: Judge; Connecticut Governor. Said, "God would graciously pour out His Spirit upon us and make the blessed Gospel in His hand effectual to a thorough reformation and general revival of the holy and peaceful religion of Jesus Christ" (236). // James Iredell: US Supreme Court Justice appointed by George Washington; Ratifier of CON. Said, "merciful Father ,,,thanksgivings ,,,for the sake of Jesus Christ,,," (226). // Gabriel Duvall: soldier, US Supreme Court Justice. Delegate to Constitution. Said, ",,,my soul ,,,Almighty Who gave it ,,,through our Savior Jesus Christ". (Will and testament, attested on Sept 21, 1840). // Jacob Broom: member of Lutheran Christian Church; Christian education; Married in a Christian Church by Pastor Girelius the same year of the Boston Tea Party (84); raised in a Quaker Christian home; joined an Episcopalian Christian Church and had his children baptized (70); wrote his son at Princeton College, AD 1794, saying, ",,,do not forget to be a Christian. I have said much to you on this,,, and I hope an indelible impression is made"; and a report of him says, "I have studied Mr. Broom's life,,, was ,,,evangelical Swedish orthodoxy ,,,as,,, accepted fact that 'the foundation of all permanent prosperity is a right regard for the Divine Being,' it is proper to say that Jacob Broom was a God-fearing man" (84). // George Mason: an Anglican; an Episcopalian Christian Church member, very studied in the Holy Bible, spoke it often in speeches, quoted Jesus in his speech to the Virginia ratifying convention, saying, "They have done what they ought not to have done, and have left undone what they ought to have done" (33). A "man of profound learning ,,,and disapproved the slave-trade" (85). // Benjamin Franklin: not a member of, but rather a regular attendee of Christian Churches; never stayed with one DEN; rather visited various ones regularly. A professing Christian. What time he used studying the "Deist" religion, was that he was simultaneously attending various different DENs, and thought this was all being a non-denominational Christian; only saying things about Deism when younger of age, and later then became more active in orthodox Christianity and Churches. He had to make a verbal profession of Christ to be in Office for Pennsylvania; and regularly attended various Christian Churches; stated that he believed in the Holy Bible, quoted it often, told others to obey it, obeyed it himself, prayed, confessed Christ Jesus as God, and contributed monies and labors to Christianity. Was ill often from gout and a large bladder stone, having to be carried in to the meetings at times (70). Dedicated, attended Church regularly, taught from the Bible, very fond of John Bunyan's Pilgrim's Progress, and his Father was planning on him to be in clergy; he loved Isaac Watts hymns (108). Admits to doubts in his youth as to the various doctrines of Christianity. He joined in with Freemasonry (part of Deism) when younger and achieved a position; always believed in God, creation, providence to some degree, good morals, eternal reward or punishment. Said he was "religiously educated as a Presbyterian"; read Cotton Mather's Christian writings; credited the Lord for helping him from poverty to working success. When younger, he was having difficulty or doubts of Christianity, including the DEN debates, because he thought it strange that Christianity claiming to be fact of the true religion, and yet "arguments" occurring; and the Calvinist doctrines, which he shares in his autobiography, were difficult problems. Supported that religion and morality were necessary to make a free self-governing society operate (70). Raised in Christian home with parents hoping he would be in Church ministry; self taught; he was a printer and printed Christian ministers messages, such as Whitefield's; said it was wonderful to see people in the Great Awakenings, sing Christian Psalms and make their behavior good (47a). Believed God was a personal God. Said, "Here is my creed. I believe in one God, the Creator of the universe ,,,governs it by His Providence ,,,He ought to be worshipped ,,,service we render to Him is in doing good to His other children ,,,soul of man is immortal ,,,treated with justice in another life respecting its conduct in this" (47b). Wrote a paper, "Articles of Belief and Acts of Religion" which says, "wise and good God ,,,Author and Owner of our system, that I propose for the Object of my praise and adoration ,,,I conceive that He has in Himself some of those passions He has planted in us ,,,given us reason whereby ,,,observing His ,,,Creation ,,,He caring for us ,,,offended when we slight Him, or neglect His glory ,,,and ,,,happy to have so wise, good and powerful a Being my Friend, let me consider in what Manner I shall make myself most acceptable to Him

,,,O Creator, O Father ,,,By Thy Wisdom hast Thou formed all things ,,,created man,,, superior to Thy other earthly Creatures ,,,and art not delighted with violent death and bloody sacrifices ,,,Thou abhorrest in Thy creatures treachery and deceit, malice, revenge, [Intemperance] and every other hurtful Vice ,,,Thou art a Lover of justice and sincerity, of friendship, benevolence and every virtue. Thou art my Friend, my Father, and my Benefactor. Praised by Thy Name, O God, forever, Amen [[note all the Christian Bible phrases and teachings]] ,,,I may be preserved from atheism and infidelity, impiety and profaneness ,,,avoid irreverence and ostentation, formality and odious hypocrisy ,,,Help me, O Father ,,,the favors I receive from heaven ,,,I thank Thee" (224). Doctrinal statements that he recommended for preaching: "one God; Father of the Universe; good, powerful, wise; omnipresent; ought to be worshipped; adoration prayer and thanksgiving both in publick and private; loves such of His creatures that they should love; do good to others; will reward them either in this world or hereafter; men's minds do not die with their bodies, but are made more happy or miserable after this life according to their actions; virtuous men ought to league together to strengthen the interest of virtue, in the world; knowledge and learning it so to be cultivated, and Ignorance dissipated; none but the virtuous are wise (224) [[these doctrines are from the Christian Bible]]. Wrote his graveyard epitaph with Christian doctrine, ",,,Lies here, food for worms; Yet the work itself shall not be lost, For it will (as he believed) appear once more, In a new, and more beautiful edition, Corrected and amended,,," (47a). Wrote the Lord's prayer from the Christian Bible: "Heavenly Father, May all revere Thee, And become Thy dutiful children and faithful subjects. May Thy laws be obeyed on earth as perfectly as ,,,in Heaven. [[here is desire for the US to be a Christian law abiding nation]]. Provide ,,,Keep us out of temptation and deliver us from Evil" (223). He notes of changing to Christian orthodoxy doctrines and away from some of the Deism doctrines. Lived with a French protestant and a catholic family at different times. Wrote a "Plan for Attaining Moral Perfection" which includes this, "Silence~ Speak not but what may benefit others or yourself; avoid trifling conversation; Justice~ Wrong none by doing injuries, or omitting the benefits that are your duty. Humility~ Imitate Jesus and Socrates." and also wrote ",,,I am so far from thinking that God is not to be worshipped, that I have compos'd and wrote a whole Book of Devotions for my own Use;" and then shared that good works could not merit salvation but in God's grace (109). Diligent to try to work on various character traits as Jesus had, using one week on each one; though intense struggles he continued; regularly attended church, Presbyterian, helped establish a Christian school, in Philadelphia, and wanted Christian religion taught; opposed lottery for finance, and had his daughter baptized (108). Wrote in letters to his daughter, "Go constantly to church ,,,devotion in the common prayer book is your principal business ,,,I wish you would never miss the prayer days,,,"; and wrote to his wife, "You spent your Sunday very well, but I think you should go oftener to church"; wrote to Catherine Ray, "Be a good girl and don't forget your catechism. Go constantly to meeting~ or church~ Till you get a good husband; then stay at home, nurse the children, and live like a Christian" (47b). Wrote about a Presbyterian clergyman, "I became one of his constant hearers, his sermons pleasing me,,,". Used his printing press to assist Christian writings extensively; stated in his older days that he still had some doubts re: Christ's divinity, but expected to see him and for now believed in all of His doctrines; continued study of subjects in the Holy Bible. // George Washington: Prayer in his circulated letter as a farewell on June 8, 1783, was mailed to the colonies. Notice it states his intention was to start the USA with God as the ruler, and for it to maintain such. Also states what the religion that the USA started with, which should continue. Also that we are not going to be a happy nation (happiness from God) as only possible with the true religion of Jesus Christ: "Almighty God; We make our earnest prayer that Thou wilt keep the US in Thy Holy protection; Thou wilt incline the hearts of the citizens to cultivate a spirit of subordination and obedience to government; and entertain a brotherly affection and love for one another and for their fellow citizens ,,,And ,,,dispose us all to do justice, to love mercy ,,,with that charity, humility, and pacific temper of mind ,,,the characteristics of the Divine Author of our blessed religion, and without a humble imitation of whose EX in these things we can never hope to be a happy nation. Grant our supplication, we beseech Thee, through Jesus Christ our Lord. Amen". Was an Anglican and/or Episcopalian Church member all of his life. Repeatedly stated that the Religion of the USA is Christian; and that it is needed for good GOV. Raised in a Christian home. +From (71)~ John Marshall, a Supreme Court Justice officer, said, GW was ",,,a sincere believer in the Christian faith, and a truly devout man"; In AD 1799, Rev J.T. Kirkland said GW ",,,habitually devout; To Christian institutions he gave the countenance of his example,,,"; In AD 1827, William White shares that Robert Lewis reported to him of witnessing GW habits of "morning and evening kneeling posture with a Bible"; GW's own words: "It is impossible to account for the creation of the universe, without the agency of a Supreme Being", and, that God is the "Author of all good" and "all things" and "beings", and "protection of Almighty God ,,,superintendence ,,,his holy keeping."; ",,,Ruler of the Universe,,," and "Arbiter of Nations,,,". // Rufus King: Episcopalian; lawyer; US senator of New York; strong supporter of GOV Checks & Balances because of sin potentiality and man's temptability (33). Attended religious schools; was a Congregationalist Christian church attendee then Episcopalian Christian Church. Stated the basis of law is God's law, which is really what the law of nature is (33). // Samuel Adams: Said, "Let divines and philosophers, statesmen and patriots, unite their endeavors ,,,by impressing the minds of men with the importance of educating their little boys and girls ,,,the fear and love of the Deity ,,,in subordination to these great principles ,,,the love of their country; of instructing them in the art of self-government, without which they never can act a wise part in the government of societies, great or small; in short, of leading them in the study and practice of the exalted virtues of the Christian system,,," (46a). Known as the "Father of the American Revolution". Mr. Jefferson said of SA: "I always considered him as more than any other member (in Congress) the fountain of our important measures" and "In meditating the matter of that address, I often asked myself, is this exactly in the spirit of the patriarch of liberty, Samuel Adams?" (112). Encyclopedia Britannica tells that SA, "did more than any other American to arouse opposition against English rule in the Colonies" (114). World Book Encyclopedia tells that SA was, ",,,the leading speaker in the cause of American Independence" (115). Probable organizer of the Boston Tea Party; organizer of independence groups; Governor of Massachusetts 1789-1793; signer of DOI, CON, and worked on various committees and conventions; insisted on a Bill or Rights. Puritan Christianity; devotion was a serious concern. Strong desire for New England to establish Puritan manners and morals (104a). Raised in the Congregational Christian Church, learned Greek and Latin, enrolled in Harvard at age 14; his parents hoping he would be in the clergy, and was reported that "Sam's morals were good and he was seldom missing from the family pew on Lord's days", but was not intensely interested in theology and metaphysics until the First Great Awakening when he was encouraged (104a). Samuel's father opened his home up to politicians which interested SA; {(104a)~ includes material from C.K. Shipton, Sibley's Harvard Graduates}. Became intensely religious, and set aside days of fasting and prayer to seek the Lord; earned only a meager wage in his life. Condemned luxury, indolence, licentiousness all his life (9). Studied John Locke (104a); It is reported that "He was never more angelic than when singing hymns in Dr. Checkley's meetinghouse", where he displayed, "an exquisite ear for music, and a charming voice ,,,organized singing societies,,," (104a). Intense desire about religious abuse from various GOV in history and England at the time, attempting to ruin true Christianity, and extending "popery" and "poor deluded Catholic reverenc'd the decree of Holy Father at Rome" (104a). Many instances of discussion about religious abuse and Christian reason to support the independence revolution (9). Declared that the US was a great nation and soon be extending proper laws for England (104a). All law comes from God, revealed in SCs and in nature; wrote to Thomas Paine, rebuking him for turning to "infidelity". // Thomas Jefferson: Made professions of Christianity. Was at times mixed up on what to do about Christianity and discerning problems at times and various questions and doubts about specific subjects of Christianity, but overall evidenced of following Christ by actions and profession. Wrote "The Life and Morals of Jesus of Nazareth". Professed himself a Christian (9). Raised by God-fearing, affectionate, hard-working parents (50). Attended Christian school, William and Mary College; 3 of his extra-biblical influences, which he mentions in a letter to Benjamin Rush, are 3 Christians, Isaac Newton, Francis Bacon, John Locke; had difficulties with the doctrine of the trinity, and wrote, "difficulty of reconciling the ideas of Unity and Trinity" (110). Wrote "truth and reason are eternal" (30). Stated that liberty and Rights need to be safeguarded while people are searching for truth on Christian doctrines, including saying, ",,,get rid ,,,of those tyrannical laws ,,,suffer an execution for heresy, or a three years' imprisonment for not comprehending the mysteries of the Trinity ,,,A single zealot may commence persecution, and better men be his victims ,,,it can never be too often repeated, that the time for fixing every essential right on a legal basis is while our rulers are honest,,," (50). In AD 1823, wrote John Adams saying, ",,,I think that every Christian sect gives a great handle to Atheism by their general dogma that, without a revelation, there would not be sufficient proof of the being of a God ,,,I hold (without appeal to revelation) that when we take view of the Universe, in its parts general or particular, it is impossible for the human mind not to perceive ,,,a conviction of design ,,,skill ,,,power in every atom of its composition ,,,it is impossible, I say, for the human mind not to believe that there is,,, cause and effect ,,,irresistible ,,,evidences of an intelligent and powerful Agent,,," (110). In AD 1813 wrote, "Of all the systems of morality ancient or modern ,,,none appear to me so pure as that of Jesus,,," (110). Yet in AD 1816, continued with problems understanding the Trinity (110). Wrote in AD 1780's, "The God who gave us life gave us liberty ,,,that these liberties are ,,,the gift of God,,,"; agreed the Bible as God's Word, "I shall need ,,,the favor of that Being in whose hands we are, who led our forefathers, as Israel of old, from their native land,,," ; wrote of God much (112). Supported Jesus as a leader and the Bible as a guide, writing, "His system of morality was the most benevolent and sublime probably that has been every taught ,,,the most innocent, the most benevolent, the most eloquent and sublime character that ever has been exhibited to man"; and wrote an explanatory paper on how Jesus differed than the Jews with 4 points that include, "corrected the deism ,,,confirming them in their belief in God, and giving them juster notions of His attributes and government ,,,2. His moral doctrines relating to kindred and friends were more pure and perfect,,,3. ,,,pushed his scrutinizes into the heart of man,,,4. ,,,taught emphatically the doctrines of a future state,,," (112). Often read of Jesus and quoted Bible vss and contemplated the doctrines of Christianity (110)(112). In AD 1825, wrote to a friend's son, "Adore God. Reverence and cherish your parents. Love your neighbor as yourself. Be just. Be true. Murmur not at the ways of Providence. So shall the life into which you have entered be the Portal to one of eternal and ineffable bliss" (110). In AD 1823, he wrote a letter about John Calvin (from where Calvinist doctrines come from), "I can never join Calvin in addressing his god. He was indeed an Atheist, which I can never be; or rather his religion was Daemonism. If ever man worshipped a false god, he did. The being described in his 5 points is not the God whom you and I acknowledge and adore, the Creator and benevolent governor of the world, but a daemon of malignant spirit,,," (110). Was regular in Christian church attendance at the Episcopal church; wrote the plan for the church in Charlottesville; was a financial contributor, and supported the clergy; assisted the Presbyterian Christian church; and replied to a man who expressed his disbelief in the Holy Bible, by saying, "Then, sir, you have studied it to little purpose"; no profanity; disliked impiety; favorite quotation to youth was from the Bible, Psalms 15; did not permit cards in his house (112). In AD 1815, states ",,,I am a real Christian, that is to say, a disciple of the doctrines of Jesus, very different form the Platonists, who call me infidel, and themselves Christians and preachers of the gospel,,," (110). Supported Christianity to be included in the USA GOV: In AD 1808 writing to a clergy, "I consider the GOV of the US as interdicted by the CON from intermeddling with religious institutions, their doctrines, discipline, or exercises. This results not only from the provision that no law shall be made respecting the establishment of free exercise of religion, but from that also which reserves the states to the powers not delegated to the US. Clearly, no power to prescribe any religious exercise, [[Christian DEN, secondary doctrines and expressions]] or to assume authority in religious discipline, [[Christianity DEN]] has been delegated to the general GOV"; and at his second Presidential Inaugural Address, stated, "In matters of religion I have considered that its free exercise is placed by the CON independent of the powers of the General Government. I have therefore undertaken on no occasion to prescribe the religious exercise suited to them, but have left them, as the CON found them, under the direction and discipline of the church or state authorities acknowledged by the several religious societies" (113).

---T--- The Doctrines that the FFoG trusted & supported were Christian: // The subject of the Trinity was studied and Thomas Jefferson, James Madison, and Benjamin Franklin expressed desires about it; and the Divinity of the Holy Spirit and of Jesus; However they all agreed eventually about these: a) God the Father; b) Providence (God's intervention and involvement in men's life on earth). Thomas Jefferson and Benjamin Franklin had desires about this doctrine in early years but later agreed to it. c) The Holy Bible is God's word; d) Jesus as God's Son; e) Salvation; f) Opposition to sin, including evil; g) Christian Churches; h) Living without sin, or evil; i) Sanctification in various definitions; j) Each professed and lived intense faith in God.

+++

-------------------- *SYMBOLS, MOMUMENTS, BUILDINGS, MEMORIALS, ALL Representations and Communication Expressions as Intended Supports for God and Christianity as the Foundational Basis of the USA; AND all These Support the CC (DOI & CON):*
------------ *((Also See Other Symbols of the USA Attached at the start of the Book))*

---T--- GREAT SEAL SYMBOL of the USA - A Christian Symbol about God [[see pictures near front of this book; various versions are all Christian]]: // Congress Legal Enactment: Official Continental Congress — June 20, 1782. // Summary Description of the Great Seal, is a Christian Symbol representing that the Nation is to be centered around God, the Lord Jesus. // The Final Edition occurrence of activities as recorded: Congress observed the submitted explanations and returned the designs to Charles Thomson on June 19, 1782, and he made a few modifications. Thus he produced the "blazon" with "Remarks and Explanation" and presented them to the Continental Congress on June 20, overnight and the next day. The Congress enacted that same Day, the report. It was the work of many minds, as C. Thomson used the previous various committees designs to include in his. // An alteration was made by Pres. Truman & people in AD 1945, ordering the eagle's head turned toward the olive branch. // One of the Seals first use was: by Pres. George Washington in some exchange of prisoners of war with Britain. // Engraving and Casting Formations: A short summary explanation as follows~ Engraving and casting formations began operating at that time as a developing science; The cast (die) was cut, for the First Great Seal, and possibly engraved by Robert Scot of Philadelphia in AD 1782. A Brass cast was in use for almost 60 years. // Definitions of the Symbol, provided by the very words of the designers: +Clouds - Christian definition: Ben Franklin's original idea was for a representation of the "divine presence and command"; as seen by Holy Scripture records of Israel coming out of Egypt; this was his first design. Clouds are in the final design. Mr. Jefferson stated, "Pharaoh sitting in an open Chariot, a Crown on his head and a Sword in his hand, passing through the divided waters of the Red Sea in pursuit of the Israelites: Rays from a Pillar of Fire in the Cloud, expressive of the divine Presence and Command, beaming on Moses who stands on the shore and extending his hand over the Sea causes it to overwhelm Pharaoh.". T. Jefferson uses Holy Scriptures and so does B. Franklin as follows. Benjamin Franklin's proposal is preserved in a note of his own handwriting as: "Moses standing on the shore, and extending his hand over the sea, thereby causing the same to overwhelm Pharaoh who is sitting in an open chariot, a crown on his head and a sword in his hand. Rays from a Pillar of Fire in the Clouds reaching to Moses, to express that he acts by Command of the Deity.". +Christian Motto for the first committee design was, "Rebellion to tyrants is obedience to God". // 2nd Committee's Design is Christian: William Barton suggested a pyramid underneath the Eye of Providence with Mottos Deo Favente ("with God's favor", or more literally, "with God favoring") and Perennis ("Everlasting"). The pyramid and Perennis motto had come from a $50 Continental Currency Bill designed by Francis Hopkinson. This also is Holy Scripture based. // The Eagle: Ben Franklin had suggested a wild turkey, representing America conduct and temper. However, rather, the Eagle was decided with the intent/ purpose that the eagle (an American Bald Eagle), is making the symbol part of America, because the bird lives in the US, and there are many of them living and in many parts of the USA geographically. The wings extending as in flight. // Glossary of Heraldic Term Symbols of color and shapes used in the Blazon of the final design submitted by Mr. Thomson include some as these: argent = silver; azure = blue; chief = top part of the shield; dexter = right; escutcheon = shield; gules = red; or = gold or yellow; paleways, pieces = vertical stripes on the shield proper = the element's natural color; sinister = left. +Glory is a Christian word, relating to the glory of God, from the Holy Bible; and to which Benjamin Franklin noted. +Pyramid: A Symbol of "Strength and Duration": The pyramid was originally suggested by William Barton, "A Pyramid of thirteen Strata, (or Steps)." W. Barton was undoubtedly influenced by the pyramid on the $50 Continental Currency Bill designed in AD 1778 by Francis Hopkinson. That is Holy Bible based. Strength representation: The three men primarily responsible for putting the pyramid on the Great Seal (Francis Hopkinson, William Barton, and Charles Thomson) all had access to books written by historians and explorers who estimated it took about between 100,000 and 360,000 workers to work for about 20 years to build the Great Pyramid of Egypt. At least this is one report that was probably considered. Observe the cost of what Americans had to endure to separate from evil governments. The battles were terrible, and it should be noted that France assisted the USA in winning the RW. The Pyramids are massive in structure. The "Great Pyramid" is a group of large stones; it is 480 feet tall, with a 750 feet base in each direction, and forms a square at the

214

bottom; contains multiples of blocks of stones with some weighing approximately 2.5 tons (on average), some over 16 tons, even over 50 tons in some areas. It is a geometric design, with sides that rise at an angle, a precise angle degree; which 4 sides coincide to the four points of the compass. The pyramid is one of the strongest accomplishments of mankind in technical and structural engineering. Duration representation, as time element: Historians, during the time of the FFOG, knew that the Egyptian pyramids had already survived many years. They were known to be a very permanent structure. They are one of the Wonders of the World. Approx. 75 pyramids exist in Egypt. The history of the Pyramid is not in itself, nor is it stated as such in the Holy Bible; nor that it is a symbol of evil worldliness, or evil, or of Egypt. There is no sure evidence as to who built the pyramids or when exactly, or how. The history that the FFOG studied had various ideas. The location of the pyramids in Egypt does not explain that the Egyptians built them; and there are pyramids in other countries. Some pyramids may have been built by the Hebrews withi Egyptian government. And some of the pyramids could have been built years earlier, and the Egyptians only took the land after the flood. Historian, William Baxter Godbey, states that Cain's relatives or such built buildings or structures, including some pyramids, with the use of dinosaurs. They harnessed the more docile dinosaurs and let them move the blocks in place. The intention/ purpose stated for the pyramid, "strength and duration" are also reminders of the Israelites coming out of Egyptian tyranny and for God. The pyramid therefore is connected to Holy Scriptures and the truth therein about good GOV & citizens & God. In both of its comparisons it is connected to God. // The Christian mottos: "Annuit Coeptis" is ("He", referring to God, "favors our undertaking"); and "Novus Ordo Seclorum" is ("The New Order of the Ages"). It is Anglicized Latin. It is taken from the Latin words annuo (nod, approve) and cœpta (beginnings, undertakings); and it is literally translated as "He approves (or has approved) [our] undertaking(s)". Mr. Thomson, also being a Latin scholar, suggested the mottos "Annuit Coeptis (He [God] has favored our undertakings)" which is the one that is now over the Eye and Novus Ordo Seclorum on the Great Seal. It may be, but is not stated by Mr. Thomson, that he selected the Latin phrases because they each have 13 letters. Recollect that there were 13 colonies, and thus the 13 Stars in the constellation above the eagle's head, 13 Stripes in the eagle's shield made of 6 red and 7 white stripes, 13 Arrows by the eagle's left talon, 13 Leaves on the Olive branch in the eagle's right talon, 13 Levels in the unfinished pyramid, and also then the 13 Letters in E Pluribus Unum, and also 13 Letters in Annuit Coeptis. +Lies and myths are told that the relation of these terms is connected to some evil. It is not true. The truth is herein. To prove such is easily done. The description of the Seal is given verbatim from Mr. Thomson's own writings submitted to Congress, as we will now show. On June 20, 1782, Congress approved Mr. Thomson's design for both sides of the Great Seal whose official description for the reverse side is quoted as: "A Pyramid unfinished. In the Zenith an Eye in a triangle surrounded with a glory proper. Over the Eye these words 'Annuit Cœptis'." Mr. Thomson states that it is connected with the Eye of Providence in a triangle surrounded by light rays in the zenith of an unfinished pyramid. More quotes from him include: "The Eye over it & the motto Annuit Coeptis allude to the many signal interpositions of providence in favour of the American cause." Some notes on translating Latin, of the verbs and nouns for proper grammar, make the combination a term that Mr. Thomson used in relation to the eye being also joined with the term "Annuit copeptis". Thomson provided his Official Explanation of the definition of this motto, and it is documented by Congress, as he wrote: "The Eye over it [the pyramid] and the motto Annuit Cœptis allude to the many signal interpositions of providence in favor of the American cause." [5] Annuit Cœptis is translated by the U.S. State Department, The U.S. Mint, U.S. Treasury as "He (God) has favored our undertakings.". // Here is the description given by C. Thomson to the Continental Congress, June 20, 1782, for the Blazon and the Seal. I parenthesized some of the sections because of size: "Blazon of the Great Seal of the US - The Secretary of the US in Congress assembled to whom were referred the several reports of committees on the device for a great seal,,, That the Device for an Armorial Achievement & Reverse of the great seal of the US in Congress assembled is as follows ,,", {"Arms -- Paleways of thirteen pieces Argent and Gules: a Chief, Azure. The Escutcheon on the breast of the American bald Eagle displayed, proper, holding in his dexter talon an Olive branch, and in his sinister a bundle of thirteen arrows, all proper, & in his beak a scroll, inscribed with this Motto. "E pluribus unum" } ,,,{"For the Crest -- Over the head of the Eagle which appears above the Escutcheon, A Glory, Or, breaking through a cloud, proper, & surrounding thirteen stars forming a Constellation, Argent, on an Azure field."} ,,,Reverse (side) ,,,{"A Pyramid unfinished. In the Zenith an Eye in a triangle surrounded with a glory proper. Over the Eye these words "Annuit Coeptis". On the base of the pyramid the numerical letters MDCCLXXVI & underneath the following motto. "novus ordo seclorum"}. ,,,"Remarks and Explanation — June 20, 1782. The shield is composed of thirteen stripes that represent the several states joined into one solid compact, supporting the chief which unites the whole and represents Congress. The stripes are kept closely united by the chief and the chief depends upon that union and the strength resulting from it. The motto E Pluribus Unum alludes to this union. The shield is born on the breast of an American Eagle without any other supporters to denote that the US of America ought to rely on their own virtue. The olive branch and arrows denote the power of peace and war which is exclusively vested in Congress. The constellation of thirteen stars denotes a new state taking its place and rank among other sovereign powers. The pyramid signifies strength and duration. The Eye over it and the motto Annuit Coeptis allude to the many signal interpositions of providence in favor of the American cause. [[God & the Holy Bible is here]] The date 1776 underneath is that of the Declaration of Independence and the words Novus Ordo Seclorum under it signify the beginning of the new American Era, which commences from that date. ,,,The Escutcheon is composed of the chief & pale, the two most honorable ordinaries. The Pieces, paly, represent the several states all joined in one solid compact entire, supporting a Chief, which unites the whole & represents Congress. The Motto alludes to this union. The pales in the arms are kept closely united by the chief and the chief depends upon that union & the strength resulting from it for its support, to denote the Confederacy of the US of America & the preservation of their union through Congress. The colours of the pales are those used in the flag of the US of America; White signifies purity and innocence, Red, hardiness & valor, and Blue, the colour of the Chief signifies vigilance, perseverance & justice. The Olive branch and arrows denote the power of peace & war which is exclusively vested in Congress. The Constellation denotes a new State taking its place and rank among other sovereign powers. The Escutcheon is born on the breast of an American Eagle without any other supporters to denote that the US of America ought to rely on their own Virtue.—Reverse. The pyramid signifies Strength and Duration: The Eye over it & the Motto allude to the many signal interpositions of providence in favour of the American cause. The date underneath is that of the Declaration of Independence and the words under it signify the beginning of the new American Era, which commences from that date.— ". // Knowledge on Symbols or Emblems in general that were considered in the designs: +Heraldic language - written description to precisely describe the appearance of the imagery. A heraldic is defined: "signal something: to give or be a sign that something is going to happen; welcome somebody or something: to welcome or announce somebody or something with enthusiasm; official messenger: art of describing coats of arms; an official messenger and representative of a king or leader in former times." (1a). +It should be noted that the king of this county was clearly stated, and designed and based, as Jesus, the Lord God of all. On the subject of Heraldry, Mr. Barton wrote in AD 1788 a letter to General George Washington: "I am likewise persuaded, Sir, that Blazonry not only merits the notice of an inquisitive mind, viewed merely as an affective science; but that Coat-Armour, the object of it, may be rendered conducive to both public and private uses, of considerable importance, in this infant nation, now rising into greatness". +Blazon defined: "To proclaim or announce something widely or ostentatiously; heraldry depict coat of arms: to create or describe a coat of arms using the traditional symbols; a blazon is the visible pictorial symbol of the Heraldry." (1a). +Definition of "Realization.": "a certain type of imagery". This was the imagery used for the USA (6a). +Spiritualism and Mysticism in Christian methods: In a right form, the Great Seal exists as an image with words. An EX based on this written description is called a "Realization.". This all proves the spiritualistic mind and heart concern of the FFOG, and that they were spiritual men, and of a Christian spirit. Charles Thomson, who submitted the final design of the Great Seal, had a project to translate the Holy Bible later in his life. // The religion of the designers of the Great Seal of the US are Christian supporters: +William Barton was raised in a Christian home with a father, Rev. Thomas Barton. William studied heraldry in England where he traveled for a while. He attended and graduated from a Christian College, the College of New Jersey. In AD 1789, Pres. George Washington nominated Mr. Barton as a Judge of the Western Territory; Barton declined. +Charles Thomson participated in the Christian religion, born in Gorteade, Ireland; a Patriot leader in Revolution; secretary of the Continental Congress (AD 1774—1789); mother died early in his life and then he migrated to the US with his father who died at sea, him being young; he and his brothers were made homeless and penniless in America; he was taken in by a blacksmith in New Castle, Delaware, and was educated in New London, Pennsylvania. In AD 1750 he became a tutor in Latin at the Philadelphia Academy; a leader of Philadelphia's Sons of Liberty; he was an aggressive assistant in the Revolutionary efforts of the AD 1770's; John Adams called him the "Samuel Adams of Philadelphia"; his efforts include the written recording of the debates of congress; Thomson's name, as secretary, appears on the first published version of the DOI in July 1776; was also considered as the Prime Minister of the US; involved in Foreign affairs; his final years was working on a translation of the Holy Bible; a very devoted Christian. +John Adams has already been clearly evidenced as Christian. +Benjamin Franklin has been proved as a very devoted Christian; his life is recorded in this Chapter in the record of the FFOG. +A mix up of William Barton with another William Barton, who was a Mason, has been suggested. The other Seal workers were Christian supporters. // Chronological History of the events of the Construction of the Great Seal Emblems: +At least 3 known various committees, made by Congress, were formed, and each of them made various different attempts to construct a Symbol. +The First Committee worked with challenges of intangible principles, ideals, and graphic symbols. 3 men served on this committee, Franklin, Adams, and Jefferson. They did not ever conclude on a symbol, but some of the symbols are yet available. One symbol made by this First Committee was a Christian Biblical theme of the Israel in the Wilderness and another of the Judgement of Hercules. Then they sought the help from a drawer, or artist, Pierre Eugene du Simitiere, who brought knowledge of heraldry and experience in designing seals. Four parts were constructed and submitted by this first committee and its consultants, and were later adopted in the final seal: The Eye of Providence; the date of the DOI DOC of independence (MDCCLXXVI); The Shield; The Latin motto, E Pluribus Unum (Out of many, one). This first committee submitted its design on Aug. 20, 1776, but the Congress ordered the report "to lie on the table," which is essentially was, "open" unfinished project, and yet unapproved. +The Second Committee: In Mar. 1780, the Congress submitted the design and reports of the first committee over to a new committee, composed of James Lovell, John Morin Scott, and William Churchill Houston. They asked Francis Hopkinson to counsel them, who also was an assistant in designing the American flag and the New Jersey State great seal. This committee did not get the project completed either. However some of their work also contributed to the final design we have today: The 13 red and white stripes, the blue shield; the constellation of 13 six pointed stars; the olive branch, a symbol of peace. Evidently Mr. Hopkinson was a large part of the contributor of these designs. +A Third Committee, May 1782, is appointed by Congress consisting of John Rutledge, Arthur Middleton, and Elias Boudinot. These fellows apparently did not much work on it. A Christian motto was suggested. They enlisted the services of William Barton, a lawyer who also had art skill, and learned in Heraldry. He suggested an eagle, not the bald, but a small crested white eagle, with wings spread. He also combined it with some of the other symbols previously, a flag, a pyramid with 13 steps unfinished, and the Eye of Providence. He provided some technical explanations. But Congress did not pass it. +June 13, 1782, Congress takes all the collected work of the previous committees to Charles Thomson, Secretary of Congress. Though not an artist, he was good at getting jobs done. He included various parts of all the previous designs. He replaced Mr. Barton's crested Imperial eagle with the native American bald eagle, making the symbol part of America (because the bird lives in large numbers in the US). The wings extending downward as though in flight. A bundle of arrows is put in the left talon, and an olive branch in the right. Then the flag, pyramid, and eye on the other. Thomson modified the crest (a device placed above the shield). In his design of the Seal's reverse, Thomson retained the pyramid and the Eye of Providence in a triangle at the zenith (the tip of an astronomical object); and also being a Latin scholar, suggested the mottos Annuit Coeptis (He [God] has favored our undertakings) over the Eye and Novus Ordo Seclorum.

---T--- *"IN GOD WE TRUST". This is a USA Statement; a Foundational Basis Statement for Supporting The USA Establishment with God:* // Introduction: "And this be our motto: 'In God is our trust.'" (Francis Scott Key). // "The Star Spangled Banner" song is our national anthem, which is where this statement is reported as coming from. // The last stanza of that song states, "Blest with vict'ry and peace, may the heav'n rescued land - Praise the Pow'r that has made and preserv'd us a nation - And conquer we must when our cause is just - And this be our motto: 'In God is our trust.' - And the Star Spangled Banner in triumph shall wave - O'er the land of the free and the home of the brave." // History of the song: Francis ("Frank") Scott Key is a contributor to the song in the time periods of AD 1814. // The fourth stanza, "And this be our motto - 'In God is our Trust!'", statement was shortened in AD 1864 to, "In God We Trust," to fit a newly designed two-cent piece. // It was historically, and for much time after starting~ an unofficial American motto. // In AD 1955, Congress ordered it placed on all US' currency. // The God here is the same God that Francis Scott Key supported in his life and the song, Christ Jesus of the Holy Trinity. // The writing of the Song occurred at the following time and events: The US was again at war with an abusive evil GOV in England, who had once again turned from good to evil. France and England were both evil GOV's at this time. In June 18, 1812, the US declared war on England. There was illegal and abusive activity with American sea shipping, whereas American crews were captured and enslaved. "Free Trade and Sailors' Rights" were in concern, and defense of National Rights for business activity and freedom, were some primary causes of the war. In August of AD 1814, an English army arrived in Chesapeake Bay, and eventually captured and torched the US capital. President Madison departed the White House without his wife, Dolly, as the attack was so quick and fierce. Dolly later fled, and, not able to take much with her, but did take a portrait of George Washington. The flames from the burning city, including the White House and capital bldg, could be seen 40 miles away in Baltimore. A rain, from God of providence, stopped the flames from completely ruining the city. Fort McHenry was the aim of attack by the British. Baltimore, seeing the flames and hearing of the attack, prepared itself and the fort for battle. One thing they did was to raise the flag that had been prepared. // What flag? This flag: Prepared previously in AD 1813, was a flag very large so it could be seen easily by all. An Officer, named "Armistead", asked for a flag that was very big so that "the British would have no trouble seeing it from a distance". A Flag maker named, Mary Young Pickersgill, was hired to design and make it. It consisted of 15 stars on a blue background and some red and white strips. Mary and her daughter, Caroline, cut the flag parts from 400 yards of wool. The size was going to be thirty by forty-two feet and had to be assembled in a borrowed business warehouse building. It was finished in Aug. 1813 and cost $405.90. // Now the battle that was occurring, as previously discussed, was a raid on the US Capital city. Mr. William Beanes was taken captive; and his freedom was requested and his life was feared for. Thus Francis Scott Key was requested for the mission; he was a Christian, Episcopalian DEN, and an attorney; also a veteran of the current war. Mr. Francis needed assistance and enlisted Colonel John Skinner, who as an American agent had experience in prisoner exchanges. President Madison approved. Hence they took a boat, with a white flag of truce, and sailed to the British fleet; and the British allowed them to board, and Commander Admiral Alexander Cochrane met with them but refused their petition. Mr. Key & Mr. Skinner then submitted letters from English soldiers, that were American prisoners, and who had been wounded, who commended the good treatment from the Americans to them as prisoners. This changed the decision of the British Officials, who then agreed to free Mr. Beanes. However, release was delayed because Mr. Key and Mr. Skinner had seen and heard too much about the English battle plans on Fort McHenry; thus Key, Skinner, and Beanes were now all 3 taken captive, and put under guard in their boat and positioned beyond the army fleet. There they had a view that enabled them to watch the battle occur. During one day the English ships fired over 1,500 shells at the fort. During such time, it was feared that the fort had fallen; Key, Skinner, and Beanes waited for opportunity to observe if the flag was yet flying. But they did not know that the British had abandoned the attack because of diminishing ammunition. As morning came, Mr. Key looked at the fort and saw the giant flag yet flying; he was encouraged, and having a pen and paper, wrote the poem "The Star Spangled Banner" closing it with "this be our motto; 'in God is our trust!'". // Mr. Key's poem was published in the Baltimore Patriot's Sept. 20, 1814 issue. // The lyrics were recommended to accompany the tune of an English song, "Anacrean in Heaven". // It was publicly performed in Oct. 1814. // The Army & Navy adopted the song as their unofficial national anthem. // Congress on Mar. 3, 1931 officiated the song making it the National Anthem. // The great motto and statement of faith, "In God We Trust" occurred also during the USA Civil War days. // These are the words to the Song: STAR SPANGLED BANNER: "O say can you see, by the dawn's early light; What so proudly we hailed at the twilight's last gleaming; Whose broad stripes and bright stars, thro' the perilous flight; O'er the ramparts we watched were so gallantly streaming; And the rocket's red glare, the bombs bursting in air; Gave proof through the night that our flag was still there; O say, does that Star-Spangled Banner yet wave; O'er the land of the free and the home of the brave; On the shore dimly seen through the mists of the deep; Where the foe's haughty host in dread silence reposes; What is that which the breeze o'er the towering steep; As it fitfully blows, half conceals, half discloses?; Now it catches the gleam of the morning's first beam; In full glory reflected now shines on the stream; Tis the Star-Spangled Banner, Oh long may it wave; O'er the land of the free and the home of the brave; And where is that band who so vauntingly swore; That the havoc of war and the battle's confusion; A home and country, shall leave us no more?; Their blood was washed out their foul foot steps pollution; No refuge could save the hireling and slave; From the terror of flight or the gloom of the grave; And the Star-Spangled Banner in triumph doth wave; O'er the land of the free and the home of the brave; Oh thus be it e'er when free men shall stand; Between their lov'd homes and war's desolation!; Blest with vict'ry and peace, may the heav'n rescued land; Praise the Pow'r that has made and preserv'd us a nation; And conquer we must when our cause is just; And this be our motto: "In God is our trust"; And the Star-Spangled Banner in triumph shall wave; O'er the land of the free and the home of the brave". Francis Scott Key. // MOTTO: this statement is also considered a USA Motto, "In God is Our Trust" and also shortened to "In God We Trust". // It is known every where, as millions read our confession of faith. Whatever the monetary currency it, it is best known that God is the God of this nation, and not the currency. // During the Civil War, eleven Protestant DENs devoted to a campaign for references of God to the U.S., including the CON and other federal DOCs. // One of the first to actions was by Rev. M. R. Watkinson (a minister of Christ's Gospel, from Pennsylvania) who wrote in the AD 1860's his concerns to GOV Official Samuel Chase, Secretary of the Treasury, which included saying, "One fact touching our currency has hitherto been seriously overlooked. I mean the recognition of the Almighty God in some form on our coins". Mr. Chase agreed; thus during the week he wrote a letter to Mint Director, James Pollack stating, "No nation can be strong except in the strength of God, or safe except in His defense. The trust of our people in God should be declared on our national coins. You will cause a device to be prepared without unnecessary delay with a motto expressing in the fewest ,,,words possible this national recognition." Mr. Pollack quickly submitted to Mr. Chase, with some designs for three new coins and two suggested mottoes. These were "Our country; our God" and "God, our Trust". Mr. Chase suggested to amend the statements saying, "I approve your mottoes, only suggesting that on that with the Washington obverse the motto should begin with 'Our', so as to read: 'Our God and our country'. And on that with the shield, it should be changed so as to read, 'In God we trust'". Congress on date, Apr. 22, 1864, approved "In God We Trust" to be struck on a new bronze two-cent piece. Congress, in the following year, also had the motto to be used on any other coins, since having enough space for it. By AD 1909 it was on most coins. All activity relating to the situation involved God, even when disagreement about putting "God" on money, which Theodore Roosevelt stated in a letter to William Boldly in Nov 1907 saying, "My own feeling in the matter is due to my very firm conviction that to put such a MOTTO on coins, or to use it in any kindred manner, not only does no good but does positive harm, and is in effect irreverence, which comes dangerously close to sacrilege ,,,It is a MOTTO which it is indeed well to have inscribed on our great national monuments, in our temples of justice, in our legislative halls, and in building such as those at West Point and Annapolis -- in short, wherever it will tend to arouse and inspire a lofty emotion in those who look thereon. But it seems to me eminently unwise to cheapen such a MOTTO by use on coins, just as it would be to cheapen it by use on postage stamps, or in advertisements." Congress then in AD 1955 ordered it put on all US' currency. Christianity was the purpose for the President's agreement. In AD 1956 the disagreements with communism were occurring. Thus the 84th Congress by joint resolution, replaced the existing motto with "In God we Trust" and signed into law on July 1956 by the President. This was intended/ purposed to differentiate between communism, which promotes Atheism, and the USA GOV, a republic, which is Christian and supports God as God of this USA Nation. Courts in 3 lawsuits, concluded the motto, though they stated it was not religious, it is nevertheless constitutional.

---T--- Flag Day, American Flag, Flag Day Memorial, and Explanation of these as follows:

---T--- *FLAG DAY HOLIDAY:* // National Holiday, June 14th every year, annually: To celebrate this National symbol of the United States, Flag Day: // Conceived in AD 1885 by Wisconsin schoolteacher B.J. Cigrand as an annual holiday; The first celebration by Cigrand and his Wisconsin public school students, commemorated the 108th anniversary of the Continental Congress first Act of passing the symbol of a national flag banner for the USA. // The Enactment of 6/14/1777 resolved that the official banner be designed with thirteen alternating red and white stripes and thirteen white stars, representing a new Constellation of the thirteen colonies, stitched on a blue background. The AD 1777 Congressional resolution started the concept for the explanation of American Flag Day by emphasizing a strong union of those thirteen colonies; by a comparison to a cloth flag~ forever linked together by the threads of a unified Republic. // "Resolved, that the flag of the United States be thirteen stripes, alternate red and white; that the union be thirteen stars, white in a blue field representing a new constellation." A Marine Committee of the Second Continental Congress, on June 14, 1777.

---T--- *AMERICAN FLAG & Explanation of the Design:* // 2 Versions of the explanation are here provided as they connect to each other. These are mostly accurate: // The usage of stripes in our flag may be connected to two pre-existing flags. An AD 1765 Sons of Liberty flag flown in Boston had nine red and white stripes, and a flag used by Capt. Abraham Markoe's Philadelphia Light Horse Troop in AD 1775 had 13 blue and silver stripes. One or both of these flags likely influenced the design of the American flag. // The most logical explanation for the colors of the American flag is that it was modeled after the first unofficial American flag, the Continental Colors. In turn the Continental Colors was probably designed using the colors of England's Union Jack. The colors of the Great Seal are the same as the colors in the American flag. To attribute definitions to these colors, Charles Thomson, who helped design the Great Seal, reported to Congress that "White signifies purity and innocence. Red hardiness and valor, and Blue... signifies vigilance, perseverance and justice." // In AD 1986 Pres. Ronald Reagan altered C. Thomson's explanation by saying "The colors of our flag signify the qualities of the human spirit we Americans cherish: red for courage and readiness to sacrifice; white for pure intentions and high ideals; and blue for vigilance and justice." // The other theories of it are unproven and have no evidence whatsoever. // Continental Colors as follows~ AD 1795-1818 Star Spangled Banner Flag: +Designed with 15 stars and 15 stripes to represent the 13 original States plus Kentucky and Vermont. +Made by Mary Pickersgill and her daughter. +The 13 stripes stand for the original 13 Colonies that became the USA. +The stripes are red and white. Red stands for bravery. +White stands for purity or goodness. +The stars are in a circle to show that they are all equal. +The background color behind the stars is blue; Blue stands for justice. // This following version is also accurate: The Explanation of the COLORS IN THE FLAG, From website: helpsaveamerica.com. THE FLAG OF THE UNITED STATES OF AMERICA, by Howard Schnauber, Credit to Fort Collins Public Library Local History Archive. "My RED stands for the blood that was shed for the freedom I represent. Yet, my red originated from the blood of Jesus who died and rose again for those who believe in Him and for whom the Pilgrims came to this country for religious freedom and for the freedom from tyrants who would not let them worship God except in a national denominational church. My people are now free to worship in the church of their choice whether it be Baptist, Methodist, Presbyterian, Calvary Chapel, Evangelical Free, Brethren, Episcopalian, Catholic, Vineyard or other denominations who believe in the One True God of the Bible. People here are even free to disbelieve or to doubt. All we ask in America is that the ones who do not believe in Jesus will not try to use the freedoms we give them to try to take away the freedoms of those of us who do believe in Jesus. Our Founders held church services in the Rotunda of the Capitol, in the Treasury Office, and in the offices of the Supreme Court. By 1867, the church in the Capitol had become the largest church in Washington, and the largest Protestant church in America. (from James Hutson, Chief of the Manuscript Division of the Library of Congress, Religion and the Founding of the American Republic, Washington, D.C., Library of Congress 1998). This, among many other historical writings and facts, is proof that the recent claims of a separation of church and state did not exist among the original intent of our Founders. "Blessed is the nation whose God is the Lord." Psalm 33:12. My BLUE stands for heaven, the eternal dwelling place of those who go to be with the eternal, everlasting Father who created us. My blue reminds me that those who want to go to heaven must believe and put their trust and belief in God's Son, the Lord Jesus Christ. Obedience to the written message that God gave to them in His Holy Book, the Bible is the proof of my people's faith in God. My WHITE reminds me that my motives must always remain pure, unselfish, without greed, & with arms outstretched to welcome all who long for freedom, justice, opportunity and equality under the law. My white reminds me that because I am the symbol of a Christian nation founded upon Christian principles and the law of God represented by God's Ten Commandments that I am only pure and righteous because I was washed white in the blood of Jesus Christ, God's Son, and Savior of all who trust in Him. "Righteousness exalts a nation, but sin is a disgrace to any people." Proverbs 14:34. May all who love me work to elect Godly men and women who will live Godly lives in private and in public, who will honor me in their homes, their hearts, and in our nation, who will make righteous laws which reflect God's righteous rules in His Holy Word, the Bible".

---T--- <u>MONUMENTS / BUILDINGS: ALL of these pertain to, & are part of God's Christian Religion:</u> // Jefferson Memorial - Wall inscription states Jefferson's warning: "God who gave us life gave us liberty. Can the liberties of a nation be secure when we have removed a conviction that these liberties are the gift of God?". // Lincoln Memorial - Wall inscription is SC from Matthew 18:7. // Washington Monument - Stone block inscriptions have 8 SCs. // USA Capitol Building - Inscriptions of SC and references to God, in many locations through the building, with official dedications that the USA is God and Holy Bible based. // Library of Congress - SC from Psalms, Proverbs and Micah on Walls. // White House - President Franklin Roosevelt has President John Adams prayer engraved on the fireplace mantel in the State Dining Room; it states, "I pray Heaven to bestow the best of blessings on this House and on all that shall hereafter inhabit it ,,,". // National Cemetery at Arlington, VA, the tomb inscription states: "Here lies in honored glory, an American soldier, known but to God."~ Titled the, Tomb of the Unknown Soldier. // USA Supreme Court Building - Words of the Ten Commandments are chiseled into the marble slabs placed above the seat of the Chief Justice Judge Seat. // State Capitol Buildings - Many State capitol buildings of the USA have SC engraftments. // Liberty Bell - A Symbol of Religious Freedom; rejuvenated in commemoration of the 50th anniversary of Pennsylvania States establishment; This State was set up under the Charter of Privileges DOC Covenant Contract agreement which insured religious freedom for the citizens. The Bell is inscribed with SC Lev25:10, "Proclaim liberty throughout all the land unto all the inhabitants thereof". // The Library of Congress, in the rotunda, has Moses with the Ten Commandments. // USA Supreme Court has Moses in facade; & also inside the courtroom is Moses with the Ten Commandments. // The Ronald Reagan Building has a statue of "Liberty of Worship" which sits on the Ten Commandments. // National Archives - a Floor memorial of The Ten Commandments. // Library of Congress North Hall, Painting called "Knowledge". // A stained glass window of George Washington praying, in the chapel in the USA Capitol. // A phrase from Lord Tennyson in the rotunda of the Library of Congress. // Washington Monument, a memorial plaque from the Free Press Methodist Episcopal Church.

++

------------- *SOME SUMMARY CONCLUSIONS* About the 1-A, R-E, R~Est:

---T--- <u>The subject then, is what is the</u> relationship to be between God, Christianity & GOV??. What can the GOV do and what can it not do with Christianity?: // CANNOT Dos: t= It cannot refuse Christianity to exist; t= It cannot limit its support, or its activities, to any one DEN (sect) exclusively; t= It cannot limit the decision of individual Spiritual Moral Creatures about DEN; t= It cannot control DEN of secondary doctrines of Christianity; t= It cannot limit Christian expressions of individual Spiritual Moral Creatures, nor DEN; t= It cannot make a law to only allow one (or a few) national Church DEN (Establishment of Religion of Christianity); t= It cannot be partial or favor "respecting" Christian DEN, secondary doctrines, and expressions by making a law; t= It cannot hinder Christianity in any way, if Christianity is not doing any sin; if someone does sin, or evil, with the name of Christian, then it is not Christian and may be opposed; However it is not to micromanage nor meddle, nor dictate, nor tyranny; careful discern is needed. // CAN DO's: t= It can be Christian respected and prefer Christian; The CC (DOI & CON) states it; it must and needs to be; law requires that Christianity be supported and increased in the Nation & worldwide; t= The REP must be Christian; because they are directly connected to the Law making; t= Spiritual Moral Creatures in employment positions not directly connected to Law Making are required to support the CC in every part; which includes Christianity; t= Christianity must be supported in its efforts as True Christianity, as a general principle; t= It must allow all DENs of Christianity; those that agree with the basic fundamental doctrines of Christianity; t= It can allow freedom individual Spiritual Moral Creatures and DEN to decide on their own about secondary doctrines of Christianity; t= It can allow freedom for all individual Spiritual Moral Creatures, and DEN, to express Christianity; for expressions; t= It (GOV) can express activities, involvement, inclusion of one or more Christian DEN, secondary doctrines, and expressions without making laws about such; t= It must oppose evil in the USA, as according to the 10 commandments; t= It must not allow false religions to have public meetings and advertisements in the USA; not to have physical buildings for meetings; t= It is to reverence the Holy Bible and make it a study of application for the Law Basis, as the Common Law shares; t= It is to apply the Laws of Love to all of its functions and be slow to anger, slow to speak, and love all Spiritual Moral Creatures and be unselfish; not self-idolatry; God 1st priority.

---T--- GOV must, therefore, support all religion that claims Christ and the Holy Bible and the basic morals of it. It must oppose all other religions to have public assemblies and advertisements in the USA. All Spiritual Moral Creatures have Right to agree with any religion (true or false); but for false religions there is no unlimited freedom for physical buildings for meeting places, nor their personal homes for public meetings; they may practice in their home but not advertise it. The Laws of the Holy Bible must be the laws of the land.

++

------------- **Chapter 6 ,,,,,,,,, DECISION MAKING PROCESS for the USA GOV -**

Please See next Chapter (Chp 7) for this Part.

++
+++

---------------- Chapter 7 ,,,,,,,,, BASIS OF LAW ----------------

---------- GOD's LAWS as THE BASIS of the LAW -----------------------------

====== [CONCLUSION]: THE FOLLOWING PROCEDURE IS THE TRUTH ON WHAT DISCERNING THOUGHTS ARE To BE HEARTILY or SPIRITUALLY AN INTENTION/ PURPOSE IN ALL MANKIND BRANCHES Of THE USA GOV (CITIZENS, JUDICIAL, CONGRESS, EXECUTIVE); These Are ABSOLUTE And UNCHANGEABLE And SELF-EVIDENT RIGHTEOUSNESS Of THOUGHTS, WILL, ATTITUDES, INTENTS/ PURPOSE, AFFECTIONS, And DESIRES For GOD:

---T--- Free Will (FW): // The USA GOV respected the FW of mankind. Hence the decision to put Christ and His laws and conscience subjects is provided. No force of the Will is to be made for the decision to be a Christian. However the USA GOV was not established for anti-Christianity, rather for Christianity. So conflicts do exist on what is agreed, and supported, and on what is disagreed, and opposed; and how to support and how to oppose. Furthermore each Spiritual Moral Creature must keep some laws that are of God. Existence & society and civilization require such; and the CC, all DOCs, and the FFOG state such.
---T--- The subject involved is what to support & what to oppose; & to what degree; & if to support or oppose then how; & if so, either way, then how much in quantity? Totally stop, total freedom, or limited either way. AND who makes the decision on what is supported and what is opposed.
---T--- Some subjects may conflict in specific areas and need careful contemplation, meditation, study, and application.
---T--- Does it support the Lord Jesus, God, Creator, Supreme Ruler, Divine Providence, God of creation natures laws; (The Same God with different names here) ??
---T--- Does it oppose the Lord Jesus, God, Creator, Supreme Ruler, Divine Providence, God of creation natures laws; (The Same God with different names here) ??
---T--- Is it an idolatrous situation to the Lord Jesus, God, Creator, Supreme Ruler, Divine Providence ??
---T--- Does it support Christ's Christian Religion in "Freedom to exercise"; to increase and be established in the land ??
---T--- Does it support the Freedom of Exercising God's Christian Religion Laws, including those of the Holy Bible ??
---T--- Does it oppose or "Prohibit" God's Christian Religion in Freedom to exercise and increase and be established in the land ??
---T--- Does it oppose or "Prohibit" the Laws of the Religion of Jesus Christ, including those in the Holy Bible ??
---T--- Does it do favor or partiality ("respecting") one Christian Denomination (sect or as called Establishment of Religion)~ for Christ; over another in the USA GOV by making Laws For it ?? Now assisting a Christian DEN (Establishment) is not Respecting such to the extent of making it a law. Hence a Christian DEN can be worked with, and without such favorism, or partiality which is done by making a law.
---T--- Does it do favor or partiality ("respecting") one of Christ's Christian secondary doctrine over another in the USA GOV by making Laws For it ?? Now assisting a Christian secondary doctrine is not Respecting to the extent of making a law; hence a Christian secondary doctrine can be worked with, and without such favor, or partiality which is done by making a law.

---T--- <u>Does it do favor or partiality</u> ("respecting") one of Christ's Christian expression over another in the USA GOV by making Laws For it ?? Now assisting a Christian expression is not Respecting to the extent of making a law; hence a Christian expression can be worked with, and without such favorism, or partiality which is done making a law.

---T--- <u>Does it Ruin or stop other Christian Denominations</u> (sects) by making laws for supporting only one DEN ?? Such is Respecting or favorism.

---T--- <u>Does it Stop, hinder, or prohibit the freedom</u> of Speech about the Christian Religion & God's Presence ??

---T--- <u>Does it Support False Religion,</u> such as Infidel, Pagan, Mohammadens (Islam), Hindu, etc, -- any religion not Christian for God ??

---T--- <u>Does it support evil or Sin as</u> God's true Religion defines it ?? Are there limits to be applied, or what limits should be applied to such; or is it to be stopped in total ?

---T--- <u>Does it support or oppose God's Basic</u> Christian Religion Doctrines or Basic Christian Assembly Activities ?? These are well defined and known. In Principle or general they include the True God, the True Mankind, and the True Basic Doctrines of God & mankind. In specific, they include the Holy Bible as God's Word, the Holy Trinity, the Divinity of Jesus & the Holy Spirit, allowance of Judaism as a lesser knowledge of current Christianity, salvation, sanctification, music, preaching, public assemblies of, organizing of, schools for, expressions of worship or joy and love, Holy Bible studies and books, godly music, the Atonement Blood, the providence of God, tithes & offerings, etc.

---T--- <u>Does it allow USA GOV Branches of Executive,</u> Congress, Judicial to have control over God's Church Denominations in their Freedom to exercise in all areas of righteousness ??

---T--- <u>Does it support False Christianity, where</u> it is sin against the Ten Commandments, or anti-Biblical in Basic Christian Doctrines; and without opposing the Freedom in secondary doctrines of Christianity ??

---T--- <u>Does it support anti- Lord Jesus Christ,</u> God, Supreme Ruler, Creator Laws in the Land ??

---T--- <u>Does it oppose Laws of</u> Lord Jesus Christ ??

---T--- <u>Does it support Laws of Lord Jesus</u> Christ, The God and Supreme Ruler ??

---T--- <u>Does it support USA GOV to Be NO Religion</u> ??; The USA GOV is to have the Christian Religion, and God. Infidelity was specifically, clearly, and obviously opposed. It must have limits. It cannot be the Law of the Land. It would be then to exclude God when the Law states in the CC, all DOCs, and by the FFOG, that God & His Religion is to be included.

---T--- <u>Law of Agreement or Disagreement:</u> Law of Support or Opposition, FOR or AGAINST, Friend or Enemy, Assist or Fight against, Help or Hinder. There EXISTS NO NEUTRAILTY -- AGREEMENT or DISAGREEMENT: +"Neutrality" concept must be according to truth. The word concept needs study. The word is not to be thought loosely; so as to claim it is defined as this, or as such, and so on. Neutrality does exist in specific subjects, IF we claim this word as it really is defined as by truth. See Chp 2 on Truth and Chp 5 on CC and Neutral sub-parts.

---T--- <u>Does it Support or AGREE with the Laws of</u> Christ Jesus the Supreme Ruler God Creator in the Desires, His Will, His Intents, His Affections, His thoughts, His Definition of Right & Wrong ??

---T--- <u>Does it Oppose or DISAGREE with the Laws of</u> Christ Jesus the Supreme Ruler God Creator in the Desires, His Will, His Intents, His Affections, His thoughts, His Definition of Right & Wrong ??

---T--- <u>Does it Force Spiritual Moral Creatures who are not Christians to internally</u> will/decide for Christ Jesus in every part of their life ?? Some parts of all Creatures life must include God; but not all.

---T--- <u>As the USA GOV, we cannot INCLUDE & EXCLUDE</u> God at the same time. We cannot oppose & support at the same time neither. Furthermore, this pertains to every decision of the laws and activities of physical material substance that occurs on the USA Soil. The Spiritual or unseen is not to be controlled by the USA GOV. However the USA GOV and State GOV was not to promote or allow evil physical activity on the USA Soil; in other words, some specific evils are not allowed any at all; and some specific evils are limited. Evil includes false religion, false Christianity that commits sin against the 10 commandments. // The USA GOV are to do & not do the following: +NOT DO~ the doctrines of Christianity are not to be meddled or controlled by. +TO DO~ Christianity is to have freedom of itself, to work it all to solutions by itself. +NOT DO~ to make or control Christianity in all its affairs and activities. +TO DO~ is to be Christian and support Christianity. +CANNOT~ include and exclude God at the same time on any decision of physical activity; this also relates that they CANNOT separate; To separate must be defined as to what THEY DO and what THEY DO NOT DO. +CANNOT exclude Christianity in everything. +TO DO~ MUST include Christianity in everything. +NOT TO DO~ If it excludes Christianity then it begins or initiates opposition. +NOT TO DO~ to oppose Christianity is to Breach and commit treason against the CC (DOI & CON). +TO DO~ physical activity is to be monitored with regards to whether it is Christian or not; This is the only area where THEY ARE TO DO is to manage all their activities; +NOT TO DO~ No anti-God or anti-Christ physical activity is to be promoted or allowed on USA Soil. // Now what is such physical activity is to come from the 10 commandments and the True God, Christ Jesus, including the Holy Bible. This is referring to businesses of selling, services, non-profit, etc. In a home, there is a different standard, or law, as discussed elsewhere. Homes have different limits and freedoms.

---T--- <u>How Do We Operate?</u> // By referring to the rules written down in the CC.

---T--- <u>What If We Do Not Know?:</u> // There are 2 ways we do not know: 1} We do not know what part the subject is related to in the CC; that the subject is not said directly in the DOI or CON or Supporting DOC. 2) The subject is said in the CC, but we do not know how to apply it.

---T--- <u>What If There is Disagreement?</u>: // God & the CC is the basis to start from; Not to exclude.

====== [CONCLUSION]: CC {DOI & CON}, And MOST OTHER SUPPORTING DOC ESTABLISH That The LAWS Of The USA GOV ARE TO BE BASED ON THE LORD JESUS CHRIST, GOD, CREATOR, SUPREME RULER, DIVINE PROVIDENCE) And HIS LAWS INCLUDING HIS HOLY BIBLE:

-------------------------------- *GENERAL Evidences* --------------------------------------

---T--- <u>Now to include God in the CC (DOI & CON)</u> is defined as including Him. Now what is He? Basically a Spirit Moral Being. It is not a value of what He looks like in the form, as Body~ (except that He does not look like a monster). Anyway He is a Will, Supreme Conscience, Affection, Emotion, Thought, Reasoning, Desire, Intent/ purpose, Judgment. Now for the CC (DOI & CON) to make a CC with God and then not include what He thinks as to what is right & evil (Supreme Conscience), and what He feels, affections & emotions, and what His will is, and what He desires, and intentions/purposes, and what His reasons and thoughts are, is to exclude Him.
---T--- <u>England, as referring to the group of Spiritual Moral Agents that supported</u> the evil in that Country, (not the group living there that opposed the evil activities), was that they opposed the true God, Christ Jesus, and only claimed these as a name, and not in Spirit or Heart. Thus they only conducted themselves under a cloak, or a falsehood of appearance; sort of like a ship that has a white flag but the Spiritual folk on board have a black heart; or a ship that has a righteous symbol on the flag but with Spiritual people with evil inside themselves.
---T--- <u>To say that we include God, as in the CC</u> (DOI & CON), and yet to say that we do not have His laws, which includes what He thinks is as the Rule Book; that is His discernment of right & evil, is to not include God and to remove Him. Every Spiritual Moral Being has a definition of what is right & evil; you yourself included. And God being God, thus the main authority, is to have the final say. And in this situation, it is on laws, or in other words, what is right or wrong. It is a total lie to include God and exclude His desires about what is right & evil. When we include another Being, then we include what makes them feel good and what makes them feel bad; that is what rules they have of the household (laws). When we place ourself in some Being's house to occupy, then we must careful ourself with the house rules, or we will lose our shelter. It is their house and to their rules (laws) must we Will to obey; intention/ purpose. We may think it is right to indulge the cookie jar a bit more frequent than the House Authority might allow. In many subjects, it is not what we think or will. This is not to say that the House Authority is to be cruel, unkind, unloving, or hateful. But if such House Authority has stated that such is the Law (rule), and to that it is evil, and other contraries are good, we may appeal to the House Authority. But if the House Authority states that there will be not further discussion on the subject, then to that we must obey.
---T--- <u>We must have laws:</u> // Some Spiritual Moral Creature(s) has to decide on what laws. // What laws to have and by what basis are they decided on. // Selfish or Self-1st-Priority Creatures, or Self-idolatry Creatures are not what we intend to support as unlimited activity. Can you totally trust such a Creature ?
---T--- <u>The fact that God & His law is to be</u> the overruling & final GOV has already been fully proven in other sections & is fully proven by the CC (DOI & CON). It is self-evidence, spiritual and conscience stated, that God is the GOV of the USA. This fact tells us that God is to be God of the USA. If God is not God, then He is not God. Thus He is either God or not God.
---T--- <u>God is FIRST Priority~ Not GOV</u> (citizens, executive, congress, judicial); & His laws were to be the Law of the Land & to be the rule in making laws. // Here is a paragraph of the DOI that has some statements about God and His laws: "We, therefore, the Representatives of the US of America, in General Congress, Assembled, appealing to the Supreme Judge of the world for the rectitude of our intentions, do, in the Name, and by Authority of the good People of these Colonies, solemnly publish and declare, That these United Colonies are, and of Right ought to be Free and Independent States; that they are Absolved from all Allegiance to the British Crown, and that all political connection between them and the State of Great Britain, is and ought to be totally dissolved; and that as Free and Independent States, they have full Power to levy War, conclude Peace, contract Alliances, establish Commerce, and to do all other Acts and Things which Independent States may of right do. And for the support of this Declaration, with a firm reliance on the protection of divine Providence, we mutually pledge to each other our Lives, our Fortunes and our sacred Honor." // This is a Sacred Intention/ purpose to have the Being of God MAGNIFIED, and LOVED for the Being that He is, in Himself. Praise and thank Him with Heart affection !!!

-------------------- *PRINCIPLE LAW and TRUTH is the LAW BASIS* --------------------

---T--- <u>Principle Law: Intending/ purpose & activating to assist some Christian DEN</u>, including a secondary doctrine or expression: // Now with Principle Law, there may be some confusion, and there may be unknown for awhile on some areas. For EX, how do you do activity for, or spend money for, supporting Christianity yet not do activity for, or spend money towards some DEN, or secondary doctrines, or expressions. In study of this, it relates to the sub-subject of "respecting" or partiality or favorism; as by making a law. Now it is well clarified; it is easy now. If N GOV activates or spends it on some Christian subject, then great. If the N GOV does not make a law for that activity or spending of money to or for that

223

DEN then it is not favoring. These sort of problems are not really very problematic. A true and loving Christian will be kind and humble. And if there is some subject that requires a specific DEN occasionally it is not a problem to such Heart Creatures.

---T--- Principle Law about Controlling or Managing Christianity is Limited: // The CC (DOI & CON) support Christianity and, obviously protect it; but also state that God is 1s priority overruling GOV. Therefore N GOV is not to control over all Christianity. Carefulness must be applied. These sort of problems are not really very problematic. A true and loving Christian will be kind and humble. Therefore Law Making requires not to be excessive nor deficient.

---T--- Principle Law about Free Exercise: // For EX these are some situations. Protection of Christianity is the desire and intention/ purpose. Thus N. GOV is not to oppose free exercise of expressions or secondary doctrines; or DEN. If any law offends, or goes against Christianity, then at that point, anti-Christ laws have started and Christians start to lose their liberty (freedom of exercise).

---T--- Principle Laws have advantages & disadvantages: // Because they are, to some degree, general, then the application can cause a sort of unclarity. Thus a potential exists to comprehend that they say what they do or do not say; and also to misapply them. // Advantages exist in the same part of them. Because they are general, provides more liberty to apply them. This should give righteousness an advantage, which is by increasing in application. // Another disadvantage is that when an evil mind & heart gets one, then they desire to do evil with it.

---T--- Law establishes what is right & what is wrong; every law states 2 things~ something that is right & something that is wrong; that is what to do that is right, and thus if not done it is wrong; or something that if did is wrong, and thus to not do it is right. What basis is used for Heart Creatures making laws? BY some thought that comes to their mind; and a word that comes from their mouth? // We have Statements from the GOV FFOG that tell us carefulness of including God.

---T--- Principle Law for including God: // We have Statements from the GOV FFOG that tell us carefulness of including God. This is part of the Checks & Balances for protection of the people. God is always right & loving; and unselfish. Spiritual Creatures who reject God are self-idolatrous, and selfish; and if they do good it is returning to self; and they have potential for increase of evil.

---T--- We have Statements from the GOV FFOG.

---T--- The Oberlin College Group of Spiritual Folk, including Charles Finney will agree to Principle Law: // They assisted the USA from slavery, from various evils, and for the continuation of God as priority. C. Finney has writings that state that the Intention must be always directed to God as a Being, for His own sake. And such includes benevolent love; this has an unselfishness about it and some other attributes. We cannot agree with selfish Moral Creatures (people with moral ability & responsibility) to place government to us.

---T--- Principle Law that the basis of N GOV & Laws are to based on God, who is the Holy Bible; because God is where the Rights of the N GOV come from to exist: // GOV itself does not have the Right to exist without God. The CC (DOI & CON) clearly includes such Principle Law.

---T--- Principle Law that the Rights of the Spiritual Moral Beings, as to live, for life, liberty, and happiness; where we get life from, is God. Therefore the GOV is only a manager under God for these. // Only an infidel rejects this. If we get life from Him, then all areas of life must be based on Him. What child cannot discern this simple fact that the statement declares, or is defined as?

---T--- Principle of War: // Defensive war is the only legal war in the USA. Aggressive or offensive war, if allowed by God, is murder. // War is a Right; because sometimes it is part of our ability to oppose evil~ if such method of war is how God decides to stop evil.

---T--- Principle Law: If we do not have a basis for law, we will go in circular reasoning: // In other words, we will go round & round & never come to any standard or truth or basis or conclusion as to what is right & wrong.

---T--- Principle Law: Truth Laws: // Principle Law is included as a Truth Law. Truth Law is the very basis of All Law. "We hold this TRUTH to be self-evident.", as per the CC.

---T--- Principle Law: Standard Cannot Be Relative Or Everyone Can Make His Own Law: // No man has right to be a law to himself; Nor GOV, which is only a group of mankind~ an administration of mankind. HSC tells this danger; and repeats it; the danger that "every way of a man is right in his own eyes"~Pro21:2.

---T--- A medical facility had some laws written for their employees; such as this: // "Legality - Be concerned that you do not violate a regulation, law or our standards of conduct and policies; fair to all concerned in the short and long term; promoting ,,,right or ethical for all concerned". Now someone is making the rules here, and that also which is right is known internally by all Spiritual Bodily Beings.

---T--- Principle Law: Cannot be Man's opinion: // FFOG Thomas Jefferson stated, "The CON ,,,is a mere thing of wax in the hands of the judiciary which they may twist and shape into any form they please" (111). Is not this the truth? Who of you will let this happen and continue? Who cannot conceive that man's opinion is not the basis for all mankind? Truth is; Rightness is; and these are of God; God is our source, not man. Are you going to idol a man ? Thomas Jefferson said such a thing was NOT to occur. Yet today Heart Creatures are idoling creatures rather than the Creator, for to make a GOV system. Are you going to put self-idolatrous creatures to make laws of evil ??

---T--- Principle Law: Same Laws for ALL Spiritual Moral Creatures; some laws only for some: // This is valuable. For groups of Spiritual Moral Creatures to live in the same geographical area they must have some common laws; laws that apply to all. EX +Stealing is one law that applies to all. +Laws about medicine applies only to medical people. // Furthermore, freedom includes personalities and special guidances from God to each individual. Surely no GOV should be dictating to families and individual's what skills, talents, vocation, and intent/ purpose, and etc. That Families

224

and personalities are to commune with God Himself; fellowship with Him; not some GOV Creatures in some place. And this is not all the subjects of that which is on an individual and/or family basis.

---T--- Principle Law: of Equality: // HSC~ "Lev 19:15, Deu 1:16-17~ "You shall do no unrighteousness in judgment: you shalt not respect the person of the poor, nor honor the person of the mighty"; "I charged your judges at that time saying, Hear the causes between your brethren, and judge righteously between every man and his brother, and the stranger that is with them. You shall not respect persons in judgment: but you shall hear the small and as well as the great".

---T--- Including God is Principle Law: // FFOG share~ +George Washington said, "It is impossible to govern the world without God and the Bible". +Abraham Lincoln said, "I believe the Bible is the best gift God has ever given to man. All the good of the Savior of the world is communicated to us through this Book".

---T--- All this is very deep in its spirit, but it is very simple in its truth, although it is very studious in its conception and feelings and complex, yet it is very simplistic; it also is very intense and yet very basic; and yet very spiritual.

---T--- Principle Law is Law Basis & Laws must support Christian laws because they are Not Evil rather Good: // Are these following laws bad?: Evil Drugs & recreational alcohol avoidance; murder; adultery; personstealing; swearing; blasphemy; profane language; pornography; stealing; endangering others; pollution; fornication; child killing (abortion); idolatry; polygamy; Racism. // Every law the FFOG made was Holy Biblically supported or referenced. // Illicit sex definition was based on the Holy Bible until after WWI (137). // Mr. Larry Cata' Backer states as paraphrased: That all societies are ordered by norms from some sources he shares; but that the USA Legal system was initially based on religion (137).

---T--- Principle Law: Law is: +either a Do or Do Not; +is either internal (spiritual) or external (body or material substance) or both.

---T--- Principle Law of Being or Personality as Source of Law: // Thus the standard or Laws must come from some personality. They do not come from material substance things, as such. They are spirit related~ that is Being related. Now thus who makes the rules, basically. And whoever makes the rules, rules. We are surely not stating dicatorship, tyranny, or cruelty. Thus the one who rules is God. Now any child knows this when they get out of bed to start their day~ Any group of Beings must have a system of rules. Now they can have one Being do it, or 2 plus Beings do it. They can decide who makes the rules by one Being's decision or 2 plus. Rules come from some personalities decision. The decision is based on their constitutional Being or on situations with maxims as a basis to them; Maxims are Principle Law. Let Us Not Be Confused Or Bewildered Or Dismayed Or Deceived !!!!!!!

---T--- Principle Law: Now a GOV consists in having some Spirit Moral Creature(s) make the decisions that all others of a geographic area abide by; or enact a~ To Do, or a To Do Not. // Dictatorship is rejected, as per the decisions for a GOV written in the CC & DOC.

---T--- Principle Law: of Limitations of Laws: // Laws are to exist: +ONLY in specific subjects; and +ONLY in specific geographic areas; and +ONLY enforced by specific ways. God is the only one who has Right to rule in every area of our life; and He is LOVE & RIGHTNESS. However we must decide on who makes the decisions for human GOV. The GOV can only relate to its jurisdiction, or geographical area and human group. That is the limits. Thus we must decide on who gets to be our manager. God is the real manager; but as in this world we must decide on a manager of 1 or 2 plus managers and what basis they will manage or system and on how the system will operate.

---T--- Relativity: // Is law relativity? Absolutely not. When you walk across the room do you want every step to be unknown and change so that if you walk forward you may go backwards? Or you may go sideways? Or you may fall down. Obviously not.

---T--- Now to shoot aerodynamic terms around, and so many concepts and multiplicity of concepts, and so many distractions and all various disconnections, is to do demons work. Then there are the Spiritual Moral Creatures with lack of knowledge, who are stumbled in so many ways, because of such. It is not so confusing as they make it, nor as it is made.

---T--- The tactics of the demons is to mankind in Hell, by any way they can: // This includes maniacism, lunaticism, and insanity. Thus an attack to the reasoning and knowledge area is included. You can accept any form of reasoning you want; but if you do not the truth you will end in Hell. This world is a place of discernment between good & evil !!!

---T--- FFOG Congress & Judicial State that The Holy Bible is the Standard; & That All of God's Law is to be the Duty of All Men: // Roger Sherman: "It is the duty of all to acknowledge that the Divine Law which requires us to love God with all our heart and our neighbor as ourselves, on pain of eternal damnation, is Holy, just, and good ,,,The revealed law of God is the rule of our duty." (245). // Joseph Story: "I verily believe that Christianity is necessary to support a civil society and shall ever attend to its institutions and acknowledge its precepts as the pure and natural sources of private and social happiness." and "One of the beautiful boasts of our municipal jurisprudence is that Christianity ,,," (183). // Noah Webster: "The moral principles and precepts found in the SCs ought to form the basis of all our civil constitutions and laws." (176). Also, "The Christian religion is the most important and one of the first things in which all children under a free GOV ought to be instructed. No truth is more evident than that the Christian religion must be the basis of any government intended to secure the rights and privileges of a free people." (175). Also, "The Christian religion ,,,is the basis, or rather the source, of all genuine freedom in GOV ,,,I am persuaded that no civil GOV of a republican form can exist and be durable in which the principles of Christianity have not a controlling influence." (188).

---T--- Principle Law of LOVE: // Love is that of God. If Love is our Principle Law, then all will be done with an unselfishness, or unself-idolatry. We will love God and Other Spiritual Moral Creatures; and love them as ourselves. HSC states this Law in many places including Deu6, Mat22:37-39.

225

---T--- <u>Principle Law: Other words or terms</u> for Principle Law is Guiding Laws or Guiding Rules: // All applications are not specified in a Principle Law, but rather it is of such a design that it can be applied to all areas of life. Thus in every subject, the principle law, or guiding rule, is applied to that area. Also it is applied as a test or guide to determine, discern, and decide, if it be good or evil; and if it be truth or lie (falsity).

---T--- <u>Principle Law:</u> of <u>Laws of Nature & of God:</u> // Truth & Law Basis: +} Do not make more of a statement than it is intended/ purposed for or states, and, +} Do not make less of a statement than it is intended/ purposed for or states. These are also included in Chp. 2 about Truth.

---T--- <u>Principle Law:</u> of <u>Problems of Laws:</u> // Laws often, sometimes more frequently, are not about good but about evil. Laws are made to stop evil. +Laws are of omission or commission: One is against not doing good; which is a law against something. And the other is against doing some wrong; and that is also against something. // The definition of good & evil: Such is based on a desire intention/ purpose. This is plainly stated by the FFOG as coming from God and His Laws, and not creatures opinion. And this then is further engaged by use of the body and/or material substance(s).

-------------------- *EVIDENCES of USING CHRISTIANITY, The TRUE GOD, JESUS CHRIST, and His HOLY BIBLE as LAW BASIS* -----------------

---T--- <u>The Laws are all referenced in the</u> Holy Scripture and part of the 10 Commandments. They are applications of such.

---T--- <u>Law of Category of Sin as Evil, Self-Evidence,</u> History of Evils, & of Opposing Evil of All Sorts: // In AD 1788 FFOG Benjamin Rush wrote David Ramsay saying, "Is not history as full of the vices of the people, as it is of the crimes of kings? What is the present moral character of the citizens of the US? I need not describe it. It proves too plainly that the people are as much disposed to vice as their rulers, and that nothing but a vigorous and efficient GOV can prevent their degenerating into savages or devouring each other like beasts of prey ,,,To look up to a GOV that establishes justice, insures order, cherishes virtue, secures property, and protects from every species of violence, affords a pleasure that can only be exceeded by looking up, in all circumstances, to an overruling providence. Such a pleasure I hope is before us, and our posterity under the influence of the new GOV,,," (97). // "looking UP", as he said, is to commune with God as 1st priority.

---T--- <u>Evil Laws & Evil Spiritual Moral Beings are Not Legal to M</u>ake Laws, Nor Be Directly Connected with Law Official Positions (not specified at this time); Nor are Evil Laws Legal in the USA: // Only a few statements from the FFOG will be given to prove this Truth(s). All of the FFOG are similar; Therefore when you read these, you read them all. +Alexander Hamilton states, "The attempt by the rulers of a nation to destroy all religious opinion and to pervert a whole people to atheism is a phenomenon of profligacy ,,,To establish atheism on the ruins of Christianity to deprive mankind of its best consolations and most animating hopes and to make gloomy desert of the universe" (170). +Thomas Jefferson (3rd Pres.), in AD 1805 stated a national prayer, "Almighty God, Who has given us this good land for our heritage: we humbly beseech Thee that we may always prove ourselves a people mindful of Thy favor and glad to do Thy will. Bless our land with honorable ministry, sound learning, and pure manners. Save us from violence, discord, and confusion, from pride and arrogance, and from every evil way. Defend our liberties, and fashion into one united people the multitude brought hither out of many kindreds and tongues. Endow with Thy spirit of wisdom those to whom in Thy Name we entrust the authority of GOV, that there may be justice and peace at home, and that through obedience to Thy law, we may show forth Thy praise among the nations of the earth. In time of prosperity fill our hearts with thankfulness, and in the day of trouble, suffer not our trust in Thee to fail; all of which we ask through Jesus Christ our Lord, Amen.". +John Adams states, "The idea of infidelity cannot be treated with too much resentment or too much horror. The man who can think of it with patience is a traitor in his heart and ought to be execrated as one who adds the deepest hypocrisy to the blackest treason" (169). +Benjamin Rush states, "I anticipate nothing but suffering to the human race while the present systems of paganism, deism, and atheism prevail in the world" (97). +Samuel Adams states, "I have a thorough contempt for all men,,, who appear to be the irreclaimable enemies of religion" (171). +Gouverneur Morris states, "The most important of all lessons (from the SCs) is the denunciation of ruin to every State that rejects the precepts of religion" (172). +John Witherspoon states, "Shun, as a contagious pestilence ,,,those especially whom you perceive to be infected with the principles of infidelity or who are enemies to the power of religion" and "Whoever is an avowed enemy of God ,,,call him an enemy to his country" (154). // Most every earlier State CON had requirements to be a Christian; and always to support Christianity. // The CC proves this because the CON is application of the DOI; and the DOI occurred because of the Intention/ purpose to Put God as Priority to Mankind and evil; and to get Rights from God; evil laws and evil spiritual moral Beings were rejected. // The Holy Bible was the Most Priority Reference for Constructing the USA GOV & National Systems. Here are Holy Scriptures about such: +It is never right to do wrong to do right. This includes lying, breaking laws, etc. This would be inclusive of right laws. Rom3:8~"And not rather, (as we be slanderously reported, and as some affirm that we say,) Let us do evil, that good may come? whose damnation is just". See here that God does not define this sort of government work, or whatever, that does evil in order to do good. It appears that Rahab lied 2 times in Jos2:4-5 (HSC). Now here KN at the time is related. However it is never right to lie; there is no such a thing as a right lie (white lie). It is never right to sin in pressure of pain/pleasure, such as TTT. God does not need the sinful methods to catch evil. Some evil may be caught or opposed by such methods; however it is never right and it will receive the anger of God and a pronouncement of guilt on all Beings who use such methods. Thus they will rather hurt themselves and be guilty to God & in danger of Hell. Such methods are stupid, foolish, and vile. +Spiritual Moral Beings are not to sin if an evil law of the society tells them to; and God is priority to evil legal systems. This is proven repeatedly in HSC. For one, Act5:29~"Then Peter and the

226

other apostles answered and said, We ought to obey God rather than men". And this is exactly what the FFOG did to oppose evil coming from some evil people; the CC has it's basis herein. +A Law Official is required to be Christian & Christian supporting; The CC states such, and so does~ Rom 13:4~"For he is the minister of God to you for good. But if you do that which is evil, be afraid". See there that they are to be a helper to God and to do Good to other Spiritual Moral Beings, and Not evil. vs 5~"but also for conscience sake". Then, that is the supporting of the heart or Spirit which includes the conscience. +The Lord Jesus does not intend for us to put anti-Christian Laws applied to Christian Lives and Christian living activities. Christian homes are Sanctified homes~ 1Cor7:14~"For the unbelieving husband is sanctified by the wife, and the unbelieving wife is sanctified by the husband". +A separation is to be applied between Christians & Non-Christians; at some points. Application of such includes, that Christians are not to have non-Christian Laws or activities applied to them. 2Cor6:14-17~"Be you not unequally yoked together with unbelievers: for what fellowship has rightness with unrightness? and what communion has light with darkness? And what concord has Christ with Belial? or what part has he that believeth with an infidel? And what agreement has the temple of God with idols? for you are the temple of the living God; as God has said, I will dwell in them, and walk in them; and I will be their God, and they shall be my people. Wherefore come out from among them, and be you SEPARATE, saith the Lord, and touch not the unclean thing; and I will receive you". Do not ask for ungodly reasoning~ 1Cor6:1-6~"Dare any of you, having a matter against another, go to law before the unjust, and not before the saints? Do ye not know that the saints shall judge the world? and if the world shall be judged by you, are you unworthy to judge the smallest matters? how much more things that pertain to this life? If then you have judgments of things pertaining to this life, set them to judge who are least esteemed in the church. Is it so, that there is not a wise man among you? no, not one that shall be able to judge between his brethren? But brother goeth to law with brother, and that before the unbelievers". In fact, God prefers that we get a Christian Spiritual Moral Being that has no official position and is thought to be the lowest position in the Church to decide for Christians rather than taking situations to the ungodly. +God hates the reasoning and the intent/ purpose of evil Spiritual Moral Beings and Rejects them and their reasoning~ Mat 4 was Jesus rejecting the Devil's evil reasoning, and even reasoning with the Holy Bible; Rom 8~"The Carnal mind is enmity (an enemy) to God"; Psa 1 says do not stand, sit, nor walk with ungodly and sinners; take not their counsel; 1Cor 10 says Do Not fellowship (commune) with sinners & ungodly; 1Joh5:18 says for the demons not to touch a Christian; Eph4 says do not give demons places for evil. +The Christian's home has the Atonement Blood over it, similar to Egypt. Exo 12:7, 1Joh1:7~"the Blood of Jesus Christ His Son cleanses us from all sin".

---T--- FFOG Congress & Judicial Branch State that The Holy Bible is the Standard with All of God's Law as the Duty of All Men: // Roger Sherman: "It is the duty of all to acknowledge that the Divine Law which requires us to love God with all our heart and our neighbor as ourselves, on pain of eternal damnation, is Holy, just, and good ,,,The revealed law of God is the rule of our duty." (245). // Joseph Story: "I verily believe that Christianity is necessary to support a civil society and shall ever attend to its institutions and acknowledge its precepts as the pure and natural sources of private and social happiness." and "One of the beautiful boasts of our municipal jurisprudence is that Christianity ,,," (183). // Noah Webster: "The moral principles and precepts found in the SCs ought to form the basis of all our civil constitutions and laws." (176). Also, "The Christian religion is the most important and one of the first things in which all children under a free GOV ought to be instructed. No truth is more evident than that the Christian religion must be the basis of any government intended to secure the rights and privileges of a free people." (175). Also, "The Christian religion ,,,is the basis, or rather the source, of all genuine freedom in GOV ,,,I am persuaded that no civil GOV of a republican form can exist and be durable in which the principles of Christianity have not a controlling influence." (188).

---T--- The Laws in the CON come from The HOLY BIBLE and therefore makes the CON a Christian & Religious DOC based on Christ; and of the which represent the US, and hence, the US is as they are, Religious, of Christ. Following are some of the laws, in the CC (DOI & CON) as enumerated in a list: // +The 10 Commandments. +Idolatry (in various forms). +Stealing (in various forms). +Covetousness (which is evil desires in general). +Dishonor to parents, posterity. +Securing freedom of righteousness. +Freedom for the Gospel to be spoken. +Murder. +Dictatorship prevention. +Lying (with the oath & affirmation). +Marriage is supported; the home & family. +Adultery & fornication. +Opposition to false religion. +Equal Rights to all creatures opposes evil desires of Race, gender, position of employment.

---T--- Stealing & murder is wrong: // CC states~ "No person shall be ,,,deprived of life, liberty, or property, without due process of law; nor shall private property be taken for public use without just compensation".

---T--- Abortion is wrong: // CC states~ "No person shall be deprived of life,,,". // Exo20:13~ "You shall not kill". // 7th Amendment is the Right to Life. // Virginia State in AD 1810 had laws declaring children in the womb are not to be killed. // The Holy Bible opposes it in Exo21; Deu19; 1Sam19; Job31; Psa94; 139; Pro6; Isa44; 49; 59; Jer1; Luk1. // James Wilson was a Judge who was put on the US Supreme Court by Pres. George Washington. He started America's first organized legal training; and taught students that, ",,,beautiful and undeviating, human life, from its commencement to its close, is protected by the Common Law. In the contemplations of law, life begins when the infant is first able to stir in the womb. By the law, life is protected" (206). // Right to life is the purpose of GOVs. John Quincy Adams says, "Ask the DOI and that will tell you that its authors hold for self-evident Truth that the right to life is the first of the unalienable rights of man ,,,to secure and not to destroy,,, governments are instituted among men" (184). // John Witherspoon says, "Some nations have given parents the power of life and death over their children ,,,we have denied the power of life and death to parents" (154). // Shapes: Now if you study shapes your learning will result that no Material Substance has ability (of any sort) to shape or make forms. A shape requires a mind; a mind to think; to intend/ purpose some specific shape of the Material Substance. EX: take a pie and think with your mind as to how you will slice the pie. Hence, in No Possible way can that pie think of how to shape its slices. HSC states, Joh5:37; Luk3:22~"the Father Himself,,,You have neither,,,seen His shape; And the Holy Ghost descended in a bodily shape like a dove on Him". God Shapes (forms) children in the womb, both body & spirit; and from the very start of the fluids (male/female) joining; Isa44:2, 24; 49:5; Jer1:5. Hence to kill the child in the womb is to touch God's shaping. Sacred shaping, not a hardness of feeling for such a subject.

---T--- <u>People-stealing is wrong:</u> // The CC states~ "No person shall be deprived of life, liberty, or property,,,".

---T--- <u>Idolatry is wrong:</u> // 1ˢᵗ Amendment of the CON & DOI (CC).

---T--- <u>Adultery is wrong:</u> // "No person shall be deprived of life ,,,property,,,". Spouses are other Spiritual Moral Being's household Family relations. It is unclean and immorality. The home & family is supported not opposed.

---T--- <u>Pres. George Washington tells that the</u> CC (DOI & CON) are laws for application; Thanksgiving Day enactment speech: // ",,,it is the duty of all nations to acknowledge the providence of Almighty God, to obey His will, to be grateful for his benefits, and humbly to implore His protection,,,".

---T--- <u>Rights are from God:</u> // GOV is not the source of our Rights. They do not create, diminish, or remove our Rights. They come from God. // GOV is to secure the Rights from God, as Spiritual Moral Servants of God~ as the CC states~ "endowed by their Creator". // GOV Cannot alter or abolish them; they have Not the Right. // Now how can a GOV secure those Rights from God and exclude or oppose God ? Or exclude His thought, intention/ purpose, affections, desires, discernment, Supreme Conscience ???

---T--- <u>Rights are from God & GOV</u> is to secure them as servants (ministers) of God (Rom13): // If GOV removes GOD and religion, then how will, or can they secure Rights that come from God ??

---T--- <u>GOV is required to secure</u> GOD as our source of Rights: // GOV cannot assist us with the Rights from God if they remove God. GOV must include God and the Supreme Conscience. God exists in the CC (DOI & CON), in the supporting DOCs, and in providence.

---T--- <u>Our GOV is a form of Theocracy; Not a form of Paganism:</u> // IF evil Beings do not like this, then they need to abide by the Laws anyway~ that is the Christian Laws; the godly laws. If some Spiritual Moral Beings become excessively evil and do not like that, and intend to do such evil, then they need to move away, as Holy Scripture states; a Right from God includes a command to all Spiritual Moral Beings to Resist them, their evil, and the demons involved; Jam 4. Opposition to evil was resisted by the CC (DOI & CON); the RW, etc. Rights for evil are limited, Not unlimited. God is what our CC (DOI & CON) teaches, not devilry evil; not demoniacs.

---T--- <u>FFOG John McHenry writes in support of</u> funding for the Bible Society: // "Neither, in considering this subject, let it be overlooked, that public utility pleads most forcibly for the general distribution of the Holy SCs. The doctrine they preach, the obligations they impose, the punishment they threaten, the rewards they promise, the stamp and image of divinity they bear, which produces a conviction of their truths, can alone secure to society, order and peace, and to our courts of justice and constitutions of GOV, purity, stability and usefulness. In vain, without the Bible, we increase penal laws and draw intrenchments around our institutions. Bibles are strong intrenchments. Where they abound, men cannot pursue wicked courses, and at the same time enjoy quiet conscience." (127).

---T--- <u>Rufus King, signer of CON, stated</u> to Missouri Senate preparing for statehood, "I hold that all laws or compacts imposing any such condition (as involuntary servitude) upon any human being are absolutely void because contrary to the law of nature, which is the law of God" (33). +Thus the basis of law is GOD.

---T--- <u>First Principles, of Self-Evidence,</u> must be our basis for Law: // We cannot base decisions on only a persons opinion. We are to start with God; Self-evidence is part of God; it is created by Him; it is truth.

---T--- <u>FFoG made a~ +] Constant, +] Priority, +] Practice~</u> of action to not enact any anti-Christian law; and never stated or encouraged any anti-Christian law or activity: // Sometimes Presidents today will claim the name of God and then enact anti-Christian laws; which, in essence is supporting demons. To intentionally/ purposefully be deceitful and do such is as a Trojan horse; or as showing oneself with a camellia color; as to work from the inside out under disguise of "right". // FFOG made laws: +For Supporting Christian holidays, prayer, fasting, Christian education, Holy Bibles for the public, churches, Christian education to Indians, etc. +To Oppose profaning of the Sabbath, blasphemy, polygamy, pornography, evil speaking against Christianity, recreational alcohol, idolatry, murder, stealing, adultery, slavery, etc. Thus the Holy Biblical laws were always supported and a basis of counseling and the rule.

---T--- <u>John Jay, (US Supreme Court Judge,</u> Governor of New York, signer of CON) said the US Law is based on Holy Bible Law: // "It is true ,,,ordinances of Moses ,,,Legal punishments ,,,inflicted by the law and magistrate, and not by unauthorized individuals. These and all other positive laws or ordinances established by Divine direction, must of necessity be consistent with the moral law ,,,Law of Moses,,,". And he continues that the reason for the US GOV is because of anti-Christian activity, that is sins and evil~ "The depravity which mankind inherited from their first parents, introduced wickedness into the world. That wickedness rendered human GOV necessary to restrain the violence and injustice resulting from it.".

---T--- <u>FFOG State God is USA Law Basis, Not Whatever Nor Anything:</u> // Gouverneur Morris states: "How can we hope for public peace and national prosperity, if the faith of governments so solemnly pledged can be so suddenly violated? ,,,private property ,,,infringed? ,,,Destroy this prop ,,,and

228

where will you turn „,? „,known to Him alone, whose divine providence exalts or depresses states and kingdoms. Not by the blind dictates of arbitrary will. [[<< note here that judicial, legislative, executive, or population majority do not have a Right to will laws whatsoever they will, but to observe God's laws >>]] „,Not by a tyrannous and despotic mandate. But in proportion to their obedience or disobedience of his just and holy laws. It is he who commands us that we abstain from wrong. It is he who tells you, 'do unto others as ye would that they should do unto you'" (11a). +Letters~ in AD 1811 from G. Morris to John Murray states, "Holy Writings"; and in AD 1813 to David B. Ogden states, "to which I reply, in the language of Holy Writ, thou shalt not do evil that good may come of it" (11a). +G. Morris also states that, "Judge, then, what would be the value of association „,The great mass of the common people have no religion but their priests, no law but their superiors, no morals but their interest. Creatures who, led by drunken curates,,," (11a); and describing the status of the French people and nation because of a large amount of activity that was godless with laws not of God (at some point in time in that Nation); also says, "„,in free governments the laws being supreme „,those „,who form the sublime and godlike idea of rescuing their fellow creatures from a slavery „,must begin by instruction,,," (11a).

---T--- CASE LAW: // This system should be not be used in totality; this is not the USA system. Cases can be studied and compared for knowledge, but are not in themselves the basis of laws.

---T--- Self-Government by the Laws of God within; Conscience & Self-Evidence: // FFOG Samuel Adams states: "Let divines and philosophers, statesmen and patriots, unite their endeavors „,by impressing the minds of men with the importance of educating their little boys and girls „,the fear and love of the Deity „,in subordination to these great principles „,the love of their country; of instructing them in the art of self-government, without which they never can act a wise part in the GOV of societies, great or small; in short, of leading them in the study and practice of the exalted virtues of the Christian system,,," (46a).

---T--- God's Laws are the Basis of Law: // In AD 1772, a member of the Boston Tea Party meetings assisted in forming GOV for the DOI, stating, "That a committee „,be appointed „,to state the Rights of the Colonists „,as men, as Christians, and as Subjects: to communicate and publish the same to the several Towns in the Province „,and to the World „,with the infringements and violations thereof,,,"; then continues stating the, "Rights of the Colonists as Men" „, "Among the natural Rights of the Colonists are these First, A Right to Life; Secondly to liberty; Thirdly to Property; together with the Right to Support and defend them „,All positive and civil laws should conform, as far as possible, to the law of natural reason and equity „,Just and true liberty, equal and impartial liberty in matters spiritual and temporal, is a thing that all men are clearly entitled to, by the eternal and immutable laws of God and nature, as well as by the law of nations, & all well grounded municipal laws, which must have their foundation in the former"; and continues, "Rights of the Colonists as Christians" which are, "„,best understood by reading -- carefully studying the institutes of the great Lawgiver and head of the Christian Church: which are to be found closely written and promulgated in the New Testament"; and that "Rights of the Colonists as Subjects" to be "The absolute Rights of Englishmen, and all freemen in or out of Civil society, are principally, personal security, personal liberty, and private property" (46a).

---T--- Magna Charta of AD 1215 Includes statements: // "„,protection of the writ of habeas corpus, the right of trial by jury, the guarantee that no person can be deprived of life, liberty or property without due process of law,,,". +This was a pattern document system for the USA system; a supporting DOC.

---T--- John Wycliffe (AD 1320-84 approx): // A theologian, member of Parliament in England, translator of the Holy Bible, reformer of the Christian Church, stood against anti-Biblical ideas and proclaimed the Holy Bible as authority, and not some men's opinions; said~ "Christ's law is best and enough, and other laws „,should not take „,but as branches of God's law" (96). He also told the English GOV that every man was responsible to God alone and the freedom of "individualism". Also stated, "This Bible is for the government of the people, by the people, for the people" (88a).

---T--- Divine Law of God IS & supersedes or is Priority before GOV law: // The CC states~ "due process of law" which includes Divine law; and that any GOV law that offends Divine Law then is void; The CC says so.

---T--- A major fact of the CC (CON & DOI) is to LIMIT the powers of the USA GOV: // Thus to say that the USA GOV can make laws at will, whatever and whenever they decide, by Congress, or executive, or judicial will, is to totally contradict that which is clearly said and proved. The USA GOV is to be submissive to the DIVINE LAWS; that of GOD and the 10 commandments and such. Otherwise the USA GOV could be wild; and make whatsoever laws they please or will; such is crazy. This is not the right function of constitutional law; which binds the USA GOV to the CC (DOI & CON); that are contract or covenant with God.

---T--- Christianity is the USA GOV laws as Holy Biblical Doctrines were used in writing of the CON: // Note the sin potentiality in the Checks & Balances system stated by George Washington in his farewell speech, "„,avoiding in the exercise of the Powers of one department to encroach upon another.--„,a real despotism, -- A just estimate of that love of power, and proneness to abuse it, which predominates in the human heart, is sufficient to satisfy us of the truth of this position.-- The necessity of reciprocal checks in the exercise of political power; by dividing and distributing it into different depositiories, & constituting each the Guardian of the Public Weal against invasions by the others, has been evinced by experiments ancient & modern; some of them in our country & under our own eyes".

---T--- The CC state~ +] "Provide for the common defense" (CON preamble) is similar to a Father with his family & +] Justice is the same term that the Holy Bible says~ He is, "a just God" & +] "promote the general welfare": These are Principle Laws for the Christian laws not to be opposed; rather supported; or the general welfare is threatened. "General welfare" is to include the spirit & body. This not of Thought

229

Government; but rather in spiritual welfare as in the doctrine of God & man and its application to the actions and external activities that occur on USA land. // The CON is intended as a Christian DOC to express the "general welfare" in the form of "blessings" as its preamble states~ "secure the Blessings of Liberty to ourselves and our Posterity". See Chp 5 for the study of this word.

---T--- <u>The USA Laws are similar to England's</u> & other European countries at various times which were based on the Holy Bible: // The Magna Carta, English Bill of Rights, and Mr. W. Blackstone's Documents. Demons attempted to destroy these. The Nazi's and various European peoples attempted in World War 2 to steal the Magna Carta, by use of a balloon and/or blimp. Why? It is written DOC that many Nazi's gave themselves to the demons, and we indeed know that they did, as any such sin to that degree will invite demons (1Joh3). These Spiritual Beings did not like the Magna Carta in England because it was a system based on the Holy Bible.

---T--- <u>Witho a basis of law we have no standard; n</u>o measurement: // Who cannot know this? We are like a ship on sea in a storm without a sail or compass and no knowledge of what we are doing and where we are going and where we came from. Self-Evidence tells us that God, Truth, Bible, Nature or Creation's God are the standards. We cannot let some human judge make his rules and lord over us on impulsive opinions~ No thank you!!! "It is better to obey God than man Acts5:29"; Referring to when one is contrary to the other.

---T--- <u>Every thought & religion or idea of existence</u> & god is not all truth or right: // Anarchy, maniacism, lunaticism, foolishness is all herein. And we know it (self-evidence); this self-evidence teaches Responsibility to us. // Some courts and legislative Branch are doing that which they do themselves as impulsiveness; & telling other Spiritual people not to do it. Taking statements of DOC, history, testimonies, and witnesses, and try to fit it in to some form of interpretation and make a law or apply a law. Yet they tell others not to do this which they do; because they know it is wrong in conscience. // Denying that the statements in the CC (DOI & CON) exist; that the DOI has the overRuling Right to the CON.

---T--- <u>Massachusetts GOV enacted in AD 1636 </u>by the General Court to make their Law Code "agreeable to the word of God"; Then in AD 1641 they enacted the "Body of Liberties" which is a legal code reading as follows: // "The free fruition of such liberties, immunities and priveledges as humanity ,,,Civilitie, and Christianitie call for as due to every man in his place and proportion ,,,tranquillitie and Stabilitie of Churches and Commonwealths. And the deniall or deprival thereof, the disturbance if not the ruine of both. 58. Civill Authoritie hath power and libertie to see the peace, ordincances and rules of Christ observed in every church according to his word ,,,. Civill Authoriteie hath power and liberties to deale with any Church member in a way of Civill Justice ,,,. If any man after legall conviction shall have or worship any other god, but the lord God, he shall be put to death. 2. If any men or women be a witch, (that is hath or consulteth with a familiar spirit), they shall be put to death. ,,,All the people of God,,, shall have full libertie to gather themselves into a Church Estaite ,,,10. We allow private meetings for edification in religion amongst Christians of all Sortes of people. So be it without just offence for number, time, place, and other circumstances." (92).

---T--- <u>John Eliot in AD 1659 constructed</u> a Civil Policy for the Rising Kingdom of Jesus Christ for the Indian Community; included stating~: // ",,,humble themselves to embrace that as the best, how mean soever it may seem to Humane Wisdom ,,,The written Word of God is the perfect System or Frame of Laws, to guide all the Moral actions of man, either towards God or man" (92).

---T--- <u>Rev John Cotton constructed a law code</u> which used the term "the Law of Nature, delivered by God"; included stating~: // "The Lord is our Judge.; The Lord is our Law-Giver.; The Lord is our King, He will save us" (92). This was used in constructing USA Systems.

---T--- <u>In AD 1985 Attorney General</u> Edwin Meese stated that we exercise, "jurisprudence of Original Intention".

---T--- <u>Justice Joseph Story of AD 1833 noted</u> illegal interpretation of the CON and stated some legal rules in the truthful observance of it; Part of those rules include: // "nature" of it; "objects" of it; "scope and design" of it; consider the "words are plain, clear and determinate"; "viewed as a whole and also viewed in its component parts"; and to beware of contradictory matters, and with all these, carefulness.

---T--- <u>God's Laws are the basis for USA</u> Laws; NOT a Law to ourselves as in Selfishness, or Self-Idolatry, Rather Self~Less~ness: // "The Laws of Nature and of Nature's God" statement in the DOI, states God as God, or the Ruler or Lawgiver. This is a term William Blackstone & John Locke used; and their reference included Rom2:14-15 (Holy Bible) referring to the conscience and creation. +The fact that it pertains to the USA law or legal system as based on God and not man is observed again by the DOI statement: "We hold these truths to be self-evident -- that all men ,,,are endowed by their Creator with certain inalienable rights; that among these are life, liberty, and the pursuit of happiness ,,,that whenever any form of GOV becomes destructive of these ends it is the right of the people to alter or abolish it, and to institute a new GOV,,,". Now observe here that specific Rights are from God, the Creator and that no GOV can remove those Rights and if they (those governing people) try to remove them, then the Rights from God are priority. Otherwise, by God they have a Right to alter or abolish such GOV (people trying to do such evil as dictators or tyranny). // It is the frequent historical EV & experience that evil Spiritual people get in to governing positions and attempt to get a multitude of evil or deceived followers and then overcome the good laws and people of the land. // This is a common occurrence with idolaters. They are a law to themselves; they are their own god; self-god; and then they want to rule others; self-worship. (Rom2:14).

---T--- <u>Alcohol, intended/ purposed for Recreational uses, is</u> ILLEGAL: // The 10th Amendment states: "After one year from the ratification of this article the manufacture, sale, or transportation of intoxicating liquors within, the importation thereof into, or the exportation thereof from the US and all territory subject to the jurisdiction thereof for beverage purposes is hereby prohibited". This is God's Christian law to prohibit recreational alcohol; and is also a violation under religious freedom of the land because it is offensive against Christianity and begins the establishment of a multitude of evils connected to it. HSC~ Eph5:18; 1Tim3:3; it is a DO NOT.

---T--- <u>Individual Rights Protected:</u> // A doctrine of Christ's Christianity is Creatures representing other Creatures for the power, or task, to make laws of the land. The Legislative (Congress) power is what law making power is. "All Legislative Powers herein granted shall be vested in a Congress of the US, which shall consist of a Senate and House of Representatives."

---T--- <u>The 7th Amendment states the use</u> of the Common Law Legal System: // "In Suits at Common Law, where the value in controversy shall exceed twenty dollars, the right of trial by jury shall be preserved, and no fact tried by a jury, shall be otherwise re-examined in any Court of the US, than according to the rules of the common law". // The Common Law system is a Holy Bible based system; for God. This is proved in this Book.

---T--- <u>Samuel Adams, known as the "Father</u> of the American Revolution", claimed that all law comes from God, and that human law is to conform to God's Law in Nature and as revealed in SC; he wrote: "The Rights of the Colonists as Christians: These may be best understood by reading -- and studying the institutes of the great Lawgiver and head of the Christian Church: which are to be found clearly written and promulgated in the New Testament--- By the Act of the British Parliament commonly called the Toleration Act, every subject in England Except Papists etc was restored to, and re-established in, his natural right to worship God according to the dictates of his own conscience. And by the Charter of the Province it is granted ordained and established (that it is declared as an original right) that there shall be liberty of conscience allowed in the worship of God, to all Christians except Papists, inhabiting or be resident within said Province or Territory. Magna Charta itself is in substance but a constrained Declaration, or proclamation, and promulgation in the name of King, Lord, and Commons of the sense the latter had of their original inherent, indefeasible natural Rights, and also those of free Citizens equally perdurable with the other. That great author that great jurist, and even that court writer Mr. Justice Blackstone holds that his recognition was justly obtained of King John sword in hand: and peradventure it must be one day sword in hand again rescued from total destruction and oblivion". +Also, In AD 1797, as governor proclaimed: "And as it is our duty to extend our wishes to the happiness of the great family of man, I conceive that we cannot better express ourselves than by humbly supplicating the Supreme Ruler of the world that the rod of tyrants may be broken into pieces, and the oppressed made free; that wars may cease in all the earth, and that the confusions that are and have been among the nations may be overruled by promoting and speedily bringing on that holy and happy period when the kingdom of our Lord and Saviour Jesus Christ may be everywhere established, and all people everywhere willingly bow to the septre of Him who is Prince of Peace" (116).

---T--- <u>The CC established a Christian National</u> System; & included Laws Based on the Holy Bible; & with State & FED orderly arrangement; including the Common Law System which is Biblical: // It was re-established in the late AD 1800's as by a Court Case, which states that the CC is to stay together, with the DOI as part of it. (261a). // The Common Law: +The Common Law was also called the Moral Law. +It was DIRECTLY included as part of the U.S. National System and Law System while the States were yet joined with the Country of England (261b). +After Independence, such Law System was named Common Law and included in the States (261b). +The FED GOV system included the Common Law in the Bill of Rights, 7th Amendment. +Many FFOG in all Branches stated that the Constitution is based on the Common Law (261c). +The Common Law is based on God's Laws, and is stated by words "the laws of nature and of nature's God". These words are part of the Religiousness of Christianity; and the study of God, as in the Principles thereof (261d). +Following are some words about the Common Law from cite (261d): "But the abstract right of individuals to withdraw from the society of which they are members, is recognized by an uncommon coincidence of opinion — by every writer, ancient and modern; by the civilian, as well as by the common-law lawyer; by the philosopher, as well as the poet: It is the law of nature, and of nature's God, pointing to 'the wide world before us, where to chose our place of rest, and providence our guide'"; "The common law is grounded upon the general customs of the realm; and includes in it the Law of Nature, the Law of God, and the Principles and Maxims of the Law: It is founded upon Reasons; and is said to be perfection of reason, acquired by long study, observation and experience, and refined by learned men in all ages"; "The law of nature is that which God at mans' creation infused into him, for his preservation and direction; and this is lex eterna and may not be changed: and no laws shall be made or kept, that are expressly against the Law of God, written in his Scripture; as to forbid what he commandeth"; "But this large division may be reduced to the common division; and all is founded on the law of nature and reason, and the revealed law of God, as all other laws ought to be".

---T--- <u>The CC is a Christian & Holy Bible Based Law System for God:</u> // Parts of the Judicial System is committing illegal acts against the USA citizens, CC, and God. // FFOG Thomas Jefferson said about judges, that "power [is] the more dangerous as they are in office for life and not responsible, as the other functionaries are, to the elective control.". AND "[T]o consider the judges as the ultimate arbiters of all constitutional questions [is] a very dangerous doctrine indeed, and one which would place us under the despotism of an oligarchy ,,,The Constitution has erected no such single tribunal. The Constitution, on this hypothesis, is a mere thing of wax in the hands of the Judiciary which they may twist and shape into any form they please." (262 a & b).

---T--- <u>The CC, as a Christian Law System, is constructed for Limited</u> GOV Rights of the Federal & State Level: // Such includes an identifying of such Relations of the Federal Level; which identification is enumerated with only seventeen Rights in which the FED GOV has to the States Independency (263); This enumeration does not give Rights from God to the Fed GOV to do everything & anything; rather it is only a few Rights given; from God. Then it identifies that all other things are the Rights to be determined by the People and the States (the Ninth & Tenth Amendments). // FFOG Thomas Jefferson states the CC System, "the States can best govern our home concerns and the general [federal] government our foreign ones. ,,,taking from the States the moral rule of their citizens and subordinating it to the general authority [federal government] ,,,would ,,,break up the foundations of the Union." (264). Also he states that if the limits breakdown of the CC, there would be an illegal GOV in the FED, with excessive Rights and the Checks & Balances System would be dysfunctional (262c). // The CC states, "The United States shall guarantee to every State in this Union a republican form of government". // The Supreme Court is making illegal Laws against the State Independency existence, against the Rights of the State Independency, against the Spiritual Moral Creatures and their votes, against the FED GOV Rights to the States which were identified and enumerated, and against the Christian Common Moral Law System, and against God, His Nature & Nature Laws.

---T--- <u>James Wilson stated in congress meetings</u> that US law must be based on Divine law; & used England as EX: // "Parliament may, unquestionably, be controlled by natural or revealed law, proceeding from divine authority". ~ this is saying that God's laws are over and above GOV or any laws therefrom.

---T--- <u>The fact (truth) is that Laws are</u> stated in the CC (DOI & CON): // Principle Laws and Stated Laws: After all, what is law but a statement of command; whether it be omission or commission; to do or not to do; some activity, such as thought, will, intention/ purpose, or body action. The supporting DOC in the earlier US construction times are to be included; they agree with the Laws in the CC (DOI & CON).

---T--- <u>Non-Christian activity Limited: // Such is Not</u> supported by the USA GOV, but rather rebuked. // An allowance is obviously given to internally agree to non-Christianity. However it is not to be enacted for laws. And not supported, practiced in actions, nor approved by the USA GOV.

---T--- <u>The Laws of the USA GOV are to</u> be centered around "GOD, CREATOR, SUPREME JUDGE, DIVINE PROVIDENCE". Notice all the EV involving God; the Creator. Such is what gives the USA GOV the Right to exist and the basis of the Rights of the people.

---T--- <u>The God is the Christian God: //</u> They stated that no other God has Right to the N GOV or USA. // It is a fact or Truth of Christianity that Christ is the only True God and that other god's are rejected by Him & Christianity.

---T--- <u>The CON is a working</u> tool based & derived from the DOI: // To separate the CON as an UNGODLY DOC is illegal; a crime.

---T--- <u>Law of Life or Existence: // That the basis of</u> N GOV Laws are to based on God, the Holy Bible; God is where the Rights of the N GOV come from to exist; and where the Rights of the people to live and who gives us life, liberty, and happiness; where we get life from. // Only an infidel rejects this. // If we get life from Him, then all of life must be based on Him. What child cannot discern this simple fact that the statement says, or is defined as?

------------------ *OPERATION of THE LAW BASIS and DIFFICULTIES* ----------------------

---T--- <u>However the difficulties are not</u> that difficult. // For EX in a situation involving various Christian DEN and the efforts on a specific subject, the following gives an application: N GOV can support any one DEN, or any one Christian secondary doctrine, or any one Christian expression without making a Law about such. Because they do not make a law about such support, then such does not favor (respecting) the specific secondary doctrine, or expression. Rather the N GOV is operating and supporting with them on a specific subject of Christianity, to assist where it is needed. This reconciles both the Principle Laws of the 1-A, R-E, R~Est. Actually such activity is needed.

----------- *JUDICIAL BRANCH REALIZES, KNOWS, and APPLIES The CHRISTIAN GODLY LAW BASIS* ---------

---T--- <u>LAWS of the TRUE GOD:</u> // Supportive and cooperation with the Laws of the True God; The DOI states~ "laws of nature and of nature's God entitle them".

---T--- <u>The Holy Bible: // Supportive</u> of the Holy Bible; the true God and the Laws of nature (creation) of the true God - "laws of nature and of nature's God entitle them".

---T--- <u>LAW: Support Statutory Law & Principle Law: //</u> "laws of nature and of nature's God entitle them"; the Holy Bible is full of Statutory Laws. The CC (CON & DOI) are Principle Laws and provide the basis for such law. And the Holy Bible is full of Principle Laws.

---T--- <u>Judicial Branch was Based on 10 Commandments:</u> // Stone vs. Graham case in 1980 of the US Supreme Court: - removal of the 10 commandments from hanging in the hallways of a public school. Illegal ruling.

---T--- <u>AD 1878, Case of Reynolds vs. US, the</u> Courts ruled against Polygamy and in support of Christian principle.

---T--- <u>AD 1947, Case of Everson vs. Board of Education:</u> // Illegal ruling by the Courts to define and make a CON change using a statement by Thomas Jefferson in a letter to a Baptist DEN (Danbury) regarding the protection of DEN; which is wrongly applied for a Separation of Church and State, or GOV; so as to remove God from GOV. This law attempted to change the CON; and separate it temporarily from connected to the DOI as the Ruling DOC. This situation is studied in Chp. 5. in a sub-part; In short, the words of some individual, as Pres. Jefferson, in only a letter of correspondence, is not a legal method to make CON changes.

---T--- <u>N. GOV does not have Rights to Exclude Christianity Religion</u> in the States: // Some intentions/purposes of the CON are stated by Thomas Jefferson, while he was an Officer of the GOV, in AD 1808, in a letter to Samuel Adams that the Fed GOV is not to dictate to the States: "I consider the GOV of the US as interdicted [prohibited] by the CON from intermeddling with religious institutions, their doctrines, discipline, or exercises. This results not only from the provisions that no law shall be made respecting the establishment or free exercise of religion, but from that also which reserves to the States the powers not delegated to the US [10th Amendment]. Certainly, no power to prescribe any religious exercise, or to assume authority in religious discipline, has been delegated to the General GOV. It must then rest with the States, as far as it can be in any human authority" (30).

---T--- Court ruling that we are a Christian Nation & that the GOV is to be Christian & that the definition of religion includes ONLY Christianity & it's DEN: // Case of 1892, Church of the Holy Trinity vs. US, US Supreme Court: The case was on a Church DEN hiring a foreigner. The Courts statement: "No purpose of action against religion can be imputed to any legislation, state or national, because this is a religious people ,,,This is a Christian nation." And Judge Brewer continues~ "This is a religious people. This is historically true. From the discovery of this continent to the present hour, there is a single voice making this affirmation ,,,the first charter ,,,propagating of Christian Religion to such People as yet live in Darkness ,,,the DOI recognizes the presence of the Divine in human affairs in these words: ("We hold these truths to be self-evident, that all men are created equal, that they are endowed by their Creator with certain unalienable Rights ,,,appealing to the Supreme Judge of the world for the rectitude of our intentions ,,,And for the support of this Declaration, with a firm reliance on the Protection of Divine Providence, we mutually pledge to each other our Lives, our Fortunes, and our sacred Honor") ,,,(p) there is no dissonance in these declarations. There is a universal language pervading them all, having one meaning; they affirm and reaffirm that this is a religious nation. These are not individual sayings, declarations of private persons: they are organic utterances; they speak the voice of the entire people ,,,we find that in Updegraph vs. The Commonwealth, it was decided that, ("Christianity, general Christianity, is, and always has been, a part of the common law ,,,not Christianity with an established church ,,,but Christianity with liberty of conscience to all men"). And in The People vs. Ruggles, Chancellor Kent, the great commentator on American law, speaking as Chief Justice of he Supreme Court of New York, said: ("The people of this State, in common with the people of this country, profess the general doctrines of Christianity, as the rule of their faith and practice ,,,We are a Christian people, and the morality of the country is deeply engrafted upon Christianity, and not upon the doctrines or worship of those impostors [other religions].") And in the famous case of Vidal vs. Girard's Executors, this Court ,,,observed: ("It is also said, and truly, that the Christian religion is a part of the common law,,,"). These, and many other matters which might be noticed, add a volume of unofficial declarations to the mass of organic utterances that this is a Christian nation". // Here also observe that the US Supreme Court included the decisions in the State courts, of other cases which said the very same thing as this case.

---T--- Court case stating we are a Christian nation, Christian GOV, Christian people, and Christian Laws, and that General Christianity is what is supported; and that religion in one statement part of the 1-A is defined as including DEN (identifying DEN as naming a "sect" or "particular Christianity" or "particular tenets"): // Case of 1824 Updegraph vs. The Commonwealth ,,,Supreme Court of Pennsylvania: Involving an individual charged with blasphemy. The court established the definition of the word, Blasphemy by using the Christian Mr. Blackstone's Law References; defining it as a sin against Christ, specifically as this: "Blasphemy against the almighty in denying his being or providence, or uttering contumelious reproaches on our Savior Christ. It is punished at common law by fine and imprisonment, for Christianity is part of the laws of the land" (10). Mr. Updegraph was found guilty. Part of the grand jury's indictment and facts of the case, stated~ "Abner Updegraph ,,,not having the fear of God before his eyes ,,,intending to scandalize, and bring into disrepute, and vilify the Christian religion and the SCs of truth, in the presence and hearing of several persons ,,,did unlawfully, wickedly and premeditative, despitefully and blasphemously say ,,,("That the Holy Scriptures were a mere fable: that they were a contradiction, and that although they contained a number of good things, yet they contained a great many lies"). To the great dishonor of Almighty God, to the great scandal of the profession of the Christian religion." ,,, and continues~ "The jury ,,,finds a malicious intention in the speaker to vilify the Christian religion and the SCs, and this court ,,,that the words were uttered by the defendant ,,,in which so serious a subject is treated with so much levity, indecency and scurrility ,,,I am sorry to hear, for it would prove a nursery of vice, a school of preparation to qualify young men for the gallows, and young women for the brothel ,,,but when spoken of in a Christian land, and to a Christian audience, the highest offence contra bonos mores; and even if Christianity was not part of the law of the land, it is the popular religion of the country, an insult on which would be indictable". And the Court makes these direct statements about that Christianity is the laws of the land: "The assertion is once more made, that Christianity never was received as part of the common law of this CHRISTIAN LAND ,,,if the argument be worth anything ,,,all the laws which have Christianity for their object ,,,cursing and swearing, and breach of the Lord's day ,,,incestuous marriages, perjury by taking a false oath upon the book, fornication and adultery ,,,. (p) We will dispose of what is considered the grand objection --the constitutionality of Christianity --for, in effect, that is the question. Christianity, General Christianity, is and always has been part of the common law ,,,not Christianity founded on any particular religious tenets; not Christianity with an established church ,,,but Christianity with liberty of conscience to all men. (p) Thus this wise legislature framed this great body of laws, for a Christian country and Christian people. This is the Christianity of the common law ,,,and thus, it is irrefragably proved, that the laws and institutions of this state are built on the foundation of reverence for Christianity ,,,In this the CON of the US has made no alteration, nor in the great body of the laws which was an incorporation of the common-law doctrine of Christianity ,,,without which no free GOV can long exist. (p) ,,,In the Supreme Court of New York it was solemnly determined, that Christianity was part of the law of the land, and that to revile the Holy SCs was an indictable offence. The case assumes, says Chief Justice Kent, that we are a Christian people, and the morality of the country is deeply engrafted on Christianity (p) Without these restraints no free GOV ,,,long exist ,,,hostile to the spirit and genius of our GOV ,,,forerunners of anarchy, and finally, despotism. (p) No free

GOV now exists in the world unless where Christianity is acknowledged, and is the religion of the country ,,,Its foundations are broad and strong, and deep ,,,it is the purest system of morality, the firmest auxiliary, and only stable support of all human laws,,,. (p) Christianity is part of the common law ,,,nor is Christianity inconsistent with our free GOV or the genius of the people. (p) ,,,it is not necessary to maintain that any man should have the right publicly to vilify the religion ,,,of the country ,,,privileges are directly opposed".

---T--- <u>Judicial court case of AD 1811, The People vs. Ruggles, Supreme Court</u> of New York: // Charges are-- The defendant was indicted ,,,for that he did ,,,wickedly, maliciously, and blasphemously, utter, and with a loud voice publish ,,,of and concerning the Christian religion, and of ,,,Jesus Christ ,,,in contempt of the Christian religion,,,. Found guilty. +The defense attorney argued: "There are no statutes concerning religion ,,,the CON allows a free toleration to all religions ,,,Judaism ,,,Mahometanism,,,"; and that the Common Law is Christian and Law of Land~ ",,,body of common law, that Christianity is part of the laws of the State, untouched and unimpaired". However that defense attorney is wrong; Our CON does not allow any religion. That is proved in Chpt 5. +The Judge reacted with Truth, saying~ ",,,without these restraints no free GOV ,,,long exist ,,,hostile to the spirit and genius of our GOV ,,,forerunners of anarchy, and finally, despotism. (p) No free government now exists in the world unless where Christianity is acknowledged, and is the religion of the country ,,,Its foundations are broad and strong, and deep ,,,it is the purest system of morality, the firmest auxiliary, and only stable support of all human laws ,,,(p) Christianity is part of the common law ,,,nor is Christianity inconsistent with our free GOV or the genius of the people. (p) ,,,it is not necessary to maintain that any man should have the right publicly to vilify the religion ,,,of the country ,,,privileges are directly opposed ,,,To construe it as breaking down the common law barriers against licentious, wanton, and impious attacks upon Christianity itself, would be an enormous PERVERSION of its meaning ,,,The Court are ,,,of opinion that the judgment ,,,blasphemy against God ,,,and profane ridicule of Christ or the Holy SCs, are offenses punishable at the common law, whether uttered by words or writings".

---T--- <u>Judicial court case of AD 1838, Commonwealth vs.</u> Abner Kneeland, Massachusetts Supreme Court. A person indicted for "blaspheming the holy name of God" and negatives against Christ: // The defendant was a pantheist and argued that the CON guarantees religious freedom, and freedom of press for writing the things. +The court upheld God & the CC, etc.; that blasphemy was an illegal act, that it includes libel against God, saying "speaking evil of a Deity ,,,to alienate the minds of others from the love and reverence of God ,,,purposely using words concerning God ,,,to impair and destroy the reverence, respect, and confidence due to Him ,,,attempt to lessen men's reverence of God by denying his existence, or his attributes as an intelligent creator, governor and judge of men,,,". +The Court also stated that the law against this evil (sin) was according to Massachusetts CON, and that other states had similar CON laws, including Maine, New York, New Hampshire. +The Court also stated that freedom of press is not freedom to crime with words~ ",,,every ,,,act ,,,criminal ,,,can be committed by the use of language ,,,if such language is printed ,,,a general license for scandal ,,,falsehood ,,,treason, assassination, and all other crimes ,,,if conveyed in printed language, would be dispunishable".

---T--- <u>Other Court Cases which occurred in</u> the AD 1800's said as follows: // Court Case states: "It would be strange that a people Christian in doctrine and worship, many of whom or whose forefathers had sought these shores for the privilege of worshipping God ,,,in purity of faith, and who regarded religion as the basis of their civil liberty and the foundation of their rights ,,,to secure ,,,freedom of conscience which they valued so highly, solemnly repudiate and put beyond the pale of the law the religion which was dear to them as life and dethrone the God who they openly and avowedly professed to believe had been their protector and guide ,,,Religious tolerance is entirely consistent with a recognized religion. Christianity may be conceded to be established religion to the qualified extent mentioned, while freedom of conscience and religious preference is secured to individuals of every other creed and profession ,,,every man left free to worship God according to ,,,conscience, or not worship him at all, as he pleases ,,,Compulsory worship of God in any form is prohibited, and every man's opinion on matters of religion ,,,is beyond the reach of the law. No man can be compelled to perform any act ,,,as a duty to God ,,,this liberty is consistent with,,,the Christian religion ,,,All agreed that the Christian religion was engrafted upon the law and entitled to protection as the basis of our morals and the strength of our GOV"~{this was related to the defense of Sabbath keeping (Sunday Business Closing); one of the 10 Commandments}. // Court Case states: "The Christian religion ,,,is recognized as constituting a part and parcel of the common law, and as such, all the institutions growing out of it, or, in any way connected to it ,,,entitled to the most profound respect and can rightfully claim the protection of the law-making power of State". // Court Case states: "We are not forgetting the public acts of our Pennsylvania ancestors abound with declarations in favor of liberty of conscience,,, They (the Founders) could not admit this liberty of conscience as a civil justification of human sacrifices, or parricide (killing one's parents or close kin), infanticide, or thuggish (religious murders), or of such modes of worship as the disgusting and corrupting rites of the Dionysian, and Aphrodisia, and Eleusinia, and other festivals of Greece and Rome. They did not mean that the pure moral customs which Christianity has introduced should be without legal protection because some pagan, or other religionist, or anti-religionist, should advocate as matter of conscience concubine, polygamy, incest, free love, and free divorce, or any of them. They did not mean ,,,phallic processions ,,,satiric dances and obscene songs and indecent statues and paintings of ancient or of modern paganism ,,,introduced under the profession of religion, or pleasure, or conscience, to seduce the young and the ignorant into a Corinthian degradation; to offend the moral sentiment of a refined Christian people; and to compel Christian ,,,with nudity and impurity of Polynesian or of Spartan women. No Christian people could possibly allow such things ,,,By our ,,,law against vice and immorality we do not mean to enforce religions ,,,But we do mean to protect our customs, not matter that they may have originated in our religion; for they are

234

essential parts of our social life. It is mere social defense „,Law can never become entirely infidel; for it is essentially founded on the moral customs of men and the very generating principle of these is most frequently religion".

---T--- <u>Judicial court case of AD 1844, Vidal vs. Girard's Executors</u>, US supreme court: // This involved the Death Will of Stephen Girard, who assigned his possessions to the city of Philadelphia, instructing them to build an orphanage and a college, but stipulated that no hiring of any Christians should occur at these. // The case is not described much here except these words that were supported: +"The purest principles of morality are to be taught. Where are they found? Whoever searches for them must go to the source „,the Bible „,There is an obligation to teach what the Bible alone can teach, viz. a pure system of morality"; +"Both in the Old and New Testaments [religious instruction's] importance is recognized „,("Thou shalt diligently teach them to thy children „,suffer little children to come unto me and forbid them not").; +"Christianity „,is not to be maliciously and openly reviled and blasphemed against, to the annoyance of believers or the injury of the public „,It is unnecessary for us „,to consider the establishment of a school or college, for the propagation of„, Deism, or any other form of infidelity. Such a case is not to be presumed to exist in a Christian country." +The Court also stated that the school and orphanage shall have the Bible taught in them, which were GOV schools and orphanages.

---T--- <u>Judicial court case of AD 1817, The Commonwealth vs. Wolf</u>, Pennsylvania Supreme Court: Regarded the Sabbath Day, the Jewish vs. the Christian. (OT vs NT). // Observe how the GOV Judicial system, judges, and laws were Christian (for Christ). True religion was applied by the Judicial statement: "Laws cannot be administered in any civilized GOV unless the people are taught to revere the sanctity of an oath, and to LOOK TO A FUTURE STATE OF REWARDS and PUNISHMENTS for the deeds of this life. It is „,utmost „,therefore „,that they should be reminded of their religious duties at stated periods „,A wise policy would naturally lead to the formation of laws calculated to sub serve those salutary purposes. The invaluable privilege of the rights of conscience secured to us by the CON „,was never intended to shelter those persons, who „,would directly oppose those laws„,". +Wise remarks made by the Judge on the Sabbath day, in that it is a wise formation to be frequently and regularly reminded of our sacred duties. +The Court connected the CON with Christianity.

---T--- <u>Christianity IS supported by Judicial branch; & by</u> the Congress laws; & is the CON basis; & it IS the basis of the Laws; & it IS superior and supersedes other Rights or religions of the land: // Judicial court case in AD 1846 of Supreme Court of South Carolina, City of Charleston vs. S.A. Benjamin: Regarding proper activity on Sunday, the Christian Sabbath, where the defendant was accused of selling some gloves at his business place. +Part of this case included about the CON giving religious Rights to a Jewish person for keeping Saturday as his Sabbath; in addition that Christian laws violate the religious Rights of others. +The GOV Sabbath law of the USA stated that~ "„,observance of the Lord's day„, Sunday „,No person „,whatsoever shall publicly expose to sale, or sell „,any goods„, whatsoever on the Lord's day". // Following are statements in the case: +"Christianity is a part of the common law of the land, with liberty of conscience to all. It HAS ALWAYS BEEN SO RECOGNIZED „,IF CHRISTIANITY is a part of the common law, its disturbance is punishable „,THE U.S. CONSTITUTION ALLOWS IT AS A PART OF THE COMMON LAW. The President is allowed „,the Legislature does not sit, public offices are closed, and the Government recognizes the day in all things „,Sunday „,recognized by our U.S. and State GOVs „,Christianity „,is the foundation of those morals and manners upon which our society is formed; it is their basis. Remove this and they would fall „,morality has grown upon the basis of Christianity"; and they continue emphasizing the Christianity of the GOV, the Nation, and the public: "The Lord's day, the day of Resurrection, is to us, who are called Christians, the day of rest after finishing a new creation. It is the day of the first visible triumph over death, hell and the grave! It was the birth day of the believer in Christ, to whom and through whom it opened up the way which, by repentance and faith, leads unto everlasting life and eternal happiness! On that day we rest, and to us it is the Sabbath of the Lord-- its decent observance, in a Christian community, is that which ought to be expected". +The judge then discerns the CON as this: "Who gave to us this noble safeguard of religious toleration„,? IT WAS CHRISTIANITY „,But this toleration „,is religious toleration „,free exercise and enjoyment of religious profession and worship, with two provisos, one of which, that which guards against acts of licentiousness, testifies to the Christian construction „,What are acts ("of licentiousness") within the meaning of this section? „,public acts „,of the community where they take place? „,public opinion „,(p) What constitutes the standard of good morals? Is it not Christianity? There certainly is none other „,moral virtue „,if that standard were abolished, lapse into „,Pagan immorality. (p) In the courts over which we preside, we daily acknowledge Christianity as the most solemn part of our administration „,witness „,hand upon the book, is sworn upon the holy „,an evidence of the part which Christianity has in the common law. (p) I agree fully to what is „,said in Updegraph v. The Commonwealth „,Christianity, general Christianity, is, and always has been, a part of the common law. Not Christianity founded on any particular religious tenets; not Christianity with an established church „,but Christianity with liberty of conscience to all men". +About the Christian laws violating other people's CON religious Rights, it was stated: "It is said that a Sunday law violates the free exercise and enjoyment of the religious „,of the Israelite. Why? It does not require him to desecrate his own Sabbath. It does not say, ("you must worship God on the Christian Sabbath"). On the contrary, it leaves „,free on all these matters „,His Sundays are spent as he pleases, so far as religion is concerned. (p) „,simply, respect us, by ceasing on this day from the pursuit of „,business „,by our Christian laws.". +Note, then, that public activity of business is not that of opposite of advanced knowledge of Christianity.

---T--- <u>Judicial court case in AD 1815 at Supreme Court of</u> Pennsylvania, The Commonwealth vs. Sharpless; & other cases: // This case regarded, "„,did exhibit „,a certain lewd „,obscene painting, representing a man in an obscene „,and indecent posture with a woman to „,other citizens„,".

235

Basically a porno case here. +Defense attorneys argued that it was a private home situation and not public. +The court presents this verdict about it: ",,,Crimes are public offences, not because they are perpetrated publicly, but because their effect is to injure the public. Burglary, thought done in secret, is a public offense. (p) ,,,it follows, that an offence may be punishable, it in its nature and by its example, it tends to the corruption of morals; although it be not committed in public. (p) Although every immoral act, such as lying, etc., is not indictable, yet where the offence charged is destructive of morality in general ,,,it is punishable at common law ,,,to corrupt the morals of people,,,". +Now the problem was that the people who owned the picture were making it available to the public, to come visit and look at it, and selling the views.

---T--- <u>Federal Judge Luther W. Youngdahl</u> of New York said, "If we are to win the cold war, we must get back to God and to get back to God we must get back to the Bible". (260b). Notice he did not say to get~ to these, rather get~ back to these. They were the start; and now we are getting away from those.

---T--- <u>Judicial Branch Cases about</u> that Christianity is the Religion of the USA & All DEN supported: // Judicial court case of AD 1799, Supreme Court of Maryland, Runkel vs. Winemiller: Regarding a minister of a Christian church being displaced. The court and all its members were in total agreement that DEN was the religion that was not to be enforced by the USA GOV but Christianity was to be enforced. The united court statement is as follows: "Religion is of general and public concern, and on its support ,,,good order of GOV, the safety and happiness of the people. By our form of GOV, the Christian religion is the established religion; and all the sects and DENs of Christians are placed upon the same equal footing, and are equally entitled to protection in their religious liberty". // Judicial court case: Charlestown vs. Benjamin, in AD 1846: The courts stated, "Christianity has reference to the principles of right and wrong ,,,it is the foundation of those morals and manners upon which our society is formed; it is their basis. Remove this and they would fall,,,". // House Judiciary Committee in AD 1854 proclaims, "Laws will not have permanence or power without the sanction of religious sentiment,,," and "Religion must be considered as the foundation on which the whole structure rests,,, there can be no substitute for Christianity" (143). // The US House of Representatives in AD 1854 proclaim~ "The great vital ,,,element in our system is the belief of our people in the pure doctrines and divine truths of the gospel of Jesus Christ" (36). // Judicial court case of AD 1889, US Supreme Court, Davis vs. Beason: Regarding the action of bigamy and polygamy. +The CON was said by some attorneys to claim that it protects "free exercise" of other religions that oppose Christianity, a violation of the 1-A, and that Christianity was the established religion which also violated the 1-A, "establishment of religion". +This is the courts verdict: "Bigamy and polygamy are crimes by the laws of all civilized and CHRISTIAN COUNTRIES. They are crimes by the laws of the US, and ,,,by the laws of Idaho. They ,,,destroy the purity of the marriage relation,,, disturb,,, families ,,,degrade women,,, debase men,,,. (p) ,,,sects which denied ,,,as part of their religious tenets ,,,marriage ,,,advocated promiscuous intercourse of the sexes ,,,this country, swift punishment would follow ,,,and no heed would be given to the pretence that ,,,their supporters could be protected ,,,by the CON of the US."

---T--- <u>Law System based on Holy Bible</u> stated by FFOG: // John Adams, ",,,a nation ,,,should take the Bible for their only law book and every member should regulate his conduct by the precepts there exhibited ,,,What a Eutopia, what a Paradise would this region be" and "I have examined all religions ,,,and the result is that the Bible is the best Book in the world." (21). // Joseph Story, "The Bible is the common inheritance, not merely of Christiandom, but of the world" (52a).

---T--- <u>Doctrine that Law is based on GOD:</u> // Rules: +He who makes the rules is God. +God is 1st priority for Rules. +It is God's definition of Good & Evil that is totally right. +We must use God's rule book. // FFOG R.J. Rushdoony shares this Truth saying: "Behind every system of law there is a god. To find the god in any system, look for the source of law in that system. If the source of law is the individual, then the individual's the god ,,,court is our god" (88).

------------------ JUDICIAL Branch HAS LIMITATIONS ~&~ THEY are NOT the ABSOLUTE LAW BASIS nor SOURCE of LAW -------------

---T--- <u>The Judicial Branch cannot, has no</u> power, no legal jurisdiction to nullify an act of Congress; that is the CC (DOI & CON). Yet the illegality is being done sometimes. They only have a Right to examine the law; and apply it; if it is in accordance to the CC (DOI & CON); and then state their opinion as to if it is or not. But no decision may be made as to make it illegal by their examination. (Art 111, sec 2, Art VI).

---T--- <u>JUDGES:</u> Holy Scripture reading: Please read Psalm 2:1-12. // Psa2:10; Pro8:16~ "Be wise now therefore, O you kings: be instructed, you judges of the earth; By me princes rule, and nobles, even all the judges of the earth." These SCs prove easily that God is the Judge over the Judges. Judges have a responsibility, and that not of ordinary, rather solemn, or divine. // Some origin of Biblical Judges is in Exo18:13-27. Moses and the society decided to have judges for small or petty cases. This was a sharing of the responsibility because every geographical area is in a different place and there are excess quantity of people. That is one system. The USA system includes local judges, state judges, Federal judges, nine Supreme Court Judges (for final appeal). These judges take an oath when sworn into employment, which includes to maintain and preserve our laws, the CC (DOI, CON, and Bill of Rights). The Bill of Rights is part of the basis of our American civil liberties as given to us with the pattern framed by the first ten amendments of the Constitution which were added in AD 1791. (260) ~paraphrased from an article by Howard McKonkey.

---T--- <u>Conclusion: Judicial Branch</u> is Not the Basis of Law Nor Source of Law.

---T--- <u>What Right does a creature judge have to say</u> or think something, and only because he thinks or says it, it should be such and such; and makes a decision which then makes it right or wrong? Such is not a Right.

---T--- <u>The Judicial Branch is to apply</u> the CC (DOI & CON). They are Not to Not apply the CC (DOI & CON). // They are to discern how to apply the CC (DOI & CON). They are to assist in the right application of the CC (DOI & CON). To not apply the CC (DOI & CON) is to treason the USA. To intently ignore the CC (DOI & CON) is to treason the USA. To reject the CC (DOI & CON) is to treason the USA. These may not all be intentional/ purposely known premeditatively.

---T--- <u>The Judicial Branch has made decisions</u> in Cases with a wrong basis. Then they use those bad decisions as a basis for other illegal decisions on other cases. Then they say it is their Right to do so. This is all illegal. Yet what is the American citizen Branch or Legislative Branch doing about it ?

<u>------------------------- CC ((DOI and CON)) is Christianity for Christ and Includes the HOLY BIBLE ; and Its RELATION to the OTHER BRANCHES is Superior and Priority, the Basis; and includes Living Spiritual Moral Hearts, (Spirits) or otherwise known as the Creature - -------------------</u>

---T--- <u>CON formation Congress Meetings:</u> // Benjamin Franklin quotes and supports using the Christian Holy Bible as a basis for the RW and formation of a new nation: "Moses lifting up his wand and dividing the red sea, and Pharoh in his chariot overwhelmed with the waters. This motto: Rebellion to tyrants is obedience to God". // Thomas Jefferson does the same: "The children of Israel in the wilderness, led by a cloud by day, and a pillar of fire by night". // Congress appointed Christian chaplains to the US Army in AD 1776. (Nation Formation times). // The Christian Holy Bible was one of the first books printed, funded, and promoted by the US as a Nation; Congress in AD 1777: "that the use of the Bible is so universal, and its importance so great ,,,your committee recommends that Congress will order the committee of Commerce to import 20,000 Bibles from Holland, Scotland, or elsewhere, in to the different parts of the States of the Union: whereupon the Congress was moved to order the committee of Commerce to import twenty thousand copies of the Bible" (58). // Congress proclaims national day of prayer and thanksgiving for victory in Battle on Nov 1, 1777 to Jesus Christ, ",,,to humble and earnest supplication that it may please God, through the merit of Jesus Christ ,,,righteousness, peace, and joy in the Holy Ghost" (58). // Congress states that help coming to the GOV is from God - "divine protection" (58). // Congress states Christ as the reason and controller for the US GOV (58). // Congress states the US and GOV exist for the intention/ purpose of communicating Christianity to the world (58). // Congress approves & funds another request for Holy Bibles to be supplied to the general public (citizens), including schools; called, "Bible of the Revolution"; printed in America in AD 1782; a US proclamation was written in the Bible, stating: "Whereupon, resolved, that the US in Congress assembled ,,,recommend this edition of the Bible to the inhabitants of the US and hereby authorize Robert Aitken to publish this,,," (58). (Amo Press in New York has a AD 1968 reprint of this).

---T--- <u>THE CC (DOI & CON) is required to be part of the basis of the Laws of the USA:</u> // This is what is said in the CON: "This CON, and the Laws of the US which shall be made in Pursuance thereof ,,,or which shall be made, under the Authority of the US, shall be the supreme Law of the Land." This statement is written 2 (Two) Times in the CON.

---T--- <u>FFOG Congress & Judicial State that The Holy Bible is the Standard;</u> and That All of God's Law is to be the Duty of All Men: // Roger Sherman~ "It is the duty of all to acknowledge that the Divine Law which requires us to love God with all our heart and our neighbor as ourselves, on pain of eternal damnation, is Holy, just, and good ,,,The revealed law of God is the rule of our duty." (245). // Joseph Story~ "I verily believe that Christianity is necessary to support a civil society and shall ever attend to its institutions and acknowledge its precepts as the pure and natural sources of private and social happiness." and "One of the beautiful boasts of our municipal jurisprudence is that Christianity ,,," (183). // Noah Webster~ "The moral principles and precepts found in the SCs ought to form the basis of all our civil constitutions and laws." (176). Also, "The Christian religion is the most important and one of the first things in which all children under a free GOV ought to be instructed. No truth is more evident than that the Christian religion must be the basis of any government intended to secure the rights and privileges of a free people." (175). Also, "The Christian religion ,,,is the basis, or rather the source, of all genuine freedom in GOV ,,,I am persuaded that no civil GOV of a republican form can exist and be durable in which the principles of Christianity have not a controlling influence." (188).

---T--- <u>Sabbath keeping Laws & Christian Sabbath Established</u> by all Branches of the FFOG; that Christianity is the Law Basis before, during, and after the times of the CC (DOI & CON): // "A day peculiar to that faith, and known to no other (27). // "It would be impossible within the limits of a lecture to point out all the ways in which that day is recognized" (27). // The USA CON requires the President to "Sundays excepted" on his "bill passing", because he receives Sunday off from employment. Similar provisions are found in the CONs of most of the States, and thirtysix had the same expression, "Sundays excepted". // Four {4} earlier CONs of Louisiana State (AD 1812, 1845, 1852, 1864) contained the Sabbath; following are statements from some: "In law Sundays are generally excluded as days upon which the performance of any act demanded by the law is not required. They are held to be ,,,non juridical"; And "in the Christian world Sunday is regarded as the 'Lord's Day' and a holiday, a day of cessation from labor"; and "By statute, enacted as far back as 1838, this day is made in Louisiana one of 'public rest.'; and "This is the policy of the State of long standing and the framers of the CON are to be considered as intending to conform to the same". // This statement is part of the USA DOCs:

237

"By express command of Congress, studies are not pursued at any Branch of the military academies, and distilleries are prohibited from operation on Sundays, while chaplains are required to hold religious services once at least on that day". // A statute in England, of 29 Charles II, tells no tradesman, artificer, workman, laborer, or other person was permitted to do or exercise any worldly labor, business or work of ordinary calling upon the Lord's Day, or any part thereof, works of necessity or charity only excepted. This statute, (with some varying), was enacted by most of the States (27). // Massachusetts had Sunday car traveling regulations. // Georgia statute illegalized freight trains operating on Sunday (a misdemeanor). // Many States declared contracts made on Sunday as invalid. // No judicial proceedings can be held on Sunday. // All legislative bodies, municipal, state or national, abstain from work on that day, even in current times. // South Carolina, court case - City Council vs. Benjamin states, "On that day we rest, and to us it is the Sabbath of the Lord — its decent observance in a Christian community is that which ought to be expected". // Pennsylvania Supreme Court: "It is not our business to discuss the obligations of Sunday any further than they enter into and are recognized by the law of the land. The common law adopted it, along with Christianity, of which it is one of the bulwarks." // In Arkansas Supreme Court, Shover vs. The State: "Sunday or the Sabbath is properly and emphatically called the Lord's Day, and is one amongst the first and most sacred institutions of the Christian religion. This system of religion is recognized as constituting a part and parcel of the common law, and as such all of the institutions growing out of it, or, in any way, connected with it, in case they shall not be found to interfere with the rights of conscience, are entitled to the most profound respect, and can rightfully claim the protection of the law-making power of the State." // The Supreme Court of Maryland, in Judefind vs. The State: "The Sabbath is emphatically the day of rest, and the day of rest ,,,the Lord's Day or Christian's Sunday. Ours is a Christian community, and a day set apart as the day of rest is the day consecrated by the resurrection of our Saviour, and embraces the twenty-four hours next ensuing the midnight of Saturday ,,,But it would scarcely be asked of a court, in what professes to be a Christian land, to declare a law unconstitutional because it requires rest from bodily labor on Sunday (except works of necessity and charity) and thereby promotes the cause of Christianity." // The subject is that it is a religious day, consecrated by the Holy Bible Commandment, "Six days shalt thou labor, and do all thy work: but the seventh day is the Sabbath of the Lord thy God: in it thou shalt not do any work, thou, nor thy son, nor thy daughter, thy man servant, nor thy maid servant, nor thy cattle, nor the stranger that is within thy gates.". This is Exodus 20. The Sabbath in Genesis was on the First Day of the Week in that time frame; and was changed to the 7th Day of the Week for part of the Old Testament. Now it is changed again to the First Day of the Week, Sunday, for the NT Saints in 1Cor16.

---T--- <u>CC (DOI & CON): 4 BASIC LAWS that ALL ELSE MUST DERIVE FROM:</u> GOD (Christianity), Thus Holy Bible; No Self-Idolatry or Selfishness; TRUTH, Thus Holy BIBLE; CREATION; CONSCIENCE; HAPPINESS; NO EVIL or SIN (which includes cults, or false religions, and every sin that is such identified). // Discern if all these agree or not.

---T--- <u>THE Christian Oath before the Christian God,</u> whether one is Christian or not. The exception that is provided is an affirmation, which is given to the Spiritual Moral Personality who disagrees about oaths to God because some of the NT SCs which are sometimes difficult to interpret; and/or maybe their knowledge is untrained about such. So an affirmation is provided for these Spiritual Moral Personalities; And this is defined for comprehension, that such an affirmation, is an "Appeal" recognizing God's Being and presence & and to tell the truth and that God has rewards & punishments.

---T--- <u>The USA GOV opposes the CON & re</u>moves the Liberty if they allow evil anti-Christian laws in the land; public activity; depends on the subject; limits etc. // Many legal Spiritual Moral Creatures deny that an atheist can hold Office in the USA; some of these are in the List of Citations.

---T--- <u>The DOCs & Congress Journals, of the CON,</u> are legal & necessary DOCs to the CON: // Thus for the definition of "religion" or "religious" or "religions", they must be included for the right and proper definitions of the words. It is totally plain that, it is a fact that Christianity was, and is, to be the True doctrine of God and mankind in the USA GOV. Thus all the supporting DOC are EV that prove that it is DEN, which is known as Establishment of Religion; in the 1-A, R-E, R~Est; and that Christianity is the USA GOV Religion; and again repeated, that religious establishment is defined as DEN, which is secondary doctrines, expressions, and organizations or establishments. // The Supporting DOC are to be included as stated by congress rules: "Each House shall keep a Journal of its Proceedings, and from time to time publish the same ,,,and the Yeas and Nays of the Members of either House on any question shall, at the Desire of one-fifth of those Present, be entered on the Journal".

---T--- <u>SACRED Honor:</u> // <u>"We pledge our</u> ,,,SACRED Honor" are the words in the DOI. What is the definition of "Sacred"? "Make a compact; consecrated to or belonging to God; Holy; of or connected with religion or religious rites; regarded with the same respect and reverence accorded holy things". This is part of forming a Covenant Compact or Contract; that is that it includes God and religion. This is a further application to them as Spiritual Moral ministers; to make themselves devoted to God. (Rom13).

---T--- <u>The Judicial Branch is Legally required</u> to abide by the CC (DOI & CON). This is called, bound; they are bound to laws of God, not selfishness nor self-idolatry, nor evil promoting. The USA DOC Rules words are~ ",,,the Judges in every State shall be bound thereby, any Thing in the Constitution or Laws of any State to the Contrary notwithstanding".

---T--- <u>Rebellion to God & His Laws is opposed:</u> // The CON states~ "No person shall be a <u>Senator</u> or Representative in Congress, or Elector of President and Vice President, or hold any office, civil or military, under the US, or under any State, who, having previously taken an oath ,,,to support the CON [[and thus DOI (CC)]] of the US, shall have engaged in insurrection or rebellion against the same,,,". Now to contradict, reverse, oppose, ban, or repeal is an act of rebellion or opposition.

---T--- <u>Art V1:</u> "This CON, and the Laws of the US which shall be made in Pursuance thereof: and all Treaties made, or which shall be made, under the Authority of the US, shall be the supreme Law of the Land".

---T--- <u>The CON does not give us</u> our Rights & Liberties; They come from God, as the DOI states: // The CON is only to guarantee those Rights and Liberties, to make the "secure" from foreign powers and GOV abuse within the US. (63). And the CON states that it is intended for such. // Life, Happiness, liberty, etc. are not subjects that Laws or paper have ability to do; only a Live Being has such ability.

---T--- <u>If any act of GOV violates the CC (DOI & CON)</u> laws then the GOV act shall be void, null, and negated, as illegal: // "that declaring void all laws that violate Eternal Justice and thus deny or destroy 'inalienable rights' given by God to men in America". (133). // "Men should not yield to Caesar the things which are God's". Mat22:21. GOV has no Right to priority of mens' spirits. "Limited Powers" is the term FFoG used. // Judges Roane, Henry, and Tyler, said as Judicial officers for the USA this~ "The supposed omnipotence of parliament ,,,is an abominable insult upon the honor and good sense of our country, as nothing is omnipotent as it relates to us, either religious or political, but the God of Heaven,,," (95). The "us" refers to the people; and also note the use of the word, "religious", as again referring to Christian DEN; this is not God Himself, but adds His religion.

---T--- <u>FFOG William Blackstone, a Christian Law Officer, influenced the USA REPs of</u> Congress & Judicial officers; & for years: // Mr. Blackstone often stated the Holy Bible vs. that, "the fear of the Lord was the beginning of wisdom" (Psa111:10; Pro1:7); and used it as a reference to the laws of God. He wrote things, which are the same as in the USA DOI & CON; which were with all probability learned from him. Such includes this: "The doctrines thus delivered we call the revealed or divine law, and they are to be found only in the holy SCs. Upon these two foundations, the law of nature and the law of revelation, depend all human laws; that is to say no human laws should be suffered to contradict these".

---T--- <u>The 10 Commandments are in the CC (DOI & CON):</u> // Idolatry is in the DOI where it states that God and our Rights are from Him, and that no evil should be allowed in the country. This is self-evident.

---T--- <u>Michael Farris is a Constitution Attorney that has a book with some</u> legal Truth in it; including this statement: "By basing our right to be a free nation upon God's law, we were also saying ,,,that we owed obedience to the law that allowed us to be ,,,a country ,,,By-laws must be interpreted to be in agreement with the Charter ,,,the Declaration of Independence ,,,the CON of the US must be in agreement with the Declaration" (69).

---T--- <u>One unknown quote (paraphrased as follows)</u> from a Christian Pamphlet said, "Americans are endowed with specific and sure inalienable rights, but if we do not put out efforts to keep them, making it public, then some people will come along and un-endow them".

---T--- <u>Here is another paragraph of the DOI that</u> has some statements about God & His laws: // "We, therefore, the Representatives of the US of America, in General Congress, Assembled, appealing to the Supreme Judge of the world for the rectitude of our intentions, do, in the Name, and by Authority of the good People of these Colonies, solemnly publish and declare, That these United Colonies are, and of Right ought to be Free and Independent States; that they are Absolved from all Allegiance to the British Crown, and that all political connection between them and the State of Great Britain, is and ought to be totally dissolved; and that as Free and Independent States, they have full Power to levy War, conclude Peace, contract Alliances, establish Commerce, and to do all other Acts and Things which Independent States may of right do. And for the support of this Declaration, with a firm reliance on the protection of divine Providence, we mutually pledge to each other our Lives, our Fortunes and our sacred Honor."

---T--- <u>James Otis, FFoG for the CON, stated the</u> "limited powers" of GOV are, "These are bounds, which by God and nature are fixed, hitherto have they a right to come, and no further ,,,These are the first principles of law and justice,,,".

---T--- <u>The total intention/ purpose of the DOI & RW</u> was to establish a "righteous" purpose for making a separate country; establishing godliness within, not pagan, not heathen, not of false religion; rather supporting the true God.

---T--- <u>AMENDMENTS & ALTERATIONS of The CON:</u> // This study is in Chp 5. Amendments are not, and do not allow, subtractions, reversals, voiding, exclusions, etc. of the DOI, nor CON~ CC.

---T--- <u>The "US Code Annotated" includes the DOI</u> under the following Legal Group of DOCs (which also includes the CON, AOC & Northwest Ordinance) for the US; and defines all these DOCs: "The Organic Laws of the US of America". Organic is that which laws are made from, a basis.

---T--- <u>Many Christian Laws are in the CC (DOI & CON):</u> // As having 2 or more witnesses to crimes in Article 3; This is similar to the Bible in 1Tim5:19, Heb10:28, Deu17:6; 19:15, 2Cor13:1. // Now this does not provide the opportunity for evil spiritual creatures, with evil intention/ purposes to join together to form a lie, or falsity. For one, an evil intention/ purpose is instantly rejected as the attribute that makes a person good or evil; this is the priority Character attribute. HSC states it in 1Cor10:31. For another, large groups of people can be wrong, even to the degree of evil. Sodom & Gomorrah is an EX. The Flood with Noah & Family is another EX; the murder of God Himself is another EX~ Jesus Christ. Gen6, 19, Luk23.

---T--- <u>Principle Law is exampled by the following:</u> // Be thankful in all things: HSC~ "1The5:18, Eph5:20 In every thing give thanks: for this is the will of God in Christ Jesus concerning you. Giving thanks always for all things unto God and the Father in the name of our Lord Jesus Christ" +What is all things, and how to be thankful and what expressions, and exactly when and where, as such, are not stated; rather only a general To

Do. But this general command, or Principle Law can be applied to a persons' general conduct and in every area of life. This Principle Law also includes a Do Not Do~ which is unthankfulness.

---T--- <u>All Branches of USA GOV are to be Christian &</u> support Christian Laws & oppose evil & are bound by oath to do so; & the people may belong to any Christian DEN whatsoever: // Executive, Judicial, Congress Branches are required to take an Oath to hold the office which states that he will defend and protect the CC (DOI & CON; with the CON only being a sub-DOC of the overruling DOI). Thus to support Christianity is required by law. DEN is not to be tested, but Christianity is. // This is about the Oath: "Before he enter on the Execution of his Office, he shall take the following Oath or Affirmation:--"I do solemnly swear (or affirm) that I will faithfully execute the Office of President of the US, and will to the best of my Ability, preserve, protect and defend the CON of the US." That is the Constitutional Law System. +And~ "The Senators and Representatives before mentioned, and the Members of the several State Legislatures, and all executive and judicial Officers, both of the US and of the several States, shall be bound by Oath or Affirmation, to support this CON". // DEN is not required as stated~ "but no religious Test shall ever be required as a Qualification to any Office or public Trust under the US." The Religious Test is that of a DEN, (Establishment of Religion ~ true Religion of Christianity), which also includes secondary doctrines and expressions. // Thus the Law Making Branches require a person to be a Christian. Spiritual Moral Creatures holding Office in parts of the Branches or related Branches that are not part of the Law Making may hold Office without being a Christian, but they must oath to support Christianity, God, and not oppose it; in every subject for public.

---T--- <u>The CON was established to protect those "inalienable rights"</u> that are from God: // From who? GOD, that is. This is a protection from GOV abuse or excess; and this includes that of democracy, or majority rule, or the popular vote or mass. A large amount of Spiritual Moral Creatures population IS NOT EQUAL to right. No. Such would depend on whether they have the Right subject, and if they agree with the Right subject. God is always right, however.

---T--- <u>Part of the CC (DOI & CON) is to protect from</u> Democracy, or popular vote, or the majority, or peer pressure, or the mass, or the crowd. They set up votes according to population and not by wherever the most people were. They also stated such. The GOV puts "checks" or controls on the majority; that only because more people say such and such, does not make it right. This would be a violation of the Laws of Divinity (God) in the DOI & CON.

---T--- <u>The Colonial Courts that existed before the DOI, and as also</u> stated in the DOI, maintained the attitude and observance that God is to be over the legal system; and should be over English Parliament that was refusing to do right by God & man: // Such Stated, "The fundamental law which God and nature have given to the people cannot be infringed". This was the GOV and judicial motto, and rule of law, also known as the "common law", which was in existence during the RW, DOI, & CON. // For any GOV currently in the USA to oppose this that was supposed to be, which was clearly stated and covenanted in the CC (DOI & CON) is an act of treason and breech of contract and law-breaking; a lie, deceit, and crime against the USA, USA GOV (citizens), and FFoG, which includes the citizens of the past. Some people do it by ignorance or unknowingly; not intentionally/ purposed; maybe they do not know at all; or have some other philosophy, or knowledge; some other knowledge system. // Reinsch shares that "the colonies were so impressed with the idea of an overruling law of nature that the laws of God and so-called natural laws were regarded as the true law, and all temporal legislation was considered to be binding only in so far as it was an expression of this natural law" (95). // God is the basis as in the CC: "When British statesmen and writers talked of a statute or action as 'unconstitutional', they meant that it was something impolitic or contrary to the spirit of the British Constitution, but not that it was something beyond the power of Parliament to enact; for Parliament was supreme. When on the other hand, James Otis, John Adams, and Samuel Adams of Massachusetts, James Wilson of Pennsylvania, Richard Bland and Richard Henry Lee of Virginia, and other leading men of the Colonies began talking, in letters and addresses, of the Stamp Tax Law, the Tea Tax Law, the Billeting Law, and other Acts of Parliament as 'unconstitutional' they were using the word in an entirely new and purely American sense, which profoundly shocked England. For the Americans meant by 'unconstitutional', Acts absolutely illegal, Acts which Parliament had no power to pass and which were to be disregarded by the courts and by the citizens of the Colonies. 'An Act against the CON is void; and act against natural equity is void,,,'" (95).

---T--- <u>Application of the Laws in the DOI & CON:</u> // Where does it state that the judicial, or for any Branch, including citizens, to be exempt from the law and that the statements of the CC do not apply? Nowhere.

---T--- <u>GOV, even of Ungodly, Heathen, Pagan,</u> or Idolatrous, have normally had laws of the 10 commandments; many of them, in their GOV legal system. No murder, stealing, etc.

---T--- <u>GOV have often had double</u> standards where they do Reasoning to justify murder or stealing or adultery (spouse stealing) or idolatry for them; yet for their citizens, be it far from them, and beware if you do not (so to speak).

---T--- <u>While proving the truths in this Book, it was</u> learned that there are other Spiritual Moral Creatures that are honest hearts; & were aware & knowledgeable of some of the same truths. // Mr. Dan Gilbert was one such sensitive personality; stated in his book following (95): "The GOV today and citizens today are doing this ,,,crushed and coerced ,,,murderous, militaristic, and materialistic machines ,,,making guinea pigs out of their children ,,,crushing their consciences and souls out of them ,,,bending them to bondage to power-mad state juggernauts ,,,using their children as raw material ,,,trying to mold a generation which will not know God,,, no comprehension of or contact with the things of the Spirit,,, godless governments exercising the powers of distortion, deformation, and destruction over their childhood which a vivisectionist wields over mongrel

240

dogs". // I will also state that more so than this is our GOV and citizens turning over to demons of devils, with their witchcraft increasing by the day, with literally thousands of all sorts of dedicated witches preying on Spiritual Moral folk of all age, from the very young to the old, creating evil desires, dedicated witches I say, literally thousands by thousands of them; including in the realm of what they are calling music & movies, equally as in Nebuchadnezzar's day when the 3 Hebrew men refused to bow, which is not what these Spiritual Moral Beings are doing today. With the electronic mezmerization, they are taken into bondage of,,, lusts. Illegally minimize, diminish, remove, negate, and disrespect the Holy Bible but allow, get this, allow on USA soil open sales of witchcraft, of all sorts of books, music, and movies. And all this, when the USA GOV (FFOG) specifically stated this is a land for God not the devil & demons, for righteousness not evil, for Jesus not Satan, for God's laws of revelation and nature (creation) not Satan's seeds of craft planted in the helpless status of little children. They banned slavery, banned recreational alcohol, banned blasphemy, banned evil GOV, banned Sabbath breaking, banned disrespect of Christ & Christianity, banned dueling, banned stealing, banned murder, but now they are banning the Holy Bible and promoting, even making rich, them who serve the evil & demons - a total illegal act on USA Soil. What a shameful and evil GOV exists today in many parts. For the good that they do, we do not reject, rather for the evil that they currently do, we reject.

---T--- <u>Now let us have one Spiritual Moral Sane Being stand up and</u> tell why the USA is promoting movies of murder as entertainment, horror movies, satanic witchcraft activity and etc. Violent cartoons or movies are not to be displayed as fun; should not even exist because it wrongs personality. Violence is not a spare time activity, not a fun or pleasure. When violence is done it is to be done carefully and with grief. Victory over evil is different, but not to be as activity for regularity; and surely not for pleasure viewing or reading. The poor society is decreasing to evil, as demoniacs are roaming and people are having "shoot-outs" and killing innocent people. This is becoming a crazy society. // This is the result of removing the CC, and promotion of evil.

---T--- <u>Self-Evidence of God, conscience, creation</u>, truth: // Where is it? It is to be, in all Spiritual Moral Creatures, including all GOV Officers.

---T--- <u>USA CC CON includes the 10 Commandments</u>, which is no murder, no stealing, etc.~ "may deprive unjustly any man or group of men of life, liberty, or property".

---T--- <u>In the Judicial Branch</u> they take an oath to support the Divine Justice. This is not a Self~Opinion; selfishness, but rather God. Such oath states~ "so help me God".

---T--- <u>The GOV officials take oath to support the</u> CC (DOI & CON). That also requires, that they support the DIVINE Covenant, that it is (contract), between God and them and the USA in general.

---T--- <u>Judicial Cases state:</u> // <u>Justice</u> Davis in the Milligan case stated: "The CON is a law for rulers and for people, equally in war and peace, and covers with its shield of protection all classes of men, at all times, and under all conditions". // Justice Holmes states, "At the foundation of our civil liberty lies the principle which denies to GOV officials an exceptional position before the law and subjects them to the same rules of conduct that are commands to the citizen". // And let us observe that this same rule is not that which the judge or GOV Official says that it is, or tells us it is, but what truth says it is. Furthermore, a judge does not say the rule applies to we, but not to themselves. Additionally, it is not that which he tells us it is, but rather that which God tells us it is. Only because a judge is so privileged to be hired in a Position, does not allow that, he then tells us all his rules that are to be on us. Judges are not to be some idol, some self-centered, self-idolatrous, some selfish Being doing the rule to make increase of the same. Or for continuing, telling us some other mans rules on us, as is what case law sometimes tries to do.

---T--- <u>CC (DOI & CON) protects all groups of Spiritual Moral Creatures</u>, which includes "races", genders, economic statuses, and abuses from the GOV.

---T--- <u>FFoG did not establish the CC (DOI & CON)</u> for it to be opposed or contradicted.

---T--- <u>Law Basis not men basis:</u> // <u>The DOI is based</u> on laws, and laws of God not on mans opinion.

---T--- <u>What is this that man puts men into "classes"</u> in the first place? Who is he that rules? No man will rule over me? I will submit to whom I will submit; and the Lord Jesus tells me about this attitude and conduct and when it applies and when it does not apply. And what Spirit Creature is there, that has such inner attitudes to step over me, and order me to do as they say, think, or opinionize? I am not for anarchy or rebellion, nor war, nor hate, nor lawlessness. I am for humility & society. But how it applies is a serious and valuable situation. 1John5:21 is God's rule, that~ "Little children, keep yourselves from idols. Amen.".

---T--- <u>In England, Lord Coke (English Jurist) is one Spiritual Moral Being that</u> our FFoG studied; they included Him; and he proclaimed that GOV rulers are under the jurisdiction of Divine Law: // Mr. Coke writes that the king is under "natural and divine law"; and if the king offended such law he was illegal. A King, named James, became angry and charged treason for any person to claim that the King is under any law but his own. However Mr. Coke stated, "the king ought not to be under any man, but under God and His law". FFOG, including Mr. George Mason, cited Mr. Coke and stated that all people, including judges, are~ "in conscience bound to disobey all enactments which contradict the laws of nature and the laws of God,,, The laws of nature are the laws of God, whose authority can be superseded by no power on earth. A legislature must not obstruct our obedience to Him [[GOD]] from whose punishment they cannot protect us. [[All Creatures are responsible to God, now & forever]]. All human laws which contradict His laws we are in conscience bound to disobey". ~Spellings were corrected in that quote. // Thus the FFOG Colonists claimed HSC such as, "We ought to obey God rather than men" Act5:29.

241

---T--- <u>GOV Officials are to respect God & His creatures</u>; to be unselfish, to do to other creatures as they would have them do to them: // "Equal" or "Equality" is in the DOI & CON. Creatures as themselves; and not tyrannicalize or dictate over them wrongly.

---T--- <u>The higher law than men, is the Law of Nature</u> and the Revealed Law, both coming from God. (included in the DOI & CON).

---T--- <u>Constitutional Law is Law Based on A</u> DOC, which in the USA is the CC; of Written Order: // All the other Branches of GOV, which includes the Spiritual Creature citizens is subordinate to the CC. // Voting Limitations of the Majority and the Branches are only parts of the "Checks & Balances", which also includes the CC as a Check & Balance part.

---T--- <u>The Judicial Branch is not primary before</u> the CC: // The Federalist Papers 78, has Alexander Hamilton in an article stating that the judicial Branch is to be a "faithful guardians of the CON". They are not to say, 'I will make the rules around here', with a haughty self centered selfish attitude.

---T--- <u>The Vote is not, nor is Congress, nor the Judicial</u> Branch primary priority to the CC; rather they are submissive, or under. Various FFOG share following: // The Federalist Papers 78 includes Alexander Hamilton stating that the judicial Branch is to be "faithful guardians of the CON"; and "The Judiciary's duty it must be to declare all acts contrary to the manifest tenor of the CON void". // James Madison states, "A law violating a CON established by the people themselves would be considered by the judges as null and void" (202). // Note that any law coming from any direction put up against (opposition to) the CC (DOI & CON) is VOID. // James Wilson states, "When they (the judges) consider its (a law's) principles and find it to be incompatible with the superior power of the CON, it is their duty to pronounce it void" (98). // And remember the CON is overruled by it's DOI starting DOC of the CC. // Laws coming from Congress put up against (opposition to) the CC (DOI & CON) are VOID and the Judges have Rights (power) to Check; or put a Check on the Congress to assure that they do not try to make laws against the CC. This does not equal that the Judicial Branch makes laws, only that they are to Check on Congress; as all Branches are to do the same to each other; and the standard is God and the CC; God is the 1ˢᵗ priority Check. // Samuel Chase states, "The Judicial power ,,,is the proper and competent authority to decide whether any law made by Congress ,,,is contrary to or in violation of the Federal CON" (203). // Luther Martin declares, "The (judges) could declare an unconstitutional law void". // James Kent, "The Judicial department is the proper power in the GOV to determine whether a statute be or be not constitutional" (204). // Joseph Story, "The power of interpreting the laws involves necessarily the function to ascertain whether they are conformable to the CON or not; and if not so conformable to declare them void and inoperative" (52). // The Judicial Branch is submissive and cannot go against the CC (DOI & CON): Alexander Hamilton in Federalist Paper #81 states, "There is not a syllable in the plan which directly empowers the national courts to construe [[interpret as they desire]] the laws according to the spirit of the CON". // The Judicial Branch is to submit to the laws of the CC (DOI & CON) and Congress, as James Madison stated, "Refusing or not refusing to execute a law ,,,makes the Judiciary department paramount in fact to the Legislature, which was never intended and can never be proper" (201). Thus note, again, that the Judicial Branch does not make the laws, only applies them in court and puts a Check on other Branches; intending/ purposing that they abide by the CC. // Thomas Jefferson shared Judiciary abuse to the CON: "I have never shrunk from ,,,that the germ of dissolution of our federal GOV is ,,,of the federal judiciary ,,,working like gravity by night and by day, gaining a little today and a little tomorrow, and advancing its noiseless step like a thief, over the field of jurisdiction, until all shall be usurped." (30).

---T--- <u>The CC (DOI & CON) is the basis of the Laws of the USA</u>: // Stated as follows in the CON: "This CON, and the Laws of the US which shall be made in Pursuance thereof ,,,or which shall be made, under the Authority of the US, shall be the supreme Law of the Land." THIS STATEMENT is written 2 (Two) Times in the CON. Supreme is defined as the "highest authority". The CON is part of the CC, as the application of the DOI; and the DOI states God is the supreme authority. Therefore the CC, (DOI & CON) are the applications of God; that was the priority intention of the USA start~ priority of God & His Laws. Is God God or Not God ?

---T--- <u>Bills are to be based on GOD: as stated in the CON:</u> // Bill: "Every Bill which shall have passed the House of Representatives and the Senate, shall, before it become a Law, be presented to the President of the US; If he approve he shall sign it, but if not he shall return it, with his Objections to that House in which it shall have originated, who shall enter the Objections at large on their Journal, and proceed to reconsider it. If after such Reconsideration 2/3 of that House shall agree to pass the Bill, it shall be sent together with the Objections, to the other House, by which it shall likewise be reconsidered, and if approved by 2/3 of that House, it shall become a Law. But in all such Cases the Votes of both Houses shall be determined by Yeas and Nays, and the Names of the Persons voting for and against the Bill shall be entered on the Journal of each House respectively. If any Bill shall not be returned by the President within ten Days (Sundays excepted) after it shall have been presented to him, the Same shall be a Law, in like Manner as if he had signed it, unless the Congress by their Adjournment prevent its Return, in which Case it shall not be a Law." // Observe here, that there is not law basis authority where it is not based on this system established by the CC (DOI & CON). The Branches were all participants with God & His Holy Bible as the Main priority participants; all as Spiritual Moral Creature Beings under the Creator.

---T--- <u>Claims: // The CON states, "The congress shall have</u> Power to dispose of and make all needful Rules and Regulations respecting the Territory or other Property belonging to the US; and nothing in this CON shall be so construed as to Prejudice any Claims of the US, or of any particular State".

242

---T--- The CC part DOI Formation required Christian Assembly of God Worship: // US Congress Articles of War, June 30, 1775: ",,,earnestly recommended to all officers and soldiers diligently to attend Divine service; and all officers and soldiers who shall behave indecently or irreverently at any place of Divine worship, shall ,,,be brought before a court-martial" (58).

---T--- CONGRESS: LAW basis is God & Christianity Religion: FFOG stated such: // James Wilson, "Human law must rest its authority ultimately upon the authority of that law which is divine ,,,Far from being rivals or enemies, religion and law are twin sisters, friends, mutual assistants." (206). // "Whereas true religion and good morals are the only solid foundations of public liberty and happiness ,,,it is hereby earnestly recommended to the several States to take the most effectual measures for the encouragement thereof." (Continental Congress, AD 1778). // Matthias Burnet, Connecticut Legislator in AD 1803, stated, "Feeble ,,,would be ,,,government, and ,,,laws ,,,without a sense of religion and the terrors of the world to come ,,,banish ,,,religion and the terrors of the world to come from society and you dissolve the sacred obligation of conscience and leave every man to do that which is right in his own eyes" (205). // Noah Webster, "Our citizens should early understand that the genuine source of correct republican principles is the Bible, particularly the New Testament, or the Christian religion." (176). // James Wilson, "All laws ,,,may be arranged in two different classes. 1) Divine. 2) Human ,,,is should always be remembered that this law, natural or revealed, made for men or for nations, flows from the same Divine source; it is the law of God ,,,Human law must rest its authority ,,,upon the authority of that law which is Divine" (206). // Alexander Hamilton, "The Law ,,,dictated by God Himself is, of course, superior in obligation to any other. It is binding over all the globe, in all countries, and at all times. No human laws are of any validity if contrary to this." (170). // Rufus King, ",,,law established by the Creator ,,,extends over the whole globe, is everywhere and at all times binding upon mankind ,,,paramount to all human control." (207). // Samuel Huntington, "While the great body of freeholders are acquainted with the duties which they owe to their God, to themselves, and to men, they will remain free. But if ignorance and depravity ,,,slavery and ruin" (98).

---T--- GOD, Creator, Supreme Ruler, Divine Providence, Lord Jesus Christ are the terms clearly stated in the DOI part of the CC; & then supported in the CON: // The CON supports such by application of the DOI with the Laws of the Christian Bible, Sabbath, Christian Oaths & Affirmations, Stealing, Murder, People-stealing, Slavery, Assisting Religion, Opposing the partiality to Christian DEN, etc. And then with a closing reference for priority of God; as including God, not excluding; closing statements and signed with reference to the support and timing of Jesus; and the fact that the CON was constructed as a DOC in support and application to the DOI. It is common knowledge that God is perfect, true, right, and to be God of all; and no idolatry against Him.

---T--- CC (DOI & CON) Support Christian Laws; Including as follows: // God. // Anti-self-idolatry; or self-1st-priority; or selfishness; or selflessness vivi selfmore. // Marriage; Marriage is man & woman; all other is perversion. // Holy Bible. // Evil opposed. // Evil is anti-Christian. // Churches are to be supported. // Liberty. // Equality. // Equality is all men are equal without any other title than that they are humans created by God. // Children & family are protected by many terms and principles including that it says "posterity"~ defined as "family or future generations". // Protects strangers in the land, Lev19:34-35. // Protects from foreign evils. // The USA GOV cannot be a Church in itself. // The USA GOV laws must support Christianity; at any time or any point, that they do not, then they break, disagree with the CC (DOI & CON) Principle Laws; at such point, they oppose and not protect. // The N GOV cannot force people to be Christians. // No Officer of any Law Making Branch as directly related can be an infidel, rather must be a Christian; as was in the State CON's, the DOI, and the CON supporting the DOI; and all the REP sent to form the USA CON were Christians at the time. // The Laws must be Christian, and in support of the CC (DOI & CON) protecting these DOC and protecting Christians. // All religion must be true and not lies; no falsities~ this applies to the FFOG and intention/ purpose of USA and such. // Infidelity, a non-believer in Christianity~ such a person may be an infidel in private, but must obey the Christian Laws of the land; he does not have to go to church assembly, but he must not do business on the Sabbath; nor disobey other laws of Christianity in public. // Laws against evil; some is to be stopped, and some is limited.

---T--- All Law Making in the USA is based on "God, Creator, Supreme Judge, Divine Providence, Lord Jesus Christ" as the Main Ruler, over the CC (DOI & CON); and over Spiritual Creature Citizens: // That is the CC that was made; and with oaths and pledges of sacred honor to God. There are no other factors in the process. These are all to work together.

---T--- CC (DOI & CON) are Holy Biblically based & the Vote (that is, a Total Democracy) IS Subordinate to God & NOT the Absolute Rule; FFOG & DOC state as follows: // About a Democracy which is that all is ruled in total by a Vote: +James Madison, "Democracies have ever been spectacles of turbulence and contention ,,,incompatible with personal security, or the rights of property ,,,short in their lives ,,,violent in their deaths" (202). +John Adams, "Remember, democracy never lasts long ,,,soon wastes, exhausts, and murders itself. There never was a democracy yet that did not commit suicide"; and "will soon degenerate into an anarchy ,,,that every man will do what is right in his own eyes and no man's life or property or reputation or liberty will be secure,,, wanton pleasures ,,,capricious will,,, execrable cruelty of one or a very few" (169a). +Fisher Ames, "A democracy is a volcano which conceals the fiery materials of its own destruction ,,,known propensity of a democracy is to licentiousness [[excessive license; evil not limited]] which the ambitious call, and ignorant believe to be liberty" (29). +Gouverneur Morris, "We have seen the tumult of democracy terminate ,,,as it has everywhere terminated, in despotism ,,,savage and wild ,,,bring down the virtuous and wise to thy level of folly and guilt" (219). +John Quincy Adams, "The experience of all former ages had shown that of all human GOVs, democracy was the most unstable, fluctuating and short-lived" (220). +Benjamin Rush, "A simple democracy ,,,is one of the greatest evils" (97). +Noah Webster,

243

"„„democracy „„there are „„tumults and disorders „„generally a bad GOV „„often the most tyrannical GOV on earth" (221). +Zephaniah Swift, "„„more a GOV resembles a pure democracy the more they abound with disorder and confusion." (141a).

--------------------------- EVIL or WRONG LAW BASIS --------------------

---T--- <u>Illegal attempts are intending/ purposing to</u> associate good & evil, so that the good is devalued or not conceived rightly, and therefore not good but evil. However they, that use such tactics, are doing the devil's (with demons on them) bidding, and are no more intelligent than the demons, as they were first at doing it, and their intellectual pride derived has been felt before by a more subtle evil Being than themselves. // Therefore to change history by stating evil deeds of a specific person(s), and then associating them with the truth & righteousness, saying therefore the truth & righteousness is not right, will only work to their own defeat; who do such. God defines it as Evil Speaking Principle Law and promises the wrong will be punished Colo3. Because for this activity, and action on their part, is an eternal cost before the True and only Judge of the Universe. It is a lie, a falsity, a wrong basis of truth, love, and righteousness. Because a person(s) fails, or is unstable in their life, or has failed, does not make truth, love, and righteousness wrong; nor is it the basis of such subjects. Those subjects and Beings last forever, eternal, and are the best pleasures, and affectionate cares now & forever.

------------------------------- GOV ACTIVITIES as EVIDENCES --------------------------

---T--- <u>Christ & Christianity is the Basis of Relations with Other Nations & A</u>ctivities of Congress: // "Journals of the Continental Congress, 1774-1789 - FEB 26, 1788. - „„Congress assembled. Present „„According to Order the Minister Plenipotentiary from most CHRISTIAN Majesty of France was introduced to a public Audience when he delivered a letter of Credence1 from his most CHRISTIAN Majesty of which the following is a translation „„Very dear great friends and Allies Particular reasons relative to the good of our service have determined us to appoint „„and more and more worthy of our good will. We PRAY you to give full faith to whatever he may say to you on our part, particularly when he shall assure you of the sincerity of our wishes for your prosperity, as well as of the constant affection and friendship which we bear to the US in general, and to each of them in particular. We PRAY GOD that he will have you very dear great friends and Allies in his HOLY keeping. Written at Versailles the 30th . Sept. 1787. [Note 2: 2 Roger Alden takes up the entry.] Your good friend and Ally (signed) Louis Ct . de Montmorin. After which he addressed Congress in a speech of which the following is a translation. Gentlemen of the Congress, The relations of friendship and Affection which subsist between the King my Master and the US, have been established on a basis which cannot but daily acquire a new degree of solidity. It is satisfactory to be mutually convinced that an Alliance formed for obtaining a glorious peace, after efforts directed by the greatest wisdom, and sustained with admirable constancy, must always be conformable to the common Interests „„The King who was the first to connect himself with the US as a Sovereign Power, to second their efforts and favour their Interests, has never ceased since that memorable period, to turn his attention to the means of proving to them his Affection „„Their success will always interest him sensibly, and there is reason to hope for it from the wisdom of the measures which they will adopt. To this solemn Assurance of Interest and Attachment on the part of the King, to the Unanimous sentiment of the Nation, and to the fervent wishes of a great number of my countrymen, who have had the advantage to be associated in the military toils, and success of the US, permit me to add „„which I have been constantly penetrated for a people who have been able to fix from their birth, the attention of the most considerable powers in Europe, and whose courage and patriotism have astonished all Nations. My happiness will be compleat, Gentlemen „„who held the place near You Gentlemen, with which I am now honored, I am far from enjoying the advantages which he derived from his talents, his knowledge, and those circumstances which placed him in the most intimate relations to you. I will endeavor to resemble him at least, by the greatest attention to promote and give success to whatever may contribute to the satisfaction, the glory, and the prosperity of the US. To which the President made the following reply. Sir „„It will always give us pleasure to acknowledge the friendship and important good offices which we have experienced from his Most CHRISTIAN Majesty and Your generous Nation; and we flatter ourselves that the same principles of magnanimity and regard to mutual convenience which dictated the connections between us, will continue to operate, and to render them still more extensive in their benefits to the two Countries. „„We consider the Alliance as involving engagements highly interesting to both parties, and we are persuaded that they will be observed with entire and mutual good faith „„that the harmony and Interest of both Nations will not be less promoted„„".
---T--- <u>Congress & Presidential overRule Judicial</u> Branch: // FFOG Thomas Jefferson states, "Nothing in the CON has given to them a right to decide for the Executive, more than to the Executive to decide for them „„The opinion which gives to the judges the right to decide what laws are constitutional, and what not „„for the legislature and the executive „„would make the judiciary a despotic branch." (30).
---T--- <u>Judicial Branch Limitations:</u> // FFOG Thomas Jefferson states, "Nothing in the CON has given to them a right to decide for the Executive, more than to the Executive to decide for them „„The opinion which gives to the judges the right to decide what laws are constitutional, and what not „„for the legislature and the executive „„would make the judiciary a despotic branch." (30).

244

---T--- THE 7 Conditions as Follows:

---T--- <u>THE 7 CONDITIONS STATED IN THE CC (DOI & CON):</u> // NOW note that this CC (DOI & CON), with clarity, with plainness, with absoluteness~ establishes the Laws of the USA to be based on; that is the Governing, or ruling organization - law making society of order - is to be based on these factors as Follows~ Law making in the USA has strictness of Love applied and various standards applied with it. // It is limited and confined. The words, "herein granted"; herein refers to inclusions & exclusions. Thus limited to that. Granted is that given from God. // It takes these following Beings (Spirits) to make Laws; they cannot work separately from each other; it is the condition: 1} Congress acceptance - "All legislative Powers herein granted shall be vested in a Congress of the US, which shall consist of a Senate and House of Representatives". +To be an Officer in the USA GOV requires one to be a Christian and not infidel nor false religion; because required by the Oath. 2} Must be in support of the CC (DOI & CON). 3} NOT in opposition to, rather IN support of the CC (DOI & CON). 4} Acceptance from the Executive branch. 5} God is to be God of the Nation which is Christianity and His Laws, the Holy Bible; No opposition to, rather to His support as God; God is the Priority Being. 6} Citizen (Every Spiritual Moral Creature) Branch. 7} The Oath requires that Christians be in the Law Making Branches in all Offices that are directly connected to making the Laws. Otherwise any GOV Offices or Positions not directly connected to Law Making or in any GOV Branch Official not directly connected to Law Making, then an oath of agreement to support and not oppose the CC is required; in every part of public activity.

---T--- <u>Of these 7 conditions, the CC (DOI & CON)</u> Rules over them all; it is the Covenant Contract; or Written Order under God for the Nation. // These DOC establish the operational foundation and operational application for every Branch; all Spiritual Moral Creatures are included as stated.

---T--- *<u>American citizens are to honor the CC (DOI &</u>* CON) as from GOD is included; & requires a pledge by them: // To oppose (which includes contradiction) is a lie and an act of Treason against the USA and the God of the USA. To become a citizen is to contract with the DOI & CON; to not be a citizen is nevertheless to be under the authority of the DOI & CON. Citizens are part of the GOV and the REP did the citizens work; and the words of the CC (DOI & CON) are pledged to.

---T--- <u>Congress (REP of Citizens) & Ci</u>tizen Branches of GOV to be Christian (or supportive) & the Law basis to be Christian is Holy Biblical & Truth; stated by FFOG: // John Adams says, ",,,I believe the Hebrews have done more to enlighten and civilize the world. Moses did more than all their legislators and philosophers ,,,Your philosophy, Condorcet, has waged a more cruel war against truth than was ever attempted by king or priest ,,,There is no such thing without a supposition of a God. There is no right or wrong in the universe without the supposition of a moral government and an intellectual and moral governor" (119). +In a discussion Mary Wollstonecraft (a liberal apologist) said, "it is time to get rid of the notions of 'the wild traditions of original sin'; and Mr. Adams replied that what she meant was, "we must get entirely clear of Christianity"; then Mary asserted that man is free to chose any scientific path. Mr. Adams replied, "it is religion and GOV that have effected this"; Mary then discussed national morality. Then Mr. Adams replied, "Whence is this morality to come? If the Christian religions and all the power of GOV has never produced it, what will? Yet this mad woman is for destroying the Christian religion". +Evil Spiritual Creatures were rejected to have unlimited influence in the US; which included David Hume, who Mr. Adams rejected by saying~ ",,,If ever there existed a wise fool, a learned idiot, a profound deep-thinking coxcomb, it was David Hume. As much worse than Voltaire and Rousseau as a sober decent libertine is worse than a rake"; and also stated, "The only equality of man that is true was taught by Jesus: Do as you would be done by,,,". // Pierre Samuel Dupont de Nemours, founder of the Dupont activity in America, conducted a study for Thomas Jefferson which proved that, "Most young Americans ,,,can read, write and cipher. Not more than four in a thousand are unable to write legibly-- even neatly"; and compared it to countries with low literacy and found that the difference was the fact that~ "in,,, countries [[where]] the Bible is read; it is considered a duty to read it to the children; and in that form of religion the sermons and liturgies in the language of the people ,,,increase and formulate ideas of responsibility"; Also he attributed the educational status was good in America because of reading the Bible and newspapers in the home (91). // Noah Webster in AD 1820 confirmed the high level of reading & writing in the USA, and likewise Frenchman Alexis de Tocqueville.

---T--- <u>Congress:</u> // <u>Congress member John Adams said</u>, "Suppose some nation in some distant Region, should take the Bible for their only law Book, and every member should regulate his conduct by the precepts there exhibited. Every member would be obliged in Conscience to temperance and frugality and industry, to justice and kindness and Charity towards his fellow men, and to Piety and Love, and reverence towards almighty God. In this Commonwealth, no man would impart his health by gluttony, drunkenness, or lust-- no man would sacrifice his most precious time to cards, or any other trifling and mean amusement --no man would steal or lie or any way defraud his neighbour, but would live in peace and good will with all men-- no man would blaspheme his maker or profane his worship, but a rational and manly, a sincere and unaffected Piety and devotion, would reign in all hearts. What a Eutopa, what a Paradise would this region be." (97a).

---T--- <u>Citizens as shared by FFOG John Adams:</u> // Christianity has "No other institution for education, no kind of political discipline, could diffuse this kind of necessary information, so universally among all ranks and descriptions of citizens. The duties and Rights of the man and the citizens are thus taught from early infancy to every creature." (97a). Also ",,,the duties of religion and morality comprehends a very extensive connection with society at large and the great interests of the public" (117).

---T--- <u>Citizens & Civilization</u>: // The most civilized countries are the most Christian countries in the world; and thus has the USA been at some times~ a good civilization.

---T--- <u>Christianity with the Holy Bible is the USA GOV Law Basis; as FFOG share</u>: // Noah Webster states, "The moral principle and precepts contained in the SCs ought to form the basis of all our civil constitutions and laws" and "All the miseries and evils which men suffer from vice, crime, ambition, injustice, oppression, slavery and war, proceed from their despising or neglecting the precepts contained in the Bible" (176). Also, "The opinion that human reason left without the constant control of Divine laws and commands will ,,,give duration to a popular government is as chimerical as the most extravagant of ideas that enter the head of a maniac ,,,Where will you find any code of laws among civilized men in which the commands and prohibitions are not founded on Christian principles? I need not specify the prohibition of murder, robbery, theft, and trespass" (175). // Joseph Story, "One of the beautiful boasts of our municipal jurisprudence is that Christianity is a part of the Common Law. There never has been a period in which the Common Law did not recognize Christianity as lying at its foundations. I verily believe Christianity necessary to the support of civil society" (183). // Daniel Webster, "The Christian religion~ its general principles~ must ever be regarded among us as the foundation of civil society" and "We seek to prevent in some measure the extension of the penal code by inspiring a salutary and conservative principle of virtue and of knowledge in an early age ,,,By general instruction we seek, as far as possible, to purify the whole moral atmosphere ,,,and to turn the strong current of feeling and opinion , as well as the censures of the law and the denunciations of religion, against immorality and crime" (147). // John Adams, "The study and practice of law,,, does not dissolve the obligations of morality and religion" (21). Also, "The moment the idea is admitted into society that property is not as sacred as the laws of God, and that there is not a force of law and public justice to protect it, anarchy and tyranny commence. If 'Thou shalt not covet,' and 'Thou shalt not steal," were not commandments of Heaven, they must be made inviolable precepts in every society, before it can be civilized or made free" (190). // Benjamin Rush, "I have always considered Christianity as the strong found of republicanism ,,,It is only necessary for republicanism to ally itself to the Christian religion to overturn all the corrupted political and religious institutions in the world" (97). // DeWitt Clinton, "The ethics, doctrines, and examples furnished by Christianity exhibit the best models for the laws." and "The sanctions of the Divine law ,,,cover the whole ,,,human action ,,,The laws which regulate our conduct are the laws of man and the laws of God" (177). // John Quincy Adams, "The law given from Sinai was a civil and municipal as well as a moral and religious code ,,,laws essential to the existence of men in society and most of which have been enacted by every nation which ever professed any code of laws. Vain indeed would be the search among the writings of profane antiquity ,,,to find so broad, so complete and so solid a basis for morality as this Decalogue (Ten Commandments) lays down." and "Human legislators can undertake only to prescribe the actions of men,; they acknowledge their inability to govern and direct the sentiments of the heart ,,,It is one of the greatest marks of Divine favor bestowed upon the children of Israel that the legislator (God) gave them rules not only of action, but for the government of the heart" (175). // William Findley, RW Soldier & US Congressman, states, "It pleased God to deliver, on Mount Sinai, a compendium of this holy law and to write it with His own hand on durable tables of stone. This law, which is commonly called the Ten Commandments or Decalogue ,,,was incorporated in the judicial law" (191). // John Witherspoon, "The Ten Commandments ,,,are the sum of the moral law" and "To PROMOTE true religion is the best and most effectual way of making a virtuous and regular people. Love to God and love to man is the substance of religion; when these prevail, civil laws will have little to do ,,,The Magistrate (or ruling part of any society) ought to encourage piety ,,,and make it an object of public esteem." and "Those who are vested with civil authority ought ,,,to promote religion and good morals among all under their government" (154). Also, "The first point of justice ,,,consists in piety; nothing certainly being so great a debt upon us as to render to the Creator and Preserver those acknowledges which are due to Him,,," (171).

---T--- <u>FFOG Congress, Executive</u>, all Declare Christianity as the Law Basis: // George Mason, "The laws of nature are the laws of God, whose authority can be superseded by no power on earth" (42). Does that say superseded by~ majority vote? or Judge? or legislature? No, it says none of those. Rather by Constitutional Law which is based on God of the Holy Bible. // Abraham Lincoln, "But for the Bible we could not know right from wrong. All things most desirable for man's welfare ,,,in it" (210). // George Washington, "Let us with caution indulge the supposition, that morality can be maintained without religion,,, reason and experience both forbid us to expect that National morality can prevail in exclusion of religious principle" (71).

---T--- <u>What is a Law System ? A system of MORALITY.</u> Now what sort of Beings do we exist as? As Spiritual Moral Beings !!

---T--- <u>Laws of God, the Gospel of Christ Jesus</u> (the Holy Bible); FFOG share: // John Quincy Adams~ "The people of the North American union, and of its constituent States, were associated bodies of civilized men and Christians in a state of nature, but not of anarchy. They were bound by the laws of God, which they all, and by the laws of the Gospel, which they nearly all, acknowledged as the rules of their conduct" (151). // Joseph Story~ "The promulgation of the great doctrines of religion, the being, and attributes, and providence of one Almighty God; the responsibility to Him for all our actions, founded on moral accountability; a future state of rewards and punishments; the cultivation of all the personal, social, and benevolent virtues; -- these never can be a matter of indifference in any well-ordered community. It is indeed difficult to conceive how any civilized society can well exist without them" (52a).

---T--- <u>Congress: Law making in the USA has~ +] strictness to some degree</u> applied; +] a Love strictness; +] and various standards applied to it: // It is limited & a Gift. The CC words, "herein granted" are identifying it is a gift to~ "granted". This is the attitude that Spiritual Moral people are to have in Employment Offices; the Employment Office has a limited amount of duties & Rights; And that is all it has; limited, not unlimited. // Laws are not done by one Branch making its own laws without any limits or regulations about what, when, where, etc. It is by the Branches working together and none can enact laws separately: The CC states, "All legislative Powers herein granted shall be vested in a Congress of the US, which shall consist of a Senate and House of Representatives"; +and must be in support of the CC (DOI & CON); +and not in opposition to the States Independency; +and gain assistance from the Presidential Branch; +and be approved by the Citizen Branch. // Legislation: is by definition, "the act or process of making a law or laws; having the power to make laws; the lawmaking branch of the GOV; to make or pass laws" (1a). // Congress is defined as: "any of various legislatures, especially the legislature of a republic" (1a). Thus again with legislature as its basis. // Neither Branch can enact laws separately. God is to be God of the Nation, and must be included; as 1ˢᵗ priority. The citizens (which is everyone), are not forced to trust Christ and follow Him; yet they must support such without changing. However, to be an Officer in Law Making Branch Offices, requires to be a Christian; and not infidel or false religion. // Every Officer in Congress or USA GOV is required to be Christian; in Law Making Positions; directly connected to Law Making. // Every Bill of Law must also have the Presidential Branch approval. // The CC cannot be opposed by Congress in making Laws. The very Congress itself would not exist without the CC. Their Right to exist is by citizens, Jesus, and the CC. Congress must abide by the Laws in the CC enforcing the CC by Laws that agree with it.

---T--- <u>Now what would an infidel have to do with</u> the CC ?? To be a USA Citizen requires that such agree to support the CC in public activities; and to some extent in private activities. They do not have to agree to accept Christ in their life and live by His Laws in private life.

---T--- <u>Citizens & Congress: Responsibility:</u> // FFOG Daniel Webster was asked, "What is the greatest thought that ever passed through your mind?"; and he said, "My accountability to God" (70).

-------------------- <u>MORE and FURTHER EVIDENCE SOURCES, Inclusive of HISTORICAL (Good Knowledge), Of LAW BASIS which FFOG UTILIZED and STUDIED and INCLUDED; of the Which are CHRIST LORD GOD BASED</u> -----------------

====== [CONCLUSION]: The MAGNA CARTA ~&~ The COMMON LAW Are LARGE PARTS Of The SOURCE Of THE USA LAW SYSTEM ~&~ ARE GODLY CHRISTIAN CENTERED LAW SYSTEMS:

---T--- <u>The Magna Carta is also included in the Common Law</u> as an influence to it and connected; as the Common Law was a developing system based on Christianity.

---T--- <u>Common law, considered with Attorney and Author John Whitehead and the Rutherford Institute, and in his book, "The Second American Revolution":</u> Mr. Whitehead has written, debated, and practiced in the area of constitutional law and human rights; his concern for the persecuted and oppressed led him, in 1982, to establish The Rutherford Institute, a nonprofit civil liberties and human rights organization. (rutherford.org). +Mr. Whitehead states that "Common Law is an age-old doctrine that developed by way of court decisions that applied the principles of the Bible to everyday situations. Judges simply decided their cases, often by making explicit reference to the Bible but virtually always within a framework of biblical values. Of these cases, rules were established that governed future cases." +Also states, "The common law was ,,,incorporated into the CON by direct reference in the Seventh Amendment. This amendment reads: "In suits at common law ,,,and no fact tried by jury, shall be otherwise re-examined in any court of the US than according to the rules of common law. By implication this means that the framers intended to be governed in practice as well as in principle by the higher law,,,". +Continuing he shares that, "Episcopalian theologian T.R. Ingram has observed that the reference point for the common law was in the Ten Commandments". Mr. Ingram said, "Christian men have always known that what we might call political liberty as part of all Christian liberty is a consequence of upholding the common law ,,,the Ten Commandments". +Mr. Whitehead states that people 'in England, such as Samuel Rutherford, wrote Christian legal DOCs which influenced the US REP in writing the CON and that the DOI and CON are covenants between the people and the GOV whereby to prevent abuse by each.'

---T--- <u>Britannica Concise Encyclopedia also states</u> the Common Law, as the Anglo-American law, and as referring to a "Body of law based on custom and general principles ,,,Common law has been administered in the courts of England since the Middle Ages; it is also found in the U.S. and in most of the British Commonwealth. It is distinguished from civil law."

---T--- <u>A note from The Free Dictionary</u> website, Copyright 1981-2005, by Gerald N. Hill & Kathleen T. Hill. All Right reserved; legaldictionary.thefreedictionary.com: "The common law became the basic law of most States due to the Commentaries on the Laws of England, completed by Sir William Blackstone in 1769, which became every American lawyer's bible. Today almost all common law has been enacted into statutes with modern variations by all the States except Louisiana which is still influenced by the Napoleonic Code. In some States the principles of common law are so basic they are applied without reference to statute."

---T--- <u>Amendment 7 of the USA</u> CON has the Common Law in it: // "Trial by Jury in Civil Cases. Ratified 12/15/1791. In Suits at common law, where the value in controversy shall exceed twenty dollars, the right of trial by jury shall be preserved, and no fact tried by a jury, shall be otherwise re-examined in any Court of the US, than according to the rules of the common law."

---T--- <u>Bill of RIGHTS:</u> // One of the Bill of Rights (BOR) is against "double jeopardy" - the right not to be compelled to give evidence against oneself; due process of law; not tried twice for the same crime; no witness against self - self incrimination; grand jury for major crimes required; much of this BOR came from English Law & The Magna Charta.

---T--- <u>Did you know that the USA law foundation</u> is based on the English Common Law, which has a Holy Biblical foundation. Holy Biblical Common Law: // I paraphrase and summarize this historical account from the source, Judge Moore's Jesus Saves Ministry, as follows (18a) in triple brackets: {[{+ // History and basis of Common Law ~ Christian heritage and Christianity of the Common Law: The Timeline: ~ The Mosaic Law around BC 1400; ~ King Brut (a migrant Trojan) built the city of 'New Troy' (now named London) ~ around BC 1150. // Timeline of starting at BC 510 and forward, includes a British King Dunvall Moelmud proclaimed God's Moral Law with all of its judicial proceedings to be the Common Law of the land. // At BC 75, 'New Troy' was renamed London by King Lludd. // Later in time, came Julius Caesar, a Roman tyrant who attacked the Briton's in war, in which the Briton's battled twice to defend them off. // The city of Westminster began from London, where kings did their crowning. This included William the Conqueror, of AD 1066 and onward. This crowning involved the Stone of Scone, also origins of earlier Iro-Scotic kings used in crowning in Scotland and also before that; even by kings in Ireland. The crowning item of 'Westminster' (according to the Encyclopedia Britannica 1929 American edition, the stone is of Iro-Scotic origin, and that tradition identifies it with Jacob's pillow at Bethel recorded in the Holy Bible, Gen28:10-22). // The magnificent Magna Carta enacted for Britain's constitution is a prime EX: of good law and liberties from ancient times; AD 1215. // After this, in Westminster, important legislative enactments came about with King Edward (the First) and Parliament; AD 1275. The first statute (titled - Westminster I) constituted a code of law - but also included some unwritten law into the written code; AD 1285, The second statute, (titled - Westminster II) established different judicial systems and systems regarding land ownership; AD 1290, The third statute, (titled - Westminster III), ceased subinfeudation. // From AD 1360 forward, came John Wycliffe, a Protestant, Reformer, whom some claim Dan12:11 relates to; Wycliffe's work, theologically and politically, assisted much advance; encouraged the sole authority of the Word of God, and to include such in government, with God and His Laws. John's patriotism, expositions opposed forms of false Christianity including a false priesthood (including the Pope), the transubstantiation, etc.; resulted in him being excommunicated and banned by the Vatican. Wycliffe was slanderously accused for the Tylerite Rebellion of AD 1381; he was able to stay alive and continued on these same missions until AD 1384 when he died. By him and his fellow workers, various people were influenced to carry on the truth, such as Huss and others in Bohemia, which influenced Martin Luther; also in England and Scotland; many people joined Wycliffe in the British Isles and became very influential (half the population of Scotland & England is reported); persecution was terrible. But remnants remained, called the Lollards, and assisted the reformation. // In AD 1470 came English Chief Justice, Sir John Fortescue; he accomplished a study of Ancient British Common Law; he traced British Law back through the BC 1190 Trojan Brut and then back to the BC 1440 Moses himself; his conclusions are that "the customs of the English are not only good, but the best.". // Then came Sir Thomas de Littleton who similarly upheld the Anglo-British law, and not the Roman nor the Roman-French, for Property, Procedure, and Persons. // In AD 1536, Welsh-British King Henry Tudor VIII achieves Union between England and Wales. // In AD 1615, Irish Articles, composed by Dr. James Ussher, from Ireland, a Puritan Archbishop, and who was later the Westminster Assembly Commissioner; a scholar, and purposed to prove the apostolic antiquity of British Christianity; thought Protestantism as a revival of Proto-Protestant Culdee Christianity, which was prevalent in Ireland and other parts of the Isles to the end of eleventh century; Ussher's AD 1615 Irish Articles influenced greatly the legal and political situations and was utilized for the Westminster Confession later on; other influences on the Westminster Assembly was in Holland and beyond, also the AD 1618-19 Synod of Dordt. // In the AD 1600's there were many Christians in the Westminster Assembly, many Puritans, and some Episcopalians, Erastians, Presbyterians, Congregationalists, a few others possibly; English, Scots, a few Irish, Welsh, and French. // History then reveals a dominant and common views of the Westminster Assembly Commissioners regarding the calling of the magistrate; names of some of these Commissioners include Burgess, Calamy, Coleman, Gillespie, Henderson, Herle, Lightfoot and Marshall (all Commissioners), and their extant works, including that of a Christonomous, which was common. Also with the work of Samuel Rutherford, including his grand document, Lex Rex. Such messages in the written content is also in Commissioners Seaman, Spurstowe, Temple, Thorowgood, Vines, Wilkinson, Wilson, Woodcock, and Dr. James Ussher material. And what is that centered message? The Law of God. It is furthermore observed in the Westminster Standards (Catechisms). // Puritan Rev. Dr. Thomas, AD 1600's, wrote to encourage a catechism with one standard for all of British Isles (Scotland, Ireland, and other geographical colonies), which includes a legal system with the 10 Commandments, the "light of Nature", the moral law (indicated to be the 10 Commandments), and of protecting human life, morality, property, veracity, and contentment. The Light of Nature is stated to be the conscience and internal laws of truth, which order humans, societies, and governments; that even after The Fall remains in all Adam's descendents hearts, and that God bound man at creation to a covenant of works. This One Catechism listed 8 rules for comprehension and application of the 10 Commandments as, "perfection; spirituality; interlockingness; contrariety; timeliness; synecdoche; enforcibility; and assistance." Also included these relations~ "Christ's Great Commandment of Love precisely, [[Mat 5:43-44; 22:38-40]] Lev19:18 and Deu6:5. Judicial laws and Cases of Moses applications are included, and refers to Christ the King and His later full reign as King, and of assistance to bringing in the Lord's kingdom, pertinent to the "Lord's Prayer". Furthermore he continues, writing for Church purity, civil magistrate overseeing and cooperation, and to wait for God's providence, the "daily bread" and the victory over all evil and enemies. Holy SC is all through the writings and systems. Responsibility is stated to be to the Church and State for members and the population of persons, regarding the practice or proclamation contrarily to the "light of nature"; because why? Because the "light of nature" and the "law of nature" are God's Lordship. It included Sabbath Laws & offenses of it. Includes~ Providential cares of Christ for Christians expressed because He is Prophet, Priest, and King; Ceremonial laws of the OT are not applicable; Christ's Great Commission, Mat28, to spread worldwide; public and officer oaths. The relation of Church & State is studied and organized that GOV is never Over the Church but each cooperating with each other, including prayer for GOV. Particpants involved include Rev. Professor Dr. Shaw & Rev. Dr. John Richard de Witt. Again Holy SC is the basis for all the writings. // At this time in the Parliament of England, existed 121 Puritan Theologians, 20 Members of the House of Commons, 10 Peers of the House of Lords; and which has Holy Bible mixed with judicial laws, sundry laws, moral duties, and a catechism~ called the, Westminster Sum of Saving Knowledge. // There were religious wars in Britain (also known as Britain's civil wars) from AD 1642-49 between Romanizers and Protesters (Anglo-Romanism and Puritan Protestantism); which Dr. B.B. Warfield identifies the two sides (groups of Beings) as because of the tyranny of Charles the First in opposition to the English Constitution, (monarchy vivi Parliament); thus the 2 groups are one with King Charles the First, and the other following the Parliament and its 'King Pym'. A similarity of this occurred again, later, because British Rulers again warred against the USA, and were tyrants, when their own laws were against their own Rulers, and nevertheless, at least including those of the Laws of God, or Laws of nature (conscience). All history is not here reported, but there was much denominational disputes and Catholicism and protestant issues, and governmental relations with church. // One event, AD 1648, occurred where the English defeated some invading Scots, who as defeated awoke to their senses, and made confessions with solemnness of public sins, breaches of covenant, treasons against God and the English, requested forgiveness, and rededicated themselves to cooperation with Britain. Then approximately the same time, the monarchy in England was ceased, with the English army overcoming 'Charles Stuart' who was sentenced with a beheading for pronounced guilty of treason. Also at this time the Clergy was making Covenant which constructed organizing with GOV and Church. The Westminster Assembly was ordained to Parliament, to which Colonial Americans were invited to attendance, so as to form a relationship between Ireland, Scotland, England, and the colonies in America after the terrible wars; and an international relationship, called the AD 1643 Solemn League and Covenant, which then included a Westminster Form of Government in AD 1645; which all includes a Westminster Confession of Faith. By AD 1646, it includes the "Light of Nature; the Necessity of Holy SC; the Triune God; Creation; Providence; the Covenant and Law of God; Christian Liberty; Oaths; the Civil Magistrate; Marriage; Property; and Councils to advise Governments." Much political relations and laws were included. // History was stated, purposed to base situations on God, and relate Common Law to God, proving that even before Moses Law, our relatives in Europe was from Noah, Japheth (Noah's son), the ancient Gomeric Cymri, was in Britain, and its law was the God-given Common Law which they learned from Japheth who learned from Noah. Japhethitic Gomer otherwise known as the Brythonic Celts and Japhethitic Javan, and otherwise known as the Greeks and the Trojans ~ vs, "would dwell in the tents of Shem" (Gen9:27). // Chief Justice Sir Edward Coke of the AD 1600's stated that all human law was originally the Common Law (Laws of God common to all people, as spiritual and of the conscience), Gen1:26-28; 2:15-24; 9:1-19, and said, "Unity and consent in such diversity of things, proceeds only from God the Fountain and Founder of all good laws and constitutions." Psalm 36:9; "diversity of things" ~ is referring to that which is observed observable in the various factors influencing the laws; the Trinity ("Multiform Maker"), ("Multiformity") as the universe, of the Triune God, has various forms, The Fall of man problematical areas, mankind's dispersion throughout the earth. // The Common Law of Britain was a better legal system than other places on earth, since it was closer to God's original Common Law for man; and J. Coke states the law is itself a light and that Solomon said the "Candle" of God is the Light of Nature and related it to Pro6:23, 20:27, thus being the conscience. // Justice Coke states that systems of law, as 2Cor6:15 apply as "If a Christian king should conquer a kingdom of an infidel ,,,ipso facto the laws of the infidel are abrogated. For they be not only against Christianity; but [also] against the Law of God and of Nature contained in the Decalogue." // Justice Coke also reports historically that "Brut(us), the first king of this land ~ as soon as he had settled himself in his kingdom ~ for the safe and peaceable government of his people, wrote a book in the Greek tongue, calling it the Law of the Britons ,,,He collected the same out of the laws of the Trojans", also known as the Darda-nians at the Darda-nelles. Genesis 38:29 & 1st Kings 4:31 & 1st Chron 2:6. "This King [Brut] ,,,died after the creation of the world 2860 years, and before the incarnation of Christ 1103 years ~ Samuel then being Judge of Israel ,,,That the laws of the Ancient Britons, their contracts and other instruments, and the records and proceedings of their judges, were written and 'sentenced' in the Greek tongue ~ it is plain and evident ,,,Our chronologers ,,,say that 441 years before the incarnation of Christ, Mulumucius ~ by some called Dunwallo Mulumucius, by some Dovenant [Moelmud or Molmutius] ~ did write two books of the laws of the Britons ,,,the Statute Law and the Common Law ,,,356 years before the birth of Christ, Martia Prova ~ queen and wife of King Gwintelin ~ wrote a book of the laws of England in the British language." // Justice Coke also shares that much of history was deeply and regrettably lost about Britain. // However we know enough to show the following facts and coordination with the Holy Bible as these following are shared by the website: 1} Our Common Law Origins with God, not in relativism or opinions; 2} The Common Law of various parts of the British Isles was existent prior to Christ's birth; 3} Britain had, with all probability, within 5 years after Calvary, received the Gospel; 4} Christianity was included in the British Common Law over these decades by Christian Culdees, and with certainty this was far advanced in time before the conquest of Britain by the Anglo ~Saxons and the subsequent semi~Romanization; 5} The British, American, and Australian legal systems have resemblances of Christian law far developed. Thus consider this Holy Bible vs., "Behold, My Servant! ,,,I have put My Spirit upon Him. He shall bring forth judgment unto the Gentiles ,,,He shall not fail ,,,He shall set judgment in the Earth: and the Isles shall wait for His Law." Isa42:1-4. // During the AD 1600's Oliver Cromwell was an effective Officer (in England) who did accomplish some Christian things and supported the Common Law, also known as Commonwealth Government, which had a written constitution where Cromwell's powers and duties were defined and stated that, "the Christian religion ,,,contained in the HSCs" was to be "the public profession of these nations" for all of the Isles and colonies; all the various members and participants, (people included are Christonomous Theologians, Gillespie, Gilbert, Owen, and others) called for a Christian government, like the Magna Charta, which teaches "liberty of conscience" and separation of powers. The Laws of Moses were also included in Law Systems constructed by~ Puritan Sir Matthew Hale (appointed a Judge of the Common Bench by Cromwell) who wrote out a Code of Common Law proclaiming "Christianity is parcel of the laws of England" ~ so that "to reproach the Christian religion" is to speak evil, and also contained an approval for the "conviction of witches". // Britain, Scotland, and Ireland were formed into one Parliament, AD 1654, and there were property Rights of sort. Excess central government power was offset by Mr. Cromwell's Commonwealth establishment of 11 military districts. Mr. Cromwell was a Puritan and opposed Romish doctrines; he declined an offer to be a king over the Isles. // In AD 1657, Parliament made an enactment titled, "Humble Petition and Advice to Protector Cromwell" which provided freedom for the existence and practice of various Christian DENs, and protection by legal punishment against public opposition to the Christian religion. // About Mr. Cromwell as follows: +threatened war against Romish Dukes for murdering and persecuting workers with John Wycliffe, also called the Waldensians and Lollards. +John Milton commended him for heroic efforts in defending the Saints +His dying prayer (AD 1658), shared that he was in covenant with God and asked God that "those who look too much upon Thy instruments" should instead "depend more upon Thyself."; also requested God's pardon for his enemies, those who want "to trample upon the dust of a poor worm" as himself, for "they are Thy people too." +He is likened by historians to George Washington, and his work is what assisted Britain to be in God's favor for the spread of Christianity and a great empire, Australia's Commonwealth government, and the advance of Puritanism in America. // After Mr. Cromwell's death, however, monarchy was somewhat reformed and King Charles, with some lies, started persecuting Christians, including Puritans, and America. // Puritan Sir Matthew Hale was Chief Justice of England at the time. // In AD 1689, British Bill of Rights or Act for Declaring Rights and Liberties was an advancement for Christianity, including Puritans; also known as "Glorious Revolution" in the British Isles; this occurred in spite of various Kings not supportive of Christianity. // In AD 1702-14 was the reign of the Protestant Queen Anne. After her was a German King in England. // Sir William Blackstone wrote his Commentaries on the Common Law of England, AD 1765. He researched history and connected the Common Law from the creation of the World, Britain's first, and through various ages and dangers, including a legal system called, 'Romanesque' Civil Law and Romish Canon Law, and said they were not godly enough to excel British Common Law. This effort was encouragement to the American colonies for the Common Law. // British Commonwealth was encouraged in Queen Elizabeth II's AD 1953 Coronation Oath and Britain's Prime Minister Thatcher, in AD 1988, who stated to the Church of Scotland that "we are a nation whose ideals are founded on the Bible." // History of Christian efforts, reveal that westward expansion of Christianity was occurring since Christ time, as Proto-Protestant Celto-British Christians reached the New World by AD 560; established colonies in North America by AD 830; Celto-Icelandic Christians were colonizing by AD 985; a colony of about 300 Culdee Christian Celto-Brythonic Welshmen under Prince Madoc was started in North America around AD 1170; British Calvinists plans for North America occurred about AD 1583. // The English Common Law with Mosaic basis was brought with the American Colonies in the AD 1600's and evidenced by AD 1629 Charter of Massachusetts, John Cotton's AD 1633 theocracy, the AD 1639 North American municipal confederations of local Government, the AD 1643 "New England Confederation" between Connecticut and Massachusetts, the "ecclesiastically con-foeder-at", the AD 1648 Cambridge Platform 'Con-soc-iation' ~ which includes the AD 1643-47 Westminster Standards, and the others in AD 1648, that of 55 New England law codes, and that all the States had Christian constitutions and catechism's at the Declaration of Independence time. End of paraphrases from (18a). +}]} }}>>> Now let it be clear, that the herebefore mentioned, is not about some geographic boundry as Britain or some people that lived somewhere, as those in Britain. This is not thoughts and feelings of "Racism" or some other folly. +This is about Divine providential and Divine intervention throughout history; the work of God assisting humanity. And He desires to do the same for all people as He loves all people equally. And we should not with all respect lose this law system that was developed. It is very obvious that the FFOG reviewed all these counselors and developed a very similar system for the USA GOV.

---T--- The Common Law is Identified and Stated 2 times in the 7th Amendment.

---T--- Many historians testify that the CC (DOI & CON) are derived from the Holy Bible, Magna Carta, English Bill of Rights, and Westminster Law system (63).

---T--- The Common Law system was included, but more prioritively was the Christian Law system, which is also the Common Law's basis; the 2 were intended/ purposed to be~ connected and known that they were connected: // Law basis: England's good Law System and history, including that of Mr. Cromwell who supported Christianity was studied and included; Although some Kings of England were sometimes actually against Christian Law and England's Law. // GOV Officials abuse of citizens and of the CC is similar to what has occurred in past times of other countries. // DOC: "The Debates in the Several State Conventions on the Adoption of the Federal CON [Elliot's Debates, Volume 1] MARYLAND. The province of Maryland was included originally in the patent of the Southern or Virginia Company; and, upon the dissolution of that company, it reverted to the crown. King Charles I., on the 20th June, 1632, granted it by patent to Cecilius Calvert, Lord Baltimore,,, The territory was bounded by a right line, drawn from Watkins's Point, on Chesapeake Bay, to the ocean, on the east; thence to that part of the estuary of Delaware, on the north, which lieth under the 40th degree, where New England is terminated; thence, in a right line, by the degree aforesaid, to the meridian of the fountain of Potomac; thence, following its course by the farther bank, to its confluence with the Chesapeake, and thence to Watkins's Point. The first emigration made under the auspices of Lord Baltimore was in 1632, and consisted of about 200 gentlemen of considerable fortune and rank, and their adherents, being chiefly Roman Catholics. "He laid the foundation of this province (says Chalmers) upon the broad basis of security to property and of freedom of RELIGION, granting, in absolute fee, fifty acres of land to every emigrant; establishing CHRISTIANITY agreeably to the old common law, [[see the Common Law system is established on Christianity]] of which it is a part, without allowing preeminence to any particular SECT. The wisdom of his choice soon converted a dreary wilderness into a prosperous colony." The first legislative assembly of Maryland, held by the freemen at large, was in 1634--1635; but little of their proceedings is known. No acts appear to have been adopted until 1638--1639, when provision was made, in consequence of an increase of the colonists, for a representative assembly, called the House of Assembly, chosen by the freemen; and the laws passed by the Assembly, and approved by the proprietary, or his lieutenant, were to be of full force. At the same session, an act, which may be considered as in some sort a Magna Charta, was passed, declaring, among other things, that "HOLY CHURCH, within this province, shall have all her rights and liberties; that the inhabitants shall have all their rights and liberties according to the great charter of England;" and that the goods of debtors, if not sufficient to pay their debts, shall be sold and distributed pro rata, saving debts to the proprietary. In 1649, an act was passed punishing blasphemy, or denying the HOLY Trinity, with death, and confiscation of goods and lands. Under the protectorate of Cromwell, roman Catholics were expressly denied any protection in the province; and all others, "who profess faith in GOD by JESUS CHRIST, though differing in judgment from the doctrine, worship, or discipline, publicly held forth," were not to be restrained from the exercise of their RELIGION. In 1696, the CHURCH of England was established in the province; and in 1702, the liturgy, and rites, and ceremonies, of the CHURCH of England, were required to be pursued in all the CHURCHes--with such toleration for dissenters, however, as was provided for in the act of William and Mary. And the introduction of the test and abjuration acts, in 1716, excluded all Roman Catholics from office. It appears to have been a policy, adopted at no great distance of time after the settlement of the colony, to provide for the public registration of conveyances of real estates. In the silence of the statute book until 1715, it is presumed that the system of descents of intestates was that of the parent country. In that year an act passed which made the estate partible among all the children; and the system thus introduced has, in its substance, never since been departed from. Maryland too, like the other colonies was early alive to the importance of possessing the sole power of internal taxation; and accordingly, in 1650, it was declared that no taxes should be levied without the consent of the General Assembly. Upon the revolution of 1688, the government of Maryland was seized into the hands of the crown, and was not again restored to the proprietary until 1716. From that period no interruption occurred until the American Revolution".

---T--- <u>Common Law:</u> // In 1938 US case Erie vs. Thompkins, the Common Law was dismissed and replaced with statutory law and case law. // Congress passes and enacts laws of the Land based on the dimensions of the CON powers provided them and after completing a process of evaluations and Checks & Balances ~ which should include the citizens in some part on interpretation. // It is not actually a legal system that is according to the USA system. // It is exclusive of God, the CC (DOI & CON) in its rightness.

---T--- <u>Common Law:</u> // Other names for it are "Divine Law". // The Judicial Case that dismissed the Common law was an illegality. The DOI, CON, and all DOC and FFOG included the Common Law to support God & the Holy Bible.

---T--- <u>The Magna Carta was originally</u> written in Latin and had a greetings "to the archbishops, bishops, abbots, earls, barons, justices, foresters, sheriffs, reeves, ministers, and to all the bailiffs, and faithful subjects". The priority here is stating that Christianity, and religion thereof, is the English GOV, and to be the basis of it. Notice that all citizens are included in "faithful subjects". Furthermore "faithful subjects" excludes evil supporters.

+++

251

---------- **Chapter 8** ,,,,,,,,,,,, **What Can We Do ???** ------------

---------- <u>WHAT WE CAN DO</u>

---T--- Listed as Follows:

T= Word of mouth. T= Not Evil Speaking; rather good speaking. T= Citizens. T= Declare Revolution Restoration. T= Refuse to pay taxes. T= Leave the nation. T= Revolution~ Total change of GOV & system. T= Reverse the judicial decisions. T= Unify. T= Educate with DOCs and Holy Bible. T= Live righteous. T= Have God as God; no idolatry as Self-idol; no selfishness; selfless vivi selfmore. T= Return to the Holy Bible for the Law Basis; Common Law. T= Republican form of GOV. T= Remain ignorant and ignore it. T= We can commune prayer with God to remove the illegal Spiritual moral creatures; remove the illegal methods enforcing the Laws. T= We may not be able to remove them and reverse or void the laws if we do not do it. T= We may not be able to get enough Christians to vote rightness. T= Vote. T= We need to gather ourselves in multitudes to do these things. T= Force may be needed. T= If we have the Laws of God and land together, the earth is the Lords, and God's laws; and if such will not abide and are doing evil, then we may ask God about such. T= God has, such as personal studies and those of for EX, William Law (248), that when children are involved, it becomes a serious and effectual desire that God contemplates the removal of such societies; Because they are hurting them, and making a society of total evil. This is a decision by God to protect the innocent, a sort of self-defense; and it crosses the line between mercy & punishment, making of such a serious situation that God decides to stop it. T= We can spread the word. T= We can enlist godly Lawyers who will take the situation. T= This is an Amendment that has been done more currently; I am not sure of the status of it.~ The Istook Amendment. At one time the Bill reads: "To secure the people's right to acknowledge God according to the dictates of conscience: The people's right to pray and to recognize their religious beliefs, heritage or traditions on public property, including schools, shall not be infringed. The GOV shall not require any person to join in prayer or other religious activity; initiate or designate school prayers, discriminate against religion, or deny equal access to a benefit on account of religion." +Although these thoughts are not totally accurate, it does contain a medium amount of truth from the CC (DOI & CON). Our GOV is not to support false religion nor false Christianity; The Free Will is not forced; but neither are the falsities provided a place to have public assembly & advertisement. Hence the Bill is in error in parts. T= An invitation is graciously provided to all from the Lord; Psa91.

+++

------------ Chapter 9 ,,,,,,,,,,,,,, GOVERNMENT SYSTEM ------------

What is included herein this Chapter are Facts or Truth that are Necessary in the Current USA GOV system. ~~ They are to be included and were part of the intention/ purpose design by the FFOG. Omission is part of lying, stealing, treason; depending on the Intention, knowledge, situations, and abilities of Spiritual Moral Creature Beings ~~ The Following is not an all-Inclusive chapter, providing all the necessary parts, but rather submits some good Basics, some necessary Basic parts; some Principles.

-- GOVERNMENT SYTSEM:

---T--- Some better clarification needed: // It is strongly recommend that clarification of the DOI and CON be made to institute properly the Christ's Christian form more clearly. Mat6:10; Luk11:2-"Your kingdom come. Your will be done in earth, as it is in heaven". These HSC were basis that the FFOG used for the USA existence~ communion (fellowship with God in personal lives, as God; and for God's will as a Christian mission nation location. Although the FFOG started and completed much, they~ +had no sure basis; +had many trials, troubles, and temptations occurring at the time; +had no complete experiential system to base on; +had the past to study, and the future to consider; +had preventive techniques, which includes any evil twisting of their work; as to include. // Hence the CC and the supporting DOCs need to be put together. As this Book proved. Hence to assist faster increase of goodness, and better prevention of evil. // For the FFOG, it was a difficult project to distinguish how to word the laws without providing statements that could be abused by the GOV; such as what occurred with the GOV they were trying to avoid. Thus they worded it the best they knew how at the time. And because it is a system of Principle Law, it makes a system both "open" and "closed" and "more applicable". The danger is that Principle Law, if it gets in control by an evil mind & heart, or even an unknowledgeable Spiritual Immoral person, or who has untrained thinking, or who is trained in a differing falsity of god, then such has potential for wrong~ both to the evil and to spiritual moral people who do not know Principle Law. // Furthermore the supporting DOCs, which are actually part of the CC, show applications of the Principle Laws in the CC, and what specific definitions there were of the CC. // The Words of the CC (DOI & CON) have provided the proof, and are supported by the Supporting Documents and Supporting Records.

-- POLITICAL PARTIES:

---T--- There are some political parties that do include some truths that are helpful. They are: Libertarian Party; Constitutional Party; Tea Party. And especially the Constitution Party, because they support the Holy SCs more quantitatively. However, the Constitution Party has had some major problems in their Platform, which are against the CC (DOI & CON); and are anti-Christian. Thus serious changes must be made before such is totally a Christian system; and as true to the USA GOV system; as pertaining to their platform at the time of AD 2011. The ability of us to enhance the political system, GOV system, that our FFOG intended/ purposed to do is very needful and right and requested by them. Although these mentioned "parties" have some truths, they all do remain short of the Gospel concerns that our FFOG affectionately, considerately, and rightly intended. This Book is not for debating these "parties". The Republican and Democratic Party both have some truths in them, the Republican more than the other.

-- ENHANCEMENT / AMENDMENTS:

---T--- <u>The FFOG had to start from a</u> level of comprehension that was somewhat lesser than ours and yet somewhat higher also. The lesser area was that they did not have as much a basis to build on; because there was no form yet, as a starting Nation; not as much as we have now that is. Although they did have the State Constitutions, the research thus far, and the historical studies of Europe, including Britain which we know did very much goodness at times and in subjects to assist them and provide a good basis. Because the State CONs had been developed, and the good laws and GOV in England had been developed on a Christian basis, there were useful models or patterns. England was in a civil rebellion, with evil people in the land attempting to reverse the Christian progress that had attempted to help. Furthermore the FFOG were in much conflict at the time to prevent and overcome evil both from the past, present war, and future prevention of any arising of Spiritual Creature Folks that would abuse the system and pervert it to evil. Hence with no full basis and all the trials, troubles, temptations of evil, and the past and future to all consider, gave them so much to work on, that it, doubtlessly, was excessively a serious amount; And in addition, the lack of any system that they co/ know by experience that would work in their situation.

-- STATEHOOD APPLICATION:

---T--- <u>God, Creator, Supreme Ruler,</u> Divine Providence, Lord Jesus Christ, Christianity, Christian DEN, secondary doctrines, expressions, is also a very needed part of State GOV.

-- CHECKS & BALANCES:

---T--- <u>Checks & Balances System:</u> // From the meetings in forming the CON, the following is a DOC of Congress Meetings Notes in the Table of Contents (Index), in AD 1778-89. What this provides, is the Checks & Balances system, including cautions which were very much intended: "Defence of its Omission not satisfactory; Precaution in granting Powers ,,,Legislative Power controlled by Vice-President's Vote ,,, Senatorial Term of Service; thirteen Councillors would destroy Presidential Responsibility,,,, President's Election on fair Principles; his Nominations ,,, States would not confederate without an equal Voice in the Formation of Treaties; Separation of Powers, ,,, Treaty-making Power, in all Countries, placed in the Executive Department; ,,, Mr. James Galloway - Congress; Apprehension that it may perpetuate itself ,,, Yeas and Nays; one fifth required ,,, Obedience to two Governments ,,, Senatorial Term; Powers of the Senate; Reference to British GOV ,,, Elections; Control by general GOV; executive, legislative, and judicial, separate, an Improvement ,,, President's Power over the Military; his Council, their Opinion to be given in Writing; EX of England ,,, Surrender of Territory without an Act of Parliament; relative Influence of the two Houses of Parliament, ,,, Rulers should be watched; Amendments proposed by the four States ... No Danger from the Apprehension of Aristocracy; Commons an Overmatch for King and Lords ... ,,, Senate's Power ought to counteract that of the House, to preserve State Sovereignty,,,, Exclusive Legislation; States will stipulate; Insult to Congress in 1783; Powers enumerated, excluded from all others; Abuse of Power; Non-Adoption out of the Union; State of the Union in 1776; anticipates the Interest of the First Congress; Importance of framing the first Code of Laws, ... ,,,, Contends for a Bill of Rights; Power, Jurisdiction, and Right, not given up, remain in the States; Objects to a Revision of Facts by Federal Court, and concurrent Jurisdiction dangerous ... ,,, Boundary of a Bill of Rights wanted ...,,, Mr.JOSEPH TAYLOR--Wording, "We, the People," an assumed Power ...,,, Powers; no Parallel between Congress and Parliament ... ,,, Mr. MACLAINE -- Distinction between a Monarchy and Republic...,,, Vice-President's Powers ...,,, Congress, its Powers limited and enumerated ...". // This only shows the titles of the subjects that were discussed and not any conclusions. It is a Table of Contents format.
---T--- <u>The Citizens are another</u> part of the USA GOV System, a Branch of it: This DOC is part of the Table of Contents from the Congress Notes in forming the CON from AD 1778 (the indexes): "Powers ought to be competent to the public Safety ... 95 -- Sovereignty of the States; Inequality of Suffrage in making Treaties, 125".
---T--- <u>EV that the GOV is</u> to be responsible to God, of the DOI. DOC portion from Table of Contents, Congress Notes AD 1778-89: "Power without Responsibility ... 119".
---T--- <u>Checks & Balances - CONGRESS</u> MEETING NOTES, 1778-89: // "They may trample on the rights of the people of North Carolina if there be not sufficient guards and checks. I only mentioned this to show that there may be misconstructions, and that, in so important a case as a constitution, every thing ought to be clear and intelligible, and no ground left for disputes."
---T--- <u>Following is a system of Checks &</u> Balances and a provision for Amending areas: // From the Congress Meeting Notes for forming of the CON, 1778-89: "I wish not to be so understood as to be so averse to this system, as that I should object to all parts of it ,,,though it appears to me that I would not have agreed to any proposal but the amendment of the Confederation. If there were any security for the liberty of the people, I would, for my own part, agree to it. But in this case, as millions yet unborn are concerned, and deeply interested in our decision, I would have the most positive and pointed security. I shall therefore hope that, before this house will proceed to adopt this CON, they will propose such

254

amendments to it as will make it complete; and when amendments are adopted, perhaps I will be as ready to accede to it as any man. One thing will make it aristocratical. Its powers are very indefinite. There was a very necessary clause in the Confederation, which is omitted in this system. That was a clause declaring that every power, &c., not given to Congress, was reserved to the states. The omission of this clause makes the power so much greater. Men will naturally put the fullest construction on the power given them. Therefore lay all restraint on them, and form a plan to be understood by every gentleman of this committee, and every individual of the community. Mr. SPAIGHT. Mr. Chairman, I am one of those who formed this CON. The gentleman says, we exceeded our powers. I deny the charge. We were sent with a full power to amend the existing system. This involved every power to make every alteration necessary to meliorate and render it perfect. It cannot be said that we arrogated powers altogether inconsistent with the object of our delegation. There is a clause which expressly provides for future amendments, and it is still in your power. What the Convention has done is a mere proposal. It was found impossible to improve the old system without changing its very form; for by that system the three great branches of GOV are blended together. All will agree that the concession of a power to a GOV so constructed is dangerous. The proposing a new system, to be established by the assent and ratification of nine states, arose from the necessity of the case. It was thought extremely hard that one state, or even three or four states, should be able to prevent necessary alterations. The very refractory conduct of Rhode Island, in uniformly opposing every wise and judicious measure, taught us how impolitic it would he to put the general welfare in the power of a few members of the Union. It was, therefore, thought by the Convention, that, if so great a majority as nine states should adopt it, it would be right to establish it. It was recommended by Congress to the state legislatures to refer it to the people of their different states. Our Assembly has confirmed what they have done, by proposing it to the consideration of the people. It was there, and not here, that the objection should have been made. This Convention is therefore to consider the CON, and whether it be proper for the GOV of the people of America; and had it been proposed by any one individual, under these circumstances, it would be right to consider whether it be good or bad. The gentleman has insinuated that this CON, instead of securing our liberties, is a scheme to enslave us. He has produced no proof, but rests it on his bare assertion-- an assertion which I am astonished to hear, after the ability with which every objection has been fully and dearly refuted in the course of our debates. I am, for my part, conscious of having had nothing in view but the liberty and happiness of my country; and I believe every member of that Convention was actuated by motives equally sincere and patriotic. (p) He says that it will tend to aristocracy. Where is the aristocratical part of it? It is ideal. I always thought that an aristocracy was that GOV where the few governed the many, or where the rulers were hereditary. This is a very different GOV from that. I never read of such an aristocracy. The first branch is representatives chosen freely by the people at large. This must be allowed upon all hands to be democratical. The next is the Senate, chosen by the people, in a secondary manner, through the medium of their delegates in the legislature, This cannot be aristocratical. They are chosen for six years, but one third of them go out every second year, and are responsible to the state legislatures. The President is elected for four years. By whom? By those who are elected in such manner as the state legislatures think proper. I hope the gentleman will not pretend to call this an aristocratical feature. The privilege of representation is secured in the most positive and unequivocal terms, and cannot be evaded. (p) The gentleman has again brought on the trial by jury. The Federal Convention, sir, had no wish to destroy the trial by jury. It was three or four days before them. There were a variety of objections to any one mode. It was thought impossible to fall upon any one mode but what would produce some inconveniences. I cannot now recollect all the reasons given. Most of them have been amply detailed by other gentlemen here. I should suppose that, if the representatives of twelve states, with many able lawyers among them, could not form any unexceptionable mode, this Convention could hardly be able to do it. (p) As to the subject of religion, I thought what had been said would fully satisfy that gentleman and every other. No power is given to the general GOV to interfere with it at all. Any act of Congress on this subject would be a usurpation. (p) No sect is preferred to another. Every man has a right to worship the Supreme Being in the manner he thinks proper. No test is required. All men of equal capacity and integrity, are equally eligible to offices. Temporal violence might make mankind wicked, but never religious. A test would enable the prevailing sect to persecute the rest. I do not suppose an infidel, or any such person, will ever be chosen to any office, unless the people themselves be of the same opinion. He says that Congress may establish ecclesiastical courts. I do not know what part of the CON warrants that assertion. It is impossible. No such power is given them. The gentleman advises such amendments as would satisfy him, and proposes a mode of amending before ratifying. If we do not adopt first, we are no more a part of the Union than any foreign power. It will be also throwing away the influence of our state to propose amendments as the condition of our ratification. If we adopt first, our representatives will have a proportionable weight in bringing about amendments, which will not be the case if we do not adopt. It is adopted by ten states already. The question, then, is, not whether the CON be good, but whether we will or will not confederate with the other states. (p) The gentleman supposes that the liberty of the press is not secured. The CON does not take it away. It says nothing of it, and can do nothing to injure it. But it is secured by the CON of every state in the Union in the most ample manner."

---T--- Checks & Balance System was a Prevention Method made against Abuse of GOV; The Method is stated in the CC (CON & DOI) & includes God: // The FFOG studied Britain GOVs and other GOVs abuse histories; and that Rights come from God; and that men are potentially abusive. // Benjamin Franklin stated that "There is scarce a king in a hundred who would not if he could, follow the EX of Pharoh, get first all the people's money, then all their lands, and then make them and their children servants forever". This is reference to HSC in Exodus. This is putting God as the 1st priority Check.

255

---T--- <u>6 Checks are required; not prioritized, only</u> listed as follows: // God, CC, Citizens, Congress, Judicial, Executive. These are the Branches which function as Checks.

---T--- <u>Abuse of powers — from Congress</u> Meeting Notes, Table of Contents (Index) portion (in forming the CON AD 1778): // "potential for evil Elections liable to Abuse ,,,62 ,,,Abuse of Parliamentary Power ,,,65".

---T--- <u>GOV system is not to be abusive on financial</u> aspects to the people: // Congress Meeting Notes for forming CON, 1788.

---T--- <u>Checks & Balances:</u> // Mr. Montesquieu wrote in <u>Spirit of the Laws</u> (AD 1748) that there should be triadic, such as legislative-executive-judicial powers for GOV. Mr. W. Blackstone wrote in AD 1765 that GOV powers are not be all centralized but kept discrete. These 2 Spiritual Moral Creature people were some of the counselors of the FFOG USA congressmen.

--- EXECUTIVE:

---T--- <u>Requirement to be a Christian:</u> // Such is a requirement because this Official Status is activated for Law Making and Law Application.

---T--- <u>This is one Branch that also functions as a Check</u> in the Checks & Balances System.

---T--- <u>The Rights or abilities of this Branch are identified.</u> Some of them are in Principle Law form.

---T--- <u>The Rights of the Executive Branch</u> (president) are given, "Granted" from God; and in agreement with the citizens. // Therefore the Spiritual Moral Creature here must not be self-idolatrous (selfish, self-centered, self-1st-priority, etc.). Who would affectionately care to commune with Spiritual Moral Beings that are self-centered ?

---T--- <u>The Rights, which are abilities, such as those</u> of the Executive Employment Position of President, are Limited; they are Not Unlimited: // To be unlimited is to have dictatorship or tyranny potentiality. Because mankind may or may not be a perfect (totally right) Being; whereas God is a Perfect Being and will never change from such.

---T--- <u>Presidential Official Position.</u> // The CC CON states~ "The executive Power shall be vested in a President of the USA".

--- CONGRESS:

---T--- <u>Meetings of these Spiritual Moral Creature Beings:</u> // They meet at least annually according to the CON of the CC.

---T--- <u>Requirement to be a Christian:</u> // Such is a requirement because this Official Status is activated for Law Making and Law Application.

---T--- <u>The Rights or abilities of this Branch are identified:</u> // Some of them are in Principle Law form.

---T--- <u>The Rights of the Congress Branch</u> are given, "Granted" from God; and in agreement with the citizens: Therefore the people here must not be self-idolatrous (selfish, self-centered, self-1st-priority, etc.). Who would affectionately care to commune with Spiritual Moral Beings that are self-centered ?

---T--- <u>The Rights, which are abilities, of the Congressional Branch,</u> the Spiritual Moral Beings that are of the Congress Group, are Limited; they are Not Unlimited: // Because, for one, mankind may or may not be a perfect (totally right) Being; whereas God is a Perfect Being and will never change from such.

--- LAWS:

---T--- <u>See chp 7 for the study on Law Making Basis & Systems.</u>

---T--- <u>Laws (Acts, Records, and</u> Judicial proceedings) of other States are to be given full faith and credit in other states. However this is limited to whether the Law is good or evil.

---T--- <u>GOV System & Law Basis:</u> // FFoG Thomas Jefferson, about the Branches, said, "Nothing in the Constitution has given to them a right to decide for the Executive, more than to the Executive to decide for them ,,,The opinion which gives to the judges the right to decide what laws are constitutional, and what not ,,,for the legislature and the executive ,,,would make the judiciary a despotic branch." (30). // Responsibility is required for the Contract (CC). This is a repeat that the Law System does not legalize the Judicial Branch to make laws; nor the Executive Branch apart from or opposing the CC.

---T--- <u>Laws are made by the CC,</u> DOCs, Congress, President, and Citizens. Nevertheless~ These all are to include God as first priority, per the CC.

---T--- <u>Requirement to be a Christian:</u> // Such is a requirement because this Official Status is activated for Law Making & Law Application. Any Official Employment Position that is connected directly to Law Making by any Branch in Judicial, Executive, Congress requires to be a Christian. All other employment positions for the GOV of the USA may or may not be a Christian; but must oath to support the CC and God and Christianity as 1st Priority; without exception.

------------------ CREATURE BEINGS NEED To Be UNSELFISH, NOT IDOLATORS, NOT SELF-1st PRIORITY, as SUCH:

---T--- <u>Principle Law of Being or Personality as Source of Law</u>: // Thus the standard or Laws must come from some Living Being. They do not come from material substance things, as such. Laws need a mind to be made, to have knowledge of such, and to apply, etc. They are spirit related~ that is Being related. Now thus who makes the rules, basically. And whoever makes the rules, rules. Thus the one who rules is God. Now any child knows this when they get out of bed to start their day; that is, any group of Beings must have a system of rules. Now they can have one Being do it, or 2 plus do it; They can decide who makes the rules by one Being's decision, or 2 plus. Rules come from some Being's decision. The decision is based on their constitutional Being or on situations with maxims as a basis to them; Maxims are Principle Laws. Let us not be confused or bewildered or dismayed or deceived !!! // It is not a good thing to have Spiritual Moral Beings that are Self-idols, or selfish, self-centered. In reality, even the simple concept is fearful to degree of fright. // Law Making Positions require to be Christian, because God must be 1st priority. The CC states it; Truth states it; True Love states it; the Principle Law of unselfishness states it.

---T--- <u>Principle Law: of Limitations of Laws</u>: // Laws are to exist: +ONLY in specific subjects; and +ONLY in specific geographic areas; and +ONLY enforced by specific ways. God is the only one who has Right to rule in every area of our life; and He is LOVE & RIGHTNESS. However we must decide on who makes the decisions for human GOV. The GOV can only relate to its jurisdiction, or geographical area and Creature Being group. That is the limits. Thus we must decide on who gets to be our manager. God is the real manager; but as in this world we must decide on a manager of 1 or 2 plus managers; and what basis they will manage or system and on how the system will operate.

---------------------------- ADMINISTRATIVE (AGENCY or etc.) GOV SYSTEMS:

---T--- <u>Administrative GOV System</u>: // This method is applied terminology; thus do not mix it to much with other similar terms or applications. // What is this method? This is a group of GOV Creature workers that are making laws, and the laws are based on these Creature Being's decisions. And then the laws are applied to some people. // What are some problems with this method? This can be a serious desire. For one, because it is getting in areas of micro-management. This has potential to become near tyranny and dictatorship. // Details about the method: What GOV is doing here, is forming a group of Creature Being's to work in a division, called an agency or administration. Such Being group is then paid by tax money. They are placed in some geographical location, in an office or such, and then assigned to a specific geographical jurisdiction. A geographical jurisdiction is an area of land and people Beings who live in such; and are required to obey some laws about some specific subjects. The Administration group of Creature Being's is given an assignment to manage specific subjects, in that jurisdictional geographical territory, such as forest, natural resources, yards of homes, noise control, building permits, etc. What this administration agency then does, is begin researching in to this geographical area, and then enacting laws on the Creature Beings who live there. This is accepted as the Law of the land. // Discernment about such method: +Some of this operation may not be necessarily wrong. +Some of this operation sometimes is not according to the GOV system that was established, because it is a very detailed application; which is an involvement in subjects that are very detailed in societies, etc. +Sometimes this method is according to the GOV system of the CC. +Sometimes there is need for some of it. // However it needs examined. Administrative Law co/ remain to the States, Cities, Counties, etc. And in what geographical areas and subjects, then is another situation. Some subjects and geographic obviously need to be managed.

--- JUDICIAL:

---T--- <u>Appointments of judges</u>: // The Executive Branch, or President makes the decision about these. The Congress has Right to get involved. No details are studied here. This is the Federal Branch. The State Branches are not studied here.

---T--- <u>The Judiciary Branch provision</u> in the CON of the CC: // "The Judges, both of the supreme and inferior Courts, shall hold their Offices during good Behavior". Note that the time of employment of Federal Judges is not unlimited, rather limited to basis of~ "during good behavior". This is opposite of evil. Now mistakes can occur, a short time of error, or intentful evil. However what evil, the degree, and the reaction is all consideracy. // "all civil Officers of the US, shall be removed from Office on Impeachment for, and Conviction of, Treason, Bribery, or other high Crimes and Misdemeanors." Judges are included in~ "All civil officers".

---T--- <u>The CON of the CC states regarding</u> jurisdiction: // "the supreme Court shall have appellate Jurisdiction ,,,with such Exceptions, and under such Regulations as the Congress shall make." // Note that the CC CON gives Congress the power to make exceptions to the jurisdiction of the Supreme Court.

---T--- <u>The CON of the CC regarding the Judge</u> duties with Oath: // "all executive and judicial Officers, both of the US and of the several States, shall be bound by Oath or Affirmation, to support this CON". // The DOI & CON is the DOC that the oath and affirmation supports; with God as 1st priority.

---T--- <u>The USA CON does not provide an Unconditional</u> lifetime appointment for federal judges. The official position is contingent, conditional, on good behavior. The Constitutional Rule of good behavior is to be enforced by Congress. // Impeachment is available in the procedure. Thus opposition to God is an offense to the CC. // Maybe a method for function, would be for Judges to correct themselves, by admitting a mistake, or repenting, or stopping and declaring that they will do it right the next time. // Furthermore, Congress is legally bound and oathed by the CC (DOI & CON) to exercise a Right to prohibit federal courts from hearing or processing cases which are not according to the CC (DOI & CON).

---T--- <u>Legislation Branch has responsibility to assure that rightful application</u> and prevention of wrong application is not done by the Judicial Branch; that they do not illegally remove parts of the CC; which includes support and involving acknowledgement of God as the sovereign source of law, liberty, and GOV.

---T--- <u>Included is a requirement of legality by the CC (DOI & CON)</u> to support Former Chief Justice Roy Moore of the Alabama Supreme Court for his defense of the display of the Ten Commandments; and to oppose those who opposed God and him.

---T--- <u>Foreign Court rulings cannot legally overturn the validity</u> of judicial rulings of the U.S.

---T--- <u>Requirement to be a Christian: //</u> <u>Such is a requirement</u> because this Official Status is activated for Law Application; and sometimes Law Making.

---T--- <u>The Rights or abilities of this Branch are identified:</u> // Some of them are in Principle Law form.

---T--- <u>The Rights of the Judicial Branch</u> are given, "Granted" from God; and in agreement with the citizens: // Therefore the people here must not be self-idolatrous (selfish, self-centered, self-1st-priority, etc.). Who would affectionately care to commune with Spiritual Moral Beings that are self-centered ?

---T--- <u>The Rights, which are abilities, of the Judicial Branch, the Spiritual</u> Moral Creature Beings that are Judges, are Limited; they are Not Unlimited: // Because mankind may or may not be a perfect (totally right) Being; whereas God is a Perfect Being and will never change from such.

--- STATE GOV SYSTEM:

---T--- <u>Statewide USA Constitution: //</u> State Sovereignty as FFOG Thomas Jefferson stated: "Taking from the States the moral rule of their citizens, and subordinating it to the general authority (Federal GOV) ,,,would,,,break up the foundation of the Union ,,,I believe the States can best govern our home concerns, and the general (Federal) GOV our foreign ones" (111). // State Sovereignty: All the States had power given to the people (Citizen Branch) and their representatives; not only the judicial and not only major population vote. There is a joining of God and the State CONs. The State CON include God and the citizen Branch. // Truth & Spirituality are supported. // State GOV systems were already in place and established; and studied and learned; and used to design and construct what was done with the USA GOV system. // From Table of Contents of Congress Notes in Forming the CON, 1778: "Sovereignty of the Federal GOV annihilates the States ,,,179 -- Powers of Congress dangerous to State Laws ,,,180". +Also~ "State Sovereignty represented in the Senate; Treaty; Laws, their Execution; Judiciary; prohibitory Provisions ought to supersede the Laws of particular States, 155 -- Federal Laws conflicting with those of the States; Legislation on Individuals instead of States ,,,Powers granted ,,,182 -- Powers of Congress; Tendency to destroy the State GOVs ,,,93 ,,,State Sovereignty".

---T--- <u>The 10th Amendment states: //</u> "The powers not delegated to the US by the CON, nor prohibited by it to the States, are reserved to the States respectively, or to the people."

---T--- <u>The CC (DOI & CON) designated</u> enumerated powers to the Federal GOV; that is specific identified Rights and areas of exercising governmental activity; and of which is limited. It is not Unlimited: // Many and much power of GOV was designated to the Branch of the States and the Branch of the citizens.

---T--- <u>The Constitution Party (A Political</u> party) that is more Holy Biblical than many other "parties" has observed with their GOV knowledge and analyzed that the "Federal GOV was given the exception": // Thus what this would be defined as, is that the exception is that which was not able to be provided by the States, and citizens. This jurisdiction, the exceptional, (that is~ the other parts or subjects), is given to the USA GOV. Therefore they are an Exceptional GOV. They are hired to do "other" duties that the States, citizens, and other systems in the States cannot or will not do.

---T--- <u>The States actually make up or construct</u> what is known to be our federal GOV.

---T--- <u>The Federal GOV has no authority</u> to enact some specific laws RE State education, natural resources, transportation, private business, housing, health care, and many other areas: // Some illegal activity is occurring in the jurisdictions that are not for the USA FED GOV. The CC says such.

---T--- <u>It is urged & pleaded that the States</u> reclaim & be provided the following: 1} Legal Rights in federal affairs and legislation according to Amendment 10, US CON, and, 2} Insist a legal cessation of the federal GOV to separate itself in operations from the authority of the CC~ including God.

---T--- <u>Article IV Section 4:</u> "The US shall guarantee to every State in this Union a Republican Form of GOV."

---T--- <u>Article IV Section 4 Clause 3.</u> "New States may be admitted by the Congress into this Union." // The Northwest Ordinance of AD 1787 (re-enacted under Constitutional authority 1789) defined that all new states appropriately admitted will enter the nation on an equal footing with the original 13 states.

---T--- It is to be recognized, and realized, that each State's membership in the Union is voluntary. This is a detailed subject of study; All the States are already members.

---T--- The Equality of every State is to be honored, as equal for all States.

---T--- States are to maintain sovereignty and not be subdued to powers of the USA GOV: // FFOG Samuel Adams states: 'I mean ,,,to let you know how deeply I am impressed with a sense of the importance of the Amendments, that the good people may clearly see the distinction --for there is a distinction --between the federal powers vested in the Congress and the sovereign authority belonging to the several states, which is the Palladium {the protector} of the private and person rights of the citizens"(116).

---T--- The Federal powers & the State powers; the system of GOV of the USA; State CON to be required for the USA Fed CON: // The USA Fed CON was deliberately incomplete so as to require the state CON's. // The word Federal is defined as: "compact; treaty; of or formed by a compact; designating or of a union of states, which each member agrees to subordinate its governmental power to that of the central authority". // The fact to be observed here is, that the federal is dependent on the States. // The original States and their CON are specifically designed intentionally/ purposed to assist the States in maintaining their own independence in much of the areas. // The FED GOV is made up of indestructible States; thus the fed GOV cannot overRule the sovereignty of the States and independence thereof. // The extent and application of national (FED) and State can be specified but is complex. // Judicial court case, Livingston vs. Van Ingen states: "When the people create a single, entire government, they grant at once all the rights of sovereignty. The powers granted are indefinite and incapable of enumeration. Everything is granted that is not expressly reserved in the constitutional charter, or necessarily retained as inherent in the people. But when a federal GOV is erected with only a portion of the sovereign power, the rule of construction is directly the reverse, and every power is reserved to the members that is not, either in express terms or by necessary implication, taken away from them, and vested exclusively in the federal head. This rule has not only been acknowledged by the most intelligent friends of the CON, but is plainly declared by the instrument itself".

--- 14th AMENDMENT:

---T--- 14th Amendment states: - "No state shall make or enforce any law which shall abridge the privileges or immunities of citizens of the US".

---T--- This 14th Am. has been illegally interpreted and applied to the States which then makes it contradict other portions of the CC (DOI & CON): // And to which it never was intended to apply. It has, in some parts, taken the jurisdictions or Rights from the States and thus also from the Citizen Creatures Branches of GOV.

---T--- The 14th Am. has been wrongly connected to the 1st Amendment.

---T--- RELIGION, 14th Amendment: // The 14th Amendment concept is sometimes illegal. // The Case of "Everson", AD 1947, was applied together with the 1st Amendment. And these 2 were applied to make God's Religious part activity illegal in public schools and public institutions, etc. Some of it was done by a court. This is all totally illegal. Following is explanation as to why it is illegal. The 14th Amendment was ratified (AD 1868) intended to provide that the slaves who had been freed during the civil war would have civil rights in every state. Now you, dear reader, ask me how that relates to the 1st Amendment in application to make God's Religion part illegal in public schools and public institutions, etc. ?? It does not. Yet a court in the USA did some of this. And they did this without a Right to make laws as such. A court in AD 1970, "Walz", said that the court in AD 1947 made a change to the USA GOV system, that was "revolutionary". Hence this is illegal. // Yet they will make legal and encourage demonolgy to untrained and innocent, or more innocent minds, of youth.

---T--- This 14th Am. has some advantages & disadvantages. However parts of its use are required by law to be reversed and re-examined.

-------------------------------- GOV SYSTEM PARTS:

---T--- THERE ARE 7 PARTS TO THE USA GOVERNMENT SYSTEM; SOME OF WHICH BELONG TO EVERY CREATURE BEING & EVERY PART of GOV: // God, Law & Its basis (CC herein), decisions with Intention/ purpose, executive, legislative, judicial, citizenship.

---T--- GOV system of some sort is required: // Holy Biblical references for GOV include the following, although there are many more in SC: Gen9; Exo9:16; Deu29; 2Chr7:14; Daniel; Psa2:10-12; 33:12; Pro8:15-16; 29:2; Jer4:2; 31:10; 33:9; Joh19:10-11; Rom13:1-7; Col1:16; 1Pet2:13-16; 1Tim2:1-9.

---T--- Government Definition: // All it is, is some Spiritual Moral Creature Beings in a position of making decisions that have intention/ purpose; and doing some specific tasks about a subject(s); usually of administrative {management of activities of the jurisdictions (functions or powers or allowances) of the official employment description} function, which applies to some group of Spiritual Moral Creature Beings in a geographical area.

---T--- GOV is NOT Unlimited: // It is not the job of some men to involve in other men's lives and manage them in every way and intrude. // HSC warn of meddlers, dictators, tyranny, idolaters, Busybodies, etc. Resist such evil, said Jesus, the Lord God. Jam 4.

JURISDICTION SITUATION:

---T--- There are 5 jurisdictions that were involved in the CC (DOI & CON); that of personal, family, Church group, State, and then Nation. // Now, based on God's Holy Bible, the personal and family structure has much liberty, or freedom, and Rights. 1Cor16:1-3; Rom12-16; 1Pet; 2Pet all with clarity provide EV that the family and individual have the Rights over land, monies, talents, time, obedience, and etc. These have a relation to laws and systems. // These jurisdictions are in the Holy Bible. // That they are to be included in the system is needful. Because they are different, and the Principles of Liberty and Happiness are related; God and religion is related. Etc. // Not only does the Holy Bible use all these different audiences (jurisdictions), but they are thought of as such; as also Christ Jesus taught of jurisdictions (Mat22:19-21); and so do other parts of the OT & NT. // FFOG John Jay was studious in the early AD 1800's; as a US Supreme Court Judge, and President of the American Bible Society; and he shared about this SB as part of it. // Decisions with Intention/ purpose, Function, and Activities are essential in these jurisdictions.

ADVANTAGE / DISADVANTAGE Law:

---T--- Whenever a Right (power) is granted (graciously given from God) to the GOV (a group of Spiritual Moral Creature Beings) then it is susceptible to abuse. It can either be used for good or evil. AND the degree (extent) to which it is used may either be lesser, balanced good, or excess. Hence, the application of such is very difficult to discern, surely sometimes at least. If the Spiritual Moral Beings are provided with such a work (a Right of managing or some activity; as steward) then what will they do with it? Or how shall it be done? Etc. Who are they? How much shall they manage? What shall they manage? Etc. Thus the Citizen Branch of the GOV can be abused by these stewards, (which are intended by the FFOG & CC to be ministers for God, Rom13); because of the disadvantages expressed; because of a power (work) to the group of Spiritual Moral Beings ~(GOV).

CITIZENSHIP LAW:

---T--- See all Chps also.

---T--- "We the people of the people for the people" is said in the CC. Citizens are part of the USA GOV. Their Creature Beings are Spiritual Moral Beings; and are plainly part of GOV: // Their rightness of spirit, and their bodies, and abilities are all part. The vote and the spirits (all people are a spirit) internal status and activity, the decisions, their intent/ purpose, the actions of the body; and activities of Being. // Responsibility is part of that which is required of the citizens. // Legislative REPs, Executive, Judicial do not have Right to do whatever the mass majority population, or as their constituents, so desire. It is a Yes, that their best welfare is to be desired, intended, and included; and bad attitudes of tyranny, excess control, and dictatorship are to be avoided. // FFOG John Adams said, "Our CON was made ONLY for a moral and religious people. It is wholly inadequate for the GOV of any other".

---T--- Citizenry is assisted by the Citizenry Definitions from the CON (of the CC): // "All persons born or naturalized in the US, and subject to the jurisdiction thereof, are citizens of the US and of the STATE wherein they reside. No State shall make or enforce any law which shall abridge the privileges or immunities of CON of the US; nor shall any STATE deprive person of life, liberty, or property without due process of law; nor deny to any person withi its jurisdiction the equal protection of the laws".

---T--- STATE CON to be included: // USA CON says, "The CON of each State shall be entitled to all Privileges and Immunities of the CON in the several States".

---T--- If the Executive, Legislative, or Judicial attempt to go outside the limitations of the CC (DOI & CON) they are committing an illegal act; which if intentionally, (as some is mistaken and/or miscomprehended), is treason, lying, and stealing against USA. This provides the Rights of the Citizen Branch to make a reversal of such.

---T--- Citizenship Requirements: // The person must agree to the CC (DOI, CON, & supporting DOCs). They do not have to decide to be a Christian. The agreement to CC Constitutional Law, includes the following, that: +} they will vote for only Christians to be in employment offices which are directly connected to making Laws; +} they will vote on laws that are related to material substance things, which will utilize such in agreement to the CC; that are used in public; and limited to degrees of evil at their home; +} they will vote for activities of body and spirit that agree to the CC; +} they will use Principle Law to discern everything in this life that is public if it agrees or not to the CC; +} they will obey the Christian Laws of the CC in public; +} they do not have to decide to be a Christian, and do not have to obey Him in their home; +} they will never do specific Evils on USA soil; such Evils are never allowed on USA soil, neither in Public nor in personal homes; some such Evils are Satanism, murder, etc.

---T--- CITIZEN Branch Responsible to Keep CC: // This Covenant Contract is to be kept by all people; it is the responsibility of the citizens; they are in the contract, based on many inclusions. And it includes the basis that the Representatives which wrote up the contract were representing the people.

---T--- <u>CITIZEN Branch Responsible to Keep CC:</u> // This contract is to be kept by the people, as it is the responsibility of the citizens; as they are in the contract, as referred to in many ways. And it includes the basis that the Representatives which wrote up the contract were representing the people. // FFoG John Jay says: "Every member of the State ought diligently to read and to study the constitution of his country ,,,By knowing their rights, they will sonner perceive when they are violated and be the better prepared to defend and assert them" (6). // FFOG also state~ "The power under the Constitution will always be in the people. It is entrusted for certain defined purposes, and for a certain limited period to representation of their own choosing and whenever it is exercised contrary to their interest or not agreeably to their wishes, their servants can, and undoubtedly will be recalled". // Hence the Rights in the CC need to match with what the Officers are doing or the People need to reject the actions of such GOV.

---T--- <u>Requirement to be a Christian or support Christianity:</u> // Such is a requirement because this is actually an Official Status. They must either be a Christian or agree to the exception provided. The exception is that, if they decide not to be a Christian, they are not free to do unlimited evil; rather they must do as the CC states. This is included in signing the CC; to support it. It is a Covenant Contract. If they do not agree and sign it, then they lose some freedoms, or abilities to participate in the GOV; and also must abide by Christian Laws. The exception for Citizens applies to those who do not decide to be a Christian; they must then agree to support Christianity and obey the Laws of the Land. // In voting all citizens must abide by the CC, which states that they must vote only for Christians who are in Official employment positions that are directly connected to making laws. Such positions are some in the Executive, Congress, and Judicial Branches. If employment positions are not directly connected to Making laws, which not all positions in the Branches are, then being a Christian is not required; but Christianity must be supported in public without exception.

-- TAXATION:

---T--- <u>Wrong activity and money is occurring:</u> // The tax system must be examined and evaluated. The N GOV branches, the activity procedures; and if it is right or not; or needed or not. God needs to be included. Such is in the CC (DOI & CON).
---T--- <u>Some rightness activity and money is occurring:</u> // For such, we can thank the Lord God & for each Spiritual Moral Creature particpating.

-- VOTE:

---T--- <u>The CC (DOI & CON) state~</u> "Governments are instituted among Men, deriving their just powers from the consent of the governed"; and~ "We the People of the US, in Order to form a more perfect Union,,,". // Thus see the vote; that is the part of GOV that includes citizens. Such is a part of to be included; it does exist; it is a truth.
---T--- <u>Intention/ Purpose of VOTE:</u> // The CC with CON statements stated about the vote prove~ +that the intention/ purpose of the "consent of the governed" is to "Secure these rights". +that This Does Not state that we are consenting to the vote or view or opinion of the majority of people. +It is to, rather, support the Principles of Truth. +It is not a total democracy; which is majority rule. // A part of Democracy is included, but not the total system. We may thank God, that a form of Democracy is included in the system; this system of Republic includes a part of Democracy. Nevertheless, that the majority of population rules, is not right in the USA system; it is an insertion that does not exist in the CC, etc. // And the fact that God is part of the CC & Nation surely resists systems that are based on population vote. Such a basis would be a mankind and number of mankind basis. Such a basis is not reality; it has not truth as reference, rather makes a relative~ or related to whomever, whenever, whatever. // Consent is only necessary to establish the GOV; not the principles of the GOV. The Principles of GOV are those of God Creator, not people creatures priority. If God is priority then people will be blessed the best. If He is not, a temporary sin pleasure may be a form of some evil pleasure, but will eventually be a curse. // The exact order or arrangement or organization of the GOV is not specified in the DOI. Those are the Basic Principle Laws to Build on, or Increase with. Thus this was why the AOC, and then later the CON, were constructed; intended/ purposed to further increase some form of organization as to how to secure the Rights of truth from God (per the DOI). This is supported by the statements. // Martin Diamond & studies agrees with this book in many parts (123). // Any organization is a possible system that may be examined, "open policy" in the DOI. But the Truth Principles, Principle Law, is not "open".
---T--- <u>Voting Right stated in CC:</u> // "Citizens right of the US to Vote shall not be denied or abridged by the US or by any STATE on account of race, color, or previous condition of servitude; Nor shall such be denied or abridged by the US or by any STATE on account of sex".
---T--- <u>The Williamsburg Charter</u> shares the following about the Vote: // "A society is only as just and free as it is respectful of this right, especially toward the beliefs of its smallest minorities and least popular communities." Now this is a Praise the Lord !!! However, rightness is a basic truth that no small or large population can be acceptable or rejected without; Thus this Charter needs to additionally include such. Nevertheless we surely do not want population rule (Mob rule) against right, or insensitive to the weak, the sick, the poor, the rich, the principles, etc.

---T--- <u>VOTE & the Power Of It; & as Connected to the CC:</u> // The vote does not void the CC (DOI & CON). // The vote is secondary to the CC; of lesser priority equally as God is priority to man. The CC states that the vote and GOV is under God~ "One nation under God"; "laws of nature and of nature's God entitle them ,,,all men are created equal ,,,that they are endowed by their Creator with certain inalienable rights; that among these are life, liberty, and the pursuit of happiness." This includes the Rights, and Rights includes the Vote; that Right comes from God. Furthermore it is also self-evident that God is over man; that God is priority. // The vote is to support the CC. // These Rights come from God, not from any other than God, as is clearly stated.

---T--- <u>Majority Population Rule is included in the CC (DOI & CON).</u> // It has Checks put on it; has limitations. Such a system is Not supported. Rather truth principle and God are the essential basis to be trusted, not popular opinion. Majority Population Rule is not supported by the FFOG; all supporting DOC state such; it was studied much. The CC has other statements in it that relate to that such system is not the GOV system of the USA.

---T--- <u>*Constitutional Law Includes a CC;*</u> & is Not a Democracy: // A Total Democracy is where the majority of the people is the law; and is without Constitutional Laws. However our CC (DOI & CON) laws are based referenced to Constitutional Laws; and on Christianity and overseers with Checks & Balances. In other words, a CC. // FFoG say such as follows: +James Madison~ "Democracies have ever been spectacles of turbulence and contention ,,,incompatible with personal security, or the rights of property ,,,short in their lives ,,,violent in their deaths" (202). +John Adams~ "Remember, democracy never lasts long,,, soon wastes, exhausts, and murders itself. There never was a democracy yet that did not commit suicide" and "will soon degenerate into an anarchy ,,,that every man will do what is right in his own eyes and no man's life or property or reputation or liberty will be secure,,, wanton pleasures ,,,capricious will ,,,execrable cruelty of one or a very few" (169a). +Fisher Ames~ "A democracy is a volcano which conceals the fiery materials of its own destruction ,,,known propensity of a democracy is to licentiousness [[excessive license]] which the ambitious call, and ignorant believe to be liberty" (29). +Gouverneur Morris~ "We have seen the tumult of democracy terminate ,,,as it has everywhere terminated, in despotism ,,,savage and wild ,,,bring down the virtuous and wise to the level of folly and guilt" (219). // These FFOG have HSC in those as you see.

---T--- <u>Not a Democracy in Totality as FFOG</u> declare: // John Quincy Adams~ "The experience of all former ages had shown that of all human governments, democracy was the most unstable, fluctuating and short-lived" (220). // Benjamin Rush~ "A simple democracy ,,,is one of the greatest evils" (97). // Noah Webster~ ",,,democracy ,,,there are ,,,tumults and disorders ,,,generally a bad GOV,,, often the most tyrannical GOV on earth" (221). // Zephaniah Swift~ ",,,more a GOV resembles a pure democracy the more they abound with disorder and confusion." (141a).

-- RELIGION:

---T--- <u>See Chp 5 and sub-parts of "Religion".</u> (Covenant Contract).

---T--- <u>USA GOV control over religion is</u> illegal: // "Certainly, no power to prescribe any religious exercise, [[Christian DEN; secondary doctrines; expressions]] or to assume authority in religious discipline, [[Christianity DEN; secondary doctrines; expressions]] has been delegated to the general GOV. It must, then, rest with the States" (111). // Establishments of Religion (per 1-A, R-E, R~Est) are DEN. The Religion is True Religion, with the True God, true Man, True Basic doctrines of God & Mankind.

---T--- <u>The USA GOV must abide by the 7 Rules, or Laws,</u> made regarding God's Religion: // 1} No anti-Christian religion to be supported to build its embassies, assembly buildings, or public activities, such as Advertisements, on USA soil; nothing more than a personal family meeting; 2} No general control over Christ's Christianity; 3} No prevention to the States for supporting any Christian DEN; 4} No prohibition for States to have Christian activity in all of GOV including their CON and their Laws; 5} No Christian DEN, such as secondary doctrine, expression, or organization to be partial, or favored, "respected"~ by making a law about them; which excludes other DEN; 6} No making of laws in GOV or public which support anti-Religion Freedoms; those opposing true Religion of Christianity; 7} No making Laws that oppose the True God as a Being in USA; nor His parts of Being~ Spirit supreme conscience, intention/ purpose, will/decision, affections & emotions & desires, thoughts of evil, etc. // These laws are studied in Chpt 5. // Law Case of Barron vs. Baltimore, AD 1833, includes Justice John Marshall stating that he could not apply the R-E to the States~ "In almost every convention by which the CON was adopted amendments to guard against the abuse of power are recommended. These amendments demanded security against the apprehended encroachments of the general (federal) governments -- not against those of the local (State) governments ,,,These amendments contain no expression indicating an intention to apply them to the State governments. This Court cannot so apply them."

---T--- <u>Most the States had already provided for equal</u> protection for all the Christian DEN: // In fact that is probably where the idea came from firstly before the USA GOV enacted and applied it: Virginia, AD 1785-86; New Jersey, North Carolina, Delaware, Maryland, all had such, long before the USA GOV. // Furthermore, when the States first started having GOV churches or DEN included in their activity, it was not to favor only one DEN more than any other; rather it was because they are finite Spiritual creatures without Knowledge as how to keep God & true Christian Religion and prevent abuses simultaneously; they do not have all-knowledge.

---T--- <u>Judicial & Citizenry & CC & Statewide Application:</u> // All the States had priority of God as a Right, and power given to the people, and their representatives; that is, they are less priority than God & State CONs & USA CC. Religion of the USA was Not given to the Judicial Branch at the State level; they do not make laws about religion. Neither was the Right or power given to popular majority vote.

---T--- <u>Prayer (Christian) is to be a</u> part of GOV: // For GOV Officials, churches, citizens, family members. To refuse to talk & listen to God is to reject God; and to reject God is to reject the CC; and thus a form of treason. // Now after all, why would Not any Spiritual Moral Being not desire, affectionately care, and decide to commune (fellowship) with such a God as such a value that He is; and so loving and right ? What better subject in life can there be ? There is none better.

---T--- <u>The operation or governmental system</u> functioned as following: // The States already made the requirement that only Christians serve as Officials connected directly to making laws; and that they were Christian States and supportive of such Christ; but not denominational, which is secondary doctrine favored, or expression favored~ by laws. Thus the Fed GOV was not to interfere with that; but support it. Therefore from that Basis also proves that the Fed GOV was to be Christian and support the Religion of Christ's Christianity; but not be dictatorship over DEN; nor DEN favored. // If the States were Christian servants, and Christian doctrine supportive, and the Holy Bible required, then why would they put anti-Christian in Fed GOV? // The USA FED CON did not, and was not to, change the States CON; Rather it was to support it. And what was it? Exclusively Christian. What Spiritual Moral Creature will speak at this moment to say that demonology is to be included? // The USA Fed CON did not change the States CON which was that the States were Christian, and sent Christian REP to the Fed office. // The States were Christian; required Officers to be Christian, required Holy Bible supporting, required no anti-Christian REP; yet did not require a specific DEN.

--------------------------------- SABBATH DAY is Holy to the LORD:

---T--- <u>The Sabbath Day of Christianity is</u> in the CON: // Such comes from the Holy Bible (1Cor16:1-3; Rev1:10; Joh20:1; Luk24:1; Mar16:2; Mat28:1). This subject has been studied and EVs provided in Chp 5 in a sub-point. Here again it is shared that Sunday's are to be provided as a day NOT to be involved with business of many subjects, including the President approving bills passed by Congress. The CON states, "Specifically it is provided that if not returned by him within ten days, "Sundays excepted," after it shall have been presented to him it becomes a law". // Furthermore, similar provisions were in the CONs of most of the States; many included the same expression, "Sundays excepted." // This Sabbath is special to Christianity and is of no other religion (27). // Freedom is allowed for Spiritual Creatures with Saturday Sabbaths (or other Sabbaths); but the Sunday Sabbath is required as applicable for these same groups as connecting to business activities.

-- GOD:

---T--- See parts on God in Chp 5 of CC (Covenant Contract).

---------------------- CC (Covenant Contract) — DOI & CON & Supporting DOCs:

---T--- See Chp 5 on CC.

-- MINISTERS or STEWARDs:

---T--- <u>The FFOG inserted in the CC (DOI & CON)</u> the Concept & Principle Law that the GOV is Spiritual Moral Creature Beings who are Ministers, which is from what the Holy Bible titles them: // The definition of Minister is: +in Greek (1c), "one who executes the commands of another, especially of a master, a servant, attendant, minister; the servant of a king; a deacon, one who, by virtue of the office assigned to him by the church, cares for the poor and has charge of and distributes the money collected for their use; a waiter, one who serves food and drink; an attendant, that is, (generally) a waiter (at table or in other menial duties); specifically a Christian teacher and pastor (technically a deacon or deaconess): - minister, servant". +In English is (1b), "Properly, a chief servant; hence, an agent appointed to transact or manage business under the authority of another; in which sense, it is a word of very extensive application. One to whom a king or prince entrusts the direction of affairs of state; as minister of state; the prime minister. In modern governments, the secretaries or heads of the several departments or branches of government are the ministers of the chief magistrate. A magistrate; an executive officer. For he is the minister of God to thee for good. Rom 13; A delegate; an embassador; the representative of a sovereign at a foreign court; usually such as is resident at a foreign court, but not restricted to such; An angel; a messenger of God; To attend and serve; to perform service in any office, sacred or secular; To afford supplies; to give things needful; to supply the means of relief; to relieve. When saw we thee hungry, or thirsty, or a stranger, or naked, or sick, or in prison, and did not minister unto thee? Mat25; In this sense, we commonly use administer". // Now to deny that this concept or position is what the FFOG, including the citizen Branch, titled it as, is to deny all the instances in which the words herein are written in the CC and all the supporting DOC. Note that there are different sorts of ministers, as in its definition above. Note that a Minister is to be under God; to be a servant of Other Spiritual Moral Creature Beings. Note that a Minister is to be unselfish, or other Creature Beings caring for; and that God is to be the priority Being. Do you desire or intend to be Ruled by a selfish or self-idolatry Being ?? Best think about if that is what you want. Note that the word Minister defined above, states that they are executive officers, servants of Governments, helpers, etc. // Holy Scripture states the GOV is ministers, such as Rom 13:6~"for they are God's ministers". And this title is repeated in HSC. // We surely do not want demonic ministers.

-------------------------------------- What Can The GOV Do By Way Of Enforce ? — Including~ A] What Rights Can Be Enforced ? ~&~ B] What Actions Can Be Opposed ~&~ C] How Do (The Total GOV of The USA; The 7 Branches) Apply The Laws Of The USA GOV (As Have Totally Been Proven) ?; What Can Be Enforced And What Cannot Be Enforced ?:

---T--- <u>Citizen participation (Fellowship, or communion)</u>: // A very caring part of GOV is such. We know the Branches of our GOV system includes citizens. Thus the Rights of enforcement, or powers, also belongs to the citizens. Therefore, when we sit down at the Round Table of discussion, we best not limit our direction of attention to some groups of Spiritual Moral Creature Beings selected to do such and such; rather also include the citizens; including small groups of citizens within the citizens; and to what they are entitled or provided Right to do, or not do. // This is not a license to meddle, taletalking, anarchy, craze, mobs, confusion, excess expressions, busybodies, etc. // This is not a license to exceed limits, nor is it an unlimited license. // It is limited. // It does not provide Right for anarchy, nor Mob Rule, nor Craziness, nor evil aggressions, nor evil methods or means, nor removing Checks, etc. // Carefulness and Love and God are the priority Rule.

---T--- <u>Societal (national) Rights of Communion</u> & idolatry: // The Rights (or powers) or areas of enforcement have been given or granted or allowed to the other Branches by the other Branches. They are not assumed or presumed powers. The powers are not given by the Branches to the other Branches without Checks put on them by the other Branches. The powers of enforcement are also not given separate from the "God, Creator, Supreme Judge, Lord Jesus, Divine Providence" of the CC (DOI & CON).

---T--- <u>"Enumerated powers" as stated</u> in the CC (CON & DOI) are these, as specific: // Defined, planned, not impulsive, not random, but very identified. // Enumerated powers (Rights) includes that they are limited powers (rights of enforcement); not unlimited. They are identified and numbered (enumerated) in a list. And the List has a limited number (enumerated) to it; it does not go on indefinitely, nor infinitely; which is unlimited; nor is it a list of multi-million Rights. Rather there are only a few in number Rights. // And it is not for confusion or craze. // God does not give mankind unlimited Rights. The Rights are not from mankind, rather from God.

---T--- <u>Cannot Force any Spiritual Moral Creature to be</u> a Christian or go to Church assembly: // God has given this to Spiritual Moral Creatures by their faculty known as the Free Will and decision. This Right is given by God for this existence known as a Temporary Time Probation Status. Eternity is hereafter. Responsibility to decide the eternal dwelling place of Heaven or Hell is to the individual & God. Children are not included in this group; they are the Rights of parents. As said in Holy SC, CC (DOI & CON), and DOCs, and etc. Nevertheless the children are owned by God ~Gen2-3; 1Cor11; Eze18:4.

---T--- <u>No one in the GOV can be in</u> opposition to the True God, Church, Bible, Truth, nor support sin or evil.

---T--- <u>"Checks" must be made to examine</u> all sin & evil in society. To what is allowed & not allowed. This is not to invade family homes, nor thoughts; rather specific evils are not allowed & others are allowed to only some degree. EX: Satanism is not allowed anywhere at anytime; but how to manage it is another subject of discussion. 7 Branches are to cooperate about such subjects.

---T--- <u>The Continual and verbal and ceremonial</u> activity must be made to declare that the USA is supportive of the True God, Church, Holy Bible, Christianity Religion, Truth, and opposed to sin and evil.

---T--- <u>No Law must be made to support</u> any law that is against the True God, the Christian Church, Christian Religion, Truth, or in support of any evil or sin.

---T--- <u>The GOV must keep a continual</u> watch of society to verbally encourage the True God, Christian Church, Christian Religion, Holy Bible, Truth, and to express its disapproval of sin (evil).

---T--- <u>Any business of sin (evil) is not legal or</u> allowed to do business activity in the USA; that is depending on what evil it is. Some evils are totally disallowed and some are limited. This is pertaining to selling, buying, corporation, organization, etc.

---T--- <u>Any business of false Christianity is not legal</u> or allowed to establish business in the USA: // This pertains to the main doctrines and body actions (expressions) that are against the 10 commandments, the Holy Trinity, the Holy Bible, Salvation, Sanctification, Atonement. This does not say that there is not, nor will not be false doctrines in Christianity. Such Christians can function on their own to discern and learn and apply them and work them through. Rather these main doctrines are the only doctrines which do not allow any disagreement on in being an Officer, or law making, or physical activity on the USA Soil. The details about other doctrines, that is of secondary, are not enforced. Salvation & Sanctification vary in some Spiritual Moral Creatures thoughts. The basic doctrines must be the same, but some variations are allowed to exist for Spiritual folk to learn and decide them; as to what is true & what is false. // That there will be error is sure. And that some groups will be wrong & some will be right is sure. And that there is allowance for this is given as a Right. This is referring to some of the basic doctrines. This is allowed by God in HSC.

As to degrees of responsibility to individuals is not given to GOV; it is not their Right from God. GOV are not God's managers of the Church nor of Christ or God; they have limited involvement for participation.

---T--- <u>The Christian Church must be consulted,</u> the Holy Bible, as to what is good & evil.

---T--- <u>All the 10 Commandments of</u> the Holy Bible must be enacted.

---T--- <u>No anti-Christian, or other</u> religion or doctrine of God is legal on USA Soil: // Spiritual Moral Creatures may agree to some idolatrous god internally; but they must abide by Christian laws (as specified). This is mainly referring to external actions and general respect for a Christian land and people and laws. Such people may not build temples, nor buildings for public meetings, nor advertise, nor be employed in Office of any USA or STATE position that is directly connected to Law Making. Any other employment position is available if they will become a USA citizen by agreeing and signing for support of the CC. They may not enact their idolatrous beliefs and doctrines in the land, or in any USA or STATE GOV.

---T--- <u>These Goodnesses & Evils of the 10 Commandments are to</u> be Illegal & Legal: // Adultery. // Divorce that is not based on adultery or desertion (and similarities) is illegal. However an exception is allowed that if they do, the guilty person will not be given a license for remarriage. Such people have liberty to do so, based on their own decision to do so, as they may do it. They have the Right to live together unmarried. Such is found in 1Cor7. But the GOV is not to license it. // Fornication. // Murder. // Stealing. // Sabbath Day is Legal; no business conducted on it, except that of medical or police military; or various such activities; which then should be rotated for the good sake of opportunity to Church assembly. // Any evil music is illegal such as rock, rapp, country music; Christians may decide to play "Christian pop rock", etc. The discernment as to the rightness of this remains in Christianity. But that which has evil words is not legal. // Pornography. // Alcohol for recreational intention/ purposes. // Dancing (as defined right). // Any activity that is not with high degree of EV Christian or Scriptural should not be allowed in the USA. // Specific drugs. Sometimes these do not need managed but rather not allowed to be grown on farms. A method to micro-management of such is not needed because it is excess GOV needs; rather if society teaches it and such knowledge is taught in schools then it will help at the home levels. And it should not be sold in stores; business. // The Christian holidays that have already been established should be legal and continued to be encouraged; businesses should close down for the most part on holidays; except military and medical; which should rotate for the good sake of all Spiritual Moral Beings. // Rights for some activities to spiritual peoples who agree to false religions do not have to be protected; they are limited; not unlimited. // For 7th Day, Saturday Sabbath Keepers, (or other Sabbaths), there is limited Rights; if they decide to not work on Saturday, they will have to find a job that does not work on that day, or request of it from the employer; and it should be provided for them. It should be a legal requirement for such to be available, because these spiritual folk have rights to exist; they may not have "light" knowledge, on the Sabbath Day; etc. The limitations of this, is only if they are a form of Judaism, or Christianity "in the making". We can sympathize with the 7th Day Adventist in some respects and encourage them to desire and seek the Lord; we can conceive, that in these situations, since the name of Christ is somewhat honored, and they may be deceived and seeking the Lord; kindness is to be expressed Gal5; do not discourage them. // Absolutely no physical harm to Spiritual Moral Creature Beings bodies is part of the USA GOV; as referring to all these legalizing and illegalizing what has thus far here been stated. However there is potential and sure harm to society in not having correct laws; as we are surely experiencing now. // The citizens must seriously take an evaluation of what to do with the acting pretending profession, competitional sports, vehicle racing, gambling, etc. // Children are to obey their parents, but not in committing sin. (Colo3 of HSC). // The proper and right way of child discipline should be legal in the USA and not opposed but encouraged. All HSC is given to families without GOV control. Mat4-7; 1Cor10; 2Cor6; Eph5; Col3; 1Cor11; 1Cor1-7. And obviously parents should do it with love & carefulness; but not micromanaged by the GOV; forms of application of physical lessonry is befitting sometimes. // The schools, if public schools are decided on by the society, then they should be Christian for God. It is a very well known fact, that children are very susceptible to evil influences and peer pressure, and deception and highly impressionable and very easily led astray. They need serious and careful guidance and not put in an ungodly school atmosphere. It has been witnessed by many Spiritual Moral Folk, that there were experiences with Christ during public school nativity scenes, and where the school choir or some Christmas Hymns were played by a recording or the band. // Creation is to be legalized and all other contrary beliefs are to be illegal; and treated as an UNright lie. (Gen1-3).

---T--- <u>Physical buildings and activities are dependent</u> on whether they are legal for the public; depending on God & the CC.

---T--- <u>Holy Bible must be our guide.</u> +Truth is stated in the CC & DOC; +the Holy Bible was the main source of knowledge and Basis of the USA by FFOG.

---T--- <u>The FFoG were Christian, expected the N GOV</u> to be Christian & Christian supporting & supported the Holy Bible, & in opposition to evil or sin in society: // Thomas Jefferson with Virginia Bill for Religious Liberty proclaimed that "to compel a man to furnish contributions of money for the propagation of opinions which he disbelieves, is sinful and tyrannical" (64). Notice his support of Christian doctrinal, TRUTH, and the words, "sinful" and "tyrannical". These are Christian words. He does not want N GOV or STATE GOV to support evil or anti-Christ practices, laws, or actions. And this situation is not applicable to "opinions", say for instance the color of the carpet. Evil has limited Rights in the USA.

---T--- <u>RIGHTS (powers) as in the CC for the</u> USA FED GOV include: // "CONGRESS: Taxation. Regulated interstate and foreign commerce (traffic, navigation, trade, shipping); power of regulation is defined as: foster, protect, control, restrain, prohibit, appropriate regard for the welfare of the public. Money and regulate its value. Establish post offices and post roads. Copyrights of writings and discoveries. Power to declare war. No export tax imposed. No preference to states with regards to ports. Money making Rights are given to states". // PRESIDENTIAL; Executive power:

"take care that laws be faithfully executed". Power of veto. Treaty making. To advise congress. Pardon power, to recommend for and approve of. Head commander of the armed forces. // JUDICIAL Powers or Rights: Pardon power". // This is not a total list, and the details of these are not stated, nor the existence or limits. Rather to show the applications of functioning together in a national society with rightness, love, and care.

---T--- Arms: // "A well regulated Militia, being necessary to the Security of a free State, the right of the people to keep and bear Arms, shall not be infringed". Such is the CC.

---T--- Taxation: RIGHTS of FED for TAXATION: // Taxes~ "The CON, in Article I, Section 8, gives Congress the power ,,,to lay and collect Taxes, Duties, Imposts, and Excises, to pay the Debts and provide for the common Defense and general Welfare of the US." In Article I, Section 9, the original DOC made clear that "no Capitation, or other direct Tax shall be laid, unless in Proportion to the Census of Enumeration herein before directed to be taken." It is moreover established that "No Tax or Duty shall be laid on Articles exported from any State." // There are good desires as to how large the USA GOV has become and the tax system. An evaluation is needed. Many Spiritual Moral Creature folk are proclaiming the current system is illegal according to the original system. It is already known that the USA GOV is supporting anti-Christian or anti-religion laws; such is an illegal use of the Citizen GOV Branch of monies. // Threat to religious freedom is potential with taxes. // FFOG Thomas Jefferson with Virginia Bill for Religious Liberty proclaimed that "to compel a man to furnish contributions of money for the propagation of opinions which he disbelieves, is sinful and tyrannical" (64). // FFOG James Madison's "Memorial and Remonstrance against Religious Assessments" states~ "a citizen to contribute three pence only of his property". Now what he was referring to here was DEN (secondary doctrines & expressions); that of forcing taxes to support only one specific DEN is also against the 1-A; The "respecting" is a partiality or favorism towards by making a law for only one or a few DEN; secondary doctrine or expression; By partiality it would be done by making a Law; excluding some DEN & including only one or a few. // N GOV did use GOV money for religious purposes at times; but it did not make a law to institutionalize the DEN. In other words, the N GOV is not to make a law to only spend money because they are Baptist. The USA can and needs to spend money to support Christianity subjects, or laws, and specific issues, as the USA N GOV; they are to support God & truth. But they are not only to support one DEN; by making a law. // FFOG Jesse Choper is right about this subject stating that our N GOV has mostly supported Christianity as a purpose to help our society (65). // Taxes from Constitutional Party website: They recommend that resources as a consideration for Management: State mainly, and some Federal; Land, roadways, police. // It is wrong to force Christians to be supporting abortion, alcohol for recreational drinking, cigarettes, pornography, schools that teach evil, Evolutionary theories (lies), homosexuality, idolatry, false religions, etc. This is a VIOLATION of the 1-A, among other things. This is causing a Spiritual Moral Creature Being to offend his conscience and it offends GOD. This is also causing a citizen to contradict or violate his oath to the CC & God of that CC. God is OverRuler of the USA.

--------------------------------- CAN THEY GOVERN And NOT GOVERN THESE ??:

---T--- This is a very serious situation also. Enumerated powers or Rights have been provided to the GOV; granted by the other Branches basically. And God is the 1st Priority Branch. The Rights they have come from God. They are Not given without "checks" on them. Land zoning, population, resources, are areas susceptible to abuse.

---T--- Women working out of the home, is a subject susceptible to abuse by the GOV: // Jurisdiction of this is not given by a central group of Spiritual Moral people. This is connected to priests of the Home jurisdiction; or the family's jurisdiction. Societal situations are involved, physical bodily health, family structures, needs, etc. Individual person and family liberty is priority in the USA. // Such is HSC which has records of bodily, mental, disabilities, etc. (Genesis with Isaac & Rebekah; with Jacob's disability; David was ill and needed medical attentions; if a person was wounded in war, the wife would care for them, etc.).

---T--- There are various subjects, that are of difficult discernment, and there needs to be loving, and careful thought and study about it.

---T--- To prioritize and maintain Christ Jesus, Creator, Supreme Ruler, Divine Providence, God as such, without idolatry, and the CC (DOI & CON).

---T--- The subject then, is what is the relationship to be between Christianity & GOV??. What can the GOV do & what can it not do with Christianity & Christ?: // This is studied in Chapter 5. However more identifications of assistance follows: // CANNOT Do's: T= It cannot refuse God's Christianity to exist; T= It cannot limit its support, or its activities, to any one DEN (sect) exclusively by making a law; T= It cannot limit the decision of individual people, nor DEN of secondary doctrines of Christianity; T= It cannot limit Christian expressions of individual people, nor DEN; T= It cannot set up (establish) a national Church DEN by making a law for such; T= It cannot be partial or favor "respecting" Christian DEN, secondary doctrines, and expressions by making a Law for such; T= It cannot hinder Christianity in any way, if Christianity is not doing a sin that is of public illegality (such as defined elsewhere); if someone does such sin, or evil, with the name of Christian, then it is not Christian and may be opposed; for EX: if a person commits murder and then says they are a Christian. // CAN DO's: T= It can and is to be Christian respected and prefer God's Christianity; The CC (DOI & CON) states it; T= The REP must be Christian; T= Christianity must be supported in its efforts as True Christianity, as a general principle; T= It must allow all DENs of Christianity; those that agree with the basic fundamental doctrines (True Basic doctrines) of Christianity; T= It can allow individual people and DEN to decide on their own about secondary doctrines of Christianity; T= It can allow freedom for all individual people, and DEN to express Christianity; T= It must oppose evil in the USA, as according to the 10 commandments;

266

some must be stopped totally and other evils must be limited; T= It must not allow false religions to advertise nor assembly publically; T= It is to reverence the Holy Bible and make it a study of application for the Law Basis, as the Common Law shares; T= It is to apply the Laws of Love to all of its functions and be slow to anger, slow to speak, and love all Spiritual Creature people and be unselfish; // At no point can God's Christianity be opposed with evil.

---T--- GOV must then support all religion that claims Christ & the Holy Bible & the basic morals of it. It must oppose all other religions by limiting them: // All individuals have Right to agree to any religion, true or false; but not for public meetings, advertisement, or organizing in the USA GOV; such is limited to their personal homes. Some false religions are not allowed at all totally; such as Satanism; including in personal homes. The Basic 10 Commandments of the Holy Bible must be the laws of the land.

++

------------- Chapter 10 ,,,,,,,,,,,,,,, EVIL is ILLEGAL in THE USA Which Is Intended To Put Limits To Or Stop EVIL, Depending On Conditions ----------------

====== [CONCLUSION]: EVIL (ALL FORMS Of SIN Or WRONG) IS OPPOSED TO THE COVENANT CONTRACT (DOI & CON); ~And~ EVIL HAS LIMITS ON IT WHICH INCLUDE THAT SOME EVIL IS TO BE STOPPED And SOME EVIL HAS LIMITS DEPENDING ON VARIOUS CONDITIONS ~~~~ {{The EVIL Identified in this Chapter Does Not Include the Evil of False Religions, Anti-Christian Religions; Those of Non-Christian Religions or Not Christian DENs; Nor Do We Identify Secondary Doctrines and Expressions of Christian DENs. Those Related Evils are Included in Chapter 5, with Religion; and the Sub-Parts.}}:

---T--- Actions to be performed about the Evils Existing Currently: // These must be reversed and decided on rightly. // Correct Laws must be enacted to make the correct GOV support or opposition to these. // Which Evils & what to do is based specficaly.
---T--- Treason: // The USA GOV is currently activating Treason against the USA GOV; this includes the CC & Citizen Branch; & God. Some Spiritual Moral Beings do it based on various strange teachings that have been slowly or slyly or subtly slipping in to the minds and hearts of Officials and citizens; and in the educational institutions, and in the legal employments; and such. Yet they are not truly legal; What is now called legal and law, is not what in reality really is such; nor is it the truth about our FFOG and what was given to us. Instead the legality is stealing. Some is not intentional, as many Spiritual Creatures have little knowledge, little ability, little time, problematic situations, do not know the subjects, have wrong learning about the subjects, etc.
---T--- Now we all desire freedom of the Free-will. We do not desire dictatorial governments: // We all are part of the GOV in the USA. Thus, when thinking of what to do and not to do, is difficult. Evil must be included in the thinking. A GOV system does not have to allow evil to allow the Free-

will. And the GOV is not limited to some small group of Spiritual Moral Creatures at some location. In a system such as the USA, evil is not to be promoted. This then allows Spiritual Moral Creatures to decide on their personal living situations. However, citizenry depends on decisions to support the CC (DOI & CON); in public activities and in degrees of personal evils committed. The personal land of a Spiritual Moral Creature is their personal decision; however it cannot be established to do evil; If they do evil in their home, then that is their decision; however it depends on what evil. Satanism is not allowed. There are HSC about such. Degrees of evil have various limits to them. Neither is evil to be as a business in the USA. It may not be sold or promoted to other Spiritual Moral folk. Some of the basic laws against evil are herein stated.

---T--- *GOOD & NOT EVIL BASIS: // Congress Meeting notes*, 1778-88 - ",,,it is very evident,,, Another thing is remarkable, - that gentlemen, as an answer to every improper part of it, tell us that every thing is to be done by our own representatives, who are to be good men. There is no security that they will be so, or continue to be so. Should they be virtuous when elected, the laws of Congress will be unalterable. ,,,The CON must be the supreme law of the land; otherwise, it would be in the power of any one state to counteract the other states, and withdraw itself from the Union. ,,,Are laws as immutable as constitutions? Can any thing be more absurd than assimilating the one to the other? The idea is not warranted by the CON, nor consistent with reason." // This is Principle Law. All should be good because the Ruling Principle is that all should be in the category of good. Therefore evil must have limits with Free-will.

---T--- Principle Law is that of GOODNESS: // This is Principle Law. All should be good because the Ruling Principle is that all should be in the category of good. Hence evil must have limits with Free-will.

---T--- Now this National system was designed based on God & Christianity because of evil: // It does not promote evil anywhere. A wrong system & wrong hearts makes, or equals (=) evil. The situations are: +} that of a Free-Will allowance; +} no evil supported by business, nor by promotion; +} it is right to provide forgiveness, mercy & Love; +} evil is to be limited; some evil is to be stopped and some evil is to be limited in other ways. // How do Nations get to have evil National systems anyway? By starting an evil system. // The USA system was planned to prevent & oppose such. How? By putting a limit on evil.

---T--- Kidnapping or man-stealing is illegal. // This pertains to the business of human traffic in any way, including slavery, and that of the home. // Protecting the parents and their children from invasion by the USA GOV is also part of stealing of children. Parents have Right to their children to raise them accordingly, and religiously as in accordance to the 1-A, R-E, R~Est. // Holy Scripture~ Col 3:20-"Children, obey your parents in all things: for this is well pleasing to the Lord".

---T--- Family & Home & Parental Abuse: // Now note here that the Home & family is the 1st Institution or group of Spiritual Moral Creatures; and that the Order is God, Husband, Wife, Children. There is no place for some strange Creature from the GOV. HSC~ "1Cor11:3 But I would have you know, that the head of every man is Christ; and the head of the woman is the man; and the head of Christ (Emmanuel) is God (the Father)". // GOV has limited Rights from God as part of the family. And it is to support God & goodness Rom 13. Not evil & demons, or anti-God.

---T--- GOV is NOT to Oppose God teachings in the Home/family Nor Support teachings against God: // Such is stated by the CC, all supporting DOC, the FFOG, the cause of the RW and the DOI, etc. // Furthermore, HSC~ 1Joh5:21-"Little children, keep yourselves from idols. Amen." // The home, family, and living shelter is to be FULL of, not limited, HSC & GOD~ Deu6:5-18-"you shall love the LORD your God with all your heart, and with all your soul, and with all your might. And these words, which I command you this day, shall be in your heart: And you shall teach them diligently to your children, and shall talk of them when you sittest in your house, and when you walkest by the way, and when you liest down, and when you risest up. ,,,And you shall write them on the posts of your house, and on your gates. And houses full of all good things ,,,when you shall have eaten and be full; Then beware lest you forget the LORD ,,,You shall fear the LORD your God, and serve him, and shall swear by his name. You shall not go after other gods, of the gods of the people which are round about you; (For the LORD your God is a jealous God among you) lest the anger of the LORD your God be kindled against you,,, You shall not tempt the LORD your God ,,,You shall diligently keep the commandments of the LORD your God, and his testimonies, and his statutes, which he hath commanded you. And you shall do that which is right and good in the sight of the LORD".

---T--- Evil or all sorts of sin; Principle Law of Evil Category: // "laws of nature and of nature's God entitle them"; "that they are endowed by their Creator with certain inalienable rights; that among these are life, liberty, and the pursuit of happiness." ~These statements of Truth in the CC (DOI & CON) are, with clarity, opposing any activity against God the Creator that is evil; and any activity against liberty to do good and also liberty~ is liberty from evil. Evil is not intended/ purposed; And so we want to be free (liberated) from it. Also happiness and evil do not go together, which is a self-evident. The conscience truth is an evidence clarified.

---T--- Adultery & Sodomy (homosexuality licenses); Licenses for evil is Wrong: // FFOG John Adams states, ",,,The Jews, the Greeks, the Romans, the Swiss, the Dutch, all lost their public Spirit, their Republican Principles and habits, and their Republican Forms of GOV, when they lost the Modesty and Domestic Virtues ,,,In vain are Schools ,,,universities instituted, if loose Principles and licentious habits are impressed upon Children in their earliest years. [Parents] are the earliest and most important Instructors of youth,,,"; also stated, ",,,Contract of marriage is not only a civil and moral Engagement, but a Sacrament, one of the most Solemn Vows and Oaths of Religious devotion. Can they then believe Religion and Morality too any thing more than a Veil, a Cloak, an hypocritical Pretext, for political purposes of decency and Conveniency." (117). // Now the problem with homosexuality is, for one, it is not a marriage according to God & His Holy Bible; nor by Nature. Therefore not only is it an anti-true-religion, but an opposition to God. // It is also a lie. To define marriage as such is to lie; This is against truth. // It is an eye-sore; any Spiritual reasonable Moral Creature can see with the eye that it is not reasonable, rather a form of insanity. // Repeated again~ To give licenses to do evil is not right. If Spiritual Immoral creatures desire to do sodomy, then they have a personal right to do such. May the Lord have mercy. However God's Society does not have a Right to provide licenses, tax incentives, nor promotion of it; public advertising, etc. We may give them some food, and assistance in living. // Sodomy is also against "natures laws". The bodies are not made as designed intended for it. Children cannot come from it. Children should not be taught to do it. Neither are the affections and desires for it Right. Such activity will undoubtedly receive the anger of the Lord in to their spirits.

---T--- PRINCIPLE LAW & WORD Definition Law, as pertaining to the CC (DOI & CON), and to all the Evidences in this Book, make a clarified Fact or Truth that all such activity must be discerned; and that all evil is to be rejected, and considered as Illegal in the USA. Evil must be limited, not supported and encouraged.

---T--- We will not provide a Total Reference of Listing of all Illegal Laws of the USA that have been enacted; rather only some parts.

---T--- As USA citizens, a pledge is done to honor the CC (DOI & CON); to become a citizen: // Thus, to oppose (which includes contradiction) is a lie and an act of Treason against the USA and to God.

---T--- Covenant or Contract Agreement: // The DOI & CON are an instrument of Agreement. // To oppose (including contradict) is to breach of contract, an illegal offense to the USA and to the God of the contracts (covenant)~ CC.

---T--- These Amendments have been wrongly connected and/or interpreted~ the 1st, the 5th, and the 14th.

---T--- Re-writing history is an illegal action of lying.

---T--- Illegality of Misinterpreting, denying, or distorting the facts of history.

---T--- Misinterpreting or distorting to make the DOCs and EV to define something which it does not say.

---T--- Alcohol, in the use or form of Recreational Alcohol, is ILLEGAL: // The 18th Amendment states: "After one year from the ratification of this article the manufacture, sale, or transportation of intoxicating liquors within, the importation thereof into, or the exportation thereof from the US and all territory subject to the jurisdiction thereof for beverage purposes is hereby prohibited". // This is God's Christian law to prohibit recreational alcohol. Note that it states Beverage Purposes. // It is also a violation under religious freedom of the land; because it is an offense against Christ & Christianity as starting oppositional evils. // Amendment 18 - Liquor Abolished. Ratified 1/16/1919. Repealed by Amendment 21, 12/5/1933. +This made the evil of recreational alcohol legal; thus is actually illegal. // Recreational Alcohol is an evil, as was stated by the FFOG (all Branches). // Medicinal and hygienic uses of alcohol, and how to control it, is different. These are allowed and supported. // The Bill should not have been ratified because, including that the Holy Bible states, recreational alcohol is an evil; and not only not to drink it, but do not even look at it, which is a first action to the indulging of it; If spiritual moral people never looked at it, they would not think of it; and then not start a desire for it, nor make it, and not drink it. HSC~ Pro23; Eph5:18. // Recreational Alcohol is the cause of many problems; serious problems, both mentally & bodily, and eternally, etc. It has a crazy effect to the mind; such is not right emotions, affections, nor healthy.

---T--- False Christianity: // This is referring to doctrines that are not of the main doctrines. A careful and seriousness about false Christianity and religious abuse is very much the reason for the USA, DOI, and CON.

---T--- Witchcraft opposed; which includes the serious degrees of it~ demonism, Satanism.

---T--- Evil music which is involved in Evil Activities, which includes some forms sometimes called, Rock, Rapp, Specific Country, etc. Evil words, and such like.// Witchcraft music, etc.

---T--- Dancing, as rightly defined, in the form of illicity sexual dancing.

---T--- There are these subjects that occurred in the earlier times of the USA, and of which may seem contradictory to the Proper Righteous Application of the USA & its GOV: Slavery, Alcohol, Women's voting Rights, Indians, and Dueling. It needs to be realized that there was difficulty, and study, for discerning on these subjects by the FFOG. The facts are as follows about activities, events, and FFOG: /////// SLAVERY: This was included in the CC by the statement of the DOI~ "all men are created equal". Now, the facts are that enough effort was not exerted to end slavery at first because some Spiritual Moral folk did not know fully of what was occurring; and others did not know whether it is right or wrong; and others thought it was an employment method; and others thought that they were not involved with it; and others intended to maintain freedom of Free-will. Now there may be other things they thought about the subject, etc. Nevertheless after the RW more effort should have been put forth to stop it. FFOG, such as George Mason, warned of national judgments from God because of national sins. FFOG George Washington, Benjamin Rush, Benjamin Franklin, and others agreed. They wanted slavery totally stopped then, or soon. In the Civil War, 600,000 lives approx. were lost, and other non-life damages. Luther Martin, (not Martin Luther) at the time of the DOI & CON desired slavery to be stopped, saying, "It ought to be considered that national crimes can only be and frequently are punished in this world by national punishments, and that the continuance of the slave trade ,,,ought to be considered as justly exposing us to the displeasure and vengeance of Him Who is equally Lord of all and Who views with equal eye the poor African slave and his American master" (254). Thomas Jefferson opposed slavery stating, "I tremble for my country when I reflect that God is just, that His justice cannot sleep forever" (40a). The Character Personality of most of the FFoG, at the time, was in opposition to slavery, or at least to abusive slavery, and wanted it stopped. Good Spiritual Moral people did not abuse the slaves. We, nor they, say that it should exist, and exist in such a definition. But the fact is that some good persons were involved in slavery, but used it as a method; and intentional purposed for it to be a method of employment and physical sustenance for the slaves. Any honest person in an unstable economic world would gladly admit that stable and secure employment is ideal and desirable; if there is a good place to live and everything is supplied, then thank the Lord God. This was the essence of the system by the good spiritual moral Beings. This is well proven and revealed by their status. The following Spiritual people did the following actions: +George Washington eventually relinquished the system and gave the spiritual moral folks (his slaves) their choice of full freedom. +Congressman Richard Bassett, a Christian Methodist, "freed his slaves and then employed them as hired labor" (33). +George Mason, was a "man of profound learning ,,,and disapproved the slave-trade" (85). As the DOI states, that "All men are created equal" and includes slaves, or all spiritual created peoples. Slavery was not legalized in the DOI nor CON. It was simply unmentioned directly; but in Principle mentioned as illegal. Furthermore, we need to realize that, any peoples involved in Satanism, as some people from all "races" or societies have been, are connected to problems with other spiritual people. The people that lived in Ireland, Druids, by some names, were enslaving people from Britain, as was St Patrick himself a slave; Satanism was involved. This is not to justify slavery, for we do not agree with it; Slavery is not agreed on. It may be a form of employment and called by the term Slavery, but this is disagreed to also. The "Race", called the "black race", also enslaved spiritual people; such as the Egyptians who enslaved the Israelites (the Egyptians are of the "black race"). Now the truth about the slavery status of the FFOG is herein. They realized it was in error~ the system of employment as such; they tried to end it many times but Britain refused (6)(30). Benjamin Franklin in AD 1773 shared with Dean Woodward that every attempt to end slavery was hindered by Britain (222). John Quincy Adams was known as the "hell-hound of abolitions" for his efforts in opposition to slavery (184). Elias Boudinot states, "Even though the sacred SCs had been quoted to justify this in iniquitous traffic ,,,It is true that the Egyptians held the Israelites in bondage for four hundred years,,, but,,, gentlemen cannot forget the consequences that followed: they were delivered by a strong hand and stretched -out arm and it ought to be remembered that the Almighty Power that accomplished their deliverance is the same yesterday, today, and ever" (185a)(28). Some of the southern States agreed to slavery. +Slavery is anti-Christian, and such Christianity was the reason that slavery was finally and totally illegal; thank the Lord for Christianity. +See such of this enactment: "Bills and Resolutions ,,,and which by its terms forever prohibits slavery or involuntary servitude ,,,except as a punishment for crime, whereof the party shall have been duly convicted,,, free citizens of the US to be so disposed of as to re-establish chattel slavery for life, or for years, against the principles of the CHRISTIAN RELIGION, of civilization, and of the CON of the US, which now recognizes no involuntary servitude, except to the law and to the officers of its administration". +Now, therefore, opposition to slavery is stated often by many FFoG people, for EX by John Dickinson, Charles Carroll, John Jay, Richard Henry Lee, Thomas Jefferson, Luther Martin, William Livingston, Henry Laurens, Noah Webster, George Mason, Benjamin Rush, Joseph Reed, James Wilson, John Witherspoon, and many members of societies, of Bible societies, and others. Much earlier than the Civil War was this enactment: Rufus King assisted a law to ban slavery that George Washington signed and thus Illinois, Indiana, Ohio, Iowa, Michigan, and Wisconsin agreed and prohibited it. Additionally is the need to study what the Holy Bible says about the subject. There are Biblical references to it in the OT, for which some sort of system was set up. The FFOG studied this, of which we will not include the details for now; except to share that God demanded the Israelites to be kind and loving to all; and that in the OT slavery is wrong. Furthermore many slaves, those that were treated kindly, were thankful for the assistance received. Such as Phillis Wheatley who wrote a poem which is titled "On Being Brought From Africa to America" which remarks this, "Twas mercy brought me from my Pagan land, Taught my benighted soul to understand That there's a God, that there's a Savior too: Once I redemption neither sought nor knew,,,". ~See there the USA as a Christian Mission Nation to other nations. Now we remind again, that the FFoG attitude was that slavery was prohibited in the statement that "all men are created equal" (DOI). /////// ALCOHOL (recreational): Alcohol had differing opinions at the time. Often it was called "spirits". It is to be totally rejected in the USA (recreational use). Only medicinal and hygienic purposes are to be allowed, or such like. The FFOG were struggling on interpretations in the Holy Bible, on the wordings, and of which some Christians stumbled. But in Holy SC it is clearly stated, "Be not drunk with wine; do not look on the wine when it is red,,, turn color" (fermenting process) Eph5:18, Pro23:31; drunk process starts as soon as it enters. And there are many other HSC. Wine in Old English Language is usually defined as~ liquid from grapes. This is not the same word used for wine of the alcohol category today. And this is not a complete study of HSC on wine used in the KJV. However, alcohol has purposes for medicinal as numbing, or cleaning, hygienic, sterilizing, etc. For recreational drinking, it was made illegal and considered evil, by the FFOG; they constructed the 18th Amendment that made it illegal within 1 yr of the CON completion. /////// WOMEN'S RIGHTS -- to Vote: This has parts about it that are considerable. +Equality ~ "all men created equal" includes women; this is the statement in the DOI part of the CC. And such was the intention and application of the FFOG. Women were highly treated with dignity and respect. Conscience is reflective of this in our Spiritual Moral Being. All Mankind includes~ males & females; they are to be treated equal. And goodness is to be expressed and NOT evil; no evil to any Creature Being is supported; rather is opposed. Females are created by God equally as males. And leadership and GOV abuse pertains to all, including women. All applications of the Principle Laws in the CC (DOI & CC) could not totally be accomplished with such limited circumstances, limited time, and with the trials, troubles, and temptations the FFOG was enduring. The Holy Biblical subject was not completely studied by some Spiritual people; keeping the home without dividing it, traveling not as common and easy, systems of voting with all the confidentiality, proving the vote, and such, and the lack of a system for all to study what issues are to be concerned about, and who the candidates are, and such are subjects that influenced the FFOG. There are Holy Biblical references that God has instructed for positions and tasks and genders; that specific individuals have. No person is more valuable, nor loved than any other to God; nor to good men (Joh3:16, Rom2:11, Eph6:9). Nor is any person more useful than anyone else, with regard to natural rights or abilities. No position makes a person more valuable or loved by God. All these categories are only a fact, and the way things are in this world, by intention/ purpose, design, circumstances, providence, and function-ability; and some for eternity. However, "all men are created equal" was the attitude of the FFoG, and for this application they had not fully been able to perfect, neither in study nor ability. For the place of men & women in society will have to be considered carefully, prayerfully, and completely; and is not fully done so in this Book; there are many exceptions to the rules in some subjects. And such subject is not in the jurisdication of some group of GOV Creatures alone, nor prioritively. It is a home or family & God jurisdiction; & Church. Women were valuable and not considered less as a Spirit Moral Being than men. FFOG John Adams stated the priority and value of women in society, ",,,The Manners of Women, are the surest Criterion by which to determine whether a Republican GOV is practicable, in a Nation or not ,,,The foundations of national Morality must be laid in private Families" (117). However because of related situations, such as including travel, children, home function, physical ability, voting technicalities and methods, and other related parts, then the application was limited for that time to the Basic Principle Laws. How could every person travel and all the votes be counted; or mailing, and every one eat and live, and such? Hence the subject was put in a Principle Law to include the women, but the study of the subject, and the method to get all the votes of all the population in a less capable society pertinent to tools, was the problem. /////// INDIANS: No true Christian would abuse another Spiritual Creature Being knowingly and intentionally. Maybe a false one, or deceived one. This Book is not a full reports on the Indian situation. Any abuse was not from the FFOG who gave us the right establishments; rather any abuse was from them who were in the same time frame working in opposition to the true establishments, which includes false religionists, or false Christians, or anti-Christians. Land situations were not clear, and no ownership was established. The Earth is owned by God, obviously, and to all mankind by delegation; that is stated in the CC, including the DOI; and in HSC. We are our brothers keeper to some extent, and we must do as the Lord Jesus has commanded which includes to love other Spiritual Beings as ourself; that is the motto of Christians. The distinction of ownership with man is a related situation of living operation, and thus he must manage the situations for existence; as to what that should be. We all must live on the Earth, and God's Christianity is the Truth and therefore how we manage such is the situation. /////// DUELING: This evidently was a strange form, of some parts of the GOV, to solve serious disagreements; of some sort. It was eventually illegalized. What cases it was applied and how applied is not discussed here; Nor a full report of it is supplied herein. It did exist in some parts; and by what Spiritual Moral folk it was supported and not supported is not discussed here. It is a form of war. It was a form of solving problems between good & evil. /////// EVALUATION of these PROBLEMS: The fact is that because some Spiritual Moral people associated with a doctrine or truth does not equal that they are: 1} Practicing it. 2} Do not have areas that are wrong elsewhere. 3} That all their doctrines or beliefs in life are right. 4} That they are not intentionally wrong in areas. 5} That they are not hypocrites, as remember we are in a world of good & evil. 6} Are not mistaken in areas; even Christian DEN make mistakes. 7} Thus none of these situations negates the truth; not even one small amount. 8} These problems do not offer excuse or reason to do evil or diminish the CC; Rather the CC is a Method of correction and assistance to these, and assisted in solving them. 9} The CC is increased by these because the CC includes God and His Love and this is the solution to all problems, or trials, troubles, temptations; God's presence and intention/ purpose to Him as a Being of Value is our solution and comfort.

---T--- Deceitfully ignoring, rejecting, or dismissing of the intention/ purposes of the FFOG of our GOV.

---T--- The USA CON states it is illegal for the USA to commit crime against the citizens of the USA, which crime is that which opposes the DOI & CON (CC).

---T--- Illegally inserting deceitful definitions in to the CON.

---T--- Libraries are Becoming Full of Illegal Material & Evil Thought Promoting: // The Lord Jesus said in Pro 23:10-12-"Remove not the old landmark; and enter not into the fields of the fatherless: For their redeemer is mighty; He shall plead their cause with you.". Here is a promise that Christ will surely defend the children; especially those that do not have proper home instruction. A Spiritual Moral creature visited a Library in search for a reading lesson for a Spiritual Moral Creature that needed to learn to read. It was desired to get a CD, or cassette, for audio lessons and then a little written accommodating booklet. However after an hour search the results were not one TRUE Christian item co/ be found; rather 5000 minimal in number~ of pagan, demonic, evil worldly, illicity fornicational, and foolish & vain materials. What corruption and fearful alarm this is for the illegalities and damage to poor, little, minds and hearts searching only for a comforting table of warmth and kindness to be expressed to them.

---T--- Demented Results: // The illegalities of the TV. The effects to children are causing problems, as observed across the USA. A group of Children had been habitually trained by TV viewing, whose parents claimed was as a "learning session"; however it was rather not helpful. In reality, the children were of highly anxious mind, and of such crazy thoughts & feelings that being with them was similar to try to comprehend an insane asylum, and control an already stampeding herd of cattle spooked by wolfs; various children have had mental, emotional, affectionate, etc. problems. Now of the Free-Will is one subject, but the publicity of advertising evil to other Spiritual Moral Creatures is a Do Not.

---T--- The pretending profession, cartoons, etc. are making recreational violence; which makes recreation of violence; an entertainment to watch fighting, killing, disagreements, strife, wars, etc. Such should never be made recreational; these subjects are to be grieved over, to avoid, to mourn about. Entry to such subjects is not to be a devalued fast folly or careless attitude; such subjects are in reality, terrible & fearful; painful to Spirit Beings. Mat5-7.

---T--- <u>Taxation System: Some parts of it are Legal & Some are not legal to the CC.</u> // Money is spent to pay them to have such a mass system that takes multiples of thousands of dollars simply to operate. A simple system would save money. Additionally they are trying to have a small group of Spiritual Moral Creature people in position make places where to spend money by making line items for credits & deductions. Now for the wrongs that are therein needs assistance, but for the right therein is thanked to them. For Christianity to get relief is right, but in other areas is excess GOV control. // Continuing on the other subject, as to spending of money. How does it help to pay Spiritual Moral Creature people to make a time costing form for filing and then pay some more GOV workers to have to study the form, requiring much time; and so now what exists, is the money that was paid in for taxes is being used up for this service. Then there may be private people that prepare taxes, being paid for preparing the form, etc. Now the creation of jobs is some philosophy; or the spending of money creates a good economy is another theory. // However this system is errorful. EX: Let us say that a private business makes $10k annually and pays $100 to a private tax preparer. The N GOV makes 5% on the income after expenses; which is actually what the $10K is per above. Now the GOV spends money to make it. So the total money generated by these 2 workers is $10,100. Then the N GOV tax form designers and the proofers all make incrementally $300, excluding costs of benefits and taxes, paper, mailing, and all administrative costs of buildings and so on, etc. Thus now a total of $10,400 has been generated. However now we have the cost of the situation. The business pays $500 (5% of $10k) to N GOV; the tax preparer pays $5 (5% of $100). So we have $505 paid to N GOV for taxes for which cost $300 for them to earn; and then the added cost additional overhead as said; of paper, mailing, admin., buildings, etc. If we put in the tax paid by the N GOV tax workers we have incrementally $15. Thus an obvious loss here. This is an EX of how the situation should be evaluated. This is not a real situation, rather only a similitude.

---T--- <u>USA GOV opposed to Evil Principles, idolatry (anti-Christ), non-truth, Evil actions or Sins as identified in Christ's Holy Bible; such as Bad GOV & GOV abuse on Other Spirit Creature folks, murder, licentiousness, rage, stealing, etc.:</u> // "Letters of Delegates to Congress: Volume 10- 6/1, 1778 – 9/30, 1778 Gouverneur Morris to the Carlisle Commissioners [June 20, 1778] ,,,Trusty and well-beloved servants of your SACRED master, in whom he is well pleased. As you are sent to America for the express purpose of treating with anybody and anything, you will pardon an address from one who disdains to flatter those whom he loves. Should you therefore deign to read this address, your chaste ears will not be offended with the language of adulation, a language you despise. I have seen your ,,,letter "to ,,,the President, and other Members of the Congress." ,,,As that body have thought your propositions unworthy their particular regard, it may be some satisfaction to your curiosity, and tend to appease the offended SPIRIT of negotiation, if one out of the many individuals on this great Continent should speak to you the sentiments of America. Sentiments which your own good sense hath doubtless suggested, and which are repeated only to convince you that, notwithstanding the narrow ground of private information on which we stand in this distant region, still a knowledge of our own rights, and attention to our own interests, and a SACRED respect for the dignity of human nature, have given us to understand the TRUE PRINCIPLES which ought, and which therefore shall, sway our conduct. You begin with the amiable expressions of humanity, the earnest desire of tranquility and peace. A better introduction to Americans could not be devised. ,,,You tell us you have powers unprecedented in the annals of your history. And England, unhappy England, will remember with deep contrition, that these powers have been rendered of no avail by a conduct unprecedented in the annals of mankind. Had your royal master condescended to listen to the PRAYER of millions,,,", You tell us that "all parties may draw some degree of consolation, and even auspicious hope, from recollection." We wish this most sincerely for the sake of all parties. America, even in the moment of subjugation, would have been consoled by conscious virtue, and her hope was and is in the justice of her cause, and THE JUSTICE OF THE ALMIGHTY. These are sources of hope and of consolation, which neither time nor chance can alter or take away. You mention "the mutual benefits and consideration of EVILs, that may naturally contribute to determine our resolutions." As to the former, you know too well that we could derive no benefit from an union with you, nor will I, by deducing the reasons to evince this, cast an insult upon your understandings. As to the latter, it were to be wished you had preserved a line of conduct equal to the delicacy of your feelings. You could not but know that men, who sincerely love freedom, disdain the consideration of all EVILs necessary to attain it. Had not your own hearts borne testimony to this TRUTH, you might have learnt it from the annals of your history. For in those annals instances of this kind at least are not unprecedented. But should those instances be insufficient, we PRAY you to read the unconquered mind of America. That the acts of Parliament you transmitted were passed with singular unanimity, we pretend not to doubt. You will pardon me, gentlemen, for observing, that the reasons ,,,You tell us you are willing "to consent to a cessation of hostilities, both by sea and land." It is difficult for rude Americans to determine whether you are serious in this proposition, or whether you mean to jest with their simplicity. Upon a supposition, however, that you have too much magnanimity to divert yourselves on an occasion of such importance to America, and perhaps not very trivial in the eyes of those who sent you, permit me to assure you, on the SACRED word of a gentleman, that if you shall transport your troops to England, where before long your Prince will certainly want their assistance, we never shall follow them thither. We are not so romantically fond of fighting, neither have we such regard for the city of London, as to commence a crusade for the possession of that HOLY land. Thus you may be certain that hostilities will cease by land. It would be doing singular injustice to your national character, to suppose you are desirous of a like cessation by sea ,,,to revive mutual affection, and renew the common benefits of naturalization." [[DOI here supported with God Given Rights]] Whenever your countrymen shall be taught wisdom by experience, and learn from past misfortunes to pursue their TRUE

272

interests ,,,To revive mutual affection is utterly impossible. We freely forgive you, but it is not in nature that you should forgive us. You have injured us too much. We might, on this occasion, give you some late instances of singular BARBARITY, committed as well by the forces of his Britannic Majesty, as by those of his generous and faithful allies, the Senecas, Onondagas and Tuscaroras. But we will not offend a courtly ear by the recital of those disgusting scenes. Besides this, it might give pain to that humanity which hath, as you observe, prompted your overtures to dwell upon the splendid victories obtained by a licentious soldiery over unarmed men in defenceless villages, their wanton devastations, their deliberate murders, or to inspect those scenes of carnage painted by the wild excesses of savage rage. These AMIABLE TRAITS OF NATIONAL CONDUCT CANNOT but revive in our bosoms that partial affection we once felt for everything which bore the name of Englishman. As to the common benefits of naturalization, it is a matter we conceive to be of the most sovereign indifference ,,,will hardly claim naturalization in either of those places as a benefit. On the other hand, such of your subjects as shall be driven by the iron hand of oppression to seek for refuge among those whom they now persecute, will certainly be admitted to the benefits of naturalization. We labour to rear an asylum for mankind, and regret that circumstances will not permit you, Gentlemen, to contribute to a design so very agreeable to your several tempers and dispositions. But further, your Excellencies say, "we will concur to extend every freedom to trade that our respective interests can require." Unfortunately there is a little difference in these interests, which you might not have found it very easy to reconcile, had the Congress been disposed to ,,,listening to terms ,,,The difference I allude to is, that it is your interest to monopolize our commerce, and it is our interest to trade with all the world ,,,By reserving to the Parliament of Great-Britain the right of determining what our respective interests require, they might extend the freedom of trade, or circumscribe it, at their pleasure, for what they might call our respective interests. But I trust it would not be to our mutual satisfaction. Your "earnest desire to stop the farther effusion of blood, and the calamities of war," will therefore lead you, on maturer reflection, to reprobate a plan teeming with discord, and which, in the space of twenty years, would produce another wild expedition across the Atlantic ,,,on behalf of my countrymen, I do most solemnly promise and assure you, that no military force shall be kept up in the different States of North-America without the consent of the general Congress, and that of the legislatures of those States. You will therefore cause the forces of your royal master to be removed, for I can venture to assure you that the Congress have not consented, and probably will not consent, that they be kept up ,,,with "perfect respect" ,,,that it will be necessary to procure very ample recommendations. For ,,,You propose to us a devise to "perpetuate our union." It might not be amiss previously to establish this union, which may be done by your acceptance of the treaty of peace and commerce tendered to you by Congress ,,,And such treaty, I can venture to say, would continue as long as your ministers could prevail upon themselves not to violate the faith of nations. You offer, to use your own language, the inaccuracy of which, considering the importance of the subject, is not to be wondered at, or at least may be excused, "in short to establish the powers of the respective legislatures in each particular State, to settle its revenue, its civil and military establishment, and to exercise a perfect freedom of legislation and internal government, so that the British States throughout North-America acting with us, in peace and war, under one common sovereign, may have the irrevokable enjoyment of every privilege that is short of a total separation of interests, or consistent with that union of force on which the safety of our common RELIGION [[Christianity; words from the Holy Bible]] and liberty depends." Let me assure you, gentlemen, that the power of the respective legislatures in each particular State is already most fully established, and on the most solid foundations. It is established on the perfect freedom of legislation and a vigorous administration of internal government ,,,We cannot perceive that our liberty does in the least depend upon any union of force with you; for we find that, after you have exercised your force against us for upwards of three years, we are now upon the point of establishing our liberties in direct opposition to it. Neither can we conceive, that, after the experiment you have made, any nation in Europe will embark in so unpromising a scheme as the subjugation of America ,,,Your Excellencies will, I hope, excuse me when I differ from you, as to our having a RELIGION in common with you: the RELIGION of America is the RELIGION of all mankind. Any person may worship in the manner he thinks most agreeable to the Deity; [[See here that Christian is the Deity; not falsity deities; worship in any manner to the Deity is referring to DEN or Sect, expression, and secondary doctrines; DEN is Establishments of Religion of God]] and if he behaves as a good citizen, no one concerns himself as to his faith or adorations, neither have we the least solicitude to exalt any one SECT or profession above another. I am extremely sorry to find in your letter some sentences, which reflect upon the character of his most CHRISTIAN Majesty. It certainly is not kind, or consistent with the principles of philanthropy you profess, to traduce a gentleman's character without affording him an opportunity of defending himself: and that too a near neighbour, and not long since an intimate brother, who besides hath lately given you the most solid additional proofs of his pacific disposition, and with an unparalleled sincerity, which would do honour to other Princes, declared to your court, unasked, the nature and effect of a treaty he had just entered into with these States. ,,,Neither is it quite according to the rules of politeness to use such terms in addressing yourselves to Congress, when you well knew that he was their good and faithful ally. It is indeed TRUE, as you justly observe, that he hath at times been at enmity with his Britannic Majesty, by which we suffered some inconveniences: but these flowed rather from our connection with you than any ill-will towards us: At the same time it is a solemn TRUTH, worthy of your serious attention, that you did not commence the present war, a war in which we have suffered infinitely more than by any former contest, a fierce, a bloody, I am sorry to add, an unprovoked and cruel war. That you did not commence this, I say, because of any connection between us and our present ally; but, on the contrary, as soon as you perceived that the treaty was in agitation, proposed terms of peace to us in consequence of what you have been pleased to denominate an insidious interposition. How then does the account stand between us. America, being at peace with all the world,,,. At present America, being engaged in a war with Great Britain ,,,For the TRUTH of these positions I appeal, gentlemen, to your own knowledge. I know it is very hard for you to part with what you have accustomed yourselves, from your earliest infancy, to call your colonies. I pity your situation, and therefore I excuse the little abberations from TRUTH which your letter contains. At the same time it is possible that you may have been misinformed. For I will not suppose that your letter was intended to delude the people of these States. ,,,To undeceive you, therefore, I take the liberty of assuring your Excellencies, from the very best intelligence, that what you call "the present form of the French offers to North-America," in other words the treaties of alliance and commerce between his most CHRISTIAN Majesty and these States, were not made in consequence of any plans of accommodation concerted in Great-Britain, nor with a view to prolong this destructive war. ,,,and the assurance given that America had reserved a right of admitting even you to a similar treaty, you must be convinced of the TRUTH of my assertions. The fact is ,,,It seems to me, gentlemen, there is something (excuse the word) disingenuous in your procedure. I put the supposition that Congress had acceded to your propositions, and then I ask two questions. Had you full power from your commission to make these propositions? Possibly you did not think it worth while to consider your commission, but we Americans are apt to compare things together, and to reason. The second question I ask is, What security could you give that the British Parliament would ratify your compacts? You can give no such security ,,,after all this, I say, we should have been at the mercy of a Parliament, which, to say no more of it, has not treated us with too great tenderness. It is quite needless to add, that even if that Parliament had ratified the conditions you proposed, still poor America was to lie at the mercy of any future Parliament, or appeal to the sword, which certainly is not the most pleasant business men can be engaged in.,,, Your nation totters on the brink of a stupendous precipice, and even delay will ruin her. You have told the Congress, "If, after the time that may be necessary to consider this communication, and transmit your answer, the horrors and devastations of war should continue, we call GOD and the world to witness that the EVILs, which must follow, are not to be imputed to Great-Britain." I wish you had spared your protestation. Matters of this kind may appear to you in a trivial light, as meer ornamental flowers of rhetoric, but they are serious things registered in the high chancery of HEAVEN. Remember the awful abuse of words like these by General Burgoyne, and remember his fate. There is one above us, who will take exemplary vengeance for every insult upon his Majesty. [[see God as most High Ruler]] You know that the cause of America is just. You know that she contends for that freedom, to which all men are entitled. That she contends against oppression, rapine, and more than savage barbarity. The blood of the innocent is upon your hands, and all the waters of the ocean will not wash it away. We again make our solemn appeal to the GOD of HEAVEN to decide between you and us. And we PRAY that in the doubtful scale of battle we may be successful, as we have JUSTICE ON OUR SIDE, and that the MERCIFUL SAVIOUR OF THE WORLD may forgive our oppressors. I am, my Lords and Gentlemen, The friend of human nature, And one who glories in the title of, An AMERICAN ,,,reprinted from the Pennsylvania Gazette, June 20, 1778 ,,,letters that Morris wrote to ,,,Carlisle commission as "An American." ,,,William Henry Drayton' Draft ,,,Henry Laurens' June 17 letter to the Carlisle commissioners,,,".

---T--- Republic; Not Democracy; Not Oligarchy: // Part of the formations of GOV that are now operating are not Republic. Changes to part forms of Democracy and Oligarchy (aristocracy, a few rule the many): // Attempting to make the vote able to overcome truth, which is a wrong Democracy; such sort of Democracy is not based on truth. Whereas a Republic, if formed right, with a basis of truth, can be based on truth. // FFOG John Adams stated, "There is no good GOV, but what is republican; for a republic is an empire of laws, and not of men"; "to constitute the best of republics, we enforced the necessity of separating the executive, legislative, and judicial powers" (8). // A Total Democracy and or a total Oligarchy are illegal forms.

---T--- Operating with false procedures and treating it as Law; For EX: Judges changing the CON.

---T--- Making laws that are illegal. // Enacted false and illegal laws then applying them to other Spiritual Moral Creatures.

---T--- Judicial actions & right system: // EX: Lets say there is a subject of good & evil, God or sin. +Now actions of Congress say "No" to evil and sin and "Yes" to God and good; +The Public vote says the same; +The CC says God and good are to be supported and evil and sin are not to be supported, rather controlled to some degree; limited. Now lets say a judge acts illegally in 2 ways: 1st} acts on his employment in an action that is disallowed by the CC for his employment. 2nd} acts to support evil & sin and rejects God & good on his employment. +Such is a form of dictatorship. No judge has Right to rule over the public, the congress, the CC, and God as such. // EX: Now lets say the subject is blue & pink. +Congress says the 2 are as they are in truth; +Public also discerns them as truth; +The dictionary says they are truth. Now then a judge comes in and says pink is blue and blue is pink. +Hence this defies the dictionary, congress, public, truth, and God. // The question is: Why do the public and congress support it? If they allow it, they support it. Why are not some actions done to put a stop to it ? // One example of this was the Abortion (kill babies) subject. The case not only had the same illegalities in it, but many more involved.

---T--- Opposed to anti-Christian activity; Principle Law: // "Letters of Delegates to Congress: Volume 8- 9/19, 1777 - 1/31, 1778 - John Adams to Abigail Adams - My best Friend York Town Octr. 25. 1777,,,This Town is a small one, not larger than Plymouth. There are in it, two German CHURCHes, the one Lutheran, the other Calvinistical. The CONGREGATIONS are pretty numerous, and their attendance upon PUBLIC WORSHIP is decent. It is remarkable that the Germans, wherever they are found, are carefull to maintain the PUBLIC WORSHIP, which is more than can be said of the other DENOMINATIONS of CHRISTIANs, this way. There is one CHURCH here erected by the joint contributions of Episcopalians and Presbyterians, but the minister, who is a missionary, is confined for Toryism, so that they have had for a long time no publick worship. ,,,Congress have appointed two Chaplains, Mr. White and Mr. Duffield, the former of whom an Episcopalian is arrived and opens Congress with PRAYERS every day. The latter is expected every hour. Mr. Duche I am sorry to inform you has turned out an Apostate and a Traytor. Poor Man! I pitty his weakness, and detest his WICKEDNESS. As to News, we are yet in a painful suspense about affairs at the northward, but from Philadelphia, We have accounts that are very pleasing. Commodore Hazelwood, with his Gallies, and Lt. Coll. Smith in the Garrison of Fort Mifflin, have behaved in a manner the most gallant and glorious. They have defended the River, and the Fort with a firmness and perseverance, which does honour to human nature. If the News from the Northward is TRUE, Mr. Howe will scarcely venture upon winter quarters in Philadelphia. We are waiting, for News, from Rhode Island. I am wearied with the life I lead, and long for the joys of my family. GOD grant I may enjoy it, in peace. Peace is my dear delight. War has no charms for me. If I live much longer in banishment I shall scarcely know my own Children. Tell my little ones, that if they will be very good, Pappa will come home. RC (MHi). ,,,2:359-60."

---T--- <u>Opposed to evil or wickedness, which is anti-Christian as Principle Law;</u> Also OPPOSED: To Sins; To Evil GOV; To Abuse from GOV; To GOV opposing God as the Main Authority; & To GOV taking God Given Rights of Citizens: // "Journals of the Continental Congress, 1774-1789, OCT 30, 1778 These US having been driven to hostilities by the oppressive and tyrannous measures of Great Britain; having been compelled to commit the essential rights of man to the decision of arms; and having been at length forced to shake off a yoke which had grown too burthensome to bear; they declared themselves free and independent. Confiding in the justice of their cause; confiding in Him, who disposes of human events; although weak and unprovoked, they set the power of their enemies at defiance. In this confidence they have continued through the various fortunes of three bloody campaigns, unawed by the power, unsubdued by the barbarity of their foes. Their virtuous citizens have borne, without repining, the loss of many things which make life desirable. Their brave troops have patiently endured the hardships and dangers of a situation fruitful in both, beyond former EX. The Congress considering themselves bound to love their enemies, as CHILDREN OF THAT BEING WHO IS EQUALLY THE FATHER OF ALL; and desirous, Since they could not prevent, at least to alleviate the calamities of war, have studied to spare those who were in arms against them, and to lighten the chains of captivity. The conduct of those serving under the king of Great Britain hath, with some few exceptions, been diametrically opposite. They have laid waste the open country, burned the defenceless villages, and butchered the citizens of America. Their prisons have been the slaughter-houses of her soldiers, their ships of her seamen; and the severest injuries have been aggravated by the grossest insult. Foiled in their vain attempt to subjugate the unconquerable SPIRIT of freedom, they have meanly assailed the representatives of America with bribes, with deceit, and the servility of adulation. They have made a mock of humanity by the wanton destruction of men. They have made a mock of RELIGION by impious appeals to GOD, whilst in the violation of his SACRED commands: They have made a mock even of reason itself, by endeavouring to prove that the liberty and happiness of America could safely be entrusted to those who have sold their own, unawed by the sense of virtue or of shame. Treated with the contempt which such conduct deserved, they have applied to individuals. They have solicited them to break the bonds of allegiance, and imbue their souls with the blackest of crimes. But fearing that none could be found through these US equal to the WICKEDNESS of their purpose, to influence weak minds they have threatened more wide devastation. While the shadow of hope remained that our enemies could be taught by our EX, to respect those laws which are held SACRED among CIVILIZED nations, and to comply with the dictates of a RELIGION which they pretend in common with us to believe and revere, they have been left to the influence of that RELIGION and that EX. But since their incorrigible dispositions cannot be touched by KINDNESS and COMPASSION, it becomes our duty by other means to vindicate the rights of humanity. We, therefore, the Congress of the US of America, do solemnly declare and proclaim, that if our enemies presume to execute their threats, or persist in their present career of barbarity, we will take such exemplary vengeance, as shall deter others from a like conduct. WE APPEAL TO THAT GOD WHO SEARCHETH THE HEARTS OF MEN, FOR THE RECTITUDE OF OUR INTENTIONS: AND IN HIS HOLY PRESENCE WE DECLARE, THAT AS WE ARE NOT MOVED BY ANY LIGHT AND HASTY SUGGESTIONS OF ANGER OR REVENGE, SO ,,,we will adhere to this our determination. Done in Congress, by unanimous consent, the thirtieth day of Oct., 1778. H. L.President. Attest ,,,C. T.Secretary.? ,,,Major General ,,,No. 158, folio 125.]".

---T--- <u>Illegal cases against the USA, CC (DOI &CON);</u> These are only a few of many that should be reversed: // 1948 McCollum vs. Board of Education. Christianity learning. // 1962 Engel vs. Vitale. Prayer to God, Christ Jesus. // 1963 School District of Abington Township vs. Schempp. Holy Bible reading. // 1968 Epperson vs. Arkansas. Religion definitions. // Lemon Test as implementation to determine violation by the Establishment Clause; a test developed by US Supreme Court in 1971, Lemon vs. Kurtzman case; to determine violations, as falsely defined. An unconstitutional wrongness by asserting they are supporting the CON. // 1980 Stone vs. Graham. Ten Commandments.

---T--- <u>Rights of CC DOI are not to be Opposed:</u> // Congress Meeting Notes, 1778-89, "They may trample on the rights of the people of North Carolina if there be not sufficient guards and checks. I only mentioned this to show that there may be misconstructions, and that, in so important a case as a constitution, every thing ought to be clear and intelligible, and no ground left for disputes."

---T--- <u>Illegalities of USA GOV against USA CC (DOI & CON)</u> with God: // Refusal to abide by the contractual conditions of the 10th amendment in the BOR which states that no powers beyond those stated. // The 9th Amendment states that the US GOV is limited to the "enumerated" Rights or powers. // The 7th amendment of the BOR, thus CON is that Common Law is the basis of law, thus the Holy Bible. // Evolving case law is illegal in the USA. // Statutory law cannot be defined as where judges or judicial law rules; or are the source of law. // Common law supports the DOI, that all is under God, truth, His Holy Bible, and against all evil with limits.

---T--- <u>Opposed to Evil, Anti-Christian, &</u> GOV Not Agreeing, or Disagreeing, to the Main Authority of GOD; & against UNTHANKFULNESS to GOD, to Our FFOG work, etc: // "Journals of the Continental Congress, 1774-1789 - AUG 3, 1784. The Committee of the States assembled: Present, nine states as yesterday. The committee, consisting of „,to his Excellency the President of Congress, dated Philadelphia, July 5, 1784, reported the draft of a letter to be signed by the chairman of the Committee of the States, and transmitted to the executive of the State of Virginia, together with a copy of said letter; which was agreed to. Sir „,It never was the idea of Congress that such Grant should be located or possession of the land taken till the general arrangements necessary for concluding a peace and establishing fixing „,public tranquility insured established „,I am Sir, Your Excellency's most obedt. and most hble. servt., Saml. Hardy „,Govr. of the state of Virginia.1 [Note 1: 1 This report, in the writing of Jacob Read, is in the Papers of the Continental Congress, No. 32, folio 141. „,Spaight)1 of the 2d instant "That a committee be appointed to prepare a proclamation for a day of solemn PRAYER and thanksgiving to Almighty GOD, to be observed throughout the US of America, on the exchange of the instruments of ratification of the Definitive Treaty of Peace, between the US of America and his Britannic Majesty; and the happy completion of the great work of Independency and peace to these US„, reported the following form of a proclamation „,By the US of America, in the Committee of the States assembled, A Proclamation. WHEREAS IT HATH PLEASED THE SUPREME RULER OF THE UNIVERSE, OF HIS INFINITE GOODNESS AND MERCY, SO TO CALM THE MINDS AND DO AWAY THE RESENTMENTS OF THE POWERS LATELY ENGAGED IN A MOST BLOODY AND DESTRUCTIVE WAR, AND TO DISPOSE THEIR HEARTS TOWARDS AMITY AND FRIENDSHIP, THAT „,A DEFINITIVE TREATY OF PEACE BETWEEN THE SAID US OF AMERICA AND HIS BRITANNIC MAJESTY, WAS SIGNED AT PARIS, ON THE 3D DAY OF SEPTEMBER, IN THE YEAR OF OUR LORD 1783; THE INSTRUMENTS OF THE FINAL RATIFICATIONS OF WHICH WERE EXCHANGED AT PASSY, ON THE 12TH DAY OF MAY, IN THE YEAR OF OUR LORD 1784, WHEREBY A FINISHING HAND WAS PUT TO THE GREAT WORK OF PEACE, AND THE FREEDOM, SOVEREIGNTY AND INDEPENDENCE OF THESE STATES, FULLY AND COMPLEATELY established: And whereas in pursuit of the great work of freedom and independence, and the progress of the contest in which the US of America have been engaged, and on the success of which the dearest and most essential rights of human nature depended, the benign interposition of DIVINE Providence hath, on many occasions, been most miraculously and abundantly manifested; and the citizens of the US have the greatest reason to return their most hearty and sincere praises and thanksgiving to the GOD of their deliverance; whose name be praised: Deeply impressed therefore with the sense of the mercies manifested to these US, and of the blessings which it hath pleased GOD, to shower down on us, of our future dependance, at all times, on his power and mercy as the only source from which so great benefits can be derived; we, the US of America, in the Committee of the States assembled, do earnestly recommend to the supreme executives of the several states, to set apart Tuesday, the 19th day of Oct. next, as a day of public PRAYER and thanksgiving, that all the people of the US may then assemble in their respective CHURCHes and congregations, to celebrate with grateful hearts, and joyful and united voices, the mercies and praises of their all-bountiful CREATOR, most HOLY, and most righteous! for his innumerable favours and mercies vouchsafed unto them; more especially that HE HATH BEEN GRACIOUSLY PLEASED so to conduct us through the perils and dangers of the war, as finally to establish the US in freedom and independency „,to lead our armies, and in our greatest difficulties and distresses hath given us unanimity to adhere to and assert our just rights and privileges; and that he hath been most graciously pleased also „,magnanimous people, as allies, to assist us in effectually supporting and maintaining them; that he hath been pleased to prosper the labour of our husbandmen; that there is no famine or want seen throughout our land: And above all, that he hath been pleased to continue to us the light of GOSPEL TRUTHS, and secured to us, in the fullest manner, the rights of CONSCIENCE in faith and worship. And while our hearts overflow with gratitude, and our lips pronounce the praises of our GREAT AND MERCIFUL CREATOR, that we may also offer up our joint and fervent supplications, that it may please him of his infinite goodness and mercy, to pardon all our SINS and offences; to inspire with wisdom and a TRUE sense of public good, all our public councils; to strengthen and cement the bonds of LOVE and AFFECTION BETWEEN ALL OUR CITIZENS; to impress them with an earnest regard for the public good and national faith and honour, and to teach them to improve the days of peace by every good work; to PRAY that he will, in a more especial manner, shower down his blessings on Louis the Most CHRISTIAN King our ally, to prosper his house, that his son's sons may long sit on the throne of their ancestors, a blessing to the people entrusted to his charge; to bless all mankind, and inspire the princes and nations of the earth with the love of peace, that the sound of war may be heard of no more; that he may be pleased to smile upon us, and bless our husbandry, fishery, our commerce, and especially our schools and seminaries of learning; and to raise up from among our youth, men eminent for virtue, learning and piety, to his service in CHURCH and state; to cause virtue and TRUE RELIGION to flourish, to give to all nations amity, peace and concord, and to fill the world with HIS GLORY. DONE BY THE US, IN THE COMMITTEE OF THE STATES ASSEMBLED, WITNESS THE HONBL SAMUEL HARDY, CHAIRMAN, THIS-- DAY OF--, IN THE YEAR OF OUR LORD, &C. AND IN THE 9TH OF THE SOVEREIGNTY AND INDEPENDENCE OF THE US OF AMERICA.1 [Note 1: 1 This report, in the writing of Jacob Read, is in the Papers of the Continental Congress, No. 32, folios 145--149.] A motion was made by Mr. [Francis] Dana, seconded by Mr. [Jonathan] Blanchard „,Mr. [Jacob] Read,".

---T--- Oppose evil, anti-Christ activity, Sin; Principle Laws: // "Letters of Delegates to Congress: Volume 13 June 1, 1779 - Sept 30, 1779 - James Lovell to Arthur Lee Dear Sir private Sepr. 22d. 1779 „,Mr. Smith-as follows Apr. 30th. „,I expect in a few hours to be able to show you whether yr honor is properly regarded here or not. If the Decision in regard to the Floridas & Mississ. are to be conveyed to Doctr. F or to a third person, your replicatory & defensive Letters have been in vain laid before men willfully blind. But I hope better things. I have Papers so arranged as to enlighten new members and make the old SIN against conviction, if they do SIN. „,".

---T--- Opposing evils, such as Slavery, Non-Christian Activity, & wrong interpretation of God's Holy Bible: // "The Debates in the Several State Conventions on the Adoption of the Federal CON [Elliot's Debates, Volume 2] - NEW HAMPSHIRE CONVENTION. [A friend has favored the editor with the following fragment, being the only speech known to be preserved in the New Hampshire Convention, on adopting the federal CON of the US.]

Page 7, Sec. 9,,, The migration or importation of such persons as any the states now existing shall think proper to admit, shall not be prohibited by Congress prior to the year 1808 ,,,Several members, on the other side, spoke in favor of it, with remarks on what Mr. Dow had said; after which, the Hon. JOSHUA ATHERTON, from Amherst, spoke as follows:-- Mr. President, I cannot be of the opinion of the honorable gentlemen who last spoke, that this paragraph is either so useful or so inoffensive as they seem to imagine, or that the objections to it are so totally void of foundation. The idea that strikes those, who are opposed to this clause, so disagreeably and so forcibly, is, hereby it is conceived (if we ratify the CON) that we become consenters to, and partakers in, the SIN and guilt of this abominable traffic, at least for a certain period, without any positive stipulation that it should even then be brought to an end. We do not behold in it that valuable acquisition so much boasted of by the honorable member from Portsmouth, "that an end is then to be put to slavery." Congress may be as much, or more, puzzled to put a stop to it then, than we are now. The clause has not secured its abolition. We do not think ourselves under any obligation to perform works of supererogation in the reformation of mankind; we do not esteem ourselves under any necessity to go to Spain or Italy to suppress the inquisition of those countries; or of making a journey to the Carolinas to abolish the detestable custom of enslaving the Africans; but, sir, we will not lend the aid of our ratification to this cruel and inhuman merchandise, not even for a day. There is a great distinction in not taking a part in the most barbarous violation of the SACRED laws of GOD and humanity, and our becoming guaranties for its exercise for a term of years. Yes, sir, it is our full purpose to wash our hands clear of it; and, however unconcerned spectators we may remain of such predatory infractions of the laws of our nature,,,".

---T--- Opposed to evil (anti-Christian activity) including evil words, evil against God's children, etc: // "Letters of Delegates to Congress: Volume 10- 6/1, 1778 — 9/30, 1778 - Henry Marchant to His Children - Dear Children, Philadelphia July 20th 1778 I recd. your endearing Letter of the 7th of July this Day and you can't conceive what a heartfelt Satisfaction it gave me; go on my dear Children and strive to excell in all useful knowledge, especially such as relates to GOD and that other world, where we are all to go. To them that behave well in this World, the next will be a world of happiness indeed-but to such as do ill here, it will be a world of EVERLASTING TORMENT. GOD grant that when we have all left this world, we may not be parted from each other in the world to come; but that all, father and mother, brother and sisters, may meet together, never to part again, but live a whole ETERNITY with GOD and CHRIST-with Abraham, Isaac & Jacob, and all other good men & women and children who have gone there before us. Remember that GOD hates a lye, and every thing that is dishonest-and that you must always be chearful and willing to do your duty to GOD and Man, and to your parents and to love one another and all good people, and that you must try to perswade naughty children to behave better and to QUIT all their WICKED WORDS and WAYS, if they would ever expect to be happy. I was pleased to see Billys Mark, he will in good time I hope learn to write his name. I wish Miss Sally & Betsy may begin to learn him his letters, and how to spell ,,,There was but two or three words misspelt, and one or two errors in grammar, and which I am sure Miss Sally could correct herself if she had had time to look it over again. For instance she spelt the word School-Skool. Miss Sally has been very industrious to have read the books She mentions twice over. I rejoice that she does not forget her BIBLE-her CATECHISM & PRAYERS. I am glad to find Mr. Pemberton has been with and that he kindly advises you. I will agree with him, that You may not make a task of your Grammar. Indeed my dear Child I know you love your book so well, that I think it needless you should task yourself with any book. I think a good and edifying book will never be a task to Miss Sally ,,,A little exercise in cyphering now and then I think is very well. I am also pleased that you take such notice of the business of the farm, and that you are able to give me so good an account of it. Your curiosity is excited to know the meaning of the tow upon some of the trees. I got some small twigs from trees of another sort of apples and pears and cut off a limb and stuck the small twiggs into it, to grow, and wrapt the Tow & clay round to keep the rain out. Mr. Webster will explain it to you further if you ask him. Are you like to have a good many pears, peaches, and apples? have you any currants? And how have You been for strawberries, huccleberries and blackberries? ,,,full powers and authority from the King of France to join with us, his advice and to assist us against our enemies-And the King of France has also sent us a great many large ships, to assist in taking the British Ships & people, and to drive them away from this good land which HEAVEN gave to Our Fore-Fathers, and to us their children, and which the KING OF ENGLAND and his WICKED people have been endeavouring to take from us-And I hope by the Blessing of GOD that we shall by & by have peace thro' all this Country, and that you may live to grow up and enjoy it with thankfulness to GOD, and never forget what great things the LORD hath done for you. Was it not for this hope my Dear Children, I could never consent to leave you & your good Mamma so long year after year. Hoping we may soon meet & praise GOD for his great goodness to us all, I remain your affectionate Father, Henry Marchant RC (RHi). Addressed: "Miss Sally, Miss Betsy, and Mr. [Billy] Marchant."

---T--- Opposes Evil or anti-Christian activity Principle Laws: // "Letters of Delegates to Congress: Volume 18- 3/1, 1781 — 8/31, 1781 - Arthur Middleton to Aedanus Burke My dr. Sir Pa. Apr. 7th. [1782] ,,,I take advantage of the return of Col. Motte to present you my Acknowledgts ,,,for yr. kind remembrance of me. The Strong Outlines you have drawn of the mellancholy real Situation of our Country in all points correspond exactly with what my anxious imagination had formed, whenever reason & reflexion led me to consider an Object allways uppermost in my mind; ,,,can restore that firm, orderly, & composed mode of proceeding so essential to establish the publick Happiness [[DOI supported by Congress as a continuing applicable DOC of USA]] which is or ought to be the wish of all. I have much confidence in the ability & integrity of the men chosen to conduct affairs. I think I know the PURITY of THEIR INTENTIONS & I trust their councills may yet lead us to prosperity. Upon mature consideration of all circumstances; of the unmerited sufferings of so many, & of the resentments necessarily rous'd in a people whom I know to be naturally generous & sensible, I rejoice that matters have been conducted with so much moderation & temper; tho' I could have wishd the idea of

Confiscation had been totally abolish'd, or at least put off till entire secure possession [of the] Country had restor'd Tranquillity, & the publick mind was free & open to the guidance of cool dispassionate reason. Your Sentiments upon the Subject are those of the Patriot & the friend of human Nature, & I wd. there had been more of your way of thinking ,,,even in cases of treason, I have been & am principled against it; I cannot approve of the inhuman sentence of visiting the SINS of the Fathers upon the guiltless women [and] children, [[Holy Bible quoted]] notwithstanding the SACRED Authority which may be quoted for it. It is a doctrine suited only to the climates of DESPOSTISM, & abhorrent to the dignified SPIRIT of pure & genuine republicanism. In the Eye of reason the individual shd. stand or fall by his own actions, & those connected should be involved in the punishment no farther, than they have been partakers in the crime. Banishment of the individual, & a deprivation of the Benefits of Citizenship & property for life are surely sufficient both as a punishment & a prevention of crimes, without reducing a whole family for the SIN of one to misery & destruction. Here my friend you have my thoughts upon an interesting subject which concerns the good of mankind ,,,see SCHGM, 26 (Oct. 1925): 190-95 ,,,on Apr. 3.JCC, 22:161 ,,,3 This day Middleton also drafted a letter ,,,"Testimony of my duty & gratitude," ,,,1754-63, 1768-71. "Next to the obedience due the Dictates of my own CONSCIENCE," Middleton continued, "it has ever lain nearest to my heart so to regulate my conduct as to wish your Approbation. I shall still be governed by the same motives, & trust I shall retain it to our Life's end-at parting with my Brother I entreated him to present my Duty to you, & to acquaint you that my mind was thoroughly at Ease with regard to my own fate; This I hoped would operate as a Balm to your affliction upon my Account. "To the many anxieties for my dearest Connections, the knowledge of your Ill health & Troubles have added grief indeed. Mr. R can tell how much I have felt for you. I am now anxious [for my?] Br[other]-in short our day seems to be crowded with Troubles ,,,Middleton's draft ,,,ScHi."

---T--- Opposing Evil Abuse to innocent Spiritual Moral Creature folks, including women & children; physical violence & anti-Christian violence & activity: // "Letters of Delegates to Congress: Volume 4- 5/16, 1776 — 8/15, 1776 - the North Carolina Council of Safety - Gentlemen Philadelphia Aug 7 [i.e. 8] 1776 ,,,We wrote you lately by the Post informing you ,,,to the Western Inhabitants of North Carolina that they might not want, as far as it was in our power to prevent it, the means of defence against ,,,The Waggoners have been detained here by some private business of their own till now, but this day they propose to set off. You will be the best Judge whether to order a guard for them thro Guildford or any other part of our Province, as their Route is by the upper Road which Mr Sharp & Alexander are well acquainted with ,,,We must most earnestly importune you to compleat the Continental Battalions ,,,in behalf of Congress to hold forth such Encouragement as will make that Task very easy. The Circumstance ,,,The secure state of your Sea Coast at present gives your Board an Opportunity to direct all your attention against your enemy ,,,The gross infernal breach of faith which they have been guilty of ,,,our Frontiers not only will ,,,disturb the peace of their neighbours ,,,But CHRISTIANITY the dear RELIGION of peace & mercy should hold ,,,we feel the resentment of men ,,,we ought not to forget the duties of the CHRISTIAN. Women and Children ,,,their weakness disarms rage ,,,the Law of nations will vindicate. We have been large upon this subject, as we have it much at heart to quiet the apprehensions of our frontiers ,,,We are Gentlemen, With great Respect, Your most Obedt Humble Servants, Wm Hooper Joseph Hewes John Penn RC (Nc-Ar). Written by Hooper and signed by Hooper, Hewes, and Penn ,,,Congress ,,,2 Washington's second letter to Hancock of Aug. 7 ,,,(Fitzpatrick), 5:382-83."

---T--- Opposes GOV abuse~ that of anti-Christian evils, such as evil pride, not praying, no devotion to Christ the God; not being the God of this nation; thus idolatry~ "Supreme Being": // "Journals of the Continental Congress, 1774-1789 — 3/19, 1782 - The Secretary at War, to whom was referred a memorial of Lieutenant Power ,,,Whereupon, Ordered ,,,On a report of a committee, consisting of Mr. [Joseph] Montgomery, Mr. [Oliver] Wolcott, and Mr. [John Morin] Scott, appointed to prepare a recommendation to the several states, to set apart a day of humiliation, fasting, and PRAYER Congress agreed to the following Proclamation: THE GOODNESS OF THE SUPREME BEING to all his rational creatures, demands their acknowledgments of gratitude and love; his absolute government of this world dictates, that it is the interest of every nation and people ardently to supplicate his mercy favor and implore his protection. When the LUST OF DOMINION or LAWLESS AMBITION excites arbitrary power to INVADE THE RIGHTS, or endeavor to WRENCH WREST from a people their SACRED and UNALIENABLE INVALUABLE PRIVILEGES, and compels them, in DEFENCE of the same, to encounter all the horrors and calamities of a bloody and vindictive war; then is that people loudly called upon to fly unto that GOD for protection, who hears the cries of the distressed, and will not turn a deaf ear to the supplication of the OPPRESSED. Great Britain, hitherto left to infatuated councils, and to pursue measures repugnant to their her own interest, and distressing to this country, still persists in the chimerical idea design of subjugating these US; which will compel us into another active and perhaps bloody campaign. The US in Congress assembled, therefore, taking into consideration our present situation, our multiplied transgressions of the HOLY laws of our GOD, and his past acts of kindness and goodness exercised towards us, which we would ought to record with me the liveliest gratitude, think it their indispensable duty to call upon the different several states, to set apart the last Thursday in April next, as a day of fasting, humiliation and PRAYER, that our joint supplications may then ascend to the throne of the RULER of the UNIVERSE, beseeching Him that he would to diffuse a SPIRIT of universal reformation among all ranks and degrees of our citizens; and make us ,,,HOLY, that so we may be an HAPPY people; that it would please Him to impart wisdom, integrity and unanimity to our counsellors; to bless and prosper the REIGN of our illustrious ally, and give success to his arms employed in the DEFENCE of THE RIGHTS of human nature; that HE WOULD SMILE upon our military arrangements by land and sea; administer comfort and consolation to our prisoners in a cruel captivity ,,,give grant us victory over our enemies; establish peace in all our borders, and give happiness to all our inhabitants; that he would prosper the labor of the husbandman, making the earth yield its increase in abundance, and give a proper season for the in gathering of the fruits thereof; that He would grant success to all engaged in lawful trade and commerce, and take under his guardianship all schools and seminaries of learning, and make them nurseries of VIRTUE and PIETY; that He would incline the HEARTS of all men to peace, and fill them with universal charity and benevolence, and that the RELIGION of our DIVINE REDEEMER, with all its benign influences, may cover the earth as the waters cover the seas. ?Done by the US in Congress assembled, &c. &c.?1 [Note 1: 1 This report ,,,committee, consisting of Mr. [Samuel] Livermore, Mr. [James] Madison, and Mr. [Abraham] Clark ,,,".

---T--- <u>Agency (or Administrative) Law Offices:</u> // This method is applied terminology; thus do not mix it to much with other similar terms or applications. // What is this method? This is a group of GOV workers that are making laws, and the laws are based on these Creature Being's decisions. And then the laws are applied to some people. // What are some problems with this method? This can be a serious desire. For one, because it is getting in areas of micro-management. This has potential to become near tyranny and dictatorship. // Details about the method: What GOV is doing here, is forming a group of Creature Being's to work in a division, called an agency or administration. This group of Being's is then paid by tax money. They are placed in some geographical location, in an office or such, and then assigned to a specific geographical jurisdiction. A geographical jurisdiction is an area of land and people Beings who live in such; and are required to obey some laws about some specific subjects. The Administration group of Creature Being's is given an assignment to manage specific subjects, in that jurisdictional geographical territory, such as forest, natural resources, yards of homes, noise control, building permits, etc. What this administration agency then does, is begin researching in to this geographical area, and then enacting laws on the Creature Beings who live there. This is accepted as the Law of the land. // Discernment about such method: +Some of this operation may not be necessarily wrong. +Some of this operation is sometimes not according to the GOV system that was established, because it is a very detailed application; which is an involvement in subjects that are very detailed in societies, etc. +Sometimes this method is according the GOV system of the CC. +Sometimes there is need for some of it. // However it needs examined & used carefully. Administrative Law co/ remain to the States, Cities, Counties, etc. And in what geographical areas and subjects, then is another situation. Some subjects and geographic obviously need to be managed.

---T--- <u>VOTE; or Majority:</u> // In spirit so in body. If thought, desire, intention, and willed, then it is acted out. +And this CON law is not to be ruled out by votes of majority population. The CON is the words of the spirit. The system was designed as CON law, not votes law. Voting is one part of it, but not the primary law making or law construction. The people of the USA are bound by the CC (DOI & CON) of the USA. Only because they vote does not make it so. This nation was established to be Christian for God.

---T--- <u>Opposes actions against The "liberty" of the CC (DOI & CON); such is a "right" from "God" the "Creator":</u> // It does not include the Right to sin, or evil, as in to publish it; The "liberty" is not a license to do evil to the public; is not a license to establish evil for the public. // A Spiritual Moral person does have liberty to reject Christianity, but not advertise evil business or organized evil.

---T--- <u>Opposes True Happiness as a Right coming from God:</u> // Evil or anti-Christian activity hurts public happiness. // Happiness is defined as a Right coming from God. Both Spiritually & bodily; The CC (DOI & CON) state this; A Right~ coming from GOD. // The Holy Bible & God's presence & such things as Christmas are EX: of happiness. // Other DOCs state the same~ "Letters of Delegates to Congress: Volume 18- 3/1, 1781 – 8/31, 1781 - Arthur Middleton to Aedanus Burke My dr. Sir Pa. Apr. 7th. [1782] ,,,I take advantage of the return of Col. Motte to present you my Acknowledgts. ,,,for yr. kind remembrance of me. The Strong Outlines you have drawn of the mellanchoy real Situation of our Country in all points correspond exactly with what my anxious imagination had formed, whenever reason & reflexion led me to consider an Object always uppermost in my mind; the picture is easily fill'd up, it is a melancholy one, & I fear with you that nothing but Time & skillfull management can restore that firm, orderly, & composed mode of proceeding so essential to establish the publick Happiness which is or ought to be the wish of all,,,".

---T--- <u>Opposes any Intentions not right; pure (defined as totally right):</u> // "Letters of Delegates to Congress: Volume 18 Mar 1, 1781 - Aug 31, 1781 - Arthur Middleton to Aedanus Burke My dr. Sir Pa. Apr. 7th. [1782 ,,,I have much confidence in the Ability & Integrity of the men chosen to conduct affairs. I think I know the PURITY of THEIR INTENTIONS,,,".

---T--- <u>Gentle Manner & Kind Affectionate consideration of Spiritual Moral Creatures</u> & Situations was to be the heart promoted in the USA GOV attitude: // "Letters of Delegates to Congress: Volume 18 Mar 1, 1781 - Aug 31, 1781 - Arthur Middleton to Aedanus Burke My dr. Sir Pa. Apr. 7th. [1782 ,,,Upon mature Consideration of all Circumstances; of the unmerited Sufferings of so many, & of the resentments necessarily rous'd in a people whom I know to be naturally generous & sensible, I rejoice that matters have been conducted with so much moderation & temper,,,".

---T--- <u>True Peace is Not to be Opposed; It is part of Happiness as a Right from God:</u> // "Letters of Delegates to Congress: Volume 18 Mar 1, 1781 - Aug 31, 1781 - Arthur Middleton to Aedanus Burke My dr. Sir Pa. Apr. 7th. [1782 ,,,had restor'd Tranquillity [[peace]],,,".

---T--- <u>Right & truthful Reasoning, Affections,</u> & Desires ("Sentiment") are only Promoted; those of God: // "Letters of Delegates to Congress: Volume 18 Mar 1, 1781 - Aug 31, 1781 - Arthur Middleton to Aedanus Burke My dr. Sir Pa. Apr. 7th. [1782 ,,,the publick mind was free & open to the guidance of cool dispassionate reason. Your sentiments upon the subject are those of the Patriot & the friend of human nature, & I wd. there had been more of your way of thinking".

---T--- <u>In the CC there IS NOT one word or statement to agree with or support evil:</u> // This would include excessive harshness to evil, as in pardoning, or not pardoning, in some situations. +Yet nevertheless, contrarily, Spiritual Moral people are using it today to support all sorts of evil, as sodomy, abortion, etc., and even Satanism and opposing God.

---T--- <u>Treason is evil; which is to oppose the CC (DOI, CON)</u> God & His Holy Bible: // "Letters of Delegates to Congress: Volume 18 Mar 1, 1781 - Aug 31, 1781 - Arthur Middleton to Aedanus Burke My dr. Sir Pa. Apr. 7th. [1782 ,,,upon a thorough Investigation of this mode of Punishment, even in Cases of Treason,,,".

---T--- <u>Wrong decisions made by Judicial Branch:</u> // We must remember that judges are Spiritual Moral human beings, as we all are. And humanity always is possible to failings, faults, and misjudgments. // However in more recent times, the American judicial system has corrupted and do not always judge rightly as previously. // Pledge of Allegiance in the USA, in all States, should contain the words "under God.". This was the Pledge earlier. // Christian prayer, Holy Bible teachings, Christmas nativity celebrations, and the Ten Commandments should be allowed in our public schools. // "We ought to obey God rather than men"-Act5:27-29. If Spiritual Moral Beings do not prioritize God 1st, then what do they prioritize~ Self Idol ?

---T--- <u>Much of our American Law is Based</u> on Old English Law, which is Based on the Ten Commandments. (260) ~paraphrased from an article by Howard McKonkey.

---T--- <u>Sin, Not part of Sin, Rather All, is stated as Not Acceptable; and Christ's</u> Holy Bible Reference is Used by FFOG GOV Branches to Identify What Sin is to be Defined as; As by the Holy Bible: // "Letters of Delegates to Congress: Volume 18 Mar 1, 1781 - Aug 31, 1781 - Arthur Middleton to Aedanus Burke My dr. Sir Pa. Apr. 7th. [1782 ,,,I have been & am principled against it; I cannot approve of the inhuman sentence of visiting the SINS of the Fathers upon the guiltless women [and] children, [[HOLY BIBLE quoted]] notwithstanding the SACRED Authority which may be quoted for it. It is a doctrine suited only to the climates of DESPOSTISM, & abhorrent to the dignified SPIRIT of pure & genuine republicanism. In the Eye of reason the individual shd. stand or fall by his own actions, & those connected should be involved in the punishment no farther, than they have been partakers in the crime. Banishment of the individual, & a deprivation of the Benefits of Citizenship & property for life are surely sufficient both as a punishment & a prevention of Crimes, without reducing a whole family for the SIN of one to misery & destruction. Here my friend you have my thoughts upon an Interesting Subject which concerns the good of mankind ,,,FC (ScHi: Middleton Papers)." // Limits are put on Evil.

---T--- <u>The Right Heart (Spirit) Condition or Status, is Not To Be Evil, as a</u> Principle Law, a Universal Generality. Heart is a word coming from the Holy Bible and its various parts are herein mentioned (heart is actually a Bible word for spirit also). // "Letters of Delegates to Congress: Volume 18 Mar 1, 1781 - Aug 31, 1781 - Arthur Middleton to Aedanus Burke My dr. Sir Pa. Apr. 7th. [1782 ,,,0"Next to the obedience due the Dictates of my own <u>CONSCIENCE,"</u> Middleton continued, "it has ever lain nearest to <u>my HEART so</u> to regulate my conduct as to wish your Approbation. I shall still be governed by the same <u>MOTIVES, & trust</u> I shall retain it to our Life's end-at parting with my Brother I entreated him to <u>present my Duty to</u> you, & to acquaint you that my mind was thoroughly at Ease with regard to my own fate; This I <u>hoped would operate as a Balm to your</u> affliction upon my Account. "To the many anxieties for my dearest Connections, the knowledge of your Ill health & Troubles have <u>added grief indeed.</u> Mr. R can tell how much I <u>have felt for</u> you. I am now anxious [for my?] Br[other]-in short our day seems to be crowded with Troubles & I flatter myself their Period is nearly closed...." Middleton's draft of the letter, partially in his personal shorthand, is in the Middleton Papers, ScHi.".

---T--- <u>Opposes bad actions regarding property & economic</u> subjects: // The grievances listed in the CC (DOI & CON) prove some of the limitations on these subjects including taxation and its abuse by the GOV. Such offences had occurred by various historical governments, including what was being experienced at those times from parts of England.

---T--- <u>Part of evil is false religions, including false Christianity;</u> and true religion is that which caused the existence of the US; Included in false Christianity was the desire not to have Catholicism in its wrong formation, given unlimited freedom: // Catholicism's creeds or doctrines, as defined then, had been, and by some Spiritual people, to expel Christian DEN and abuse them; and be dominant in the geographical territory. Thus Catholicism was reprimanded to be cautionary of its loyalties and doctrines but allowed to be exercised; God says no evil in the country. And so Catholics do have part truths and do have some concern about Jesus Christ and the Holy Bible and doing right. Thus in this manner they were cautioned to exist in the US. Included in assisting the US GOV was some individuals that claimed to be Catholic. These individuals did not support to the previous creeds of abusive Catholics and so mannered themselves to be good citizens, and conduct themselves in rightness of Christian laws for Christ, and not oppose Christian DEN nor abuse them.

---T--- <u>Opposed to Evil that is Against Christ, & the Holy Bible, & prayer, & excluding God</u> in America; & against anti-Christian laws; limits on Evil: // "Letters of Delegates to Congress: Volume 10- 6/1, 1778 — 9/30, 1778; Gouverneur Morris to the Carlisle Commissioners - [June 20, 1778] ,,,William Eden, and George Johnstone. Trusty and well-beloved servants of your SACRED MASTER, in whom HE is well pleased. ,,,the President, and other Members of the Congress ,,,As that body have thought your propositions unworthy ,,,and tend to appease the offended SPIRIT of negotiation, if one out of the many individuals on this great Continent should speak to you the sentiments of America. Sentiments which your own good sense hath doubtless suggested, and which are repeated only to convince you that ,,,knowledge of our own rights, and attention to our own interests, and a SACRED respect for the dignity of human nature, have given us to understand the TRUE principles which ought, and which therefore shall, sway our conduct. You begin with the amiable expressions of humanity, the earnest desire of tranquility and peace. A better introduction to Americans could not be devised. [[England commits evils against the God given Rights of Americans]] For the sake of the latter, we once laid our liberties at the feet of your Prince, and even your armies have not eradicated the former from our bosoms. You tell us you have powers unprecedented in the annals of your history. And England, unhappy England, will remember with deep contrition, that these powers have been rendered of no avail by a conduct unprecedented in the annals of mankind. [[evil against God & Christianity which is part of USA's main intention]] Had your royal master condescended to listen to the PRAYER of millions, he had not thus have sent you. Had moderation swayed what we were proud to call mother country, "her full-blown dignity would not have broken down under her." You tell us that "all parties may draw some degree of consolation, and even auspicious hope, from recollection." We wish this most sincerely for the sake of all parties. America, even in the moment of subjugation, would have been consoled by CONSCIOUS VIRTUE, and her hope was and is in the justice of her cause, and the justice of the ALMIGHTY. These are sources of hope and of consolation, which neither time nor chance can alter or take away. You mention "the mutual benefits and consideration of EVILs, that may naturally contribute to determine our resolutions." [[evil against freedom & truth]] As to the former, you know too well that we could derive no benefit from an union with you, nor will I, by deducing the reasons to evince this, cast an insult upon your understandings. As to the latter, it were to be wished you had preserved a line of conduct equal to the delicacy of your feelings. You could not but know that men, who sincerely love freedom, disdain the consideration of all EVILs necessary to attain it. Had not your own hearts borne testimony to this TRUTH, you might have learnt it from the annals of your history. For in those annals instances of this kind at least are not unprecedented. But should those instances be insufficient, we PRAY you to read the unconquered mind of America. That the acts of Parliament you transmitted were passed with singular unanimity, we pretend not to doubt. You will pardon me, gentlemen, for observing, that the reasons of that unanimity are strongly marked in the report of a Committee of Congress, agreed to on the 22d of April last ,,,and referred to in a late letter from Congress to Lord Viscount Howe and Sir Henry Clinton. ,,,[[evils of war; of barbarious acts; no right intention~ without cause]] You tell us you are willing "to consent to a cessation of hostilities, both by sea and land." It is difficult for rude Americans to determine whether you are serious in this proposition, or whether you mean to jest with their simplicity. Upon a supposition, however, that you have too much magnanimity to divert yourselves on an occasion of such importance to America, and perhaps not very trivial in the eyes of those who sent you, permit me to assure you, on the SACRED word of a gentleman, that if you shall transport your troops to England, where before long your Prince will certainly want their assistance, we never shall follow them thither. We are not so romantically fond of fighting, neither have we such regard for the city of London, as to commence a crusade for the possession of that HOLY land. Thus you may be certain that hostilities will cease by land. It would be doing singular injustice to your national character, to suppose you are desirous of a like cessation by sea. ,,,the very flourishing state of your commerce, notwithstanding our weak efforts to interrupt it, clearly shew that you can exclude us from the sea. The sea your kingdom. [[evil in not allowing America freedom to travel & conduct commerce business]] You offer "to restore free intercourse, to revive mutual affection, and renew the common benefits of naturalization." Whenever your countrymen shall be taught wisdom by experience, and learn from past misfortunes to pursue their TRUE interests in future we shall readily admit every intercourse which is necessary for the purposes of commerce, and usual between different nations. To revive mutual AFFECTION is utterly impossible. We FREELY FORGIVE YOU, but it is not in nature that you should forgive us. You have injured us too much. We might, on this occasion, give you some late instances of singular barbarity, committed as well by the forces of his Britannic Majesty, as by those of his generous and faithful allies, the Senecas, Onondagas and Tuscaroras. But we will not offend a courtly ear by the recital of those disgusting scenes ,,,obtained by a licentious soldiery over unarmed men in defenceless villages, their wanton devastations, their deliberate murders, or to inspect those scenes of carnage painted by the wild excesses of savage rage. These amiable traits of national conduct cannot but revive in our bosoms that partial affection we once felt for everything which bore the name of Englishman. [[Some Spiritual Moral people went away from God & somehow bad people got in GOV in England]] As to the common benefits of naturalization, it is a matter we conceive to be of the most SOVEREIGN indifference. ,,,These will hardly claim naturalization in either of those places as a benefit. On the other hand, such of your subjects as shall be driven by the iron hand of Oppression to seek for refuge among those whom they now persecute, will certainly be admitted to the benefits of naturalization. We labour to rear an asylum for mankind, and regret that circumstances will not permit you, Gentlemen, to contribute to a design so very agreeable to your several tempers and dispositions. But further, your Excellencies say, "we will concur to extend every freedom to trade that our respective interests can require." Unfortunately there is a little difference in these interests, which you might not have found it very easy to reconcile, had the Congress ,,,The difference I allude to is, that it is your interest to monopolize our commerce, and it is our interest to trade with all the world ,,,Your "earnest desire to stop the farther effusion of blood, and the calamities of war," ,,,We cannot but admire the generosity of soul, which prompts you "to agree that no military force shall be kept up in the different States of North-America without the consent of the general Congress or particular Assemblies." ,,,I do most solemnly promise and assure you, that ,,,and that of the legislatures of those States ,,,I am to assure you (which I do with "perfect respect") that it will be necessary to procure very ample recommendations. [[evil against Christ & the Christian religion; freedom of Christian DEN; & God-Given Rights]] You propose to us a devise to "perpetuate our union." It might not be amiss previously to establish this union, which may be done by your acceptance of the treaty of peace and commerce tendered to you by Congress. ,,,And such treaty, I can venture to say, would continue as long as your ministers could prevail upon themselves not to violate the faith of nations. You offer, to use your own language, the inaccuracy of which, considering the importance of the subject, is not to be wondered at, or at least may be excused, "in short to establish the powers of the respective legislatures in each particular State, to settle its revenue, its civil and military establishment, and to exercise a perfect freedom of legislation and internal government, so that the British States throughout North-America acting with us, in peace and war, under one common sovereign, may have the irrevocable enjoyment of every privilege that is short of a total separation of interests, or consistent with that union of force on which the safety of our common

RELIGION and liberty depends." Let me assure you, gentlemen, that the power of the respective legislatures in each particular State is already most fully established, and on the most solid foundations. It is established on the perfect freedom of legislation and a vigorous administration of internal government. As to the settlement of the revenue, and the civil and military establishment, these are the work of the day, for which the several legislatures are fully competent. I have also the pleasure to congratulate your Excellencies, that the country, for the settlement of whose government, revenue, administration, and the like, you have exposed yourselves to the fatigues and hazards of a disagreeable voyage, and more disagreeable negociation, hath abundant resources wherewith to defend her liberties now ,,,every proposition which you may agree to ,,,You are solicitous to prevent a total separation of interests ,,,We cannot perceive that our liberty does in the least depend upon any union ,,,for we find that, after you have exercised your force against us for upwards of three years, we are now upon the point of establishing our liberties in direct opposition to it. Neither can we conceive, that, after the experiment you have made, any nation in Europe will embark in so unpromising a scheme as the subjugation of America ,,,Your Excellencies will, I hope, excuse me when I differ from you, as to our having a RELIGION in common with you: the RELIGION of America is the RELIGION of all mankind. Any person may worship in the manner he thinks most agreeable to the Deity; and if he behaves as a good citizen, no one concerns himself as to his faith or adorations, neither have we the least solicitude to exalt any one SECT or profession above another. [[Note that worship methods are allowed to be variable & also the name of the organization, which is Christian DEN; yet Only the one True Deity is allowed]] I am extremely sorry to find in your letter some sentences, which reflect upon the character of his most CHRISTIAN Majesty. It certainly is not kind, or consistent with the principles of philanthropy you profess, to traduce a gentleman's character without affording him an opportunity of defending himself: and that too a near neighbour, and not long since an intimate brother, who besides hath lately given you the most solid additional proofs of his pacific disposition, and with an unparalleled sincerity, which would do honour to other Princes, declared to your court, unasked, the nature and effect of a treaty he had just entered into with these States. ,,,Neither is it quite according to the rules of politeness to use such terms in addressing yourselves to Congress, when you well knew that he was their good and faithful ally. It is indeed TRUE, as you justly observe, that he hath at times been at enmity with his Britannic Majesty, by which we suffered some inconveniences: but these flowed rather from our connection with you than any ill-will towards us: At the same time it is a solemn TRUTH, worthy of your serious attention, that you did not commence the present war, a war in which we have suffered infinitely more than by any former contest, a fierce, a bloody, I am sorry to add, an unprovoked and cruel war. That you did not commence this, I say, because of any connection between us and our present ally; but, on the contrary, as soon as you perceived that the treaty was in agitation, proposed terms of peace to us in consequence of what you have been pleased to denominate an insidious interposition. How then does the account stand between us. America, being at peace with all the world ,,,At present America, being engaged in a war with Great Britain, will probably obtain the most honourable terms of peace, in consequence of her friendly connection with France. For the TRUTH of these positions I appeal, gentlemen, to your own knowledge. I know it is very hard for you to part with what you have accustomed yourselves, from your earliest infancy, to call your colonies. I pity your situation, and therefore I excuse the little abberations from TRUTH ,,,in other words the treaties of alliance and commerce between his most CHRISTIAN Majesty and these States ,,,and the assurance given that America had reserved a right of admitting even you to a similar treaty, you must be convinced of the TRUTH of my assertions ,,,and persuaded us to give to the common enemy of man the precious jewel of our liberties; after all this, I say, we should have been at the mercy of a Parliament, which, to say no more of it, has not treated us with too great tenderness ,,,I believe that in every kingdom, state, or empire there must be, from the necessity of the thing, one supreme legislative power, with authority to bind every part in all cases, the proper object of human laws. I believe that to be bound by laws, to which he does not consent by himself or by his representative, is the direct definition of a slave. I do therefore believe, that a dependence on Great Britain, however the same may be limited or qualified, is utterly inconsistent with every idea of liberty, for the defence of which I have solemnly pledged my life and fortune to my countrymen; and this engagement I will SACREDly adhere to so long as I shall live. Amen ,,,away with your fleets and your armies, acknowledge the independence of America ,,,You have told the Congress, "If, after the time that may be necessary to consider this communication, and transmit your answer, the horrors and devastations of war should continue, we call GOD and the world to witness that the EVILs, which must follow, are not to be imputed to Great-Britain." I wish you had spared your protestation. Matters of this kind may appear to you in a trivial light, as meer ornamental flowers of rhetoric, but they are serious things registered in the high chancery of HEAVEN. Remember the awful abuse of words like these by General Burgoyne, and remember his fate. There is one above us, who will take exemplary vengeance for every insult upon his Majesty. You know that the cause of America is just. You know that she contends for that freedom, to which all men are entitled. That she contends against oppression, rapine, and more than savage barbarity. The blood of the innocent is upon your hands, and all the waters of the ocean will not wash it away. We again make our solemn appeal to the GOD of HEAVEN to decide between you and us. And we PRAY that in the doubtful scale of battle we may be successful, as we have justice on our side, and that the merciful SAVIOUR of the world may forgive our oppressors. I am, my Lords and Gentlemen, The friend of human nature ,,,An AMERICAN. ,,,as "An American." The other three appeared in the Pennsylvania Packet on July 21, Sept. 19,,,".

---T--- Opposition to Subjects of Principle Laws of Self Evidence, Spirituality, Conscience, and Righteousness; which would be Biblical & Christ Caring.

---T--- Opposition to stopping evils, such as witchcraft.

---T--- <u>Because a Larger Number of Spiritual Moral Folk is evil is No Right to Support Evil or Not</u> Have Limitations on Evil; Because such is what the DOI & CON (CC) is All About; It included to counteract the Majority of an Evil GOV or Evil Majority persecuting them: // Somehow in England a majority of soldiers and GOV became evil and did evil.

---T--- <u>It is Impossible that the FFOG constructed a place for evil or opposing activities to CC</u> because this would be an opposite and ruin all they intended/ purposed & accomplished: // What fool would do such? A hypocrite is a fake, and whomever pretends to be good while purposely doing bad in some areas have various evil motives. However the FFoG were generally constant in goodness, and expressed such work, and risked their lives and possessions.

---T--- <u>Not Support of Evil by FFOG:</u> // John Witherspoon states, "He is the best friend to American liberty who is the most sincere and active in promoting true and undefiled religion, and who sets himself with the greatest firmness to bear down profanity and immorality of every kind. Whoever is an avowed enemy of God, I ,,,call him an enemy to his country." (154a). // Samuel Adams said, "While the people are virtuous they cannot be subdued; but once they lose their virtue they will be ready to surrender their liberties to the first external or internal invader."

---T--- <u>Demonism or Satanism with Evil is Opposed:</u> // Now what intention/ purpose would some demon care for to engage in communication with me or you ?? Such is one very good reason why such is opposed. HSC: +states in Psal 1 that it is not good to use your body with such; Do Not stand, walk, sit with those evil Beings; +1Cor 10 states Do Not agree in communication with them; agree with their subjects and open to unlimited listening & talking; +2Cor 10:5 states Do Not agree to think with them; they intend/ purpose to consume your mind; +Eph 6 states Do put on Armor provided by God; and what is the main subject of the Armor~ The Being of God & communion (fellowship) with Him. God is our friend, not the demons; no better friend can you know than God.

---T--- <u>Principle Law against Evil:</u> // Here is an EX of Principle Laws frequently used by the FFoG and in USA DOCs: // Nor cruel and unusual punishments inflicted. This is in the CON. Notice it does not say any specific form of cruelty or punishments in the statement. But does that make the statement not apply? No. Does it make it less demanding? No. Does that give us Right to bend the rules, dismiss, ignore, or refuse? No. No evil in that general category; that area.

---T--- <u>Serious Physical & Spiritual And Providential Consequences of Sin:</u> // Warning!!! Job's friends (HSC) had the false doctrine that the sickness of Job was because of sin; possibly agreed to the doctrine that all sickness, except that leading to death, was because of sin. That doctrine is not true. All sickness and death is not the direct result of sin committed. This is not a study of all the reasons (intentions/purposes) for physical illness. However it is true that physical and spiritual problems are caused by sin, and that they will be eventually. The following list IS or CAN BE the result of sin committed; Intentional sin: +re-crucifies Christ -Heb6:4-6; Joh3:16; 1Cor11:27-31. +Puts in danger of physical death -Heb6:4-6; 1Cor11:26-32; Joh5:14; Num12:4-15; Act5; 1Kin13; 1Pet3:10-11; Noah's flood (Gen6-8). +Can cause a shortening of our physical life -1Pet3:10-11. +Puts in danger of physical illness -Heb6:4-6; 1Cor11:26-32; Joh5:14; Num12:4-15. +Zacharias in Luk1. +Always Results in spiritual death -Gen2-3; Jam1:14-16; 1Joh3; Rom6. +Puts in danger of eternal Hell -Jam1:15; Heb10:26; Rom6:23. +Gives place to the demons; degrees of, even cause of physical health -Eph4:27; Mat12:45; Luk11:26. +Can bring chastisement -1Cor11; Heb12:1-15; Egyptians in Exodus. +Brings trouble, anguish, problems -Rom2:9; 1Pet3:10-11. +Includes guilt and condemnation; feel bad. +Is major, not a minor thing -Luk19:17; Mat12:36; Jam2:10; 1Cor5:6; Gal5:9. +Everyone who sins has a potential curse -Rev3-5. +Condemnation and anger of God abiding on them~ Psa50; Joh3:36. +Every sin is punished -Exo23:7; Heb6; Gen2-3; Nah1:3; Rom1:18 (Christ had to pay it). +Hardens the heart -Heb3-4 (terrible to have our senses, feelings, thoughts, reasoning, affections, all hardened; like stone). +Conscience damage occurs in the connection with God, and may burn it -1Tim4:2. +Mental capacity can be damaged; reprobate mind; reasoning capacity; dishonesty -Mar2:8; Rom1:28.

---T--- <u>Sin Crucifies Christ:</u> // A=} Why was Christ crucified in history past, in the first place? Did not they act out in the body what they first did as a spirit? They first thought, judged, reasoned, felt, intended, and willed to kill Him - internal sin? What was the cost & consequences? The crucifixion of Christ !! What is the cost & consequence of sin now ? The re-crucifixion of Christ out of your Being !! Do you want to pay the cost ? (Heb6 states this Truth; repentance is possible as the words in the KJV are a continuing time tense).

---T--- <u>Willful Intentional Sin, Including Willful Doubtful Subjects,</u> Tramples on Jesus & Blood. Intents/purposes are the part of our Being that causes Self to move the Will. Without them, Self does not move the will to decisions: // The Fear (respect & reverence; fear affection) for the Lord is the beginning of wisdom; fear to do evil against the Lord, in other words. Notice the connecting consequences of willful intentional/ purpose sin (including willful doubtful sin) in this section of statements (Heb10:26-29): +the Cause or problem: For if we sin willfully after that we have received the knowledge of the truth. +the consequences or effects: This is the main consequence which we want to emphasize; the others are only mechanical results, and secondary results, whereas these are at the Being Person, this first one, striking at the heart (spirit), and the body, with HURT -WHO hath trodden under foot the Son of God (tramples Jesus under foot; sin re-crucifies Christ, Heb6); AND hath counted the blood of the covenant, wherewith he was sanctified, an unholy thing (trampling under foot, abusing the blood of Jesus); AND hath done despite to the Spirit of grace (insults or hurts the Holy Spirit and grace -remember Paul's conversion (in Acts of HSC) "Why are you persecuting Me" ?; AND how much sorer punishment, suppose you, shall he be thought worthy; AND there remaineth no more sacrifice for sins (Jesus blood was not and will not apply to unrepented willful sin); AND But a certain fearful looking for of judgment and fiery indignation, which shall devour the adversaries (puts one in danger of eternal Hell); AND died without mercy (puts one in line receiving an eternal curse, is a rejection of mercy and an insult to God);

283

AND Sensitivity to the Spirit of God, a tender heart and mind to Thought (Jesus) or Truth (Jesus) or Feelings (Jesus or the Holy Spirit) and not harden our hearts when we hear His voice (Heb3-4), that is Him the Thought, Truth, Feeling, Affection, etc ~ Prioritively Intention/ purpose God as a Being valuable to You; then do all with that~ 1Cor10:31.

---T--- <u>DO INIQUITY SIN ~or~ DO NO INIQUITY SIN</u>: // Let us exalt Jesus clarifying, that intentional/ purposeful sin, guilt, brings condemnation. The Lord Jehovah tells how to get saved (into heaven; and not Hell). 1Joh3:6-9 tell us how to start and stay saved or right: "whosoever if born of God doth not commit sin; whosoever abideth in him sinneth not". Repent of, stop sinning, and abide, or commune (fellowship) with Him, without sin. Intentional iniquity is not part of the status of salvation (or rightness with God). A person can repent if they do it before it is too late in time. // 4 Holy Scriptures for learning knowledge of God as a Being; It is the intention of them to direct our attention to God's presence. 1] Psa66:18~"If I regard iniquity in my heart, the Lord will not hear me". 2] Psa119:3~"They also do no iniquity: they walk in his ways". 3] Rev22:13-14: Is the preparation for and entrance in to Heaven, rather than Hell~ "I am Alpha and Omega, the beginning and the end, the first and the last. Blessed are they that do His commandments, that they may have right to the tree of life, and may enter in through the gates into the city". 4] Mat13:41-43~"The Son of man shall send forth his angels, and they shall gather out of his kingdom all things that OFFEND and THEM WHICH DO INIQUITY and cast them into a furnace of fire; there shall be wailing and gnashing of teeth. Then shall the righteous shine forth,,,". +Observe here, the righteous are they that DO NOT OFFEND or DO NOT INIQUITY. But those NOT in a SAVED status are they WHICH DO OFFEND or DO INIQUITY. +A Grammar Law, Word Definition Law states~ Iniquity is defined as: "violation of law; illegality; wickedness; unrighteous; not submissive to law; transgression of law; lawless". +Christ is telling us: =by Offense, is Spiritual Moral Beings who influence other spiritual moral Beings to sin (this would be by either 1-encouragement with words or expressions, or by sinning against, or by some actions). =And by "Iniquity" is the persons' sin(s) itself. +Grammar (Word Law or Statement Law) Law makes the situation clarified with the Statement Law. It is not an (and, if) statement; it is an (either, or) statement or Status of Being. Observe: EITHER [a} Heaven, Saved, are the RIGHTEOUS (DO NOT OFFEND and DO NOT INIQUITY)] - or - [b} Hell, Condemned, (DO OFFEND, DO INIQUITY)]. +Difference Law (which also applies) states it clearly; that the difference between those who went to heaven & Hell is offense and iniquity; those who currently have an offense or do iniquity on the books of Heaven. The same conditional requirements made at the Final Judgment Event, in this SC, are the same of us to get saved (right) today -- "go and sin no more" Joh5:14; 8:11. Are we going to have FAITH in JESUS here or harden our heart??? Consider this statement by FFOG Puritan Nathaniel Ward: "Nothing is easier than to tolerate when you do not seriously believe that differences matter."

---T--- <u>Intention/ Purpose with Decision of Will</u>: // Our good friends from previous times, such as the Salvation Army, Methodists and Wesley's, John Fletcher, Thomas Akempis & the Common Brethren, William Law, Jeremy Taylor, and Charles Finney & the Oberlin College Group (in older times) have identified the Lord's True Doctrine about a priority subject. And we include all their co-assistants such as their wives, & the unnamed. // This Intention/ purpose Principle is additionally where it tells of the other side of Love, which is right fear: Love does not rejoice in evil, rather hates it and fears to do such; and fears God's ability and the pain from evil; and from doing evil. // Part of God's commandments are to put God 1st and to Love Him as is in Gen~Deu. Deu 6 is only 1 HSC of many in that part, which in vs5~"And you shall love the LORD your God with all your heart, and with all your soul, and with all your might". This says to have God's word on every material substance thing, and all your body actions and etc. Now what is this activity in reality?? Note vs7-8~"and shall talk of them when you sittest in your house, and when you walkest by the way, and when you liest down, and when you risest up. And you shall bind them for a sign on your hand, and they shall be as frontlets between your eyes". What is this except that the intent/ purpose is the constant subject; now what is that constant subject? It is to love God; God's presence; God's Being, or Person. Now it is a SETLWHM, or First Truth that to love another Being is to love them for what they are as a Being and without any selfish intention to get or etc. That Being is loved, and for simply Being the Being they are; they are loved, for their own sake. Such is love. Therefore the intent/ purpose is the subject of activity here and is the constant aimed subject to have God's presence in all activities of life; when you sit down think of God, when rise, when eat, when walk, when sleep, etc. think of God's presence; and that you love Him simply because He is a valuable Being in Himself. // Now similarly is the HSC in Eccl 12 that has those Love commandments included in them~ if you think of what it is referring to. And to love God & put Him 1st is said as simply because He is God; He is valuable, as a Being. Ecc 12:13-14 says, "Let us hear the conclusion of the whole matter: Fear God, and keep his commandments: for this is the whole duty of man. For God shall bring every work into judgment, with every secret thing, whether it be good, or whether it be evil". Thus communion with God as intent/ purpose in all subjects and God will be joyful with you, rather than bring you to be put in the eternal prison.

---T--- <u>GOODNESS PRINCIPLE</u>: // Mr. Charles Finney & the Oberlin College Group, identified this principle in HSC. His teachings shared to include this for our intention/ purpose. First is to Being, and then include this also. // HSC on Goodness Principle Law: +Eph2:10-"For we are his workmanship, created in Christ Jesus to GOOD WORKS, which God hath before ordained that we should walk in them". +Php2:13-"For it is God which worketh in you both to will and to do of his GOOD PLEASURE". +Php4:7-9-"And the peace of God, which passeth all understanding, shall keep your hearts and minds through Christ Jesus. Finally, brethren, whatsoever things are true, whatsoever things are honest, whatsoever things are just, whatsoever things are pure, whatsoever things are lovely, whatsoever things are of GOOD REPORT; if there be any virtue, and if there be any praise, think on these things. Those things, which you have both learned, and received, and heard, and seen in me, do: and the God of peace shall be with you". +Col1:10-11-"That you may walk worthy of the Lord to all pleasing, being fruitful in every good work, and increasing in the knowledge of God;

Strengthened with all might, according to his glorious power, to all patience and longsuffering with joyfulness". +Psa23:6-"Surely GOODNESS and mercy shall follow me ALL the days of my life: and I will dwell in the house of the LORD for ever".

---T--- <u>Love & Selfishness Or Self-Idolatry Or Self-Priority:</u> // Parts of HSC in 1Cor13 include the opposition to Self-idolatry or self-priority or self-more Creature Beings. It includes: +Talking with unselfish Love intentions~ "though I speak ,,,and have not charity, I am become as sounding brass, or a tinkling cymbal". +Knowledge & trust in God with unselfish Love intentions~ "though I have the gift of prophecy, and understand all mysteries, and all knowledge; and though I have all faith ,,,and have not charity, I am nothing". +Giving or good deeds done with unselfish Love intentions~ "though I bestow all my goods to feed the poor, and though I give my body to be burned, and have not charity, it profiteth me nothing. // Love with non-self-1st priority includes Charity Does Not Seek It's Own by~ +"suffereth long; +is kind; +envieth not; +vaunteth not itself; +not puffed up; +not behave itself unseemly; +not easily provoked; +thinketh no evil; +Rejoiceth not in iniquity; +rejoiceth in the truth". These are Principle Law words. // True Love is Eternal & the Greatest~ 1Cor13:13-"And now abideth faith, hope, charity, these three; but the greatest of these is charity". // 1Joh4:8-"God is Love". // Charles Finney & the older times Oberlin College Group has some good studies on Benevolent Love & Selfishness. It has some good attributes that are part of love & of selfishness which helps your Personality develop to a support of right and opposition to evil.

---T--- <u>Illegality of Evil opposition to Christianity</u>, the Holy Bible; to the Laws of God: // FFOG George Washington writes: "Let us unite ,,,imploring the Supreme Ruler of nations, to spread his holy protection over these US: to turn the machinations of the wicked to the confirming of our CON: to enable us at all times to root out internal sedition, and put invasion to flight: to perpetuate to out country that prosperity, which his goodness has already conferred, and to verify the anticipation of this government being a safeguard to human rights" (71).

---T--- <u>The CC LAW that Righteousness is to be supported is </u>also inclusive that evil is opposed: // FFOG George Washington encouraged others by His faithfulness~ +while his brotherly was dying; +and while Mr. Washington's personal physical health problem of Rheumatism Arthritis; +also when his mother and sister were very ill; +and yet attended the Congressional Convention meetings (66).

---T--- <u>Opposition To All Evil; It is Limited; which includes any Anti-Christian Activity:</u> // "Journals of the Continental Congress, 1774-1789: Saturday, Mar 16, 1776: Mr. W[illiam] Livingston ,,,was agreed to as follows: In times of impending calamity and distress; when the liberties of America are imminently endangered by the secret machinations and open assaults of an insidious and vindictive administration, it becomes the indispensable duty of these hitherto free and happy colonies, with TRUE PENITENCE OF HEART, AND THE MOST REVERENT DEVOTION, publickly to acknowledge the over RULING PROVIDENCE OF GOD; to CONFESS AND DEPLORE OUR OFFENCES AGAINST HIM [[anti-Christian ~ evil]]; and to supplicate his interposition for averting the threatened danger, and prospering our STRENUOUS EFFORTS IN THE CAUSE OF FREEDOM, VIRTUE [[righteousness is encouraged]], and posterity. The Congress, therefore, considering the warlike preparations of the British Ministry to subvert our INVALUABLE RIGHTS and PRIVILEDGES, [[the Rights & priviledges referring to the CC, where God is the Main Ruler & the Christian Bible our Guide Book]] and to reduce us by fire and sword, by the savages of the wilderness, and our own domestics, to the most abject and ignominious bondage: Desirous, at the same time, TO HAVE PEOPLE OF ALL RANKS AND DEGREES DULY IMPRESSED WITH A SOLEMN SENSE OF GOD'S SUPERINTENDING PROVIDENCE, and of their duty [[duty to whom? To God, to man, to self, that's to whom]], DEVOUTLY TO RELY, IN ALL THEIR LAWFUL ENTERPRIZES [[laws are considered; those of God]], ON HIS AID AND DIRECTION, Do earnestly recommend, that Friday, the Seventeenth day of May next, be observed by the said colonies as a day of humiliation, fasting, and PRAYER; that we may, with united hearts, confess and bewail our manifold SINS and transgressions [[any anti-Christian activity, which is evil]], and, by a sincere repentance and amendment of life [[quit all evil & do righteousness]], appease his righteous displeasure, and, THROUGH THE MERITS AND MEDIATION OF JESUS CHRIST, obtain his pardon and forgiveness; humbly imploring his assistance to frustrate the cruel purposes of our unnatural enemies; and by inclining their hearts to justice and benevolence, prevent the further effusion of kindred blood. But if, continuing deaf to the voice of reason and humanity, and inflexibly bent, on desolation and war, they constrain us to repel their hostile invasions by open resistance, that it may please the Lord of Hosts [[Holy Biblical reference as the Lord of Hosts, or of the Angelic]], the GOD of Armies, to animate our officers and soldiers with invincible fortitude, to guard and protect them in the day of battle, and to crown the continental arms, by sea and land, with victory and success: Earnestly beseeching him to bless our civil rulers, and the representatives of the people, in their several assemblies and conventions; to preserve and strengthen their union, to inspire them with an ardent, disinterested love of their country; to give wisdom and stability to their counsels; and direct them to the most efficacious measures for establishing the rights of America on the most honourable and permanent basis--That he would be graciously pleased to bless all his people in these colonies with health and plenty, and grant that a SPIRIT of incorruptible patriotism, and of pure undefiled RELIGION, may universally prevail; and this continent be speedily restored to the blessings of peace and liberty, and enabled to transmit them inviolate to the latest posterity. And it is recommended to CHRISTIANs [[little Christ's]] of all DENOMINATIONs, to assemble for public worship, and abstain from servile labour on the said day".

---T--- <u>Opposed Evil GOV, false religion, cults</u> & idolatrous activity; as the FFOG & Congress studied History of evil doctrines of God & evil GOV; intents very detailed & concerned, not passive; involved Christ in their activities: // Benjamin Franklin spoke at a Congress meeting for the CON on June 8, 1787 and appealed for prayer to Christ: ",,,four or five weeks close attendance & continual reasonings with each other -- our different sentiments on almost every question ,,,We have gone back to ancient history for models of GOV, and examined the different forms of those

285

Republics which ,,,formed either the seeds of their dissolution now no longer exist. And we have viewed modern states all round Europe, but find none of their Constitutions suitable to our circumstances.".

---T--- <u>No religion except Christian of Christ is supported</u> & all others are evil because they are false; all DEN are acceptable: // The remarks in the following quotation require carefulness in interpreting as they are only summary statements without a conclusion; they state the subject about the discussion; and are without the conclusions about the subject. Thus if it says "pagan in the US", it does not refer to say that the Pagan religion is to be allowed to advertise or positive publicity, rather is only a remark as to what subject was discussed: // "Henry Abbott-- RELIGION; opposed to an exclusive Establishment; no RELIGIOUS Test; PAGAN or Deist may obtain Office; OATH; by whom are we to swear? Jupiter ... 191 and, RELIGION; conceived that Jews, MAHOMETANS, and PAGANs, are invited to the US ,,,199 ,,,conduct of our rulers, and that, in a Christian country, it would be at least decent to hold out some distinction between the professors of Christianity and downright infidelity or paganism." And "The seventh article declares, that the ratification of nine states shall be sufficient for the establishment of this CON, between the states ratifying,,, making treaties, they might make a treaty engaging with foreign powers to adopt the Roman Catholic religion in the US, which would prevent the people from worshipping God according to their own consciences. The worthy member ,,,from Halifax has in some measure satisfied ,,,mind on this subject. But others may be dissatisfied. Many wish to know what religion shall be established. I believe a majority of the community are Presbyterians. I am, for my part, against any exclusive establishment; but if there were any, I would prefer the Episcopal. The exclusion of religious tests is by many thought dangerous and impolitic. They suppose that if there be no religious test required, pagans, deists, and mahometans might obtain offices among us, and that the senators and representatives might all be pagans. Every person employed by the general and state GOVs is to take an oath to support the former. Some are desirous to know how and by whom they are to swear, since no religious tests are required--whether they are to swear by Jupiter, Juno, Minerva, Proserpine, or Pluto. We ought to be suspicious of our liberties. We have felt the effects of oppressive measures, and know the happy consequences of being jealous of our rights. I would be glad some gentleman would endeavor to obviate these objections, in order to satisfy the religious art of the society. Could I be convinced that the objections were well founded, I would then declare my opinion against the CON,,,".

---T--- <u>Illegal court cases have involved the following:</u> // +Children, +free exercise of religion in secondary doctrines and expressions, +ownership of children, +freedom of speech, +personal appearance, +Christmas Nativity scenes and such like, +invocations, +prayers and chaplain prayers, +10 commandments.

---T--- <u>DOC of USA states that equality</u> & consideration be given to States, a Self-Evidence, a Righteous subject, a Just Cause: Commerce: // "The Congress shall have Power ,,,to regulate commerce with foreign Nations, and among the several States, and with the Indian Tribes,,, No preference shall be given by any Regulation of ,,,or Revenue to the Ports of one State over those of another."

---T--- <u>Causes of the RW included wrongful</u> taxation; wrongful British GOV dictation in social and religious life.

---T--- <u>The REP could not do everything & could</u> not think of every application & take care of the total world's problems; Thus they established Principle Laws whereby that every application could be included through such: // They could not state every application. They intended to not leave openness for evil interpretations or abuse of such statements. Principle Law was the method; and the Basic Principle Law Subjects.

---T--- <u>Because some of the FFOG USA GOV Officers did</u> not always decide with knowledge and with exacting directives on religion does not eliminate the DOI Statements and all the other facts of truth.

---T--- <u>There was problems in interpreting & applying~</u> +the exact specifications on how to apply the Checks & Balances system, +the problem with N GOV becoming abusive towards Christ and the people, +the GOV supporting Christian Law, +and all these without setting up a future and potential danger for misinterpretation.

---T--- <u>Not sufficient time was allotted to the FFoG</u> for all applications & for sufficient implementation of the CC (DOI & CON). // The CON was drafted in less than 100 working days (63).

---T--- <u>Enacted illegal laws & putting them in to society:</u> Legalizing abortion. // FFOG William Blackstone stated the Right to life: "A man's limbs,,, cannot be wantonly destroyed or disabled without a manifest breach of civil liberty" (10). // Abortion methods include some ways the babies are killed as that of~ +a vacuum sucking the baby out of the womb which tears the child apart; +by salt which burns the baby to death; +by a knife which cuts the baby in pieces and then discarded; +by pulling the baby out of the womb and trashing the child. // The Christian Beacon, July 27, 1972, said, "Any woman who will demand laws allowing her to abort her baby is less civilized than the animals, for no animal, not even a mother snake, will reject her babies" (260).

---T--- <u>Pres. Abraham Lincoln opposed evil & states that the USA is constructed as</u> the same, saying, "I know that the Lord is always on the side of the right; but it is my constant anxiety and prayer that I and this Nation be on the Lord's side".

---T--- <u>Providing Rights unlimited</u> for witches and warlocks.

---T--- <u>Refusal to observe the legal definition</u> of "religion" & "Establishment of Religion"; & make falsities (lies): // The dictionary used at the time is a supporting DOC. // Cross reference to other supporting DOCs proves what they intended/ purposed as Religion & Establishment of Religion. // See Chpt 5. // It all proves that false religions are not allowed public activity of assembly and advertisement; for business. Proves that only Christianity & DEN is legal for such public assembly & advertisements. // Gouverneur Morris (CON signer) wrote, "religion is the only solid basis of

286

good morals; therefore education should teach the precepts of religion, and the duties of man towards God,,,". // FFOG Alexander Hamilton defined "religion" and wrote to James Bayard: "In my opinion the present CON is the standard to which we are to cling ,,,channel itself provided for amendments ,,,let an association be formed to be denominated, 'The Christian Constitutional Society', its object to be first: the support of the Christian religion, second: the support of the US". // John Adams (signer of DOI, CON, President of USA) stated: "We have no GOV armed with power capable of contending with human passions unbrideld by morality and religion. Avarice, ambition, revenge, or gallantry, would break the strongest cords of our CON,,, Our CON was made only for a moral and religious people. It is wholly inadequate to the GOV of any other" (21).

---T--- Illegal Avoiding to include God & the Doctrine of Sinfulness of Man in the CC & DOCs: // Federalist #15 states: "Why has GOV been instituted at all? Because the passions of men will not conform to the dictates of reason and justice without constraint". // Federalist #55 states: "As there is a degree of depravity in mankind which requires a certain degree of circumspection and distrust, so there are other qualities in human nature which justify a certain portion of estem and confidence". // Donald Lutz states: ",,,and the most fundamental assumption (of the CON) is that the American people are a virtuous people" (17). // FFOG John Adams states: "We have no GOV armed with power capable of contending with human passions unbrideld by morality and religion. Avarice, ambition, revenge, or gallantry, would break the strongest cords of our CON,,, Our CON was made only for a moral and religious people. It is wholly inadequate to the GOV of any other" (21).

---T--- Illegal Removal of the CON from the DOI of Which Legally the CON is to be the application of the DOI with the DOI OverRuling it; Illegally Using the CON to oppose the DOI; separating the 2 DOCs: // See Chapter 5. // Also briefly we will include the following: // The CON is placed under the statements in DOI where we have "God" as the Ruler. // Sinfulness of man was included in the CON where a Checks & Balances System was designed; existence of wrong power; existence of evil; citizens must be protected against GOV powers of evil. These are what the FFOG had experienced, history had experienced, and what they were experiencing at present with Britain. John Adams said of any man who held power is as "a ravenous beast". // The Federalist Papers (#10 & 47) state ~"enlightened men may not always be in control"; "Government needs to be divided into various branches to check each other". // Gouverneur Morris, CON signer, wrote, "religion is the only solid basis of good morals; therefore education should teach the precepts of religion, and the duties of man towards God,,,". // The AOC is the historical DOC which the CON was a modification of. The AOC states: "and whereas it has pleased the Great Governor of the World to incline the hearts of the legislatures we respectively represent in Congress to approve of, and to authorize us to ratify the said Articles of Confederation and perpetuate union". It puts God as the OverRuler. // FFOG Alexander Hamilton at CON meetings states: "I sincerely esteem it a system which without the finger of God, never could have been suggested and agreed upon by such a diversity of interests". // FFOG James Madison wrote in Federalist Paper #37: "It is impossible for the man of pious reflection not to perceive in it a finger of the Almighty hand which has been so frequently and signally extended to our relief in the critical stages of the revolution." // Note the common subject of God in all these; that the DOI overrules with God.

---T--- Illegally Claiming that Separation of Church & State is in the CON: // The judicial Branch has not power to change the CON and make a sinful statement in a case. What was intended/ purposed and defined in all other USA DOCs (CC included), of the FFOG, is that~ +Christianity is supported; +N GOV is not to be exclusive of some DEN by making a law to only have one DEN; which is partially or favoring, ("respecting"); +N GOV cannot control Christianity in everything. Also see Chpt. 5. // Mr. James Madison's draft of the religious clauses in the First Amendment state: "The civil rights of none shall be abridged on account of religious belief or worship, nor shall any national religion be established, nor shall the full and equal rights of conscience be in any manner, or on any pretext infringed" (22). "National Religion" is that of DEN; "belief" is secondary doctrines and worship is expressions; such are part of Christianity. The CC already establishes the True God, mankind, and the Basic true doctrines of God & Mankind as the USA Religion; the True Religion. Mr. Madison supported the CC, and including the DOI. Civil Rights are that of being a human Being; Rights to exist are given without any DEN connection. Religion is used in 2 differing ways. Establishing is referring to DEN; The USA is not to favor one DEN; by making a law for it. // A rule of law cannot be made from a figure of speech from a letter; such as when T. Jefferson said only in letter~ "wall of separation between Church and State". Furthermore he did not say that GOV and Christianity should be separated. The study of Mr. Madison & Mr. Jefferson is in Chp 5., in the Sub-Part, titled Religion.

---T--- Illegal use of USA supporting DOCs for misinterpretation & application: // Whether intentional or not, or mistaken.

---T--- Illegal assertion for a Right to wrongly include & apply the supporting DOCs of the USA: // Such as the letter by Thomas Jefferson with the Danbury Baptist Church (studied in Chp 5); this letter is misinterpreted. Additionally then at the same time, a refusal is activated to use other supporting DOCs of the USA; and many which contradict misinterpretations that exist about various subjects. Then the nerve to tell the citizens the same.

---T--- Illegality of Evil Intention/ purpose of actions and activity of the Hearts (Spirit) GOV; the Spiritual Moral Beings they are with consciences.

---T--- There has never existed a separation of Church & State; the DOI (of the CC) puts God over the State & in the State: // The GOV has always included Christ's Christianity; from the start; and operated by the Laws of God. Such Evidences could go on exceedingly.

---T--- Illegally refusing to recognize that God's Christianity, the Holy Bible, Truth, and the Christian Religion was that of the GOV and its Intention/ purpose: // Such support is proved by the operation and system of the GOV with the States: // Massachusetts had a State church (the Congregational Church) until AD 1833. // Other States in AD 1789 had State Christian Churches also. // The statements do not dictate anti-God or atheist GOV.

---T--- <u>Illegal rejection of True Knowledge of Our Being & Existence:</u> // <u>The Function or Operation</u> of Our Spiritual Moral Being is Exactly Defined and Described in the Holy Bible and Found at No Other Source.

---T--- <u>Illegal refusal to Apply the Holy Bible words</u> included in the CC (DOI & CON); & in the supporting DOC: // "conscience" for EX; We would not have as much KN about our conscience if it were not for the Holy Bible; the word's definition comes from God.

---T--- <u>Illegal refusal to realize & apply the</u> fact that the RW was based on religious principles and God was included; it is stated for a Right before God to defend themselves against an evil GOV.

---T--- <u>Refusal of the Laws of Truth.</u>

---T--- <u>Illegal allowance of judges to change</u> the CON when the CON states that the legislature has the Right to change (amend) the CON; & only limited changes by legislature are legal: // FFOG Montesquieu said, "of the three powers above mentioned, the judiciary is next to nothing"(20). // FFOG A. Hamilton in The Federalist #78, stated: "the interpretation of laws is the proper and peculiar province of the courts". +The Judicial Branch has interpretational Rights only.

---T--- <u>Illegal Refusal to Observe the</u> States Religious Activity & Support of Christianity & Opposition to Unlimited Evil; The States Represented the Federal GOV Congress, etc.: // Massachusetts State CON of GOV is similar to the USA; yet done 7 yrs earlier. +Rev Samuel Cooper preaches a sermon on the Massachusetts CON enactment day: "Virtue is the spirit of a republic; for where all power is derived from the people, all depends on their good disposition. If they are impious, factions and selfish; if they are abandoned to idleness, dissipation, luxury, and extravagance; if they are lost to the fear of God, and the love of their country, all is lost ,,,we seem called by heaven to make a large portion of this globe a seat of knowledge and liberty, of agriculture, commerce, and arts, and what is more important than all of Christian piety and virtue". This proves that citizen knowledge was public about the GOV working with and in cooperation with and including Christianity with Christ.

---T--- <u>Allowing Judges to make laws</u> when it is only the legislature, the CC, and the Public vote, which legally have the power to make or create laws.

---T--- <u>Illegal Removal of "God, Creator,</u> Supreme Judge, Divine Providence" from Priority in the USA: // In AD 1776 people were very familiar with terms "divine providence".

---T--- <u>Formation of a Different Basis for Law that is Illegal:</u> // England historically and afterwards, and obviously, was not always a bad country in its GOV and army. They have offered much. Much of USA law is based on that which was designed in Britain. The Magna Carta of AD 1215 is a wonderful legal Biblical system. Then in AD 1688 Britain had the "Glorious Revolution of 1688"; which added an attachment to the Magna Carta. Then in AD 1689 they added the "Bill of Rights". And the English citizens then enjoyed more Rights under their Monarchy than all other people on Earth. // John Locke & William Blackstone, both Christian, political, and governmental workers in England, contributed to the USA legal DOCs, who next to the Holy Bible were 2 of the other 3 most utilized sources (9). +William Blackstone said "Christianity was part of the laws of the land" for Britain. +Edmund Burke (British jurist), AD 1775, said that W. Blackstone's Commentaries were the interest of America. Knowledge Material used most commonly besides the Holy Bible in the forming of US GOV DOCs, comes from Mr. Blackstone's. (9). +US Supreme Court Justice, Associate Justice James Iredell, AD 1799, talks of W. Blackstone in relation to the subject of the First Amendment of the CON: "We derive our principles of law originally from England ,,,in my opinion, no where more happily or just expressed than by the great Author of the Commentaries on the Laws of England, which book deserves more particular regard on this occasion, because for nearly 30 years it has been the manual of almost every student of law in the US, and its uncommon excellence has also introduced it into the libraries, and often to the favorite reading of private gentlemen" (18). // The Holy Bible was the major source used by the writers of the DOI & CON; and members of the US GOV. Donald S. Lutz & Charles S. Hyneman studied 15,000 DOCs (political material, monographs, newspaper articles, pamphlets), and approx. 2,200 related writing publications, including books, all relating to AD 1760-1805 of America's founding, and discovered that of all the citations or references to other sources, the most frequent source was, at 34%, the Holy Bible (17). Then after that, there was Charles Montesquieu, William Blackstone, John Locke (17). And these 3 studious fellows were all serious Christians. // US Supreme Court said in AD 1897: "The first official action of this nation declared the foundation of government in these words, ""We hold these truths to be self-evident, that all men are created equal, that they are endowed by their Creator with certain unalienable rights, that among these are life, liberty, and the pursuit of happiness." ,,,While such declaration of principles may not have the force of organic law, or be made the basis of judicial decisions as to the limits of right and duty, and while in all cases references must be had to the organic law of the nation for such limits, yet the latter is but the body and the letter of which the former is the thought and the spirit, and it is always safe to read the letter of the Constitution in the Spirit of the Declaration of Independence". Regarding that statement the following needs also known: +We have a full admission that the CON is to be interpreted and derives and comes from and is to not contradict the DOI. +Furthermore it includes a part truth and also includes a falsity. To say that the DOI statements "may not have the force of organic law" is to say a lie; one of obviously not intentful, rather there is deficiency of knowledge. We observe that they had a consciousness of the doubtfulness of the remark, in that they said, "MAY NOT" rather than "DOES NOT"; they show they were aware of their insecurity to state an absolute law, and so without clarity, said "may not". Also Organic Law is defined as: "As a tool or instrument for a specific purpose". Thus Law is purposed. +The DOI Statements are true; the Judicial Branch here admits that the DOI statements are true; even Principle Law will apply here that these Principles apply to every area of life or law, and cannot be contradicted and must agree with every law; that laws are written by the use of statements, and verbal statements, and communicated as such. +They admit to God, truth, creation, laws of God, laws of the Bible. +"Laws of Nature's God" was known to be God's will in the Holy SC; and Conscience. +"Law of Nature" is God's existence and guide by Creation and Providence, as defined. +W. Blackstone explains on laws in a work titled, "Of the Nature of Laws in General" saying~ "Law, in its most general and comprehensive sense, signifies a rule of action, and is applied indiscriminately to all kinds of action, whether animate or inanimate, rational or irrational, thus we say, the laws of motion, of gravitation, of optics, or mechanics, as well as the laws of nature and of nations. And it is that rule of action which is prescribed by some superior, and which the inferior is bound to obey. Thus when the Supreme Being formed the universe, and created matter out of nothing, He impressed certain principles upon that matter, from which it can never depart, and without which it would cease to be. When He put that matter into motion, He established certain laws of motion, to which all moveable bodies must conform. Man considered as a creature, must necessarily be subject to the laws of his creator, for he is an entirely dependent being. A being, independent of any other, has no rule to pursue but such as He prescribes to Himself ,,,it is necessary that he (the dependent being) should in all points conform to his makers will. This will of His maker is called the LAW OF NATURE. (p) So when God created man, and endowed him with free will ,,,He laid down certain immutable laws of human nature, whereby that free will is in some degree regulated and restrained, and gave him also the faculty of reason to discover the purport of those laws ,,,are found upon comparison to be ,,,a part of the original law of nature ,,,but we are not from thence to conclude that the knowledge of these truths ,,,attainable by reason, in its corrupted state ,,,until revealed,,,". Thus W. Blackstone defines laws of "nature" , "laws of natures God" to include the Holy Bible, creation, laws originate with God, reasoning, reasoning alone is not sufficient, spirit (inanimate); said GOV that deny these citizen Rights, which are God given, may be overthrown and are illegal; states "that man should pursue his own happiness" but says not in license to evil but happiness is "inseparably interwoven the laws of eternal justice with the happiness of each individual that the latter cannot be obtained but by observing the former" and thus "happiness".

---T--- <u>The Total Basis of Fighting for Independence was Based on a Right from God:</u> // FFOG did not want to fight or kill or die; And if they did do so, they wanted to be Right before God in doing so. The CC states: "We hold these truths to be self-evident, that all men are created equal, that they are endowed by their Creator with certain unalienable rights, that among these are life, liberty, and the pursuit of happiness." // A RW statement from Patrick Henry~ "give me liberty or give me death"; he also included God as the Right to defense by saying~ "There is a just God who presides over the destinies of nations, and who will raise up friends to fight our battles for us". // Mr. James Madison states in his writings that the CON was not all his own work but involved many people; thus the agreement for Rights from God for the USA.

---T--- <u>Illegally Omit & then Redefine the DOI</u> Statements regarding "nature": // Part of Thomas Jefferson's contribution to the DOI was studying the word of Nature. His research included that of the Dutch Revolution from Spain. The Dutch instigated a declaration of their independence using "rights of nature". It is stated as this: "Every man knows that subjects are not created by God for princes, but princes for the sake of their subjects,,," (8). // Patrick Henry said, "Sir, we are not weak, if we make a proper use of the means which the God of nature hath placed in our power. Three millions of people, armed in the Holy cause of liberty, and in such a country as that which we possess, are invincible by any force which our enemy can send against us ,,,Forbid it, Almighty God! I know not what course others may take; but as for me, give me liberty or give me death" (13). // Observe "nature" here, and how God was the cause and Holy cause in the DOI with the intention/ purpose of the country.

---T--- <u>Illegality of Claiming a Standard and then Refusal to</u> Submit to that Very Standard.

---T--- <u>Illegality of Hiding & Avoiding the Most Valuable Existence of the Eternal Future</u> of Heaven & Hell; which includes more time than the existence of Earth: // This is a very extreme injustice to a society of Spiritual Moral Beings who must go to such existence after death; their need is for knowledge~ much of it and speedily receive it. Hence it is a very extreme necessity to do what the FFOG did to prove they cared. // Charlie Peace told the Chaplain of a Legal Court in England that if Hell is true, then "even if England were covered with broken glass from coast to coast, I would walk over it, if need be, on hands and knees and think it worth while living, just to save one soul from an eternal hell like that!". // To encourage Spiritual Eternal Beings to do evil, thus to prepare for Hell, is a extremely low evil action(s) by any neighbor doing such; including any GOV.

---T--- <u>Spiritual Moral Students have recorded brain waves during statuses</u> of either right or wrong with God; & it is part of the construction of our Being in conscience: // A dying lady praying to God recorded electrical brain waves which was on the positive side of the meter, and in size of a multiple times stronger than a broadcasting station sending signals around the world. A dying man was enticed to disobey one of the 10 commandments in a hospital; his brain waves recorded the same level, (as the lady said above), but it was on the negative side. (260d).

---T--- <u>Illegality of Excluding the Holy Bible & God as the Standard:</u> // Senator John McClellan pleas to return to Old-Fashioned Morality saying: "Apathy must go; It needs to be replaced by the outraged righteousness of a people who rose to greatness in this world through the spiritual values that their forefathers wrote into the Declaration of Independence and the Constitution of the United States,,, there is no better way to stop the advance of crime into every structure of our society. The entire nation must be roused and morally armed against the criminal army. Every honest man will be required to do his share, no matter how small a contribution his circumstances may permit him to make. The fight must be waged,,, among the youth of the nation. Their parents must give them,,, the fundamentals to differentiate right from wrong; appreciation and understanding of the true values of life,,, and churches,,, schools,,, community organizations,,, children societies, and probation officers double and redouble their efforts,,,,. If the leaders of crime continue their inroads upon our society and their degradations upon our national wellbeing,,,, this country will,,, rule by a group of gangsters,,,". (260e).

---T--- Louis Harris took polls in 1964 and reported that 94% of USA citizens want prayer restored to schools. (260c).

---T--- Evil teachings of fornication in the Public Schools.

---T--- Evil fornication perversions are one of the most common problems that Spiritual Moral folk are supporting. // Nudity is included. Such magazines were banned at one time in Victoria Texas. // // Spiritual Immoral Beings exposing parts of skin & bone tissue in public as if it was the right desire; and others looking at that tissue; which may as well equal sticks & stone savages~ Jer3;8-9; Eze23:14. // Mrs. Claire Collins Harvey, president of a Christian womens organization (Church Women United) said in an interview that, "ours is a sick, sick society", and, worsening "moral fiber of America"; and concerned about the USA problems of pornography and venereal diseases. (260f). // Benjamin Spock said, "Civilization is the product of restraint on natural impulse". The related article tells that great civilizations have been destroyed by unrestrained appetites, going to such excesses until characters were so corrupted survival was destroyed. Sweden is a current example as they made sex education compulsory, then gonorrhea increased, young people suffering it also, divorce tripling, marriage decreasing, illegitimate children increasing, teen pregnancies increasing, abortion increasing, and a very saddening 150% increase of teen suicide. (260g).

---T--- What most people call life is really & actually death, according to God. John1-17. // It has been said that "there is no greater curse than A Privilege (Right) abused".

---T--- Evil is agreed & supported as right; & that it has Rights, when it does not have Rights; rather limited Rights: // Congressman John R. Rarick of the State of LA. shared that, "the mothers and dads are already incensed at the indencies and violence purveyed to their children through the TV, movies, and even the radio,,, turning off the TV and staying away from the movies to shield their children,,, new attack vie the class room and the textbook. Today we find the classrooms of America have been turned into a battle ground to subvert the mind of our youth."

---T--- Such evils is known to have been opposed by our FFOG.

---T--- Illegal Cloths: In the earlier years of the USA as a Nation, more value was on cloths, in the right way. Women were urged to wear long sleeves. After World War II & early 1950's, there seemed to be a change towards 3/4 sleeves. We do want to say, that this is not intended to make laws on sleeves. Rather to share that some degree of clothing is to be illegal; in public. There are now laws legalizing pornography, or nudity, and swim suits in public, etc. Swimsuits are basically underwear. Anywhere there is nudity and immodesty there is a ruin of societies. Holy Scripture records Christ delivering a Person who had demons inside; the demons had him unclothed and Christ helped him get fully clothed (Mark5).

---T--- Illegal refusing to accept the true historical GOV involvement, participation, & supporting of the Christian Great Awakening Movements that occurred in America & Europe: // British Historian, Paul Johnson, states that 3 of 4 Americans were involved in these; and that, "as we have seen, America had been founded primarily for religious purposes, and the Great Awakening had been the original dynamic of the continental movement for independence. The Americans were overwhelmingly church going, much more so than the English whose rule they rejected." (7). // Part of one Christian Great Awakening occurred during the Independence Times~ that is the DOI times approx. The churches assisted the GOV and the GOV assisted the churches; including the pastors. Some groups of Christians were given a title called the "black regiment"; they wore a black overcoat and assisted the RW efforts; and included various ministers; they preached against England and its evils and assisted the DOI development. Many of the churches and the pastors were in charge and participated and initiated the "minute men" military. (2). // Churches preached that "resistance to tyranny is obedience to God". This Truth encouraged the GOV and public to have a basis for which to be justified; that of being Right with God, and in doing such included then to defend oneself from the evils of the British GOV. // The Churches enlisted the ministry as the most educated of the land (2). // Election Day sermons preached (2). // Rev Samuel West, minister of Congregational Church, helped John Adams write the Massachusetts CON, which is Christian based (2). // The Minute Men were groups of men who could fight at a minutes notice; often called and led by a Pastor or deacon; met in the center of town; instead of lining up armies, they would hide behind trees, hills, rocks, and fight with whatever they could find; they had few guns and so they relied on sticks, rocks, and such. A famous group of Minute Men were from the Lexington Church. The British attempted to seize the town of Lexington because it had gunpowder and a fortress; and also to kill 2 lead men, Samuel Adams & John Hancock, who were lodged in the home of Rev Jonas Clark, minister of the Lexington Church. Paul Revere, that night, made his famous midnight ride warning, "The British are coming, the British are coming!". The Americans were extremely outnumbered and the British army very disciplined. However only 7 Americans were killed, 9 wounded; some that died here were elderly men who chose to pay with their lives rather than die of old age in their home. Jonas Clark said the British army, "was "more like murderers and cut-throats, than the troops of a Christian King, without provocation, without warning, when no war was proclaimed, they draw the sword of violence,,," (Jonas Clark, Commentary on the Battle of Lexington, 1776). // Churches provided moral and spiritual basis for the country.

---T--- Excessive false Christianity is to be opposed: // Such is limited not unlimited. Allowances for a specific degree and range of Christianity is allowed because of reasons (intentions/purposes) as identified in the previous Chapters on the CC and others. Unlimited doctrines and applications or activity has not been given a Right. If it was unlimited the USA would return to the same problem for which caused it to become a separate Nation; and it would contradict our CC. +Note the danger of wrong Catholicism. Abraham Lincoln says, "The (Roman Catholic) priests, the nuns

290

and the monks, who daily land on our shores under the pretext of teaching their religion, instructing in their schools, taking care of the sick in their hospitals, are nothing else but the emissaries of the pope, to undermine our institutions, alienate the hearts of our people from the Constitution and our laws, destroy our public schools, and prepare a reign of anarchy here as they have done in Ireland, in Spain, and wherever there are people that want to be free.,,, Is it right to give the priviledge of citizenship to men who are the sworn and public enemies of our Constitution, our laws, our liberty, and our life?,,, Two supreme powers cannot exist in the same territory.,,,, I am for liberty of conscience for its noblest, broadest, highest sense. But I cannot give liberty to the Pope, or his followers, the Papists, so long as they tell me their conscience orders them to,,, [[do such and such]]". (260a).

---T--- <u>Evil Laws & Evil Spiritual Moral Beings are Not Legal to</u> Make Laws, Nor Be Directly Connected with Law Official Positions (not specified at this time); Nor are Evil Laws Legal in the USA: // Only a few statements from the FFOG will be given to prove this Truth(s). These are the same as all of the FFOG. Therefore when you read these, you read them all. +Alexander Hamilton states, "The attempt by the rulers of a nation to destroy all religious opinion and to pervert a whole people to atheism is a phenomenon of profligacy ,,,To establish atheism on the ruins of Christianity to deprive mankind of its best consolations and most animating hopes and to make gloomy desert of the universe" (170). +Thomas Jefferson (3rd Pres.), in AD 1805 stated a national prayer, "Almighty God, Who has given us this good land for our heritage: we humbly beseech Thee that we may always prove ourselves a people mindful of Thy favor and glad to do Thy will. Bless our land with honorable ministry, sound learning, and pure manners. Save us from violence, discord, and confusion, from pride and arrogance, and from every evil way. Defend our liberties, and fashion into one united people the multitude brought hither out of many kindreds and tongues. Endow with Thy spirit of wisdom those to whom in Thy Name we entrust the authority of GOV, that there may be justice and peace at home, and that through obedience to Thy law, we may show forth Thy praise among the nations of the earth. In time of prosperity fill our hearts with thankfulness, and in the day of trouble, suffer not our trust in Thee to fail; all of which we ask through Jesus Christ our Lord, Amen.". +John Adams states, "The idea of infidelity cannot be treated with too much resentment or too much horror. The man who can think of it with patience is a traitor in his heart and ought to be execrated as one who adds the deepest hypocrisy to the blackest treason" (169). +Benjamin Rush states, "I anticipate nothing but suffering to the human race while the present systems of paganism, deism, and atheism prevail in the world" (97). +Samuel Adams states, "I have a thorough contempt for all men,,, who appear to be the irreclaimable enemies of religion" (171). +Gouverneur Morris states, "The most important of all lessons (from the SCs) is the denunciation of ruin to every State that rejects the precepts of religion" (172). +John Witherspoon states, "Shun, as a contagious pestilence ,,,those especially whom you perceive to be infected with the principles of infidelity or who are enemies to the power of religion" and "Whoever is an avowed enemy of God ,,,call him an enemy to his country" (154). // +Every Earlier State CON had requirements to be a Christian & support Christianity. // The CC proves this because the CON is application of the DOI; and the DOI occurred because of the Intention/ purpose to Put God as Priority to Mankind and evil; and to get Rights from God; evil laws and evil spiritual moral Beings were rejected. // The Holy Bible was the Most Priority Reference for Constructing the USA GOV & National Systems. Here are Holy Scriptures about such: +It is never right to do wrong to do right. This includes lying, breaking laws, etc. This would be inclusive of right laws. Rom3:8~"And not rather, (as we be slanderously reported, and as some affirm that we say,) Let us do evil, that good may come? whose damnation is just". See here that God does not call this sort of GOV work, or whatever, that does evil in order to do good. It appears that Rahab lied 2 times in Jos2:4,5 (HSC). Now here KN at that time is related; & her training & newness as a Saint. However it is never right to lie; there is no such a thing as a right lie (white lie). It is never right to sin in pressure of pain/pleasure, such as TTT. God does not need the sinful methods to catch evil. Some evil may be caught or opposed by such methods. However it is never right and it will receive the anger of God and a pronouncement of guilt on all Beings who use such methods. Such methods are stupid, foolish, and vile. +Spiritual Moral Beings are not to sin if an evil law of the society tells them to; and God is priority to evil legal systems. This is proven repeatedly in HSC. For one, Act5:29~"Then Peter and the other apostles answered and said, We ought to obey God rather than men". And this is exactly what the FFOG did to oppose evil coming from some evil people; the CC has it's basis herein. +A Law Official is required to be Christian & Christian supporting; The CC states such, and so does~ Rom13:4~"For he is the minister of God to you for good. But if you do that which is evil, be afraid". See there that they are to be a helper to God and to do Good to other Spiritual Moral Beings, and Not evil. vs 5~"but also for conscience sake". See here the supporting of the heart or Spirit which includes the conscience. +The Lord Jesus does not intend for us to take Christian Lives and Christian living activities to get training from Non-Christian Spiritual Moral Beings. Christian homes are Sanctified homes~ 1Cor7:14~"For the unbelieving husband is sanctified by the wife, and the unbelieving wife is sanctified by the husband". A separation is to be applied between Christians & Non-Christians~ 2Cor6:14-17~"Be you not unequally yoked together with unbelievers: for what fellowship has rightness with unrightness? and what communion has light with darkness? And what concord has Christ with Belial? or what part has he that believeth with an infidel? And what agreement has the temple of God with idols? for you are the temple of the living God; as God has said, I will dwell in them, and walk in them; and I will be their God, and they shall be my people. Wherefore come out from among them, and be you SEPARATE, saith the Lord, and touch not the unclean thing; and I will receive you". Do not ask for ungodly reasoning~ 1Cor6:1-6~"Dare any of you, having a matter against another, go to law before the unjust, and not before the saints? Do you not know that the saints shall judge the world? and if the world shall be judged by you, are you unworthy to judge the smallest matters? how much more things that pertain to this life? If then you have judgments of things pertaining to this life, set them to judge who are least esteemed in the church. Is it so, that there is not a wise man among you? no, not one that shall be able to judge between his brethren?. But brother goeth to law with brother, and that before the unbelievers". In fact, God prefers that we get a Christian Spiritual Moral Being that has no official position and is thought to be the lowest position in the Church to decide for Christians rather than taking situations to the ungodly. +God hates the reasoning and the intent/ purpose of evil spiritual moral Beings and Rejects them and their reasoning~ Mat 4 was Jesus rejecting the Devil's evil reasoning, and even reasoning with the Holy Bible; Rom 8 says~'The Carnal mind is enmity (an enemy) of God'; Psa1 says 'do not stand, sit, nor walk with ungodly and sinners; take not their counsel'; 1Cor10 says 'Do Not fellowship (commune) with sinners & ungodly'. +The Christian's home has the Atonement Blood over it, similar to Egypt. Exo12:7; 1Joh1:7~"the Blood of Jesus Christ His Son cleanses us from all sin".

---T--- <u>Illegality of refusing historical DOCs and evidence;</u> and doing such with disrespect or irreverence to God.

---T--- <u>Illegally removing the written laws and God</u>'s law that are in the CC (DOI & CON); and replacing it illegally with the vote; which is an illegal act and illegal operation.

---T--- <u>VOTE, and the power of it</u>: // The vote does not void the CC (DOI & CON). // The vote is to be secondary to the CC (DOI & CON). // The vote is to support the CC (DOI & CON). // The vote and GOV is under God. Note what the CC DOI states~ "One nation under God"; "laws of nature and of nature's God entitle them ,,,all men are created equal ,,,that they are endowed by their Creator with certain inalienable rights; that among these are life, liberty, and the pursuit of happiness.". Notice the Rights come from God; and furthermore it is also self-evident that God is over man, and comes from God. // These Rights come from God, and none but Him; as is clearly stated.

---T--- <u>Illegality of putting falsities to word definitions;</u> of not using the true definitions of words; and thus breaking the Laws of Language (communication, DOCs, evidence, grammar, word laws).

++

-------------------- ,,,,,,,,,,,,, CLOSING CHAPTER -------------------

---T--- <u>Sanctification</u>: // The main intention/ purpose and focus of Sanctification is the spirit and Joining with the Holy Spirit; in communion with the Lord. This includes all the parts of our Being (spirit), which are the conscience, affections & emotions, desires, intents (motives), will, reasoning, etc. Other Holy Bible words for it are: Gal2:20; 3:27; Eph4:24; Col3:10~"I am crucified with Christ: nevertheless I live; yet not I, but Christ liveth in me"; "Perfection"; Put on Christ; put on new man". It is to have all parts of the Being regulated by the Will & Reasoning Truth Laws and right Intent/purpose; which is Totally submitted to Christ & Truth; to have all intents (Intent/purpose) directed to Him & Truth. You must decide the right Intention/ purpose which is that God is 1st priority, only because He is God and as a Being valuable to you; thus you love Him. Then apply this in all subjects of your life. {Mat22:37-40; 1Cor10:31}. This is your 1st priority main Intent/ purpose. Do not put anything before such; not self-satisfaction, not the subject, not the body, not the law, not other spiritual moral Beings, not self, etc. All Spiritual Moral Beings main subject is to get God, get the main 1st priority intention/ purpose for everything, Deu6:5; Mat22:37-40; 1Cor13; 1Cor10:31; this includes doing all because you love God; do it for Him only because He is God and for the good of His Being as valuable to you. Then commune (fellowship) with Him and do all subjects with that 1st priority Intent/ purpose & Being. All should be directed for getting that done. // ACTIONS as follows: // Be sure you started your salvation status~ that you are saved~ all past sin acts forgiven and thus justified. Walk in light (knowledge) and keep attention on Jesus (as Peter when walking on the water Mat14); conscious attention to Him in front of you, and the Holy Spirit with you. // Any confessions & restitutions remaining that need done that are known; and that can be done? // Attitude Preparation & maintenance: Seek, priority, great desire of Intention/

purpose, want~ hunger and thirst for rightness and God, humility; and Intention/ purpose; to put all evil out and Him in. It is good to begin to learn oneself with communing with the Lord and experiences with Him as a Spirit. Expressions received from Him. // To gain a good basis of KN for comprehension, it is good to study a couple of books on guidance and communion (fellowship). 2Cor 10:5 & Isa 26:3 & Psa 16:8 assist this. // Consecration & Commitment: Study and search and preparation: +Make a list of all. All of your Being that you consecrate, such as your body, mind, spirit, decisions, desires, emotions, affections, will, conscience, intentions/ purposes, and etc. +Sin acts are not to be consecrated, but forgiven. +Sinful status or desires, affections, evil desires (lusts), Intents/purposes, and so on, are not to be consecrated, but put to death~ stop them, hate them, replace them; stop the subject, start a new or different subject. // After some time of that consecration and commitment, which is however long you reason by conscience and truth, and also by God's guidance of spiritual communication and the SCs; maybe a few hours, maybe a few days, etc. +Put everything on the altar. // Use some time asking the Lord if there is anything that He wants to communicate to you that needs to be included. // Then put all other things that are unknown on a list titled, the Unknown List. This includes all deficiency in KN, sin acts, anything unknown or not conscious of having not included on the list that is known. Commit this to the Lord in trust feelings and thoughts to Him; of intention/ purpose; and by a decision of the Will. +With all your heart (will) by force against all; violence; stretch every nerve, press with vigor; zeal. // There are only 3 hindrances~ which would include~ 1} Spirit things internally (sinful desires, or Intents/purposes, evil affections, will/decisions, thinking), 2} or sin acts, 3} or not knowing what to do. Then once these are known, faith and commitment can be done. // Self must die~ be crucified. That is your Being and your set of rules (laws). These are not the standard to live by any longer. Rather: a} God is to be God, no idol, and b} His rules (laws) are that which are to be obeyed, and c} His presence is highly desired, the Intent/ purpose, decided by will constantly, & communed with (fellowship). // Now is the time of crucifixion. Where you clarify within your reasoning, and will, and affections that you Intention/ purpose want all that which is on the list to die; and that you Intention/ purpose want Christ and the Holy Ghost; no sin in desire, affection, emotion, thought, intent, will, etc. You make this decision and review the list with hate. Cannot put on new over old; put off old by putting on new; which is Christ; the old affections is put out, and a new affection is put in. The old is dead, it is not thought about, no thinking evil, no desire and enjoyment of it, and the new is thought of, desired, and loved. The wrong Intent/ purpose is stopped, and a new put in. // Confession of your need. // A clear conscience is all that is needed before taking the Faith procedure. If you made a total consecration and commitment, which included requesting the Lord to communicate to you anything else that you may have missed or unknown, then your conscience should be clear. // Faith procedure: Get a promise and rely on it as from God, and claim your sanctification based on the promise. He says "now" is the time (2Cor 6). He says we will not be ashamed if we do trust His promise (Rom 9:33). His promise is how He feels and thinks and wills about us; what He intends/purposes. Thus trust Him on that. He says that if we do not trust Him we will be guilty for not trusting Him. What an invitation and assistance to trust Him. He will do it if we simply apply our will, desire, Intent/ purpose, and trust in Him, with a feeling of trust and will/ decision, desire, Intent/ purpose. // Think thoughts of Faith and will and desire them intently with Intent/ purpose to the Lord, and make the decision to claim the promise. Many promises are available. Promises that do not have the word sanctification in them are also useful; as long as it intends, or part of such. Many are like that. Christ's atoning, including blood, gives you the right, earns it for you. And Christ gives you the promise. // Faith Fight: Unless you fight a regiment of devils with bravery you will never get sanctified, said W. Godbey. Stay with your committal and crucifixion which is on the altar and think thoughts that the promise is True. Casting down every thought that is contrary to faith thoughts (2Cor 10:5). Note what are faith thoughts. Dare not take a doubt. God wants and asks you to trust Him and is hurt if you do not. Looking after feeling is a trick of the devil to cheat you out of it. FACT, FAITH, FEELING is the order. Affections and emotions and expressions from the Lord will come. Commune with the Lord and He will express Himself constantly in a small expression and occasionally in large expressions. Remind yourself and share it with God that you have fully done all the conditions of consecration, commitment, crucifixion, of desire, intent (Intent/ purpose), affection, thought, will, emotion, and decision. Verbally say, 'I do not care if I feel any different; I am all the Lords'; say it; repeat it over and over. // Trust and wait for God to bring you His Witness (Expression). When He will bring it, we do not know, but He will, for He has promised. This may be peace, or affections of love or comfort; joy; or such and can include various other expressions. A clear conscience is good enough to make the fact clear, as long as you trust the promise and have done the conditions. // Priority is to commune with the Lord constantly in intents (Intent/ purpose), desire, will, affections, emotions, thoughts, reasonings, and decisions of the Will. //Make verbal communications to Spiritual Moral Beings that you are trusting God has sanctified you, based on the promise. 1Tim6:12. // Ignore doubts, keep the will committed, desire and intents for God, and conscious attention on the Lord in front of you; communing with the Lord constantly; and Holy Spirit; affections loving the Lord; peace and every thought to God. // If you stumble, get up and get immediately returning at it, make the decision again, and decide more fervency, desire, and discipline; concentrate on your intention/ purpose. // Continue to learn to commune with Jesus and the Holy Ghost and prayer and receive guidance with Him; and apply all parts of your Being. // Constant watch on emotions, affections, desires, thoughts, intents, and these submitting to your will and reasoning. Walk in Love, with the will, reasoning, intents, desires, affections, and thoughts. // Use time learning occasionally to wail, mourn, weep and the Lord will come and comfort you (Mat5:3-4; Jam4). // You must decide the right Intent/ purpose (intent) which is that God is 1st priority, only because He is God and as a Being is valuable; thus you love Him. Then apply this in all subjects of your life. {Mat22:37-40; 1Cor10:31}. This is your 1st priority main Intent/ purpose. Do not put anything, before such; not self-satisfaction, not the subject, not for the body itself (body-idolatry), not the law, not other spiritual moral agents, not self, etc.

<u>++++ CLOSING REMARKS:</u>

////On the Great Seal Emblem of the USA, in many Supporting DOCs, in the Meetings for the CC (DOI & CON), was the inclusion of Holy SC. One of those, as is shown at the start of this book, is the Record of Israel & Egypt; where Israel came out and away from the tyranny of the GOV of Egypt. This is in Exodus through Deuteronomy. Here are some of the SC which the US GOV intended/ purposed seriously to include in establishing the USA on a right basis; they are~ Lev26; Exo28; Deu6-7. Essentially these Scriptures are the basis of the Great Seal. They tell that God is to be first priority and there should be no idols; and that the commandments of the Lord should be obeyed and not disobeyed; furthermore they state that blessings or problems will result for obedience or disobedience. One of the blessing or problems relates to the land; It shares that the land will be blessed if the Lord is obeyed. Psalms 96 says~"Sing to the Lord, all the world,,, Praise Him. Proclaim every day the good news that He [[the Lord]] has saved us. Proclaim His glory to the nations, His mighty deeds to all peoples. The gods of all other [[falsity gods]] nations are only idols, but the Lord created the heavens. Say to all the nations, 'The Lord is King!' ,,, Be glad, earth and sky! Roar, sea, and every creature in you; be glad, fields, and everything in you! The trees in the woods will shout for joy when the LORD comes to rule the earth. He will rule the peoples of the world with justice and fairness". (Good News Bible version).

//// Our heart's can be encouraged with a self-evidence more clarified than it was at first, and more evident and more conscious to all, and to the desirous folk. A more responsible liberty, and a more responsibility to be happy, will depend on having a clear conscience. Some Spiritual heart folk may reply, 'that is only your opinion'. What then of such a reply; is that accurate? No it is a Lie that has tried to damage the minds and hearts of many. Such citizen Branch is to encourage Christianity, as in the past, and then activate themselves to laws and governmental agencies and activities. Engaging and encouraging confusion across the land causes divisions that cause dysfunction. Cannot serve both the demons or evil, or be anti-God to extreme, and God; and then expect right function Luk16:13. Demonology is not to be supported by USA GOV; and surely does not have the CC (DOI & CON) support. This CC overRules group(s) of Spiritual Folk who promote evil or idolatry in any form. To this will be some Reasoning Tests together, such as including an internal (Spirit) self-evidence of responsibility of the conscience. Christ, the Messiah, had worked long and hard to keep Himself on the Earth; "The Earth is the Lord's and the fullness thereof"~Psa24:1. An historical event and activity report of a battle, is shared, as paraphrased, that occurred in Europe when aggressors without cause, without kind consideration, without proper evaluation, without proper negotiation, and without proper respect and love of their brother, aggressed on them. The reaction to this, was a little group of Spiritual Moral Beings researching to learn of answers for defense; defense for their selves, wives, little ones, and their things. The decision was made to call Christian meetings; thus they did and some prayed hard enough and rightly enough to get an answer from the Supreme Ruler, Christ Jesus; one person said the Lord had instructed them to go out and shout "Hallelujah" 3 times at the battle. Hence when the time of battle confrontation was coerced on them, they did so; and the murdering aggressors could not run fast enough the opposite direction. Thus no one should ever overlook or lightly consider the great intervention costing of the Lord Jesus. Pres. Abraham Lincoln shared about the Civil War, "We here highly resolve that these dead shall not have died in vain; that this nation, under God, shall have a new birth of freedom, and that government of the people, by the people, for the people shall not perish from the earth". Pres. John Adams with clarity stated the value of heart rightness and of the importance of other people, by saying this~ "Posterity! You will never know how much it cost the present generation to preserve your freedom! I hope you will make good use of it! If you do not, I shall repent in Heaven that I ever took half the pains to preserve it!". Christ, the Lord God worked much to provide us this USA Nation. Now what of Christ's Work in the Country, and how does He feel and think of our FFOG and of His Own work ?? I heard reported that Christ Jesus gets alerted at the children, when other Beings insert them with evil thoughts, feelings, affections, and the likes. Observe Christ's highest joy, 3Joh1:4~"I have no greater joy than these things, to hear that my children walk in the truth". Also 1Joh5:21~"Little children, keep yourselves from idols. Amen". It is Holy Bible, no doubt, which you may easily find in God's heart. An Eleanor (Adams-Henderson-Deeter), possible relative of Samuel & John Adams, once told me that she 'would not want to offend the Eagle'. Why? Because it is an unbeatable bird, a terrific soldier of the air, a 'ferocious fighter against enemies'. This is HSC about the Eagle, Jer48:40~"For so says Jehovah: Behold, he shall fly like an eagle and shall spread his wings,,,". Now note what God thinks of past efforts: Heb6:10~"For God is not unrighteous to forget your work and labor of love, which you have showed toward his name ~KJV; For God is not unjust so as to overlook your work and the love that you have shown for his name ~ESV". That loving NAME was righteously included, and in many ways, the kind~ "God, Creator, Supreme Ruler, Divine Providence, Lord Jesus Christ". To Him we owe our heartfelt obedience, thankfulness, and gratitude; intention/ purpose priority. God teaches us lessons on pain. What are they? It may be better said, 'how can they be missed?'. They are missed, nevertheless. And as Rom 1-3 says, that Spiritual Moral people should look around and think of the decaying body that they exist in, and how time converts to eternity, and how children should be taught by various methods of such subjects. If Spiritual Moral people cannot learn to Not desire and intend/ purpose evil, then if they cannot learn anything else, plead they learn to attend to lessons of pain. "The fear of the Lord is the beginning of knowledge and wisdom"~ Pro1:7; Psa111:10. This is found in Holy SC multiple times. It is a lesson of pain. The anger of the Lord does not feel good in our affections and conscience. And evil did not effect Sodom & Gomorrah good, nor the Flood people of Noah. Freedom is what "God, Creator, Supreme Judge, Divine Providence, Lord Christ Jesus" has stated it is~ "the truth shall set you free" and "I am the Truth,

294

the Way, the Life, and no man cometh to the Father but by Me"~Joh8:32; 14:6. God, Christ Jesus, is the religion of the FFOG, including the USA GOV. The USA States GOV IS NOT to be idolatrous; thus selfish.

//// A kind recommendation for a grand experience is to go get a cup of hot chocolate or coffee and then prepare the heart; maybe also get a donut or cookie. Then we may with our family or such, gather together for a praise to the best Being of all. A good song (hymn or psalm), such as one that has the word "King" in it; of which there are many. Also these 2 songs, "Love Divine", or "Seek Ye First the Kingdom of God" are recommended for some time to express ourself to Him; and then have communion with Him, trusting for reactions from the most High. Is He not the most kindest, loving Being of all ??

//// If you affectionately care, you may decide the right Intention/ purpose which is that God is 1st priority, only because He is God, and as a Being that is valuable; thus you love Him. Then apply this in all subjects of your life. {Mat22:37-40; 1Cor10:31}. This is your 1st priority Intent/ purpose. Do not put anything before such; not self-satisfaction, not the subject, not for the body itself (body-idolatry), not the law, not other Spiritual Moral Beings, not self, etc. // Now this is the most needed subject: +Let me share what C. Finney says (copyright free){as paraphrased}: Selfishness; Self-Idolatry or Self-Centeredness; The first thing is to change the {intention/ purpose} and then the sinner can cease from outward (body) sin; Indeed, if the {intention/ purpose} be changed, many of the same acts which were before sinful will become holy. While the selfish end {intention/ purpose} continues, whatever a sinner does, is selfish. Whether he eats, drinks, labors, preaches, or, in short, whatever he does, is to promote some form of self-direction. The end {intention/ purpose} being wrong, all is, and must be, wrong. But let the end {intention/ purpose} be changed; let benevolence {good willing to God, others, self} take the place of selfishness, and all is right. With this end {intention/ purpose} in view {in consciousness; similar to looking at a visual view} the mind is absolutely incapable of doing anything or of choosing anything, except as a means of promoting the good of the universe; {which is God & other Beings}. (end of Finney's). Therefore to start, decide that you want God; to love Him most of all; & to love other Beings as yourself. Decide for an Intent/ purpose that you will include Him in everything, (God is in all your thoughts~ Psa 10:4); and that all your subjects that you do will include such intent/ purpose; that it will be as your 1st Priority Total intention/ purpose; that of God; only because He is God; for the good of Him as a Being that is valuable to you. Then start applying this in all parts of your life~ decisions of the will, desires, etc. {Eze18:31; 36:26; Mat12:33; 22:37-40; Rom 6:all; 8:13; 8:all; 12:1-2; Jam 1:21; 4:8; Deu6:5; 30:15, 19; Psa 34:14; Isa 1:16-17; 55:7; Eph4:22-247; Col3:5-9, 17; 1Pet1:14; 2:1; 4:2-4; 2Pet1:4; Phi4:13; 1Cor10:31}. This is the main decision~ that of the right intention/ purpose; which is that God is 1st priority, only because He is God and as His Being is valuable; thus you love Him. Then apply this in all subjects of your life. This is a change from self-idolatry, or selfishness, from self-centeredness, to God & Love. This is your 1st Priority Total intention/ purpose. Do not put anything, before such; not self-satisfaction, not the subject, not the body, not the law, not other people, not self, not ulterior intentions, not other or different intentions, etc. All Spiritual Moral Agents main subject is to get God, get the main 1st priority intention/ purpose for everything; which is do all because you love God, do it for Him only because He is God and for the good of His Being as valuable to you. Then commune (fellowship) with Him; and do all subjects with that 1st priority intention/ purpose & Being. All should be directed for getting that done. It is a SETLWHM {Self-Evidence Truth Law Written on Heart & Mind}; a First Truth~ that such an intention/ purpose should be decided. // C. Finney has identified the Goodness Principle and the Love Principle. Love includes all right Personality Traits or Attributes; and in balance; as a unit; working together. Goodness is what God does to all Beings. Goodness is a Principle Law word. It is to be part of the intention/ purpose. Such is to aim at a Being; not a rule or law, or material substance, etc. Although laws are part of it, the Being is to be the real value to us, because of themselves; without a selfish return receiving; The Being is the subject. Although there is always a pleasure and receiving from doing right, it is not the priority; rather it is because of the Laws of Love, and rightness that such is part of it; because it is that Love always effects for pleasure of heart or spirit. But pleasure is to be defined rightly. It can be a clear conscience, or having denied self for other Beings, etc. Nevertheless the 1st Priority is the Other Being themselves; as a value to us.

++

LIST OF CITATIONS:

(1a) All normal and English Definitions came from Webster's New World Dictionary of the American Language, 2nd College Ed. David B. Guralnik, Editor in Chief. United States. William Collins & World Pub. Co. 1972, 1978.

(1b) Noah Webster's 1828 Dictionary of the American Language.

(1c) Joseph Thayer. Thayer's Greek Definitions. (lexicon). First printing 1889. Digital Version: Rick Meyers, e ~ Sword, 5902 Parham Rd., Franklin, TN. 37064. United States. website: e-sword.net.

(2) David Gibbs. One Nation Under God: Ten Things Every Christian Should Know About the Founding of America. Seminole, Florida: Christian Law Assoc. 2005.

(2a) David Gibbs. Understanding the Constitution: Ten Things Every Christian Should Know about the Supreme Law of the Land. Seminole, FL: Christian Law Assoc. 2006.

(3) David Barton. Separation of Church & State: What the Founders Meant. Aledo, TX: Wallbuilders Press. 2007.

(4) David Barton. The Myth of Separation. Aledo, TX. Wallbuilder Press. 1992.

(5) David Barton. Original Intent: The Courts, the Constitution, and Religion, 5th Ed., TX: Aledo. Wallbuilders Press. 2008.

(5a) David Barton. The Wallbuilders.com. Website.

(6) John Jay. The Correspondence and Public Papers of John Jay. Henry P. Johnston, ed. 1890. NY: Burt Franklin, 1970.

(6a) Website, GreatSeal.com.

(7) Paul Johnson. A History of the American People. New York: Harper Collins Publishers, 1997.

(8) George Bancroft. History of the US of America, From the Discovery of the Continent. NY: D. Appleton and Company, 1890.

(9) John Eidsmoe. Christianity and the Constitution. Grand Rapids: Baker Book House, 1987.

(10) Sir William Blackstone. Commentaries on the Laws of England. Philadelphia: J.B. Lippincott and Co. 1879.

(11) Jared Sparks, ed. The Writings of George Washington, 12 Vols. Boston: American Stationer's Co. 1837, NY. F, Andrew's, 1834-1847.

(11a) Jared Sparks, ed. Quoted Gouverneur Morris. The Life of Gouverneur Morris, w/ Selections from His Correspondence and Miscellaneous Papers. Boston: Gray and Bowen, 1832.

(12) George Washington. The Writings of Washington. 1778.

(12a) George Washington. Address of George Washington, President of the US. Baltimore: George and Henry S. Keatings. 1796.

(12b) George Washington. Address of George Washington, President of the US and Late Commander and Chief of the American Army to the People of the US Preparatory to His Declination. Baltimore: Christopher Jackson, 1796.

(13) The Annuals of America. Chicago et al: Encyclopedia Britannica, 1976.

(14) Annals of Congress, 1789-1791. Washington, D.C: Gales & Seaton, 1843.

(14a) US Library of Congress. All Documents of the US. Specific one mentioned in text.

(15) Compton's Pictured Encyclopedia and Fact-Index, Vol. 15, 26. Washington's Farewell Address.

(16) Mecklenburg County, Declaration of Independence, May, 20, 1775. Raleigh, North Carolina Register Apr. 30, 1819. Charles W. Eliot, LL.D., ed. American Historical Documents 1000-1904. NY: P.F. Collier & Son Co. The Harvard Classics, 1910.

(17) Donald S. Lutz. The Origins of American Constitutionalism. Baton Rouge: Louisiana State University Press, 1988.

(18) Chief Justice Roy S. Moore. Our Legal Heritage. Montgomery, AL: The Administrative Office of Courts, June 2001.

(18a) Website - http://ten-commandments.us/ The Jesus Saves Ministry, 1271 Eastland Rd. Sparta, TN 38583 Teleph: 931-935-2110 or 1-877-210-5266. [Judge Moore is involved w/ this].

(19) Alexander Hamilton, April 16-21, 1802 Letter to James Bayard, Claude G. Bowers, Jefferson and Hamilton: The Struggle for Democracy in America. Boston: Houghton Mifflin Co. 1925/1937.

(20) Charles Montesquieu. Spirit of Laws. Vol 1.

(21) John Adams. The Works of John Adams - Second President of the US: w/ a Life of the Author, Notes, and Illustrations. Boston: Little, Brown, & Co. 1854.

(21a) John Adams. The Works of John Adams - Second President of the US: w/ a Life of the Author, Notes, and Illustrations. Charles Francis Adams, ed., Boston: Little, Brown, & Co. 1850.

(22) Robert Cord. Separation of Church and State: Historical Fact and Current Fiction. NY: Lambeth Press. 1982. [quote in (2)].

(23) William J. Federer. America's God and Country. Encyclopedia of Quotations. St. Louis, MO: Amerisearch, Inc. 1994.

(24) Gorton Carruth and Eugene Ehrich. The Harper Book of American Quotations. New York: Harper & Row, Publishers, 1988.

(25) John Fiske. The Beginnings of New England. Boston: Houghton, Mifflin & Co. 1898. Charter of New Haven Colony, April 3, 1644.

(26) Catherine Drinker Bowen. Miracle at Philadelphia: The Story of the Constitutional Convention May to September 1787. Boston et al: An Atlantic Monthly Press Book, a division of Little, Brown, and Co. 1966. { Translated in (2) }.

(27) David J. Brewer, Justice. The US: A Christian Nation. Philadelphia, PA: The John C. Winston Co. 1905.

(28) Debates and Proceedings in the Congress of the US. Washington, DC: Gales & Seaton, 1834.

(29) Fisher Ames. <u>Works of Fisher Ames</u>. Boston: T.B. Wait & Co. 1809.

(30) Albert Ellery Bergh, ed., quotes Thomas Jefferson. <u>The writings of Thomas Jefferson</u>. Washington, DC: The Thomas Jefferson Memorial Assoc., 1904, 1907.

(31) <u>Sources and Documents Illustrating the American Revolution 1764-88 and the Formation of the Federal Constitution.</u> S.E. Morrison, ed. NY: Oxford University Press, 1923.

(32) <u>The Constitutions of All the US According to the Latest Amendments.</u> Lexington, KY: Thomas To. Skillman, 1817.

(33) M.E. Bradford. <u>A Worthy Company</u>. NH: Plymouth Rock Foundation, 1982.

(34) Steve C. Dawson. <u>God's Providence in America's History</u>. Rancho Cordova, CA: Steve C. Dawson, 1988.

(35) <u>Church and State in American Law: Cases and Materials.</u> John J. McGrath, ed. Milwaukee: The Bruce Pub. Co. 1962.

(36) B.F. Morris. <u>The Christian Life and Character of the Civil Institutions of the US.</u> Philadelphia: George W. Childs 1864.

(37) Edwin Gaustad. <u>Faith of Our Fathers.</u> San Fancisco: Harper & Row, 1987.

(38) Anson Phelps Stokes. <u>Church and State in the US</u>. NY: Harper & Brothers, 1950.

(39) Christopher Collier. <u>Roger Sherman's Connecticut</u>. Middletown, CT: Wesleyan University Press, 1979.

(40) Thomas Jefferson. <u>Jefferson Writings</u>. Merrill D. Peterson, ed. NY: Literary Classics of the US, Inc., 1984.

(40a) Thomas Jefferson. <u>Notes on State of Virginia</u>. Philadelphia. Mathew Carey. 1794.

(41) J. Wingate Thornton. <u>The pulpit of the American Revolution</u>. 1860. Reprinted NY: Burt Franklin 1970.

(42) Russ Walton. <u>Biblical Principles of Importance to Godly Christians</u>. NH: Plymouth Rock Foundation. 1984.

(43) Peter G. Mode. <u>Sourcebook and Bibliographical Guide for American Church History</u>. Menasha, WI: George Banta Pub. Co. 1921.

(44) Franklin B. Dexter, ed. <u>Documentary History of Yale University</u>. NY: Amo Press. The New York Times, 1969.

(45) Selim H. Peabody, ed. <u>American Patriotism: Speeches, Letters, and Other Papers Which Illustrate the Foundation, the Development, the Preservation of the US of America</u>. NY: American Book Exchange, 1880.

(46) Verna M. Hall & Rosalie J. Slater. <u>The Bible and the Constitution of the US of America</u>. San Francisco: Foundation for American Christian Education, 1983.

(46a) Verna M. Hall. <u>The Christian History of the Constitution of the US of America</u>. San Francisco, Foundation for American Christian Education, 1960; 1966; 1976; 1993. ~Also <u>Christian Self-Government w/ Union</u>.

(47) Benjamin Franklin; Richard Price ed. <u>Works of the Late Doctor Benjamin Franklin Consisting of His Life, Written by Himself, Together w/ Essays, Humorous, Moral & Literary, Chiefly in the Manner of the Spectator</u>. Dublin: P. Wogan, P. Byrne, J. Moore, and W. Jones, 1793.

(47a) Benjamin Franklin. <u>The Autobiography of Benjamin Franklin.</u> NY: Books, Inc., 1791.

(47b) Albert Henry Smyth, ed. <u>The Writings of Benjamin Franklin</u>. NY: Macmillan, 1905-07.

(48) Richard B. Morris. <u>The Encyclopedia of American History</u>. Bicentennial ed. NY: Harper and Row. 1976.

(49) Saul K. Padover. <u>The Complete Madison</u>. NY: Harper and Bros., 1953.

(49a) Saul Padover. <u>The Washington Papers</u>. NY: Harper and Bros., 1955.

(49b) Saul Padover. <u>The Mind of Alexander Hamilton</u>. NY: Harper and Bros, 1958.

(50) Saul Padover. <u>Jeffeson, A Great American's Life and Ideas.</u> NY: Mentor Books, 1942, 1970.

(51) Michael J. Malbin. <u>Religion and Politics, The Intentions of the Authors of the First Amendment</u>. Washington, DC: American Enterprise Institute for Public Policy Research, 1978.

(52) Joseph Story. <u>Commentaries on the Constitution of the US</u>, 2nd ed. Boston: Charles C. Little and James Brown, 1851.

(52a) Joseph Story. <u>A Familiar Exposition of the Constitution of the US.</u> NY: Harper and Brothers, 1854.

(53) Thomas M. Cooley. <u>Constitutional Limitations</u>. Boston: Little, Brown, and Co., 1868.

(54) <u>Public Statues at Large.</u> Reference can be made to the various Congress meetings within these documents.

(55) <u>Documents, Legislative and Executive, of the Congress of the US</u>. Refer to subject noted w/ them.

(56) <u>American State Papers.</u> Washington D.C.; Gales and Seaton, 1834.

(57) US Office of Indian Affairs, <u>Annual Reports of the Commissioner of Indian Affairs</u>.

(58) <u>Journals of the Continental Congress.</u>

(59) John and Abigail Adams. <u>Letters of John Adams Addressed to His Wife</u>. Charles Francis Adams, ed. Boston: Charles C. Little and James Brown, 1841.

(60) <u>The Journals of each Provincial Congress of Massachusetts</u>. William Lincoln ed. Boston: Dutton & Wentworth, 1838.

(61) <u>Journal of the First Session of the Senate of the US of America, Begun and Held at the City of New York, March 4, 1798</u>. Washington, DC: Gales & Seaton, 1820.

(62) James Madison. <u>Notes of Debates in the Federal Convention of 1787</u>. Reprinted NY: W.W. Norton & Co. 1987.

(62a) Fredrick Nyneyer. <u>First Principles in Morality and Economics: Neighborly Love and Ricardo's Law of Association</u>. South Holland: Libertarian Press. 1958. { as cited in (4) }.

(63) Sol Bloom. <u>The Story of the Constitution</u>. Washington D.C. US Constitutional Sesquicentennial Commission. 1937.

(64) Mr. Hening, <u>Statutes of Virginia., 1823.</u> Cf. ~and also: Mark De Wolf Howe, <u>The Garden and the Wilderness; religion and government in American constitutional history</u>. Chicago: Chicago Universtiy Press. 1965.

(65) Jesse H. Choper. <u>Securing Religious Liberty; Principle for Judicial Interpretation of the Religion Clauses</u>. Chicago, Ill. University of Chicago Press, 1995.

(66) W. Cleon Skousen. <u>The Making of America</u>. Washington, DC: The National Center for Constitutional Studies, 1985.

(67) Daniel P. Marsh. <u>Unto the Generations</u>. Buena Park, CA: ARC, 1968.

(68) Dr. Ed Rowe. <u>The ACLU and America's Freedom</u>. Washington: Church League of America, 1984.

(69) Michael Farris. <u>The Real Meaning of the Declaration of Independence</u>. Concerned Women for America News, Vol. 8, July 1986, pp 3, 16.

(70) Tim LaHaye. <u>Faith of Our Founding Fathers</u>. Brentwood, TN: Wolgemuth & Hyatt, Pub. Inc. 1987.

(71) John F Schroeder, ed. <u>Maxims of Washington</u>. MT Vernon: Mt Vernon Ladies Association, 1942.

(72) W. Herbert Burk, B.D. <u>Washington's Prayers</u>. Norristown, PE: Published for the Benefit of the Washington Memorial Chapel, 1907.

(73) Martin E. Marty. <u>Pilgrims in Their Own Land: 500 Years of Religion in America</u>. Boston: Little , Brown and Co. 1984.

(74) Charles C. Jones. <u>Biographical Sketches of the Delegates from Georgia</u>. Tustin, CA: American Biography Service. { in cite (70) }.

(75) Gaillard Hunt. <u>James Madison and Religious Liberty</u>. Washington: American Historical Assoc. Government Printing Office, 1902. { in cite (70) }.

(76) William C. Rives. <u>History of the Life and Times of James Madison</u>. Boston: Little, Brown. { in cite (70) }.

(77) William T. Hutchinson & William M. Rachal. <u>The Papers of James Madison.</u> Chicago: Univ. of Chicago, 1912. { in cite (70) }.

(78) A.D. Wainwright, ed., Madison and Witherspoon: <u>Theological Roots of American Political Thought</u>. The Princeton University Library Chronicle, Spring, 1961. { in cite (70) }.

(79) A.M. Schlesinger. <u>The State of the Union Messages of the Presidents, 1790-1966</u>. NY: Chelsea House-Robert Hector, 1966; ~and Also~ Adrienne Koch. <u>Madison's Advice to My Country</u>. Princeton: Princeton University Press, 1966. { noted in cite (70) }.

(80) Frederick Horner. <u>History of the Blair, Banister and Braxton Families</u>. Philadelphia: J.B. Lippincott Co. 1898. { noted in cite (70) }.

(81) Lewis Henry Boutell. <u>The Life of Roger Sherman</u>. Chicago: A.C. McClure & Co., 1896. { noted in cite (70) }.

(82) Dorothy McGee. <u>Framers of the Constitution</u>. NY: Dodd, Mead, 1968. { noted in cite (70) }.

(83) Allan M. Hamilton. <u>The Intimate Life of Alexander Hamilton</u>. Philadelphia: Richard West, 1979. { noted in cite (70) }.

(84) Rev William Campbell. _Papers of the Historical Society of Delaware._ Wilmington: Historical Society of Delaware, 1909. { noted in cite (70) }.

(85) Martha J. Lamb. Ed., _The Framers of the Constitution, A Magazine of American History_. NY: Historical Pub. Co., 1985. { noted in cite (70) }.

(86) Patrick Henry. _Speech before Virginia Ratifying Convention_, 1788. Reprinted in Storing, The Anti-Federalist.

(87) Zoltan Harasett quotes John Adams. _John Adams and the Prophets of Progress_. Cambridge: Harvard Univ. Press, 1952.

(88) R. J. Rushdoony. _Law and Liberty. Fairfax, Virginia_: Thoburn Press, 1971.

(88a) Rousas John Rushdoony. _The Institutes of Biblical Law_. The Presbyterian and Reformed Pub. Co. 1973.

(89) Forrest McDonald, ed., _Empire and Nation_. Englewood Cliffs, NJ: Prentice-Hall, 1962. { noted in cite (70) }.

(90) Martin Luther. _Secular Authority: To What Extent It Should Be Obeyed_, 1523. Reprinted in _Works of Martin Luther_. Grand Rapids: Baker Book House, 1982.

(91) Pierre Samuel DuPont de Nemours. _National Education in the United Staes of America_. Newark: Univ. of Delaware Press 1923; quoted in R.J. Rushdoony. _The Messianic Character of American Education_. Nutley, NJ: Prague Press, 1963 { noted in cite (9) }.

(92) Benjamin Fletcher Wright. _Massachusetts Colonial Records_ ~and also _American Interpretations_ ~and also _John Eliot: Massachusetts Historical Collection, 3rd ser_. Russell & Russell, 1962. { noted in cite (9) }.

(93) John Cotton, quoted by Perry Miller and Thomas Herbert Johnson. _The Puritans, Vol 1 & 2_. NY: Harper and Row, 1963, reprinted in 1965.

(94) Grotius. _The Truth of the Christian Religion_ ~and also~ _Universe: Divine Law and a Quest for Harmony_. Quoted by William Vasilio Sotirovich. NY: Vantage Press. 1978.

(95) Dan Gilbert. _The Biblical Basis for the Constitution_. San Diego, CA: The Danielle Pub., 1936.

(96) John Wycliff, quoted by Herbert E. Winn, ed., _Wycliff Select English Writings_. Oxford University Press, 1929.

(97) L. H. Butterfield, ed. _Letters of Benjamin Rush,_ 1951. Princeton University Press. { noted in cite (46) }.

(97a) L. H. Butterfield, ed, Quotes John Adams. _Diary and Autobiography of John Adams_. Cambridge, Mass: The Belknap Press of Harvard University Press, 1962. ~and Also _Adams Family Correspondence_. 1963.

(98) Jonathon Elliot, ed. _The Debates in the Several State Conventions on the Adoption of the Federal Constitution, 2nd_ ed. Washington, D.C., 1836.

(99) S. Gerald Sandler. _Lockean Ideas in Jefferson's Bill for Establishing Religious Freedom. Journal of the History of Ideas_., 1960.

(100) Paul F. Boller. _George Washington and Religion_. Dallas, Southern Methodist University Press, 1963. { noted in cite (9) }.

(101) Richard B. Morris. _Alexander Hamilton and the Founding of the Nation_. NY: Dial Press, 1957. { noted in cite (9) }.

(102) Broadus Mitchell. _Alexander Hamilton: Youth to Maturity_, 1755-1788. NY: MacMillan, 1957. { noted in cite (9) }.

(103) Alexander Hamilton. Quoted by Nathan Schachner. _Alexander Hamilton_. NY: Barnes & Co. 1946, 1961. { noted in cite (9) }.

(104) John C. Miller. _Alexander Hamilton: Portrait in Paradox_. NY: Harper, 1959.

(104a) John C. Miller. _Sam Adams: Pioneer in Propaganda_. Stanford: Stanford University Press, 1936, 1960.

(105) Frank Monaghan. _John Jay; Defender of Liberty_. Indianapolis: Bobbs-Merrill, 1935, 1972 who quotes, William Jay. _The life of John Jay_. NY: Harper, 1833.

(105a) William Jay. _The life of John Jay, with Selections from His Correspondence and Miscellaneous Papers_. NY: J. & J. Harper. 1833.

(106) Norman Cousins. _In God We Trust: The Religious Beliefs and Ideas of the American Founding Fathers_. NY: Harper & Bros. 1958. John Jay to the American Bible Society.

(107) Gouverneur Morris; quoted by Henry Cabot Lodge. _Historical and Political Essays_. NY: Houghton & Mifflin, 1892. { as in cite (9) }.

(108) Melvin H. Buxbaum. _Benjamin Franklin and the Zealous Presbyterians_. Univ. Park: Pennsylvania State Univ. Pres, 1975.

(109) Carl Van Doren, ed. Quoted Benjamin Franklin. _The Letters of Benjamin Franklin & Jane Mecom_. London: Princeton University press, 1950.

(110) Adams Dickinson, ed., _Jefferson's Extracts from the Gospels_. Princeton: Princeton University Press, 1983.

(111) Thomas Jefferson Randolph, ed. Quotes Thomas Jefferson. _Memoir, Correspondence, and Miscellanies from the Papers of Thomas Jefferson_. Boston: Grey & Bowen, 1830. ~And Also: Thomas Jefferson. _The Papers of Thomas Jefferson_. Ed. Barbara B. Oberg. Princeton, NJ. Princeton University Press. 2006.

(112) M. Richard Maxfield, K. DeLynn Cook, W. Cleon Skousen., Quote Thomas Jefferson. _The Real Thomas Jefferson, 2nd ed_., Washington D.C.: National Center for Constitutional Studies, 1981, 1983.

(113) John W. Whitehead. _The Separation Illusion_. Milford, Michigan: Mott Media, 1977.

(114) Encyclopedia Britannica: Macropaedia: _Knowledge in Depth, Adams Samuel_.

(115) World Book Encyclopedia, _Adams, Samuel._

(116) William V. Wells. _The Life and Public Services of Samuel Adams_, 1865. { noted in cite (104a) and all in cite (9) }. ~and Also~ _Will & Testament of Samuel Adams_, attested Dec 29, 1790.

(117) Page Smith. _John Adams_. Garden City: Doubleday, 1962, 1963.

(118) Stewart Mitchell. Quoted Abigail Adams in a letter to Mary Cranch, Feb 7, 1801. _New Letters of Abigail Adams, 1788-1801_, reprinted. Boston: Houghton Mifflin, 1947.

(119) Zoltan Haraszti. Quoted John Adams. _John Adams and the Prophets of Progress_. Cambridge, Mass: Harvard University Press, 1952. ~and Also included Mary Wollstonecraft. (1794). _Historical and Moral View of the Origin and Progress of the French Revolution_. Reprinted by Zoltan Haraszti.

(120) Norine Dickson Campbell. _Patrick Henry: Patriot and Statesman_. Old Greenwich, Connecticut: Devin-Adair, 1969, 1975,. Quotes Patrick Henry. _Sketches of the Life and Character of Patrick Henry_. William Wirt Henry ed. NY: M"Elrath and Sons, 1835.

(121) Roger Sherman Boardman. _Roger Sherman: Singer and Statesman_. NY: Da Capo Press, 1971.

(122) Marvin R. Zahniser. _Charles Cotesworth Pinckney: Founding Father_. Chapel Hill, NC: Univ. of North Carolina Press, 1967.

(123) Martin Diamond. _The Public Interest_. No. 41, Fall 1975, pp. 39-55, at 46ff. { noted in cite (9) }.

(124) David C. Mearns. _The Story Up to Now_. Washington, D.C.: The Library of Congress, 1947.

(125) Vincent Wilson, Jr., _The Book of the Founding Fathers_. Brookeville, MD: American History Research Associates, 1974.

(126) J. A. Stevens. _The Magazine of American History_. NY: A.J. Baines & Co., 1878.

(127) Bernard C. Steiner. _One Hundred and Ten Years of Bible Society_. Maryland: Maryland Bible Society, 1921.

(128) Brantz Mayer. _Baltimore Past and present, 1729-1970_. Washington, D.C.: Library of Congress.

(129) A.E. Miller and the Vestry of the St Phillips Church. _A Sermon Preached at St Phillips Church, August 21, 1825, by Christopher E. Gadsen, On the Occasion of the Decease_. Charleston: published by the vestry, printed by A.E. Miller, 1825.

(130) John Neal. _Trinity College Historical Society Papers, Series 13_. NY: AMS Press, 1915.

(131) Horace Binney. _The Leaders of the Bar of Philadelphia_. Philadelphia: Henry Ashmead (printer), 1886.

(132) 2 references here: H.M. Timkcom. _The Republicans and Federalists in Pennsylvania_. Philadelphia: University of Pennsylvania, 1950. ~And Also: K.R. Rossman. _Thomas Mifflin_. Chapel Hill, NC: University of North Carolina Press, 1952.

(133) Albert J. Beveridge. _The Life of John Marshall_. Boston: Houghton Mifflin, 1919.

(134) Stephen K. McDowell and Mark A. Beliles. _America's Providential History._ Charlottesville, VA: Providence Press, 1988.

(134a) Stephen K. McDowell and Mark A. Beliles. _America's Providential History_. Charlottesville, VA: Providence Press, 1988. Quote from Moody Adams. _America is Too Young to Die_. 1976. { as cited in (4) }.

(135) Richard J. Neuhaus. _Law and Religion: A Critical Anthology (A New Order of Religious Freedom)_. Ed. by Stephen M. Feldman. NY: NY Univ. Press, 2000.

(136) Stephen M. Feldman. _Law and Religion: A Critical Anthology (A Christian America and the Separation of Church and State)_. Ed. by Stephen M. Feldman. NY: NY Univ. Press, 2000.

137) Larry Cata' Backer. Law and Religion: A Critical Anthology (There Can Be Only One: Law, Religion, Grammar, and Social Organization in the US). Ed. by Stephen M. Feldman. NY: NY University Press, 2000.

138) The Debates in the Several State Conventions on the Adoptions of the Federal Constitutions. Jonathan Elliot, Ed., Washington, DC: Jonathan Elliot, 1836.

139) The Constitutions of the Several Independent States of America. Boston: Norman and Bowen. 1785 (New Hampshire, 1783).

139a) The Federal and State Constitutions, Colonial Charters, and Other Organic Laws. Francis Newton Thorpe, Ed. Washington: Government Printing Office. 1909.

140) A Constitution or Frame of Government Agreed Upon By the Delegates of the People of the State of Massachusetts-Bay. Boston: Benjamin Edes & Sons, 1780.

141) Zephaniah Swift. The Correspondent. Windham: John Byrne, 1793.

141a) Zephaniah Swift. A System of Laws of the State of Connecticut. Windham: John Byrne, 1796.

142) Kate Mason Rowland. Life of Charles Carroll of Carrollton. NY: G.P. Putnam's Sons, 1890.

143) Reports on Committees of the House of Representatives Made During the First Session of the Thirty-Third Congress. Washington, DC: A.O.P. Nicholson, 1854.

144) Reports on Committees of the Senate of the United States Made for the Second Session of the Thirty-Second Congress. Washington, DC: Robert Armstrong, 1853.

145) Benjamin Rush. Essays, Literary, Moral & Philosophical. Philadelphia: Thomas & Samuel F. Bradford, 1798.

146) Reports of the Proceedings and Debates of the Convention of 1821, Assembled for the Purpose of Amending The Constitution of the State of New York. Albany: E. and E. Hosford, 1821.

147) Daniel Webster. Mr. Webster's Speech in Defence of the Christian Ministry and in Favor of the Religious Instruction of the Young. Delivered in the Supreme Court of the US, February 10, 1844, in the Case of Stephen Girard's Will. Washington: Printed by Gales and Seaton, 1844.

147a) Daniel Webster. The Works of Daniel Webster. Boston: Little, Brown & Co., 1853.

148) James Coffield Mitchell. The Tennessee Justice's Manual and Civil Officer's Guide. Nashville: Mitchell and C. C. Norvell, 1834.

149) Josiah Bartlett, Proclamation for a Day of Fasting and Prayer, March 17, 1792.

150) John Dickinson. The Political Writings of John Dickinson. Wilmington: Bonsal and Niles, 1801. ~And also: From the Last Will & Testament of John Dickinson, attested March 25, 1808.

151) John Quincy Adams. An Addres Delievered at the Request of the Committee of Arrangements for Celebrating the Anniversary of Independence at the City of Washington on the Fourth of July 1821. Cambridge: Hilliard and Metcalf, 1821.

152) Francis Hopkinson. The Miscellaneous Essays and Occasional Writings of Philadelphia: T. Dobson, 1792.

153) Hugh Moore. Memoir of Col. Ethan Allen. Plattsburgh, NY: O.R. Cook, 1834.

154) John Witherspoon, D.D. The Works of John Witherspoon. Edinburgh: J. Ogle, 1815.

154a) John Witherspoon. The Works of Rev. John Witherspoon. Philadelphia: William W. Woodward, 1802.

154b) John Witherspoon. The Holy Bible. Introduction to the Holy Bible. Trenton: Isaac Collins, 1791.

155) House Journals, 1775: A Journal of the,,, House of Representatives. Watertown, MA, 1776.

156) The New Annual Register or General Repository of History, Politics, and Literature, for the Year, 1783. London: G. Robinson, 1784.

157) New Hampshire Gazette. Portsmouth, May 26, 1791. ~Also Documentary History of the Supreme Court.

158) The Documentary History of the Supreme Court, Vol. II p. 412, from the Newport Mercury. Rhode Island, June 25, 1793.

159) Columbian Centinel. Boston, May 16, 1792. ~Also Documentary History of the Supreme Court.

160) John Quincy Adams. Memoirs of John Quincy Adams. Charles Francis Adams, ed. Philadelphia: J.B. Lippincott and Co., 1874.

161) John Quincy Adams. Memoirs of John Quincy Adams. Charles Francis Adams, ed. Philadelphia: J.B. Lippincott and Co., 1874. ~Also~ James Hutson. Religion in the Founding of the American Republic. Washington, DC: Library of Congress, 1998. ~Also~ Abijah Bigelow. American Antiquarian Society. Proceedings, 1810-1815 (1930). ~Also~ William Cutler and Julia Cutler. Life, Journal, and Correspondence of Rev. Mannasseh Cutler. Cincinnati: Colon Robert Clarke & Co., 1888. ~Also~ The Federal Orrery (Boston), July 2, 1795.

162) John E. O'Conner. William Paterson: Lawyer and Statesman. New Brunswick: Rutgen University Press, 1979.

163) John Quincy Adams. An Answer to Paine's ~ "Rights of Man". London: John Stockdale, 1793.

163a) John Quincy Adams. A Discourse on Education Delievered at Braintree, Thursday, October 24th, 1839. Boston: Perkins & Marvin. 1840.

164) A. G. Arnold. The Life of Patrick Henry of Virginia. Auburn and Buffalo: Miller, Orton and Mulligan, 1854.

165) Robert Treat Paine, The Papers of Robert Treat Paine. Stephen T. Riley and Edward W. Hanson, editors. Boston: Massachusetts Historical Society, 1992.

166) Samuel Worchester. A Sermon Preached in Boston on the Anniversary of the American Society for Educating Pious Youth for the Gospel Ministry. Andover: Flagg & Gould, 1816.

167) Appleton's Cyclopedia of American Biography: "Cotton Mather Smith".

168) Henry Otis Dwight. The Centennial History of the American Bible Society. NY: MacMillan Co., 1916.

169) John Adams. Papers of John Adams. Cambridge, MA: Belknap Press, 1983.

169a) John Adams. Papers of John Adams. Robert J. Taylor, ed., Cambridge, MA: Belknap Press, 1977.

170) Alexander Hamilton. The Papers of Alexander Hamilton. Harold C. Syrett, Ed. NY: Columbia University Press, 1977.

171) Samuel Adams. The Writings of Samuel Adams. Harry Alonzo Cushing, ed. NY: G. P. Putnam's Sons, 1908. ~àlso~ various and multiple fasting and prayer day Proclamations by Governor Samuel Adams, Massachusetts, including some but not all, as March 10, 1793, March 15, 1796, and March 20, 1797.

172) Collections of the New York Historical Society for the Year 1821. NY: E. Bliss and E. White, 1821.

173) Edwards Beardsley. Life and Times of William Samuel Johnson. Boston: Houghton, Mifflin and Co., 1886.

174) The Speeches of the Different Governors to the legislature of the State of New York, Commencing w/ Those of George Clinton and Continued Down to the Present Time. Albany: J. B. Van Steenbergh, 1825.

175) Noah Webster. A Collection of Papers on Political, Literary, and Moral Subjects. New York: Webster and Clark, 1843.

176) Noah Webster. History of the United States. New Haven: Durrie & Peck, 1832.

177) William W. Campbell. The Life and Writings of DeWitt Clinton. NY: Baker and Scribner, 1849.

178) John Quincy Adams. Letters of John Quincy Adams to His Son on the Bible and Its Teachings. Auburn: James M. Alden, 1850. And also at: New York: Derby, Miller & Company. 1848.

179) William Wirt Henry. Sketches of the Life and Character of Patrick Henry. Philadelphia: James Webster, 1818.

179a) William Wirt Henry Ed., Quotes Patrick Henry. Patrick Henry: Life, Correspondence and Speeches. New York: Charles Scribner's Sons, 1891.

180) Daniel Webster. Address Delivered at Bunker Hill, June 17, 1843, on the Completion of the Monument. Boston: T. R. Marvin, 1843. ~and Also~ W. P. Strickland, History of the American Bible Society from its Organization to the Present Time. New York: Harper and Brothers, 1849.

181) John Jay. John Jay: The Winning of the Peace. Unpublished Papers 1780-1784. Richard B. Morris, ed. NY: Harper & Row Pub., 1980.

182) Noah Webster. The Holy Bible,,, With Amendments of the Language. New Haven: Durrie & Peck, 1833.

183) Joseph Story. Life and Letters of Joseph Story. William W. Story, Ed. Boston: Charles C. Little and James Brown, 1851.

184) John Quincy Adams. An Oration Delivered Before the Inhabitants of the Town of Newburyport at Their Request on the Sixty-First Anniversary of the Declaration of Independence, July 4, 1837. Newburyport: Charles Whipple, 1837. ~and Also~ An Oration Addressed to the Citizens of the Town of Quincy, on the Fouth of July, 1831, the Fifty Fifth Aniversary of the Independence of the United States of America. Boston: Richardson, Lord, and Holbrook. 1831.

185) From Will of Elias Boudinot available from New Jersey State Archives. ~and Also~ George Adams Boyd. Elias Boudinot: Patriot and Statesman. Princeton: Princeton University Press, 1952.

185a) George Adams Boyd. Elias Boudinot: Patriot and Statesman. Princeton: Princeton University Press, 1952.

299

(186) Bernard C. Steiner. The Life and Correspondence of James McHenry. Cleveland: The Burrows Brothers, 1907. From Charles Carroll, Nov 4, 1800.

(187) Jared Sparks. Lives of William Pinkney, William Ellery, and Cotton Mather. NY: Harper and Brothers, 1860. From the Library of American Biography.

(188) K. Alan Snyder. Defining Noah Webster: Mind and Morals in the Early Republic. NY: University Press of America, 1990.

(189) J. J. Boudinot, Ed. Quotes Elias Boudinot. The Life, Public Services, Addresses, and Letters of Elias Boudinot. Boston: Houghton, Mifflin & Co., 1896.

(190) John Adams. A Defense of the Constitution of Government of the United States of America. Philadelphia: William Young, 1797.

(191) William Findley. Observations on "The Two Sons of Oil". Pittsburgh: Patterson & Hopkins, 1812.

(192) Charles C. Jones. Biographical Sketches of the Delegates from Georgia to the Continental Congress. Boston and New York: Houghton, Mifflin and Co., 1891.

(193) Independent Chronicle. Boston: Nov 2, 1780, last page. ~and Also~ Abram English Brown. John Hancock, His Book. Boston: Lee and Shepard Pub., 1898.

(194) Henry Laurens. The Papers of Henry Laurens. George C. Rogers, Jr. and David R. Chesnut, editors. Columbia: University of South Carolina Press, 1980.

(195) The Connecticut Courant. Hartford. June 7, 1802. "A report of the Committee,,, to the General Assembly of the State of Connecticut" by Oliver Ellsworth.

(196) William Livingston, The Papers of William Livingston. Trenton: New Jersey Historical Commission, 1979. An address from John Hart, Oct 5, 1776.

(197) James Otis. The Rights of the British Colonies Asserted and Proved. London: J. Williams and J. Almon, 1766.

(198) James D. Richardson. A Compilation of the Messages and Papers of the Presidents, 1789-1897. Published by Authority of Congress, 1899.

(199) Samuel Adams. From a Fast Day Proclamation issued by Governor Samuel Adams. Massachusetts, March 20, 1797.

(200) Jonathon Trumbull. By His Excellency Jonathon Trumbull, Esq. Governor and Commander in Chief In and Over the State of Connecticut. A Proclamation. Hudson and Goodwin, 1807.

(201) James Madison. Letters and Other Writings of James Madison. New York: R. Worthington, 1884.

(202) James Madison. The Papers of James Madison. Henry D. Gilpin, ed., Washington, DC: Langtree & O'Sullivan, 1840.

(203) The Documentary History of the Supreme Court of the United States, 1789-1800. Maeva Marcus, ed., NY: Columbia University Press, 1990., Samuel Chase's "Charge to the Grand Jury of the Circuit Court for the District of Pennsylvania".

(204) James Kent. Commentaries on American Law. NY: O. Halsted. 1826.

(205) Matthias Burnet. An Election Sermon, Preached at Hartford, on the day of the Anniversary Election, May 12, 1803. Hartford: Hudson and Goodwin, 1803.

(206) James Wilson. The Works of the Honourable James Wilson. Bird Wilson, ed., Philadelphia: Lorenzo Press, 1804.

(207) Rufus King. The Life and Correspondence of Rufus King. Charles R. King, ed., NY: G.P. Putnam's Sons, 1900.

(208) Noah Webster. Letters to a Young Gentleman Commencing His Education. New Haven: S. Converse, 1823.

(209) Jedidiah Morse's Election Sermon given at Charleston, Mass. On Apr 25, 1799. from Evans collection compiled by the American Antiquarian Society. ~and Also~ Jedidiah Morse. A Sermon, Exhibiting the Present Dangers and Consequent Duties of the Citizens of the United States of America. Delivered at Charlestown, April 25, 1799, The Day of the National Fast. MA: Printed by Samuel Etheridge, 1799.

(210) Abraham Lincoln. The Collected Works of Abraham Lincoln, Roy P. Basler, ed., New Brunswick,, NJ: Rutgers Union Press, 1853. ~and Also~ Clarence E. Macartney. Lincoln and the Bible. NY: Abingdon-Cokesbury Press, 1949.

(211) Independent Chronicle. Boston: Feb 22, 1787 and Nov 2, 1780.

(212) Nathanael Greene. The Papers of General Nathanael Greene. Richard K. Showman, ed., Chapel Hill: University of North Carolina Press, 1976.

(213) Richard Henry Lee. The Letters of Richard Henry Lee. James Curtis Ballagh, ed., NY: MacMillan Co., 1911-1914.

(214) Gouverneur Morris. A Diary of the French Revolution. Boston: Houghton Mifflin Co., 1939.

(215) United States Oracle. Portsmouth, NH: May 24, 1800.

(216) David Ramsay. An Oration, Delivered in St. Micahel's Church Before the Inhabitants of Charleston, South-Carolina, on the Fourth of July, 1794. Charleston: W.P. Young, 1794. ~and Also~ David Ramsay. The History of the American Revolution. Dublin: William Jones, 1795.

(217) A Selection of Orations and Eulogies,,, In Commemoration of the Life,,, of George Washington. Charles Humbphre Atherton, ed., Amherst: Samuel Preston, 1800.

(218) John Sanderson. Biography of the Signers to the Declaration of Independence. Philadelphia: R. W. Pomeroy, 1824. (Vol. IX, p. 333), Thomas Stone to his son, October 1787.

(219) Gouverneur Morris. An Oration Delivered on Wednesday, Jun 29, 1814. New York: Van Winkle and Wiley, 1814.

(220) John Quincy Adams. The Jubilee of the Constitution. A Discourse Delivered at the Request of the New York Historical Socidty, in the City of New York, on Tuesday, the 30th of April 1839. NY: Samuel Colman, 1839.

(221) Noah Webster. The American Spelling Book. Boston: Isaiah Thomas and Ebenezer T. Andrews, 1794.

(222) Jared Sparks, ed. The Works of Benjamin Franklin. Boston: Tappan, Whittemore and Mason, 1840.

(223) William B. Willcox, ed. The Papers of Benjamin Franklin. New Haven: Yale University Press, 1972.

(224) Leonard Labaree, ed. The Papers of Benjamin Franklin. New Haven: Yale University Press, 1959.

(225) George Grant. The Laws Crusader: the Untold Story of Christopher Columbus. Wheaton, IL: Crossway Books, 1992.

(226) James Iredell. The Papers of James Iredell. Don Higginbotham, ed. Raleigh, NC: North Carolina Division of Archives and History, 1976.

(227) William Kent. Memoirs and Letters of James Kent. Boston: Little, Brown, and Company, 1898.

(228) Letters of Delegates to Congress: 1775 -- 1800. Paul H. Smith, ed., Washington DC: Library of Congress, 1995.

(229) Gunning Bedford. Funeral Oration Upon the Death of General George Washington. Wilmington: James Wilson, 1800.

(230) Charles W. Upham. The Life of Timothy Pickering. Boston: Little, Brown, and Company, 1873.

(231) Mary Orne Pickering. Life of John Pickering. Boston: 1887.

(232) Collected Letters of John Randolph of Roanoke to Dr. John Brockenbrough. Kenneth Shorey, ed., New Brunswick: Transaction Books, 1988.

(233) Hugh A. Garland. The Life of John Randolph of Roanoke. New York: D. Appleton & Co., 1853.

(234) Jonathan Trumbull. Proclamation for a Day of Fasting and Prayer, March 9, 1774.

(235) Last will and testament of Jonathan Trumbull, Sr., attested on Jan 29, 1785.

(236) Jonathan Trumbull. Governor of Connecticut, A Proclamation for a Day of Public Thanksgiving, October 12, 1770.

(237) Letter from John Adams to Benjamin Rush, from Quincy, Massachusetts, dated December 21, 1809.

(238) John Adams and John Quincy Adams. The Selected Writings of John and John Quincy Adams. Adrienne Koch and William Peden, editors. New York: Alfred A. Knopf, 1946.

(239) Life of John Quincy Adams. W. H. Seward, ed., Auburn, NY: Derby, Miller & Company, 1849.

(240) Elias Boudinot. The Age of Revelation, or the Age of Reason Shewn to be An Age of Infidelity. Philadelphia: Asbury Dickins, 1801.

(241) Jacob Broom. A letter to his son dated Feb 24, 1794. Written in Wilmington, Delaware. { A letter in possession of cite (5) }.

(242) Lewis A. Leonard. Life of Charles Carroll of Carrollton. New York: Moffit, Yard & Co, 1918.

(243) Benjamin Franklin. Works of Benjamin Franklin. John Bigelow, ed., NY: G.P. Putnam's Sons, 1904.

(244) Benjamin Rush. The Autobiography of Benjamin Rush. George W. Corner, ed., Princeton: Princeton Univ. Press, 1948.

(245) Correspondence Between Roger Sherman and Samuel Hopkins. (in 1790). Worcester, MA: Charles Hamilton, 1889.

(246) Aaron Merritt (A. M.) Hills, DD., LLD. Fundamental Christian Theology, A Systematic Theology. Salem, OH: Schmul Publishing Co. Reprint 1980 from Approx. Late AD 1800's ~ early 1900's.

(247) Timothy Dwight. Travels in New England and New York. New Haven, Timothy Dwight. 1822. { as cited in (3) }.

(248) William Law. <u>Works — Comprehensive</u>. AD 1700's. Digital version: CD of books and commentaries: Wesleyan Heritage Library, 1690 Old Harmony Dr NW, Concord, NC 28027. Tele. (704) 782-4377.

(249) <u>The Founders' Bible; The Origin of the Dream of Freedom</u>. General Eds. Brad Cummings & Lance Wubbels. Shiloh Road Publishers, LLC. Newbury Park, CA. 2012. Includes: <u>The New American Standard Bible</u>. Lockman Foundation. 1995.

(250) Thomas Paine. <u>The Writings of Thomas Paine</u>. Ed. Moncure Daniel Conway (New York & London: Putnam's Sons). 1896.

(251) Diana Fontaine (Maury) Corbin, Ed. <u>A Life of Matthew Fontaine Maury</u>. London: Sampson Low, Marston, Searle & Rivington. 1888. ~and Also~ Stephen McDowell. <u>Matthew Fontaine Maury; the Pathfinder of the Seas</u>. Charlottesville, VA. Providence Biblical Worldview University. 2011.

(252) Town of Pryor vs. Williamson, OK Supreme Court, 1959.

(253) John Marrant. <u>A Narrative of the Lord's Wonderful Dealings with John Marrant</u>. Rev. William Albridge, Ed. Gilbert & Plummer. London. 1785.

(254) Luther Martin. <u>The General Information Delivered to the Legislature of the State of Maryland Relative to the Proceedings of the General Convention Lately Held at Philadelphia</u>. Philadelphia. Eleazor Oswald. 1788. { as in cite (138) }.

(255) <u>The Evangelical Guardian by an Association of Ministers of the Associate Reformed Synod of the West</u>. Rev. D. MacDill. Rossville, OH: J. M. Christy. 1845.

(256) Hezekiah Niles. <u>Principles and Acts of the Revolution in America</u>. Baltimore: William Ogden Niles. 1822.

(257) John Marshall. <u>The Papers of John Marshall</u>. Charles Hobson, Ed. Chapel Hill: University of North Carolina Press. 2006.

(258) Roy Tilman Williams. <u>The Perfect Man</u>. (chpt, "Politics"). Publishing House Of The Pentecostal Church Of The Nazarene. Kansas City, MO. 1913. Digital version available on 2 different CD's which are very good libraries of books and commentaries: 1} <u>Wesleyan Heritage Library</u>, 1690 Old Harmony Dr NW, Concord, NC 28027. Tele. #704-782-4377. 2} God's Acres, <u>Voice of the Nazarene CD</u>, 520 Forrest Ave., Houston PA 15342 USA.

(259) William Baxter Godbey. <u>Patriotism and Politics</u>. Published by God's Revivalist Office; No publication date or copyright. Digital version: A CD which is a very good library of books and commentaries: God's Acres, <u>Voice of the Nazarene CD</u>, 520 Forrest Ave., Houston PA 15342 USA.

(260) <u>Voice of the Nazarene Publication</u>. CD Version. <u>Voice of the Nazarene CD</u>, 520 Forrest Ave., Houston PA 15342 USA. {a} Article <u>Knighthood of Catholicism</u>. {b} 1962-1963 issue. {c} in Nov. 1967 issue; from Oct. 30, 1964 Chicago Daily News. {d} article by Jerome Stowell. {e} in Sept. 1969 issue, in Senator's book, Crime Without Punishment. {f} 1974 issue. {g} 1983 Nov-Dec issue. {h} 1988 may-June issue. {i} article by Stephen A. Coston, Sr.

(261 a,b,c,d) ~{a}~ Gulf, Colorado and Santa Fe Railway Company v. Ellis, 165 U. S. 150, 160 (1897). ~{b}~ 1} Zephaniah Swift. <u>A System of the Laws of the State of Connecticut</u>. Windham: John Byrne, 1795, Vol. I, pp. 1-2, <u>Of Law and Government</u>. 2} Henry Campbell Black. <u>A Law Dictionary Containing Definition of the Terms and Phrases of American and English Jurisprudence, Ancient and Modern</u>. St. Paul: West Publishing Co., 1910, pp. 226-227, s.v. <u>Common Law</u>. 3} John Bouvier. <u>Law Dictionary, Adapted to the Constitution and Laws of the United States of America, and of the Several States of the American Union</u>. Philadelphia: J.B. Lippincott, 1892, Vol. I, pp. 348-349. 4} Alexander M. Burrill. <u>A Law Dictionary and Glossary</u>. New York: Baker, Voorhis & Co., 1867, Vol. I, pp. 324-326. ~{c}~ Following are only few of many: 1} U.S. v. Coolidge, 1 Gall. 488 (1813). 2} U.S. v. Wonson, 1 Gall. 5 (1812). 3} Robinson v. Campbell, 16 U.S. 3 Wheat. 212 (1818). 4} Alexander M. Burrill. <u>A Law Dictionary and Glossary</u>. New York: Baker, Voorhis & Co., 1871, Vol. I, pp. 324-326. 5} Thomas M. Cooley. <u>A Treatise on the Constitutional Limitations which Rest Upon the Legislative Power of the States of the American Union</u>. Boston: Little, Brown, and Company, 1871, pp. 21-25, <u>The Formation and Amendment of State Constitutions</u>. 6} Theron Metcalf & Jonathan Perkins. <u>Digest of the Decisions of the Courts of Common Law and Admiralty in the United States</u>. Boston: Charles C. Little and James Brown, 1860, Vol. I, p. 532, s.v. <u>Common Law</u>. 7} John Bouvier. <u>Law Dictionary, Adapted to the Constitution and Laws of the United States of America, and of the Several States of the American Union</u>. Philadelphia: J.B. Lippincott, 1892, Vol. I, pp. 348-349; etc. ~{d}~ 1} Alexander M. Burrill. <u>A Law Dictionary and Glossary</u>. New York: Baker, Voorhis & Co., 1867, Vol. I, p. 325. 2} A. J. Dallas. <u>Reports of Cases Ruled and Adjudged in the Several Courts of the United States and of Pennsylvania Held at the Seat of the Federal Government</u>. Philadelphia: J. Ormrod, 1799, Vol. III, p. 139, Talbot, Appellant, versus Janson, Appellee, et al. which says: "But the abstract right of individuals to withdraw from the society of which they are members, is recognized by an uncommon coincidence of opinion — by every writer, ancient and modern; by the civilian, as well as by the common-law layer; by the philosopher, as well as the poet: It is the law of nature, and of nature's [G]od, pointing to 'the wide world before us, where to chuse our place of rest, and providence our guide';". 3} Giles Jacob. <u>A New Law Dictionary</u>. New York: Frederick C. Brightly, 1905, s.v. "Common Law" which says: "The common law is grounded upon the general customs of the realm; and includes in it the Law of Nature, the Law of God, and the Principles and Maxims of the Law: It is founded upon Reasons; and is said to be perfection of reason, acquired by long study, observation and experience, and refined by learned men in all ages". 4} Giles Jacob & T. E. Tomlins. <u>The Law-Dictionary: Explaining the Rise, Progress, and Present State of the English Law</u>. Philadelphia: Fry and Kammerer, 1811, Vol. IV, p. 89, s.v. "law" which says: "The law of nature is that which God at mans' creation infused into him, for his preservation and direction; and this is lex eterna and may not be changed: and no laws shall be made or kept, that are expressly against the Law of [G]od, written in his Scripture; as to forbid what he commandeth, & c. 2 Shep. Abr. 356". 5} William Nicholson. <u>American Edition of the British Encyclopedia or Dictionary of Arts and Sciences</u>. Philadelphia: Mitchell, Ames, and White, 1821, Vol. VII, s.v. "Law" which says "But this large division may be reduced to the common division; and all is founded on the law of nature and reason, and the revealed law of God, as all other laws ought to be". 6} Joseph Story. <u>Commentaries on the Constitution of the United States</u>. Boston: Hilliard, Gray, and Company, 1833, Vol. III, p. 724, 1867. 7} <u>Testimony of Distinguished Laymen to the Value of the Sacred Scriptures</u>. New York: American Bible Society, 1854, pp. 51-53, Justice John McLean, November 4, 1852. 8} Samuel W. Bailey. <u>Homage of Eminent Persons to the Book</u>. New York, 1869, p. 54, Joseph Hornblower, chief justice of New Jersey. 9} Case: Updegraph v. The Commonwealth, 11 S. & R. 394, 399 (Sup. Ct. Pa. 1824). 10} Case: Richmond v. Moore, 107 Ill. 429, 1883 WL 10319 (Ill.), 47 Am.Rep. 445 (Ill. 1883). 11} Case: State v. Mockus, 14 ALR 871, 874. Maine Sup. Jud. Ct., 1921. 12} Case: Cason v. Baskin, 20 So.2d 243, 247 (Fla. 1944) (en banc). 13} Case: Stollenwerck v. State, 77 So. 52, 54 (Ala. Ct. App. 1917) (Brown, P. J. concurring). 14} Case: Gillooley v. Vaughn, 110 So. 653, 655 (Fla. 1926), citing Theisen v. McDavid, 16 So. 321, 323 (Fla. 1894). 15} Case: Rogers v. State, 4 S.E.2d 918, 919 (Ga. Ct. App. 1939). 16} Case: Brimhall v. Van Campen, 8 Minn. 1 (1858). 17} Case: City of Ames v. Gerbracht, 189 N.W. 729, 733 (Iowa 1922). 18} Case: Ruiz v. Clancy, 157 So. 737, 738 (La. Ct. App. 1934), citing Caldwell v. Henmen, 5 Rob. 20. 19} Case: Beaty v. McGoldrick, 121 N.Y.S.2d 431, 432 (N.Y. Sup. Ct. 1953). 20} Ex parte Mei, 192 A. 80, 82 (N.J. 1937). 21} Case: State v. Donaldson, 99 P. 447, 449 (Utah 1909). 22} Case: De Rinzie v. People, 138 P. 1009, 1010 (Colo. 1913). 23} Case: Addison v. State, 116 So. 629 (Fla. 1928). 24} Case: State v. Gould, 46 S.W.2d 886, 889-890 (Mo. 1932). 25} Case: Doll v. Bender, 47 S.E. 293, 300 (W.Va. 1904) (Dent, J. concurring). 26} Many others can be found. 27} Joseph Story. <u>A Discourse Pronounced upon the Inauguration of the Author, as Dane Professor of Law in Harvard University, on the Twenty-Fifth Day of August, 1829</u>. Boston: Hilliard, Gray, Little, and Wilkins, 1829, pp. 20-21. 28} John Adams. <u>The Works of John Adams</u>. Charles Francis Adams, ed. Boston: Charles C. Little and James Brown, 1851, Vol. III, p. 439, "On Private Revenge," originally published in the Boston Gazette, September 5, 1763. 29} James Wilson. <u>The Works of the Honourable James Wilson</u>. Bird Wilson, ed. Philadelphia: Lorenzo Press, 1804, Vol. I, p. 104, "Of the General Principles of Law and Obligation". 30} Case: Church of the Holy Trinity v. United States, 143 U.S. 457, 470-471 (1892). 31} Case: Shover v. State, 10 Ark. 259, 263 (1850). 32} Case: People v. Ruggles, 8 Johns 225 (1811). 33} <u>Reports of the Proceedings and Debates of the Convention of 1821, assembled for the purpose of amending the Constitution of the State of New York, Nathaniel H. Carter and William L. Stone, reporters</u>. Albany: E. and E. Hosford, 1821, p. 576, October 31, 1821. 34} Charles B. Galloway. <u>Christianity and the American Commonwealth</u>. Nashville: Publishing House Methodist Episcopal Church, 1898, pp. 170-171. 35} Case: Lindenmuller v. The People, 33 Barb 548, 560-564, 567 (Sup. Ct. NY 1861). 36} Case: Strauss v. Strauss, 148 Fla. 23, 3 So.2d 727 (Sup.Ct.Fla. 1941). {{these citations were all borrowed from website, <u>wallbuilders.com</u>, in an article titled <u>Statement on the Supreme Court Decision</u>, written by David Barton, dated 6/27/15. It was regarding the illegal judiciary application to legalize homosexual marriage in the US}}.

(262 a,b,c) ~{a}~ Thomas Jefferson. <u>Writings of Thomas Jefferson</u>. Albert Ellery Bergh, ed. Washington D. C.: Thomas Jefferson Memorial Association, 1904, Vol. XV, p. 277, to William Charles Jarvis on September 28, 1820. Also: ~{b}~ Vol. XV, p. 215, to Judge Spencer Roane on September 6, 1819. Also ~{c}~ Vol. XV, p. 332, to Charles Hammond on August 18, 1821. {{these citations were borrowed from website, <u>wallbuilders.com</u>, in an article titled <u>Statement on the Supreme Court Decision</u>, written by David Barton, dated 6/27/15. It was regarding the illegal judiciary application to legalize homosexual marriage in the US}}.

(263) Article I, Section 1 lists fifteen powers permissible to the federal government; two additional federal powers are added through constitutional amendments, thus bringing the total number of constitutionally-authorized federal jurisdictions to seventeen. {{this citation was borrowed from website, <u>wallbuilders.com</u>, in an article titled <u>Statement on the Supreme Court Decision</u>, written by David Barton, dated 6/27/15. It was regarding the illegal judiciary application to legalize homosexual marriage in the US}}.

(264) Thomas Jefferson. <u>Memoir, Correspondence, and Miscellanies, From the Papers of Thomas Jefferson</u>. Thomas Jefferson Randolph, editor. Boston: Gray and Bowen, 1830, Vol. IV, p. 374, to Judge William Johnson on June 12, 1823. {{this citation was borrowed from website, <u>wallbuilders.com</u>, in an article titled <u>Statement on the Supreme Court Decision</u>, written by David Barton, dated 6/27/15. It was regarding the illegal judiciary application to legalize homosexual marriage in the US}}.

(265) False (non-true) Religions are to be limited in the US. Books & Articles which also agree with my conclusions that Islam is to be limited in the U.S. include the following: {a} Dave Miller, Ph. D. <u>Were the Founding Fathers "Tolerant" of Islam?</u>." Apologetics Press, 230 Landmark Dr., Montgomery, AL. 36117, U.S.A. Ph. (334) 272-8558; www.apologeticspress.org. {b} Bob Eschliman. <u>Common Sense: The Framers Were Unanimous About Islam</u>. Dec. 2015. Charisma Magazine. 600 Rinehart Rd., Lake Mary, FL 32746 www.charismamag.com; ph: 407-333-0600 {c} John Locke. <u>A Letter Concerning Toleration</u>. AD 1689. Translated by William Popple.

(266 a, b) ~{{a}}~ Digital version: <u>Truth in Heart CD</u>. Website: Truth in Heart.com and a CD of books & commentaries available, Tele. #989-637-4179. ~{{b}}~ Anthony Sheffield. <u>A Good Educational Reference Course of God, Communion of God's Presence, Truth, Spirit, Heart, Holy Bible, Fundamental Doctrines, Love: A Good Study with Good Knowledge, with quality and quantity of Evidences for Positive Increase of Complete Comprehension</u>. {Isa26:3; Pro2:1-5; 3:5-6; Eze14:23; Joh14-17; 1Cor10:31; 13; 2Cor6; 10:4-5; Col3:17, 23; 2Pet1; Mat11:28-30; Heb11:6}.

<u>Help of Intention/ purpose to Love God; Christ said Build your Personality; He desires to be your friend that has all-ability, knows all, is unselfish, is good, and to be with you all the time.</u>

Printed in the United States
by Baker & Taylor Publisher Services